What Went Right/What Went Wrong: Ford Motor Co. and Exide Batteries: Are Country Managers Here to Stay?

What Went Wrong? GM, Nissan, and the Value of the Dollar 1980–1988

Are Dirty Dishes Mobile? Dixan, Joy, Dawn, and Generic *Patti Scala* from Scala S.p.A.

Big Mac Index of Purchasing Power Parity

MERCOSUR Averts a Trade War

President Bush's 2002 Steel Tariffs: Justified Sanctions or Hypocritical Protectionism?

Intel's Chip Market Access Improves in Japan

Network Externalities at Microsoft and Apple: A Role for Protective Tariffs?

If Europe, What About One Currency for NAFTA?

Household Iron Manufacturer in Mexico Becomes Major Engine Block Supplier to Detroit: Cifunsa SA

EU Ban on Some Parallel Imports Pleases European but not U.S. and Japanese Manufacturers

PART III: PRODUCTION AND COST

Chapter 7: Production Economics

Managerial Challenge: What Went Wrong in California's Deregulation of Electricity?

An Illustrative Production Function: Deep Creek Mining Company

Increasing Returns at Sony and Intel

What Went Right/What Went Wrong: Boeing Assembly Plant

Isocost Determination: Deep Creek Mining Company

Cost Minimization: Deep Creek Mining Company

GM's A-Frame Supplier Achieves 99.998 Percent Technical Efficiency

What Went Right/What Went Wrong: How Exactly Have Computerization and Information Technology Lowered Costs at Chevron and Merck?

Technical and Allocative Efficiency in Commercial Banks versus Power Plants

Increasing Returns to Scale at the Wellington Company

Time-Series Analysis: U.S. Manufacturing Sector

Cross-Sectional Analysis: U.S. Manufacturing Industries

Empirical Estimation of a Production Function for Major League Baseball

Appendix 7A: Maximization of Production Output Subject to a Cost Constraint

Production Decisions and Linear Programming

Chapter 8: Cost Analysis

Managerial Challenge: US Airways' Cost Structure

Opportunity Costs at Bentley Clothing Store

Inventory Valuation at Westside Plumbing and Heating

Short-Run Cost Functions: Deep Creek Mining Company

Average Cost Per Kilowatt Hour in Underutilized Power Plants

Refuse Collection and Disposal in Orange County

Economies of Scale: Superscale Money-Center versus Community Banks

Flexibility and Operating Efficiency: Ford Motor Company's Flat Rock Plant

⊕ How Japanese Companies Deal with the Problems of Size

Aluminum-Intensive Vehicle Lowers the Minimum Efficient Scale at Ford

Chapter 9: Applications of Cost Theory

Managerial Challenge: Product Costing and CAM-I and ABC

What Went Right/What Went Wrong: Boeing: Rising Marginal Cost of 747s

Short-Run Cost Functions: Multiple-Product Food Processing

Short-Run Cost Functions: Electricity Generation

Long-Run Cost Functions: Electricity Generation

Scale Economies in the Traditional Cable Industry: Time-Warner

Economies of Scale and Survivor Technique: Steel Production

Break-Even Analysis: Allegan Manufacturing Company

Fixed Costs and Production Capacity at General Motors

Operating Leverage: Allegan Manufacturing Company

Business Risk Assessment: Allegan Manufacturing Company

Appendix 9A: Mass Customization and the Learning Curve

Learning Curves: Emerson Corporation

Percentage of Learning: Emerson Corporation

PART IV: PRICING AND OUTPUT DECISIONS: STRATEGY AND TACTICS

Chapter 10: Prices, Output, and Strategy: Pure and Monopolistic Competition

Managerial Challenge: Resurrecting Apple Computer?

What Went Right/What Went Wrong: Xerox

Rawlings Sporting Goods Waves Off the Swoosh Sign

Think Small to Grow Big: Southwest Airlines

Dell Cost Leadership Strategy Dominates PC Assembly

The E-Commerce of Sandwiches at 7-Elevens in Japan

Relevant Market for Web Browsers: Microsoft's Internet Explorer

Potential Entry at Office Depot/Staples

Eli Lilly Poses a Threat of Potential Entry for Zeneca

Objective versus Perceived Product Differentiation: Xerox

Price Competition at the Soda Fountain: PepsiCo Inc.

Contribution Margins at Hanes Discourage Discounting

Intensity of Rivalry at Northwest Airlines

Profit Maximization in Pure Competition (Short Run): Adobe Corporation

North Sea and West Texas Oil Fields Continued to Produce Despite Prices Below *ATC*

What Went Right/What Went Wrong: The Dynamics of Competition at Amazon.com

Long-Run Price and Output Determination: Video Magic, Inc.

Optimal Advertising: Flow Motors Ford

Ford and P&G Tie Ad Agency Pay to Sales

Optimal Advertising Intensity at Kellogg and General Mills

Credible Product Replacement Claims: Dooney & Bourke

Customers for Life at Sewell Cadillac

Efficient Uncut Diamond Sorting: DeBeers

Chapter 11: Price and Output Determination: Monopoly and Dominant Firms

Managerial Challenge: Dominant Microprocessor Company Lagging Behind Next Trend

The Mickey Mouse Monopoly: Disney

Impermanent Control of Denver Airport Hub: United Airlines

What Went Right at Microsoft but Wrong at Apple Computer?

What Went Right/What Went Wrong: Pilot Error at Palm

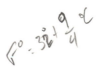

10TH EDITION

Managerial Economics

Applications, Strategy, and Tactics

James R. McGuigan
JRM Investments

R. Charles Moyer
Babcock Graduate School of Management
Wake Forest University

Frederick H. deB. Harris
Babcock Graduate School of Management
Wake Forest University

THOMSON
™
SOUTH-WESTERN

Australia · Canada · Mexico · Singapore · Spain · United Kingdom · United States

SOUTH-WESTERN
THOMSON LEARNING ™

Managerial Economics: Applications, Strategy, and Tactics, 10e

James R. McGuigan, R. Charles Moyer, and Frederick H. deB. Harris

VP/Editorial Director:
Jack W. Calhoun

VP/Editor-in-Chief:
Michael P. Roche

Acquisitions Editor:
Michael Worls

Senior Developmental Editor:
Susanna C. Smart

Developmental Editor:
Amy Ray

Executive Marketing Manager:
Lisa L. Lysne

Production Editor:
Chris Hudson

Technology Project Editor:
Peggy Buskey

Media Editor:
Pam Wallace

Manufacturing Coordinator:
Sandee Milewski

Production House:
settingPace

Printer:
QuebecorWorld
Versailles, Kentucky

Internal Designer:
Rik Moore

Cover Designer:
Lisa Albonetti

Cover Images:
© PhotoDisc, Inc.

For permission to use material
from this text or product,
submit a request online at
http://www.thomsonrights.com.

For more information
contact South-Western,
5191 Natorp Boulevard,
Mason, Ohio 45040.
Or you can visit our Internet site
at http://www.swlearning.com

BRIEF CONTENTS

Preface   xiii

PART I

Introduction   1

1   Introduction and Goals of the Firm   2

2   Fundamental Economic Concepts   29

2A   Differential Calculus Techniques in Management   52

PART II

Demand and Forecasting   71

3   Demand Analysis   72

3A   Indifference Curve Analysis of Demand   116

4   Estimation of Demand   127

4A   Problems in Applying the Linear Regression Model   170

5   Business and Economic Forecasting   186

6   Managing Exports   233

6A   International Parity Conditions   289

PART III

Production and Cost   293

7   Production Economics   294

7A   Maximization of Production Output Subject to a Cost Constraint   338

7B   Production Decisions and Linear Programming   340

8   Cost Analysis   345

8A   Long-Run Costs with a Cobb-Douglas Production Function   378

9   Applications of Cost Theory   382

9A   Mass Customization and the Learning Curve   417

PART IV

Pricing and Output Decisions: Strategy and Tactics   423

10   Prices, Output, and Strategy: Pure and Monopolistic Competition   424

11   Price and Output Determination: Monopoly and Dominant Firms   476

12   Price and Output Determination: Oligopoly   505

13   Game-Theoretic Rivalry: Best-Practice Tactics   547

13A   Capacity Planning and Pricing Against a Low-Cost Competitor: A Case Study of Piedmont Airlines and People Express   597

14   Pricing Techniques and Analysis   601

14A   Revenue Management   638

14B   Pricing of Joint Products and Transfer Pricing   653

PART V

Organizational Architecture and Institutional Economics   671

15   Contracting, Governance, and Organizational Form   672

16   Optimal Mechanism Design   712

16A   Externalities   749

17   Government Regulation   762

PART VI

Long-Term Investment Decisions and Risk Management   797

18   Long-Term Investment Analysis   798

19   Decisions Under Risk and Uncertainty   839

Appendix A: The Time Value of Money   A-1

Appendix B: Tables   B-1

Check Answers to Selected End-of-Chapter Exercises   C-1

Index   I-1

CONTENTS

Preface   xiii

PART I

Introduction   1

CHAPTER 1
Introduction and Goals of the Firm   2

Chapter Preview   2

**Managerial Challenge: Executive Performance
Bonus Plan: Salomon Smith Barney**   3

What Is Managerial Economics?   4

Managerial Economics and Economic Theory   5

The Decision-Making Model   5

The Role of Profits   6

Objective of the Firm   9

Separation of Ownership and Control:
The Problem of Agency   14

Implications of Shareholder Wealth Maximization   17

**What Went Right/What Went Wrong: Eli Lilly
Depressed by Loss of Prozac Patent**   18

**What Went Right/What Went Wrong: Saturn
Corporation**   19

Goals in the Public Sector and the Not-for-Profit
Enterprise   23

**International Perspectives: Managing in a Global
Competitive Economy**   24

Summary   25

Exercises   26

Case Exercise: Reducing Greenhouse Gases   27

Case Exercise: Reforming the Former Soviet
Economy   27

CHAPTER 2
Fundamental Economic Concepts   29

Chapter Preview   29

**Managerial Challenge: Revenue Management
at Delta Airlines**   30

Marginal Analysis   31

The Net Present Value Concept   34

Meaning and Measurement of Risk   38

**What Went Right/What Went Wrong: Long-Term
Capital Management (LTCM)**   43

The Relationship Between Risk and Return   46

Summary   48

Exercises   49

Case Exercise: The Toro Company and the
Probability of Snow   50

APPENDIX 2A
Differential Calculus Techniques in
Management   52

Relationship between Marginal Analysis and
Differential Calculus   52

**Managerial Challenge: A Skeleton in the Stealth
Bomber's Closet**   53

Applications of Differential Calculus to
Optimization Problems   60

Partial Differentiation and Multivariate
Optimization   64

Summary   66

Exercises   67

PART II

Demand and Forecasting   71

CHAPTER 3
Demand Analysis   72

Chapter Preview   72

**Managerial Challenge: Health-Care Reform and
Cigarette Taxes**   73

Demand Relationships: The Demand Schedule and
the Demand Curve   74

Demand Relationships: The Demand Function   76

Price Elasticity of Demand   81

CONTENTS

International Perspectives: Free Trade and the Price Elasticity of Demand: Nestlé Yogurt 97

Income Elasticity of Demand 98

Cross Elasticity of Demand 101

Other Demand Elasticity Measures 104

Combined Effect of Demand Elasticities 105

Summary 106

Exercises 107

Case Exercise: Polo Golf Shirt Pricing 115

APPENDIX 3A
Indifference Curve Analysis of Demand 116

Indifference Curves 116

Managerial Challenge: New Product Pricing at Motorola 117

Budget Lines 118

Graphical Determination of the Optimal Combination 119

Graphical Derivation of the Demand Function 120

Income and Substitution Effects 122

Algebraic Determination of the Optimal Combination 123

Exercises 125

Case Exercise: Value-In-Use of DVDs 126

CHAPTER 4
Estimation of Demand 127

Chapter Preview 127

Managerial Challenge: Demand for Public Transportation 128

Demand Estimation Using Marketing Research Techniques 128

Statistical Estimation of the Demand Function 131

What Went Right/What Went Wrong: Excess Fiber Optic Capacity at Global Crossing Inc. 135

Simple Linear Regression Model 136

Multiple Linear Regression Model 150

Summary 155

Exercises 156

Case Exercise: Demand Estimation 166

Case Exercise: Soft Drinks 168

APPENDIX 4A
Problems in Applying the Linear Regression Model 170

Introduction 170

Nonlinear Regression Models 180

Summary 182

Exercises 182

CHAPTER 5
Business and Economic Forecasting 186

Chapter Preview 186

Managerial Challenge: What Went Wrong? Demand for Sport Utility Vehicles at Ford Motor Co. 187

Significance of Forecasting 187

Selection of a Forecasting Technique 188

Alternative Forecasting Techniques 190

Deterministic Time-Series Analysis 190

Smoothing Techniques 198

Barometric Techniques 204

Survey and Opinion-Polling Techniques 207

Econometric Models 211

Stochastic Time-Series Analysis 216

Forecasting with Input-Output Tables 220

International Perspectives: Long-Term Sales Forecasting by General Motors in Overseas Markets 220

Summary 221

Exercises 222

Case Exercise: South Pole Ice Cream Company 229

Case Exercise: Cruise Ship Arrivals in Alaska 229

Case Exercise: Lumber Price Forecast 230

Case Exercise: Bush Recession Forecast 231

CHAPTER 6
Managing Exports 233

Chapter Preview 233

Managerial Challenge: Export Market Pricing at Toyota 234

Introduction 234

Import-Export Sales and Exchange Rates 235

CONTENTS

International Perspectives: Collapse of Export and Domestic Sales at Cummins Engine 238

The Market for U.S. Dollars as Foreign Exchange 239

Foreign Exchange Risk Management 243

International Perspectives: Toyota and Honda Buy U.S. Assembly Capacity 244

Determinants of Long-Run Trends in Exchange Rates 246

Purchasing Power Parity 251

What Went Right/What Went Wrong: Ford Motor Co. and Exide Batteries: Are Country Managers Here to Stay? 252

International Trade: A Managerial Perspective 260

Free Trade Areas: The European Union and NAFTA 270

Trade Deficits and the Balance of Payments 279

Summary 283

Exercises 285

Case Exercise: The Value of the U.S. Dollar, 1998, the Euro, 2000, and the U.S. Dollar, 2003 286

Case Exercise: U.S. Energy Policy, Oil Imports, and the Price of Gasoline 287

APPENDIX 6A
International Parity Conditions 289

Introduction 289

PART III
Production and Cost 293

CHAPTER 7
Production Economics 294

Chapter Preview 294

Managerial Challenge: What Went Wrong in California's Deregulation of Electricity? 295

The Production Function 296

Production Functions with One Variable Input 299

What Went Right/What Went Wrong: Boeing Assembly Plant 303

Determining the Optimal Use of the Variable Input 307

Production Functions with Two Variable Inputs 309

Determining the Optimal Combination of Inputs 313

Determining the Cost-Minimizing Production Process 317

What Went Right/What Went Wrong: How Exactly Have Computerization and Information Technology Lowered Costs at Chevron and Merck? 320

Returns to Scale 323

Summary 330

Exercises 331

Case Exercise: Production Function: Wilson Company 336

APPENDIX 7A
Maximization of Production Output Subject to a Cost Constraint 338

Exercise 339

APPENDIX 7B
Production Decisions and Linear Programming 340

Algebraic Formulation of the Constrained Output-Maximization Problem 340

Graphical Representation and Solution of the Output-Maximization Problem 341

Exercise 344

CHAPTER 8
Cost Analysis 345

Chapter Preview 345

Managerial Challenge: US Airways' Cost Structure 346

The Meaning and Measurement of Cost 347

Short-Run Cost Functions 351

Long-Run Cost Functions 359

Economies and Diseconomies of Scale 363

International Perspectives: How Japanese Companies Deal with the Problems of Size 367

Summary 369

Exercises 370

Case Exercise: Cost Analysis 376

CONTENTS

APPENDIX 8A

Long-Run Costs with a Cobb-Douglas Production Function — 378

Exercises — 380

CHAPTER 9

Applications of Cost Theory — 382

Chapter Preview — 382

Managerial Challenge: Product Costing and CAM-I and ABC — 383

Types of Cost Functions — 383

Short-Run Cost-Output Relationships — 384

What Went Right/What Went Wrong: Boeing: Rising Marginal Cost of 747s — 388

Long-Run Cost-Output Relationships — 391

Break-even Analysis versus Contribution Analysis — 397

Linear Break-even Analysis — 399

Summary — 409

Exercises — 410

Case Exercise: Cost Functions — 413

Case Exercise: Charter Airline Operating Decisions — 414

APPENDIX 9A

Mass Customization and the Learning Curve — 417

Learning Curve Relationship — 417

Estimating the Learning Curve Parameters — 419

The Percentage of Learning — 420

Exercise — 421

PART IV

Pricing and Output Decisions: Strategy and Tactics — 423

CHAPTER 10

Prices, Output, and Strategy: Pure and Monopolistic Competition — 424

Chapter Preview — 424

Managerial Challenge: Resurrecting Apple Computer? — 425

Introduction — 426

Competitive Strategy — 427

What Went Right/What Went Wrong: Xerox — 428

Porter's Five Forces Strategic Framework — 432

A Continuum of Market Structures — 442

Price-Output Determination Under Pure Competition — 445

Price-Output Determination Under Monopolistic Competition — 451

What Went Right/What Went Wrong: The Dynamics of Competition at Amazon.com — 452

Selling and Promotional Expenses — 455

Competitive Markets under Asymmetric Information — 458

Solutions to the Adverse Selection Problem — 463

Summary — 467

Exercises — 469

Case Exercise: Apple Computer — 475

Case Exercise: Saving Sony Music — 475

CHAPTER 11

Price and Output Determination: Monopoly and Dominant Firms — 476

Chapter Preview — 476

Managerial Challenge: Dominant Microprocessor Company Lagging Behind Next Trend — 477

Monopoly Defined — 478

Sources of Market Power for a Monopolist — 478

What Went Right/What Went Wrong: Pilot Error at Palm — 483

Price and Output Determination for a Monopolist — 484

Optimal Markup, Contribution Margin, and the Contribution Margin Percentage — 487

Regulated Monopolies — 492

What Went Right/What Went Wrong: Public Service Company of New Mexico — 494

The Economic Rationale for Regulation — 495

Summary — 498

Exercises — 499

Case Exercise: Differential Pricing of Pharmaceuticals: The HIV/AIDS Crisis — 503

CONTENTS

CHAPTER 12

Price and Output Determination: Oligopoly **505**

Chapter Preview 505

Managerial Challenge: Are Nokia's Margins on Cell Phones Collapsing? 506

Oligopolistic Market Structures 507

Interdependencies in Oligopolistic Industries 510

Ignoring Interdependencies 512

Cartels and Other Forms of Collusion 513

International Perspectives: The Organization of Petroleum Exporting Countries (OPEC) Cartel 523

Price Leadership 524

The Kinked Demand Curve Model 529

Avoiding Price Wars 530

What Went Right/What Went Wrong: Good-Better-Best Product Strategy at Kodak 532

Oligopolistic Rivalry and Game Theory 535

Summary 542

Exercises 543

Case Exercise: Cell Phones Displace Mobile Phone Satellite Networks 546

CHAPTER 13

Game-Theoretic Rivalry: Best-Practice Tactics **547**

Chapter Preview 547

Managerial Challenge: Price Differentials in Computers: IBM, Compaq, and Dell 548

Business Strategy Games 548

Business Rivalry as a Sequential Game 555

Credible Threats and Commitments 558

Entry Deterrence and Accommodation 567

Simultaneous Games 576

Escape from Prisoner's Dilemma 580

Summary 591

Exercises 593

International Perspectives: Case Exercise: Superjumbo Dilemma 596

APPENDIX 13A

Capacity Planning and Pricing Against a Low-Cost Competitor: A Case Study of Piedmont Airlines and People Express **597**

Airline Entry Strategy 597

Large-Scale Accommodation 598

Exercises 600

CHAPTER 14

Pricing Techniques and Analysis **601**

Chapter Preview 601

Managerial Challenge: Pricing of Apple Computers: Market Share Versus Current Profitability 602

Conceptual Framework for Proactive, Systematic-Analytical, Value-Based Pricing 602

Intertemporal Pricing in Target Market Segments 603

Price Discrimination 606

What Went Right/What Went Wrong: $19.95 for "Unlimited Access" at America Online 609

Optimal Discriminating Price Levels 613

Mathematics of Price Discrimination 615

Pricing of Multiple Products 620

Pricing in Practice 623

Other Pricing Strategies 628

Summary 632

Exercises 633

APPENDIX 14A

Revenue Management **638**

The Concept of Revenue Management 638

Revenue Management Decisions 643

Summary 651

Exercises 652

APPENDIX 14B

Pricing of Joint Products and Transfer Pricing **653**

Joint Products in Fixed Proportions 653

Joint Products in Variable Proportions 655

Transfer Pricing 657

CONTENTS

International Perspectives: Transfer Pricing, Taxes, and Ethics 665

Summary 666

Exercises 666

Case Exercise: Transfer Pricing 668

PART V

Organizational Architecture and Institutional Economics 671

CHAPTER 15

Contracting, Governance, and Organizational Form 672

Chapter Preview 672

Managerial Challenge: Controlling the Vertical: Ultimate TV 673

Introduction 674

The Role of Contracting in Cooperative Games 674

Corporate Governance and the Problem of Moral Hazard 682

What Went Right/What Went Wrong: Moral Hazard and Holdup at Enron and Worldcom 685

The Principal-Agent Model 685

What Went Right/What Went Wrong: Why Have Restricted Stock Grants Replaced Executive Stock Options at Microsoft? 694

Choice of Efficient Organizational Form 694

International Perspectives: Economies of Scale and International Joint Ventures in Chip Making 697

What Went Right/What Went Wrong: Cable Allies Refuse to Adopt Microsoft's WebTV as an Industry Standard 698

Vertical Integration 699

What Went Right/What Went Wrong: Dell Replaces Vertical Integration with Virtual Integration 702

Licensing, Patents, and Trade Secrets 702

What Went Right/What Went Wrong: Technology Licenses Cost Palm Its Lead in PDAs 704

What Went Right/What Went Wrong: Motorola: What They Didn't Know Hurt Them 706

Summary 707

Exercises 708

Case Exercise: Borders Books and Amazon.com Decide to Do Business Together? 710

Case Exercise: Designing a Managerial Incentive Contract 710

Library Exercise: Vertical Integration at GM-Fisher Body 711

CHAPTER 16

Optimal Mechanism Design 712

Chapter Preview 712

Managerial Challenge: Fidelity/W. R. Hambrecht Open Dutch Auction for IPOs 713

The Concept of an Optimal Mechanism Design 714

Optimal Queue Service Rules 717

Auction Design and Information Economics 719

Incentive-Compatible Revelation Mechanisms 735

International Perspectives: Joint Venture in Memory Chips: IBM, Siemens, and Toshiba 740

International Perspectives: Whirlpool's Joint Venture in Appliances Improves Upon Maytag's Outright Purchase of Hoover 742

Summary 743

Exercises 745

Case Exercise: Spectrum Auction 746

Case Exercise: Division of Investment Banking Fees 747

Case Exercise: Debugging Computer Software: Intel 747

APPENDIX 16A

Externalities 749

Externalities and Bargaining 749

Other Solutions to the Externality Problem 754

Externalities and Urban Renewal 757

Summary 759

Exercises 759

CHAPTER 17

Government Regulation 762

Chapter Preview 762

Managerial Challenge: Deregulation and the Coase Theorem 763

CONTENTS

Market Structure, Conduct, and Performance	764
Antitrust Regulation Statutes and Their Enforcement	771
Antitrust Prohibition of Selected Business Decisions	774
Command and Control Regulatory Constraints: An Economic Analysis	778
Governmental Protection of Business	784
What Went Right/What Went Wrong: Aventis	785
International Perspectives: The U.S. Sugar Import Quota	786
Summary	788
Exercises	789
Case Exercise: Price Fixing of Auction House Commissions	794
Case Exercise: Microsoft Tying Arrangements	794
Case Exercise: Music Recording Industry Blocked from Consolidating	794

PART VI

Long-Term Investment Decisions and Risk Management 797

CHAPTER 18

Long-Term Investment Analysis 798

Chapter Preview	798
Managerial Challenge: What Went Right? What Went Wrong? Are Fat Margins About to Plummet at Nokia?	799
The Nature of Capital Expenditure Decisions	800
A Basic Framework for Capital Budgeting	800
The Capital Budgeting Process	802
Estimating the Firm's Cost of Capital	810

Cost-Benefit Analysis	817
Steps in Cost-Benefit Analysis	819
Objectives and Constraints in Cost-Benefit Analysis	820
Analysis and Valuation of Benefits and Costs	822
The Appropriate Rate of Discount	825
Cost-Effectiveness Analysis	827
Summary	829
Exercises	830
Case Exercise: Cost-Benefit Analysis	836
Case Exercise: Industrial Development Tax Relief and Incentives	838

CHAPTER 19

Decisions Under Risk and Uncertainty 839

Chapter Preview	839
Managerial Challenge: Multigenerational Effects of Ozone Depletion and Greenhouse Gases	840
Risk and Decision Analysis	841
Decision Making under Uncertainty	855
Managing Risk and Uncertainty	857
What Went Right/What Went Wrong: Conglomerate Diversification Misapplied: Gillette	861
Summary	865
Exercises	865

Appendix A: The Time Value of Money	**A-1**
Appendix B: Tables	**B-1**
Check Answers to Selected End-of-Chapter Exercises	**C-1**
Index	**I-1**

Managerial economics is concerned with resource-allocation, strategic, and tactical decisions that are made by analysts, managers, and consultants in the private, public, and not-for-profit sectors of the economy. Managerial economic techniques seek to achieve the objectives of the organization in the most efficient manner, while considering both explicit and implicit constraints.

The book is organized around the twin themes of product-line rivalry and shareholder wealth maximization, and the major emphasis is on analytical tools and managerial insights.

PEDAGOGICAL APPROACH: THEORY-IN-CONTEXT

Managerial Economics is an applied branch of microeconomics. Along a continuum of pedagogical methods from abstract theory lecturing at one extreme to pure case teaching at the other, our theory-in-context approach fits squarely in the middle. Conceptual frameworks based on microeconomic theory provide the ever-present skeletal backbone of discipline-specific knowledge. But because of our emphasis on real-world business applications, new economic theory in this text is always motivated first with a deep fact-situation context.

Teaching potential managers with this approach is far preferable to teaching either applications alone or theory alone. Theory-in-context not only stimulates student interest at the inception of the learning process, but also promotes mastery of challenging analytical tools and facilitates the acquisition of complex managerial insights. Perhaps most importantly, theory-in-context empowers students to spot analogous real-world situations and apply appropriate tools and insights outside of the classroom and beyond the final exam.

Real-world management decision problems seldom have simple, uniquely correct answers that apply to all future contingencies. To convey some of this complexity, we have incorporated a feature entitled *What Went Right/What Went Wrong* at a variety of companies. Also, we continue to motivate the topics in each chapter with a *Managerial Challenge* taken from the business press or our own management consulting experience. The individual topics within chapters are then illustrated with 300 real-world applications, in-depth examples, or case exercises. We have deliberately doubled the number of such applications, examples, and exercises relative to other books while retaining a focus on rigorous analytical tools. We believe this theory-in-context approach elicits the students' commitment to the lifelong learning required for best-practices management throughout their careers. An appreciation for best practices, the application of careful analysis, and a healthy dose of managerial insight provide the winning formula for students who can make a difference as employees and managers.

COURSE CONTENT

Our surveys of adopters in a wide variety of universities and degree programs suggest a great diversity in uses for the book. The very broad topical coverage is intended to give instructors a great deal of flexibility in designing a course suited to the needs of their students.

NEW TO THIS EDITION

The tenth edition has been heavily revised and updated to streamline the presentation, to provide additional contemporary applications, and to enhance student learning. Many new topics and a new part have been added to reflect recent developments especially in the field of organizational architecture. The changes include the following:

Part I: Introduction

Chapter 1—Introduction and Goals of the Firm

This chapter includes expanded discussions on:

- incomplete markets in pollution byproducts
- asymmetric information
- recontracting costs as caveats to maximizing shareholder value

Chapter 2—Fundamental Economic Concepts

This chapter has been shortened by 16 pages, and the material on risk and decision analysis has been moved to a chapter that appeared in earlier editions titled, "Decisions Under Risk and Uncertainty," which we've restored to this edition as Chapter 19. In addition, some of the material from former Web Chapter A in the previous edition has been moved to a new appendix in Chapter 2 titled, "Differential Calculus Techniques in Management."

Part II: Demand and Forecasting

Chapter 4—Estimation of Demand

This chapter has been shortened by 11 pages. The material on problems in applying the linear regression model (autocorrelation, heteroskedasticity, specification and measurement errors, multicollinearity, and simultaneous relationships) has been moved to Appendix 4A. New applications in this chapter include:

- fiber optic capacity
- estimating demand for new automobiles

Chapter 6—Managing Exports

This chapter has been updated extensively. New applications include:

- country managers
- hedging
- purchasing power parity
- steel tariffs
- euro optimal currency area
- price differentials across Europe
- parallel importing

Part III: Production and Cost

Chapter 7—Production Economics

The material on statistical estimation of production functions has been condensed and the chapter shortened by 5 pages. New applications include:

- California's energy crisis
- increasing returns in information-economy businesses
- lean production techniques at Boeing's assembly plants

Part IV: Pricing and Output Decisions: Strategy and Tactics

Chapter 10—Prices, Output, and Strategy: Pure and Monopolistic Competition

This chapter contains a new section on competitive strategy (components of a business model and generic types of strategy), and an expanded discussion on the dynamics of adjustment in a competitive industry. Additionally, the first one-third of Chapter 11 in the ninth edition (on asymmetric information and a game theoretic analysis of competitive equilibrium in a lemons market) has been moved to the end of this chapter to consolidate all of the material on the analysis of cost curves in competitive environments. The chapter also includes the following new applications:

- Xerox's closed architecture
- Rawlings' product differentiation
- Dell's cost leadership
- 7–Eleven Japan

Chapter 11—Price and Output Determination: Monopoly and Dominant Firms

The regulated monopoly material has been moved to Chapter 17, "Government Regulation." The following new material is featured in Chapter 11:

- an expanded discussion of network effects and declining costs in computer components (external economies of scale)
- new case exercise on pharmaceutical pricing across nations

Chapter 12—Price and Output Determination: Oligopoly

New applications include:

- Nokia's cell phone margins
- Hewlett-Packard's dominance in the printer market
- cartels and major league baseball
- barometric firm price leadership in the airline industry
- the unsuccessful launch of Motorola's Iridium worldwide wireless phone

Chapter 13—Game-Theoretic Rivalry: Best-Practice Tactics

The new sections in this chapter include:

- new applications to model upgrades (the practice of versioning)
- fractional ownership and the tactical advantages of leasing
- brinksmanship and wars of attrition
- case exercise on building superjumbo airliners

Chapter 14—Pricing Techniques and Analysis

This chapter has been entirely rewritten and has been shortened 14 pages by moving the material on joint products and transfer pricing to new Appendix 14B. The chapter includes the following:

- new material on bundling
- new material on differential retail pricing
- new material on product life cycle pricing
- new material on the pricing of online products

Part V (new): Organizational Architecture and Institutional Economics

Chapter 15—Contracting, Governance, and Organizational Form
This new chapter includes the following discussions:

- the role of contracting in manufacturer-distributor and other cooperative games
- other functions of commercial contract
- governance mechanisms and the problem of moral hazard
- contract renewals and the hold-up problem
- the principal-agent model
- screening and sorting managerial talent with performance-based contracts
- choosing an efficient organizational form
- vertical integration
- licensing, patents, and trade secrets
- case exercise on designing a performance-based executive compensation contract

Chapter 16—Optimal Mechanism Design
This new chapter includes the following discussions:

- mechanism design
- auction design and information economics
- information revelation in common-value auctions
- the winner's curse in private-value auctions
- strategic underbidding and the second-highest sealed bid auction
- revenue equivalence of auction types
- incentive compatible revelation mechanisms
- cost revelation in joint ventures and partnerships
- optimal incentives contracts
- implementation of IC contracts
- case exercise on investment banking fees
- case exercise on spectrum auction design

Chapter 17—Government Regulation
This chapter has been thoroughly updated. Among the new topics and updated discussions are:

- the contestability of airline markets
- the federal government's case against Microsoft
- import beer competition in Mexico
- the settlement of California's class action suit against Microsoft
- 1997 merger guidelines
- the consolidation merger denials in satellite TV
- air pollution attainment restrictions on business growth

Part VI: Long-Term Investment Decisions and Risk Management

Chapter 19: Decisions Under Risk and Uncertainty

The revision of this chapter, which appeared in previous editions, includes the following new material:

- hybrid utility functions and prospect theory
- framing effects and full-line forcing
- disability insurance and utility theory

ORGANIZATION OF THE TEXT

Part I of the book provides an overview of managerial economics, establishes shareholder wealth, and introduces the fundamental economic concepts of marginal analysis, net present value, risk, and decision analysis. Part II examines the areas of demand analysis and forecasting techniques in domestic and export markets. A unique feature of the book is an extensive chapter on international business economics, import/export trade, and an introduction to international finance. Part III deals with production and cost analysis, including linear programming concepts for the production process choices that characterize real-world operations management. Part IV focuses on price determination and capacity choice in theory and practice. The strategic framework of Michael Porter and the new tactical insights from sequential business games are highlighted. The unique features here include more extensive material on applied game theory than in other managerial economics books and an extensive treatment of yield management in an appendix to the chapter on pricing. Part V includes coverage of organization architecture including corporate governance, choice of organization form, and optimal mechanism design. The chapter on economic regulation includes an extensive discussion of externalities and optimal abatement. Part IV addresses capital budgeting, cost-benefit analysis, and decision-making under risk.

Although the primary focus of the book is on private sector management, the text is written with the recognition that many students of economics and business management pursue careers in the public and not-for-profit sectors of the economy. Consequently, we have included a discussion of the philosophy of public involvement in the economy, the objective of public and not-for-profit organizations, and coverage of specific analytical tools that are of use in these sectors.

STUDENT PREPARATION

The text is designed for use by upper-level undergraduates and first-level graduate students in departments of economics, schools of business management, public administration, and information technology. Students are presumed to have a background in the basic principles of economics. Prior course work in statistics and quantitative methods is desirable but not essential because all of the concepts employed in the text or Web chapter are fully developed within the text. The book makes occasional use of elementary concepts of differential calculus after a review of these basic concepts. However, in all cases where calculus is employed, one or more alternative approaches, such as graphical, algebraic, or tabular analysis, are also presented. Spreadsheet applications have become so prominent in the practice of managerial economics that we now explain many concepts of optimization in this context.

PEDAGOGICAL FEATURES OF THE TENTH EDITION

The tenth edition of *Managerial Economics* makes extensive use of pedagogical learning aids to enhance student learning. The key features of the book are:

1. **Part Openers.** Each major section of the book opens with a brief discussion of the material contained in the following chapters. The relationship of the material in the section to the goal of shareholder wealth maximization and efficient resource allocation is illustrated with a schematic diagram appearing on the first page of each part opener.

2. **Managerial Challenges.** Each chapter opens with a Managerial Challenge illustrating a real-life economic analysis problem faced by managers that is related to the material to be covered in the chapter. Many of these challenges have been updated with more contemporary illustrations.

3. **What Went Right/What Went Wrong.** Most chapters contain a What Went Right/What Went Wrong feature that allows students to relate real-world business decisions to what they have learned, and to show how management decisions can have positive and negative outcomes.

4. **Chapter Glossaries.** In the margins of the text, new terms are defined as they are introduced. The placement of the glossary terms next to the location where the term is first used reinforces the importance of these new concepts and aids in later studying.

5. **Chapter Preview.** Each chapter begins with a Chapter Preview that briefly summarizes the major issues that are covered in the chapter.

6. **International Perspectives.** Throughout the book, special International Perspectives sections are provided that illustrate the application of managerial economics concepts to problems faced by managers in an increasingly global economy.

7. **Extensive Use of Examples.** More than 300 real-world applications and examples derived from actual practice are provided and highlighted throughout the text. These examples help the tools and concepts to come alive and thereby enhance student learning. They are listed on the inside front and back covers to highlight the prominence of this feature of the book.

8. **Point-by-Point Summaries.** Each chapter ends with a detailed, point-by-point summary of important concepts from the chapter.

9. **Diversity of Presentation Approaches.** Important analytical concepts are presented in several different ways, including tabular analysis, graphical analysis, and algebraic analysis. When elementary differential calculus is used, at least one alternative mode of analysis also is presented for the student.

10. **Exercises.** Each chapter contains a large problem analysis set. Check answers to selected problems color coded in blue boldface type are provided at the end of the text. Problems that can be solved using Excel are highlighted with an Excel icon.

11. **Short Case Exercises.** Many chapters include short case problems that extend the concepts and tools developed in the text.

12. **Internet Margin Notes.** Internet addresses in the margins tie applications and examples to the sites of companies being discussed or to other relevant sites. Students gain not only the additional information and data found at the sites, but also the experience of using the Web to find financial and economic information.

13. **Internet Exercises.** Exercises at the ends of most chapters provide further practice on the Internet by having students apply information and/or data from the Web sites to a problem or question posed in the exercise.

ANCILLARY MATERIALS

A complete set of ancillary materials is available to adopters to supplement the text, including the following:

- The textbook Support Web site is at http://mcguigan.swlearning.com. The Web chapter, "Linear Programming Applications," is available at this site. The *Managerial Economics* Web site also provides instructor resources, student resources like online quizzing, Internet application links and updates, and a Talk-to-the-Author link.

- The Economic Applications Web site (http://econapps.swlearning.com) includes South-Western's dynamic Web features: EconNews, EconDebate, and EconData Online. Organized by pertinent economic topics, and searchable by topic or feature, these Web features are easy to integrate into the classroom. EconNews, EconDebate, and EconData all deepen your understanding of theoretical concepts through hands-on exploration and analysis for the latest economic news stories, policy debates, and data. These features are updated on a regular basis. The Economic Applications Web site is complimentary to every new book buyer via an access card packaged with the book. Used book buyers can purchase access at the site.

- An *Instructor's Manual* and *Test Bank*, prepared by the authors, contain suggested answers to the end-of-chapter exercises and cases. The authors have taken great care to provide an error-free manual for instructors to use. The manual is available both in a hard copy form and on the Web site (http://mcguigan.swlearning.com) in MS Word to make it easy for instructors to provide portions of these solutions to students, if they desire. The Test Bank, containing a large collection of true-false, multiple choice, and numerical problems, is available to adopters. The Test Bank is also available on the Web site.

- *ExamView* software for the Test Bank is available to simplify the preparation of quizzes and exams. *ExamView* contains all of the questions in the printed test bank and is an easy-to-use test creation software compatible with Microsoft Windows. Instructors can add or edit questions, instructions, and answers, and select questions by previewing them on the screen; selecting them randomly, or selecting them by number. Instructors can also create and administer quizzes online, whether over the Internet, a local area network (LAN), or a wide area network (WAN).

- A revised and updated *Study Guide,* prepared by Professor Richard D. Marcus at the University of Wisconsin-Milwaukee, is available for purchase by students. The Study Guide provides valuable assistance to students when they are reviewing and applying the material presented in the text.

- Two *PowerPoint Presentation* packages are available for the student as a study aid, and for the instructor as a lecture aid. One package, prepared by Richard D. Marcus at the University of Wisconsin-Milwaukee, provides lecture aids covering many of the most important topics from the text. These slides can be customized by instructors to meet their specific course needs. The second PowerPoint package consists of key tables and figures from the book.

- *Excel for Economics* is an interactive spreadsheet package, created by Thomas Palm, Professor Emeritus, Portland State University. *Excel for Economics* lifts static, printed textbook models, equations, and graphs, and changes them to dynamic spreadsheets. Users can enter numerical values and change them at will in *what-if* entries that simulate managerial decision-making. Multiple linked spreadsheets can be used simultaneously, and calculations and graphing are done automatically to allow the student to focus on the meanings, implications, and applicability of the decisions.

ACKNOWLEDGMENTS

A number of reviewers, users, and colleagues have been particularly helpful in providing us with many worthwhile comments and suggestions at various stages in the development of this and earlier editions of the book. Included among these individuals are:

William Beranek, J. Walter Elliott, William J. Kretlow, William Gunther, J. William Hanlon, Robert Knapp, Robert S. Main, Edward Sussna, Bruce T. Allen, Allen Moran, Edward Oppermann, Dwight Porter, Robert L. Conn, Allen Parkman, Daniel Slate, Richard L. Pfister, J.P. Magaddino, Richard A. Stanford, Donald Bumpass, Barry P. Keating, John Wittman, Sisay Asefa, James R. Ashley, David Bunting, Amy H. Dalton, Richard D. Evans, Gordon V. Karels, Richard S. Bower, Massoud M. Saghafi, John C. Callahan, Frank Falero, Ramon Rabinovitch, D. Steinnes, Jay Damon Hobson, Clifford Fry, John Crockett, Marvin Frankel, James T. Peach, Paul Kozlowski, Dennis Fixler, Steven Crane, Scott L. Smith, Edward Miller, Fred Kolb, Bill Carson, Jack W. Thornton, Changhee Chae, Robert B. Dallin, Christopher J. Zappe, Anthony V. Popp, Phillip M. Sisneros, George Brower, Carlos Sevilla, Dean Baim, Charles Callahan, Phillip Robins, Bruce Jaffee, Alwyn du Plessis, Darly Winn, Gary Shoesmith, Richard J. Ward, William H. Hoyt, Irvin Grossack, William Simeone, Satyajit Ghosh, David Levy, Audie Brewton, Simon Hakim, Patricia Sanderson, David P. Ely, Albert A. O'Kunade, Doug Sharp, Arne Dag Sti, Walker Davidson, David Buschena, George M. Radakovic, Harpal S. Grewal, Stephen J. Silver, Michael J. O'Hara, Luke M. Froeb, Dean Waters, Jake Vogelsang, Lynda Y. de la Viña, Audie R. Brewton, Paul M. Hayashi, Richard D. Marcus, and Lawrence B. Pulley, Tim Mages, and Paul M. Hayashi, Robert Brooker, Richard D. Evans, Carl Emomoto, William Simeone, Charles Leathers, and Marshall Medoff.

People who were especially helpful in the preparation of the tenth edition include Gary Brester, Stephan Gohmann, L. Joe Moffitt, Satyajit Ghosh, Christopher Erickson, Antoine El Khoury, and Steven Rock.

We are also indebted to Richard D. Marcus, Bob Hebert, Sarah E. Harris, and Wake Forest University for the support they provided and owe thanks to our faculty colleagues for the encouragement and assistance provided on a continuing basis during the preparation of the manuscript. We wish to express our appreciation to the members of the South-Western/Thomson Learning staff—particularly, Lisa Lysne, Amy Ray, Chris Hudson, and Michael Worls—for their help in the preparation and promotion of this book. We also wish to express our appreciation for the sound advice and extensive assistance of settingPace during the production of the text. Most of all we would like to thank our editor, Susanna Smart, who is a constant source of excellent advice and encouragement. Susan's high standards of performance and her total knowledge of the publishing field have helped immensely with this project.

We are grateful to the Literary Executor of the late Sir Ronald A. Fisher, F.R.S.; to Dr. Frank Yates, F.R.S.; and to Longman Group, Ltd., London, for permission to reprint Table III from their book *Statistical Tables for Biological, Agricultural, and Medical Research* (6th ed., 1974).

James R. McGuigan
R. Charles Moyer
Frederick H. deB. Harris

James R. McGuigan

James R. McGuigan owns and operates his own numismatic investment firm. Prior to this activity, he was Associate Professor of Finance and Business Economics in the School of Business Administration at Wayne State University. He also taught at the University of Pittsburgh.

McGuigan received his undergraduate degree from Carnegie-Mellon University. He earned an M.B.A. at the Graduate School of Business at the University of Chicago, and his Ph.D. from the University of Pittsburgh.

In addition to his interests in economics, he has co-authored books in financial management, including *Contemporary Financial Management,* with R. Charles Moyer. His research articles on options have been published in the *Journal of Financial and Quantitative Analysis.*

R. Charles Moyer

R. Charles Moyer is Dean Emeritus, and holds the GMAC Insurance Chair in Finance, at the Babcock Graduate School of Management, Wake Forest University. Previously, he was Professor of Finance and Chairman of the Department of Finance at Texas Tech University. Professor Moyer has also taught at the University of Houston, Lehigh University, and the University of New Mexico, and spent a year at the Federal Reserve Bank of Cleveland.

Moyer earned his B.A. in Economics from Howard University, and his M.B.A. and Ph.D. in Finance and Managerial Economics from the University of Pittsburgh.

In addition to this text, Moyer has also co-authored *Contemporary Financial Management,* and *Financial Management with Lotus 1-2-3.* He has been published in many leading journals, including *Financial Management, Journal of Financial and Quantitative Analysis, Journal of Finance, Financial Review, Journal of Financial Research, International Journal of Forecasting,* and many others.

Frederick H. deB. Harris

Frederick H. deB. Harris is the John B. McKinnon Professor of Managerial Economics and Finance at the Babcock Graduate School of Management, Wake Forest University. His specialties are pricing tactics and capacity planning. Professor Harris has taught managerial economics courses in three business schools in the U.S. and Europe. He holds a B.A. in Economics from Dartmouth College and a Ph.D. in Financial Economics from the University of Virginia.

Professor Harris has published widely in financial and economics journals including the *Review of Economics and Statistics, Journal of Financial and Quantitative Analysis, Journal of Financial Markets,* and *Journal of Industrial Economics.* From 1988–1993, he served on the Board of Associate Editors of the *Journal of Industrial Economics.* In addition, Professor Harris often benchmarks the revenue management functions of large companies and writes about his findings in management practice journals like *Marketing Management* and the *Journal of Operations Management.*

Awards and recognitions include several awards for "Best Academic Publication of the Year," Babcock School Professor of the Year, and Most Popular Courses designations. Additionally, *Inc.* Magazine (2000) and *Business Week's Guide to the Best Business Schools* (1997–2003) identify Professor Harris as among Outstanding Faculty.

I
Introduction

ECONOMIC ANALYSIS AND DECISIONS

1. Demand Analysis and Forecasting
2. Production and Cost Analysis
3. Pricing Analysis
4. Capital Expenditure Analysis

ECONOMIC, POLITICAL, AND SOCIAL ENVIRONMENT

1. Business Conditions (Trends, Cycles, and Seasonal Effects)
2. Factor Market Conditions (Capital, Labor, Land, and Raw Materials)
3. Competitors' Responses
4. External, Legal, and Regulatory Constraints
5. Organizational (Internal) Constraints

Cash Flows

Risk

Firm Value (Shareholders' Wealth)

Part I (Introduction) presents an overview of managerial economics analysis and introduces some key economic concepts and tools. In the first chapter, the goals of the enterprise (both the for-profit firm and the not-for-profit organization) are developed; the decision-making process and the philosophy of optimization are introduced; the role of profit is discussed; and the relationship between managerial economics techniques and accounting, finance, marketing, operations management, and labor relations are highlighted. Chapter 2 reviews fundamental economic concepts, including marginal analysis, net present value, risk versus return analysis, and the measurement of risk. Appendix 2A provides a self-contained introduction to optimization and constrained optimization techniques, including applications of basic calculus. Linear programming applications appear later, to support the discussion of production and cost.

1

Introduction and Goals of the Firm

CHAPTER PREVIEW Managerial economics is the application of microeconomic theory and methodology to decision-making problems faced by private, public, and not-for-profit institutions. Managerial economics assists decision makers (managers) in efficiently allocating scarce resources, planning corporate strategy, and executing effective tactics. Economic profit is defined and the role of profits in allocating resources in a free enterprise system is examined. The primary normative goal of the firm, namely, shareholder wealth maximization, is developed along with a discussion of how managerial decisions influence shareholder wealth. Next, the problems associated with the separation of ownership and control and agency relationships in large corporations are explored. Finally, appropriate normative goals to guide resource-allocation decisions in public sector and not-for-profit enterprises are discussed.

MANAGERIAL CHALLENGE

Executive Performance Bonus Plan: Salomon Smith Barney[1]

Separation of ownership (shareholders) and control (management) in large corporations permits managers to pursue goals, such as maximization of their own personal welfare, that are not always in the long-term interests of shareholders. As the result of pressure from large institutional shareholders and recent tax law changes,[2] a growing number of corporations are seeking to forge a closer alliance between the interests of shareholders and managers by structuring compensation plans that have a larger proportion of the manager's compensation in the form of performance-based bonuses.

One such plan, devised by Salomon Brothers, the investment banking predecessor of Salomon Smith Barney, paid the chairman, Deryck C. Maughan, an annual base salary of $1 million plus an annual performance bonus of up to $24 million. This bonus was based on Salomon's overall rate of return on equity and its rate of return *relative* to the firm's five major competitors.[3] The following table shows the possible performance bonuses that the chairman could earn. For example, if Salomon's annual return on equity was 5 percent, and was not different from the average rate of return of the

Annual bonus, in millions of dollars

Salomon Brothers' return on equity minus the average of five competitors						
+10	$1	$2.5	$7	$12	$17	$24
+5	$0.5	$2	$6	$9	$12	$17
0	$0	$1.5	$5	$7	$9	$12
−5	$0	$1	$4	$6	$8	$10
−10	$0	$0.5	$3	$4	$5	$7
	5%	10%	15%	20%	25%	30%

Salomon Brothers' return on equity

Source: Salomon Brothers Inc. proxy statements, U.S. Securities and Exchange Commission

MANAGERIAL CHALLENGE

five rival investment banking firms, then the Salomon chairman would earn no performance bonus. On the other hand, the payment of the maximum $24 million bonus would require the firm to have a very extraordinary year—Salomon's return on equity would have to be 30 percent (or more), and this rate of return would have to be 10 (or more) percentage points above the average of its five major competitors.

The objectives of the firm and how to motivate managers to pursue these objectives are some of the topics discussed in this chapter.

http://

You can access financial information as well as the annual report for Salomon Smith Barney on the Internet at http://www.smithbarney.com/career_center/our_company

---

[1] Michael Siconofli, "Salomon's Chief Stands to Hit the Jackpot," *Wall Street Journal*, May 5, 1994, p. C1.

[2] Changes in the tax laws (1993) bar publicly held corporations from deducting (in computing taxable income) compensation of more than $1 million for each of its top executives, unless it is based on performance goals approved by shareholders.

[3] These competitors are Merrill Lynch, Morgan Stanley, Bear Sterns, J. P. Morgan, and Bankers Trust.

WHAT IS MANAGERIAL ECONOMICS?

Managerial economics deals with the application of microeconomic reasoning to real-world decision-making problems faced by private, public, and not-for-profit institutions. Managerial economics extracts from microeconomic theory those concepts and techniques that enable a decision maker to select strategic direction, to allocate efficiently the resources of the organization, and to respond effectively to tactical issues. That is, all managers seek to do the following:

> To identify the alternative means of achieving given objective(s), and then to select the alternative that accomplishes the objective(s) in the most resource efficient manner, taking into account the constraints and the likely actions and reactions of interdependent rival decision makers.

For example, consider the following stylized decision problem:

DECISION PROBLEM: CAPACITY EXPANSION AT HONDA AND TOYOTA MOTORS

Example

http://

Learn more about Toyota's operations by accessing their website at http://www.toyota.com/about/operations

To reduce the trade imbalance between Japan and the U.S. and purchase foreign assets while the yen remains strong in the currency markets, Honda North America and Toyota Motors wish to expand their already substantial assembly operations in the United States. Both companies face increasing demand for their U.S.-manufactured vehicles, especially the Toyota Camry and the Honda Accord. Camrys and Accords rate extremely high in consumer reports of durability and reliability, and the demand for used Accords is so strong that they depreciate only 38 percent in their first four years. Other competing vehicles may depreciate as much as 65 percent in the same period. Toyota and Honda have identified two possible strategies (S1 and S2) to meet the growing demand for Camrys and Accords. Strategy S1 represents an internal expansion of capacity at Toyota's Princeton, Indiana, plant and Honda's Marysville,

Ohio, plant. Strategy S2 represents the purchase of a surplus plant now owned by General Motors. The objective of Toyota's and Honda's managers is to maximize the value today (present value) of expected future returns (profit) from the capacity expansion. This problem can be summarized as follows:

Objective function: Maximize (present value) profit (S1, S2)

In this example, the following decision rule can be created:

Decision rule: Choose strategy S1 if Profit (S1) > Profit (S2)

Choose strategy S2 if Profit (S1) < Profit (S2)

MANAGERIAL ECONOMICS AND ECONOMIC THEORY

As in the simple example given above, most decisions made by managers usually involve questions of resource allocation within the organization in both the short and the long run. In the short run, a manager may be interested in estimating demand and cost relationships to make decisions about the price to charge for a product and the quantity of output to produce. The areas of microeconomics dealing with demand theory and with the theory of cost and production are obviously useful in making decisions on such matters. Macroeconomic theory also enters into decision making when a manager attempts to forecast future demand based on forces influencing the overall economy.

In the long run, decisions must be made about expanding or contracting production and distribution facilities, developing and marketing new products, and possibly acquiring other firms. Basically, these decisions require the organization to make capital expenditures; that is, expenditures made in the current period that are expected to yield returns in future periods. Economists have developed a theory of capital budgeting that can be used in deciding whether to undertake specific capital expenditures.

THE DECISION-MAKING MODEL

The ability to make good decisions is the key to successful managerial performance. All decision making shares several common elements. First, the decision maker must establish or identify the objectives of the organization. The failure to identify organizational objectives correctly can result in the complete rejection of an otherwise well-conceived and well-implemented plan. Later sections of this chapter deal with the objectives of the capitalist publicly-owned firm.

Next, the decision maker must identify the problem requiring a solution. For example, the manager of a brewing plant in Milwaukee may note that the plant's profit margin on sales has been decreasing. This could be caused by pricing errors, labor force problems, or the use of outdated production equipment. Once the source or sources of the problem are identified, the manager can move to an examination of potential solutions. If the problem is the use of technologically inefficient equipment, two possible solutions are (1) updating and replacing the plant's equipment or (2) building a completely new plant. The choice between these alternatives depends on the relative costs and benefits, as well as other organizational and societal constraints that may make one alternative preferable to another. For example, the decision to build a new brewery in a suburban area may face opposition by community activists, whereas locating in an industrial park may garner property tax relief and free road and sewer infrastructure.

Figure 1.1   The Decision-Making Process

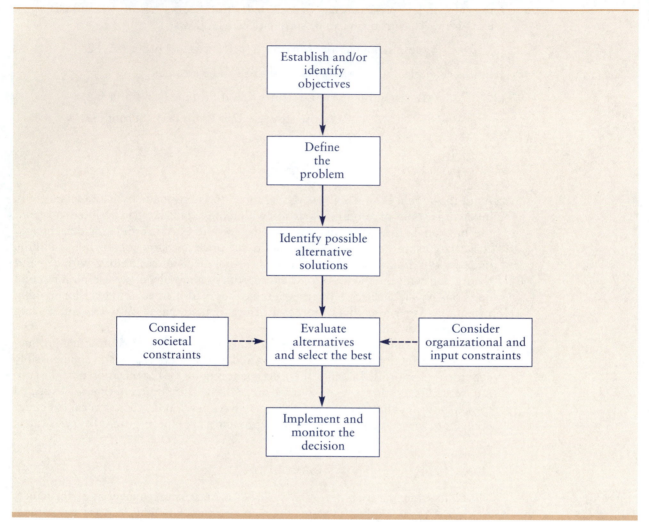

The final step in the process, after all alternatives have been identified and evaluated and the best alternative has been chosen, is the implementation of the decision. This phase often requires constant monitoring to ensure that results are as expected. If they are not, corrective action needs to be taken when possible. This five-step decision-making process is illustrated in Figure 1.1.

THE ROLE OF PROFITS

Economic Profit
The difference between total revenue and total economic cost. Economic cost includes a "normal" rate of return on the capital contributions of the firm's partners.

Economic profit is the difference between total revenue and total economic cost. *Total revenue* is measured as the sales receipts of a firm, that is, price times quantity sold. The *economic cost* of any activity may be thought of as the highest valued alternative opportunity that is forgone. To attract economic resources to some activity, the firm must pay a price for these factors (labor, capital, and natural resources) that is sufficient to convince the owners of these resources to sacrifice other alternatives and commit the resources to this use. Thus, economic costs may be thought of as *opportunity costs,* or the costs of attracting a resource from its next best alternative use. Accordingly, the term *economic cost* in this book refers to all costs, both explicit and implicit, including a normal return (profit) for owners of the financial resources. In a general sense, economic profit may be defined as the *difference between total revenue and total economic cost.*[4] When we refer to profit maximization in this book, we mean an objective of maximizing the economic profit of the firm.

Why Are Profits Necessary?

In a free enterprise system, economic profits play an important role in guiding the decisions made by the thousands of competing independent economic units. The existence of profits determines the type and quantity of goods and services that are produced and sold, as well as the demand for various factors of production—labor, capital, and natural resources. Because of the important role played by profits in our system, we will review several theories of profit.

Risk-Bearing Theory of Profit   Some economists have argued that economic profits above a normal rate of return are necessary to compensate the owners of the firm for the risk they assume when making their investments. Because a firm's shareholders are not entitled to a fixed rate of return on their investment—that is, they are residual claimants to the firm's resources—they need to be compensated for this risk in the form of a higher rate of return.

Example

http://
The website for Circus Circus Casinos, Inc. is http://www.circuscircus.com

RISK AND PROFITABILITY: CIRCUS CIRCUS

The relationship between risk and profit levels can be seen in the case of Circus Circus, the Las Vegas hotel and casino operator. During 1994 Circus Circus earned a return on net worth of about 20.5 percent, compared with a mean return on net worth of 12.5 percent for all firms in the hotel/gaming industry and of 15.0 percent for all industrial, retail, and transportation firms followed by *Value Line.* The hotel and gaming industries are subject to substantial swings in profitability over time. Firms operating in these industries also are subject to severe competitive pressures. In addition, Circus Circus is financed with a high proportion of debt (50 percent of total capital), compared with an average of 39 percent for the other firms followed by *Value Line.* Other firms in this industry did not perform as well as Circus Circus during 1994. Mirage Resorts earned 11.5 percent on net worth, Hilton earned 10.5 percent, and Bally earned 2.5 percent. Firms that operate in a high-risk industry such as this one require the incentive of high potential profits to attract capital. The high returns of Circus Circus came with high risk, however. By 1996, the return to net worth fell by half to 10.2 percent, then to 7.4 percent in 1998. Finally in 2000, profitability returned to the 12.0 percent hotel and casino average.

The risk-bearing theory of profits is explained in the context of normal profits, where *normal* is defined in terms of the relative risk of alternative investments. Normal profits for a high-risk firm, such as a casino operator, should be higher than normal profits for firms of lesser risk, such as water utilities. Indeed, the industry average return

---

[4] The concepts of economic costs and profits are discussed in more detail in Chapter 8.

on net worth for the hotel/gaming industry was 12 percent in 2000, compared with 10 percent for the water utility industry.

Dynamic Equilibrium (Friction) Theory of Profit   According to the dynamic equilibrium or friction theory of profit, there exists a long-run equilibrium normal rate of profit (adjusted for risk) that all firms should tend to earn. At any point in time, however, an individual firm or the firms in a specific industry might earn a rate of return above or below this long-run normal return level. This can occur because of temporary dislocations (shocks) in various sectors of the economy. For example, U.S. firms that produced oil and natural gas experienced a dramatic increase in profits in response to supply shortages following the invasion of Kuwait by Iraq in 1990 and during the general strike in Venezuela in 2002. Rates of return rose substantially. However, those high returns declined shortly after the war and strike ended, when market conditions led to excess supplies.

Similarly, if a new, inexpensive, and readily available energy source were to be discovered, oil prices would decline substantially. Over time, some producers would leave this increasingly unprofitable market until a normal rate of profit was restored for the remaining firms. The inability of our economic system to adjust instantaneously to changes in market conditions may result in short-term profits above or below normal levels.

Monopoly Theory of Profit   In some industries, one firm is effectively able to dominate the market and potentially earn above-normal rates of return for a long period of time. This ability to dominate the market may arise from economies of scale (a situation in which one large firm can produce additional units of output at a lower cost than can smaller firms), control of essential natural resources, control of critical patents, or governmental restrictions that prohibit competition. The conditions under which a monopolist can earn above-normal profits are discussed in greater depth in Chapter 11.

Innovation Theory of Profit   The innovation theory of profit suggests that above-normal profits are the reward for successful innovations. Firms that develop unique, high-quality products (such as Microsoft in the computer software industry) or firms that successfully identify unique market opportunities (such as Federal Express) are rewarded with the potential for above-normal profits. Indeed, the U.S. patent system is designed to ensure that these above-normal return opportunities furnish strong incentives for continued innovation.

Managerial Efficiency Theory of Profit   Closely related to the innovation theory is the managerial efficiency theory of profit. This theory maintains that above-normal profits can arise because of the exceptional managerial skills of well-managed firms. The ability to earn above-normal profits by exercising high-quality managerial skills is a continuing incentive for greater efficiency in any economic system.

No single theory of profit can explain the observed profit rates in each industry, nor are these theories necessarily mutually exclusive. Profit performance is invariably the result of many factors, including differential risk, innovation, managerial skills, the existence of monopoly power, and chance occurrences. The important thing to remember is that profit and profit opportunities play a major role in determining the efficient allocation of resources in any economy. Without the market signals that profits give, it would be necessary to develop alternative schemes on which to base resource-allocation decisions. These alternatives are often highly bureaucratic and frequently lack the responsiveness to changing market conditions that a free enterprise system provides.

OBJECTIVE OF THE FIRM

One common economic model of the firm assumes that the objective of the owners of the firm is to maximize profits. This profit-maximization model of firm behavior has been extremely rich in its decision-making implications. The marginal (and incremental) decision rules that have been derived from profit maximization provide very useful guidelines for making a wide range of resource-allocation decisions. For example, if incremental cost is defined as the change in total cost resulting from a decision, and if incremental revenue is defined as the change in total revenue resulting from a decision, then any business decision is profitable if one of these results occurs:

1. It increases incremental revenue more than incremental costs.
2. It decreases some incremental costs more than it increases others (assuming revenues remain constant).
3. It increases some incremental revenues more than it decreases others (assuming costs remain constant).
4. It reduces incremental costs more than incremental revenue.

The Shareholder Wealth-Maximization Model of the Firm

The simple profit-maximization model of the firm has provided decision makers with useful insights. However, the profit-maximization model is limited because it does not incorporate the time dimension in the decision process and it does not consider risk. The **shareholder wealth**-maximization model of the firm overcomes these limitations.

Shareholder Wealth
A measure of the value of a firm. Shareholder wealth is equal to the value of a firm's common stock, which, in turn, is equal to the present value of all future cash returns expected to be generated by the firm for the benefit of its owners.

The shareholder wealth-maximization goal states that the objective of a firm's management should be to maximize the *present value* of the *expected future* cash flows to the equity owners (shareholders). For simplicity, at this point let us consider cash flows to be the same as profits. Hence, the value of a firm's stock is equal to the present value of all expected future profits, discounted at the shareholders' required rate of return, or

$$V_0 \cdot (\text{Shares Outstanding}) = \frac{\pi_1}{(1 + k_e)^1} + \frac{\pi_2}{(1 + k_e)^2} + \frac{\pi_3}{(1 + k_e)^3} + \ldots + \frac{\pi}{(1 + k_e)}$$

$$V_0 \cdot (\text{Shares Outstanding}) = \sum_{t=1}^{\infty} \frac{\pi_t}{(1 + k_e)^t} \qquad [1.1]$$

where V_0 is the current (present) value of a share of stock, π_t represents the profits expected in each of the future periods (1 through ∞), and k_e equals the investors' required rate of return. Equation 1.1 assumes that the reader is familiar with the concept of discounting and present values. (A review of this concept is found in Appendix A at the end of the book.) For the purposes of analysis here, it is only necessary to recognize that $1 received one year from today is generally worth less than $1 received today because $1 today can be invested at some rate of interest, for example, 15 percent, to yield $1.15 at the end of one year. Thus, an investor who requires (or has an opportunity to earn) a 15 percent annual rate of return on an investment would place a current value of $1 on $1.15 expected to be received in one year.

Equation 1.1 explicitly considers the *timing* of future profits. By discounting all future profits at the required rate of return, k_e, Equation 1.1 recognizes that a dollar received in the future is worth less than a dollar received immediately.

Equation 1.1 also provides a conceptual basis for evaluating differential levels of *risk*. For example, if a series of future profits is highly uncertain (i.e., the profits are likely to diverge substantially from their expected values), the discount rate, k_e, can be increased to account for this risk. Thus, the greater the risk associated with receiving a future benefit (profit), the lower the value placed by investors on that benefit. The shareholder wealth-maximization model of the firm is therefore capable of dealing with the two primary shortcomings of the static profit-maximization model—i.e., equilibrium adjustment for differential timing of cash flows and for differential risk.

SHAREHOLDER WEALTH MAXIMIZATION: BERKSHIRE HATHAWAY CORPORATION

Warren E. Buffett, chairman and CEO of Berkshire Hathaway, Inc., has described the long-term economic goal of Berkshire Hathaway as follows: "to maximize the average annual rate of gain in intrinsic business value on a per-share basis."[5] Berkshire's book value per share has increased from $19.46 in 1964, when he acquired the firm, to $46,727 at the end of 2002, a compound annual rate of growth of about 22 percent. The growth rate in the market value of Berkshire's shares has been even greater, with the market value per share reaching $67,800 at the end of 2002. Berkshire's directors are all major stockholders. At least four of the directors have over 50 percent of their family's net worth invested in Berkshire. Insiders own over 47 percent of the firm's stock. Buffet's firm has placed a high premium on the goal of maximizing shareholder wealth, that is, maximizing the value of the owners' portion of the firm.

Additional insight regarding the achievement of the shareholder wealth-maximization goal can be gained by decomposing the profit concept, π, into its important elements. Profit in period t, π_t, is equal to total revenue (TR_t) minus total costs (TC_t), or

$$\pi_t = TR_t - TC_t \qquad [1.2]$$

Similarly, total revenue in period t equals price per unit (P_t) times quantity sold (Q_t), or

$$TR_t = P_t \cdot Q_t \qquad [1.3]$$

Total cost in period t equals variable cost per unit (V_t) times the number of units of output (Q_t) plus fixed costs in period t, or

$$TC_t = V_t \cdot Q_t + F_t \qquad [1.4]$$

By combining Equations 1.2, 1.3, and 1.4 with Equation 1.1, we get

$$V_0 \cdot (\text{Shares Outstanding}) = \sum_{t=1}^{\infty} \frac{P_t \cdot Q_t - V_t \cdot Q_t - F_t}{(1 + k_e)^t} \qquad [1.5]$$

The integrative nature of the wealth-maximization model is illustrated in Figure 1.2. The term $P_t \cdot Q_t$ represents the total revenue generated by the firm. From a decision-making perspective, this value is dependent on the firm's demand function (discussed in Chapters 3–4) and the firm's pricing decisions (see Chapters 10–16).

---

[5] *Annual Report*, Berkshire Hathaway, Inc., 2002.

Figure 1.2   Determinants of Firm Value

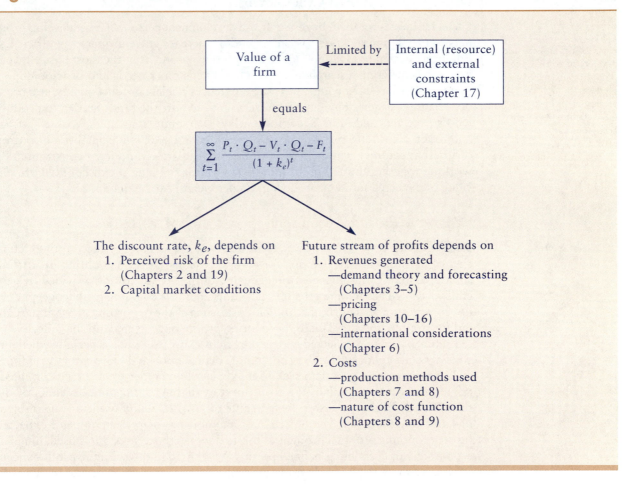

$$\sum_{t=1}^{\infty} \frac{P_t \cdot Q_t - V_t \cdot Q_t - F_t}{(1 + k_e)^t}$$

The discount rate, k_e, depends on
1. Perceived risk of the firm
   (Chapters 2 and 19)
2. Capital market conditions

Future stream of profits depends on
1. Revenues generated
   —demand theory and forecasting
   (Chapters 3–5)
   —pricing
   (Chapters 10–16)
   —international considerations
   (Chapter 6)
2. Costs
   —production methods used
   (Chapters 7 and 8)
   —nature of cost function
   (Chapters 8 and 9)

The firm's costs, both fixed (F_t) and variable (V_t) are discussed in Chapters 8–9. In addition, the choice of investments made by the firm—the capital budgeting decisions—determines what proportion of total cost will be fixed and what proportion will be variable. A firm that chooses a capital-intensive production technology will tend to have a higher proportion of fixed costs than will a firm that chooses a more labor-intensive technology. Capital budgeting decisions are considered in Chapter 18.

The discount rate, k_e, that investors use to value the stream of income generated by a firm is determined by the perceived risk of the firm and by conditions in the financial markets, including the level of expected inflation. Risk and its relationship to required rates of return are discussed in Chapters 2 and 19. International considerations (e.g., exchange rates and tariffs) can affect a firm's revenues (and costs). These issues are discussed in Chapter 6.

In making its pricing, output, production, and cost decisions, management is faced with several legal, behavioral, value-based, and environmental constraints on its actions. These constraints are briefly considered in the next section and discussed in greater detail in Chapter 17.

Example

http://

Firms such as IBM can also develop the expertise to produce complementary products through the acquisition process. You can learn about IBM's recent acquisitions at http://www.ibm.com/investor/data/irdasa.phtml

RESOURCE-ALLOCATION DECISIONS AND SHAREHOLDER WEALTH MAXIMIZATION: IBM CORPORATION

Consider the case of IBM. Its research and development personnel must develop products that will appeal to its customers and/or increase current operating efficiency. Engineers design production facilities to produce products in the most cost-efficient manner. Marketing researchers try to identify customer needs and provide important information about competitors that influences pricing, product quality, and product feature decisions. Financial managers must acquire the funds needed to produce IBM's products and fund its capital outlays. Personnel managers work to attract and retain a cost-effective workforce. These decisions are made against a backdrop of internal resource constraints, government regulation, and legal constraints. By working together toward the common goal of maximizing the discounted present value of expected future profits, shareholder wealth can be maximized.

Economic Profits, Accounting Profits, and Cash Flows

The economic profit concept we are using is *not* the same as the accounting definition of earnings, or net income, for several reasons. First, accounting profits are subject to ambiguous interpretation because of the broad latitude provided by generally accepted accounting principles. In addition, the accounting profit concept does not consider some important economic costs, such as the opportunity cost of the capital invested by owners. Finally, accounting profit concepts may not be reflective of the actual *cash flows* collected and paid by a company over time, especially when one considers differential methods of computing depreciation and of inventory valuation.

In practice, managers who seek to maximize shareholder wealth focus on maximizing the present value of the cash flows available to the equity owners of the firm. The definition of cash flow available to a firm's equity owners is unambiguous and consistent with the objective of maximizing the present value of expected future economic profits. Throughout this text, when the term *profit* is used, it means economic, not accounting-defined profits. When used in this way, the profit concept is consistent with the cash flow concept and will lead to shareholder wealth-maximizing decisions by managers.

Managerial Actions to Influence Shareholder Wealth

A tangible measure of shareholder wealth is the price of the firm's stock. Many factors ultimately influence the stock price. Some of these factors are largely outside the direct control of managers; others can be directly influenced. The top panel of Figure 1.3 enumerates some of the economic environment factors outside the direct control of managers (e.g., antitrust policy or the yen/dollar exchange rate), but managers must be aware of how these factors constrain their chosen business policies.

The policy decision areas are enumerated in the next panel of Figure 1.3. Managers make choices regarding the products to be produced, the technology used to produce them, the marketing effort and distribution channels, and the selection of employees and their compensation. In addition, managers establish investment policies, the ownership structure of the firm, the capital structure (use of debt) of the firm, working capital management policies, and dividend policies. Managers also initiate restructuring events, such as mergers, spinoffs, and alliances, in an attempt to increase capitalized value. The decisions made in these key policy decision areas determine the amount, timing, and risk of the firm's expected cash flows. Participants in the financial markets evaluate the profits expected by the firm in relation to alternative streams

Figure 1.3   Factors Affecting Stock Prices

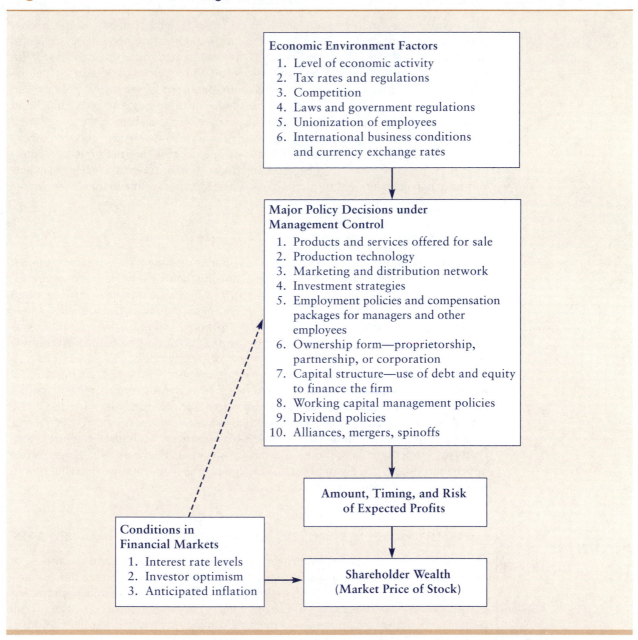

Economic Environment Factors

1. Level of economic activity
2. Tax rates and regulations
3. Competition
4. Laws and government regulations
5. Unionization of employees
6. International business conditions and currency exchange rates

Major Policy Decisions under Management Control

1. Products and services offered for sale
2. Production technology
3. Marketing and distribution network
4. Investment strategies
5. Employment policies and compensation packages for managers and other employees
6. Ownership form—proprietorship, partnership, or corporation
7. Capital structure—use of debt and equity to finance the firm
8. Working capital management policies
9. Dividend policies
10. Alliances, mergers, spinoffs

Conditions in Financial Markets

1. Interest rate levels
2. Investor optimism
3. Anticipated inflation

Amount, Timing, and Risk of Expected Profits

Shareholder Wealth (Market Price of Stock)

of profits expected from other firms and ultimately establish the price of the firm's stock. The value of a firm's stock is influenced at any point in time by general conditions in the financial markets, including the level of interest rates, anticipated inflation rates, and the level of investor optimism regarding the future.

The focus of this book is on making resource allocation, strategic, and tactical decisions that can improve the amount, the timing, or the risk profile of a firm's profit stream in accordance with legal, environmental, and ethical constraints, thus leading to increases in shareholder wealth.

SEPARATION OF OWNERSHIP AND CONTROL: THE PROBLEM OF AGENCY

The marginal (or incremental) decision criteria, derived from the static profit-maximization and dynamic shareholder wealth-maximization objectives, are useful in cases where alternative decisions are easily enumerated and outcomes (costs and revenues) associated with these alternatives can be estimated. These cases include scheduling for optimal production, determining an optimal inventory policy given some pattern of sales, buying or leasing a machine, or refunding an outstanding bond issue. In other cases, however, where the alternatives are less clear or the incremental effects are debatable, economists have frequently found a divergence between theory and practice. What are the reasons for this divergence? As the small business enterprise grew and expanded into the modern corporation of today, the roles of ownership and management became increasingly separated,[6] permitting managers to pursue their own self-interests.

Divergent Objectives

Separation of ownership and control has permitted managers to "satisfice," or seek acceptable levels of performance while maximizing their own welfare. For example, in the early 1980s, Exxon managers diversified the general administrative function of the company into product lines, such as computer software development, where Exxon had little or no competitive advantage. Although wild fluctuations in the executive bonuses that were tied to quarterly earnings did smooth out, the diversification decision resulted in a decline in the value of Exxon stock.

Maximization of their own personal welfare can also lead management to minimize (or limit) the amount of risk incurred by the firm, because unfavorable outcomes can lead to their dismissal or possible bankruptcy for the firm. Likewise, the desire for job security is cited as one reason management often opposes takeover merger offers by other companies. Giving senior management "golden parachute" contracts to compensate them if they lose their positions as the result of a merger is one approach designed to ensure that they will act in the interests of shareholders in merger decisions, rather than in their own interests.

Example

EXECUTIVE COMPENSATION AND SHAREHOLDER WEALTH MAXIMIZATION

How should corporations structure the compensation (i.e., salary and incentives) of officers and directors to motivate these managers to make decisions that maximize shareholder wealth? One approach, such as the Salomon Smith Barney example cited earlier in the Managerial Challenge, is to offer managers cash bonuses based on the overall performance of the firm or division in the firm. Another approach is to offer executives options to buy stock in the company at some predetermined price. If the firm prospers, then both the owners and managers reap the rewards of higher stock prices. However, this options approach does not always lead to a long-term wealth-maximization perspective on the part of managers. Instead of retaining their ownership interest in the company, executives sometimes exercise the options and sell the stock relatively quickly.

Several corporations have tried an alternative approach by requiring (or strongly encouraging) management to own stock in the company. Kodak, for example,

[6] Adolf Berle and Gardiner C. Means, *The Modern Corporation and Private Property* (New York: Macmillan, 1932).

requires 40 of its top executives to invest one to four times their base salary in Kodak stock.[7] General Motors instituted a similar plan by requiring its top 65 executives to hold General Motors common stock equivalent in market value to the manager's annual salary.[8] Other companies that have instituted either mandatory or voluntary stock ownership guidelines include Xerox, CSX, Union Carbide, and Hershey Foods. A survey found that nearly 10 percent of U.S. firms with sales exceeding $5 billion require senior executives to hold common stock in the company.[9] This requirement appears to be a growing trend—over 50 percent of the CEOs of 561 major corporations believe executives should be required to own significant amounts of stock in the companies where they are employed.[10]

The trend toward long-term, performance-based compensation plans is not limited just to a firm's top layer of managers. For example, in 1989 PepsiCo announced a stock option plan for all of its 100,000 employees who work 30 hours or more per week—from truck drivers to plant managers. The average large firm now has 300 to 400 of its top employees covered by stock option plans, up from about 100 employees just 10 years ago.[11] In addition, the size of the long-term compensation received by managers has grown dramatically. For example, Michael Eisner received over $20.2 million in long-term compensation (in addition to his $750,000 salary) as a reward for increasing Walt Disney's market value over tenfold to $22.7 billion during his 10 years as chairman.[12]

The growth of performance-based compensation plans is an attempt to realign the interests of managers with those of stockholders, and thereby avoid costly inefficiencies that can arise because of a divergence of interests.

Agency Problems

The existence of divergent objectives between owners and managers leads to an agency problem. **Agency relationships** exist when one or more individuals (the principals) delegate decision-making authority to another individual (the agent).[13] In the context of managerial economics, the most important agency relationship is the relationship between stockholders (owners) and managers.

Stockholders and Managers   Inefficiencies that arise because of agency relationships are called *principal-agent problems,* or just *agency problems.* The concern by some managers for long-run survival (job security), rather than shareholder wealth maximization, is an example of an agency problem. Another example is the consumption of on-the-job perquisites (such as the use of company airplanes, limousines, and

---

Agency Relationship
A basis for delegating decision-making authority from principals to agents.

---

[7] Grace M. Kang, "Now, a Big Job at Kodak Means You'll Buy a Big Stake," *Business Week,* February 1, 1993, p. 26.

[8] Robert L. Simison, "GM in Bid to Retain Talent, Awards Hefty Raises to 3,400 Top Executives," *Wall Street Journal,* March 3, 1994, p. A2.

[9] Joann S. Lublin, "Buy or Bye," *Wall Street Journal,* April 21, 1993, p. R9.

[10] Ibid., p. R9.

[11] Jolie Solomon, "Pepsi Offers Stock Options to All, Not Just Honchos," *Wall Street Journal,* June 28, 1989.

[12] "That Eye-Popping Executive Pay," *Business Week,* April 25, 1994, pp. 52–58.

[13] See Amir Barnea, R. Haugen, and L. Senbet, *Agency Problems and Financial Contracting* (Englewood Cliffs, NJ: Prentice-Hall, 1985), for an overview of the agency problem issue. See also Michael Jensen and William Meckling, "Theory of the Firm: Managerial Behavior, Agency Costs, and Ownership Structure," *Journal of Financial Economics,* October 1976, pp. 305–360, and Eugene Fama, "Agency Problems and the Theory of the Firm," *Journal of Political Economy,* April 1980, pp. 288–307.

luxurious offices) by managers who have no (or only a partial) ownership interest in the firm. Managers' shirking of responsibilities is also an agency-related problem.

Two common factors that give rise to all principal-agent problems are the unobservability of some manager-agent action and the presence of random disturbances in team production. The job performance of parking gate attendants and piecework garment workers is easily monitored, but the work effort of salespeople and manufacturer's trade representatives may not be observable at less-than-prohibitive cost. Directly observing the managerial input is even more problematic because managers contribute what one might call "creative ingenuity." Creative ingenuity in making the company's decisions is inherently unobservable; owners know it when they see it, but often do not recognize when it is missing. As a result, the managerial input is inseparable from good and bad luck in explaining fluctuations in company performance. Owners therefore find it difficult to know when to reward managers and when to blame them for poor performance.

Managerial motivations to act in the interests of stockholders include the structure of their compensation package, the threat of dismissal, and the threat of takeover by a new group of owners. Remaining agency problems reduce the value of the firm's shares in the marketplace and increase the likelihood of takeovers.

Example

AGENCY PROBLEMS AND CORPORATE TAKEOVERS: RJR NABISCO

When managers do not have a significant ownership stake in the firm they manage, the potential exists for shareholder resources to be diverted from their most productive uses to provide perquisites for managers that are inconsistent with the most efficient allocation of resources. When this happens, pressure may build for a change in management. For example, in 1988 RJR Nabisco was a firm that had become bloated with resources that were frequently being allocated in an unwise manner. The executive beach homes in Florida; the gargantuan airplane hangar in Atlanta for the firm's extensive fleet of corporate aircraft; the expensive, but failed, "smokeless" cigarette, Premier; and the trail of failed former acquisitions had left RJR Nabisco with substantially less value in the marketplace than was possible with better management. Recognizing this, Kohlberg Kravis Roberts & Co. (KKR) initiated an unfriendly takeover bid and paid a record $25 billion to acquire RJR Nabisco in early 1989. This represented a price of about $109 per share, compared with a pretakeover price in the range of $50 to $55. The deal was heavily leveraged with debt. The new owners moved quickly to sell many of RJR's poorly performing assets, slash operating expenses, reduce the company's workforce, and cancel the Premier project.

Agency Costs
Costs associated with resolving conflicts of interest among shareholders, managers, and lenders. Agency costs include the cost of monitoring and bonding performance, the cost of constructing contracts designed to minimize agency conflicts, and the loss in efficiency resulting from unresolved agent-principal conflicts.

To mitigate these agency problems, the firm incurs several **agency costs,** which include the following:

1. Expenditures to structure executive compensation in such a way as to align the incentives for management with shareholder interests, such as direct grants of stock or deferred stock options, discussed in Chapter 15.
2. Expenditures to monitor management's actions, such as internal audits and accounting oversight boards.
3. Bonding expenditures to protect the owners from managerial dishonesty.
4. The opportunity cost of lost profits arising from complex organizational structures designed to limit managerial discretion, but which prevent timely responses to opportunities.

Example

AGENCY COSTS AND CORPORATE RESTRUCTURING: O.M. SCOTT & SONS

The existence of high agency costs associated with the separation of ownership from management has prompted many firms to financially restructure themselves to achieve higher operating efficiencies. For example, in December 1986, the lawn products firm O.M. Scott & Sons, prior to that time a subsidiary of ITT, was purchased by the Scott managers in a highly financially leveraged buyout (often referred to as an LBO). Faced with the heavy interest and principal burdens of the debt-financed transaction and having the potential to profit from more efficient operation of the firm, the new owner-managers quickly put in place accounting controls and operating procedures designed to improve Scott's performance. By monitoring inventory levels more closely and negotiating more aggressively with suppliers, the firm was able to reduce its average monthly working capital investment from an initial level of $75 million to $35 million. At the same time, sales increased from $160 million to a new level of $200 million.[14] One of the motivations for LBO transactions is to reduce agency costs.

IMPLICATIONS OF SHAREHOLDER WEALTH MAXIMIZATION

Critics of aligning management interests with equity owner interests often allege that shareholder wealth maximization focuses on short-term payoffs to the exclusion of long-term investment. The evidence suggests just the opposite. Near-term cash flows can explain only a small fraction of the capitalized market value reflected in a firm's share price. For example, only 18 percent of 1988 share values of NYSE stocks can be explained by the first five years of expected dividends and only 35 percent by the entire first ten years.[15] Shareholder wealth maximization is long term, not short term, in focus. Moreover, it is forward looking, not merely extrapolative. For example, despite consistent upward trends in cash flows and stock price appreciation over the previous ten years, declining share prices of tobacco companies in 1990–1992 anticipated the ongoing switch to generic cigarettes and the additional smoking location restrictions announced in 1992–1994. This also illustrates another implication of shareholder wealth maximization. Managers must manage change, sometimes radical change in competition (e.g., in airlines), technology (e.g., in broad-band signal compression), and regulation (e.g., in pharmaceuticals), and they must do so three and four steps ahead of current events. Even in periods of relative stability in the business environment, they must focus continuously on change-management questions, like whether to ramp up or phase out capacity in particular product lines. Wealth-maximizing managers must anticipate change and proactively plan for all relevant contingencies.

Shareholder wealth maximization is also an explicitly dynamic objective reflecting the currently available public information regarding a company's expected future cash flows and foreseeable risks. As such, it reflects the strategic investment opportunities a management team develops, not only the firm's preexisting positive net present value investments. Amgen, a biotechnology company, had shareholder value of $42 million in 1983 despite no sales, no cash flow, no capital assets, no patents, and poorly protected trade secrets. In 1999, Amgen had sales of over $6.35 billion and cash flow of $2.5 billion annually. In general, only about 85 percent of shareholder value can be explained by even 30 years of cash flows. The remainder reflects

---

[14] A more complete discussion of the Scott experience can be found in Brett Duval Fromson, "Life After Debt: How LBOs Do It," *Fortune,* March 13, 1989, pp. 91–92.

[15] J. R. Woolridge, "Competitive Decline: Is a Myopic Stock Market to Blame?" *Journal of Applied Corporate Finance,* Spring 1988, pp. 26–36.

WHAT WENT RIGHT   WHAT WENT WRONG

Eli Lilly Depressed by Loss of Prozac Patent[16]

Pharmaceutical giants like GlaxoSmithKline, Merck, Pfizer, and Eli Lilly expend an average of $802 million over 12.3 years to research, develop, test for efficacy and side effects, conduct clinical trials on, and then produce and market a new drug. Only 4 in 100 candidate molecules or screening compounds lead to investigational new drugs (INDs). Only 5 in 200 INDs display sufficient efficacy in animal testing to warrant human trials. Clinical failure occurs in 6 of 10 human trials, and only half of the FDA-proposed drugs are ultimately approved. In sum, the joint probability of successful drug discovery and development is just $0.04 \times 0.025 \times 0.4 \times 0.5 = 0.0002$, two hundredths of one percent. Those few patented drugs that do make it to the pharmacy shelves, especially the blockbusters with several billion dollars in sales, must contribute enough operating profit to recover the cost of all the R & D failures.

In 2000, one of the key extension patents for Eli Lilly's blockbuster drug for the treatment of depression, Prozac, was overturned by a regulator and a U.S. federal judge. Within one month, Eli Lilly lost 70 percent of Prozac's sales to the generic equivalents. Although this company has several other blockbusters, Eli Lilly's share price plummeted 32 percent. CEO Sidney Taurel said he had made a mistake in not rolling out Prozac's successor drugs when the extension patent was challenged. Taurel then moved quickly to establish a new management concept throughout the company. Now, each new Eli Lilly drug is assigned a team of scientists, marketers, and regulatory experts who oversee the entire life cycle of the product from research inception to patent expiration. The key function of these cross-functionally integrated teams is contingency analysis; crisis management is out, and scenario planning is in.

───────────

[16] C. Kennedy, F. Harris, and M. Lord, "Differential Pricing, Public Policy and Public Affairs in Pharmaceuticals," and "Eli Lilly: Bloom and Blight," *The Economist*, October 26, 2002, p. 60.

the capitalized value of strategic options to expand some profitable lines of business, to cancel and abandon others, and to retain but delay investment until more information becomes available on still other projects.

Shareholder wealth-maximizing behavior as the objective of management is also distinguishable from satisficing behavior.[17] Satisficers strive to "hit" their sales targets, return on investment targets, or safety targets; they are not wealth maximizers. Rather than seeking to achieve an incremental moving standard such as 97 percent, 99 percent, 99.9 percent error-free takeoffs and landings from O'Hare Airport, or 9 percent, 11 percent, 12.1 percent return on investment, the shareholder wealth-maximizing manager commits himself or herself to continuous marginal improvements in accordance with an unambiguous rule of rational life. In particular, any time the marginal benefits of an action exceed their marginal cost, just do it! We discuss this optimization approach to marginal decision-making analysis further in Chapter 2 and Appendix 2A. In general, then, shareholder wealth maximization implies that management should seek to develop a forward-looking, dynamic, and long-term outlook; anticipate and manage change; acquire strategic investment opportunities;

───────────

[17] Herbert Simon stated the case for satisficing behavior in "Theories of Decision-Making in Economic and Behavioral Science" reprinted in E. Mansfield, *Microeconomics: Selected Readings*, 5th ed. (New York: Norton, 1985).

WHAT WENT RIGHT   WHAT WENT WRONG

Saturn Corporation[18]

When General Motors rolled out the "different kind of car company" in 1991, J.D. Powers rated product quality 8 percent ahead of Honda, and customers liked the no-haggle selling process. Saturn achieved the 200,000 unit sales enjoyed by the Honda Civic and the Toyota Corolla in two short years and caught the 285,000 volume of the Ford Escort by 1995. Making interpersonal aspects of customer service the number-one priority and possessing superior inventory and MIS systems, Saturn dealerships proved very profitable and quickly developed a reputation for some of the highest customer loyalty in the industry.

However, with pricing of the base Saturn model $1,200 below the $12,050 rival Japanese compacts, the GM parent earned only $400 profit margin per vehicle. In a typical year this meant GM was recovering only about $100 million of its $3 billion investment, a 3 percent return on investment. At GM's 11 percent cost of capital, each Saturn was losing approximately $1,000. These figures compare to a $3,300 profit margin per vehicle in some of GM's other divisions. Consequently, cash flow was not reinvested in the Saturn division, products were not updated, and the models stagnated. By 1997, sales were slumping at −9 percent and in 1998 they fell an additional 20 percent.

Three problems appear responsible for Saturn's downturn. First, managers at GM never adopted a change-management view of what would be required to transfer the first-time Saturn owners to their more profitable GM divisions. The corporate strategy was that price-conscious young Saturn buyers would eventually trade up to Buick and Oldsmobile. Instead, middle-aged loyal Saturn owners sought to trade up within Saturn, and finding no sporty larger models from their different kind of car company, they preferred larger Japanese imports like the Honda Accord and Toyota Camry. Second, Saturn projected a continuing popularity of the small economy car because of high gasoline prices. However, by 1997 oil prices had declined to 1974 levels of $1/gallon and the market moved to SUVs, sport wagons, and minivans. In addition, exchange rates fluctuated sharply between 1995 and 1998 with the dollar appreciating from 94 to 130 yen per U.S. dollar. This made it possible for Honda and Toyota to discount the dollar prices of Civics, Accords, Corollas, and Camrys without reducing the yen revenue from these exports. Companies like Saturn whose products are exposed to competition from foreign producers must plan product introductions and marketing campaigns to account for these oil price and exchange rate cycles in the global competitive environment.

[18] Based on M. Cohen, "Saturn's Supply-Chain Innovation," *Sloan Management Review,* Summer 2000, pp. 93–96. "Small Car Sales Are Back" and "Why Didn't GM Do More for Saturn?" *BusinessWeek,* September 22, 1997, pp. 40–42, and March 16, 1998, p. 62.

and maximize the present value of expected cash flows to owners, as allowed by legal, ethical, and regulatory constraints.

Necessary Conditions

In order for managers to focus exclusively on maximizing shareholder value, three conditions must hold: complete markets, no significant asymmetric information, and known recontracting costs.

Complete Markets   For all the effects of management decisions to influence a company's cash flows, there must be liquid markets for the firm's inputs, products, and by-products. For example, if a market in transferable pollution allowances (pollution permits) establishes a price for sulfur dioxide (acid rain) emissions, then managers of power plants can make wealth-maximizing decisions about whether to install smokestack scrubbers or purchase additional pollution permits. Economically profitable pollution abatement will occur, and over time the number of pollution permits issued and pollution released into the environment can be reduced.

Similarly, more complete futures and options markets for crude oil and coffee bean inputs allow Texaco and Starbuck's Coffeehouses to plan with more accurate cash flow analyses and more accurate cost projections. For a small 3–5 percent expense known in advance, wealth-maximizing managers can employ these "derivative markets" to hedge against unexpected cost increases and reduce the respective cost-covering prices of gasoline and cappuccino.

Example

http://

The EPA keeps track of allowance transactions and holdings by way of the Allowance Tracking System. Learn more about the mechanics of how allowance trading occurs, current allowance prices, and trade volumes, at

http://www.epa.gov/ airmarkets/

TRADABLE POLLUTION PERMITS AT DUKE POWER[19]

Sulfur dioxide (SO_2) by-products of burning high-sulfur coal in power plants and other heavy industry have raised the acidity of eastern forests from Maine to Georgia to levels 25 times higher than in California's Napa Valley or Rocky Mountain National Park. Dead trees, peeling paint, and stone decomposition on buildings and monuments have been the result. To elicit substantial pollution abatement at the least cost, the Clean Air Act of 1990 created a market in the rights to emit SO_2. The result was tradable pollution permits or allowances (TPAs) issued by the Environmental Protection Agency to 467 known SO_2 polluters for approximately 70 percent of pre-existing emissions. The utilities then began to trade the allowances. Low-abatement-cost plants sold allowances, and high-abatement-cost plants bought allowances. As a result of the growing completeness of this market, electric utilities like Duke Power now know what expense line to incorporate in their cash flow projections for the SO_2 by-products of operating with high-sulfur coal. Recently, the TPAs have sold for $131/ton, and a single utility plant operation may require 15,000 tons of permits or more. The continuous tradeoff between installing pollution abatement equipment (e.g., smokestack scrubbers), utilizing higher cost alternative fuels (e.g., low-sulfur coal and natural gas), or paying the current market price of these EPA-issued pollution permits can now be analyzed directly.

Of course, what would be really useful for wealth-maximizing managers to know is the forecasted future cost of the permits relative to the life cycle cost of pollution abatement equipment. Futures and forward markets in pollution allowances have emerged to assist polluters in making these determinations. It is now possible to hedge the cost of pollution permits by buying today a futures contract for the delivery of a TPA in, for instance, 1, 2, or 3 years. This locks in the expense of the SO_2 by-product over that time frame. Should the TPA permits become more expensive, the futures contract holder will receive a rise in contract value, which simply offsets the increase in cost of the permit. Should the TPA permits become cheaper, the futures contract holder will suffer a decline in contract value, which again simply offsets the reduced cost of the permits. For about 3–5 percent of the value at risk, the power utility can "lock in" its future by-product expense.

No Asymmetric Information   A second necessary condition if managers intend to focus exclusively on maximizing shareholder wealth is that all information must be symmetrically known. Monitoring and coordination problems within the corporation

[19] Based on "Cornering the Market," *Wall Street Journal*, June 5, 1995, p. B1, and *Economic Report of the President*, February 2000 (Washington, DC: U.S.G.P.O., 2000), pp. 240–264.

and contracting problems between sellers and buyers often arise because of asymmetric information. Line managers and employees can misunderstand what senior executives intend. A Food Lion memo challenging employees to find a thousand different ways to save 1 percent of their own costs elicited unintended shortcuts in food preparation and storage that posed a hazard to public health. Often, asymmetric information also causes customers to rationally discount products such as used cars or computer components for which quality information is often unverifiable at the point of purchase. Reputation with customers, workers, and the surrounding tax jurisdiction is one way companies deal with the problem of asymmetric information, and managers must attend to these effects of reputation on shareholder value. We address the managerial implications of asymmetric information in Chapter 10.

Known Recontracting Costs   Finally, to focus exclusively on the discounted present value of cash flows to shareholders necessitates that managers obtain not only sales revenue and expense estimates but also future recontracting costs for pivotal inputs. Owners of professional baseball teams have recently emphasized the importance of known recontracting costs (with star players) to the value of their franchises. In another instance, Westinghouse entered into long-term contracts to maintain and resupply fuel rods to nuclear power plants without such knowledge. Thereafter, the market price of uranium quadrupled. Although Westinghouse was allowed to breach its contracts to the nation's power suppliers, Westinghouse's reputation suffered and its capitalized value declined. Complete derivative markets for hedging commodity price risk can go a long way toward solving these problems introduced by recontracting costs. For example, if Westinghouse had purchased forward contracts for uranium, it could have locked in the projected cost of its uranium requirements. In the absence of such a lock-in, a pivotal input can always "hold up" the firm's owners when the time comes for contract renewals, and managers must anticipate and mitigate these recontracting problems.

Example

LOW EARTH ORBIT SPACE JUNK: LOCKHEED[20]

Satellite orbital paths are becoming congested with space junk. The U.S. Air Force's Space Command tracks 8,500 objects that are 10 centimeters or larger in low earth orbit (6–125 miles up) and 1 meter or larger in geosynchronous orbit (20,000 miles up). However, a collision with an object as small as 0.5 centimeter will depressurize the space shuttle resulting in "mission loss." In July 1996, Cerise, a French satellite, tumbled out of orbit after colliding with small pieces of an exploded Arienne 4 French rocket. The vastness of interstellar space is just that—vast—but geosynchronous and low earth orbits are becoming congested. About 70 to 100 new commercial and military satellites are launched per year worldwide at a cost of about $8,000 to $25,000 per pound. Lockheed Martin is testing an X-33 rocket that will reduce this cost to $1,000 per pound. As companies like Aeroastro and Kelly Space develop still cheaper launch systems that can achieve escape velocity, the congestion will surely worsen.

The problem is that satellite orbital paths are common property resources like deep sea fisheries. No company or nation has an incentive to economize on their use in order to achieve maximum sustainable yield because no one can appropriate the benefits of doing so. No property rights are specified, assigned, or enforced. As a result, each producer has an incentive to overutilize the resource. When congestion occurs, the costs

---

[20] Based on "To Boldly Dump," *The Economist,* March 29, 1997, p. 87, and "They're Going Crazy in Space," *BusinessWeek,* July 28, 1997, p. 89.

are widespread, but the catastrophic accident costs fall upon isolated parties. Who owes what to whom when a future Cerise plows into a Westinghouse satellite has not been determined. This lack of private property rights and the consequentially incomplete market prevents all but the most vague analysis of projected cash flows.

Motorola contracted with Teledesic to launch a swarm of 924 new communication satellites into low earth orbit. Before they do so, Teledesic's managers will need to press for the privatization of the common property resources associated with satellite orbital paths. Markets can then emerge to price the paths. This will enable meaningful recontracting cost analysis of the projected cash flow expense for replacing a satellite.

Example

FCC Auction Introduces a Market in Spectrum Rights

A similar congestion problem was solved recently when the Federal Communications Commission (FCC) auctioned off the electro-magnetic spectrum in urban areas. Radio, television, and broadband cellular phone frequencies were once common property available to anyone who wished to transmit signals. As demand by broadcasters and cellular phone users in a geographic area grew, the FCC assigned unique blocks of frequencies closer and closer to one another and kept a watchful eye on all the signal interference. However, the FCC was powerless to stop the growing congestion and resulting signal degradation. Only when Congress empowered the FCC to auction off the electromagnetic spectrum did the projected cost of clear signal quality become identifiable. The auctions then created an incentive for the development of innovative communications technologies to reduce cost. For example, the 1995 auction of broadband frequencies for personal communication systems coincided with the announcement of signal compression technology to mitigate the signal interference problem.

To the extent that markets are incomplete, information is asymmetric, or recontracting costs are unknown, managers must attend to these matters rather than simply focus on projected cash flows. In so doing, their efforts will raise shareholder value.

Residual Claimants

A growing consensus believes that the primary duty of management and the board of directors of a company is to the shareholders themselves. Shareholders have a residual claim on the firm's net cash flows after all expected contractual returns have been paid. All the other stakeholders (employees, customers, bondholders, banks, suppliers, the surrounding tax jurisdictions, the community in which plants are located, etc.) have *contractual* expected returns. If expectations created by those contracts are not met, any of these stakeholders has access to the full force of the contract law in securing whatever they are due. Shareholders have contractual rights, too, but those rights simply entitle them to whatever is left over, i.e., to the residual. As a consequence, when shareholder owners hire a CEO and a board, they create a fiduciary duty to husband the company's resources in such a way as to maximize the net present value of these residual claims. This is what constitutes the objective of shareholder wealth maximization.

Be very clear, however, that the value of any company's stock is quite dependent on reputation effects. Underfunding a pension plan or polluting the environment results in massive losses of capitalized value because the financial markets anticipate (correctly) that such a company will have reduced future cash flows. Labor costs to attract new employees will rise; tax jurisdictions will reduce the tax preferences offered in new plant locations; customers may boycott; and the public relations, lobbying, and legal costs of such a company will surely rise. All this implies that wealth-maximizing managers must be very carefully attuned to stakeholder interests precisely because it is in their shareholders' best interests to do so.

GOALS IN THE PUBLIC SECTOR AND THE NOT-FOR-PROFIT ENTERPRISE

The value-maximization objective developed for private sector firms is not an appropriate objective in the public sector or in not-for-profit (NFP) organizations.[21] These organizations pursue a different set of objectives because of the nature of the goods or services they supply and the manner in which they are funded.

There are three characteristics of NFP organizations that distinguish them from for-profit enterprises and influence decision making in the enterprise. First, no one possesses a right to receive profit or surpluses in an NFP enterprise. The absence of a profit motive can have a serious impact on the incentive to be efficient. Second, NFP enterprises are exempt from taxes on corporate income. Finally, many NFP enterprises benefit from the fact that donations to them are tax deductible. These tax benefits give NFP enterprises an advantage when competing with for-profit enterprises.

Not-for-profit organizations include performing arts groups, museums, libraries, hospitals, churches, volunteer organizations, cooperatives, credit unions, labor unions, professional societies, foundations, and fraternal organizations. Some of these organizations offer services to a group of clients, such as the patients of a hospital. Others provide services primarily to members, such as the members of a country club or credit union. Finally, some NFP organizations produce public benefits, as does a local symphony or theater company.

Public sector (government) agencies tend to provide services with a significant *public-good* character. In contrast to private goods like bite-sized candy bars, **public goods** may be consumed by more than one person at the same time and entail high transaction costs of excluding those who do not pay. Examples of public goods include national defense and flood control. If an antiballistic missile shield or a flood control project is constructed, those behind the shield cannot be excluded from its protection even if they refuse to contribute to the cost. Even if one could exclude those who do not pay, the indivisibility in consumption of a public good makes the incremental cost (and therefore the efficient price) of another participant quite low. Some goods, such as recreational facilities and the performing arts, have both private- and public-good characteristics. For example, concerts and parks may be shared (within limits) and are partially nonexcludable since quality performing arts and recreational facilities convey prestige and quality-of-life benefits to the entire community.[22] The more costly the exclusion, the more likely the good or service will be provided by the public sector rather than the private sector. Portrait artists and personal fitness trainers offer pay-as-you-go private fee arrangements. On the other hand, chamber music fans and tennis court users often organize in consumption-sharing and cost-sharing clubs, while open-air symphony concerts and large parks usually necessitate some public financing.

Public Goods
Goods that may be consumed by more than one person at the same time with little or no extra cost, and for which it is expensive or impossible to exclude those who do not pay.

---

[21] This section draws heavily on Burton A. Weisbrod, *The Nonprofit Economy* (Cambridge, MA.: Harvard University Press, 1988).

[22] William J. Baumol and W. G. Bowen, *Performing Arts: The Economic Dilemma* (Brookfield, VT: Ashgate Publishing Co., 1993).

Not-for-Profit Objectives

For NFP organizations that rely heavily on external contributions, the overriding objective is to satisfy current and prospective contributors. It is common to find an NFP organization that seeks to satisfy its contributors by (1) efficiently managing its resources, (2) increasing its capacity to supply high-quality goods or services, and (3) providing a rewarding work environment for its administrators.

The Efficiency Objective

Cost-Benefit Analysis
A resource-allocation model that can be used by public sector and not-for-profit organizations to evaluate programs or investments on the basis of the magnitude of the discounted costs and benefits.

Whatever set of objectives the organization decides to pursue, these objectives should be pursued in the most resource-efficient fashion possible. The model that has been developed to provide a framework for the allocation of public and NFP resources among competing uses primarily has been the **cost-benefit analysis** model. This model is the analogue to the capital budgeting model in the private sector. Benefits and costs associated with investments are estimated and discounted by an appropriate discount rate, and projects are evaluated on the basis of the magnitude of the discounted benefits in relation to the costs. Because government and NFP organization spending is normally constrained by a budget ceiling, the criterion actually used in evaluating expenditures for any public purpose may be one of the following:

1. Maximize benefits for given costs
2. Minimize costs while achieving a fixed level of benefits
3. Maximize net benefits (benefits minus costs)

Chapter 18 discusses the capital budgeting techniques that are appropriate for investment decision-making in the public and NFP sector.

Although cost-benefit analysis can serve as a guide to a more efficient allocation of resources by a public agency or an NFP institution, such analysis typically does not consider the effect of a proposed project on income distribution. Concern for these matters must be introduced at a later stage in the analysis, generally through the political process.

International Perspectives

http://

You can find information on international trade, balance of payments, and direct investment at the Internet site for the Bureau of Economic Analysis, U.S. Department of Commerce: http://www.bea.doc.gov/bea/di1.htm

MANAGING IN A GLOBAL COMPETITIVE ECONOMY

U.S. manufacturers face serious economic challenges from firms located in Japan, Korea, other countries in the Far East, the European Community, Canada, Mexico, Brazil, and others. As other economies have developed and trade barriers have been lowered, American firms have found themselves facing increasingly intense competition from abroad. The U.S. foreign trade deficit (i.e., the dollar value of exports minus imports) has grown from an annual level of approximately $200 billion during the late 1990s to well over $500 billion in 2003.

Many industries have seen substantial portions of industry output move overseas, either to foreign firms or subsidiaries of U.S. firms. For example, in 1980 nearly 94 percent of the computers bought in the United States were made in the United States. By 1990, that figure had declined to less than 66 percent. The figure is even lower if one counts the foreign component contents of U.S.-assembled computers. Dramatic domestic market share declines have been experienced in the machine tool, semiconductor, telephone equipment, and apparel industries. Indeed, very few industries have witnessed increases in the domestically produced portion of their U.S. market share.

Another challenge for U.S. manufacturers, however, is the increased competition from foreign firms that have set up plants in the United States. From 1986 to 1996, a relatively weak U.S. dollar induced foreigners to purchase not only Cadillacs and IBM PCs, but also dollar-denominated *assets*. The buying spree included not only T-bills, bonds, and stocks, but also real estate and factories. This trend reduced the U.S.-owned share of U.S. production capacity in the cement industry, for example, from 90 percent in 1979 to 30 percent in 1989. Domestic automobile manufacturers also face substantial competition from domestic plants owned by foreign firms from Japan and Europe; by 1997, 20 percent of all U.S. automobile production was foreign-owned, compared to 3 percent in 1985.

Sustained international trade deficits necessarily result in either asset sales or borrowing. As a result, since 1985 the U.S. has been a net debtor nation. On the one hand, this situation is attractive; Americans receive more foreign goods today in exchange for U.S. promissory notes to repay tomorrow. Although a shrinking U.S. manufacturing sector implies limited employment prospects in the short term, in the longer term one has the prospect of higher income trading partners buying more American exports. Freer international trade may, that is, increase incomes and employment in the U.S. as well as in our major trading partners (Japan, Mexico, Canada, and China).

The study of managerial economics is important for future managers who face the growing challenge of global competition. Many times U.S. managers can learn from the successful experiences of their foreign competitors, like the "just-in-time" inventory management techniques and quality management practices adapted from successful Japanese firms. Chapter 6 addresses import-export trade especially in U.S., Japanese, and European companies. Throughout the text we will highlight specific issues and opportunities that face managers in a global, competitive economy.

SUMMARY

- *Managerial economics* is the application of economic theory and analytical tools to decision-making problems faced by private, not-for-profit, and public institutions. Increasingly, these decision-making problems have an international dimension.

- Managerial economics draws on microeconomic theory and macroeconomic models to assist managers in making optimal resource-allocation decisions.

- *Economic profit* is defined as the difference between *total revenues* and *total economic costs*. Economic costs include a normal rate of return on the capital contributed by the firm's owners. Economic profits exist to compensate investors for the risk they assume, because of temporary disequilibrium conditions that may occur in a market, because of the existence of monopoly power, and as a reward to firms that are especially innovative or highly efficient.

- As an overall objective of the firm, the *shareholder wealth-maximization* model is very appealing. It is flexible enough to account for differential levels of risk and timing differences in the receipt of benefits and the incurring of future costs. Because shareholder wealth is defined in terms of the value of the stock, this goal provides a precise measure of performance, which is free from the problems associated with using various accounting measures.

- Managers may not always behave in a manner consistent with the shareholder wealth-maximization objective. The agency costs associated with preventing or at least mitigating these deviations from the owner-principal's objective are substantial.

- Shareholder wealth-maximization implies forward-looking, long-run-oriented, dynamic strategies that anticipate change in a risky market environment. Managers can focus on maximizing the discounted present value of the firm's cash flows if three conditions hold: complete markets, no asymmetric information, and known recontracting costs. Otherwise, they must attend to these complications as well.

- *Not-for-profit* enterprises exist to supply a good or service desired by their primary contributors. Public sector organizations often provide services having significant public-good characteristics; that is, they may be consumed by more than one person at a time with little additional cost, and the transaction cost of excluding those who do not pay exceeds the benefits that are derived by charging the efficient price.
- Regardless of their specific objectives, both public and private institutions should seek to furnish their goods or services in the most resource-efficient manner. The marginal decision rules from the profit-maximization model apply.

EXERCISES

1. In the period leading up to the war in Iraq, oil prices increased significantly, as did the profits earned by many oil companies. Some politicians argued that these profits were undeserved, and they called for price rollbacks and/or increased taxes. Discuss the pros and cons of these proposals in the context of the various theories of profit.

2. In 2000, firms in the drug industry earned an average return on net worth of 25.0 percent, compared with an average return of 15.0 percent earned by over 1,400 firms followed by *Value Line*. Which theory or theories of profit do you think best explain(s) the performance of the drug industry?

3. Try to define, in as operational a manner as possible, the objectives that your college or university seeks to pursue.
   a. How may success in achieving these objectives be measured?
   b. To what extent do the objectives of various subunits of your college or university complement (or contradict) each other?
   c. Who are the major constituencies served by your university? What role do they play in the formation of these objectives?
   d. You may want to talk with some of your school's administrators and compare their views on the college's goals and objectives with your own.

4. In the context of the shareholder wealth-maximization model of a firm, what is the expected impact of each of the following events on the value of the firm?
   a. New foreign competitors enter the market.
   b. Strict pollution control requirements are implemented by the government.
   c. A previously nonunion workforce votes to unionize.
   d. The rate of inflation increases substantially.
   e. A major technological breakthrough is achieved by the firm, reducing its costs of production.

5. After the invasion of Kuwait by Iraq, the price of jet fuel used by airlines decreased dramatically. As the CEO of Delta Airlines, you have been presented with the following options to deal with this problem:
   a. Reduce airfares to reflect the expense reduction.
   b. Increase the number of flights per day in some markets.
   c. Make long-term contracts to buy jet fuel at a fixed price for the next two years and set airfares to a level that will cover these costs.

   Evaluate these options in the context of the decision-making model presented in the text.

6. How would each of the following actions be expected to affect shareholder wealth?

   a. RJR Nabisco sells its Del Monte division for over $1 billion.

   b. Ford Motor Company pays $2.5 billion for Jaguar.

   c. General Motors offers large rebates to stimulate sales of its automobiles.

   d. Rising interest rates cause the required returns of shareholders to increase.

   e. Import restrictions are placed on the Japanese competitors of Chrysler.

   f. There is a sudden drop in the expected future rate of inflation.

   g. A new, labor-saving machine is purchased by Wonder Bread and results in the layoff of 300 employees.

7. Use a search engine such as http://www.yahoo.com or http://www.newsindex.com to find articles on CEO compensation. In September 1996, Towers Perrin reported that only about 27 percent of typical CEO compensation in large U.S. corporations was in the form of salary, while annual and long-term incentive pay made up 66 percent, with the remainder of compensation being in the form of benefits. Has this changed since 1996?

   Use the information that you find at the site you select to write a two-paragraph executive summary of current practices in CEO incentive compensation, and relate your findings to the agency problem mentioned in the chapter.

CASE EXERCISES

REDUCING GREENHOUSE GASES

The U.N. Kyoto Protocol of December 1997 obligates the United States to reduce by approximately 25 percent the emission of carbon dioxide and other greenhouse gases between 2000 and 2010. Brazil, China, India, and Mexico were all exempted from the agreement. Kyoto's regulatory quota system[23] was rejected by the U.S.

QUESTION

1. Assuming a reduction in greenhouse gases is desirable, how could a tradable permit system accomplish that goal?

REFORMING THE FORMER SOVIET ECONOMY

The failure of the state-controlled, centrally planned economies of the Eastern European countries and of the former Soviet Union to produce adequate quantities of high-quality products that are desired by consumers has led to major economic and political reform in these countries. East Germany ceased to exist as an independent nation-state in a little over one year and was merged into a united Germany in late 1990. Economic and political pressures have led to major changes in the organization of the economies (and governments) of Hungary, Poland, Rumania, and the Soviet Union itself.

The failure of state-controlled economies that did not permit the private ownership of property or capital and did not permit competition among profit-seeking enterprises can be viewed as a reflection of a major agency problem. Plant managers had little to gain from more efficient operations. There was neither the pressure from competitors nor from potential takeovers by a more efficient group of owner-managers, as is true in Western economies. Furthermore, as state-chartered monopolies, there was no risk of failure of the enterprise.

---

[23] Based on "Letting the Free Market Clear the Air," *Business Week,* November 6, 2000, pp. 200–204.

The Soviet Union finally collapsed under the pressure of a failed economic system and political reforms that permitted open criticism of the government. President Yeltsin of Russia quickly moved to reform the economic system. Price controls were lifted on most goods and services, state subsidies were eliminated, and steps were taken that should lead to the international convertibility of the currency, the ruble. These steps were designed to increase the accountability of managers to the new owners, add an important element of competition to the former Soviet economy, and increase the efficiency of economic enterprises in the former Soviet Union. This ambitious plan to privatize the former Soviet economy raises a host of interesting challenges for managers.

QUESTIONS

1. When state-owned enterprises are sold, how should their value be established?

2. Should the value be based on the cost of the assets in place, the past earning power of the enterprise, or the future earning potential in a competitive economy?

3. How can the future earning capacity of privatized enterprises be estimated?

4. Propose a compensation plan for managers of the privatized oil and gas companies in the former Soviet Union.

2

Fundamental Economic Concepts

CHAPTER PREVIEW A few fundamental economic concepts provide cornerstones for all of the analysis in managerial economics. Four of the most important are marginal analysis, net present value, the meaning and measurement of risk, and the trade-offs that must be made between risk and return. Marginal analysis tools are central when a decision maker is seeking to optimize some objective, such as profits or shareholder wealth. Appendix 2A develops the relationship between marginal analysis and differential calculus. The net present value concept provides the linkage between the long-term decisions made by a firm and the shareholder wealth-maximization objective. Because most economic decisions involve an element of risk, the meaning and measurement of risk is an important concept for managers. Risk-return analysis is important to an understanding of the many trade-offs that managers must make as they plan new products, expand capacity, or change prices. In Chapter 18, we will see how managers incorporate explicit probability information about the risk of various outcomes into individual choice models, decision trees, risk-adjusted discount rates, simulation analysis, and scenario planning.

MANAGERIAL CHALLENGE

Revenue Management at Delta Airlines[1]

Airlines face highly cyclical demand; Delta reported a net loss of $958 million amidst the 2002 recession, but a profit of $920 million in the 1997 expansion. Demand also fluctuates day to day. One of the ways Delta copes with random demand is through revenue management techniques. Revenue or "yield" management (RM) is an integrated demand-management, order-booking, and capacity-planning process that focuses on marginal analysis.

To win orders in a service industry *without slashing prices* requires that companies create perceived value for segmented classes of differentiated customers. Business travelers on airlines, for example, want and will pay for last-minute responsiveness to their change orders. Other business travelers demand exceptional delivery reliability and on-time performance. In contrast, most vacation excursion travelers want commodity-like service at rock-bottom prices. Although only 15–20 percent of most airlines' seats are in the business segment, 65–75 percent of the profit contribution on a typical flight comes from this group. The problem is that airline capacity must be planned and allocated well in advance of customer arrivals, often before demand is fully known, yet unsold inventory perishes at the moment of departure. This same management challenge faces hospitals, consulting firms, TV stations, and printing businesses, all of whom must acquire and schedule capacity before the demands for elective surgeries, next week's crisis management team, Thursday's network TV ads, or the afternoon press run are fully known.

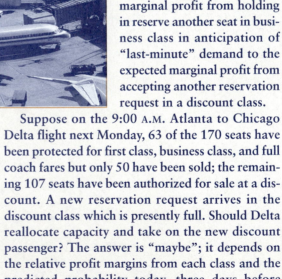

One approach to minimizing unsold inventory and yet capturing all last-minute high-profit business is to auction off capacity to the highest bidder. The auction for free-wheeling electricity works just that way: power companies bid at quarter 'til the hour for excess supplies that other utilities agree to deliver on the hour. However, in airlines (like many other service businesses) prices cannot be adjusted quickly as the moment of departure approaches. Instead, revenue managers employ large historical databases to predict segmented customer demand in light of current arrivals on the reservation system. They then compare the expected marginal profit from holding in reserve another seat in business class in anticipation of "last-minute" demand to the expected marginal profit from accepting another reservation request in a discount class.

Suppose on the 9:00 A.M. Atlanta to Chicago Delta flight next Monday, 63 of the 170 seats have been protected for first class, business class, and full coach fares but only 50 have been sold; the remaining 107 seats have been authorized for sale at a discount. A new reservation request arrives in the discount class which is presently full. Should Delta reallocate capacity and take on the new discount passenger? The answer is "maybe"; it depends on the relative profit margins from each class and the predicted probability today, three days before departure, of excess demand (beyond 63 seats) next Monday in the business classes.[2]

If the $721 full coach fare has a $500 profit margin and the $155 discount fare has a $100 profit margin, the seat in question should not be reallocated from

MANAGERIAL CHALLENGE

business to discount customers when the probability of "stocking out" in business is greater than 0.20. For example, if the probability is 0.25, the expected marginal profit from holding an empty seat for another potential business customer is $125, whereas the marginal profit from selling that seat to the discount customer is only $100. Even an advance-payment no-refund seat request from the discount class should be refused. Every company has some viable orders that should be refused; excess capacity in business class is not "idle capacity" but rather a predictable revenue opportunity waiting to happen.

In this chapter, we introduce the methods of "marginal analysis" that can be used to solve an airline's seat allocation decision problem. Chapter 14 discusses the price discrimination analysis that underlies revenue management, and Appendix 14A applies the techniques of revenue management.

http://

Talus Solutions, formerly Aeronomics Inc., specializes in revenue management. Visit their Web site at http://www.talussolutions.com for case studies and industry information. Some other firms that use revenue management are listed at http://www.abovetheweather.com

[1] Based on Robert Cross, *Revenue Management* (New York: Broadway Books, 1995), and Frederick Harris and Peter Peacock, "Hold My Place Please: Yield Management Improves Capacity Allocation Guesswork," *Marketing Management,* Fall, 1995, pp. 34–46.

[2] Appendix 14A explains how these demand assessments take into account the likely incidence of cancellations and no-shows—i.e., an optimal level of overbooking.

MARGINAL ANALYSIS

Marginal Analysis
A basis for making various economic decisions that analyzes the additional (marginal) benefits derived from a particular decision and compares them with the additional (marginal) costs incurred.

Marginal analysis is one of the most useful concepts of economic decision making. Resource-allocation decisions typically are expressed in terms of the marginal conditions that must be satisfied to attain an optimal solution. The familiar profit-maximization rule for the firm of setting output at the point where "marginal cost equals marginal revenue" is one such example. Long-term investment decisions (capital expenditures) also are made using marginal analysis decision rules. If the expected return from an investment project (that is, the *marginal return* to the firm) exceeds the cost of funds that must be acquired to finance the project (the *marginal cost* of capital), then the project should be undertaken. Following this important marginal decision rule leads to the maximization of shareholder wealth.

In the marginal analysis framework, resource-allocation decisions are made by comparing the marginal (or incremental) benefits of a change in the level of an activity with the marginal (or incremental) costs of the change. *Marginal benefit* is defined as the change in total benefits that are derived from undertaking some economic activity, such as additional shipbuilding at Tenneco Shipyards. For example, the marginal revenue (a benefit) derived from producing and selling one more supertanker is equal to the difference between total revenue, assuming the additional unit is not sold, and total revenue including the additional sale. Similarly, *marginal cost* is defined as the change in total costs that occurs from undertaking some economic activity, such as the production of an additional ship design. Recall from the previous chapter that total (economic) costs include opportunity costs, and therefore may not necessarily always be equal to the cash outlays alone.[3] Perhaps the Tenneco design team has an opportunity for higher net profit as subcontractors on Boeing projects. If so, Tenneco's routine ship-design work should be contracted out to lower cost firms.

[3] The concept of economic cost is examined in more detail in Chapter 8.

→ A change in the level of an economic activity is desirable if the marginal benefits exceed the marginal costs. This is equivalent to saying that the increase in total revenues, for example, exceeds the increase in total costs. Therefore, in decisions involving the expansion of an economic activity, the optimal level occurs at the point where the marginal benefits are equal to the marginal costs. If we define *net marginal return* as the *difference* between marginal benefits and marginal costs, then an equivalent optimality condition is that the level of the activity should be increased to the point where the net marginal return is zero.

Example

MARGINAL ANALYSIS AND CAPITAL BUDGETING DECISIONS: SARA LEE CORPORATION

The capital budgeting decision problem facing a typical firm, such as Sara Lee Corporation, can be used to illustrate the application of marginal analysis decision rules. Sara Lee has the following schedule of potential investment projects (all assumed to be of equal risk) available to it:

Project	Investment Required ($ Million)	Expected Rate of Return	Cumulative Investment ($ Million)
A	$25.0	27.0%	$25.0
B	15.0	24.0	40.0
C	40.0	21.0	80.0
D	35.0	18.0	115.0
E	12.0	15.0	127.0
F	20.0	14.0	147.0
G	18.0	13.0	165.0
H	13.0	11.0	178.0
I	7.0	8.0	185.0

Sara Lee has estimated the cost of acquiring the funds needed to finance these investment projects as follows:

Block of Funds ($ Million)	Cost of Capital	Cumulative Funds Raised ($ Million)
First $50.0	10.0%	$50.0
Next 25.0	10.5	75.0
Next 40.0	11.0	115.0
Next 50.0	12.2	165.0
Next 20.0	14.5	185.0

The expected rate of return on the projects listed above can be thought of as the marginal (or incremental) return available to Sara Lee as it undertakes each additional investment project. Similarly, the cost-of-capital schedule may be thought of as the marginal cost of acquiring the needed funds. Following the marginal analysis rules means that Sara Lee should invest in additional projects as long as the expected rate of return on the project exceeds the marginal cost of capital funds needed to finance the project.

Project A, which offers an expected return of 27 percent and requires an outlay of $25 million, is acceptable because the marginal return exceeds the marginal cost of capital (10.0 percent for the first $50 million of funds raised by Sara Lee). In fact, an examination of the tables indicates that projects A through G all meet the marginal analysis test because the marginal return from each of these projects exceeds the marginal cost of capital funds needed to finance these projects. In contrast, projects H and I should not be undertaken because they offer returns of 11 and 8 percent, respectively, compared with a marginal cost of capital of 14.5 percent for the $20 million in funds needed to finance these projects.

In summary, marginal analysis instructs decision makers to determine the additional (marginal) costs and additional (marginal) benefits associated with a proposed action. *Only if the marginal benefits exceed the marginal costs* (that is, if net marginal benefits are positive) should the action be taken.[4]

Total, Marginal, and Average Relationships

Economic relationships can be presented using tabular, graphic, and algebraic frameworks. Let us first use a tabular presentation. Suppose that the total profit π_T of a firm is a function of the number of units of output produced Q, as shown in columns 1 and 2 of Table 2.1. Marginal profit, which represents the change in total profit resulting from a one-unit increase in output, is shown in column 3 of the table. (A Δ is used to represent a "change" in some variable.) The marginal profit $\Delta\pi(Q)$ of any level of output Q is calculated by taking the difference between the total profit at this level $\pi_T(Q)$ and at one unit below this level $\pi_T(Q - 1)$.[5] In comparing the marginal and total profit functions, we note that for increasing output levels, the marginal profit values remain positive as long as the total profit function is increasing. Only when the total profit function begins decreasing—that is, at $Q = 10$ units—does the marginal profit become negative. The average profit function values $\pi_A(Q)$, shown in column 4 of Table 2.1, are obtained by dividing the total profit figure $\pi_T(Q)$ by the output level Q. In comparing the marginal and the average profit function values, we see that the average profit function $\pi_A(Q)$ is increasing as long as the marginal profit is greater than the average profit; that is, up to $Q = 7$ units. Beyond an output level of $Q = 7$ units, the marginal profit is less than the average profit and the average profit function values are decreasing.

By examining the total profit function $\pi_T(Q)$ in Table 2.1, we see that profit is maximized at an output level of $Q = 9$ units. Given that the objective is to maximize total profit, then the optimal output decision would be to produce and sell 9 units. If the marginal analysis decision rule discussed earlier in this section is used, the same (optimal) decision is obtained. Applying the rule to this problem, the firm would expand production as long as the *net* marginal return—that is, marginal revenue minus marginal cost (marginal profit)—is positive. From column 3 of Table 2.1, we can see that the marginal profit is positive for output levels up to $Q = 9$. Therefore, the marginal profit decision rule would indicate that 9 units should be produced— the same decision that was obtained from the total profit function.

---

[4] Strictly speaking, an action may also be undertaken if marginal benefits equal marginal costs. In this case, the firm's change in profit will be just equal to zero, and the manager will be indifferent to taking the action.

[5] Appendix 2A expands upon the idea that the total profit function can be maximized by identifying the level of activity at which the marginal profit function goes to zero.

Table 2.1   Total, Marginal, and Average Profit Relationships

(1) Number of Units of Output Per Unit of Time Q	(2) Total Profit $\pi_T(Q)$ ($\$$)	(3) Marginal Profit $\Delta\pi(Q) = \pi_T(Q) - \pi_T(Q-1)$ ($\$$/Unit)	(4) Average Profit $\pi_A(Q) = \pi_T(Q)/Q$ ($\$$/Unit)
0	−200	0	—
1	−150	50	−150.00
2	−25	125	−12.50
3	200	225	66.67
4	475	275	118.75
5	775	300	155.00
6	1,075	300	179.17
7	1,325	250	189.29
8	1,475	150	184.38
9	1,500	25	166.67
10	1,350	−150	135.00

The relationships among the total, marginal, and average profit functions and the optimal output decision also can be represented graphically. A set of *continuous* profit functions, analogous to those presented above in Table 2.1 for discrete integer values of output (Q), is shown in Figure 2.1. At the break-even output level Q_1, both total profits and average profits are zero. The marginal profit function, which equals the *slope* of the total profit function, takes on its maximum value at an output of Q_2 units. This point corresponds to the *inflection point*. Below the inflection point, total profits are increasing at an increasing rate, and hence marginal profits are increasing. Above the inflection point, up to an output level Q_4, total profits are increasing at a decreasing rate and consequently marginal profits are decreasing. The average profit function, which represents the slope of a straight line drawn from the origin 0 to each point on the total profit function, takes on its maximum value at an output of Q_3 units. The average profit necessarily equals the marginal profit at this point. This follows because the slope of the $0A$ line, which defines the average profit, is also equal to the slope of the total profit function at point A, which defines the marginal profit. Finally, total profit is maximized at an output of Q_4 units where marginal profit equals 0. Beyond Q_4 the total profit function is decreasing, and consequently the marginal profit function takes on negative values.

The Net Present Value Concept

To achieve the objective of shareholder wealth maximization, a set of appropriate decision rules must be specified. We just saw that the decision rule of setting *marginal revenue (benefit) equal to marginal cost* (MR = MC) provides a framework for making many important resource-allocation decisions. The MR = MC rule is best suited for situations when the costs and benefits occur at approximately the same time.

Figure 2.1   Total, Average, and Marginal Profit Functions

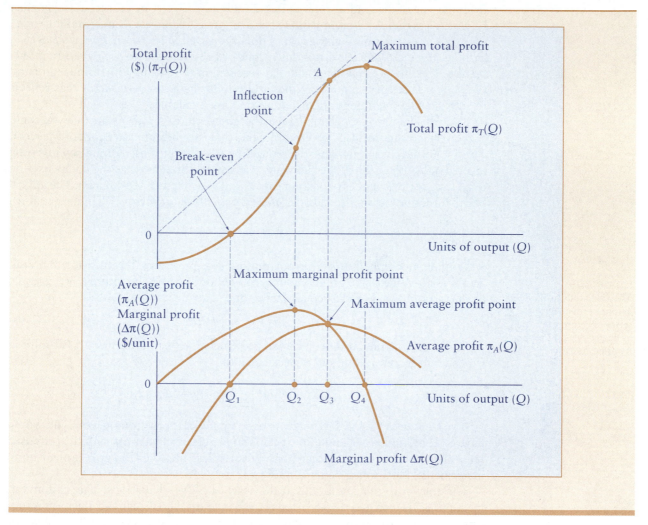

Many economic decisions require that costs be incurred immediately but result in a stream of benefits over several future time periods. In these cases, the *net present value* (NPV) *rule* provides appropriate guidance for decision makers.

Determining the Net Present Value of an Investment

To understand the NPV rule, consider the following situation. You have just inherited $1 million. Your financial advisor has suggested that you use these funds to purchase a piece of land near a proposed new highway interchange. Your advisor, who is also a state road commissioner, is certain that the interchange will be built and that in one year the value of this land will increase to $1.2 million. Hence, you believe initially that this is a riskless investment. At the end of one year you plan to sell the land. You are being asked to invest $1 million today in the anticipation of receiving $1.2 million a year from today, or a profit of $200,000. You wonder whether this profit represents a sufficient return on your investment.

You feel it is important to recognize that there is a one-year difference between the time you make your outlay of $1 million and the time you receive $1.2 million from the sale of the land. A return of $1.2 million received one year from today must be worth less than $1.2 million today because you could invest your $1 million today to earn interest over the coming year. *A dollar received in the future is worth less than a dollar in hand today because a dollar today can be invested to earn a return immediately.* Therefore, to compare a dollar received in the future with a dollar in hand today, it is necessary to multiply the future dollar by a *discount factor* that reflects the alternative investment opportunities that are available.

Instead of investing your $1 million in the land venture, you are aware that you could also invest in a one-year U.S. government bond that currently offers a return of 5 percent. The 5 percent return represents the return (the opportunity cost) forgone by investing in the land project. The 5 percent rate also can be thought of as the compensation to an investor who agrees to postpone receiving a cash return for one year. The appropriate discount factor, also called a *present value interest factor (PVIF)*, is equal to

$$PVIF = \frac{1}{1 + i}$$

Present Value
The value today of a future amount of money or a series of future payments evaluated at the appropriate discount rate.

where i is the compensation for postponing receipt of a cash return for one year. The **present value** (PV_0) of an amount received one year in the future (FV_1) is equal to that amount times the discount factor, or

$$PV_0 = FV_1 \times (PVIF) \qquad [2.1]$$

In the case of the land project, the present value of the promised $1.2 million expected to be received in one year is equal to

$$PV_0 = \$1.2 \text{ million} \left(\frac{1}{1 + 0.05} \right) = \$1,142,857$$

If you invested $1,142,857 today to earn 5 percent for the coming year, you would have $1.2 million at the end of the year. You are clearly better off with the proposed land investment (assuming that it really is riskless like the U.S. government bond investment). How much better off are you?

The answer to this question is at the heart of NPV calculations. The land investment project is worth $1,142,857 today to an investor who demands a 5 percent return on this type of investment. You, however, have been able to acquire this investment for only $1,000,000. Thus your present wealth has increased by undertaking this investment by $142,857 ($1,142,857 present value of the projected investment opportunity payoffs minus the required initial investment of $1,000,000). The NPV of this investment is $142,857. In general, the NPV of an investment is equal to

$$NPV = \text{Present value of future returns} - \text{Initial outlay} \qquad [2.2]$$

This example was simplified by assuming that the returns from the investment were received exactly one year from the date of the initial outlay. The NPV rule can be generalized to cover returns received over any number of future time periods. In Appendix A the present value concept is developed in more detail so that it can be applied in more complex investment settings.

Net Present Value and Shareholder Wealth Maximization

The NPV of an investment made by a firm represents the contribution of that investment to the value of the firm and, accordingly, to the wealth of shareholders. The net present value concept is used to evaluate the *cash flows* generated from the firm's activities. Hence, the NPV concept plays a central role in the achievement of shareholder wealth maximization.

Market Efficiency   A central theme of much of the financial economics thinking and research has been the *efficiency* of the capital markets. The more efficient capital markets are, the more likely it is that resources will find their highest value (risk-adjusted) uses.

In an efficient capital market, stock prices provide an unbiased estimate of the true value of an enterprise. Stock prices reflect a *present value* estimate of the firm's *expected cash flows*, evaluated at an appropriate *required rate of return*. The required rate of return is determined by conditions in the financial markets, including the supply of funds from savers, the investment demand for funds, and expectations regarding future inflation rates. The required rate of return on a security also depends on the seniority of the security, the maturity of that security, the business and financial risk of the firm issuing the security, the risk of default, and the marketability of the security. The *efficiency of the capital markets* is the important "glue" that bonds the present value of a firm's net cash flows—discounted at the appropriate risk-adjusted required rate of return—to shareholder wealth as measured by the market value of a company's common stock.

Sources of Positive Net Present Value Projects

What causes some projects to have a positive NPV and others to have a negative NPV? When product and factor markets are other than perfectly competitive, it is possible for a firm to earn above-normal profits (economic rents) that result in positive net present value projects. The reasons why these above-normal profits may be available arise from conditions that define each type of product and factor market and distinguish it from a perfectly competitive market. These reasons include the following barriers to entry and other factors:

1. Buyer preferences for established brand names.
2. Ownership or control of favored distribution systems (such as exclusive auto dealerships or airline hubs).
3. Patent control of superior product designs or production techniques.
4. Exclusive ownership of superior natural resource deposits.
5. Inability of new firms to acquire necessary factors of production (management, labor, equipment).
6. Superior access to financial resources at lower costs (economies of scale in attracting capital).
7. Economies of large-scale production and distribution arising from
   a. Capital-intensive production processes.
   b. High initial start-up costs.

These factors can permit a firm to identify positive net present value projects for internal investment. If the barriers to entry are sufficiently high (such as a patent on key technology) so as to prevent any new competition or if the start-up period for competitive ventures is sufficiently long, then it is possible that a project may have a positive net present value. However, in assessing the viability of such a project, the manager or analyst must consider the likely period of time when above-normal returns can be earned before new competitors emerge and force cash flows back to a more normal level. It is generally unrealistic to expect to be able to earn above-normal returns over the entire life of an investment project.

Risk and the NPV Rule

The land investment example above assumed that the investment was riskless. Therefore, the rate of return used to compute the discount factor and the net present value was the riskless rate of return available on a U.S. government bond having a one-year maturity. What if you do not believe your investment advisor who says that the construction of the new interchange is a certainty, or you are not confident about your advisor's estimate of the value of the land in one year? To compensate for the perceived risk of this investment, you decide that you require a 15 percent rate of return on your investment. Using a 15 percent required rate of return in calculating the discount factor, the present value of the expected $1.2 million sales price of the land is $1,008,696 [$1.2 million times (1/1.15)]. Thus, the NPV of this investment declines to $8,696. The increase in the perceived risk of the investment results in a dramatic decline in its NPV.

A primary problem facing managers is the difficulty of evaluating the risk associated with investments and then translating that risk into a discount rate that reflects an adequate level of risk compensation. In the next section of this chapter we discuss the risk concept and the factors that affect investment risk and influence the required rate of return on an investment.

MEANING AND MEASUREMENT OF RISK

We begin the discussion of risk analysis by defining several key terms and concepts. Although the examples presented here deal primarily with investment decisions, the ideas are applicable to all other types of economic decisions, such as those of pricing and production.

The Meaning of Risk-Free and Risky Investments

Risk implies a chance for some unfavorable outcome to occur. From the perspective of security analysis or the analysis of an investment project, risk is the *possibility that actual cash flows (returns) will be less than forecasted cash flows (returns)*. More generally, **risk** refers to the chance that you will encounter an outcome that differs from the expected outcome. When a range of potential outcomes is associated with a decision and the decision maker is able to assign probabilities to each of these possible outcomes, risk is said to exist.

Risk
A decision-making situation in which there is variability in the possible outcomes, and the probabilities of these outcomes can be specified by the decision maker.

An investment decision is said to be *risk free* if the outcome (dollar returns) from the initial investment is known with certainty. A good example of a risk-free investment is U.S. Treasury securities. There is virtually no chance that the Treasury will fail to redeem these securities at maturity or that the Treasury will default on any interest payments owed.[6]

In contrast, US Airways bonds constitute a *risky* investment opportunity because it is possible that US Airways will default on one or more interest payments and will lack sufficient funds at maturity to redeem the bonds at face value.

In summary, *risk* refers to the potential variability of outcomes from a decision. The more variable these outcomes are, the greater the risk.

---

[6] Note that this discussion of risk deals with *dollar returns* and ignores such other considerations as potential losses in purchasing power. In addition, it assumes that securities are held until maturity, which is not always the case. Sometimes a security must be sold before maturity and at such times the seller may suffer a capital loss (selling for less than face value) because of changes in the level of interest rates.

Probability Distributions

Probability
The percentage chance that a particular outcome will occur.

The **probability** that a particular outcome will occur is defined as the relative frequency or *percentage chance* of its occurrence. Probabilities may be either objectively or subjectively determined. An objective determination is based on past outcomes of similar events, whereas a subjective determination is merely an opinion made by an individual about the likelihood that a given event will occur. In the case of decisions that are frequently repeated, such as the drilling of developmental oil wells in an established oil field, reasonably good objective estimates can be made about the success of a new well. In contrast, for totally new decisions or one-of-a-kind investments, subjective estimates about the likelihood of various outcomes are necessary. The fact that many probability estimates in business are at least partially subjective does not diminish their usefulness.

Example

http://

The annual report for the US Airways Corporation can be found at http://investor.usairways.com

PROBABILITY DISTRIBUTIONS AND RISK: US AIRWAYS BONDS

Consider an investor who is contemplating the purchase of US Airways bonds. That investor might assign the probabilities associated with the three possible outcomes from this investment, as shown in Table 2.2. These probabilities are interpreted to mean that a 30-percent chance exists that the bonds will not be in default over their life and will be redeemed at maturity, a 65-percent chance of interest default during the life of the bonds, and a 5-percent chance that the bonds will not be redeemed at maturity. In this example, no other outcomes are deemed possible.

Using either objective or subjective methods, the decision maker can develop a probability distribution for the possible outcomes. Table 2.3 shows the probability distribution of net cash flows for two sample investments. The lowest estimated annual net cash flow (NCF) for each investment—$200 for Investment I and $100 for Investment II—represents pessimistic forecasts about the investments' performance; the middle values—$300 and $300—could be considered normal performance levels; and the highest values—$400 and $500—are optimistic estimates.

Expected Values

Expected Value
The weighted average of the possible outcomes where the weights are the probabilities of the respective outcomes.

From this information, the expected value of each decision alternative can be calculated. The **expected value** is defined as the weighted average of the possible outcomes. It is the value that is expected to occur on average if the decision (such as an investment) were repeated a large number of times.

Table 2.2   Possible Outcomes from Investing in US Airways Bonds

Outcome	Probability
No default, bonds redeemed at maturity	0.30
Default on interest for one or more periods	0.65
No interest default, but bonds not redeemed at maturity	0.05
	1.00

Table 2.3 · Probability Distributions of the Annual Net Cash Flows (NCF) from Two Investments

Investment I		Investment II	
Possible NCF	Probability	Possible NCF	Probability
$200	0.2	$100	0.2
300	0.6	300	0.6
400	0.2	500	0.2
	1.0		1.0

Table 2.4   Computation of the Expected Returns from Two Investments

Investment I			Investment II		
r_j	p_j	$r_j \times p_j$	r_j	p_j	$r_j \times p_j$
$200	0.2	$ 40	$100	0.2	$ 20
300	0.6	180	300	0.6	180
400	0.2	80	500	0.2	100
Expected value: $\bar{r}_I = \$300$					$\bar{r}_{II} = \$300$

Algebraically, the expected value may be defined as

$$\bar{r} = \sum_{j=1}^{n} r_j p_j \qquad [2.3]$$

where $\bar{r}$ is the expected value; r_j is the outcome for the jth case, where there are n possible outcomes; and p_j is the probability that the jth outcome will occur. The expected cash flows for Investments I and II are calculated in Table 2.4 using Equation 2.3. In this example both investments have expected values of annual net cash flows equaling $300.

Standard Deviation: An Absolute Measure of Risk

Standard Deviation
A statistical measure of the dispersion or variability of possible outcomes.

The **standard deviation** is a statistical measure of the dispersion of a variable about its mean. It is defined as the square root of the weighted average squared deviations of individual outcomes from the mean:

$$\sigma = \sqrt{\sum_{j=1}^{n} (r_j - \bar{r}_j)^2 p_j} \qquad [2.4]$$

where σ is the standard deviation.

The standard deviation can be used to measure the variability of a decision alternative. As such, it gives an indication of the risk involved in the alternative. The larger the standard deviation, the more variable the possible outcomes and the riskier the decision alternative. A standard deviation of zero indicates no variability and thus no risk.

Table 2.5 shows the calculation of the standard deviations for Investments I and II. These calculations show that Investment II appears to be *riskier* than Investment I because the expected cash flows from Investment II are *more variable*.

This example dealt with a *discrete* probability distribution of outcomes (net cash flows) for each investment; that is, a *limited* number of possible outcomes were identified and probabilities were assigned to them. In reality, however, many different outcomes are possible for each investment decision, ranging from losses each year to annual net cash flows in excess of the optimistic estimates of $400 and $500. To indicate the probability of *all* possible outcomes, it is necessary to construct a *continuous* probability distribution. Conceptually, this involves assigning probabilities to each possible outcome such that the sum of the probabilities over possible outcomes totals 1.0 (see Figure 2.2). This figure shows that Investment I has a tighter probability distribution and smaller standard deviation, indicating a lower variability of returns, and Investment II has a flatter distribution and larger standard deviation, indicating higher variability and, by extension, more risk.

Normal Probability Distribution

The outcomes from many decisions can be estimated by assuming that they follow the *normal* probability distribution. This assumption is often correct or nearly correct, and it greatly simplifies the analysis. The normal probability distribution is characterized by a symmetrical, bell-like curve. If the expected continuous probability distribution

Table 2.5   Computation of the Standard Deviations for Two Investments

	i	r_i	$\bar{r}$	$r_i - \bar{r}$	$(r_i - \bar{r})^2$	p_i	$(r_i - \bar{r})^2 p_i$
Investment I	1	$200	$300	$-100	$10,000	0.2	$2,000
	2	300	300	0	0	0.6	0
	3	400	300	100	10,000	0.2	2,000

$$\sum_{i=1}^{3} (r_i - \bar{r})^2 p_i = \$4,000$$

$$\sigma = \sqrt{\sum_{j=1}^{n} (r_i - \bar{r})^2 p_i} = \sqrt{4,000} = \underline{\$63.25}$$

	i	r_i	$\bar{r}$	$r_i - \bar{r}$	$(r_i - \bar{r})^2$	p_i	$(r_i - \bar{r})^2 p_i$
Investment II	1	$100	$300	$-200	$40,000	0.2	$8,000
	2	300	300	0	0	0.6	0
	3	500	300	200	40,000	0.2	8,000

$$\sum_{i=1}^{3} (r_i - \bar{r})^2 p_i = \$16,000$$

$$\sigma = \sqrt{\sum_{j=1}^{n} (r_i - \bar{r})^2 p_i} = \sqrt{16,000} = \underline{\$126.49}$$

Figure 2.2   Continuous Probability Distributions for Two Investments

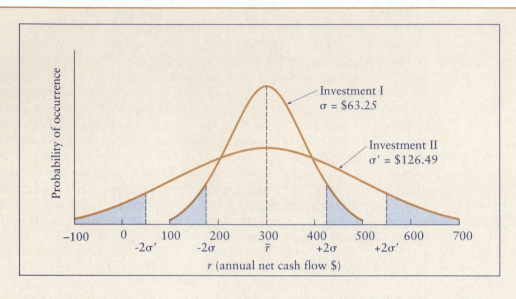

for the possible outcomes is approximately normal, a table of the *standard normal probability function* (Table 1 in Appendix B at the end of this book) can be used to compute the probability of occurrence of any particular outcome. From this table, for example, it is apparent that the actual outcome should be between plus and minus 1 standard deviation from the expected value 68.26 percent of the time,[7] between plus and minus 2 standard deviations 95.44 percent of the time, and between plus and minus 3 standard deviations 99.74 percent of the time (see Figure 2.3). So a "3 sigma event" occurs less than 1 percent of the time with a relative frequency 0.0026 (i.e., 1.0 − 0.9974), and a "9 sigma event" occurs almost never, with a relative frequency less than 0.0001. Nevertheless, extraordinary events can and do happen (see box on LTCM).

The number of standard deviations z that a particular value of r is from the mean $\bar{r}$ can be computed as

$$z = \frac{r - \bar{r}}{\sigma} \qquad [2.5]$$

Table 1 in Appendix B and Equation 2.5 can be used to compute the probability of an annual net cash flow for Investment I being less than some value r—for example, $205. First, the number of standard deviations that $205 is from the mean must be calculated. Substituting the mean and the standard deviation from Tables 2.4 and 2.5 into Equation 2.5 yields

$$z = \frac{\$205 - \$300}{\$63.25}$$

$$= -1.50$$

---

[7] For example, Table 1 indicates a probability of 0.1587 of a value occurring that is greater than $+1\sigma$ from the mean *and* a probability of 0.1587 of a value occurring that is less than -1σ from the mean. Hence the probability of a value *between* $+1\sigma$ and -1σ is 68.26 percent—that is, $1.00 - (2 \times 0.1587)$.

WHAT WENT RIGHT   WHAT WENT WRONG

Long-Term Capital Management (LTCM)[8]

LTCM operated from June 1993–September 1998 as a hedge fund that invested highly leveraged private capital in arbitrage trading strategies on the financial derivative markets. LTCM's principal activity was examining interest rate derivative contracts throughout the world for evidence of very minor mispricing and then betting enormous sums on the subsequent convergence of those contracts to predictable equilibrium prices. Since the mispricing might be only several cents per thousand dollars invested, LTCM often risked millions or even billions on one bet. With sometimes as many as 100 independent bets spread across dozens of different government bond markets, LTCM appeared globally diversified. In a typical month, 60 such convergence strategies with positions in several thousand counterparty contracts would make money and another 40 strategies with a similar number of counterparties would lose money. Steadily, the profits mounted. From approximately $1 billion net asset value (equity) in February 1994, LTCM reached $7 billion of net asset value in January 1998. LTCM then paid out $2.4 billion in a one-time distribution to non-partners which equaled a 40 percent annual compound return on their investment (ROI). Shortly thereafter, in August 1998 the remaining $4.6 billion equity shrank by 45 percent, and then 1 month later shrank by another 82 percent to less than $500 million. In September 1998, the hedge fund was taken over by 14 Wall Street banks who inserted $3.6 billion to cover the firm's debts and assumed 90 percent of the ownership. What went wrong?

One potential explanation is that such events are fully expected in an enterprise so risky that it returns a 40 percent ROI. Anticipated risk and expected return *are* highly positively correlated. However, LTCM's annual return had a standard deviation from June 1993 to June 1998 of only 11.5 percent per year as compared to 10 percent for the S&P 500 stocks. In this respect, LTCM's return volatility was quite ordinary. Another potential explanation is that

LTCM's $129 billion on the June 1998 balance sheet was overwhelmed by excessive off-balance sheet assets and liabilities. Although the absolute size of the numbers is staggering (e.g., $1.2 trillion in interest rate swaps, $28 billion in foreign exchange derivatives, and $36 billion in equity derivatives), LTCM's 9 percent ratio of on-balance sheet to off-balance sheet assets was similar to that of a typical securities firm (about 12 percent) or bank (about 15 percent). Even LTCM's high financial leverage ($129 billion assets to $4.7 billion equity = 26 to 1) was customary practice for derivatives traders.

What appears to have gone wrong for LTCM was that the default of the Russian government debt in August 1998 set in motion a truly extraordinary sequence of events. Investors around the globe took a "flight to quality" and quickly bid up the price of U.S. Treasury securities, which set off general turmoil in the bond markets across the world. Within 1 month, interest rate volatility stood at a standard deviation of 36 percent per year when 3 percent would have been typical. LTCM was caught on the wrong side of many interest rate derivative positions as the contract prices adjusted to this extraordinary volatility. Liquidity dried up altogether in some contracts, and no trade was available at any price. LTCM had "stress tested" their trading positions against so-called "3 sigma events" (a one-day loss of $35 million) that occur with less than 1 percent frequency in normal probability distributions but this August–September 1998 volatility proved to be a 9 sigma event (i.e., a one-day loss of $553 million). With massive investments highly leveraged and exposed to a 9 sigma event, LTCM was unable to sell off many of its money-losing positions at any positive price and hemorrhaged $2 billion in 1 month.

---

[8] R. Lowenstein, *When Genius Failed*, Random House, 2000; Remarks by Dave Modest, NBER Conference, May 1999; and "Case Study: LTCM," eRisk, 2000.

Figure 2.3 A Sample Illustration of Areas Under the Normal Probability Distribution Curve

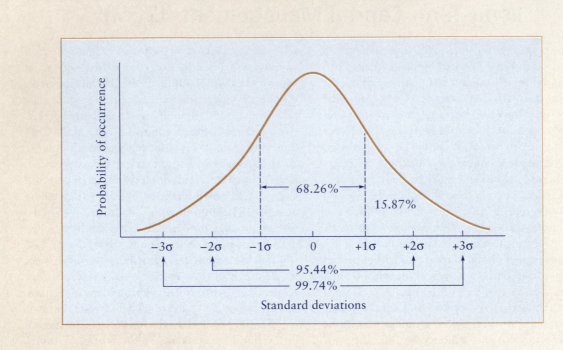

In other words, the annual cash flow value of $205 is 1.5 standard deviations *below* the mean. Reading from the 1.5 row in Table 1 gives a value of 0.0668, or 6.68 percent. Thus a 6.68 percent probability exists that Investment I will have annual net cash flows less than $205. Conversely, there is a 93.32 percent probability (1 − 0.0668) that the investment will have a cash flow greater than $205.

A Practical Approach for Estimating Standard Deviations

Most business decisions have outcomes best represented by a continuous probability distribution of possible outcomes, not the discrete distribution of outcomes, such as those shown in Tables 2.2 and 2.3. Under these circumstances, a simple technique can be used to derive the standard deviation of possible outcomes. Assuming that the distribution of possible outcomes is approximately normally distributed, information can be developed in a form useful for making the necessary computations.

For example, the individual responsible for making estimates of the expected return and risk from a decision, such as an investment project or the pricing of a new product, could be asked to supply the following information:

1. Estimate the most optimistic outcome. The most optimistic outcome is defined to be an outcome that would not be exceeded more than 5 percent (or any other prespecified percentage) of the time.
2. Estimate the most pessimistic outcome. The most pessimistic outcome is defined to be an outcome that you would not expect to do worse more than 5 percent of the time.

3. With a normal distribution, the expected value will be midway between the most optimistic and the most pessimistic estimate.
4. Calculate the value of one standard deviation from Appendix B, Table 1.

Example

ESTIMATION OF THE STANDARD DEVIATION: PROCTER & GAMBLE

When pricing a new product, the product manager of Procter & Gamble estimates that the most optimistic (not expected to be exceeded more than 5 percent of the time) price the firm can charge is $5.00 per unit. The most pessimistic (not expected to be less than this amount more than 5 percent of the time) estimate of the price that can be charged is $3.50. Assuming normality, the expected price is $4.25. From Table 1 in Appendix B, the *z*-value that leaves 5 percent in either tail of the normal distribution is approximately 1.645 standard deviations (σ) to the right or left of the expected value. This *z*-value corresponds to the distance between the expected value and either the most optimistic or the most pessimistic estimate of price. Hence, the probability of a price of at least $5.00 is equal to the probability of a *z*-value *greater* than +1.645. To calculate the standard deviation (σ) of this distribution, use the most optimistic outcome ($5.00), the expected outcome ($4.25), and the *z*-value:

$$z = 1.645 = \frac{(\$5.00 - \$4.25)}{\sigma}$$

$$\sigma = \frac{\$0.75}{1.645}$$

$$= \$0.46$$

In this case the expected value is $4.25 with a standard deviation of $0.46.

Coefficient of Variation: A Relative Measure of Risk

The standard deviation is an appropriate measure of risk when the decision alternatives being compared are approximately equal in size (that is, have similar expected values of the outcomes) and the outcomes are estimated to have symmetrical probability distributions. Because the standard deviation is an *absolute* measure of variability, however, it is generally not suitable for comparing alternatives of differing size. In these cases the **coefficient of variation** provides a better measure of risk.

Coefficient of Variation
The ratio of the standard deviation to the expected value. A relative measure of risk.

The coefficient of variation (*v*) considers relative variation and thus is well suited for use when a comparison is being made between two unequally sized decision alternatives. It is defined as the ratio of the standard deviation σ to the expected value $\bar{r}$, or

$$v = \frac{\sigma}{r} \tag{2.6}$$

In general, when comparing two equally sized decision alternatives, the standard deviation is an appropriate measure of risk. When comparing two unequally sized alternatives, the coefficient of variation is the more appropriate measure of risk.

Example

RELATIVE RISK MEASUREMENT: ARROW TOOL COMPANY

Arrow Tool Company is considering two investments, T and S. Investment T has expected annual net cash flows of $100,000 and a standard deviation of $20,000, whereas Investment S has expected annual net cash flows of $4,000 and a $2,000 standard deviation. Intuition tells us that Investment T is less risky because its *relative* variation is smaller. As the coefficient of variation increases, so does the relative risk of the decision alternative. The coefficients of variation for Investments T and S are computed as

Investment T:

$$v = \frac{\sigma}{\bar{r}}$$

$$= \frac{\$20,000}{\$100,000}$$

$$= 0.20$$

Investment S:

$$v = \frac{\sigma}{\bar{r}}$$

$$= \frac{\$2,000}{\$4,000}$$

$$= 0.5$$

Cash flows of Investment S have a larger coefficient of variation (0.50) than do cash flows of Investment T (0.20); therefore, even though the standard deviation is smaller, Investment S is the *more* risky of the two alternatives.

THE RELATIONSHIP BETWEEN RISK AND RETURN

Understanding the trade-off between risk and required (or expected) rates of return is integral to effective decision making. For example, investors who purchase shares of common stock hope to receive returns that will exceed those that might be earned from alternative investments, such as a savings account, U.S. government bonds, or high-quality corporate bonds. Investors recognize that the expected return from common stock over the long run tends to be higher than the expected return from less risky investments. To receive higher returns, however, investors must be prepared to accept a higher level of risk.

Risk and Required Return

The relationship between risk and required return on an investment in either a physical asset or financial asset (security) can be defined as

Required return = Risk-free return + Risk premium   [2.7]

The risk-free rate of return refers to the return available on an investment with no risk of default. For debt securities, no default risk means that promised interest and principal payments are guaranteed to be made. The best example of risk-free securities are short-term U.S. government securities, such as Treasury bills. There is no risk of default on these securities because the U.S. government always can print more money. Of course, if the government recklessly prints money to pay its obligations, the purchasing power of the money will decline. So, risk-free returns equal the real rate of interest plus the expected rate of inflation. Nevertheless, the buyer of a U.S. government bond always is assured of receiving the promised *principal* and *interest* payments.

A *risk premium* is a potential "reward" that an investor can expect to receive from making a risky investment. The risk may arise for any number of reasons. The borrower firm may default on its contractual repayment obligations (a default risk premium). The investor may have little seniority in presenting claims against a bankrupt borrower (a seniority risk premium). The investor may be unable to sell his security interest (a liquidity risk premium), or debt repayment may occur early (a maturity risk premium). Finally, the return the investor receives may be highly volatile, exceeding expectations during one period and plummeting below expectations during the next period. Investors generally are considered to be *risk averse*; that is, they expect, on average, to be compensated for any and all of these risks they assume when making an investment.

RISK-RETURN TRADE-OFFS IN STOCKS AND BONDS

Investors require higher rates of return on securities subject to default risk. Bond rating agencies, such as Moody's, Standard and Poor's, Duff and Phelps, and Fitch, provide evaluations of the default risk of many corporate bonds in the form of bond ratings. Moody's, for example, rates bonds on a 9-point scale from Aaa through C, where Aaa-rated bonds have the lowest expected default risk. As can be seen in Table 2.6, the yields on bonds increase as the risk of default increases, reflecting the positive relationship between risk and required returns. Over time, the spread between the required returns on bonds having various levels of default risk varies, reflecting the economic prospects and the resulting probability of default.

The risk versus return trade-off also can be illustrated by examining the returns *achieved* by investors in various securities over long periods of time. Table 2.7 shows the realized returns (and the standard deviation of those returns) from small company common stock (highest risk), the common stocks in the S & P 500 index (next highest risk), long-term corporate bonds (third highest risk), long-term U.S. government bonds (fourth highest risk), intermediate-term government bonds (fifth highest risk), and U.S. Treasury bills (lowest risk). The realized returns and the standard deviation (risk) of these returns over the period 1926–2002 are consistent with our expectation that there is a positive relationship between risk and return.

Table 2.6   Relationship Between Default Risk and Required Returns

Security	Yield
U.S. Treasury bonds (25 year +)	5.06%
Aaa-rated corporate bonds	6.49
Aa-rated bonds	6.93
A-rated bonds	7.18
Baa-rated corporate bonds	7.80

Source: Board of Governors of the Federal Reserve System, *Federal Reserve Bulletin* (Washington, DC, July 2002), p. A26.

Table 2.7   Relationship Between Realized Returns and Risk of Various Investments (1926–2002)

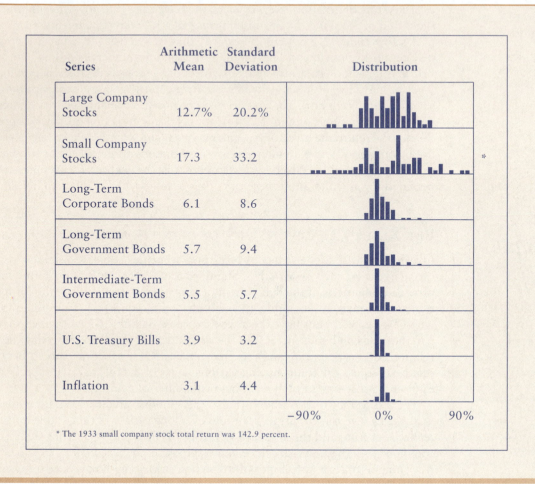

Series	Arithmetic Mean	Standard Deviation	Distribution
Large Company Stocks	12.7%	20.2%	
Small Company Stocks	17.3	33.2	*
Long-Term Corporate Bonds	6.1	8.6	
Long-Term Government Bonds	5.7	9.4	
Intermediate-Term Government Bonds	5.5	5.7	
U.S. Treasury Bills	3.9	3.2	
Inflation	3.1	4.4	

                                    −90%   0%   90%

* The 1933 small company stock total return was 142.9 percent.

Source: *Stocks, Bonds, Bills and Inflation: 2002 Yearbook* (Chicago: Ibbotson Associates, Inc., 2002). Table 2–1, p. 31. Data reproduced with permission of Ibbotson Associates. All rights reserved.

SUMMARY

- The *marginal analysis* concept requires that a decision maker determine the additional (marginal) costs and additional (marginal) benefits associated with a proposed action. If the marginal benefits exceed the marginal costs (that is, if the net marginal benefits are positive), the action should be taken.

- The *net present value* of an investment is equal to the present value of expected future returns (cash flows) minus the initial outlay.

- The net present value of an investment equals the contribution of that investment to the value of the firm and, accordingly, to the wealth of shareholders. The net present value of an investment depends on the return required by investors (the firm), which, in turn, is a function of the perceived risk of the investment.

- *Risk* refers to the potential variability of outcomes from a decision alternative. It can be measured either by the *standard deviation* (an absolute measure of risk) or *coefficient of variation* (a relative measure of risk).

- A positive relationship exists between risk and required rates of return on securities and physical asset investments. Investments involving greater risks must offer higher expected returns.

EXERCISES

1. The Ajax Corporation has the following set of projects available to it:

Project*	Investment Required ($ Million)	Expected Rate of Return
A	500	23.0%
B	75	18.0
C	50	21.0
D	125	16.0
E	300	14.0
F	150	13.0
G	250	19.0

*Note: All projects have equal risk.

Ajax can raise funds with the following marginal costs:

First $250 million	14.0%
Next 250 million	15.5
Next 100 million	16.0
Next 250 million	16.5
Next 200 million	18.0
Next 200 million	21.0

Use the marginal cost and marginal revenue concepts developed in this chapter to derive an optimal capital budget for Ajax.

2. The demand for MICHTEC's products is related to the state of the economy. If the economy is expanding next year (an above-normal growth in GNP), the company expects sales to be $90 million. If there is a recession next year (a decline in GNP), sales are expected to be $75 million. If next year is normal (a moderate growth in GNP), sales are expected to be $85 million. MICHTEC's economists have estimated the chances that the economy will be either expanding, normal, or in a recession next year at 0.2, 0.5, and 0.3, respectively.

    a. Compute expected annual sales.

    b. Compute the standard deviation of annual sales.

    c. Compute the coefficient of variation of annual sales.

3. Two investments have the following expected returns (net present values) and standard deviation of returns:

Project	Expected Returns	Standard Deviation
A	$ 50,000	$ 40,000
B	$250,000	$125,000

Which one is riskier? Why?

4. An investment project has expected annual net cash flows of $100,000 with a standard deviation of $40,000. The distribution of annual net cash flows is approximately normal.

   a. Determine the probability that the annual net cash flows will be negative.

   b. Determine the probability that the annual net cash flows will be less than $20,000.

5. The manager of the aerospace division of General Aeronautics has estimated the price it can charge for providing satellite launch services to commercial firms. Her most optimistic estimate (a price not expected to be exceeded more than 10 percent of the time) is $2 million. Her most pessimistic estimate (a lower price than this one is not expected more than 10 percent of the time) is $1 million. The price distribution is believed to be approximately normal.

   a. What is the expected price?

   b. What is the standard deviation of the launch price?

   c. What is the probability of receiving a price less than $1.2 million?

6. Amgen, Inc. uses state-of-the-art biotechnology to develop human pharmaceutical and diagnostic products. During 1983 and 1984 Amgen had losses of $4.9 million and $7.8 million, respectively. The firm barely broke even between 1985 and 1987 and had sizable losses ($8.2 million) in 1988. On the strength of royalty income from the sale of its Epogen product, a stimulator of red blood cell production, profits increased steadily from $19 million in 1989 to $355 million in 1993 to $670 million in 1996. Profits were expected to exceed $900 million per year by 1998–1999, according to forecasts prepared by the *Value Line Investment Survey*. *Value Line* rated the safety (a risk measure) of Amgen to be "average."

   a. Discuss the past, present, and projected performance of Amgen in the context of risk-return trade-offs.

   b. Amgen's 1993 return on equity (net income ÷ shareholders' equity) was about 30 percent. In 1993, its projected return on equity was 28.5 percent for 1995 and 22.5 percent during 1997–1999. The 1989 return on equity was 10.2 percent, and the 1985–1987 return on equity was about 0.9 percent. Do you believe Amgen is now earning "excessive profits" from its Epogen product? Why or why not?

CASE EXERCISE

THE TORO COMPANY AND THE PROBABILITY OF SNOW[10]

The Toro Company makes snow blowers that remove snow from walks and driveways. According to Richard Pollick, marketing director at Toro, "We found that the big barrier to buying one of our machines was the fear that there wouldn't be enough snow to justify the cost."

The company designed a promotional campaign to overcome this problem. It agreed to refund the entire price of its machines purchased before December 10 if the snowfall during the ensuing winter was less than 20 percent of the 40-year average for the purchase location. In effect, then, the customer would get the snowblower free! If the snowfall was less than 50 percent of the 40-year average, then Toro would refund

---

[10] Based on Bill Richards, "Executives at Toro Are Dreaming of a White Winter—Very White," *Wall Street Journal,* December 12, 1983.

part of the purchase price. According to the marketing director, this promotion led to significantly increased early season sales.

After the program ended, company management began to monitor closely reports from 172 weather stations located in the northern part of the country. Toro also hedged its bets by purchasing weather insurance from Good Weather International, a New York company. In the event of low snowfall amounts, Good Weather would reimburse Toro for its losses.

The probability that Good Weather would have to reimburse Toro under this agreement was very small. In almost half a century of data, Minneapolis *never* had a winter with a snowfall less than 20 percent of the average. Also, the city had less than 50 percent of its average snowfall only four times.

QUESTIONS

1. What factors might have led Toro management to consider purchasing this type of insurance?

2. What factors would the managers at Good Weather have to consider in determining a price to charge Toro for this protection?

Differential Calculus Techniques in Management

Decision analysis involves determining the action that best achieves a desired goal or objective. This means finding the action that optimizes (that is, maximizes or minimizes) the value of an objective function. For example, we may be interested in determining the output level that maximizes profits. In a production problem, the goal may be to find the combination of inputs that minimizes the cost of producing a desired level of output. In a capital budgeting problem, the objective may be to select those projects that maximize the net present value of the investments chosen. There are many techniques for solving optimization problems such as these. This appendix focuses on the use of differential calculus to solve certain types of optimization problems.

RELATIONSHIP BETWEEN MARGINAL ANALYSIS AND DIFFERENTIAL CALCULUS

In Chapter 2, marginal analysis was introduced as one of the fundamental concepts of economic decision making. In the marginal analysis framework, resource-allocation decisions are made by comparing the marginal benefits of a change in the level of an activity with the marginal costs of the change. A change should be made as long as the marginal benefits exceed the marginal costs. By following this basic rule, resources can be allocated efficiently and profits or shareholder wealth can be maximized.

Initially, let us assume that the objective we are seeking to optimize, Y, can be expressed algebraically as a function of *one* decision variable, X,

$$Y = f(X) \qquad\qquad [2A.1]$$

Recall that marginal profit is defined as the change in profit resulting from a one-unit change in output. In general, the marginal value of any variable Y, which is a function of another variable X, is defined as the change in the value of Y resulting from a one-unit change in X. The marginal value of Y, M_y, can be calculated from the change in Y, ΔY, that occurs as the result of a given change in X, ΔX:

$$M_y = \frac{\Delta Y}{\Delta X} \qquad\qquad [2A.2]$$

When calculated with this expression, different estimates for the marginal value of Y may be obtained, depending on the size of the change in X that we use in the computation. The true marginal value of a function (e.g., an economic relationship) is obtained from Equation 2A.2 when ΔX is made as small as possible. If ΔX can be thought of as a continuous (rather than a discrete) variable that can take on fractional values,[11] then in calculating M_y by Equation 2A.2, we can let ΔX approach zero. In

---

[11] For example, if X is a continuous variable measured in feet, pounds, and so on, then ΔX can in theory take on fractional values such as 0.5, 0.10, 0.05, 0.001, 0.0001 feet or pounds. When X is a continuous variable, ΔX can be made as small as desired.

MANAGERIAL CHALLENGE

A Skeleton in the Stealth Bomber's Closet[12]

In 1990 the U.S. Air Force publicly unveiled its newest long-range strategic bomber—the B-2 or "Stealth" bomber. This plane is characterized by a unique flying wing design engineered to evade detection by enemy radar. The plane has been controversial because of its high cost. However, a lesser known controversy relates to its fundamental design.

The flying wing design originated from a secret study that concluded that a plane's maximum range could be achieved if virtually all the volume were contained in the wing. A complex mathematical appendix was attached to the study.

However, Joseph Foa, now an emeritus professor of engineering at George Washington University, discovered that a fundamental error had been made in the initial report. It turned out that the original researchers had taken the first derivative of a complex equation and found

PHOTO CREDIT: © PHOTODISC, INC.

that it had two solutions. The original researchers mistakenly concluded that the all-wing design was the one that maximized range, when, in fact, it *minimized* range.

In this chapter we introduce some of the same optimization techniques applied to the Stealth bomber project. We develop tools designed to maximize profits or minimize costs. Fortunately, the mathematical functions we deal with in this chapter and throughout the book are much simpler than those that confronted the original "flying wing" engineers. We introduce techniques that can be used to check whether a function, such as profits or costs, is being minimized or maximized at a particular level of output.

[12] Based on W. Biddle, "Skeleton Alleged in the Stealth Bomber's Closet," *Science*, May 12, 1989, pp. 650–651.

Derivative
A measure of the marginal effect of a change in one variable on the value of a function. Graphically, it represents the slope of the function at a given point.

concept, this is the approach taken in differential calculus. The **derivative**, or, more precisely, *first derivative*,[13] dY/dX, of a function is defined as the *limit* of the ratio $\Delta Y/\Delta X$ as ΔX approaches zero; that is,

$$\frac{dY}{dX} = \lim_{\Delta X \to 0} \frac{\Delta Y}{\Delta X}$$

[2A.3]

Graphically, the first derivative of a function represents the *slope* of the curve at a given point on the curve. The definition of a derivative as the limit of the change in Y (that is, ΔY) as ΔX approaches zero is illustrated in Figure 2A.1(a). Suppose we are interested in the derivative of the $Y = f(X)$ function at the point X_0. The derivative dY/dX measures the slope of the tangent line ECD. An estimate of this slope,

---

[13] It is also possible to compute second, third, fourth, and so on, derivatives. Second derivatives are discussed later in this chapter.

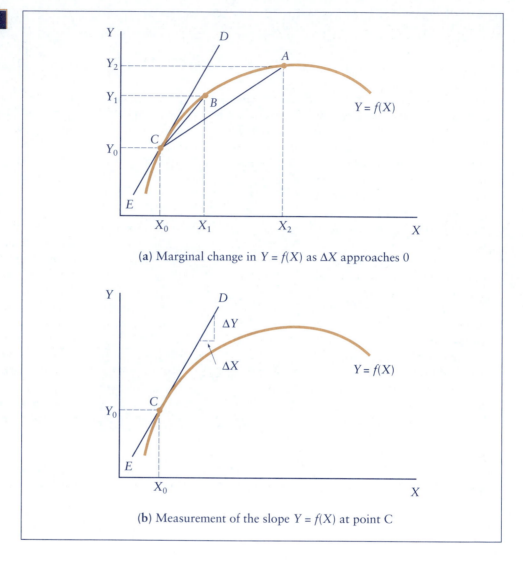

(a) Marginal change in $Y = f(X)$ as ΔX approaches 0

(b) Measurement of the slope $Y = f(X)$ at point C

albeit a poor estimate, can be obtained by calculating the marginal value of Y over the interval X_0 to X_2. Using Equation 2A.2, a value of

$$M_y' = \frac{\Delta Y}{\Delta X} = \frac{Y_2 - Y_0}{X_2 - X_0}$$

is obtained for the slope of the CA line. Now let us calculate the marginal value of Y using a smaller interval, for example, X_0 to X_1. The slope of the CB line, which is equal to

$$M_y'' = \frac{\Delta Y}{\Delta X} = \frac{Y_1 - Y_0}{X_1 - X_0}$$

gives a much better estimate of the true marginal value as represented by the slope of the ECD tangent line. Thus we see that the smaller the ΔX value, the better the estimate of the slope of the curve. Letting ΔX approach zero allows us to find the slope of the $Y = f(X)$ curve at point C. As shown in Figure A.1(b), the slope of the

ECD tangent line (and the $Y = f(X)$ function at point *C*) is measured by the change in *Y*, or rise, ΔY, divided by the change in *X*, or run, ΔX.

Process of Differentiation

The process of differentiation—that is, finding the derivative of a function—involves determining the limiting value of the ratio $\Delta Y/\Delta X$ as ΔX approaches zero. Before offering some general rules for finding the derivative of a function, we illustrate with an example the algebraic process used to obtain the derivative without the aid of these general rules. The specific rules that simplify this process are presented in the following section.

Example

PROCESS OF DIFFERENTIATION: PROFIT MAXIMIZATION AT ILLINOIS POWER

Suppose the profit, π, of Illinois Power can be represented as a function of the output level Q using the expression

$$\pi = -40 + 140Q - 10Q^2 \qquad [2A.4]$$

We wish to determine $d\pi/dQ$ by first finding the marginal-profit expression $\Delta\pi/\Delta Q$ and then taking the limit of this expression as ΔQ approaches zero. Let us begin by expressing the new level of profit $(\pi + \Delta\pi)$ that will result from an increase in output to $(Q + \Delta Q)$. From Equation 2A.4, we know that

$$(\pi + \Delta\pi) = -40 + 140(Q + \Delta Q) - 10(Q + \Delta Q)^2 \qquad [2A.5]$$

Expanding this expression and then doing some algebraic simplifying, we obtain

$$\begin{aligned}(\pi + \Delta\pi) &= -40 + 140Q + 140\Delta Q - 10[Q^2 + 2Q\Delta Q + (\Delta Q)^2] \\ &= -40 + 140Q - 10Q^2 + 140\Delta Q - 20Q\Delta Q - 10(\Delta Q)^2 \qquad [2A.6]\end{aligned}$$

Subtracting Equation 2A.4 from Equation 2A.6 yields

$$\Delta\pi = 140\Delta Q - 20Q\Delta Q - 10(\Delta Q)^2 \qquad [2A.7]$$

Forming the marginal-profit ratio $\Delta\pi/\Delta Q$, and doing some canceling, we get

$$\begin{aligned}\frac{\Delta\pi}{\Delta Q} &= \frac{140\Delta Q - 20Q\Delta Q - 10(\Delta Q)^2}{\Delta Q} \qquad [2A.8] \\ &= 140 - 20Q - 10\Delta Q\end{aligned}$$

Taking the limit of Equation 2A.8 as ΔQ approaches zero yields the expression for the derivative of Illinois Power's profit function (Equation 2A.4)

$$\begin{aligned}\frac{d\pi}{dQ} &= \lim_{\Delta Q \to 0} [140 - 20Q - 10\Delta Q] \qquad [2A.9] \\ &= 140 - 20Q\end{aligned}$$

If we are interested in the derivative of the profit function at a particular value of Q, Equation 2A.9 can be evaluated for this value. For example, suppose we want to know the marginal profit, or slope of the profit function, at $Q = 3$ units. Substituting $Q = 3$ in Equation 2A.9 yields

$$\underset{\text{profit}}{\text{Marginal}} = \frac{d\pi}{dQ} = 140 - 20(3) = \$80 \text{ per unit}$$

Rules of Differentiation

Fortunately, we do not need to go through this lengthy process every time we want the derivative of a function. A series of general rules, derived in a manner similar to the process just described, exists for differentiating various types of functions.

Constant Functions   A constant function can be expressed as

$$Y = a \qquad\qquad\qquad\qquad\text{[2A.10]}$$

where *a* is a constant (that is, *Y* is independent of *X*). The derivative of a constant function is equal to zero:

$$\frac{dY}{dX} = 0 \qquad\qquad\qquad\qquad\text{[2A.11]}$$

For example, consider the constant function

$$Y = 4$$

which is graphed in Figure 2A.2(a). Recall that the first derivative of a function (*dY/dX*) measures the slope of the function. Because this constant function is a horizontal straight line with zero slope, its derivative (*dY/dX*) is therefore equal to zero.

Power Functions   A power function takes the form of

$$Y = aX^b \qquad\qquad\qquad\qquad\text{[2A.12]}$$

where *a* and *b* are constants. The derivative of a power function is equal to *b* times *a,* times *X* raised to the (*b* − 1) power:

FIGURE 2A.2   Constant, Linear, and Quadratic Functions

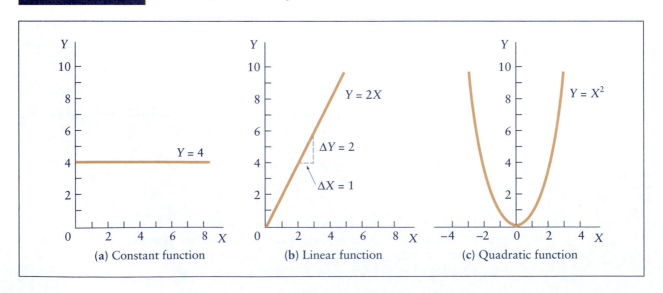

(a) Constant function   (b) Linear function   (c) Quadratic function

$$\frac{dY}{dX} = b \cdot a \cdot X^{b-1}$$

[2A.13]

A couple of examples are used to illustrate the application of this rule. First, consider the function

$$Y = 2X$$

which is graphed in Figure 2A.2(b). Note that the slope of this function is equal to 2 and is constant over the entire range of X values. Applying the power function rule to this example, where $a = 2$ and $b = 1$, yields

$$\frac{dY}{dX} = 1 \cdot 2 \cdot X^{1-1} = 2X^0$$

$$= 2$$

Note that any variable raised to the zero power, e.g., X^0, is equal to 1.

Next, consider the function

$$Y = X^2$$

which is graphed in Figure 2A.2(c). Note that the slope of this function varies depending on the value of X. Application of the power function rule to this example yields ($a = 1$, $b = 2$):

$$\frac{dY}{dX} = 2 \cdot 1 \cdot X^{2-1}$$

$$= 2X$$

As we can see, this derivative (or slope) function is negative when $X < 0$, zero when $X = 0$, and positive when $X > 0$.

Sums of Functions   Suppose a function $Y = f(X)$ represents the sum of two (or more) separate functions, $f_1(X)$, $f_2(X)$, that is,

$$Y = f_1(X) + f_2(X)$$

[2A.14]

The derivative of Y with respect to X is found by differentiating each of the separate functions and then adding the results:

$$\frac{dY}{dX} = \frac{df_1(X)}{dX} + \frac{df_2(X)}{dX}$$

[2A.15]

This result can be extended to finding the derivative of the sum of any number of functions.

Example

RULES OF DIFFERENTIATION: PROFIT MAXIMIZATION AT ILLINOIS POWER (continued)

As an example of the application of these rules, consider again the profit function for Illinois Power, given by Equation 2A.4, which was discussed earlier:

$$\pi = -40 + 140Q - 10Q^2$$

In this example Q represents the X variable and π represents the Y variable; that is, $\pi = f(Q)$. The function $f(Q)$ is the sum of *three* separate functions—a constant function, $f_1(Q) = -40$, and two power functions, $f_2(Q) = 140Q$ and $f_3(Q) - 10Q^2$. Therefore, applying the differentiation rules yields

$$\frac{d\pi}{dQ} = \frac{df_1(Q)}{dQ} + \frac{df_2(Q)}{dQ} + \frac{df_3(Q)}{dQ}$$

$$= 0 + 1 \cdot 140 \cdot Q^{1-1} + 2 \cdot (-10) \cdot Q^{2-1}$$

$$= 140 - 20Q$$

This is the same result that was obtained earlier in Equation 2A.9 by the differentiation process.

Product of Two Functions   Suppose the variable Y is equal to the product of two separate functions $f_1(X)$ and $f_2(X)$:

$$Y = f_1(X) \cdot f_2(X) \tag{2A.16}$$

In this case the derivative of Y with respect to X is equal to the sum of the first function times the derivative of the second, plus the second function times the derivative of the first.

$$\frac{dY}{dX} = f_1(X) \cdot \frac{df_2(X)}{dX} + f_2(X) \cdot \frac{df_1(X)}{dX} \tag{2A.17}$$

For example, suppose we are interested in the derivative of the expression

$$Y = X^2(2X - 3)$$

Let $f_1(X) = X^2$ and $f_2(X) = (2X - 3)$. By the above rule (and the earlier rules for differentiating constant and power functions), we obtain

$$\frac{dY}{dX} = X^2 \cdot \frac{dY}{dX}[(2X - 3)] + (2X - 3) \cdot \frac{dY}{dX}[X^2]$$

$$= X^2 \cdot (2 - 0) + (2X - 3) \cdot (2X)$$

$$= 2X^2 + 4X^2 - 6X$$

$$= 6X^2 - 6X$$

$$= 6X(X - 1)$$

Quotient of Two Functions   Suppose the variable Y is equal to the quotient of two separate functions $f_1(X)$ and $f_2(X)$:

$$Y = \frac{f_1(X)}{f_2 X} \tag{2A.18}$$

For such a relationship the derivative of Y with respect to X is obtained as follows:

$$\frac{dY}{dX} = \frac{f_2(X) \cdot \dfrac{df_1(X)}{dX} \cdot - f_1(X) \cdot \dfrac{df_2(X)}{dX}}{[f_2(X)]^2} \tag{2A.19}$$

As an example, consider the problem of finding the derivative of the expression

$$Y = \frac{10X^2}{5X - 1}$$

Letting $f_1(X) = 10X^2$ and $f_2(X) = 5X - 1$, we have

$$\frac{dY}{dX} = \frac{(5X - 1) \cdot 20X - 10X^2 \cdot 5}{(5X - 1)^2}$$

$$= \frac{100X^2 - 20X - 50X^2}{(5X - 1)^2}$$

$$= \frac{50X^2 - 20X}{(5X - 1)^2}$$

$$= \frac{10X(5X - 2)}{(5X - 1)^2}$$

Functions of a Function (Chain Rule)   Suppose Y is a function of the variable Z, $Y = f_1(Z)$; and Z is in turn a function of the variable X, $Z = f_2(X)$. The derivative of Y with respect to X can be determined by first finding dY/dZ and dZ/dX and then multiplying the two expressions together:

$$\frac{dY}{dX} = \frac{dY}{dZ} \cdot \frac{dZ}{dX}$$

$$= \frac{df_1(Z)}{dZ} \cdot \frac{df_2(X)}{dX} \qquad\qquad [2A.20]$$

To illustrate the application of this rule, suppose we are interested in finding the derivative (with respect to X) of the function

$$Y = 10Z - 2Z^2 - 3$$

where Z is related to X in the following way:[14]

$$Z = 2X^2 - 1$$

First, we find (by the earlier differentiation rules)

$$\frac{dY}{dX} = 10 - 4Z$$

$$\frac{dY}{dX} = 4X$$

and then

$$\frac{dY}{dX} = (10 - 4Z) \cdot 4X$$

---

[14] Alternatively, one can substitute $Z = 2X^2 - 1$ into $Y = 10Z - 2Z^2 - 3$ and differentiate Y with respect to X. The reader is asked to demonstrate in Exercise 10 that this approach yields the same answer as the chain rule.

	Function	Derivative
TABLE 2A.1	1. Constant Function	
Summary of Rules for Differentiating Functions	$Y = a$	$\dfrac{dY}{dX} = 0$
	2. Power Function	
	$Y = aX^b$	$\dfrac{dY}{dX} = b \cdot a \cdot X^{b-1}$
	3. Sums of Functions	
	$Y = f_1(X) + f_2(X)$	$\dfrac{dY}{dX} = \dfrac{df_1(X)}{dX} + \dfrac{df_2(X)}{dX}$
	4. Product of Two Functions	
	$Y = f_1(X) \cdot f_2(X)$	$\dfrac{dY}{dX} = f_1(X) \cdot \dfrac{df_2(X)}{dX} + f_2(X) \cdot \dfrac{df_1(X)}{dX}$
	5. Quotient of Two Functions	
	$Y = \dfrac{f_1(X)}{f_2 X}$	$\dfrac{dY}{dX} = \dfrac{f_2(X) \cdot \dfrac{df_1(X)}{dX} - f_1(X) \cdot \dfrac{df_2(X)}{dX}}{[f_2(X)]^2}$
	6. Functions of a Function	
	$Y = f_1(Z)$, where $Z = f_2(X)$	$\dfrac{dY}{dX} = \dfrac{dY}{dZ} \cdot \dfrac{dZ}{dX}$

Substituting the expression for Z in terms of X into this equation yields

$$\frac{dY}{dX} = [10 - 4(2X^2 - 1)] \cdot 4X$$

$$= (10 - 8X^2 + 4) \cdot 4X$$

$$= 40X - 32X^3 + 16X$$

$$= 56X - 32X^3$$

$$= 8X(7 - 4X^2)$$

These rules for differentiating functions are summarized in Table 2A.1.

APPLICATIONS OF DIFFERENTIAL CALCULUS TO OPTIMIZATION PROBLEMS

The reason for studying the process of differentiation and the rules for differentiating functions is that these methods can be used to find optimal solutions to many kinds of maximization and minimization problems in managerial economics.

Maximization Problem

First-Order Condition
A test to locate one or more maximum or minimum points of an algebraic function.

As you recall from the discussion of marginal analysis, a necessary (but not sufficient) condition for finding the maximum point on a curve (for example, maximum profits) is that the marginal value or slope of the curve at this point must be equal to zero. We can now express this condition within the framework of differential calculus. Because the derivative of a function measures the slope or marginal value at any given point, an equivalent necessary condition for finding the maximum value of a function $Y = f(X)$ is that the derivative dY/dX at this point must be equal to zero. This is known as the **first-order condition** for locating one or more maximum or minimum points of an algebraic function.

Example

FIRST-ORDER CONDITION: PROFIT MAXIMIZATION AT ILLINOIS POWER (continued)

Using the profit function (Equation 2A.4)

$$\pi = -40 + 140Q - 10Q^2$$

discussed earlier, we can illustrate how to find the profit-maximizing output level Q by means of this condition. Setting the first derivative of this function (which was computed previously) to zero, we obtain

$$\frac{d\pi}{dQ} = 140 - 20Q$$
$$0 = 140 - 20Q$$

Solving this equation for Q yields $Q^* = 7$ units as the profit-maximizing output level. The profit and first derivative functions and optimal solution are shown in Figure 2A.3. As we can see, profits are maximized at the point where the function is neither increasing nor decreasing; in other words, where the slope (or first derivative) is equal to zero.

FIGURE 2A.3

Profit and First Derivative Functions

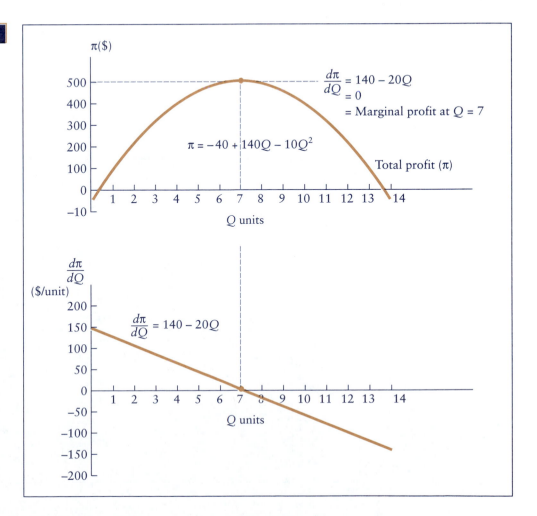

Second Derivatives and the Second-Order Condition

Setting the derivative of a function equal to zero and solving the resulting equation for the value of the decision variable does not guarantee that the point will be obtained at which the function takes on its maximum value. (Recall the Stealth bomber example at the start of the Appendix.) The slope of a U-shaped function will also be equal to zero at its low point and the function will take on its *minimum* value at the given point. In other words, setting the derivative to zero is only a *necessary* condition for finding the maximum value of a function; it is not a *sufficient* condition. Another condition, known as the **second-order condition,** is required to determine whether a point that has been determined from the first-order condition is either a maximum point or minimum point of the algebraic function.

This situation is illustrated in Figure 2A.4. At both points A and B the slope of the function (first derivative, dY/dX) is zero; however, only at point B does the function take on its maximum value. We note in Figure 2A.4 that the marginal value (slope) is continually *decreasing* in the neighborhood of the maximum value (point B) of the $Y = f(X)$ function. First the slope is positive up to the point where $dY/dX = 0$, and thereafter the slope becomes negative. Thus we must determine whether the

Second-Order Condition
A test to determine whether a point that has been determined from the first-order condition is either a maximum point or a minimum point of the algebraic function.

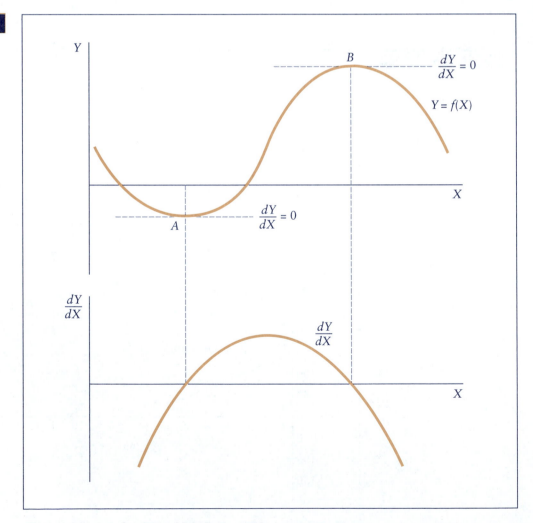

FIGURE 2A.4

Maximum and Minimum Values of a Function

slope's marginal value (slope of the slope) is declining. A test to see whether the marginal value is decreasing is to take the derivative of the marginal value and check to see if it is negative at the given point on the function. In effect, we need to find the derivative of the derivative—that is, the *second derivative* of the function—and then test to see if it is less than zero. Formally, the second derivative of the function $Y = f(X)$ is written as d^2Y/dX^2 and is found by applying the previously described differentiation rules to the first derivative. A *maximum point is obtained if the second derivative is negative; that is, $d^2Y/dX^2 < 0$.*

Example

SECOND-ORDER CONDITION: PROFIT MAXIMIZATION AT ILLINOIS POWER (continued)

Returning to the profit-maximization example, the second derivative is obtained from the first derivative as follows:

$$\frac{d\pi}{dQ} = 140 - 20Q$$

$$\frac{d^2\pi}{dQ^2} = 0 + 1 \cdot (-20) \cdot Q^{1-1}$$

$$= -20$$

Because $d^2\pi/dQ^2 < 0$, we know that a maximum-profit point has been obtained.

An opposite condition holds for obtaining the point at which the function takes on a minimum value. Note again in Figure 2A.4 that the marginal value (slope) is continually *increasing* in the neighborhood of the minimum value (point *A*) of the $Y = (X)$ function. First the slope is negative up to the point where $dY/dX = 0$, and thereafter the slope becomes positive. Therefore, we test to see if $d^2Y/dX^2 > 0$ at the given point. *A minimum point is obtained if the second derivative is positive; that is, $d^2Y/dX^2 > 0$.*

Minimization Problem

In some decision-making situations, cost minimization may be the objective. As in profit-maximization problems, differential calculus can be used to locate the optimal points.

Example

COST MINIMIZATION: KEYSPAN ENERGY

Suppose we are interested in determining the output level that minimizes average total costs for KeySpan Energy, where the average total cost function might be approximated by the following relationship (Q represents output):

$$C = 15 - .040Q + .000080Q^2$$

Differentiating *C* with respect to *Q* gives

$$\frac{dC}{dQ} = -.040 + .000160Q$$

Setting this derivative equal to zero and solving for Q yields

$$0 = .040 + .000160Q$$
$$Q^* = 250$$

Taking the second derivative, we obtain

$$\frac{d^2C}{dQ^2} = + .000160$$

Because the second derivative is positive, the output level of $Q = 250$ is indeed the value that minimizes average total costs.

Summarizing, we see that *two* conditions are required for locating a maximum or minimum value of a function using differential calculus. The *first-order* condition determines the point(s) at which the first derivative dY/dX is equal to zero. Having obtained one or more points, a *second-order* condition is used to determine whether the function takes on a maximum or minimum value at the given point(s). The second derivative d^2Y/dX^2 indicates whether a given point is a maximum ($d^2Y/dX^2 < 0$) or a minimum ($d^2Y/dX^2 > 0$) value of the function.

PARTIAL DIFFERENTIATION AND MULTIVARIATE OPTIMIZATION

Thus far in the chapter, the analysis has been limited to a criterion variable Y that can be expressed as a function of *one* decision variable X. However, many commonly used economic relationships contain two or more decision variables. For example, a *demand function* relates sales of a product or service to such variables as price, advertising, promotion expenses, price of substitutes, and income.

Partial Derivatives

Consider a criterion variable Y that is a function of two decision variables X_1 and X_2.[15]

$$Y = f(X_1, X_2) \qquad [2A.21]$$

Partial Derivative
A measure of the marginal effect of a change in one variable on the value of a multivariate function, while holding constant all other variables.

Let us now examine the change in Y that results from a given change in either X_1 or X_2. To isolate the marginal effect on Y from a given change in X_1—that is, $\Delta Y/\Delta X_1$—we must hold X_2 constant. Similarly, if we wish to isolate the marginal effect on Y from a given change in X_2—that is, $\Delta Y/\Delta X_2$—the variable X_1 must be held constant. A measure of the marginal effect of a change in any one variable on the change in Y, holding all other variables in the relationship constant, is obtained from the **partial derivative** of the function. The partial derivative of Y with respect to X_1 is written as $\partial Y/\partial X_1$ and is found by applying the previously described differentiation rules to the $Y = f(X_1, X_2)$ function, where the variable X_2 is treated as a constant. Similarly, the partial derivative of Y with respect to X_2 is written as $\partial Y/\partial X_2$ and is found by applying the differentiation rules to the function, where the variable X_1 is treated as a constant.

---

[15] The following analysis is not limited to two decision variables. Relationships containing any number of variables can be analyzed within this framework.

Example

PARTIAL DERIVATIVES: INDIANA PETROLEUM COMPANY

To illustrate the procedure for obtaining partial derivatives, let us consider the following relationship in which the profit variable, π, is a function of the output level of two products (heating oil and gasoline) Q_1 and Q_2:

$$\pi = -60 + 140Q_1 + 100Q_2 - 10Q_1^2 - 8Q_2^2 - 6Q_1Q_2 \qquad [2A.22]$$

Treating Q_2 as a constant, the partial derivative of π with respect to Q_1 is obtained:

$$\frac{\partial \pi}{\partial Q_1} = 0 + 140 + 0 + 2 \cdot (-10) \cdot Q_1 - 0 - 6Q_2$$

$$= 140 - 20Q_1 - 6Q_2 \qquad [2A.23]$$

Similarly, with Q_1 treated as a constant, the partial derivative of π with respect to Q_2 is equal to

$$\frac{\partial \pi}{\partial Q_1} = 0 + 0 + 100 - 0 + 2 \cdot (-8) \cdot Q_2 - 6Q_1$$

$$= 100 - 16Q_2 - 6Q_1 \qquad [2A.24]$$

Example

PARTIAL DERIVATIVES: DEMAND FUNCTION FOR SHIELD TOOTHPASTE

Partial derivatives can be very useful in demand analysis, especially in quantitative studies. Suppose the demand for Shield toothpaste is estimated as tubes per year,

$$Q = 14.6 - 2.2P + 7.4A \qquad [2A.25]$$

where Q = quantity sold, P = selling price, and A = advertising campaigns, the partial derivatives of Q with respect to P and A are

$$\frac{\partial Q}{\partial P} = -2.2 \text{ and } \frac{\partial Q}{\partial A} = 7.4$$

To take another example, for the multiplicative exponential demand function

$$Q = 3.0P^{-.50}A^{.25}$$

The partial derivative of Q with respect to P is

$$\frac{\partial Q}{\partial P} = 3.0A^{.25}(-.50P^{-.50-1})$$

$$= -1.5P^{-1.50}A^{.25}$$

Similarly, the partial derivative of Q with respect to A is

$$\frac{\partial Q}{\partial P} = 3.0P^{-.50}(.25A^{.25-1})$$

$$= .75P^{-.50}A^{-.75}$$

Maximization Problem

The partial derivatives can be used to obtain the optimal solution to a maximization or minimization problem containing two or more X variables. Analogous to the first-order conditions discussed earlier for the one-variable case, we set *each* of the partial derivatives equal to zero and solve the resulting set of simultaneous equations for the optimal X values.

Example

PROFIT MAXIMIZATION: INDIANA PETROLEUM COMPANY (continued)

Suppose we are interested in determining the values of Q_1 and Q_2 that maximize the company's profits given in Equation 2A.22. In this case, each of the two partial derivative functions (Equations 2A.23 and 2A.24) would be set equal to zero:

$$0 = 140 - 20Q_1 - 6Q_2$$
$$0 = 100 - 16Q_2 - 6Q_1$$

This system of equations can be solved for the profit-maximizing values of Q_1 and Q_2.[16] The optimal values are $Q_1^* = 5.77$ units and $Q_2^* = 4.08$ units.[17] The optimal total profit is equal to

$$\pi^* = -60 + 140(5.77) + 100(4.08) - 10(5.77)^2 - 8(4.08)^2 - 6(5.77)(4.08) = 548.45$$

SUMMARY

- *Marginal analysis* is useful in making decisions about the expansion or contraction of an economic activity.
- *Differential calculus,* which bears a close relationship to marginal analysis, can be applied whenever an algebraic relationship can be specified between the decision variables and the objective or criterion variable.
- The *first derivative* measures the slope or rate of change of a function at a given point and is equal to the limiting value of the marginal function as the marginal value is calculated over smaller and smaller intervals, that is, as the interval approaches zero.
- Various rules are available (see Table 2A.1) for finding the derivative of specific types of functions.
- A necessary, but not sufficient, condition for finding the maximum or minimum points of a function is that the first derivative be equal to zero. This is known as the *first-order condition.*
- A *second-order condition* is required to determine whether a given point is a maximum or minimum. The *second derivative* indicates that a given point is a maximum if the second derivative is less than zero or a minimum if the second derivative is greater than zero.
- The *partial derivative* of a multivariate function measures the marginal effect of a change in one variable on the value of the function, holding constant all other variables.

---

[16] The second-order conditions for obtaining a maximum or minimum in the multiple-variable case are somewhat complex. A discussion of these conditions can be found in most basic calculus texts.

[17] Exercise 11 at the end of this appendix requires the determination of these optimal values.

EXERCISES

1. Defining Q to be the level of output produced and sold, suppose that a firm's total revenue (TR) and total cost (TC) functions can be represented in tabular form as shown below.

Output (Q)	Total Revenue (TR)	Total Cost (TC)	Output (Q)	Total Revenue (TR)	Total Cost (TC)
0	0	20	11	264	196
1	34	26	12	276	224
2	66	34	13	286	254
3	96	44	14	294	286
4	124	56	15	300	320
5	150	70	16	304	356
6	174	86	17	306	394
7	196	104	18	306	434
8	216	124	19	304	476
9	234	146	20	300	520
10	250	170			

a. Compute the marginal revenue and average revenue functions.

b. Compute the marginal cost and average cost functions.

c. On a single graph, plot the total revenue, total cost, marginal revenue, and marginal cost functions.

d. Determine the output level in the *graph* that maximizes profits (that is, profit = total revenue − total cost) by finding the point where marginal revenue equals marginal cost.

e. Check your result in part (d) by finding the output level in the *tables* developed in parts (a) and (b) that likewise satisfies the condition that marginal revenue equals marginal cost.

2. Consider again the total revenue and total cost functions shown in tabular form in the previous problem.

a. Compute the total, marginal, and average profit functions.

b. On a single graph, plot the total profit and marginal profit functions.

c. Determine the output level in the graph and table where the total profit function takes on its maximum value.

d. How does the result in part (c) in this exercise compare with the result in part (d) of the previous exercise?

e. Determine total profits at the profit-maximizing output level.

3. Differentiate the following functions:

a. $TC = 50 + 100Q − 6Q^2 + .5Q^3$

b. $ATC = 50/Q + 100 − 6Q + .5Q^2$

c. $MC = 100 − 12Q + 1.5Q^2$

d. $Q = 50 − .75P$

e. $Q = .40X^{1.50}$

4. Differentiate the following functions:
   a. $Y = 2X^3/(4X^2 - 1)$
   b. $Y = 2X^3(4X^2 - 1)$
   c. $Y = 8Z^2 - 4Z + 1$, where $Z = 2X^2 - 1$ (differentiate Y with respect to X)

5. Defining Q to be the level of output produced and sold, assume that the firm's cost function is given by the relationship

$$TC = 20 + 5Q + Q^2$$

Furthermore, assume that the demand for the output of the firm is a function of price P given by the relationship

$$Q = 25 - P$$

   a. Defining total profit as the difference between total revenue and total cost, express in terms of Q the total profit function for the firm. (*Note:* Total revenue equals price per unit times the number of units sold.)
   b. Determine the output level where total profits are maximized.
   c. Calculate total profits and selling price at the profit-maximizing output level.
   d. If fixed costs increase from $20 to $25 in the total cost relationship, determine the effects of such an increase on the profit-maximizing output level and total profits.

6. Using the cost and demand functions in Exercise 5:
   a. Determine the marginal revenue and marginal cost functions.
   b. Show that, at the profit-maximizing output level determined in part (b) of the previous exercise, marginal revenue equals marginal cost. This illustrates the economic principle that profits are maximized at the output level where marginal revenue equals marginal cost.

7. Determine the partial derivatives with respect to all of the variables in the following functions:
   a. $TC = 50 + 5Q_1 + 10Q_2 + .5Q_1Q_2$
   b. $Q = 1.5L^{.60} K^{.50}$
   c. $Q_A = 2.5P_A^{-1.30} Y^{.20} P_B^{.40}$

8. Bounds Inc. has determined through regression analysis that its sales (S) are a function of the amount of advertising (measured in units) in two different media. This is given by the following relationship (X = newspapers, Y = magazines):

$$S(X,Y) = 200X + 100Y - 10X^2 - 20Y^2 + 20XY$$

   a. Find the level of newspaper and magazine advertising that maximizes the firm's sales.
   b. Calculate the firm's sales at the optimal values of newspaper and magazine advertising determined in part (a).

9. The Santa Fe Cookie Factory is considering an expansion of its retail piñon cookie business to other cities. The firm's owners lack the funds needed to undertake the expansion on their own. They are considering a franchise arrangement for the new outlets. The company incurs variable costs of $6 for each pound of cookies sold. The fixed costs of operating a typical retail outlet are

estimated to be $300,000 per year. The demand function facing each retail outlet is estimated to be

$$P = \$50 - .001Q$$

where P is the price per pound of cookies and Q is the number of pounds of cookies sold. [*Note:* Total revenue equals price (P) times quantity (Q) sold.]

a. What price, output, total revenue, total cost, and total profit level will each profit-maximizing franchise experience?

b. Assuming that the parent company charges each franchisee a fee equal to 5 percent of total revenues, recompute the values in part (a) above.

c. The Santa Fe Cookie Factory is considering a combined fixed/variable franchise fee structure. Under this arrangement each franchisee would pay the parent company $25,000 plus 1 percent of total revenues. Recompute the values in part (a) above.

d. What franchise fee arrangement do you recommend that the Santa Fe Cookie Factory adopt? What are the advantages and disadvantages of each plan?

10. Show that the optimal solution to the set of simultaneous equations in the Indiana Petroleum example are $Q_1^* = 5.77$ and $Q_2^* = 4.08$.

II
Demand and Forecasting

ECONOMIC ANALYSIS AND
DECISIONS

1. **Demand Analysis and
   Forecasting**
2. Production and Cost Analysis
3. Pricing Analysis
4. Capital Expenditure Analysis

ECONOMIC, POLITICAL, AND
SOCIAL ENVIRONMENT

1. **Business Conditions (Trends,
   Cycles, and Seasonal Effects)**
2. Factor Market Conditions (Capital,
   Labor, Land, and Raw Materials)
3. Competitors' Responses
4. External, Legal, and Regulatory
   Constraints
5. Organizational (Internal)
   Constraints

Cash Flows

Risk

**Firm Value
(Shareholders' Wealth)**

Part II (Demand and Forecasting) considers the elements determining the demand for a firm's output. Chapter 3 develops the theory of demand and introduces the elasticity properties of the demand function. Chapter 4 examines the procedures that may be used in making empirical estimates of the demand relationships developed in Chapter 3. Business and economic forecasting is the topic in Chapter 5. We consider forecasting at both the level of the firm and the overall economy. Chapter 6 examines the deter-minants of exchange rates, trade policy, and other factors crucial for effectively managing import-export trade. Understanding the determinants of both domestic and export demand is central to estimating the level and risk of the cash flows facing a firm. Forecasts of future economic activity and assessments of the impact of differing levels of economic activity on the demand of a firm are important inputs in the pricing, production, and resource-allocation decisions that wealth-maximizing managers must make.

3

Demand Analysis

CHAPTER PREVIEW Demand analysis serves two major managerial objectives. First, it provides the insights necessary to effectively manipulate demand. Second, it helps forecast sales and revenues. This chapter develops the theory of demand and introduces the elasticity properties of the demand function. The chapter begins by examining only the relationship between price and unit sales, thereby assuming that the other factors that influence demand, such as income levels and advertising, remain unchanged or are held constant. Later the effects of these other factors are added to the analysis.

One of the most important concepts from the theory of demand is the concept of elasticity. The price elasticity of demand is a measure of the responsiveness of quantity demanded to a change in one of the factors influencing demand, such as price, advertising, income levels, and the prices of substitute or complementary goods. The appendix to the chapter employs consumer indifference curves to develop the relationship between cost-of-living price indices and new product introductions.

A thorough understanding of demand theory and its applications is central to effective, wealth-maximizing decision making by a firm's managers because demand relationships determine the revenue portion of a firm's cash flow stream.

MANAGERIAL CHALLENGE

Health-Care Reform and Cigarette Taxes[1]

Between 1982 and 1992, Canadians experienced the dramatic effect that a substantial price increase could have on cigarette consumption. When the government raised the cigarette taxes enough to push the price per pack over $4, adult smoking declined by 38 percent and teenage smoking declined even more (by 61 percent). In 1997, a similar U.S. excise tax increase funded the "Tobacco settlement." Philip Morris, Reynolds Tobacco, Liggett, and other cigarette manufacturers agreed to pay $368 billion over 25 years to achieve immunity from civil liability in class action suits. The State Attorneys General had sued the cigarette manufacturers to recover the additional Medicare and Medicaid costs of smoking-related illnesses. Under the settlement, the average price of $1.43 per pack rose by 62 cents to $2.05 (35 percent). Some critics of the proposal insisted at the time that the tobacco tax should be higher (perhaps as much as $1.50 higher) to deter young smokers from acquiring the habit. The stated objective for reducing teenage smoking was 30 percent in 5 years and 50 percent in 7 years.

One important element of the debate regarding the "optimal" cigarette tax increase depends on how sensitive consumption is to changes in price. A measure of this sensitivity is the price elasticity of demand. In general, the price elasticity of demand represents the percentage change in quantity demanded that occurs as a result of some percentage change in price. Economists have estimated the price elasticity of adult cigarette demand to be −0.4,

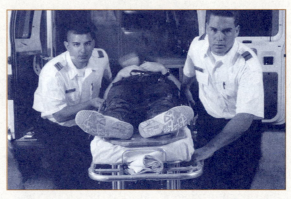

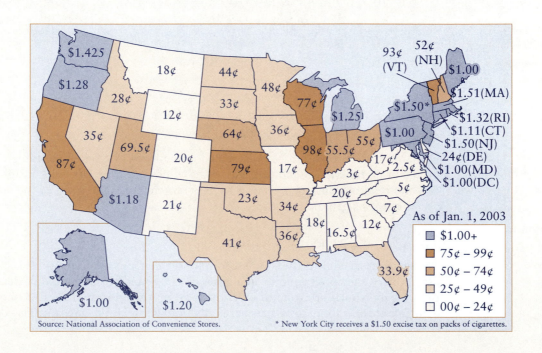

$1.425
$1.28
18¢
44¢
48¢
93¢ (VT)
52¢ (NH)
$1.00
28¢
12¢
33¢
77¢
$1.51(MA)
$1.50*
35¢
69.5¢
64¢
36¢
$1.25
$1.32(RI)
87¢
20¢
98¢   55.5¢
55¢
$1.00
$1.11(CT)
79¢
17¢
17¢
$1.50(NJ)
$1.18
21¢
23¢
34¢
3¢
2.5¢
24¢(DE)
$1.00(MD)
41¢
18¢   16.5¢   12¢
20¢
5¢
$1.00(DC)
36¢
7¢

As of Jan. 1, 2003

33.9¢

■ $1.00+
■ 75¢ – 99¢
■ 50¢ – 74¢
□ 25¢ – 49¢
□ 00¢ – 24¢

$1.00

$1.20

Source: National Association of Convenience Stores.   * New York City receives a $1.50 excise tax on packs of cigarettes.

MANAGERIAL CHALLENGE

indicating that for a 10 percent increase in price, quantity demanded can be expected to decline by 4 percent. For teenagers, however, the price elasticity is thought to be fifty percent higher—namely, −0.6—indicating that for a 10 percent increase in price, quantity demanded can be expected to decline by 6 percent. So, a 35 percent change in price would result in a 21 percent decline in teen smoking, far below the stated goal of 30 percent.[2]

As a result, in 1999 Congress decided to raise the federal excise tax another 60 cents. State legislatures got involved as well, such that by 2002 the average price per pack reached $3.28 nationwide. In some states, the price is much higher. New York, Massachusetts, New Jersey, Washington, Rhode Island, Oregon, Michigan, and Arizona all impose more than $1 in state excise tax (see map on previous page).

In the ongoing debate over the amount of cigarette tax required for health care cost recovery, policy makers faced a difficult set of trade-offs. On the one hand, if the primary objective is to generate income to fund health-care costs, the tax should be set such that it will maximize tax revenue. On the other hand, if the primary objective is to discour-

age smoking, a much higher tax could be justified. In either case, however, knowledge of the true price elasticity of demand is an essential element of this important policy decision. In this chapter, we investigate how to estimate such demand relationships.

http://

The National Center for Policy Analysis Internet site provides additional information on cigarette tax policy at the following address:
http://www.public-policy.org/,ncpa/ba/ba231.html
The Internet site for the Federation of Tax Administrators lists current state excise tax rates for cigarettes at the following address:
http://www.taxadmin.org/fta/rate/cigarett.html

---

[1] Based in part on "Add $2 to the Cost of a Pack of Cigarettes" and "And Even Teen Smokers May Kick the Habit," *BusinessWeek,* March 15, 1993, p. 18; "Critics Question Tobacco Pact's Effect on Teen Smoking," *Wall Street Journal,* August 19, 1997, p. A20; "Major Makers of Cigarettes Raise Prices," *Wall Street Journal,* August 31, 1999, p. A3; and "Politicians Are Hooked on Cigarette Taxes," *Wall Street Journal,* February 20, 2002, p. A2.

[2] The 35 percent price increase in the U.S. can be calculated by dividing the $0.62 tax increase by the average of the original $1.43 and the post-tax $2.05 price.

DEMAND RELATIONSHIPS: THE DEMAND SCHEDULE AND THE DEMAND CURVE

Demand relationships can be represented in the form of a schedule (table), graph, or algebraic function. Each of these forms of presentation provides insights into demand relationships. This section focuses on schedules and graphs; the next section discusses algebraic functions.

The Demand Schedule Defined

The demand schedule is the simplest form of the demand relationship. It is merely a list of prices and corresponding quantities of a commodity that would be demanded by some individual or group of individuals at uniform prices.[3] Table 3.1 shows the demand schedule for regular-size pizzas at a local Pizza Hut restaurant. This demand

---

[3] The terms *commodity, good,* and *product* are used interchangeably throughout the text to describe both physical goods and services. Prices are assumed to be uniform across all buyers.

Table 3.1   Simplified Demand Schedule: Pizza Hut Restaurant

Price of Pizza ($/Unit)	Quantity of Pizzas Sold (Units Per Time Period)
10	50
9	60
8	70
7	80
6	90
5	100

schedule indicates that *if* the price of pizzas were $9.00, consumers would purchase 60 pizzas. Note that the lower the price, the greater the quantity of pizzas that would be demanded. This inverse or negative relationship between price and quantity demanded is generally referred to as the "law of demand." At lower prices, people are able and willing to purchase more of a commodity than at a higher price.

Constrained Utility Maximization and Demand

The concept of demand is based on the theory of consumer choice. Each consumer faces a constrained optimization problem, where the objective is to choose among the combinations of goods that maximize his or her satisfaction or utility, subject to a constraint on the amount of funds available (i.e., budget) to purchase these goods. Think of a food and entertainment budget allowance from your employer while you are traveling on an extended business trip or, alternatively, a set of friends who share these expenses while rooming together. In this constrained utility-maximizing framework, economists have identified two basic reasons for the increase in quantity demanded as the result of a price reduction. These factors are known as the *income* and *substitution effects*.

Income Effect   When the price of a good—for example, steak—declines, the effect of this decline is that the real income or purchasing power of the consumer has increased. This is known as the *income effect*. For example, if an individual normally purchases two pounds of steak per week at $5 per pound, a price decline to $4 per pound would enable the consumer to purchase the same amount of steak for $2 less per week. This savings of $2 represents an increase in real income of $2, which may be used to purchase greater quantities of steak (as well as other income-superior goods) each week. Sometimes the income effect of a price reduction is miniscule because so little of the household's budget is expended on the good (consider salt), but at other times the change in purchasing power is enormous. Consider a young family who spends 40 percent of their disposable income on apartment housing.

Substitution Effect   When the price of a good—such as steak—declines, it becomes less expensive in relation to other goods—for example, chicken. As a result of the price decline, the rational consumer can increase his or her satisfaction (or utility) by purchasing more of the good whose price has declined and less of the other goods. This is known as the *substitution effect*.

For example, suppose that the prices of steak and chicken are $5 and $2 per pound, respectively. Furthermore, assume that an individual purchases two pounds of steak and two pounds of chicken per week for a total expenditure of $14. Suppose that the price of steak declines to $4 per pound. As a result of this price decrease, an individual who has a preference for steak may decide to increase his or her consumption of steak to three pounds per week and decrease his or her consumption of chicken to one pound per week—which requires the same total expenditure of $14 per week. Thus we see that a decrease in the price of steak (relative to that of chicken) has led to an increase in the demand for steak.

In summary, because of the combined impact of the income and substitution effects, a decline in the price will always have an impact on the quantity demanded. For income-superior goods for which more is preferred to less as income rises (e.g., single-family housing), both the substitution and income effects dictate an increase in quantity demanded at lower prices. For income-inferior goods like efficiency apartments, mackerel, and subcompact cars,[4] the income and substitution effects have opposite and partially offsetting impacts on the quantity demanded. The net effect of both actions, even in the case of inferior goods, is that more will likely be demanded at lower prices.

Individual and Market Demand Curves

The expenditure decisions made by each individual determine his or her own demand curve. The market demand curve for a good is equal to the sum of the individual demands. As shown in Figure 3.1, for two individuals, the market demand curve is obtained through the horizontal summation of the quantities demanded at each price.[5] For example, at a price of $5 per unit, consumers 1 and 2 would purchase 20 and 15 units, respectively, yielding a market demand of 35 units. Other points on the market demand curve are obtained in a similar manner. Market demand is generally of more interest than individual demand relationships to the firm's managers because the market demand curve serves as a basis for making many pricing and output decisions.

DEMAND RELATIONSHIPS: THE DEMAND FUNCTION

The demand curve specifies the relationship between prices and the quantity of a good or service that will be demanded at those prices at some point in time, *holding constant the influence of all other factors*. A number of these other factors may effect a change in the shape as well as the position of the demand curve as time passes. Decision variables that management will often consider include the design and packaging of products, the amount and distribution of the firm's advertising budget, the size of the sales force, promotional expenditures, the time period of adjustment for any price changes, and taxes or subsidies. Algebraically, the **demand function** can be represented as

Demand Function
The relationship that exists during some period of time between the number of units of a good or service that consumers are willing to buy and a given set of conditions that influence the willingness to purchase, such as price, income level, and advertising.

$$Q_D = f\ (P,\ P^S,\ P^C,\ Y,\ A,\ A^C,\ N,\ C^P,\ P^E,\ T^A,\ T/S\ \ldots) \qquad [3.1]$$

Determinents that shift Demand (handwritten annotation)

---

[4] "Inferior goods" are those that are consumed less as income rises, and vice versa.

[5] For goods that can be shared, like pools, concerts, and flood control projects, market demand is the vertical summation of the willingness to pay of the individual demanders.

Figure 3.1   Individual and Market Demand Curves

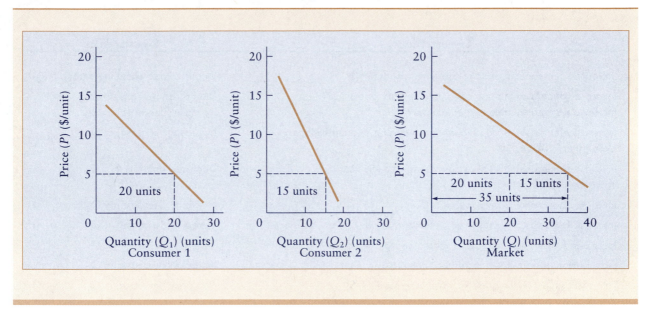

where Q_D = quantity demanded of the good or service

P = price of the good or service $(-)$

P^S = price of **substitute goods** or services

P^C = price of **complementary goods** or services

Y = income of consumers

A = advertising expenditures (and other marketing expenditures)

A^C = competitors' advertising expenditures on the good or service

N = population (and other demographic factors)

C^P = consumer tastes and preferences for the good or service

P^E = expected (future) changes in price

T^A = adjustment time period

T/S = taxes or subsidies

Substitute Goods

Two goods are substitutes if the quantity demanded of one *increases* (decreases) when the price of the other *increases* (decreases), assuming all other factors affecting demand remain unchanged.

Complementary Goods

Two goods are complementary if the quantity demanded of one *decreases* (increases) when the price of the other *increases* (decreases), assuming all other factors affecting demand remain unchanged.

This representation of the demand function indicates that quantity demanded is a function of a number of different factors (i.e., independent variables). Table 3.2 summarizes some of the factors that affect the shape and/or position of the demand curve. For export products, Chapter 6 shows how other variables such as the foreign exchange rate may be equally important in explaining demand.

The demand schedule or demand curve merely deals with the price-quantity relationship. *Changes in the price (i.e., P) of the good or service will result only in movement along the demand curve, whereas changes in any of the other independent variables (i.e., P^S, P^C, Y, A, A^C, N, C^P, P^E, . . .) in the demand function result in a shift of that curve.*

This is illustrated graphically in Figure 3.2. The initial demand relationship is line DD'. If the original price were P_1, quantity Q_1 would be demanded. If the price declined to P_2, the quantity demanded would increase to Q_2. If, however, changes occurred in the other independent variables, we would expect to have a shift in the

Table 3.2   Partial List of Factors Affecting Demand

Demand Factor	Expected Effect
Increase (decrease) in price of substitute goods[a] (P^S)	Increase (decrease) in demand (Q_D)
Increase (decrease) in price of complementary goods[b] (P^C)	Decrease (increase) in Q_D
Increase (decrease) in consumer income levels[c] (Y)	Increase (decrease) in Q_D
Increase (decrease) in the amount of advertising and marketing expenditures (A)	Increase (decrease) in Q_D
Increase (decrease) in level of advertising and marketing by competitors (A^C)	Decrease (increase) in Q_D
Increase (decrease) in population (N)	Increase (decrease) in Q_D
Increase (decrease) in consumer preferences for the good or service (C^P)	Increase (decrease) in Q_D
Expected future price increases (decreases) for the good (P^E)	Increase (decrease) in Q_D
Time period of adjustment increases (decreases) (T^A)	Increase (decrease) in Q_D
Taxes (subsidies) on the good increase (decrease) (T/S)	Decrease (increase) in Q_D

[a] Two goods are substitutes if an increase (decrease) in the price of Good 1 results in an increase (decrease) in the quantity demanded of Good 2, holding other factors constant, such as the price of Good 2, other prices, income, and so on, or vice versa. For example, margarine may be viewed as a rather good substitute for butter. As the price of butter increases, more people will decrease their consumption of butter and increase their consumption of margarine.

[b] Goods that are used in conjunction with each other, either in production or consumption, are called *complementary goods*. For example, DVDs are used in conjunction with DVD players. An increase in the price of DVD players would have the effect of decreasing the demand for DVDs, *ceteris paribus*. In other words, two goods are complementary if a decrease in the price of Good 1 results in an increase in the quantity demanded of Good 2, *ceteris paribus*. Similarly, two goods are complements if an increase in the price of Good 1 results in a decrease in the quantity demanded of Good 2.

[c] The case of inferior goods—that is, those goods that are purchased in smaller total quantities as income levels rise—will be discussed below in a consideration of the concept of income elasticity.

entire curve. If, for example, a tax reduction were approved and consumer disposable income increased, the new demand curve might become D_1D_1'. At any price, P_1, along D_1D_1', a greater quantity, Q_3, will be demanded than at the same price on the original curve DD'. Similarly, if the prices of substitute products were to decline, the demand curve would shift downward and to the left. At any price, P_1, along the new curve D_2D_2', a smaller quantity, Q_4, would be demanded than at the same price on either DD' or D_1D_1'.

In summary, movement *along* a demand curve is often referred to as *a change in the quantity demanded,* while holding constant the effects of factors other than price that affect demand. A shift of the entire demand curve is often referred to as *a change in demand* and is always caused by some demand factor, other than price.

Example

COMPLEMENT STRATEGY AT GENERAL MOTORS AND INTEL[6]

Identifying, developing, and managing relationships with complement products in order to increase demand for one's own product has become a key element of corporate strategy. The other five forces of competition (threat of substitutes, intensity

[6] Adam Brandenberg and Barry Nalebuff explain this role of complementary products in *Co-Opetition* (New York: Bantam Books, 1996).

Figure 3.2   Shifts in Demand

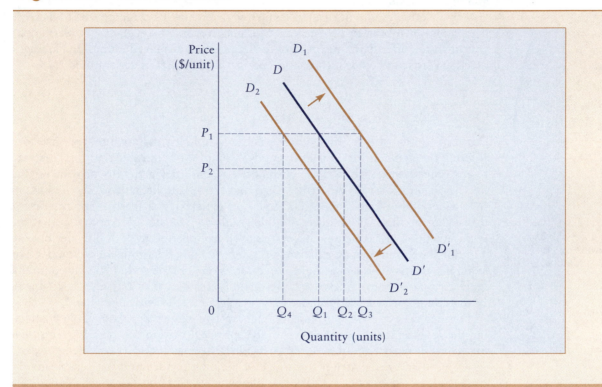

http://

You can access financial and product line information on General Motors at the following Internet address: http://www.gm.com/flash_homepage/

of rivalry, threat of entry, power of buyers, and power of suppliers) are much more difficult to influence.[7] To eliminate the competition from substitute products requires a never-ending upstaging of new imitators and can seldom provide sustainable competitive advantage. To cooperate effectively with rivals often constitutes a violation of the antitrust laws of the United States or the tougher antitrust laws of the European Union. To erect permanent barriers to entry requires the best product differentiation ad campaigns and relationship marketing. And, after improving coordination with vertical integration and total quality management, the remaining power of buyers and suppliers is often beyond a firm's control. Consequently, many companies today seek to develop complementary products as a driver of demand for their own products.

General Motors (GM) invests heavily in and thereby expands the capacity of high-end auto loans (GMAC) and specialty auto insurance (GMAC Insurance). GM does so not because these are particularly profitable assets on their own, but rather because reduced time and inconvenience in arranging such loans and insurance are strong complements to the sale of very profitable Suburbans, Cadillacs, and other luxury cars and trucks. Similarly, Intel engineers responsible for designing computer chips now regularly outpace the demands of current PC applications for speed and computation capacity. So, Intel has entered into a joint venture with ProShare to accelerate the development of inexpensive interactive video, desktop video conferencing,

---

[7] Michael Porter's five forces of competition model is described in Chapter 10 (see Figure 10.2).

and video telephone. These new complementary technologies will require much larger and faster computer chips.

Other examples that illustrate a company's astute use of complements to increase demand for their primary products are Michelin tires and travel guides, Borders books and in-store coffee bars, inexpensive reading glasses displayed alongside Hallmark greeting cards, and convenience stores or fast food outlets in gas stations.

Other Factors Affecting Demand

Durable Goods   Up to this point it has been implicitly assumed that we are considering the demand for consumer goods to be of a nondurable nature. These are goods purchased largely to meet current needs, and they generally provide service on a short-term basis. Food items, Christmas trees, and virtually all services fall in this category, but housing and DVD players are clearly different. One reason for this is that by their very nature, **durable goods** *may be stored.* Another is that the replacement of a durable item may be delayed from period to period by performing additional maintenance on existing items or by merely tolerating an old model. For example, an automobile may be repaired (or its out-of-date styling merely endured); an electric range may be fixed (at considerably less cost than buying a new range); or the discomforts of old furniture may be tolerated for "one more year."

Obsolescence in style, convenience, and prestige value play a larger role in affecting the replacement of durables than does physical deterioration. Also, *consumer expectations* regarding future levels of income, the availability of complements, and future product price play a major role in explaining the demand for durable goods. For example, a consumer may ask the following sorts of questions when embarking on a personal computer purchase:

- Will new products soon make my computer obsolete?
- Will my income be sufficient and steady enough to make the payments on the computer?
- Are prices likely to rise or fall over the next year?
- Will adequate software be available over the economic working life of my PC?

Because these expectational factors come into play in evaluating replacement demand, demand for durable goods is more volatile, and its analysis is more complex than a similar analysis for nondurables.

Derived Demand for Producer's Goods   **Producer's goods** differ from consumer goods in that they are not produced for direct consumption but rather are the raw materials, capital equipment, and parts that are combined to produce a consumer good (or some other producer's good). As such, the demand for producer's goods may be thought of as a *derived demand* because it is derived from some ultimate consumer desire. For example, the demand for aluminum, a raw material, is dependent on consumer desires and tastes for those products that are wholly or partially composed of aluminum, such as home siding and rain gutters, and for those services that are dependent on aluminum, such as plane travel.

Therefore, when analyzing derived demand for producer's goods, an account must be taken of two new sets of factors. First, we must consider the criteria or specifications used by the purchasing agent of the producing company that guide the agent in selecting one material, machine, process, or product over competitive alternatives.

Durable Good
A good that yields benefits to the owner over a number of future time periods.

Producer's Good
A good that is not produced for direct consumption, but rather is the raw material or capital equipment that is used to produce a consumer good (or some other producer's good).

Second, and perhaps more important, we must take account of the significant factors affecting the demand for the ultimate consumer goods for which the producer's goods are inputs.

Exchange Rate Considerations   In addition to the above determinants of demand, the demand for goods traded in foreign markets is also influenced by external factors such as exchange rate fluctuations. When Microsoft sells computer software overseas, it prefers to be paid in U.S. dollars. This is because a company like Microsoft incurs few offshore expenses beyond advertising and therefore cannot simply match payables and receivables in a foreign currency. To accept Italian lire, French francs, or Australian dollars in payment for software purchase orders would introduce an exchange rate risk exposure for which Microsoft would want to be compensated in the form of higher prices on its software. Consequently, the foreign exports of Microsoft are typically transacted in U.S. dollars and are therefore tied inextricably to the price of the dollar against other currencies. As the value of the dollar rises, offshore buyers must pay a larger amount of their own currency to obtain the dollars required to pay for Microsoft's software, and this decreases the export demand. Similarly, a lower value of the dollar reduces the lira or franc price of the product, raising the export demand for Microsoft software. Even in a large domestic market like the United States, companies often find that these export demand considerations are key determinants of their overall demand.

Example

http://

The U.S. International Trade Administration provides news and other information on international trade issues affecting U.S. companies at the following Internet address:
http://www.ita.doc.gov/media/

EXCHANGE RATE IMPACTS ON DEMAND: CUMMINS ENGINE COMPANY

Cummins Engine Company of Columbus, Indiana, is the largest independent manufacturer of new and replacement diesel engines for heavy trucks and for construction, mining, and agricultural machinery. GMC, Ford, and Daimler-Benz are their major competitors, and 38 percent of sales occur offshore. The Cummins and Daimler-Benz large diesel truck engines sell for approximately $40,000 and DM100,000, respectively. Three times in the last two decades Cummins has suffered substantial declines in cash flow—i.e., during the recessions of 1990–1991 and 2000–2002 and during the expansionary period 1982–1985.

In the earliest period, the price of the dollar against the mark (i.e., the dollar exchange rate quoted in deutschmarks) rose from DM2.43 to a high of DM2.94. This meant that a $40,000 Cummins diesel engine that had sold for DM97,200 in Munich in 1982 became DM117,600, whereas the DM100,000 Mercedes diesel that had been $41,152 declined to $34,014 in Detroit. Cummins faced two unattractive options, either of which would reduce cash flow. It could either cut its profit margins and maintain unit sales, or maintain margins but have both offshore and domestic unit sales collapse. The company chose to cut margins and maintain sales. By 1987 the dollar's value had declined and Cummins' performance improved. In the interim, demand for Cummins engines was very adversely affected by the temporary appreciation of the dollar.

PRICE ELASTICITY OF DEMAND

From a decision-making perspective, the firm needs to know the effect of changes in any of the independent variables in the demand function on the quantity demanded. Some of these variables are under the control of management, such as price, advertising, product quality, and customer service. For these variables, management must know the effects of changes on quantity to assess the desirability of instituting the change. Other variables, including income, prices of competitors' products, and expectations of consumers regarding future prices, are outside the direct control of the firm. Nevertheless, effective demand management requires that the firm be able to measure the impact of changes in these variables on the quantity demanded.

Price Elasticity Defined

The most commonly used measure of the responsiveness of quantity demanded to changes in any of the variables that influence the demand function is *elasticity*. In general, *elasticity* may be thought of as a ratio of the percentage change in one quantity (or variable) to the percentage change in another, *ceteris paribus* (all other things remaining unchanged). In other words, how responsive is some dependent variable to changes in a particular variable? With this in mind, we define the **price elasticity of demand** (E_D) as the ratio of the percentage change in quantity demanded to a percentage change in price:

ceteris paribus
Latin for "all other things held constant."

Price Elasticity
The ratio of the percentage change in quantity demanded to the percentage change in price, assuming that all other factors influencing demand remain unchanged. Also called *own* price elasticity.

$$E_D = \frac{\%\Delta Q}{\%\Delta P}, \text{ ceteris paribus} \qquad [3.2]$$

where ΔQ = change in quantity demanded
ΔP = change in price

Because of the normal inverse relationship between price and quantity demanded, the sign of the price elasticity coefficient will be negative. Occasionally, price elasticities are referred to as absolute values. In the passages that follow, the use of absolute values will be indicated where appropriate.

Arc Price Elasticity

The *arc* price elasticity of demand is a technique for calculating price elasticity between two prices.[8] It indicates the effect of a change in price, from P_1 to P_2, on the quantity demanded. The following formula is used to compute this elasticity measure:

$$E_D = \frac{\dfrac{Q_2 - Q_1}{\left(\dfrac{Q_2 + Q_1}{2}\right)}}{\dfrac{P_2 - P_1}{\left(\dfrac{P_2 + P_1}{2}\right)}} = \frac{Q_2 - Q_1}{P_2 - P_1} \cdot \frac{P_2 + P_1}{Q_2 + Q_1} = \frac{\Delta Q}{\Delta P}\frac{P_2 + P_1}{Q_2 + Q_1} \qquad [3.3]$$

where Q_1 = quantity sold before a price change
Q_2 = quantity sold after a price change
P_1 = original price
P_2 = price after a price change

---

[8] As we will see in the following section dealing with "point price elasticities," the price elasticity of a straight-line demand curve is different at each point on the demand curve. Hence an "arc price elasticity" computed between two prices may be thought of as an "average" of the various point elasticities between the two prices.

The fraction $(Q_2 + Q_1)/2$ represents average quantity demanded in the range over which the price elasticity is being calculated. $(P_2 + P_1)/2$ also represents the average price over this range.

Rearranging Equation 3.3 shows that the elasticity measurement depends on the inverse of the *slope* of the ordinary demand curve (i.e., the sensitivity of demand in the target market to price *changes*)

$$\frac{Q_2 - Q_1}{P_2 - P_1}$$

as well as the *position* on the curve (i.e., the price point positioning) where elasticity is calculated

$$\frac{P_2 + P_1}{Q_2 + Q_1}$$

Because the slope remains constant over the entire schedule (*assuming linearity*), but the value of $(P_2 + P_1)/(Q_2 + Q_1)$ changes, depending on where on the demand curve elasticity is being calculated, *the value of the elasticity measure generally changes throughout the length of the demand curve*. Price elasticity at higher prices and small volume is therefore larger (in absolute value) than price elasticity for the same product and same demanders at lower price points and large volume.

To illustrate, consider the demand schedule shown in Table 3.3 for men's Levi's jeans in a local Sears store. Calculate the price elasticity between an original price of $19 (14 units are demanded) and a new price of $18. Substituting the relevant data from Table 3.3 into Equation 3.3 yields

$$E_D = \frac{\dfrac{16 - 14}{(16 + 14)/2}}{\dfrac{\$18 - \$19}{(\$18 + \$19)/2}}$$

$$= -2.46$$

Table 3.3   Demand Schedule: Levi's Jeans

Price, P ($/Unit)	Quantity Sold, Q_D (Units Per Period)
20	12
19	14
18	16
17	18
16	20
12	28
11	30

A price elasticity of demand coefficient of -2.46 means that a 10 percent increase (decrease) in price can be expected to result in a 24.6 percent decrease (increase) in quantity demanded, *ceteris paribus*.

Now assume the original price was $12, and a new price of $11 is set. Determine the price elasticity of demand. Employing Equation 3.3 and the relevant data from Table 3.3 yields

$$E_D = \frac{\dfrac{30 - 28}{(30 + 28)/2}}{\dfrac{\$11 - \$12}{(\$11 + \$12)/2}} = -0.79$$

A price elasticity of demand of -0.79 means that a 10 percent increase (decrease) in price can be expected to result in a 7.9 percent decrease (increase) in quantity demanded, *ceteris paribus*.

We can also use Equation 3.3 to compute a price that would have to be charged to achieve a particular level of sales. Consider the NBA Corporation, which had monthly basketball shoe sales of 10,000 pairs (at $100 per pair) before a price cut by its major competitor. After this competitor's price reduction, NBA's sales declined to 8,000 pairs a month. From the past experience NBA has estimated the price elasticity of demand to be about -2.0 in this price-quantity range. If the NBA wishes to restore its sales to 10,000 pairs a month, determine the price that must be charged.

Letting $Q_2 = 10,000$, $Q_1 = 8,000$, $P_1 = \$100$, and $E_D = -2.0$, the required price, P_2, may be computed using Equation 3.3:

$$-2.0 = \frac{\dfrac{10,000 - 8,000}{(10,000 + 8,000)/2}}{\dfrac{P_2 - \$100}{(P_2 + \$100)/2}}$$

$$P_2 = \$89.50$$

A price cut to $89.50 would be required to restore sales to 10,000 pairs a month.

Example

PRICE ELASTICITY OF DEMAND: THE *MACON TELEGRAPH* [9]

The *Macon Telegraph* newspaper is the principal sponsor of the Macon Labor Day Road Race, a 5K and 10K running event held annually in Macon, Georgia. The entry fee for the race in 1990 was $12 per runner. The fee was raised to $20 per runner for the 1991 race, in hopes of increasing revenues from the race. Prior to the race, there were complaints that the fee was too high for that kind of race and that it precluded many families from being able to afford entry fees.

The newspaper learned a lesson in price elasticity for running events from this experience. In 1990 the race attracted 1,600 runners, and thus generated income of $19,200. In 1991, under similar weather conditions, the race attracted only 900 runners, and thus generated income of only $18,000. Because a $(\$20 - \$12)/\$16 = 50$ percent increase in price resulted in a massive $(-700/1250) = 56$ percent decrease in quantity demanded, the total revenue *declined*, and the price elasticity of demand over this range is "elastic" (greater than 1.0 in absolute value). Specifically, the price elasticity can be estimated as

---

[9] Based on Margaret Chivers, "They Voted with Their Feet," *Running Journal*, October 1991, pp. 1–2.

$$E_D = [(Q_2 - Q_1)/(Q_2 + Q_1)]/[(P_2 - P_1)/(P_2 + P_1)]$$
$$= [(900 - 1{,}600)/(900 + 1{,}600)]/[(\$20 - \$12)/(\$20 + \$12)]$$
$$= -1.12$$

That is, the $\%\Delta Q_D = -56$ percent is 1.12 times as large as the $\%\Delta P = 50$ percent; the demand percentage decrease exceeded the price percentage increase.

In this case, the strategy of raising the price backfired because the newspaper misunderstood or incorrectly estimated the price elasticity of demand.

Point Price Elasticity

The preceding formulas measure the *arc elasticity* of demand; that is, elasticity is computed over a discrete range of the demand curve or schedule. Because elasticity is normally different at each point on the curve, arc elasticity is a measure of the average elasticity over that range.

By employing some elementary calculus, the elasticity of demand at any *point* along the curve may be calculated with the following expression:

$$E_D = \frac{\partial Q_D}{\partial P} \cdot \frac{P}{Q_D} \qquad [3.4]$$

where $\dfrac{\partial Q_D}{\partial P}$ = the partial derivative of quantity with respect to price (the inverse of the slope of the demand curve)

Q_D = the quantity demanded at price P

P = the price at some specific point on the demand curve

The partial derivative of quantity with respect to price, $\partial Q_D/\partial P$, is merely an indication of the rate of change in quantity demanded as the price changes. This incremental change ratio is analogous to the

$$\frac{Q_2 - Q_1}{P_2 - P_1} = \frac{\Delta Q}{\Delta P}$$

discrete change ratio in the arc elasticity measure.

The daily demand function for Christmas trees at sidewalk seasonal sales lots in mid-December can be used to illustrate the calculation of the point price elasticity. Suppose that demand can be written algebraically as quantity demanded per day:

$$Q_D = 45{,}000 - 2{,}500P + 2.5Y \qquad [3.5]$$

If one is interested in determining the point price elasticity when the price (P) is equal to \$40 and per capita disposable personal income (Y) is equal to \$30,000, taking the partial derivative of Equation 3.5 with respect to P yields

$$\frac{\partial Q_D}{\partial P} = -2{,}500 \text{ trees per dollar}$$

Substituting the relevant values of P and Y into Equation 3.5 gives

$$Q_D = 45{,}000 - 2{,}500(40) + 2.50(30{,}000) = 20{,}000$$

From Equation 3.4 one obtains

$$E_D = -2{,}500 \frac{\text{trees}}{\$} \left(\frac{\$8}{10{,}000 \text{ trees}}\right) = -2.0$$

PRICE ELASTICITY OF DEMAND: THE CASE OF HORSE RACE PARI-MUTUEL BETTING[10]

Faced with tight budgets and the need to raise additional revenues, many states have turned to various forms of state-operated legalized gambling. One of the earliest forms of betting, and still among the most prevalent, is the pari-mutuel wagering system of horse racing. The state revenue from horse race betting comes from a tax (called the "takeout rate") on the total of money wagered (called the "handle"). If the demand for horse race wagering is price inelastic, then states could increase their tax revenues by increasing the takeout rate. In contrast, if demand is price elastic, then increases in the takeout rate are likely to lead to declines in state revenues.

Two tracks in New York City lost revenue when they cut the takeout rate from 17 percent to 14 percent. With an inelastic demand, a reduction in "price" results in a decline in total revenue. At 22 other racetracks, in 21 instances, increases in the takeout rate resulted in increases in total revenues to both the state and the racing industry. These revenue effects suggest an inelastic demand for racetrack betting, insensitive to price increases.

Interpreting the Price Elasticity: Relationship between the Price Elasticity and Revenues

Once the price elasticity of demand has been calculated, it is necessary to interpret the meaning of the number obtained. The elasticity coefficient may take on *absolute values* over the range from 0 to ∞ (infinity). Values in the indicated ranges are described in Table 3.4.

When demand is *unit* elastic, a percentage change in price P is matched by an *equal* percentage change in quantity demanded Q_D. When demand is *elastic*, a percentage change in P is exceeded by the percentage change in Q_D. For *inelastic* demand, a percentage change in P results in a smaller percentage change in Q_D. The theoretical extremes of perfect elasticity and perfect inelasticity are illustrated in Figure 3.3. AAA-grade January wheat sells on the Kansas City spot market with perfectly elastic demand facing any particular grain dealer; Panel A illustrates this case. Heroin addicts have almost perfectly inelastic demand; their quantity demanded is fixed no matter what the price, as indicated in Panel B. However, these extremes are rarely encountered. Rather, they illustrate the limits of price elasticity.

The price elasticity of demand indicates the effect a change in price will have on the total revenue that is generated. Because total revenue *TR* is equal to price (average revenue), *P*, times the number of units sold, Q_D, we may determine, from our knowledge of demand elasticity, the effect on total revenue when price changes.

When demand elasticity is less than 1 in absolute value (i.e., inelastic), an increase (decrease) in price will result in an increase (decrease) in total consumer expenditures $(P \cdot Q_D)$. This occurs because an inelastic demand indicates that a given percentage increase in price results in a smaller percentage decrease in quantity sold, the net effect being an increase in the total expenditures, $P \cdot Q_D$. Table 3.5 illustrates this point. When demand is *inelastic*—that is, $|E_D| < 1$—an increase in price from \$2 to \$3, for example, results in an increase in total revenue from \$18 to \$24.[11]

---

[10] Based on Donn R. Pescatrice, "The Inelastic Demand for Wagering," *Applied Economics* 12 (1980), pp. 1–10.

[11] The symbol $|E_D| < 1$ indicates that we are talking about the absolute value of the elasticity coefficient, rather than its actual negative value. This symbol (| |) is used whenever we refer to absolute values.

Table 3.4   Price Elasticity of Demand in Absolute Values

Range	Description
$E_D = 0$	Perfectly inelastic
$0 < |E_D| < 1$	Inelastic
$|E_D| = 1$	Unit elastic
$1 < |E_D| < \infty$	Elastic
$|E_D| = \infty$	Perfectly elastic

Figure 3.3   Perfectly Elastic and Inelastic Demand Curves

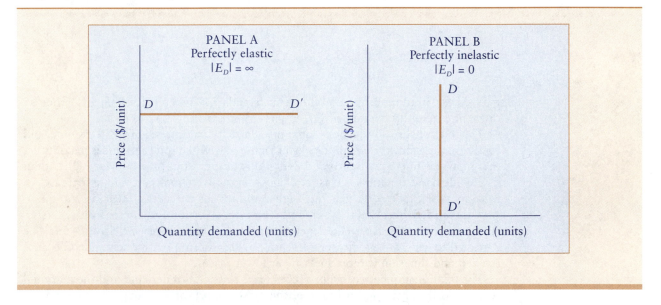

In contrast, when demand is *elastic*—that is, $|E_D| > 1$—a given percentage increase (decrease) in price is more than offset by a larger percentage decrease (increase) in quantity sold. An increase in price from $9 to $10 results in a reduction in total consumer expenditure from $18 to $10 (again see Table 3.5).

When demand is *unit elastic,* a given percentage change in price is exactly offset by the same percentage change in quantity demanded, the net result being a constant total consumer expenditure. If the price is increased from $5 to $6, total revenue would remain constant at $30, because the decrease in quantity demanded at the new price just offsets the price increase (see Table 3.5). When the price elasticity of demand $|E_D|$ is equal to 1 (or is unit elastic), the total revenue function is

Table 3.5   Relationship between Elasticity and Marginal Revenue

Price, P ($/Unit)	Quantity, Q_D (Units)	Elasticity E_D	Total Revenue $P \cdot Q_D$ ($)	Marginal Revenue ($/Unit)
10	1		10	
9	2	−6.33	18	8
8	3	−3.40	24	6
7	4	−2.14	28	4
6	5	−1.44	30	2
5	6	−1.00	30	0
4	7	−0.69	28	−2
3	8	−0.46	24	−4
2	9	−0.29	18	−6
1	10	−0.15	10	−8

maximized. In the example, total revenue equals $30 when price P equals either $5 or $6 and quantity demanded Q_D equals either 6 or 5.

The relationship among price, quantity, elasticity measures, marginal revenue, and total revenue is illustrated graphically in Figure 3.4. When total revenue is maximized, marginal revenue equals zero and demand is unit elastic. At any price higher than P_2, the demand function is elastic. Hence, successive equal percentage increases in price may be expected to generate higher and higher percentage decreases in quantity demanded because the demand function is becoming increasingly elastic. Alternatively, successive equal percentage reductions in price below P_2 may be expected to generate ever lower percentage increases in quantity demanded because the demand function is more inelastic at lower prices.

The relationship between a product's price elasticity of demand and the marginal revenue at that price point is one of the most important in managerial economics. This relationship can be derived by analyzing the change in revenue resulting from a price change. To start, **marginal revenue** is defined as the change in total revenue resulting from lowering price to make an additional unit sale. Lowering price from P_1 to P_2 in Figure 3.4 to increase quantity demanded from Q_1 to Q_2 results in a change in the initial revenue P_1AQ_10 to P_2BQ_20. The difference in these two areas is illustrated in Figure 3.4 as the two shaded rectangles. The horizontal shaded rectangle is the loss of revenue caused by the price reduction $(P_2 - P_1)$ over the previous units sold Q_1. The vertical shaded rectangle is the gain in revenue from selling $(Q_2 - Q_1)$ additional units at the new price P_2. That is, the change in total revenue from lowering the price to sell another unit can always be written as follows:

Marginal Revenue
The change in total revenue that results from a one-unit change in quantity demanded.

$$MR = \frac{\Delta TR}{\Delta Q} = \frac{P_2(Q_2 - Q_1) + (P_2 - P_1)Q_1}{(Q_2 - Q_1)} \qquad [3.6]$$

Figure 3.4   Price Elasticity over Demand Function

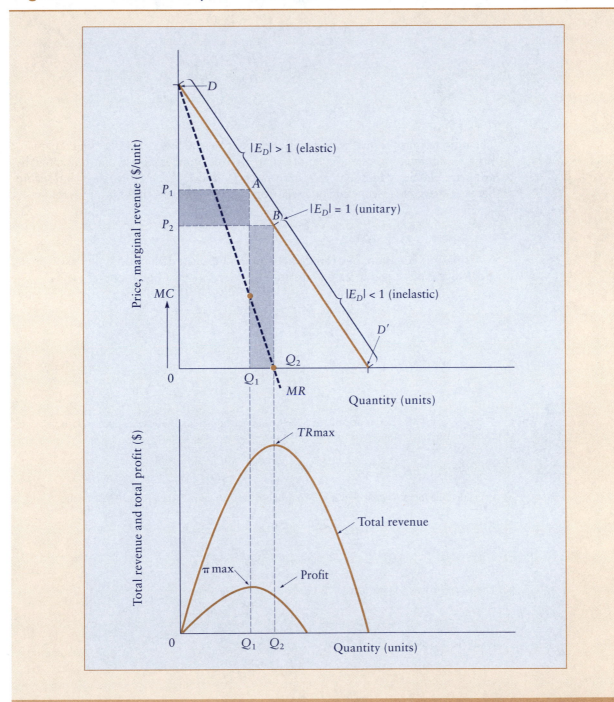

where $P_2(Q_2 - Q_1)$ is the vertical shaded rectangle and $(P_1 - P_2)Q_1$ is the horizontal shaded rectangle. Rearranging, we have

$$MR = P_2 + \frac{(P_2 - P_1)Q_1}{(Q_2 - Q_1)}$$

$$= P_2\left(1 + \frac{(P_2 - P_1)Q_1}{(Q_2 - Q_1)P_2}\right)$$

$$MR = P_2\left(1 + \frac{\Delta P Q_1}{\Delta Q P_2}\right)$$

The ratio term is the inverse of the price elasticity at the price point P_2 using the quantity Q_1. For small price and quantity changes, this number closely approximates the arc price elasticity in Equation 3.3 between P_1 and P_2. Therefore, the relationship between marginal revenue and price elasticity can be expressed algebraically as follows:[12]

$$MR = P\left(1 + \frac{1}{E_D}\right) \tag{3.7}$$

Using this equation, one can demonstrate that when demand is unit elastic, marginal revenue is equal to zero. Substituting $E_D = -1$ into Equation 3.7 yields

$$MR = P\left(1 + \frac{1}{-1}\right)$$

$$= P(0)$$

$$= 0$$

---

[12] This equation also can be derived from the definitions of marginal revenue and price elasticity using calculus. Marginal revenue is equal to the first derivative of total revenue:

$$MR = \frac{d(TR)}{dQ_D} = \frac{d(P \cdot Q_D)}{dQ_D}$$

Using the rule for taking the derivative of a product (see Appendix 2A, Equation 2A.20) yields

$$MR = P \cdot \frac{dQ_D}{dQ_D} + Q_D \frac{dP}{dQ_D}$$

$$= P + Q_D \frac{dP}{dQ_D}$$

This equation may be rewritten as

$$MR = P\left(1 + \frac{Q_D}{P} \cdot \frac{dP}{dQ_D}\right)$$

Recalling that the point price elasticity of demand is

$$E_D = \frac{dQ_D}{dP} \cdot \frac{P}{Q_D}$$

it can be seen that the term $\frac{Q_D}{P} \cdot \frac{dP}{dQ_D}$ is the reciprocal of the point price elasticity measure.

Hence, substituting $\frac{1}{E_D}$ for $\frac{Q_D}{P} \cdot \frac{dP}{dQ_D}$ results in Equation 3.7:

$$MR = P\left(1 + \frac{1}{E_D}\right)$$

Example

AUTHORS PRESS PUBLISHING COMPANIES TO INCREASE SALES REVENUE

Entertainment and publishing companies pay composers, playwrights, and authors a fixed percentage of realized sales revenue as a royalty. The two groups often differ as to the preferred price and unit sales. Referring to Figure 3.4, total revenue can be increased by lowering the price anytime the quantity sold is less than Q_2. That is, at any price above P_2 (where marginal revenue remains positive), the total revenue will continue to climb only if prices are lowered and additional units sold. Composers, playwrights, patent holders, and authors often therefore press their licensing agents and publishers to lower prices whenever marginal revenue remains positive—i.e., to the point where demand is unit elastic. The publisher, on the other hand, will wish to charge higher prices and sell less quantity because operating profits arise from marginal revenue in excess of marginal cost. Unless marginal cost is zero, the publisher always wants a positive marginal revenue and therefore a price greater than P_2 (for example, P_1). A commission-based sales force and the senior management have this same conflict; sales people often develop ingenious hidden discounts to try to circumvent a company's list pricing policies. Lowering the price from P_1 to P_2 to set $|E_D| = 1$ will always maximize sales revenue (and therefore, maximize total commissions).

The fact that total revenue is maximized (and marginal revenue is equal to zero) when $|E_D| = 1$ can be shown with the following example.

Example

TOTAL REVENUE, MARGINAL REVENUE, AND ELASTICITY: CUSTOM-TEES, INC.

Custom-Tees, Inc., operates a kiosk in Hanes Mall where it sells custom-printed T-shirts. The demand function for the shirts is

$$Q_D = 150 - 10P \qquad [3.8]$$

where P is the price in dollars per unit and Q_D is the quantity demanded in units per period.

The inverse demand curve can be rewritten in terms of P as a function of Q_D.

$$P = 15 - \frac{Q_D}{10} \qquad [3.9]$$

Total revenue (*TR*) is equal to price times quantity sold.

$$TR = P \cdot Q_D$$

$$= \left(15 - \frac{Q_D}{10}\right) Q_D$$

$$= 15Q_D - \frac{Q_D^2}{10}$$

Marginal revenue (*MR*) is equal to the first derivative of total revenue with respect to Q_D:

$$MR = \frac{d(TR)}{dQ_D}$$

$$= 15 - \frac{Q_D}{5}$$

To find the value of Q_D where total revenue is maximized, set marginal revenue equal to zero:[13]

$$MR = 0$$

$$15 - \frac{Q_D}{5} = 0$$

$$Q_D^* = 75 \text{ units}$$

Substituting this value into Equation 3.9 yields

$$P^* = 15 - \frac{75}{10} = \$7.50 \text{ per unit}$$

Thus, total revenue is maximized at $Q_D^* = 75$ and $P^* = \$7.50$. Checking:

$$E_D = \frac{\partial Q_D}{\partial P} \cdot \frac{P}{Q_D} = (-10) \frac{(7.5)}{75} = -1$$

$$|E_D| = 1$$

In addition to showing that $|E_D| = 1$ when the total revenue function is at its maximum, this example also demonstrates that marginal revenue MR is equal to zero when total revenue is maximized. This finding is not surprising when we remember that the definition of marginal revenue is the increase in total revenue resulting from the sale of one additional unit. Beyond the output level where total revenue is maximized, marginal revenue becomes negative and total revenue declines; that is, $|E_D| < 1$.[14]

Importance of Elasticity-Revenue Relationships

Elasticity is often the key to marketing plans. A product-line manager will attempt to maximize sales revenue by allocating a marketing expense budget among price promotions, advertising, retail displays, trade allowances, direct mail, and in-store couponing. Knowing whether and at what magnitude demand is responsive to each of these marketing initiatives depends on careful estimates of the various demand elasticities of price, advertising, displays, etc.

Example

http://

You can reach Volkswagen on the Internet at http://www.vw.com/

VW INVASION OF NORTH AMERICA

When Volkswagen entered the U.S. market with their basic no-frills automobile, the Beetle, European excess inventory had stockpiled at ports and road terminals awaiting export to a new market. Consequently, VW focused for a time on any demand stimulus that would increase revenue. In the U.S. market, VW had no dealer network and initially provided sales and service only at the docks in New Jersey; Charleston, SC; and Houston, TX. General Motors and Ford were developing

---

[13] To be certain one has found values for P and Q_D, where total revenue is maximized rather than minimized, check the second derivative of TR to see that it is negative. In this case $d^2 TR/dQ_D^2 = -1/5$, so the total revenue function is maximized.

[14] Additional applications of the relationship among price, marginal revenue, and elasticity (Equation 3.7) are examined in the discussions of pricing by monopolists (Chapter 11) and the practice of price discrimination (Chapter 14).

compact cars as well, so VW decided to enter the market at a ridiculously low promotional price of $800 (approximately $6,000 in 2004 U.S. dollars). Two years later, a 25-percent price increase was introduced. Although VW lost some potential customers at $1000 who were willing to pay between $800 and $999, the extra $200 per car on all the cars they continued to sell (see Figure 3.5) easily offset the revenue loss at old $800 prices from a few lost sales. (Compare the two shaded areas in Figure 3.5.) The price elasticity of demand was in the inelastic range of demand. By 1960, VW had raised the price another 20 percent to $1,200, and again revenue rose. Finally, in 1964 at $1,350, the extra receipts from the $150 price increase across all remaining sales were just sufficient to offset the loss in revenue from the lost sales. At $1,350, price elasticity had reached the unit elastic price point (see Figure 3.5). Volkswagen then proceeded to build a U.S. dealer network. These changes increased the potential size of the market in the United States and shifted the demand for Volkswagen products to the right. At $1,350 with a dealer network and a larger quantity base, the measured price elasticity then declined (again into the inelastic range), and Volkswagen was again in a position to raise price.

In 1968, 562,000 Beetles were sold at a price of $1,500, and revenue again increased (to $843 million). Although the product remained very inexpensive ($1,500 in 1968 is about $9,000 today), the Highway Safety Act of 1996, plus Ralph Nader's crusade against small rear-engine cars, plus low gasoline prices caused consumers to begin losing interest in Beetles and start buying large numbers of Mustangs, Camaros, and a new more powerful Super Beetle. In 1969, revenue and price of the Beetle increased one last time. At $1,800, revenue was $968 million ($1,800 × 538,000 units sold). That is, demand remained in the inelastic range since a price increase from $1,500 to $1,800 resulted in higher total revenue.

Figure 3.5   Raising Price with Demand in the Inelastic Range

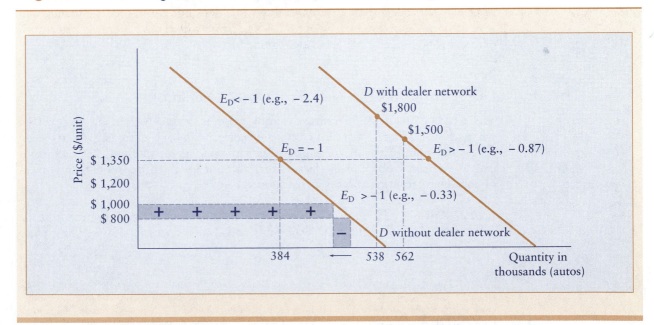

One managerial insight that this example illustrates is that firms should always seek to raise prices for any products in the inelastic range of their demand. To lower prices in such a range would both *increase* costs (of producing and distributing additional output) and *decrease* revenue. It is better to approach unit elasticity by raising prices, and thereby increase revenue and save the production and distribution costs. In fact, profit-maximizing firms will carry these price increases right on into the elastic range beyond the point of maximum revenue and unit elasticity (above and beyond point B at P_2 and Q_2 in Figure 3.4). Starting from the other direction at zero output, a profit-maximizing firm will lower price to increase revenue as long as the incremental change in total revenue (the MR in Figure 3.4) exceeds the change in total variable cost (labeled height MC). That is, the profit-maximizing output will always occur in the elastic region of the firm's demand—for example, at a price above the unit elastic price point.

As we saw earlier, unit elasticity is also of special significance for commission-based employees or anyone whose paycheck rises as sales revenue increases. In general, composers, playwrights, patent holders, authors, and e-business content providers want to maximize revenue. Because operating profits occur only when marginal revenue is in excess of marginal cost, managers want higher prices with somewhat reduced revenue, much reduced costs, and therefore higher profits. One solution to this incentives conflict is to involve the content providers in the company's profit-sharing plan.

PRICE ELASTICITY ESTIMATES FOR COFFEE VARY BY PRICE

A study by Huang, Siegfried, and Zardoshty on the demand for coffee confirms the relationship between price levels and the price elasticity of demand shown in Figure 3.4.[15] After studying coffee demand for the period 1963–1977, they found that the price elasticity of demand for that period ranged from −0.10 for price levels prevailing throughout most of the period to −0.89 for the peak price level. Thus, coffee users are nearly nine times more sensitive to price changes at high prices than at low price levels. Because these are market-level, not firm-level, elasticity estimates, observing price elasticities less than 1.0 in absolute value does not contradict the managerial insight that is conveyed by Figure 3.5—i.e., *firms* will always increase price until demand is no longer in the inelastic region.

Factors Affecting the Price Elasticity of Demand

The market demand for furniture, a durable good, is extremely price elastic (−3.04), whereas the market demand for caffeinated coffee (−0.16) is extremely price inelastic. As shown in Table 3.6, other price elasticities vary greatly among different products and services. Some of the factors that account for the differing responsiveness of consumers to price changes are examined below.

Availability and Closeness of Substitutes   The most important determinant of the price elasticity of demand is the availability and closeness of substitutes. The greater

[15] Cliff J. Huang, J.J. Siegfried, and Farangis Zardoshty, "The Demand for Coffee in the United States, 1963–1977," *Quarterly Review of Economics and Business* 20, no. 2 (Summer 1980), pp. 36–50. Another more recent estimate of the demand elasticity for coffee can be found in Albert A. Okunade, "Functional Forms and Habits Effects in the U.S. Demand for Coffee," *Applied Economics* (November 1992).

Table 3.6   Empirical Price Elasticities

Commodity (Good/Service)	Price Elasticity of Market Demand
Alcoholic beverages (consumed at home)	
Beer	−.84[e]
Wine	−.55[e]
Liquor	−.50[e]
Apparel	
Market	−1.1[m]
Firms	−4.1[m]
Coffee	
Regular	−.16[b]
Instant	−.36[b]
Credit charges on bank cards	−2.44[l]
Dental visits	
Adult males	−.65[g]
Adult females	−.78[g]
Children	−1.40[g]
Food	
Market	−1.0[n]
Firms	−3.8[n]
Furniture	−3.04[m]
Glassware/China	−1.20[c]
Household appliances	−.64[c]
International air transportation	
United States/Europe	−1.25[h]
Canada/Europe	−.82[h]
Outdoor recreation	−.56[f]
School lunches	−.47[d]
Shoes	−.73[c]

(continued)

[a] D. Cracknell and M. Knott, "The Measurement of Price Elasticities—The BT Experience," *International Journal of Forecasting* 11 (1995), pp. 321–329.

[b] Cliff J. Huang, John J. Siegfried, and Farangis Zardoshty, "The Demand for Coffee in the United States, 1963–1977," *Quarterly Review of Economics and Business* 20, no. 2 (Summer 1980), pp. 36–50.

[c] H. S. Houthakker and Lester D. Taylor, *Consumer Demand in the United States,* 2d ed. (Cambridge, Mass.: Harvard University Press, 1970).

[d] George A. Braley and P. E. Nelson, Jr., "Effect of a Controlled Price Increase on School Lunch Participation: Pittsburgh, 1973," *American Journal of Agricultural Economics* (February 1975), pp. 90–96.

[e] Dale Heien and Greg Pompelli, "The Demand for Alcoholic Beverages: Economic and Demographic Effects," *Southern Economic Journal* (January 1989), pp. 759–769.

[f] Russel L. Gum and W. E. Martin, "Problems and Solutions in Estimating the Demand for and Value of Rural Outdoor Recreation," *American Journal of Agricultural Economics* (November 1975), pp. 558–566.

[g] Willard G. Manning, Jr. and Charles E. Phelps, "The Demand for Dental Care," *The Bell Journal of Economics* 10, no. 2 (Autumn 1979), pp. 503–525.

[h] J. M. Cigliano, "Price and Income Elasticities for Airline Travel: The North Atlantic Market," *Business Economics* (September 1980), pp. 17–21.

[i] C. E. Ferguson and M. Polasek, "The Elasticity of Import Demand for Raw Apparel Wool in the United States," *Econometrica* 30 (1962), pp. 670–699.

[j] H. Knipscheer, L. Hill, and B. Dixon, "Demand Elasticities for Soybean Meal in the European Community," *American Journal of Agricultural Economics* (May 1982), pp. 249–253.

[k] Daniel B. Suits, "Agriculture," in *Structure of American Industry,* 7th ed., ed. W. Adams (New York: Macmillan, 1986).

[l] J. Starvins, "Can Demand Elasticity Explain Sticky Credit Card Rates?" *New England Economic Review* (July/August 1996), pp. 43–54.

[m] Richard D. Stone and D.A. Rowe, "The Durability of Consumers' Durable Goods," *Econometrica* 28 (1960), pp. 407–416.

[n] M. D. Shapiro, "Measuring Market Power in U.S. Industry," NBER Working Paper, No. 2212, 1987.

Table 3.6 Continued

Commodity (Good/Service)	Price Elasticity of Market Demand
Soybean meal	−1.65 [i]
Telephones	−0.10 [a]
Textiles	
Market	−1.5 [m]
Firms	−4.7 [m]
Tires	−0.60 [c]
Tobacco products	−.46 [c]
Tomatoes	−2.22 [k]
Wool	−1.32 [i]

the number of substitute goods, the more price elastic is the demand for a product because a customer can easily shift to a substitute good if the price of a product in question increases. The availability and closeness of substitutes relates not only to different products, such as beef and chicken, but also to the availability of the same product from different producers. For example, the demand for Chevrolets is likely to be very price elastic because of the ready availability of close substitutes such as Fords, Toyotas, and Hondas. Intravenous feeding solution has few (if any) substitutes for hospital patients in shock or otherwise unable to digest food, but the price elasticity of demand for Johnson & Johnson's bandaids is high because numerous companies offer a nearly identical product.

Durable Goods   The demand for durable goods tends to be more price elastic than the demand for nondurables. This is true because of the ready availability of a relatively inexpensive substitute in many cases—for instance, the repair of a used television, car, or refrigerator, rather than buying a new one. In addition, consumers of durable goods are often in a position to wait for a more favorable price, a sale, or a special deal when buying these items.

Percentage of Budget   The demand for relatively high-priced goods tends to be more price elastic than the demand for inexpensive items because expensive items account for a greater proportion of a person's expenditures than do low-priced items. Consequently, we would expect the demand for automobiles to be more price elastic than the demand for children's toys. The greater the percentage of the budget spent on a good, the larger the purchasing power released by any given price reduction or absorbed by any given price increase. And the larger this "income effect," the greater the price elasticity for normal goods. German households often spend as much as 20–30 percent of their disposable income on cars; French households do the same with food, but spend half as much as Germans on automobile transportation. Therefore, *ceteris paribus,* we would expect the price elasticity of demand for standard sedan autos to be higher in Germany than in France.

Time Frame of Analysis   Over time, the demand for many products tends to become more elastic because of the increase in the number of effective substitutes that become available. For example, in the short run, the demand for gasoline may be relatively price inelastic because the only available alternatives are not taking a trip or using some form of public transportation. Over time, as consumers replace their cars, they find another excellent substitute for gasoline—namely, more fuel-efficient vehicles. Also, other product alternatives may become available, such as electric cars or cars powered by natural gas.

Another reason the time frame of analysis affects the elasticity involves transaction costs. Almost all purchases necessitate a certain transportation and time expense on the part of both buyer and seller. In addition, to respond to a price decrease, potential customers must first learn about the discount and then incur the cost of adjusting their own schedules to complete a purchase during the sale period. Because both search and adjustment costs for consumers are higher if sale prices last only a few minutes, the demand response to price changes is diminished the shorter the time period of adjustment. Predictable end-of-model-year promotions in the auto industry lasting throughout the month of August stimulate much more elastic demand than unannounced "Midnight Madness" sales that last only a few hours.

Example

http://

The Internet site maintained by the U.S. Census Bureau contains information on housing, home ownership, and affordability. The site address is
http://www.census.gov/hhes/www/housing.html

DETERMINANTS OF PRICE ELASTICITY OF DEMAND FOR HOUSING IN SAN FRANCISCO, KANSAS CITY, AND HOUSTON[16]

Residents of San Francisco spend 39.7 percent of their after-tax income on housing, while residents of Kansas City and Houston spend only 18.4 percent and 18.7 percent, respectively. This difference in the allocation of a typical household's budget implies that the increase in a San Franciscan's purchasing power for all goods and services, if housing costs in general fall by 10 percent, will be more than twice as large as the increase in purchasing power enjoyed by a Kansas Citian or Houstonian for the same 10 percent decline in housing costs. The demand for all "normal" or income-superior goods (i.e., goods whose demand increases with greater income available) should rise more in San Francisco than in Kansas City or Houston. Since housing is an income-superior good, one might expect the percentage increase in demand for housing in San Francisco to be larger than in Kansas City or Houston for an equal percentage reduction in price in all three locations.

Recall that this reasoning assumes that all other factors influencing quantity demanded have remained unchanged. If this assumption (*ceteris paribus*) is not met, the elasticity measure may be quite different. This warning applies to all elasticity calculations and analysis.

International Perspectives

FREE TRADE AND THE PRICE ELASTICITY OF DEMAND: NESTLÉ YOGURT

The 1990s were characterized by an explosion of free-trade agreements among important trading partners. The Europe 1992 plan virtually eliminated trade barriers, and goods now flow freely and without tariffs from one European country to another. Increasing standardization of products in these markets will further reduce trading barriers. On the North

---

[16] Based on "The Home Front," *Wall Street Journal*, July 11, 1997, p. B6.

American continent, the North American Free Trade Agreement (NAFTA) was ratified in the United States, Canada, and Mexico. In 1994, the General Agreement on Tariffs and Trade (GATT) was implemented, leading to a worldwide reduction in tariffs and other trade barriers.

What are the implications of these reduced trade barriers for estimates of price elasticity of demand? Free trade results in an effective increase in the number of substitute goods that are available to consumers and businesses in any country. Consequently, as barriers to free trade come down, the demand will become more price elastic for goods that historically have not been able to flow easily (without significant tariffs or quotas) between countries. Nestlé's yogurt and custard products now travel from manufacturing sites in the British Midlands to Milan in 17 hours, whereas the customs processing and transportation bottlenecks once required 38 hours. Similarly, iron forging of crankshafts and engine blocks for U.S. auto companies now occurs primarily in Mexico. The winners in this globalization process should be consumers, who will have a wider variety of products to choose from at competitive prices. The losers will be those firms that cannot compete in a global market on the basis of cost, quality, and service.

INCOME ELASTICITY OF DEMAND

Among the variables that affect demand, income is often one of the most important. One can also compute an income elasticity of demand, which is analogous to the price elasticity of demand.

Income Elasticity Defined

Income Elasticity
The ratio of the percentage change in quantity demanded to the percentage change in income, assuming that all other factors influencing demand remain unchanged.

Income elasticity of demand measures the responsiveness of a change in quantity demanded of some commodity to a change in income. It can be expressed as

$$E_y = \frac{\%\Delta Q_D}{\%\Delta Y}, ceteris\ paribus \qquad [3.10]$$

where ΔQ_D = change in quantity demanded
ΔY = change in income

Various measures of income can be used in the analysis. One commonly used measure is consumer disposable income, calculated on an aggregate, household, or per capita basis.

Arc Income Elasticity

The *arc* income elasticity is a technique for calculating income elasticity between two income levels. It is computed as

$$E_y = \frac{\dfrac{Q_2 - Q_1}{(Q_2 + Q_1)/2}}{\dfrac{Y_2 - Y_1}{(Y_2 + Y_1)/2}} = \frac{\Delta Q}{\Delta Y} \frac{(Y_1 + Y_2)}{(Q_1 + Q_2)} \qquad [3.11]$$

where Q_2 = quantity sold after an income change
Q_1 = quantity sold before an income change
Y_2 = new level of income
Y_1 = original level of income

For example, assume that an increase in disposable personal income in Rhode Island from $1.00 billion to $1.10 billion is associated with an increase in boat sales in the state from 5,000 to 6,000 units. Determine the income elasticity over this range. Substituting the relevant data into Equation 3.11 yields

$$E_y = \frac{\dfrac{6,000 - 5,000}{(6,000 + 5,000)/2}}{\dfrac{\$1.10 - \$1.00}{(\$1.10 + \$1.00)/2}} = \frac{1,000}{\$0.10} \frac{(\$2.10)}{(11,000)}$$

$$= 1.91$$

Thus, a 1 percent increase in income would be expected to result in a 1.91 percent increase in quantity demanded, *ceteris paribus*.

Point Income Elasticity

The arc income elasticity measures the responsiveness of quantity demanded to changes in income levels over a range. In contrast, the *point* income elasticity provides a measure of this responsiveness at a specific point on the demand function. The point income elasticity is defined as

$$E_y = \frac{\partial Q_D}{\partial Y} \cdot \frac{Y}{Q_D} \qquad\qquad [3.12]$$

where Y = income

   Q_D = quantity demanded of some commodity

   $\dfrac{\partial Q_D}{\partial Y}$ = the partial derivative of quantity with respect to income

The algebraic demand function for Christmas trees (Equation 3.5) introduced earlier in the chapter can be used to illustrate the calculation of the point income elasticity. Suppose one is interested in determining the point income elasticity when the price is equal to $40 and per capita personal disposable income is equal to $30,000. Taking the partial derivative of Equation 3.5 with respect to Y yields

$$\frac{\partial Q_D}{\partial Y} = 2.50$$

Recall from the point price elasticity calculation described earlier in the chapter that substituting P = $40 and Y = $30,000 into Equation 3.5 gave Q_D equal to 10,000 units. Therefore, from Equation 3.12, one obtains

$$E_y = 2.50 \left(\frac{\$30,000}{20,000} \right) = 3.75$$

Thus, from an income level of $30,000, one could expect demand for Christmas trees to increase by 37.5 percent for each 10 percent increase in per capita disposable income, *ceteris paribus*.

Interpreting the Income Elasticity   For most products, income elasticity is expected to be positive; that is, $E_y > 0$. Such goods are referred to as *normal* or *income-superior goods*. Those goods having a calculated income elasticity that is negative are called *inferior goods*. Inferior goods are those that are purchased in smaller absolute quantities as the income of the consumer increases. Such food items as canned mackerel, dried beans, or subcompact autos are frequently cited as examples of inferior goods. They may compose a large part of a low-income diet or transportation budget, but may virtually disappear as income levels increase.

Income elasticity is typically defined as being *low* when it is between 0 and 1 and *high* if it is greater than 1. Goods that are normally considered luxury items generally have a high income elasticity, whereas goods that are necessities (or perceived as necessities) have low income elasticities.

Knowledge of the magnitude of the income elasticity of demand for a particular product is especially useful in relating forecasts of economic activity. In industries that produce goods having high income elasticities (such as new furniture), a major increase or decrease in economic activity will have a significant impact on demand. Knowledge of income elasticities is also useful in developing marketing strategies for products. For example, products having a high income elasticity can be promoted as being luxurious and stylish, whereas goods having a low income elasticity can be promoted as being economical.

Example | INCOME ELASTICITIES: EMPIRICAL ESTIMATES

Estimates of the income elasticity of demand have been made for a wide variety of goods and services, as shown in Table 3.7. Note that the income elasticities for goods that are often perceived as necessities (e.g., many food items, housing) are less than 1.0, whereas the income elasticities for items that are usually viewed as luxuries (e.g., European travel) are greater than 1.0.

Table 3.7   Empirical Income Elasticities

Commodity (Good/Service)	Income Elasticity
International air transportation	1.91[a]
Apples	1.32[b]
Beef	1.05[b]
Chicken	.28[b]
Dental visits	
Adult males	.61[c]
Adult females	.55[c]
Children	.87[c]
Housing (low-income renters)	.22[d]
Milk	.50[a]
Oranges	.83[a]
Potatoes	.15[a]
Tomatoes	.24[a]

[a] J. M. Cigliano, "Price and Income Elasticities for Airline Travel: The North Atlantic Market," *Business Economics* (September 1980), pp. 17–21.

[b] Daniel B. Suits, "Agriculture," in *Structure of American Industry*, 7th ed., ed. W. Adams (New York: Macmillan, 1986).

[c] Willand G. Manning, Jr. and Charles E. Phelps, "The Demand for Dental Care," *The Bell Journal of Economics* 10, no. 2 (Autumn 1979), pp. 503–525.

[d] Elizabeth A. Roistacher, "Short-Run Housing Responses to Changes in Income," *American Economic Review* (February 1977), pp. 381–386.

CROSS ELASTICITY OF DEMAND

Another variable that often affects the demand for a product is the price of a related (substitute or complementary) product.

Cross Price Elasticity Defined

Cross Price Elasticity
The ratio of the percentage change in the quantity demanded of Good A to the percentage change in the price of Good B, assuming that all other factors influencing demand remain unchanged.

The **cross price elasticity** of demand, E_x, is a measure of the responsiveness of changes in the quantity demanded (Q_{DA}) of Product A to price changes for Product B (P_B).

$$E_x = \frac{\%\Delta Q_{DA}}{\%\Delta P_B}, \text{ ceteris paribus} \qquad [3.13]$$

where ΔQ_{DA} = change in quantity demanded of Product A
ΔP_B = change in price of Product B

Arc Cross Price Elasticity

The *arc* cross price elasticity is a technique for computing cross elasticity between two price levels. It is calculated as

$$E_x = \frac{\dfrac{Q_{A2} - Q_{A1}}{(Q_{A2} + Q_{A1})/2}}{\dfrac{P_{B2} - P_{B1}}{(P_{B2} + P_{B1})/2}} = \frac{\Delta Q_A}{\Delta P_B} \frac{(P_{B2} + P_{B1})}{(Q_{A2} + Q_{A1})} \qquad [3.14]$$

where Q_{A2} = quantity demanded of A after a price change in B
Q_{A1} = original quantity demanded of A
P_{B2} = new price for Product B
P_{B1} = original price for Product B

For example, suppose the price of butter P_B increases from \$1 to \$1.50 per pound. As a result, the quantity demanded of margarine Q_A increases from 500 pounds to 600 pounds a month at a local grocery store. Compute the arc cross price elasticity of demand. Substituting the relevant data into Equation 3.14 yields

$$E_x = \frac{\dfrac{600 - 500}{(600 + 500)/2}}{\dfrac{\$1.50 - \$1.00}{(\$1.50 + \$1.00)/2}} = \frac{100}{\$0.50} \frac{(\$2.50)}{(1,100)}$$

$$= 0.45$$

This indicates that a 10 percent increase in the price of butter will lead to a 4.5 percent increase in the quantity demanded of margarine, which is, of course, a butter substitute.

Point Cross Price Elasticity

In similar fashion, the *point* cross price elasticity between Products A and B may be computed as

$$E_x = \frac{\partial Q_A}{\partial P_B} \cdot \frac{P_B}{Q_A} \qquad [3.15]$$

where P_B = price of Product B

Q_A = quantity demanded of Product A at price point P_B

$\dfrac{\partial Q_A}{\partial P_B}$ = the partial derivative of Q_A with respect to P_B

Interpreting the Cross Price Elasticity

If the cross price elasticity measured between Products A and B is *positive* (as might be expected in our butter/margarine example or between such products as plastic wrap and aluminum foil), the two products are referred to as *substitutes* for each other. The higher the cross price elasticity, the closer the substitute relationship. A *negative* cross price elasticity, on the other hand, indicates that two products are *complementary*. For example, a significant decrease in the price of DVD players would probably result in a substantial increase in the demand for DVDs.

Antitrust and Cross Price Elasticities

The number of close substitutes may be an important determinant of the degree of competition in a market. The fewer and poorer the number of close substitutes that exist for a product, the greater the amount of monopoly power that is possessed by the producing or selling firm. An important issue in antitrust cases involves the appropriate definition of the relevant product market to be used in computing statistics of market control (e.g., market share). A case involving DuPont's production of cellophane was concerned with this issue. Does the relevant product market include just the product cellophane or is it the much broader flexible packaging materials market? The Supreme Court found the cross price elasticity of demand between cellophane and other flexible packaging materials to be sufficiently high so as to exonerate DuPont from a charge of monopolizing the market.[17] Had the relevant product been considered to be cellophane alone, DuPont would have clearly lost, because it produced 75 percent of all celophane output and its only licensee, Sylvania, produced the rest. But when other flexible packaging materials were included in the product market definition, DuPont's share dropped to an acceptable 18 percent level. The importance of the definition of the relevant product market and the determination of the cross price elasticity of demand among close substitute products has often been emphasized by the Courts.[18]

Example

WHY PAY MORE FOR FAX PAPER AND STAPLES AT STAPLES?[19]

Just what constitutes an available substitute has as much to do with the cross price elasticity of rival firm supply as it does with the cross price elasticity of demand. In a hotly contested recent merger proposal, the Federal Trade Commission (FTC) has

---

[17] U.S. *v.* DuPont, 351 U.S. 377 (1956).

[18] See, for example, U.S. *v.* Alcoa, 148 F.2d., 416, 424; Times Picayune Publishing Co. *v.* U.S., 345 U.S. 594; Continental Can Co. *v.* U.S., 378 U.S., 441, 489. See John E. Kwoka and Lawrence J. White, *The Antitrust Revolution: Economics, Competition, and Policy* (New York: Oxford University Press, 1999) for a further discussion of some of the economic issues involved in antitrust laws.

[19] Based on "FTC Votes to Bar Staples' Bid for Rival," *Wall Street Journal,* March 11, 1997, p. A3.

http://
Read more about the FTC case against Office Depot and Staples by searching the FTC Internet site under the keyword "Staples" at the following address:
http://www.ftc.gov

argued that office superstores like OfficeMax, Office Depot, and Staples are a separate relevant market from other smaller office supply retailers. Office Depot had 46 percent of the $13.22 billion in 1996 superstore sales of office supplies; Staples had 30 percent, and OfficeMax had the remaining 24 percent. Office Depot and Staples proposed to merge, thereby creating a combined firm with 76 percent of the market. Such mergers have been disallowed many times under the Sherman Antitrust Act's prohibition of monopolization.

The two companies insisted, however, that their competitors included not only OfficeMax but all office supply distribution channels, including small paper goods specialty stores, department stores, discount stores like Target, warehouse clubs like Sam's Club, office supply catalogs, and some computer retailers. This larger office supply industry is very fragmented, easy to enter (or exit), and huge; 1996 sales topped $185 billion. By this latter standard, the proposed merger involved admittedly the largest players in the industry, but companies with only 3–5 percent market shares. Under this alternative interpretation of the relevant market, Office Depot and Staples should be allowed to proceed with their merger.

Have superstores like Home Depot and Lowes in do-it-yourself building supplies, PetSmart in pet supplies, and Office Depot, OfficeMax, and Staples created a new time-saving customer shopping experience and demand pattern in towns where they are clustered? Office supply products are search goods for which customers *can* detect quality prior to purchase and locate just the quality-price combination they desire. Brand name reputations should therefore have little effect on repeat purchase shopping patterns at Office Depot and Staples. Is this case devoid of a rationale for antitrust action? Have successful entrepreneurs simply created a new segment within the traditional relevant market for office products? The FTC undertook two sets of experiments to advise the commissioners who voted to deny the proposed merger. Prices for everything from paper clips to fax paper were sampled in 40 cities and towns where Office Depot and Staples competed and in other similar locations where only one of the superstores was present. The prices were significantly higher in the single store markets. Apparently, despite an enormous rival supply of traditional office product retailers, target customers (like clerks responsible for securing resupply) are willing to pay more for staples at Staples.

As Wal-Mart has demonstrated in other search good categories, shoppers will flock to a superstore despite numerous closer small retailers. So, despite the enormous pre-existing supply of traditional rivals and the exceptional ease of entry (and exit) at small scale, competition for superstore retailers comes only from other superstore retailers. As a result, the Sherman Act warrants denying the proposed merger in office supply superstores. Although Toys "R" Us or Wal-Mart can become "category killers" on their own sales growth, the FTC has decided to bar superstore mergers as a route to near-monopoly status.

An Empirical Illustration of Price, Income, and Cross Elasticities

A study by Chapman, Tyrrell, and Mount examined the elasticity of energy use by residential, commercial, and industrial users during the period 1946–1972.[20] They hypothesized that the demand for electricity was determined by the price of electricity, income levels, and the price of a substitute good—natural gas.

---

[20] D. Chapman, T. Tyrrell, and T. Mount, "Electricity Demand Growth and the Energy Crisis," *Science*, November 17, 1972, p. 705.

Table 3.8   Electricity-Use Elasticities

	Price Elasticity	Income Elasticity	Cross Elasticity (Gas)
Residential market	−1.3	0.3	0.15
Commercial market	−1.5	0.9	0.15
Industrial market	−1.7	1.1	0.15

Table 3.8 summarizes the electricity-use elasticities with respect to price, income, and natural gas prices. As shown in the table, price elasticity of demand for electricity is relatively elastic in all markets, with the highest price elasticity being in the industrial market. The significant decline in the growth rate of demand for electricity since the energy crisis-induced price increases is consistent with these results. For example, many assembly plants, foundries, and other heavy industrial users switched to self-generated power with natural gas-fired turbines. The income elasticity figures indicate that electricity use tends to increase with increases in income. The positive cross-elasticity shows that electricity and natural gas are, indeed, substitute goods.

OTHER DEMAND ELASTICITY MEASURES

Price, income, and cross-elasticity measures are the most common applications of the elasticity concept to demand analysis. However, elasticity is a general concept; we will discuss some less common elasticities.[21]

Advertising Elasticity

Advertising elasticity measures the responsiveness of sales to changes in advertising expenditures. It is measured by the ratio of the percentage change in sales to a percentage change in advertising expenditures. The higher the advertising elasticity coefficient, the more responsive sales are to changes in the advertising budget. An awareness of this elasticity measure may assist advertising or marketing managers in their determination of appropriate levels of advertising outlays relative to price promotions or display and packaging expenditures.

---

[21] In addition to demand elasticities, one can also define a price elasticity of *supply*. The price elasticity of supply measures the responsiveness of quantity supplied by producers to changes in prices. An inelastic supply function is one whose price elasticity coefficient is less than unity. It indicates that a 1 percent change in price will lead to a less than 1 percent change in quantity supplied. An elastic supply function has an elasticity coefficient greater than unity, indicating that a 1 percent change in price will result in a greater than 1 percent change in quantity supplied. Because producers are normally willing to supply more at higher prices, the sign of the price elasticity coefficient of supply will normally be positive.

Elasticity of Price Expectations

In an inflationary environment or in projecting durable goods demand (houses, for example), the elasticity of price expectations may provide helpful insights. It is defined as the percentage change in *future* prices expected as a result of current percentage price changes. A coefficient that exceeds unity indicates that buyers expect future prices to rise (or fall) by a greater percentage amount than current prices. A positive coefficient that is less than unity indicates that buyers expect future prices to increase (or decrease) but by a lesser percentage amount than current price changes. A zero coefficient indicates that consumers feel that current price changes have no influence on future changes. Finally, a negative coefficient indicates that consumers believe an increase (decrease) in current prices will lead to a decrease (increase) in future prices.

A positive coefficient of price expectations (especially one greater than unity) suggests that current price increases may shift the demand function to the right. This may result in the same or greater sales at the higher prices, as consumers try to beat future price increases by stockpiling the commodity. The stockpiling that occurs when crops freeze (e.g., coffee beans in South America) or otherwise appear in short supply (e.g., crude oil during the Venezuelan general strike of 2002) can be explained, at least in part, by the effects of a high elasticity of price expectations.

COMBINED EFFECT OF DEMAND ELASTICITIES

When two or more of the factors that affect demand change simultaneously, one is often interested in determining their combined impact on quantity demanded. For example, suppose that a firm plans to increase the price of its product next period and anticipates that consumers' incomes will also increase next period. Other factors affecting demand such as advertising expenditures and competitors' prices are expected to remain the same in the next period. From the formula for the price elasticity (Equation 3.2), the effect on quantity demanded of a price increase would be equal to

$$\%\Delta Q_D = E_D(\%\Delta P)$$

Similarly, from the formula for the income elasticity (Equation 3.10), the effect on quantity demanded of an increase in consumers' incomes would be equal to

$$\%\Delta Q_D = E_y(\%\Delta Y)$$

Each of these percentage changes (divided by 100 to put them in a decimal form) would be multiplied by current period demand (Q_1) to get the respective changes in quantity demanded caused by the price and income increases. Assuming that the price and income effects are *independent* and *additive,* the quantity demanded next period (Q_2) would be equal to current period demand (Q_1) plus the changes caused by the price and income increases:

$$Q_2 = Q_1 + Q_1 [E_D(\%\Delta P)] + Q_1[E_y(\%\Delta Y)]$$

or

$$Q_2 = Q_1 [1 + E_D(\%\Delta P) + E_y(\%\Delta Y)] \qquad [3.16]$$

The combined use of income and price elasticities, illustrated here for forecasting demand, can be generalized to include any of the elasticity concepts that were developed in the preceding sections of this chapter.

Plan: % ΔP = 10%

expect % ΔY = 6%

E_D = -1.3 (elastic)

E_Y = 2 (luxury good)

Q_D = 2 million watches

PRICE AND INCOME EFFECTS: THE SEIKO COMPANY

Suppose Seiko is planning to increase the price of its watches by 10 percent in the coming year. Economic forecasters expect <u>real disposable personal income</u> to increase by 6 percent during the same period. From past experience, the price elasticity of demand has been estimated to be approximately −1.3 and the income elasticity has been estimated at 2.0. These elasticities are assumed to remain constant over the range of price and income changes anticipated. Seiko currently sells 2 million watches per year. Determine the forecasted demand for next year (assuming that the percentage price and income effects are independent and additive). Substituting the relevant data into Equation 3.16 yields

$$Q_2 = 2,000,000 \, [1 + (-1.3)(.10) + (2.0)(.06)]$$
$$= 1,980,000 \text{ units}$$

The forecasted demand for next year is 1.98 million watches assuming that other factors that influence demand, such as advertising and competitors' prices, remain unchanged. In this case, the positive impact of the projected increase in household income is more than offset by the decline in quantity demanded associated with a price increase.

SUMMARY

- Demand relationships can be represented in the form of a schedule (table), graph, or algebraic function. Each of these methods of presentation provides insights into the demand concept.

- The demand curve is typically downward sloping, indicating that consumers are willing to purchase more units of a good or service at lower prices.

- Changes in price result in *movement* along the demand curve, whereas changes in any of the other variables in the demand function result in *shifts* of the entire demand curve. Thus "changes in quantity demanded along" a particular demand curve result from price changes. In contrast, when one speaks of "changes in demand," one is referring to shifts in the entire demand curve.

- Some of the factors that cause a shift in the entire demand curve are changes in the income level of consumers, the price of substitute and complementary goods, the level of advertising, competitors' advertising expenditures, population, consumer preferences, time period of adjustment, taxes or subsidies, and price expectations.

- Elasticity refers to the responsiveness of one economic variable to changes in another, related variable. Thus *price elasticity* of demand refers to the percentage change in quantity demanded associated with a percentage change in price, holding constant the effects of other factors thought to influence demand. Demand is said to be relatively price *elastic* if a given percentage change in price results in a greater percentage change in quantity demanded. Demand is said to be relatively price *inelastic* if a given percentage change in price results in a lesser percentage change in quantity demanded.

- When demand is unit elastic, marginal revenue equals zero and total revenue is maximized. When demand is elastic, an increase (decrease) in price will result in a decrease (increase) in total revenue. When demand is inelastic, an increase (decrease) in price will result in an increase (decrease) in total revenue.

- Prices should always be increased in the inelastic region of the firm's demand because lower price points would result in reduced revenue, despite increased unit sales.
- *Income elasticity* of demand refers to the percentage change in quantity demanded associated with a percentage change in income, holding constant the effects of other factors thought to influence demand.
- *Cross elasticity* of demand refers to the percentage change in quantity demanded of Good *A* associated with a percentage change in the price of Good *B*.
- An understanding of the magnitude of various elasticity measures for a product can be extremely helpful when forecasting demand and formulating marketing or operations plans.

EXERCISES

1. Jenkins Photo Company manufactures an automatic camera that currently sells for $90. Sales volume is about 2,000 cameras per month. A close competitor, the B.J. Photo Company, has cut the price of a similar camera it makes from $100 to $80. Jenkins' economist has estimated the cross elasticity of demand between the two firms' products at about 0.4, given current income and price levels.

   What impact, if any, will the action by B.J. have on total revenue generated by Jenkins, if Jenkins leaves its current price unchanged?

2. The Potomac Range Corporation manufactures a line of microwave ovens costing $500 each. Its sales have averaged about 6,000 units per month during the past year. In August, Potomac's closest competitor, Spring City Stove Works, cut its price for a closely competitive model from $600 to $450. Potomac noticed that its sales volume declined to 4,500 units per month after Spring City announced its price cut.

   a. What is the arc cross elasticity of demand between Potomac's oven and the competitive Spring City model?

   b. Would you say that these two firms are very close competitors? What other factors could have influenced the observed relationship?

   c. If Potomac knows that the arc price elasticity of demand for its ovens is −3.0, what price would Potomac have to charge to sell the same number of units it did before the Spring City price cut?

3. The price elasticity of demand for personal computers is estimated to be −2.2. If the price of personal computers declines by 20 percent, what will be the expected percentage increase in the quantity of computers sold?

4. The Olde Yogurt Factory has reduced the price of its popular Mmmm Sundae from $2.25 to $1.75. As a result, the firm's daily sales of these sundaes have increased from 1,500/day to 1,800/day. Compute the arc price elasticity of demand over this price and consumption quantity range.

5. The subway fare in your town has just been increased from a current level of 50 cents to $1.00 per ride. As a result, the transit authority notes a decline in ridership of 30 percent.

   a. Compute the price elasticity of demand for subway rides.

   b. If the transit authority reduces the fare back to 50 cents, what impact would you expect on the ridership? Why?

6. The demand for mobile homes in Azerpajama, a small, oil-rich sheikdom, has been estimated to be $Q_D = 250,000 - 35P$. If this relationship remains approximately valid in the future:

   a. How many mobile homes would be demanded at a price of $2,000? $4,000? $6,000?

   b. What is the *arc* price elasticity of demand between $2,000 and $4,000? Between $4,000 and $6,000?

   c. What is the *point* price elasticity of demand at $2,000, $4,000, and $6,000?

   d. If 25,000 mobile homes were sold last year, what would you expect the average price to have been?

   e. In a move to increase his popularity (and in the face of rapidly accumulating oil royalties), Sheik Archie has decided to subsidize the price of mobile homes and offer them to all who want them at a price of only $1,000. As the sheik's chief adviser, how many homes would you expect to be bought at this bargain-basement price? At this price, how confident are you of the estimated demand equation?

   f. Without subsidy, what is the highest theoretical price that anyone would pay for a mobile home in the sheikdom?

7. A number of empirical studies of automobile demand have been made yielding the following estimates of income and price elasticities:

Study	Income Elasticity	Price Elasticity
Chow	+3.0	−1.2
Alkinson	+2.5	−1.4
Roos and Von Szeliski	+2.5	−1.5
Suits (as reworked)	+3.9	−1.2

Assume that income and price effects on automobile sales are *independent* and *additive*. Assume also that the auto companies intend to increase the average price of an automobile by about 6 percent in the next year and that next year's disposable personal income is expected to be 4 percent higher than this year's. If this year's automobile sales were 11 million units, how many would you expect to be sold under each pair of price and income demand elasticity estimates?

8. A typical consumer behaved in the following manner with respect to purchases of butter over the past eight years:

Year	Price of Butter ($/Pound)	Quantity of Butter Purchased (Pounds)	Real Income (Dollars)	Price of Margarine ($/Pound)
1	$.95	200	$11,000	$.65
2	1.10	180	11,000	.65
3	1.10	190	11,500	.65
4	1.10	200	11,500	.90
5	1.15	170	11,500	.90
6	.99	190	11,500	.90
7	.99	175	10,500	.90
8	.99	150	10,500	.65

Compute all meaningful price, income, and cross-elasticity coefficients. (Remember that the effects of other factors need to be held constant when computing any one of these coefficients.)

9. If the marginal revenue from a product is $15 and the price elasticity of demand is −1.2, what is the price of the product?

10. Excess inventory overhang in some markets like autos and clothing results in short-run price adjustment to clear the market. In other markets, however, such as restaurant food and milk, inventory overhang leads to a slashing of production orders with little or no price change. Why do some markets adopt the one adjustment mechanism while others adopt just the opposite?

11. The demand function for bicycles in Holland has been estimated to be

$$Q = 2,000 + 15Y - 5.5P$$

where Y is income in *thousands* of euros, Q is the quantity demanded in units, and P is the price per unit. When $P = 150$ euros and $Y = 15(000)$ euros, determine the following:

a. Price elasticity of demand
b. Income elasticity of demand

12. Two goods have a cross price elasticity of +1.2.

a. Would you describe these goods as substitutes or complements?
b. If the price of one of the goods increases by 5 percent, what will happen to the demand for the other product, holding constant the effects of all other factors?

13. In an attempt to increase revenues and profits, a firm is considering a 4 percent increase in price and an 11 percent increase in advertising. If the price elasticity of demand is −1.5 and the advertising elasticity of demand is +0.6, would you expect an increase or decrease in total revenues?

14. During 2000 the demand for a firm's product has been estimated to be

$$Q = 1,000 - 200P$$

During 2001 the demand for that same firm's product has been estimated to be

$$Q = 1,150 - 225P$$

If the price was $2 during 2000 and $3 during 2001, has the price elasticity of demand for this product been increasing or decreasing?

15. Between 1999 and 2000, the quantity of automobiles produced and sold declined by 20 percent. During this period the real price of cars increased by 5 percent, real income levels declined by 2 percent, and the real cost of gasoline increased by 20 percent. Knowing that the income elasticity of demand is +1.5 and the cross price elasticity of gasoline and cars is −0.3,

a. Compute the impact of the decline in real income levels on the demand for cars.
b. Compute the impact of the gasoline price increase on the demand for cars.
c. Compute the price elasticity of the demand for cars during this period.

16. Compute the price elasticity of demand and the income elasticity of demand at the prices and income specified in the following demand function:

$$Q = 25 - 4P + 6I$$

   a. When $I = 10$ and $P = 4$
   b. When $I = 4$ and $P = 6$

17. The demand function for school lunches in Pittsburgh has been estimated to be

$$Q = 16,415.21 - 262.743P$$

   where Q = lunches served
       P = price in cents

   a. Compute the point elasticity of demand for school lunches at a price of
      (i) 40 cents per lunch
      (ii) 50 cents per lunch
   b. What is the arc price elasticity of demand between prices of 40 cents and 50 cents?

18. Over the past six months Heads-Up Hair Care, Inc., has normally had sales of 500 bottles of A-6 Hair Conditioner per week. On the weeks when Heads-Up ran sales on its B-8 Hair Conditioner, cutting the price of B-8 from $10 to $8, sales of A-6 declined to 300 bottles.
   a. What is the arc cross elasticity of demand between A-6 and B-8?
   b. If the price of B-8 were increased to $12, what effect would you expect this to have on the quantity demanded of A-6?
   c. What does the evidence indicate about the relationship between B-8 and A-6?

19. The income elasticity of demand for residential use of electricity has been estimated as 0.3. If the price of electricity is expected to remain constant and the price of substitute goods is expected to remain constant, what would you expect to happen to the demand for electricity by residential customers if disposable personal income were expected to decline by 10 percent over the next year?

20. A study of the long-term income elasticity of demand for housing by renters is in the range of 0.8 to 1.0, whereas the income elasticity for owner-occupants is between 0.7 and 1.15.
   a. If income levels are expected to increase at a compound annual rate of 4 percent per year for the next five years, forecast the impact of this increase in income levels on the quantity of housing demanded in the two markets (rental and owner-occupants) in five years (assume that the price of housing does not change over this period).
   b. What would be the impact of price increases during this period on the levels of demand forecasted in part (a)?

21. Given the following demand function:

Price P ($)	Quantity Q_D (Units)	Arc Elasticity E_D	Total Revenue ($)	Marginal Revenue ($/Unit)
$12	30	n.a.	_____	n.a.
11	40	_____	_____	_____
10	50	_____	_____	_____
9	60	_____	_____	_____
8	70	_____	_____	_____
7	80	_____	_____	_____
6	90	_____	_____	_____
5	100	_____	_____	_____
4	110	_____	_____	_____

a. Compute the associated arc elasticity, total revenue, and marginal revenue values.

b. On separate graphs, plot the demand function, total revenue function, and marginal revenue function.

22. The Stopdecay Company sells an electric toothbrush for $25. Its sales have averaged 8,000 units per month over the last year. Recently, its closest competitor, Decayfighter, reduced the price of its electric toothbrush from $35 to $30. As a result, Stopdecay's sales declined by 1,500 units per month.

a. What is the arc cross elasticity of demand between Stopdecay's toothbrush and Decayfighter's toothbrush? What does this indicate about the relationship between the two products?

b. If Stopdecay knows that the arc price elasticity of demand for its toothbrush is −1.5, what price would Stopdecay have to charge to sell the same number of units as it did before the Decayfighter price cut? Assume that Decayfighter holds the price of its toothbrush constant at $30.

c. What is Stopdecay's average monthly total revenue from the sale of electric toothbrushes before and after the price change determined in part (b)?

d. Is the result in part (c) necessarily desirable? What other factors would have to be taken into consideration?

23. The demand for renting motorboats in a resort town has been estimated to be $Q_D = 5,000 − 50P$ where Q_D is the quantity of boats demanded (boat-hours) and P is the average price per hour to rent a motorboat. If this relationship holds true in the future:

a. How many boat-hours will be demanded at rental prices of $10, $20, and $30 per hour?

b. What is the *arc* price elasticity of demand between $10 and $20? Between $20 and $30?

c. What is the *point* price elasticity of demand at $10, $20, and $30?

d. If the number of boat rental hours was 4,250 last year, what would you expect the average rental rate per hour to have been?

24. The following table gives hypothetical data for the weekly purchase of sirloin steak by a college fraternity house. Compute all meaningful arc elasticity

Week	Price per Pound of Steak	Quantity of Steak Purchased (Pounds)	Income (Member Dues)	Price per Pound of Hamburger
1	$2.50	100	$500	$.90
2	2.60	95	500	.90
3	2.60	100	550	.90
4	2.60	105	550	.95
5	2.50	115	550	.95
6	2.50	105	550	.90
7	2.50	100	500	.90
8	2.65	90	500	.90
9	2.65	110	500	1.00
10	2.65	90	400	1.00

coefficients (price, cross, and income). Remember that the effects of the other factors must be held constant when computing any of these elasticities.

25. "Because of the American love affair with driving the automobile, increases in the price of gasoline will not affect consumption." What type of demand curve is implied by this statement? Do you believe this is true? Why?

26. Some proposals for tax reform would eliminate the interest deduction for second homes. Explain the impact this would have on the disposable income of owners of second homes and on the price of second homes in the marketplace.

27. If the price of DVD players declines by 20 percent and the total revenue from the sale of DVD players rises, what can you say about the price elasticity of demand for DVD players? Will this price reduction necessarily lead to an increase in profits for DVD player manufacturers?

28. The Genessee Transportation Company operates an urban bus system in the city of Genessee, Pennsylvania. Economic analysis performed by the firm indicates that two major factors influence the demand for its services: fare levels and downtown parking rates. Table 1 presents information available from 2002 operations. Forecasts of future fares and daily parking rates are presented in Table 2.

TABLE 1

Average Daily Transit Riders (2002)	Round-Trip Fare	Average Downtown Parking Rate
5,000	$1.00	$5.50

TABLE 2

Year	Round-Trip Fare	Average Parking Rates
2003	$1.00	$6.50
2004	$1.25	$6.50

Genessee's economists supplied the following information so that the firm can estimate ridership in 2003 and 2004. Based on past experience, the coefficient of cross elasticity between bus ridership and downtown parking rates is estimated at 0.2, given a fare of $1.00 per round trip. This is not expected to change for a fare increase to $1.25. The price elasticity of demand is currently estimated at −1.1, given daily parking rates of $5.50. It is estimated, however, that the price elasticity will change to −1.2 when parking rates increase to $6.50. Using these data, estimate the average daily ridership for 2003 and 2004.

29. Many states offer drivers an opportunity to express their individuality with their automobile license plates. For the privilege of having your license plate imprinted with your own custom message—such as SINGLE, PISCES, AG OF 81, PLIBIT, MY BENZ, B-PHIT—drivers normally pay a small premium to the state.

   In 1965 when vanity license plates were introduced in Texas, they could be acquired for a mere $10 over the cost of a normal license plate. By 1985 the price had jumped to $25. At this price 154,000 Texans invested in "their own automotive identity." As Texas entered the oil price recession of the mid-80s, however, legislative leaders frantically scrambled for new sources of revenue. In 1986 the Texas legislature tripled the price to $75. Sales tumbled to only 56,000 custom plates. Faced with this sudden decline in demand, the legislature cut the price to $40 for 1987. The Texas legislators learned a quick lesson in the concept of price elasticity.

   a. What assumptions do you believe led the legislature to increase the price in 1986?

   b. Compute the arc price elasticity of demand between $25 and $75, assuming no other factors affecting the demand for license plates changed between 1985 and 1986. Given this calculation, why do you feel the legislature cut the price to $40 for 1987?

   c. What other factors should be considered in future pricing decisions by the legislature?

30. The Reliable Aircraft Company manufactures small, pleasure-use aircraft. Based on past experience, sales volume appears to be affected by changes in the price of the planes and by the state of the economy as measured by consumers' disposable personal income. The following data pertaining to Reliable's aircraft sales, selling prices, and consumers' personal income were collected:

Year	Aircraft Sales	Average Price	Disposable Personal Income (in Constant 2003 Dollars—Billions)
2003	525	$7,200	$610
2004	450	8,000	610
2005	400	8,000	590

   a. Estimate the arc price elasticity of demand using the 2003 and 2004 data.

   b. Estimate the arc income elasticity of demand using the 2004 and 2005 data.

   c. Assume that these estimates are expected to remain stable during 2006. Forecast 2006 sales for Reliable assuming that its aircraft prices remain constant at 2005 levels and that disposable personal income will increase by $40 billion. Also assume that arc income elasticity computed in (b) above is the best available estimate of income elasticity.

d.   Forecast 2006 sales for Reliable given that its aircraft prices will increase by $500 from 2005 levels and that disposable personal income will increase by $40 billion. Assume that the price and income effects are *independent* and *additive* and that the arc income and price elasticities computed in parts (a) and (b) are the best available estimates of these elasticities to be used in making the forecast.

31. In 1998 the fare on Chicago's transit system was 60 cents per ride. This resulted in 711.6 million trips being taken on the system. In 1999 the fare was increased to 80 cents and ridership declined to 692.4 million trips.

a.   Compute the arc price elasticity of demand for transit ridership in Chicago assuming that all other factors influencing demand remained constant during this period.

b.   Based on your answer to part (a), do you believe the fare increase was a rational action for the Chicago Transit Authority?

c.   What other factors do you feel may have had an impact on ridership during this period? Do you believe the decline in ridership experienced in 1999 tends to overstate or understate the actual impact of the fare increase?

d.   In 2000 the fare increased to 90 cents and ridership declined to 640 million trips. Compute the arc price elasticity between 1999 and 2000. How can you account for the differences between the 1998–1999 elasticity coefficient and the 1999–2000 elasticity coefficient?

32. A Department of Energy report showed that during the period between March 1990 and March 1995, energy consumption per U.S. household dropped 9 percent. During the same period, energy prices rose by 24 percent.

a.   Assuming all other factors influencing demand remained constant during this period, what was the price elasticity of demand for household energy consumption?

b.   What other factors may have influenced the results for this period?

c.   If household energy consumption had been increasing at a rate of 2 percent per year before this price increase, what impact would this have had on the computed price elasticity?

http://

Further Research on the Proposed Office Depot–Staples Merger

33. In late June 1997 a federal district court in Washington, D.C., granted the Federal Trade Commission's (FTC's) request for a preliminary injunction blocking the Staples–Office Depot merger. The antitrust case involving Staples was significant in part for the role of econometric analysis of the pricing behavior of Staples.

Access the Federal Trade Commission Internet site at http://www.ftc.gov. Search under the "Staples" keyword and read the summary of econometric analysis. By how much did the FTC's empirical analysis determine that average office supply prices would rise as a consequence of the merger between Office Depot and Staples? A key issue of contention in the case was that Staples charged higher prices in those geographical markets that lacked an Office Depot outlet. What were the alternative methods used by the FTC and the merging firms to determine whether or not an Office Depot and a Staples outlet were in the same geographical market? How did these differences in measurement of geographical market affect the pricing behavior estimated by the FTC and by the merging firms?

CASE EXERCISE

POLO GOLF SHIRT PRICING

Complete the following demand and total revenue spreadsheet for daily sales of a golf shirt in each of Ralph Lauren's discount stores. What price maximizes sales revenue? What price maximizes operating profit? Why? Who would pursue the first objective? How could Ralph Lauren's managers provide an incentive for profit-maximizing behavior?

Quantity Sold	Uniform Price	Total Revenue	Marginal Revenue	Variable Cost
0	$50.00	$0	$0	$28
1	$48.00	$48	$48	$28
2	$46.00	$92	$44	$28
3	$45.00	$135	$43	$28
4	$44.00	$176	$41	$28
5	$42.00	$210	$34	$28
6	$40.00	$240	$30	$28
7	$38.31	$268	$28	$28
8	$36.50	$292	$24	$28
9	$34.50	$311	$19	$28
10	_____	_____	$16	$28
11	_____	_____	$13	$28
12	_____	_____	$10	$28
13	_____	_____	$7	$28
14	_____	_____	$4	$28
15	_____	_____	$0	$28
16	_____	_____	($1)	$28
17	_____	_____	($4)	$28
18	_____	_____	($7)	$28

Appendix 3a

Indifference Curve Analysis of Demand

INDIFFERENCE CURVES

The derivation of a consumer's demand function is based on indifference curves and budget lines. *Indifference curves* reveal the consumer's consumption preferences, or utility, for various combinations of goods. *Budget lines,* which are based on the prices of various goods and on the consumer's income, limit the choices available for consumption.

Consider the situation of a consumer who wishes to allocate an available sub-budget of income between two commodities, restaurant food (*F*) and entertainment (*E*). The utility, *U*, or satisfaction the consumer receives from the two goods, can be expressed as

$$U = f(Q_F, Q_E) \qquad \text{[3A.1]}$$

where Q_F and Q_E are the respective quantities of food and entertainment consumed. The utility received from consuming various combinations of goods *F* and *E* can be ranked in an ordinal fashion. That is, it is possible to indicate that a consumer prefers 8 restaurant meals and 3 movies per month to an alternative combination, such as 10 meals and 1 movie. This notion of ordinal utility can be depicted by *indifference*

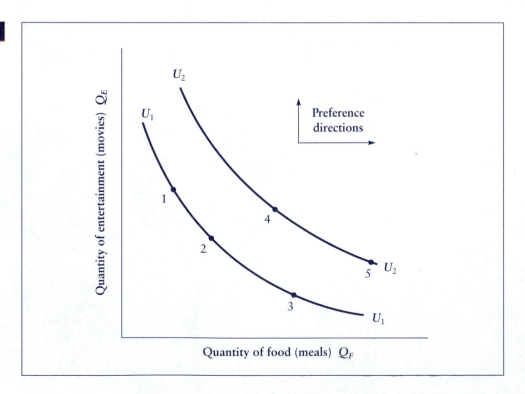

FIGURE 3A.1

Indifference Curves

MANAGERIAL CHALLENGE

New Product Pricing at Motorola[22]

What's a cell phone worth? When cell phones first began replacing two-way mobile radios in 1983, one of the hardest questions for Motorola to answer was what price elasticity of demand would characterize the new product. Clearly, no close substitutes existed. Returning to one's car to check in with the office or regularly calling the office from a pay phone imposed substantial inconvenience relative to a small light cell phone carried in one's coat pocket. Consumers would presumably pay substantially higher prices for the convenience of the new technology. But how much higher and what sensitivity would the new demand exhibit to price promotions? These are difficult questions requiring careful analysis when an extensive history of product sales and price data are present. They are virtually impossible to answer with new products, not yet introduced.

One approach to estimating the value of a new product is to conduct marketing research experiments that benchmark the product against other similar technologies. Thus, when digital technology made pagers a practical extension of cell phones in 1992, it was possible to ask cell phone users what extra amount per month they would pay to have access to a pager. Similarly, buyers of Cheerios, a ready-to-eat cereal, can be surveyed about their willingness to pay extra for Apple Cinnamon Cheerios, and music cassette buyers were probably asked the same question about music CDs. Often, however, the technological leaps associated with new product introductions make these comparisons infeasible. In 1972, few engineers could assess their willingness to pay for pocket calculators relative to slide rules. In 1981, few secretaries could assess their improved efficiency with electronic word processors rather than manual typewriters. Some other method was required to identify the extra quality and value contributed by the new products.

In this appendix, we will see how the techniques of indifference curve analysis can identify the value of a new product. These methods have application in measuring the effect of higher quality products on the cost of living and in pricing decisions affecting new product introductions.

http://

Motorola's Internet site can be accessed at
http://www.mot.com/

---

[22] Based on "It Overstates Inflation," *BusinessWeek*, June 9, 1997, pp. 68–69, and "Now Prices Can be 'Virtual' Too," *The Economist*, June 14, 1997, p. 88.

curves. An indifference curve is a plotting of points representing various combinations of two goods, for example F and E, such that the consumer is *indifferent* among any combinations along a specific indifference curve.

Figure 3A.1 shows two indifference curves, U_1 and U_2. The consumer is indifferent among combinations 1, 2, and 3 on curve U_1, but prefers any combination of E and F, such as points 4 and 5 on curve U_2 to any combination available on curve U_1. The most important properties of indifference curves are:

1. Any combination of commodities lying on an indifference curve (U_2, for example) that is above and to the right of another indifference curve (such as U_1) is the preferred combination.
2. Indifference curves have a negative (downward) slope to the right, indicating that more of E can only be obtained by consuming less of F.
3. Indifference curves never intersect.

4. Indifference curves are convex to the origin. The absolute value of the slope of an indifference curve is the marginal rate of substitution of F for E. The convex shape of an indifference curve indicates that the slope diminishes as one moves to the right; i.e., the consumer is willing to give up fewer and fewer units of E to gain an increasing number of units of F. This is consistent with the law of diminishing marginal utility, which states that the additional satisfaction, or marginal utility, derived from successive units of a good is thought to decline.

BUDGET LINES

In choosing the amount of goods F and E that maximizes his or her utility, the consumer is limited by the amount of income available to purchase these goods. The consumer faces an $(F + E)$ subbudget of the household budget constraint, of the form

$$M = P_F Q_F + P_E Q_E \qquad [3A.2]$$

where M represents the amount of income available to the consumer to be spent on goods F and E. P_F and P_E represent the price of a unit of F and E, respectively. The amount spent on F—$P_F Q_F$—plus the amount spent on E—$P_E Q_E$—equals the total amount of income available, M. This budget line is shown in Figure 3A.2. It intersects the y-axis (vertical) at M/P_E—the number of movies consumed if the entire subbudget is spent on movies. The budget line intersects the x-axis (horizontal) at M/P_F—the number of meals consumed if all of the subbudget is spent on F. Any combination of meals and movies lying on or below the budget line is available to the consumer. Any household that prefers more meals and movies to less will select for consumption some combination of F and E which lies on the subbudget constraint— i.e., a consumption bundle which exhausts the subbudget.

Knowing that all interior combinations of food and entertainment (below the budget constraint) are less preferred than the chosen combination (F_1, E_1) allows a

FIGURE 3A.2

Using Budget Lines to Reveal Consumer Preference

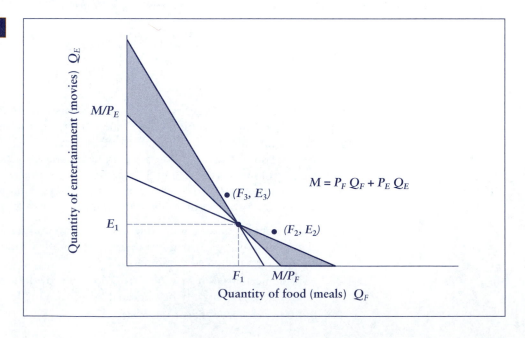

practical mechanism for locating a regular buyer's indifference curve. In a so-called revealed preference experiment, a household agrees to keep a diary of their food and entertainment consumption over an extended time period. Various coupon and subsidy schemes change the effective price of items the household buys regularly. If a consumption experimenter lowers the price of food and raises the price of entertainment such that the household now can select between (F_1, E_1) or any other combination allowed by the new flatter budget line in Figure 3A.2, and if the household responds that they still prefer (F_1, E_1), the new shaded area of consumption choices has been identified as less preferred. Conducting the same experiment in reverse (i.e., with increased food prices and lower entertainment prices along the steepest budget constraint in Figure 3A.2), another shaded set of consumption bundles less preferred than (F_1, E_1) can be identified. Continuing in this fashion until the household switches to a new subsidized food combination like (F_2, E_2) or a new subsidized entertainment combination like (F_3, E_3) reveals the shape and location of the household's indifference curve. These techniques are important in pricing new products and in measuring the cost of living before and after new product introductions.

GRAPHICAL DETERMINATION OF THE OPTIMAL COMBINATION

Given the indifference curves and budget constraint, the consumer's problem is to choose the combination of F and E that *maximizes* the utility derived without overspending the budget. Because a consumer's satisfaction increases with combinations

FIGURE 3A.3

Optimal Combination

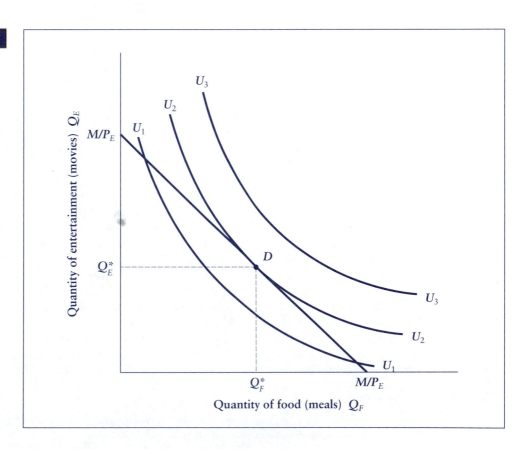

moving upward and/or to the right, utility is maximized at the point of *tangency* between the budget constraint and the highest consumer indifference curve, as illustrated in Figure 3A.3. Given three possible indifference curves and a budget constraint, the optimal combination of goods F and E for this consumer is given at point D. At this point the consumer can achieve a U_2 level of satisfaction by consuming Q_F^* units of F and Q_E^* units of E. These levels provide the highest utility without violating the budget constraint.

At the point of tangency of the indifference curve (U_2) and the budget line in Figure 3A.3, the slope[23] of the indifference curve is equal to the slope of the budget line. The slope ($\Delta Q_E/\Delta Q_F$) of the budget line is equal to the ratio of the price of commodity $F(P_F)$ to the price of commodity $E(P_E)$; that is

$$\frac{\Delta Q_E}{\Delta Q_F} = \frac{(M/P_E - 0)}{(M/P_F - 0)} = \frac{P_F}{P_E} \qquad [3A.3]$$

The slope of the indifference curve ($\Delta Q_E/\Delta Q_F$) at any point measures the consumer's *marginal rate of substitution* (MRS) of commodity E for commodity F (holding utility constant). This slope is equal to the ratio of the marginal utility of F ($MU_F = \partial U/\partial Q_F$) to the marginal utility of E ($MU_E = \partial U/\partial Q_E$), that is

$$\frac{\Delta Q_E}{\Delta Q_F} = MRS = \frac{MU_F}{MU_E} \qquad [3A.4]$$

At the optimum (tangency) point, setting Equation 3A.3 equal to Equation 3A.4 yields

$$\frac{MU_F}{MU_E} = \frac{P_F}{P_E} \qquad [3A.5]$$

or

$$\frac{MU_F}{P_F} = \frac{MU_E}{P_E} \qquad [3A.6]$$

GRAPHICAL DERIVATION OF THE DEMAND FUNCTION

A consumer's demand function for a good can be derived graphically based on his or her indifference curves and budget line.

Consider a consumer whose indifference curves and budget line are shown in Figure 3A.4. Assume the consumer has $350 to spend on products F and E. The initial price of E is $5 per movie and the initial price of F is $10 per restaurant meal. Under these conditions, the consumer could acquire 70 movies or 35 meals or any other combination thereof (illustrated by the lower budget line). Three indifference curves are plotted, U_1, U_2, and U_3. Given the income constraint of $350 and the initial prices of F ($10) and E ($5), the consumer would choose combination X on curve U_1. At this point the consumer would acquire 16 units of F. Hence at a price of $10 per unit, the consumer would demand 16 meals. This point is now plotted on the lower panel of Figure 3A.4 as point X'.

If the price of F declines to $5, a new budget line is defined which intersects the Q_F axis at 70 units. The new optimum occurs at point Y with 35 units of F being demanded at a price of $5. This point is plotted on the lower panel at Y'.

---

[23] Note that the slopes of the indifference curves and budget line are both negative. In the remainder of this appendix, slope will be taken to mean *absolute value*.

Finally, at a price of $3.50 for a unit of F, a new optimum point occurs at Z with 64 units of F being demanded. By plotting in the lower panel of Figure 3A.4 the three prices and associated quantities demanded, the familiar demand curve, D_F, for food is derived. This is illustrated by the curve that connects points X', Y', and Z'.

FIGURE 3A.4

Derivation of a
Demand Function

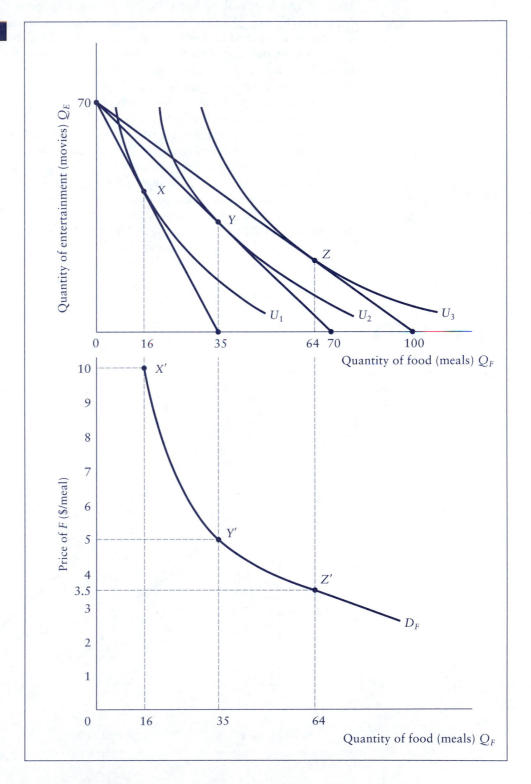

INCOME AND SUBSTITUTION EFFECTS

Indifference curve analysis can also be used to illustrate the income and substitution effects of a price decline. Consider the case of a consumer who consumes food and entertainment with an initial budget constraint given in Figure 3A.5 as XV. The consumer will buy Q_1 units of F and Q_4 units of E, as indicated at Point 1.

If the price of food declines such that the new budget line becomes XV', Point 2 represents the new optimum for the consumer. This point falls on the higher of the two indifference curves, U_2, plotted on the figure. Given the new lower price for food, the consumer demands Q_2 units of F.

Next, we construct a new, artificial budget line, ZW, which is parallel to XV' and tangent to the original indifference curve U_1. From the original optimal combination of food and entertainment, Point 1, to the artificial optimum, Point 3, "real" income of the consumer has remained the same in the sense that the consumer experiences the same utility at Point 1 and Point 3. The change in quantity demanded for F from Q_1 to Q_3 may be thought of as representing the "pure" substitution effect of food for entertainment resulting from the price reduction for food. In contrast, the increased consumption of food measured from Points Q_3 to Q_2 may be thought of as the "pure" income effect. This is so because the only difference between ZW and XV' is the level of income that each reflects. In summary, a decline in price for food results in the consumer demanding $Q_3 - Q_1$ more units of food because of the substitution effect, and $Q_2 - Q_3$ more units of food because of the income effect for an income-superior good.

FIGURE 3A.5

Income and Substitution Effects for Income-Superior Goods

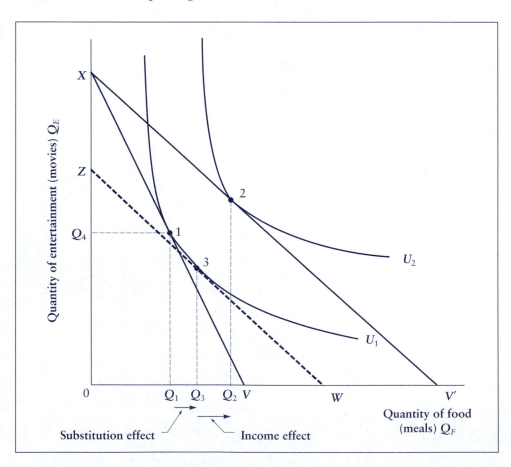

ALGEBRAIC DETERMINATION OF THE OPTIMAL COMBINATION

The determination of the optimal combination of goods F and E that maximizes a consumer's utility subject to a budget constraint can also be obtained algebraically using Lagrangian multiplier techniques. The objective is to maximize utility, represented by Equation 3A.1,

$$U = f(Q_F, Q_E)$$

subject to the budget constraint, represented by Equation 3A.2,

$$M = P_F Q_F + P_E Q_E$$

We begin by forming the Lagrangian function

$$U_\lambda = f(Q_F, Q_E) - \lambda (P_F Q_F + P_E Q_E - M) \qquad [3A.7]$$

Differentiating Equation 3A.7 with respect to Q_F, Q_E, and λ and setting the derivatives equal to 0 yields

$$\frac{\partial U_\lambda}{\partial Q_F} = \frac{\partial f}{\partial Q_F} - \lambda P_F = 0 \qquad [3A.8]$$

$$\frac{\partial U_\lambda}{\partial Q_E} = \frac{\partial f}{\partial Q_E} - \lambda P_E = 0 \qquad [3A.9]$$

$$\frac{\partial U_\lambda}{\partial \lambda} = -P_F Q_F - P_E Q_E + M = 0 \qquad [3A.10]$$

Recognizing that $\partial f/\partial Q_F = MU_F$ and $\partial f/\partial Q_E = MU_E$, we substitute these quantities into Equations 3A.8 and 3A.9 to give

$$MU_F = \lambda P_F$$

$$\lambda = \frac{MU_F}{P_F} \qquad [3A.11]$$

and

$$MU_E = \lambda P_E$$

$$\lambda = \frac{MU_E}{P_E} \qquad [3A.12]$$

Setting Equation 3A.11 equal to Equation 3A.12 yields the optimality condition (Equation 3A.6):

$$\frac{MU_F}{P_F} = \frac{MU_E}{P_E}$$

Example

MEASURING THE VALUE OF CELLULAR PHONES[24]

When Motorola introduced the cellular phone, the quality of telecommunications services clearly rose. The difficult question was what value to place on this enhanced convenience for "staying in touch." Public as well as private managers are interested

---

[24] Based on "It Overstates Inflation," *Business Week*, June 9, 1997, pp. 68–69; "Costing a Packet," *The Economist*, May 6, 1996, p. 75; and J. Hausman, "Cellular Telephones: New Products and the CPI," NBER Working Paper, No. 5982, March 1997.

in such a question because quality enhancements offered by new products like cellular phones, open-heart surgery, and central air conditioning all lower the cost of living. Official cost-of-living indices for medical services, housing, and telecommunications determine everything from hospital cost reimbursements to wage indexation agreements in union bargaining, and therefore become embedded in the underlying rate of inflation. Estimating correctly the value of these quality improvements from a new product became a serious issue in boardrooms, on Wall Street, and in congressional debates about social security cost-of-living adjustments.

To calculate the value of a new product consumed at P_{NP} in the quantity Q_{NP} (on the horizontal axis), consider the following procedure with a representative household or business which chooses between two-way-radio mobile phones and cellular phones. Raise the price of the new cellular phone service until the last most valuable use is discouraged and quantity demanded falls to zero. Figure 3A.6 illustrates this idea as a steepening of the initial budget constraint whose x-intercept is M/P_{NP} until the preferred quantity declines from Q_{NP} to zero at Point $2'$. Identify the price that is high enough to accomplish the collapse of all new product sales as P_{MAX}, the "virtual price" beyond which no one would purchase the new cellular phone product. Then, maintaining relative prices at this P_{MAX} level (namely, P_{MAX}/P_{RADIO}), calculate the purchasing power required to leave the household as well off as they

FIGURE 3A.6

Value of a New Product

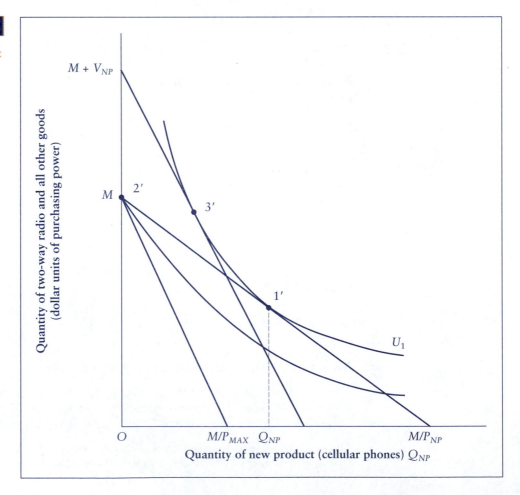

were with Q_{NP} at Point 1' on U_1. After subtracting the money income of the household (M), the additional dollars required to restore utility to the level U_1 associated with current sales of the new product is the value of the enhanced quality attributable to the new product.

Graphically, in Figure 3A.6, hold utility constant at U_1 while raising cellular phone prices to P_{MAX} as indicated by the shape of the budget constraint from M to M/P_{MAX}. Along U_1 the tangency at Point 3' identifies $M + V_{NP}$ as the amount of purchasing power required. Subtracting M from the y-intercept of the budget constraint tangent at 3' leaves V_{NP}. Therefore, V_{NP} is the additional value attributable to the new cellular phone product.

With revealed preference techniques for identifying the household's indifference curve data and linear programming to identify the budget constraints in question, estimates of V_{NP} for cellphones are obtainable for both Motorola's pricing analysts and the cost-of-living analysts in the Bureau of Labor Statistics.

EXERCISES

1. Suppose an individual's utility (that is, satisfaction) received from two goods can be represented by the following relationship:

$$U = f(Q_A, Q_B) = 2Q_A + 2Q_B - .5Q_A^2 + Q_AQ_B - .6Q_B^2$$

where Q_A and Q_B are the amounts consumed of the respective goods. Furthermore, assume that the cost per unit of good A is $4 and the cost per unit of good B is $6. The individual has $48 available to spend on the two goods and desires to maximize the utility received from consumption of the two goods subject to his budget constraint.

   a. Formulate the problem in a programming format.

   b. Convert this constrained optimization problem into an unconstrained problem by forming the Lagrangian function.

   c. Solve this unconstrained problem using the techniques of differential calculus.

   d. Defining $MU_A = \partial f/\partial Q_A$ and $MU_B = \partial f/\partial Q_B$ to be the marginal utility functions, show that the ratio of the marginal utilities

$$\frac{MU_A}{MU_B}$$

   evaluated at optimal values of Q_A and Q_B obtained in part (c) is equal to the ratio of the prices of the two goods. This illustrates the economic principle that in equilibrium the ratio of the prices of two goods must be equal to the ratio of the marginal utilities (i.e., Equation 3A.5).

   e. Give an economic interpretation of the value of the Lagrangian multiplier (λ) obtained in part (b).

2. Ms. Jones consumes three products, A, B, and C. She has decided that her last purchase of A gave her 8 units of satisfaction, her last purchase of B gave her 10 units of satisfaction, and her last purchase of C gave her 5 units of satisfaction. The prices of A, B, and C are $4, $5, and $3 per unit, respectively.
   As a rational consumer, what should Ms. Jones purchase?

CASE EXERCISE

VALUE-IN-USE OF DVDS

Discuss alternative methods of estimating the value of DVDs. What established products would you ask consumers to compare to DVDs? What advantages would marketing researchers focus on as the sources of new product value for a DVD over an earlier product you have chosen. Sketch how a revealed preference experiment and indifference curve analysis could be used to estimate the value of a DVD.

Estimation of Demand

CHAPTER PREVIEW The preceding chapter developed the theory of demand, including the concepts of price elasticity, income elasticity, and cross price elasticity of demand. A manager who is contemplating an increase in the price of one of the firm's products needs to know the impact of this increase on quantity demanded, total revenue, and profits. Is the demand elastic, inelastic, or unit elastic with respect to price over the range of the contemplated price increase? What will happen to demand if consumer incomes increase or decrease as a result of an economic expansion or contraction? Managers in profit-seeking enterprises face these types of magnitude questions about empirical demand relationships every day.

Governments and not-for-profit institutions are also faced with similar questions. What will be the impact of an increase in bridge tolls? Will automobile commuting decrease by 5, 10, or 20 percent? What effect will a tuition increase have on local state university revenues? Will a sales tax increase boost revenue enough to cover a projected budget shortfall? This chapter discusses some of the techniques and problems associated with making such estimates. The more knowledgeable a manager is regarding the empirical demand relationships, the more likely that manager will be to take actions that can maximize the profits and cash flows accruing to the firm.

MANAGERIAL CHALLENGE

Demand for Public Transportation[1]

Port Authority Transit (PAT) provides public transportation services to the residents of Allegheny County (Pittsburgh and suburbs). It operates a fleet of 925 buses and 71 light rail vehicles and trolleys in providing 88 million rides per year (see graph on page 129). In June 1990 PAT adopted a $173.7 million budget for the next fiscal year. By state law PAT is required to operate on a balanced budget. PAT's cash base fare is $1.10. Fares cover only part of its costs—with the balance of its revenues coming from federal, state, and county subsidies.

As a result of the first Iraq-Kuwait crisis beginning in August 1990, the cost of diesel fuel (used to operate buses) increased from $0.61 per gallon to $1.09 per gallon—which produced a projected $3.2 million budget deficit. (Each 1-cent increase in the price of diesel fuel costs PAT more than $100,000 per year, because its vehicles use more than 10 million gallons annually.)

Faced with this projected deficit and the need to balance its budget, PAT could attempt to either reduce costs or increase revenues. Cutting costs is difficult because most administrative expenses (e.g., salaries) are relatively fixed in the short run. Likewise, hourly wage rates paid to drivers and mechanics are set by union contracts and cannot be lowered unilaterally. Service cutbacks are possi-

ble; however, this may also reduce revenues and thus be counterproductive. Instead of attempting to reduce costs, the executive director of PAT proposed a 15-cent increase in fares to offset the increased cost of diesel fuel.

In analyzing the effects of this fare increase, a number of issues had to be addressed. For example:

- How would the fare (price) increase affect demand and overall revenues?
- What other factors, besides fares, could affect demand?

Examination of the data in the graph on the following page gives some possible answers to these questions. Note that ridership declined every year (i.e., 1969, 1971, 1976, 1980, 1982, and 1990) that PAT raised fares. Note also that ridership increased during the mid to late 1970s when there were gasoline shortages and (relatively) higher gasoline prices. Finally, note that ridership declined in the early 1980s—a period during which there was higher unemployment, population declines, and (relatively) lower gasoline prices.

Econometric models can be developed that incorporate price and other relevant variables in explaining demand for various goods and services. Such models can be used to make forecasts of demand (and revenues) based on expected changes in any of the relevant variables. This chapter focuses

(continued)

DEMAND ESTIMATION USING MARKETING RESEARCH TECHNIQUES

Before examining some of the statistical techniques that are useful in estimating demand relationships, this section looks at three different marketing research methods that can be used in analyzing demand. These techniques are consumer surveys, focus groups, and market experiments.

MANAGERIAL CHALLENGE

on the techniques that are used in developing such models.

http://

The U.S. Department of Transportation maintains the National Transportation Library on the Internet, which contains travel demand forecasting studies. The site address is

http://ntl.bts.gov/index.cfm

————

[1] Based on an article in *The Pittsburgh Press* by Joe Grata, October 26, 1990, p. A1.

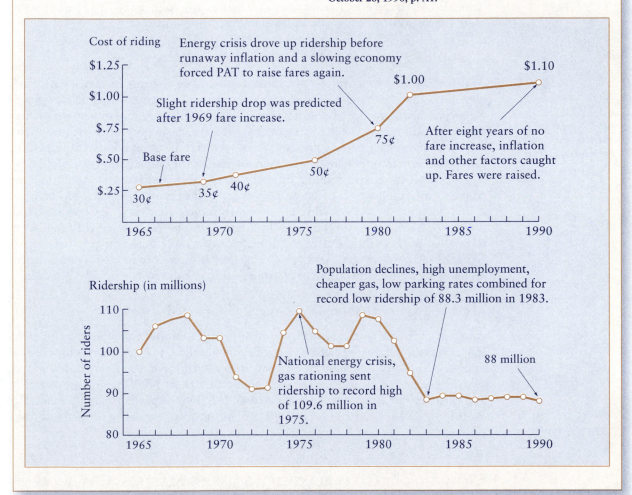

Cost of riding

Energy crisis drove up ridership before runaway inflation and a slowing economy forced PAT to raise fares again.

$1.10

$1.00

Slight ridership drop was predicted after 1969 fare increase.

75¢

After eight years of no fare increase, inflation and other factors caught up. Fares were raised.

Base fare

35¢ 40¢ 50¢

30¢

$1.25 $1.00 $.75 $.50 $.25

1965 1970 1975 1980 1985 1990

Ridership (in millions)

Population declines, high unemployment, cheaper gas, low parking rates combined for record low ridership of 88.3 million in 1983.

National energy crisis, gas rationing sent ridership to record high of 109.6 million in 1975.

88 million

Number of riders

110 100 90 80

1965 1970 1975 1980 1985 1990

http://

Access the Council of American Survey Research Organizations on the Internet at

http://www.casro.org/

Consumer Surveys

Consumer surveys involve questioning a sample of consumers to determine such factors as their willingness to buy, their sensitivity to price changes or relative price levels, and their awareness of advertising campaigns. Consumer surveys can provide a great deal of useful information to a firm. However, many consumers are not able or not willing to give accurate answers to these types of questions. For example, can you specify what your response would be to a 25-cent rise in the price of hamburgers at your favorite fast-food restaurant? How many fewer hamburgers would you buy per month? Do you know how many you buy now? The approach of direct consumer interviewing has many potential pitfalls.

This is not to say that nothing can be learned from consumer interviews. Consumer expectations about future business and credit conditions may provide significant insights into the consumers' propensity to purchase many items, especially durable goods. Using a little imagination and asking less direct questions may also offer insights. If questioning reveals that consumers are unaware of price differences among several competing goods, it might be concluded that at least within the current range of prices, consumers are not terribly price conscious; that is, demand may be price inelastic. Also, the effectiveness of advertising campaigns may be tested by sampling the awareness of a group of consumers to the campaign.

Consumer Focus Groups

Focus Group
A market research technique employing close observation of discussion among target consumers.

Another means of recording consumer responses to changes in factors affecting demand is through the use of consumer **focus groups.** In these situations, for example, experimental groups of consumers are given a small amount of money with which to buy certain items. The experimenter can observe the impact on actual purchases as price, prices of competing goods, and other variables are manipulated.[2] Then the group of consumers are closely observed discussing the choices they made and why.

Of course, the costs of setting up and running such a clinic are substantial, and consequently the number of consumers actually participating is likely to be quite small. Second, the participants are generally aware that their actions are being observed, and hence they may seek to act in a manner somewhat different from normal—the "Hawthorne effect." For example, an individual taking part in a consumer clinic may suspect that the experimenter is interested in sensitivity to prices and may be significantly more price conscious than otherwise would be the case.

Market Experiments in Test Stores

Another approach that is sometimes used to garner information about the demand function is the *market experiment,* which examines the way consumers behave in real market situations. A firm may vary one or more of the determinants of demand, such as price or advertising or the presence of an NFL or NBA logo on a sweatshirt, and observe the impact on quantity demanded. This approach may be especially useful in developing a feel for the price or promotion elasticity of demand for a product.

ESTIMATION OF CROSS ELASTICITY: SIMMONS MATTRESS COMPANY

The Simmons Mattress Company conducted an experiment involving the relative prices of its mattresses. Two identical types of mattresses, some with the Simmons label and others with an unknown brand name, were offered for sale at the same

[2] The use of laboratory experimentations to estimate demand elasticities is illustrated in J.F. Engle, *Consumer Behavior* (Hinsdale, IL: Dryden Press, 1993).

prices and varying price spreads to determine cross elasticity. It was found that with identical prices, Simmons outsold the unknown brand 15 to 1; with a $5 premium over the unknown label, Simmons's margin was reduced to 8 to 1; and with a 25 percent premium over the unknown label, sales were about the same.

Market experimentation has several serious shortcomings. Because of the expense, few well-controlled experiments are conducted, so results can be unreliable. Observed changes that occur in an uncontrolled experiment may be due to all sorts of disturbance factors, such as unusually bad weather, competitive advertising or competitive price reductions, and even local strikes or large layoffs that change consumer incomes significantly. The duration of these experiments is likely to be short, and the number of possible variations in parameters, such as price or advertising outlays, is likely to be small. Hence long-run decisions must be made on the basis of a few short-run observations.

In spite of these limitations, direct market experimentation may be useful in a number of situations. For example, statistical demand studies may be impossible when the marketing of a new product is being considered and no price-output data are available. Also, market experiments may provide important data for verifying the results of a statistical study. The information that a statistical demand analysis can provide, however, is generally more comprehensive and often significantly lower in cost than the alternatives outlined above.

STATISTICAL ESTIMATION OF THE DEMAND FUNCTION

Effective decision making requires the empirical measurement of economic relationships. For example, when forecasting demand, the manager must have a quantitative estimate of the responsiveness of quantity demanded to changes in variables such as price, income levels, and advertising expenditures. *Econometrics* is a collection of statistical techniques available for empirically measuring such relationships. The principal econometric techniques used in measuring demand relationships are *regression* and *correlation analysis*. The simple (two-variable) linear regression model and the more complex cases of multiple linear regression models and nonlinear models (discussed in Appendix 4A) are developed.

VARIABLE IDENTIFICATION AND DATA COLLECTION: SHERWIN-WILLIAMS COMPANY

Example ·

http://

Sherwin-Williams Company can be found on the Internet:
http://www.sherwin-williams.com/default.asp

Sherwin-Williams Company is attempting to develop a multivariate linear regression demand model for its line of exterior house paints. The company's chief economist feels that the most important variables affecting paint sales (Y) (measured in gallons) are

1. Promotional expenditures (A) (measured in dollars). These include expenditures on advertising (radio, TV, and newspapers), in-store displays and literature, and customer rebate programs.
2. Selling price (P) (measured in dollars per gallon).
3. Disposable income per household (M) (measured in dollars).

The chief economist decides to collect data on the variables in a sample of 10 company sales regions that are roughly equal in population.[3] Data on paint sales, promotional expenditures, and selling prices were obtained from the company's marketing department. Data on disposable income (per capita) were obtained from the Bureau of Labor Statistics. The data are shown in Table 4.1.

Specification of the Model

The next step is to specify the form of the equation, or regression relation, that indicates the relationship between the independent variables and the dependent variable(s). Normally the specific functional form of the regression relation to be estimated is chosen to depict the true demand relationships as closely as possible. Many alternatives and variations may be tried. Because there is often no *a priori* reason for expecting one form to model the true relationship better than another, many variations are usually estimated to obtain the best fit between the data for the dependent and independent variables. A clue to which functional form should initially be tried may be gained by graphing such relationships as the dependent variable over time (when working with time-series data) and each independent variable against the dependent variable. The results of this preliminary analysis often will tell, for example, whether a linear equation is most appropriate or whether logarithmic, exponential, or other transformations are more appropriate.[4]

Table 4.1   Sherwin-Williams Company Data

Sales Region	Sales (Y) (×1,000 gallons)	Promotional Expenditures (A) (×$1,000)	Selling Price (P) ($/gallon)	Disposable Income (M) (×$1,000)
1	160	150	15.00	19.0
2	220	160	13.50	17.5
3	140	50	16.50	14.0
4	190	190	14.50	21.0
5	130	90	17.00	15.5
6	160	60	16.00	14.5
7	200	140	13.00	21.5
8	150	110	18.00	18.0
9	210	200	12.00	18.5
10	190	100	15.50	20.0

(handwritten annotations: Dependent Variable over Sales (Y); Independent over Promotional Expenditures (A); Independent over Selling Price (P); independent over Disposable Income (M))

---

[3] A sample size of 10 observations was chosen to keep the arithmetic simple. Much larger samples are used (when the data are available) in actual applications. The desired accuracy and the cost of sampling must be weighed in determining the optimal sample size to use in a given problem.

[4] See Appendix 4A for a discussion of these transformations. See also any standard econometrics text, such as R.S. Pindyck and D.L. Rubinfeld, *Econometric Models and Economic Forecasts*, 4th ed. (New York: McGraw-Hill, 1999) for additional information concerning some of the alternative functional forms that may be tried.

Linear Model   A linear demand model for Sherwin-Williams paint would be specified as follows:

$$Q = \alpha + \beta_1 A + \beta_2 P + \beta_3 M + \epsilon \qquad [4.1]$$

where α, β_1, β_2, and β_3 are the parameters of the model and ϵ is the error term. The values of the parameters are estimated using the regression techniques described later in the chapter. An error term is included in the model to reflect the fact that the relationship is not an exact one, i.e., the observed demand value may not always be equal to the theoretical value. Based on economic theory, one would hypothesize that price (P) would have a negative impact on gallons of paint sold (Q) (i.e., as the price rises, quantity demanded declines, holding constant all other variables) and that promotional expenditures (A) and income (M) would have a positive impact on paint sales.

The parameter estimates may be interpreted in the following manner. The constant or intercept term, α, has little economic significance in Equation 4.1 because it represents the quantity of paint demanded when all the independent variables (i.e., promotional expenditures, price, and income) are equal to zero. However, if we rearrange Equation 4.1 to solve for price (P), the intercept of the resulting *inverse demand function* identifies the maximum price that can be charged.

The value of each β coefficient provides an estimate of the change in quantity demanded associated with a *one-unit* change in the given independent variable, holding constant all other independent variables. The β coefficients are equivalent to the partial derivatives of the demand function:

$$\beta_1 = \frac{\partial Q}{\partial A}, \quad \beta_2 = \frac{\partial Q}{\partial P}, \quad \beta_3 = \frac{\partial Q}{\partial M} \qquad [4.2]$$

Thus, each independent variable has a *constant marginal impact* on quantity demanded, regardless of the level of the other independent variables (i.e., regardless of the point on the demand curve where it is measured). Note also that the elasticity of demand with respect to each independent variable is *not* constant, but instead varies with the point on the demand curve where it is measured. This can be shown as follows for the price variable. Recall from Chapter 3 that the point price elasticity of demand was defined as

$$E_D = \frac{\partial Q}{\partial P} \cdot \frac{P}{Q} \qquad [4.3]$$

Now substitute Equation 4.2 into this expression to yield

$$E_D = \beta_2 \cdot \frac{P}{Q} \qquad [4.4]$$

Equation 4.4 shows that price elasticity is a function of both price sensitivity and price point positioning.

Linear demand equations have been used extensively in empirical work because of their ease of estimation and the realism with which they approximate many true demand relationships.

Multiplicative Exponential Model   Another commonly used demand relationship is the multiplicative exponential model. In the Sherwin-Williams example, such a model would be specified as follows:

$$Q = \alpha A^{\beta_1} P^{\beta_2} M^{\beta_3} \qquad [4.5]$$

This model is popular because of both its ease of estimation and its intuitive appeal. For instance, Equation 4.5 may be transformed to a simple linear relationship in logarithms (adding an error term) as follows:

$$\log Q = \log \alpha + \beta_1 \log A + \beta_2 \log P + \beta_3 \log M + \epsilon \qquad [4.6]$$

and the parameters $\log \alpha$, β_1, β_2, and β_3 can be easily estimated by any regression package.

The intuitive appeal of this multiplicative exponential functional form is based on the fact that the marginal impact of a change in price on quantity demanded is dependent not only on the price change, but also on the level of promotional expenditures and income.

Demand functions in the multiplicative exponential form possess the useful feature that the *elasticities are constant* over the range of data used in estimating the parameters and are equal to the estimated values of the respective parameters.

In the Sherwin-Williams example again, the price elasticity of demand is defined as

$$E_D = \frac{\partial Q}{\partial P} \cdot \frac{P}{Q} \qquad [4.7]$$

Differentiating Equation 4.5 with respect to price results in

$$\frac{\partial Q}{\partial P} = \beta_2 \alpha A^{\beta_1} P^{\beta_2 - 1} M^{\beta_3} \qquad [4.8]$$

Hence,

$$E_D = \beta_2 \alpha A^{\beta_1} P^{\beta_2 - 1} M^{\beta_3} \left(\frac{P}{Q} \right) \qquad [4.9]$$

Substituting Equation 4.5 for Q in Equation 4.9 and canceling and combining terms where possible yields

$$E_D = \beta_2$$

The property of constant elasticity means that a given percentage change in one of the independent variables, such as price or income, will result in the same proportionate percentage change in quantity demanded at all points on the demand curve. This is a peculiar property of the multiplicative exponential demand function in comparison with the more typical linear demand function. As was shown earlier, the elasticity of a linear function changes over the entire range of the demand curve. However, pricing analysts at Sherwin-Williams may be able to tell us that the percentage change in quantity demanded for either a 10-percent price increase or a 10-percent price cut is a constant 15 percent. If so, a multiplicative exponential demand model is appropriate.

The cautions against extrapolating the results from the estimated equation too far beyond the values of the data used in obtaining the original parameter estimates are just as applicable for the multiplicative or any other specified form of the demand equation as for the linear equation. For example, prior to 1980, the growth in peak electric demand was exponential. Utility companies planned additions to capacity to meet this demand growth. However, this exponential growth relationship ceased to hold after 1980, resulting in massive overbuilding of electric generating capacity and increasing the pressure to restructure the industry to bring the forces of competition to bear on the situation.

WHAT WENT RIGHT   WHAT WENT WRONG

Excess Fiber Optic Capacity at Global Crossing Inc.[5]

By 2002, the capacity of U.S. fiber optic networks to transmit high-speed data and voice signals had outstripped telecom demand so much that 97 percent of the installed capacity in the U.S. was idle "silent fiber." Indeed if all telecom network traffic in the U.S. were routed through Chicago, only one-quarter of that city's fiber optic capacity would be in use. With all this excess capacity in the market, fiber optic network providers like Global Crossing Inc. saw their pricing power collapse. A one-megabyte data connection between New York and Los Angeles that in 1995 had sold for as much as $12,000 per year declined by 2001 to $3,000 and by 2002 to $1,200. As their sales revenue plummeted, fifty telecom network companies sought bankruptcy protection from their creditors.

How did this extreme excess capacity situation develop? On the one hand, innovations in signal compression technology outpaced the growth of the market. Between 1995 and 2003, advances like dense wave divisional multiplexing (DWDM) tech-

nology expanded the transmission capacity of a single strand of fiber optic cable from 25,000 one page e-mails per second to 25 million per second, a thousandfold increase. In addition, however, telecom network providers like Global Crossing and WorldCom were wildly optimistic about the growth of telecom traffic, fueled by the projected growth of the Internet, so they continued to lay additional cable. UUNet, a subsidiary of WorldCom, forecasted that Internet use would continue to double every 100 days. This exponential tenfold growth per year (1000 percent) was an extrapolation of the sales growth UUNet actually experienced in 1995–1996. When the U.S. Department of Commerce and the Federal Communications Commission repeated this forecast, network providers continued to buy and bury redundant fiber optic cable. Between 2001 and 2002, U.S. fiber optic total capacity grew from 8,000 gigabytes per second to 80,000, but by 2003 the growth rate of demand had slowed (from 1000 percent) to only

Figure 4.1

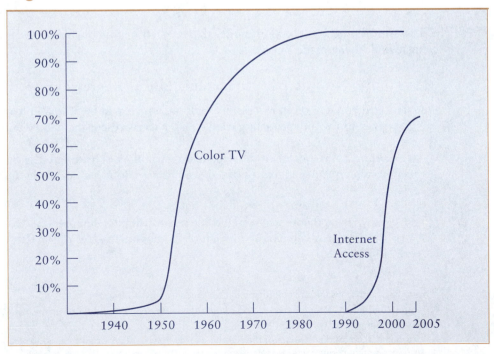

WHAT WENT RIGHT WHAT WENT WRONG

40 percent per year. Their failure to forecast this demand slowdown proved disastrous to Global Crossing and many other network providers.

Much like the adoption of color television, the penetration of the Internet into the American household has followed a classic S-shaped pattern of exponential growth by the early adopters (1994–1996), then linear growth, and eventually fractional growth. This S-shaped penetration curve is drawn in Figure 4.1. It took both color television and the Internet only 8 years (1947 to 1955 for color TVs and 1993 to 2001 for direct Internet access) to reach approximately 60 percent of U.S. households. However, color television adoptions then hit a wall, requiring another thirty years (1955 to 1985) to achieve 98 percent penetration.

Similarly with the Internet, customers who did not adopt early are resistant to adopt now for several reasons: 1) the challenge for aging Americans of learning the user interface is much greater than for turning on a color TV, 2) the Internet is often available at work for some personal use during break time, and 3) there is limited availability of movies and other entertainment through high-speed Internet lines. Consequently, demand growth will likely continue to slow.

---

[5] Based on "Adoption Rate of Internet by Consumers Is Slowing," "Has Growth of the Net Flattened," "Behind the Fiber Glut," and "Innovation Outpaced the Marketplace," *Wall Street Journal*, July 16, 2001, pp. B1 and B8; July 26, 2001, p. B1; and September 26, 2002, p. B1.

SIMPLE LINEAR REGRESSION MODEL

The analysis in this section is limited to the simple case of one independent and one dependent variable, where the form of the relationship between the two variables is *linear*.[6]

$$Y = \alpha + \beta X + \epsilon \qquad [4.10]$$

The simple linear regression model that is used in this problem involves several basic underlying assumptions.

Assumptions Underlying the Simple Linear Regression Model

A standard convention in regression analysis, which will be followed here, is to use X to represent the independent variable and Y to represent the dependent variable.[7]

Assumption 1   The value of the dependent variable Y is postulated to be a random variable, which is dependent on fixed (i.e., nonrandom) values of the independent variable X.[8]

Assumption 2   A theoretical straight-line relationship (see Figure 4.2) exists between X and the expected value of Y for each of the possible values of X. This theoretical regression line

---

[6] Nonlinear relationships are considered in the Appendix for this chapter.

[7] Capitalized letters X and Y represent the *name* of the random variables. Lowercase x and y represent *specific values* of the random variables.

[8] Stochastic (i.e., random) values of the right-hand side independent variable are addressed in Appendix 4A under simultaneous equations relationships.

Figure 4.2   Theoretical Regression Line

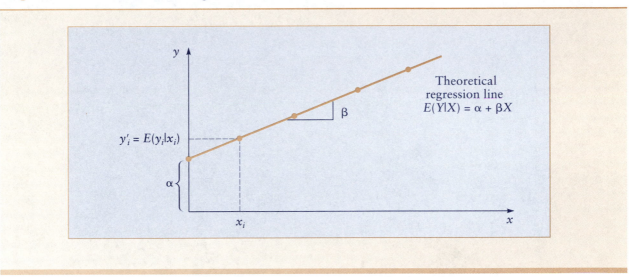

$$E(Y|X) = \alpha + \beta X \qquad [4.11]$$

has a slope of β and an intercept of α. The regression coefficients α and β constitute population parameters whose values are unknown, and we desire to estimate them.

Assumption 3   Associated with each value of X is a probability distribution, $p(y|x)$, of the possible values of the random variable Y. When X is set equal to some value x_i, the value of Y that is observed will be drawn from the $p(y|x_i)$ probability distribution and will not necessarily lie on the theoretical regression line. As illustrated in Figure 4.3, some values of $y|x_i$ are more likely than others, and the mean $E(y|x_i)$ lies on the theoretical regression line. If ϵ_i is defined as the *deviation* of the *observed* y_i value from the theoretical value y_i', then

$$y_i = y_i' + \epsilon_i \qquad [4.12]$$
$$y_i = \alpha + \beta x_i + \epsilon_i$$

or, in general, the *linear regression relation* becomes (as illustrated in Figure 4.4)

$$Y = \alpha + \beta X + \epsilon \qquad [4.13]$$

where ϵ is a zero mean *stochastic disturbance* (or *error*) *term*.

Assumption 4   The disturbance term (ϵ_i) is assumed to be an independent random variable [that is, $E(\epsilon_i \epsilon_j) = 0$ for $i \neq j$] with an expected value equal to zero [that is, $E(\epsilon_i) = 0$] and with a constant variance equal to σ_ϵ^2 [that is, $E(\epsilon_i^2) = \sigma_\epsilon^2$ for all i]. Furthermore, to perform the statistical tests of significance (i.e., *t*-tests and *F*-tests) later in the chapter, we also must assume that the disturbance term (ϵ_i) follows the normal probability distribution.

Together, Assumptions 1 and 4 imply that the disturbance term is expected to be uncorrelated with the independent variables in the regression model.

Figure 4.3   Conditional Probability Distribution of Dependent Variable

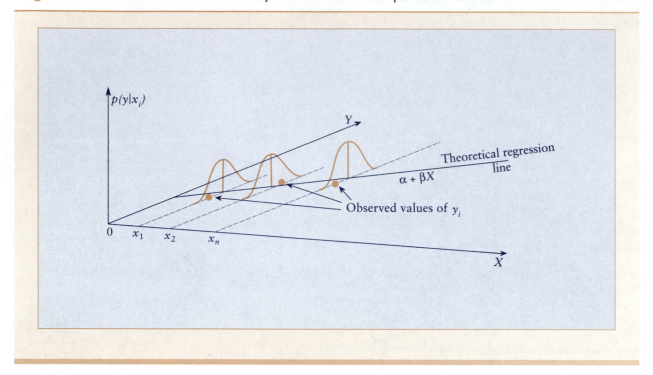

Figure 4.4   Deviation of the Actual Observations about the Theoretical Regression Line

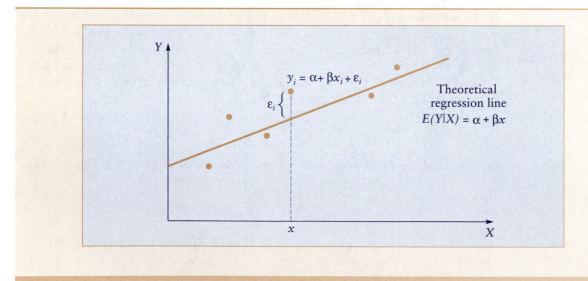

Estimating the Population Regression Coefficients

Once the regression model is specified, the unknown values of the population regression coefficients α and β are estimated by using the *n* pairs of sample observations (x_1, y_1), (x_2, y_2), . . ., (x_n, y_n). This process involves finding a *sample regression line* that best fits the sample of observations the analyst has gathered.

The sample estimates of α and β can be designated by *a* and *b*, respectively. The estimated or predicted value of *Y*, $\hat{y}_i$, for a given value of *X* (see Figure 4.5) is

$$\hat{y}_i = a + bx_i \qquad\qquad [4.14]$$

Letting e_i be the *deviation* of the *observed* y_i value from the *estimated value* $\hat{y}_i$, then

$$y_i = \hat{y}_i + e_i$$

$$= a + bx_i + e_i \qquad\qquad [4.15]$$

or, in general, the *sample regression equation* becomes

$$Y = a + bX + e \qquad\qquad [4.16]$$

Although there are several methods for determining the values of *a* and *b* (that is, finding the regression equation that provides the best fit to the series of observations), the best known and most widely used is the method of *least squares*. The objective of least-squares analysis is to find values of *a* and *b* that *minimize* the sum of the squares of the e_i deviations. (By squaring the errors, positive and negative errors cumulate and do not cancel each other.) From Equation 4.15, the value of e_i is given by

$$e_i = y_i - a - bx_i \qquad\qquad [4.17]$$

Figure 4.5   Deviation of the Observations about the Sample Regression Line

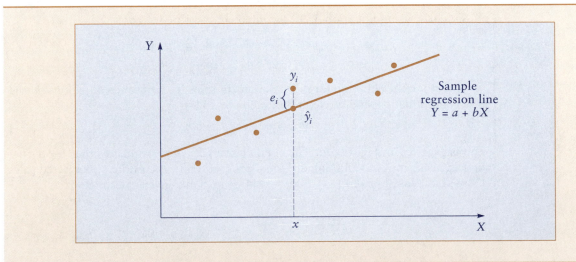

Squaring this term and summing over all n pairs of sample observations, one obtains

$$\sum_{i=1}^{n} e_i^2 = \sum_{i=1}^{n} (y_i - a - bx_i)^2 \qquad [4.18]$$

Using calculus, the values of a and b that minimize this sum of squared deviations expression are given by

$$b = \frac{n\Sigma x_i y_i - \Sigma x_i \Sigma y_i}{n\Sigma x_i^2 - (\Sigma x_i)^2} \qquad [4.19]$$

$$a = \bar{y} - b\bar{x} \qquad [4.20]$$

where $\bar{x}$ and $\bar{y}$ are the arithmetic means of X and Y, respectively (that is, $\bar{x} = \Sigma x/n$ and $\bar{y} = \Sigma y/n$) and where the summations range over all the observations ($i = 1, 2, \ldots, n$).

Example

ESTIMATING REGRESSION PARAMETERS: SHERWIN-WILLIAMS COMPANY (continued)

Returning to the Sherwin-Williams Company example, suppose that only promotional expenditures are used to predict paint sales. Using the notation of the simple linear regression model, Y will be used to represent paint sales and X to represent promotional expenditures. The regression model can be represented by Equation 4.13, discussed earlier. If promotional expenditures are used to predict paint sales in a given metropolitan area, then estimates of α and β must be calculated from the sample data presented earlier in Table 4.1. These data are reproduced here in columns 1–3 of Table 4.2 and shown graphically in Figure 4.6.

The estimated slope of the regression line is calculated as follows using Equation 4.19:

$$b = \frac{10(229,100) - (1,250)(1,750)}{10(180,100) - (1,250)^2}$$

$$= .433962$$

Similarly, using Equation 4.20, the intercept is estimated as

$$a = 175 - .433962(125)$$

$$= 120.75475$$

Therefore, the equation for estimating paint sales (in thousands of gallons) based on promotional expenditures (in thousands of dollars) is

$$Y = 120.755 + .434X \qquad [4.21]$$

and is graphed in Figure 4.6. The coefficient of X (.434) indicates that for a one-unit increase in X ($1,000 in additional promotional expenditures), expected sales (Y) will increase by .434 ($\times$ 1,000) = 434 gallons in a given sales region.

Table 4.2 Worksheet for Estimation of the Simple Regression Equation:
Sherwin-Williams Company

Sales Region (1)	Promotional Expenditures (× $1,000) (2)	Sales (× 1,000 gal) (3)	(4)	(5)	(6)
i	x_i	y_i	$x_i y_i$	x_i^2	y_i^2
1	150	160	24,000	22,500	25,600
2	160	220	35,200	25,600	48,400
3	50	140	7,000	2,500	19,600
4	190	190	36,100	36,100	36,100
5	90	130	11,700	8,100	16,900
6	60	160	9,600	3,600	25,600
7	140	200	28,000	19,600	40,000
8	110	150	16,500	12,100	22,500
9	200	210	42,000	40,000	44,100
10	100	190	19,000	10,000	36,100
Total	1,250	1,750	229,100	180,100	314,900
	Σx_i	Σy_i	$\Sigma x_i y_i$	Σx_i^2	Σy_i^2

$$\bar{x} = \Sigma x_i/n = 1,250/10 = 125$$
$$\bar{y} = \Sigma y_i/n = 1,750/10 = 175$$

Figure 4.6 Estimated Regression Line: Sherwin-Williams Company

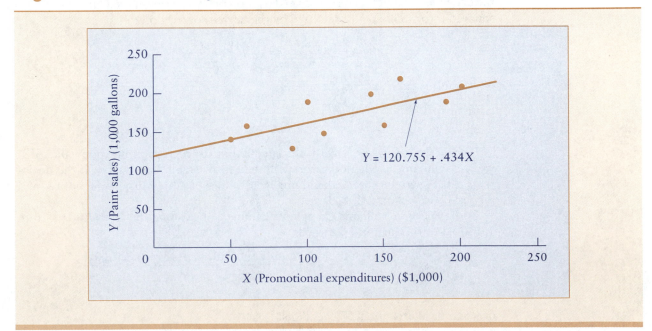

$Y = 120.755 + .434X$

Using the Regression Equation to Make Predictions

A regression equation can be used to make predictions concerning the value of Y, given any particular value of X. This is done by substituting the particular value of X, namely, x_p, into the sample regression equation (Equation 4.14):

$$\hat{y} = a + bx_p$$

where, as you recall, $\hat{y}$ is the hypothesized expected value for the dependent variable from the probability distribution $p(Y|X)$.[9]

Suppose one is interested in estimating Sherwin-Williams' paint sales for a metropolitan area with promotional expenditures equal to $185,000 (i.e., $x_p = 185$). Substituting $x_p = 185$ into the estimated regression equation (Equation 4.21) yields

$$\hat{y} = 120.755 + .434\,(185)$$
$$= 201.045$$

or 201,045 gallons.

Caution must be exercised in using regression models for prediction, particularly when the value of the independent variable lies *outside* the range of observations from which the model was estimated. In many cases the linear relationship is not valid for extremely large or small values of the independent variable. For example, suppose we want to estimate paint sales for a sales region with promotional expenditures equal to $300,000 (i.e., $x_p = 300$). Because this value of X falls well outside of the series of observations for which the regression line was calculated, we cannot be certain that the prediction of paint sales based on the linear regression model would be reasonable. Such factors as diminishing returns and the existence of saturation levels can cause relationships between economic variables to be nonlinear.

Standard Error of the Estimate
The standard deviation of the error term in a linear regression model.

A measure of the accuracy of estimation with the regression equation can be obtained by calculating the standard deviation of the errors of prediction (also known as the **standard error of the estimate**). The error term e_i was defined earlier in Equation 4.17 to be the difference between the observed and predicted values of the dependent variable. The standard deviation of the e_i term is based on the summed squared error (SSE) Σe_i^2 normalized by the degrees of freedom:

$$s_e = \sqrt{\frac{\Sigma e_i^2}{n-2}} = \sqrt{\frac{\Sigma(y_i - a - bx_i)^2}{n-2}}$$

or, when this expression is simplified,

$$s_e = \sqrt{\frac{\Sigma y_1^2 - a\Sigma y_i - b\Sigma x_i y_i}{n-2}} \qquad [4.22]$$

If the observations are tightly clustered about the regression line, the value of s_e will be small and prediction errors will tend to be small. Conversely, if the deviations e_i between the observed and predicted values of Y are fairly large, both s_e and the prediction errors will be large.

In the Sherwin-Williams Company example, substituting the relevant data from Table 4.2 into Equation 4.22 yields

$$s_e = \sqrt{\frac{314,900 - 120.75475(1,750) - .433962(229,100)}{10-2}}$$
$$= 22.799$$

or a standard error of 22,799 gallons.

---

[9] The expected value of the error term (e) is zero, as indicated earlier in Assumption 4.

The standard error of the estimate (s_e) can be used to construct prediction *intervals* for *y*.[10] An *approximate* 95 percent prediction interval is equal to[11]

$$\hat{y} \pm 2s_e \qquad\qquad [4.23]$$

Returning to the Sherwin-Williams Company example, suppose we want to construct an approximate 95 percent prediction interval for paint sales in a sales region with promotional expenditures equal to \$185,000 (i.e., $x_p = 185$). Substituting $\hat{y} = 201.045$ and $s_e = 22.799$ into Equation 4.23 yields

$$201.045 \pm 2(22.799)$$

or a prediction interval from 155.447 to 246.643 (that is, from 155,447 gallons to 246,643 gallons).

Inferences about the Population Regression Coefficients

For repeated samples of size *n*, the sample estimates of α and β—that is, *a* and *b*—will tend to vary from sample to sample. In addition to prediction, often one of the purposes of regression analysis is testing whether the slope parameter β is equal to some particular value β_0. One standard hypothesis is to test whether β is equal to zero.[12] In such a test the concern is with determining whether *X* has a significant effect on *Y*. If β is either zero or close to zero, then the independent variable *X* will be of no practical benefit in predicting or explaining the value of the dependent variable *Y*. When $\beta = 0$, a one-unit change in *X* causes *Y* to change by zero units, and hence *X* has no effect on *Y*.

To test hypotheses about the value of β, the sampling distribution of the statistic *b* must be known.[13] It can be shown that *b* has a *t*-distribution with $n - 2$ degrees of freedom.[14,15] The mean of this distribution is equal to the true underlying regression coefficient β, and an estimate of the standard deviation can be calculated as

$$s_b = \sqrt{\frac{s_e^2}{\Sigma x_i^2 - (\Sigma x_i)^2/n}} \qquad\qquad [4.24]$$

---

[10] An *exact* $(1 - k)$ percent prediction interval is a function of both the sample size (*n*) and how close x_p is to $\bar{x}$ and is given by the following expression:

$$\hat{y} \pm t_{k/2,n-2} s_e \sqrt{1 + \frac{1}{n} + \frac{(x_p - \bar{x})^2}{\Sigma(x_i - \bar{x})^2}}$$

where $t_{k/2,n-2}$ is the value from the *t*-distribution (with $n - 2$ degrees of freedom) in Table 2 of the Statistical Tables (Appendix B) in the back of the book.

[11] For large *n* ($n > 30$), the *t*-distribution approximates a normal distribution and the *t*-value for a 95 percent prediction interval approaches 1.96 or approximately 2. For most applications, the approximation methods give satisfactory results.

[12] The intercept parameter, α, is of less interest in most economic studies and will be excluded from further analysis.

[13] In addition to testing hypotheses about β, one can also calculate confidence intervals for β. See L. Lardaro, *Applied Econometrics* (New York: HarperCollins, 1993), pp. 225–226, for a discussion of the procedures for calculating confidence intervals.

[14] A *t*-test is usually used to test for the significance of individual regression parameters when the sample size is relatively small (30 or less). For larger samples, tests of statistical significance may be made using the standard normal probability distribution, which the *t*-distribution approaches in the limit.

[15] *Degrees of freedom* are the number of observations beyond the minimum necessary to calculate a given regression coefficient or statistic. In a regression model, the number of degrees of freedom is equal to the number of observations less the number of parameters (α and βs) being estimated. For example, in a simple (two-variable) regression model, a minimum of two observations is needed to calculate the slope (β) and intercept (α) parameters—hence the number of degrees of freedom is equal to the number of observations minus two.

where s_e is the standard deviation of the error terms from Equation 4.22.

Suppose that we want to test the null hypothesis:

$$H_0: \beta = \beta_0$$

against the alternative hypothesis:

$$H_a: \beta \neq \beta_0$$

at the k percent level of significance.[16] We calculate the statistic

$$t = \frac{b - \beta_0}{s_b} \qquad [4.25]$$

and the decision is to reject the null hypothesis, if t is either less than $-t_{k/2,n-2}$ or greater than $+ t_{k/2,n-2}$ where the $t_{k/2,n-2}$ value is obtained from the t-distribution (with $n - 2$ degrees of freedom) in Table 2 (Appendix B).[17] Business applications of hypothesis testing are well advised to keep k small (i.e., no larger than 1 percent or 5 percent). One cannot justify building a marketing plan around advertising and retail displays incurring millions of dollars of promotional expense unless the demand estimation yields a very high degree of confidence that promotional expenditures actually "drive" sales (i.e., $\beta \neq 0$).

In the Sherwin-Williams Company example, suppose that we want to test (at the $k = .05$ level of significance) whether promotional expenditures are a useful variable in predicting paint sales. In effect, we wish to perform a statistical test to determine whether the sample value—that is, $b = .433962$—is significantly different from zero. The null and alternative hypotheses are

$$H_0: \beta = 0 \text{ (no relationship between } X \text{ and } Y)$$
$$H_a: \beta \neq 0 \text{ (linear relationship between } X \text{ and } Y)$$

Because there were 10 observations in the sample used to compute the regression equation, the sample statistic b will have a t-distribution with $8(=n-2)$ degrees of freedom. From the t-distribution (Table 2 of Appendix B), we obtain a value of 2.306 for $t_{.025,8}$. Therefore, the decision rule is to reject H_0—in other words, to conclude that $\beta \neq 0$ and that a statistically significant relationship exists between

---

[16] The *level of significance* (k) used in testing hypotheses indicates the probability of making an incorrect decision with the decision rule—that is, rejecting the null hypothesis when it is true. For example, with $H_0: \beta \geq 0$, setting k equal to .05 (i.e., 5 percent) indicates that there is one chance in 20 that we will conclude that an effect exists when no effect is present—i.e., a 5-percent chance of "false positive" outcomes. Medical researchers trying to identify statistically significant therapies that could save lives and research and development (R&D) researchers trying to identify potential blockbuster products worry more about reducing the risk of "false negatives"—i.e., of concluding they have nothing when their research could save a life or a company. Medical and R&D researchers therefore often perform hypothesis tests with $k = 0.35$ (i.e., with 65 percent confidence that the null hypothesis $\beta = 0$ should be rejected). Only 65, not 95, percent of the time will they conclude that $\beta = 0$ when in fact β might well be positive. Ultimately, the question of what significance level to choose must be decided by the relative cost of false positives and false negatives in a given situation.

[17] *One-tail* tests can also be performed. To test $H_0: \beta \leq \beta_0$ against $H_a: \beta > \beta_0$, one calculates t using Equation 4.25 and rejects H_0 at the k level of significance of $t > t_{k,n-2}$, where $t_{k,n-2}$ is obtained from the t-distribution (Table 2 of Appendix B) with $n - 2$ degrees of freedom. Similarly, to test $H_0: \beta \geq \beta_0$ against $H_a: \beta < \beta_0$, one calculates t using Equation 4.25 and rejects H_0 at the k level of significance if $t < -t_{k,n-2}$.

promotional expenditures and paint sales—if the calculated value of t is either less than -2.306 or greater than $+2.306$.

Using Equation 4.24, s_b is calculated as

$$s_b = \sqrt{\frac{(22.799)^2}{180,100 - (1,250)^2/10}}$$

$$= .14763$$

The calculated value of t from Equation 4.25 becomes

$$t = \frac{.433962 - 0}{.14763}$$

$$= 2.939$$

Because this value is greater than $+2.306$, we reject H_0. Therefore, based on the sample evidence, we conclude that at the 5-percent level of significance a linear, positive relationship exists between promotional expenditures and paint sales.

Correlation Coefficient

In correlation analysis we analyze the extent to which high (or low) values of one variable tend to be associated with high (or low) values of the other variable. The measure of the degree of association between two variables is called the *correlation coefficient*. Given n pairs of observations from the population, $(x_1, y_1), (x_2, y_2), \ldots, (x_n, y_n)$, the sample correlation coefficient is defined as

$$r = \frac{\Sigma(x_i - \bar{x})(y_i - \bar{y})}{\sqrt{\Sigma(x_i - \bar{x})^2 \Sigma(y_i - \bar{y})^2}}$$

and, when this expression is simplified, it is calculated as

$$r = \frac{n\Sigma x_i y_i - \Sigma x_i y_i}{\sqrt{[n\Sigma x_i^2 - (\Sigma x_i)^2][n\Sigma y_i^2 - (\Sigma y_i)^2]}} \qquad [4.26]$$

The value of the correlation coefficient (r) ranges from $+1$ for two variables with perfect positive correlation to -1 for two variables with perfect negative correlation. In Figure 4.7, (a) and (b) illustrate two variables that exhibit perfect positive and negative correlation, respectively. Very few, if any, relationships between economic variables exhibit perfect correlation. Figure 4.7 (c) illustrates zero correlation—no discernible relationship exists between the observed values of the two variables. A positive correlation coefficient indicates that high values of one variable tend to be associated with high values of the other variable, whereas a negative correlation coefficient indicates just the opposite—high values of one variable tend to be associated with low values of the other variable.

The Sherwin-Williams Company example discussed earlier can be used to illustrate the calculation of the sample correlation coefficient. Substituting the relevant quantities from Table 4.2 into Equation 4.26, we obtain a value of

$$r = \frac{10(229,100) - (1,250)(1,750)}{\sqrt{[10(180,100) - (1,250)^2][10(314,900) - (1,750)^2]}}$$

$$= .72059 \text{ or } .721$$

Figure 4.7   Correlation Coefficient

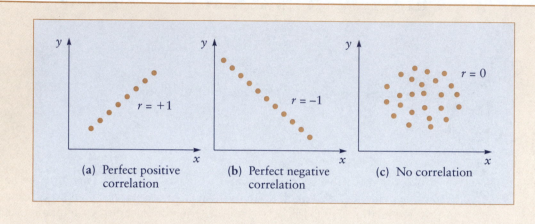

(a) Perfect positive correlation   (b) Perfect negative correlation   (c) No correlation

for the correlation between the sample observations of promotional expenditures and paint sales.[18]

Correlation analysis is useful in exploratory studies of the relationships among economic variables. The information obtained in the correlation analysis can then be used as a guide in building regression models.

The Analysis of Variance

The section entitled "Estimating the Population Regression Coefficients" on page 139 illustrated a method for testing the statistical significance of individual regression coefficients. Now we will examine some techniques for evaluating the overall "fit" of the regression model to the sample of observations.

We begin by examining a typical observation (y_i) in Figure 4.8. Suppose we want to predict the value of Y for a value of X equal to x_i. While ignoring the regression line for the moment, what error is incurred if we use the average value of Y (that is, $\bar{y}$) as the best estimate of Y? The graph shows that the error involved, labeled the "total deviation," is the difference between the observed value (y_i) and $\bar{y}$. Suppose we now use the sample regression line to estimate Y. The best estimate of Y, given $X = x_i$, is $\hat{y}_i$. As a result of using the regression line to estimate Y, the estimation error has been reduced to the difference between the observed value (y_i) and $\hat{y}_i$. In the graph, the total deviation ($y_i - \bar{y}$) has been partitioned into two parts—the unexplained portion of the total deviation ($y_i - \hat{y}_i$) and that portion of the total deviation explained by the regression line ($\hat{y}_i - \bar{y}$); that is,

$$\text{Total deviation} = \text{Unexplained error} + \text{Explained error}$$
$$(y_i - \bar{y}) = (y_i - \hat{y}_i) + (\hat{y}_i - \bar{y})$$

---

[18] Statistical techniques exist for testing whether the degree of correlation within the population is significantly different from zero. See D.R. Anderson, D.J. Sweeney, and T.A. Williams, *Statistics for Business and Economics,* 6th ed. (St. Paul, MN: West, 1997), for a discussion of these techniques.

Figure 4.8   Partitioning the Total Deviation

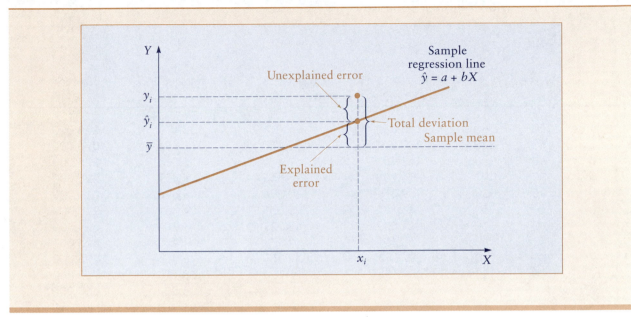

If we decompose the total error of each observation in the sample using this procedure and then sum the squares of both sides of the equation, we obtain (after some algebraic simplification):[19]

$$\text{Total SS} = \text{Unexplained SS} + \text{Explained SS}$$

$$\text{SST} = \Sigma e_i^2 + \text{SSR} = \text{SSE} + \text{SSR}$$

$$\Sigma(y_i - \overline{y})^2 = \Sigma(y_i - \hat{y}_i)^2 + \Sigma(\hat{y}_i - \overline{y})^2 \qquad [4.27]$$

This equation indicates that the total of the squared deviations from the mean, summed over all the observations in the sample, can be partitioned into two independent parts—the Unexplained SS and the Explained SS.

By using this sum-of-squares analysis, we can now illustrate two techniques for evaluating the overall explanatory power of the regression equation. One measure of the fit of the regression line to the sample observations is the sample **coefficient of determination.** The coefficient of determination (r^2) is equal to the ratio of the Explained SS to the Total SS:

Coefficient of Determination
A measure of the proportion of total variation in the dependent variable that is explained by the independent variable(s).

$$r^2 = \frac{X\hat{y}_i - \overline{y}C^2}{Xy_i - \overline{y}C^2} = \frac{\text{SSR}}{\text{SST}} \qquad [4.28]$$

It measures the proportion of the variation in the dependent variable that is explained by the regression line (the independent variable). The coefficient of determination ranges in value from 0—when none of the variation in Y is explained by the regression—to 1—when all the variation in Y is explained by regression.

---

[19] A standard convention in statistics is to let the prefix "SS" represent the "Sum of Squares" as illustrated by SSE, the sum of squared errors.

Table 4.3   Calculation of the Explained, Unexplained, and Total SS for the Sherwin-Williams Company

i	x_i	y_i	$\hat{y} =$ 120.75475 + .433962 x_i	Explained SS $(\hat{y}_i - \bar{y})^2$	Unexplained SS $(y_i - \hat{y}_i)^2$	Total SS $(y_i - \bar{y})^2$
1	150	160	185.849	117.702	668.171	225.000
2	160	220	190.189	230.696	888.696	2,025.000
3	50	140	142.453	1,059.317	6.017	1,225.000
4	190	190	203.208	795.665	174.451	225.000
5	90	130	159.811	230.696	888.696	2,025.000
6	60	160	146.792	795.665	174.451	225.000
7	140	200	181.509	42.373	341.917	625.000
8	110	150	168.491	42.373	341.917	625.000
9	200	210	207.547	1,059.317	6.017	1,225.000
10	100	190	164.151	117.702	668.171	225.000
				4,491.506	4,158.504	8,650.000*
				$\Sigma (\hat{y}_i - \bar{y})^2$	$\Sigma (y_i - \hat{y}_i)^2$	$\Sigma (y_i - \bar{y})^2$

* "Total SS" differs slightly from the sum of "Explained SS" and "Unexplained SS" because of rounding.

Table 4.3 shows the calculation of the Explained, Unexplained, and Total SS for the Sherwin-Williams Company example that was introduced earlier.[20] The Explained SS is 4,491.506 and the Total SS is 8,650.000, and therefore, by Equation 4.28 the coefficient of determination is

$$r^2 = \frac{4,491.506}{8,650.000}$$

$$= .519$$

The regression model, with promotional expenditures as the sole independent variable, explains about 52 percent of the variation in paint sales in the sample. Note also that, in the simple linear regression model, the coefficient of determination is equal to the square of the correlation coefficient, i.e., $r^2 = .519 = (r)^2 = (.72059)^2$.

A second technique for evaluating the explanatory power of the regression equation is an F-test of the sources of variation within the sample data.[21] Using the sum-of-squares framework discussed above, an analysis of variance table is constructed, as shown in Table 4.4. The F-ratio

$$F = \frac{SSR}{SSE/d.f.}$$ [4.29]

---

[20] Only two of the three SS need to be calculated in the manner shown in Table 4.3, because the third SS can be obtained from Equation 4.27 once the other two SS are calculated.

[21] For the multiple linear regression model, the F-test is used to test the hypothesis that *all* the regression coefficients are zero.

then can be used to test whether the estimated regression equation explains a significant proportion of the variation in the dependent variable. The decision is to reject the null hypothesis of no relationship between X and Y (that is, no explanatory power) at the k level of significance if the calculated F-ratio is greater than the $F_{k,1,n-2}$ value obtained from the F-distribution in Table 3 of the Statistical Tables (Appendix B).

An analysis of variance table for the Sherwin-Williams Company example appears in Table 4.4. Forming the F-ratio, we obtain

$$F = \frac{4,491.506}{4,158.5/8}$$

$$= 8.641$$

The comparable value of $F_{.05,1,8}$ from the F-distribution (Table 3 of Appendix B) is 5.32. Therefore, we reject, at the .05 level of significance, the null hypothesis that there is no relationship between promotion expenditures and paint sales. In other words, we conclude that the regression model *does* explain a significant proportion of the variation in paint sales in the sample.

Association and Causation

Based on the finding of a statistically significant regression relationship, one may be tempted to conclude that a causal economic relationship exists—the independent variable being the cause and the dependent variable being the effect. However, *the presence of association (correlation)* does not necessarily imply causation. Statistical tests can establish only whether association exists between the variables. The existence of a cause-and-effect economic relationship can only be inferred from economic reasoning.

An association relationship may not imply a causal relationship for many reasons. First, even a 95-percent statistically significant association between two variables may result from 5-percent pure chance. Second, the association between two variables may be the result of the influence of a third common factor. For example, although per capita expenditures for food and clothing exhibit a close relationship over time, one cannot conclude that increases in food expenditures cause increases in clothing expenditures. The high degree of association between these two variables can be

---

Table 4.4   Analysis of Variance Table for Regression Model

Source of Variation		Sum of Squares	Degrees of Freedom
Regression	$\left(\begin{array}{c}\text{explained}\\\text{variation}\end{array}\right)$	$SSR = \Sigma(\hat{y}_i - \bar{y})^2$ $= 4,491.5$	1
Error	$\left(\begin{array}{c}\text{unexplained}\\\text{variation}\end{array}\right)$	$SSE = \Sigma(y_i - \hat{y}_i)^2$ $= 4,158.5$	$n - 2$
Total		$SST = \Sigma(y_i - \bar{y})^2$ $= 8,650$	$n - 1$

attributed to a third variable—namely, per capita income. As per capita income increases over time, people tend to spend more on both food and clothing. Finally, both variables may be the cause and the effect at the same time. In other words, a simultaneous or interdependent relationship may exist between the variables. One could, for example, hypothesize that a person's income is a function of his or her level of education—the more years of schooling the person has, the higher will be the income. However, one could instead argue that the opposite relationship is also true—namely, that education level is a function of income. A higher income increases the likelihood that a person will be able to afford additional college or professional education.

MULTIPLE LINEAR REGRESSION MODEL

A linear relationship containing two or more independent variables is known as a *multiple linear regression model*. In the (completely) general multiple linear regression model, the dependent variable Y is hypothesized to be a function of m independent variables $X_1, X_2, \ldots, X_m$, and to be of the form

$$Y = \alpha + \beta_1 X_1 + \beta_2 X_2 + \ldots + \beta_m X_m + \epsilon \qquad [4.30]$$

In the Sherwin-Williams Company example, paint sales (Y) were hypothesized to be a function of three variables—promotional expenditures (A), price (P), and household disposable income (M) (see Equation 4.1):

$$Q = \alpha + \beta_1 A + \beta_2 P + \beta_3 M + \epsilon$$

Assumptions Underlying the Multiple Linear Regression Model

In addition to satisfying a set of four assumptions similar to those for the simple linear regression model, the application of the least-squares estimation procedure to the multiple linear regression model requires two further assumptions.

Assumption 5   The number of observations (n) must exceed the number of parameters to be estimated ($m + 1$).

Assumption 6   No exact linear relationships can exist between any of the independent variables. A definitional relationship or identity—for example, cash in the register is equal to initial cash plus receipts—cannot be estimated unless there is some source of randomness in the data. For example, the clerk on duty may commit occasional errors in making change.

Use of Computer Programs

Using matrix algebra, procedures similar to those explained for the simple linear regression model can be employed for calculating the estimated regression coefficients (α and βs) of Equation 4.30, and for testing the statistical significance of the individual independent variables and overall explanatory power of the regression equation. In most practical applications of multiple regression analysis, generalized computer programs are used to perform these procedures.

Although many different programs are available for doing multiple regression analysis, the output of these programs is fairly standardized. The output normally includes the estimated regression coefficients, t-statistics of the individual coefficients, R^2, analysis of variance, and F-test of overall significance. The particular program that is illustrated here is MYSTAT.[22]

Putting the data in Table 4.1 for the Sherwin-Williams Company along with the appropriate control statements into the MYSTAT program yields the output shown in Figure 4.9.

Estimating the Population Regression Coefficients

From the computer output (coefficient column) the following regression equation is obtained:

$$Y = 310.245 + 0.008A - 12.202P + 2.677M \qquad [4.31]$$

The coefficient of the P variable (-12.202) indicates that, *all other things being equal,* a \$1.00 price increase will reduce expected sales by $-12.202 \times 1,000 = 12,202$ gallons in a given sales region.

Using the Regression Model to Make Forecasts

As in the simple linear regression model, the multiple linear regression model can be used to make point or interval forecasts. Point forecasts can be made by substituting

Figure 4.9   Computer Output: Sherwin-Williams Company

Dep var:	SALES (Y)	N: 10	Multiple R:	.889	Multiple R squared:	.790

Adjusted multiple R squared:	.684	Standard error of estimate:	17.417

Variable	Coefficient	Std error	Std coef	Tolerance	T	P(2 tail)
CONSTANT	310.245	95.075	0.000	.	3.263	0.017
PROMEXP (X_1)	0.008	0.204	0.013	0.3054426	0.038	0.971
SELLPR (X_2)	-12.202	4.582	-0.741	0.4529372	-2.663	0.037
DISPINC (X_3)	2.677	3.160	0.225	0.4961686	0.847	0.429

Analysis of Variance

Source	Sum-of-squares	DF	Mean-square	F-ratio	P
Regression	6829.866	3	2276.622	7.505	0.019
Residual	1820.134	6	303.356		

[22] MYSTAT is a product of Systat, Inc., Evanston, IL.

the particular values of the independent variables into the estimated regression equation.

In the Sherwin-Williams example, suppose we are interested in estimating sales in a sales region where promotional expenditures are \$185,000 (i.e., $A = 185$), selling price is \$15.00 (P), and disposable income per household is \$19,500 (i.e., $M = 19.5$). Substituting these values into Equation 4.31 yields

$$\hat{y} = 310.245 + .008(185) - 12.202(15.00) + 2.677(19.5) = 180.897$$

or 180,897 gallons. Whether to include one, two, or all three independent variables in predicting $\hat{y}$ depends on the mean prediction error (e.g., here $185,000 - 180,897 = 4,103$) in this and subsequent out-of-sample forecasts.

The standard error of the estimate (s_e) from the output in Figure 4.8 can be used to construct prediction intervals for Y. An *approximate* 95-percent prediction interval is equal to

$$\hat{y} \pm 2s_e$$

For a sales region with the characteristics cited in the previous paragraph (i.e., $A = 185$, $P = \$15.00$, and $M = 19.5$), an *approximate* 95-percent prediction interval for paint sales is equal to

$$180.897 \pm 2(17.417)$$

or from 146,063 to 215,731 gallons.

Inferences about the Population Regression Coefficients

Most regression programs test whether *each* of the independent variables (Xs) is statistically significant in explaining the dependent variable (Y). This tests the null hypothesis:

$$H_0: \beta_i = 0$$

against the alternative hypothesis:

$$H_a: \beta_i \neq 0$$

The decision rule is to reject the null hypothesis at the k level of significance if the t-value (labeled T) from the computer output ($t = b/s_b$) is either less than $-t_{k/2,n-m-1}$ or greater than $+t_{k/2,n-m-1}$ where the $t_{k/2,n-m-1}$ value is obtained from the t-distribution (with $n - m - 1$ degrees of freedom) in Table 2 (Appendix B).[23]

To test the null hypothesis of no relationship between paint sales (Y) and each of the independent variables at the .05 significance level, we would reject the null hypothesis if the respective t-value for each variable is less than $-t_{.025,6} = -2.447$ or greater than $t_{.025,6} = +2.447$. As shown in Figure 4.9, only the calculated t-value for the P variable is less than -2.447. Hence, we can conclude that only selling price (P) is statistically significant (at the .05 level) in explaining paint sales. This inference might determine that marketing plans for this type of paint should focus on price and not on the effects of promotional expenditures or the disposable income of the target households.

---

[23] Rather than having to look up the $t_{k/2,n-m-1}$ in the table, MYSTAT calculates the significance level at which one can reject the null hypothesis ($\beta_i = 0$). For example, if we are testing the null hypothesis at the $k = .05$ significance level, we would reject the null hypothesis (no relationship between Y and X_i) if the P (2 tail) value from the computer output is less than .05.

The Analysis of Variance

Techniques similar to those described for the simple linear regression model are used to evaluate the *overall* explanatory power of the multiple linear regression model.

The multiple coefficient of determination (r^2) is a measure of the overall "fit" of the regression model. The squared multiple R value of .790 in Figure 4.9 indicates that the three-variable regression equation explains 79 percent of the total variation in the dependent variable (paint sales).

The *F*-value (labeled *F*-ratio in the computer output of Figure 4.9) is used to test the hypothesis that all the independent variables ($X_1, X_2, \ldots, X_m$) together explain a significant proportion of the variation in the dependent variable (Y). One is using the *F*-value to test the null hypothesis:

$$(H_0: \text{All } \beta_i = 0)$$

against the alternative hypothesis:

$$H_a: \text{At least one } \beta_i \neq 0$$

In other words, we are testing whether at least one of the explanatory variables contributes information for the prediction of Y. The decision is to reject the null hypothesis at the k level of significance if the *F*-value from the computer output is *greater* than the $F_{k,m,n-m-1}$ value from the *F*-distribution (with m and $n-m-1$ degrees of freedom). Table 3 (Appendix B) provides *F*-values.

In the Sherwin-Williams example, suppose we want to test whether the three independent variables explain a significant (at the .05 level) proportion of the variation in income. The decision rule is to reject the null hypothesis (no relationship) if the calculated *F*-value (7.505 in Figure 4.9) is greater than $F_{.05,3,6} = 4.76$. Rather than having to look up the $F_{.05,3,6}$ critical value in tables of the *F*-distribution, MYSTAT calculates the significance level at which we can reject the null hypothesis (H_0: All $\beta_i = 0$) and prints the result in the column labeled *P*. Because $F = 7.505$ has a *P*-value of 0.019, we reject the null hypotheses and conclude that the independent variables *are* useful in explaining paint sales with $(1 - 0.019) = 98.1$ percent confidence.

Example

ESTIMATED DEMAND FOR NEW AUTOS[24]

New car registrations of recently purchased autos vary over time in predictable ways. This economic theory reasoning can identify the explanatory variables to include in an empirical model of new car demand. First, any consumer durable demand increases with rising population of the target customer group. Therefore, one must either control for population size as an explanatory variable or, alternatively, divide registrations by population, thereby creating a dependent variable of new car demand per capita, as in Table 4.5. Second, many new car purchases are financed, so minimum cash deposit requirements (Minimum Deposit) and auto financing rates (Interest Rate) are as important as the sale price (Price) in triggering a decision to purchase during one month rather than another. Third, one would expect changes in disposable income (Income) to affect a household's decision to replace its prior car. Higher household income would be associated with increased demand for superior models. Geopolitical events like the OPEC oil crisis with its attendant gas shortages, time-consuming

---

[24] Based on "An Econometric Model of New Car Demand in the UK," *Managerial and Decision Economics*, 7 (1986), pp. 19–23.

queues at the pump, and price spikes should also affect demand since gasoline is the primary complement in consumption of automobiles. Finally, as with other fad items, the introduction of popular new models enhances subsequent purchase decisions, so higher auto sales last period should have a positive effect on additional auto sales this period. These positive lagged effects of past sales should dampen as one gets further away from the product introductions that triggered the initial surge in sales.

Table 4.5 reports the empirical results. These are double log transform models sometimes known as multiplicative exponential models, like Equations 4.5 and 4.6. Thus, the dependent variable and each of the explanatory variables are in logarithms,[25] and therefore the parameter estimates themselves can be interpreted as elasticities—price elasticity of demand, income elasticity of demand, interest rate elasticity of demand, minimum deposit elasticity of demand, etc.

The British researchers who performed this study found, first of all, that market demand for new car registrations per capita was price inelastic (-0.341), suggesting some substantial pricing power for many models. Next, a minimum deposit elasticity of -0.105 means that a 20-percent increase in cash deposit leads to a 2.1-percent decrease in demand (i.e., $0.2 \times -0.105 = 0.021$). As expected, a 50-percent increase in auto financing rates from, say, 6 percent to 10 percent, leads to a 22-percent decline in auto demand (i.e., $0.5 \times -0.436 = -0.22$). Autos appear to be income elastic (1.947) such that a 10-percent increase in disposable income results in a 19.5-percent rise in auto demand. Gas shortages and high prices for the complement gasoline led to a 14-percent reduction in auto demand during the 1974–1975 OPEC oil embargo. Finally, one period lagged demand, New Auto$_{t-1}$, had a significant positive effect on current purchases with the coefficient being between 0 and 1, as expected.[26] Overall, this model explained 96 percent of the time-series variation in new car sales per capita.

[25] There is one exception: the 0/1 Oil Crisis Dummy variable is added to the regression model directly, without taking logs, since the logarithm of zero is equal to negative infinity and is therefore an undefined value in the regression programs.

[26] In contrast, a coefficient greater than 1 (or less than -1) on the lagged dependent variable would imply inherently unstable dynamics of exponentially accelerating demand growth (or decay).

Table 4.5   OLS Estimates of the Determinants of the U.K. Per Capita
Demand for New Autos

Explanatory Variables	Coefficient
Constant	−15.217
	(−5.66)[a]
log Price	−0.341
	(−2.25)[b]
log Minimum Deposit	−0.105
	(−1.78)[c]
log Interest Rate	−0.436
	(−5.31)[a]
log Income	1.947
	(10.94)[a]
Oil Crisis Dummy	−0.146
	(−4.45)[a]
log New Car$_{t-1}$	0.404
	(3.24)[a]
Adjusted R^2	0.965
Durbin-Watson	2.11
F	91.62
N	20

Notes: *t*-statistics in parentheses. Hypotheses tests are one-tailed.
[a,b,c] Statistical significance at the 1%, 5%, and 10% levels, respectively.

SUMMARY

- Empirical estimates of the demand for relationships are essential if the firm is to achieve its goal of shareholder wealth maximization. Without good estimates of the demand function facing a firm, it is impossible for that firm to make profit-maximizing price and output decisions.

- Consumer surveys involve questioning a sample of consumers to determine such factors as their willingness to buy, their sensitivity to price changes or levels, and their awareness of promotional campaigns.

- Focus groups make use of carefully directed discussion among groups of consumers. The results may be influenced by significant experimental bias.

- Market experiments observe consumer behavior in real-market situations. By varying product characteristics, price, advertising, or other factors in some markets but not in others, the effects of these variables on demand can be determined. Market experiments are very expensive.

- Statistical techniques are often found to be of great value and relatively inexpensive as a means to make empirical demand function estimates. Regression analysis is often used to estimate statistically the demand function for a good or service.

- The linear model and the multiplicative exponential model are the two most commonly used functional relationships in demand studies.

- In a *linear* demand model, the coefficient of each independent variable provides an estimate of the change in quantity demanded associated with a one-unit change in the given independent variable, holding constant all other variables. This marginal impact is constant at all points on the demand curve. The elasticity of a linear demand model with respect to each independent variable (e.g., price elasticity and income elasticity) is not constant, but instead varies over the entire range of the demand curve.

- In a multiplicative exponential demand model, the marginal impact of each independent variable on quantity demanded is not constant, but instead varies over the entire range of the demand curve. However, the elasticity of a multiplicative exponential demand model with respect to each independent variable is constant and is equal to the estimated value of the respective parameter.

- The objective of *regression analysis* is to develop a functional relationship between the dependent and independent (explanatory) variable(s). Once a functional relationship (that is, regression equation) is developed, the equation can be used to make forecasts or predictions concerning the value of the dependent variable.

- The *least-squares* technique is used to estimate the regression coefficients. Least squares minimizes the sum of the squares of the differences between the observed and estimated values of the dependent variable over the sample of observations.

- The *t*-test is used to test the hypothesis that a specific independent variable is useful in explaining variation in the dependent variable.

- The *F*-test is used to test the hypothesis that *all* the independent variables (X_1, $X_2, \ldots, X_m$) in the regression equation explain a significant proportion of the variation in the dependent variable.

- The *coefficient of determination* (r^2) measures the proportion of the variation in the dependent variable that is explained by the regression equation (that is, the entire set of independent variables).

- The presence of association does not necessarily imply causation. Statistical tests can only establish whether or not an association exists between variables. The existence of a cause-and-effect economic relationship should be inferred from economic reasoning.

EXERCISES

1. Consider the Sherwin-Williams Company example discussed in this chapter (see Table 4.1). Suppose one is interested in developing a simple regression model with paint sales (Y) as the dependent variable and selling price (P) as the independent variable.

   a. Determine the estimated regression line.

   b. Give an economic interpretation of the estimated intercept (a) and slope (b) coefficients.

   c. Test the hypothesis (at the .05 level of significance) that there is no relationship (that is, $\beta = 0$) between the variables.

   d. Calculate the coefficient of determination.

   e. Perform an analysis of variance on the regression, including an *F*-test of the overall significance of the results (at the .05 level).

f.   Based on the regression model, determine the best estimate of paint sales in a sales region where the selling price is $14.50. Construct an *approximate* 95-percent prediction interval.

g.   Determine the price elasticity of demand at a selling price of $14.50.

2.   In a study of the demand for life insurance, Executive Insurers, Inc., is examining the factors that affect the amount of life insurance held by executives. The following data on the amount of insurance and annual incomes of a random sample of 12 executives were collected.

Observation	Amount of Life Insurance ($\times$ $1,000)	Annual Income ($\times$ $1,000)
1	90	50
2	180	84
3	225	74
4	210	115
5	150	104
6	150	96
7	60	56
8	135	102
9	150	104
10	150	108
11	60	65
12	90	58

a.   Given the nature of the problem, which would be the dependent variable and which would be the independent variable?

b.   Plot the data.

c.   Determine the estimated regression line. Give an economic interpretation of the slope (*b*) coefficient.

d.   Test the hypothesis that there is no relationship (i.e., $\beta = 0$) between the variables.

e.   Calculate the coefficient of determination.

f.   Perform an analysis of variance on the regression, including an *F*-test of the overall significance of the results.

g.   Determine the best estimate, based on the regression model, of the amount of life insurance held by an executive whose annual income is $80,000. Construct an *approximate* 95-percent prediction interval.

3.   The Pilot Pen Company has decided to use 15 test markets to examine the sensitivity of demand for its new product to various prices, as shown in the table on the next page. Advertising effort was identical in each market. Each market had approximately the same level of business activity and population.

a.   Using a linear regression model, estimate the demand function for Pilot's new pen.

b.   Evaluate this model by computing the coefficient of determination and by performing a *t*-test of the significance of the price variable.

c.   What is the price elasticity of demand at a price of 50 cents?

Test Market	Price Charged	Quantity Sold (thousands of pens)
1	50¢	20.0
2	50¢	21.0
3	55¢	19.0
4	55¢	19.5
5	60¢	20.5
6	60¢	19.0
7	65¢	16.0
8	65¢	15.0
9	70¢	14.5
10	70¢	15.5
11	80¢	13.0
12	80¢	14.0
13	90¢	11.5
14	90¢	11.0
15	40¢	17.0

4. In a study of housing demand, the county assessor is interested in developing a regression model to estimate the market value (i.e., selling price) of residential property within his jurisdiction. The assessor feels that the most important variable affecting selling price (measured in thousands of dollars) is the size of house (measured in hundreds of square feet). He randomly selected 15 houses and measured both the selling price and size, as shown in the table below.

Observation i	Selling Price ($\times$ \$1,000) Y	Size ($\times$ 100 ft^2) X_2
1	65.2	12.0
2	79.6	20.2
3	111.2	27.0
4	128.0	30.0
5	152.0	30.0
6	81.2	21.4
7	88.4	21.6
8	92.8	25.2
9	156.0	37.2
10	63.2	14.4
11	72.4	15.0
12	91.2	22.4
13	99.6	23.9
14	107.6	26.6
15	120.4	30.7

a. Plot the data.
b. Determine the estimated regression line. Give an economic interpretation of the estimated slope (b) coefficient.

c. Determine if size is a statistically significant variable in estimating selling price.

d. Calculate the coefficient of determination.

e. Perform an *F*-test of the overall significance of the results.

f. Construct an *approximate* 95-percent prediction interval for the selling price of a house having an area (size) of 15 (hundred) square feet.

5. The supply function for Gooseberry Patch Dolls has been estimated to be

$$Q_s = -35,000 + 4,000P + 2,000T$$

where *T* is a trend variable with a value $T = 0$ during 1990, $T = 1$ during 1991, $T = 2$ during 1992, and so on. *P* is the price per doll and Q_s is the quantity supplied.

In the 1990s, actual price and quantity sold were as follows:

Year	Price	Quantity Sold
1990	$15.00	25,000
1991	14.00	23,100
1992	13.50	22,700
1993	13.20	24,100
1994	12.50	22,700
1995	12.00	23,200
1996	12.00	24,600
1997	11.50	25,700
1998	11.20	25,800
1999	11.00	26,800

a. Plot the supply curves year by year by first letting $T = 0$ for 1990, then setting $T = 1$ for 1991, and so on.

b. On the same graph with the 10 supply curves, plot the actual price and quantity sold data.

c. Estimate the demand function using the preceding data and a simple regression routine. What is the slope of the regression line?

d. What assumptions must you make to be confident about the demand function estimated in part (c)?

6. a. Fill in the missing information (blanks) in the following multiple regression computer output on the next page.

b. Determine which of the variables (if any) are statistically significant (at the .05 level).

c. Determine whether the independent variables explain a significant (.05 level) proportion of the variation in the dependent variable.

DEPENDENT VARIABLE: SALES

VARIABLE	DF	PARAMETER ESTIMATE	STANDARD ERROR	T-RATIO
INTERCEPT	1	_____	1.105	2.205
PRICE	1	−.3750	_____	−1.570
INCOME	1	_____	.140	2.780
ADVERTISING	1	−6.2500	1.950	_____

SOURCE OF VARIATION	DF	SUM OF SQUARES	MEAN SQUARES	
REGRESSION	_____	1187.343	_____	
RESIDUAL	_____	_____	18.625	
TOTAL	25	_____		

R-SQUARE: _____

F-RATIO: _____

7. Cascade Pharmaceuticals Company developed the following regression model, using time-series data from the past 33 quarters, for one of its nonprescription cold remedies:

$$Y = -1.04 + .24X_1 - .27X_2$$

where Y = quarterly sales (in thousands of cases) of the cold remedy

X_1 = Cascade's quarterly advertising (×$1,000) for the cold remedy

X_2 = competitors' advertising for similar products (×$10,000)

Here is additional information concerning the regression model:

$$s_{b_1} = .032 \qquad s_{b_2} = .070$$

$$R^2 = .64 \qquad s_e = 1.63 \qquad F\text{-statistic} = 31.402$$
$$\text{Durbin-Watson } (d) \text{ statistic} = .4995$$

a. Which of the independent variables (if any) appear to be statistically significant (at the .05 level) in explaining sales of the cold remedy?

b. What proportion of the total variation in sales is explained by the regression equation?

c. Perform an F-test (at the .05 level) of the overall explanatory power of the model.

d. How do the results in part (d) affect your answers to parts (a), (b), and (c)?

e. What additional statistical information (if any) would you find useful in the evaluation of this model?

8. The following equation was estimated as the demand function for gasoline (number of observations equals 100, and standard errors are in parentheses):

$$\ln Q = 3.95 - 0.582 \ln P + 0.401 \ln Y - 0.211 \ln P_c$$
$$\qquad\qquad\quad (0.105) \qquad (0.195) \qquad (0.156)$$

where Q = gallons of gas demanded, P = price per gallon of gasoline, Y = income level of consumers, and P_c = an index of the price for automobiles.

a. Interpret the coefficients of the various variables in the preceding demand equation.

b. How much confidence do you have in each of these coefficient estimates?

9. In an article entitled "A Coherence Approach to Estimates of Price Elasticities in the Vacation Travel Market," Taplin reports the following regression equation for vacation leisure travel expenditures in Australia.[27] The dependent variable in the equation (X_1) is dollars spent on vacation travel overseas. The independent variables are household disposable income in dollars per week (Y) and age of household head in years (Z).

$$\log X_1 = -0.6858 + 0.7407 \log Y + 0.6267 \log Z$$
$$(2.181) \qquad\qquad (0.432)$$
$$r^2 = 0.519$$

(*Note: t*-values in parentheses; 8 degrees of freedom.)

a. What interpretation would you give to the coefficient of the Y variable; that is, 0.7407?

b. What interpretation would you give to the coefficient of the Z variable; that is, 0.6267?

c. What conclusions can you draw about the significance of the income variable and the age variable?

d. What interpretation can you give to r^2 from this equation?

10. Moyer Winery is the maker of a high-quality champagne. A linear regression model used to estimate the demand function for Moyer's champagne yielded the following results:

$$Q_D = 10,425 - 2,910P_x + .028A + 11,100P_{op}$$
$$(1,010) \quad (0.004) \quad (3,542)$$

where Q_D = quantity of Moyer champagne demanded

P_x = price of Moyer champagne

A = Moyer Winery advertising in dollars

P_{op} = percentage of the U.S. population over 21 years of age

a. Determine the point price elasticity for prices of $5 and $10, when $A =$ $1,000,000 and P_{op} = .05.

b. Determine the point advertising elasticity at an advertising level of $2,000,000, if price remains at $5 and P_{op} = .05.

c. The standard error for each coefficient is given in parentheses. If you know that the demand function was estimated using 25 observations, can you reject at the 95-percent confidence level the hypothesis that there is no relationship between each of the independent variables and Q_D?

11. General Cereals is using a regression model to estimate the demand for Tweetie Sweeties, a whistle-shaped, sugar-coated breakfast cereal for children. The following (multiplicative exponential) demand function is being used:

$$Q_D = 6,280P^{-2.15}A^{1.05}N^{3.70}$$

[27] John Taplin, "A Coherence Approach to Estimates of Price Elasticities in the Vacation Travel Market," *Journal of Transport Economic Policy* 14 (1980).

where Q_D = quantity demanded, in 10 oz. boxes

$\quad$ P = price per box, in dollars

$\quad$ A = advertising expenditures on daytime television, in dollars

$\quad$ N = proportion of the population under 12 years old

a. Determine the point price elasticity of demand for Tweetie Sweeties.
b. Determine the advertising elasticity of demand.
c. What interpretation would you give to the exponent of N?

12. The demand for gasoline sold by the Black Gold Refining Company has been estimated as

$$Q_B = .22P_B^{-.95}I^{1.4}A_B^{.3}P_C^{.2}P_{op}^{.6}$$

where Q_B = number of gallons of gas sold each month (millions)

$\quad$ P_B = price per gallon charged by Black Gold

$\quad$ I = level of per capita disposable personal income in Black Gold's market area

$\quad$ A_B = dollar amount of advertising expenditures made by Black Gold

$\quad$ P_C = price per gallon charged by competitors

$\quad$ P_{op} = driving age population in Black Gold's market area

a. What interpretation can you give to the exponents of P_B, I, A_B, P_C, P_{op}?
b. Are these values consistent with your expectations?
c. If Black Gold ceased advertising, what would be the impact on demand according to this demand equation? What problem does this illustrate in an interpretation of demand functions?

13. The demand for haddock has been estimated as[28]

$$\log Q = a + b \log P + c \log I + d \log P_m$$

where Q = quantity of haddock sold in New England

$\quad$ P = price per pound of haddock

$\quad$ I = a measure of personal income in the New England region

$\quad$ P_m = an index of the price of meat and poultry

If $b = -2.174$, $c = .461$, and $d = 1.909$,

a. Determine the price elasticity of demand.
b. Determine the income elasticity of demand.
c. Determine the cross price elasticity of demand.
d. How would you characterize the demand for haddock?
e. Suppose disposable income is expected to increase by 5 percent next year. Assuming all other factors remain constant, forecast the percentage change in the quantity of haddock demanded next year.

---

[28] F.W. Bell, "The Pope and the Price of Fish," *American Economic Review* (December 1958).

14. An estimate of the demand function for household furniture produced the following results:

$$F = .0036Y^{1.08}R^{0.16}P^{-0.48} \qquad r^2 = .996$$

where F = furniture expenditures per household

Y = disposable personal income per household

R = value of private residential construction per household

P = ratio of the furniture price index to the consumer price index

a. Determine the point price and income elasticities for household furniture.

b. What interpretation would you give to the exponent for R? Why do you suppose R was included in the equation as a variable?

c. If you were a furniture manufacturer, would you have preferred to see the analysis performed in physical (constant dollar) sales units rather than actual dollar units? If you change F to constant dollar terms, what other variable should you also change?

15. The following demand function has been estimated for product A:

$$Q_A = aP_A^b I^c P_B^d P_{op}^c A_B^f A_A^g$$

where Q_A = quantity of A demanded in units

P_A = price of A

P_B = price of B

I = per capita income

P_{op} = total population

A_A = advertising expenditures for A

A_B = advertising expenditures for B

a. Determine the cross price elasticity between A and B. Determine the price elasticity of A. Determine the income elasticity of A.

b. How would you interpret the values for e, f, and g?

c. If $c = -.8$, what could you say about product A?

d. If $f = -.3$ and $d = .9$, what can you say about products A and B?

16. You wish to design an experiment aimed at estimating the price elasticity of demand for your firm's new Convertible Monster (CONMON) toy. The toy currently sells for $14.95 and is sold exclusively at FloorMart discount stores throughout the country. Design an experiment that will enable you to estimate the price elasticity of demand for these toys at the lowest possible cost to your firm.

17. Consider again the Sherwin-Williams Company example discussed in this chapter (see Table 4.1). Suppose one is interested in developing a multiple regression model with paint sales (*Y*) as the dependent variable and promotional expenditures (*A*) and selling price (*P*) as the independent variables.

   a. Determine the estimated regression line.

   b. Give an economic interpretation of the estimated slope (*b*s) coefficients.

   c. Test the hypothesis (at the .05 level of significance) that there is no relationship between the dependent variable and each of the independent variables.

   d. Determine the coefficient of determination.

   e. Perform an analysis of variance on the regression, including an *F*-test of the overall significance of the results (at the .05 level).

   f. Based on the regression model, determine the best estimate of paint sales in a sales region where promotional expenditures are $80(000) and the selling price is $12.50.

   g. Determine the point promotional and price elasticities at the values of promotional expenditures and selling price given in part (*f*).

18. Executive Insurers, Inc. (see Exercise 2) feels the use of more independent variables might improve the overall explanatory power of the regression model. In the following table, data are shown on two additional variables (age of the executive and number of children) for the random sample of 12 executives, along with the original data from Exercise 2:

Observation	Amount of Life Insurance ($\times$$1,000)	Annual Income ($\times$$1,000)	Age (Years)	Number of Children
1	90	50	34	2
2	180	84	40	4
3	225	74	46	3
4	210	115	63	3
5	150	104	62	4
6	150	96	54	2
7	60	56	31	1
8	135	102	57	3
9	150	104	40	3
10	150	108	42	4
11	60	65	45	2
12	90	58	35	1

   a. Determine the estimated regression equation with the three explanatory variables shown in the table.

   b. Give an economic interpretation of each of the regression coefficients.

   c. Which of the independent variables (if any) are statistically significant (at the .05 level) in explaining the amount of insurance held by executives?

   d. What proportion of the total variation in the amount of insurance is explained by the regression model?

   e. Perform an *F*-test (at the .05 significance level) of the overall explanatory power of the model.

f. Construct an *approximate* 95-percent prediction interval for the amount of insurance held by an executive whose annual income is $90,000, whose age is 50, and who has three children.

19. The county assessor (see Exercise 4) feels that the use of more independent variables in the regression equation might improve the overall explanatory power of the model.

In addition to size, the assessor feels that the total number of rooms, age, and whether or not the house has an attached garage might be important variables affecting selling price. This data for the 15 randomly selected dwellings is shown in the table below.

a. Using a computer regression program, determine the estimated regression equation with the four explanatory variables shown in the table below.

b. Give an economic interpretation of each of the estimated regression coefficients.

c. Which of the independent variables (if any) are statistically significant (at the .05 level) in explaining selling price?

d. What proportion of the total variation in selling price is explained by the regression model?

e. Perform an *F*-test (at the .05 significance level) of the overall explanatory power of the model.

f. Construct an *approximate* 95-percent prediction interval for the selling price of a 15-year-old house having 1,800 square feet, 7 rooms, and an attached garage.

Observation i	Selling Price (×$1,000) Y	Size (×100 ft²) X_1	Total No. of Rooms X_2	Age X_3	Attached Garage (No = 0, Yes = 1) X_4
1	65.2	12.0	6	17	0
2	79.6	20.2	7	18	0
3	111.2	27.0	7	17	1
4	128.0	30.0	8	18	1
5	152.0	30.0	8	15	1
6	81.2	21.4	8	20	1
7	88.4	21.6	7	8	0
8	92.8	25.2	7	15	1
9	156.0	37.2	9	31	1
10	63.2	14.4	7	8	0
11	72.4	15.0	7	17	0
12	91.2	22.4	6	9	0
13	99.6	23.9	7	20	1
14	107.6	26.6	6	23	1
15	120.4	30.7	7	23	1

20. The techniques discussed in this chapter are used by a large number of commercial market research companies, many who provide free information on the Internet. For example, the company Computer Industry Forecasts provides market data on software, peripherals, computers, communications equipment,

and the Internet. The analyses they provide include sales and shipment forecasts, planned purchases, and market shares.

Access the Computer Industry Forecasts Internet site at http://www.info. com. Use these free back issues to perform an economic profile of a sector of the computer industry listed in each issue, such as personal computers. Your profile should include forecast U.S. and worldwide shipments, market share by channel (brand name), and retail sales (for example, subdivided into home, school, and commercial).

CASE EXERCISES

DEMAND ESTIMATION

Early in 1993, the Southeastern Transportation Authority (STA), a public agency responsible for serving the commuter rail transportation needs of a large Eastern city, was faced with rising operating deficits on its system. Also, because of a fiscal austerity program at both the federal and state levels, the hope of receiving additional subsidy support was slim.

The board of directors of STA asked the system manager to explore alternatives to alleviate the financial plight of the system. The first suggestion made by the manager was to institute a major cutback in service. This cutback would result in no service after 7:00 P.M., no service on weekends, and a reduced schedule of service during the midday period Monday through Friday. The board of STA indicated that this alternative was not likely to be politically acceptable and could only be considered as a last resort.

The board suggested that because it had been over five years since the last basic fare increase, a fare increase from the current level of $1 to a new level of $1.50 should be considered. Accordingly, the board ordered the manager to conduct a study of the likely impact of this proposed fare hike.

The system manager has collected data on important variables thought to have a significant impact on the demand for rides on STA. These data have been collected over the past 24 years and include the following variables:

1. Price per ride (in cents)—This variable is designated P in Table 1. Price is expected to have a negative impact on the demand for rides on the system.

2. Population in the metropolitan area serviced by STA—It is expected that this variable has a positive impact on the demand for rides on the system. This variable is designated T in Table 1.

3. Disposable per capita income—This variable was initially thought to have a positive impact on the demand for rides on STA. This variable is designated I in Table 1.

4. Parking rate per hour in the downtown area (in cents)—This variable is expected to have a positive impact on demand for rides on the STA. It is designated H in Table 1.

TABLE 1					
Data on Transit Ridership	**Year**	**Weekly Riders (Y) (×1,000)**	**Price (P) per Ride (Cents)**	**Population (T) (×1,000)**	**Income (I)**	**Parking Rate (H) (Cents)**
	1966	1,200	15	1,800	2,900	50
	1967	1,190	15	1,790	3,100	50
	1968	1,195	15	1,780	3,200	60
	1969	1,110	25	1,778	3,250	60
	1970	1,105	25	1,750	3,275	60
	1971	1,115	25	1,740	3,290	70
	1972	1,130	25	1,725	4,100	75
	1973	1,095	30	1,725	4,300	75
	1974	1,090	30	1,720	4,400	75
	1975	1,087	30	1,705	4,600	80
	1976	1,080	30	1,710	4,815	80
	1977	1,020	40	1,700	5,285	80
	1978	1,010	40	1,695	5,665	85
	1979	1,010	40	1,695	5,800	100
	1980	1,005	40	1,690	5,900	105
	1981	995	40	1,630	5,915	105
	1982	930	75	1,640	6,325	105
	1983	915	75	1,635	6,500	110
	1984	920	75	1,630	6,612	125
	1985	940	75	1,620	6,883	130
	1986	950	75	1,615	7,005	150
	1987	910	100	1,605	7,234	155
	1988	930	100	1,590	7,500	165
	1989	933	100	1,595	7,600	175
	1990	940	100	1,590	7,800	175
	1991	948	100	1,600	8,000	190
	1992	955	100	1,610	8,100	200

The transit manager has decided to perform a multiple regression on the data to determine the impact of the rate increase.

QUESTIONS

1. What is the dependent variable in this demand study?

2. What are the independent variables?

3. What are the expected signs of the variables thought to affect transit ridership on STA?

4. Using a multiple regression program available on a computer to which you have access, estimate the coefficients of the demand model for the data given in Table 1.

5. Provide an economic interpretation for each of the coefficients in the regression equation you have computed.

6. What is the value of the coefficient of determination? How would you interpret this result?

7. Calculate the price elasticity using 1992 data.

8. Calculate the income elasticity using 1992 data.

9. If the fare is increased to $1.50, what is the expected impact on weekly revenues to the transit system if all other variables remain at their 1992 levels?

SOFT DRINKS

Demand can be estimated with experimental data, time-series data, or cross-section data. Sara Lee Corporation generates experimental data in test stores where the effect of an NFL-licensed Carolina Panthers logo on Champion sweatshirt sales can be carefully monitored. Demand forecasts usually rely on time-series data. In contrast, cross-section data appear in Table 2. Soft drink consumption in cans per capita per year is related to six-pack price, income per capita, and mean temperature across the 48 contiguous states in the United States.

QUESTIONS

1. Estimate the demand for soft drinks using a multiple regression program available on your computer.

2. Interpret the coefficients and calculate the price elasticity of soft drink demand.

3. Omit price from the regression equation and observe the bias introduced into the parameter estimate for income.

4. Now omit both price and temperature from the regression equation. Should a marketing plan for soft drinks be designed that relocates most canned drink machines into low-income neighborhoods? Why or why not?

TABLE 2

Soft Drink Demand Data

	Cans/Capita/Yr	6-Pack Price	Income/Capita	Mean Temp.
Alabama	200	2.19	11.7	66
Arizona	150	1.99	15.3	62
Arkansas	237	1.93	9.9	63
California	135	2.59	22.5	56
Colorado	121	2.29	17.1	52
Connecticut	118	2.49	24.3	50
Delaware	217	1.99	25.2	52
Florida	242	2.29	16.2	72
Georgia	295	1.89	12.6	64
Idaho	85	2.39	14.4	46
Illinois	114	2.35	21.6	52
Indiana	184	2.19	18	52
Iowa	104	2.21	14.4	50
Kansas	143	2.17	15.3	56
Kentucky	230	2.05	11.7	56
Louisiana	269	1.97	13.5	69
Maine	111	2.19	14.4	41
Maryland	217	2.11	18.9	54
Massachusetts	114	2.29	19.8	47
Michigan	108	2.25	18.9	47
Minnesota	108	2.31	16.2	41
Mississippi	248	1.98	9	65
Missouri	203	1.94	17.1	57
Montana	77	2.31	17.1	44
Nebraska	97	2.28	14.4	49
Nevada	166	2.19	21.6	48
New Hampshire	177	2.27	16.2	35
New Jersey	143	2.31	21.6	54
New Mexico	157	2.17	13.5	56
New York	111	2.43	22.5	48
North Carolina	330	1.89	11.7	59
North Dakota	63	2.33	12.6	39
Ohio	165	2.21	19.8	51
Oklahoma	184	2.19	14.4	82
Oregon	68	2.25	17.1	51
Pennsylvania	121	2.31	18	50
Rhode Island	138	2.23	18	50
South Carolina	237	1.93	10.8	65
South Dakota	95	2.34	11.7	45
Tennessee	236	2.19	11.7	60
Texas	222	2.08	15.3	69
Utah	100	2.37	14.4	50
Vermont	64	2.36	14.4	44
Virginia	270	2.04	14.4	58
Washington	77	2.19	18	49
West Virginia	144	2.11	13.5	55
Wisconsin	97	2.38	17.1	46
Wyoming	102	2.31	17.1	46

Appendix 4a

Problems in Applying the Linear Regression Model

INTRODUCTION

When the simple linear and multiple linear regression models were discussed in Chapter 4, several assumptions were made about the nature of the relationships among the variables. Questions naturally arise on the applicability or validity of these assumptions in the actual analysis of economic relationships and data. How can we determine if the assumptions are being violated in a given situation? How does the violation of the assumptions affect the parameter estimates and prediction accuracy of the model? What methods (if any) exist for overcoming the difficulties caused by the inapplicability of the assumptions in a given situation?

Econometrics provides answers to some, but not all, of these questions. A thorough treatment of them is beyond the scope of this introductory chapter. The (more limited) objective in this section is to make the reader aware of some of the potential problems that can arise in actual applications of the regression models and to suggest possible techniques for overcoming some of these problems. Some of the problems that may invalidate the regression results include the following:

1. Autocorrelation
2. Heteroscedasticity
3. Specification and measurement errors
4. Multicollinearity
5. Simultaneous equation relationships and the identification problem
6. Nonlinearities

All of these problems are discussed in this appendix.

Autocorrelation

In many economic modeling and prediction problems, empirical data are in the form of a *time series*—a series of observations taken on the variables at different points in time. For example, we may be interested in predicting total (domestic U.S.) television sales by using disposable income as the independent variable. The data used to calculate estimates of the regression parameters (that is, a and b) might consist of a series of yearly (or quarterly) measurements of the number of television sets sold and disposable income for a period of 10 to 15 years. In working with time-series data, a problem known as autocorrelation can arise.

Recall that one of the assumptions underlying the regression model (specifically, Assumption 4) is that the disturbance term e_t must be an independent random variable. In other words, we assume that each successive error, e_t, is independent of earlier and later errors so that the regression equation produces no predictable pattern in the successive values of the disturbance term. The existence of a significant pattern in the successive values of the error term constitutes **autocorrelation.** Successive values of

Autocorrelation
An econometric problem characterized by the existence of a significant pattern in the successive values of the error terms in a linear regression model.

the disturbance term can exhibit either positive or negative autocorrelation. Positive autocorrelation, as shown in Figure 4A.1 (a), is inferred whenever successive positive (or negative) disturbances tend to be followed by disturbances of the *same* sign. Negative autocorrelation, as shown in Figure 4A.1 (b), is inferred whenever successive positive (or negative) disturbances tend to be followed by disturbances of the *opposite* sign.

Negative autocorrelation reflects an undershooting and overshooting process like purchases of storable consumer goods. If a household buys too much breakfast cereal one week, that household will probably buy less than average the next week, and again more than average the following week. Financial market returns can also exhibit such patterns. Returns temporarily above capital market equilibrium values will set in motion arbitrage activity that corrects (perhaps overcorrects) the return back toward the trend.

Positive autocorrelation can result from several factors. One is the existence of cyclical and seasonal variation in economic variables. The overall growth of the economy coupled with business cycles causes most economic time series to have an overall upward trend with periodic upturns and downturns around this trend. Likewise, seasonal patterns can cause weekly, monthly, or quarterly data to rise and fall in a predictable manner each year. Another cause of positive autocorrelation is self-reinforcing trends in consumer purchase patterns, for example, in fashion retailing. If Hermes scarves are in fashion, each successive week of sales data will be further above trend than the previous week until the fad slows and the Hermes look goes out of fashion. Either positive or negative autocorrelation may also result if significant explanatory variables are omitted from the regression equation or if nonlinear relationships exist.

As a safeguard when working with time-series data, the disturbances (e_t values) should be examined for randomness. Statistical tests are also available to check for autocorrelation. One commonly used technique is the Durbin-Watson statistic. It is calculated as follows:[29]

$$d = \frac{\sum_{t=2}^{n}(e_t - e_{t-1})^2}{\sum_{t=1}^{n}e_t^2} \qquad \text{[4.A1]}$$

FIGURE 4A.1   Types of Autocorrelation (Numbers 1, 2, 3, . . . , 10 refer to successive time periods.)

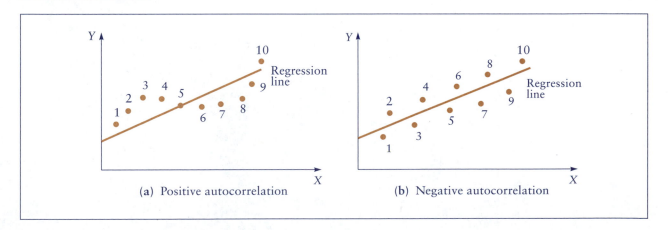

(a) Positive autocorrelation   (b) Negative autocorrelation

[29] Most computer regression programs will compute the Durbin-Watson statistic when specified by the user in the control statements.

where e_t is the estimated error term in period t and e_{t-1} is the error term in period $t - 1$. The Durbin-Watson statistic tests for first-order autocorrelation, that is, whether the error in period t is dependent on the error in the preceding period $t - 1$. The value of d ranges from 0 to 4. If there is *no* first-order autocorrelation, the expected value of d is 2. Values of d less than 2 indicate the possible presence of *positive* autocorrelation, whereas values of d greater than 2 indicate the possible presence of *negative* autocorrelation.

Formal hypothesis tests for first-order autocorrelation can be performed using the d statistic and the Durbin-Watson table (Table 6 in Appendix B). The critical value of d from the table (at the .025 significance level for a one-tail test, that is, a test for positive autocorrelation or a test for negative autocorrelation, or at the .05 significance level for a two-tail test) is a function of both the number of observations (n) and the number of independent variables (m). The decision rules are summarized in Figure 4A.2.

For example, suppose we wish to test for the presence of positive autocorrelation (at the .025 level of significance) in a regression equation with four independent variables (not counting the constant term) estimated from 25 observations. For $m = 4$ and $n = 25$, the values of d_L and d_U are 0.94 and 1.65, respectively (see Table 6, Appendix B). If the calculated d value is less than $d_L = 0.94$, one would *reject H_0* and conclude that there is statistically significant evidence of the presence of positive autocorrelation. If the calculated d value is between 0.94 and 1.65, no conclusion could be drawn concerning the possible presence of positive autocorrelation. Finally, if the calculated d value is greater than 1.65, one would *not reject H_0* and conclude that there is *no* statistically significant evidence of the presence of positive autocorrelation.

FIGURE 4A.2				
		One-tail Tests		**Two-tail Tests***
Testing for the Presence of First-Order Autocorrelation	**Type of Autocorrelation**	**Positive Autocorrelation**	**Negative Autocorrelation**	**Positive and Negative**
	Hypothesis			
	Null	H_0: No Positive autocorrelation	H_0: No negative autocorrelation	H_0: No positive or negative autocorrelation
	Alternative	H_a: Positive autocorrelation	H_a: Negative autocorrelation	H_a: Positive or negative autocorrelation
	Decision Rule			
	Reject H_0	$d < d_L$	$d > (4 - d_L)$	$d < d_L$ or $d > (4 - d_L)$
	Do not reject H_0	$d > d_U$	$d < (4 - d_U)$	$d_U < d < (4 - d_U)$
	Test is inconclusive	$d_L \leq d \leq d_U$	$(4 - d_U) \leq d \leq (4 - d_L)$	$d_L \leq d \leq d_U$ or $(4 - d_U) \leq d \leq (4 - d_L)$
	(No conclusion can be made concerning the possible presence of autocorrelation)			

*Note that for a two-tail test, the significance level is double that shown in Table 6 in Appendix B.

The presence of autocorrelation leads to several undesirable consequences in the regression results. First, although the estimates of α and β will be unbiased, the least-squares procedure will misestimate the sampling variances of these estimates. [An estimator is unbiased if its expected value is identical to the population parameter being estimated. The computed a and b values are unbiased estimators of α and β, respectively, because $E(a) = \alpha$ and $E(b) = \beta$.] In particular, the standard error (s_e in Equation 4.22) will either be inflated or deflated depending on whether we have positive or negative autocorrelation. As a result, the use of the t-statistic to test hypotheses about these parameters may yield incorrect conclusions about the importance of the individual predictor (that is, independent) variables. Second, overall measures of the fit and explanatory power of the regression model, such as the coefficient of determination (r^2) and F-test, will no longer provide reliable information about the significance of the economic relationships obtained. Finally, the use of the regression equation for prediction purposes will yield predictions with unnecessarily large sampling variances.

Several procedures are available for dealing with autocorrelation.[30] If one can determine the functional form of the dependence relationship in the successive values of the residuals, then the original variables can be transformed by a lag structure to remove this pattern. Another technique that may help to reduce autocorrelation is to include a new linear trend or time variable in the regression equation.[31] A third procedure is to calculate the first differences in the time series of each of the variables (that is, $Y_{t+1} - Y_t$, $X_{1,t+1} - X_{1,t}$, $X_{2,t+1} - X_{2,t}$, and so on) and then calculate the regression equation using these transformed variables. A fourth method is to include additional variables of the form X_1^2 or $X_1 X_2$ in the regression equation. Usually one of these procedures will yield satisfactory results consistent with the independent errors assumption.

Heteroscedasticity

In developing the ordinary least-squares regression model, another of the assumptions (Assumption 4) is that the error terms have a constant variance. In other words, we assume that the observations have uniform variability about the theoretical regression line. This property is referred to as *homoscedasticity*. Departure from this assumption is known as **heteroscedasticity,** which is indicated whenever there is a systematic relationship between the absolute magnitude of the error term and the magnitude of one (or more) of the independent variables. Graphic or tabular comparisons between the absolute values of disturbance terms and the values of each of the independent variables will help to detect the existence of significant heteroscedasticity.

The presence of heteroscedasticity causes the estimate of the variance of the error terms (s_e) to be dependent on the particular set of values of the independent variables that was chosen. Another set of observations may yield a much different estimate of this variance. As a result, tests of the statistical significance of the individual regression coefficients (the t-test) and overall explanatory power of the regression equation (the F-test, r^2) may prove to be misleading.

One form of heteroscedasticity occurs when the variance of the error term increases with the size of the independent variable, such as in the case illustrated in Figure 4A.3.

Heteroscedasticity
An econometric problem characterized by the lack of a uniform variance of the error terms about the regression line.

[30] See R. Pindyck and D. Rubinfeld, *Econometric Models and Econometric Forecasting* (Boston, MA: Irwin/McGraw-Hill, 1998) for a much more detailed discussion of procedures for dealing with autocorrelation.

[31] A linear trend variable is one in which each observation in the time series is given a successively larger integer value, such as 1, 2, 3, . . . , n, when n is the number of observations.

FIGURE 4A.3

Illustration of
Heteroscedasticity

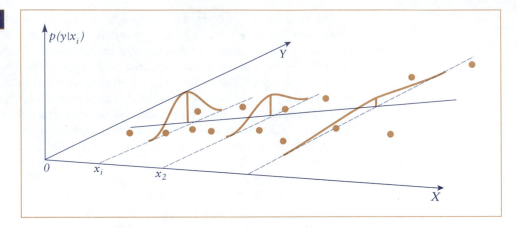

For example, consider a regression model in which savings by households is postulated to be a function of household income. In this case it is likely that more variability will be found in the savings of high-income households compared with low-income households simply because high-income households have more money available for potential savings. Another example arising frequently with cross-sectional sales data is that the error variance with large-size retail stores, divisions, or firms exceeds the error variance for smaller entities. In many cases this form of heteroscedasticity can be reduced or eliminated by dividing all the variables in the regression equation by the independent variable that is thought to be causing the heteroscedasticity and then applying the least-squares analysis to the resulting set of transformed variables. This transformation, however, *does* alter the form of the hypothesized relationship among the variables and thus may be inappropriate in some situations. Another method for dealing with heteroscedasticity is to take logarithms of the data. Again, this transformation alters the form of the hypothesized relationship among the variables. More advanced, generalized least-squares techniques can account for the nonuniform error variance and preserve the original, hypothesized relationship.

Specification and Measurement Errors

Specification errors can result whenever one or more significant explanatory variables are not included in the regression equation. If the omitted variable is moderately or highly correlated with one of the explanatory variables included in the regression equation, then the effect of the missing variable will be represented in the coefficient (b value) of the included variable. This may lead to overestimating or underestimating the economic effect of the explanatory variable included in the regression equation, that is, a bias in the least-squares estimates of the theoretical regression coefficients (α, β). Even if the missing variable is independent of (that is, uncorrelated with) all the other explanatory variables included in the regression equation, then the effect of the omitted variable will be to increase the magnitude of the residual errors and the resulting estimated standard deviation of the residuals (s_e). The omission of a significant explanatory variable from a time series regression equation (e.g., a time trend) may also produce autocorrelation problems.[32]

---

[32] Inclusion of irrelevant explanatory variables has a similar effect on the standard error of the residuals (s_e).

The formulation of a correctly specified model must therefore occupy a prominent role in the estimation of any economic relation. Sometimes relevant variables must be omitted because the estimation is supporting decisions that must be taken prior to complete data availability. When this occurs, a close proxy variable is often available and should be substituted for the omitted variable. The closer the proxy, the better the estimation. When no proxy is available, the direction of bias in the estimated parameters should be diagnosed. The misestimated parameter for X_1 (b_1) may be written as the sum of the true parameter (β_1) plus the effect of the omitted variable j,

$$b_1 = \beta_1 + \beta_j r_{1,j} \qquad\qquad [4.A2]$$

If one knows that the likely sign of the correlation coefficient between the omitted variable and the included explanatory variable ($r_{1,j}$) is positive, and if the hypothesized effect of the omitted variable on the dependent variable (β_j) is positive, the estimated parameter will be positively biased. For example, omitting household income from a demand estimation of luxury car rentals is likely to positively bias the parameter on the price variable, since higher income and the price paid for a luxury car for a week are probably positively correlated and since household income itself is hypothesized to be a positive determinant of luxury car rentals. On the other hand, if the likely correlation between the omitted and the explanatory variable is negative or the hypothesized effect of the omitted variable on the dependent variable is negative, the estimated parameter will be negatively biased. In the Sherwin-Williams paint demand data, the correlation coefficient between disposable income and price is -0.514 (see Figure 4A.4). Omitting DISPINC from that demand estimation in Figure 4.9 would lead to a negative bias in the estimated effect of price on sales. Although these diagnoses of the omitted variable bias can never replace a fully and correctly specified model, they do allow much more informed decision making based on incomplete data.

The estimation of the parameters of the regression equation requires that a series of measurements be made on both the dependent and independent variables that are to be included in the relationship. Despite the many precautions taken, errors in the measurement of economic variables can arise. For example, the values of many economic variables (such as unemployment, GNP, and prices) are obtained from samples, and sampling error is inherent in the data. Also, data based on a complete census of the population can contain errors caused by missing observations, interviewer biases, recording errors, and so forth. Finally, proxy variables always introduce some measurement error. Measurement errors in the dependent variable do not affect the validity of the assumptions underlying the regression model or the parameter estimates obtained by the least-squares procedure because these errors become part of the overall residual or unexplained error. However, measurement error in the explanatory variables introduces a stochastic component in the Xs and may cause the values of the error term e_i to be correlated with the observed values of these explanatory variables. Consequently, the assumption that the disturbance terms are independent random variables (Assumption 4) is violated, and the resulting least-squares estimates of the regression coefficients (α, β) are biased.

Simultaneous equation estimation techniques discussed in a later section are one method of dealing with stochastic explanatory variables. Measurement error can also be modeled, if the form of the error in the X variables can be specified.[33]

---

[33] See Lardaro, *Applied Econometrics,* for some suggested procedures for overcoming the problems presented by measurement error.

	SALES Y	PROMEXP X_1	SELLPR X_2	DISPINC X_3
SALES Y	1.000			
PROMEXP X_1	0.721	1.000		
SELLPR X_2	−0.866	−0.739	1.000	
DISPINC X_3	0.615	0.710	−0.514	1.000

Multicollinearity

Whenever a high degree of intercorrelation exists among some or all of the explanatory variables in the regression equation, it becomes difficult to determine the separate influences of each of the explanatory variables on the dependent variable because the standard deviations (s_b) of their respective regression coefficients become large. Whenever two or more explanatory variables are highly correlated (or collinear), the t-test is no longer a reliable indicator of the statistical significance of the individual explanatory variables. Under such a condition, the least-squares procedure tends to yield highly unstable estimates of the regression coefficients from one sample to the next. The presence of **multicollinearity**, however, does not necessarily invalidate the use of the regression equation for prediction purposes. Provided that the intercorrelation pattern among the explanatory variables persists into the future, the equation can produce reliable forecasts of the value of the dependent variable.

A number of techniques exist for dealing with multicollinearity. One technique is to alter the model by removing all but one of the set of highly intercorrelated variables. For example, consider the variables that were used to explain paint sales in the Sherwin-Williams example discussed earlier. The correlation coefficients between each of the variables are shown in Figure 4A.4. The correlation coefficients between each of the possible pairs of explanatory (independent) variables are shown in the enclosed area of the table. Note the high degree of intercorrelation (in absolute value terms) between promotional expenditures and selling price and between promotional expenditures and disposable income, indicating that the standard deviations of the estimates of these three regression coefficients may be inflated. Therefore, the analyst may want to consider dropping one of these variables from the regression.[34]

When working with time-series data, another technique is to use cross-sectional data to obtain independent estimates of some of the regression parameters. Finally, the elimination of trends, through deflation procedures such as using a trend variable or first differences, will often reduce the multicollinearity problem.

Simultaneous Equation Relationships and the Identification Problem

Many economic relationships are characterized by simultaneous interactions. For example, recognition of simultaneous relationships is at the heart of marketing plans. The optimal advertising expenditure for a product line like Hanes Her Way hosiery depends on sales (i.e., on the quantity Hanes expects to sell). However, sales obviously also depend on advertising; a particularly effective ad campaign that just happens

Multicollinearity
An econometric problem characterized by a high degree of intercorrelation among some or all of the explanatory variables in a regression equation.

---

[34] The analyst must carefully observe the effect of this procedure on the other parameters, however, because removing a partially collinear but relevant explanatory variable introduces omitted variable bias into the estimation.

to match a random swing in customer fashion will drive sales substantially upward. And this sales boost will increase spending on advertising. Sales (i.e., demand) and advertising are simultaneously determined.

In attempting to estimate the parameters of simultaneous equation relationships with single equation models, one encounters the **identification problem.** For example, in developing demand functions from empirical data, one is faced with the simultaneous relationship between the demand function and the supply function. Suppose demand can be written as a function of price (P), income (M), and a random error ϵ_1,

Identification Problem
A difficulty encountered in empirically estimating a demand function by regression analysis. This problem arises from the simultaneous relationship between two functions, such as supply and demand.

$$Q_d = \beta_1 + \beta_2 P + \beta_3 M + \epsilon_1 \qquad [4A.3]$$

and supply can be written as a function of price, input costs (I), and a random error ϵ_2,

$$Q_s = \alpha_1 + \alpha_2 P + \alpha_3 I + \epsilon_2 \qquad [4A.4]$$

or, rearranging,

$$P = \frac{-\alpha_1}{\alpha_2} + \frac{1}{\alpha_2}(Q_s - \epsilon_2) - \frac{\alpha_3}{\alpha_2} I \qquad [4A.5]$$

Since quantity demanded will equal quantity supplied in market-clearing equilibrium (i.e., $Q_d = Q_s$), we can substitute Equation 4A.3 for Q_s in 4A.5 to obtain

$$P = \frac{-\alpha_1}{\alpha_2} + \frac{1}{\alpha_2}(\beta_1 + \beta_2 P + \beta_3 M + \epsilon_1 - \epsilon_2) - \frac{\alpha_3}{\alpha_2} I \qquad [4A.6]$$

$$P = \frac{1}{\alpha_2 - \beta_2}(-\alpha_1 + \beta_1 + \beta_3 M + \epsilon_1 - \epsilon_2 - \alpha_3 I). \qquad [4A.7]$$

The price variable in this rearranged supply function, Equation 4A.7, is quite obviously a stochastic explanatory variable; observed values of P will be correlated with the disturbance term in the demand function ϵ_1. An ordinary least-squares regression of Equation 4A.3 therefore violates Assumption 4 that disturbance terms must be independent of the Xs—i.e., $E(P_i \epsilon_i) = 0$. As a result, the price coefficient in Equation 4A.3 (β_2) will be biased.

To see the problem this poses when estimating the shape of an empirical demand function, note that one may observe only one actual price-output combination at any point in time. If one sought to estimate the demand curve for computer memory chips, one might observe historical data on quantity bought (sold) and the price at a specific time. A next step would be to plot these data on a graph, as shown in Figure 4A.5. Is the line DD', drawn by connecting the four observed price-output combinations, equivalent to the demand curve for memory chips? Usually not. Although it does have the traditional negative slope of a demand curve, one cannot conclude that it represents the true demand-price relationship.

To see why this is so, recall that the price-output combinations actually observed result from an interaction of the supply and demand curves at a point in time. This is illustrated in Figure 4A.6. If $D_1, D_2, D_3,$ and D_4 represent the true demand curves at four different points in time and $S_1, S_2, S_3,$ and S_4 the corresponding supply curves, one would have been seriously misled to conclude that the true demand relationship was depicted by DD' and was generally inelastic, when in fact demand was quite elastic and shifting (as was the supply curve). During the four successive time periods in which price-output combinations were observed, both the demand and supply curves had shifted. Recall from Chapter 3 that to obtain a true estimate of the actual demand curve, one must hold constant the effects of all other variables in the demand functions, allowing only price and quantity demanded to vary.

FIGURE 4A.5

Quantity of Computer
Memory Chips
Purchased (Sold)

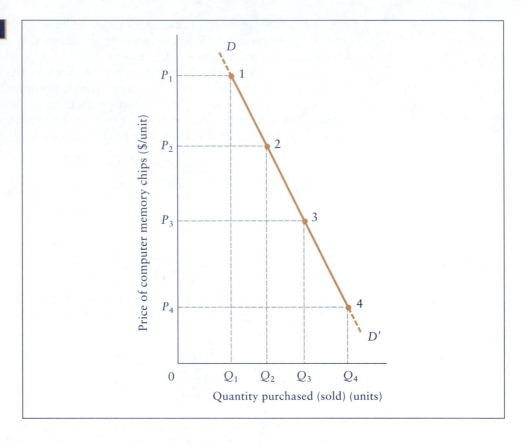

FIGURE 4A.6

Quantity of Computer
Memory Chips
Purchased (Sold) with
Shifting Supply and
Demand

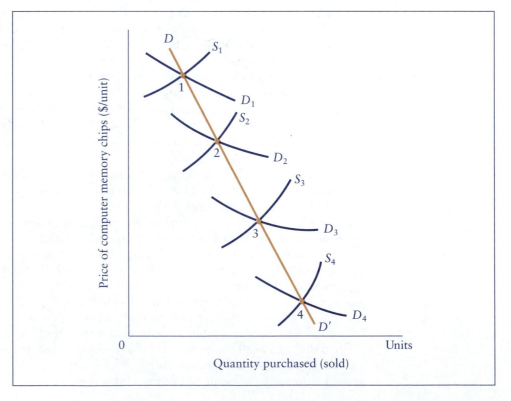

Under what circumstances may valid empirical estimates of the demand curve be made? If both curves retain their original shape and position from one time period to the next, nothing can be learned of the true demand curve because all observed price-output combinations will coincide, or at least be closely clustered. If, however, the supply curve shifts but the demand curve remains constant, observed price-output combinations will trace out the true demand curve. This is illustrated in Figure 4A.7. If, for example, technological advances were being introduced in the production of computer memory chips during Periods 1, 2, 3, and 4, then the supply curve would shift downward and to the right, from S_1 to S_4, tracing out the actual demand curve.

A final possibility is that both curves have shifted during the time period under consideration, but one has enough information to *identify* how each curve has shifted. When simultaneous relationships such as this occur, the ordinary least-squares (OLS) curve-fitting techniques discussed earlier in this chapter may very well *break down and yield results that bear little or no relationship to the actual equation being sought.* Separating the effects of simultaneous relationships in demand analysis requires that more than just price-output data be available. In other words, other variables, such as income and advertising which may cause a shift in the demand function, must also be included in the model. Alternative statistical estimation techniques, such as two-stage least-squares (2SLS), must often be used to separate supply curve shifts from shifts in the demand curve.[35]

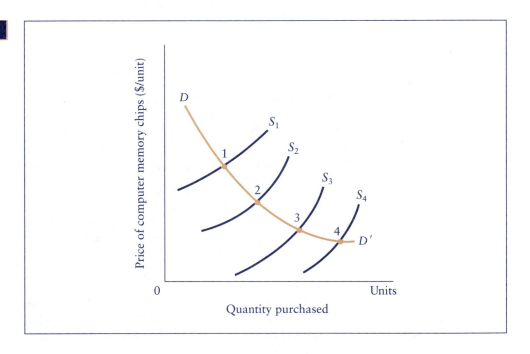

FIGURE 4A.7

Quantity of Computer Memory Chips Purchased (Sold) with Stable Demand and Shifting Supply

[35] A discussion of these alternative estimation procedures is beyond the scope of this book. The reader is referred to R. Pindyck and D. Rubinfeld, *Econometric Methods and Forecasting*, 3rd ed., Chapter 12 (Boston, MA: Irwin/McGraw-Hill, 1998), for a further discussion of the identification problem and alternative estimation techniques. See also Ernst R. Berndt, *The Practice of Econometrics: Classic and Contemporary* (Reading, MA: Addison-Wesley Publishing Company, 1991), especially Chapter 8.

NONLINEAR REGRESSION MODELS

Although the relationships among many economic variables can be satisfactorily represented using a linear regression model, situations do occur in which a nonlinear model is clearly required to portray adequately the relationship over the relevant range of observations. For example, many economic time series tend to exhibit a constant percentage rate of growth and thus yield a nonlinear relationship when plotted against time.

Various models are available to deal with these situations. Through an appropriate transformation of the variables in the model, the standard linear regression procedures can be used to estimate the values of the parameters of these models. The transformations that are discussed here include the semilogarithmic transformation, the double-log transformation, reciprocal transformation, and polynomial transformations. These transformations normally can be handled with an appropriate instruction to the regression analysis computer program.

Semilogarithmic Transformation

Sometimes, the relationship between one or more of the independent variables and the dependent variable can be estimated best by taking the logarithm of one or more of the independent variables.[36] This transformation is often useful when problems of heteroscedasticity exist with respect to one of the independent variables. For example, cross-section regression models, which use firm size as one of the independent variables, often take the log of firm size because of the potential problems caused by including in the same equation firms of $10 million in assets with firms of $10 billion in assets.

A semilog transformation is of the form

$$Y = a + b \log S + cX + dZ \qquad \text{[4A.8]}$$

where Y is the dependent variable, X and Z are independent variables expressed in a normal form, and $\log S$ is an independent variable expressed in a logarithmic form. Standard least-squares techniques can be used to estimate Equation 4A.8.

Double-Log Transformation

In Chapter 4, we saw that a multiplicative exponential model (see Equation 4.5 and Table 4.5) is often used in demand studies. Likewise, as will be seen later in Chapter 7, such models are useful for relating the quantities of various inputs used in a production process to the quantity of output obtained. A three-variable exponential regression function can be represented as

$$Z = AV^{\beta_1}W^{\beta_2} \qquad \text{[4A.9]}$$

where V and W are the explanatory variables; A, β_1, and β_2 are the parameters to be estimated. Multiplicative exponential functions such as these can be transformed to linear relationships. In Equation 4A.9, taking logarithms of both sides of the equation yields

$$\log Z = \log A + \beta_1 \log V + \beta_2 \log W$$

---

[36] It is possible to transform many, but not all, nonlinear forms into a linear expression.

By defining the following transformations: $Y = \log Z$, $\alpha = \log A$, $X_1 = \log V$, $X_2 = \log W$, and adding an error term ϵ, the following multiple linear regression model is obtained:

$$Y = \alpha + \beta_1 X_1 + \beta_2 X_2 + \epsilon$$

Again, least-squares procedures can be used to estimate these regression coefficients.

CONSTANT ELASTICITY DEMAND: PEPSI

Example

If the data on soft drinks in Case Exercise 2 at the end of Chapter 4 (see Table 2) represent firm-level unit sales, marketing analysts in the company (PepsiCo, Inc.) may confirm that price elasticity coefficients have been very similar at several price points in recent years. If the same results of nearly-constant elasticity estimates have arisen from detailed studies of income elasticity in upper- and lower-income neighborhoods, then a demand specification like Equation 4A.9 and a double-log estimation of the data in Table 2 would be indicated. Results of such an estimation are listed below:

$$\text{Log } Q = 0.3986 - 3.196 \text{ LogPrice} + 0.221 \text{ LogIncome} + 1.119 \text{ LogTemperature}$$

$$(0.43) \qquad (4.92) \qquad\qquad (1.19) \qquad\qquad\qquad (4.23)$$

$$SSE = 0.111 \qquad R^2 = 0.671$$

Numbers in parentheses are *t*-score statistics.

Reciprocal Transformation

Another transformation, which is useful in relationships that exhibit an asymptotic behavior, is the reciprocal transformation. The two possible cases are shown in Figure 4A.1. In Figure 4A.8 (a) the relationship is of the form

$$Y = \alpha + \frac{\beta}{Z} \qquad\qquad [4A.10]$$

and in Figure 4A.8 (b) it is of the form

$$Y = \alpha - \frac{\beta}{Z} \qquad\qquad [4A.11]$$

FIGURE 4A.8

Reciprocal
Transformations

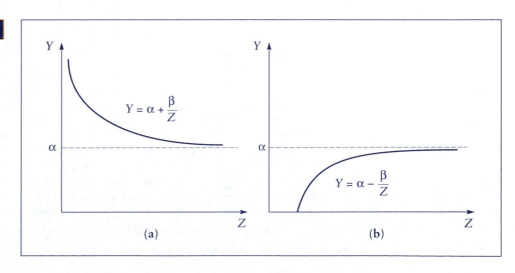

Defining the transformation $X = 1/Z$, Equations 4A.10 and 4A.11 yield the following respective simple linear regression models:

$$Y = \alpha + \beta X + \epsilon$$

and

$$Y = \alpha - \beta X + \epsilon$$

whose parameters can be estimated by the usual least-squares procedures.

Polynomial Transformation

As will be seen in Chapter 8, the cost-output function for a firm is often postulated to follow a quadratic or cubic pattern. This type of relationship can be represented by means of a *polynomial function*. For example, a third-degree (that is, cubic) polynomial function can be represented as

$$Y = \alpha + \beta_1 Z + \beta_2 Z^2 + \beta_3 Z^3 \qquad [4A.12]$$

Letting $X_1 = Z$, $X_2 = Z^2$, $X_3 = Z^3$, Equation 4A.12 can be transformed into the following multiple linear regression model:

$$Y = \alpha + \beta_1 X_1 + \beta_2 X_2 + \beta_3 X_3$$

Standard least-squares procedures can be used in estimating the parameters of this model.

The transformations discussed illustrate the possibilities that are available to the model builder. These various transformations may, of course, be combined and used in the same equation. Further discussions of these and other more complex transformations are found in most econometrics books.

SUMMARY

- Various methodological problems can occur when applying the single-equation linear regression model. These include autocorrelation, heteroscedasticity, specification and measurement errors, multicollinearity, simultaneous equation relationships, and nonlinearities. Many of these problems can invalidate the regression results. In some cases, methods are available for detecting and overcoming these problems.

- Because of the simultaneous equation relationship that exists between the demand function and the supply function in determining the market-clearing price and quantity, analysts must exercise great care when estimating and interpreting empirical demand functions.

EXERCISES

1. Suppose an appliance manufacturer is doing a regression analysis, using quarterly *time-series* data, of the factors affecting its sales of appliances. A regression equation was estimated between appliance sales (in dollars) as the dependent variable and disposable personal income and new housing starts as the independent variables. The statistical tests of the model showed large t-values for both independent variables, along with a high r^2 value. However, analysis of the residuals indicated that substantial autocorrelation was present.

   a. What are some of the possible causes of this autocorrelation?

b.   How does this autocorrelation affect the conclusions concerning the significance of the individual explanatory variables and the overall explanatory power of the regression model?

c.   Given that a person uses the model for forecasting future appliance sales, how does this autocorrelation affect the accuracy of these forecasts?

d.   What techniques might be used to remove this autocorrelation from the model?

2.   Suppose the appliance manufacturer discussed in Exercise 1 also developed another model, again using time-series data, where appliance sales was the dependent variable and disposable personal income and retail sales of durable goods were the independent variables. Although the r^2 statistic is high, the manufacturer also suspects that serious multicollinearity exists between the two independent variables.

a.   In what ways does the presence of this multicollinearity affect the results of the regression analysis?

b.   Under what conditions might the presence of multicollinearity cause problems in the use of this regression equation in designing a marketing plan for appliance sales?

3.   In the case exercise at the end of Chapter 4 on soft drink demand, what problem might arise if the given data are for Pepsi and the researcher decides to add the price of Coca-Cola in each state to the model?

4.   A product manager has been reviewing selling expenses (that is, advertising, sales commissions, and so on) associated with marketing a line of household cleaning products. The manager suspects that there may be some sort of diminishing marginal returns relationship between selling expenses and the resulting sales generated by these expenditures. After examining the selling expense and sales data for various regions (all regions are similar in sales potential) shown in the following table and graph, however, the manager is uncertain about the nature of the relationship.

Region	Selling Expense ($000)	Sales (100,000 units)	Log (selling expense)	Log (sales)
A	5	1	3.6990	5.0000
B	30	4.25	4.4771	5.6284
C	25	4	4.3979	5.6021
D	10	2	4.0000	5.3010
E	55	5.5	4.7404	5.7404
F	40	5	4.6021	5.6990
G	10	1.75	4.0000	5.2430
H	45	5	4.6532	5.6990
I	20	3	4.3010	5.4771
J	60	5.75	4.7782	5.7597

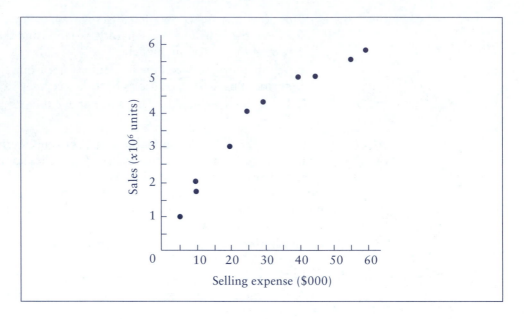

a. Using the linear regression model
$$Y = \alpha + \beta X$$
where Y is sales and X is selling expenses, estimate α, β, and the r^2 statistic by the least-squares technique.

b. Using the exponential function model
$$Y = \alpha X^\beta$$
apply the double-logarithmic transformation to obtain a linear relationship that can be estimated by the least-squares technique.

c. Applying the least-squares technique, estimate α, β, and the r^2 statistic for the transformed (linear) model in part (b). (Note that the logarithms of the X and Y variables needed in the calculations are given in the table.)

d. Based on the r^2 statistics calculated in parts (a) and (c), which model appears to give a better fit of the data?

e. What implications does the result in part (d) have for the possible existence of a diminishing marginal returns relationship between sales and selling expenses as suggested by the manager?

f. What other transformations of the variables might we try to give a better fit to the data?

Note: The following problems require the use of a multiple regression computer program, such as JMP, Minitab, SAS, SPSS, MYSTAT, or Excel.

5. a. Using the data in Table 4.1 for the Sherwin-Williams Company, estimate a multiplicative exponential demand model (see Equation 4.5) for paint sales.

    b. Compare the results in part (a) (i.e., parameter estimates, standard errors, statistical significance) with the linear model developed in the chapter.

6. The following table presents data on sales (S), advertising (A), and price (P):

Observation	Sales (S)	Advertising (A)	Price (P)
1	495	900	150
2	555	1,200	180
3	465	750	135
4	675	1,350	135
5	360	600	120
6	405	600	120
7	735	1,500	150
8	435	750	150
9	570	1,050	165
10	600	1,200	150

a. Estimate the following demand models:
   (i) $S = \alpha + \beta_1 A + \beta_2 P$
   (ii) $S = \alpha A^{\beta_1} P^{\beta_2}$

b. Determine whether the estimated values of β_1 and β_2 are statistically significant (at the .05 level).

c. Based on the value of R^2 and the F-ratio, which model gives the best fit?

7. The county assessor (see Exercise 19) is concerned about possible multicollinearity between the size (X_1) and total number of rooms (X_2) variables. Calculate the correlation coefficient between these two variables.

5

Business and Economic Forecasting

CHAPTER PREVIEW   "With over 50 cars already on sale here, the Japanese auto industry isn't likely to carve out a big slice of the U.S. market for itself."
—*Business Week*, 1958

"TV won't be able to hold on to any market it captures after the first six months. People will soon get tired of staring at a plywood box every night."
—20th Century Fox's Daryl F. Zanuck, 1946

One of the central concerns of managers in all enterprises is forecasting the future demand for their products, forecasting the cost of producing their products, and forecasting the price at which their products will be sold. As the quotes above indicate, forecasting is often difficult. The forecasts at the firm level depend on the performance of the overall economy, including the growth rate in gross national product, the level of interest rates, the rate of unemployment, the value of the dollar in foreign exchange markets, and the rate of inflation. These macroeconomic forecasts are provided by economists employed by the government, large firms, and economic forecasting organizations. The forecasting models used to forecast the future macroeconomic environment are very complex and require considerable judgment in their use. Other forecasting techniques are more suitable for use at the firm level. In this chapter we discuss several classes of forecasting techniques and consider the strengths and weaknesses of each, including time-series analysis, smoothing techniques, barometric techniques, survey and opinion-polling techniques, and econometric methods. Because the value of a firm depends on expected levels of future cash flows, accurately forecasting the components of these future cash flows is very important if managers wish to make shareholder wealth-maximizing decisions.

MANAGERIAL CHALLENGE

What Went Wrong? Demand for Sport Utility Vehicles at Ford Motor Co.

The demand for motor vehicles underwent several important changes during the 1990s. The proportion of total vehicles sold in the United States that were traditional passenger cars declined substantially as light-duty pickup trucks, minivans, and sport utility (four-wheel drive) vehicles increased in popularity. Indeed, this change in consumer vehicle preferences may be responsible for the survival of the Chrysler Corporation (now Daimler-Chrysler), which popularized the minivan and Jeep products. The profit margin on trucks, minivans, and sport utility vehicles tends to be much larger than on traditional passenger cars.

In 1994, Ford Motor Company announced a substantial increase in its capacity to produce its popular sport utility vehicle, the Explorer. Ford had been running its factories consistently on overtime to meet the surging demand. Ford hoped that its capacity expansion would be a very profitable investment and announced substantial price increases for the 1995 Explorer relative to its 1994 model predecessor.

Industry analysts questioned the wisdom of these price increases in the face of GM's dramatic increase in capacity. Furthermore, General Motors and Chrysler had just introduced the redesigned Blazer, the Tahoe, and the Grand Cherokee. Honda was planning a competitive entry in this segment of the market as well.

Ford analysts prepared forecasts of demand that took into account responses of competitors. However, this is often quite difficult because past patterns of demand may not hold in the future. Instead, new product introductions change the structure of the demand relationship.

In this chapter, we discuss several commonly used quantitative forecasting methods, including time-series analysis and econometric techniques. Other methods, such as survey and opinion-polling techniques and market experiments, can provide additional information that will be useful in reducing the error in making forecasts.

J.D. Power and Associates is an international market research firm that specializes in the automobile industry. You can read their most recent forecasts on the Internet at http://jdpower.com

SIGNIFICANCE OF FORECASTING

IBM chairman Thomas Watson once said, "I think there's a world demand for about five computers." This quote illustrates the difficulty managers face, yet accurately forecasting future business prospects is one of their most important functions. Sales forecasts are necessary to plan the proper future levels of production. The financial manager requires estimates of not only future sales revenue but also disbursements and capital expenditures. Forecasts of credit conditions must also be made so that the cash needs of the firm may be met at the lowest possible cost.

Public administrators and managers of not-for-profit institutions must also forecast. City government officials, for example, forecast the level of services that will be required of their various departments during a budget period. How many police officers will be needed to handle the public-safety problems of the community? How many streets will require repair next year, and how much will this cost? What will next year's school enrollment be at each grade level? The hospital administrator must forecast the health care needs of the community and the amount and cost of charity patient care.

Obviously, good forecasting is essential to reduce uncertainty, but sometimes when the potential gains or losses are small and the decision has a short-run impact, an appropriate forecast may simply be based on the assumption that the future will be like the past. At other times, when the costs of an erroneous forecast increase and extend over many periods, the use of more formal and sophisticated methodology becomes justifiable.

Example

http://

Domino's Pizza has extended its "pizza meter" to politics, sporting events, and television programming. Access the Domino's Pizza Internet site at
http://www.dominos.com

UNCONVENTIONAL FORECASTING: DOMINO'S PIZZA AND THE PENTAGON

At the Pentagon, Domino's usually delivers an average of three pizzas a night. On Sunday, January 13, 1991, the number of pizzas ordered reached 20. By Monday, two days before the First Gulf War began with Iraq, 50 pizzas were ordered. Tuesday the number grew to 101, and Wednesday, the night the war began, the number hit 125. Similar patterns of pizza ordering occurred at the CIA and the White House prior to the event. This pattern in pizza ordering in Washington has received such close attention from the press that it has been named the "Domino Principle." One wonders whether pizza deliveries to the Pentagon should become classified information.

SELECTION OF A FORECASTING TECHNIQUE

The forecasting technique used in any particular situation depends on a number of factors.

Hierarchy of Forecasts

The highest level of economic aggregation that is normally forecast is that of the national economy. The usual measure of overall economic activity is gross national product (GNP); however, a firm may be more interested in forecasting some of the specific components of GNP. For example, a machine tool firm may be concerned about expected plant and equipment expenditures. Retail establishments are concerned about future levels and changes in disposable personal income rather than the overall GNP estimate.

The next levels in the hierarchy of economic forecasts are the industry sales forecast, followed by individual firm sales forecasts. A simple, single firm forecast might take the industry sales estimate and relate this to the expected market share of the individual firm. Future market share might be estimated on the basis of historical market shares as well as on changes that are anticipated because of new marketing strategies, new products and model changes, and relative prices.

Within the firm, a hierarchy of forecasts also exists. Managers often estimate company-wide or regional dollar sales and unit sales by product line. These forecasts are used by operations managers in planning orders for raw materials, employee-hiring needs, shipment schedules, and production runs. In addition, marketing managers use sales forecasts to determine optimal sales force allocations, to set sales goals, and to plan promotions. The sales forecast also constitutes a crucial part of the financial manager's forecast of the cash needs of the firm. Long-term forecasts for the economy, the industry, and the firm are used in planning long-term capital expenditures for plant and equipment and for charting the general direction of the firm.

Criteria Used in the Selection of a Forecasting Technique

Some forecasting techniques are quite simple, rather inexpensive to develop and use, and best suited for short-term projections, whereas others are extremely complex, require significant amounts of time to develop, and may be quite expensive. The technique used in any specific instance depends on a number of factors, including the following:

1. The cost associated with developing the forecasting model compared with potential gains resulting from its use
2. The complexity of the relationships that are being forecast
3. The time period of the forecast (long-term or short-term)
4. The accuracy required of the model
5. The lead time necessary for making decisions dependent on the variables estimated in the forecast model

Evaluating the Accuracy of Forecasting Models

In determining the accuracy, or reliability, of a forecasting technique, one is concerned with the magnitude of the differences between the observed (actual) (Y) and the forecasted values ($\hat{Y}$) of the variable(s) being examined. Various measures of model accuracy are available. For example, in the discussion of regression analysis in the previous chapter, the coefficient of determination, or R^2, was used as a measure of the "goodness of fit" in evaluating the explanatory power of a regression equation. In this chapter, the average forecast error, or root mean square error,

$$\text{RMSE} = \sqrt{\frac{1}{n}\Sigma(Y_t - \hat{Y}_t)^2} \qquad [5.1]$$

is used to evaluate the accuracy of a forecasting model (where n is the number of observations). The smaller the value of the RMSE, the greater the accuracy of the forecasting model.[1]

---

[1] Sometimes alternative forecasting models incorporate variables with very different scale. For example, one model may address GNP in trillions of U.S. dollars whereas another may address industry sales in $ millions. To compare the relative accuracy of such models, one can use Theil's U statistic to make the necessary scaling adjustments as follows,

$$U = \frac{\text{RMSE}}{\sqrt{\frac{1}{n}\Sigma Y} + \sqrt{\frac{1}{n}\Sigma \hat{Y}}} \qquad [5.2]$$

where RMSE is as defined in Equation 5.1. U varies from 0 to 1; the closer to 0, the better the accuracy of the forecasting model.   (footnote continues on page 190)

ALTERNATIVE FORECASTING TECHNIQUES

The managerial economist may choose from a wide range of forecasting techniques. These can be classified in the following general categories:

- Deterministic time-series analysis
- Smoothing techniques
- Barometric techniques
- Survey and opinion-polling techniques
- Econometric models
- Stochastic time-series analysis
- Forecasting with input-output tables

The remaining sections of this chapter examine these forecasting techniques.

DETERMINISTIC TIME-SERIES ANALYSIS

Time-Series Data
A series of observations taken on an economic variable at various past points in time.

Data collected for use in forecasting the value of a particular variable may be classified into two major categories—time-series or cross-sectional data. **Time-series data** are defined as a sequential array of the values of an economic variable at different points in time. **Cross-sectional data** are an array of the values of an economic variable observed at the same time. Data collected in a census are cross-sectional because they consist of a series of observations taken at approximately the same time across many individuals in the population. No matter what type of forecasting model is being used, one must decide whether time-series or cross-sectional data are most appropriate.

Cross-Sectional Data
Series of observations taken on different observation units (for example, households, states, or countries) at the same point in time.

Components of a Time Series

In the analysis of time-series data (see Figure 5.1a, b), time (in years, months, and so on) is represented on the horizontal axis and the values of the variable are on the vertical axis. The variations that are evident in the time series in Figure 5.1 can be decomposed into four components:

Secular Trends
Long-run changes (growth or decline) in an economic time-series variable.

1. *Secular trends.* These are long-run trends that cause changes in an economic data series [*solid line* in Panel (a) of Figure 5.1]. For example, in empirical

---

Theil's U reflects three sources of error in competing forecasting models: bias, variance replication failure, and the remaining unsystematic error.

The bias component, $(E(\hat{Y}) - E(Y))^2$ / RMSE, captures the systematic error in the average value that arises from using the forecast to predict the actual data. The bias component should be as close to zero as possible. The variance replication component, $(\sigma_Y - \sigma_{\hat{Y}})^2$ / RMSE, measures the ability of the forecasting model to reproduce the magnitude of the variance in the underlying data. For example, forecasts of the money supply process are notoriously inaccurate in part because the actual M^s is extremely volatile relative to forecasting models of Federal Reserve behavior in controlling the money supply. Sometimes the reverse problem presents itself; the forecasted path of hurricanes fluctuates widely while the actual track is usually quite stable. Again, high values of the variance replication failure (VRF) component of the forecast error are undesirable and suggest the need for a different forecasting model. The third, unsystematic error component of Theil's U statistic is $2(1 - \rho) \sigma_Y \sigma_{\hat{Y}}$ where ρ is the correlation coefficient between $\hat{Y}$ and Y. Since this factor represents correlated disturbances between the stochastic processes underlying the forecasted and actual data series, they cannot be avoided. Ideally, bias and variance replication failure would equal zero, and the unsystematic component of Theil's U statistic would dominate. For several illustrations of these three components of forecast error in business settings, see R. Pindyck and D. Rubinfeld, *Econometric Models and Economic Forecasts,* 4th ed., Irwin/McGraw-Hill, 1998, pp. 212–214.

Figure 5.1   Secular, Cyclical, Seasonal, and Random Fluctuations in Time-Series Data

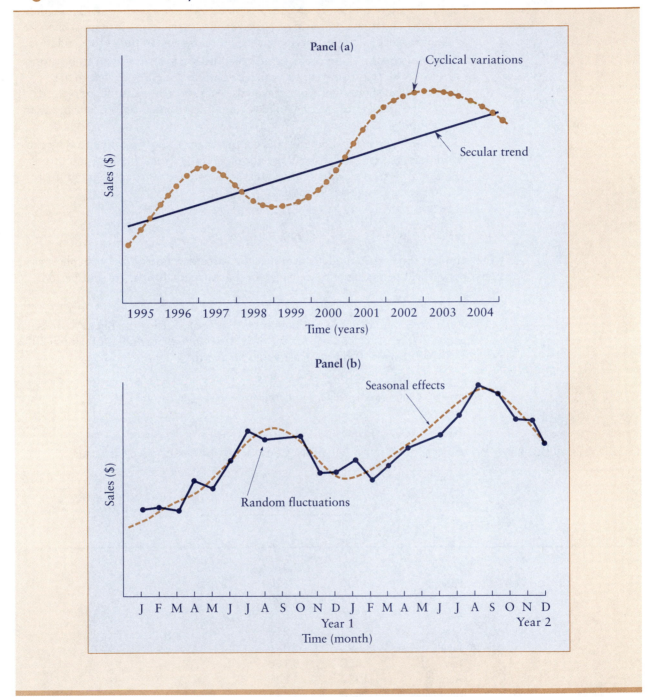

demand analyses, such factors as increasing population size or evolving consumer tastes may result in trend increases or decreases of a demand series over time.

2. *Cyclical variations.* These are major expansions and contractions in an economic series that are usually greater than a year in duration [*broken line*

in Panel (a) of Figure 5.1]. For example, the housing industry appears to experience regular expansions following contractions in demand. When cyclical variations are present, regression estimates using the raw data will be distorted due to the presence of positive autocorrelation. Care must then be taken to specify an appropriate lag structure to remove the autocorrelation.[2]

3. *Seasonal effects.* These cause variations during a year that tend to be more or less consistent from year to year. The data in Panel (b) of Figure 5.1 (*broken line*) show significant seasonal variation. For example, two-thirds of Hickory Farms' (a retailer of holiday food gifts) annual sales occur between November and January.

4. *Random fluctuations.* Finally, an economic series may be influenced by random factors that are by and large not predictable [*solid line* in Panel (b) of Figure 5.1], such as wars, natural disasters, and extraordinary government actions like a wage-price freeze.

Seasonal Effects
Variations in a time series during a year that tend to appear regularly from year to year.

Some Elementary Time-Series Models

The simplest time-series model states that the forecast value of the variable for the next period will be the same as the value of that variable for the present period:

$$\hat{Y}_{t+1} = Y_t \qquad [5.3]$$

For example, consider the sales data shown in Table 5.1 for the Buckeye Brewing Company. To forecast monthly sales, the model uses *actual* beer sales for March 2003 of 2,738 (000) barrels as the forecast value for April.

[2] Tests for diagnosing the presence of autocorrelation are discussed in Appendix 4A.

Table 5.1   Buckeye Brewing Company's Monthly Beer Sales (thousands of barrels)

Month	Year 2001	2002	2003
January	2,370	2,446	2,585
February	2,100	2,520	2,693
March	2,412	2,598	2,738
April	2,376	2,533	
May	3,074	3,250	
June	3,695	3,446	
July	3,550	3,986	
August	4,172	4,222	
September	3,880	3,798	
October	2,931	2,941	
November	2,377	2,488	
December	2,983	2,878	

Where changes occur slowly and the forecast is being made for a relatively short period in the future, such a model may be quite useful. However, because Equation 5.3 requires a knowledge of this month's sales, the forecaster may be faced with the task of speeding up the collection of actual data. Another problem with this model is that it makes no provision for incorporating the effects of known changes in the marketplace that may affect sales. Special promotions by the firm (or its competitors) could cause such great distortion in the observed values of the variable from one period to the next that past data will be of little use in predicting future values.

Further examination of the Buckeye beer sales data in Table 5.1 indicates a slight upward trend in sales—beer sales in most months are higher than in the same month of the previous year. Second, we note that sales are somewhat seasonal—beer sales are high during the summer months and low during the winter. The tendency for recent increases to trigger further increases in beer sales may be incorporated by adjusting Equation 5.3 slightly to yield this equation:

$$\hat{Y}_{t+1} = Y_t + (Y_t - Y_{t-1}) \qquad [5.4]$$

For example, Buckeye's sales forecast for April 2003 using this model would be

$$Y_{t+1} = 2{,}738 + (2{,}738 - 2{,}693)$$
$$= 2{,}783(000) \text{ barrels}$$

Other forecasting models that incorporate trends and seasonal effects such as these are discussed below.

Secular Trends

Long-run changes in an economic time series can follow a number of different types of trends. Three possible cases are shown in Figure 5.2. A *linear* trend is shown in Panel (a). Panels (b) and (c) depict *nonlinear* trends. In Panel (b), the economic time series follows a *constant rate of growth* pattern. The earnings of many corporations follow this type of trend. Panel (c) shows an economic time series that exhibits a declining rate of growth. Sales of a new product may follow this pattern. As market saturation occurs, the rate of growth will decline over time.

Figure 5.2   Time-Series Growth Patterns

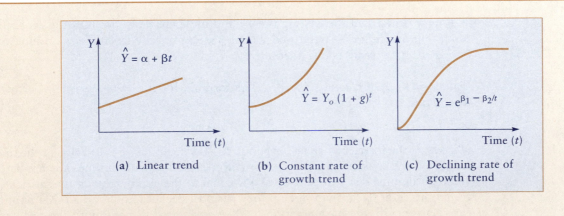

(a) Linear trend

(b) Constant rate of growth trend

(c) Declining rate of growth trend

Linear Trends   A linear time trend may be estimated by using *least-squares* regression analysis to provide an equation of a straight line of "best fit." (See Chapter 4 for a further discussion of the least-squares technique.) The equation of a linear time trend is given in the general form

$$\hat{Y}_t = \alpha + \beta t \qquad [5.5]$$

where $\hat{Y}_t$ is the forecast or predicted value for period t, α is the y intercept or constant term, t is a unit of time, and β is an estimate of this trend factor. Typically, some year, quarter, or month is identified as the starting time period (i.e., $t = 0$).

LINEAR TREND FORECASTING: PRIZER CREAMERY

Suppose one is interested in forecasting monthly ice cream sales of the Prizer Creamery for 2005. A least-squares trend line could be estimated from the ice cream sales data for the past four years (48 monthly observations), as shown in Figure 5.3. Assume that the equation of this line is calculated to be

$$\hat{Y}_t = 30,464 + 121.3\, t$$

where $\hat{Y}_t$ = predicted monthly ice cream sales in gallons in month t
$30,464$ = number of gallons sold when $t = 0$
t = time period (months) (where December 2000 = 0, January 2001 = 1, February 2001 = 2, March 2001 = 3, . . .)

The coefficient (121.3) of t indicates that sales may be expected to increase by 121.3 gallons on the average each month. Based on this trend line and ignoring any seasonal effects, forecasted ice cream sales for August 2005 ($t = 56$) would be

$$Y_{56} = 30,464 + 121.3(56)$$
$$= 37,257 \text{ gallons}$$

This *seasonally unadjusted* forecast is given by the August 2005 point (⊙) on the trend line in Figure 5.3. As can be seen in the graph, ice cream sales are subject to seasonal variations. Later in this section we will show how this seasonal effect can be incorporated into the forecast.

Linear time trend forecasting is easy and inexpensive to do, but it is generally too simple and inflexible to be used in many forecasting circumstances. Constant rate of growth time trends is one alternative.

Constant Rate of Growth Trends   The formula for the constant rate of growth forecasting model is

$$\hat{Y}_t = Y_0(1 + g)^t \qquad [5.6]$$

where $\hat{Y}_t$ is the forecasted value for period t, Y_0 is the initial ($t = 0$) value of the time series, g is the constant growth rate per period, and t is a unit of time. The predicted value of the time series in period t ($\hat{Y}_t$) is equal to the initial value of the series (Y_0) compounded at the growth rate (g) for t periods. Because Equation 5.6 is a nonlinear relationship, the parameters cannot be estimated directly with the ordinary least-squares method. However, taking logarithms of both sides of the equation gives

$$\log \hat{Y}_t = \log Y_0 + \log(1 + g) \cdot t$$

or

$$\hat{Y}'_t = \alpha + \beta t \tag{5.7}$$

where $\hat{Y}'_t = \log \hat{Y}_t$, $\alpha = \log Y_0$, and $\beta = \log(1 + g)$. Equation 5.7 is a linear relationship whose parameters can be estimated using standard linear regression techniques.

For example, suppose that annual earnings data for the Fitzgerald Company for the past 10 years have been collected and that Equation 5.7 was fitted to the data using least-squares techniques. The annual rate of growth of company earnings was estimated to be 6 percent. If the company's earnings this year ($t = 0$) are $600,000, then next year's ($t = 1$) forecasted earnings would be

$$\hat{Y}_1 = 600,000(1 + .06)^1$$
$$= \$636,000$$

Figure 5.3 Prizer Creamery: Monthly Ice Cream Sales

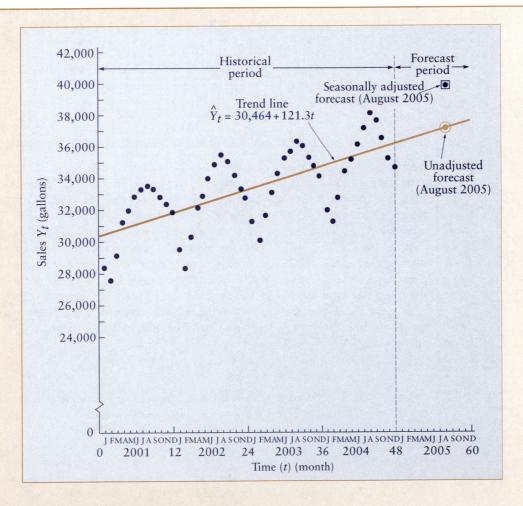

Similarly, forecasted earnings for the year after next ($t = 2$) would be

$$\hat{Y}_2 = 600{,}000(1 + .06)^2$$
$$= \$674{,}160$$

Declining Rate of Growth Trends   The curve depicted in Figure 5.2, panel (c) is particularly useful for representing sales penetration curves in marketing applications. Using linear regression techniques, one can specify a semilog estimating equation,

$$\ln \hat{Y}_t = \beta_1 - \beta_2(1/t)$$

and recover the β_1 and β_2 parameters of this nonlinear diffusion process as a new product diffuses across a target population. β_1 and β_2 measure how quickly a new product or new technology or brand extension penetrates and then slowly (ever more slowly) saturates a market.

Seasonal Variations

When *seasonal* variations are introduced into a forecasting model, its short-run predictive power may be improved significantly. Seasonal variations may be estimated in a number of ways.

Ratio to Trend Method   One approach is the *ratio to trend method*. This method assumes that the trend value is *multiplied by* the seasonal effect.

Example

SEASONALLY ADJUSTED FORECASTS: PRIZER CREAMERY (continued)

Recall in the Prizer Creamery example discussed earlier that a linear trend analysis (Equation 5.5) yielded a sales forecast for August 2000 of 37,257 gallons. This estimate can be adjusted for seasonal effects in the following manner. Assume that over the past four years (1996–1999) the trend model predicted the August sales patterns shown in Table 5.2 and that actual sales are as indicated. These data indicate that, on the average, August sales have been 7.0 percent higher than the trend value. Hence, the August 2000 sales forecast should be seasonally adjusted *upward* by 7.0 percent to 39,865. The seasonally adjusted forecast is shown by the point (□) above the trend line in Figure 5.3. If however, the model predicted February 2000 ($t = 50$) sales to be 36,529, but similar data indicated February sales to be 10.8 percent below trend on the average, the forecast would be adjusted *downward* to $36{,}529(1 - .108) = 32{,}584$ gallons.

Dummy Variables   Another approach for incorporating seasonal effects into the linear trend analysis model is the use of *dummy variables*. A dummy variable is a variable that normally takes on one of two values—either 0 or 1. Dummy variables, in general, are used to capture the impact of certain qualitative factors in an econometric relationship, such as sex—male-0 and female-1. This method assumes that the seasonal effects are added to the trend value. If a time series consists of quarterly data, then the following model could be used to adjust for seasonal effects:

$$\hat{Y}_t = \alpha + \beta_1 t + \beta_2 D_{1t} + \beta_3 D_{2t} + \beta_4 D_{3t} \qquad [5.8]$$

Table 5.2   Prizer Creamery's August Ice Cream Sales

(August)	Forecast	Actual	Actual/Forecast
1996	31,434	33,600	1.0689
1997	32,890	35,600	1.0824
1998	34,346	36,400	1.0598
1999	35,801	38,200	1.0670
2000	37,257	–	–
			Sum = 4.2781

Adjustment factor = 4.2781/4 = 1.0695 (i.e., 1.07)

---

where $D_{1t} = 1$ for first-quarter observations and 0 otherwise, $D_{2t} = 1$ for second-quarter observations and 0 otherwise, $D_{3t} = 1$ for third-quarter observations and 0 otherwise, and α and β are parameters to be estimated using least-squares techniques. In this model the values of the dummy variables (D_{1t}, D_{2t}, D_{3t}) for observations in the fourth quarter of each year (base period) would be equal to zero. In the estimated model the value $\beta_2 D_{1t}$ represents the impact of a first-quarter observation (D_1) on values of the forecast, Y_t, relative to the forecast from the omitted class (4th quarter), when D_{2t} and D_{3t} take values of 0.

Example

DUMMY VARIABLES AND SEASONAL ADJUSTMENTS: VALUE-MART COMPANY

The Value-Mart Company (a small chain of discount department stores) is interested in forecasting quarterly sales for next year (20X4) based on Equation 5.8. Using quarterly sales data for the past eight years (19X6–20X3), the following model was estimated:

$$\hat{Y}_t = 22.50 + 0.250\,t - 4.50\,D_{1t} - 3.20\,D_{2t} - 2.10\,D_{3t} \qquad [5.9]$$

where $\hat{Y}_t$ = predicted sales ($ million) in quarter t

22.50 = quarterly sales ($ million) when $t = 0$

t = time period (quarter) (where the fourth quarter of 20X0 = 0, first quarter of 20X1 = 1, second quarter of 20X1 = 2, . . .)

The coefficient of t (0.250) indicates that sales may be expected to increase by $0.250 million on the average each quarter. The coefficients of the three dummy variables (−4.50, −3.20, and −2.10) indicate the change (i.e., reduction because the coefficients are negative) in sales in Quarters 1, 2, and 3, respectively, because of seasonal effects. Based on Equation 5.9, Value-Mart's quarterly sales forecasts for 20X4 are shown in Table 5.3.

The introduction of these trend and seasonality factors into a forecasting model should significantly improve the model's ability to predict short-run turning

Table 5.3 Value-Mart's Quarterly Sales Forecast (20X4)

Quarter	Time Period t	Dummy variable			Sales Forecast ($ Million) $\hat{Y} = 22.50 + .250t - 4.50 D_{1t} - 3.20 D_{2t} - 2.10 D_{3t}$
		D_{1t}	D_{2t}	D_{3t}	
1	33	1	0	0	26.25
2	34	0	1	0	27.80
3	35	0	0	1	29.15
4	36	0	0	0	31.50

points in the data series, provided the historical causal factors have not changed significantly.[3]

The models of time-series forecasting discussed in this section may have substantial value in many areas of business. However, the business forecaster must not rely too heavily on time-series models alone. These models do not seek to relate changes in a data series to the causes underlying observed values in the series, so they are highly susceptible to making poor predictions when the underlying causal factors change. For example, the nation's money supply series has at times proved very useful for forecasting inflationary pressure in the economy. But narrow definitions of the nation's money supply have gradually broadened to include bank-card lines of credit, which may have become a more important measure of household purchasing power. Inflation forecasts based on narrow money supply measures today would yield large errors between the actual and predicted inflation (see Figure 5.4 on the next page).

SMOOTHING TECHNIQUES

Smoothing techniques are another type of time-series forecasting model which assumes that an underlying pattern can be found in the historical values of a variable that is being forecast. It is assumed that these historical observations represent not only the underlying pattern but also random variations. By taking some form of an average of past observations, smoothing techniques attempt to eliminate the distortions arising from random variation in the series and to base the forecast on a smoothed average of several past observations.

In general, smoothing techniques work best when a data series tends to change slowly from one period to the next with few turning points. Housing price forecasts would be a good application for smoothing techniques. Gasoline price forecasts would not. Smoothing techniques, like many other time-series forecasting models, are cheap to develop and inexpensive to operate.

---

[3] See more extensive discussion of these issues in F. Diebold, *Elements of Forecasting,* 2nd ed., Cincinnati: South-Western College Publishing.

Figure 5.4   Actual and Expected Inflation

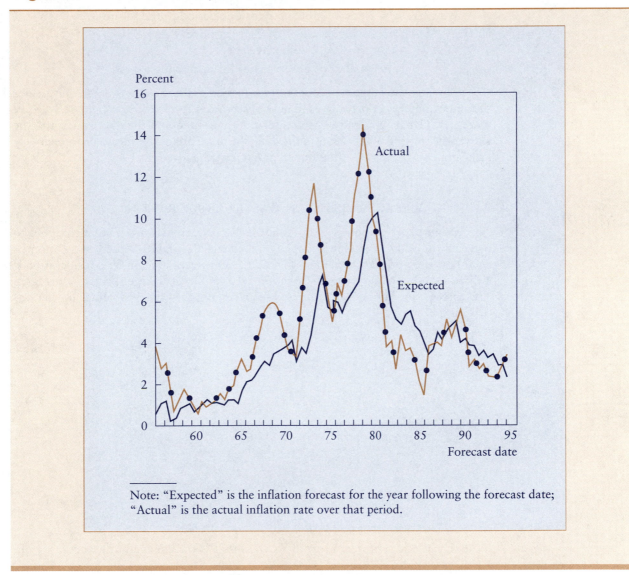

Note: "Expected" is the inflation forecast for the year following the forecast date; "Actual" is the actual inflation rate over that period.

Source: Federal Reserve Bank of Philadelphia, *Business Review,* May/June 1996.

Moving Averages

Moving averages are one of the simplest of the smoothing techniques. If a data series possesses a large random factor, a trend analysis forecast like those discussed in the previous section will tend to generate forecasts having large errors from period to period. In an effort to minimize the effects of this randomness, a series of recent observations can be averaged to arrive at a forecast. This is the moving average method. A number of observed values are chosen, their average is computed, and this average serves as a forecast for the next period. In general, a moving average may be defined as

$$\hat{Y}_{t+1} = \frac{Y_t + Y_{t-1} + \ldots + Y_{t-N+1}}{N}$$ [5.10]

where $\hat{Y}_{t+1}$ = forecast value of Y for one period in the future
Y_t, Y_{t-1}, Y_{t-N+1} = observed values of Y in periods $t, t - 1, \ldots,$
$t - N + 1$, respectively
N = number of observations in the moving average

The greater the number of observations N used in the moving average, the greater the smoothing effect because each new observation receives less weight ($1/N$) as N increases. Hence, generally, the greater the randomness in the data series and the slower the turning point events in the data, the more preferable it is to use a relatively large number of past observations in developing the forecast.

Example

MOVING AVERAGE FORECASTS: WALKER CORPORATION

The Walker Corporation is examining the use of various smoothing techniques to forecast monthly sales. The company collected sales data for the last 12 months (2000) as shown in Table 5.4 and Figure 5.5. One technique under consideration is a three-month moving average. Equation 5.10 can be used to generate the forecasts. The forecast for Period 4 is computed by averaging the observed values for Periods 1, 2, and 3.

$$\hat{Y}_4 = \frac{Y_3 + Y_2 + Y_1}{N}$$ [5.11]

$$= \frac{1,925 + 1,400 + 1,950}{3}$$

$$= 1,758$$

Similarly, the forecast for Period 5 is computed as

$$\hat{Y}_5 = \frac{Y_4 + Y_3 + Y_2}{N}$$ [5.12]

$$= \frac{1,960 + 1,925 + 1,400}{3}$$

$$= 1,762$$

Note that if one subtracts $\hat{Y}_4$ from $\hat{Y}_5$, the result is the change in the forecast from $\hat{Y}_4$, or

$$\Delta \hat{Y}_4 = \hat{Y}_5 - \hat{Y}_4$$ [5.13]

$$= \frac{Y_4 + Y_3 + Y_2}{N} - \frac{Y_3 + Y_2 + Y_1}{N}$$

$$= \frac{Y_4}{N} - \frac{Y_1}{N}$$

Adding this change to $\hat{Y}_4$, the following alternative expression for $\hat{Y}_5$ can be derived:

$$\hat{Y}_5 = \hat{Y}_4 + \frac{Y_4}{N} - \frac{Y_1}{N}$$ [5.14]

or, in general,

$$\hat{Y}_{t+1} = \hat{Y}_t + \frac{Y_t}{N} - \frac{Y_{t-N}}{N}$$ [5.15]

which indicates that each moving average forecast is equal to the past forecast, $\hat{Y}_t$, plus the weighted effect of the most recent observation, Y_t/N, minus the weighted effect of the oldest observation that has been dropped, Y_{t-N}/N. As N becomes larger, the smoothing effect increases because the new observation, Y_t, has a small impact on the moving average.

As shown in Table 5.4, Walker's forecast for January 2001 ($t = 13$) is $2,283(000). Note also that the root mean square error (RMSE) of the three-month (N) moving average period is $561(000).

The choice of an appropriate moving average period, that is, the choice of N, should be based on a comparison of the results of the model in forecasting past observations. For example, the forecaster might try a three-period average, a five-period average, and a seven-period average, and compare the accuracy of the alternatives. The best moving average is chosen on the basis of the value of N that minimizes the root mean square error (Equation 5.1).

First-Order Exponential Smoothing

One criticism of moving averages as smoothing techniques is that they normally give equal weight (a weight of $1/N$) to all observations used in preparing the forecast, even though intuition often indicates that the most recent observation probably

---

Table 5.4   Walker Corporation's Three-Month Moving Average Sales Forecast Table

t	Month	Sales ($1,000) Actual Y_t	Forecast $\hat{Y}_t$	Error $(Y_t - \hat{Y}_t)$	$(Y_t - \hat{Y}_t)^2$
1	January 2000	1,950	—	—	—
2	February	1,400	—	—	—
3	March	1,925	—	—	—
4	April	1,960	1,758	202	40,804
5	May	2,800	1,762	1,038	1,077,444
6	June	1,800	2,228	−428	183,184
7	July	1,600	2,187	−587	344,569
8	August	1,450	2,067	−617	380,689
9	September	2,000	1,617	383	146,689
10	October	2,250	1,683	567	321,489
11	November	1,950	1,900	50	2,500
12	December	2,650	2,067	583	339,889
13	January 2001	*	2,283	—	—
				Sum =	2,837,257

$$\text{RMSE} = \sqrt{2,837,257/9} = \$561(000)$$

Figure 5.5   Walker Corporation's Three-Month Moving Average Sales Forecast Chart

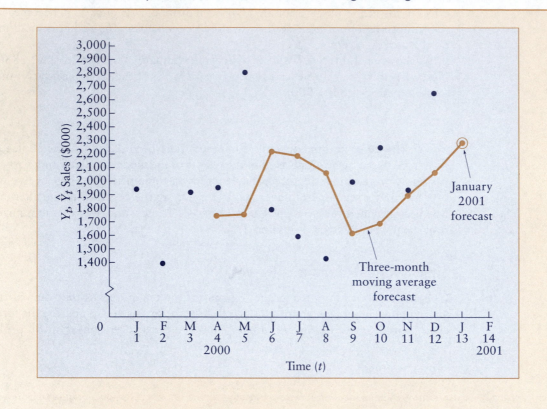

contains more immediately useful information than more distant observations. Exponential smoothing is designed to overcome this objection.[4]

Consider the following alternative forecasting model:

$$\hat{Y}_{t+1} = wY_t + (1 - w)\hat{Y}_t \qquad [5.16]$$

This model weights the most recent observation by w (some value between 0 and 1 inclusive), and the past forecast by $(1 - w)$. A large w indicates that a heavy weight is being placed on the most recent observation.[5]

Using Equation 5.16, a forecast for $\hat{Y}_t$ may also be written as

$$\hat{Y}_t = wY_{t-1} + (1 - w)(\hat{Y}_{t-1}) \qquad [5.17]$$

By substituting Equation 5.17 into 5.16, we get

$$\hat{Y}_{t+1} = wY_t + w(1 - w)Y_{t-1} + (1 - w)^2\hat{Y}_{t-1} \qquad [5.18]$$

---

[4] More complex double exponential smoothing models generally give more satisfactory results than first-order exponential smoothing models when the data possess a linear trend over time. See Newbold and Bos, *Introductory Business Forecasting*.

[5] The greater the amount of serial correlation (correlation of values from period to period), the larger will be the optimal value of w.

By continuing this process of substitution for past forecasts, we obtain the general equation

$$\hat{Y}_{t+1} = wY_t + w(1 - w)Y_{t-1} + w(1 - w)^2 Y_{t-2}$$
$$+ w(1 - w)^3 Y_{t-3} + \ldots \qquad [5.19]$$

Equation 5.19 shows that the general formula (Equation 5.16) for an exponentially weighted moving average is a weighted average of all past observations, with the weights defined by the geometric progression:

$$w, (1 - w)w, (1 - w)^2 w, (1 - w)^3 w, (1 - w)^4 w, (1 - w)^5 w, \ldots \qquad [5.20]$$

For example, a w of 2/3 would produce the following series of weights:

$$w = .667$$
$$(1 - w)w = .222$$
$$(1 - w)^2 w = .074$$
$$(1 - w)^3 w = .024$$
$$(1 - w)^4 w = .0082$$
$$(1 - w)^5 w = .0027$$

With a high initial value of w, heavy weight is placed on the most recent observation, and rapidly declining weights are placed on older values.

Another way of writing Equation 5.16 is

$$\hat{Y}_{t+1} = \hat{Y}_t + w(Y_t - \hat{Y}_t) \qquad [5.21]$$

This indicates that the new forecast is equal to the old forecast plus w times the error in the most recent forecast. A w that is close to 1 indicates a quick adjustment process for any error in the preceding forecast. Similarly, a w closer to 0 suggests a slow error correction process.

It should be apparent from Equations 5.16 and 5.21 that exponential forecasting techniques can be very easy to use. All that is required is last period's forecast, last period's observation, plus a value for the weighting factor, w. The optimal weighting factor is normally determined by making successive forecasts using past data with various values of w and choosing the w that minimizes the root mean square error (RMSE) given in Equation 5.1.

Example

EXPONENTIAL SMOOTHING: WALKER CORPORATION (continued)

Consider again the Walker Corporation example discussed earlier. Suppose that the company is interested in generating sales forecasts using the first-order exponential smoothing technique. The results are shown in Table 5.5. To illustrate the approach, an exponential weight w of .5 will be used. To get the process started, one needs to make an initial forecast of the variable. This forecast might be a weighted average or some simple forecast, such as Equation 5.3:

$$\hat{Y}_{t+1} = Y_t$$

The latter approach will be used. Hence the forecast for Month 2 made in Month 1 would be \$1,950(000) ($\hat{Y}_{t+1} = 1,950$). The Month 3 forecast value is (using Equation 5.21)

$$\hat{Y}_3 = 1,950 + .5(1,400 - 1,950)$$
$$= 1,950 - 275 = \$1,675(000)$$

Similarly, the Month 4 forecast equals

$$\hat{Y}_4 = 1,675 + .5(1,925 - 1,675)$$
$$= \$1,800(000)$$

The remaining forecasts are calculated in a similar manner.

As can be seen in Table 5.5, Walker's sales forecast for January 2001 using the first-order exponential smoothing technique is $2,322(000). Also, the root mean square error of this forecasting method (with $w = .50$) is $491(000).

BAROMETRIC TECHNIQUES

http://

National Bureau of
Economic Research on the
Internet is located at
http://www.nber.org

The time-series forecasting models discussed above assume that future patterns in an economic time series may be predicted by projecting a repeat of past patterns, but very few economic time series exhibit consistent enough cyclical variations to make simple projection forecasting reliable. For example, Table 5.6 conveys why the prediction of a business cycle's turning point proves to be so difficult. Although the duration of postwar U.S. business cycles averages 61 months (from peak to peak), two cycles have lasted 100 months or more, while others have been as short as 32 and even 18 months. Economists, however, have long recognized that if it were possible to isolate sets of time series that exhibited a close correlation, and if one or more of these time series normally *led* (in a consistent manner) the time series in which the forecaster had interest, then this leading series could be used as a predictor or barometer.

Table 5.5   Walker Corporation: First-Order Exponential Smoothing Sales Forecast

		Sales ($1,000)		Error	
t	Month	Actual Y_t	Forecast $\hat{Y}_t$	$(Y_t - \hat{Y}_t)$	$(Y_t - \hat{Y}_t)^2$
1	January 2000	1,950	—	—	—
2	February	1,400	1,950	−550	302,500
3	March	1,925	1,675	250	62,500
4	April	1,960	1,800	160	25,600
5	May	2,800	1,880	920	846,400
6	June	1,800	2,340	−540	291,600
7	July	1,600	2,070	−470	220,900
8	August	1,450	1,835	−385	148,225
9	September	2,000	1,642	358	128,164
10	October	2,250	1,821	429	184,041
11	November	1,950	2,036	−86	7,396
12	December	2,650	1,993	657	431,649
13	January 2001	—	2,322	—	—
				Sum =	2,648,975

$$RMSE = \sqrt{2,648,975/11} = \$491(000)$$

Table 5.6   Duration of U.S. Business Cycles (in months)

		Contraction*	Expansion†	Business Cycle‡	
Oct 1945	Nov 1948	8	37	88	45
Oct 1949	July 1953	11	45	48	56
May 1954	Aug 1957	10	39	55	49
Apr 1958	Apr 1960	8	24	47	32
Feb 1961	Dec 1969	10	106	34	116
Nov 1970	Nov 1973	11	36	117	47
Mar 1975	Jan 1980	16	58	52	74
July 1980	July 1981	6	12	64	18
Nov 1982	July 1990	16	92	28	108
Mar 1991		8	–	100	–
Average post-war cycle		11	50	61	61

*Months from previous peak to trough.
†Months from trough to next peak.
‡Months from previous trough to next trough and months from previous peak to next peak.
Source: http://osec.doc.gov/ *Survey of Current Business,* October 1994, Table C-51.

Although the concept of leading or barometric forecasting is not new,[6] current barometric forecasting is based largely on the work done at the National Bureau of Economic Research. The barometric forecasting model developed there is used primarily to identify potential future changes in *general business conditions,* rather than conditions for a specific industry or firm.

Leading, Lagging, and Coincident Indicators

Economic indicators may be classified as leading, coincident, or lagging indicators, depending on their timing relative to business cycle peaks and troughs (see Figure 5.6). The *Business Conditions Digest,* a monthly publication of the U.S. Department of Commerce, has identified 11 series that tend to lead the peaks and troughs of business cycles, 4 series of roughly coincident indicators of economic activity, and 7 series that tend to lag the peaks and troughs of economic activity. Table 5.7 lists the title of each series and the mean lead or lag of the series in relation to peaks and troughs of economic activity.

The rationale for the use of many of the series listed in this table is obvious. Many of these series represent commitments to future levels of economic activity. Building permits precede housing starts, and orders for durable goods precede their actual production. For some of the other indicators, the nature of the causal relationships involved is not quite so clear. The value of any particular time series as a predictor of future changes in another series depends on a number of factors. First, the user must be concerned with the success of the series in predicting the turning

---

[6] Andrew Carnegie used to count the number of smoke-belching chimneys in Pittsburgh to forecast the level of business activity and consequently the demand for steel.

Figure 5.6   Barometric Indicators

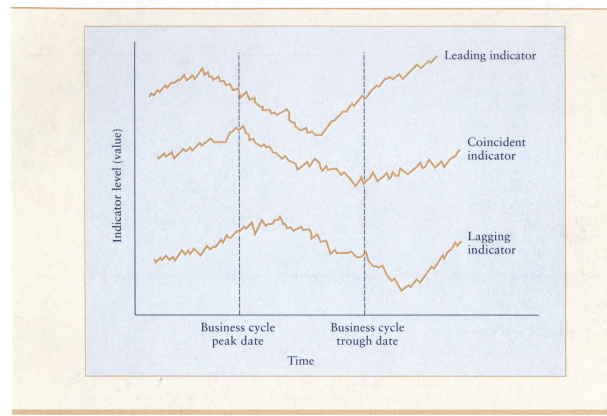

The main value of leading and lagging indicators is in predicting the *direction* of future change in economic activity. These indicators reveal little or nothing about the *magnitude* of the changes.

points in economic activity. Even the best series exhibit only 80- to 90-percent accuracy. In addition, a series is more valuable not only if it consistently leads (lags) business cycles but also if it lacks a large variability in the *length* of the lead (lag). Finally, a series that is free of large random or seasonal fluctuations should be rated high because it will not give as many false signals.

The main value of leading and lagging indicators is in predicting the *direction* of future change in economic activity. These indicators reveal little or nothing about the *magnitude* of the changes.

Example

http://

The Index of Leading Economic Indicators can be accessed at http://www.conference-board.org/

For descriptions of recent revisions in this index, see http://www.tcb-indicators.org/

LEADING INDICATORS CHANGE[7]

The Index of Leading Economic Indicators is constantly under scrutiny by both private and public forecasting agencies. When any series appears outdated or begins to generate misleading signals, a replacement can often emerge from a consensus of best practices in business forecasting. Recently, three of the series in Table 5.7 have been ranked "Poor" at predicting recessions and recoveries in the last decade by the Conference Board, a prominent trade association of major corporations that collects, analyzes, and distributes business cycle data. Two of the three (i.e., manufacturers' unfilled orders for durables and the change in sensitive materials

[7] Based on "Makeup of Leading Indicators May Shift," *Wall Street Journal*, August 11, 1996, p. A2.

prices) may be removed from the Index and replaced by the interest rate spread between 10-year Treasury bond yields and 3-month Treasury bill yields. The interest rate spread is an attempt to capture the effects of monetary policy on the business cycle. A long-bond yield at least 1.21 percent higher than the T-bill yield implies less than a 0.05 probability of recession four quarters ahead. If the Federal Reserve tightens credit, however, such that short-term interest rates rise 0.82 percent above long-term rates, the probability of recession increases to 50 percent and more. For example, at an interest rate spread of 2.40 percent, the probability of recession four quarters ahead rises to 90 percent. This new indicator of credit conditions should effectively supplement the generally poor third predictor, the M2 measure of the nation's money supply. If inventory policies or oil price hikes return to a position of prominence in business planning, then the manufacturers' unfilled orders and sensitive materials price series can easily be restored to the Index at a later date.

Diffusion and Composite Indexes

To overcome some of the weaknesses associated with forecasting based on leading series, economists have developed the *diffusion index*. The primary advantage of this index is that it reduces the chances of making a false prediction based on a short-term fluctuation in one series alone. When all indicators in the index are rising, the diffusion index equals 100; when all are falling, it equals 0; and when one-fourth are rising, it equals 25. During business cycle expansions, the National Bureau of Economic Research has found that this index is normally above 50 percent, and during contractions it is normally below 50 percent. Diffusion indexes may be constructed using any combination of indicator series that the forecaster feels is appropriate.

Composite indexes, which are weighted averages of several indicators, are also designed to overcome the problem of making false predictions based on short-term fluctuations in a single series. The performances of the composite indexes for the 11 leading, 4 coincident, and 7 lagging indicators are summarized in Table 5.7. For example, consider the composite index of 4 coincident indicators (listed at line 920 in Table 5.7). This index missed the July 1990 peak by one month (-1 meaning one month late) but exactly coincided with the March 1991 business cycle trough.

SURVEY AND OPINION-POLLING TECHNIQUES

Survey and opinion-polling techniques are other forecasting tools that may be helpful in making short-period forecasts. These techniques may be used for forecasting the overall level of economic activity, or they may be used within the firm for forecasting future sales. The rationale for the use of survey and opinion-polling techniques is that certain attitudes having an impact on economic decisions may be identified in advance of the actual implementation of the decision. If individuals who are responsible for making these decisions are polled, they may provide insights into their intended actions. Business firms normally plan additions to plant and equipment well in advance of the actual expenditures; consumers plan expenditures for autos, vacations, and education in advance of the actual purchase; and governments at all levels prepare budgets indicating priorities and amounts of intended expenditures.

Table 5.7   Cyclical Leads (−) and Lags (+) for Leading, Coincident, and Lagging Indicators (length in months)

Series No.	Series Title	July 1990	July 1981	Jan. 1980	Nov. 1973	Dec. 1969	Apr. 1960	Aug. 1957	July 1953	Nov. 1948	Mean
	At Reference Peaks [1]										
	LEADING INDICATORS										
1	Average weekly hours, manufacturing	−15	−7	−10	−7	−14	−11	−21	−3	−11	−11.0
5	Average weekly initial claims for unemployment insurance (inverted)[2]	−22	0	−16	−9	−11	−12	−23	−10	−13	−12.9
8	Manufacturers' new orders in 1987 dollars, consumer goods and materials	−2	−2	−13	−8	−13	−13	−25	−3	−5	−9.3
32	Vendor performance, slower deliveries diffusion index	+1	−3	−9	0	−4	−14	−28	−12	−7	−8.4
20	Contracts and orders for plant and equipment in 1987 dollars	−7	−3	−10	−1	−11	−13	−9	−5	−7	−7.3
29	Building permits, new private housing units	−21	−10	−19	−11	−10	−17	−30	−8	−13	−15.4
92	Change in manufacturers' unfilled orders in 1987 dollars, durable goods (smoothed)[3]	−3	−6	−13	−6	−7	−12	−19	−26	−3	−10.6
99	Change in sensitive materials prices (smoothed)[3]	+2	−7	−7	+3	−10	−17	−17	−9	n.a.	−7.8
19	Index of stock prices, 500 common stocks	−1	−8	NST	−10	−12	−9	−13	−6	−30	−11.1
106	Money supply M2 in 1987 dollars	−7	NST	−24	−10	−11	NST	−16	NST	−17	−14.2
83	Index of consumer expectations	−18	−2	−38	−15	−10	−2	−9	−5	n.a.	−12.4
910	Composite index of 11 leading indicators	−18	−8	−15	−9	−11	−11	−20	−5	−7	−11.6
940	Ratio, coincident index to lagging index	−4	−4	−15	−11	−9	−12	−27	−9	−10	−11.2
	COINCIDENT INDICATORS										
41	Employees on nonagricultural payrolls	−1	0	+2	+11	+3	0	−5	−1	−2	+0.8
51	Personal income less transfer payments in 1987 dollars	−3	+1	0	0	NST	+1	0	−1	−1	−0.4
47	Index of industrial production	+2	0	+2	0	−2	−3	−5	0	−4	−1.1
57	Manufacturing and trade sales in 1987 dollars	−4	−6	−10	0	−2	−3	−6	−3	+1	−3.7
920	Composite index of 4 coincident indicators	−1	+1	0	0	−2	−3	−5	0	−1	−1.2
	LAGGING INDICATORS										
91	Average duration of unemployment (inverted)[1]	−13	+5	−6	−2	−2	+2	+1	+2	0	−1.4
77	Ratio, manufacturing, and trade inventories to sales in 1987 dollars	+6	+15	+5	+16	+11	+9	+8	+5	+8	+9.2
62	Change in index of labor cost per unit of output, manufacturing (smoothed)[3]	+8	+6	+5	+16	+1	+10	+6	+6	0	+6.4
109	Average prime rate charged by banks	−14	+1	+3	+10	+2	+3	+4	+7	NST	+2.0
101	Commercial and industrial loans outstanding in 1987 dollars	0	+14	+2	+10	+8	NST	+1	−1	+3	+4.6
95	Ratio, consumer installment credit to personal income	−10	NST	−7	+5	NST	+8	+5	+5	NST	+1.0
120	Change in Consumer Price Index for services (smoothed)[3]	+2	+2	+5	+11	+4	−6	−5	n.a.	n.a.	+1.9
930	Composite index of 7 lagging indicators	−8	+3	+3	+13	+3	+3	+4	+5	NST	+3.1

[1] NOTE: Reference peaks and troughs are the cyclical turning points in overall business activity; specific peaks and troughs are the cyclical turning points in individual series. This table lists, for the composite indexes and their components, the leads (−) and lags (+) of the specific peaks and troughs in relation to the corresponding reference peaks and troughs. See National Bureau of Economic Research pamphlets for information on the selection of cyclical peaks and troughs; they are available at http://www.nber.org.

n.a. Not available. Data needed to determine a specific turning point are not available.

NST No specific turn. No specific turning point is discernible in the data.

Table 5.7 Cyclical Leads (−) and Lags (+) for Leading, Coincident, and Lagging Indicators (length in months) (continued)

Series No.	Series Title	At Reference Troughs[1]									
		Mar. 1991	Nov. 1982	July 1980	Mar. 1975	Nov. 1970	Feb. 1961	Apr. 1958	May 1954	Oct. 1949	Mean
	LEADING INDICATORS										
1	Average weekly hours, manufacturing	+1	−1	0	0	−2	−2	0	−1	−6	−1.2
5	Average weekly initial claims for unemployment insurance (inverted)[1]	0	−2	−2	0	−1	0	0	+4	0	−0.1
8	Manufacturers' new orders in 1987 dollars, consumer goods and materials	0	−1	−2	0	0	0	−2	−7	−4	−1.8
32	Vendor performance, slower deliveries diffusion index	0	−8	−2	−1	+1	−11	−4	−6	−7	−4.2
20	Contracts and orders for plant and equipment in 1987 dollars	+3	+4	−2	+9	−1	+1	−1	−2	−6	+0.6
29	Building permits, new private housing units	−2	−13	−3	0	−10	−2	−2	−8	−9	−5.4
92	Change in manufacturers' unfilled orders in 1987 dollars, durable goods (smoothed)[2]	+20	−2	−1	+1	−3	−9	−2	−5	−4	−0.6
99	Change in sensitive materials prices (smoothed)[2]	0	−5	0	−2	−2	−1	−4	−4	−4	−2.4
19	Index of stock prices, 500 common stocks	−5	−4	NST	−3	−5	−4	−4	−8	−4	−4.6
106	Money supply M2 in 1987 dollars	−2	NST	−2	−2	−7	NST	−3	NST	−15	−5.2
83	Index of consumer expectations	−5	−8	−4	−1	−6	−3	+1	−6	n.a.	−4.0
910	Composite index of 11 leading indicators	−2	−10	−2	−1	−1	−2	−2	−4	−4	−3.1
940	Ratio, coincident index to lagging index	−2	−10	−2	0	−8	−1	0	−5	0	−2.9
	COINCIDENT INDICATORS										
41	Employees on nonagricultural payrolls	+11	0	0	+1	0	0	+1	+3	0	+1.8
51	Personal income less transfer payments in 1987 dollars	+8	0	0	−1	NST	−2	0	−1	−3	+0.1
47	Index of industrial production	0	+1	0	0	0	0	0	−1	0	0
57	Manufacturing and trade sales in 1987 dollars	−2	+1	−1	0	0	−1	0	−5	−3	−1.2
920	Composite index of 4 coincident indicators	0	+1	0	0	0	0	0	+2	0	+0.3
	LAGGING INDICATORS										
91	Average duration of unemployment (inverted)[1]	+19	+8	+6	+10	+19	+5	+6	+12	+8	+10.3
77	Ratio, manufacturing, and trade inventories to sales in 1987 dollars	+36	+14	+6	+44	+27	+14	+13	+12	+9	+17.4
62	Change in index of labor cost per unit of output, manufacturing (smoothed)[2]	+6	+10	+7	+8	+12	+7	+6	+11	+1	+9.7
109	Average prime rate charged by banks	+35	+8	+1	+25	+16	+57	+4	+14	NST	+17.9
101	Commercial and industrial loans outstanding in 1987 dollars	+24	+11	+8	+18	+15	NST	+4	+3	−1	+10.2
95	Ratio, consumer installment credit to personal income	+21	0	NST	+11	NST	+9	+7	+6	NST	+9.0
120	Change in Consumer Price Index for services (smoothed)[2]	+18	+2	+3	+5	+27	+5	+8	n.a.	n.a.	+9.7
930	Composite index of 7 lagging indicators	+36	+7	+3	+21	+15	+6	+4	+9	NST	+9.3

Source: *Survey of Current Business*, U.S. Department of Commerce, October 1994, no. C52.

[2] This series is inverted; i.e., low values are peaks and high values are troughs.

[3] This series is smoothed by an autoregressive-moving-average filter developed by Statistics Canada

Survey techniques furnish a substantial amount of qualitative information that may be useful in economic forecasting. These techniques are usually used to supplement the other quantitative forecasting methods discussed in this chapter. The greatest value of survey and opinion-polling techniques is that they may help to uncover changes in past relationships that the quantitative techniques assume will remain stable. If consumer tastes are changing or if business executives begin to lose confidence in the economy, survey techniques may be able to uncover these trends before their impact is felt.

Forecasting Economic Activity

Some of the best-known surveys available from private and governmental sources include the following:

http://
You may contact the *Survey of Current Business* on the Internet at
http://www.bea.doc.gov/bea/pubs.htm

1. *Plant and equipment expenditure plans*—Surveys of business intentions regarding plant and equipment expenditures are conducted by McGraw-Hill, the National Industrial Conference Board, the U.S. Department of Commerce, *Fortune* magazine, the Securities and Exchange Commission, and a number of individual trade associations. The McGraw-Hill survey, for example, is conducted twice yearly and covers all large corporations and many medium-sized firms. The survey reports plans for expenditures on fixed assets, as well as for expenditures on research and development. More than 50 percent of all new investment is accounted for by the McGraw-Hill survey.

   The Department of Commerce–Bureau of Economic Analysis plant and equipment expenditures survey is conducted quarterly and published regularly in the *Survey of Current Business*. The sample is larger and more comprehensive than that used by McGraw-Hill.

   The National Industrial Conference Board surveys capital appropriations commitments made by the board of directors of 1,000 manufacturing firms. The survey picks up capital expenditure plans that are to be made sometime in the future and for which funds have been appropriated. It is especially useful to firms that sell heavily to manufacturers and may aid in picking turning points in plant and equipment expenditures. This survey is published in the *Survey of Current Business*.

http://
The Institute for Supply Management is located on the Internet at
http://www.ism.ws

2. *Plans for inventory changes and sales expectations*—Business executives' expectations about future sales and their intentions about changes in inventory levels are reported in surveys conducted by the U.S. Department of Commerce, McGraw-Hill, Dun and Bradstreet, and the National Association of Purchasing Agents. The National Association of Purchasing Agents survey, for example, is conducted monthly, using a large sample of purchasing executives from a broad range of geographical locations and industrial activities in manufacturing firms.

http://
The University of Michigan's Survey Research Center can be found on the Internet at
http://www.isr.umich.edu/src/

3. *Consumer expenditure plans*—Consumer intentions to purchase specific products—including household appliances, automobiles, and homes—are reported by the Survey Research Center at the University of Michigan and by the Census Bureau. The Census Bureau survey, for example, is aimed at uncovering varying aspects of consumer expenditure plans, including income, holdings of liquid and nonliquid assets, the likelihood of making future durable goods purchases, and consumer indebtedness.

Sales Forecasting

Opinion polling and survey techniques are also used on a micro level within the firm for forecasting sales. Some of the variations of opinion polling that are used include the following:

1. *Sales force polling*—Some firms survey their own salespeople in the field about their expectations for future sales by specific geographical area and product line. The idea is that the employees who are closest to the ultimate customers may have significant insights to the state of the future market.

2. *Surveys of consumer intentions*—Some firms conduct their own surveys of specific consumer purchases. Such surveys are common in durable goods industries but too expensive or infeasible for less expensive items. Consider an auto dealer who pursues a "customer for life" relationship with his or her target market. Such a dealer or a furniture company may conduct a mail survey of a sample of consumers to estimate consumers' intentions of purchasing replacement autos or furniture.

ECONOMETRIC MODELS

Another forecasting tool that is available to the managerial economist is econometric modeling. Econometrics is a combination of theory, statistical analysis, and mathematical model building to explain economic relationships. Econometric models may vary in their level of sophistication from the simple to the extremely complex. Econometric techniques for demand estimation were discussed in detail in Chapter 4.

Advantages of Econometric Forecasting Techniques

Forecasting models based on econometric methodology possess a number of significant advantages over time-series analysis (e.g., trend projection) models, barometric models, and survey or opinion poll-based techniques. The most significant advantage of econometric models is that they identify independent variables (such as price or advertising expenditures in a demand model) that the manager may be able to manipulate.

Another advantage of econometric models is that they predict not only the direction of change in an economic series, but also the magnitude of that change. This represents a substantial improvement over the trend projection models, which failed to identify turning points, and the barometric models, which did not forecast the magnitudes of expected changes.

A third advantage of econometric models is their adaptability. On the basis of a comparison between forecast values and actual values, the model can be modified (that is, existing parameters may be reestimated and new variables or relationships developed) to improve future forecasts.

Single-Equation Models

The simplest form of econometric model is the single-equation model, as was developed for explaining the demand for Sherwin-Williams house paint in Chapter 4. Once the parameters of the demand equation are estimated, the model can be used to make forecasts of demand for house paint in a given region.

Example

SINGLE-EQUATION FORECASTS: THE DEMAND FOR GAME-DAY ATTENDANCE IN THE NFL[8]

Welki and Zlatoper report a model that explains the major determinants of the demand for game-day attendance at National Football League games. A forecasting model such as this might be used by a team to plan the most opportune times for special promotions and to predict demand for items sold at the stadium concession outlets. The following variables were used in the estimated model:

ATTENDANCE	game attendance
PRICE	average ticket price (1991 dollars)
INCOME	real per capita income (1987 dollars)
COMPCOST	price of parking at one game (1991 dollars)
HMTMRECORD	season's winning proportion of the home team prior to game day
VSTMRECORD	season's winning proportion of the visiting team prior to game day
GAME	number of regular season games played by the home team
TEMP	high temperature on game day
RAIN	dummy variable 1 = rain, 0 = no rain
DOME	dummy variable 1 = indoors, 0 = outdoors
DIVRIVAL	dummy variable 1 = teams are in same division, 0 = teams are not in same division
CONRIVAL	dummy variable 1 = conference game, 0 = nonconference game
NONSUNDAY	dummy variable 1 = game day is not Sunday, 0 = game day is Sunday
SUNNIGHT	dummy variable 1 = game moved to Sunday night for coverage on ESPN, 0 otherwise
BLACKOUT	dummy variable = 1 if game is blacked out for local TV, 0 otherwise

The estimated values of the coefficients for each of these variables are shown in the table on the next page.

These results indicate that weather conditions have little impact on the attendance at games. Fans appear to favor games played outdoors rather than in domed stadiums. Conference and divisional rivalries do not appear to impact demand greatly. Higher prices negatively impact attendance, but demand appears to be inelastic at current price levels. The quality of the team, as measured by its winning percentage, has a significant positive impact on attendance. A model similar to this could be used as the basis for forecasting demand for any type of athletic event.

Structural Equation Models

Although in many cases single-equation models may accurately specify the relationship that is being examined, frequently the interrelationships may be so complex that a system of several structural equations becomes necessary. Some of the more important terms encountered in a discussion of such models are the following:

---

[8] Andrew M. Welki and Thomas J. Zlatoper, "U.S. Professional Football: The Demand for Game-Day Attendance in 1991," *Managerial and Decision Economics* (September/October 1994), pp. 489–495.

Independent Variable	Expected Sign	Estimated Coefficient	T-Statistic
INTERCEPT		98053.00	11.49
PRICE	−	−642.02	−3.08
INCOME	?	−1.14	−3.12
COMPCOST	−	574.94	1.34
HMTMRECORD	+	16535.00	6.38
VSTMRECORD	?	2588.70	1.05
GAME	?	−718.65	−3.64
TEMP	?	−66.17	−1.27
RAIN	−	−2184.40	−1.23
DOME	?	−3171.70	−1.66
DIVRIVAL	+	−1198.00	−0.70
CONRIVAL	?	−1160.00	−0.58
NONSUNDAY	+	4114.80	1.74
SUNNIGHT	+	804.60	0.28
BLACKOUT	−	−5261.00	−3.15

Endogenous Variables
The variables that the econometric model seeks to explain or predict through the solution of a system of equations.

Exogenous Variables
The variables that are explained or determined by factors external to the econometric model.

Endogenous and Exogenous Variables   **Endogenous variables** are those that the model seeks to explain via the solution to the system of equations. **Exogenous variables** are either predetermined or determined by factors external to the model and may include such things as the level of government expenditures or the level of exports. If corporate investment were expressed as a function of corporate profits last year, the corporate profit variable would be considered a predetermined exogenous variable. Variables considered exogenous in one model may be endogenous in another.

Structural and Definitional Equations   An econometric model consists of two types of equations: *structural* (or *behavioral*) equations and *definitional* equations. A structural equation explains the relationship between a particular endogenous variable and other variables in the system. In contrast, definitional equations specify relationships that are true by definition. The statement that gross national product (*GNP*) equals consumption expenditures (*C*) plus gross capital investment (*I*) plus government expenditures (*G*) is an example of a definitional equation.

Example

MULTIPLE-EQUATION MODELS: THE U.S. ECONOMY

An econometric model based on a system of equations can best be illustrated by examining a simple model of the national economy:

$$C = \alpha_1 + \beta_1 Y + \epsilon_1 \tag{5.22}$$
$$I = \alpha_2 + \beta_2 P_{t-1} + \epsilon_2 \tag{5.23}$$
$$T = \beta_3 GNP + \epsilon_3 \tag{5.24}$$
$$GNP = C + I + G \tag{5.25}$$
$$Y = GNP - T \tag{5.26}$$

where C = consumption expenditures

I = investment

P_{t-1} = profits, lagged one period

GNP = gross national product

T = taxes

Y = national income

G = government expenditures

Equations 5.22, 5.23, and 5.24 are behavioral or structural equations, whereas Equations 5.25 and 5.26 are identities or definitional equations. Once the system of equations has been specified, the next task is to estimate the value of the parameters (α_1, α_2, β_1, β_2, β_3) based on historical data. The ϵ disturbances (or error terms) are included in Equations 5.22, 5.23, and 5.24 to reflect the fact that the theoretical relationships are not exact. To make unbiased estimates of the model's parameters, one must assume that the disturbance terms are randomly distributed with an expected value of zero. Once parameters of a system of equations have been estimated,[9] forecasts may be generated by substituting known or estimated values for the exogenous variables into the system and solving for the endogenous variables.

---

[9] See, for example, Ernest R. Berndt, *The Practice of Econometrics,* Reading, MA: Addison-Wesley Publishing Co., 1991, Chapter 8.

Table 5.8 Characteristics of Three Econometric Models of the U.S. Economy

	Model		
Characteristic	Wharton Econometric Forecasting Associates	Chase Econometric Associates	Townsend-Greenspan
Approximate number of variables forecasted	10,000	700	800
Forecast horizon (quarters)	2	10–12	6–10
Frequency of model updates (times per year)	12	12	4
Date model forecast first regularly issued	1963	1970	1965
Forecasting techniques			
(a) Econometric model	60%	70%	45%
(b) Judgment	30%	20%	45%
(c) Time-series methods	–	5%	–
(d) Current data analysis	10%	5%	10%

Source: Stephen K. McNees, "The Recent Record of Thirteen Forecasters," *New England Economic Review,* September–October 1981, pp. 5–21.

Complex Models of the U.S. Economy   A number of complex multiple-equation econometric models of the U.S. economy have been developed and are used to forecast business activity. Information on three of these models and the forecasting techniques they employ is summarized in Table 5.8. As can be seen, some of the large econometric models still rely heavily on the judgment of their staffs of economists.

Example

COMPARATIVE FORECASTING ACCURACY: TWO VAR MODELS[10]

Vector autoregression (VAR) was introduced in the early 1980s as an alternative to the large structural forecasting models used at Data Resources Inc. and Wharton Econometrics. Each VAR model illustrated below consists of six variables: real gross national product (*RGNP*), the implicit price deflator for GNP (*PGNP*), the unemployment rate (*RU*), gross private domestic investment (*GPDI*), the three-month Treasury bill rate (*TBILL*), and the money supply (*M1*). *RGNP, PGNP, GPDI,* and *M1* are used in natural log form. The first VAR model includes six lags of each variable, requiring the estimation of 37 *right-hand-side* variables for each equation. The second VAR model includes two lags of each variable, requiring the estimation of only 13 *right-hand-side* variables for each equation. Both VAR models are estimated with OLS.

Table 5.9 compares the forecasting performance of the two models over 20 successive, eight-quarter-ahead experimental forecasts. The first forecasts are for 1984:1Q through 1985:4Q, having estimated each model with data through 1983:4Q. The second forecasts are for 1984:2Q through 1986:1Q, having estimated each model with data through 1984:1Q, and so on.

The forecasting accuracy of each model is based on the root mean square error (RMSE) in forecasting each variable over Steps 1 through 8.

$$\text{RMSE}_s = \sqrt{\frac{1}{T}\sum_{t=1}^{T}(Y_t - {}_s\hat{Y}_t)^2}$$

where Y_t is the actual value at time t, ${}_s\hat{Y}_t$ is the forecast made s quarters earlier, and T is the number of forecasts made ($T = 20$). This simply means that, for each variable and forecast in Steps 1 through 8, the absolute error of the forecast is computed and stored. We then reestimate the model with one additional observation, forecast and compute the absolute error for each variable at each step, store each amount again, and so on. Once the 20 eight-quarter-ahead forecasts are completed, the program then averages the 20 absolute errors at each step for each variable.

Table 5.9 shows that the two-lag VAR model clearly outperforms the six-lag VAR model. The two-lag VAR model is more accurate in 40 of 48 cases compared with the six-lag model, and substantially more accurate in most cases. RMSE is smaller for the two-lag model of every series except M1.

Consensus Forecasts: The Livingston Surveys

Joseph A. Livingston and the Federal Reserve Bank of Philadelphia conduct a semi-annual survey of leading U.S. economists regarding their forecasts of unemployment, inflation, stock prices, and economic growth. The 50 to 60 economists who are

http://

The Livingston survey is maintained by the Philadelphia Federal Reserve Bank:
http://www.phil.frb.org/econ/liv/index.html

---

[10] These forecasts were developed at the Center for Economic Studies, Babcock School, Wake Forest University, by Professor Gary Shoesmith.

Table 5.9   Squared Forecast Errors for Eight-Quarter-Ahead VAR Models and RMSE

Forecast Step	1	2	3	4	5	6	7	8	RMSE
VAR (Lags = 6)									
RGNP	1.04	1.94	2.44	2.99	3.66	4.17	4.58	5.13	1.80
PGNP	0.36	0.85	1.52	2.31	3.17	4.05	4.91	5.81	1.69
RU	0.25	0.50	0.78	1.09	1.38	1.57	1.72	1.89	1.07
GPDI	4.19	8.18	9.96	11.39	12.18	12.14	10.74	10.24	3.14
TBILL	0.88	2.05	3.05	3.93	4.77	5.56	6.18	6.57	2.03
M1	0.71	1.66	3.07	4.53	5.83	7.41	8.89	10.48	2.31
VAR (Lags = 2)									
RGNP	0.60	0.95	1.10	1.38	1.86	2.20	2.49	2.76	1.29
PGNP	0.33	0.76	1.28	1.88	2.58	3.33	4.17	5.05	1.56
RU	0.16	0.28	0.31	0.32	0.37	0.44	0.60	0.79	0.64
GPDI	2.94	5.10	6.13	6.67	6.85	7.01	6.85	7.15	2.46
TBILL	0.83	1.64	2.32	3.00	3.65	4.23	4.72	5.16	1.79
M1	0.80	2.02	3.46	5.01	6.45	8.05	9.52	11.15	2.41

regularly surveyed represent a cross section from large corporations and banks, labor unions, government, investment banking firms, and universities. In addition to providing a broad consensus forecast of the economy, the Livingston surveys have been used by researchers as direct measures of economic expectations when testing various economic theories. The Livingston surveys also have been used to test theories regarding the way expectations are formed.

As a broad-based consensus forecast, the Livingston survey tends to be more stable over time than any individual forecast. Figure 5.7 indicates the record of the Livingston forecasts in predicting major expansions and recessions. As can be seen, economists have tended to predict relatively moderate recessions and expansions. Referring to Figure 5.4, there is evidence that economists have tended to underestimate both increases and decreases in the inflation rate. However, forecasts of inflation are improving.[11]

STOCHASTIC TIME-SERIES ANALYSIS

Finally, consider two forecasting approaches that capitalize on the interdependencies in business data: stochastic time-series analysis and input-output analysis. Deterministic time-series analysis, discussed earlier, was concerned with extrapolating deterministic past trends in the data (e.g., seasonal effects and population growth time trends). In contrast, stochastic time-series analysis attempts to remove deterministic time trends and instead model, estimate, and hopefully replicate the stochastic process generating any remaining patterns in the data across successive

---

[11] Based on Herb Taylor, "The Livingston Surveys: A History of Hopes and Fears," *Business Review,* Federal Reserve Bank of Philadelphia, May/June 1996, pp. 15–25.

Figure 5.7   Livingston Forecasts of GNP Growth

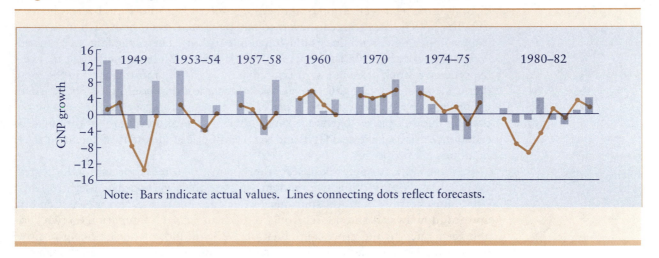

Note: Bars indicate actual values. Lines connecting dots reflect forecasts.

time periods—i.e., any remaining autocorrelation patterns. Autocorrelation was discussed in Appendix 4A.

Consider a simple autoregressive first-order process with positive drift α,

$$y_t = \alpha + \beta y_{t-1} + \varepsilon_t \qquad \overset{iid}{\varepsilon} \sim N(0, \sigma_\varepsilon^2) \qquad [5.27]$$

where $\beta = 1$ by hypothesis and where ε_t is a pure white noise disturbance drawn independently each period from a zero-mean, constant-variance normal probability distribution (an iid, independent and identically distributed, disturbance). As illustrated in Figure 5.8 Panel (a), when α equals zero, such a series has no tendency to revert

Figure 5.8   Random Walks Illustrated

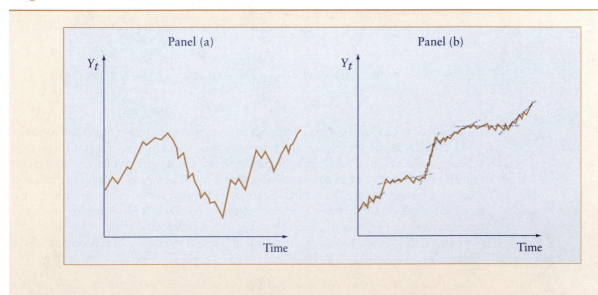

to any particular value (no "mean reversion"). In contrast, such series wander, and are inherently unforecastable, and therefore the last realization of y_t is the best prediction of the next realization of the series. Similarly, when α is non-zero, the level of y_t has no tendency to mean revert to any particular trend line; each innovation can result in a new trend line as illustrated in Panel (b). This is the famous "random walk" model applicable to the level of stock prices. Under the efficient markets hypothesis, a stock price like y_t in Equation 5.27 is "fully informative" in the sense that it incorporates all publicly available information that could possibly be useful in forecasting next period's stock price. For business forecasters, the difficulty is that commodity prices, exchange rates, interest rates, and possibly other macroeconomic variables like real GNP and the overall price index may also exhibit these random walk properties.

Random walk variables pose several problems for forecasting with OLS regression analysis. For one thing, two random walk variables with positive (negative) drift will almost certainly exhibit spurious correlation. Because each series is trending upward (downward) and not reverting to its mean, an OLS estimation on two variables generated by the process in Equation 5.27 will indicate a significant positive relationship between the variables when none exists. For example, even though real GNP and the overall price index of the economy (the GNP price deflator) have random shocks that may be totally unrelated, and even though real growth and inflation may have unrelated structural determinants (e.g., population growth versus monetary expansions), the t score in a simple OLS regression of real GNP on the price index can easily be as high as 12.0 (i.e., 99-percent confidence in a positive relationship). This can be very misleading to the forecaster seeking leading indicators for use in a business plan; imagine selling your firm's senior officers on the idea that because inflation is up, the firm can expect substantial real growth in demand next period. You might well be sent on an extended unpaid leave or even fired.

Of course, not all business time series exhibit these random walk properties. For example, a firm's profitability and earnings *do* mean revert in response to competitive entry and exit whenever they move substantially above or below the risk-adjusted mean for the industry, and therefore profits and earnings are not a random walk.[12] Hence, it is crucial to know whether the data one is working with were, or were not, generated by a random walk process.

The second problem posed by random walks is that the level of y_T after a number of periods T is

$$y_T = y_0 + \sum_{i=0}^{T} (\alpha + \varepsilon_{T-i}) \qquad [5.28]$$

$$= y_0 + T\alpha + \Sigma\, \epsilon_t \qquad [5.29]$$

the cumulative sum of the drift parameter plus all the white noise errors up to period T. Another way of describing this phenomenon is to say that all innovations to random walk variables result in *permanent* effects; the shocks just continue to cumulate and don't wash out as the time series lengthens. Therefore, "trends" in business data have two meanings. Some trends are deterministic like the upward and downward sales trends for bathing suits in the spring and summer versus fall and winter seasons. Other trends, however, are stochastic; stochastic trends are the permanent effects of innovations in a random walk process like Equation 5.27. Since

---

[12] See E. Fama and K. French, "Forecasting Profitability and Earnings," *Journal of Business*, April 2000, pp. 164–175.

these $\Sigma \, \varepsilon_t$ do not cancel out, it is appropriate to think of them as trends too. The problem is that the variance of y_T as the time series lengthens is equal to $T\sigma_\varepsilon^2$—that is, the variance of the stock price or interest rate has no limit! This makes it quite difficult to reduce root mean square error (RMSE) with the forecasting techniques we have seen so far. For example, even long lag structures in VAR regression models of stock price changes often have R^2 as low as 0.02 to 0.05 and very large RMSEs.

Although many advanced techniques beyond the scope of this text are motivated by the random walk stochastic process,[13] two simple methods we have already introduced at least partially address both of the above complications. First, all random walk-like processes have very long, slowly decaying autocorrelation functions. The first-order autoregressive AR(1) random walk process with drift α in Equation 5.27 is said to be *integrated of order one*—written I(1)—because the coefficient on the first autoregressive lag is by hypothesis $\beta = 1$. Indeed, this particular first-order autocorrelation function never decays. Consequently, the Durbin-Watson statistic introduced in Equation 4A.1 and Figure 4A.2 can be used to detect the presence of severe autocorrelation in such variables. The DW statistic will definitely fall well below 2.0 for data generated by Equation 5.27—i.e., below d_L for positively autocorrelated series and above $(4-d_L)$ for negatively autocorrelated series generated by a process like Equation 5.27 with $\beta = -1$. So, one can use the DW statistic as a diagnostic instrument to detect the possibility of a non-mean-reverting, random walk process.

Moreover, the I(1) property of an AR(1) random walk implies that taking the first difference of the price or interest rate series in Equation 5.27,

$$\Delta y_t = \alpha + (\beta - 1) \, y_{t-1} + \varepsilon_t \qquad [5.30]$$

would leave us with a process that did mean revert—i.e., a process that reverted to the drift parameter α—if in fact $\beta = 1$. It is straightforward to estimate the first difference of the time series in Equation 5.30 or, more generally, to estimate a vector autoregression in first differences,

$$\Delta y_t = \alpha + (\beta - 1) \, y_{t-1} + \sum_{t=1}^{\infty} \Delta y_{t-1} + \varepsilon_t \qquad [5.31]$$

Cointegrated Time Series
Stochastic series with a common order of integration and exhibiting an equilibrium relationship such that they do not permanently wander away from one another.

and conclude whether the null hypothesis $\beta = 1$ is true or false.[14] If true, any series with these properties should be differenced and incorporated into the forecasting regressions as first differences, not as levels.[15] If the situation as described in Equations 5.28, 5.29, and 5.30 pertains to both the dependent and an explanatory variable, the entire forecasting model should be specified in first differences. In that case, these two series are said to be **cointegrated** and will exhibit a nonspurious co-movement with one another that could prove quite important to achieving the standard forecasting objective of low RMSE.

---

[13] Several useful introductions to additional techniques in stochastic time-series analysis are F. Diebold, *Elements of Forecasting*, South-Western, 1998; W. Enders, *Applied Econometric Time-Series*, John Wiley and Sons, 1995; and William Greene, *Econometric Analysis*, 3rd ed., Prentice-Hall, 1997, Chapter 18.

[14] These tests can be performed with the *t*-statistic on the $(\beta - 1)$ parameter on y_{t-1} but require using a modified set of Dickey-Fuller critical values. See Appendix B, Table 7.

[15] If $\beta = 1$ is rejected, each series in question should be differenced again, and the second differences tested in exactly the same fashion. If in that case $\beta = 1$, second differences would be incorporated rather than first differences. If neither first nor second differences indicate a I(1) or 1(2) series, the forecaster proceeds using the levels of the original data.

FORECASTING WITH INPUT-OUTPUT TABLES

Another forecasting approach that capitalizes on the cross-sectional interdependence between various intermediate product and final product industries is *input-output analysis*. Input-output analysis enables the forecaster to trace the effects of an increase in demand for one product to other industries. An increase in the demand for automobiles will first lead to an increase in the output of the auto industry. This in turn will lead to an increase in the demand for steel, glass, plastics, tires, and upholstery fabric. In addition, secondary impacts will occur as the increase in the demand for upholstery fabric, for example, requires an increase in the production of fibers used to make the fabric. The demand for machinery may also increase as a result of the fabric demand, and so the pattern continues. Input-output analysis permits the forecaster to trace through all the interindustry effects that occur as a result of the initial increase in the demand for automobiles. The Bureau of Economic Analysis of the U.S. Department of Commerce produces a complicated set of tables specifying the interdependence among the various industries in the economy.[16]

International Perspectives

LONG-TERM SALES FORECASTING BY GENERAL MOTORS IN OVERSEAS MARKETS[17]

General Motors has an extensive forecasting system for both its North American and its overseas operations that is implemented by the Corporate Product Planning and Economics Staff. The process generates short- and long-term forecasts of the U.S. vehicle market and long-term forecasts for overseas markets. A discussion of the overseas forecasting process follows.

General Motors produces forecasts for motor vehicle sales in nearly 60 countries. These countries vary in the number of cars per 1,000 people (car density), from less than 10 to over 500. The primary factor used to explain the growth in car density is the level of and changes in income in each country. In the first step of the forecasting process, the macroeconomic relationship between key economic variables, including income levels and motor vehicle sales, is estimated. Specifically, estimates are made of the income elasticity of demand in each country. The second step attempts to monitor changes over time in the relationships established in Step 1.

The third step consists of consultations between the Product Planning and Economics Staff and the Marketing Staffs of each GM overseas operation. The objective of this phase is to identify any special factors in each country that might require a significant modification in the forecasts generated from the econometric models. For example, in the early and mid-1980s, it was felt that certain voluntary restraint policies that had been adopted by the Japanese government would hold down demand by up to 50 percent, relative to the forecasts from the econometric model. When these policy barriers were removed, car sales increased greatly, returning to levels predicted by the econometric model.

The final step provides models of alternative future scenarios that reflect the impact of major changes in the economic environment for which full information is unavailable. For example, GM developed an alternative model scenario that reflected the impact of the creation of a single West European market and the dissolution of the former

---

[16] The most recent input-output tables may be found for 85 industries in "Annual Input-Output Accounts for the U.S. Economy, 1996: Requirements Tables," *Survey of Current Business*, January 2000, pp. 37–86.

[17] This section was adapted from Richard DeRoeck, "Sales Forecasting at General Motors," *International Institute of Forecasters Newsletter*, December 1990, pp. 2–4.

Soviet-bloc countries. More recently, GM developed a scenario plan for the opening of the Chinese market; it predicted more sales by 2010 in the fast-growing markets of China and India than all other foreign sales combined.

The types of sales forecasting models that are available to managers of global corporations are really no different than those available to domestic firms. However, deriving cash flow forecasts from foreign sales necessitates modeling (and managing) the exchange rate risk exposure. Forecasting models for use by a multinational firm are discussed in the next chapter on managing exports.

SUMMARY

- A forecast is a prediction concerning the future.
- The choice of a forecasting technique depends on the cost of developing the forecasting model relative to the potential benefits to be derived, the complexity of the relationship being forecast, the time period for the forecast, the accuracy required of the model, and the lead time required to obtain inputs for the forecasting model.
- Data used in forecasting may be in the form of a time series—that is, a series of observations of a variable over a number of past time periods—or they may be cross-sectional—that is, observations are taken at a single point in time for a sample of individuals, firms, geographic regions, communities, or some other set of observable units.
- Deterministic time-series forecasting models are based on an extrapolation of past values into the future. Time-series forecasting models may be adjusted for seasonal, secular, and cyclical trends in the data. Stochastic time-series forecasting models investigate the randomness generating process in the underlying data.
- When a data series possesses a great deal of randomness, *smoothing techniques,* such as moving averages and exponential smoothing, may improve the forecast accuracy.
- Neither trend analysis models nor smoothing techniques are capable of identifying major future changes in the direction of an economic data series.
- *Barometric techniques,* which employ leading, lagging, and coincident indicators, are designed to forecast changes in the direction of a data series but are poorly suited for forecasting the magnitude of the change.
- *Survey and opinion-polling techniques* are often useful in forecasting such variables as business capital spending and major consumer expenditure plans and for generating product-specific or regional sales forecasts for a firm.
- *Econometric methods* seek to explain the reasons for a change in an economic data series and to use this quantitative, explanatory model to make future forecasts. Econometric models are one of the most useful business forecasting tools, but they tend to be expensive to develop and maintain.
- Trends in business data are either deterministic or stochastic. Stochastic trends like those introduced by random walk variables require careful diagnosis and special methods.
- The ultimate measure of the effectiveness of a forecast is not its level of mathematical or theoretical sophistication, but rather its ability to generate cost-effective estimates of the future that are sufficiently accurate to meet the needs of the decision maker.

EXERCISES

1. An economist for Pittsburgh Brewing Company has hypothesized a forecasting model in which the sales in any particular month are directly proportional to the square of the wages of Pittsburgh steelworkers in the previous month, plus a random error.

   a. If S = sales, W = steelworkers' wages, t = time, and e = the random error term, formulate an equation to forecast this month's sales and another equation to forecast next month's sales.

   b. If the random errors average out to zero, and if sales this month are $900,000 and wages last month were $2,000, what should next month's sales be if this month's wages decline to $1,800?

2. The forecasting staff for the Prizer Corporation has developed a model to predict sales of its air-cushioned-ride snowmobiles. The model specifies that sales S vary jointly with disposable personal income Y and the population between ages 15 and 40, Z, and *inversely* with the price of the snowmobiles P. Based on past data, the best estimate of this relationship is

$$S = k \frac{YZ}{P}$$

   where k has been estimated (with past data) to equal 100.

   a. If Y = $11,000, Z = $1,200, and P = $20,000, what value would you predict for S?

   b. What happens if P is reduced to $17,500?

   c. How would you go about developing a value for k?

   d. What are the potential weaknesses of this model?

3. Forecast errors can usually be reduced by increasing the amount of time and money spent on preparing the forecast. Under what circumstances might such an increase in expenditures not be undertaken by profit-maximizing managers?

4. Stowe Automotive is considering an offer from Indula to build a plant making automotive parts for use in that country. In preparation for a final decision, Stowe's economists have been hard at work constructing a basic econometric model for Indula to aid the company in predicting future levels of economic activity. Because of the cyclical nature of the automotive parts industry, forecasts of future economic activity are quite important in Stowe's decision process.

   Corporate profits (P_{t-1}) for all firms in Indula were about $100 billion. *GNP* for the nation is composed of consumption C, investment I, and government spending G. It is anticipated that Indula's federal, state, and local governments will spend in the range of $200 billion next year. On the basis of an analysis of recent economic activity in Indula, consumption expenditures are assumed to be $100 billion plus 80 percent of national income. National income is equal to *GNP* minus taxes T. Taxes are estimated to be at a rate of about 30 percent of *GNP*. Finally, corporate investments have historically equaled $30 billion plus 90 percent of last year's corporate profits (P_{t-1}).

a. Construct a five-equation econometric model of the state of Indula. There will be a consumption equation, an investment equation, a tax receipt equation, an equation representing the *GNP* identity, and a national income equation.

b. Assuming that all random disturbances average to zero, solve the system of equations to arrive at next year's forecast values for *C, I, T, GNP,* and *Y.* (*Hint:* It is easiest to start by solving the investment equation and then working through the appropriate substitutions in the other equations.)

5. a. Fred's Hardware and Hobby House expects its sales to increase at a constant rate of 8 percent per year over the next three years. Current sales are $100,000. Forecast sales for each of the next three years.

   b. If sales in 1990 were $60,000 and they grew to $100,000 by 1994 (a four-year period), what was the actual annual compound growth rate?

6. Metropolitan Hospital has estimated its average monthly bed needs as

$$N = 1,000 + 9X$$

where X = time period (months); January 2003 = 0
   N = monthly bed needs

Assume that no new hospital additions are expected in the area in the foreseeable future. The following monthly seasonal adjustment factors have been estimated, using data from the past five years:

Month	Adjustment Factor
January	+5%
April	−15%
July	+4%
November	−5%
December	−25%

a. Forecast Metropolitan's bed demand for: January, April, July, November, and December of 2005.

b. If the following actual and forecast values for June bed demands have been recorded, what seasonal adjustment factor would you recommend be used in making future June forecasts?

Year	Forecast	Actual
2003	1,045	1,096
2002	937	993
2001	829	897
2000	721	751
1999	613	628
1998	505	560

7. A firm experienced the demand shown in the table below in the 1990s.

Year	5-Year Moving Demand	3-Year Moving Average	Exponential Smoothing Average	Exponential Smoothing ($w = .9$)	($w = .3$)
1990	800	xxxxx	xxxxx	xxxxx	xxxxx
1991	925	xxxxx	xxxxx	—	—
1992	900	xxxxx	xxxxx	—	—
1993	1025	xxxxx	—	—	—
1994	1150	xxxxx	—	—	—
1995	1160	—	—	—	—
1996	1200	—	—	—	—
1997	1150	—	—	—	—
1998	1270	—	—	—	—
1999	1290	—	—	—	—
2000	*	—	—	—	—

*Unknown future value to be forecast.

    a. Fill in the table by preparing forecasts based on a five-year moving average, a three-year moving average, and exponential smoothing (with a $w = .9$ and a $w = .3$). *Note:* The exponential smoothing forecasts may be begun by assuming $\hat{Y}_{t+1} = Y_t$.

    b. Using the forecasts from 1995 through 1999, compare the accuracy of each of the forecasting methods based on the RMSE criterion.

    c. Which forecast would you have used for 2000? Why?

8. The economic analysis division of Mapco Enterprises has estimated the demand function for its line of weed trimmers as

$$Q_D = 18,000 + 0.4N - 350P_M + 90P_S$$

where N = number of new homes completed in the primary market area

    P_M = price of the Mapco trimmer

    P_S = price of its competitor's Surefire trimmer

In 2006, 15,000 new homes are expected to be completed in the primary market area. Mapco plans to charge $50 for its trimmer. The Surefire trimmer is expected to sell for $55.

    a. What sales are forecast for 2006 under these conditions?

    b. If its competitor cuts the price of the Surefire trimmer to $50, what effect will this have on Mapco's sales?

    c. What effect would a 30-percent reduction in the number of new homes completed have on Mapco's sales (ignore the impact of the price cut of the Surefire trimmer)?

9. The sales of Cycle City, a large motorcycle and moped distributor, grew significantly during the 1990s. This past history of sales growth is indicated in the table below:

Year	Sales
1990	$100,000
1991	130,000
1992	166,400
1993	209,664
1994	259,983
1995	317,180
1996	380,615
1997	449,126
1998	520,986
1999	593,924
2000	665,195

a.   What was the compound annual rate of growth in sales for Cycle City over this ten-year period?

b.   Based on your answer in Part (a), what sales would you have forecasted for the next year (2001)?

c.   Graph the growth in sales over the ten years. What happened to the rate of growth over this period?

d.   Based on your answer to Part (c), what sales would you have forecasted for 2001?

10.   The Questor Corporation has experienced the following sales pattern over a ten-year period:

Year	Sales ($000)
19X0	121
19X1	130
19X2	145
19X3	160
19X4	155
19X5	179
19X6	215
19X7	208
19X8	235
19X9	262
19Y0	*

*Unknown future value to be forecast.

a.   Compute the equation of a trend line (similar to Equation 5.5) for these sales data to forecast sales for the next year. (Let 1990 = 0, 1991 = 1, etc., for the time variable.) What does this equation forecast for sales in the year 2000?

b.   Use a first-order exponential smoothing model with a w of 0.9 to forecast sales for the year 2000.

11. The following table provides corporate average bond yields for each month of 1994:

Month	Yield
January	12.92%
February	12.88
March	13.33
April	13.59
May	14.13
June	14.40
July	14.32
August	13.78
September	13.56
October	13.33
November	12.88
December	12.74

a. Use the models in Equations 5.3, 5.4, 5.5, plus a three-month moving average to forecast the interest rate for January 1995.

b. Compare the results of each of these forecasts with the actual January 1995 figure of 12.64 percent.

12. Bell Greenhouses has estimated its monthly demand for potting soil to be the following:

$$N = 400 + 4X$$

where N = monthly demand for bags of potting soil

X = time periods in months (March 2003 = 0)

Assume this trend factor is expected to remain stable in the foreseeable future. The following table contains the monthly seasonal adjustment factors, which have been estimated using actual sales data from the past five years:

Month	Adjustment Factor
March	+2%
June	+15%
August	+10%
December	−12%

a. Forecast Bell Greenhouses' demand for potting soil in March, June, August, and December 2005.

b. If the following table shows the forecasted and actual potting soil sales by Bell Greenhouses for April in five different years, determine the seasonal adjustment factor to be used in making an April 2005 forecast.

Year	Forecast	Actual
2005	500	515
2004	452	438
2003	404	420
2002	356	380
2001	308	320

13. Savings-Mart (a chain of discount department stores) sells patio and lawn furniture. Sales are seasonal, with higher sales during the spring and summer quarters and lower sales during the fall and winter quarters. The company developed the following quarterly sales forecasting model:

$$\hat{Y}_t = 8.25 + .125t - 2.75D_{1t} + +.25D_{2t} + 3.50D_{3t}$$

where $\hat{Y}_t$ = predicted sales ($ million) in quarter t

　　8.25 = quarterly sales ($ million) when $t = 0$

　　　　t = time period (quarter) where the fourth quarter of 19X0 = 0, first quarter of 1991 = 1, second quarter of 1991 = 2, . . .

$$D_{1t} = \begin{cases} 1 \text{ for first-quarter observations} \\ 0 \text{ otherwise} \end{cases}$$

$$D_{2t} = \begin{cases} 1 \text{ for second-quarter observations} \\ 0 \text{ otherwise} \end{cases}$$

$$D_{3t} = \begin{cases} 1 \text{ for third-quarter observations} \\ 0 \text{ otherwise} \end{cases}$$

Forecast Savings-Mart's sales of patio and lawn furniture for each quarter of 1996.

14. The demand for tea has been estimated as

$$Q = 7,000 - 550P + 210I + 425P_c$$

where Q = thousands of pounds of tea sold

　　P = price per pound of tea

　　I = per capita disposable personal income in thousands of dollars

　　P_c = price per pound of coffee

a. If next year's tea price is forecast to be $3, per capita disposable personal income is estimated to be $15,000 (that is, 15), and the price per pound of coffee is estimated to be $4, compute the expected quantity demanded for the coming year.

b. Economic forecasters think there is a high probability of a major recession next year that would reduce per capita income to $13,000 (13). In addition, a frost in Brazil is likely to increase the price of coffee to $7 per pound. What impact would these changes in the economic outlook have on the demand for tea?

15. A university is typically required to prepare operating budgets well in advance of actually receiving its revenues and incurring the expenditures. An important source of revenue is student tuition, which is obviously a function of the number

of students enrolled. A university was having problems in preparing accurate budgets because past forecasts of enrollment, made each February before the start of the academic year in September, were subject to considerable error. One aspect of the problem was determining the relationship between the numbers of applications received by February 1 and the number of new students entering the university the following September. The data tabulated below were collected on September registrations and February 1 applications.

Year	Number of Applications Received by February 1 (hundreds)	Number of New Students Enrolled in September (hundreds)
1990	28	24
1991	26	20
1992	28	18
1993	28	22
1994	36	32
1995	36	33
1996	42	34
1997	46	34
1998	46	35
1999	50	38

a. Given the nature of the forecasting problem, which variable would be the dependent variable and which would be the independent variable?

b. Plot the data.

c. Determine the estimated regression line. Give an economic interpretation of the slope (β) coefficient.

d. Test the hypothesis that there is no relationship (that is, $\beta = 0$) between the variables.

e. Calculate the coefficient of determination.

f. Perform an analysis of variance on the regression, including an F-test of the overall significance of the results.

g. Suppose 4,200 applications are received by February 1. What is the best estimate, based on the regression model, of the number of new students that will be enrolled in the following September? Construct an approximate 95-percent prediction interval.

h. Suppose that as the result of changes in the deadlines for scholarship and loan selection requests, applications received by February 1 increase to 6,000. What would be the estimate of enrollment for the following September?

i. Would the estimate of enrollment in part (h) be reliable? Why or why not?

16. Use the monthly series on the Consumer Price Index (all items) from the previous 2 years to produce a forecast of the CPI for each of the next 3 years. Is the precision of your forecast greater or less at 36 months ahead than at 12 months ahead? Why? Compare your answer to that of the Dismal Scientist, a company that provides economic data, analysis, and forecasts on the Internet at http://www.dismal.com/.

http://
http://www.dismal.com/

SOUTH POLE ICE CREAM COMPANY

Monthly sales ($\times$ $100,000) of the South Pole Ice Cream Company are shown in the table below.

Month	2000	2001	2002
January	2.30	2.65	3.30
February	2.60	2.80	3.60
March	2.70	3.00	3.60
April	2.85	3.20	4.20
May	3.25	3.85	4.20
June	3.30	3.90	5.00
July	3.25	3.80	—
August	3.35	3.90	—
September	3.20	3.60	—
October	3.10	3.55	—
November	2.75	3.30	—
December	2.65	3.20	—

QUESTIONS

1. Plot the data on a graph with time on the horizontal axis and sales ($\times$ $100,000) on the vertical axis.

2. Fit a linear trend equation to the data using the least-squares method. (*Note:* This can be done using either a calculator or a computer.)

3. Based on your answer to Question 2, forecast (seasonally unadjusted) sales for each of the last six months of 2002.

4. Calculate seasonally adjusted monthly sales by the ratio to trend method for the last six months of 2002.

CRUISE SHIP ARRIVALS IN ALASKA

The summer months bring warm weather, megafauna (bears), and tourists to the coastal towns of Alaska. Skagway at the top of the Inland Passage was, in the 19th century, the entrance to the Yukon. Today this town attracts multiple cruise ships per day; literally thousands of passengers disembark into a town of 800 for a taste of the Alaskan frontier experience between 10 A.M. and 5 P.M. Some ride steam trains into the mountains, others wander the town spending money in galleries, restaurants, and souvenir shops. The Skagway Chamber of Commerce is trying to decide which transportation mode in the table on the next page should receive the highest priority in the tourist promotions for next season.

QUESTIONS

1. Plot the raw data on arrivals for each transportation mode against time, all on the same graph. Which mode is growing the fastest? Which the slowest?

2. Plot the logarithm of arrivals for each transportation mode against time, all on the same graph. Which now appears to be growing the fastest?

Logarithms are especially useful for comparing series with two divergent scales since 10-percent growth always looks the same, regardless of the starting level. When absolute levels matter, the raw data is more appropriate, but when growth rates are what's important, log scales are better.

3. Now create an index number to represent the growth of arrivals in each transportation mode by dividing the first (smallest) number in each column into the remaining numbers in the column. Plot these index numbers for each transportation mode against time, all in the same graph. Which is growing the fastest?

4. In attempting to formulate a model of the passenger arrival data on cruise ships over time would a nonlinear (perhaps a multiplicative exponential) model be preferable to a linear model of cruise ship arrivals against time? What about in the case of the passenger arrivals by ferry against time?

5. Estimate the double-log (log linear) time trend model for log cruise ship arrivals against log time. Estimate a linear time trend model of cruise ship arrivals against time. Calculate the root mean square error between the predicted and actual value of cruise ship arrivals. Is the root mean square error greater for the double log time trend model or for the linear time trend model? Which is a better model?

Skagway Visitor Arrival Statistics				
Year	Cruise	Ferry	Highway	Air
1983	48,066	25,288	72,384	3,500
1984	54,907	25,196	79,215	3,750
1985	77,623	31,522	89,542	4,000
1986	100,695	30,981	91,908	4,250
1987	119,279	30,905	70,993	4,953
1988	115,505	31,481	74,614	5,957
1989	112,692	29,997	63,789	7,233
1990	136,512	33,234	63,237	4,799
1991	141,284	33,630	64,610	4,853
1992	145,973	37,216	79,946	7,947
1993	192,549	33,650	80,709	10,092
1994	204,387	34,270	81,172	10,000
1995	256,788	33,961	87,977	17,000
1996	299,651	35,760	86,536	20,721
1997	438,305	27,659	91,849	11,466
1998	494,961	31,324	100,784	20,679
1999	525,507	31,467	92,291	15,963

Source: *The Skagway News,* Nov. 16, 1999

LUMBER PRICE FORECAST

QUESTIONS

1. One of the most important variables that must be forecasted accurately to project the cost of single-family home construction is the price of Southern pine framing lumber. Use the following data to forecast two- and four-year-ahead lumber prices. Compare the forecast accuracy of at least two alternative forecasting methods.

Lumber Price Index

1999	176.3	1980	95.2
1998	168.4	1979	99.0
1997	182.7	1978	90.9
1996	168.7	1977	77.9
1995	162.7	1976	67.7
1994	168.9	1975	58.3
1993	163.2	1974	60.5
1992	137.5	1973	58.3
1991	123.9	1972	47.6
1990	121.7	1971	41.9
1989	118.9	1970	37.4
1988	111.5	1969	41.3
1987	105.8	1968	37.3
1986	100.7	1967	32.9
1985	100.0	1966	33.0
1984	101.3	1965	31.6
1983	101.2	1964	31.4
1982	93.8		
1981	96.4		

BUSH RECESSION FORECAST

QUESTIONS

1. Using the data in the following table, provide an estimate of real GNP for eight quarters of the first Bush Presidency (i.e., 1989:1 to 1990:4). This requires a procedure much longer than was needed for the lumber price forecast. Begin with a single-variable, four-lag forecasting model of the price series (PGNP) and the interest rate series (TBILL), deleting insignificant lags as indicated by the results. Then build a forecasting model of the RGNP series using significant lags of this dependent variable and of the PGNP and TBILL forecasted series.

2. Compare your forecast to the actual data from the *Survey of Current Business*: 4096, 4112, 4130, 4133, 4151, 4155, 4170, and 4148. Did your model predict the recession that began in 1990:4?

Historical Data: Real GNP (Billions of Constant 1982 Dollars); Implicit Price Deflator for GNP (1982 = 100); 3-Month T-Bill Rate (%)

Time	RGNP	PGNP	TBILL
79:1	3181.70	76.100	9.35767
79:2	3178.70	77.800	9.37233
79:3	3207.40	79.400	9.63133
79:4	3201.30	81.000	11.80370
80:1	3233.40	82.700	13.45870
80:2	3157.00	84.600	10.04930
80:3	3159.10	86.500	9.23533
80:4	3199.20	89.000	13.70970
81:1	3261.10	91.300	14.36900
81:2	3250.20	92.800	14.82900
81:3	3264.60	94.900	15.08730
81:4	3219.00	96.700	12.02270
82:1	3170.40	98.200	12.89500
82:2	3179.90	99.400	12.35900
82:3	3154.50	100.800	9.70533
82:4	3159.30	101.700	7.93500
83:1	3186.60	102.500	8.08133
83:2	3258.30	103.300	8.41900
83:3	3306.40	104.200	9.18667
83:4	3365.10	105.400	8.79333
84:1	3451.70	106.500	9.13333
84:2	3498.00	107.300	9.84333
84:3	3520.60	108.200	10.34330
84:4	3535.20	109.000	8.97333
85:1	3577.50	109.700	8.18333
85:2	3599.20	110.600	7.52333
85:3	3635.80	111.300	7.10333
85:4	3662.40	112.200	7.14667
86:1	3721.10	112.400	6.88667
86:2	3704.60	113.200	6.13000
86:3	3712.40	114.600	5.53333
86:4	3733.60	115.100	5.34000
87:1	3781.20	116.100	5.53333
87:2	3820.30	117.000	5.73333
87:3	3858.90	118.000	6.03333
87:4	3920.70	118.500	6.00333
88:1	3970.20	119.300	5.76000
88:2	4005.80	120.600	6.23000
88:3	4036.10	122.000	6.99333
88:4	4069.30	123.400	7.70333

6

Managing Exports

CHAPTER PREVIEW Today, business plans involve supply chain management, production operations, and targeted marketing on several continents. Most companies, whether American, Dutch, German, Japanese, Brazilian, or Korean, engage in foreign direct investment and manufacture abroad. Some companies outsource manufacturing to low-wage partners, affiliates, or operating divisions in places like China, Mexico, Portugal, Indonesia, and the Caribbean. Others buy parts and supplies or assembled components from foreign firms. And almost all manufacturers produce an export product to sell abroad. Indeed, export markets are increasingly the primary source of sales growth for many manufacturers. Careful analysis and accurate forecasting of these international purchases and international sales provide pivotal information for capacity planning, for production scheduling, and for pricing, promotion, and distribution plans in many companies.

In this chapter, we investigate the relationship between exchange rates and import/export sales. International trade plus capital flows determine long-term trends in exchange rates, which we analyze with standard demand and supply tools in the market for U.S. dollars as foreign exchange (FX). Purchasing power parity conditions provide a way to assess these FX trends and incorporate export sales in business scenario planning. We then explore the reasons for and patterns of trade in the world's economy with special attention to regional trading blocs, like the European Union and NAFTA. The chapter closes with perspectives on the U.S. trade deficit. Our attention throughout is focused on the special challenges for individual companies that arise out of global competition and the growing importance of the import/export sector in the U.S. economy.

MANAGERIAL CHALLENGE

Export Market Pricing at Toyota[1]

On January 5, 1994, the U.S. dollar exchanged for ¥113. A 1994 Toyota Celica ST Coupe made in Japan and shipped to Eastern U.S. dealers sold for $16,968—i.e., each sale realized revenue approximately equal to ¥2 million (i.e., ¥1,917,384). Just 16 months later on April 19, 1995, the dollar was worth only ¥80. This 34-percent decline in the value of the dollar and corresponding 34-percent appreciation of the yen made Japanese exports to the United States potentially much more expensive. To recover costs and maintain their 1994 profit margin, Toyota was presented with the prospect of pricing that same Toyota Celica ST Coupe at $23,967—i.e., ¥1,917,384 ÷ (¥80/U.S.$). Since domestic U.S. producers of comparable small sporty cars had raised prices only 5–10 percent over the intervening period, Toyota faced a tough decision. Increase the car's price well ahead of the competition and try to limit the erosion of market share by emphasizing manufacturing quality and service or, alternatively, reduce margins and protect current market share.

As we shall see in this chapter, different companies react in different ways to the challenges presented by such severe currency fluctuations. GM and Ford tend to maintain margins. In contrast, Toyota chose to increase the 1995 Celica ST Coupe price by only 2 percent to $17,285, despite the consequential 32-percent decline in realized yen per unit sale. Because of these pricing and related decisions, between 1994 and 1997 Toyota's share of the U.S. passenger car market jumped from 8.5 percent to 10.5 percent, while the Big Three's share of the U.S. passenger car market fell from 64.6 percent to 61.1 percent.

The U.S. International Trade Administration provides news and other information on international trade issues affecting U.S. companies at the following Internet address: http://www.ita.doc.gov/media

---

[1] Based on G. Gardner, "The Fading Big Three Car Market," *Ward's Automotive World*, September 1997, pp. 41–46; and Jack Gillis, *The Car Book*, 1997.

INTRODUCTION

Around the globe, the reduction of trade barriers and the opening of markets to foreign imports has increased the competitive pressure on manufacturers who once dominated their domestic industries. Tennis shoes and dress footwear once produced in large factories in Britain and the United States now come from Korea, China, and Italy. Automobiles once dominated by Ford, General Motors, and Chrysler now come in large numbers from Japan. Boeing and Microsoft are the largest U.S. exporters. In retailing, McDonald's operates in over 100 foreign countries, Wal-Mart sells $200 billion overseas, and both General Motors and Coca-Cola's international sales will soon exceed those in the United States. Exports have become the key to growth for many leading manufacturing firms, service companies, and franchise retailers.

Figure 6.1   U.S. Exports and Imports as Percentage of GNP

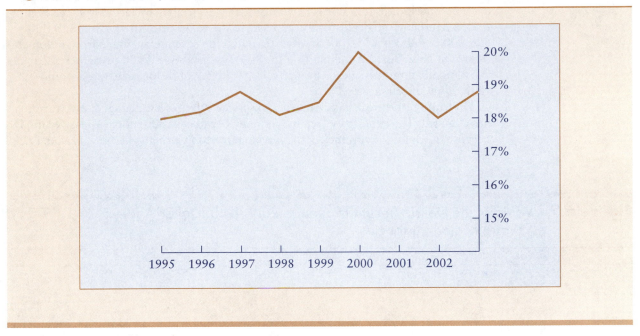

Source: *Economic Report of the President.*

Similarly, outsourcing parts, components, and supplies to foreign companies has become standard "supply chain management" practice for U.S. manufacturers. For a minivan, DaimlerChrysler may decide to cast engine blocks in Mexico, acquire electronics from Taiwan, tool ball bearings in Germany, and locate final assembly in Canada. Wood furniture "made in the U.S.A." now includes foreign components equal to 38 percent of the total value added, whereas imports constituted only 18 percent as recently as 1992.[2] So, when 32 percent of Canadian output and 25 percent of Mexican, Singaporan, Malaysian, and Hong Kong's output flows into the U.S., much of that import flow is components and supplies, not consumer electronics and Japanese autos. Overall, Figure 6.1 shows that in 2000, the dollar value of import plus export transactions totaled one fifth of the dollar value of all U.S. output. This explains in large measure why 26 percent of U.S. corporate profits in 2003 came from overseas operations.[3] The world of business has truly become a matter of managing in the global economy.

IMPORT-EXPORT SALES AND EXCHANGE RATES

Export and import sales are very sensitive to changes in exchange rates. A Jeep Grand Cherokee automobile that retails in New York for $30,000 can be transported to Munich for about €300. In 1999, if the U.S. dollar exchanges for 0.85 euros, the Jeep dealer in Munich must charge $30,000 × €0.85/$ = €25,500 to replace the U.S. dollar revenue from a forgone domestic sale in America. Including the

---

[2] "Made Elsewhere," *Winston-Salem Journal,* March 25, 2002, p. B1.

[3] "Dollar's Dive Helps U.S. Companies," *Wall Street Journal,* April 21, 2003, p. A2.

transportation cost, a Jeep in Munich would therefore retail for €25,800. Now suppose the exchange rate changes, and the value of the euro trends downward for an extended period. If 1.18 euros exchange for a U.S. dollar by late 2000 (see Figure 6.2), a Munich Jeep dealer will need to raise the retail price to (1.18 × $30,000 = €35,400 + €300 = €35,700) in order to match the revenue available from a domestic sale in New York. If competition for SUVs is stiff, this €9,900 price increase may substantially diminish sales. Alternatively, a rollback of the price increase would substantially reduce margins.

No feature of the car has changed. No service offering has changed. No warranty has changed. The exports by Jeep to Germany became €9,900 more expensive simply because the domestic currency of the foreign buyers in Germany became weaker. Price

Figure 6.2   Value of the Dollar: Recent Exchange Rates (U.S. Dollar Against Several Major Currencies)

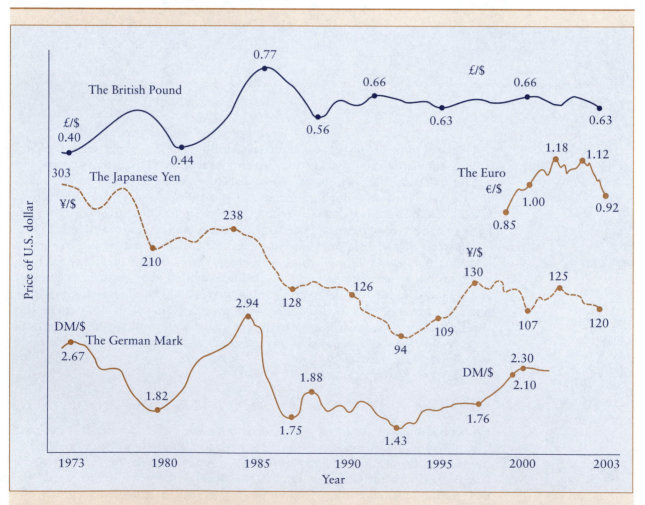

increases of this magnitude in export markets caused by changes in long-term trend exchange rates are common. Over the 1970s, 1980s, and 1990s, exchange rates were four times more volatile than interest rates and ten times more volatile than inflation rates. Figure 6.2 shows that £/$ and DM/$ exchange rates in the mid-1980s and the €/$ exchange rate between 1999 and 2003 were particularly volatile. Analyzing and forecasting the cash flow effects of such changes provides key information for the marketing, operations, and merger plans of companies like Boeing, Microsoft, and DaimlerChrysler.

Foreign Exchange Translation Risk Exposure
An accounting adjustment in the home currency value of foreign assets or liabilities.

Such operating risk exposures necessitate substantial risk management initiatives and are distinguished from two other less significant types of foreign exchange risk exposure. **Translation risk exposure** occurs when a company's foreign assets (or liabilities) are affected by exchange rate movements. Accordingly, the accounting books in the home country must translate these balance sheet adjustments back into home country currency. A 100-million-deutsche mark ball-bearing plant owned by Jeep-Chrysler and located in Germany may need to be written down on the company's U.S. balance sheet when the deutsche mark falls from 0.5618 $/DM (i.e., 1.76 DM/$) in 1997 to 0.4762 $/DM (i.e., 2.10 DM/$) in the year 1999 (again, see Figure 6.2). This $8,560,000 translation risk exposure, $(0.5618 - 0.4762) \times$ DM 100,000,000, is often and easily offset with balance sheet hedges (i.e., a merger or acquisition designed to match the magnitude of company liabilities to those of the company assets held by the foreign subsidiary). Then an $8.56 million reduction in liabilities leaves the net asset position of the foreign subsidiary unchanged. During a financial crisis, when companies worry about violating their bond covenants against excessive balance sheet debt, translation risk exposure receives more attention. This was especially true during the "Asian crisis" in 1998–2000.

Foreign Exchange Transaction Risk Exposure
A change in cash flows resulting from contractual commitments to pay in or receive foreign currency.

Transaction risk exposure is a much more generally significant problem in managing exports. Transaction risk exposure occurs when a purchase agreement or sales contract (a specific "transaction") commits the company to make future payables or accept future receivables in a foreign currency. Over the time period between executing the contract and actually making or receiving the payments, the company has foreign exchange transaction risk exposure. Many financial derivatives like foreign exchange forward contracts, FX swap contracts, and FX options contracts have emerged to assist corporate treasurers in laying off this transaction risk exposure for a modest risk premium known and fixed in advance. A later section discusses the use of these derivative instruments to construct covered hedges that lay off the transaction risk exposure.

Foreign Exchange Operating Risk Exposure
A change in cash flows from foreign or domestic sales resulting from currency fluctuations.

Finally, exchange rate fluctuations that result in substantial changes in the operating cash flow of foreign subsidiaries, like those befalling Toyota in the Managerial Challenge and Daimler-Jeep-Chrysler in the above illustration, are examples of **foreign exchange operating risk exposure.** Operating risk exposures are more difficult to forecast than transaction risk exposures and more difficult to lay off than translation risk exposures. As a result, operating risk exposures necessitate still more managerial attention and careful analysis. For one thing, the deterioration of export revenues from sales in foreign subsidiaries is just one side of the problem that a rising domestic currency poses. In addition, depending on the viability of global competition, operating risk exposures may entail a substantial deterioration of domestic sales as well, because competing import products become cheaper in the home market. These relationships are well illustrated by the export and domestic business of the Cummins Engine Co. of Columbus, Indiana.

International Perspectives

http://

Access current quarterly financial statements and annual reports for Cummins Engine Company (including information on international sales) at the following Internet site:
http://www.cummins.com

http://

Current exchange rates and other financial information can be found on the Internet at
http://quote.yahoo.com/

COLLAPSE OF EXPORT AND DOMESTIC SALES AT CUMMINS ENGINE[4]

Cummins Engine Co. is the world's leading producer of replacement diesel engines for trucks. Like the sales of all capital equipment manufacturers, Cummins' sales are highly cyclical, declining steeply in economic downturns. If households buy fewer appliances, clothing, and furniture, less shipping by truck is required to deliver supplies, refill inventories in warehouses, and restock store shelves. Less shipping means less truck mileage, and less truck mileage means a slower replacement demand for diesel engines. For example, in the short steep recession of 1982, Cummins's dollar sales fell off 20 percent and cash flow declined 55 percent. As the U.S. economy improved during 1983–1984, Cummins's sales recovered to record levels. By 1985, the U.S. economy was booming with real GNP growth at 5.8 percent. Yet that year, Cummins's sales declined 8 percent, operating margins declined 44 percent, and cash flow declined 51 percent. What went wrong?

Cummins Engine sells 38 percent of its replacement diesel engines in the export market and its biggest competitor is the Mercedes-Benz diesel. What deutsche mark or pound price a Cummins engine can sell for in Munich or London (and still recover its cost plus a small profit) is as important to Cummins's cash flow as steel costs or their wage bargain with the United Machinists union. A $40,000 Cummins diesel sold for approximately DM 72,000 in 1978, 1988, and again in 1998. In each of these years, the exchange rate between the deutsche mark and the U.S. dollar stood at approximately 1.8—i.e., 1.8 deutsche marks per dollar. In one intervening time period, however, the dollar appreciated substantially against the mark. Between 1980–1985, the value of the dollar soared almost 47 percent from DM 1.82 to DM 2.94 (see Figure 6.2). Similar exchange rate movements occurred against the British pound, against which the U.S. currency appreciated 54 percent (from £0.44/$ to £0.77/$).[5]

The effect of the massive 1980–1985 dollar appreciation on Cummins's export sales was catastrophic. For a German trucking company to buy a $40,000 Cummins diesel engine at the dollar's peak in 1985 required not $1.82 \times \$40,000 = $ DM 72,600 but rather $2.94 \times \$40,000 = $ DM 117,600! This enormous DM price increase of the Cummins export product (attributable solely to the change in exchange rates) made substitute products, like a domestic DM 100,000 Mercedes-Benz diesel, much more attractive to German buyers than before the change in the exchange rate. Moreover, Mercedes-Benz perceived a real opportunity to sell their own diesel in Cummins's home territory in the United States. An import diesel made by Mercedes-Benz (which had sold in Columbus, Cleveland, and Chicago for DM 100,000/1.82 = $54,945 in 1980) could now sell for just DM 100,000/2.94 = $34,014. Consequently, not only did Cummins's export sales collapse, but so did Cummins's domestic sales (and margins). The steep appreciation of the dollar in this 1980–1985 period put U.S. manufacturers of traded goods, like autos, VCRs, airplanes, and diesel engines, at a very big disadvantage. The same pattern emerged between 1997–2002 (again, see Figure 6.2), and the U.S. trade deficit skyrocketed.

---

[4] Based on *Value Line Investment Survey, Part III: Ratings and Reports,* various issues.

[5] Exchange rate percentage changes are calculated as the difference from one period to the next divided by the average exchange rate over the period. For example £0.44 per U.S. dollar to £0.77 equals a 0.33/60.5 = 54 percent change. Similarly, DM 1.82 to DM 2.94 equals a 1.12/2.38 or 47 percent change. The reason for this midpoint procedure is that when the DM/$ exchange rate returns by 1988 to very nearly its original level (i.e., see DM 1.88 for 1988 in Figure 6.2), the midpoint calculation yields a downward adjustment of −44 percent, nearly equal and opposite to the +47 percent rise.

The U.S. dollar weakened throughout 2002–2003 (see Figure 6.2), especially against the euro, which appreciated 25 percent—i.e., $(0.92 - 1.18) \div ((0.92 + 1.18)/2) = -0.26/1.05 = .2476$. This made American exports much less expensive in euros, resulting in booming European sales. IBM reported 11% sales growth in 2003 Q1, 7 percent attributed to currency fluctuations. Similarly, Colgate-Palmolive and Microsoft, respectively, reported two-thirds of a 20-percent sales increase in Europe and nine-tenths of a 12-percent sales increase in Europe, the Middle East, and Africa were attributable to the lower in-country prices resulting from a weaker U.S. dollar.[6]

THE MARKET FOR U.S. DOLLARS AS FOREIGN EXCHANGE

Since American manufacturers, like Cummins Engine, incur many of their expenses at domestic manufacturing sites in the United States, American manufacturers tend to require that export purchase orders be made payable in U.S. dollars. This receivables policy requires that Munich dealers wishing to buy Cummins diesels transact simultaneously in the foreign exchange and diesel markets. To buy a Cummins diesel, Munich companies (or their financial intermediaries) will supply euros and demand dollars to secure the currency required for the dollar-denominated purchase order and payment draft awaited by the Cummins shipping department. This additional demand for the dollar and the concurrent additional supply of marks drive the price of the dollar higher than it otherwise would have been. Thus, the equilibrium exchange rate in euros per dollar rises (i.e., the price of the dollar as foreign exchange exhibited in Figure 6.2 rises). In general, any such unanticipated increase in export sales results in an appreciation of the domestic currency.

Similarly, any unanticipated decrease in export sales results in a depreciation of the domestic currency. For example, Boeing experienced a collapse of export sales in competition with Europe's Airbus as the dollar appreciated during 1997–2001, just as Cummins had experienced in competition with Mercedes diesels during 1983–1985. After 1985, Figure 6.2 shows that the dollar did reverse course and depreciate from DM 2.94 per dollar to DM 2.17 per dollar by 1986. Likewise, the dollar reversed course in 2001 and nosedived 25 percent against the euro during 2002–2003. These downward price trends of the dollar assisted Cummins in stabilizing its sales and cash flows both at home and abroad. With the dollar worth fewer euros, American imports priced in dollars by Mercedes-Benz and Airbus sales reps in the United States became more expensive, while American exports priced in euros by Cummins and Boeing sales reps in Germany became cheaper. This automatic self-correcting adjustment of flexible exchange rates in response to trade flow imbalances is one of the primary arguments for adopting a freely fluctuating exchange rate policy.

Import/Export Flows and the Transaction Demand for a Currency

To examine these effects more closely, let's turn the argument around and trace the currency flows when Americans increase their demand for imported goods. Suppose an unexpectedly large number of baby boomers wish to recapture their youth by purchasing sporty Miata or BMW convertibles. The Mazda and BMW dealers would have some inventory stock on hand. But, in anticipation of some custom orders, the dealers' banks would have a carefully selected amount of foreign currency on hand

---

[6] "Dollar's Dive Helps U.S. Companies," *Wall Street Journal*, April 21, 2003, p. A2.

to support the necessary purchase order transactions with BMW headquarters in Munich. Our interest lies in tracing the consequences of an unanticipated upswing in American demand for these imported convertibles. What exactly happens in the currency markets in that case?

First, just as Cummins Engine prefers to be paid in U.S. dollars, so too BMW wishes to be paid in euros. Therefore, BMW purchase orders must be accompanied by euro cash payments. The local BMW dealer in Charlotte therefore requests a wire transfer from her banker at Bank of America. BOA debits the dollar account of the dealer, then authorizes payment from the euro cash balances of BOA and presents a wire transfer for an equivalent sum (minus fees) to the Munich branch of Deutsche Bank for deposit in the BMW account. Both import buyer and foreign seller have done business in their home currencies and exchanged a handsome new car. And the merchandise trade account of the U.S. balance of payments would show one additional import transaction valued at the BMW convertible's purchase price.

If Bank of America anticipated fewer such import transactions and euro requests than actually occurred, the bank's foreign currency portfolio would now be out of balance. Euro balances must be restored to support future export transactions. Bank of America therefore goes (electronically) into the interbank foreign currency markets and demands euros. Although the American bank might pay with any currency in excess supply in its foreign currency portfolio, it would normally pay in U.S. dollars. In particular, if no other unanticipated import or export flows (and no unanticipated capital flows) have occurred, BOA would pay in U.S. dollars. Therefore, unanticipated demand by Americans for German imports both raises the demand for euros and (as the flip side of that same transaction) increases the supply of U.S. dollars.

Equilibrium Price of the U.S. Dollar

In the market for U.S. dollars as foreign exchange (see Figure 6.3), the supply curve shifts to the right. This shift of market supply represents Bank of America and many other correspondent banks supporting import transactions by selling dollars to acquire other foreign currencies. The equilibrium price on the y-axis of Figure 6.3 is the price of the dollar expressed in amounts of any foreign currency—for example, British pounds per U.S. dollar, yen per U.S. dollar, or euros per U.S. dollar. As the supply of U.S. dollars increases S_{1985} to S_{1986}, the equilibrium price of the dollar declines.

For example, as imports of Mercedes-Benz replacement diesel truck engines and other German imports increased in 1985–1986, the supply of U.S. dollars in the foreign currency market had to increase. Again, American consumers and companies needed to acquire marks to purchase German imports. U.S. financial intermediaries supplied dollars to acquire the foreign currency their local customers requested. Thus, the spectacular dollar appreciation of the previous four years slowed and the dollar began to depreciate (see Figure 6.2). The dollar's price decline is expressed quite naturally as a falling exchange rate in Figure 6.3, for example, DM 2.94 per U.S. dollar in 1985 to DM 2.17 per U.S. dollar in 1986 and eventually all the way to DM 1.75/$ in 1988.

Speculative Demand, Government Transfers, and Coordinated Intervention

The U.S. dollar depreciation of 1985–1988 reflects factors besides transaction demand. In general, currency value depends upon transaction demand, speculative demand, government transfers, and central bank interventions. Transfers can involve

Figure 6.3   Market for U.S. Dollars as Foreign Exchange (Depreciation of the Dollar, 1985–1988)

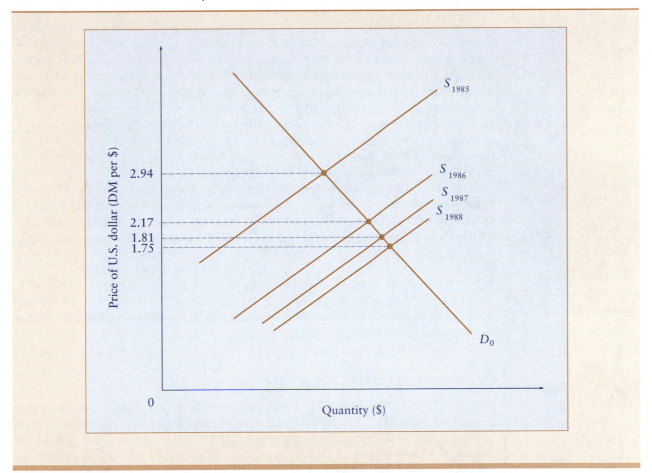

Sterilized Interventions
Central bank transactions in the foreign exchange market accompanied by equal offsetting transactions in the government bond market, in an attempt to alter short-term interest rates without affecting the exchange rate.

either debt repayment (reducing the supply of a currency as a debtor nation takes money out of circulation and returns it to the lender nation's treasury) or foreign aid (increasing the supply of a currency). Interventions can be sterilized or unsterilized. **Sterilized interventions** involve offsetting transactions in the relevant government bond market. For example, the Federal Reserve might sell dollars in the foreign currency markets, but then turn around and acquire dollars by selling an equal dollar volume of T-bonds, leaving the supply of dollars in international exchange essentially unchanged.

What is the proportionate weight of each of these factors in determining the equilibrium value of a currency? An important first perspective is that only one out of five foreign exchange transactions supports an import or export trade flow; four out of five support international capital flows. In mid-1998, for example, the average *daily* volume of foreign currency transactions in the 43 largest foreign currency markets had a dollar value of $1.5 trillion. The average *daily* volume of world exports was $25 billion. So, the dollar volume of currency flows far outstrips the dollar volume of trade flows, by 60 to 1. Most foreign currency transactions therefore reflect international capital flows, much of which is speculative and transitory.

Intervention in the foreign currency markets by any one central bank therefore has almost no chance of affecting the equilibrium value of a currency. Take the Bank of Japan, for instance. In September 2002, the central bank of Japan had official reserves of foreign currencies equal (at existing exchange rates) to $440 billion and further reserves of gold equal to $7 billion.[7] By comparison, the European Central Bank in this same month had $230 billion in foreign currency reserves and $115 billion in gold reserves. China had $240 billion in reserves, while the U.S. Federal Reserve had $70 billion in currency and $75 billion in gold. Suppose the Bank of Japan decided to try to initiate a depreciation of the yen to improve the competitiveness of their export sector. Investing half of their entire reserves ($220 billion), the Bank of Japan's intervention could be easily overwhelmed in one day by the sheer enormity of the $1.5 trillion mobile capital awash in the international capital markets. Indeed, the official reserves of all the developed countries *total* only $1.8 trillion, approximately equal to *one day's worth* of foreign currency transactions.

It takes coordinated intervention by several large central banks with deep reserves to permanently affect a currency's value. One such coordinated intervention occurred as a result of the Plaza Accords in 1985 when the G-7 nations (the United States, Britain, Japan, Germany, France, Italy, and Canada) agreed to a sustained sale of dollars from their reserves over 1986 and 1987. It was this coordinated intervention that contributed to the steep decline of the dollar from DM 2.94/$ to DM 1.75/$ over 1986 and 1987, illustrated in Figure 6.2. In September 2000, the Bank of England, the European Central Bank, the Bank of Japan, and the U.S. Federal Reserve Bank again all sold dollars to stem dollar appreciation when DM/$ reached 2.30 and euros/$ reached 1.18. Again, see Figure 6.2.

Example

COORDINATED INTERVENTION TO SUPPORT THE EURO

Beginning Friday, September 22, 2000, several central banks joined the European Central Bank in selling U.S. dollars and buying euros to support the European Union's new currency. Since its inception in January 1999, the euro had fallen almost 20 percent to $0.85 per euro, or 1.18 euros per U.S. dollar. With Intel, Sun Microsystems, Hewlett-Packard, IBM, and Oracle all experiencing fully 30 percent of worldwide sales in Europe, the U.S. Federal Reserve was motivated by concern about projected declines in the U.S. export sector if dollar appreciation continued. One of Intel's chief competitors, Siemens of Germany, reported record chip sales the same day that Intel warned that earnings would slump because of weaker demand in Europe. That Friday, Intel stock declined in value 23 percent (or $97 billion). The central banks of Japan and England had similar reasons to avoid export sector collapses by intervening to support the euro. Coordinated intervention for several days resulted in a 7 percent appreciation of the euro.

Short-Term Exchange Rate Fluctuations

The transaction demand determinants of long-term annual trends in exchange rates are fundamentally different from the determinants of day-to-day exchange rate fluctuations. Short-term exchange rate movements from week to week, day to day, or even hour to hour are determined by arbitrage activity in the international capital markets and by speculative demand, rather than by the transaction demand determinants of

[7] "Official Reserves," *The Economist*, September 21, 2002, p. 97.

Arbitrage
Buying cheap, and selling elsewhere for an immediate profit.

Speculation
Buying cheap, and selling later for a delayed profit (or loss).

trade flows and long-term capital flows. Speculative demand is driven by volatile investor expectations of what other investors are likely to do. **Arbitrage** is the act of buying real assets, commodities, stocks, bonds, loans, or even televisions and radios cheaply and selling them at higher prices later. If the buying and selling prices and terms of delivery can be arranged simultaneously, then the transaction is one of pure arbitrage. If the second transaction is delayed, we often call the activity **speculation**. Arbitrage activity is triggered by temporary violations of arbitrage equilibrium conditions, such as the situation when real rates of return (adjusted for any differences in risk) do not equilibrate. When such conditions do not hold, opportunities for arbitrage profits exist, and arbitrage activity will appear quickly, proceed at huge volume, and continue until the relevant arbitrage equilibrium conditions are reestablished.

To illustrate, if the real rate of return differs across economies on government bonds and bills of equal maturity and equal risk (for example, 3-year bills are paying 3.1 percent in the U.S. and 1.7 percent in Germany), investors will sell German bills, driving their price down. This raises the rate of return implied by a fixed interest coupon on the remaining lower face value of the German bonds. The loanable funds released from the German market will then buy U.S. T-bills, driving their price up and their interest rate of return down. Another way to think about it is that an arbitrager with no principal but good credit can borrow funds in Germany at little more than 1.7 percent real interest cost by selling short the German 3-year bills and lend the loan proceeds in the U.S. T-bill market at 3.1 percent by buying a T-bill. Again, such arbitrage activity will quickly develop and continue at a brisk pace until risk-adjusted real rates of return are equalized in the two economies.

The sheer magnitude of the mobile capital committed to this financial arbitrage between nations is astounding. Again, the dollar value of the international capital flow *per day* in the world's capital markets is $1.5 trillion. These enormous floodtides of arbitrage capital quickly (within hours or even minutes) close the window of arbitrage profit opportunity in FX trading.

FOREIGN EXCHANGE RISK MANAGEMENT

Internal Hedge
A balance sheet offset to foreign currency cash flows.

To reduce the potentially wide swings in net assets and cash flows from currency fluctuations, companies use internal hedges and financial hedges.[8] **Internal hedges** may be either operating hedges (such as matching anticipated foreign sales receipts with foreign expenses in that same currency) or balance sheet hedges (such as buying foreign plants). Operating hedges address operating risk exposure, which 72 percent of all U.S., Asian, and U.K. companies consider an important focus of FX risk management.[9] Balance sheet hedges address primarily translation risk exposure by matching assets and liabilities in various countries and their respective currencies. Fewer than 25 percent of all U.S., Asian, and U.K. companies consider translation risk important. *Financial hedges* address primarily transaction risk exposure by setting up positions in financial derivative contracts to offset cash flow losses from currency fluctuations. For example, over 93 percent of U.S., Asian, and U.K. companies employ forward contracts to manage transaction risk exposure.

---

[8] Kenneth A. Froot et al., "A Framework for Risk Management," *Journal of Applied Corporate Finance*, 3, Fall 1994, pp. 22–31.

[9] Andrew P. Marshall, "Foreign Exchange Risk Management in Multinational Companies," *Journal of Multinational Financial Management*, 10, 2000, pp. 185–211.

But such hedging isn't cheap. Goldman Sachs estimates that financial hedges for $100 million of risk exposure cost about $5.2 million, approximately 5 percent of the value at risk. As the dollar appreciated steeply against the euro in 2000, Goodyear concluded that the hedging cost was prohibitive and ended up reporting a $68 million profit on European operations rather than the $97 million they would have earned without currency fluctuations.[10] In contrast, Coca-Cola hedged their euro net cash flow and lost not a penny.

Internal Hedges

The FX transactions required to purchase a BMW would have been unnecessary if BMW had set up an internal hedge in the form of offsetting payables in U.S. dollars. For example, the North American subsidiary of BMW might have simply accepted purchase orders with payment in U.S. dollars and then used those same dollars to cover BMW marketing expenses owed in the United States. Or BMW might have used the U.S. dollar receivables to buy American parts and supplies or fixed assets. For example, in 1995, BMW built a Spartanburg, SC, plant to assemble their 325 model convertibles. Such offsetting positions in payables and receivables is a way of balancing BMW assets and liabilities in U.S. dollars.

With an internal hedge provided by a German ball-bearing plant, Cummins Engine could accomplish the same thing. In part because the U.S. dollar rose steadily against the deutsche mark from 1995 to 2000, Chrysler-Jeep invested in Daimler in November 1998 to form DaimlerChrysler.

International Perspectives

TOYOTA AND HONDA BUY U.S. ASSEMBLY CAPACITY[11]

When a manufacturer's home currency is strong, foreign direct investment in overseas plant and equipment is especially attractive. As the yen rocketed from ¥238 per U.S. dollar in 1985 to ¥94 per U.S. dollar in 1993 (see Figure 6.2), Honda and Toyota employed the strengthening yen to acquire U.S. manufacturing capacity. A $1 billion U.S. assembly plant would cost ¥94 billion in 1993, down from ¥238 billion 10 years earlier. At the same time, the U.S. demand for the Toyota Camry and Honda Accord outpaced the capacities of the Japanese manufacturers, and the Japanese share of the North American market rose from 20 percent to 30 percent. In the late 1980s and early 1990s, the U.S. Congress responded with "voluntary import restraints" on Japanese cars and imposed a 25 percent tariff on Japanese light trucks.

In part to ease the trade policy pressure, to exempt their cars and trucks from U.S. tariffs, and to improve the delivery time and reliability for their most popular models, Toyota and Honda each built four assembly plants in North America. Nissan also built one plant in the United States and one plant in Mexico, and Mazda and Mitsubishi each built one plant in the United States. The combined capacity of these 12 Japanese-owned factories is 3.2 million vehicles a year, 18 percent of the total 17.2 million North American auto manufacturing capacity. By 1996, Honda assembled in North America 80 percent (and Toyota assembled 60 percent) of their vehicles sold in North America. Both Honda and Toyota plan to expand their light truck and minivan assembly capacity still further in the United States and Canada.

[10] "Business Won't Hedge the Euro Away," *BusinessWeek*, December 4, 2000, p. 157.

[11] Based on "Japanese Carmakers Plan Major Expansion of American Capacity," *Wall Street Journal*, September 24, 1997, p. A1, and "Detroit Is Getting Sideswiped by the Yen," *BusinessWeek*, November 11, 1996, p. 54.

By acquiring plants and equipment in North America while the yen was appreciating against the dollar, Honda and Toyota clearly acquired fixed assets at very favorable home currency cost. At the same time, however, these transactions established a substantial internal hedge that complemented other cost-cutting measures initiated by Toyota and Honda. Thus, despite the plummeting yen value of the dollar receivables on each Camry sold, the purchase of less expensive U.S. parts and assembly plants provided a cost savings. As the value of the dollar declined and the yen rose, these low-cost dollar payables for U.S. parts and U.S. assembly plants made it possible to hold price increases on Corollas, Camrys, and Accords to a minimum. As a result, the Toyota Camry has become the highest volume model of any car sold in the United States.

Covered Hedges: Forwards, Options, and Swaps

http://

Learn about currency futures and options at the following Internet site maintained by the Chicago Mercantile Exchange: http://www.cme.com/prd/fx/

In addition to internal hedges, any company can reduce the transaction risk exposure of exchange rate fluctuations by establishing a short position in the foreign currency forward or option market to hedge the domestic cash flow from their export sales receipts. For example, suppose Cummins Engine had sales contracts with their German dealers for future delivery in 2001 of €5 million of diesel engines. Cummins has risk exposure to a decline in the value of these export sales receipts. So, to lay off this exchange rate risk, in 2000 Cummins might have sold a euro forward contract in the foreign exchange derivative markets to establish a hedge. Cummins's transaction is described as a covered hedge because Cummins anticipates euro receivables (from their German dealers) equal to the amount of their short forward position. That is, their contract sales receipts "cover" their obligation to deliver as a seller of euro forward contracts.

Example

CUMMINS ENGINE GOES SHORT

Selling forward contracts in 2000 that agree to deliver €5 million at some prespecified forward price (say, $1.00/€) and future settlement date in 2001 would make money for Cummins Engine if the dollar appreciated and the euro declined in value. For example, at €1.18 per dollar in 2001 (i.e., $0.85/€), Cummins is entitled to receive $1.00/€, deliverable by purchasing the European currency in the spot market for $0.85. Therefore, Cummins cancels its position and can collect from the futures market settlements process a gain of $0.15/€ × 5 million euros = $750,000 on their forward contract. This cash flow would be just sufficient to cover their $1.00 to $0.85 per euro loss in value on the 5 million euros received in 2001 from their German dealers. As intended, these two cash flows from a covered hedge just offset one another.

Besides setting up internal hedges or short forward positions, Cummins Engine could also have entered into a currency-swap contract with a German company like BMW to exchange their anticipated future streams of dollar and euro cash flows from export sales. BMW would swap a prespecified amount of their anticipated dollar receipts from auto sales in North America for a prespecified amount of Cummins's anticipated euro sales receipts in Germany.[12] However, these swap contract alternatives to demanding payment in their domestic (home) currency impose some costs on BMW

---

[12] At each future settlement date in a swap contract, the difference between the spot market exchange rate and the forward rates prespecified at the start of the swap contract actually determine who pays whom. For complete explanations of the use of forwards, options, and swap contracts in managing foreign exchange risk, see C. Eun and B. Resnick, *International Finance,* 3rd. Ed. (Burr Ridge, IL: Irwin, 2003).

and Cummins Engine. Therefore, BMW generally will offer its best fixed price on an export transaction to an American or other foreign buyer on a purchase order payable in euros. And for the same reason, the best fixed price from Cummins Engine generally will be available on a purchase order payable only in U.S. dollars.

Of course, the problem facing the managers of the BMW 3-series and the Cummins Engine diesel is more serious than a mere transaction risk exposure on constant receivables in their respective foreign subsidiaries or dealerships. In addition, a steeply rising home currency also means a likely decline in both foreign and domestic *unit* sales. As we shall see, some companies react to this *operating risk exposure* from domestic currency appreciation by slashing margins to maintain market share abroad, whereas others sacrifice foreign market share to maintain margins. Understanding the magnitude, the timing, and the forces that set in motion these exchange-rate-induced swings in sales and profits is crucial for effectively managing export businesses in pursuit of the maximization of capitalized value.

DETERMINANTS OF LONG-RUN TRENDS IN EXCHANGE RATES

Short-term movements in FX rates are caused by speculative demand. Sometimes the current events set speculators off in support of a currency (a long position), sometimes the reverse (a short position). Behaviorally, each speculator tries to guess what the other will do, and much herd-like stampeding occurs.

Long-run trends in FX rate are different. Quarter-to-quarter or year-to-year trends depend on three factors: real growth rates, real interest rates, and anticipated inflation rates. We now discuss each of these determinants.

The Role of Real Growth Rates

As we have seen, a primary determinant of the year-to-year exchange rate fluctuations in Figure 6.2 is the net direction of trade flows. Unanticipated increases in imports lower a local currency's value, whereas unanticipated increases in exports raise a local currency's value. The stimulus underlying such trade flow imbalances may be either business cycles, productivity increases, or the introduction of protectionist trade barriers. In a business-cycle or productivity-based expansion, consumption (including import consumption) increases; in a contraction, import consumption decreases.

Example

EUROPEAN SLOWDOWN DECREASES DUPONT EXPORTS[13]

"Beggar thy neighbor" trade policies provided a rallying cry for the mercantilist centuries (1500–1750), during which punitive tariffs and other forms of protectionism isolated city, state, and national economies. Today, however, rather than attempting self-sufficiency, most nations are better off recognizing mutual interdependence, encouraging both import and export activities, and specializing in accordance with comparative advantage. In that freer trade environment, growing neighbors are the best neighbors.

In the late 1990s, an economic slowdown in Europe undercut the export sales of American manufacturers and U.S. multinationals. Not only Cummins Engine (28 percent), Sun Microsystems (36 percent), and DuPont (39 percent), but even

---

[13] "Weak Growth in Europe Threatens U.S. Exports," *Wall Street Journal*, March 11, 1999, p. A1.

Wrigley Chewing Gum (41 percent) and McDonald's (37 percent) realized a large proportion of their 1997 revenue in Europe. Across all S&P 500 U.S. companies, 21 percent of 1997 sales revenue arose from European sales. After several years of steady increases, import demand by households and companies flattened in Germany and France, and it actually declined in Italy and the United Kingdom during 1998. The industrial sector was particularly hard hit; chemicals shipments from the U.S. to Europe, for example, declined 20 percent on a year-to-year basis.

During the years 1994, 1995, and 1996, U.S. gross domestic product (GDP) grew at 4.0 percent, 2.7 percent, and 3.7 percent, respectively. The United States had a healthy but slowing economy. Japanese real GDP, on the other hand, exhibited only 0.6 and 1.5 percent growth in 1994 and 1995 but 5.0 percent growth in 1996. Canada and Mexico also experienced stronger growth over this period—Canada from 1.7 percent in 1996 to 4.0 percent in 1997 and Mexico from 6.4 percent to 8.8 percent. British growth rates rose as well. These growth-rate trends among the five largest U.S. trading partners led to increased exports from the United States of goods like computer software, PCs, grains, aircraft, professional services, and diesel engines, while causing decreased imports into the United States of goods like autos and consumer electronics.

As exports from the United States rose, foreign buyers had to acquire dollars to complete transactions with U.S. companies like Microsoft, IBM, ADM, Boeing, McKinsey, and Cummins Engine. In the market for dollars as foreign exchange, this increases the demand for dollars; D_{1995} in Figure 6.4 shifts out to D_{1997}. At the same time, decreased purchases of foreign imports by Americans decreases the supply of dollars. That is, in the market for dollars as foreign exchange, S_{1995} shifts left to S_{1997}. Both factors cause an appreciation of the U.S. dollar, such as occurred in 1996–1997. In sum, the increase in exports and decrease in imports led to a rise in the price of the dollar against the yen from an average ¥94 per dollar in 1993 to ¥109 per dollar in 1995, and ¥130 per dollar in 1998. The rise in ¥/$ exchange rates over this period in Figure 6.2 mirror these market demand and supply shifts shown in Figure 6.4.

More recently, in 1998–2000, Table 6.1 shows that the U.S. economy grew at 4.3 percent, 4.1 percent, and 5.0 percent. The Japanese economy slowed dramatically at real GDP growth rates of −2.8 percent, 1 percent, and 1.7 percent, while the German economy grew at largely unchanged real rates of 2.6, 2.7, and 3.4 percent. The anemic real growth in Japan (−2.8, 1.0, 1.7 percent) contributed to a markedly reduced consumer spending by Japanese households and an especially reduced spending on U.S. imports. Consequently, the ¥/$ exchange rate reversed its 1994–1998 upward trend. As shown in Figures 6.2 and 6.4, after appreciating from 94 ¥/$ in 1993 to 130 ¥/$ in 1998, the value of the dollar then declined to 107 ¥/$ by 2000. This depreciation of the U.S. dollar occurred not because the supply of dollars had increased as shown in Figure 6.3, but rather because the demand for dollars by potential foreign customers of American exports had declined from 1998–2000.

The Role of Real Interest Rates

The second factor determining long-run trends in exchange rates is comparable interest rates adjusted for inflation. The higher the real rate of interest in an economy, the greater the demand for the financial assets offered by that economy. If a Japanese, German, or Swiss investor or financial institution can earn higher returns

Figure 6.4   Market for U.S. Dollars as Foreign Exchange (Appreciation Against the Yen, 1995−1998; Depreciation in 2000)

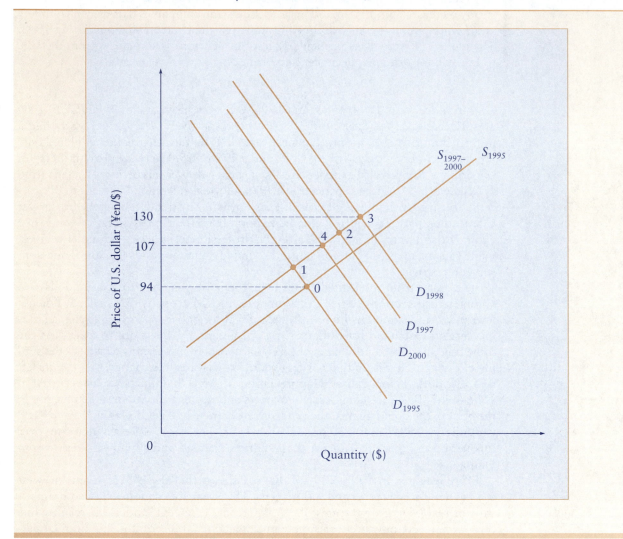

(for equivalent risk) from U.S. bonds than from German or Japanese bonds, foreign owners of capital will move quickly toward U.S. financial markets as foreign port-folios are rebalanced to incorporate more U.S. assets. Since the New York Federal Reserve Bank auctioning off new T-bills; Salomon Brothers underwriting a new issue of DuPont bonds; Merrill-Lynch selling T-bills, T-bonds, and DuPont bonds in the secondary (resale) market; and the New York Stock Exchange settlements depart-ment all require payment in U.S. dollars, the foreign investor who desires U.S. finan-cial assets must first acquire U.S. dollars to complete her transactions. So, a higher real interest rate in the United States (relative to German, Japanese, and British rates) implies international capital inflow into the United States and an increased demand for and appreciation of U.S. dollars.

What really matters in triggering these international capital flows is an investor's expectation of the domestic value of the foreign interest earned when capital invested

Table 6.1   Transaction Determinants of Long-Term Exchange Rate Trends

	United States			Germany			Japan		
	Real GDP	Real r	PPI	Real GDP	Real r	PPI	Real GDP	Real r	PPI
1994	4.0	2.0	1.7	2.3	3.5	2.5	0.6	1.5	0.2
1995	2.7	2.1	2.3	1.7	3.2	2.0	1.5	1.3	−0.6
1996	3.7	2.7	2.8	0.8	1.4	1.0	5.0	0.5	−1.4
1997	4.5	3.4	−1.2	2.4	1.4	1.8	1.4	0.5	0.2
1998	4.3	3.9	−0.1	2.6	2.5	0.5	−2.8	0.1	0.3
1999	4.1	2.78	3.0	2.7	0.75	3.9	1.0	0.5	−0.9
2000	5.0	3.61	3.8	3.4	1.59	7.1	1.7	0.2	−0.2
2001	0.3	0.65	2.0	0.6	2.21	−0.5	−0.3	−4.0	−0.7
2002	2.2	0.02	−1.4	0.5	1.95	3.0	−0.5	−3.8	−0.9

Sources: *Economic Report of the President 2003; The Economist,* various issues.
Notes: Real GDP refers to the growth rate of gross domestic product adjusted for price changes by the GDP deflator. Real r refers to the short-term interest rate on government debt minus the annual percentage change in consumer prices. PPI is the annual percentage change in producer prices.

overseas in bonds, for example, is redeemed and converted back from the foreign to the investor's home currency. Nominal interest rates minus consumer inflation rates in the foreign country approximate this post-redemption return. In September 1997, 90-day T-bill rates in the United States stood at 5.6 percent, up from 5.2 percent a year earlier. With consumer inflation in the United States running at 2.2 percent in the third quarter of 1997, down from 2.5 percent a year earlier, the real rate of return in the United States was rising—i.e., 5.2 − 2.5 = 2.7 percent in the third quarter of 1996 versus 5.6 − 2.2 = 3.4 percent in the third quarter of 1997 (see Table 6.1). In contrast, real rates of interest in Germany on government-issued 90-day bills were lower relative to U.S. rates and unchanged from 1996 to 1997 (i.e., 3.1 − 1.7 = 1.4 percent in 1996 and 3.3 − 1.9 = 1.4 percent in 1997). Japanese 90-day real rates were also lower relative to U.S. rates and unchanged from 1996 to 1997 (i.e., 0.5 percent in both 1996 and 1997).

The same interest rate differentials attracted foreign capital to the United States at the end of the century. In mid-1999, U.S. 3-month T-bills yielded 4.78 percent with a 2 percent inflation forecast, returning therefore 2.78 percent after adjusting for inflation. A year later in mid-2000, the real rate of return had risen to 3.61 percent in the United States (i.e., 6.71 − 3.1). In Germany (and throughout much of the euro area), short-term interest rates also rose over this period from 2.65 percent to 4.69 percent, but so did anticipated inflation, growing from 1.9 percent in mid-1999 to 3.1 percent in mid-2000. Consequently, the real rate of short-term interest in Germany increased from 0.75 percent (i.e., 2.65 − 1.9) to just 1.59 percent (4.69 − 3.1). With 202 basis points favoring investment in U.S. assets (3.61 − 1.59), foreign capital literally flooded into the T-bill and other U.S. short-term money instruments.

As shown in Figure 6.5, the exchange rate responded in the predicted fashion as the dollar appreciated steeply against the deutsche mark (and the euro) in 2000. In particular, these real interest rate differentials favoring investment in the United States increase the foreign demand for U.S. financial assets, and increased foreign demand for U.S. financial assets raises the demand for U.S. dollars. For example, between 1996 and 2000, European companies and investment funds like BPA Amoco, British Telecom, BASF, Bayer and UBS-Warburg invested $650 billion in foreign direct investment (FDI) in the United States. This four-year figure exceeds half the entire FDI by the U.S. in Europe over the past 50 years. When this enormous capital flow occurs, again referring to Figure 6.5, the demand for the dollar increases against the German mark and the euro. In 2002, real interest rates in the U.S. fell to 0.02, the lowest rate in 40 years, and predictably the dollar collapsed against the euro (again see Figure 6.2).

Figure 6.5 Market for U.S. Dollars as Foreign Exchange (Appreciation Against DM and Euro, 1996–2000; Depreciation in 2001–2003)

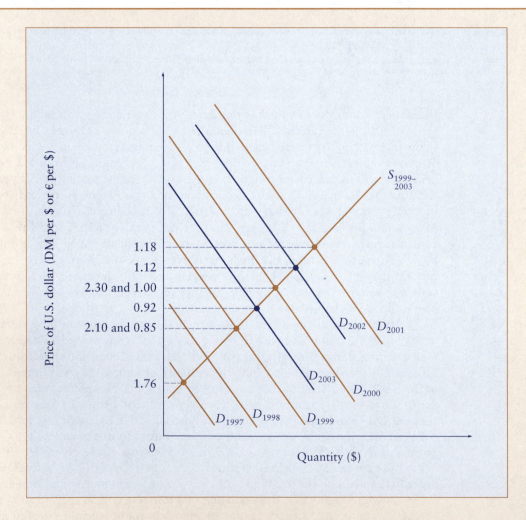

The Role of Expected Inflation

Inflationary expectations provide an important third determinant of long-term trends in exchange rates. Suppose you were entering into a long-term contract to replace the diesel engines installed in a fleet of trucks over the next three to five years. Would you be inclined to approach and enter into negotiation with Cummins Engine, where recent material costs have been low, cost-saving productivity increases have been substantial, and union bargaining pressure may be declining? Or would you approach a substitute supplier like Mercedes-Benz, where all those factors are reversed, suggesting the strong possibility of an upsurging inflationary trend underlying the costs of a German diesel engine?

Cost inflation is usually compared across economies by examining an index of producer prices or wholesale prices. From 1996 to 1997, the percentage change in producer prices in the United States was -1.2 percent (negative), whereas in Germany producer prices increased by 1.8 percent. Clearly, the lower price in a long-term fixed price contract for replacement diesels will be available from Cummins, the company in a country experiencing cost-push deflation. In general, when producer price inflation is low in one country relative to another, export sales on traded goods like diesel engines increase.[14]

These trade flows swell U.S. exports and German imports, thereby putting upward pressure on the DM/$ exchange rate. In Figure 6.5, demand for the dollar again shifts to the right (i.e., D_{1997} to D_{1998}), and the dollar appreciates still further. Indeed, the relative purchasing power parity (PPP) hypothesis says that goods arbitrage of this sort will continue until the DM/$ exchange rate adjusts upward sufficiently to reflect entirely the inflation differential. That is, between the United States and Germany, a 3.5-percent differential in the producer price index favoring the United States should, according to PPP, raise the value of the dollar 3.5 percent against the mark. We discuss purchasing power parity in the next section.

PURCHASING POWER PARITY

When there are no significant costs or other barriers associated with moving goods or services between markets, then the price of each product should be the same in each market. This conclusion is known as the *law of one price*. When the different markets represent different countries, the law of one price says that prices will be the same in each country after making the appropriate conversion from one currency to another. Alternatively, one can say that exchange rates between two currencies will equal the ratio of the price indexes between the countries. In international finance and trade, this relationship is known as the absolute version of purchasing power parity.

Absolute purchasing power parity implies that a doubling of UK prices for a Dickens novel (and other traded goods) will result in a depreciation of the British currency by 50 percent. For example, if after a sustained period of British inflation, one needs £20 to buy a Dickens novel that before the inflation cost £10, and if German publishers will continue to print and sell that same novel (in English) for DM 10, the novel will be exported to Britain, driving down the pound. Such imports by

---

[14] Eventually, if producer price inflation differentials between the United States and Germany persist, import-export companies that specialize in capital equipment transactions between the U.S. and Germany will join the surging demand for American products and buy replacement diesels cheaply in the United States for resale at a profit in Germany. This goods arbitrage activity is discussed in the next section.

WHAT WENT RIGHT   **WHAT WENT WRONG**

Ford Motor Co. and Exide Batteries: Are Country Managers Here to Stay?[15]

As export growth outstripped domestic growth for many U.S. firms in the 1990s, multinationals like Ford Motor, Procter and Gamble, and Exide Batteries wrestled with the question of whether to organize worldwide operations by product line or by country. That is, should operations and marketing decisions be controlled by global business units for Tide detergent, Pampers diapers, and Crest toothpaste, or should country managers in Spain, Germany, and China call the shots on input contracts, manufacturing standards, assembly location, pricing, and promotion?

By developing global product lines, Ford Motor claimed $5 billion in savings from 1995–1998 when it eliminated overlapping plants, standardized suppliers, realized volume discounts on components, and brought new products to market faster. A consolidated worldwide design team and centralized manufacturing authority saved money. However, Ford Europe's market share slipped from 13 percent in 1995 to 8.8 percent in 1999; untargeted marketing and inflexible pricing divorced from local market conditions were to blame.

Exide pursued the same path from 1998–2002 by organizing global business units around its automotive, industrial, and network telecom batteries. Major plants were spread out as far as China, Brazil, and Germany. When forming supply chains, these disparate origins for the subassembly components of Exide's final product can often cut labor costs tenfold and shorten lead times from three months to five weeks. Yet, Exide found that some regional sales team activities continued to make sense, and so the North American industrial battery operation has again become a separate division. As a result, relationship marketing between Exide–North America and Ford headquarters in Detroit secured a major new account in automotive batteries for Exide.

---

[15] "Place vs. Product: It's Tough to Choose A Management Model," *Wall Street Journal*, June 21, 2001, p. A1, and "The World as a Single Machine," *The Economist*, June 20, 1998, pp. 3–18.

the British will persist until the exchange rate reflecting the price of the British pound declines from DM 10/£10 = 1.0 deutsche mark per pound to DM 10/£20 = 0.5 deutsche mark per pound.

Relative Purchasing Power Parity
A relationship between differential inflation rates and long-term trends in exchange rates.

A less restrictive form of the law of one price is known as **relative purchasing power parity** (PPP). The relative PPP principle states that in comparison to a period when exchange rates between two countries are in equilibrium, changes in the differential rates of inflation between two countries will be offset by equal, but opposite, changes in the future spot exchange rate. For example, if prices in the United States rise by 4 percent per year and prices in Europe rise by 6 percent per year, then relative PPP asserts that the euro will weaken relative to the U.S. dollar by approximately 2 percent.

The exact relative purchasing power parity relationship is

$$\text{Relative PPP:} \quad \left(\frac{S_1}{S_0}\right) = \left(\frac{1 + \pi_h}{1 + \pi_f}\right) \qquad [6.1]$$

where S_1 is the expected future spot rate at time period 1, S_0 is the current spot rate, π_h is the expected home country (U.S.) inflation rate, and π_f is the expected foreign country inflation rate. Using the previous example, if U.S. prices are expected to rise by 4 percent over the coming year, prices in Europe are expected to rise by 6 percent during the same time, and the current spot exchange rate (S_0) is \$0.60/€, then the expected spot rate in one year (S_1) will be

$$S_1/\$0.60 = (1 + 0.04)/(1 + 0.06)$$
$$S_1 = \$0.5887$$
$$= \$0.60 \, (1 - 0.0189)$$

The higher European inflation rate can be expected to result in a decline in the future spot value of the euro relative to the dollar by 1.89 percent.[16]

The dashed lines in Figure 6.6 indicate purchasing power parity between the deutsche mark and the U.S. dollar, accounting for cumulative inflation in the United States and Germany from 1973–2000. Over this period, the consumer price index in Germany rose from 67.1 to 137.2 (a 104-percent increase), and the consumer price index in the U.S. rose from 49.3 to 166.7 (a 238-percent increase). Starting from a March 1973 exchange rate of DM 2.81/\$, the predicted equilibrium exchange rate in 2000 implied by the hypothesis of relative purchasing power parity would be (DM 2.81/\$1.00) × (204/338) = 1.70, close to the actual 1997 exchange rate of DM 1.76/\$ but far below the 2000 exchange rate of 2.30. Therefore, referring again to Figure 6.6, the dollar was substantially above its purchasing power parity level in 1984–1986, and again in 1999–2001. In each case, a subsequent sharp decline in value against European currencies ensued. Between 2001 and 2003, for example, the dollar lost 25 percent of its value against the euro (see Figure 6.2).

Figure 6.6   Purchasing Power Parity (DM/\$, 1973–2000)

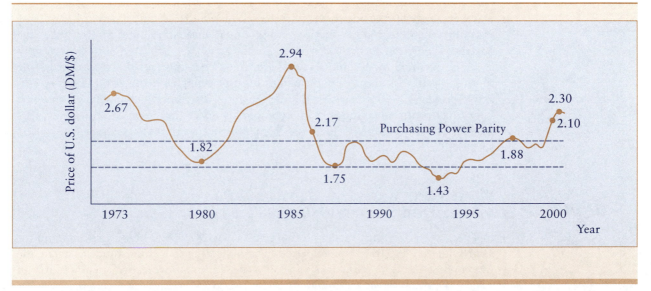

---

[16] Several other parity conditions in international finance are discussed in R. C. Moyer, W. Kretlow, and J. McGuigan, *Contemporary Financial Management,* 9th ed. (Cincinnati, OH: South-Western, 2003), Chapter 21.

Qualifications of PPP

Purchasing power parity calculations can be very sensitive to the starting point for the analysis. In 1972, the DM/$ exchange rate averaged DM 3.19/$, whereas in 1973 the average value of the dollar fell to DM 2.67/$. The 1972 starting point implies a 2000 exchange rate predicted by PPP of DM 1.93/$, while the 1973 starting point implies a predicted 2000 exchange rate of only DM 1.70/$. Clearly, the difference is nontrivial, and many such applications of the PPP hypothesis will hinge on which year the analyst chooses to start. Figure 6.6 indicates this qualification by displaying a band of exchange rates within which PPP holds.

Purchasing power parity has several other qualifications as well. For the full PPP adjustments to take place in exchange rates as domestic prices inflate, the traded goods must be nearly identical in quality and use in the two economies. Cross-cultural differences (e.g., the Islamic aversion to Western clothing for women) can short-circuit these adjustments. In addition, both economies must have similar trade policies. If Europe has much higher agricultural subsidies and trade barriers than the U.S., that policy may prevent the trade flows and subsequent exchange rate adjustments hypothesized by PPP. Similar qualifications apply to differences in value-added taxes and other sales taxes across economies. Finally, the markups and profit margins arising from the degree of competition in an economy must be comparable for purchasing power parity to hold. Despite these caveats, purchasing power parity has proved to be a useful benchmark for assessing trends in currency values.

No one would ever execute a currency arbitrage trade based on the predictions of the purchasing power parity hypothesis. Currency arbitrage is triggered by unanticipated events that generate very temporary profit opportunities lasting only several hours or a few days. The trade flows predicted by PPP in response to inflation differentials, on the other hand, are a much longer-term process requiring several quarters or even years. Companies with a substantial proportion of their sales abroad must identify these longer-term trends in exchange rates, and purchasing power parity proves useful for just that purpose. For example, a realization that the dollar was well above purchasing power parity levels in 1984–1985 and again in 1999–2001 should have influenced production and pricing policies in the mid-1980s and at the dawn of the new century.

Being attuned to the international business environment does not allow fine tuning, but it does allow better medium-term planning of production volume, proactive pricing, targeted marketing, and segmented distribution channels, all of which may offer profit advantages. Some companies make these considerations a focus of their business plans and prosper in international markets; others are less successful.

Example

WHAT WENT WRONG? GM, NISSAN, AND THE VALUE OF THE DOLLAR 1980–1988[17]

In 1980, with exchange rates at ¥226/$ and DM 1.82/$, the Buick Century sold for approximately $10,000. Nissan priced their competing four-door standard sedan, the Maxima, at ¥2,250,000, or $9,956. As the dollar appreciated spectacularly in 1980–1984 against the German mark (i.e., 1.82 to 2.94) and appreciated somewhat

---

[17] Based on "General Motors and the Dollar," Harvard Business School, Publishing Division, Harvard University, 1989, and "Foreign-Owned Plants Produce Growing Share of U.S. Autos," *Investors Business Daily,* March 30, 1998, p. A4.

against the yen (i.e., 226 to 238), GM took four price increases averaging 10.2 percent per year across all its models, which added 48 percent ($1.102^4 = 1.48$) to the domestic (dollar) price of cars like the Century. Nissan took four price increases averaging 13.8 percent, which added 68 percent to the dollar price of a Maxima sold in the U.S. The dollar had risen 5 percent, so Nissan's effective price increase in their home currency was 63 percent in yen (68 percent − 5 percent). For GM, the export price to Japan was 53 percent (48 percent + 5 percent) higher.

Consider, however, the net price increases for GM products in deutsche marks. Because the dollar had risen 47 percent against the mark in 1980–1984, the net price increase for overseas sales in Germany in 1985 was a whopping 95 percent (48 percent + 47 percent) higher in deutsche marks. The Opel Division of General Motors found it difficult to explain to potential German customers why asking prices should essentially double in so short a period. Accordingly, Opel received permission to roll back many of these price increases.

In the subsequent period, 1985–1988, the dollar depreciated almost as spectacularly as it had risen in 1980–1984 (i.e., −44 percent against the mark and −60 percent against the yen). It is instructive to examine how Nissan and GM reacted when their roles in managing the exchange rate trends reversed. Now, Nissan had to deal with a strengthening currency and the deterioration of export sales that might follow, the same problem GM had faced in 1980–1984. Nissan's response was to slash their profit margins by taking only 5.7-percent per-year dollar price increases (i.e., $1.057^4 = 1.25 = 25$ percent price increase) at a time when their currency was steeply appreciating by 60 percent. Over this four-year period, therefore, the net receipts in yen from selling a Maxima in the U.S. export market declined by 35 percent (25 percent − 60 percent). That is, the 25-percent additional dollars charged were worth so much less yen that the net receipts in the home currency actually fell by 35 percent. General Motors, in this 1985–1988 time period, took 7.2 percent price increases, raising dollar receipts 32 percent ($1.072^4 = 1.32$).

Altogether, between 1980 and 1988, the cumulative dollar price increases on the competing cars were similar. A $10,000 GM car rose in price to $19,479, and a competing $9,956 Nissan car rose in price to $20,837. However, the exchange rate trend from ¥226/$ in 1980 to ¥128/$ in 1988 reveals that the Japanese accepted a much smaller price increase in their home currency. Multiplying $20,837 by ¥128 to the dollar identifies the Nissan gross receipts on an export Maxima in 1988 as ¥2,667,136. This figure represents only a *cumulative* 20-percent yen price increase over the eight years, while GM's cumulative dollar price increase was 95 percent. Not surprisingly, the Japanese share of the U.S. new car market grew rapidly over this period, from 19.8 percent to 23.7 percent. General Motors' market share plummeted from 45.9 percent in 1980 to 36.1 percent in 1988.

Why did GM and Nissan have such different pricing and markup policies? One might suspect that costs were higher in the United States during 1980–1988. In fact, the unit labor costs in auto manufacturing were lower in the United States than in Japan over this period. Perhaps Nissan sought greater sales volume to realize scale economies or take advantage of learning curve-related reductions in unit cost as cumulative volume increased. Total quality initiatives in Japanese manufacturing in this period did realize much-heralded cost savings on the assembly plant floor as more vehicles passed quality inspections without requiring rework. And cost savings from manufacturing quality initiatives are related to volume. Nissan's plant in Smyrna, Tennessee, is heralded as the most efficient assembly line in America, with worker productivity almost 35 percent higher than the average GM plant. Finally, Toyota, Honda, and Nissan certainly are export-driven companies. Between 1985 and 1988,

Nissan generated 50 percent of its sales abroad (fully 45 percent in the United States alone).

General Motors, in contrast, had 72-percent domestic sales, 12-percent export sales, and 16-percent sales from overseas production divisions. Consequently, GM does not focus marketing and operations planning on export sales. Every company should, however, always analyze their import market competition. Fundamentally, GM simply maintained higher net profit margins (i.e., 3.2-percent return on sales) over 1980–1988, while Nissan cut net margins (i.e., from 2.4 percent to 1.2 percent) to achieve market penetration and realize cost savings on greater production volume. Nissan's response to ¥/$ exchange rate fluctuations is typical of Japanese manufacturers, who tend to absorb approximately half of any unfavorable exchange rate moves (appreciations of the yen) by reducing margins.

The Appropriate Use of PPP: An Overview

What, then, is the appropriate role of purchasing power parity in managing international business? First, one should be aware that PPP is a very long-run proposition that depends on cross-national arbitrage in goods and services. Arbitrage activities are motivated whenever the price of auto tires or canned green beans in one economy departs markedly from the price of similar goods in another economy, not far distant. In such circumstances, entrepreneurs emerge to buy cheap in one location and sell dear in the other, but goods arbitrage takes time. Goods arbitrage requires logistical infrastructure like freight terminals, distribution networks or reliable relationships, and effective transnational marketing campaigns. Until all these matters can be resolved, international markets remain somewhat segmented, thereby preventing the complete convergence of prices of identical products between the United States and Japan, between EU countries, between the United States and the United Kingdom, and even between the United States and Canada. Unlike arbitrage in financial markets, the goods arbitrage underlying PPP may take months, years, or even decades. As a result, the variance of prices for like goods across countries is larger (often ten times larger) than the variance of prices through time within an economy.[18]

In the short run, therefore, when the prices of traded goods in the United States diverge from those in the United Kingdom, nominal exchange rates may not respond to fully offset the price differentials, as predicted by PPP. Instead, price stickiness in traded goods combined with the lemming-like behavior of herds of FX (foreign exchange) speculators leads to more volatile nominal exchange rates than would characterize a fully-adjusting price regime. In particular, nominal exchange rates may overshoot or undershoot their equilibrium levels in adjusting to demand or monetary shocks. To avoid the problem of comparing prices across countries at these contemporaneous exchange rates that may bias the assessment, many analysts perform cross-border comparisons of price levels or trade statistics using purchasing power parity estimates for at least the prior 10- to 15-year period.

For example, if one observes that 10 feet of 0.019-gauge gutter pipe sells in do-it-yourself stores in the United States for $3.36 and that in 2000 the value of the British pound is $1.80/£ (i.e., £0.56/$), it might be very misleading to calculate that

---

[18] C. Engel and J.H. Rogers, "How Wide Is the Border?" *American Economic Review,* 86 (1996), pp. 1112–1125 and "Goods Prices and Exchange Rates," *Journal of Economic Literature,* 35 N (1997), pp. 1243–1272.

identically-priced gutter pipe should sell for £1.88 in the U.K. (i.e., $3.36 × £0.56/$). Even if the British are paying £2.10, the apparent arbitrage profit of (£2.10 − £1.88) × $1.80/£ = $0.40 per 10 feet may not be available. Consequently, rushing out to organize the distribution and export of gutter pipe for sale in Great Britain every time the exchange rate overshoots does not make sense. Instead, one could multiply the $3.36 U.S. price by a £0.65/$ purchasing power parity value of the pound over 1985–2000 (see Figure 6.2). This would imply that gutter pipe in British stores selling for as much as £2.18 would not be overpriced relative to the United States.

Example

ARE DIRTY DISHES MOBILE?
DIXAN, JOY, DAWN, AND GENERIC *PATTI SCALA* FROM SCALA S.P.A.

Sometimes purchasing power parity (PPP) fails to characterize the price of identical items for sale in different currencies because some complementary factors in consumption or production are immobile. Especially unique land is one immobile factor; dirty dishes are another. In July 2001, after a 35% two-year appreciation of the U.S. dollar to 2,284 lire and 1.18 euros, Tuscan villagers found themselves serving mountains of *primi patti* (first dishes) of various pastas to throngs of U.S. tourists. As a result, dirty dishes piled up in many Italian sinks.

As elsewhere, dirty dishes in Italy eventually require *patti scala* (dish soap), and Scala S.p.A. from Castrocielo, France, supplies lemon-scented generic Patti Scala throughout the grocery stores of Tuscany. Generic Patti Scala at 1,900 lire competes directly against Dixan, a popular branded dish soap at 2,600 lire, both in regular size 750-ml plastic containers. What is extraordinary at first glance about these Italian prices is that in July 2001, 1,900 lire and 2,600 lire equated to $0.84 and $1.14, respectively, much less than the price of equivalent dish soaps in U.S. stores (e.g., Harris Teeter sells 750 ml of generic dish soap for $1.80; Joy, Palmolive, and Dawn sell for $1.99, $2.49, and $2.79 in roughly comparable sizes (see Table 6.2 below). Does this imply that Joy, Palmolive, and Dawn should anticipate massive erosion of their U.S. market share because of lower priced Dixan imports from Italy?

The answer is definitely no, for three reasons. First, of course, customers of Joy, Palmolive, and Dawn in the U.S. do not recognize the Dixan brand. A massive advertising and promotional campaign by Dixan would be necessary to overcome the brand name barriers to entry in the U.S. market. International arbitrage in goods and full attainment of PPP is partially prevented by the customer-switching costs imposed by these brand names. Most branded products compete in at least partially segmented domestic markets.

Second, even in the absence of branded products, PPP may fail to hold in the generic dish soap market because dirty dishes are immobile. Although the chemical ingredients, lemon scents, and hand softeners in Scala S.p.A.'s Patti Scala are virtually identical to those in Harris Teeter Dish Soap, American dirty dishes are permanently located in the U.S., and Tuscan dirty dishes are permanently located in Italy. Thus, despite the availability of surplus Patti Scala at 1,900 lire in Italy, the immobile dirty dish complements in consumption are located in the U.S. One must therefore incorporate a transportation cost into these price comparisons. A delivered price of Patti Scala in the U.S. would be 1,900/2,284 lire = $0.84, plus perhaps 30% shipping cost—i.e., $1.09. Transportation costs explain a substantial portion of the observed price differential between identical products priced in different currencies.

Finally, why should the prices of generic dish soap products shipped into another currency's domestic market in the summer of 2001 differ by as much as $1.09 to

$1.80? The answer lies in recognizing that relative purchasing power parity is a hypothesis about long-term price dynamics. Exchange rates often overshoot their equilibrium levels, and consequently the ratio of retail prices in one economy to the exchange-rate-adjusted retail prices in another economy should be computed over several years. For example, two years earlier the Italian lira was much stronger than in the summer 2001; specifically, in June 1999 the U.S. dollar exchanged for just 1,665 lire, versus 2,248 lire in June 2001. With the suggested retail prices of Patti Scala and Dixan the same in 1999 as in 2001, Patti Scala at (1,900/1,650 lire =) $1.15 + 30 percent transportation cost = $1.48 for 750 ml. (i.e., $0.0020 per ml.) is right in line with Harris Teeter's $0.0022-per-ml. price of $1.80 for 828 ml. of generic dish soap. Furthermore, Dixan at (2,600/1,665 lire =) $1.56 + 30 percent transportation cost = $2.03 for 750 ml. is nearly identical to Joy's $1.99 price for 740 ml. of branded dish soap.

In conclusion, successful brand name campaigns, complementary factory immobility, and temporary exchange rate overshooting may create a persistent gap between the final product prices of like products sold in different currencies.

Table 6.2   Competing Dish Soap Products in the U.S. and Italy

Branded Products	June 2001 Price	Unit Volume (ml.)
Joy	$1.99	740
Palmolive	$2.49	739
Dawn	$2.79	740
Dixan (June 2001)	$1.14 (2,600 lire) + 30% shipping = $1.45	750
Dixan (June 1999)	$1.56 (2,600 lire) + 30% shipping = $2.03	750
Generic Products		
Harris Teeter Dish Soap	$1.80	828
Patti Scala (June 2001)	$0.84 (1,900 lire) + 30% shipping = $1.09	750
Patti Scala (June 1999)	$1.15 (1,900 lire) + 30% shipping = $1.48	750

Example

BIG MAC INDEX OF PURCHASING POWER PARITY[19]

Big Mac hamburgers sold in 120 countries around the world are as close to identical as the MacDonald's parent corporation can make them, yet individual country managers have complete discretion in setting the price. In 1974, the Big Mac sold for approximately $1.00 in the United States and DM 2.50 in Germany. In that same year, 2.50 German marks exchanged for one U.S. dollar in the foreign currency markets. The Big Mac index of PPP (i.e., DM 2.50/$1.00) just equalled the actual exchange rate.

[19] Based on "McCurrencies: Where's the Beef?" *The Economist*, April 27, 1996, p. 110; "Big MacCurrencies," *The Economist*, April 9, 1994, p. 88; and "Big MacCurrencies," *The Economist*, April 3, 1999.

By 1996, the cost of a Big Mac in downtown Munich had risen to $4.90, slightly higher than implied by the 93-percent cumulative German inflation between 1974–1996 (i.e., 1.93 × DM 2.50 = DM 4.82). In 1996 in Atlanta, on the other hand, the Big Mac sold for $2.36, considerably lower than implied by the 219-percent cumulative U.S. inflation 1974–1996 (i.e., 3.19 × $1.00 = $3.19). Consequently, the Big Mac index of purchasing power parity (i.e., DM 4.90/$2.36 = 2.08) at the end of 1996 implied that the U.S. dollar should exchange for DM 2.08. With the actual exchange rate at DM 1.76/$1, PPP implied that the dollar was substantially undervalued. Sustained dollar appreciation against the mark in 1997–2000 from DM 1.76/$ to DM 2.30/$ suggests that "burger economics" may have some merit.

The Big Mac relationships are not a perfect application of the relative PPP hypothesis for several reasons: (1) because the German VAT tax exceeds the U.S. sales tax, (2) because downtown land rents and utilities in Munich approach those in midtown Manhattan and exceed those in Atlanta, and (3) because the degree of fast food industry competition facing a Munich MacDonald's is lower than that facing an Atlanta MacDonald's. Also, of course, a prepared Big Mac cannot be purchased in Munich for effective resale in Atlanta; goods arbitrage with perishable commodities is infeasible. Nevertheless, such PPP measures can help evaluate trends in currency value, like the 1997–2000 appreciation of the dollar against the deutsche mark, shown in Figure 6.6.

When the dollar reached DM 2.10/$ in 1999, the Big Mac index of PPP predicted that any additional increases in dollar value would constitute overshooting. Sure enough, as conveyed in Figure 6.2, no sooner had the U.S. dollar risen to DM 2.30/$ in 2001 than it collapsed 20 percent during 2002–2003 against many of the DM and other European currencies (i.e., from €1.12/$ to €0.92/$). Even the trade-weighted index value of the dollar declined (see Figure 6.7), despite the fact that Canada, Mexico, and Japan are more prominent than Germany in this trade-weighted exchange rate index.

Trade-Weighted Exchange Rate Index

Figure 6.7 shows the value of the U.S. dollar against the currencies of the United States' largest trading partners from 1973–2003. This trade-weighted exchange rate, sometimes called the effective exchange rate (EER), calculates the weighted average value of the dollar against 19 currencies, where the weights are determined by the volume of import plus export trade between the U.S. and each of its trading partners. The EER for the United States is defined as

$$\text{EER}^\$_t = \sum_i \text{eI}^\$_{it} \text{w}_{it} \qquad [6.2]$$

where w_{it} is the relative proportion of total import and export trade from and to country i in time period t (say, 5 percent or more precisely, the relative weight 0.05 for the U.K. in 2003) and where $\text{eI}^\$_{it}$ is the exchange rate index for the dollar in period t against the currency of country i. For Britain, $\text{eI}^\$_{\pounds 03}$ is calculated as the £/$ exchange rate in 2003 divided by the £/$ exchange in the base year, multiplied by 100—i.e., (£0.63/$ ÷ £0.40/$) × 100 = 1.58 × 100 = 158. From 1995–2001, the trade-weighted U.S. dollar appreciated substantially. All three factors determining long-run trends in exchange rates were involved. Real growth rates in the United States declined over this period relative to several of the United States' largest trading partners. Real interest rates on U.S. T-bills were high and rising relative to those

Figure 6.7   Trade-Weighted Effective Exchange Rate Index, U.S. Dollar (1973–2003)

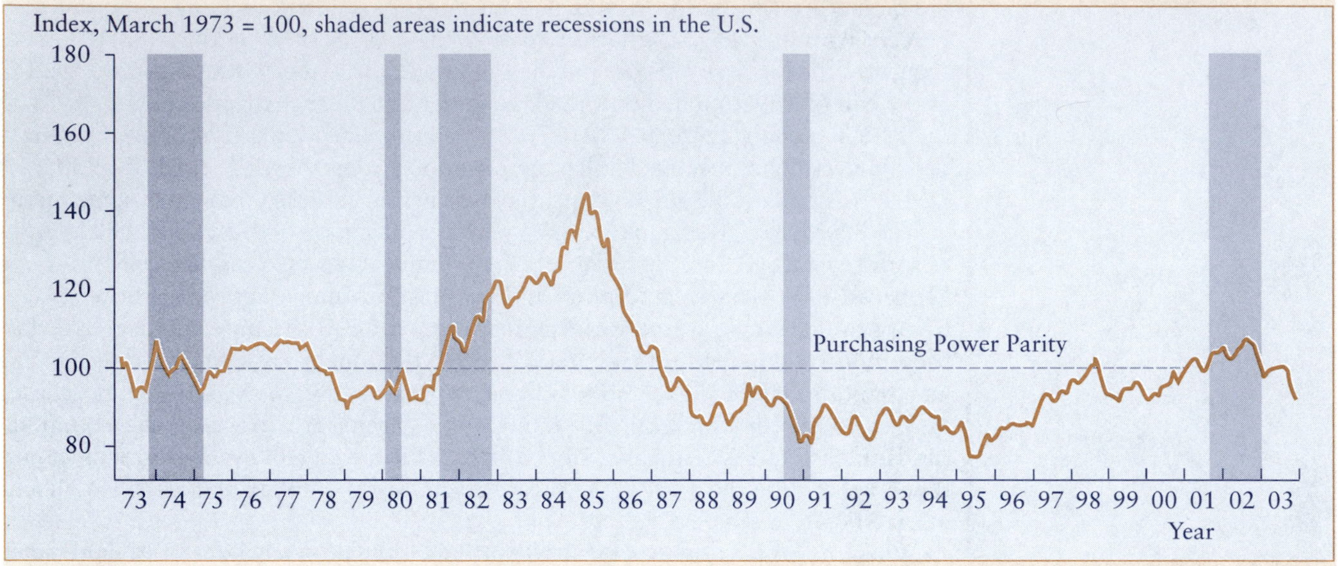

Index, March 1973 = 100, shaded areas indicate recessions in the U.S.

Purchasing Power Parity

Year

Source: *National Economic Trends,* Federal Reserve Bank of St. Louis, quarterly.

same trading partners. And finally, cost inflation in the U.S. producer price index was at a post-World War II low relative to the United States' largest trading partners. So, U.S. export trade rose dramatically and capital flowed into the U.S.

As it was for their Japanese and European competitors in the 1980s, export trade provided the engine of growth for many U.S. companies in the 1990s. Panel (a) of Figure 6.8 shows that from the 1960s to the late 1990s, the share of exports relative to U.S. GDP grew from 4 percent to 12 percent. By 1992, merchandise exports represented a 19-percent share of real U.S. GDP growth. Between 1992 and 1997, the contribution of exports to GDP growth doubled (see Figure 6.8, Panel (b)). Decay of the U.S. export sector since 1998 suggests that the value of the dollar has again reached a level so high that it will dampen export sales. However, at its highest recent values of ¥134 in mid-1998 and DM 2.30 in mid-2000, the U.S. dollar was still well below its spectacular 1985 peak of ¥238 and DM 2.94. This multicultural historical perspective, reflected in Figure 6.7, can be quite useful for assessing the relative strength of a currency.

INTERNATIONAL TRADE: A MANAGERIAL PERSPECTIVE

Shares of World Trade and Regional Trading Blocs

The United States is both the largest exporter and the largest importer in the world's economy. Thus, the United States has the largest share of bilateral world trade (15 percent). The next five countries with the largest shares of world trade in 2001 were

Figure 6.8   Growth of Export Sector in U.S. Economy

Percent of GDP, 1960–2002   Growth of export sector in U.S. economy

Panel (a)

Panel (b)

□ Export contribution
■ Real GDP growth

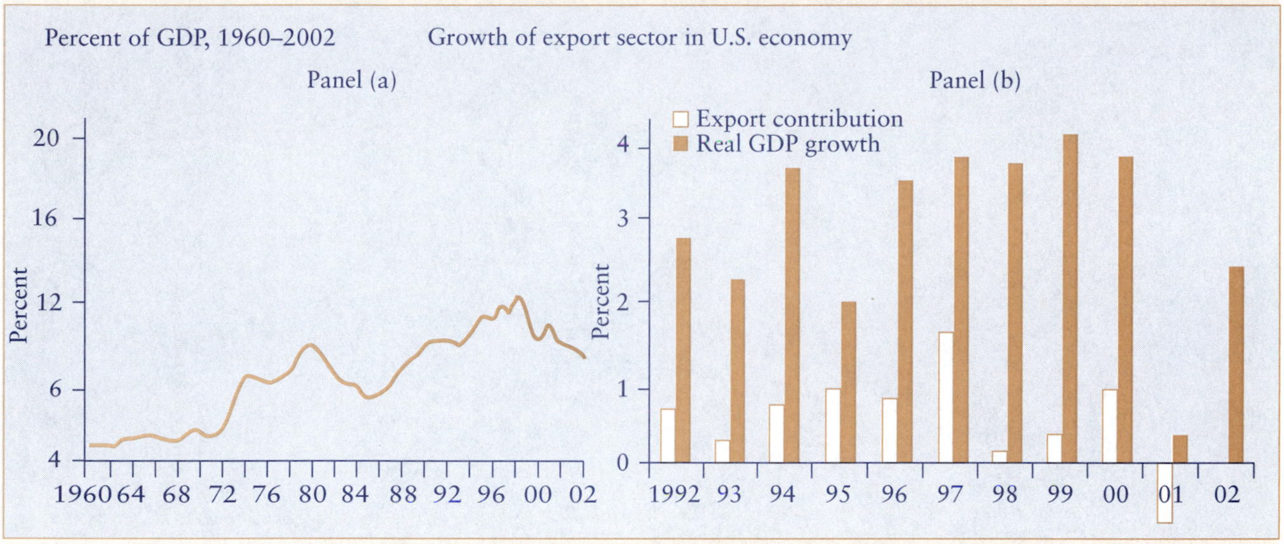

Source: U.S. Department of Commerce, Bureau of Economic Analysis

Germany (8 percent), Japan (6 percent), France (5 percent), Britain (5 percent), and Italy (4 percent). Although these largest trading nations are predominantly Western-developed economies, the next 10 largest trading nations are rapidly developing Asian economies: China (4 percent), Canada (4 percent), the Netherlands (4 percent), Hong Kong China (3 percent), Belgium (3 percent), South Korea (2 percent), Mexico (2 percent), Singapore (2 percent), Spain (2 percent), and Taipai (2 percent). Altogether, the World Trade Organization (WTO) includes 179 nations who have agreed to share trade statistics and coordinate the liberalization of trade policy (i.e., the opening of markets). In the last decade of the 20th century, not only capitalism but also free trade spread across the world economy.

Figure 6.9 shows that over the last two decades the import (and to a lesser extent, export) trade flows to and from the United States have grown to represent fully 25 percent of GDP. Nevertheless, the United States remains an economy dominated by domestic activity where exports equaled only 10 percent of GDP in 2002. Elsewhere, some nations, especially in Asia, are export-driven. South Korean exports were 34 percent of 2002 GDP; Taiwanese exports were 53 percent of GDP; Indonesian exports were 50 percent of GDP; Malaysian exports were 93 percent of GDP! In Europe, German exports were 35 percent of 2002 GDP. And within North America, Mexican and Canadian exports were 34 percent and 43 percent of 2002 GDP, respectively.

Most nations continue to protect with tariffs and other trade barriers some infant or politically sensitive industries. France, for example, remains a largely agricultural polity and therefore lowers its agricultural trade barriers only after great hand-wringing and extended periods of tough negotiations with its European neighbors. Until recently, the United States imposed import restraints on Japanese automobiles and maintained 30-percent tariffs on textiles, apparel, and carbon steel imports. Fortunately, regional trading blocs like the European Union (EU) and the North

Figure 6.9   U.S. Imports and Exports as a Percentage of GDP

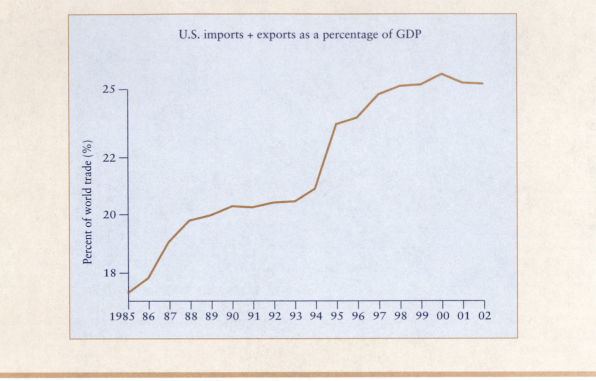

http://www.osec.doc.gov/
Source: U.S. Department of Commerce

American Free Trade Agreement (NAFTA) were highly successful in the 1990s at removing trade barriers, negotiating multilateral reductions in tariffs, and promoting free trade as a mechanism of peaceful competition between nations.

Across the world economy, six such regional trading blocs have emerged (see Figure 6.10). In South America, Argentina, Brazil, Paraguay, Uruguay, Bolivia, and Chile have formed one trading block (MERCOSUR). The Andean group (Venezuela, Peru, Colombia, Bolivia, and Ecuador) has formed another; both are attempts to mirror the NAFTA free trade agreements of Canada, the United States, and Mexico. Seven Southeast Asian (ASEAN) and 16 trans-Pacific economies including Japan and Mexico (APEC) have also formed trading blocs. From 1980–1999, trade *within* these trading blocs swelled as a percentage of the member states' total trade, especially in NAFTA, MERCOSUR, and the Andean Community (see Table 6.3). For example, Canada-U.S.-Mexico trade grew from 33 percent to 47 percent between 1993 and 2000, while Japan-U.S. trade shrank from 15 percent to 10 percent of U.S. trade.[20] In addition, with fully 88 percent of Mexican trade now involving its two NAFTA partners, 34 nations in Central and South America, Canada, Mexico, and the U.S. have agreed in principle to form by 2005 a Free Trade Area of the Americas (FTAA) with 800 million people and combined output equal to $12 trillion.

http://
Access the MERCOSUR
Internet site at
http://www.mercosur.com.
ar/portal/

---

[20] "Trade in the Americas," *The Economist*, April 21, 2001, pp. 20–24.

Figure 6.10   Regional Trading Zones (Percentage of World Trade)

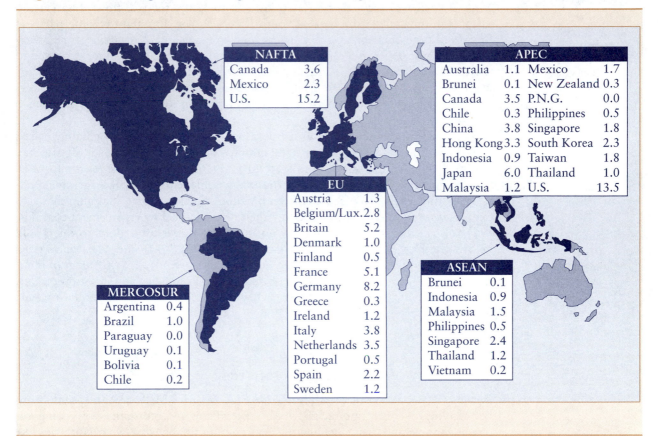

NAFTA	
Canada	3.6
Mexico	2.3
U.S.	15.2

APEC			
Australia	1.1	Mexico	1.7
Brunei	0.1	New Zealand	0.3
Canada	3.5	P.N.G.	0.0
Chile	0.3	Philippines	0.5
China	3.8	Singapore	1.8
Hong Kong	3.3	South Korea	2.3
Indonesia	0.9	Taiwan	1.8
Japan	6.0	Thailand	1.0
Malaysia	1.2	U.S.	13.5

EU	
Austria	1.3
Belgium/Lux.	2.8
Britain	5.2
Denmark	1.0
Finland	0.5
France	5.1
Germany	8.2
Greece	0.3
Ireland	1.2
Italy	3.8
Netherlands	3.5
Portugal	0.5
Spain	2.2
Sweden	1.2

MERCOSUR	
Argentina	0.4
Brazil	1.0
Paraguay	0.0
Uruguay	0.1
Bolivia	0.1
Chile	0.2

ASEAN	
Brunei	0.1
Indonesia	0.9
Malaysia	1.5
Philippines	0.5
Singapore	2.4
Thailand	1.2
Vietnam	0.2

Source: WTO Web site, 2002.

Table 6.3   Intraregional Trade as a Percent of a Region's World Trade

	1980	1990	1999
European Union	57	66	61
NAFTA	33	37	47
MERCOSUR	13	14	22
Andean	4	5	10
ASEAN	14	14	18

Source: International Monetary Fund, *Direction of Trade Statistics.*

Example

MERCOSUR AVERTS A TRADE WAR

MERCOSUR was formed as a free trade area to secure the free flow of goods and services in the cone at the base of South America. The dominant trading partners Brazil and Argentina joined with Uruguay and Paraguay and pledged under the Treaty of Asunción in 1991 to avoid punitive tariffs and import quotas (later extended to the associate members Chile and Bolivia). These commitments were sorely tested during a recession in 1998–1999. GDP growth plummeted from 7.1 percent to −3 percent in Brazil, while Argentina slowed from 8.6 percent to 1.8 percent but continued to grow.

To jump-start its economy, Brazil devalued the *real* (which immediately raised the cost of imports by 40 percent) and adopted an industrial policy of offering tax breaks, free land, and other subsidies to any Argentine automobile parts suppliers, shoe manufacturers, and corporate farms that would move to Brazil. Argentina retaliated by threatening to place tariffs on Brazilian textile exports, claiming that said exports were so heavily subsidized that their prices fell below replacement cost. The WTO allows any member to impose antidumping duties on export products sold below cost. However, under MERCOSUR's procedures, Brazil and Argentina agreed instead to negotiate a reduction in the subsidies and a removal of the threat of punitive tariffs while attempting to harmonize their fiscal policies and inflation targets, much like the European Union experience with the Maastricht Treaty. A nasty trade war was narrowly averted.

Comparative Advantage and Free Trade

Within a regional trading bloc like EU, NAFTA, MERCOSUR, or APEC, each member can improve its economic growth by specializing in accordance with comparative advantage and then engaging in free trade. Intuitively, low-wage countries like Spain, Mexico, Puerto Rico, China, and Thailand enjoy a cost advantage in the manufacture of labor-intensive goods such as garment sewing and the provision of labor-intensive services like coupon or insurance claims processing. Suppose one of these economies also enjoys a cost advantage in more capital-intensive manufacturing like auto assembly. One of the powerful insights of international microeconomics is that in such circumstances, the low-cost economy should not produce both goods, but rather it should specialize in that production for which it has the lower relative cost, while buying the other product from its higher-cost trading partner. Let's see how this **law of comparative advantage** in bilateral trade reaches such an apparently odd conclusion.

Law of Comparative Advantage
A principle defending free trade and specialization in accordance with lower relative cost.

Consider the bilateral trade between the United States and Japan in automobile carburetors and computer memory chips. Suppose the cost of production of carburetors in Japan is ¥10,000 compared to $120 in the United States. At an exchange rate of 100 yen to the dollar, the Japanese dollar price of $100 is lower than the U.S. price of $120. Suppose, in addition, that memory chips cost ¥8,000 in Japan compared to $300 in the United States. Again, the dollar price of the Japanese product (i.e., $80) is lower than the price of the U.S. product. Japan is said to enjoy an absolute cost advantage in the manufacture of both products. However, Japan is 83 percent (i.e., $100/$120) as expensive in producing carburetors as the United States while being only 27 percent (i.e., $80/$300) as expensive in producing memory chips. Japan is said to have a comparative advantage in memory chips and should specialize in the manufacture of that product.

Real Terms of Trade
Comparison of relative costs of production across economies.

The gains from specialization in accordance with comparative advantage and subsequent trade are best demonstrated using the real terms of trade. **Real terms of trade** identify what amounts of labor effort, material, and other resources are required to produce a product in one economy relative to another. In Japan, the manufacture of memory chips requires the sacrifice of resources capable of manufacturing 0.8 carburetors (see Table 6.4), whereas in the United States the manufacture of a memory chip requires the sacrifice of 2.5 carburetors. That is, Japan's relative cost of memory chips (in terms of carburetor production that must be forgone) is less than a third as great as the relative cost of memory chips in the United States. On the other hand, U.S. carburetor production requires the resources associated with only 0.4 U.S. memory chips, while Japanese carburetor production requires the sacrifice of 1.25 Japanese memory chips. The U.S. relative cost of carburetors is much lower than that of the Japanese. Said another way, the Japanese are particularly productive in using resources to manufacture memory chips, and the United States is particularly productive in using similar resources to produce carburetors. Each country has a comparative advantage: the Japanese in producing memory chips and the United States in producing carburetors.

Assess what happens to the total goods produced if each economy specializes in production in accordance with comparative advantage and then trades to diversify its consumption. Assume that the United States and Japan produced one unit of each product initially, that labor is immobile, that no scale economies are present, and that the quality of both carburetors and both memory chips is identical. If the Japanese cease production of carburetors and specialize in the production of memory chips, they increase memory chip production to 2.25 chips (see Table 6.4). Similarly, if the United States ceases production of memory chips and specializes in the production of carburetors, it increases carburetor production to 3.5 carburetors.

Table 6.4   Real Terms of Trade and Comparative Advantage

	Absolute Cost, U.S.	Absolute Cost, Japan
Automobile carburetors	$120	¥10,000
Computer memory chips	$300	¥8,000
	Relative Cost, U.S.	Relative Cost, Japan
Automobile carburetors	$120/$300 = 0.4 Chips	¥10K/¥8K = 1.25 Chips
Computer memory chips	$300/$120 = 2.5 Carbs	¥8K/¥10K = 0.8 Carbs
	Gains from Trade, U.S.	Gains from Trade, Japan
Initial Goods	1.0 Carb + 1.0 Chip	1.0 Carb + 1.0 Chip
After specialization:		
Carburetors produced	(1.0 + 2.5) Carbs	0
Memory chips produced	0	(1.0 + 1.25) Chips
Trade	+1.0 Chip	+1.5 Carb
	−1.5 Carb	−1.0 Chip
Net goods	2.0 Carbs + 1.0 Chip	1.5 Carbs + 1.25 Chips

In these circumstances, the United States could offer Japan 1.5 carburetors for a memory chip, and both parties would end up unambiguously better off. The United States would enjoy a residual domestic production after trade of 2.0 carburetors plus the import of one memory chip. And the Japanese would enjoy a residual domestic production after trade of 1.25 memory chips plus the import of 1.5 carburetors. As demonstrated in Table 6.4, each economy would have replaced all the products they initially produced, plus each would enjoy additional amounts of both goods—i.e., unambiguous gains from trade.

Import Controls and Protective Tariffs

In the Mercantilist period from 1500 to 1750, many nations rejected free-trade policies and instead attempted to restrain the purchase of foreign imports in order to expand the production of their domestic industries (as Brazil attempted in 1999). To bar imports, some nations adopted "beggar thy neighbor" policies such as protective tariffs that raised the domestic prices of foreign goods. Others tried direct import controls like a maximum allowable quota of a specific type of foreign import. England, for example, banned the export of Cotswold wool to French cloth manufacturers in Flanders in hopes of retaining the cloth weaving, finishing, and dyeing industries in Britain. When expensive unsold British cloth accumulated, Flanders cloth imports were restricted. Between 1500 and 1603, the unintended consequence of these import-export quotas was a 500 percent inflation in cloth prices in Britain.

A few of these ill-advised import control ideas even survive to the present day—e.g., the U.S. voluntary import restraint agreement with Japanese automobile manufacturers in the mid-1980s. Again, the net results of import controls were not as expected. Toyota and Honda simply built assembly plants all over the U.S., and still more GM, Ford, and Chrysler workers were laid off. In general, national income and employment in the country barring imports eventually falls relative to the potential income available under freer trade policies. Even mercantilist Brazil agreed and reversed its 1999 mercantilist trade policy.

The reason why hinges on an understanding of exchange rates and trade balances. Import controls lead inevitably to a reduction in the supply of a nation's currency in the foreign exchange market. For example, when some American households are prohibited from completing import purchases of Toyotas and Hondas they would otherwise have bought, those households fail to request the yen they would have needed to accomplish the import purchases. Accordingly, they also fail to supply the U.S. dollars that would have been exchanged for the requisite foreign currency. A reduction in the supply of dollars, all other things being the same, implies that the dollar must appreciate; therefore, reduced imports implies a rise in value of the domestic currency. However, this exchange rate adjustment raises the price of American exports since the number of yen, DM, or lire a foreign buyer must pay to acquire dollar-denominated goods and services inevitably rises, and U.S. exports then decline. These consequences normally unfold even if the domestic producers attempt to offset their currency's appreciation with reduced profit margins. Ultimately, therefore, the attempt to improve domestic output and raise national income by imposing import controls often results in a collapse of the export sector sufficient to worsen the trade balance (exports minus imports) and actually decreases national income.

Free trade and open markets offer the prospect of higher national income. Developing countries with open economies grew by 4.5 percent per year in the 1970s and 1980s, whereas those with import controls and protective tariffs grew by only 0.7 percent per year. Rich country comparisons also favored free trade: 2.3 percent to, again, 0.7 percent. In the 1990s, this gap widened still further. Those developing countries whose import plus export trade as a percentage of GDP ranked in the top 50th percentiles of developing countries had GDP growth per person of 5 percent. Those in the bottom 50th percentiles saw GDP growth per person actually shrink by 1 percent.[21] Clearly, globalization and trade enhance prosperity, even in the lesser developed countries.

Example

PRESIDENT BUSH'S 2002 STEEL TARIFFS: JUSTIFIED SANCTIONS OR HYPOCRITICAL PROTECTIONISM?[22]

Despite its heavy weight and high transportation cost, steel is sourced from factories around the globe. At $350/ton, sheet steel from Brazil and South Korea can be shipped to the U.S. for $70/ton and still sell $55 below the $475/ton cost of the big integrated hot-rolled steel producers in the U.S. like Bethlehem and Republic Steel (see Table 6.5). As a result, 15 of 17 such integrated U.S. producers who convert iron ore in blast furnaces using 160,000 United Steel Workers (USW) are operating under bankruptcy protection from their creditors. Their market share has fallen from 80 percent in 1976 to 40 percent today. The U.S. is ranked fourth in world steel production after the E.U., China, and Japan (see Figure 6.11).

Only AK Steel, U.S. Steel, Nucor, and other mini-mill producers are profitable. Nucor employs one third as many workers as the integrated mills, using less expensive electric arc furnaces. In addition, because Nucor starts with scrap metal, not iron ore, their principal input cost is highly correlated with final steel sheet and steel slab prices, a highly effective internal hedge. For example, when slab steel prices sank from $300 to $200 recently, the price of Nucor's scrap steel input plummeted to all-time lows as well. Finally, a nonunion workforce allows Nucor to avoid the so-called "legacy costs" of the USW contracts with the integrated steel producers (i.e., detailed work rules that stifle innovation and extraordinary health care benefits). In short, U.S. integrated mill steel-making is a highly competitive business that makes use of a high-priced artificially scarce factor, namely, unionized steel workers. In such circumstances, international trade theory predicts internal consumption of domestic production with little export trade and massive foreign imports.

Yet, the USW is a powerful political lobby, and U.S. International Trade Commission hearings plus World Trade Organization (WTO) antidumping rules and dispute resolution procedures provided the vehicle for Presidents Ford and Bush to consider imposing tariff sanctions to protect the domestic steel industry. In March 2002, Bush decided to impose quotas on Brazilian steel and 30 percent tariffs on steel slab and steel sheet from other nations for three years. Predictably, such trade restrictions will increase the cost of steel supplies in the U.S. Precision Technologies of Houston estimated it would raise their costs $3 million on $57 million in sales of high-stress steel tubing for the drilling industry.

There *are* several valid arguments for trade restrictions (import quotas or tariffs): (1) to protect *infant industries* until they reach minimum efficient scale, (2) to offset government subsidies provided to foreign competitors with one's own *countervailing duties,* and (3) to impose antidumping sanctions for foreign goods sold below their domestic cost. Chilean salmon, Argentine honey, and Brazilian frozen orange juice concentrate and slab steel have all been subject to U.S. antidumping duties in recent years. The Brazilians, in particular, claim that their export prices

[21] "Globalization, Growth and Poverty," World Bank report, December 2001.

[22] Based on "Rust Never Sleeps," *The Economist,* March 9, 2002, p. 61; "U.S. Companies Cry Foul," *Wall Street Journal,* March 19, 2002, p. A2; "U.S. Protectionism Imperils Free Trade Talks with Latins," *Wall Street Journal,* March 20, 2002, p. A15; and "WTO Trade Negotiations Hit a Snag," *Wall Street Journal,* March 18, 2003, p. A2.

simply reflect a countervailing reduction relative to their domestic cost in order to offset the enormous $30 billion in farm subsidies that the U.S. makes available to its agriculture. Although the U.S. does spend $20,000 per full-time farmer to subsidize agricultural products (third behind Switzerland's $27,000 and Japan's $23,000), this says nothing about steel.

The WTO has undertaken as part of its Doha round of trade talks to begin sorting out these claims and counterclaims on agricultural subsidies and steel duties. Whether the U.S. will ultimately be sustained in imposing antidumping sanctions on $8 billion of steel or whether foreign nations will be sustained in their countervailing duties to offset the massive U.S. agricultural subsidies remains to be seen. This WTO process will likely take two years; in the meantime, the U.S. steel industry has time to get back on its feet. For its part, Brazil has taken the position that a Free Trade Area of the Americas (FTAA) is a nonstarter until the U.S. abuse of antidumping sanctions ends.

The Case for Strategic Trade Policy

Although the logic of free trade has dominated academic debate since 1750, and the 20th century saw the repeal of many import controls and tariffs, a few exceptions are worth noting. The WTO has very effectively spearheaded the negotiation of *mutual* trade liberalization policies. However, *unilateral* reduction of tariffs when trading partners stubbornly refuse to relax import controls or open their domestic markets seldom makes sense. The United States has found it necessary to threaten tariffs on Japanese consumer electronics, for example, in order to negotiate successfully the opening of Japanese markets to U.S. cellular phones and computer chips. This threat bargaining and negotiated mutual reduction of trade barriers illustrates

Table 6.5   Sheet Steel, $ Cost per Ton

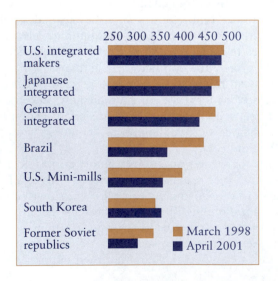

Source: *World Steel Dynamics*, 2002.

Figure 6.11   World Steel Production, 2001

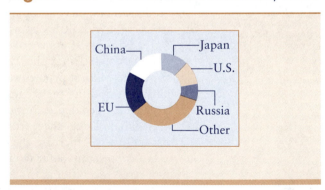

Source: *The Economist*, February 16, 2002.

the concept of strategic trade policy, whereby one nation anticipates and reacts to another nation's trade policies.

In the spring of 1999, continued EU import controls on U.S.-based Dole and Chiquita bananas from Central America led the United States to impose WTO-sanctioned duties on $180 million of European products from Louis Vuitton plastic handbags and British cashmere sweaters to French Roquefort cheese and foie gras. The British and French former colonies in the Caribbean like St. Lucia enjoy approximately $150 million in banana farm profits as a result of the EU's quota limiting U.S. bananas. But the cost to EU consumers has been estimated at $2 billion in higher priced fruit. Strategic trade policy by the U.S. was required to induce the EU to relax its import controls.

Example

INTEL'S CHIP MARKET ACCESS IMPROVES IN JAPAN[23]

In the mid-1980s, Japanese semiconductor producers grabbed much of the world market in the dynamic random access memory chips (DRAMs) used in personal computers. Through a combination of very aggressive pricing and an almost closed home market, Japanese semiconductors achieved massive economies of scale and much reduced average total cost. When the retail price of PCs declined steeply in 1986, it became largely unprofitable for American and European manufacturers like Intel to produce basic memory chips.

In 1986 and again in 1991, U.S. trade representatives negotiated five-year trade agreements with the Japanese to open their markets to U.S. semiconductors. The trade negotiations were precipitated by an international dumping complaint that proved many Japanese chips had been sold in the U.S. and Europe below cost. The U.S. Department of Commerce then imposed punitive tariffs on Japanese chips, laptop computers, and televisions. To avoid these higher tariffs, the Japanese then agreed to open access to their domestic market and set a 20-percent target for foreign memory chip sales in Japan. Intel Corp., Siemens, and other producers expanded, and the Japanese producers Sharp and Toshiba cut production. Although the Japanese did not renew the chip access accords when the second round expired in 1995, the U.S., German, and Japanese semiconductor manufacturers have formed joint ventures to codesign and jointly manufacture subsequent generations of flash memory chips. In this instance, strategic trade policy opened markets and expanded the national income of all the participating nations.

Increasing Returns

Another motivation for strategic trade policy arises in markets where domestic producers encounter increasing returns. Suppose the Boeing Corp. and Airbus find that learning curve effects in airframe manufacturing offer a one-percent reduction in *variable* cost for every market share point above 30 percent. A firm with a 40-percent market share of the world output in a 737 generation of aircraft will experience variable costs only 90 percent as great as smaller competitors. A firm with 50-percent market share will experience variable costs only 80 percent as great as smaller competitors, and so forth. These circumstances are very rare indeed in the industrial sector of the economy, since they imply that diminishing returns in production

---

[23] Based on "America Chips Away at Japan," *The Economist,* March 27, 1993; and "Foreign Chip Sales Up in Japan," *Financial Times,* December 16, 1994.

are more than offset by economies of scope or learning curve advantages at higher output. However, where such circumstances exist, some nations attempt to jump-start the preemptive development of new aircraft models with public subsidies to research and development (a so-called industrial policy). Others impose import controls or protective tariffs to assure the attainment of the 30-percent market share baseline volume required to trigger the emergence of learning curve advantages. This, too, entails strategic trade policy.

Example

NETWORK EXTERNALITIES AT MICROSOFT AND APPLE: A ROLE FOR PROTECTIVE TARIFFS?

The information economy has a higher incidence than the industrial economy of these increasing returns phenomena. Frequently, in the information economy context, cost reductions at larger market share are associated with externalities in the installation of a network or the adoption of a technical standard. As the installed base of Windows software expands, Microsoft finds it increasingly less difficult to convince new customers to adopt their product. Computer users find it much easier to exchange documents and explain new applications, for example, if their PCs employ the same operating system. As a result, the marketing cost to secure the next adoption from a marginal buyer actually declines the larger the market share that Windows attains. The same thing holds for Apple's operating system. The greater the installed base, the more software the independent programmers will write for use on a Mac. The more software available for use on a Mac, the lower the variable cost to Apple of successfully marketing the next PC.

Should strategic trade policy in the United States protect a company with the possibility of achieving increasing returns? Microsoft and Apple pose a good case in point. *Without* import controls and protective tariffs, Microsoft successfully achieved a larger dollar volume of export trade than any other American company. Had the U.S. competitor been Apple alone, a serious question would have arisen. Could Apple have secured a 30-percent-plus market share in the absence of import controls and protective tariffs against a foreign Microsoft?

Is it an appropriate role of the government to pursue such cost advantages for one domestic company or an alliance of domestic companies? Or should government pursue the consumer interest of lowest prices wherever that product is produced? These are the questions hotly debated in strategic trade policy today. The case exercise on reciprocal protectionism at the end of Chapter 14 looks at these strategic trade policy questions in the context of Boeing and Airbus.

http://
The European Union on the Internet:
http://europa.eu.int/

FREE TRADE AREAS: THE EUROPEAN UNION AND NAFTA

Free Trade Area
A group of nations which has agreed to reduce tariffs and other trade barriers.

Free trade and specialization in accordance with comparative advantage leaves economies vulnerable to trade interruptions and punitive tariffs on essential inputs. Nevertheless, the European Union provides an example of what can be accomplished. Starting with the Treaty of Rome in 1957, 12 original European Community members established the groundwork for a **free trade area** which they subsequently consolidated in the Single Europe Act of 1986. Between 1986 and 1992, 12 very dissimilar European economies realized 5-percent additional cumulative growth of GDP attributable to the increased intra-European trade.

Increased specialization in accordance with comparative advantage has the relatively low-wage Spaniards and Portuguese assembling high value-added German components for BMWs and Blaupunkt radios. Reduced trade barriers at borders have cut transportation time. The English Channel ferry now unloads in 15 minutes rather than the previous $1\frac{1}{2}$ hours, and yogurt from Nestlé's subsidiary in Birmingham, England, now speeds across Europe to target customers in Milan in 11 hours rather than the previous 38. Reduced intra-European tariffs on foodstuffs, beer, wine, and autos have markedly reduced the cost of living. Although corporate tax rates still differ from 45 percent in Italy and Germany to 30 percent in Ireland, wide differences in value-added taxes have been reconciled at uniform 17 percent rates in most cases. Just the mere act of exchanging money, which employed 1 in every 200 full-time employees in Europe, became much more efficient with a single European currency.

Optimal Currency Areas

How far and wide a single currency should be adopted as the official monetary unit depends on a complex mix of economic, social, and political factors. The benefits of a single currency are the avoidance of exchange rate risk on intraregional trade and the reduction of conversion costs. Since one in every 200 employees in Europe worked in currency conversion itself, the release of these resources to more productive uses was seen as significant. Similarly, hedging does cost 5 percent of the value at risk, and remember that the total value of world trade (equal to almost $3 trillion per year) pales in comparison to the total value of worldwide currency trading (equal to $1.5 trillion *per day*). Companies like the German pharmaceutical firm Hoeschst AG estimated that it would save over DM 10 million in covered forward hedge contract costs previously incurred to lay off risk exposure on European currencies. Competitiveness was also enhanced when European auto companies secured volume purchase discounts from their cheapest suppliers rather than spreading their parts purchases across Europe as an internal hedge, matching expenditures in local currencies to their anticipated car revenues.

On the political side, Margaret Thatcher's election as British Primer Minister in 1979 was perceived as a mandate to roll back the powers of the state. Two years later when Mitterand returned to power in France, his mandate was just the opposite. he promptly nationalized 36 banks and all the leading companies in chemicals, glass, aluminum, electronics, and armaments, thereby raising the state's share of national output from 15 percent to 30 percent. Not surprisingly, these two EU members differ on the perceived costs of a single European-wide central bank. Whether these costs outweigh the benefits and therefore the boundary of an optimal currency area hinges on three factors: the magnitude of trade, the mobility of labor, and the correlation of macroeconomic shocks between countries within the proposed currency area.

Example

IF EUROPE, WHAT ABOUT ONE CURRENCY FOR NAFTA?[24]

Should the Mexican peso, the Canadian dollar, and the U.S. dollar be replaced by a single currency for NAFTA, just as eleven European currencies were replaced in 1999 by the euro? Even as early as 1992, every nation of the European Union traded more with other EU members than with the rest of the world (see Table 6.6). In

---

[24] See O. Blanchard and J. Wolfers, "The Role of Shocks and Institutions in the Rise of European Unemployment," *Economic Journal*, March 2000; R. Mundell, "Threat to Prosperity" *Wall Street Journal*, March 30, 2000, p. A30; and M. Chriszt, "Perspectives on a North American Currency Union," *Fed Atlanta Economic Review*, 2000(4), pp. 29–36.

some cases (Belgium, Luxembourg, and Ireland), exports make up a majority of their GDP, and the countertrade patterns that underlay the hopes and dreams of the Treaty of Rome have clearly emerged. Similarly, in NAFTA countries, exports plus imports account for 70 percent of GDP in Canada and 58 percent in Mexico, with 79 percent of Canadian trade and 88 percent of Mexican trade involving the U.S.

However, two critical social and political factors limit the effectiveness of the European currency union, and three of the European Union's fifteen members (Britain, Sweden, and Denmark) decided to opt out. With monetary policy constrained to reflect European-wide perceptions about the need for credibility in fighting inflation, and with fiscal policy constrained by rigid guidelines for membership in the currency union, labor mobility must adjust rapidly to stabilize swings in unemployment caused by localized market conditions. For example, with Italy in a slump, Germany and France growing slowly, and Ireland and Portugal booming, a common monetary policy and little fiscal autonomy require that labor move quickly from Continental Europe to the fringes of the EU. Although such mobility occurs easily in the United States where a family can find schools, houses, and language in one state very similar to a state they leave, the same cannot be said in Europe. Relocation costs in the United States of $25,000 are one third as great as in Europe. Canadian-American migration patterns, all the innumerable Mexican guest workers spread throughout the U.S., and new immigrant alien households spread along the California-Mexico and Texas-Mexico borders attest to the mobility of capital and labor in NAFTA.

In addition, of course, most cultural differences are enormous from one corner of the EU to another. While European professionals have trained in foreign capitals and accepted diversity in mannerisms and cultural practices for centuries, working-class Europeans tend to be more culturally prejudicial. Thus, even those who would take the initiative to cross national and cultural borders in pursuit of transitory jobs typically will experience less than full acceptance as "guest workers." Knowing this, fewer unemployed or underemployed European workers desire to relocate than would be the case in the United States. Thus, the average level of European unemployment has increased from less than 2 percent in the 1960s to 12 percent in 2002.

Europe's many separate labor markets cause common macroeconomic shocks to result in a growing dispersion of unemployment rates from 4 percent in Switzerland to 20 percent in Spain. European countries differ in the strength of their unions, payroll taxes, minimum wages, layoff restrictions, and unemployment insurance. A one-size-fits-all monetary policy and little fiscal autonomy may be inappropriate for both Europe and North America. Although Canadian macroeconomic shocks and responses are highly correlated with the U.S., Mexico is a petroleum exporter with business cycles more similar to Venezuela than to the U.S. For the same reason that Britain opted out of a common currency, so should Mexico.

The European Union's free trade and single currency agreements occurred in a region where the output per capita differs by 100 percent between wealthy Milan, Munich, and the Rhineland versus poor Greece, Southern Italy, Spain, and Portugal. Manufacturing-unit-labor cost runs close to $36 an hour in Sweden, $30 an hour in Germany, $20 an hour in Spain, and only $14 an hour in Greece. Marketing plans are just as divergent. The peak penetration of TV into Spanish households (20-percent viewership) occurs at 2 to 4 in the afternoon. Only 5 percent of Spanish households are tuned in from 6 to 8 in the evening when the 22-percent peak British viewership is "watching the telly." The Swiss pay 78 pence per mile for intracoun-

Table 6.6   Countertrade Within the European Union

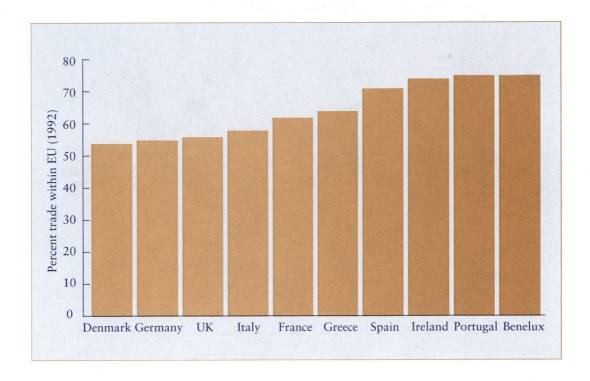

Source: *International Monetary Fund Yearbook,* various issues.

try air travel, whereas the British pay 13 pence per mile. The Spanish consider packaged pet food a luxury and purchase yogurt through the pharmacy. Milanese brag about overpaying for a Sony television, while Munich shoppers search for days to find 5-percent discounts on Sony products. In short, few pan-European marketing plans succeed. Yet, intra-European trade dominates the landscape. Italy, Germany, and France do 55 to 60 percent of their total trade with other European countries (see Table 6.6), and Spain does 70 percent. Ireland, Portugal, and Benelux do close to 80 percent. Even Britain trades more with their regional trading bloc partners than with the rest of the world combined.

Largest U.S. Trading Partners: The Role of NAFTA

Canada, not Japan, is by far the largest trading partner of the United States with almost twice the share (23.6 percent) of American goods exported there than anywhere else in the world's economy (see Figure 6.12). U.S. exports to Canada include everything from merchandise, like Microsoft's software and DaimlerChrysler's automobile components for assembly at an automated minivan plant in Ontario, to professional services like strategic management consulting by McKinsey & Co. Canada is also the largest source of U.S. imports (18 percent), with natural resources and

http://
You can access current information on U.S. trading partners and other trade issues on the Internet at the following site maintained by the Federal Reserve Bank of St. Louis:
http://www.stls.frb.org/ publications/index.html/ #data

Figure 6.12   Largest U.S. Trading Partners

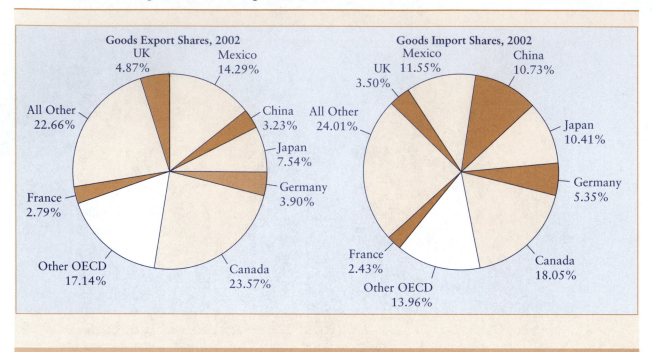

Source: *National Economic Trends, Federal Reserve Bank of St. Louis.*

finished goods manufacturing leading the list. Japanese goods like Toyota and Honda autos, Sony consumer electronics, Canon copiers, and Fuji film constitute 12.8 percent of total U.S. imports, and the Japanese absorb 8 percent of U.S. exports, primarily aircraft, chemicals, computers, timber, corn, and coal.

Mexico consumes and assembles a 14.3-percent share of U.S. exports (up 50 percent since 1996) and provides 11.5 percent of U.S. imports. Mexico supplies large quantities of auto parts, steel, and oil to the United States. From 1993–2003, following the passage of NAFTA, Mexican tariffs declined from 40 percent to 16 percent, and exports to the U.S. increased from 67 percent to 89 percent of total Mexican exports. NAFTA also reduced the trade barriers for American companies like General Motors and Wal-Mart. Wal-Mart now operates 520 retail stores across Mexico. U.S.-owned manufacturing and processing plants have long employed semiskilled labor at $2/hour in Mexico. This trade activity mirrors the labor-intensive assembly that German manufacturing companies perform in Spain and Portugal. For example, with untariffed import of subassemblies NAFTA lowered Mexican production costs for heavy equipment assembler Freightliner by $2,500 per truck between 1992 and 1998, enough to warrant opening a second **maquiladora** assembly plant in Mexico. NAFTA's million and a half new Mexican employment opportunities have caused wage rates to begin to rise. Consequently, some of the call center, data processing, and electronics manufacturing jobs have now moved to still lower wage areas in Argentina, India, and China, respectively.

Maquiladora
A foreign-owned assembly plant in Mexico that imports and assembles duty-free components for export and allows owners to pay duty only on the "value added."

Example

HOUSEHOLD IRON MANUFACTURER IN MEXICO BECOMES MAJOR ENGINE BLOCK SUPPLIER TO DETROIT: CIFUNSA SA[25]

Since its passage in 1994, the North American Free Trade Agreement (NAFTA) has made Mexico into a leading outsourcing location for the worldwide auto parts industry. Duty-free access to the U.S. for auto subassemblies like transmissions and wiring harnesses, plus a growing sector of skilled nonunionized workers, induced GM, Ford, DaimlerChrysler, and Volkswagen as well as Mexican firms like San Luis Corp. and Grupo Industrial Saltillo SA to invest $18 billion in auto plants and equipment between 1994–2000.

Cifunsa SA is a Grupo subsidiary which specialized immediately after WWII in the manufacture of metal castings for household appliances, especially hand irons. Today, Cifunsa has converted its aluminum and steel casting expertise to the production of engine blocks. Indeed, Cifunsa has the dominant position as a supplier of engine monoblocks to the North American car companies. Other Mexican metal casters play a major role in supplying heavy axles and coil springs for trucks and SUVs. Many windshields installed on U.S.-assembled cars and trucks also come from Mexico. Although some of this import-export trade is motivated by lower wage rates at Mexican than at comparable U.S. parts suppliers, another factor is the desire of the American and European car companies to decrease their dependence on unionized plants. A 1998 strike at GM's Delphi subsidiary lasted almost eight weeks. Even the Saturn assembly plant in Spring Hill, TN, suffered its first strike in 1998.

Germany is the fifth largest trading partner of the United States. Germany exports principally motor vehicles and parts (e.g., Mercedes-Benz diesel engines), specialized machinery, and chemicals to the United States; Germany imports aircraft, computers, motor vehicles and parts (e.g., Cummins engines), and scientific equipment from the United States. Trade with Germany is prominent in the U.S. business press, but it represents less than one-half of the U.S. trade with Mexico and less than one-quarter of the U.S. trade with Canada.

A Comparison of the EU and NAFTA

Between the EU and NAFTA regional trading blocs, NAFTA has the larger share of world population (6.2 percent compared to 5.0 percent in 2002) and the larger share of world output (24.5 percent compared to 15.7 percent in 2002), but the EU has the larger share of world trade (31.2 percent compared to 17.2 percent in 2002). Recall, however, that much of the EU trade is with other members inside the regional *trading bloc.*

This countertrade pattern within the trading bloc does not characterize the United States. Table 6.7 shows that although Mexico's share of U.S. exports tripled from 4.4 percent before NAFTA to 13.5 percent after NAFTA, the majority of U.S. export trade (100 percent − 24.0 percent to Canada − 13.5 percent to Mexico = 62.5 percent) goes elsewhere in the world economy.

Another important perspective can be obtained by considering competitiveness in the world economy. EU unit-labor costs and intermediate costs declined between 1987 and 1994 in motor vehicles and electrical equipment; these are Germany's

---

[25] Based on "Mexico Is Becoming Auto-Making Hot Spot," *Wall Street Journal,* June 23, 1998 [See EconNews Online: International Trade/Manufacturers Migrate to Mexico on the SWCP Economics Website]; and "Mexico Becomes a Leader in Car Parts," *Wall Street Journal,* March 30, 1999, p. A21.

Table 6.7 Destination of U.S. Goods Exports

1970–1975		1998–2003	
Country	Share (Percent)	Country	Share (Percent)
Canada	21.4	Canada	24.0
Japan	10.2	Mexico	13.5
Germany	5.4	Japan	9.4
United Kingdom	4.9	United Kingdom	5.2
Mexico	4.4	Germany	3.9
Netherlands	3.9	Korea	3.8
France	3.1	Taiwan	3.2
Italy	2.9	Netherlands	2.9
Brazil	2.7	France	2.8
Belgium-Luxembourg	2.3	China	2.4

Source: Federal Reserve Bank of St. Louis, *Review,* March/April 1999, p. 35. http://stls.frb.org/publications/index.html#data

two largest export categories to Britain and the United States. However, Japanese and U.S. costs in these industries declined even further. In other cases, like aerospace equipment, basic chemicals, and office machinery, EU competitiveness suffered still more. Between 1990 and 2002, the U.S. share of world exports rose from 11.7 percent to 13.9 percent and Japan's share shrank slightly from 8.5 percent to 7.8 percent. In that same period, the German, French, Italian, and British shares all declined; e.g., the Western European share of world exports plummeted from 28.6 percent to 22.3 percent.

The EU allocates "structural funds" to upgrade roads, bridges, and port infrastructure in less developed regions of Europe. Between 2000 and 2006, €42 billion will go to Spain, €28 billion to southern Italy, €27 billion to former East Germany, and €20 billion to Greece and Portugal. But these redistributive efforts, restrictive labor laws, and social programs in Europe impose a heavy burden on manufacturing competitiveness. Six weeks' paid vacation in Germany is now standard, and the Germans spend 8.4 percent of GDP on pension payments. Compare two weeks' paid vacation in the United States and the 5 percent of GDP Americans spend on pension payments. Opting out of the EU's social program has allowed the British economy to stay almost head-to-head with U.S. total labor costs. As a consequence, although wages for time worked in the U.S., British, and German manufacturing sectors are very similar (approximately $15 per hour), labor costs for holiday and leave pay add $5.70 an hour in Germany and only $1.03 an hour in the United States. When pensions and health care coverage are included, the total labor cost in Germany rises to $27.70 an hour versus $20.75 an hour in the United States. These massive cost differentials suggest that the world competitiveness of many European manufacturers remains in doubt.

In addition, workers on the senior management councils of German corporations often vote against plant closings. Plant closing legislation in Japan and the United States, on the other hand, has sensibly left the ultimate decision-making and contracting authority with boards of directors. Also, French labor law makes it nearly impossible to lay off and furlough workers. Consequently, few entrepreneurial businesses in France proceed beyond very small sole proprietorships. One interesting development in France has been the emergence of foreign subsidiaries operating under less restrictive EU labor regulations. Consequently, despite the marketing power of a "made in Germany" label on an automobile, Mercedes-Benz builds its Swatch minicar in France.[26]

What all this demonstrates is that the institutional arrangements in the country surrounding a company are as important to its ultimate competitive success as the business plan, the quality of management decisions, and the commitment of dedicated employees. The enhanced competitive pressure arising from free trade and the opening of markets has served to accentuate the disadvantages of inefficient institutional arrangements. Rather than struggle against regulations that raise costs, global supply chain managers just take their business elsewhere.

Gray Markets, Knockoffs, and Parallel Importing

The prices charged for identical goods varied widely across Europe both before and after the formation of the Common Market (see Table 6.8). In 1998, a Ford Mondeo cost 50 percent more in Germany than in Spain. To lower overall consumer prices

Table 6.8   Price Differentials in Europe

Largest Mean Difference by Country			
1992	1.5-Liter Coca-Cola	Ecu 0.69 (Belgium)	Ecu 1.45 (Denmark)
	Heinz Catsup	Ecu 0.86 (UK)	Ecu 1.92 (Spain)
	Clothes Washer	Ecu 407 (UK)	Ecu 565 (Italy)
	Portable TV	DM 434 (Germany)	DM 560 (Italy)
	VCR	DM 1383 (Germany)	DM 1873 (Spain)
1998	Big Mac	Ecu 1.75 (Spain)	Ecu 2.10 (Belgium)
	Ford Mondeo	DM 32,000 (Spain)	DM 48,000 (Germany)

Percent Standard Deviation Across Europe, Euro-11 price index, pretax		
1998	Household Insurance	51%
	Coca-Cola	29%
	Local Phone Service	25%
	Yogurt	20%
	Gasoline	14%
	Big Mac	12%
	Levi 501 Jeans	10%
	VW Golf	5%

Note: Less mobile goods tend to have higher price variations across countries.
Source: *Financial Times, The Economist,* various issues.

[26] Two useful surveys on these issues are "Business in Europe Survey," *The Economist,* November 23, 1996, and "Survey of the World Economy," *The Economist,* September 20, 1997.

and to improve competitiveness throughout the Union, the European Commission (EC) has often adopted policies that encourage price competition. Goods arbitragers who want to buy Black and Decker power tools in Spain and sell them in Germany or buy Kawaski motorcycles in Holland and sell them in Britain are encouraged to do so. Volkswagen was fined €15 million for refusing to supply Northern Italian VW dealers that sold cars to large numbers of Munich weekenders who had traveled across the Alps for the Verona opera (and the inexpensive German car prices in Italy). The EC also has eliminated any contractual link between product sales and after-market service; any government-certified repair shop can purchase parts to perform VW, Nikon, or IBM maintenance and service. The problem, of course, is that such gray markets may lead to counterfeit sales and substandard service passed off as branded sales and authorized service.

Example

EU BAN ON SOME PARALLEL IMPORTS PLEASES EUROPEAN BUT NOT U.S. AND JAPANESE MANUFACTURERS[27]

Manufacturers often seek to maintain different prices in different franchise territories (perhaps countries) for identical branded goods like Levi jeans, Nike shoes, Microsoft Windows, or Sony CDs. A recent ruling of the European Court of Justice (the ECJ) held that copyright and trademark protection for Silhouette sunglasses, an Austrian export product, was infringed by an Austrian retailer who purchased the sunglasses at deep discount in Bulgaria and reimported the product for sale in Austria at prices below those suggested by the manufacturer. Sourcing a product cheaply wherever it can be purchased around the world and then backshipping at discounted prices into the high-valued markets is a commonplace occurrence for many trading companies. The policy question for those who must decide on fair versus unfair trade practices becomes whether the discounted product can be effectively distinguished by customers from knockoff counterfeit products and whether the brand-name reputation of the manufacturer is thereby diminished.

Prior EU rulings had allowed such "parallel imports," which occur any time a foreign export product is purchased in one EU country for resale in another EU country. For example, Tesco, a British retailer, purchased Levi jeans and Nike shoes overseas and offered them for sale at a discount in Britain where the Levi- and Nike-authorized distribution channels had much higher price points. Similarly, Merck pharmaceuticals produced in Germany and sold at substantial discount in Spain were backshipped into Germany by discount German retailers without prohibition (*Merck* v. *Primecrown* and *Beecham* v. *Europharm,* 1995). What was new about the Silhouette case was that Silhouette was itself an EU manufacturer, and the sourcing was obtained outside the European Union. The ECJ decided to extend to *European* brand-name products (like Silhouette sunglasses) intellectual property protection not extended to *foreign* brand-name products.

In addition to this new European rule weakening international property rights to brand names and trademarks, Japan's high court has recently prohibited computer software sales in violation of manufacturer-authorized distribution agreements. Under

---

[27] Based on "Set-back for Parallel Imports," *BBC World Service,* July 16, 1998; "Parallel Imports," *Financial Times,* May 20, 1996; "Music Market Indicators," *The Economist,* May 15, 1999; D. Wilkinson, "Breaking the Chain: Parallel Imports and the Missing Link," *European Intellectual Property Review,* 1997; and "Prozac's Maker Confronts China Over Knockoffs," *Wall Street Journal,* March 25, 1998, p. B9.

bilateral trade pressure from the U.S., Japan supported Microsoft's international intellectual property rights. However, at the very same time, Japan allowed the parallel importing of gray-market Steinway pianos and some music CDs. As the world's largest exporter in the $38.7-billion music industry and the $90 billion computer software industry, the United States has threatened retaliation unless major trading partners aggressively punish violators of international copyright and trademark protection. After the $13.2-billion and $6.5-billion markets in the United States and Japan, the third-, fourth-, and fifth-largest markets for cassettes, videos, and CDs are Britain, Germany, and France (i.e., 33 percent of total world sales). Clearly, the status of parallel import policy is in flux, and businesses must plan accordingly.

The price impact of a policy prohibiting parallel imports can be enormous. Australians carefully protect intellectual property by aggressively prosecuting gray-market sellers of music CDs. Cheap imitations and counterfeit substitutes are rare indeed, but popular music CDs sell for $6.33 more in Australia than in other Far Eastern economies. The United Kingdom and China, therefore, choose the opposite policy for selected products. The English obtain almost 10 percent of their pharmaceuticals and over 30 percent of their wine, liquor, and beer through parallel importing. China permits the copying of patented medicines. Eli Lilly's Prozac, an antidepressant, sells for $1.73 per capsule, but a chemically identical "knockoff" from Shanghai Zhong Qi Pharmaceutical and Jiangsu Changzhov Pharmaceutical sells for $1.02 per capsule under the brand name You Ke.

TRADE DEFICITS AND THE BALANCE OF PAYMENTS

Current Account
A balance of payments tabulation of import-export goods, services, factor income, and net transfers.

International trade is just one component of a country's balance of payments with the rest of the world. Capital flows and transfer payments (like foreign aid) are other important components. The U.S. balance of payments is divided into a current account and a capital account. Table 6.9 shows that the **current account** is composed of a trade balance (*exports minus imports*), a factor income balance (*receipts minus payments*) plus unilateral transfers. Only once in the last 30 years has the U.S. generated a trade surplus (see Figure 6.13). Instead, typically the services trade surplus (e.g., from exporting/selling oil fields development at Haliburton) is overwhelmed by a massive merchandise trade deficit. In 2002, U.S. net exports of −$484.4 billion in merchandise plus $48.8 billion in services led to a −$435.6-billion trade *deficit* (4.3 percent of U.S. GDP).

Similarly, interest and dividend *receipts* by Americans on their overseas assets plus foreign-paid wages of U.S. labor (e.g., consultants at McKinsey working on overseas assignments) were smaller than comparable *payments* to foreigners, so the U.S. had a small negative factor income balance of −$11.8 billion—i.e., the U.S. was a *net debtor*.[28] And as usual, given its wealth and continuing beneficence in foreign aid and debt relief, the U.S. in 2002 was a *net donor* nation to the tune of −$56 billion.

Trade deficits combined with net debtor and net donor status necessarily imply a U.S. current account deficit. To balance its international payments, the U.S. must therefore conduct either asset sales to foreigners or increased borrowing from foreigners as described in the capital account. The net inflow to the capital account occurs through the issue of massive quantities of U.S. Treasury bonds and bills

---

[28] Technically, net debtor status refers to the balance of interest and dividend receipts minus payments only. However, since these overseas capital income flows are approximately 100 times as large as the overseas labor income flows, the factor income balance effectively refers to net creditor or net debtor status of a nation.

Table 6.9   Composition of Current Account, 2002 United States, $ billions

Merchandise Trade:

Exports	682.6
Imports	− 1,167.0
Merchandise Trade Deficit	− 484.4

Services Trade:

Exports	289.3
Imports	− 240.5
Services Trade Surplus	48.8

Trade Balance−435.6 (Deficit)

Foreign Investment and Labor Income

Receipts	244.7
Payments	− 256.5

Factor Income Balance−11.8 (Net Debtor)

Unilateral Transfers

− 56.0

Transfers Balance−56.0 (Net Donor)

Current Account Total   **−503.4 (Deficit)**

Source: *Economic Report of the President*, February 2003.

(bought especially by the Japanese) and through foreign acquisition of U.S. companies like Vodaphone's $66 billion purchase of Air Touch Communications and BP's $55 billion purchase of Amoco.

Perspectives on the Export Sector in the United States

The $971-billion export sector in the United States compares to a $10,506-billion gross *domestic* product (GDP) in 2002. That is, U.S. exports are approximately 10 percent of the U.S. gross national product (GNP). For some quarterly growth statistics and for some companies like Cummins Engine and Boeing Aircraft, these annual averages can be very misleading. Fully 34 percent of Cummins's sales are export sales, and 43 percent of the *growth* in U.S. GNP in the third quarter of 1997 occurred in the export sector. By way of perspective, in export-oriented countries like Belgium or Singapore, the export sector constitutes 50 percent or more of the nation's GNP. Still, in the U.S., consumer demand (domestic consumption) is the key to growth (see Figure 6.13), and of course, imports are a part of consumer demand.

Figure 6.14 shows that in every year since 1980–1981, the dollar value of foreign imports sold in the United States exceeded the value of U.S. exports sold abroad and converted to dollar values at the prevailing exchange rates. Leading up to,

Figure 6.13   Components of U.S. GNP, 2003, U.S. $ Trillions

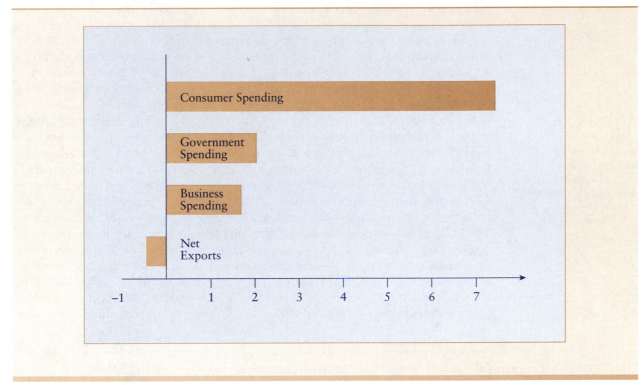

Figure 6.14   U.S. Trade Balance (Exports-Imports) as a Percentage of GDP

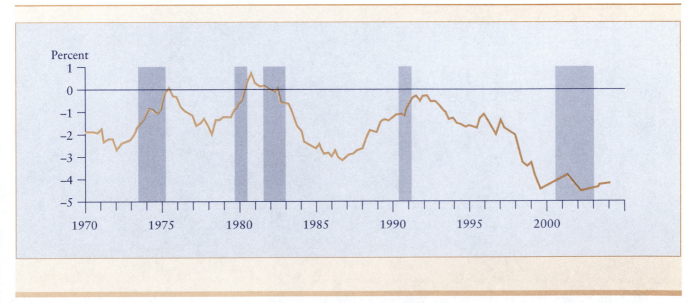

Source: *Review*, Federal Reserve Bank of St. Louis.

during, and after the 1991–1992 recession, U.S. import demand slowed and U.S. trade flows almost balanced. Over the 10-year expansion 1992–2001, the U.S. trade deficit increased to record levels. The competitiveness of U.S. manufacturers in world markets continued to improve, and the U.S. export sector therefore continued to grow, but the volume of U.S. imports grew even faster. Recall that in this period, the price of U.S. exports rose sharply and the price of U.S. imports plummeted as the dollar appreciated from DM 1.43/$ to DM 2.30/$. During the Bush II recession in 2001–2003, import demand growth has again slowed, as consumer confidence varied, enough to stabilize the trade deficit at 4 percent to 5 percent of GDP.

Several factors have contributed to this doubling of the U.S. trade deficit relative to the 2.4 percent thirty-year average. First, U.S. manufacturers like Bali bras and Ford Motor Co. increasingly outsource the production of components and subassemblies to lower wage Caribbean and Mexican locations. These goods show up in the trade statistics as imports when they return for final assembly to the United States. Between 1998–2000, literally 60 percent of total fixed investment in the United States was for information technology (i.e., computers, servers, telecommunications equipment). The Japanese are particularly successful in supplying components like liquid crystal displays, laser diodes, and silicon chips to these industries. The importance of the investment in new technology bought from abroad versus increased import consumption of cars, wine, and DVD players can be determined by examining Figure 6.15. In 1990, the proportion of capital goods imports was 22 percent of total U.S. merchandise imports. At the end of the 20th century, U.S. merchandise imports for

http://
You can find more information on international trade and the balance of payments at http://www.bea.doc.gov/ bea/di/home/bop.htm

Figure 6.15   Capital Goods Imports/Total Merchandise Imports, United States

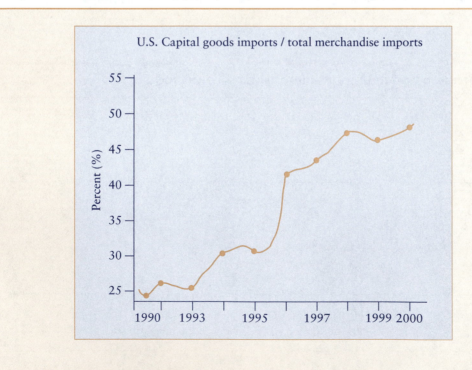

Source: *Review,* Federal Reserve Bank of St. Louis.
http://www.stls.frb.org/publications/index.html/#data

consumption had declined, and capital goods imports were almost 50 percent of total imports. Finally, Figure 6.7 shows that the U.S. dollar displayed a sustained appreciation against all the major trading partners' currencies for almost a decade during 1995–2002. Ultimately, as we have seen in this chapter, such trends in exchange rates have a significant detrimental effect on net export trade flows.

SUMMARY

- Export sales are very sensitive to changes in exchange rates. Exports become more expensive (cheaper) in the foreign currencies of the importing countries when the domestic (i.e., home) currency of the manufacturer strengthens (weakens).

- Major currencies are traded in the foreign exchange markets; there are markets for U.S. dollars as foreign exchange, British pounds as foreign exchange, German deutsche marks as foreign exchange, etc. Demand and supply in these markets reflects the speculative and transactions demands of investors, import-export dealers, corporations, financial institutions, the International Monetary Fund, central bankers, and governments throughout the global economy.

- Companies often demand payment and offer their best fixed-price quotes in their domestic currency because of transaction risk exposure and operating risk exposure to exchange rate fluctuations. Alternatively, such companies can manage the risk of exchange rate fluctuations themselves by setting up internal or financial hedges involving forward, option, or currency swap contracts.

- Internal hedges may be either balance sheet hedges addressing translation risk or operating hedges matching anticipated foreign sales receipts with anticipated expenses in that same foreign currency. Financial hedges often address transaction risk exposure by setting up positions in financial derivative contracts to offset cash flow losses from currency fluctuations. Such hedging costs about 5 percent of the value at risk.

- Foreign buyers (or their financial intermediaries) usually must acquire deutsche marks to execute a purchase from Mercedes-Benz, U.S. dollars to execute a purchase from General Motors, or yen to execute a purchase from Toyota. Each buyer in these international sales transactions usually supplies their own domestic currency. Additional imports by Americans of Japanese automobiles would normally therefore result in an increased demand for the yen and an increased supply of dollars in the foreign currency markets, i.e., a dollar depreciation.

- Long-term trends in exchange rates are determined by transaction demand, government transfer payments, and central bank or IMF interventions.

- Three transaction demand factors are expected cost inflation, real (inflation-adjusted) growth rates, and real (inflation-adjusted) interest rates. The lower the expected cost inflation, the lower the real growth rate, and the higher the real rate of interest in one economy relative to another, the higher the exports, the lower the import demand, and the higher the demand for financial instruments from that economy. All three determinants imply an increased demand or decreased supply of the domestic currency, i.e., a currency appreciation.

- Consumer price inflation serves as a good predictor of the combined effect of all three transaction demand factors on post-redemption returns to foreign asset holders. Projected changes in consumer inflation therefore directly affect international capital flows which can easily overwhelm the effect of trade flows on exchange rates.

- The relative strength of a currency is often measured as an effective exchange rate index, a weighted average of the exchange rates against major trading partners, with the weights determined by the volume of import plus export trade.

- Free trade increases the economic growth of both industrialized and developing nations. Tariffs, duties, and import quotas sometimes play a role in strategic trade policy to force multilateral reduction of tariffs, open markets, or secure increasing returns.

- Trade restrictions (quotas or tariffs) may be warranted under special circumstances to protect infant industries, to offset government subsidies with countervailing duties, or to impose antidumping sanctions on foreign imports sold at a price below their domestic cost.

- Speculative demand especially influences short-term changes in exchange rates. Since the total dollar volume of foreign-currency trading worldwide is $1.5 trillion *per day,* these short-term fluctuations can be quite volatile.

- International capital flows and the flow of tradable goods across nations respond to arbitrage opportunities. Arbitrage trading ceases when parity conditions are met. One such condition is relative purchasing power parity.

- Relative purchasing power parity (PPP) hypothesizes that a doubling of consumer prices in one economy will lead to trade flows that cut in half the value of the currency. Over long periods of time and on an approximate basis, exchange rates do appear related to differential rates of inflation across economies. PPP serves a useful benchmark role in assessing long-term trends in exchange rates.

- The European Union (EU) and the North American Free Trade Agreement (NAFTA) are two of several large trading blocs which have organized to open markets to free trade. The EU is the largest producer of world output with very dissimilar economies which have reduced trade barriers and specialized in accordance with comparative advantage. Marketing across the EU must address clusters of very different consumers.

- Whether a nation should join a (single) currency union depends on: (1) the magnitude of intra-regional trade, (2) the mobility of labor, and (3) the correlation of macroeconomic shocks.

- The United States is both the largest single-nation exporter and the largest importer in the world economy. The largest trading partner of the United States is Canada, followed by Mexico, Japan, U.K., and Germany. The U.S. share of world trade (14 percent) has grown in recent years, while that of Germany and other EU nations has declined. Extensive social programs, supplemental labor costs, and institutions that discourage business formation in Europe seem responsible for these trends.

- The trade flows of the United States are often in deficit (i.e., imports exceed exports); the last time there was a trade surplus in the United States was during the recession of 1981–1982. The balance of trade deficit of the United States is normally offset by international capital flows into the United States plus the occasional transfer of official reserves. The balance of payments accounts reflect this accounting identity.

- The U.S. 2002 trade deficit was generated by $485 billion more merchandise imported into the United States than exported. Services generated a $49 billion trade surplus. In recent years, these trade deficits have been approximately 5 percent of a $10 trillion gross domestic product in the United States.

EXERCISES

1. If the U.S dollar depreciates 20 percent, how does this affect the export and domestic sales of a U.S. manufacturer? Explain.

2. If the U.S. dollar were to appreciate substantially, what steps could a domestic manufacturer like Cummins Engine Co. of Columbus, Indiana, take in advance to reduce the effect of the exchange rate fluctuation on company profitability?

3. After an unanticipated dollar appreciation has occurred, what would you recommend a company like Cummins Engine do with its strong domestic currency?

4. What is the difference between transaction demand, speculative demand, and autonomous transactions by central banks, the World Bank, and the IMF in the foreign exchange markets? Which of these factors determines the long-term quarterly trends in exchange rates?

5. Would increased cost inflation in the United States relative to its major trading partners likely increase or decrease the value of the U.S. dollar? Why?

6. If the domestic prices for traded goods rose 50 percent over ten years in Japan and 100 percent over that same ten years in the United States, what would happen to the yen/dollar exchange rate? Why?

7. If Boeing's dollar aircraft prices increase 20 percent and the yen/dollar exchange rate declines 15 percent, what effective price increase is facing Japan Air Lines for the purchase of a Boeing 747? Would Boeing's margin likely rise or fall if the yen then depreciated and competitor prices were unchanged? Why?

8. Unit labor costs in Germany approach $30 per hour, whereas in Britain unit labor costs are only $17 per hour. Why would such a large difference persist between two members of the EU free trade area?

http://
Simulated Currency Trading

9. If U.S. citizens and corporations earn more investment income on their foreign investments than is paid to foreigners on their U.S. investments, and if foreigners purchase more U.S. securities, loans, and real assets than U.S citizens and corporations purchase abroad, will the U.S. be a net importer or net exporter? Explain.

10. From 2000 (Q4) to 2002 (Q4) the net foreign direct investment in U.S. equities declined steadily from $87 billion to $9 billion per quarter. How does a reduced flow of international capital into the U.S. stock markets affect the dollar's exchange rate, and why? Would expectations of continuing withdrawals from U.S. markets have any additional effect on exchange rates, and why?

11. Unit labor costs in Spain and Portugal rose 3.5 percent from a low base in 1999–2001, while producer price indices also rose 2.6 percent and 6.0 percent, respectively. In contrast, unit labor costs in Germany declined 1.5 percent and producer prices were unchanged. What effect should these factors, by themselves, have on export trade, and why?

12. The Chicago Mercantile Exchange (CME) has developed an Internet site with a simulation that helps people learn more about how to trade currency futures and options. Access this site at http://www.cme.com/market/cfot/simulation/. Once you are there, first read the material provided by the CME on how to trade

currency futures and options. When you are ready, click the button to start the simulation.

13. What three factors determine whether two economies with separate fiscal and monetary authorities should form a currency union? Give an illustration of each factor using NAFTA economies.

CASE EXERCISES

THE VALUE OF THE U.S. DOLLAR, 1998, THE EURO, 2000, AND THE U.S. DOLLAR, 2003

1. Analyze the following data on inflation rates, interest rates, and growth rate forecasts to determine what the likely long-term trend movement of the U.S. dollar would have been during 1998–1999 against the German deutsche mark. Would you have expected the DM/$ exchange rate to increase or decrease? Why?

	1996, %	1997, %	Forecasted 1998, %
U.S. nominal interest rate (90-day bills)	5.23	5.43	
German nominal interest rate (90-day bills)	3.18	3.40	
Quarterly U.S. consumer inflation	2.2	1.5	
Quarterly German consumer inflation	2.1	2.3	
U.S. real growth rate of GDP	3.7	4.5	2.5
German real growth rate of GDP	0.8	2.4	2.9
U.S. producer price index	2.8	−1.2	
German producer price index	1.0	1.8	

2. Analyze the following data on inflation rates, interest rates, and growth rate forecasts to determine what the likely long-term trend movement of the euro would have been during 2000 against the U.S. dollar. Would you have expected the euro/$ exchange rate to increase or decrease? Why?

	1998, %	1999, %	Forecasted 2000, %
U.S. nominal interest rate (90-day bills)	5.5	5.3	
Euro-11 nominal interest rate (90-day bills)	3.8	3.0	
U.S. consumer inflation	1.6	2.2	
Euro-11 consumer inflation	1.1	1.1	
U.S. real growth of GDP	4.3	4.2	3.9
Euro-11 real growth of GDP	2.3	2.5	3.3
U.S. producer price index	0.0	3.0	
Euro-11 producer price index	1.0	1.0	

3. The U.S. economy is projected to grow at 2.5 percent in 2003, and the European economy is projected to grow at 1.0 percent. Usually the American economy does *lead* out of world business cycle downturns. To further assure this development, the U.S. Federal Reserve lowered the rate at which federal banks borrow short term from the Fed. As a result of the new Fed policy, 3-month T-bill rates are likely to decline as well from about 2 percent in 2002 to 1.6 percent in

2003. The euro area 3-month bonds are yielding 3.25 percent. Inflationary expectations for consumer prices in the U.S. and Europe over the next several quarters are 2.2 percent and 1.6 percent, respectively. Producer costs (as measured by the producer price and wholesale price index) are falling in both the U.S. and Europe at −1.9 and −0.3 percent, respectively. Analyze how each of the above-mentioned factors will affect the €/$ exchange rate, which presently stands at near-parity 1.01 € per $.

U.S. ENERGY POLICY, OIL IMPORTS, AND THE PRICE OF GASOLINE[29]

From 1973–2003, U.S. dependence on foreign oil grew as oil imports rose from 40 percent to 60 percent of U.S. oil consumption (19.5 million barrels per day). Over this 30-year period, inflation-adjusted retail gasoline prices in the U.S. were highly volatile, but they started and finished at approximately the same $1.50 per gallon (see the figure below). At times in the interim, retail gasoline cost as much as $2.20 per gallon (in 1980–1981) and at other times as little as $1.10 per gallon (in 1998). One hundred percent input price variation of this sort can easily cause profitable business plans in transportation industries (e.g., trucking and airlines) to run huge deficits.

Average U.S. Retail Gasoline Price per Barrel (Constant 1996 U.S. Dollars)

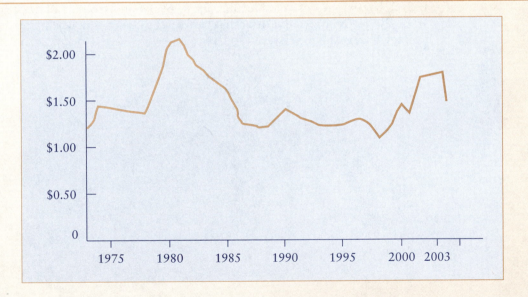

Source: U.S. Department of Energy.

[29] Based on "Why the U.S. Is Still Hooked on Oil Imports," *Wall Street Journal*, March 18, 2003, p. A1, and "Iraq's Crude Awakening," *Time*, May 18, 2003, p. 49.

You work at an oil company, and your chief operating officer (COO) has asked that you prepare a study detailing the likely sources of future price variation.

U.S. energy policy has contributed to some of the peaks and troughs of retail gasoline prices. President Carter championed a synthetic fuel oil program using coal and shale in 1979–1980, but that initiative was quickly dismissed as uneconomic when President Reagan took office. More stringent fuel efficiency standards for autos were imposed by the U.S. Congress in 1983 and again in 1997. More recently, in 2002, President Bush backed a $1.7-billion publicly-funded research effort to develop hydrogen-powered fuel cells as a substitute for gasoline engines in automobiles.

The successes and failures of the Organization of Petroleum Exporting Countries (OPEC) cartel have also been involved in explaining peaks and troughs of U.S. gasoline prices. Although only 20 percent of U.S. crude oil imports come from the Persian Gulf, members of OPEC effectively set the price by controlling two thirds of proven reserves, possessing 90 percent of excess capacity to pump and pipe and ship additional crude oil, and by developing by far the lowest-priced operations. Incremental barrels of crude oil that cost $1.00 to extract in Iraq and $2.50 in Saudi Arabia cost fully $5 in the North Sea oil fields and $10 in the U.S.

As 50 percent of the inputs for the production of gasoline for cars and trucks in North America come from crude oil imports, you hypothesize that the price of U.S. retail gasoline will also fluctuate in accordance with the value of the U.S. dollar in foreign exchange markets. As the dollar appreciates, import prices decline, and thus gasoline retail prices decline. As the dollar depreciates, import prices rise, and thus gasoline retail prices rise. Using Figure 6.7, analyze the changes in the value of the U.S. dollar in various years leading up to peaks and troughs of gas prices from 1973–2003. Analyze the relationship between U.S. energy policy initiatives and the average U.S. gasoline price.

Appendix 6a

International Parity Conditions

INTRODUCTION

Chapter 6 focused on long-term trends of exchange rates and international trade flows. This appendix sketches the forces that determine the short-term flows of international capital. Further discussion of the equilibrium conditions in international finance can be found in Chapter 21 of R. Charles Moyer, James R. McGuigan, and William J. Kretlow, *Contemporary Financial Management,* 9th edition (Mason, OH: South-Western/Thomson Learning, 2003).

Between 2000 (Q2) and 2001 (Q3), U.S. business loan demand collapsed, and as a result, the price of short-term loanable funds borrowed by the U.S. Treasury shrank dramatically from 6.5 percent to 3.7 percent. And this downward interest rate trend continued, such that by 2002 (Q3), the nominal yield on 90-day Treasury bills (T bills) had fallen below 200 basis points (i.e., 2 percent) to just 1.7 percent. That is, the 90-day promissory obligations of the U.S. Treasury to repay in $1,000 units up to $1 million sold at such a small discount relative to their face value that the implied yield fell to 1.7 percent.[30] In contrast, 90-day euro area government bills in 2002 (Q3) yielded 3.3 percent interest. Since these debt contracts obligate the issuer to make a certain known interest payment when due, and since neither the U.S. Treasury nor any of the euro area governments has any significant default risk, 1.7 percent and 3.3 percent are characterized as "risk-free" returns.

For a foreign investor, however, one risk of cash flow loss remained. To obtain the higher eurobill's 3.3 percent interest, a foreign investor (perhaps an American) could invest $100,000 for 90 days in eurobills and expect a $(1 + .033)^{.25}$ return. However, the eurobill would pay its interest obligation in euros! So, unless the American investor had previously planned a summer vacation in Europe (or had some other use for the euros), two foreign exchange transactions would be necessary to obtain the higher 3.3 percent eurobill interest. First, the American investor would convert her $100,000 to euros at the spot exchange rate (e_0), say at par 1.0 U.S.$ per euros in August 2002. Using the euros (€) to buy a €100,000 eurobill for E99,192,[31] said investor would then be entitled 90 days later to receive the €100,000 principal plus interest. At the end of the transaction, she would then convert the euros back to U.S. dollars at whatever exchange rate existed on day t + 90. And of course, the value of the €100,000 receivables due could well have declined over the 90-day holding period of the investment, cutting into the 3.3 percent interest return or even making the net return in U.S. dollars turn negative.

To avoid this exchange rate risk exposure, the American investor could engage in *covered interest arbitrage.* After spending $99,192 in the spot market to acquire euros at the $1/€ spot rate e_0 and then buying the eurobill, she could immediately sell her

---

[30] An auction sale price of $99,579 for a $100,000 T bill implies a 1.7 percent interest return if the principal is repaid 1/4 of a year later because $100,000/\$99,579 = \$(1 + .017)^{.25}$.

[31] $99,192 = 100,000/(1 + 0.033)^{.25}$.

€100,000 receivables due in 90 days in the forward market for euros to reacquire U.S. dollars. With all this selling forward of euros by foreign investors pouring into the eurobills and desiring to cover their long position in euro receivables, the forward rate $/€ (the price of the euro) will decline. Just how much it will now decline is a function of just how much the spot rate rose earlier as foreign capital bought euros in the spot market to secure the higher eurobill interest. That in turn depends on how divergent the interest rates between the U.S. T bill and the eurobill became before setting off a floodtide of covered interest arbitrage. The *interest rate parity* condition says that the equilibrium exchange rate emergent from 90-day-forward buying and selling transactions f_{90} will differ from the spot rate as a percentage of the spot rate by approximately the difference in the two yields:

$$(f_{90} - e_0)/e_0 = [r_{US} - r_{EMU}] \qquad \text{[6A.1]}$$

where f and e are the U.S. dollar value of the euro, $/€. That is, $(f_{90} - 1.0)/1.0 = [1.017 - 1.033] = -.016$; i.e., the forward rate f_{90} for the dollar value of the euro will *fall* until it becomes 1.6 percent lower than the current spot exchange.[32] Under the expectation theory of interest rates, this forward rate for day 90 is an unbiased estimate of the expected future spot rate on day 90. So, the dollar value of the euro $/€, which had previously risen sharply as divergent interest rates set off a flow of international capital into euro-denominated investments, is expected to fall 1.6 percent over the next 90 days.

Across developed countries with free movement of capital within well-established capital markets, therefore, nominal interest rate differentials for investments of comparable risk seldom persist. The reason is that covered interest arbitrage sets off a floodtide of capital *into* those economies with higher interest rates and *out of* those economies with lower real interest rates. Increased supply of loanable funds in the euro area in our previous example and decreased supply of loanable funds in the United States raises the nominal interest rate (the price of loanable funds) in the euro area and lowers it in the United States. At times the daily flow of such capital transactions exceeds 1.5 *trillion dollars*.[33] Because of this enormous mobility of short-term capital investment across international borders, divergent interest rates quickly converge, often within a few hours or days.

In summary, if EMU-member governments have been paying 3.3 percent on 90-day bills and the U.S. Treasury has been paying 1.7 percent on 90 day T bills, and everything else that might matter is the same, the currently high spot rate of the euro will be expected to depreciate by approximately 1.6 percent against the U.S. dollar over the next 90 days. These relationships between interest rate differentials and expected future changes in spot exchange rates are described on the left side of Figure 6A.1.

In the above example, we have said little about why the 90-day T bill and 90-day eurobill rates might have differed by as much as 1.6 percent. A famous monetary economist, Irving Fisher, hypothesized that nominal interest rates for risk-free investments differ primarily because of differences in expected inflation rates. The *international Fisher effect* states that a nominal interest rate r in one currency area equals the real rate of interest i plus the expected consumer inflation rate in that currency area:

$$r = i + \text{Ex}(\%\Delta\text{CPI}) \qquad \text{[6A.2]}$$

---

[32] Or, more precisely, $e_{90}/e_0 = [(1 + r_{EMU})/(1 + r_{US})]\,1.015733$, where e is the U.S.$ value of the euro ($/€).

[33] Just ten days of international capital flow across all currency markets is the same order of magnitude as the capitalized value of all the NYSE-listed stocks, $15 trillion.

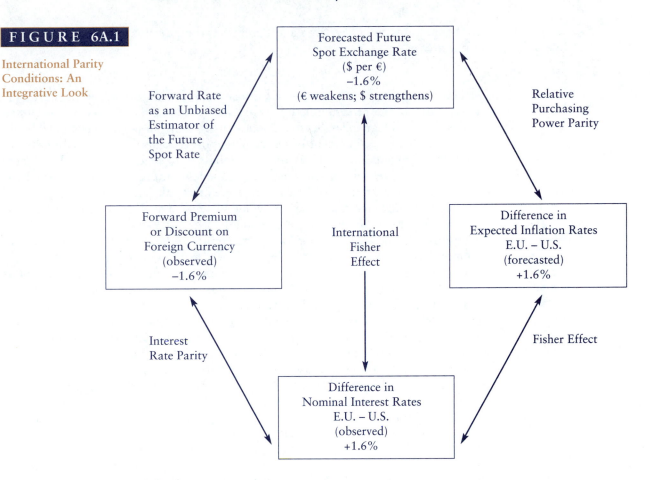

FIGURE 6A.1

International Parity
Conditions: An
Integrative Look

Forecasted Future
Spot Exchange Rate
($ per €)
−1.6%
(€ weakens; $ strengthens)

Forward Rate
as an Unbiased
Estimator of
the Future
Spot Rate

Relative
Purchasing
Power Parity

Forward Premium
or Discount on
Foreign Currency
(observed)
−1.6%

International
Fisher
Effect

Difference in
Expected Inflation Rates
E.U. – U.S.
(forecasted)
+1.6%

Interest
Rate Parity

Fisher Effect

Difference in
Nominal Interest Rates
E.U. – U.S.
(observed)
+1.6%

Assume: U.S. nominal interest rate = 1.7%
EU nominal interest rate = 3.3%
Time horizon = 90 days

In our previous example, perhaps the expected inflation rate in the euro area was 1.6 percent higher than the expected inflation rate in the United States. In that case, the inflation-adjusted *real rate of interest* in the two currency areas would be identical. For example, if the Ex(%ΔCPI)$_{US}$ = 0.5 percent and the Ex(%ΔCPI)$_{EMU}$ = 2.1 percent, then the real rate of interest in the U.S. would be $1.7 − 0.5 = 1.2$ percent, whereas the real rate of interest in the euro area would be $3.3 − 2.1 =$ also 1.2 percent.

It is this inflation-adjusted real rate of interest that ultimately motivates a foreign investor to move capital from one currency area to another. This motivation is a rational basis for interest rate arbitrage because, as we have seen, the net return to a foreign capital investment is the nominal interest return minus the expected change in the spot exchange rate at the time the bill is redeemed. And it turns out that the inflation differential is a very good forecast of the expected change in the spot exchange rate over the holding period of an investment. Another international parity condition defines this relationship between inflation rates and future changes in the spot exchange rate. In particular, *relative purchasing power parity (relative PPP)* states that arbitrage in traded goods between currency areas will cause spot exchange rates to change by the difference in the inflation rates in the two currency areas:

$$(e_{90} - e_0)/e_0 = [\text{Ex}(\%\Delta\text{CPI})_{\text{US}} - \text{Ex}(\%\Delta\text{CPI})_{\text{EMU}}] \qquad [6\text{A}.3]$$

So, if 2.1 percent inflation were forecast for the next 90 days in the euro currency area and 0.5 percent inflation were forecast for the next 90 days in the United States, relative PPP implies that the American investor in our previous example should anticipate losing 1.6 percent of her return upon redemption as she converts her euro principal and interest back into U.S. dollars at the end of 90 days. If so, there was little or no reason for the foreign capital investment in the first place since the real rates of interest in the two currencies were identical. Again, in our above example, the real rate of interest in the U.S. would be $1.7 - 0.5 = 1.2$ percent, whereas the real rate of interest in the euro area would be $3.3 - 2.1 =$ also 1.2 percent. These relationships between inflation rate differentials and expected future changes in spot exchange rates are described on the right side of Figure 6A.1.

All three international adjustment processes are simultaneously at work achieving the international parity conditions that characterize international capital flows. Covered interest arbitrage will cause forward exchange rates and expected future spot exchange rates to reflect interest rate differentials in accordance with *interest rate parity,* goods arbitrage will cause expected future spot exchange rates to reflect inflation differentials in accordance with relative *purchasing power parity,* and international capital flows will cause divergent interest rates on investments of comparable risk to converge. The timing goes like this: *Spot* exchange rates for the higher-interest currency will rise to reflect the floodtide of foreign investment capital into the higher-interest currency area. *Forward* rates for the higher-interest currency will then decline to reflect the foreign investors covering their long positions in the higher-interest currency. All of this will happen very quickly and once it does, the flow of international capital will stop, since no further covered interest parity can be profitable. More gradually, if the higher interest rates in the euro area are reflecting higher expected inflation, then the euro spot exchange rates will in fact decline over time to reflect the expected inflation and reduced exports from the higher-interest currency area. If, instead, the higher interest rates in the euro area are reflecting new investment opportunities, then the euro quickly appreciates in the spot market; the euro spot rate then gradually drifts lower as interest rates fall, reflecting the increased supply of investment capital into the euro area. In both cases, the time path of the $/€ exchange rate is an early spike in the value of the euro followed by a gradual descent.

III
Production and Cost

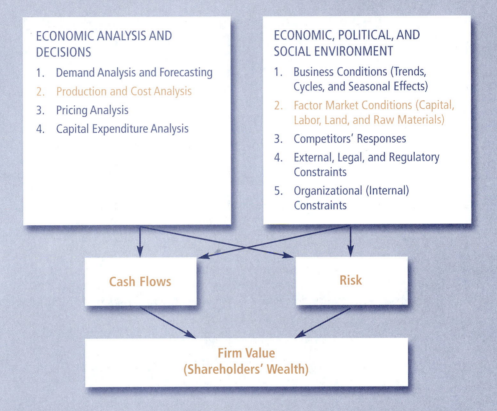

ECONOMIC ANALYSIS AND
DECISIONS

1. Demand Analysis and Forecasting
2. Production and Cost Analysis
3. Pricing Analysis
4. Capital Expenditure Analysis

ECONOMIC, POLITICAL, AND
SOCIAL ENVIRONMENT

1. Business Conditions (Trends,
   Cycles, and Seasonal Effects)
2. Factor Market Conditions (Capital,
   Labor, Land, and Raw Materials)
3. Competitors' Responses
4. External, Legal, and Regulatory
   Constraints
5. Organizational (Internal)
   Constraints

Cash Flows

Risk

Firm Value
(Shareholders' Wealth)

Part III deals with the production and cost analysis decisions facing managers of an economic enterprise. In Chapter 7 the theory of production decisions is developed using primarily graphical tools of analysis. Production decisions include the determination of the type and amount of resources—such as land, labor, materials, capital equipment, and managerial skills—that are used in the production of a desired amount of output. The objective is to combine these inputs in the most efficient manner to produce the output of the enterprise. Appendix 7A examines constrained optimization techniques, using calculus techniques to assist production decision making. Appendix 7B looks at real-world process choice decisions in a linear programming framework. In Chapter 8 the theory of cost analysis is developed. Cost measures are combined with revenue estimates to determine optimal (wealth-maximizing) levels and mixes of output. Chapter 9 discusses the applications of cost theory, including the measurement of short- and long-run cost relationships, the use of break-even and contribution analysis, and operating leverage concepts. The learning curve concept, as applied to manufacturing, is developed in Appendix 9A.

Production Economics

CHAPTER PREVIEW Managers are required to make resource allocation decisions about production operations, marketing, financing, and personnel. Although these decisions are interrelated, it is useful to discuss each of them separately. Production decisions determine the type and amount of inputs—such as land, labor, raw and processed materials, factories, machinery, equipment, and managerial talent—to be used in the production of a desired quantity of output. The production manager's objective is to minimize cost for a given output or, in other circumstances, to maximize output for a given input budget. First, we analyze the choice of a single variable input with fixed input prices. Later, we analyze the optimal multi-input combination with changing input prices and introduce the concept of returns to scale.

What Went Wrong in California's Deregulation of Electricity?[1]

Large-scale electric power plants entail huge capital investments, with pollution abatement technology in coal-fired plants and redundant safety devices in nuclear plants running into the hundreds of millions of dollars. Pacific Gas and Electric's (PG&E) Diablo Canyon nuclear power plant near Santa Barbara cost $5.8 billion. But these larger scale coal- and nuclear-powered plants have an advantage in variable input costs over smaller scale natural gas- and fuel oil-powered plants. The operating cost in 1999 was only about $20 per megawatt hour (mwh) for coal and nuclear inputs, versus $35/mwh for natural gas and fuel oil inputs. In addition, the smaller plants necessitate that a utility regularly buy electricity in the spot market to meet unexpected peak demand. In 2001, California wholesale electricity prices varied tremendously from $40/mwh to often $200/mwh; in fact, eleven times between June 2000 and June 2001 the peak-hour daily price rose above $400/mwh.

The trade-off between investing in low-fixed-cost natural gas- and fuel oil-powered plants with higher and much more volatile variable costs versus high-fixed-cost coal- and nuclear-powered plants with lower and stable variable costs has come into focus during the electricity deregulation crisis in California. In 1998, California implemented legislation to decouple electricity generation and distribution, allowing large retail and industrial customers to purchase electricity from alternative providers like Duke Energy in San Diego. As a result, two California utilities, Pacific Gas and Electric and Southern Cal Edison, scaled back their generating plant expansion plans and began to purchase 25 percent of their power in wholesale spot markets from bottlenecked long-distance transmission line suppliers and from numerous small-scale

fuel oil and natural gas independent generating plants. It has been estimated that as much as 55 percent of the variation in peak-hour daily wholesale prices is attributable to extraordinary transmission line fees and old inefficient plants fired up to meet the last 5 percent of peak demand. Unfortunately, between 2000 and 2001, natural gas prices quadrupled, and the monthly average wholesale price of electricity in California shot up from $25–$50 to $198–$231/mwh. California Edison and PG&E were restrained by a $54/mwh price cap from passing through to their retail customers over $11 billion in higher wholesale costs. Not surprisingly, therefore, only $\frac{1}{2}$ of 1 percent of Californians elected to switch away from their traditional utility providers, whereas 12 percent of Pennsylvanians, 5 percent of Ohioans, 3 percent of New Yorkers, and 30 percent of British citizens did so within two years after electricity market deregulation.

In March 2001, the independent transmission line operator for the power grid in California announced rolling blackouts across the state to balance deficient supply against peak period demand. Only then did the California Public Utility Commission approve a 46 percent increase in retail electricity rates. Still PG&E declared bankruptcy, and the State of California has been forced to arrange a very expensive long-term bailout. In light of this California "energy nightmare," three Western states (Montana, Nevada, and Oregon) and six others across the country then moved to revise or delay their electricity deregulation initiatives. Fourteen states, including Florida, Georgia, and North and South Carolina, have rejected electricity deregulation altogether, and 11 others are continuing to study the issues.

MANAGERIAL CHALLENGE

One new approach is to charge customers a variable rate per mwh to reflect differential cost at different hours of the day, days of the week, and seasons of the year. We discuss such real-time differential pricing in Chapter 14. Another new approach is *distributed generation* by extremely small-scale diesel generators or natural gas-fired microturbine generators in factories and photovoltaic cells (solar panels) in households. Operating costs of the microturbines are $70–$120/mwh, whereas solar panels cost $220–$400/mwh, both much higher than utility-supplied electricity. Yet, the capital cost that must be recovered is less than 1/1000 of traditional power plants. La Quinta Motels recently saved $20,000 in one year with a microturbine at one of its Dallas properties. Like co-generation of steam for heat and electricity for

lighting, these distributed generation systems offer the added advantage of increased reliability, reducing projected brownout and blackout periods from hours to seconds per year. Puget Sound Energy, the largest investor-owned utility in the state of Washington, recently began installing microturbines in substations near growing neighborhoods that are forecasted to be sources of peak demand on capacity. In this chapter, we will study the dilemma of whether to substitute higher cost variable inputs for fixed inputs.

---

[1] Based on "The Lessons Learned" and "Think Small," *Wall Street Journal*, September 17, 2001, pp. R4, R13, R15 and R17; "Are Californians Starved for Energy?" *Wall Street Journal*, September 16, 2002, p. A1; and "How to Do Deregulation Right," *BusinessWeek*, March 26, 2001, p. 112.

---

http://

You can access more information on production economics in Lesson 6 at the following Internet site: http://www.bus.okstate.edu/ecls/price/ICS/ECON3113W/framed/econ3113w.htm

The economic theory of production consists of a formal framework to assist the manager in deciding how to combine most efficiently the various inputs[2] needed to produce the desired output (product or service), given the existing technology. This technology consists of available production processes, equipment, labor and management skills, and information-processing capabilities. Production analysis is often applied by managers in assigning costs to the various feasible output levels and in communicating with plant engineers the operations plans of the company.

THE PRODUCTION FUNCTION

Production Function
A mathematical model, schedule (table), or graph that relates the maximum feasible quantity of output that can be produced from given amounts of various inputs.

Input
A resource or factor of production, such as a raw material, labor skill, or piece of equipment, that is employed in a production process.

The theory of production is centered around the concept of a production function. A **production function** relates the maximum quantity of output that can be produced from given amounts of various inputs for a given technology. It can be expressed in the form of a mathematical model, schedule (table), or graph. A change in technology, such as the introduction of more automated equipment or the substitution of skilled for unskilled workers, results in a new production function. The production of most outputs (goods and services) requires the use of large numbers of **inputs.** The production of a house, for example, requires the use of many different labor skills (carpenters, plumbers, and electricians), raw materials (lumber, cement, bricks, and insulating materials), and types of equipment (bulldozers, saws, and cement mixers). Also, many production processes result in more than one output. For example, in the meat-processing industry, the slaughtering of a steer results in the

---

[2] The terms *input, factor,* and *resource* are used interchangeably throughout the chapter. They all have the same meaning in production theory.

joint output of various cuts of meat, hides, and fertilizer. To simplify the analysis and to illustrate the basic theory, the following discussion is limited to a two-input, one-output production function.

Letting L and K represent the quantities of two inputs (labor L and capital K) used in producing a quantity Q of output, a **production function** can be represented in the form of a mathematical model, such as

$$Q = \alpha L^{\beta_1} K^{\beta_2} \qquad\qquad [7.1]$$

Cobb-Douglas Production Function
A particular type of mathematical model, known as a multiplicative exponential function, which is used to represent the relationship between the inputs and the output.

where α, β_1, and β_2 are constants. This particular multiplicative exponential model is known as the **Cobb-Douglas production function** and is examined in more detail later in the chapter. Production functions also can be expressed in the form of a *schedule* (or table), as illustrated in the following ore-mining example.

Example

AN ILLUSTRATIVE PRODUCTION FUNCTION: DEEP CREEK MINING COMPANY

The Deep Creek Mining Company uses capital (mining equipment) and labor (workers) to mine uranium ore. Various sizes of ore-mining equipment, as measured by its brake horsepower (b.h.p.) rating, are available to the company. The amount of ore mined during a given period is a function only of the number of workers assigned to the crew operating a given piece of equipment. The data in Table 7.1 show the amount of ore produced (measured in tons) when various sizes of crews are used to operate the equipment. In this example, the two inputs are labor, L—that is, number of workers—and capital, K—that is, size of drilling equipment—and the output Q is the number of tons of ore produced with the given combination of inputs.

A two-input, one-output production function at Deep Creek Mining can also be represented *graphically* as a three-dimensional production surface, where the height of the square column associated with each input combination in Figure 7.1 indicates the amount of iron ore output produced.

Table 7.1   Total Output Table—Deep Creek Mining Company

		Capital Input K (b.h.p., Brake Horsepower)							
		250	500	750	1,000	1,250	1,500	1,750	2,000
Labor Input L	1	1	3	6	10	16	16	16	13
(Number of	2	2	6	16	24	29	29	44	44
Workers)	3	4	16	29	44	55	55	55	50
	4	6	29	44	55	58	60	60	55
	5	16	43	55	60	61	62	62	60
	6	29	55	60	62	63	63	63	62
	7	44	58	62	63	64	64	64	64
	8	50	60	62	63	64	65	65	65
	9	55	59	61	63	64	65	66	66
	10	52	56	59	62	64	65	66	67

Figure 7.1   Production Function—Deep Creek Mining Company

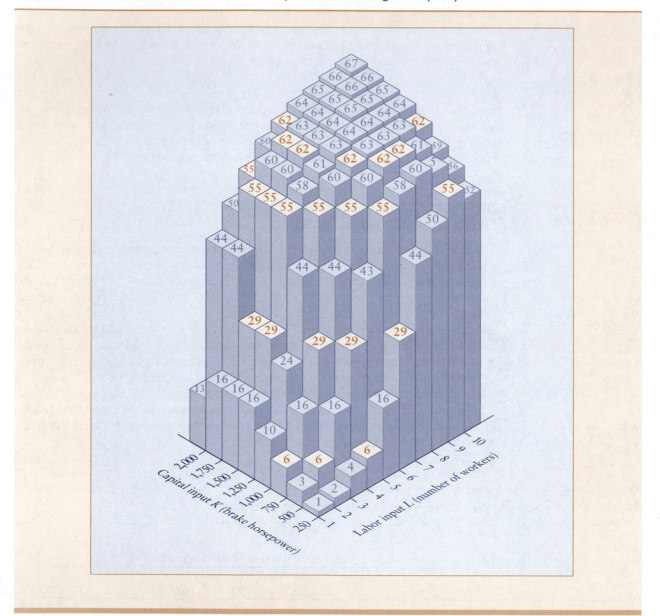

Fixed and Variable Inputs

In deciding how to combine the various inputs (L and K) to produce the desired output, inputs are usually classified as being either fixed or variable. A *fixed* input is defined as one required in the production process but whose quantity employed in the process is constant over a given period of time regardless of the quantity of output produced. The costs of a fixed input must be incurred regardless of whether the production process is operated at a high or a low rate of output. A *variable* input is defined as one whose quantity employed in the process changes, depending on the desired quantity of output to be produced.

The **short run** corresponds to the period of time in which one (or more) of the inputs is fixed. This means that to increase output, the firm must employ more of the variable input(s) with the given quantity of fixed input(s). Thus, for example, with an auto assembly plant of fixed size and capacity, the firm can increase output only by employing more labor, such as by paying workers overtime or by scheduling additional shifts.

As the time period under consideration (the planning horizon) is lengthened, however, more of the fixed inputs become variable. Over a planning horizon of about six months, most firms could acquire or build additional plant capacity and order more manufacturing equipment. Production facilities would no longer be a fixed factor. In lengthening the planning horizon, a point is eventually reached where all inputs are variable. This period of time is called the **long run.**

In the short run, because some of the inputs are fixed, only a subset of the total possible input combinations is available to the firm. By contrast, in the long run, all possible input combinations are available to the firm. Consequently, in the long run the firm can choose between increasing production through the use of more labor (overtime or hiring more workers) or through plant expansion, depending on which combination of labor and plant size is most efficient at producing the desired output.

In developing some of the concepts of production theory, a production function with one fixed and one variable input is examined first. The objective of the analysis is to determine how to combine different quantities of the variable input with a given amount of the fixed input to produce various quantities of output most efficiently. The total, average, and marginal products are defined and illustrated, and the law of diminishing returns and marginal revenue product are discussed. Then a slightly more complex situation is considered: a production function with two variable inputs is used to illustrate the pivotal multi-input concepts of isoquants and returns to scale.

PRODUCTION FUNCTIONS WITH ONE VARIABLE INPUT

Suppose, in the Deep Creek Mining Company example of the previous section, that the amount of capital input K—that is, the size of mining equipment—employed in the production process is a fixed factor. Specifically, suppose that the firm owns or leases a piece of mining equipment having a 750-b.h.p. rating. Depending on the amount of labor input L used to operate the 750-b.h.p. equipment, varying quantities of output will be obtained, as shown in the *750* column of Table 7.1 and again in the Q column of Table 7.2.

Marginal and Average Product Functions

Once the total product function is given (in tabular, graphic, or algebraic form), the marginal and average product functions can be derived. The **marginal product** is defined as the incremental change in total output ΔQ that can be produced by the use of one more unit of the variable input ΔL, while K remains fixed. The marginal product is defined as[3]

$$MP_L = \frac{\Delta Q}{\Delta L} \text{ or } \frac{\partial Q}{\partial L} \qquad [7.2]$$

for discrete and continuous changes, respectively.

---

[3] Strictly speaking, the ratio $\Delta Q/\Delta L$ represents the *incremental* product rather than the *marginal* product. For simplicity, we continue to use the term *marginal* throughout the text, even though this and similar ratios are calculated on an incremental basis.

Table 7.2   Total Product, Marginal Product, Average Product, and Elasticity—Deep Creek Mining Company (Capital input, brake horsepower = 750)

Labor Input (Number of Workers)	Total Product TP_L (= Q) (Tons of Ore)	Marginal Product of Labor, MP_L ($\Delta Q \div \Delta L$)	Average Product of Labor, AP_L (Q ÷ L)	Production Elasticity, E_L ($MP_L \div AP_L$)
0	0	—	—	—
1	6	+ 6	6	1.0
2	16	+10	8	1.25
3	29	+13	9.67	1.34
4	44	+15	11	1.36
5	55	+11	11	1.0
6	60	+ 5	10	.50
7	62	+ 2	8.86	.23
8	62	0	7.75	0.0
9	61	−1	6.78	−.15
10	59	−2	5.90	−.34

The marginal product of labor in the ore-mining example is shown in the third column of Table 7.2 and as MP_L in Figure 7.2.

Average Product
The ratio of total output to the amount of the variable input used in producing the output.

The **average product** is defined as the ratio of total output to the amount of the variable input used in producing the output. The average product of labor is

$$AP_L = \frac{Q}{L} \qquad [7.3]$$

The average product of labor for the Deep Creek ore-mining example is shown in the fourth column of Table 7.2.

The discussion of the theory of demand in Chapter 3 introduced the concept of price elasticity of demand. Similarly in production analysis, it is useful to define the **elasticity of production** as the percentage change in output Q resulting from a given percentage change in the amount of the variable input L with K remaining constant. This responsiveness of output to changes in the given input is equal to

Elasticity of Production
A measure of proportionality between changes in the variable input(s) and the resulting change in output.

$$E_L = \frac{\%\Delta Q}{\%\Delta L}$$

$$= \frac{\frac{\Delta Q}{Q}}{\frac{\Delta L}{L}} \qquad [7.4]$$

Rearranging terms yields

$$E_L = \frac{\frac{\Delta Q}{\Delta L}}{\frac{Q}{L}} = \frac{\Delta Q}{\Delta L} \times \frac{L}{Q}$$

Figure 7.2   Total Product, Marginal Product of Labor, and Average Product of Labor
Deep Creek Mining Co.

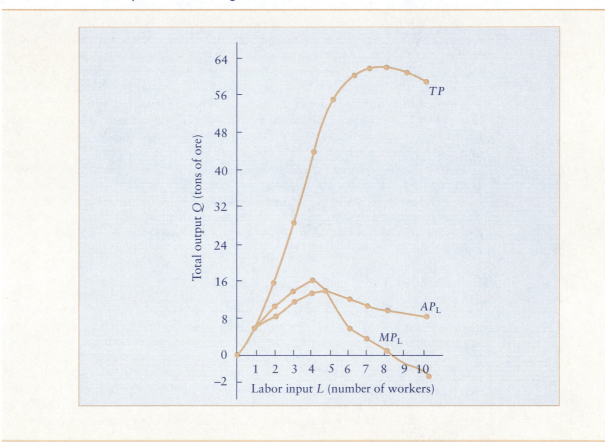

or, because $MP_L = \Delta Q / \Delta L$ and $AP_L = Q/L$:

$$E_L = \frac{MP_L}{AP_L} \qquad\qquad [7.5]$$

which shows that the elasticity of production is equal to the ratio of the marginal product to the average product of input L.

The elasticity of production for the Deep Creek ore-mining example is shown in the fifth column of Table 7.2. A production elasticity greater than (less than) 1.0 indicates that output increases more than (less than) proportionately with a given percentage increase in the variable input.

Law of Diminishing Marginal Returns

The tabular production function just discussed illustrates the production law of diminishing marginal returns. Initially, the assignment of more workers to the crew operating the mining equipment (the fixed factor) allows greater labor specialization in the use of the equipment. As a result, the marginal output of each worker added to the crew at first increases, and total output increases at an increasing rate. Thus, as listed in Table 7.2 and graphed in Figure 7.2, the addition of a second worker to the crew results in 10 additional tons of output; the addition of a third worker results in 13 additional tons of output; and the addition of a fourth worker yields 15 additional tons. However, in adding more workers to the crew, a point is eventually reached where the marginal increase in output for each worker added to the crew begins to decline. This occurs because only a limited number of ways exist to achieve greater labor specialization and because each additional worker introduces crowding effects. Thus, the addition of a fifth worker to the crew yields a marginal increase in output of 11 additional tons, compared with the marginal increase of 15 additional tons for the fourth worker. Similarly, the additions of the sixth and seventh workers to the crew yield successively smaller increases of 5 and 2 tons, respectively.

With enough additional workers, the marginal product of labor becomes zero or even negative. Note that the eighth, ninth, and tenth workers listed in Table 7.2 have marginal products of 0, −1, and −2 tons, respectively. Some work is just more difficult to accomplish when superfluous personnel are present. Such crowding effects can overwhelm the small additional output from the extra worker or other variable inputs.

Increasing Returns with Network Effects

The law of diminishing marginal returns is *not* a mathematical theorem, but an empirical assertion that has been observed in almost every economic production process as the amount of the variable input increases. An interesting exception occurs, however, with selling effort after the adoption of a new industry standard (e.g., digital HDTV) and with **network effects.** The greater the installed base of a network product, like Microsoft NT, the larger the number of compatible network connections and therefore the more possible value added for a new customer. Consequently, as Microsoft NT's installed base increases, their selling efforts become increasingly more productive.

Example

INCREASING RETURNS AT SONY AND INTEL

A manufacturer's product line costs usually now include marketing and distribution activities as well as the labor and material direct costs of standard production and assembly. The reason is that, like service firms, many manufacturers today compete on customer inquiry systems, change order responsiveness, delivery schedule conformance, product reliability, and technological updates, not just on product delivery and warranty repairs. Qualifying for and actually winning a customer order often requires quality characteristics and support services beyond the physical unit of production. For example, Ford Motor wants all its manufacturing suppliers to meet the ISO9000 manufacturing quality standards for continuous improvement processes. Wal-Mart requires that their fashion clothing suppliers deliver shipments just in time (JIT) for planned departure from Wal-Mart distribution centers. Disney chooses gift item manufacturers who can alter production schedules on short notice in order to provide much greater change-order responsiveness than traditional make-to-order manufacturing of Mickey Mouse coffee mugs.

At times, these additional marketing and distribution activities can exhibit increasing returns and declining cost. For example, securing the adoption of an industry stan-

WHAT WENT RIGHT   WHAT WENT WRONG

Boeing Assembly Plant[4]

The Boeing Company assembles wide-body aircraft (747s, 767s, and 777s) at their 4.3-million-square-foot Everett, Washington, assembly plant, the largest building in the world. Fifteen railcars a day deliver parts that are directed to 5 assembly lines by 100 forklifts and 26 overhead cranes cruising on 31 miles of networked track. The variable inputs in this production process are millions of parts and thousands of skilled assemblers.

As Boeing ramped up production from 244 aircraft deliveries in 1995 to 560 in 1999, the Everett plant went to three shifts of 6,000, 4,000 and 1,500 workers and twice as many parts poured in, but crowding effects descended on the Everett plant. Although final assembly continued to take its normal 21 workdays, overtime was required to maintain this roll-out schedule, in large part because of lost, defective, and reworked parts. At times, piles of redundant parts would appear on the shop floor, while at other times, shortages of seats and electronic gear caused delays. As a result, work-in-progress inventory skyrocketed and work orders got out of sequence. By late 1997, overtime was running almost a billion dollars over budget, and the production operations at Everett were "hopelessly snarled."

To resolve the problem, in 1999 Boeing scrapped its antiquated parts-tracking system and adopted lean production techniques. It cut parts order sizes and outsourced subassembly work away from bottlenecked points on the final assembly line. By 2001, a continuous stream of fewer parts arrived at autonomous worker cells just in time, as required to complete a smoothly flowing assembly process for 527 aircraft deliveries.

[4] "Boeing's Secret," *BusinessWeek,* May 20, 2002, pp. 113–15; "Gaining Altitude," *Barron's,* April 29, 2002, pp. 21–25; and Everett plant tours.

dard favorable to one's own product (e.g., digital high-definition television—HDTV) involves promotional and other selling efforts which grow *more productive* the larger the product's market share. The greater the installed base of Sony digital TV receivers, the more programs are produced to be transmitted with this technology, and the more programs available, the easier and cheaper it is to secure the next household's adoption of the innovation.

A similar reason for increasing returns at Microsoft is that the more adoptions Microsoft Windows secures, the more Windows-compatible applications will be introduced by independent software developers. And the more applications introduced, the greater the chance will be for further adoptions. To give another example, the higher the Intel Pentium processor's market share goes, the lower the promotional costs required to trigger another adoption. The only limiting factor in the adoption of such innovations is the appearance of still newer technologies (e.g., networked computers need much less processing power than stand-alone PCs). Normal sales penetration or saturation curves (like the MP_L curve in Figure 7.2) exhibit initially increasing marginal returns to promotional expenses followed by eventually diminishing marginal returns. However, with the adoption of new industry standards or a network technology, increasing returns can persist.

When Microsoft managed to achieve a critical level of adoption for the Windows graphical user interface (GUI), the amount of marketing and promotional expenditure required to secure the next adoption actually began to fall.[5] Selling efforts are generally subject to diminishing returns, but when the number of other users of a network-based device reaches a 30–40-percent share, the next 40–50 share points are cheaper and cheaper to promote. Then, beyond a market share of 80–90 percent, diminishing returns again set in, and securing the final adopters becomes increasingly expensive. These relationships are depicted in Figure 7.3. From 0-percent to 30-percent market share, the selling efforts required to achieve each additional share point have a diminishing effect on the probability of adoption by the next potential user (note the reduced slope of the sales penetration curve). Consequently, additional share points become more and more expensive over this range. Beyond the 30-percent *inflection point,* however, each additional share point of users connected to Windows leads to an increasing probability of adoption by another user; hence a decrease in the marketing expense required to secure another unit sale (note the increased slope of the sales penetration curve in this middle range). These network-based effects of compatibility with other users reflect increased value to the poten-

Figure 7.3   Increasing Returns in Securing Adoption of a New Technology

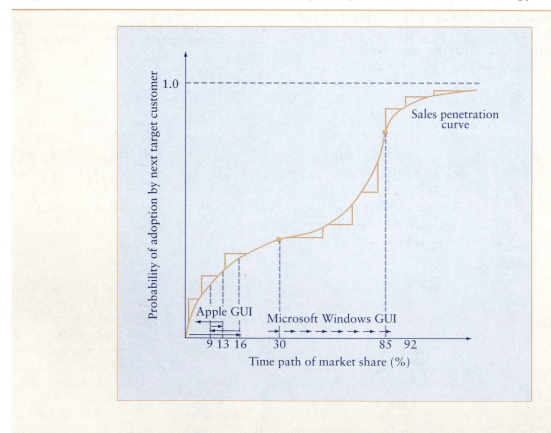

[5] Based on "The Theory That Made Microsoft: Increasing Returns," *Fortune,* April 29, 1996, pp. 65–68.

tial adopter. The same thing occurs when an ever-increasing number of independent software vendors (ISVs) write applications for an operating system like Windows that has achieved more than 30-percent acceptance in the marketplace and has therefore effectively become an industry standard.

Eventually at 85 percent, share points again become increasingly more expensive because selling efforts have again become subject to diminishing returns. That is, at 85 percent, Microsoft encountered a second inflection point. Over the middle 30–85 percent range of the sales penetration curve, Microsoft's increasing returns made an 85-percent monopoly control of the operating system market highly likely. Whatever customer relationships preexisted, once Microsoft achieved a 30-percent share, increasing returns in marketing its product offering introduced a disruptive technology that displaced other competitors. Inexorably, Microsoft's share grew to 92 percent, and other products collapsed. Netscape's Internet search engine experienced exactly this same sort of displacement by Microsoft's Internet Explorer when Microsoft achieved 30 percent-plus penetration by bundling Internet Explorer with Windows, effectively giving away the search engine for free to reach the middle sales penetration range of increasing returns.

Producing Information Services in the "New Economy"

It is insightful to compare the production economics of old-economy companies that produce *things* to new-economy companies that produce *information*. Things, when sold, the seller ceases to own. Information, when sold, the seller can sell again (at least until the information spillovers from earlier sales and the difficulty in excluding those who do not pay overwhelm the target market). Things must be replicated through expensive manufacturing processes. Information is replicable at almost zero incremental cost. Things exist in one location. Information can exist simultaneously in many locations. The production and marketing of things are subject to eventually diminishing returns. The marketing (and maybe the production) of information is subject to increasing returns. That is, the more people who use my information, the more likely it is that another person will want to acquire it (for any given marketing cost) or, said another way, the cheaper it is to secure another sale. Things often involve economies of scale in production. Information is produceable by small companies at comparably low costs. Things focus a business on supply-side thinking and the high costs of distribution. Information products focus a business on demand-side thinking and have almost no costs of distribution. By getting the next customer to adopt, one can set in motion a "virtuous circle" of higher customer value, lower overhead costs, and lower prices and costs for the next customer. Hence, Microsoft evolved to dominate an information-oriented business like computer network software. Chapter 11 discusses increasing returns as a source of dominant firm market power.

Relationship Between Total, Marginal, and Average Product

In contrast to Figure 7.2, which illustrates discrete choices for the single variable input (labor), Figure 7.4 illustrates a production function (TP) with a continuous single variable input. Several relationships among the TP, AP, and MP curves can be seen in the graph. In the first region labeled "Increasing returns," the TP function (total output) is increasing at an *increasing rate*. Because the MP curve measures the slope of the TP curve ($MP = \partial Q/\partial L$), the MP curve is increasing up to L_1. In the region labeled "Decreasing returns," the TP function is increasing at a *decreasing rate*,

Figure 7.4 Relationships Among Total, Average, and Marginal Product Curves

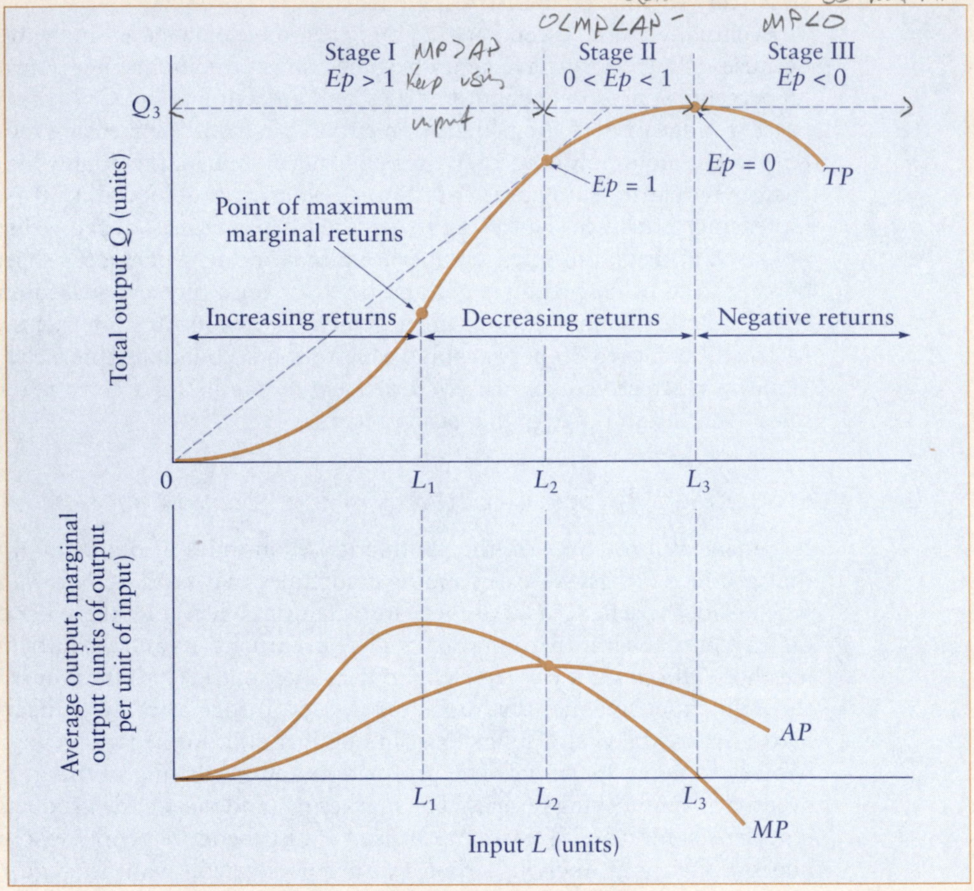

and the MP curve is decreasing up to L_3. In the region labeled "Negative returns," the TP function is *decreasing*, and the MP curve continues decreasing, becoming negative beyond L_3. An inflection point occurs at L_1. Next, if a line is drawn from the origin 0 to any point on the TP curve, it can be seen that the slope of this line, Q/L, is at a maximum when the line touches the TP curve at an input value of L_2. The slope of this line, Q/L, measures the average product AP. Hence we see that the AP curve reaches a maximum at this point.[6]

---

[6] Note also that the marginal product MP equals the average product AP at L_2. This follows because the marginal product MP is equal to the slope of the TP curve ($MP = \partial Q/\partial L$), and at L_2 the average product AP is also equal to the slope of the TP curve.

Consider, for example, the following analogy: A baseball player's batting *average* for the season is 0.250. If that player has an excellent night at bat (his *marginal* performance) and goes 4 for 4 (1.000), then his season average will be pulled up. On the other hand, if he goes hitless, this poor *marginal* performance will pull down his season average. If he goes 1 for 4, this marginal performance will have no impact on his season average (marginal performance equals average performance). Hence the MP curve will always intersect with the AP curve when it is at a maximum. As we will see in the next chapter, a firm's marginal cost curve always intersects the average cost curve at its minimum point, for the same reason.

Three Stages of Production

In analyzing the production function, economists have identified three different stages of production based on the relationships among the *TP, AP,* and *MP* functions. Stage I is defined as the *range of* L *over which the average product is increasing.* This occurs from the origin (0) up to L_2 and represents the region of net gains from specialization. Stage II corresponds to the *range of* L *from the point at which the average product is at a maximum* (L_2) *to the point where the marginal product* (MP) *declines to zero* (L_3). The endpoint of Stage II thus corresponds to the point of maximum output on the *TP* curve. Stage III encompasses the *range of* L *over which the total product is declining* or, equivalently, *the marginal product is negative.* Stage III thus corresponds to all values of L greater than (i.e., to the right of) L_3, where crowding effects overwhelm any output attributable to additional workers.

The determination of the optimal quantity of labor input L to be used in producing a given amount of output Q is described in the next section; however, one can eliminate several values of L from consideration at this point. First, the rational producer would not operate the production process over the range of values of input L contained in Stage III. In Stage III an excessive amount of the variable input, relative to the fixed input K, is being used to produce the desired output. In other words, because the marginal product of input L is negative beyond L_3, using more than L_3 units would cause a *reduction* in total output. Any desired output (up to the maximum obtainable with the given amount of the fixed input, that is, Q_3) could be produced by using less than L_3 units of the variable input. No manager would ever knowingly increase labor expenses to hire additional workers whose presence reduces output (e.g., Stage III). Even if the variable input were free, the rational producer would not wish to proceed into Stage III. By the same token, no manager whose productivity per worker is rising due to the gains from specialization (i.e., *AP* increasing in Stage I) should stop adding workers as long as the incremental cost for additional workers remains constant.

In general, then, how much of the variable input to employ over the remaining range of potentially optimal input choice (Stage II) depends on variable input costs. If labor costs are high, as in a United Auto Workers' assembly plant, production may proceed just a short distance into Stage II in hiring labor. If labor costs are lower in a nonunionized plant, for example, labor hiring may proceed well across Stage II to include relatively low-level productivity workers, like apprentices.

Of course, some input costs are subsidized (e.g., job training programs), and others may be effectively negative such that revenues actually increase the more the input is used. For example, in order to ensure that dredge spoil once removed does not flow back into harbors and navigable waterways, the U.S. Army Corps of Engineers will actually pay concrete block manufacturers for every cubic yard of the muddy slurry used in the production process. Too much of the dredge spoil slurry, in combination with concrete mix and sand, results in more cracked blocks leaving the kilns. However, with a negative price on the input, the manufacturers employ dredge spoil into the range of Stage III production. Such exceptions prove the general rule that optimal production with a single variable input and positive input prices necessitates restricting input choices to Stage II.

DETERMINING THE OPTIMAL USE OF THE VARIABLE INPUT

With one of the inputs (K) fixed in the short run, the producer must determine the optimal quantity of the variable input (L) to employ in the production process.

http://
For further reading on marginal revenue product, see David Friedman's Internet textbook at: http://www.daviddfriedman.com/Academic/Price_Theory/PThy_Chapter_9/PThy_Chapter_9.html

Such a determination requires the introduction into the analysis of product (output) prices and factor costs. Therefore, the analysis begins by defining marginal revenue product and marginal factor cost.

Marginal Revenue Product

Marginal revenue product (MRP_L) is defined as *the amount that an additional unit of the variable input adds to total revenue,* or

$$MRP_L = \frac{\Delta TR}{\Delta L} \qquad [7.6]$$

where ΔTR is the change in total revenue associated with the given change (ΔL) in the variable input, and MRP_L is equal to the marginal product of L (MP_L) times the marginal revenue (MR_Q) resulting from the increase in output obtained:

$$MRP_L = MP_L \cdot MR_Q \qquad [7.7]$$

Consider again the Deep Creek Mining Company example (Table 7.2) of the previous section where K (capital) is fixed at 750 b.h.p. Suppose that the firm can sell all the ore it can produce at a price of $10 per ton (that is, in a *perfectly competitive market*). The marginal revenue product of labor (MRP_L) is computed using Equation 7.7 and is shown in Table 7.3.[7] Note that in a perfectly competitive market, marginal revenue is equal to the selling price. Sometimes in practice this concept is referred

Table 7.3   Marginal Revenue Product and Marginal Factor Cost—Deep Creek Mining Company

Labor Input L (Number of Workers)	Total Product $Q = (TP_L)$ (Tons of Ore)	Marginal Product of Labor MP_L (Tons Per Worker)	Total Revenue $TR = P \cdot Q$ ($)	Marginal Revenue $MR_Q = \frac{\Delta TR}{\Delta Q}$ ($/Ton)	Marginal Revenue Product $MRP_L = MP_L \cdot MR_Q$ ($/Worker)	Marginal Factor Cost MFC_L ($/Worker)
0	0	—	0	—	—	—
1	6	6	60	10	60	50
2	16	10	160	10	100	50
3	29	13	290	10	130	50
4	44	15	440	10	150	50
5	55	11	550	10	110	50
6*	60	5	600	10	50	50
7	62	2	620	10	20	50
8	62	0	620	10	0	50

* Indicates the optimal input level.

---

[7] Input levels in Stage III ($MP_L < 0$) have been eliminated from consideration.

to as the marginal value added. In Europe, for example, each level of production from raw material to finished goods distribution is taxed on the marginal value added.

Marginal Factor Cost

Marginal Factor Cost (MFC_L)
The amount that an additional unit of the variable input adds to total cost.

Marginal factor cost (MFC_L) is defined as *the amount that an additional unit of the variable input adds to total cost,* or

$$MFC_L = \frac{\Delta TC}{\Delta L}$$ [7.8]

where ΔTC is the change in cost associated with the given change (ΔL) in the variable input.

In the ore-mining example, suppose that the firm can employ as much labor (L) as it needs by paying the workers $50 per period ($C_L$). In other words, the labor market is assumed to be *perfectly competitive.* Under these conditions, the marginal factor cost (MFC_L) is equal to C_L, or $50 per worker. It is constant regardless of the level of operation of the mine (see the last column of Table 7.3).

Optimal Input Level

Given the marginal revenue product and marginal factor cost, we can compute the optimal amount of the variable input to use in the production process. Recall from the discussion of marginal analysis in Chapter 2 that an economic activity (for example, production) should be expanded as long as the marginal benefits (revenues) exceed the marginal costs. The optimal level occurs at the point where the marginal benefits are equal to the marginal costs. For the short-run production decision, the optimal level of the variable input occurs where

$$MRP_L = MFC_L$$ [7.9]

As can be seen in Table 7.3, the optimal input is $L = 6$ workers because $MRP_L = MFC_L = 50 at this point. At less than six workers, $MRP_L > MFC_L$ and the addition of more labor (workers) to the production process will increase revenues more than it will increase costs. Beyond six workers the opposite is true—costs will increase more than revenues.

PRODUCTION FUNCTIONS WITH TWO VARIABLE INPUTS

Using the Deep Creek Mining Company example, suppose now that both capital—as measured by the maximum brake horsepower rating of the equipment—and labor—as measured by the number of workers—are variable inputs to the ore-mining process. The firm can choose to operate the production process using any of the capital-labor combinations shown previously in Table 7.1.

Production Isoquants

Production Isoquant
An algebraic function or a geometric curve representing all the various combinations of two inputs that can be used in producing a given level of output.

A production function with two variable inputs can be represented graphically by a set of two-dimensional production isoquants. A **production isoquant** is either a geometric curve or an algebraic function representing all the various combinations of the two inputs that can be used in producing a given level of output. In the Deep Creek example, a production isoquant shows all the alternative ways in which the number of workers and various sizes of mining equipment can be combined to produce any

Figure 7.5   Production Isoquants—Deep Creek Mining Company

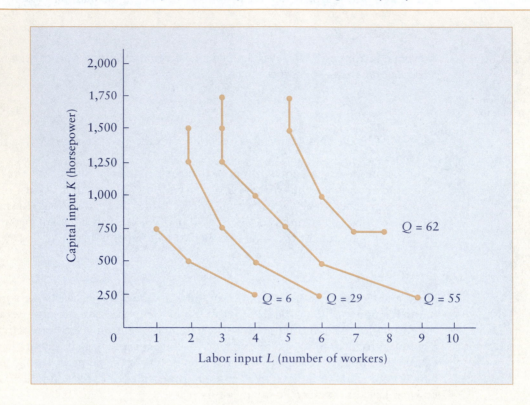

desired level of output (tons of ore). Several of the production isoquants for the ore-mining example are shown in Figure 7.5. For example, an output of 6 tons can be produced using any of three different labor-capital combinations—1 worker and 750 b.h.p. equipment, 2 workers and 500 b.h.p. equipment, or 4 workers and 250 b.h.p. equipment. Similarly, as seen in the graph, an output of 62 tons can be produced using any one of five different labor-capital combinations.

Although each isoquant indicates how quantities of the two inputs may be *substituted* for one another, these choices are normally limited for two reasons: first, some input combinations in Figure 7.5 employ an excessive quantity of one input. Just as more than 8 workers result in negative marginal returns in choosing a single variable input for Deep Creek Mining (see Figure 7.2), so too here with 750-b.h.p. machinery, the eighth worker contributes no additional output along the isoquant $Q = 62$ in Figure 7.5. The presence of a ninth worker would necessitate additional capital equipment simply to maintain output at 62 tons. That is, in the absence of additional capital equipment, the crowding effects introduced by the ninth worker would actually reduce output. Similarly, more than 1,750-b.h.p. machinery would result in negative marginal returns with only 5 workers; another 250 horsepower (from 1,750 to 2,000 b.h.p.) would require an additional (sixth) worker just to maintain output at 62 tons. Because all such inefficient mixes of capital and labor increase the input requirements (and therefore costs) without increasing output, they should be excluded from consideration in making input substitution choices.

Second, input substitution choices are also limited by the technology of production, which often involves machinery that is not divisible. Although one can find smaller and larger mining equipment, not every brake horsepower machine listed on the K axis of Figure 7.5 will be available. The industrial engineering of mining operations often requires that we select from three or four possible fixed proportions production processes involving a particular size mining drill and a particular size labor force to run it. We discuss the concept of a fixed proportions production process in the next section.

Marginal Rate of Technical Substitution

In addition to indicating the quantity of output that can be produced with any of the various input combinations that lie on the isoquant curve, the isoquant also indicates the *rate* at which one input may be substituted for another input in producing the given quantity of output. Suppose one considers the meaning of a shift from point A to point B on the isoquant labeled "$Q = 29$" in Figure 7.6. At point A, 3 workers and a 750-b.h.p. machine are being used to produce 29 tons of output, whereas at point B, 4 workers and a 500-b.h.p. machine are being used to produce the same amount of output. In moving from point A to point B, one has substituted one additional unit of labor for 250 units of capital. The rate at which capital has been replaced with labor in producing the given output is equal to 250/1 or

Figure 7.6   Production Isoquant Curve—Deep Creek Mining Company

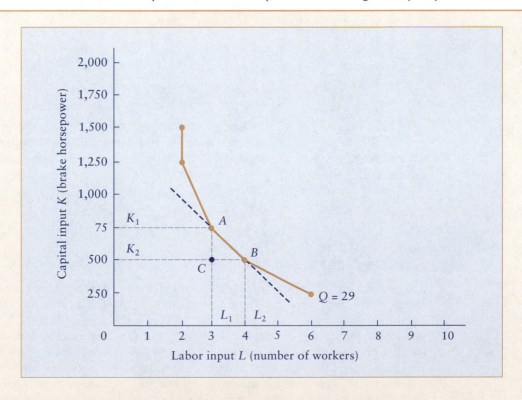

Marginal Rate of
Technical Substitution
The *rate* at which one
input may be substituted
for another input in
producing a given quantity
of output.

250 units of capital per unit of labor. The rate at which one input may be substituted for another input in the production process, while total output remains constant, is known as the **marginal rate of technical substitution,** or *MRTS*.

The rate of change of one variable with respect to another variable is given by the slope of the curve relating the two variables. Thus, the rate of change of input K with respect to input L—that is, the rate at which K may be substituted for L in the production process—is given by the slope of the curve relating K to L—that is, the slope of the isoquant. The slope of the AB segment of the isoquant in Figure 7.6 is equal to the ratio of AC to CB. Algebraically, $AC = K_1 - K_2$ and $CB = L_1 - L_2$; therefore, the slope is equal to $(K_1 - K_2) \div (L_1 - L_2)$. Because the slope is negative and one wishes to express the substitution rate as a positive quantity, a negative sign is attached to the slope:

$$MRTS = -\frac{K_1 - K_2}{L_1 - L_2} = -\frac{\Delta K}{\Delta L} \qquad [7.10]$$

In the Deep Creek Mining Company example, $\Delta L = 3 - 4 = -1$, $\Delta K = 750 - 500 = 250$. Substituting these values into Equation 7.10 yields

$$MRTS = -\frac{250}{-1} = 250$$

Therefore, along $Q = 29$ between input combinations A and B, 250 b.h.p. substituted for one worker.

It can be shown that the *MRTS* is equal to the ratio of the marginal products of L and K by using the definition of the marginal product (Equation 7.2). This definition yields $\Delta L = \Delta Q/MP_L$ and $\Delta K = \Delta Q/MP_K$. Substituting these expressions into Equation 7.10 (and dropping the minus sign) yields

$$MRTS = \frac{\Delta Q/MP_K}{\Delta Q/MP_L}$$

$$MRTS = \frac{MP_L}{MP_K} \qquad [7.11]$$

For the Deep Creek Mining Company example, $MP_L = \Delta Q/\Delta L = (29 - 16)/(4 - 3) = 13$, $MP_K = \Delta Q/\Delta K = (29 - 16)/(750 - 500) = 13/250$. Substituting these values into Equation 7.11 yields $MRTS = 250$, the same result as the above direct calculation:

$$MRTS = \frac{13}{13/250} = 250$$

Perfect Substitute and Complementary Inputs

Production inputs vary in the degree to which they can be substituted for one another in a given process. The extreme cases are *perfect substitutes* and *perfect complements*. Isoquants for these two cases are shown in Figure 7.7. The isoquants for inputs that are *perfect substitutes* for one another consist of a series of parallel lines, as shown in Panel (a). Examples of perfect substitutes are the use of alternative fuels (inputs), such as fuel oil or natural gas in the production of electricity, or the use of soybeans or oats in the production of nutrients in animal feeds. The isoquants for inputs that are *perfect complements* for one another consist of a series of right angles, as shown in Panel (b). Such inputs are said to have

Figure 7.7 Production Isoquants: Perfect Substitute and Complementary Inputs

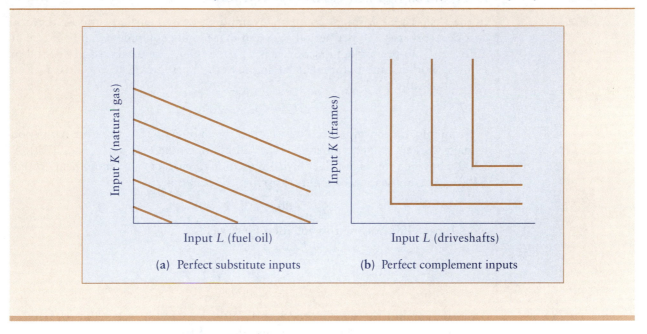

(a) Perfect substitute inputs

(b) Perfect complement inputs

zero substitutability. Examples of perfect complements include component parts that must be combined in fixed proportions, such as driveshafts and frames for automobiles or foundations and roofs for houses.

Most production inputs fall somewhere between the extreme cases of perfect complements and perfect substitutes. For most production functions, isoquants are convex to the origin, as shown earlier in Figure 7.6. This shape implies that the production inputs are imperfectly substitutable and that the rate of substitution declines as one input is substituted for another.

DETERMINING THE OPTIMAL COMBINATION OF INPUTS

As shown in the previous section, a given level of output can be produced using any of a large number of possible combinations of two inputs. The firm needs to determine which combination will minimize the total costs for producing the desired output.

Isocost Lines

The total cost of each possible input combination is a function of the market prices of these inputs. Assuming that the inputs are supplied in perfectly elastic input markets, the per-unit price of each input will be constant, regardless of the amount of the input that is purchased. Letting C_L and C_K be the per-unit prices of inputs L and K, respectively, the total cost (C) of any given input combination is

$$C = C_L L + C_K K$$

[7.12]

Example

ISOCOST DETERMINATION:
DEEP CREEK MINING COMPANY (continued)

In the Deep Creek Mining Company example discussed earlier, suppose that the cost per worker is $50 per period ($C_L$) and that mining equipment can be leased at a price of $.20 per brake horsepower per period (C_K). The total cost per period of using L workers and equipment having K brake horsepower to produce a given amount of output is

$$C = 50L + .20K \qquad [7.13]$$

From this relationship, it can be seen that the mining of 55 tons of ore per period using 5 workers and equipment having 750 b.h.p. would cost $50(5) + .20(750) = \$400$. However, this is not the only combination of workers and equipment costing $400. Any combination of inputs satisfying the equation

$$\$400 = 50L + .20K$$

would cost $400. Solving this equation for K yields

$$K = \frac{\$400}{.20} - \frac{50}{.20}L$$
$$= \$2,000 - 250L$$

Thus, the combinations $L = 1$ and $K = 1,750$; $L = 2$ and $K = 1,500$; $L = 3$ and $K = 1,250$ (plus many other combinations) all cost $400.

The combinations of inputs costing $400 can be represented as the line in Figure 7.8 labeled "$C = \$400$." This line is called an *isocost* line, because it shows all the combinations of inputs having *equal* total costs. An isocost line exists for every possible total cost C. Solving Equation 7.13 for K gives the equation of each isocost line in Figure 7.8. Note that only the y-intercept $C/.20$ changes as one moves from one isocost line to another.

$$K = \frac{C}{.20} - 250L \qquad [7.14]$$

That is, all the isocost lines are parallel, each one having a slope of -250. In general, the set of isocost lines consists of the set of equations given by the solution of Equation 7.12 for various values of C:

$$K = \frac{C}{C_K} - \frac{C_L}{C_K}L \qquad [7.15]$$

http://

You can access more information on the optimal combination of inputs in Lesson 7 at the following Internet site:

http://www.bus.okstate.edu/ ecls/price/ICS/ECON3113W/ framed/econ3113.htm

Once the isoquants and isocosts are specified, it is possible to solve for the optimum combination of inputs. The production decision problem can be formulated in two different ways, depending on the manner in which the production objective or goal is stated. One can solve for the combination of inputs that either

1. minimizes total cost subject to a given constraint on output, or
2. maximizes output subject to a given total cost constraint.

Constrained cost minimization in Option 1 is the dual problem to the constrained output maximization problem in Option 2.

Figure 7.8   Isocost Lines—Deep Creek Mining Company

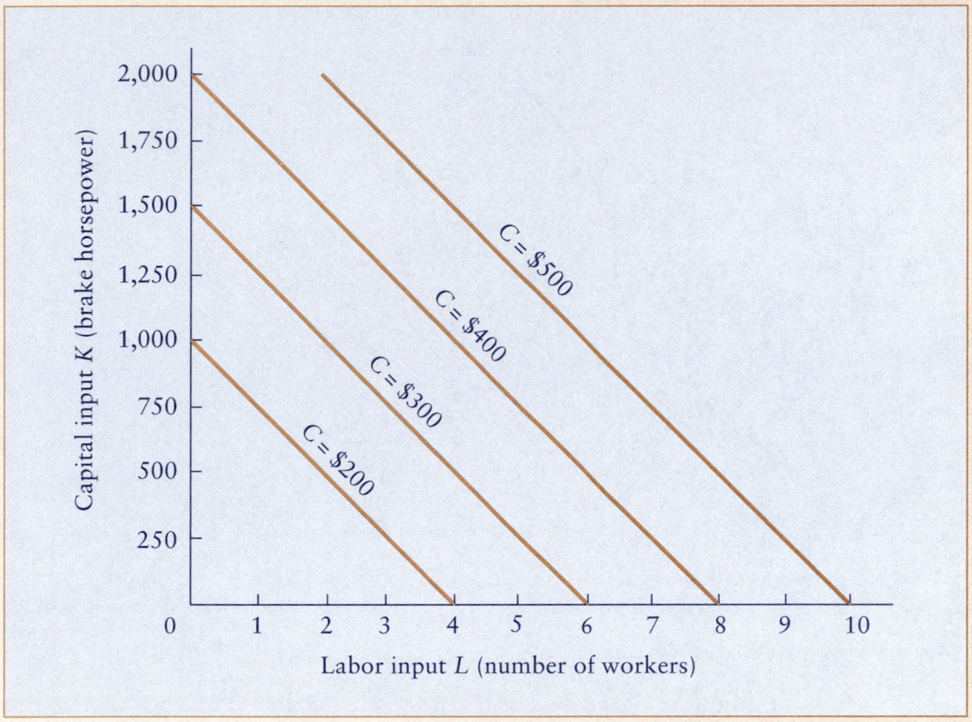

Minimizing Cost Subject to an Output Constraint

Consider first the problem in which the director of operations desires to release to production a number of orders for at least $Q^{(2)}$ units of output. As shown in Figure 7.9, this constraint requires that the solution be in the feasible region containing the input combinations that lie either on the $Q^{(2)}$ isoquant or on isoquants that fall above and to the right having larger output values (the shaded area). The total cost of producing the required output is minimized by finding the input combinations within this region that lie on the lowest cost isocost line. Combination D on the $C^{(2)}$ isocost line satisfies this condition. Combinations E and F, which also lie on the $Q^{(2)}$ isoquant, yield higher total costs because they fall on the $C^{(3)}$ isocost line. Thus, the use of L_1 units of input L and K_1 units of input K will yield a (constrained) minimum cost solution of $C^{(2)}$ dollars.

At the optimal input combination, the slope of the given isoquant must equal the slope of the $C^{(2)}$ lowest isocost line. As in the previous section, the slope of an isoquant is equal to dK/dL and

$$-\frac{dK}{dL} = MRTS = \frac{MP_L}{MP_K}$$ [7.16]

Figure 7.9   Cost Minimization Subject to an Output Constraint

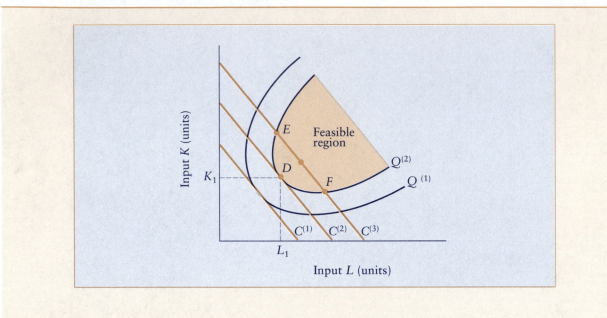

Taking the derivative of the isocost equation (Equation 7.15), the slope of the isocost line is given by

$$\frac{dK}{dL} = -\frac{C_L}{C_K} \qquad [7.17]$$

Multiplying Equation 7.17 by (−1) and setting the result equal to Equation 7.16 yields

$$-\frac{dK}{dL} = -\left(-\frac{C_L}{C_K}\right)$$

$$= \frac{MP_L}{MP_K}$$

Thus, the following equilibrium condition, the "equimarginal criterion"

$$\frac{MP_L}{MP_K} = \frac{C_L}{C_K}$$

or, equivalently,

$$\frac{MP_L}{C_L} = \frac{MP_K}{C_K} \qquad [7.18]$$

must be satisfied in order for an input combination to be an optimal solution to the problem of minimizing cost subject to an output constraint. Equation 7.18 indicates that the marginal product per dollar input cost of one factor must be equal to the marginal product per dollar input cost of the other factor.

Figure 7.10   Output Maximization Subject to a Cost Constraint

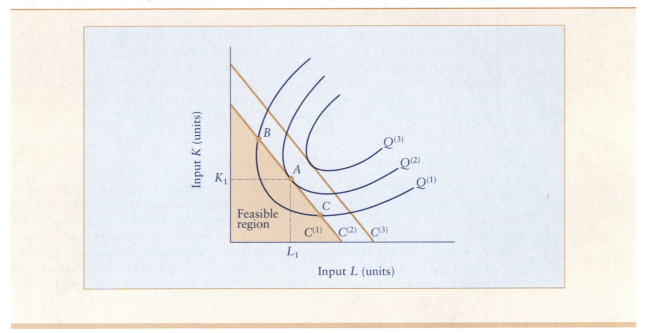

Note that the logic of this optimality condition is equivalent to that developed in Chapter 4 for consumer demand choices that maximize utility subject to a household budget constraint. Also note in Figure 7.10 that maximizing output subject to a feasible region demarcated by the $Q^{(2)}$ cost constraint yields exactly the same (L_1, K_1) optimal input combination that satisfies the equimarginal criterion.

DETERMINING THE COST-MINIMIZING PRODUCTION PROCESS

The previous section analyzed the least-cost combination of divisible inputs in variable proportions production, where one input substituted continuously for another. However, Deep Creek Mining's production choices involve indivisible capital equipment, such as one small or one large mining drill and a predetermined number of workers to run it. Similarly, an auto fender stamping machine in an assembly plant must be used in fixed proportion to a certain quantity of labor and sheet metal supplies. And 3 hours of setup, maintenance, and cleaning may be required to support a 5-hour printing press run. Three additional hours of work by maintenance personnel would be required for a second press run, and a third shift of maintenance workers would be required for 24-hour printing operations. Although a higher output rate can be achieved by scaling up all the inputs, each of these production processes is one of fixed, not variable, proportions.

Linear programming techniques are available to determine the least-cost process for fixed proportions production. The Deep Creek Mining Company example can be used to illustrate the graphic approach to finding such a solution.

Example

COST MINIMIZATION: DEEP CREEK MINING COMPANY (continued)

Suppose one is interested in finding the combination of labor input and capital equipment that minimizes the cost of producing at least 29 tons of ore. Assume that the isocost lines are the ones defined by Equation 7.13 and graphed in Figure 7.8 earlier in this section. Figure 7.11 combines several isoquants and isocost lines for the ore-mining problem. The shaded area in the graph represents the set of feasible input combinations, that is, those labor and capital production processes that yield at least $Q = 29$ tons of output. Processes M_2 and M_3 minimize the cost of producing 29 tons at $300. M_1 imposes higher costs of $350.

Production Processes and Process Rays

Production Process
A fixed-proportions production relationship.

A **production process** can be defined as one in which the inputs are combined in fixed proportion to obtain the output. By this definition, a production process can be represented graphically as a ray through the origin having a slope equal to the ratio of the number of units of the respective resources required to produce one unit of output. Three production process rays for Deep Creek Mining are shown in Figure 7.11. Along Process Ray M_1, the inputs are combined in the ratio of two workers to a 1,250 b.h.p. drilling machine. Hence, Ray M_1 has a slope of 625 b.h.p. per mine worker.

Figure 7.11   A Fixed Proportions Production Decision—Deep Creek Mining Company

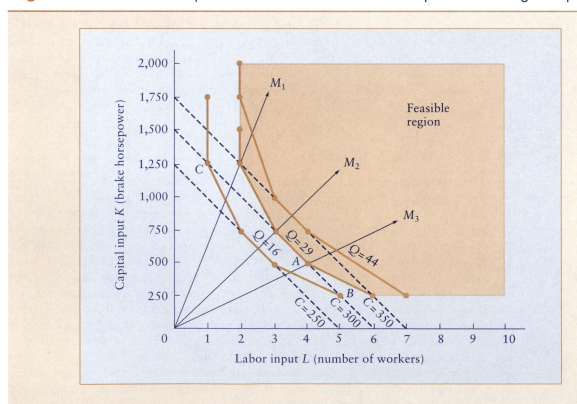

Operating multiple production processes like M_1, M_2, and M_3 can offer a firm flexibility in dealing with unusual orders, interruptions in the availability of resources, or binding resource constraints. However, not all fixed proportions production processes are equally efficient. The firm will prefer to use one or two production processes exclusively if they offer the advantage of substantial cost savings. Mine 1 employs process M_1 to produce 29 tons with 2 workers and a 1,250 b.h.p. drilling machine at a total cost of 50 (2) + .20 (1,250) = \$350 or \$350/29 = \$12.07 per ton. Mine 2 uses a more labor-intensive process (M_2) with 3 workers and a smaller 750 b.h.p. machine and incurs a lower total cost of \$300. Mine 2 is the benchmark operation for Deep Creek in that this M_2 process produces 29 tons at minimum cost—specifically, \$300/29 = \$10.34 per ton.

Measuring the Efficiency of a Production Process

Mine 1 with production process M_1 is said to be allocatively inefficient because it has chosen the wrong input mix; the mine has allocated its input budget incorrectly. Its 1,250-b.h.p. machine is too large for the number of workers hired and the output desired. By producing 29 tons of output for \$350 relative to the lowest cost benchmark at \$300, process M_1 exhibits only \$300/\$350 = 85.7 percent **allocative efficiency.**

In addition to allocative inefficiency involving the incorrect input mix, a production operation can also exhibit technical inefficiency. For example, the industrial engineering indicated by the production isoquants in Figure 7.11 suggests that the process M_3 also should be capable of producing 29 tons. The "C = \$300" isocost line is tangent to the boundary of the feasible region (i.e., the "Q = 29" isoquant) at not only 3 workers and a 750-b.h.p. machine (M_2), but also at 4 workers and 500-b.h.p. machine (M_3). In principle, both production processes yield the desired 29 tons of ore at a minimum total cost of \$300 and will thereby satisfy the condition in Equation 7.18.

However, suppose Mine 2 has been unable to achieve more than 27 tons of output. Although it has adopted a least-cost process, Mine 2 would then be characterized as *technically inefficient*. In particular, Mine 2 exhibits only 27 tons/29 tons = 93 percent **technical efficiency** despite its least-cost process. However, 93-percent technical efficiency may be inadequate. Benchmark plants often do substantially better, with many processes meeting 98 percent and 99 percent of their production goals. In addition, as technically inefficient plants approach the current standard of excellence, continuous quality improvement initiatives may raise the standards.

Allocative Efficiency
A measure of how closely production achieves the least-cost input mix or process, given the desired level of output.

Technical Efficiency
A measure of how closely production achieves maximum potential output given the input mix or process.

Example

GM's A-Frame Supplier Achieves 99.998 Percent Technical Efficiency

Just-in-time delivery systems have accentuated the need for very high reliability and technical efficiency to produce on time as promised with near zero defects. One A-frame supplier to General Motors assembly plants has reduced defective parts to five per million (i.e., 0.002 of 1 percent) and has agreed to pay a \$4,000 *per minute* "charge back" for any late deliveries resulting in assembly line delays. Such a company must constantly monitor and proactively solve production problems before they arise in order to ensure near 100-percent technical efficiency.

WHAT WENT RIGHT   WHAT WENT WRONG

How Exactly Have Computerization and Information Technology Lowered Costs at Chevron and Merck?[8]

In processing insurance claims or typesetting newspapers and magazines, it is clear how computerization has made output per worker higher and therefore lowered unit labor cost. Personal computers have decreased many-fold the time and talent required to perform routine work done previously with paper forms and time-consuming repetitive human tasks. However, not every business uses large numbers of PCs. How have computerization and information technology raised productivity and lowered cost so widely across other industries?

One key seems to be enhanced analytical and R&D capability provided by computers and information technology (IT) systems. Chevron Corporation once spent anywhere from $2 million to $4 million each to drill 10 to 12 exploratory wells before finding oil. Today, Chevron finds oil once in every five wells. The reason for the cost savings in the exploration and development of oil fields is a new technology that allows Chevron to display three-dimensional graphs of the likely oil and gas deposits.

In addition, the new processors allow more calculation-intensive simulation modeling. Using only seismic data as inputs, Chevron can now model how the oil and gas deposits will shift and flow as a known field is pumped out. This allows a much more accurate location of secondary wells in known oil fields. As a result, overall production costs have shrunk 16 percent industrywide since 1991.

Pharmaceutical research and development has experienced a similar benefit from computerization. Drug industry basic research always starts with biochemical or biogenetic modeling of the disease mechanism. In the past, once a mechanism for Hodgkins disease or pancreatic cancer became well understood, researchers at Merck and other drug companies experimented on known active compounds one by one in time-consuming chemical trials. Successful therapies emerged only after human trials on the promising compounds that showed efficacy with few side effects. Total time to introduction of a new pharmaceutical was often longer than a decade.

Today, the first stage of the basic research process remains much the same, but the second stage of dribbling chemicals into a petri dish has stopped. Instead, machines controlled and automated by microchips perform thousands of reactions at once and tally the results. Human researchers then take the most likely reagents and perform much more promising experiments that culminate in human trials. The total time to discovery has been cut by more than two thirds, and all attendant costs have declined sharply.

---

[8] Based on "The Innovators: The Rocket Under the High Tech Boom," *Wall Street Journal*, March 30, 1999.

Overall Production Efficiency
A measure of technical and allocative efficiency.

Overall production efficiency is defined as the product of technical, scale, and allocative efficiency. If a 100-percent scale-efficient plant has 93 percent technical efficiency and 85.7 percent allocative efficiency, then its overall production efficiency is $0.93 \times 0.857 = 0.797$, or 79.7 percent. Your job as an operations manager might be to decide which least-cost process Mine 1 in Figure 7.11 should now adopt. Because M_2 and M_3 are both allocatively efficient for 29 tons of output, but process M_2 has experienced technical inefficiency problems resulting in an inability to realize its maximum potential output, Process M_3 would be preferred.

TECHNICAL AND ALLOCATIVE EFFICIENCY IN COMMERCIAL BANKS VERSUS POWER PLANTS[9]

Wave after wave of bank merger activity may be motivated by the potential for substantial improvements in operating efficiency. Combining loan officers, facilities, and deposits of various kinds, the representative commercial bank in the United States produces only 63 percent of the current-status loans (i.e., loans not in default) that the most efficient benchmark banks produce. The problem (and opportunity for improvement) is twofold. First, some banks adopt inefficient processes. Linear programming studies show that allocative efficiency in U.S. commercial banking averages only 81 percent, meaning that the least-cost process is 19 percent cheaper. But one bank may not find another bank's deposit acquisition, borrower screening, or loan monitoring process easy to imitate.

When several banks do manage to adopt identical least-cost processes, yet one produces larger or more current-status loans than the others, the maximum feasible potential output in that type of institution can be identified. Technical efficiency then measures the observed bank output divided by the maximum potential output of a benchmark bank with identical processes. The smaller a bank's comparative output, the lower the technical efficiency. The representative commercial bank in the United States is only 78 percent technically efficient.

Bank takeovers, buyouts, and mergers often result in a concerted effort to improve allocative and technical efficiency. After these restructurings, technical and allocative efficiency often improves enough, the ratio of noninterest operating expenses to total bank income often declines enough, and capitalized value often rises enough to allow recovery of a merger premium of up to 20–30 percent paid by the new owners in excess of the bank's premerger value.

In contrast to this 63 percent overall efficiency problem/opportunity in commercial banking, the overall production efficiency of natural gas-fired power plants averages 87 percent. Some tiny plants with only 99 mwh output are 94 percent efficient, and some giant plants with 1,834 peak output are 92 percent efficient. Deregulation may favor the smaller facilities at the expense of utility company market share, given these results.

Effect of a Change in Input Prices

As shown above, the optimal combination of inputs in both the cost-minimization and output-maximization problems is a function of the relative prices of the inputs, that is, C_L and C_K. As the price of input L rises, one would expect the firm to use less of this input and more of the other input K in the production process, all other things being equal. This shift is demonstrated in Figure 7.12. The firm is interested in minimizing the cost of producing a given quantity of output $Q = 29$. Initially, the prices of inputs are $C_L = \$50$ and $C_K = \$0.20$ resulting in the isocost line $C = 300$. Given these conditions, the firm would operate at tangency Point A—using 4 units of labor input and 500 units of the capital input. Now suppose that the price of labor is increased to $300 itself. This has the effect of increasing the slope of the isocost lines, as shown in the graph. A $300 input budget, before the labor

[9] Based on D. Wheelock and P. Wilson, "Evaluating the Efficiency of Commercial Banks," *St. Louis Federal Reserve Review,* July/August 1995, pp. 39–52, and A. Kleit and D. Terrell, "Measuring Potential Efficiency Gains from Deregulation of Electricity Generation," *Review of Economics and Statistics,* August 2001, pp. 523–550.

Figure 7.12   Effect of a Change in Input Prices

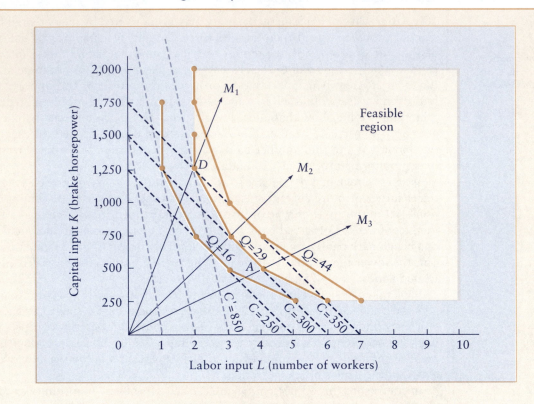

price increase, purchased 1,500-b.h.p. machinery or six workers; now $300 purchases the same 1,500-b.h.p. machine or just one worker. To produce $Q = 29$ units of output at minimum cost, the firm would operate at input combination D using a 1,250-b.h.p. machine and two workers. Cost for 29 tons of ore has risen from $300 to $580 (1,250 $\times$ $0.2 + 2 \times$ $300 = $850), but the cost is far less than if the original process at A had been continued. In that case, cost for 29 tons would have risen from $300 to $1,300 (i.e., 500 $\times$ $0.2 + 4 \times$ $300 = $1,300). Oftentimes, these *input substitution effects* are reinforced by a negative *output effect*—that is, higher input costs are passed through (as higher prices) to consumers who respond by cutting back their consumption. As less output than $Q = 29$ is ordered, the amount of sixfold-more-expensive labor hired may fall substantially below 2 workers.

From this analysis, one can see that as the price of one input increases, the firm will substitute away from this input and use more of the relatively less expensive input. Since the Industrial Revolution, this phenomenon has been observed in the shift toward more capital-intensive production processes (that is, greater use of labor-saving equipment) because the price of labor has increased relative to the price of capital. In 1984, DaimlerChrysler Corporation decided to assemble their most successful product, the minivan, in an automated Canadian factory, in part because of rising union wages and restrictive workplace rules in their Detroit assembly plants. In another case, Audi has begun replacing steel structural components in automobile models like the A8 and A2 with lighter aluminum. High-quality steel costs $500 per ton, and aluminum, which is twice as strong per unit weight, has recently fallen in price from $2,500 to $1,300 per ton. At this reduced price, many aluminum-intensive vehicles are under design at Ford Motor Co.

This and the previous sections have been concerned with the effect on production output of arbitrary changes in either or both of the two inputs and in finding the optimal combination of inputs. The following section examines the effects on output of proportional changes in both inputs simultaneously, in other words, an investigation of the effects of a change in the overall scale of production.

RETURNS TO SCALE

This section begins with a definition of returns to scale, followed by discussions of measurement of returns to scale, homogeneous production functions, and the economic rationale for increasing and decreasing returns to scale.

Definition of Returns to Scale

Returns to Scale
The proportionate increase in output that results from a given proportionate increase in *all* the inputs employed in the production process.

An increase in the scale of production consists of a simultaneous proportionate increase in *all* the inputs used in the production process. The proportionate increase in output that results from the given proportionate increase in all the inputs is defined as the physical **returns to scale.** Suppose, in the Deep Creek Mining Company example, one is interested in determining the effect on the number of tons of ore produced (output) of a 1.50-factor increase in the scale of production from a given labor-capital combination of 4 workers and equipment having 500 b.h.p. A 1.50-factor increase in the scale of production would constitute a labor-capital combination of $4 \times 1.5 = 6$ workers and equipment having $500 \times 1.5 = 750$ b.h.p. From Table 7.1, note that the labor-capital combination of 4 workers and 500 b.h.p. yields 29 tons of output, whereas the combination of 6 workers and 750 b.h.p. yields 60 tons of output. Output has increased by the ratio of $60/29 = 2.07$. Thus, a 1.50-factor increase in input use has resulted in more than a 1.50-factor output increase (specifically, 2.07) in the quantity of output produced. Clearly, this relationship between the proportionate increases in inputs and outputs is not required to be the same for all increases in the scale of production. Another 1.50-factor increase in the scale of production from 6 workers and 500 b.h.p. to 9 workers and 750 b.h.p. results in an increase in output from 55 to 61 tons—an increase by a factor of only 1.10.

Measurement of Returns to Scale

An increase in the scale of production can be represented graphically in a two-dimensional isoquant map, as is shown in Figure 7.13. Increasing the scale of production by a factor of $\lambda = 2$ from the combination of 10_1 units of input L and 100_1 units of input K to 20 units of input L and 200 units of K results in an increase in the quantity of output from $Q^{(1)}$ to $Q^{(2)}$. Three possible relationships that can exist between the increase in inputs and the increase in outputs are as follows:

1. *Increasing* returns to scale: Output increases by *more than* λ; that is, $Q^{(2)} > \lambda Q^{(1)}$.

2. *Decreasing* returns to scale: Output increases by *less than* λ; that is, $Q^{(2)} < \lambda Q^{(1)}$.

Figure 7.13   Production Isoquants Exhibiting Increasing, Decreasing, and Constant Returns to Scale

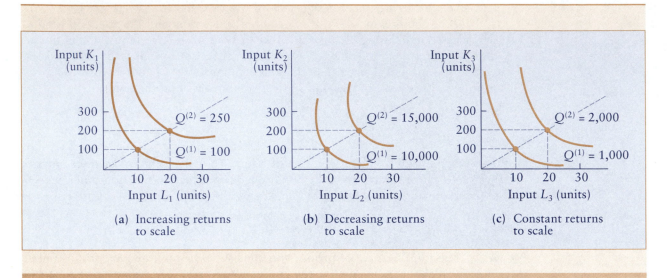

(a) Increasing returns to scale

(b) Decreasing returns to scale

(c) Constant returns to scale

3. *Constant* returns to scale: Output increases by *exactly* λ; that is, $Q^{(2)} = \lambda Q^{(1)}$.

Figure 7.13 illustrates three different production functions that exhibit these three types of returns to scale. In Panel (a), showing increasing returns to scale, doubling input L from 10 to 20 units and input K from 100 to 200 units yields more than double the amount of output—an increase from 100 to 250 units. In Panel (b), showing decreasing returns to scale, a similar doubling of two inputs, L and K, yields less than double the amount of output—an increase from 10,000 to 15,000 units. Finally, in Panel (c), showing constant returns to scale, a similar doubling of inputs L and K yields exactly double the amount of output—an increase from 1,000 to 2,000 units.

Example

INCREASING RETURNS TO SCALE AT THE WELLINGTON COMPANY

Suppose one is interested in determining the returns to scale for the following production function of the Wellington Company:

$$Q = 10LK - 2L^2 - K^2 \qquad [7.19]$$

First, increase each of the inputs by a factor of λ; that is $L' = \lambda L$ and $K' = \lambda K$. Next, substitute these values into the production function as follows:

$$\begin{aligned} Q_0 &= 10(\lambda L)(\lambda K) - 2(\lambda L)^2 - (\lambda K)^2 \\ &= 10\lambda^2 LK - 2\lambda^2 L^2 - \lambda^2 K^2 \\ &= \lambda^2(10LK - 2L^2 - K^2) \\ &= \lambda^2 Q \end{aligned}$$

Because output increases by *more than* λ—by a factor of λ^2—Wellington's production function exhibits *increasing* returns to scale.

Homogeneous Production Functions and Returns to Scale

Many of the algebraic production functions used in analyzing production processes, such as the Cobb-Douglas multiplicative exponential function (Equation 7.1), are said to be homogeneous. Homogeneous functions have certain mathematical properties that make them desirable in modeling production processes. If each input in the production function is multiplied by an arbitrary constant λ and if this constant can be factored out of the function, then the production function is defined as *homogeneous*.

One can also measure the degree of homogeneity of a production function. A production function $Q = f(L,K)$ is said to be *homogeneous of degree n* if

$$f(\lambda L, \lambda K) = \lambda^n f(L,K) \text{ for } \lambda \neq 0 \qquad [7.20]$$

where λ is some constant. The following production function of the Fletcher Company

$$f(L,K) = .6L + .2K \qquad [7.21]$$

is homogeneous of degree 1.0 because

$$\begin{aligned} f(\lambda L, \lambda K) &= .6(\lambda L) + .2(\lambda K) \\ &= \lambda^1(.6L + .2K) \\ &= \lambda^1 f(L,K) \end{aligned}$$

If the degree of homogeneity (n) is equal to 1.0, then the production function is said to be *linearly homogeneous*. In this linear homogeneous case, when one doubles the inputs, output doubles.

The degree of homogeneity (n) indicates the type of returns to scale (i.e., increasing, decreasing, or constant) that characterizes a homogeneous production function. If $n = 1$, as with the Fletcher Co. in Equation 7.21, the production function exhibits constant returns to scale; if $n > 1$ the production function exhibits increasing returns to scale; and if $n < 1$ the production function exhibits decreasing returns to scale. The nonlinear production function of the Wellington Company represented by Equation 7.19, which has a degree of homogeneity (n) equal to 2.0, exhibits increasing returns to scale. Here, when one doubles the inputs ($\lambda = 2$), output increases by a factor of 4 (λ^2).

Increasing and Decreasing Returns to Scale

In addition to satisfying the law of diminishing marginal returns discussed earlier, a firm's production function is often characterized by first increasing and then decreasing physical returns to scale. A number of industrial engineering arguments have been presented to justify this characteristic of the production function. The major argument given for initial increasing returns, as the scale of production is first increased, is the opportunity for *specialization in the use of capital and labor*. As the scale of production is increased, equipment that is more efficient in performing a limited set of tasks can be substituted for less efficient all-purpose equipment. Similarly, the efficiency of workers in performing a small number of related tasks is greater than that of less highly skilled, but more versatile, workers. Practical limits on the degree of specialization, however, may prevent increasing returns from being realized in producing ever-larger quantities of output.

A principal argument given for the existence of decreasing returns to scale is the increasingly complex *problems of coordination and control* faced by management as the scale of production is increased. Limitations on the ability of management to transmit and receive information (such as decisions and reports on performance) may diminish the effectiveness of management in exercising control and coordination of increasingly larger scales of production. As a result, proportionate increases in all of the inputs of the production process, including the input labeled "management," may eventually yield less than proportionate increases in total output.

The Cobb-Douglas Production Function

The Cobb-Douglas production function is a homogeneous function with a degree of homogeneity (n) equal to ($\beta_1 + \beta_2$):

$$Q = \alpha L^{\beta_1} K^{\beta_2} \qquad\qquad [7.22]$$

This can be shown as follows. Multiplying L and K by a constant λ yields

$$
\begin{aligned}
f(\lambda L, \lambda K) &= \alpha(\lambda L)^{\beta_1}(\lambda K)^{\beta_2} \\
&= \alpha(\lambda^{\beta_1} L^{\beta_1})(\lambda^{\beta_2} K^{\beta_2}) \\
&= \lambda^{\beta_1 + \beta_2}(\alpha L^{\beta_1} K^{\beta_2}) \\
&= \lambda^{\beta_1 + \beta_2} f(L, K)
\end{aligned}
$$

Because the exponent of λ is equal to ($\beta_1 + \beta_2$), the degree of homogeneity is equal to ($\beta_1 + \beta_2$). Depending on whether $n = \beta_1 + \beta_2$ is less than, equal to, or greater than 1, the Cobb-Douglas production function will exhibit decreasing, constant, or increasing returns, respectively.

   The multiplicative exponential Cobb-Douglas function can be estimated as a linear regression relation by taking the logarithm of Equation 7.22 to obtain

$$\log Q = \log \alpha + \beta_1 \log L + \beta_2 \log K. \qquad\qquad [7.23]$$

Thus, once the parameters of the Cobb-Douglas model are estimated, the sum of the exponents of the labor (β_1) and capital (β_2) variables can be used to test for the presence of increasing, constant, or decreasing returns to scale.

Empirical Studies of the Cobb-Douglas Production Function

Since the original production function studies of Cobb-Douglas, literally dozens of similar studies have been undertaken.[10] Using time-series data, production functions have been developed for entire economies (for example, the United States, Norway, Finland, and New Zealand); geographical regions (Massachusetts, and Victoria and New South Wales in Australia); and major sectors of the economy (manufacturing, mining, and agriculture). Also, Cobb-Douglas functions have been estimated for various sectors of an economy using cross-sectional industry data (the United States, Australia, and Canada) and for various industries using cross-sectional data on firms within an industry (railroads, coal, clothing, chemicals, electricity, milk, and rice).

   This section examines three production function studies that illustrate the basic methodology used and the type of results obtained: first, a study employing aggregate time-series data on the economy; second, a study using cross-sectional data on individual industries; and third, a study that develops a production function for major league baseball.

---

[10] See R.G. Chambers, *Applied Production Analysis* (New York: Cambridge University Press, 1988).

Example

TIME-SERIES ANALYSIS: U.S. MANUFACTURING SECTOR

In their original study Cobb-Douglas fitted a production function of the form in Equation 7.21 to indices of production Q, labor L, and capital K in the U.S. manufacturing sector for the period from 1899 to 1922. Q was an index of physical volume of manufacturing; L was an index of the average number of employed wage earners only (that is, salaried employees, officials, and working proprietors were excluded); and K was an index of the value of plants, buildings, tools, and machinery reduced to dollars of constant purchasing power. With the sum of the exponents restricted to one (constant returns to scale), the following function was obtained:

$$Q = 1.01 \, L^{.75}K^{.25} \qquad [7.24]$$

In later studies Cobb-Douglas made several modifications that altered their results somewhat. These modifications included revisions in the output and labor indices, removing the secular trend from each index by expressing each yearly index value as a percentage of its overall trend value, and dropping the assumption of constant returns to scale. With these modifications the estimated production function for the manufacturing sector was

$$Q = .84 \, L^{.63}K^{.30} \qquad [7.25]$$

These results are fairly typical of other time-series and cross-sectional production functions developed from data collected on the U.S. manufacturing sector in the early 20th century. A 1-percent increase in labor input results in about a $\frac{2}{3}$-percent increase in output, and a 1-percent increase in capital input results in approximately a $\frac{1}{3}$-percent increase in output. Also, as in this function, the sum of the exponents (that is, elasticities) of the labor and capital variables is typically slightly less than 1. Although this would seem to indicate the presence of decreasing returns to scale in the broadly defined manufacturing sector, statistically speaking the sum of the exponents was not significantly different from 1.0.

Example

CROSS-SECTIONAL ANALYSIS: U.S. MANUFACTURING INDUSTRIES

In a study of more recent vintage, Moroney used cross-sectional data to estimate Cobb-Douglas production functions for 18 U.S. manufacturing industries.[11] Using aggregate data on plants located within each state, the following three-variable model was fitted:

$$Q = \alpha \, L_p^{\beta_1} L_n^{\beta_2} K^{\beta_3} \qquad [7.26]$$

where Q is the value added by the production plants, L_p is production worker work-hours, L_n is nonproduction work-years, and K is gross book values of depreciable and depletable assets.[12] The results for several of the industries are shown in Table 7.4. The sum of the exponents ($\beta_1 + \beta_2 + \beta_3$), that is, elasticities, ranged from a low of .947 for petroleum to a high of 1.109 for furniture. In 13 of the 18 industries studied, the statistical tests showed that the sum of the exponents was not

[11] John R. Moroney, "Cobb-Douglas Production Functions and Returns to Scale in U.S. Manufacturing Industry," *Western Economic Journal* 6, no. 1 (December 1967), pp. 34–51.

[12] "Book values" of assets are the *historic* values of these assets as they appear on the balance sheet of the firm. Book values may differ significantly from current replacement values and hence may overstate or understate the actual amount of capital employed in the firm. Nonproduction workers are management and other staff personnel.

Table 7.4   Production Elasticities for Several Industries

Industry	Capital Elasticity* β_1	Production Worker Elasticity β_2	Nonproduction Worker Elasticity β_3	Sum of Elasticities $\beta_1 + \beta_2 + \beta_3$
Food and beverages	.555 (.121)	.439 (.128)	.076 (.037)	1.070* (.021)
Textiles	.121 (.173)	.549 (.216)	.335 (.086)	1.004 (.024)
Furniture	.205 (.153)	.802 (.186)	.103 (.079)	1.109* (.051)
Petroleum	.308 (.112)	.546 (.222)	.093 (.168)	.947 (.045)
Stone, clay, etc.	.632 (.105)	.032 (.224)	.366 (.201)	1.029 (.045)
Primary metals	.371 (.103)	.077 (.188)	.509 (.164)	.958 (.035)

Number in parentheses below each elasticity coefficient is the standard error.

*Significantly greater than 1.0 at the .05 level (one-tailed test).

Source: John R. Moroney, "Cobb-Douglas Production Functions and Returns to Scale in U.S. Manufacturing Industry," *Western Economic Journal* 6, no. 1 (December 1967), Table 1, p. 46.

significantly different from 1.0. This evidence supports the hypothesis that most manufacturing industries exhibit constant returns to scale.

Example

EMPIRICAL ESTIMATION OF A PRODUCTION FUNCTION FOR MAJOR LEAGUE BASEBALL[13]

Team sports such as major league baseball are similar to other enterprises in that they attempt to provide a product (team victories) by employing various inputs (skills of team members). In acquiring team members through trades, the free agent market, and minor leagues/colleges, the owner is faced with various input trade-offs. For example, a baseball team owner may have to decide whether to trade a starting pitcher to obtain a power hitter or whether to sign a free agent relief pitcher (and release another player from the roster). These decisions are all made in the context of an intuitive baseball production function, possibly subject to various constraints (e.g., budgetary limits, league rules).

In an attempt to quantify the factors that contribute to the team's success, a Cobb-Douglas production function was developed using data from the 26 major league baseball teams in 1977. Output (Q) was measured by team victories. Inputs (X_1, X_2, X_3, etc.) from five different categories were included in the model:

[13] Charles E. Zech, "An Empirical Estimation of a Production Function: The Case of Major League Baseball," *The American Economist*, vol. XXV, no. 2 (Fall 1981), pp. 19–23.

- *Hitting.* This factor involves two different subskills—hitting frequency, as measured by the team *batting average,* and hitting with power, as measured by the team's *home runs.*
- *Running.* One measure of speed is a team's *stolen base total.*
- *Defense.* This factor also involves two subskills—catching those chances that the player is able to reach, as measured by *fielding percentage,* and catching difficult chances that many players would not be able to reach, as measured by *total chances accepted.* Because these two variables are highly correlated with one another (i.e., multicollinear), separate regressions were run with each variable.
- *Pitching.* The most obvious measure of the pitching factor is the team's earned run average (ERA). However, ERA depends not only on pitching skill, but also on the team's defensive skills. A better measure of pure pitching skills is the *strikeouts-to-walks* ratio for the pitching staff.
- *Coaching.* Teams often change managers when they are performing unsatisfactorily, so this is thought to be an important factor. However, the ability of a manager (coach) is difficult to measure. Two different measures are used in this study—the manager's *lifetime won-lost percentage* and *number of years spent managing in the major leagues.* Separate regressions are run with each variable.

Finally, a dummy variable ($NL = 0$, $AL = 1$) was used to control for any differences between leagues, such as the designated hitter rule.

The results of four regressions are shown in Table 7.5. Several conclusions can be drawn from these results:

1. Hitting average contributes almost six times as much as pitching to a team's success. This tends to contradict conventional wisdom, which says that pitching is the most important part of the game.

Table 7.5 Empirical Estimates of Baseball Production Functions

Variable	Equation 1	Equation 2	Equation 3	Equation 4
Constant	.017	.018	.010	.008
League dummy	−.002	−.003	.004	.003
Batting average	2.017*	1.986*	1.969*	1.927*
Home runs	.229*	.299*	.208*	.215*
Stolen bases	.119*	.120*	.110*	.112*
Strikeouts/walks	.343*	.355*	.324*	.334*
Total fielding chances	1.235	1.200		
Fielding percentage			5.62	5.96
Manager W/L percentage		−.003		−.004
Manager years	−.004		−.002	
$\bar{R}^2$ (coef. of determination)	.789	.790	.773	.774

*Statistically significant at the .05 level.
Source: Charles Zech, op. cit.

2. Home runs contribute about twice as much as stolen bases to a team's success.

3. Coaching skills are not significant in any of the regression equations.

4. Defensive skills are not significant in any of the regression equations.

5. Finally, the sums of the statistically significant variables in each of the four equations range from 2.588 to 2.709. Because these are all much greater than 1.0, the baseball production functions examined all exhibit *increasing returns to scale*. Better ballplayers and better managers yield more than proportional increases in games won.

SUMMARY

- A *production function* is a schedule, graph, or mathematical model relating the maximum quantity of output that can be produced from various quantities of inputs.

- For a production function with one variable input, the *marginal product* is defined as the incremental change in total output that can be produced by the use of one more unit of the variable input in the production process.

- For a production function with one variable input, the *average product* is defined as the ratio of total output to the amount of the variable input used in producing the output.

- The *law of diminishing marginal returns* states that, with all other productive factors held constant, the use of increasing amounts of the variable factor in the production process beyond some point will result in diminishing marginal increases in total output. *Increasing returns* can arise with *network effects*.

- In the short run, with one of the productive factors fixed, the optimal output level (and optimal level of the variable input) occurs where marginal revenue product equals marginal factor cost. *Marginal revenue product* is defined as the amount that an additional unit of the variable input adds to total revenue. *Marginal factor cost* is defined as the amount that an additional unit of the variable input adds to total cost.

- A *production isoquant* is either a geometric curve or algebraic function representing all the various combinations of inputs that can be used in producing a given level of output.

- The *marginal rate of technical substitution* is the rate at which one input may be substituted for another input in the production process, while total output remains constant. It is equal to the ratio of the marginal products of the two inputs.

- In the long run, with both inputs being variable, minimizing cost subject to an output constraint (or maximizing output subject to a cost constraint) requires that the production process be operated at the point where the marginal product per dollar input cost of each factor is equal.

- The degree of *technical efficiency* of a production process is the ratio of observed output to the maximum potentially feasible output for that process, given the same inputs.

- The degree of *allocative efficiency* of a production process is the ratio of total cost for producing a given output level with the least cost process to the observed total cost of producing that output.

- Physical *returns to scale* is defined as the proportionate increase in the output of a production process that results from a given proportionate increase in all the inputs.
- The Cobb-Douglas production function, which is used extensively in empirical studies, is a multiplicative exponential function in which output is a (nonlinear) monotonically increasing function of each of the inputs.
- The Cobb-Douglas production function has various properties that allow one to draw conclusions, based on parameter estimates, about returns to scale.

EXERCISES

1. In the Deep Creek Mining Company example described in this chapter (Table 7.1), suppose again that labor is the variable input and capital is the fixed input. Specifically, assume that the firm owns a piece of equipment having a 500-b.h.p. rating.

    a. Complete the following table:

Labor Input L (No. of Workers)	Total Product $TP_L\ (= Q)$	Marginal Product MP_L	Average Product AP_L	Elasticity of Production E_L
1	___	___	___	___
2	___	___	___	___
3	___	___	___	___
4	___	___	___	___
5	___	___	___	___
6	___	___	___	___
7	___	___	___	___
8	___	___	___	___
9	___	___	___	___
10	___	___	___	___

    b. Plot the (i) total product, (ii) marginal product, and (iii) average product functions.

    c. Determine the boundaries of the three stages of production.

2. From your knowledge of the relationships among the various production functions, complete the following table:

Variable Input L	Total Product $TP_L\ (= Q)$	Average Product AP_L	Marginal Product MP_L
0	0	–	–
1	___	___	8
2	28	___	___
3	___	18	___
4	___	___	26
5	___	20	___
6	108	___	___
7	___	___	−10

3. Suppose the short-run total product curve (TP_L) is a linear function of the variable input over some range of values. Determine the shape of the corresponding marginal product (MP_L) and average product (AP_L) functions.

4. The amount of fish caught per week on a trawler is a function of the crew size assigned to operate the boat. Based on past data, the following production schedule was developed:

Crew Size (Number of Men)	Amount of Fish Caught per Week (Hundreds of Pounds)
2	3
3	6
4	11
5	19
6	24
7	28
8	31
9	33
10	34
11	34
12	33

a. Over what ranges of workers are there (i) increasing, (ii) constant, (iii) decreasing, and (iv) negative returns?

b. How large a crew should be used if the trawler owner is interested in maximizing the total amount of fish caught?

c. How large a crew should be used if the trawler owner is interested in maximizing the average amount of fish caught per person?

5. Consider Exercise 4 again. Suppose the owner of the trawler can sell all the fish he can catch for $75 per 100 pounds and can hire as many crew members as he wants by paying them $150 per week. Assuming that the owner of the trawler is interested in maximizing profits, determine the optimal crew size.

6. Consider the following short-run production function (where L = variable input, Q = output):

$$Q = 6L^2 - .4L^3$$

a. Determine the marginal product function (MP_L).

b. Determine the average product function (AP_L).

c. Find the value of L that maximizes Q.

d. Find the value of L at which the marginal product function takes on its maximum value.

e. Find the value of L at which the average product function takes on its maximum value.

f. Plot the (i) total, (ii) marginal, and (iii) average product functions for values of $L = 0, 1, 2, 3, \ldots, 12$.

7. Consider the following short-run production function (where L = variable input, Q = output):

$$Q = 10L - .5L^2$$

Suppose that output can be sold for $10 per unit. Also assume that the firm can obtain as much of the variable input (L) as it needs at $20 per unit.

a. Determine the marginal revenue product function.

b. Determine the marginal factor cost function.

c. Determine the optimal value of L, given that the objective is to maximize profits.

8. In the Deep Creek Mining Company example described in this chapter (Table 7.1), suppose one is interested in maximizing output subject to a cost constraint. Assume that the per-unit prices of labor and capital are $45 and $.24 respectively. Total costs (the sum of labor and capital costs) are constrained to $360 or less.

a. Using graphical isoquant-isocost analysis, determine the optimal combination of labor and capital to employ in the ore-mining process and the optimal output level.

b. Determine the optimal combination of labor and capital and optimal output level if the per-unit prices of labor and capital are $60 and $.18, respectively.

9. Suppose that as the result of recent labor negotiations, wage rates are *reduced* by 10 percent in a production process employing only capital and labor. Assuming that other conditions (for example, productivity) remain constant, determine what effect this decrease will have on the desired proportions of capital and labor used in producing the given level of output at minimum total cost. Illustrate your answer with an isoquant-isocost diagram.

10. The production schedule below was developed for a production process (where the entries represent output measured in units):

Labor Input L (Worker Hours)	Capital Input K (Machine Hours)							
	1	2	3	4	5	6	7	8
1	39	55	69	81	91	99	105	109
2	57	72	86	96	105	112	117	120
3	73	88	99	109	117	123	127	129
4	87	100	111	120	127	132	135	136
5	99	111	121	129	135	139	141	141
6	109	120	129	136	141	144	145	144
7	117	127	135	141	145	147	147	145
8	123	132	139	144	147	148	147	144
9	127	135	141	145	147	147	145	141
10	129	136	141	144	145	144	141	136

a. Plot isoquants for 99, 109, 117, 129, 136, 141, 145, and 147 units of output.

b. Assume that labor costs are $10 per worker hour and machine costs are $15 per machine hour. Determine the maximum output that can be obtained given a cost constraint of $120.

11. A firm uses two variable inputs, labor (L) and raw materials (M), in producing its output. At its current level of output:

$$C_L = \$10/\text{unit} \qquad MP_L = 25$$
$$C_M = \$2/\text{unit} \qquad MP_M = 4$$

a. Determine whether the firm is operating efficiently, given that its objective is to minimize the cost of producing the given level of output.

b. Determine what changes (if any) in the relative proportions of labor and raw materials need to be made to operate efficiently.

12. Suppose that a firm's production function is given by the following relationship:

$$Q = 2.5 \sqrt{LK} \qquad (\text{i.e., } Q = 2.5L^{.5}K^{.5})$$

where Q = output
    L = labor input
    K = capital input

a. Determine the percentage increase in output if labor input is increased by 10 percent (assuming that capital input is held constant).

b. Determine the percentage increase in output if capital input is increased by 25 percent (assuming that labor input is held constant).

c. Determine the percentage increase in output if *both* labor and capital are increased by 20 percent.

13. Based on the production function parameter estimates reported in Table 7.4:

a. Which industry (or industries) appears to exhibit decreasing returns to scale (ignore the issue of statistical significance)?

b. Which industry comes closest to exhibiting constant returns to scale?

c. In which industry will a given percentage increase in capital result in the largest percentage increase in output?

d. In what industry will a given percentage increase in production workers result in the largest percentage increase in output?

14. Given the following production function:

$$Q = 1.40L^{.70}K^{.35}$$

a. Determine the elasticity of production with respect to

    (i)   Labor (L)
    (ii) Capital (K)

b. Give an economic interpretation of each value determined in Part (a).

15. Consider the following Cobb-Douglas production function for the bus transportation system in a particular city:

$$Q = \alpha L^{\beta_1}F^{\beta_2}K^{\beta_3}$$

where L = labor input in worker hours
    F = fuel input in gallons
    K = capital input in number of buses
    Q = output measured in millions of bus miles

Suppose that the parameters (α, β_1, β_2, and β_3) of this model were estimated using annual data for the past 25 years. The following results were obtained:

$$\alpha = .0012 \qquad \beta_1 = .45 \qquad \beta_2 = .20 \qquad \beta_3 = .30$$

a.   Determine the (i) labor, (ii) fuel, and (iii) capital-input production elasticities.

b.   Suppose that labor input (worker hours) is increased by 2 percent next year (with the other inputs held constant). Determine the approximate percentage change in output.

c.   Suppose that capital input (number of buses) is decreased by 3 percent next year (that is, certain older buses are taken out of service). Assuming that the other inputs are held constant, determine the approximate percentage change in output.

d.   What type of returns to scale appears to characterize this bus transportation system (ignore the issue of statistical significance)?

e.   Discuss some of the methodological and measurement problems one might encounter in using time-series data to estimate the parameters of this model.

16. Determine whether each of the following production functions exhibits increasing, constant, or decreasing returns to scale:

a. $Q = 1.5L^{.70}K^{.30}$

b. $Q = .4L + .5K$

c. $Q = 2.0LK$

d. $Q = 1.0L^{.6}K^{.5}$

17. Determine if the following production functions are homogeneous and, if so, the degree of homogeneity:

a. $Q = 2L^{.7} + 3K^{.7}$

b. $Q = 2L^{.5}K^{.5}$

c. $Q = \dfrac{2L^3 + 3K^3}{6L^2 - 2K^2}$

d. $Q = 3L^2K^2 - .1L^3K^3$

e. $Q = 2L^{.8} + 3K^{.7}$

18. Show that elasticity of production for capital input is constant and equal to β_2 for the Cobb-Douglas production function (Equation 7.22).

19. *Extension of the Cobb-Douglas Production Function*—The Cobb-Douglas production function (Equation 7.22) can be shown to be a special case of a larger class of production functions having the following mathematical form:[14]

$$Q = \gamma[\partial K^{-\rho} + (1 - \partial)L^{-\rho}]^{-\nu/\rho}$$

where γ is an efficiency parameter which shows the output that results from given quantities of inputs; ∂ is a distribution parameter ($0 \le \partial \le 1$) that indicates the division of factor income between capital and labor; ρ is a substitution parameter that is a measure of substitutability of capital for labor (or vice versa) in the production process; and ν is a scale parameter ($\nu > 0$) that indicates the type of returns to scale (increasing, constant, or decreasing). Show that when $\nu = 1$, this function exhibits constant returns to scale. (*Hint:* Increase

---

[14] See R.G. Chambers, *Applied Production Analysis* (Cambridge: Cambridge University Press, 1988).

capital K and labor L each by a factor of λ—$K^* = (\lambda)K$ and $L^* = (\lambda)L$—and show that output Q also increases by a factor of λ-$Q^* = (\lambda)(Q)$.)

20. Lobo Lighting Corporation currently employs 100 unskilled laborers, 80 factory technicians, 30 skilled machinists, and 40 skilled electricians. Lobo feels that the marginal product of the last unskilled laborer is 400 lights per week, the marginal product of the last factory technician is 450 lights per week, the marginal product of the last skilled machinist is 550 lights per week, and the marginal product of the last skilled electrician is 600 lights per week. Unskilled laborers earn $400 per week, factory technicians earn $500 per week, machinists earn $700 per week, and electricians earn $750 per week.

    Is Lobo using the lowest cost combination of workers to produce its targeted output? If not, what recommendations can you make to assist the company?

21. Consider the following short-run cubic production functions, holding constant the firm's capital inputs:

$$Q = -0.005\,L^3 + 0.30L^2$$

where: Q = units of output

   L = units of labor input

   a. What output is produced when $L = 0$?
   b. What is the average product of labor?
   c. What is the marginal product of labor?
   d. At what level of labor input is the marginal product of labor maximized?
   e. At what level of labor input is the marginal product of labor equal to the average product of labor? What happens to total product of labor at this point?

http://
Electric Utility Deregulation

22. Access the Internet site maintained by Strategic Energy Ltd: http://www.sel.com/SE_Frames.html. Research the status of electric utility deregulation in your state. Find out how deregulation has affected plant-level economies of scale in electricity generation.

CASE EXERCISE   PRODUCTION FUNCTION: WILSON COMPANY

Economists at the Wilson Company are interested in developing a production function for fertilizer plants. They have collected data on 15 different plants that produce fertilizer (see the following page).

QUESTIONS

1. Estimate the Cobb-Douglas production function $Q = \alpha L^{\beta_1} K^{\beta_2}$ where Q = output; L = labor input; K = capital input; and α, β_1, and β_2 are the parameters to be estimated. (*Note:* If the regression program on your computer does not have a logarithmic transformation, manually transform the preceding data into the logarithms before entering the data into the computer.)

2. Test whether the coefficients of capital and labor are statistically significant.

3. Determine the percentage of the variation in output that is "explained" by the regression equation.

4. Determine the labor and capital production elasticities and give an economic interpretation of each value.

5. Determine whether this production function exhibits increasing, decreasing, or constant returns to scale (ignore the issue of statistical significance).

Plant	Output (000 Tons)	Capital ($000)	Labor (000 Worker Hours)
1	605.3	18,891	700.2
2	566.1	19,201	651.8
3	647.1	20,655	822.9
4	523.7	15,082	650.3
5	712.3	20,300	859.0
6	487.5	16,079	613.0
7	761.6	24,194	851.3
8	442.5	11,504	655.4
9	821.1	25,970	900.6
10	397.8	10,127	550.4
11	896.7	25,622	842.2
12	359.3	12,477	540.5
13	979.1	24,002	949.4
14	331.7	8,042	575.7
15	1064.9	23,972	925.8

Appendix 7a

Maximization of Production Output Subject to a Cost Constraint

Using graphical analysis, we illustrated in the chapter that the following condition (Equation 7.18)

$$\frac{MP_L}{C_L} = \frac{MP_K}{C_K}$$

must be satisfied in determining the combination of inputs (L and K) that minimizes total cost subject to an output constraint. It turns out that the same result arises in maximizing output subject to a cost constraint, the mathematical dual of the earlier constrained minimization problem.

Given the production function to identify potential output possibilities,

$$Q = f(L,K) \tag{7A.1}$$

and the cost constraint

$$C = C_L L + C_K K \tag{7A.2}$$

we define an artificial variable λ (lambda) and form the Lagrangian function

$$L_Q = Q - \lambda(C_L L + C_K K - C) \tag{7A.3}$$

Differentiating L_Q with respect to L, K, and λ and setting the (partial) derivatives equal to zero (condition for a maximum) yields

$$\frac{\partial L_Q}{\partial L} = \frac{\partial f(L,K)}{\partial L} - \lambda C_L = 0 \tag{7A.4}$$

$$\frac{\partial L_Q}{\partial K} = \frac{\partial f(L,K)}{\partial K} - \lambda C_K - 0 \tag{7A.5}$$

$$\frac{\partial L_Q}{\partial \lambda} = C_L L + C_K K - C = 0 \tag{7A.6}$$

Recognizing that $\dfrac{\partial f(L,K)}{\partial L} = MP_L$ and $\dfrac{\partial f(L,K)}{\partial K} = MP_K$, solve Equations 7A.4 and 7A.5 for λ yields

$$\lambda = \frac{MP_L}{C_L} \tag{7A.7}$$

$$\lambda = \frac{MP_K}{C_K} \tag{7A.8}$$

Setting Equations 7A.7 and 7A.8 equal to each other gives the optimality condition

$$\frac{MP_L}{C_L} = \frac{MP_K}{C_K} \tag{7A.9}$$

EXERCISE

1. The output (Q) of a production process is a function of two inputs (L and K) and is given by the following relationship:

$$Q = .50LK - .10L^2 - .05K^2$$

The per-unit prices of inputs L and K are \$20 and \$25, respectively. The firm is interested in maximizing output subject to a cost constraint of \$500.

a. Formulate the Lagrangian function:
$$L_Q = Q - \lambda(C_L L + C_K K - C)$$

b. Take the partial derivatives of L_Q with respect to L, K, and λ, and set them equal to zero.

c. Solve the set of simultaneous equations in Part (b) for the optimal values of L, K, and λ.

d. Based on your answers to Part (c), how many units of L and K should be used by the firm? What is the total output of this combination?

e. Give an economic interpretation of the λ value determined in Part (c).

f. Check to see if the optimality condition (Equation 7A.9) is satisfied for the solution obtained above.

Production Decisions and Linear Programming

Appendix 7A developed the duality between input cost minimization subject to an output constraint and output maximization subject to an input budget constraint using calculus techniques. But as we saw in Chapter 7, not all production decisions are well suited to the smooth functions and marginal choices calculus was designed to analyze. Instead, some production decisions necessitate discrete choices of machinery (e.g., mining equipment or aircraft of various sizes) involved in a fixed proportions production process. For those production decisions, linear programming analysis is more appropriate.

Figure 7.12 illustrated the linear programming approach using graphs to solve a plant manager's constrained cost minimization problem. This appendix again uses graphs to solve the dual, a constrained output maximization problem. When stated in this form, the production isoquant framework can be used to illustrate optimal input substitution (refer again to Equation 7.18) as a practical, real-world choice between alternative production processes.

ALGEBRAIC FORMULATION OF THE CONSTRAINED OUTPUT-MAXIMIZATION PROBLEM

Lumins Lamp Company can employ capital (machine-hours) and labor (work-hours) in any of three different production processes (P_1, P_2, and P_3) to manufacture a certain type of lamp. Each process involves a different combination of labor and capital—process P_1 requires 1 machine-hour of capital and 4 work-hours of labor to produce each lamp; process P_2 requires 2 machine-hours and 2 work-hours to produce each lamp; and process P_3 requires 5 machine-hours and 1 work-hour to produce each lamp. But only 5 machine-hours of capital and 8 work-hours of labor are available per day to manufacture these lamps.

Define Q_1, Q_2, and Q_3 to be the number of lamps produced per day by Processes P_1, P_2, and P_3, respectively. Given that the objective is to maximize output subject to the input (capital and labor) constraints, the problem can be formulated in the linear-programming framework as follows:

Max	$Q_1 + Q_2 + Q_3$	(objective function)	[7B.1]
Subject to	$Q_1 + 2Q_2 + 5Q_3 \leq 5$	(capital constraint)	[7B.2]
	$4Q_1 + 2Q_2 + Q_3 \leq 8$	(labor constraint)	[7B.3]
	$Q_1, Q_2, Q_3, \geq 0$	(nonnegativity constraint)	[7B.4]

The objective function represents the total output from the three production processes. The first two constraints represent the respective limitations on the inputs available to operate the three production processes. The coefficients of the Q_i variables in these constraints represent the number of units of the given resource required to manufacture one lamp by the ith production process. For example, the coefficient of Q_3 in the capital constraint indicates that 5 machine-hours of capital are required to produce one lamp using Process P_3. The other coefficients have similar interpretations. The final constraint rules out negative production quantities.

GRAPHICAL REPRESENTATION AND SOLUTION OF THE OUTPUT-MAXIMIZATION PROBLEM

The linear-programming problem just described can be illustrated and solved graphically, using *process rays* to represent the production processes, *production isoquants* to represent the objective function, and a *feasible region* to represent the resource constraints.

Each production process is assumed to exhibit *constant returns to scale*. This means that output along each ray increases proportionately with increases in the inputs. For example, at Point A on Process Ray P_1 in Figure 7B.1, one machine-hour of capital and four work-hours of labor are used to produce one unit of output. Doubling the amount of capital and labor yields two units of output (Point B), and tripling the amount of capital and labor yields three units of output (Point C).

The production isoquants for the example problem can be constructed by drawing straight lines between the points of equal output on *adjacent* process rays. Four production isoquants representing output levels Q of 1, 2, 3, and 4 lamps,

FIGURE 7B.1

Alternative Production Processes as Represented by Process Rays

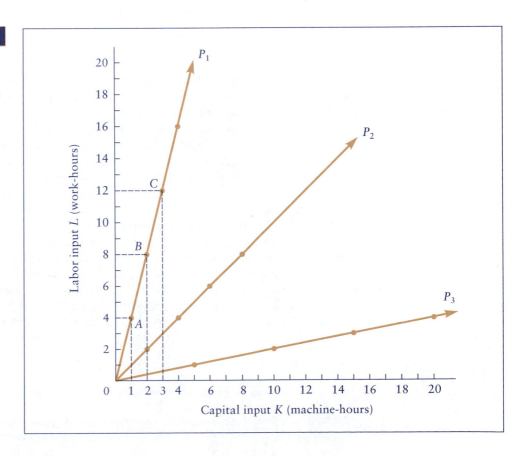

FIGURE 7B.2

Production Isoquants

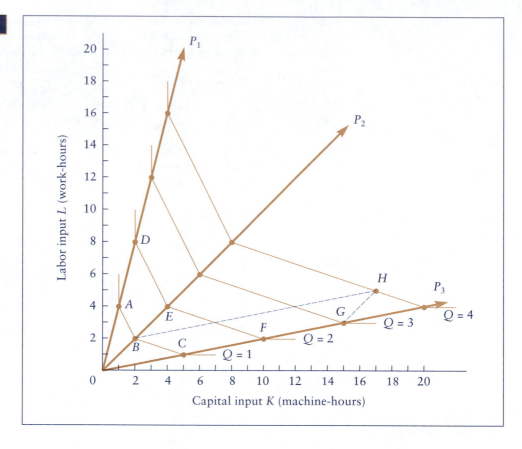

respectively, are shown in Figure 7B.2.[15] Note that these linear-programming production isoquants have the same basic shape as the isoquants of production theory. Note also that the linear-programming production isoquants have parallel line segments between adjacent process rays. For example, line segment *AB* is parallel to *DE*, and line segment *BC* is parallel to *EF*. This occurs because the coefficients of the Q_i variables in the resource constraints are constants.

As indicated earlier, points *along* each process ray represent the output obtained if the two inputs (labor and capital) are combined in the ratio of the respective number of units of each resource required to produce a given unit of output. However, the points that lie on isoquants *between* adjacent process rays have a slightly different interpretation. These points represent a combination of output from each of the adjacent production processes. For example, Point *H* on the "*Q* = 4" isoquant in Figure 7B.2 represents a production combination using both Processes P_2 and P_3. The quantity of output that is produced by each process can be obtained by constructing a parallelogram such as the one shown in Figure 7B.2.[16] A line is drawn from Point *H* parallel to Process Ray P_2, intersecting Process Ray P_3 at Point *G*. Another line is drawn from Point *H* parallel to Process Ray P_3, intersecting Process Ray P_2 at

---

[15] Production isoquants for *noninteger* output levels also can be constructed, although none are shown here.

[16] See William J. Baumol, *Economic Theory and Operations Analysis,* 4th ed. (Englewood Cliffs, NJ: Prentice-Hall, 1977), footnote 5, p. 305, for a geometrical proof of this assertion.

point B. From the parallelogram $0BHG$, we can determine both the quantity of output produced by each process and the respective amount of inputs used in each process.

In this case, the firm should produce one unit of output using P_2, because Point B is on the "$Q = 1$" isoquant, and three units of output using Process P_3, because Point G is on the "$Q = 3$" isoquant. This combination will yield the four units of output. At Point B, 2 machine-hours of capital and 2 work-hours of labor are used in Process P_2; and at Point G, 15 machine-hours of capital and 3 work-hours of labor are used in Process P_3. Total capital and labor resources used in producing the 4 units of output are 17 machine-hours and 5 work-hours, respectively. All other points that lie between process rays can be interpreted in a similar manner.

Feasible Region

The feasible region consists of all the capital and labor input combinations that simultaneously satisfy all constraints of the linear-programming problem. The shaded parallelogram $0ABC$ shown in Figure 7B.3 represents the feasible region for the example problem. Because a maximum of 5 machine-hours of capital is available per day to produce lamps, only input combinations on or to the left of the BC line represent possible solutions to the linear-programming problem. Similarly, because a maximum of 8 work-hours of labor is available per day, possible solutions must lie on or below the AB line.

FIGURE 7B.3

Solution of Output-Maximization Problem

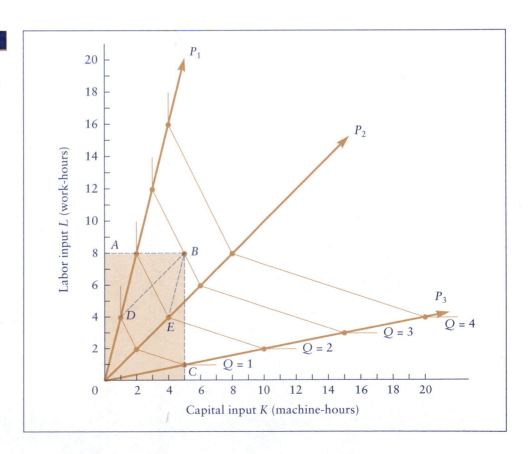

Optimal Solution Combining Two Fixed Proportions Processes[17]

The combination of production processes that maximizes output subject to the resource constraints occurs at the point on the boundary of the feasible region that lies on the highest production isoquant. For the example problem shown in Figure 7B.3, the optimal solution occurs at Point B. At Point B, three units of output (lamps) are obtained by using 5 machine-hours of capital and 8 work-hours of labor. Constructing the parallelogram $0DBE$ shows that one unit of output should be produced using Process P_1 and two units of output using Process P_2. Production Process P_1 should employ 1 machine-hour of capital and 4 work-hours of labor, and Process P_2 should use 4 machine-hours of capital and 4 work-hours of labor.

EXERCISE

1. In the Lumins Lamp Company output-maximization problem described in this appendix, assume that production resources are limited to 14 machine-hours of capital and 6 work-hours of labor.

    a. Formulate the problem algebraically in the linear-programming framework.

    b. Determine graphically the optimal amount of resources (capital and labor) to employ in each of the production processes and the total output to be obtained.

---

[17] This same optimal solution combining two processes can also be obtained algebraically using the simplex (or related) methods. See Web Chapter B on linear programming techniques.

8

Cost Analysis

CHAPTER PREVIEW Economic cost refers to the cost of attracting a resource from its next best alternative use (the opportunity cost concept). Managers seeking to make the most efficient use of resources to maximize value must be concerned with both short-run and long-run opportunity costs. Short-run cost-output relationships help managers to plan for the most profitable level of output, given the capital resources that are immediately available. Long-run cost-output relationships involve attracting additional capital to expand or contract the plant size and the scale of operations.

MANAGERIAL CHALLENGE

US Airways' Cost Structure

US Airways Corporation (USAir) was formed through the merger of several diverse regional airlines, including Allegheny, Mohawk, Lake Central, Pacific Southwest, and Piedmont Airlines. Although these mergers led to a "national" competitor in the airline industry, USAir's market strength was in the Northeast, where it faced relatively little direct competition. In 1994, USAir had a major or dominant presence in Pittsburgh, Charlotte, Philadelphia, the Baltimore/Washington area, New York, and Boston.

US Airways possesses a diverse fleet of aircraft, unlike the much more successful Southwest Airlines, which flies only one type of plane, the Boeing 737. This diversity results in higher costs of maintenance and crew training and a much more complex crew scheduling problem. In addition, USAir is burdened with very restrictive work rules that increase labor costs, which account for 40 percent of operating costs. The net result is that USAir's cost per available seat mile is the highest in the industry—in excess of 11 cents per available seat mile. This compares to a cost of slightly over 9 cents for United Airlines, about 7.5 cents for Continental Airlines, and 7 cents for Southwest.

Because of the traditionally weak competition in its Northeast market stronghold, USAir had the highest average passenger fare received for each revenue passenger mile flown: 18.8 cents, compared with 14.21 cents for United, 15.18 cents for American, 12.76 cents for Continental, and 12.37 cents for Southwest.

The combination of high fares and very high costs per available seat mile invited competition.

After emerging from bankruptcy with a new, lower cost structure, Continental announced a major restructuring of its route system to compete head on with USAir in much of its core business area. In addition, Southwest Air began to enter some of USAir's traditional markets (particularly Baltimore/Washington). Since 1995, the combination of this competitive pressure and USAir's own very high costs led to mounting losses that threatened its viability as an ongoing enterprise. Stockholder equity tumbled from a high of $15 per share to less than $1 per share.

As a result of massive losses due to the downturn in travel after September 11, 2001, and its high cost structure, USAir declared bankruptcy in 2002. After taking various steps to reduce costs, including negotiating lower wage contracts with its employee unions, the carrier emerged from bankruptcy in 2003. Cost control is a difficult problem in any corporation. It is, however, especially difficult in a heavily-unionized capital-intensive industry such as airlines.

In this chapter we consider many of the important cost relationships that are essential to a firm's long-term competitive success.

http://

The Air Transport Association of America has produced an on-line airline handbook about airline economics and costs. The web address is
http://www.air-transport.org/public/handbook/default.htm

The Meaning and Measurement of Cost

In its most elementary form, cost simply refers to the sacrifice incurred whenever an exchange or transformation of resources takes place. This association between forgone opportunities and economic cost applies in all circumstances. However, the appropriate manner to measure costs is a function of the purpose for which the information is to be used.

Accounting Versus Economic Costs

Accountants have been primarily concerned with measuring costs for *financial reporting purposes*. As a result, they define and measure cost by the *historical outlay of funds* that takes place in the exchange or transformation of a resource. Thus, whenever *A* sells a product or commodity to *B*, the *price* paid by *B*, expressed in dollars, measures the accounting cost of the product to *B*. When *A* exchanges labor services for money or other items of value, the *wages* that *A* receives represent the accounting cost of *A*'s services to the employer. Similarly, the *interest* paid to the bondholder or lending institution is used to measure the accounting cost of funds to the borrower.

Economists have been mainly concerned with measuring costs for *decision-making purposes*. The objective is to determine the present and future costs of resources associated with various alternative courses of action. Such an objective requires a consideration of the opportunities forgone (or sacrificed) whenever a resource is used in a given course of action. So, although both the accounting cost and the economic cost of a product will include such *explicit* costs as labor, raw materials, supplies, rent, interest, and utilities, economists will also include the **opportunity costs** of time and capital that the owner-manager has invested in the enterprise. The opportunity cost of the owner's time is measured by the most attractive salary or other form of compensation that the owner could have received by applying his or her talents, skills, and experience in the management of a similar (but second-best) business owned by someone else. Similarly, the opportunity cost of the capital is measured by the profit or return that could have been received if the owner had chosen to employ capital in the second-best (alternative) investment of comparable risk.

Opportunity Costs
The value of a resource in its next best alternative use. Opportunity cost represents the return or compensation that must be forgone as the result of the decision to employ the resource in a given economic activity.

Example

Opportunity Costs at Bentley Clothing Store

Robert Bentley owns and operates the Bentley Clothing Store. A traditional income statement for the business is shown in Panel (a) of Table 8.1. The mortgage on the store has been paid and therefore no interest expenses are shown on the income statement. Also, the building has been fully depreciated and thus no depreciation charges are shown. From an *accounting* standpoint and from the perspective of the Internal Revenue Service, Bentley is earning a *positive accounting profit* of $190,000 (before taxes).

However, consider the store's profitability from an *economic* standpoint. Economic profit is defined as the difference between total revenues and total economic costs. Algebraically, economic profit is given by

$$\text{Economic profit} = \text{Total revenues} - \text{Explicit costs} - \text{Implicit costs} \qquad [8.1]$$

As indicated earlier in the chapter, implicit costs include the opportunity costs of time and capital that the entrepreneur has invested in the firm. Suppose that Bentley could

Table 8.1 Profitability of Bentley Clothing Store

(a) Accounting Income Statement

Net sales		$650,000
Less: Cost of goods sold		250,000
Gross profit		400,000
Less: Expenses		
Employee compensation*	150,000	
Advertising	30,000	
Utilities and maintenance	20,000	
Miscellaneous	10,000	
Total		210,000
Net profit before taxes		$190,000

(b) Economic Profit Statement

Total revenues		$650,000
Less: Explicit costs		
Cost of goods sold	250,000	
Employee compensation*	150,000	
Advertising	30,000	
Utilities and maintenance	20,000	
Miscellaneous	10,000	
Total		460,000
Accounting profit before taxes		190,000
Less: Implicit costs		
Salary (manager)	130,000	
Rent on building	88,000	
Total		218,000
Economic profit (or loss) before taxes		($ 28,000)

*Employee compensation does not include any salary to Robert Bentley.

go to work as a clothing department manager for a large department or specialty store chain and receive a salary of $130,000 per year. Also assume that Bentley could rent his building to another merchant for $88,000 (net) per year. Under these conditions, as shown in Panel (b) of Table 8.1, Bentley is earning a *negative economic profit* (−$28,000 before taxes). By renting his store to another merchant and going to work as manager of a different store, he could make $28,000 more than he is currently earning from his clothing store business. Thus, accounting profits, which do not include opportunity costs, are not always a valid indication of the economic profitability (or loss) of an enterprise.

When one recognizes that such first-best and second-best uses change over time, it becomes clear that the historical outlay of funds to obtain a resource at an earlier date (the accounting cost basis) may not be the appropriate measure of opportunity cost in a decision problem today. For example, consider the following three cases of a substantive distinction between economic cost and accounting cost.

Capital Asset
A durable input that depreciates with use, time, and obsolescence.

Depreciation Cost Measurement   The production of a good or service typically requires the use of licenses and plant and equipment. As these **capital assets** are used, their service life is expended; the assets wear out or become obsolete. Depreciation is the cost of using these assets in producing the given output. If the Phillips Tool Company owns a machine that has a current market value of $8,000 and is expected to have a value of $6,800 after one more year of use, then the opportunity cost of using the machine for one year (the economist's measure of depreciation cost) is $8,000 − $6,800 = $1,200. Assuming that 2,000 units of output were produced during the year, the depreciation cost would be $1,200 ÷ 2,000 units = $.60 per unit.

Unfortunately, it is often very difficult, if not impossible, to determine the service life of a capital asset and the future changes in its market value.[1] Some assets are unique (patents); others are not traded in liquid resale markets (plants); and still others are rendered obsolete with little predictability (computers). To overcome these measurement problems with economic depreciation cost, accountants have adopted certain procedures for allocating a portion of the acquisition cost of an asset to each accounting time period, and in turn to each unit of output that is produced within that time period. This is typically done by estimating the service life of the asset and then arbitrarily assigning a portion of the historical cost of the asset against income during each year of the service life. If the machine is purchased by Phillips for $10,000 and is expected to have a 10-year life and no salvage value, the straight-line method of depreciation[2] ($10,000 ÷ 10 = $1,000) would calculate the depreciation cost of this asset each year. Assuming that 2,000 units of output are produced in a given year, then $1,000 ÷ 2,000 = $.50 would be allocated to the cost of each unit produced by Phillips. Note from this example that the straight-line method described for allocating depreciation costs is arbitrary, and the calculated accounting depreciation cost does not equal the economic depreciation cost actually incurred, if in fact the market value of the machine drops to $6,800 after one year.

Inventory Valuation   Whenever materials are stored in inventory for a period of time before being used in the production process, the accounting and economic costs may differ if the market price of these materials has changed from the original purchase price. The accounting cost is equal to the actual *acquisition* cost, whereas the economic cost is equal to the current *replacement* cost. As the following example illustrates, the use of the acquisition cost can lead to incorrect production decisions.

---

[1] This concept of the future cost of the partially consumed asset is termed the *replacement cost* of the asset rather than the *historical acquisition cost* of the asset.

[2] The *straight-line* depreciation method allocates an equal amount of the cost of the asset to each period during the life of the asset. Other *accelerated* depreciation methods are also used.

Example

INVENTORY VALUATION AT WESTSIDE PLUMBING AND HEATING

Westside Plumbing and Heating Company is offered a contract for $100,000 to provide the plumbing for a new building. The labor and equipment costs are calculated to be $60,000 for fulfilling the contract. Westside has the materials in inventory to complete the job. The materials originally cost the firm $50,000; however, prices have since declined and the materials could now be purchased for $37,500. Material prices are not expected to increase in the near future and hence no gains can be anticipated from holding the materials in inventory. The question is: Should Westside accept the contract? An analysis of the contract under both methods for measuring the cost of the materials is shown in Table 8.2. Assuming that the materials are valued at the acquisition cost, the firm should not accept the contract because an apparent loss of $10,000 would result. By using the replacement cost as the value of the materials, however, the contract should be accepted, because a profit of $2,500 would result.

To see which method is correct, examine the income statement of Westside at the end of the accounting period. If the contract *is not* accepted, then at the end of the accounting period the firm will have to reduce the cost of its inventory by $12,500 ($50,000 − $37,500) to reflect the lower market value of this unused inventory. The firm will thus incur a loss of $12,500. If the contract *is* accepted, then the company will make a profit of $2,500 on the contract, but will also incur a loss of $12,500 on the materials used in completing the contract. The firm will thus incur a *net* loss of only $10,000. Hence, acceptance of the contract results in a smaller overall loss to Westside than does rejection of the contract. For decision-making purposes, replacement cost is the appropriate measure of the cost of materials in inventory, and Westside should accept the contract.

Sunk Cost of Underutilized Facilities   The Dunbar Manufacturing Company recently discontinued a product line and was left with 50,000 square feet of unneeded warehouse space. The company rents the entire warehouse (200,000 square feet) from the owner for $1,000,000 per year (i.e., $5 per square foot) under a long-term (10-year) lease agreement. A nearby company that is expanding its operations offered to rent the 50,000 square feet of unneeded space for one year for $125,000 (i.e., $2.50

Table 8.2   Effect of Inventory Valuation Methods on Measured Profit—Westside Plumbing and Heating Company

	Acquisition Cost	Replacement Cost
Value of contract	$100,000	$100,000
Costs		
Labor, equipment, and so on	60,000	60,000
Materials	50,000	37,500
	110,000	97,500
Profit (or loss)	($10,000)	$ 2,500

Table 8.3   Warehouse Rental Decision—Dunbar Manufacturing Company

	Decision	
	Do Not Rent	Rent
Total lease payment	$1,000,000	$1,000,000
Less: Rent received on unused space	–	125,000
Net cost of warehouse to Dunbar Manufacturing Company	$1,000,000	$ 875,000

per square foot). Should Dunbar accept the offer to rent the unused space, assuming that no other higher offers for the warehouse space are expected?

One could argue that Dunbar should reject the offer because the additional rent (revenue) of $2.50 per square foot is less than the lease payment (cost) of $5 per square foot. Such reasoning, however, will lead to an incorrect decision. The lease payment ($5 per square foot) represents a **sunk cost** that must be paid regardless of whether or not the other company rents the unneeded warehouse space. As shown in Table 8.3, renting the unneeded warehouse space *reduces* the net cost of the warehouse from $1,000,000 to $875,000, a savings of $125,000 per year to Dunbar. The relevant comparison is between the incremental revenue ($125,000) and the incremental costs ($0 in this case). Thus, sunk costs (such as the lease payment of $5 per square foot in this example) should not be considered relevant costs because such costs are unavoidable, independent of the course of action chosen.

Sunk Cost
A cost incurred regardless of the alternative action chosen in a decision-making problem.

Conclusions   Several conclusions can be drawn from this discussion of the concept of cost:

1. Costs can be measured in different ways, depending on the purpose for which the cost figures are to be used.
2. The costs appropriate for financial reporting purposes are not always appropriate for decision-making purposes. Typically, changes and modifications have to be made to reflect the opportunity costs of the various alternative actions that can be chosen in a given decision problem. The *relevant cost* in economic decision-making is the opportunity cost of the resources rather than the historical outlay of funds required to obtain the resources.
3. Sunk costs, which are incurred regardless of the alternative action chosen, should not be considered in making decisions.
4. The opportunity costs of a given action in a decision problem are sometimes highly subjective, but often the more objective accounting cost estimates may be arbitrary.

SHORT-RUN COST FUNCTIONS

In addition to measuring the costs of producing a given quantity of output, economists are also concerned with determining the behavior of costs as output is varied over a range of possible values. The relationship between cost and output is expressed in terms of a **cost function**—a schedule, graph, or mathematical relationship showing the minimum achievable cost of producing various quantities of output.

The discussion in Chapter 7 concerning the inputs used in the production process distinguished between fixed and variable inputs. A fixed input was defined as an input that is required in the production process, but whose quantity used in the process is constant over a given period of time regardless of the level of output produced. Short-run questions relate to a situation in which one or more of the inputs to the production process is fixed. Long-run questions relate to a situation in which *all* inputs are variable; that is, no restrictions are imposed on the amount of a resource that can be employed in the production process.

The actual period of time corresponding to the long run for a given production process will depend on the nature of the inputs employed in the production process. Generally, the more capital equipment used relative to labor and other inputs (that is, the more **capital intensive** the process), the longer will be the period of time required to increase significantly all the factors of production and the scale of operations. A period of five or more years may be required for a new or expanded electric utility-generating facility, steel mill, or oil refinery to be constructed and put into operation. Before the expansion is completed (i.e., in the short run), increases in production output can only be achieved by operating existing production facilities at higher rates of use through the utilization of greater amounts of labor and other variable inputs. In comparison, a service-oriented production process (such as an employment agency, trucking company, consulting firm, or government agency), which uses a relatively small amount of capital equipment, may have a long-run planning horizon of only a few months. This is especially true if the company rents or short-term leases much of its equipment. Such a company can abruptly change the scale of operations as business conditions dictate.

Associated with the short-run and long-run planning periods are short-run and long-run cost functions. This section discusses the development and interpretation of short-run costs and cost functions. The next section contains a similar discussion of cost functions associated with long-run decisions.

Total Cost Function

The total cost of producing a given quantity of output is equal to the sum of the costs of each of the inputs used in the production process. In discussing short-run cost functions, it is useful to classify costs as either *fixed* or *variable costs*. **Fixed costs** represent the costs of all the inputs to the production process that are fixed or constant over the short run. These costs will be incurred regardless of whether a small or large quantity of output is produced during the period. **Variable costs** consist of the costs of all the variable inputs to the production process. Whereas variable costs may not change in direct proportion to the quantity of output produced, they will increase (or decrease) in some manner as output is increased (or decreased).[3]

Cost Function
A mathematical model, schedule, or graph that shows the cost (such as total, average, or marginal cost) of producing various quantities of output.

Capital-Intensive Cost Function
A characteristic of costs associated with a high proportion of fixed to variable inputs, usually due to extensive investment in plant and equipment.

http://
You can access more information on cost functions and their relationship with production in Lesson 6 at the following website: http://www.bus.okstate.edu/ecls/price/ICS/ECON3113W/framed/econ3113w.htm

Fixed Costs
The costs of inputs to the production process that are constant over the short run.

Variable Costs
The costs of the variable inputs to the production process.

[3] A third category, *semivariable costs*, can also be considered. Semivariable costs are costs that increase (decrease) in a stepwise manner as output is increased (decreased). Semivariable costs are constant when output varies within a given range. They increase or decrease only when output moves outside this range. The rental cost of a fleet of delivery trucks is an example. Over a wide range of output, delivery expenses are fixed. At some output level, however, the firm will require bigger delivery trucks.

Example

SHORT-RUN COST FUNCTIONS: DEEP CREEK MINING COMPANY

To illustrate the nature of short-run costs and show how the short-run cost function can be derived from the production function for the firm, consider again the Deep Creek Mining Company example that was discussed in Chapter 7. It was assumed that two inputs, capital and labor, are required to produce or mine ore. Various-sized pieces of capital equipment, as measured by their brake horsepower rating K, are available to mine the ore. Each of these pieces of equipment can be operated with various-sized labor crews L. The amount of output (tons of ore) that can be produced in a given period with each capital-labor input combination is shown again in Table 8.4. It was also assumed that the rental cost of using the mining equipment per period is \$.20 per brake horsepower and that the cost of each worker (labor) employed per period is \$50. This yielded the following total cost equation for any given combination of labor L and capital K (Equation 7.21):

$$C = 50L + .20K$$

Suppose that Deep Creek has signed a lease agreeing to rent, for the next year, a 750-brake-horsepower piece of mining equipment (capital). During the ensuing year (the short run), the amount of capital that the company can employ in the ore-mining process is fixed at 750 brake horsepower. Therefore, for each period a fixed cost of \$.20 × 750 = \$150 will be incurred, regardless of the quantity of ore that is produced. The firm must operate the production process at one of the capital-labor combinations shown in the third column of Table 8.4. Output can be increased (decreased) by employing more (less) labor in combination with the given 750-brake-horsepower capital equipment. Labor is thus a variable input to the production process.

The short-run cost functions for Deep Creek are shown in Table 8.5.[4] The various possible output levels Q and the associated capital-labor input combinations L

Table 8.4   Production Function—Deep Creek Mining Company

		Capital Input K (Brake Horsepower)							
		250	500	750	1,000	1,250	1,500	1,750	2,000
	1	1	3	6	10	16	16	16	13
	2	2	6	16	24	29	29	44	44
	3	4	16	29	44	55	55	55	50
Labor Input L	4	6	29	44	55	58	60	60	55
(Number of	5	16	43	55	60	61	62	62	60
Workers)	6	29	55	60	62	63	63	63	62
	7	44	58	62	63	64	64	64	64
	8	50	60	62	63	64	65	65	65
	9	55	59	61	63	64	65	66	66
	10	52	56	59	62	64	65	66	67

[4] The rational producer would not employ more than seven workers in the short run because the use of additional workers will not result in any increase in the quantity of ore that is produced. That is, labor has a negative marginal value added beyond seven workers.

Table 8.5   Short-Run Cost Functions—Deep Creek Mining Company

Output	Variable Cost		Fixed Cost		Total Cost	Average Fixed Cost	Average Variable Cost	Average Total Cost	Marginal Cost
	Labor Input	$VC =$	Capital Input		$TC =$				
Q	L	$\$50 \cdot L$	K	$FC = \$150$	$FC + VC$	$AFC = \dfrac{FC}{Q}$	$AVC = \dfrac{VC}{Q}$	$ATC = \dfrac{TC}{Q}$	$MC = \dfrac{\Delta TC}{\Delta Q}$
0	0	$\$\ 0$	750	$\$150$	$\$150$	—	—	—	—
6	1	50	750	150	200	$\$25.00$	$\$8.33$	$\$33.33$	$\dfrac{50}{6} = \$8.33$
16	2	100	750	150	250	9.38	6.25	15.63	$\dfrac{50}{10} = 5.00$
29	3	150	750	150	300	5.17	5.17	10.34	$\dfrac{50}{13} = 3.85$
44	4	200	750	150	350	3.41	4.55	7.95	$\dfrac{50}{15} = 3.33$
55	5	250	750	150	400	2.73	4.55	7.27	$\dfrac{50}{11} = 4.55$
60	6	300	750	150	450	2.50	5.00	7.50	$\dfrac{50}{5} = 10.00$

and K are obtained from Table 8.4. The short-run variable cost VC is equal to $\$50$ times the number of workers (L) employed in the mining process. The short-run fixed cost FC is equal to the rental cost of the 750-brake-horsepower equipment ($\$150$). The total cost in the short run is the sum of the fixed and variable costs:

$$TC = FC + VC \qquad\qquad [8.2]$$

In Figure 8.1 the three curves from the data given in Table 8.5 are plotted. Note that the TC curve has an identical shape to that of VC, being shifted upward by the FC of $\$150$.

Average and Marginal Cost Functions

Once the total cost function is determined, one can then derive the average and marginal cost functions. The average fixed cost AFC, average variable cost AVC, and average total cost ATC are equal to the respective fixed, variable, and total costs divided by the quantity of output produced:

$$AFC = \frac{FC}{Q} \qquad\qquad [8.3]$$

$$AVC = \frac{VC}{Q} \qquad\qquad [8.4]$$

Figure 8.1   Short-Run Variable, Fixed, and Total Cost Functions— Deep Creek Mining Company

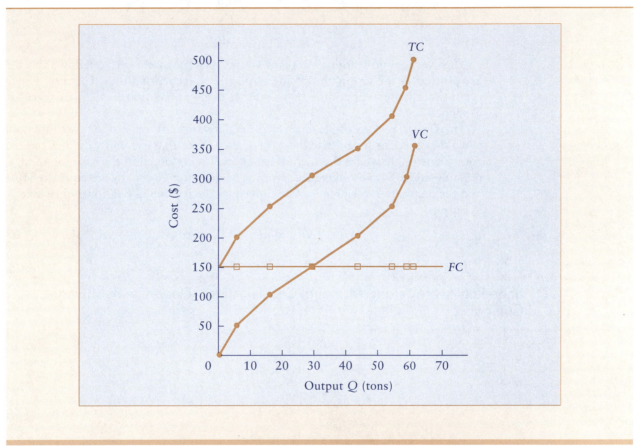

$$ATC = \frac{TC}{Q} \qquad\qquad [8.5]$$

Also,

$$ATC = AFC + AVC \qquad\qquad [8.6]$$

Marginal Cost

The incremental increase in total cost that results from a one-unit increase in output.

Marginal cost is defined as the incremental increase in total cost that results from a one-unit increase in output, and is calculated as[5]

$$MC = \frac{\Delta TC}{\Delta Q} \qquad\qquad [8.7]$$
$$= \frac{\Delta VC}{\Delta Q}$$

---

[5] Technically, the ratio $\Delta TC/\Delta Q$ represents the *incremental* cost associated with a discrete change in output by more than one unit rather than the *marginal* cost associated with *one* additional unit of output.

or, in the case of a continuous *TC* function, as

$$MC = \frac{d(TC)}{dQ}$$ [8.8]

$$= \frac{d(VC)}{dQ}$$ [8.9]

The average and marginal costs for Deep Creek that were calculated in Table 8.5 are plotted in the graph shown in Figure 8.2. Except for the *AFC* curve, which is continually declining, note that all other average and marginal cost curves are U-shaped.

The Deep Creek example illustrated the derivation of the various cost functions when the cost data are given in the form of a schedule (that is, tabular data). Consider another example where the cost information is represented in the form of an algebraic function. Suppose fixed costs for the Manchester Company are equal to $100, and the company's variable costs are given by the following relationship (where Q = output):

$$VC = 60Q - 3Q^2 + .10Q^3$$ [8.10]

Figure 8.2   Short-Run Average and Marginal Cost Functions—Deep Creek Mining Company

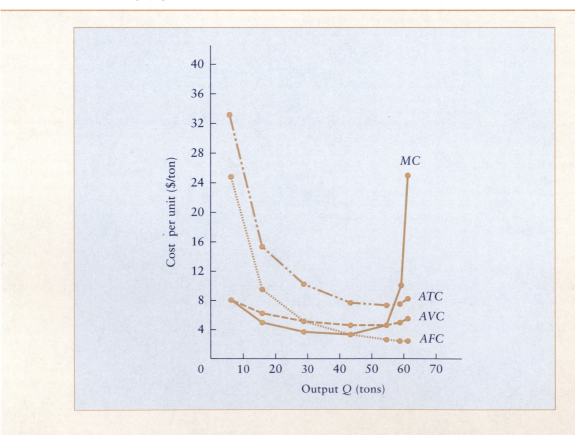

Given this information, one can derive the total cost function using Equation 8.2:

$$TC = 100 + 60Q - 3Q^2 + .10Q^3$$

Next, *AFC*, *AVC*, and *ATC* can be found using Equations 8.3, 8.4, and 8.5, respectively, as follows:

$$AFC = \frac{100}{Q}$$

$$AVC = 60 - 3Q + .10Q^2$$

$$ATC = \frac{100}{Q} + 60 - 3Q + .10Q^2$$

Finally, Manchester's marginal cost function can be obtained by differentiating the variable cost function (Equation 8.10) with respect to Q:

$$MC = \frac{d(VC)}{dQ} = 60 - 6Q + .30Q^2$$

Relationships among the Various Cost and Production Curves

http://

For further reading on the relationships between various cost and product curves, see David Friedman's Internet textbook at:
http://www.daviddfriedman. com/Academic/Price_ Theory/PThy_Chapter_9/ PThy_Chapter_9.html

To investigate further the properties of and relationships among the various cost and production curves, assume now that the cost and production curves can be represented by smooth continuous functions, as shown in Figure 8.3. Also assume that input L is the variable factor, with an associated variable cost VC; that the per-unit price of each of the factors of production (i.e., C_L and C_K) is *constant* over all usage levels; and that input K is the fixed factor, with an associated fixed cost FC. First, note that variable costs (and total costs) initially increase at a decreasing rate as output Q is increased up to Q_1. Correspondingly, the marginal cost function MC is declining. Over this range of output, the marginal product of the variable input L is increasing. Because it has been assumed that the unit cost of L is constant, an increasing marginal product for input L necessarily implies that the marginal cost function must be declining.[6] The minimum point on the MC curve at Q_1 corresponds to the maximum point on the MP_L curve at L_1. Beyond Q_1, variable (and total) costs increase at an increasing rate and, correspondingly, the marginal cost curve is increasing. Over this range of output, the marginal product of L is decreasing and, for reasons analogous to those just noted, marginal cost must necessarily be rising.

Examining the average variable cost curve, *AVC*, in Figure 8.3, note that it is declining over output levels to Q_2 and is increasing thereafter. The shape of the average variable cost function, like the shape of the marginal cost function, is closely related to the production function defined in Chapter 7. *Given that the unit cost of the variable input is constant,* an increasing (and then decreasing) average product for input L necessarily implies that the average variable cost will be decreasing (and then increasing).[7] The minimum point on the *AVC* curve at Q_2 corresponds to the

---

[6] The relationship can be shown algebraically in the following way: MC is defined as $\Delta TC/\Delta Q$, which is also equal to $\Delta VC/\Delta Q$. ΔVC is equal to $C_L\Delta L$, where C_L is the unit cost of the variable input L. Thus, $MC = C_L(\Delta L/\Delta Q)$. However, the marginal product of input L, MP, was defined in Equation 7.2 as $\Delta Q/\Delta L$, or, in reciprocal form, $1/MP = \Delta L/\Delta Q$. Substituting $1/MP$ in the relationship for MC, we obtain $MC = C_L(1/MP)$. Because the marginal productivity of L is increasing, the marginal cost must be decreasing.

[7] This relationship can be shown using the previously defined expressions for the average product AP and average variable cost AVC. AVC is equal to VC/Q. VC is equal to $C_L \cdot L$ where C_L is the unit cost of the variable input. Thus, $AVC = (C_L \cdot L)/Q$. The average product is defined as Q/L or, in reciprocal form, $1/AP = L/Q$. Substituting this in the expression for AVC, we obtain $AVC = C_L(1/AP)$. Thus, if the average product is increasing, the average variable cost must be decreasing, and vice versa.

Figure 8.3   Short-Run Cost and Production Functions

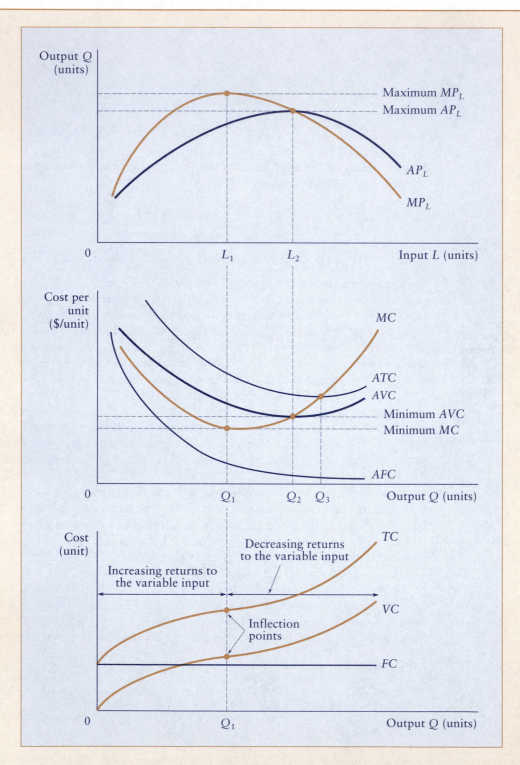

maximum point on the AP_L curve at L_2. Note also in Figure 8.3 that the marginal cost curve intersects the average variable cost function at its minimum value. This necessarily follows because the marginal product curve intersects the average product curve at its maximum value.

The average total cost curve, which is equal to the sum of the vertical heights of the average fixed cost and average variable cost curves, likewise initially declines and subsequently begins rising beyond some level of output. At a level of output of Q_3 the average total cost curve is at its minimum value.

As discussed in the previous chapter, more intensive use of the variable inputs (specialization) in combination with fixed inputs to the production process is believed to yield initially more than proportionate increases in output. Subsequently, due to the law of diminishing returns, more intensive use yields less than proportionate increases. This reasoning is used to explain the U-shaped pattern of the *ATC*, *AVC*, and *MC* curves. Initially, specialization in the use of the variable resources results in increasing returns and declining average and marginal costs. Eventually, however, the gains from specialization are overwhelmed by crowding effects, and then marginal and average costs begin increasing.

LONG-RUN COST FUNCTIONS

Over the long-run planning horizon, using the available production methods and technology, the firm can choose the plant size, types and sizes of equipment, labor skills, and raw materials that, when combined, yield the lowest cost of producing the desired amount of output. Once the optimum combination of inputs is chosen to produce the desired level of output at least cost, some of these inputs (plant and equipment) become fixed in the short run. If demand increases unexpectedly and the firm wishes to produce not Q_1, as planned, but rather Q_2 as shown in Figure 8.4, it may have little choice but to lay on additional variable inputs like overtime labor and expedite the rush-order delivery of supplies to meet its production goals. Of course, such arrangements are expensive, and short-run average cost will temporarily rise to C_2. Should this demand persist, a larger fixed input investment in plant and equipment is warranted. Then, unit cost can be reduced to C_2'. Another short-run average cost function like SAC_2 exists for this new set of inputs. In theory, there exists an optimum combination of inputs and a minimum total cost for each level of output. Associated with the fixed inputs in each of these optimum combinations is a short-run average cost function. Several of these other short-run average cost functions (SAC_3, SAC_4) are shown in Figure 8.4. The long-run average cost function consists of the *lower boundary* or *envelope* of all these (infinitely many) short-run curves. No other combination of inputs exists for producing each level of output Q at an average cost below the cost that is indicated by the *LAC* curve.[8]

Optimal Capacity Utilization: Three Concepts

Given the relationship between the short-run and long-run average cost functions can be further illustrated by examining in more detail the effect on costs of an expansion in output from Q_1 to Q_2 in Figure 8.4. Assume that the firm has been

---

[8] From the graph one can see that the long-run average cost of producing any given level of output, in general, does *not* occur at the point where short-run average costs are minimized. Only at the output level Q_3, corresponding to the minimum cost point on the *LAC* curve, does the long-run average cost equal the minimum short-run average cost.

Figure 8.4   Long-Run and Short-Run Average Cost Functions

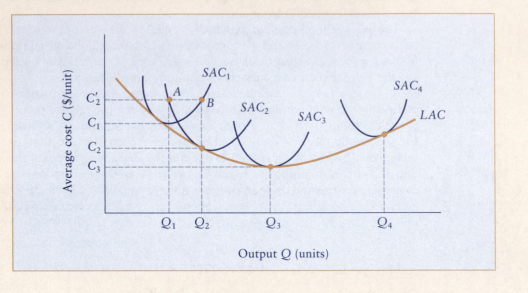

Optimal Output for a Given Plant Size
Output rate that results in lowest average total cost for a given plant size.

producing Q_1 units of output using a plant of size "1," having a short-run average cost curve of SAC_1. The average cost of producing Q_1 units is therefore C_1, and Q_1 is the optimal output for the plant size represented by SAC_1. **Optimal output for a given plant size** is a short-run concept of capacity utilization. Suppose that the firm wishes to expand output to Q_2. What will the average cost be of producing this higher volume of output? In the short run, as we saw earlier, the average cost would be C'_2. However, in the long run, it would be possible for the firm to build a plant of size "2," having a short-run average cost curve of SAC_2. With this larger plant, the average cost of producing Q_2 units of output would be only C_2. Thus, because the firm has more options available to it in the long run, average total cost of any given output generally can be reduced. SAC_2 represents the **optimal plant size for the output rate** Q_2. However, even these inputs and costs of production that are fixed in the short run can be altered in the long run to obtain a still more efficient allocation of resources. Only when optimal output increases to Q_3, where the firm will build the universally least-cost **optimal plant size** represented by SAC_3, will further opportunities for cost reduction cease. This is a long-run concept of optimal capacity utilization, given the technology in place at this plant.

Optimal Plant Size for a Given Output Rate
Plant size that results in lowest average total cost for a given output.

Optimal Plant Size
Plant size that achieves minimum long-run average total cost.

Example

AVERAGE COST PER KILOWATT HOUR IN UNDERUTILIZED POWER PLANTS[9]

Under pressure from regulators, the electric power industry has opened its customer distribution systems to freewheeled electricity. That means that a factory in Ohio can choose to buy contract electricity from Michigan, New York, or Virginia power

[9] Based on M. Maloney, R. McCormick, and R. Sauer, *Customer Choice, Consumer Value: An Analysis of Retail Competition in America's Electric Industry* (Washington, DC: Citizens for a Sound Economy, 1996).

companies. With the new competition, the price of electricity is certain to decline, and consumption will increase. However, excess capacity is present in much of the power industry today, and higher-cost electric utilities will soon find themselves priced out of the market. After all, price per kilowatt hour ranges from 4 cents in some states to almost 12 cents in others. As more efficient power plants are constructed, some estimates show the price of electricity falling by 1.8 cents using conventional coal-fired steam turbine technology and by as much as 3.0 cents using nuclear and other technologies. These savings imply an $18.00 to $30.00 reduction per month in the residential electricity bill for a customer who switches to the lower-cost firms.

The flip side, however, is that firms left behind will find themselves with "stranded costs" too high to retain customers, yet too low to shutter the facility and close the power plant. Instead, such underutilized plants will likely come on line during peak demand and at other times be relegated to stand-by status. Unfortunately, this under-utilization will raise the already-high average cost per kilowatt hour (say, C_2 at Q_2 on SAC_2), still further to C'_2 at the lower output Q_1 on SAC_1 in Figure 8.4.

Expansion Path
The input combinations that minimize cost for a given level of output.

Short-run average total cost (SAC) with underutilization of capacity at Point A or SAC with overutilization of capacity at Point B in Figure 8.4 is always higher than the minimum average total cost in the long run (LAC) when the production manager can vary plant and equipment, matching capacity to his or her output requirements. The LAC can be obtained using the **expansion path** of input combinations that satisfy the condition:

$$\frac{MP_L}{C_L} = \frac{MP_K}{C_K} \qquad [8.11]$$

Recall from the previous chapter that this equimarginal condition must be satisfied in order for a given input combination to be an optimal solution to either the output-maximization or cost-minimization problem.

As shown in Figure 8.5, the expansion path can be represented by a line that connects these various tangency points between the isoquants and isocost lines,[10] and the long-run total cost function can be obtained from the corresponding cost and output values. Thus, for example, from Point 1 in Figure 8.5 one obtains the cost-output combination $(C_1, Q^{(1)})$, which is then plotted in Figure 8.6. The cost-output combinations $(C_2, Q^{(2)})$ and $(C_3, Q^{(3)})$ are obtained in a similar manner. Connecting these points yields the long-run total cost (LTC) curve shown in Figure 8.6. The long-run average cost (LAC) and long-run marginal cost (LMC) curves are defined and calculated in a manner similar to their short-run counterparts:[11]

$$LAC = \frac{LTC}{Q} \qquad [8.12]$$

$$LMC = \frac{\Delta LTC}{\Delta Q} \qquad [8.13]$$

[10] As in the development of the short-run cost functions in the previous section, it is assumed that the per-unit price of each input is constant regardless of the quantity used in the production process. We comment further on this assumption in the next section.

[11] Alternatively, the long-run cost function can be derived algebraically from the production function. Such a derivation for the Cobb-Douglas production function is examined in Appendix 8A.

Figure 8.5   Expansion Path

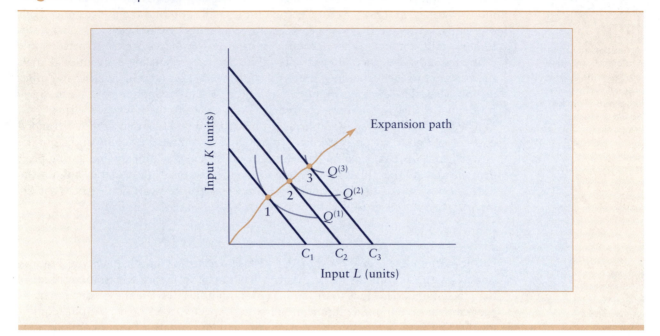

Figure 8.6   Long-Run Total Cost Function

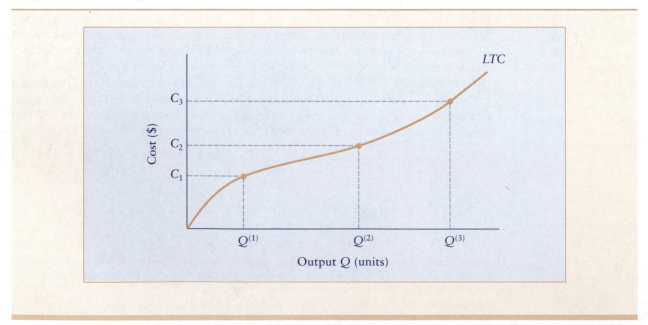

ECONOMIES AND DISECONOMIES OF SCALE

The long-run average cost function is hypothesized to decline over lower ranges of capacity (scale economies) and rise over higher ranges of capacity (scale diseconomies).

Internal Economies of Scale

Declining long-run average costs are usually attributed to three possible sources of **internal economies of scale:**

Internal Economies of Scale
Declining long-run average costs as the rate of output for a product, plant, or firm is increased.

- Product-level economies—internal economies of scale related to the output of one product
- Plant-level economies—internal economies of scale related to the total output (of multiple products) of one plant
- Firm-level economies—internal economies of scale related to the total output of a firm's operations.

http://

Access more information on U.S. corporations and economies of scale at the following Internet site: http://www.themanage mentor.com/kuniverse/ kmailersuniverse/ sm_kmailers/MS_ Competitive.htm

Product-Level Economies   A number of different sources of scale economies are associated with producing larger volumes of a single product. As discussed in the previous chapter, increasing physical returns to scale can be realized from *greater specialization in the use of capital and labor.* As the scale of production is increased, special-purpose equipment, which is more efficient in performing a limited set of operations, can be substituted for less efficient general-purpose equipment. Likewise, as the scale of production is increased, the production process can be broken down into a series of smaller tasks, and workers can be assigned to the tasks for which they are most qualified. Workers are then able to acquire additional proficiency through higher repetition of the tasks to which they are assigned.

In manufacturing, a related phenomenon called the **learning curve effect** is often observed; that is, the amount of labor input and the associated fringe benefit costs required to produce each unit of output decreases for successive increases in the cumulative volume of output (e.g., during long production runs of 767 airframes at Boeing). The learning curve concept is discussed further in Appendix 9A. In general, internal economies of scale can be distinguished from learning curve effects or volume discounts (so-called **external economies of scale**) because the latter always result from increases in cumulative volume of output no matter how small the output rate per unit time period. As such, they may well not be associated with any change in scale. Instead, purchasing manages may be simply buying things less frequently in bigger volumes or the workers may have acquired learning curve advantages because the company had been operating longer than similar-scale new competitors.

Learning Curve Effect
Declining unit cost attributable to greater cumulative volume.

External Economy of Scale
Volume discounts in purchasing inputs.

Plant-Level Economies   Sources of scale economies at the plant level include capital investment, overhead, and required reserves of maintenance parts and personnel. With respect to *capital investment,* capital costs tend to increase less than proportionately with the productive capacity of a plant, particularly in such process-type industries as petroleum refining and chemicals. For example, a pipeline with twice the radius of another pipeline can be constructed for perhaps as little as twice the cost, yet have four times the capacity (i.e., $\pi(2r)^2 = 4\pi r^2$ versus πr^2) of the smaller one. Another source of scale economies is overhead costs, which include such items as administrative costs (e.g., management salaries) and other indirect expenditures (e.g., heating and lighting expenses). Overhead costs can be spread over a higher volume of output in a larger plant, thus reducing average costs per unit. Finally, scale economies can be realized in equipment maintenance. *Reserves of replacement parts and maintenance personnel* needed to deal with randomly occurring equipment breakdowns normally increase less than proportionately with increases in the size of the plant.

Example

REFUSE COLLECTION AND DISPOSAL IN ORANGE COUNTY

Private for-profit trash collectors in California have demonstrated the scale economies of landfills. The environmental safety issues at a landfill require enormous investment in environmental impact studies, lining the site, monitoring for seepage and leeching of toxins, and scientific follow-up studies. Spreading these overhead costs across a larger rate of output has led an Orange County company to seek refuse as far away as the northern suburbs of San Diego, almost an hour down the California coast. The trucks from Orange County pass right by several municipal landfills en route. However, the fees charged for dumping at these intermediate sites are much higher. Apparently, the variable transportation costs of hauling a ton of trash prove to be less than the higher start-up costs and environmental monitoring costs per ton at smaller-scale landfills. By state law, all of these municipalities must charge a dumping fee that covers their fully-allocated cost, so reduced long-run average total cost provides a substantial price advantage for the large-scale Orange County site.

Economies of Scope
Economies that exist whenever the cost of producing two (or more) products jointly by one plant or firm is less than the cost of producing these products separately by different plants or firms.

The cost of a particular product can be affected by the interactions between product-level and plant-level economies. **Economies of scope** are present whenever the cost of producing two (or more) products jointly by one plant or firm is less than the cost of producing these products separately by different plants or firms.[12] Economies of scope occur whenever inputs can be shared in the production of different products. For example, in the airline industry, the cost of transporting both passengers and freight on a single airplane is less than the cost of using two airplanes to transport passengers and freight separately.

http://
Access information on economies of scope in the global advertising and marketing services business at the following Internet site:
http://papers.nber.org/papers/W9965

Firm-Level Economies   In addition to product-level and plant-level economies of scale, there are other scale economies associated with the overall size of the firm. Often these latter scale economies can only be realized by the large multiproduct, multiplant firm. One possible source of firm-level scale economies is in *distribution*. For example, multiplant operations may permit a larger firm to maintain geographically dispersed plants. Delivery costs are often lower for a geographically dispersed multiplant operation compared with one (larger) plant.

Another possible source of scale economies to the firm is in *raising capital funds*. Because flotation costs increase less than proportionately with the size of the security (stock or bond) issue, average flotation costs per dollar of funds raised is smaller for larger firms.[13] Similar scale economies also exist in *marketing and sales promotion*. These scale economies can take such forms as (1) quantity discounts in securing advertising media space and time, or (2) the ability of the large firm to spread the fixed costs of advertising preparation over greater output. In addition, the large

---

[12] See William J. Baumol, John C. Panzer, and Robert D. Willig, *Contestable Markets and the Theory of Industry Structure* (New York: Harcourt Brace Jovanovich, 1982), Chapter 4.

[13] *Flotation costs* are the costs paid to the investment underwriter or securities dealer who arranges the sale of the securities issue to investors.

firm may be able to achieve a relatively greater degree of brand recognition and brand loyalty from its higher level of sales promotion expenditures over an extended period of time.

A final source of firm-level scale economies is in *technological innovation*. Unlike smaller firms, large firms can afford sizable research and development (R&D) laboratories and costly specialized equipment and research personnel. Also, the large firm is better able to undertake a diversified portfolio of R&D projects and can thus reduce the risk associated with the failure of any one (or small number) of the projects. The smaller firm, in contrast, may be unwilling to undertake a large R&D project, because failure of the project could result in bankruptcy.

Example

ECONOMIES OF SCALE: SUPERSCALE MONEY-CENTER VERSUS COMMUNITY BANKS

There is a growing number of very large money-center banks in the United States, 1,000 times larger than the typical community bank in smaller towns and cities. Shaffer and David have examined the economies of scale in these superscale banks, which range in size from $2.5 billion to $120.6 billion in assets.[14] Their results indicate that long-run average costs decline until superscale banks range between $15 billion and $37 billion in assets. The superscale banks have come to dominate credit card issuance, corporate lending, and custodial asset management (see Figure 8.7), perhaps because of the massive information technology investments required in these

Figure 8.7   Bank Market Shares in Four Businesses, 2000

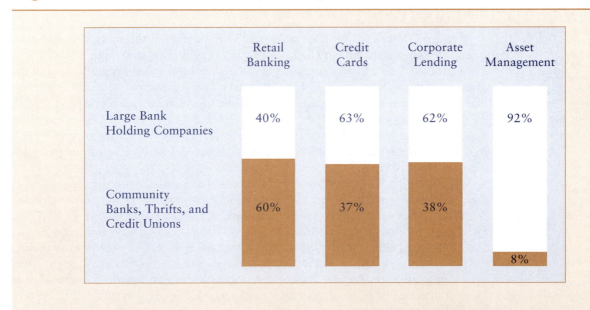

---

[14] S. Shaffer and E. David, "Economies of Superscale in Commercial Banking," *Applied Economics* 23 (1991), pp. 283–293.

businesses. In contrast, community banks thrift institutions, and credit unions dominate retail banking, where diseconomies of scale (rising long-run average costs) set in beyond $50 million in assets.[15]

Diseconomies of Scale

Rising long-run average costs at higher rates of output are attributed to **diseconomies of scale.** A primary source of diseconomies of scale associated with an individual production plant is *transportation costs.* Another possible source of plant diseconomies is labor requirements; higher wage rates or costly worker recruiting and relocation programs may be required to attract the necessary personnel, particularly if the plant is located in a sparsely populated area. Finally, large-scale plants are often inflexible operations designed for long production runs of one product.

Diseconomies of scale at the firm level result from *problems of coordination and control encountered by management* as the scale of operations is increased. First, the size of management staffs and their associated salary costs may rise more than proportionately as the scale of the firm is increased. Also, less direct and observable costs may occur, such as the losses arising from delayed or faulty decisions and weakened or distorted managerial incentives. Contemporary examples of these problems include General Motors and AT&T.

The following two examples examine the problems associated with large size—the first one looks at diseconomies of scale at the plant level, and the second one (in the *International Perspectives* section) focuses on the issue of coordination and control in large multiproduct, multiplant corporations.

FLEXIBILITY AND OPERATING EFFICIENCY: FORD MOTOR COMPANY'S FLAT ROCK PLANT[16]

Ford Motor Company spent an estimated $200 million in the early 1970s to construct a massive plant in Flat Rock, Michigan, to build cast iron engine blocks. The plant produced V8 blocks exclusively on five ultra-high-speed assembly lines at the rate of 8,000 blocks per day. In 1981, however, Ford executives decided to close the Flat Rock plant and move production to an older Cleveland engine block plant. Ford's Cleveland plant had ten smaller and slower production lines; the Cleveland plant was clearly the less efficient of the two factories. However, Ford executives realized it would cost less to convert Cleveland's smaller production lines to building five types of smaller six- and four-cylinder engines.

When Flat Rock was designed in the 1960s, Ford could count on long V8 production runs of perhaps one million units of its most popular Ford Mustang model. But in the 1980s variety in the product line became the key business strategy. By 1998, Ford's top-selling Explorer (383,852 units), Taurus (357,162 units), and Escort (283,898 units) reflected the fragmented auto marketplace. Only the F-series pickup (746,111 units) warranted Flat Rock's massive scale. As George Booth, iron-operations manager for the casting division at Ford, explained, "Flat Rock was built to make a few parts at very high volumes. But the plant turned out to be very inflexible for conversion to making new types and different sizes of engine blocks. "Sometimes you really can be too big."

---

[15] T. Gilligan, M. Smirlock, and W. Marshall, "Scale and Scope Economies in the Multi-Product Banking Firm," *Journal of Monetary Economics* 13 (1984), pp. 393–405.

[16] Based on articles in *The Economist,* January 13, 2001, p. 58; *AI,* February 1998; and *Wall Street Journal,* September 16, 1981.

International Perspectives

HOW JAPANESE COMPANIES DEAL WITH THE PROBLEMS OF SIZE[17]

Many large, successful U.S. corporations, such as General Electric, Hewlett-Packard, Sara Lee, and Johnson and Johnson, are attempting to deal with the problems of size by decentralizing their operations. These companies are setting up independent business units, each with its own profit-and-loss responsibility, thereby giving managers more flexibility and freedom in decision making.

Like their counterparts in the United States, Japanese corporations are largely collections of hundreds of individual companies. For example, Matsushita Electrical Industrial Company consists of 161 consolidated units. Another example is Hitachi, Ltd., which is composed of 660 companies, with the stock of 27 of these companies being publicly traded. James Abegglen, an expert on Japanese management, has observed that "As something new comes along, . . . it gets moved out to a subsidiary so the elephant does not roll over and smother it. If all goes well, it becomes a successful company on its own. If not, it gets pulled back in."

Overall Effects of Scale Economies and Diseconomies

For some industries like textile and furniture manufacturing, long-run average costs for the firm remain constant over a wide range of output once scale economies are exhausted; many plant sizes are consistent with least cost production. In other industries like steel ingot production and engine block casting, long-run average costs rise at very large scale. The possible presence of both economies and diseconomies of scale leads to the hypothesized long-run average cost function for a typical manufacturing firm being U-shaped with a flat middle area, as shown in Figure 8.8. Up

Figure 8.8   Long-Run Average Cost Function and Scale Economies

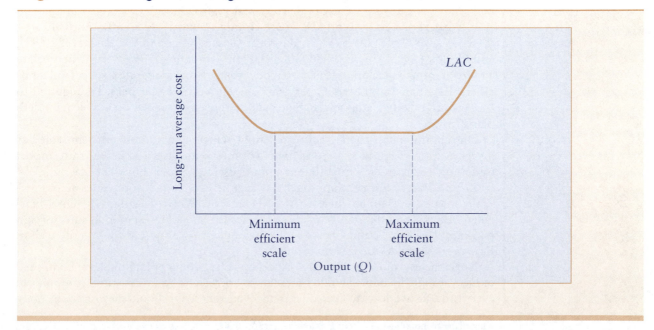

[17] Based on an article entitled "Is Your Company Too Big?" *Business Week*, March 17, 1989, pp. 84–94.

Minimum Efficient Scale (MES)
The smallest scale at which minimum costs per unit are attained.

to some **minimum efficient scale (MES)**, that is, the smallest scale at which minimum long-run average total costs are attained, economies of scale are present. In most industries, it is possible to increase the size of the firm significantly beyond the MES without incurring diseconomies of scale, as shown in Figure 8.8. Over this range, average costs per unit are relatively constant. However, expansion beyond the maximum efficient scale eventually will result in problems of inflexibility, lack of managerial coordination, and rising long-run average costs.

Example

ALUMINUM-INTENSIVE VEHICLE LOWERS THE MINIMUM EFFICIENT SCALE AT FORD[18]

The aluminum space-frame automobile Ford is designing (or the A2 that Audi has already brought to market) is not even half as heavy as conventional steel and sheet metal cars of today. In addition to phenomenal increases in gas mileage and markedly reduced CO_2 emissions, aluminum-intensive vehicles will change the scale economies of auto assembly dramatically. Aluminum space frame components are cast, forged, and extruded into different thicknesses depending upon where strength is needed. Aluminum does not require the massive body-stamping machines that for decades have been employed to bend sheet metal into hoods, trunks, and fenders and to hydraulically press steel plate into floor pan and door pillar shapes. Consequently, the tens of millions of dollars of fixed asset investment for this largest piece of capital equipment on the auto assembly line will no longer be needed.

Since a body-stamping machine has a physical working life of 600,000 vehicles, this single piece of equipment has been the source of substantial scale economies in the production of most auto models. Of the 197 models sold in the United States and Western Europe, only the top-selling Ford Focus (902,008), F-series pickup (869,001), VW Golf (795,835), Opel Astra (770,003), Chevy pickup (644,084), Renault Megane (598,434), Renault Clio (496,733), Opel Corsa (459,510), Peugeot 206 (457,521), Toyota Camry (448,162), Fiat Punto (445,535), Dodge Ram pickup (428,930), Ford Explorer (428,772), Honda Accord (425,160), Ford Taurus (368,327), VW Polo (349,579), Ford Ranger pickup (348,353), VW Passat (322,493), and Honda Civic (316,332) had sufficient sales volume in 1999 to fully depreciate a body-stamping machine within two model years. Most moderately successful models sell less than 100,000 units per year. Therefore, a six-year period is required to "wear out" a body-stamping machine making repetitive presses on a typical model's platform.

One common approach to this problem of achieving minimum efficient scale has been to export the product beyond limited domestic markets and sell the same model under different names in different countries (e.g., Ford Focus/Fiesta and VW Golf/Bora/Vento). Another approach has been to consolidate companies across several continents (DaimlerChrysler-Mitsubishi, Ford-Volvo-Mazda, GM-Opel-Fiat-Isuzu-Suzuki, and Renault-Nissan) to get access for domestic models into foreign markets. The Jeep Grand Cherokee, for example, was projected to do quite well in European Mercedes-Benz showrooms.

Nevertheless, most managers of model-specific product planning have continued to face a tough dilemma. Should they change body shapes and structural components every three to five years to keep their model "current"? Or should they forgo the body

---

[18] Based on "Aluminum Cars," *The Economist*, April 15, 2000, p. 89; *Consumer Report*, April 1997, p. 26; "The Global Gambles of GM," *The Economist*, June 24, 2000, p. 67; and "Daimler-Chrysler Merger," *Wall Street Journal*, May 8, 1998, p. A10.

style changes and fully depreciate their model's body-stamping machines over a six-year period or longer? The former decision necessitates scrapping a machine with substantial physical working life remaining and recovering the capital equipment investment with a much higher unit cost per vehicle. This classic economy of scale issue is avoided with aluminum space frame production. While 10 percent more costly on average than the typical steel and sheet metal vehicle, the minimum efficient scale of an aluminum intensive auto assembly process is only 50,000 cars. As illustrated in Figure 8.9, a marketing plan for smaller volume niche products like the Chevrolet Corvette, Ford Mustang, and Jeep Wrangler can achieve minimum efficient scale at Point *A* with these new aluminum production techniques. Previously with sheet metal and steel automobiles, production runs at this reduced scale resulted in unit costs at Point *B,* more than twice as large as a 300,000-unit vehicle (compare Point *C*).

Figure 8.9   Minimum Efficient Scale in Autos

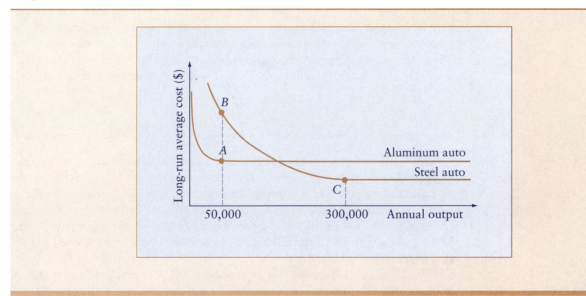

SUMMARY

- *Cost* is defined as the sacrifice incurred whenever an exchange or transformation of resources takes place.
- Different approaches are used in measuring costs, depending on the purposes for which the information is to be used. For financial reporting purposes, the historical outlay of funds is usually the appropriate measure of cost, whereas for decision-making purposes, it is often appropriate to measure cost in terms of the opportunities forgone or sacrificed.
- A *cost function* is a schedule, graph, or mathematical relationship showing the minimum achievable cost (such as total, average, or marginal cost) of producing various quantities of output.
- Short-run *total costs* are equal to the sum of *fixed* and *variable costs.*

- *Marginal cost* is defined as the incremental increase in total cost that results from a one-unit increase in output.

- The short-run average variable and marginal cost functions of economic theory are hypothesized to be U-shaped, first falling and then rising as output is increased. Falling short-run unit costs are attributed to the gains available from specialization in the use of capital and labor. Rising short-run unit costs are attributed to diminishing returns in production.

- The theoretical long-run average cost function is often found to be L-shaped. This is due to the frequent presence of scale economies and frequent absence of scale diseconomies. *Economies of scale* are attributed primarily to the nature of the production process or the factor markets, whereas *diseconomies of scale* are attributed primarily to problems of coordination and inflexibility in large-scale organizations.

- Volume discounts in purchasing inputs and learning curve effects, both of which result from a larger cumulative volume of output, can be distinguished from scale effects, which depend on the firm's rate of output per unit time period. Learning curve advantages often, therefore, arise in small-scale plants able to make long production runs.

- *Minimum efficient scale* is achieved by a rate of output sufficient to reduce long-run average total cost to the minimum possible level. Smaller rates of output imply smaller plant sizes to reduce unit cost, albeit to higher levels than would be possible if a firm's business plan could support minimum efficient scale production.

EXERCISES

1. Kay Evans has just completed her B.S. degree and is considering pursuing doctoral (Ph.D.) studies in economics. If Kay takes a job immediately after graduation, she can earn $35,000 during the first year, with an anticipated raise of $4,000 per year over the next five years. If Kay pursues the doctorate, five more years of school are required. Kay has been offered an assistantship paying $9,500 per year plus tuition. Books and computer purchases needed for her study will cost an average of $1,500 per year. These costs will not be incurred if Kay takes a job immediately. Upon graduation, Kay expects an annual income level of $55,000 during her first year of teaching. The growth rate in Kay's teaching salary is expected to equal the growth rate of the income she would make if she did not pursue the Ph.D. How should Kay evaluate her decision to pursue a Ph.D.? What other information do you need? What factors other than salary should be considered?

2. US Airways owns a piece of land near the Pittsburgh International Airport. The land originally cost US Airways $375,000. The airline is considering building a new training center on this land. US Airways has determined that the proposal to build the new facility is acceptable if the original cost of the land is used in the analysis, but the proposal does not meet the airline's project acceptance criteria if the land cost is above $850,000. A developer has recently offered US Airways $2.5 million for the land. Should US Airways build the training facility at this location? (Ignore taxes.)

3. Howard Bowen is a large cotton farmer. The land and machinery he owns has a current market value of $4,000,000. Bowen owes his local bank $3,000,000.

Last year Bowen sold $5,000,000 worth of cotton. His variable operating costs were $4,500,000; accounting depreciation was $40,000, although the actual decline in value of Bowen's machinery was $60,000 last year. Bowen paid himself a salary of $50,000, which is not considered part of his variable operating costs. Interest on his bank loan was $400,000. If Bowen worked for another farmer or a local manufacturer, his annual income would be about $30,000. Bowen can invest any funds that would be derived, if the farm were sold, to earn 10 percent annually. (Ignore taxes.)

a. Compute Bowen's accounting profits.

b. Compute Bowen's economic profits.

4. Mary Graham has worked as a real estate agent for Piedmont Properties for 15 years. Her annual income is approximately $100,000 per year. Mary is considering establishing her own real estate agency. She expects to generate revenues during the first year of $2,000,000. Salaries paid to her employees are expected to total $1,500,000. Operating expenses (i.e., rent, supplies, utility services) are expected to total $250,000. To begin the business, Mary must borrow $500,000 from her bank at an interest rate of 15 percent. Equipment will cost Mary $50,000. At the end of one year, the value of this equipment will be $30,000, even though the depreciation expense for tax purposes is only $5,000 during the first year.

a. Determine the (pretax) accounting profit for this venture.

b. Determine the (pretax) economic profit for this venture.

c. Which of the costs for this firm are explicit and which are implicit?

5. In the ore-mining example described earlier in the chapter (Table 8.4), suppose again that labor (L) is a variable input and capital (K) is a fixed input. Specifically, assume that the firm has a piece of equipment having a 500-brake-horsepower rating.

a. Complete the table shown below.

b. Plot the variable, fixed, and total cost functions on one graph.

c. Plot the marginal, average variable, average fixed, and average total cost functions on another graph.

Output Q	Input X	Variable Cost VC	Input Y	Fixed Cost FC	Total Cost TC	Avg. Variable Cost AVC	Avg. Fixed Cost AFC	Avg. Total Cost ATC	Marginal Cost MC
___	0	___	___	___	___	___	___	___	___
___	1	___	___	___	___	___	___	___	___
___	2	___	___	___	___	___	___	___	___
___	3	___	___	___	___	___	___	___	___
___	4	___	___	___	___	___	___	___	___
___	5	___	___	___	___	___	___	___	___
___	6	___	___	___	___	___	___	___	___
___	7	___	___	___	___	___	___	___	___
___	8	___	___	___	___	___	___	___	___

6. From your knowledge of the relationships among the various cost functions, complete the following table.

Q	TC	FC	VC	ATC	AFC	AVC	MC
0	125						
10							5
20				10.50			
30			110				
40	255						
50						3	
60							3
70				5			
80			295				

7. Economists at General Industries have been examining operating costs at one of its parts manufacturing plants in an effort to determine if the plant is being operated efficiently. From weekly cost records, the economists developed the following cost-output information concerning the operation of the plant:

   a. AVC (average variable cost) at an output of 2,000 units per week is $7.50.
   b. At an output level of 5,000 units per week, AFC (average fixed cost) is $3.
   c. TC (total cost) increases by $5,000 when output is increased from 2,000 to 3,000 units per week.
   d. TVC (total variable cost) at an output level of 4,000 units per week is $23,000.
   e. AVC (average variable cost) decreases by $.75 per unit when output is increased from 4,000 to 5,000 units per week.
   f. AFC plus AVC for 8,000 units per week is $7.50 per unit.
   g. ATC (average total cost) decreases by $.50 per unit when output is decreased from 8,000 to 7,000 units per week.
   h. TVC increases by $3,000 when output is increased from 5,000 to 6,000 units per week.
   i. TC decreases by $7,000 when output is decreased from 2,000 to 1,000 units per week.
   j. MC (marginal cost) is $16 per unit when output is increased from 8,000 to 9,000 units per week.

   Given the preceding information, complete the following cost schedule for the plant on the next page. *Hint:* Proceed sequentially through the list, *filling in all the related entries before proceeding to the next item of information in the list.*

8. Consider the following variable cost function (Q = output):

$$VC = 200Q - 9Q^2 + .25Q^3$$

Fixed costs are equal to $150.

Output (Units Per Week)	TFC	TVC	TC	AFC	AVC	ATC	MC
0	___	___	___	x	x	x	x
1,000	___	___	___	___	___	___	___
2,000	___	___	___	___	___	___	___
3,000	___	___	___	___	___	___	___
4,000	___	___	___	___	___	___	___
5,000	___	___	___	___	___	___	___
6,000	___	___	___	___	___	___	___
7,000	___	___	___	___	___	___	___
8,000	___	___	___	___	___	___	___
9,000	___	___	___	___	___	___	___

    a. Determine the total cost function.

    b. Determine the (i) average fixed, (ii) average variable, (iii) average total, and (iv) marginal cost functions.

    c. Determine the value of Q at which point the average variable cost function takes on its minimum value. *Hint:* Take the first derivative of the AVC function, set the derivative equal to 0, and solve for Q. Also use the second derivative to check for a maximum or minimum.

    d. Determine the value of Q at which point the marginal cost function takes on its minimum value.

9. Consider Exercise 8 again.

    a. Plot the (i) AVC and (ii) MC functions on a single graph for the values of $Q = 2, 4, 6, \ldots, 24$.

    b. Based on the cost functions graphed in Part (a), determine the value of Q that minimizes (i) AVC and (ii) MC.

    c. Compare your answers in Part (b) with those obtained earlier in 8(c) and 8(d).

10. Suppose a firm's variable cost function is given by the relationship

$$VC = 150Q - 10Q^2 + .5Q^3$$

where Q is the quantity of output produced.

    a. Determine the output level Q at which point the *average* variable cost function takes on its minimum value.

    b. What are the values of the variable cost and average variable cost functions at the output level in Part (a)?

    c. Determine the output level Q at which point the *marginal* cost function takes on its minimum value.

    d. What are the value of the variable cost and marginal cost functions at the output level in Part (c)?

11. A manufacturing plant has a potential production capacity of 1,000 units per month (capacity can be increased by 10 percent if subcontractors are employed). The plant is normally operated at about 80 percent of capacity. Operating the plant above this level significantly increases variable costs per unit because of the need to pay the skilled workers higher overtime wage rates. For output levels up to 80 percent of capacity, variable cost per unit is $100. Above 80 and up to 90 percent, variable costs on this *additional* output *increase* by 10 percent. When output is above 90 and up to 100 percent of capacity, the *additional* units cost an *additional* 25 percent over the unit variable costs for outputs up to 80 percent of capacity. For production above 100 percent and up to 110 percent of capacity, extensive subcontracting work is used and the unit variable costs of these *additional* units are 50 percent above those at output levels up to 80 percent of capacity. At 80 percent of capacity, the plant's fixed costs per unit are $50. Total fixed costs are not expected to change within the production range under consideration. Based on the preceding information, complete the following table.

Q	TC	FC	VC	ATC	AFC	AVC	MC
500	_____	_____	_____	_____	_____	_____	_____
600	_____	_____	_____	_____	_____	_____	_____
700	_____	_____	_____	_____	_____	_____	_____
800	_____	_____	_____	_____	_____	_____	_____
900	_____	_____	_____	_____	_____	_____	_____
1,000	_____	_____	_____	_____	_____	_____	_____
1,100	_____	_____	_____	_____	_____	_____	_____

12. The Blair Company has three assembly plants located in California, Georgia, and New Jersey. Currently, the company purchases a major subassembly, which becomes part of the final product, from an outside firm. Blair has decided to manufacture the subassemblies within the company and must now consider whether to rent one centrally located facility (for example, in Missouri, where all the subassemblies would be manufactured) or to rent three separate facilities, each located near one of the assembly plants, where each facility would manufacture only the subassemblies needed for the nearby assembly plant. A single, centrally located facility, with a production capacity of 18,000 units per year, would have fixed costs of $900,000 per year and a variable cost of $250 per unit. Three separate decentralized facilities, with production capacities of 8,000, 6,000, and 4,000 units per year, would have fixed costs of $475,000, $425,000, and $400,000, respectively, and variable costs per unit of only $225 per unit, owing primarily to the reduction in shipping costs. The current production rates at the three assembly plants are 6,000, 4,500, and 3,000 units, respectively.

a. Assuming that the current production rates are maintained at the three assembly plants, which alternative should management select?

b. If demand for the final product were to increase to production capacity, which alternative would be more attractive?

c. What additional information would be useful before making a decision?

13. Kitchen Helper Company has decided to produce and sell food blenders and is considering three different types of production facilities ("plants"). Plant *A* is a labor-intensive facility, employing relatively little specialized capital equipment. Plant *B* is a semiautomated facility that would employ less labor than *A* but would also have higher capital equipment costs. Plant *C* is a completely automated facility using much more high-cost, high-technology capital equip-

ment and even less labor than *B*. Information about the operating costs and production capacities of these three different types of plants is shown in the following table.

	Plant Type		
	A	B	C
Unit variable costs			
Materials	$3.50	$3.25	$3.00
Labor	4.50	3.25	2.00
Overhead	1.00	1.50	2.00
Total	$9.00	$8.00	$7.00
Annual fixed costs			
Depreciation	$ 60,000	$100,000	$200,000
Capital	30,000	50,000	100,000
Overhead	60,000	100,000	150,000
Total	$150,000	$250,000	$450,000
Annual capacity	75,000	150,000	350,000

    a. Determine the average total cost schedules for each plant type for annual outputs of 25,000, 50,000, 75,000, ... , 350,000. For output levels beyond the capacity of a given plant, assume that multiple plants of the same type are built. For example, to produce 200,000 units with Plant *A*, three of these plants would be built.

    b. Based on the cost schedules calculated in Part (a), construct the long-run average total cost schedule for the production of blenders.

14. Sisneros has just completed his MBA degree and is considering pursuing doctoral (Ph.D.) studies in economics. If Sisneros takes a job immediately after his MBA, he could earn $60,000 during the first year, with an anticipated raise of $5,000 per year over the next four years. If Sisneros pursues the doctorate, four more years of school are required. Sisneros has been offered an assistantship paying $14,000 per year plus tuition. Books and computer purchases needed for his study will cost an average of $2,000 per year. These costs will not be incurred if Sisneros takes a job immediately. Upon graduation, Sisneros expects an annual income level of $75,000 during his first year of teaching. The growth rate in Sisneros' teaching salary is expected to equal the growth rate of the income he would make if he did not pursue the Ph.D. How should Sisneros evaluate his decision to pursue a Ph.D.? What other information do you need? What factors other than salary should be considered?

15. The ARA Railroad owns a piece of land along one of its right-of-ways. The land originally cost ARA $100,000. ARA is considering building a new maintenance facility on this land. ARA has determined that the proposal to build the new facility is acceptable if the original cost of the land is used in the analysis, but the proposal does not meet the railroad's project acceptance criteria if the land cost is above $500,000. An investor has recently offered ARA $1 million for the land. Should ARA build the maintenance facility at this location?

http://

Stranded Costs and Electric
Utility Deregulation

16. One of the most controversial policy issues in the area of electric utility deregulation is the treatment of so-called "stranded costs." There are several sites
on the Internet that describe stranded costs, including the following:

http://www.rapmaine.org/stranded.html
http://www.local.org/stranded.html
http://www.afce.org/position/p&p.htm
http://www.eia.doe.gov/cneaf/electricity/chg_str/chapter8.html

Describe how the different treatments of stranded costs (shareholders pay,
ratepayers pay) affect an electric utility's cost structure.

CASE EXERCISE

COST ANALYSIS

The Leisure Products (LP) Company manufactures lawn and patio furniture. Most
of its output is sold to do-it-yourself warehouse stores (for example, Lowe's Home
Improvement) and to retail hardware and department store chains (for example, True
Value and JC Penney), who then distribute the products under their respective brand
names. LP is not involved in direct retail sales. Last year the firm had sales of $35
million.

One of LP's divisions manufactures folding (aluminum and vinyl) chairs. Sales of
the chairs are highly seasonal, with 80 percent of the sales volume concentrated in
the January–June period. Production is normally concentrated in the September–May
period. Approximately 75 percent of the hourly workforce (unskilled and semiskilled
workers) is laid off (or takes paid vacation time) during the June–August period of
reduced output. The remainder of the workforce, consisting of salaried plant management (line managers and supervisors), maintenance, and clerical staff, are retained
during this slow period. Maintenance personnel, for example, perform major over-
hauls of the machinery during the slow summer period.

LP planned to produce and sell 500,000 of these chairs during the coming year
at a projected selling price of $7.15 per chair. The cost per unit was estimated as
follows:

Direct labor	$2.25
Materials	2.30
Plant overhead*	1.15
Administrative and selling expense*	.80
TOTAL	$6.50

*These costs are allocated to each unit of output based on the projected annual production of 500,000 chairs.

A 10-percent markup ($.65) was added to the cost per unit in arriving at the firm's
selling price of $7.15 (plus shipping).

In May, LP received an inquiry from Southeast Department Stores concerning
the possible purchase of folding chairs for delivery in August. Southeast indicated
that they would place an order for 30,000 chairs if the price did not exceed $5.50
each (plus shipping). The chairs could be produced during the slow period using
the firm's existing equipment and workforce. No overtime wages would have to be
paid to the workforce in fulfilling the order. Adequate materials were on hand (or
could be purchased at prevailing market prices) to complete the order.

LP management was considering whether to accept the order. The firm's chief
accountant felt that the firm should *not* accept the order because the price per chair

was less than the total cost and contributed nothing to the firm's profits. The firm's chief economist argued that the firm should accept the order *if* the incremental revenue would exceed the incremental cost.

The following cost accounting definitions may be helpful in making this decision:

- Direct labor—labor costs incurred in converting the raw material into the finished product.
- Material—raw materials that enter into and become part of the final product.
- Plant overhead—all costs other than direct labor and materials that are associated with the product, including wages and salaries paid to employees who do not work directly on the product but whose services are related to the production process (such as line managers, maintenance, and janitorial personnel); heat; light; power; supplies; depreciation; taxes; and insurance on the assets employed in the production process.
- Selling and distribution costs—costs incurred in making sales (for example, billing and salespeople's compensation), storing the product, and shipping the product to the customer. (In this case the customer pays all shipping costs.)
- Administrative costs—items not listed in the preceding categories, including general and executive office costs, research, development, engineering costs, and miscellaneous items.

QUESTIONS

1. Calculate the incremental (that is, marginal) cost per chair to LP of accepting the order from Southeast.

2. What assumptions did you make in calculating the incremental cost in Question 1? What additional information would be helpful in making these calculations?

3. Based on your answers to Questions 1 and 2, should LP accept the Southeast order?

4. What additional considerations might lead LP to reject the order?

Appendix 8a

Long-Run Costs with a Cobb-Douglas Production Function

In Chapter 8, the shape of the firm's long-run unit cost structure (the *LAC*) was shown to depend on whether economies or diseconomies of scale were present. *A priori* hypotheses about the shape of the firm's *LAC* can be derived, before examining cost data, by postulating a production function for the firm. Consider the Cobb-Douglas production function

$$Q = \alpha L^{\beta_1} K^{\beta_2} \qquad [8A.1]$$

where L is the amount of labor, K is the amount of capital used in producing Q units of output, and α, β_1, and β_2 are constants. The total cost of employing L units of labor and K units of capital in a production process is equal to

$$C = C_L L + C_K K \qquad [8A.2]$$

where C_L and C_K are the per-unit prices of labor and capital, respectively. Using Lagrangian multiplier techniques, one can determine the total cost (C) of producing any level of output.

The objective is to minimize the total cost (C) of producing a given level of output $Q = Q_0$. We begin by forming the Lagrangian function

$$L_C = C + \lambda(Q - Q_0) \qquad [8A.3]$$
$$= C_L L + C_K K + \lambda(\alpha L^{\beta_1} K^{\beta_2} - Q_0) \qquad [8A.4]$$

Differentiating L_C with respect to L, K, and λ and setting these derivatives equal to zero yields

$$\frac{\partial L_C}{\partial L} = C_L + \lambda(\beta_1 \alpha L^{\beta_1 - 1} K^{\beta_2}) = 0 \qquad [8A.5]$$

$$\frac{\partial L_C}{\partial K} = C_K + \lambda(\beta_2 \alpha L^{\beta_1} K^{\beta_2 - 1}) = 0 \qquad [8A.6]$$

$$\frac{\partial L_C}{\partial \lambda} = \alpha L^{\beta_1} K^{\beta_2} - Q_0 = 0 \qquad [8A.7]$$

Solving these equations yields the following cost-minimizing values of L and K:

$$L* = \left(\frac{Q_0}{\alpha}\right)^{1/(\beta_1 + \beta_2)} \left(\frac{\beta_1 C_K}{\beta_2 C_L}\right)^{\beta_2/(\beta_1 + \beta_2)} \qquad [8A.8]$$

$$K* = \left(\frac{Q_0}{\alpha}\right)^{1/(\beta_1 + \beta_2)} \left(\frac{\beta_1 C_L}{\beta_2 C_K}\right)^{\beta_1/(\beta_1 + \beta_2)} \qquad [8A.9]$$

Substituting Equation 8A.8 for L and Equation 8A.9 for K in Equation 8A.2 and doing some algebraic operations gives the total cost (C) of producing any level of output (Q):

$$C = C_L^{\beta_1/(\beta_1 + \beta_2)} C_K^{\beta_2/(\beta_1 + \beta_2)} \left[\left(\frac{\beta_2}{\beta_1}\right)^{\beta_1/(\beta_1 + \beta_2)} + \left(\frac{\beta_2}{\beta_1}\right)^{-\beta_2/(\beta_1 + \beta_2)}\right] \left(\frac{Q}{\alpha}\right)^{1/(\beta_1 + \beta_2)}$$

This cost equation indicates that total costs are a function of the output level (Q), the per-units costs of labor (C_L) and capital (C_K), and the parameters (α, β_1, and β_2) of the Cobb-Douglas production function.

Several examples can be used to illustrate the implied shapes of the firm's long-run average cost (LAC) and long-run total cost (LTC). In the following examples, assume that $\alpha = 4.0$ and that the per-unit costs of labor (C_L) and capital (C_K) are \$2 and \$8, respectively.

Constant Returns

$\beta_1 = .50$, $\beta_2 = .50$ (Because $\beta_1 + \beta_2 = 1.0$, this is an example of *constant* returns to scale.)

$$LTC = (2)^{.50}(8)^{.50} [1 + 1] \left(\frac{Q}{4.0}\right)^1$$

$$= 2.0Q$$

$$LAC = \frac{C}{Q} = \frac{2.0Q}{Q}$$

$$= 2.0$$

These LAC and LTC functions are graphed in Panel (a) of Figure 8A.1. Note that when the Cobb-Douglas production function exhibits constant returns to scale, total costs increase linearly with output and average total costs are constant, or independent of output.

Decreasing Returns

$\beta_1 = .25$, $\beta_2 = .25$ (Because $\beta_1 + \beta_2 < 1.0$, this is an example of *decreasing* returns to scale.)

$$LTC = (2)^{.50}(8)^{.50} [1 + 1] \left(\frac{Q}{4.0}\right)^2$$

$$= .50Q^2$$

$$LAC = .50Q$$

These cost functions are graphed in Panel (b) of Figure 8A.1. Note that when the Cobb-Douglas production function exhibits decreasing returns to scale, total costs increase more than proportionately with output and average total costs rise as output increases (i.e., decreasing returns to scale).

Increasing Returns

$\beta_1 = 1.0$, $\beta_2 = 1.0$ (Because $\beta_1 + \beta_2 > 1.0$, this is an example of *increasing* returns to scale.)

$$LTC = (2)^{.50}(8)^{.50} [1 + 1] \left(\frac{Q}{4.0}\right)^{.50}$$

$$= 4.0 \, Q^{.50}$$

$$LAC = \frac{4.0}{Q^{.50}}$$

These cost functions are graphed in Panel (c) of Figure 8A.1. Note that when the Cobb-Douglas production function exhibits increasing returns to scale, total costs

FIGURE 8A.1   **Long-Run Average Cost and Long-Run Total Cost Functions for a Cobb-Douglas Production Function**

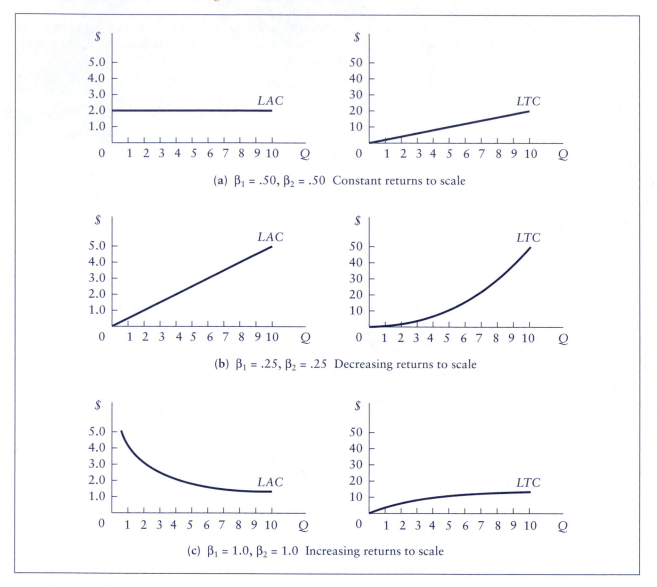

(a) $\beta_1 = .50$, $\beta_2 = .50$ Constant returns to scale

(b) $\beta_1 = .25$, $\beta_2 = .25$ Decreasing returns to scale

(c) $\beta_1 = 1.0$, $\beta_2 = 1.0$ Increasing returns to scale

increase less than proportionately with output and average total costs fall as output increases (i.e., increasing returns to scale).

EXERCISES

1. Determine how many units of labor (L^*) and capital (K^*) are required to produce five units of output (Q_0) for the production function given in the

    a. Constant returns example.

    b. Decreasing returns example.

    c. Increasing returns example.

2.   Recompute your answers to Exercise 1, assuming that the per-unit cost of labor increases from $C_L = \$2$ to $C_L' = \$4$. How has the increase in the labor rate affected the optimal proportions of labor and capital used in the production process?

3.   Determine the total cost of producing five units of output (Q_0) for the production function given in the

   a.   Constant returns example.
   b.   Decreasing returns example.
   c.   Increasing returns example.

4.   Use the data in Table 8.4 and a multiple regression analysis program on your computer to estimate a Cobb-Douglas production function of the form shown in Equation 8A.1. Do you observe increasing, decreasing, or constant returns to scale?

9

Applications of Cost Theory

CHAPTER PREVIEW This chapter examines some of the techniques that have been developed for estimating the cost functions of actual production processes and firms. In the short run, a knowledge of the firm's cost function is essential when deciding whether to accept an additional order, perhaps at less than "full cost"; whether to schedule overtime for workers; or whether to temporarily suspend operations but not close the plant. In the long run, a knowledge of cost-function relationships will determine the capital investments to make, the production technology to adopt, the markets to enter, and the new products to introduce. Because capital expenditures often cannot be reversed without significant losses, it is essential that a value-maximizing manager gather the cost information needed to make these long-term investment decisions. The first part of the chapter examines various techniques for empirically estimating short-run and long-run cost functions. The second part of the chapter deals with break-even and contribution analysis—an application of cost theory that is useful in examining the profitability of a firm's operations. Appendix 9A discusses mass customization and learning curves.

MANAGERIAL CHALLENGE

Product Costing and CAM-I and ABC[1]

Measurement of a company's costs and cost-output relationships is one of the most important and difficult tasks faced by managers. Accurate cost information is crucial in making all resource-allocation decisions within the company.

In the late 1980s, Computer-Aided Manufacturing-International (CAM-I), a research cooperative, formed a cost management group to look at such issues as investment justification, product costing, total life-cycle costs of products, and measurement of manufacturing performance. Members of the cost management group included large U.S. and European manufacturers, large accounting firms, and the Department of Defense.

The cost accounting methods promoted by CAM-I differ significantly from traditional methods. For example, consider the general overhead rate. This cost category includes everything except direct labor and materials. Components of overhead include engineering, administration, energy, and depreciation of capital equipment. Overhead costs typically account for 50 percent or more of production costs. In most companies overhead costs are allocated over all products manufactured by the company.

The problem with this approach is that companies that make many different products do not know how much it costs to make any one product. The solution is to attempt to determine the costs of every operation, including overhead functions, and allocate them according to how much time it takes to process a product by each operation. American Airlines recently spent $3 million to find the direct cost of an occupied seat on each city-pair route.

When this activity-based cost (ABC) system was implemented at an automobile-stamping plant it was found that the calculated total production costs for individual products were off by as much as plus or minus 60 percent. As a consequence, the plant was making a number of components it could have bought more cheaply, and it was outsourcing and purchasing several components it would have been cheaper to produce. Management of the stamping plant now feels that these new ABC-based estimates of direct cost may be one of its most potent competitive weapons.

Activity-Based Costing
A method of allocating direct fixed cost to time on task or other activities closely related to actual production events.

http://
You can learn more about the CAM-I Cost Management Systems Program on the Internet at
http://www.apics.org/sigs/articles/fall.Reman.htm

[1] Based on an article entitled "How the New Math of Productivity Adds Up," *BusinessWeek*, June 6, 1988, pp. 100–113.

TYPES OF COST FUNCTIONS

A *cost function* is a schedule, graph, or mathematical relationship showing the total, average, or marginal cost of producing various quantities of output. Two different cost functions can be defined and derived—the *short-run* and the *long-run* cost functions. The short-run cost function is relevant to decisions in which one or more of the inputs to the production process are fixed or incapable of being altered. To make optimal pricing and production decisions, the firm must have a knowledge of the shape and characteristics of its short-run cost function. For example, to decide whether to accept or refuse an order offered at some particular price, the firm must identify exactly what variable cost and direct fixed costs the order entails. In contrast, the long-run cost function is associated with the longer-term planning period in which all the inputs to the production process are variable and no restrictions are placed on the amount of an input that can be employed in the production process. Consequently, all costs including indirect fixed costs like headquarters facility costs are avoidable. To make optimal investment decisions on everything from new production facilities to new product introductions, the firm must have a knowledge of the behavior of its long-run cost function.

SHORT-RUN COST-OUTPUT RELATIONSHIPS

This section discusses the problems inherent in the statistical estimation of short-run cost functions and hypothesized cost-output relationships, and gives some examples of short-run cost functions.

Problems in Estimating Short-Run Cost Functions[2]

In seeking to measure statistically the static cost function of economic theory, one usually attempts to take observations of the dynamic actual cost function at different points in time. These observations must be taken in a way that allows one to estimate the average relationship between cost and output over a wide range of output values. Most of the problems in cost studies are associated with the following:

- Differences in the methods by which firms define and measure costs
- Accounting for other variables (in addition to the output level) that influence costs, like total (cumulative) volume or the costs associated with batch production runs versus frequent change orders

Differences in Cost Definition and Measurement   Recall from the discussion of the issues that arise in measuring cost in Chapter 8 that differences exist between the economic and accounting concepts of cost. Economic cost is represented by the value of opportunities forgone, whereas accounting cost is measured by the outlays that are incurred. Some oil and mining companies like Deep Creek Mining record the cost of their own crude oil, coal, or gas shipped downstream to their refining and processing operations at the world market price contemporaneous with the shipment (i.e., at their opportunity cost). Other companies account for these same resources at their out-of-pocket cost. If extraction costs are low (e.g., with West Texas intermediate crude or Persian Gulf oil), the two cost methods will diverge since the higher cost of the marginal producer (e.g., an oil platform in the North Sea) determines the market price.

---

[2] Much of this discussion is based on the work of Joel Dean, who pioneered the development of statistical cost functions. See Joel Dean, *Statistical Cost Estimation* (Bloomington, IN: Indiana University Press, 1976), pp. 3–35, for a more expanded treatment of the problems associated with the measurement of cost functions.

To measure variable costs (i.e., costs that vary with output), some companies employ direct accounting costs. "Direct" costs include materials, supplies, direct labor costs, and any direct fixed costs avoidable by refusing the batch order in question—e.g., the lawn furniture rented by a caterer for a client's garden party. Direct costs exclude all overhead and any other (indirect) fixed cost—i.e., any fixed cost that must be allocated. For batch decisions about whether to accept an order for a proposed charter air flight, a special production run, or a customer's proposed change order, these estimates of variable plus direct fixed costs are just what is needed.

Another cost measurement issue arises with depreciation, the decline in value of a capital asset. Conceptually, depreciation can be divided into two components—*time depreciation* represents the decline in value associated with the passage of *time,* and *use depreciation* represents the decline in value associated with *use.* For example, annual body style changes in the automobile industry, or technical progress in speed and memory of personal computers, renders products and production processes obsolete. Note that such time depreciation is completely independent of the rate of output at which the asset (for example, plant and equipment) is operated.

Because only use depreciation varies with the rate of output, only use depreciation is relevant in determining the shape of the cost-output relationship. However, accounting data on depreciation are seldom broken down into the two components, and it is therefore usually impossible to measure use depreciation costs separately. Also, the depreciation of the value of an asset over its life cycle is usually determined by tax regulations rather than by economic criteria. As a result, the depreciation costs allocated to any period may misstate true economic depreciation costs. Finally, capital asset values (and their associated depreciation costs) are often stated in terms of historical costs rather than in terms of replacement costs. In periods of rapidly increasing price levels, this will tend to understate true economic depreciation costs. These limitations need to be kept in mind when interpreting the cost-output relationship for a firm with numerous capital assets, like an airline.

Accounting for Other Variables   In addition to being a function of the output level of the firm, cost is a function of other factors, such as output mix, the size of manufacturing lots, employee absenteeism and turnover, production methods, factor prices, and managerial efficiency.

A number of methods can be used to try to control for these other factors and thereby isolate the cost-output relationship itself, such as the following:

- Selecting an appropriate time period for analysis in which the other factors remain constant
- Preadjusting the cost-output data to remove the effects of these other variables
- Using multiple regression analysis to hold constant the effects of these other variables

Each of these methods is examined below in more detail.

Selecting an Appropriate Time Period for Analysis   The cost-output observations should be collected during a period in which no major changes in the product, plant, equipment, or work methods are taking place. Likewise, managerial methods and policies should remain constant during the collection period; for example, no major cost-cutting programs should be instituted during the period.

Once the time period for analysis has been selected, it must be divided into a series of observation periods for collection of cost-output data. Several factors have to be *balanced* in choosing the length of the observation period. Use of a short observation period like a day or week will ensure that the output rate within the period will be approximately constant and will permit a large number of cost-output observations to be collected, thereby improving the statistical reliability of the results. The use of a long observation period, however, will minimize any errors and discrepancies that occur in allocating costs to the various time periods and in matching output with its associated costs. The ideal length of the observation period will vary with different situations and will depend in part on the detail and frequency of accounting records that are maintained by the firm and that are available to the investigator.

Altering the Cost-Output Data   The effects of some of the other influencing variables can be removed from the cost-output data through various standard preadjustment procedures.

Whenever wage rates or raw material prices change significantly over the period of analysis, one can deflate the cost data to reflect these changes in factor prices. Provided suitable price indices are available or can be constructed, costs incurred at different points in time can be restated as dollars of equivalent purchasing power.[3] It is preferable to use separate indices to deflate each of the various cost categories (for example, wages, raw materials, and utilities) rather than using a single index to deflate total costs.

If a time lag exists from the time a cost is incurred to the time it is reported, other adjustments are required. Maintenance cost is an example. Maintenance to equipment during peak periods of production can sometimes be postponed until subsequent periods of normal or below-normal operation. As a result, the higher costs of maintenance, which are incurred during periods of peak output due to more wear and tear on equipment, will not be recorded until later periods. A procedure for reallocating costs among different reporting periods is required in these situations.

Using Multiple Regression Analysis   If the effects of some of the other variables that influence costs cannot be removed by either of the preceding methods, a third possible method is to hold constant the effect of these variables using multiple regression techniques. For example, suppose a firm believes that, all other influencing factors remaining constant, costs should decline gradually over time as a result of innovative worker suggestions. One way to incorporate this effect into the cost equation would be to include time t as an additional explanatory variable:

$$C = f(Q, t) \qquad\qquad [9.1]$$

Other possible explanatory variables include the number of product lines, the number of customer segments, and the number of distribution channels.[4]

---

[3] Two assumptions are implicit in this approach: No substitution takes place between the inputs as prices change, and changes in the output level have no influence on the prices of the inputs. For more automated plants that incorporate only maintenance personnel, plant engineers, and material supplies, these assumptions fit the reality of the production process.

[4] Other more advanced econometric procedures, which are beyond the scope of this text, have been used in dealing with the methodological problems encountered in cost studies. See, for example, A. Sinan Cebenoyan, "Scope Economies in Banking: The Hybrid Box-Cox Function," *The Financial Review* 25, no. 1 (February 1990), pp. 115–125; and H. Fried, C. A. Knox Lovell, and S. Schmidt, *The Measurement of Productive Efficiency: Techniques and Applications* (Cambridge: Oxford University Press, 1993).

Estimation of Empirical Cost-Output Relationships in the Short Run

Polynomial Function   The total cost function in the short run (*STC*), as hypothesized in economic theory, is an S-shaped curve that can be represented by a cubic relationship:

$$STC = a + bQ + cQ^2 + dQ^3 \qquad [9.2]$$

The familiar U-shaped marginal and average cost functions then can be derived from this relationship. The associated marginal cost function is

$$MC = \frac{d(STC)}{dQ} = b + 2cQ + 3dQ^2 \qquad [9.3]$$

and the average total cost function is

$$ATC = \frac{STC}{Q} = \frac{a}{Q} + b + cQ + dQ^2 \qquad [9.4]$$

The cubic total cost function and its associated marginal and average total cost functions are shown in Figure 9.1(a). The use of a polynomial function allows one to test statistically for effects of including higher powers of the output variable (Q^2 or Q^3) in the equation. Polynomial functions are easy to fit with standard least-squares regression techniques, as described in Chapter 4.

If the results of a regression analysis indicate that the cubic term (Q^3) is not statistically significant, then short-run total cost can be represented by a quadratic relationship like

$$STC = a + bQ + cQ^2 \qquad [9.5]$$

http://

To see how economic cost concepts are applied in the military, access the Defense Resources Management Institute's handbook of unit cost management at the following site maintained by the Naval Postgraduate School:

http://www.nps.navy.mil/ ~drmi/unitcost.htm

Figure 9.1   Polynomial Cost-Output Relationships

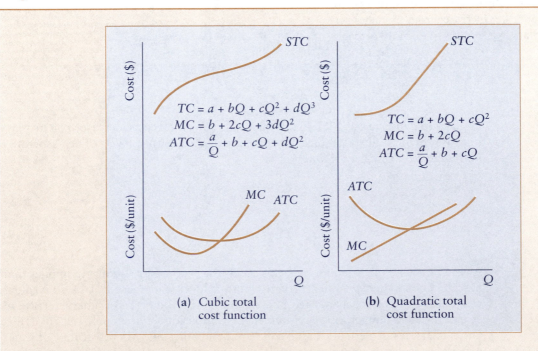

$$TC = a + bQ + cQ^2 + dQ^3$$
$$MC = b + 2cQ + 3dQ^2$$
$$ATC = \frac{a}{Q} + b + cQ + dQ^2$$

$$TC = a + bQ + cQ^2$$
$$MC = b + 2cQ$$
$$ATC = \frac{a}{Q} + b + cQ$$

(a) Cubic total cost function

(b) Quadratic total cost function

WHAT WENT RIGHT   WHAT WENT WRONG

Boeing: Rising Marginal Cost of 747s[5]

Boeing and Airbus provide all the wide-bodied jets the world needs. Boeing 747s, 767s, and 777s typically have a 60–70 percent share of the worldwide market, but Airbus accepted a majority of the new orders in 1994–1995 and doubled their output rate from 126 to 232 planes per year. Some analysts think Boeing should have given up even more of the wide-body order flow.

One reason is that until very recently, incremental orders at Boeing necessitated redrawing and duplicating the thousands of engineering diagrams that determine how 200,000 employees assemble any particular customer's plane. Rather than doing mass customization from common platforms, Boeing assembles one plane at a time with new drawings for each $150 million wide-body ordered. Eventually, incremental variable costs must rise as designers and shop floors get congested with new instructions and new diagrams.

With a backorder running to almost 1,000 planes companywide in the mid-1990s, Boeing boosted production from 180 to 560 commercial jets per year. At the Everett, Washington final assembly plant for Boeing wide-bodies, just north of Seattle, thruput was increased from 15 planes per month to 21 planes per month—i.e., by 40 percent.

To increase production rates this much typically requires splitting bottlenecked assembly stations into parallel processes entailing the hiring of additional assembly workers and massive overtime. Alternatively, a company like Boeing can secure a 40-percent increase in the production rate of final assembly by contracting out more subassemblies. Either splitting bottlenecked assembly stations or contracting out subassemblies substantially increases Boeing's variable costs.

In the late 1990s, wide-body prices did not rise because of intense competitive pressure from Airbus, but Boeing's marginal cost certainly did. As a result, for a while in the late 1990s, every Boeing 747 plane delivered had a price less than its marginal cost—i.e., a negative gross profit margin. Of course, eventually such orders must be refused. In 2000, Boeing did slow the production thruput rate at Everett back to 15 wide-bodies per month in order to return the wide-body product lines to profitability. Today, the well-equipped 747-400 aircraft earns as much as $45 million operating profit above variable cost.

---

[5] Based on "Boeing's Trouble," *Wall Street Journal*, December 16, 1998, p. A23, and Everett, Washington site visit.

---

as illustrated in Figure 9.1 (b). In this quadratic case, total costs increase at an increasing rate throughout the typical operating range of output levels. The associated marginal and average cost functions are

$$MC = \frac{d(STC)}{dQ} = b + 2cQ \qquad [9.6]$$

$$ATC = \frac{STC}{Q} = \frac{a}{Q} + b + cQ \qquad [9.7]$$

As can be seen from Equation 9.6, this quadratic total cost relationship implies that marginal costs increase linearly as the output level is increased. Rising marginal cost (such as Boeing experienced in assembling wide-body jets) is characteristic of essentially all manufacturing environments. Information services companies like IBM Global Services or network-based software companies like Microsoft may at times experience declining marginal cost.

Figure 9.2   Logarithmic Cost-Output Relationship

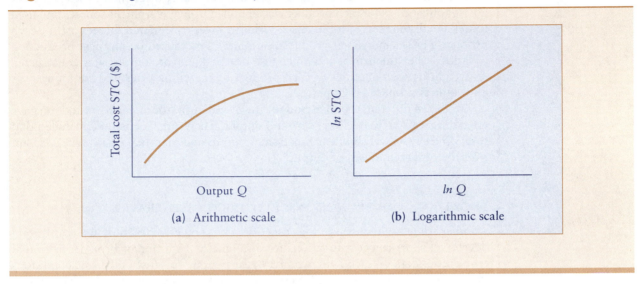

(a) Arithmetic scale   (b) Logarithmic scale

Logarithmic Function   A logarithmic function also can be used to represent empirical cost-output relationships. A simple cost relationship could take the form

$$lnSTC = a + b \, lnQ \qquad\qquad [9.8]$$

where *lnSTC* and *lnQ* are the respective natural logarithms of short-run total cost and output, respectively, and *a* and *b* are the parameters to be estimated by regression analysis.[6] Such a relationship is shown in Figure 9.2. In actual applications, for a multiproduct, multi-input firm or production process, the equation can become much more complex with the addition of linear, quadratic, and cross-product terms for all the different products and input prices.

Examples of Statistically Estimated Short-Run Cost Functions

Short-run cost functions have been estimated for firms in a large number of different industries—for example, food processing, furniture, railways, gas, coal, electricity, hosiery, steel, and cement.[7]

Example

SHORT-RUN COST FUNCTIONS: MULTIPLE-PRODUCT FOOD PROCESSING

In a study of a British food processing firm, Johnston constructed individual cost functions for 14 different products and an overall cost function for the firm.[8] Weekly data for nine months were obtained on the physical production of each type of product and total direct costs of each product (subdivided into the four categories of materials, labor, packing, and freight). Indirect costs (such as salaries, indirect labor,

---

[6] A *natural* logarithm, *lnX*, is a logarithm to the base "*e*," where *e* = 2.71828. . . . A logarithm to the base 10 is represented as log *X*.

[7] See A.A. Walters, "Production and Cost Functions: An Econometric Survey," *Econometrica* 31, no. 1–2 (January/April 1963), pp. 1–66, for a summary of these studies.

[8] See Jack Johnston, *Statistical Cost Analysis* (New York: McGraw-Hill, 1960), pp. 87–97.

factory charges, and laboratory expenses) remained fairly constant over the time period studied and were excluded from the analysis. A price index for each category of direct costs for each product was obtained from government sources and used to deflate all four sets of input costs, yielding a weekly deflated direct cost for each product. For the individual products, output was measured by physical production (quantity). For the firm as a whole, an index of aggregate output was constructed by weighting the quantities of each product by its selling price and summing over all products produced each period.

For the 14 different products and for the overall firm, the linear cost function gave an excellent fit between direct cost and output. Therefore, Johnston concluded that total direct costs were a linear function of output and marginal costs were constant over the observed ranges of output.

Example

SHORT-RUN COST FUNCTIONS: ELECTRICITY GENERATION[9]

Another study by Johnston of the costs of electric power generation in Great Britain developed short-run cost functions for a sample of 17 different firms from annual cost-output data on each firm over a 20-year period. To satisfy the basic conditions underlying the short-run cost function, only those firms whose capital equipment remained constant in size over the period were included in the sample. The output variable was measured in kilowatt-hours (kwh). The cost variable was defined as the "working costs of generation" and included (1) fuel; (2) salaries and wages; and (3) repairs and maintenance, oil, water, and stores. This definition of cost does not correspond exactly with variable costs since it includes some fixed costs (i.e., scheduled maintenance costs even at zero output). Each of the three cost categories was deflated using an appropriate price index. A cubic polynomial function with an additional linear time trend variable was fitted to each of 17 sets of cost-output observations.

The results of this study did *not* lend support to the existence of a nonlinear cubic or quadratic cost function. The cubic term, Q^3, was not statistically significant in any of the regressions, and the quadratic term, Q^2, was statistically significant in only 5 of the 17 cost equations. Among the five regressions with statistically significant quadratic terms, the sign of the Q^2 term was negative in four cases. This result is contrary to economic theory, which postulates steadily increasing AVC and MC functions for a quadratic total cost function.

A typical linear total cost function (for firm 8) is given by

$$C = 18.3 + 0.889Q - 0.639T$$

where C = variable costs of generation, Q = annual output (millions of kilowatt-hours), and T = time (years). The equation "explained" 97.4 percent of the variation in the cost variable.

The results of the two preceding studies are similar to those found in many other cost studies—namely, that short-run total costs tend to increase *linearly* over the ranges of output for which cost-output data are available. In other words, short-run average costs tend to decline and marginal costs tend to be constant over the "typ-

---

[9] Ibid, pp. 44–63.

ical" or "normal" operating range of the firm. At higher rates of output, we would expect to see exponentially increasing total cost and rising marginal cost. But, of course, this is exactly the circumstance firms try to avoid. Recall Boeing's experience in producing too many 747s per month.

LONG-RUN COST-OUTPUT RELATIONSHIPS

The long-run cost function consists of the least-cost combination of inputs for producing any level of output when *all* of the inputs to the production process are variable. As is indicated in Figure 9.3, the theoretical long-run average cost function (*LAC*) consists of the lower boundary, or envelope, of the various short-run average cost functions (*SAC*).

Statistical Estimation of Long-Run Cost Functions

Long-run costs can be estimated over a substantial period of time in a single plant (time-series data) or with multiple plants operating at different rates of output (cross-sectional data). The use of cross-sectional data assumes that each firm is operating as efficiently as possible given its fixed plant and equipment inputs—i.e., that the four firms having the four short-run average cost functions labeled SAC_1, SAC_2, SAC_3, and SAC_4 in Figure 9.3 are operating at points *A*, *B*, *C*, and *D*, respectively. The use of time-series data assumes that input prices, the production technology, and the products offered for sale remain unchanged. Both methods, therefore, require heroic assumptions, but cross-sectional data are more prevalent in estimating long-run cost functions.

Figure 9.3   Long-Run Average Cost Function

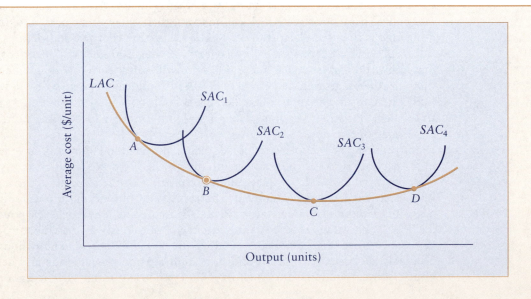

LONG-RUN COST FUNCTIONS: ELECTRICITY GENERATION

In his study of electrical power generation by British firms, Johnston developed long-run cost functions using both time-series and cross-sectional data. In the time-series analysis, a cubic cost function with a linear trend variable was fitted to each of 23 firms whose capital equipment had *not* remained constant over the 1928–1947 period. The cubic term was not statistically significant in any of the regression equations, and the quadratic term was statistically significant in only six of the regression equations. Among these six equations, the sign of the Q^2 term was positive in three cases and negative in three cases. Regardless of whether a linear time trend was included in the regression model, a linear model between cost and output tended to give the best fit.

In a cross-sectional study of U.S. electric utility companies, Christensen and Greene used a logarithmic model to test for the presence of economies and diseconomies of scale.[10] The long-run average cost curve (*LAC*) using data on 114 firms is shown in Figure 9.4. The bar below the graph indicates the number of firms in each interval. Below 19.8 billion kwh (left arrow in graph), significant economies of scale were found to exist. The 97 firms in this range accounted for 48.7 percent of the total output. Between 19.8 and 67.1 billion kwh (right arrow in the graph), no significant economies of scale were present. The 16 firms in this range accounted for 44.6 percent of the total output. Above 67.1 billion kwh, diseconomies of scale (one firm and 6.7 percent of total output) were found.

Determinants of the Optimal Scale of Operation

The size at which a company should attempt to establish its operations depends on the extent of the scale economies and the extent of the market. Some firms can operate at minimum unit cost with very small scale. Consider a licensed street vendor of leather coats. Each additional sale entails variable costs for the coat, a few minutes of direct labor effort to answer potential customers' questions, and some small allocated cost associated with the step-van or other vehicle where the inventory is stored and hauled from one street sale location to another. Ninety-nine percent of the operating cost is the variable cost of an additional leather coat per additional sale. Ten sales will incur costs dominated by 10 leather coats, 100 sales will incur costs dominated by 100 leather coats, and 1,000 sales will still incur costs dominated by the 1,000 leather coats required to make the sales. Long-run average cost will be essentially flat, constant at approximately the wholesale cost of a leather coat. As a result, in leather coat street vending, a small-scale operation will be just as efficient as large-scale operations.

In contrast, the hydroelectric power plants, depicted in Figure 9.4, have few variable costs of any kind. Instead, essentially all the costs are fixed costs associated with buying the land that will be flooded, constructing the dam, and purchasing the huge electrical generator equipment. Thereafter, the only variable inputs required are a few lubricants and maintenance workers. Consequently, a hydroelectric power plant has long-run average total costs that decline continuously as the company spreads its fixed cost over additional sales by supplying power to more and more households. Similarly, electric distribution lines (the high-tension power grids and neighborhood electrical conduits) are a high-fixed-cost and low-variable-cost operation. In the

---

[10] L.R. Christensen and W.H. Greene, "Economies of Scale in U.S. Electric Power Generation," *Journal of Political Economy* 84, no. 4 (August 1976).

Figure 9.4   Average Cost Function for U.S. Electric Utility Firms

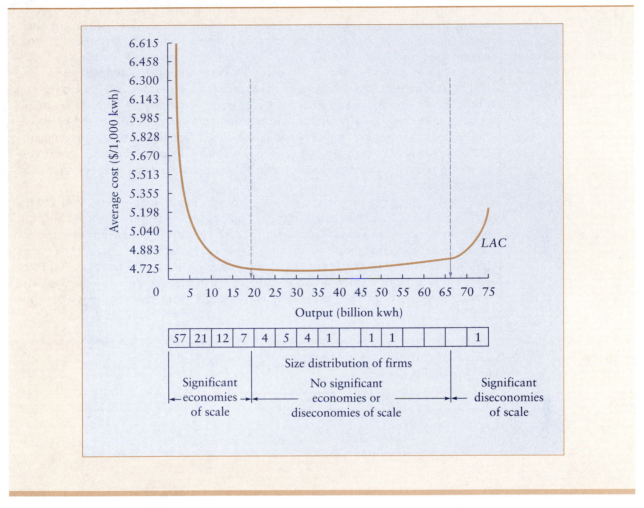

electrical utility industry, large-scale operations therefore incur lower unit cost than small-scale operations, as demonstrated in Figure 9.4.

Example

SCALE ECONOMIES IN THE TRADITIONAL CABLE INDUSTRY: TIME-WARNER[11]

Telephone landlines and traditional cable TV have cost characteristics similar to electric utilities. Once the wires have been put in place, the incremental cost of extending TV or telephone service to another household is very small. The extent of the scale economies in such industries may warrant licensing only one cable company or one local telephone service provider. Municipalities have historically issued an exclusive service contract to such public utilities. The rationale was that one firm could service the whole market at much lower cost than several firms dividing the market and

[11] See W. Emmons and R. Prager, "The Effects of Market Structure in the U.S. Cable Television Industry," *Rand Journal of Economics,* 28(4), Winter 1997, pp. 732–750.

http://

The following Internet site provides a policy analysis of economies of scale in electricity distribution in the context of electric utility deregulation:

http://www.local.org/compfran.html

failing therefore to realize all of the available scale economies. However, remember that the optimal scale of operation of any facility, even a declining cost facility, is limited by the extent of the market. The cable TV industry has always been limited by the availability of videocassette recorders as an inexpensive convenient entertainment substitute. As a result, the potential scale economies suggested by industrial engineering studies of cable TV operations have never been fully realized.

In addition, both telephone and cable TV companies are now facing new wireless alternative technologies. Satellite-based digital television and cell phones have cut deeply into the market once reserved exclusively for monopoly-licensed communications companies. As a result, the average unit cost in these cable-based businesses has increased from B to A as volume has declined (see Figure 9.5). Consequently, the price required to break even has necessarily risen. Of course, the higher the cost-covering price, the more customers cable TV and telephone companies lose to wireless alternatives.

"Freewheeling" in the electrical utility industry has similar effects. When industrial and commercial electricity buyers (e.g., a large assembly plant or hospital) were allowed in January 2003 to contract freely with low-cost power suppliers many states away, the local public utility experienced "stranded costs." That is, the high initial fixed costs of constructing dams, power plants, and distribution lines were left behind as sales volume declined and local customers chose to do business elsewhere. If the costs involved are mostly variable, the local power utilities can simply

Figure 9.5   Fixed Costs Stranded by Freewheeling Electricity and Satellite-Based TV Signals

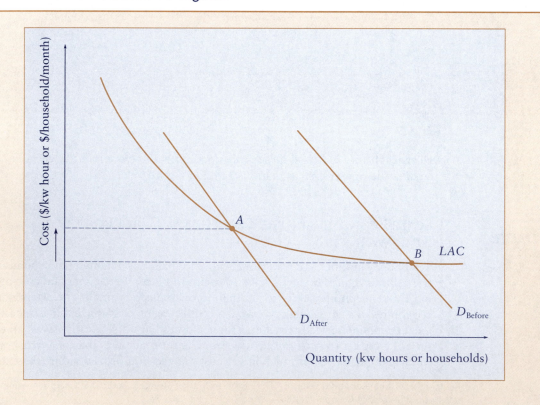

cut costs and operate profitably at smaller scale. Unfortunately, however, the costs are mostly fixed and unavoidable, so unit costs rise as the number of customers served declines. Consequently, the advantages of additional competition for lowering prices to consumers may be offset by the rise in unit costs caused by reduced scale. Jointly these effects are projected to cause a net reduction of only $2 in cable and $9 per month in monthly electric bills, despite the enormously increased competition.[12]

Example

ECONOMIES OF SCALE AND SCOPE IN BANKING

A number of empirical studies have attempted to estimate economies of scale and scope in the banking industry, which includes commercial banks, savings and loan associations, and credit unions. A survey article by Jeffrey Clark compiled the results of 13 of these studies.[13] Possible sources of production economies in financial institutions include the following:

- Specialized labor—A larger depository institution may be able to employ more specialized labor (e.g., computer programmers, cash managers, investment specialists, and loan officers) in producing its services. If the expertise of these workers results in the processing of a higher volume of deposit and loan accounts per unit of labor, then there will be lower per-unit labor costs at larger institutions as compared with smaller ones.

- Computer and telecommunications technology—Once the large setup, or fixed, costs are incurred, computer and electronic funds transfer systems can be used to process additional transactions at small additional costs per transaction. Spreading the fixed costs over a higher volume of transactions may permit the larger firm to achieve lower average total costs.

- Information—Credit information about loan applicants must be gathered and analyzed before lending decisions are made. However, once gathered, this credit information can be reused, usually at little additional cost, in making decisions about lending to the institution's customers. For example, credit information gathered in making mortgage loans can also be used in making automobile and other personal loans. Thus, larger financial institutions, which offer a wide array of different types of credit, may realize economies of scope in information gathering. That is, the cost of mortgage and auto installment lending done jointly is lower than the total cost of both when each is done separately.

All the studies reviewed by Clark employed a logarithmic cost function. The following conclusions were derived:

- There is some evidence of economies of scope between consumer and mortgage lending.

- There are significant overall (i.e., firm-specific) economies of scale only at relatively low levels of output (less than $100 million in deposits). Beyond that, most studies found an L-shaped long-run average cost curve—average total cost falls steeply at low levels of output and then tends to flatten out and become horizontal. In this respect, banking *LAC* closely mirrors the shape of the *LAC* in manufacturing.

---

[12] M. Maloney and R. McCormick, *Customer Choice, Consumer Value,* Citizens for a Sound Economy Foundation, Washington, DC, 1996.

[13] Jeffrey A. Clark, "Economies of Scale and Scope at Depository Financial Institutions: A Review of the Literature," Federal Reserve Bank of Kansas City, *Economic Review* (September/October 1988), pp. 16–33.

Engineering Cost Techniques

Engineering Cost Technique
A method of estimating cost functions by deriving the least-cost combination of labor, capital equipment, and raw materials required to produce various levels of output, using only industrial engineering information.

Engineering cost techniques provide an alternative to estimating long-run cost functions with accounting cost data. Using knowledge of production facilities and technology (such as machine speeds, worker productivity, and physical input-output transformation relationships), the engineering approach attempts to determine the least-cost combination of labor, capital equipment, and raw materials required to produce various levels of output. Engineering methods offer a number of advantages over statistical methods in examining economies of scale. First, it is generally much easier with the engineering approach to hold constant such factors as input prices, product mix, and product efficiency, allowing one to isolate the effects on costs of changes in output. Second, use of the engineering method avoids some of the cost-allocation and depreciation problems encountered when using accounting data. The primary disadvantage of engineering methods is that they deal only with the technical aspects of the production process or plant. The managerial and entrepreneurial aspects such as marketing the product and administering the organization are not included in the analysis.

In a study designed to isolate the various sources of scale economies within a plant, Haldi and Whitcomb collected data on the cost of individual units of equipment, the initial investment in plant and equipment, and operating costs (namely, labor, raw materials, and utilities). They noted that "in many basic industries such as petroleum refining, primary metals, and electric power, economies of scale are found in very large plant sizes (often the largest built or contemplated)."[14] Few (if any) firms were observed operating beyond these minimum efficient scale plant sizes.

Survivor Technique

Survivor Technique
A method of estimating cost functions from the shares of industry output coming from each size class over time. Size classes whose shares of industry output are increasing (decreasing) over time are presumed to be relatively efficient (inefficient) and have lower (higher) average costs.

George Stigler invented the **survivor technique** for determining the optimum size (or range of sizes) of firms within an industry without having access to their cost data.[15] This method involves classifying the firms in an industry by size and calculating the share of industry output coming from each size class over time. If the share of industry output of a given class decreases over time, then this size class is presumed to be relatively inefficient and to have higher average costs. Conversely, an increasing share of industry output over time indicates that the size class is relatively efficient and has lower average costs. The rationale for this approach is that competition will tend to eliminate those firms whose size is relatively inefficient, allowing to survive only those size firms with lower average costs.

Despite its appeal, the survivor technique does have one serious limitation. Because the technique does not use actual cost data in the analysis, there is no way to assess the *magnitude* of the cost differentials between firms of varying size and efficiency.

Example

SURVIVOR TECHNIQUE: STEEL PRODUCTION

The survivor technique has been used to examine the long-run cost functions in steel ingot production by open-hearth or Bessemer processes. Based on the data in Table 9.1, Stigler developed the sleigh-shaped long-run average cost function for steel

---

[14] J. Haldi and D. Whitcomb, "Economies of Scale in Industrial Plants," *Journal of Political Economy* 75, no. 1 (August 1967), pp. 373–385.

[15] G.J. Stigler, *The Organization of Industry* (Homewood, IL: Richard D. Irwin, 1968), Chapter 7. For other examples of the use of the survivor technique, see H.E. Ted Frech and Paul B. Ginsburg, "Optimal Scale in Medical Practice: A Survivor Analysis," *Journal of Business* (January 1974), pp. 23–26.

ingot production shown in Figure 9.6. Because of the declining percentages at very low levels of output and at extremely high levels of output, Stigler concluded that both were relatively inefficient size classes. The intermediate size classes (from 2.5 to 27.5 percent of industry capacity) represented the range of optimum size because these size classes grew or held their shares of capacity. Stigler also applied the survivor technique to the automobile industry and found an L-shaped average cost curve, indicating that there was no evidence of diseconomies of scale at large levels of output.

One final note of caution: The concept of average costs per unit of output (i.e., "unit costs") so prominent in our recent discussion of scale economies is seldom useful for managerial decision making. Get in the habit of avoiding the use of unit costs in your decision problem reasoning. Reserve unit costs for describing, debating, and planning issues related to scale economies and diseconomies alone.

BREAK-EVEN ANALYSIS VERSUS CONTRIBUTION ANALYSIS

Break-even Analysis
A technique used to examine the relationship among a firm's sales, costs, and operating profits at various levels of output.

Many of the planning activities that take place within a firm are based on anticipated levels of output. The study of the interrelationships among a firm's sales, costs, and operating profit at various anticipated output levels is known as **break-even analysis.**

Break-even analysis is based on the revenue-output and cost-output functions of microeconomic theory. These functions are shown together in Figure 9.7. Total revenue is equal to the number of units of output sold multiplied by the price per unit. Assuming that the firm can sell additional units of output only by lowering the price, the total revenue curve *TR* will be concave (inverted U shaped), as indicated in Figure 9.7. The total cost curve *TC* shown in the figure is a static short-run cost

Table 9.1   Distribution of Steel Ingot Capacity by Relative Size of Company

Company Size (Percentage of Total Industry Capacity)	Percentage of Industry Capacity			Number of Companies		
	1930	1938	1951	1930	1938	1951
Under ½	7.16	6.11	4.65	39	29	22
½ to 1	5.94	5.08	5.37	9	7	7
1 to 2½	13.17	8.30	9.07	9	6	6
2½ to 5	10.64	16.59	22.21	3	4	5
5 to 10	11.18	14.03	8.12	2	2	1
10 to 25	13.24	13.99	16.10	1	1	1
25 and over	38.67	35.91	34.50	1	1	1

Source: George J. Stigler, "The Economies of Scale," *Journal of Law and Economics* (October 1958). Reprinted by permission.

Figure 9.6   Long-Run Average Costs of Steel Ingot Production

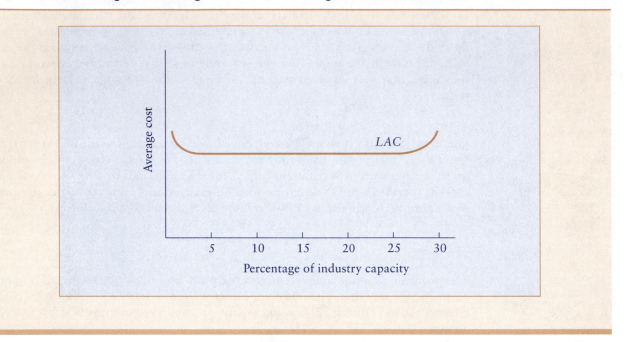

Figure 9.7   Generalized Break-Even Analysis

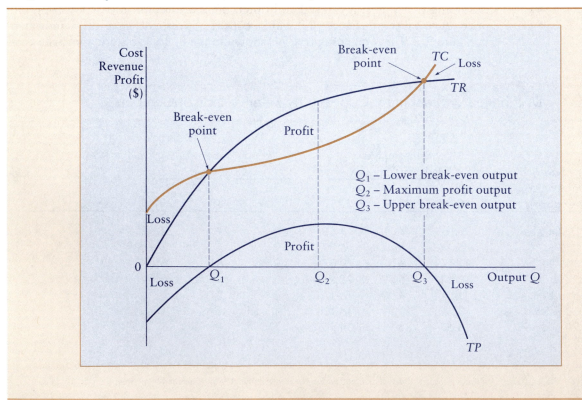

function analogous to that shown earlier in Chapter 8 (Figure 8.3). It indicates the relationship between costs and output for a given production process in which one or more of the factors of production (for example, plant and production technology) are fixed.[16] Short-run total costs consist of a fixed-cost component and a variable-cost component.

The difference between total revenue and total cost at any level of output represents the total profit that will be obtained. In Figure 9.7, total profit TP at any output level is given by the vertical distance between the total revenue TR and total cost TC curves. A break-even situation (zero profit) occurs whenever total revenue equals total cost. In Figure 9.7, note that a break-even condition occurs at two different output levels—Q_1 and Q_3. Below an output level of Q_1, losses will be incurred because $TR < TC$. Between Q_1 and Q_3, profits will be obtained because $TR > TC$. At output levels above Q_3, losses will occur again because $TR < TC$. Total profits are maximized within the range of Q_1 to Q_3; the vertical distance between the TR and TC curves is greatest at an output level of Q_2.

LINEAR BREAK-EVEN ANALYSIS

Break-even analysis is one of the most frequently used techniques of business planning. We discuss both the graphical and algebraic methods of solving break-even problems.

Graphical Method

Over the output range Q_1 to Q_2 in Figure 9.7, the linearity of total cost and total revenue can be assumed as a simplifying approximation. Constant selling price per unit and a constant variable cost per unit yield the linear TR and TC functions illustrated in Figure 9.8, which shows a basic linear break-even chart. Total cost is computed as the sum of the firm's fixed costs F, which are independent of the output level, and the variable costs, which increase at a constant rate of VC per unit of output. Earnings before interest and taxes, or $EBIT$, is equal to the difference between total revenues (TR) and total (*operating*) costs (TC). Note that this measure of profits *excludes* financing costs (e.g., interest on debt) as well as taxes.[17]

The break-even point occurs at point Q_b in Figure 9.8, where the total revenue and the total cost functions intersect. If a firm's output level is below this break-even point—that is, if $TR < TC$—it incurs *operating losses*, defined as a *negative EBIT*. If the firm's output level is above this break-even point—that is, if $TR > TC$—it realizes *operating profits*, defined as a *positive EBIT*.

Algebraic Method

To determine a firm's break-even point algebraically, one must set the total revenue and total (operating) cost functions equal to each other and solve the resulting equation for the break-even volume.

---

[16] An additional assumption of break-even analysis is that all the units produced during the period are sold during the period or that all production is in response to firm orders; that is, no inventory-planning decisions are required.

[17] See R. Charles Moyer, James R. McGuigan, and William J. Kretlow, *Contemporary Financial Management*, 9th ed. (Cincinnati, OH: South-Western Publishing Company, 2003), Chapter 13, for a discussion of how financial leverage (i.e., use of fixed cost sources of financing) can be incorporated into the analysis.

Figure 9.8   Linear Break-Even Analysis Chart

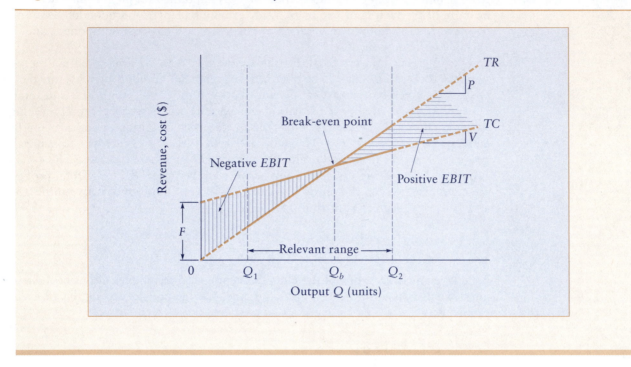

Total revenue is equal to the selling price per unit times the output quantity:

$$TR = P \times Q \qquad [9.9]$$

Total (operating) cost is equal to fixed plus variable costs, where the variable cost is the product of the variable cost per unit times the output quantity:

$$TC = F + (V \times Q) \qquad [9.10]$$

Setting the total revenue and total cost expressions equal to each other and substituting the break-even output Q_b for Q results in

$$TR = TC$$

or

$$PQ_b = F + VQ_b \qquad [9.11]$$

Finally, solving Equation 9.11 for the break-even output Q_b yields[18]

$$PQ_b - VQ_b = F$$
$$(P - V)Q_b = F$$
$$Q_b = \frac{F}{P - V} \qquad [9.12]$$

---

[18] Break-even analysis also can be performed in terms of dollar *sales* rather than *units* of output. The break-even dollar sales volume S_b can be determined by the following expression:

$$S_b = \frac{F}{1 - V/P}$$

where V/P is the variable cost ratio (that is, the variable cost per dollar of sales).

Contribution Margin
The difference between price and variable cost per unit.

The *difference* between the selling price per unit and the variable cost per unit, $P - V$, is referred to as the **contribution margin.** It measures how much each unit of output contributes to meeting fixed costs and operating profits. Thus, the break-even output is equal to the fixed cost divided by the contribution margin.

Example

BREAK-EVEN ANALYSIS: ALLEGAN MANUFACTURING COMPANY

Assume that Allegan manufactures one product, which it sells for $250 per unit ($P$). Variable costs ($V$) are $150 per unit. The firm's fixed costs (F) are $1,000,000. Substituting these figures into Equation 9.12 yields the following break-even output:

$$Q_b = \frac{\$1,000,000}{\$250 - \$150}$$
$$= 10,000 \text{ units}$$

Allegan's break-even output can also be determined graphically, as shown in Figure 9.9.

Another illustration would be to use break-even analysis to approve or reject a batch sale promotion. Suppose that in the previous example, the $1,000,000 is a trade rebate to elicit better shelf location for Allegan's product. If the estimated effect of this promotion is additional sales of 9,000 units, which is less than the break-even output, the change in total contributions will fall below the $1 million promotion cost—i.e., ($250 − $150) × 9,000 < $1,000,000. Therefore, the promotion plan should be rejected.

Figure 9.9   Linear Break-Even Analysis Chart for the Allegan Manufacturing Company

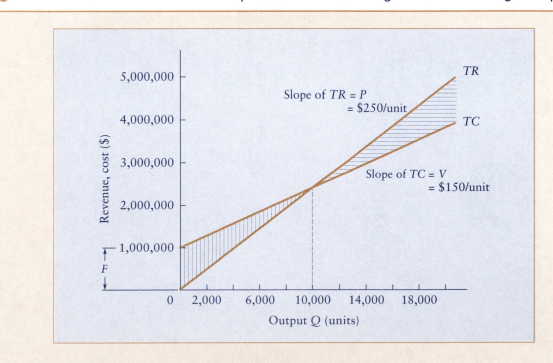

Because a firm's break-even output is dependent on a number of variables—in particular, the price per unit, variable (operating) costs per unit, and fixed costs—the firm may wish to analyze the effects of changes in any one (or more) of the variables on the break-even output. For example, it may wish to consider either of the following:

1. Changing the selling price
2. Substituting fixed costs for variable costs

Assume that Allegan increased the selling price per unit P' by $25 to $275. Substituting this figure into Equation 9.12 gives a new break-even output.

$$Q'_b = \frac{\$1,000,000}{\$275 - \$150}$$
$$= 8,000 \text{ units}$$

This can also be seen in Figure 9.10, in which an increase in the price per unit increases the slope of the total revenue function TR' and reduces the break-even output.

Rather than increasing the selling price per unit, Allegan's management may decide to substitute fixed costs for variable costs in some aspect of the company's operations. For example, as labor wage rates increase over time, many firms seek to reduce operating costs through automation, which in effect represents the substitution of fixed-cost capital equipment for variable-cost labor. Suppose Allegan determines that it can reduce labor costs by $25 per unit by leasing $100,000 of additional equip-

Figure 9.10   Linear Break-Even Analysis Chart for the Allegan Manufacturing Company Showing the Effects of a Price Increase

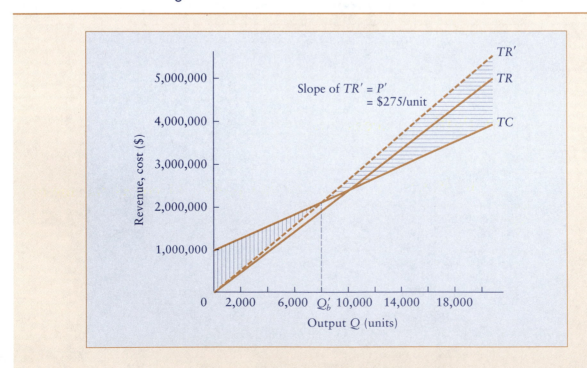

ment. Under these conditions, the firm's new level of fixed costs F' would be $1,000,000 + $100,000 = $1,100,000. Variable costs per unit V' would be $150 − $25 = $125. Substituting $P = $250 per unit, $V' = $125 per unit, and $F' = $1,100,000 into Equation 9.12 yields a new break-even output:

$$Q'_b = \frac{\$1,100,000}{\$250 - \$125}$$

$$= 8,800 \text{ units}$$

As we can see in Figure 9.11, the effect of this change in cost fixity of the operations is to raise the intercept on the vertical axis, decrease the slope of the total (operating) cost function TC', and reduce the break-even output.

Example

FIXED COSTS AND PRODUCTION CAPACITY AT GENERAL MOTORS[19]

In 1988 GM announced that it would reduce automobile production capacity to match current sales. The downsizing was to take place over a 5-year period. It represented the first time in its 80-year history that the company had significantly shrunk

Figure 9.11   Linear Break-Even Analysis Chart for the Allegan Manufacturing Company Showing the Effects of Substituting Fixed Costs for Variable Costs

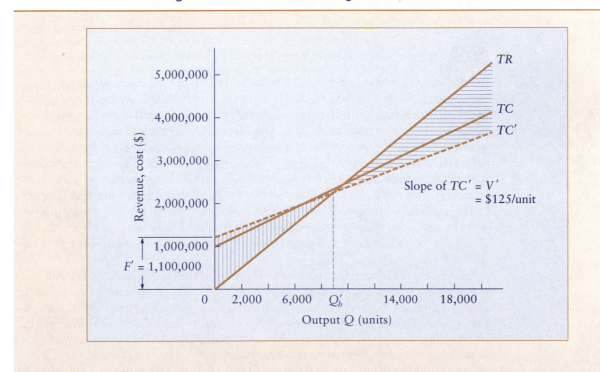

[19] Jacob M. Schlesinger, "GM to Reduce Capacity to Match Its Sales," *Wall Street Journal*, April 25, 1988, p. 2; Lawrence Ingrassia and Joseph B. White, "GM Plans to Close 21 More Factories, Cut 74,000 Jobs, Slash Capital Spending," *Wall Street Journal*, December 19, 1991, p. A3; and "A Duo of Dunces," *The Economist*, March 9, 2002, p. 63.

its capacity. As part of its decision to reduce its size, GM needed to cut $12.5 billion to $13 billion out of its fixed-cost base in 1990 compared with 1986 levels: the company planned to close ten of its U.S. automobile assembly lines.

In the past GM had alternated between (1) producing all the cars it could produce and then using costly clearance sales to attract buyers (e.g., $3.3 billion in buyers' incentives in 1988 alone) and (2) reducing output by running plants below capacity through a slowdown in the pace of the assembly line or elimination of an entire shift. The new strategy called for the company to use 100 percent of its American automobile production capacity by 1992—meaning that all of its plants would be operated five days a week with two shifts per day. When automobile demand increased above this capacity level, overtime and third-shift operations and new production efficiencies would be used to boost production. This is the strategy that Ford had been following for some time. Ford, rather than maintaining sufficient capacity to meet demand at the high end of the cycle and laying off workers when demand was low, geared its capacity to the low end of the cycle and strained to meet demand when sales were high.

In effect, GM and Ford were trading off lower fixed costs over the entire business cycle against (the possibility of) having to incur higher variable costs (e.g., use of higher cost overtime and third-shift operations) during periods of strong demand. As a consequence, GM's break-even output point declined sharply. This strategic redirection was prescient indeed because excess capacity has again become a serious problem. In March 2002, GM admitted it had almost three months of excess capacity in North America alone, over one million cars.

Break-Even versus Contribution Analysis

Break-even analysis assumes that all types of cost except the narrowly defined incremental variable cost (V) of additional unit sales are avoidable and asks the question of whether there are sufficient unit sales available at the contribution margin ($P - V$) to cover all these relevant costs. If so, this allows the firm to earn a net profit. These questions normally arise at entry and exit decision points where a firm can avoid essentially all its costs if the firm decides to stay out or get out of a business. Contribution analysis, in contrast, applies to questions like whether or not to adopt an advertising campaign, introduce a new product, shut down a plant temporarily, or close a whole division. What distinguishes these contribution analysis questions is that some fixed costs are now unavoidable and irrelevant to the decision (indirect fixed costs), while other fixed costs are newly committed as a result of the decision (direct fixed costs).

Contribution Analysis
A comparison of the additional operating profits to the direct fixed costs attributable to a decision.

More generally, contribution analysis always asks whether there is enough additional revenue from the ad campaign, the new product, or the projected sales of the plant or division to cover the additional fixed plus variable costs. That is, **contribution analysis** answers the question of whether there are sufficient gross operating profits resulting from the incremental sales (ΔQ) attributable to the ad, the new product, or the plant/division sales to offset the proposed increase in fixed cost. In other words, are the total contributions to fixed cost increased by an amount greater than the increase in direct fixed cost avoidable by the decision?

$$(P - V)\,\Delta Q > \Delta \text{ Total Fixed Cost} \qquad\qquad [9.13]$$
$$> \Delta \text{ Indirect Fixed Cost} + \Delta \text{ Direct Fixed Cost}$$
$$> 0 + \Delta \text{ Direct Fixed Cost}$$

Such decisions are not break-even decisions because they ignore (abstract from) the indirect fixed costs that, by definition, cannot be avoided by rejecting the ad campaign or new product introduction proposal or by closing the plant or division. For example, headquarters facility cost and other corporate overhead are indirect fixed costs that cannot be avoided by any of these decisions. So, corporate overhead is not a relevant cost in making these decisions, and corporate overhead is therefore ignored in the contribution analysis done to support making such decisions. Of course, corporate overhead is prominent in the above examples of break-even analysis done to decide how or whether to enter a business in the first place. The case exercise on charter airline operating decisions at the end of this chapter illustrates the use of contribution as distinguished from break-even analysis.

Some Limitations of Break-Even and Contribution Analysis

Break-even analysis has a number of other limitations that arise from the *assumptions* made in constructing the model and developing the relevant data. The application of break-even analysis is of value only to the extent that these assumptions are valid.

Constant Selling Price and Variable Cost per Unit   In the break-even analysis model, the assumptions of a constant selling price and variable cost per unit yield *linear* relationships for the total revenue and total cost functions. In practice, these functions tend to be nonlinear for the reasons discussed earlier. The assumption of a constant selling price and variable cost per unit is probably valid over some relevant range of output levels; however, consideration of output levels outside this range will normally require modifications in the break-even chart.

Composition of Operating Costs   Another assumption of break-even analysis is that costs can be classified as either fixed or variable. In fact, some costs are partly fixed and partly variable (e.g., utility bills). Furthermore, some fixed costs increase in a stepwise manner as output is increased—they are *semivariable*—and are constant only over relatively narrow ranges of output. For example, machinery maintenance is scheduled after 10 hours or 10 days or 10 weeks of use. These direct fixed costs must be considered variable if a batch production decision entails this much use.

Multiple Products   The break-even model also assumes that a firm is producing and selling either a *single* product or a *constant mix* of different products. In many cases the product mix changes over time, and problems can arise in allocating fixed costs among the various products.

Uncertainty   Still another assumption of break-even analysis is that the selling price and variable cost per unit, as well as fixed costs, are known at each level of output. In practice, these parameters are subject to uncertainty. Thus, the usefulness of the results of break-even analysis depends on the accuracy of the estimates of these parameters.

Inconsistency of Planning Horizon   Finally, break-even analysis is normally performed for a planning period of one year or less; however, the benefits received from some costs may not be realized until subsequent periods. For example, research and development costs incurred during a specific period may not result in new products for several years. For break-even analysis to be a dependable decision-making tool, a firm's operating costs must be matched with resulting revenues for the planning period under consideration.

Operating Leverage[20]

Operating leverage involves the use of assets having fixed costs. A firm uses operating leverage in the hope of earning returns in excess of the fixed costs of the assets, thereby increasing the returns to the owners of the firm. A firm's **degree of operating leverage** (DOL) is defined as the multiplier effect resulting from the firm's use of fixed operating costs. More specifically, DOL can be computed as the *percentage change* in earnings before interest and taxes (EBIT) resulting from a given *percentage change* in sales (output):

$$\text{DOL at } X = \frac{\text{Percentage change in EBIT}}{\text{Percentage change in Sales}}$$

This can be rewritten as follows:

$$\text{DOL at } X = \frac{\dfrac{\Delta\text{EBIT}}{\text{EBIT}}}{\dfrac{\Delta\text{Sales}}{\text{Sales}}} \qquad [9.14]$$

where ΔEBIT and ΔSales are the changes in the firm's EBIT and Sales, respectively. Because a firm's DOL differs at each sales level, it is necessary to indicate the sales point, X, at which operating leverage is measured. The degree of operating leverage is analogous to the elasticity of demand concept (for example, price and income elasticities) because it relates percentage changes in one variable (EBIT) to percentage changes in another variable (sales). Equation 9.14 requires the use of two different values of sales and EBIT. Another equation (derived from Equation 9.14) that can be used to compute a firm's DOL more easily is

$$\text{DOL at } X = \frac{\text{Sales} - \text{Variable costs}}{\text{EBIT}} \qquad [9.15]$$

The variables defined in the previous section on break-even analysis can also be used to develop a formula for determining a firm's DOL at any given output level. Because sales are equivalent to TR (or $P \times Q$), variable cost is equal to $V \times Q$, and EBIT is equal to total revenue (TR) less total (operating) cost, or $(P \times Q) - F - (V \times Q)$, these values can be substituted into Equation 9.15 to obtain the following:

$$\text{DOL at } Q = \frac{(P \cdot Q) - (V \cdot Q)}{(P \cdot Q) - F - (V \cdot Q)}$$

or

$$\text{DOL at } Q = \frac{(P - V)Q}{(P - V)Q - F} \qquad [9.16]$$

---

[20] This section can be omitted without loss of continuity.

Example

OPERATING LEVERAGE: ALLEGAN MANUFACTURING COMPANY (continued)

In the earlier discussion of break-even analysis for the Allegan Manufacturing Company, the parameters of the break-even model were determined as $P = \$250$/unit, $V = \$150$/unit, and $F = \$1,000,000$. Substituting these values into Equation 9.16 along with the respective output (Q) values yields the DOL values shown in Table 9.2. For example, a DOL of 6.00 at an output level of 12,000 units indicates that, from a base output level of 12,000 units, EBIT will increase by 6.00 percent for each 1 percent increase in output.

Note that Allegan's DOL is largest (in absolute value terms) when the firm is operating near the break-even point (that is, where $Q = Q_b = 10,000$ units). Note also that the firm's DOL is negative below the break-even output level. A negative DOL indicates the percentage *reduction* in operating *losses* that occurs as the result of a 1 percent *increase* in output. For example, the DOL of -1.50 at an output level of 6,000 units indicates that, from a base output level of 6,000 units, the firm's operating *losses* will be *reduced* by 1.5 percent for each 1 percent *increase* in output.

A firm's DOL is a function of the nature of the production process. If the firm employs large amounts of equipment in its operations, it tends to have relatively high fixed operating costs and relatively low variable operating costs. Such a cost structure yields a high DOL, which results in large operating profits (positive EBIT) if sales are high and large operating losses (negative EBIT) if sales are depressed.

Business Risk
The inherent variability or uncertainty of a firm's operating earnings (earnings before interest and taxes).

Business Risk

Business risk refers to the inherent variability or uncertainty of a firm's EBIT. It is a function of several factors, one of which is the firm's DOL. The DOL is a measure of how sensitive a firm's EBIT is to changes in sales. The greater a firm's DOL, the

---

Table 9.2   DOL at Various Output Levels for Allegan Manufacturing Company

Output Q	Degree of Operating Leverage DOL
0	0
2,000	-0.25
4,000	-0.67
6,000	-1.50
8,000	-4.00
10,000	(undefined) Break-even level
12,000	$+6.00$
14,000	$+3.50$
16,000	$+2.67$
18,000	$+2.25$
20,000	$+2.00$

larger the change in EBIT will be for a given change in sales. Thus, *all other things being equal,* the higher a firm's DOL, the greater the degree of business risk.

Other factors can also affect a firm's business risk, including the variability or uncertainty of sales. A firm with high fixed costs and very stable sales will have a high DOL, but it will also have stable EBIT and, therefore, low business risk. Public utilities and pipeline transportation companies are examples of firms having these operating characteristics.

Another factor that may affect a firm's business risk is uncertainty concerning selling prices and variable costs. A firm having a low DOL can still have high business risk if selling prices and variable costs are subject to considerable variability over time. A cattle feedlot illustrates these characteristics of low DOL but high business risk; both grain costs and the selling price of beef at times fluctuate wildly.

In summary, a firm's DOL is only one of several factors that determine the firm's business risk.

Break-Even Analysis and Risk Assessment

The information generated from a break-even analysis can also be used to assess the business risk to which a firm is exposed. If one adds to this set of information the *expected* (mean) level of sales (in units) for some future period of time, the standard deviation of the distribution of sales, and an assumption about how actual sales are distributed, one can compute the probability that the firm will have operating losses (that is, it will sell fewer units than the break-even level) and the probability that the firm will have operating profits (that is, it will sell more units than the break-even level).

The probability of having operating losses (that is, the probability of selling fewer than Q_b units) can be computed using the following equation and the standard normal probability distribution as

$$z = \frac{Q_b - \overline{Q}}{\sigma_Q}$$

[9.17]

where the probability values are from Table 1 in Appendix B, $\overline{Q}$ is the expected unit sales, σ_Q is the standard deviation of unit sales, and Q_b is (as defined earlier) the break-even unit sales. The probability of operating profits (that is, the probability of selling more than Q_b units) is equal to one minus the probability of operating losses.

Example

BUSINESS RISK ASSESSMENT:
ALLEGAN MANUFACTURING COMPANY (continued)

For the Allegan Manufacturing Company discussed earlier, suppose that expected sales are 15,000 units with a standard deviation of 4,000 units. Recall that the break-even volume was 10,000 units. Substituting $Q_b = 10,000$, $\overline{Q} = 15,000$, and $\sigma_Q = 4,000$ into Equation 9.17 yields

$$z = \frac{10,000 - 15,000}{4,000}$$

$$= -1.25$$

In other words, the break-even sales level of 10,000 units is 1.25 standard deviations *below* the mean. From Table 1 in Appendix B, the probability associated with

−1.25 standard deviations is .1056 or 10.56 percent. Thus, there is a 10.56 percent chance that Allegan will incur operating losses and an 89.44 percent chance (100 percent minus the 10.56 percent chance of losses) that the firm will record operating profits (that is, it will sell more than the break-even number of units of output).

SUMMARY

- In estimating the behavior of short-run and long-run cost functions for firms, the primary methodological problems are (1) differences in the manner in which economists and accountants define and measure costs, and (2) accounting for other variables (in addition to the output level) that influence costs.

- Many statistical studies of *short-run* cost-output relationships suggest that total costs increase linearly (or quadratically) with output, implying constant (or rising) marginal costs over the observed ranges of output.

- Many statistical studies of *long-run* cost-output relationships indicate that long-run cost functions are L-shaped. Economies of scale (declining average costs) occur at low levels of output. Thereafter, long-run average costs remain relatively constant over large ranges of output. Diseconomies of scale are observed in only a few cases, probably because few firms can survive with costs attributable to excessive scale.

- *Engineering cost techniques* are an alternative approach to statistical methods in estimating long-run cost functions. With this approach, knowledge of production facilities and technology is used to determine the least-cost combination of labor, capital equipment, and raw materials required to produce various levels of output.

- The *survivor technique* is a method of determining the optimum size of firms within an industry by classifying them by size and then calculating the share of industry output coming from each size class over time. Size classes whose share of industry output is increasing over time are considered to be more efficient and to have lower average costs.

- *Break-even analysis* is used to examine the relationship among a firm's revenues, costs, and operating profits (EBIT) at various output levels. Frequently the analyst constructs a break-even chart based on linear cost-output and revenue-output relationships to determine the operating characteristics of a firm over a limited output range.

- The *break-even point* is defined as the output level at which total revenues equal total costs of operations. In the linear break-even model, the break-even point is found by dividing fixed costs by the difference between price and variable cost per unit, the *contribution margin*.

- *Contribution analysis* is used to examine operating profitability when some fixed costs (indirect fixed costs) cannot be avoided and other direct fixed costs can be avoided by a decision. Decisions on advertising, new product introduction, shutdown, and downsizing are often made by doing a contribution analysis.

- *Operating leverage* occurs when a firm uses assets having fixed operating costs. The *degree of operating leverage* (DOL) measures the percentage change in a firm's EBIT resulting from a 1-percent change in sales (or units of output). As a firm's fixed operating costs rise, its DOL increases.

- *Business risk* refers to the variability of a firm's EBIT. It is a function of several factors, including the firm's DOL and the variability of sales. All other things being equal, the higher a firm's DOL, the greater is its business risk.

EXERCISES

1. Suppose one estimates, from cost-output data using multiple regression techniques, the following total cost function:

$$TC = \$140{,}000 + \$250Q + \$1.50Q^2$$

Explain why one cannot necessarily infer that fixed costs are equal to $140,000.

2. A study of 86 savings and loan associations in six northwestern states for 1975 yielded the following cost function:[21]

$$C = 2.38 - .006153Q + .000005359Q^2 + 19.2X_1$$
$$(2.84) \quad (2.37) \quad\quad (2.63) \quad\quad\quad (2.69)$$

where C = average operating expense ratio, expressed as a percentage and defined as total operating expense ($ million) divided by total assets ($ million) times 100 percent

  Q = output, measured by total assets ($ million)

  X_1 = ratio of the number of branches to total assets ($ million)

Note: The number in parentheses below each coefficient is its respective *t*-statistic.

a. Which variable(s) is(are) statistically significant in explaining variations in the average operating expense ratio?

b. What type of cost-output relationship (e.g., linear, quadratic, or cubic) is suggested by these statistical results?

c. Based on these results, what can we conclude about the existence of economies or diseconomies of scale in savings and loan associations in the Northwest?

3. Referring to Exercise 2 again:

a. Holding constant the effects of branching (X_1), determine the level of total assets that minimizes the average operating expense ratio.

b. Determine the average operating expense ratio for a savings and loan association with the level of total assets determined in Part (a) and

    (i) 1 branch

    (ii) 10 branches

4. A study of the costs of electricity generation for a sample of 56 British firms in 1946–1947 yielded the following long-run cost function:[22]

$$AVC = 1.24 + .0033Q + .0000029Q^2 - .000046QZ - .026Z + .00018Z^2$$

where AVC = average variable cost (that is, working costs of generation), measured in pence per kilowatt-hour. (A pence was a British monetary unit, being equal to—at that time—two U.S. cents.)

  Q = output, measured in millions of kilowatt-hours per year

  Z = plant size, measured in thousands of kilowatts

---

[21] Holton Wilson, "A Note on Scale Economies in the Savings and Loan Industry," *Business Economics* (January 1981), pp. 45–49.

[22] Johnston, *Statistical Cost Analysis*, op. cit., Chapter 4.

    a. Determine the long-run variable cost function for electricity generation.

    b. Determine the long-run marginal cost function for electricity generation.

    c. Holding plant size constant at 150,000 kilowatts, determine the short-run average variable cost and marginal cost functions for electricity generation.

    d. For a plant size equal to 150,000 kilowatts, determine the output level that minimizes short-run average variable costs.

    e. Determine the short-run average variable cost and marginal cost at the output level obtained in Part (d).

5. Assuming that all other factors remain unchanged, determine how a firm's break-even point is affected by each of the following:

    a. The firm finds it necessary to reduce the price per unit because of increased foreign competition.

    b. The firm's direct labor costs are increased as the result of a new labor contract.

    c. The Occupational Safety and Health Administration (OSHA) requires the firm to install new ventilating equipment in its plant. (Assume that this action has no effect on worker productivity.)

Refer to the following data when working Exercises 6–9 below.

East Publishing Company is doing an analysis of a proposed new finance text. The following data have been obtained:

Fixed costs (per edition):	
Development (reviews, class testing, etc.)	$15,000
Copyediting	4,000
Selling and promotion	7,500
Typesetting	23,500
Total	$50,000
Variable costs (per copy):	
Printing and binding	$ 6.65
Administrative costs	1.50
Salespeople's commission (2% of selling price)	.55
Author's royalties (12% of selling price)	3.30
Bookstore discounts (20% of selling price)	5.50
Total	$ 17.50
Projected selling price	$ 27.50

6. Using the data presented above:

    a. Determine the company's break-even volume for this book in

       (i) Units

      (ii) Dollar sales

    b. Develop a break-even chart for the text.

    c. Determine the number of copies East must sell to earn a (operating) profit of $30,000 on this text.

d. Determine total (operating) profits at sales levels of

   (i) 3,000 units

   (ii) 5,000 units

   (iii) 10,000 units

7. Determine the degree of operating leverage (DOL) and give an economic interpretation of the value at the following sales levels:

a. 3,000 units

b. 7,000 units

8. Suppose expected sales (per edition) are 10,000 units with a standard deviation of 2,000 units:

a. Determine the probability that East will incur operating losses on the finance text.

b. Determine the probability that East will have operating profits on the proposed text.

9. Suppose East feels that $27.50 is too high a price to charge for the new finance text. It has examined the competitive market and determined that $25 would be a better selling price. What would the break-even volume be at this new selling price?

10. Cool-Aire Corporation manufactures a line of room air conditioners. Its break-even sales level is 33,000 units. Sales are approximately normally distributed. Expected sales next year are 40,000 units with a standard deviation of 4,000 units.

a. Determine the probability that Cool-Aire will incur an operating loss.

b. Determine the probability that Cool-Aire will operate above its break-even point.

11. McKee Corporation has annual fixed costs of $12 million. Its variable cost ratio is .60.

a. Determine the company's break-even dollar sales volume.

b. Determine the dollar sales volume required to earn a target profit of $3 million.

12. Smithton Company's sales in 2001 were $5 million. Its fixed costs were $1.5 million and its variable cost ratio was .60.

a. Determine the company's DOL.

b. Based on your answer to Part (a), forecast the percentage change in Smithton's EBIT for 2002, assuming that fixed costs and the variable cost ratio remain the same and that sales increase by 3 percent.

http://

The Structure of Airline
Costs

13. The Air Transport Association of America has produced an on-line Airline Handbook that provides information on airline economics and the structure of airline costs. Access this Internet site at http://www.air-transport.org/public/Handbook/Default.htm. Summarize the major components of airline costs.

CASE EXERCISES

COST FUNCTIONS

The following cost-output data were obtained as part of a study of the economies of scale in operating a public high school in Wisconsin:[23]

Pupils in Average Daily Attendance (A)	Midpoint of Values in Column A (B)	Operating Expenditure per Pupil (C)	Number of Schools in Sample (D)
143−200	171	$531.9	6
201−300	250	480.8	12
301−400	350	446.3	19
401−500	450	426.9	17
501−600	550	442.6	14
601−700	650	413.1	13
701−900	800	374.3	9
901−1,100	1,000	433.2	6
1,101−1,600	1,350	407.3	6
1,601−2,400	2,000	405.6	7

QUESTIONS

1. Plot the data in columns B and C in an output (enrollment)-cost graph and sketch a smooth curve that would appear to give a good fit to the data.

2. Based on the scatter diagram in Question 1, what kind of mathematical relationship would appear to exist between enrollment and operating expenditures per pupil? In other words, do operating expenditures per pupil appear to (i) be constant (and independent of enrollment), (ii) follow a linear relationship as enrollment increases, or (iii) follow some sort of nonlinear U-shape (possibly quadratic) relationship as enrollment increases?

As part of this study, the following cost function was developed:

$$C = f(Q, X_1, X_2, X_3, X_4, X_5)$$

where C = operating expenditures per pupil in average daily attendance (measured in dollars)

Q = enrollment (number of pupils in average daily attendance)

X_1 = average teacher's salary

X_2 = number of credit units ("courses") offered

X_3 = average number of courses taught per teacher

X_4 = change in enrollment between 1957 and 1960

X_5 = percentage of classrooms built after 1950

Variables X_1, X_2, and X_3 were considered measures of teacher qualifications, breadth of curriculum, and the degree of specialization in instruction, respectively. Variable X_4 measured changes in demand for school services that

---

[23] John Riew, "Economies of Scale in High School Operation," *Review of Economics and Statistics* 48, no. 3 (August 1966), pp. 280–287.

could cause some lagging adjustments in cost. Variable X_5 was used to reflect any differentials in the costs of maintenance and operation due to the varying ages of school properties. Statistical data on 109 selected high schools yielded the following regression equation:

$$C = 10.31 - .402Q + .00012Q^2 + .107X_1 + .985X_2 - 15.62X_3$$
$$(.063)^* \quad (.000023)^* \quad (.013)^* \quad (.640) \quad (11.95)$$
$$+ .613X_4 - .102X_5$$
$$(.189)^* \quad (.109)$$
$$r^2 = .557^*$$

Notes:

(1) The numbers in parentheses are the standard deviations of each of the respective coefficients (b's).

(2) An asterisk (*) indicates that the result is statistically significant at the .01 level.

3. What type of cost-output relationship (linear, quadratic, cubic) is suggested by these statistical results?

4. What variables (other than enrollment) would appear to be most important in explaining variations in operating expenditures per pupil?

5. Holding constant the effects of the other variables (X_1 through X_5), determine the enrollment level (Q) at which average operating expenditures per pupil are minimized. (*Hint:* Find the value of Q that minimizes the $\partial C/\partial Q$ function.)

6. Again, holding constant the effects of the other variables, use the $\partial C/\partial Q$ function to determine, for a school with 500 pupils, the reduction in per-pupil operating expenditures that will occur as the result of adding one more pupil.

7. Again, holding the other variables constant, what would be the saving in per-pupil operating expenditures of an increase in enrollment from 500 to 1,000 students?

8. Based on the results of this study, what can we conclude about the existence of economies or diseconomies in operating a public high school?

CHARTER AIRLINE OPERATING DECISIONS

Firm-specific demand in the *scheduled airline industry* is segmented by customer class and is highly uncertain so that an order may not lead to realized revenue and a unit sale. Airlines respond to this dynamic, highly competitive environment by tracking reservations at preannounced fares and reassigning capacity to the various market segments ("buckets") as business travelers, vacationers, and convention groups book the flights above or below expected levels several days and even weeks before scheduled departure. This systems management process combining marketing, operations, and finance is referred to as revenue management or yield management and is the subject of Appendix 14A.

The *charter airline business*, on the other hand, is much less complicated because capacity requirements are known far in advance and confirmed orders lead to realized revenue. We consider below three decisions for a charter airline: (1) the entry/exit break-even decision, (2) the operate/shut down decision to fly/not fly a charter that has been proposed, and (3) the output decision as to how many incremental seats to sell if the airline decides to operate the charter flight.

Suppose the following costs for a 10-hour round-trip flight apply to the time frame and expenses of an unscheduled 5-hour charter flight from New York to Oakland (and return) on a 3-year-old Boeing 757 with 180 occupied seats.[24] Some costs have been aggregated up to the flights level from a seat-level decision. Others have been allocated down to the flights level from an entry/exit company-level decision. Still other costs vary with the go/no go flight-level decision itself. Your job is to analyze each cost item and figure out the "behavior of cost"—i.e., with what decision that cost varies.

Fuel and Landing Fees	$5,200
Quarterly airframe maintenance re: FAA certificate	$1,000
Unscheduled engine maintenance per 10 flight hours	$1,200
Pro rata time depreciation for 3rd year of airframe	$7,200
Flight pay for pilots per round-trip flight	$4,200
Long-term hangar facility lease	$6,600
Annual aircraft engine operating lease	$7,100
Base salaries of headquarters personnel	$2,000
Food service with seat-by-seat JIT delivery at each departure	$900
Airport ground crew baggage handling for each flight arrival	$450

QUESTIONS

1. What are the variable costs for the decision to send one more person aboard a charter flight that is already 80 percent booked?

2. In making an entry/exit decision, if competitive pressure is projected to force the price down to $300, what is the break-even unit sales volume this company should have projected as part of its business plan before entering this market and should reconsider each time it considers leaving (exiting) this business altogether?

3. Identify the indirect fixed, direct fixed, and variable costs for the go/no go decision to operate rather than not fly the charter service for a particular one of many such charters this month.

4. If one were trying to decide whether to operate (fly) or not fly an unscheduled round trip charter flight, what would be the total indirect fixed costs?

5. In the same choice situation, what would be the total direct fixed costs plus variable costs of the flight?

6. Charter contracts are very negotiable, and charter carriers receive many contract offers which do not promise $300 prices or 80-percent-full planes. Should the airline accept a charter flight proposal from a group which offers to guarantee the sale of 90 seats at $250? Why or why not?

7. What are the total contributions of the charter flight with 90 seats at $250 per seat?

8. What are the net income losses this period if the airline refuses the charter, stays in business, but temporarily shuts down? What are the net income losses if it decides to operate and fly the charter that has been proposed?

---

[24] The aerodynamics of the plane and its fuel efficiency do change as the number of seats occupied falls below 180, but you may ignore this effect.

9. What is the segment-level contribution of a separate group that is willing to join the 90-seat-at-$250-per-seat charter on the same plane and same departure, but only wishes to pay $50 per seat for 10 seats?

10. Should you accept their offer? What problems do you anticipate if both charter groups are placed on the 757?

Appendix 9a

Mass Customization and the Learning Curve[25]

Mass customization is a new trend in operations management designed to standardize at least some of the production processes associated with fulfilling custom orders. Lee Jeans' customers can choose their own back pocket stitching and number of prior stone washings at a mall kiosk, but then Lee actually assembles the custom order from stockpiles of subassemblies produced with long production runs. The customer is pleased with the special attention, yet Lee Jeans maintains high-volume production. Especially in manufacturing, the quantity of resources (inputs) required to complete each successive unit of output is often observed to decrease as the *cumulative* volume of output increases. This **learning curve effect** of cumulative volume in reducing unit cost is distinguished from scale economies and increasing returns to scale that are associated with the flow rate of thruput (i.e., the output per unit time period).[26] Such learning effects are most commonly observed in the behavior of labor costs. The number of work-hours necessary to obtain one unit of output may decline for a variety of reasons as more units of the product are produced. These factors include increased familiarization with the tasks by workers and supervisors, improvements in work methods and the flow of work, and the need for fewer skilled workers as the tasks become more repetitive. Raw material costs per unit may also be subject to the learning curve effect if less scrap and waste occur as workers become more familiar with the production process. Most other variable costs are not subject to the learning process, however. For example, transportation costs per unit normally do not decline with greater cumulative volume.

The learning curve principle was first applied in airframe manufacturing, shipbuilding, and appliance manufacturing. Forecasts of declining personnel and raw material costs based on the learning curve have been used in scheduling production, in setting prices, and in evaluating the price quotations of input suppliers.

Learning Curve Effect
The amount of inputs, such as labor, and associated costs required to produce each unit of output is observed to decrease with greater cumulative volume.

LEARNING CURVE RELATIONSHIP

The learning curve relationship is usually expressed as a constant percentage. This percentage represents the proportion by which the amount of an input (or cost) per unit of output is reduced each time production is doubled. For example, consider a production process in which labor input and costs follow an 80-percent learning curve. Assume that the *first* unit requires labor costs of $1,000 to produce. Based on the learning curve relationship, the *second* unit costs $1,000 × .80 = $800, the *fourth* unit costs $800 × .80 = $640, the *eighth* unit costs $640 × .80 = $512, the *sixteenth* unit costs $512 × .80 = $409.60, and so on.

---

[25] An excellent survey on mass customization is found in M. Agrawal, T.V. Kumaresh, and G.A. Mercer, "The False Promise of Mass Customization," *McKinsey Quarterly,* November 3, 2001. See also "A Long March," *The Economist,* July 14, 2001, pp. 63–65.

[26] Other names given to the learning curve relationship include learning-by-doing, progress curve, experience curve, and improvement curve.

This learning curve relationship is shown in Figures 9A.1 and 9A.2. When plotted on an *arithmetic scale,* as shown in Figure 9A.1, the cost-output relationship is a curvilinear function. When plotted on a *logarithmic scale,* as shown in Figure 9A.2, the cost-output relationship is a linear function.

The learning curve relationship can be expressed algebraically as follows:

$$C = aQ^b \tag{9A.1}$$

where C is the input cost of the Qth unit of output, Q is consecutive units of output produced, a is the theoretical (or actual) input cost of the first unit of output, and b is the rate of reduction in input cost per unit of output. Because the learning curve

FIGURE 9A.1

Learning Curve:
Arithmetic Scale

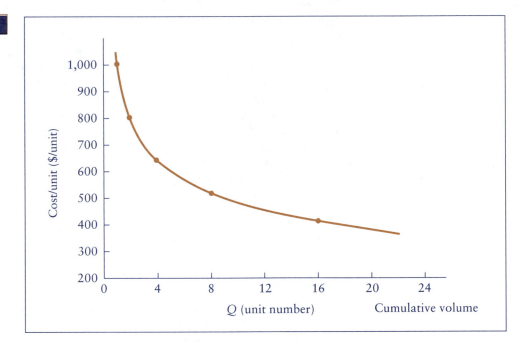

FIGURE 9A.2

Learning Curve:
Logarithmic Scale

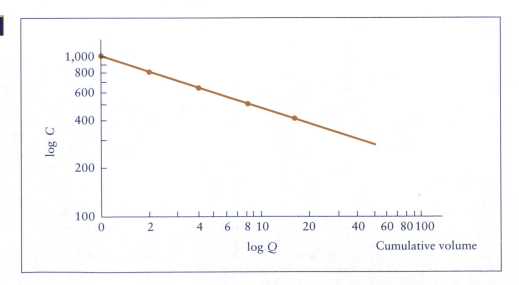

is downward sloping, the value of b is normally negative. It should be noted that b is *not* the same as the learning curve percentage. Taking logarithms of both sides of Equation 9A.1 yields

$$\log C = \log a + b \log Q \qquad [9A.2]$$

When the learning curve is expressed in logarithmic form, b represents the slope of the function.

ESTIMATING THE LEARNING CURVE PARAMETERS

Application of the learning curve in forecasting costs requires that one first determine the values of the log a and b parameters in Equation 9A.2. In the absence of any historical cost-output data for the production process, one would have to make subjective estimates of these parameters based on prior experience with similar types of production operations. For a production process that has been operating for a period of time and for which historical cost-output data are available, however, statistical methods can be used to estimate the parameters. One such method is the *least-squares* technique of regression analysis.[27] In the learning curve equation (Equation 9A.2), log C is the dependent variable and log Q is the independent variable. Applying the least-squares procedure to the series of cost-output observations yields the following equations for estimating the learning curve parameters:

$$b = \frac{n\Sigma(\log Q_i \log C_i) - (\Sigma\log Q_i)(\Sigma\log C_i)}{n\Sigma(\log Q_i)^2 - (\Sigma\log Q_i)^2} \qquad [9A.3]$$

$$\log a = \frac{\Sigma\log C_i - b\Sigma\log Q_i}{n} \qquad [9A.4]$$

where n is the number of observations.

Example

LEARNING CURVES: EMERSON CORPORATION

The Emerson Corporation, a manufacturer of airplane landing gear equipment, is trying to develop a learning curve model to help forecast labor costs for successive units of one of its products. From past data, the firm knows that labor costs of the 25th, 75th, and 125th units were $800, $600, and $500, respectively. Develop the learning curve equation from these data and use the resulting model to predict labor costs for the 200th unit of output. The preliminary calculations needed to determine log a and b are shown in Table 9A.1. Substituting the column totals from the last row of Table 9A.1 into Equations 9A.3 and 9A.4 provides the following estimates of the learning curve parameters:

$$b = \frac{3(14.92704) - (5.36991)(8.38021)}{3(9.86711) - (5.36991)^2}$$

$$= -.28724$$

$$\log a = \frac{8.38021 - (-.28724)(5.36991)}{3}$$

$$= 3.30755$$

[27] The *least-squares* technique is described in Chapter 4.

TABLE 9A.1

Learning Curve: Preliminary Calculations

Observation i	Q_i (Unit No.)	C_i (Dollars)	Log Q_i	Log C_i	$(\text{Log } Q_i)^2$	$(\text{Log } C_i)^2$	$(\text{Log } Q_i) \times (\text{Log } C_i)$
1	25	800	1.39794	2.90309	1.95423	8.42793	4.05834
2	75	600	1.87506	2.77815	3.51585	7.71811	5.20920
3 ($=n$)	125	500	2.09691	2.69897	4.39703	7.28444	5.65950
Sum			5.36991	8.38021	9.86711	23.43048	14.92704

The learning curve equation for labor costs is

$$\log C = 3.30755 - .28724 \log Q \qquad \text{[9A.5]}$$

Using this model, the estimated cost of the 200th unit of output is obtained as follows:

$$\log C = 3.30755 - .28724 \log 200$$
$$= 3.30755 - .28724(2.30103)$$
$$= 2.64660$$
$$C = \$443.20$$

THE PERCENTAGE OF LEARNING

The percentage of learning, which is defined as the proportion by which an input (or its associated cost) is reduced when output is doubled, can be estimated as follows:

$$L = \frac{C_2}{C_1} \times 100\% \qquad \text{[9A.6]}$$

where C_1 is the input (or cost) for the Q_1 unit of output and C_2 is the cost for the $Q_2 = 2Q_1$ unit of output.

Example

PERCENTAGE OF LEARNING: EMERSON CORPORATION (continued)

To illustrate the calculation of the percentage of learning, consider the Emerson Corporation example again. Using the learning curve model developed earlier (Equation 9A.5), labor costs for the $Q_1 = 50$th unit of output are $C_1 = \$659.98$ and labor costs for the $2Q_1 = 100$th unit of output are $C_2 = \$540.84$. Substituting these values into Equation 9A.6 yields

$$L = \frac{\$540.84}{\$659.98} \times 100\%$$
$$= 81.9\%$$

The percentage of learning for labor costs in the production of these landing gear units is thus approximately 82 percent—indicating that labor costs decline by about 18 percent each time output is doubled.

EXERCISE

1. Ajax Controls Company uses a learning curve to estimate labor costs for its products. The firm recently introduced a new line of process control devices and has collected the following cost data:

Unit No.	Labor Cost
100	$1,250
300	1,000
600	850

a. Determine the learning curve for the labor costs required to produce this product.

b. What is the percentage of learning for labor costs?

c. Estimate the labor costs of the 800th unit based on the learning curve developed in Part (a).

IV

Pricing and Output Decisions: Strategy and Tactics

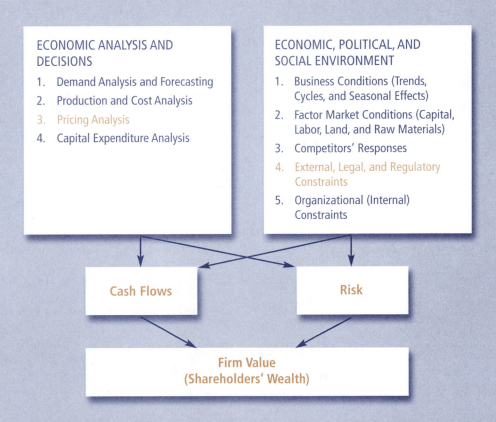

ECONOMIC ANALYSIS AND DECISIONS

1. Demand Analysis and Forecasting
2. Production and Cost Analysis
3. Pricing Analysis
4. Capital Expenditure Analysis

ECONOMIC, POLITICAL, AND SOCIAL ENVIRONMENT

1. Business Conditions (Trends, Cycles, and Seasonal Effects)
2. Factor Market Conditions (Capital, Labor, Land, and Raw Materials)
3. Competitors' Responses
4. External, Legal, and Regulatory Constraints
5. Organizational (Internal) Constraints

Cash Flows

Risk

Firm Value (Shareholders' Wealth)

In the previous chapters we developed the theories and modeling techniques useful in analyzing demand, production, and cost relationships in a firm. In this part we consider the profit-maximizing price-output decisions, especially as they relate to the firm's strategic choices in competitive markets (Chapter 10). Asymmetric information conditions as well as ideal full information exchanges are discussed. Chapters 11 and 12 consider price and output determination in dominant-firm monopoly and oligopoly markets. Chapter 13 presents a game-theoretic framework for analyzing rival response tactics.

Chapter 14 examines value-based (not cost-based) differential pricing in theory and practice, and Appendix 14A presents the concept of revenue management. Appendix 14B addresses specialized pricing problems including pricing for the multiproduct firm, pricing of joint products, and transfer pricing.

Prices, Output, and Strategy: Pure and Monopolistic Competition

CHAPTER PREVIEW Stockholder wealth-maximizing managers seek a pricing and output strategy that will maximize the present value of the future profit stream to the firm. The determination of the wealth-maximizing strategy depends on the production capacity, cost levels, demand characteristics, and the potential for immediate and longer-term competition. In this chapter we provide an introduction to competitive strategic analysis and discuss Michael Porter's Five Forces strategic framework. The implications of asymmetric information and the resulting problem of adverse selection in competitive markets are also discussed.

MANAGERIAL CHALLENGE

Resurrecting Apple Computer?[1]

Despite superior products, Apple Computer has discovered that competitive advantages may not be sustainable when products are imitated successfully. In the 1980s Apple's Macintosh revolutionized personal computing by introducing the graphical user interface. However, by 1997 Apple had been surpassed by competitors. Microsoft had come to dominate the PC operating system business with Microsoft Windows enjoying a 92-percent market share. IBM and then Compaq, Packard-Bell, and Dell had come to dominate the PC assembly business. Apple remained the market leader in only the education, graphics design, and publishing submarkets. Since 55 percent of all PC and operating systems sales are in industry, 33 percent are in the home, 7 percent in government, and only 5 percent are in education, Apple's market share slipped from 9.6 percent in 1993 to 5.2 percent in 1996 to 2.6 percent in 1997.

One problem was pricing, and another was distribution. Personal computer assembly of outsourced components is now a small minimum-efficient-scale business necessitating perhaps only 200,000 unit sales. For example, Dell Computers assembles whatever components the buyer wants and delivers by direct mail order. With little inventory and just-in-time manufacturing from a masterfully managed supply chain of component suppliers, Dell became the most profitable company in the personal computer industry, and in 1998, Dell's market share of 9 percent surpassed IBM; by 2000 Dell had 20 percent. Soon other component assemblers like Gateway entered this direct-to-the-consumer channel, and sales in the direct channel grew at twice the industry growth rate.

With few outsourced components and relatively high in-house manufacturing costs, large overhead, and extensive R&D, Apple's least expensive product offering was $1,700, while "comparable" IBM machines were $1,100 and Dell's PCs were as low as $800. Apple also continued to sell primarily through retail outlets like Computree, a national chain of independent multi-product dealers, even though the emergence of mass merchandisers like Best Buy and the direct-to-customer channel had radically changed the nature of PC distribution.

In addition, Apple had stale product design and closed architecture. Connectivity to IBM and the Windows operating systems had been resisted by Apple. This closed architecture strategy proved disastrous for exploiting the numerous complementary relationships available with the huge installed base of initially DOS-based IBM and later Windows- and Intel-based Microsoft customers. An installed base of customers attracts independent software vendors to write applications programs. Without compatibility to this Wintel installed base, Apple's software stagnated.

In 1999, Steve Jobs regained the leadership of the company intent on restoring the brand image of the once highly innovative Apple machines. The spiffy Imac PC made a good start, allowing market share to climb back to 5 percent. What prices to charge, distribution channels to use, and alliances to form had to be decided.

---

[1] Based on *Apple Computer 1992, 1995 (A), 1996, and 1997,* Harvard Business School Publishing; and "The Road Ahead," *Wall Street Journal,* November 18, 2000, p. A3.

INTRODUCTION

Competitive strategic analysis provides a framework for thinking proactively about threats to a firm's business model, about new business opportunities, and about the future reconfigurations of the firm's resources, capabilities, and core competencies.

Figure 10.1 displays the components of a business model in the context of a firm's prerequisite knowledge and strategic decisions. All successful business models begin by identifying *target markets*—i.e., what businesses one wants to enter and stay in. Physical assets, human resources, and intellectual property (like patents and licenses) sometimes limit the firm's capabilities, but business models are as unbounded as the ingenuity of entrepreneurial managers in finding ways to address new business opportunities. Next, all successful business models lay out a *value proposition* grounded in customer expectations of perceived value, and then identify what part of the *value chain* leading to end products the firm plans to create. Business models always must clarify *how and when revenue will be realized* and analyze the sensitivity of *gross and net margins* to various possible changes in the firm's cost structure. In spec-

Figure 10.1 The Strategy Process

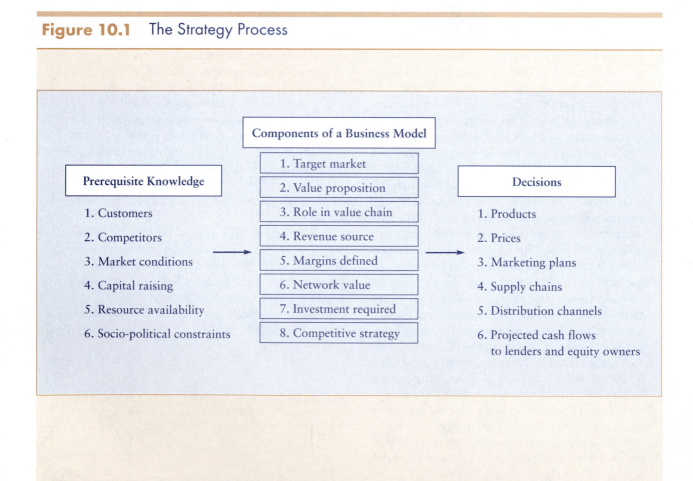

Prerequisite Knowledge	Components of a Business Model	Decisions
1. Customers	1. Target market	1. Products
2. Competitors	2. Value proposition	2. Prices
3. Market conditions	3. Role in value chain	3. Marketing plans
4. Capital raising	4. Revenue source	4. Supply chains
5. Resource availability	5. Margins defined	5. Distribution channels
6. Socio-political constraints	6. Network value	6. Projected cash flows to lenders and equity owners
	7. Investment required	
	8. Competitive strategy	

Source: Adapted from H. Chesbrough, *Open Innovation* (Cambridge, MA: Harvard University Press, 2003).

ifying the *required investments,* business models also assess the potential for creating *value in network relationships* with complementary businesses and in joint ventures and alliances. Finally, all successful business models develop a competitive strategy.

COMPETITIVE STRATEGY

The essence of competitive strategy is threefold: resource-based capabilities, business processes, and adaptive innovation.[2] First, competitive strategy analyzes how the firm can secure differential access to key resources like patents or distribution channels. From humble beginnings as an Internet bookseller that contracted out its warehousing and book delivery service, Amazon managed to become the preferred fulfillment agent for Internet sales in general. That is, Amazon acquired enough regular customers searching for CDs, office products, tools, and toys that companies like Toys"R"Us adopted Amazon as their Internet sales channel. Second, competitive strategy designs business processes that are difficult to imitate and capable of creating unique value for the target customers. The high-frequency point-to-point streamlined operations of Southwest Airlines prove very difficult for hub-and-spoke airlines to imitate, and as a result in 2002 Southwest had a market capitalization equal to that of all the major U.S. carriers combined. Similarly, both Dell and Compaq had $12 billion in net sales and approximately $1 billion in net income in 1998. But Compaq had $6 billion in net operating assets (i.e., inventories plus net plant and equipment plus working capital for net accounts receivable) while Dell had $2 billion. How could Dell produce the same net income with one third as much plant and equipment, inventories, and working capital? The answer is that Dell created a direct-to-the-customer sales process; it builds to order with subassembly components bought just in time from outside contractors, and it realizes cash from a sale within 48 hours. These value-creating business processes generated 50 percent ($1B/$2B) return on investment at Dell, whereas the comparable ROI at Compaq was just 16 percent ($1B/$6B).[3]

Finally, competitive strategy provides a road map for sustaining a firm's profitability through innovation. As industries emerge, evolve, and morph into other product spaces (e.g., think of calculators and mobile phones), firms must anticipate these changes and plan how they will sustain their positioning in the industry, and ultimately migrate their business to new industries. IBM, the dominant mainframe leasing company in the 1970s, reinvented itself twice—first in the 1980s as a PC manufacturer, and a second time in the 1990s as a systems solution provider. In contrast, some firms like Xerox or Kodak become entrenched in outdated competitive strategic positions.

Generic Types of Strategy[4]

Strategic thinking initially focuses on *industry analysis* and in which industries it would be attractive to do business. Michael Porter's Five Forces model (discussed below) illustrates this approach. Soon thereafter, however, strategists want to conduct

---

[2] This section is based on H. Chesbrough, *Open Innovation* (Boston, MA: Harvard Business Press, 2003), pp. 73–83.

[3] Return on invested capital is defined as net income divided by net operating assets (i.e., net plant and equipment plus inventories plus net accounts receivable.)

[4] This section is based in part on C. deKluyver and J. Pearce, *Strategy: A View from the Top* (Upper Saddle River, NJ: Prentice-Hall, 2003).

WHAT WENT RIGHT   WHAT WENT WRONG

Xerox[5]

Xerox invented the chemical paper copier and thereafter realized phenomenal 15-percent compound growth rates throughout the 1960s and early 1970s. When their initial patents expired, Xerox was ready with a plain paper copier (PPC) that established a first-mover technology advantage, but ultimately they failed to receive any broad patent extension.[6] Xerox's target market was large corporations and government installations who valued high-quality, high-volume leased machines with an enormous variety of capabilities and full service/ maintenance contracts, even though supplies and usage fees were expensive.

Unable to compete on product capabilities, Japanese competitors Cannon and Ricoh realized that tremendous market potential lay in small businesses where affordability per copy was a major value proposition issue. Installation and service were outsourced to highly competitive independent dealer networks, and the smaller volume copy machine itself was sold at very low initial cost with self-service replacement cartridges being the principal source of profitability.

As with later events in the development of the Xerox Star Workstation in 1981, Xerox insisted on closed architecture software and built all of its copier components in house rather than pursuing partnerships that could reduce cost and trigger a larger installed base of machines. Competitors pursued just the opposite open architecture and partnership strategy to achieve network effects and drive down costs.

Between 1975 and 1985, Xerox copier sales more than doubled from $4 billion to $9 billion while those of Canon grew 25-fold from $87 million to $2.2 billion. During this "lost decade," Xerox's market share fell to 40 percent worldwide, and Canon and Ricoh both became $2-billion firms in a copier business that Xerox had totally dominated only 15 years earlier. Failure to adapt its once-dominant business model had doomed Xerox to nearly second-rank status.

---

[5] Based on Chesbrough, op. cit., and on C. Bartlett and S. Ghoshal, *Transnational Management* (Boston, MA: Irwin-McGraw-Hill, 1995), Case 4-1.

[6] In fact, because of Xerox's 93-percent monopoly of the copier industry in 1971, the U.S. Federal Trade Commission forced Xerox in 1975 to license its PPC technology at low royalty rates.

---

competitor analysis to learn more about how firms can sustain their relative profitability in a group of related firms. Efforts to answer these questions are often described as competitive *strategic positioning*. Finally, strategists try to isolate what *core competencies* any particular firm possesses as a result of its *resource-based capabilities* in order to identify *sustainable competitive advantages* vis-a-vis their competitors in a relevant market.

Profitability clearly depends on the ability to create sustainable competitive advantages. Any one of three generic types of strategies may suffice. A firm may establish a product differentiation strategy, a lowest-delivered-cost strategy, or an information technology (IT) strategy. *Product differentiation strategy* usually involves competing on capabilities, branding, or product endorsements. Xerox in copiers and Kodak in paper and chemicals for film development compete on product capabilities. Coca-Cola is by far the world's most widely recognized brand, with almost 80 percent of sales outside the U.S., but it is followed closely by Marlboro, Gillette, P&G's Pampers, Nestle, Nescafe, and Kellogg's, all with more than 50 percent of their sales outside their home markets. All of these branded products command a price premium worldwide simply because of the product image and lifestyle associated with their successful branding.

RAWLINGS SPORTING GOODS WAVES OFF THE SWOOSH SIGN[7]

Another type of product differentiation strategy is based on endorsements. Even though Rawlings baseball gloves had sales in 2002 of only $175 million and competed against heavily-branded Nike with annual sales of $9 billion, Rawlings gloves are used by more than 50 percent of major leaguers, such as Mike Piazza, Jeff Bagwell, and Gary Sheffield. These superstars receive only $10,000 to $20,000 for licensing their autographs to Rawlings for engraving on Little League gloves. But player after player can talk about a feature of Rawlings' equipment that keeps them coming back year after year. Rawlings is very attentive to this feedback and will lengthen the webbing or stiffen the fingers on a new model in just a few weeks to please their celebrity endorsers. Quick adaptation to the vagaries of the consumer marketplace is a requisite part of any product differentiation strategy.

Which of the three generic types of strategy (differentiation, cost, or IT) will be most effective depends in part on a firm's choice of *competitive scope*—that is, the number and type of product lines and market segments, the number of geographic locations, and the network of horizontally and vertically integrated businesses in which the company decides to invest. For example, in 1999 the most profitable clothing retailer in the U.S. (The Gap) undertook to expand its competitive scope by opening a new chain of Old Navy stores. Old Navy's bargain-priced khakis, jeans, and sweaters immediately began cannibalizing sales at its mid-priced parent. Even fashion-conscious teens could see little reason to pay $16.50 for a Gap-emblazoned t-shirt when Old Navy's branding offered style and a nearly identical product for $12.50. The configuration of a firm's resource capabilities, its business opportunities relative to its rivals, and a detailed knowledge of its customers intertwine to determine the preferred competitive scope.

Competitive scope decisions are especially pivotal for cost-based strategy. A firm like Southwest Airlines with a *focused cost strategy* must limit its business plan to focus narrowly on point-to-point, medium distance, nonstop routes.

THINK SMALL TO GROW BIG: SOUTHWEST AIRLINES

Southwest adopts operations processes for ticket sales, boarding, plane turnaround, crew scheduling, flight frequency, maintenance, and jet fuel hedging that deliver exceptionally reduced operating costs to target customers in their price-sensitive market niche. Anything that works against this focus must be jettisoned from the business plan. Southwest has clearly accomplished its goal. As air travel plummeted in the months following the September 11, 2001 attacks on the World Trade Center, only Southwest had a break-even that was low enough to continue to make money. Southwest can cover all of its costs at 64-percent load factors (unit sales/seat capacity). Since September 11, American Airlines, United, Delta, US Airways, and America West have all been operating well below their break-even points of 84 percent to 94 percent.

---

[7] Based on "I've Got It," *Wall Street Journal*, April 1, 2002, p. A1.

In contrast, Dell Computers' *cost leadership strategy* allows it to address a wide scope of PC product lines at prices that make its competitors wish to exit the market, as IBM did in 1999.

Example

DELL COST LEADERSHIP STRATEGY DOMINATES PC ASSEMBLY[8]

Dell sells over the phone and over the Internet direct to the consumer, then assembles and delivers mass-customized PCs usually within 48 hours. In contrast, Compaq's large dealer network requires 35 days to convert a sale into realized cash. Even rival mail-order company Gateway takes 16 days. Having no dealer network and realizing cash quickly might be processes to imitate, but Michael Dell pushed the just-in-time approach down his supply chain. Every company that builds critical components for Dell must warehouse within fifteen minutes travel time of a Dell factory. Consequently, Dell does not even order components until the customer commits to a purchase. Even after developing Internet distribution channels, Compaq's slower production process requires that subassembly components sit on the shelves for months. Less inventories at Dell means tying up less working capital, and less working capital means lower cost.

Between 1990 and 1998, Dell drove PC prices down, and as a result even Dell's gross margin (the difference between net sales revenue and the direct costs of goods sold as a percentage of net sales revenue) also fell, from 33 percent to 23 percent. However, Dell's net profit margin actually increased from 8 percent to 11 percent over this period. How could this happen? Dell's selling, general, and administrative expense (SG&A) declined from 21 percent of sales to 9 percent of sales. Again, less overhead means lower cost, and lower cost can mean higher profitability, even in an era of steeply falling prices.

The overall effect of this cost leadership strategy on market share, profits, and capitalized value has been stunning. Between 1996 and 2001, Dell's market share in PC shipments grew from 7 percent to 24 percent. Dell's net income increased tenfold from $260 million in 1996 to $2.3 billion in 2001. And Dell's market capitalization grew from $6 billion to $70 billion, which was the fastest growing valuation among NYSE-listed companies in several of those years.

Finally, firms can seek their sustainable competitive advantage among relevant market rivals by pursuing an *information technology strategy*. Southland Corporation's 7-Eleven convenience stores in 6,000 locations across Japan provide a good example.

Example

THE E-COMMERCE OF SANDWICHES AT 7-ELEVENS IN JAPAN[9]

Japanese officeworkers put in very long hours, often arriving at 8 A.M. and staying well into the evening. In the midst of this long day, most take a break to go out on the street and pick up lunch. Boxed lunches, rice balls, and sandwiches are the routine offerings, but the fashion-conscious Japanese want to be seen eating what's

---

[8] Based on "The New Economy Is Stronger Than You Think," *Harvard Business Review,* November/December 1999, pp. 104–105; Chesbrough, op. cit., p. 55; and "How Dell Fine Tunes Its Pricing," *Wall Street Journal,* June 8, 2001, p. A1.

[9] Based on "Over the Counter Commerce," *The Economist,* May 26, 2001, pp. 77–78.

"in" this week. This situation makes an excellent opportunity for Southland Corporation's 7-Eleven stores, which became the biggest retailer in Japan in 2001. Half of sales revenue comes from these lunch items, and 7-Eleven Japan is twice as profitable as the second highest retailer, the clothing outlet Fast Retailing. The key to 7-Eleven Japan's success has been electronic commerce and its information technology strategy.

7-Eleven Japan collects sales information by proprietary satellite communication networks from 8,500 locations three times a day. Like other retailers, 7-Eleven Japan uses the data for merchandising studies to improve its product packaging and shelf placements with laboratory-like experiments in matched-pair stores throughout the country. But there is more, much more. 7-Eleven has built systems to analyze the entire data inflow in just 20 minutes. 7-Eleven Japan is interested in what sells this morning and what sold yesterday evening (and the local weather) as a forecast of what sandwiches to prepare for the lunch crowd rush hour today. As customers become more fickle, product fashion cycles in sandwiches are shortening from 7 weeks to, in some cases, as little time as 10 days. 7-Eleven Japan forecasts the demand item by item, store by store, on a daily basis.

Of course, such short-term demand forecasting would be useless if food preparation were a production-to-stock process with many weeks of lead time required. Instead, supply chain management practices are closely monitored and adapted continuously with electronic commerce tools. Delivery trucks carry bar code readers that upload instantaneously to headquarters databases. Orders for a particular sandwich at a particular store are placed before 10 A.M., processed through the supply chain to all component input companies in less than 7 minutes, and delivered by 4 P.M. for the next day's sales. Most customers praise the extraordinary freshness, quality ingredients, and minimal incidence of out-of-stock items. All this competitive advantage over rival grocers and noodle shops has led to consistent price premiums for 7-Eleven's in-house brand.

In conclusion, competitive strategy can secure higher profitability if a company configures its resource-based capabilities, business processes, and adaptive innovations in such as way as to obtain a sustainable competitive advantage. Whether cost-based strategy, product differentiation strategy, or information technology strategy provides the most effective route to competitive advantage depends in large part on the firm's strategic focus. IT-based strategy is especially conducive to broad target market initiatives. 7-Eleven Japan, for example, drives traffic in its convenience stores by allowing Internet buyers to pick up their web purchases and pay at the 7-Eleven counter. Is 7-Eleven Japan a convenience store, or an Internet fulfillment agent like Amazon, or a warehouse and distribution company? In some sense, 7-Eleven Japan is all of these. Unlike Southwest Airlines' focused cost strategy, 7-Eleven Japan has a much broader IT-based strategy that conveys a competitive advantage in all of these relevant markets.

The Relevant Market Concept

A *relevant market is a group of firms that interact with each other in a buyer-seller relationship.* Relevant markets often have both spatial and product characteristics. For example, the market for Microsoft's Windows operating system is worldwide, whereas the market for Minneapolis-origin air travel is confined to suppliers in the upper Midwest. Similarly, the market for large, prime-rate commercial loans includes large banks and corporations from all areas of the United States, whereas the market for a particular brand of bagged cement is confined to a 250-mile radius around the plant.

The *market structure* within these relevant markets varies tremendously. The four largest producers of breakfast cereals control 86 percent of the total industry output—a *concentrated* market. In contrast, the market for concrete block and brick is *fragmented*—with the largest four firms accounting for only 8 percent of the total output. Recently, the share of the total output produced by the largest four firms in the women's hosiery industry has grown from 32 percent to 58 percent. These differences in market structures and changes in market structure over time have important implications for the determination of price levels, price stability, and the likelihood of sustained profitability in these relevant markets.

PORTER'S FIVE FORCES STRATEGIC FRAMEWORK

Michael Porter[10] has developed a conceptual framework for identifying the threats from competition in a relevant market. Incumbent firms attempt to secure competitive advantages through their choice of management strategy. Porter's Five Forces Framework conceptualizes management strategy in terms of the likelihood of sustained profitability for a particular industry or line of business. Figure 10.2 displays Porter's Five Forces: the threat of substitutes, the threat of entry, the power of buyers, the power of suppliers, and the intensity of rivalry.

Threat of Substitutes

First, incumbent profitability is determined by the threat of substitutes. Is the product generic, like AAA-grade January wheat, two-bedroom apartments, and office supplies, or is it branded, like Gillette razors, Coca-Cola, and Campbell's soup? The more brand loyalty, the less the threat of substitutes and the higher the incumbent's profitability will be. Also, the more distant the substitutes outside the relevant market, the less price responsive will be demand, and the larger will be the optimal markups and profit margins. As video conferencing equipment improves, the margins in business air travel will decline. A video conferencing projector and sound system now leases for just $279 *per month*. Iced tea, coffee, and fruit drinks are not perceived by consumers as offering the lifestyle choice associated with "the Pepsi Generation." However, flavored and unflavored bottled water products may erode the loyalty of cola drinkers. If so, cola profitability will continue to decline.

The closeness or distance of substitutes often hinges not only on consumer perceptions created by advertising, but also on segmentation of the customers into separate distribution channels. Pantyhose distributed through convenience stores has many fewer substitutes at 9:00 P.M. the night before a business trip than does pantyhose sold through the department store distribution channels. Consequently, the threat of substitutes is reduced, and the profit margin on convenience store pantyhose is high. Similarly, one-stop service and nonstop service in airlines are different products with different functionality. United's one-stop service from Chicago provides a distant substitute for Minneapolis-origin air travelers. Consequently, Northwest Airlines enjoys high margins on nonstop service from Minneapolis.

---

[10] Michael Porter, *Competitive Strategy* (Cambridge, MA: The Free Press, 1998). See also Cynthia Porter and Michael Porter, eds., *Strategy: Seeking and Securing Competitive Advantage* (Cambridge, MA: Harvard Business School Publishing, 1992).

Figure 10.2   Porter's Five Forces Strategic Model

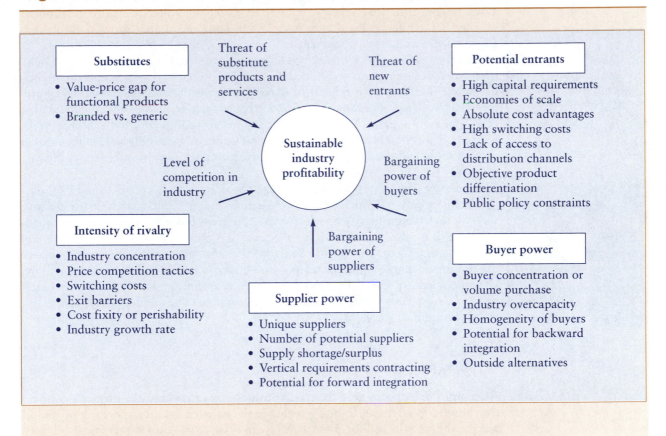

Source: Adapted from M. Porter, *Competitive Strategy* (Cambridge, MA: *The Free Press*, 1998).

Example

RELEVANT MARKET FOR WEB BROWSERS: MICROSOFT'S INTERNET EXPLORER[11]

One of the recurring antitrust policy questions in the 1990s was the definition of the relevant market for computer software. In 1996, Netscape's user-friendly and pioneering product Navigator had an 82-percent share of the Internet browser market. But during 1996–1999, Microsoft's Internet Explorer made swift inroads. Bundling Explorer with its widely adopted Windows 97 operating system, Microsoft marketed an integrated software package pre-installed on PCs. Microsoft quoted higher prices for Windows 98 alone than for Windows with Internet Explorer and threatened PC

---

[11] Based on "U.S. Sues Microsoft over PC Browser," and "Personal Technology," *Wall Street Journal*, October 21 and 30, 1997; "Microsoft's Browser: A Bundle of Trouble," *The Economist*, October 25, 1997; and *U.S. News and World Report*, Business and Technology, December 15, 1997.

assemblers like Compaq and Gateway with removal of their Windows 97 license unless they mounted Explorer as a desktop icon. Because most PC customers do want Windows pre-installed on their machines, Explorer penetrated deep into the browser market very quickly. By the start of 2000, some estimates showed Explorer's market share as high as 59 percent.

If the relevant market for these products is an integrated PC operating system (OS), then Microsoft simply incorporated new web browser technology into an already dominant Windows OS product. An analogy might be the interlock between an automobile's ignition and steering system to deter auto theft. If, on the other hand, Internet browsers are a separate relevant market, like stereo equipment for an automobile, then Microsoft should not be entitled to employ anticompetitive practices like refusals to deal to extend their dominance of PC operating systems into this new software market.

Microsoft's spectacular growth in sales of Windows 98 was not the issue. Winning a near monopoly of 85-percent market share in the previously fragmented OS software industry indicated a superior product, a great business plan, and good management. But allowing Microsoft to extend that market power into a new line of business using tactics that would be ineffective and self-defeating in the absence of the dominant market share in the original business, is just what the antitrust laws were intended to prevent. The European antitrust authorities have pursued this objective; a U.S. Appeals Court has allowed Microsoft to continue aggressive marketing tactics without sanction.

Threat of Entry

A second force determining the likely profitability of an industry or product line is the threat of potential entrants. The higher the barriers to entry, the more profitable an incumbent will be. Barriers to entry can arise from several factors. First, consider high capital costs. The bottling and distribution business in the soft drink industry necessitates a $50 million investment. Although a good business plan with secure collateral will always attract loanable funds, unsecured loans become difficult to finance at this size. Few potential entrants with the necessary capital implies a lesser threat of entry and higher incumbent profitability.

Second, economies of scale and absolute cost advantages can provide another barrier to entry. In the traditional cable TV industry, the huge infrastructure cost of laying wire throughout the community deterred multiple entrants. The first-mover had a tremendous scale economy in spreading fixed cost across a large customer base. Absolute cost advantage arises with proprietary IT technology that lowers cost (e.g., at 7-Eleven Japan). Of course, new wireless technology for satellite-based TV may soon lower this barrier, and then numerous suppliers of TV content will exhibit similar unit cost. These new threats of entry imply lower industry profitability.

Third, if customers are brand loyal, the costs of inducing a customer to switch to a new entrant's product may pose a substantial barrier to entry. Year after year, hundreds of millions of dollars of cumulative advertising in the cereal industry maintains the pulling power of the Tony the Tiger Frosted Flakes brand. Unadvertised cereals go unnoticed. To take another example, airlines raise the switching costs for their regular customers when they issue frequent flyer giveaways. Committing seat capacity to promotional giveaways raises barriers to entry. A new entrant therefore has a very high cost associated with becoming an effective entry threat in these markets.

Example

http://

Read more about the FTC case against Office Depot and Staples by searching the FTC Internet site under the keyword "Staples" at the following address:

http://www.ftc.gov/

POTENTIAL ENTRY AT OFFICE DEPOT/STAPLES[12]

In 1997 Office Depot and Staples proposed to merge. Their combined sales in the $13 billion office supply superstore industry totaled 76 percent. Potential competitors included not only OfficeMax but all small paper goods specialty stores, department stores, discount stores such as Kmart, warehouse clubs like Sam's Club, office supply catalogs, and some computer retailers. This larger office supply industry is very fragmented, easy to enter, and huge; 1996 sales topped $185 billion. By this latter standard, the proposed merger involved two firms with a combined market share of only 9 percent.

The profit margins of Office Depot, OfficeMax, and Staples are significantly higher where only one office supply superstore locates in a town. This would suggest that the small-scale office suppliers offer little threat of entry into the superstore market. The exceptional ease of entry (and exit) at small scale moderates the markups and profit margins of incumbent specialty retailers like stationery stores, but not office supply superstores. High capital requirement and scale economies in warehousing and distribution appear responsible for the barriers to entry in the office supply superstore market.

Access to distribution channels is another potential barrier that has implications for the profitability of incumbents. The shelf space in grocery stores is very limited; all the slots are filled. A new entrant would therefore have to offer huge trade promotions (i.e., free display racks or slot-in allowances) to induce grocery store chains to displace one of their current suppliers. A related barrier to entry has emerged in the satellite television industry where Direct TV and Echostar control essentially all the channel slots on satellites capable of reaching the entire U.S. audience. Government regulatory agencies also can approve or deny access to distribution channels. For example, the FDA approves prescription drugs for certain therapeutic uses but not for others. The FDA also approves or denies exceptions to the Orphan Drug Act that gives firms patent-like exclusive selling rights when public policy pressure warrants. Biogen's highest sales product, Avonex (a weekly injection for multiple sclerosis patients), received an exception to the Orphan Drug Act. Other similarly situated firms have been denied approval; such a barrier to entry may prove insurmountable.

Example

ELI LILLY POSES A THREAT OF POTENTIAL ENTRY FOR ZENECA[13]

Preexisting competitors in related product lines provide a substantial threat of entry in the prescription drug industry. Eli Lilly markets a pharmaceutical product, Evista, long approved by the FDA for the treatment of osteoporosis. Preliminary tests suggested a therapeutic potential for Evista in the prevention of breast cancer. Lilly promptly released an Evista study in which the incidence of developing cancer over a three-year period was reduced 55 percent in 10,575 women with high-risk factors for developing breast cancer. Zeneca Group PLC then sued to stop Lilly trade representatives from making any such product claims. In 2000, Zeneca's cancer

---

[12] Based on "FTC Rejects Staples' Settlement Offer," *Wall Street Journal*, April 7, 1997, p. A3; and J. Baker, "Econometric Analysis in *FTC* v. *Staples*," *Journal of Public Policy and Marketing*, 18(1), Spring 1999, pp. 11–21.

[13] "Zeneca Sues Eli Lilly Over Evista Promotion," *Wall Street Journal*, February 26, 1999, p. B6.

treatment Novaldex became the first drug ever approved for reducing the risk of breast cancer in presently healthy women. Zeneca's lawsuit may slow Lilly's marketing efforts, but the real barrier to entry would have been an FDA denial of the therapeutic use. Without it, Novaldex faces a formidable direct competitor.

Finally, a barrier to entry may be posed by product differentiation. If the differences between products are objective (e.g., dot matrix quality in a copier or shutter speed technology in a camera), the entrant can reverse engineer the copier or camera. Perceived product differentiation is actually harder to imitate and poses therefore a more effective barrier.

Example

OBJECTIVE VERSUS PERCEIVED PRODUCT DIFFERENTIATION: XEROX

Shielded from competition by patents on its landmark dry paper copier, Xerox enjoyed a virtual monopoly and 15-percent compound earnings growth through the 1960s and early 1970s. During this period, its research lab in Palo Alto, California, spun off one breakthrough device after another. One year it was the graphical user interface that Apple later brought to market as a user-friendly PC. In 1979, Xerox scientists and engineers developed the Ethernet, a first local area network for connecting computers and printers. Yet, Xerox was able to commercialize almost none of these R&D successes. As a result, Japanese copier companies like Canon and Ikon reverse engineered the Xerox product, imitated its processes, and ultimately developed better and cheaper copiers.

Especially with the increasing globalization of commerce, objective product differentiation is always subject to reverse engineering, violations of intellectual property, and offshore imitation even of patented products. In contrast, product differentiation based on customer perceptions of lifestyle images and product positioning (e.g., Coca-Cola) can erect barriers to entry that allow incumbent firms to better survive competitive attack. In sum, the higher any of these barriers to entry, the lower the threat of potential entrants and the higher the potential industry profitability will be.

Power of Buyers and Suppliers

The profitability of incumbents is determined in part by the bargaining power of buyers and suppliers. Buyers may be highly concentrated, like Boeing, Lockheed, and Airbus in the purchase of large aircraft engines, or extremely fragmented, like the restaurants that are customers of wholesale grocery companies. If industry capacity approximately equals or exceeds demand, concentrated buyers can force price concessions which reduce incumbent profitability. On the other hand, fragmented buyers have little bargaining power unless excess capacity and inventory overhang persist.

Unique suppliers may also reduce industry profitability. The Coca-Cola Co. establishes exclusive franchise arrangements with independent bottlers. No other supplier can provide the secret ingredients in the concentrate syrup. Bottler profitability is therefore rather low. In contrast, Coke's own suppliers are numerous; many potential sugar and flavoring manufacturers would like to win the Coca-Cola account, and the syrup inputs are nonunique commodities. These factors raise the likely profitability of the concentrate manufacturers because of the lack of power among their suppliers.

Supply shortages, stockouts, and a backorder production environment can alter the relative power of buyers and suppliers in the value chain. One of the few levers a supplier has against huge category-killer retailers like Toys"R"Us to prevent their expropriating all the net value is to refuse to guarantee on-time delivery for triple orders of popular products. A deeply discounted wholesale price should never receive 100 percent delivery reliability.

Finally, buyers and suppliers will have more bargaining power and reduce firm profitability when they possess more outside alternatives and can credibly threaten to vertically integrate into the industry. HMOs can negotiate very low fees from primary care physicians precisely because the HMO has so many outside alternatives.

Intensity of Rivalrous Tactics

In the global economy, few companies can establish and maintain dominance in anything beyond niche markets. Reverse engineering of products, imitation of advertising images, and offshore production at low cost imply that General Motors (GM) cannot hope to rid itself of Ford and DaimlerChrysler, and Coca-Cola cannot hope truly to defeat Pepsi. Instead, to sustain profitability in such a setting, companies must avoid intense rivalries and elicit passive, more cooperative responses from close competitors. The intensity of the rivalry in an industry depends on several factors: industry concentration, the degree of price competition, switching costs, the presence of exit barriers, the industry growth rate, and the ratio of fixed to total cost (termed the **cost fixity**) in the typical cost structure.

Cost Fixity
A measure of fixed to total cost that is correlated with gross profit margins.

What firms and what products offer close substitutes for potential customers in the relevant market determines the degree of industry concentration. One measure of industry concentration is the sum of the market shares of the four largest or eight largest firms in an industry. The larger the market shares and the smaller the number of competitors, the more interdependence each firm will perceive, and the less intense the rivalry. The ready-to-eat cereal industry has more intense rivalry than the soft drink industry, in part because Kelloggs (37 percent), General Mills (25 percent), Post (15 percent), and Quaker Oats (8 percent) together enjoy 85 percent of the market. When two firms enjoy 60–90 percent of industry shipments (e.g., Pepsi and Coke), the transparent interdependence can lead to reduced intensity of rivalry if the firms tacitly collude. Similarly, because Titleist and Spalding dominate the golf ball market, the rivalrous intensity is less than in the fragmented golf club business.

Sustainable profitability is increased by tactics that focus on nonprice rather than price competition. Airlines are more profitable when they can avoid price wars and focus their competition for passengers on service quality—e.g., delivery reliability, change-order responsiveness, and schedule convenience. But trunk route airlines between major U.S. cities provide generic transportation with nearly identical service quality and departure frequency. Consequently, fare wars are frequent, and the profitability of trunk airline routes is therefore low. In contrast, long-standing rivals Coca-Cola and Pepsi have never discounted their cola concentrates. This absence of "gain-share discounting" and a diminished focus on price competition tactics in general increases the profitability of the concentrate business. Airlines tried to control gain-share discounting by introducing "frequent flyer" programs to increase the customers' *switching cost* from one competitor to another. This idea to reduce the intensity of rivalry worked well for a time, until business travelers joined essentially all the rival frequent flyer programs.

Example

PRICE COMPETITION AT THE SODA FOUNTAIN: PEPSICO INC.[14]

Soft drinks are marketed through several distribution channels at different prices. Independent beverage resellers, vending machine companies, and company-owned bottlers supply supermarkets, convenience stores, and vending machines, which accounted for 31 percent, 12 percent, and 11 percent, respectively, of all soft drink sales in 1996. Shelf slots in the store channels are full, and bottlers compete on stocking services and retailer rebates for prime shelf space and vending machine locations in an attempt to grow their brands. With 34 percent and 32 percent market shares in the stores, the Coca-Cola- and PepsiCo-owned bottlers attempt to avoid head-to-head price competition, which would simply lower profits for both firms, and instead seek predictable patterns of company-sponsored once-every-other-week discounts. Where independent beverage resellers have established a practice of persistent gain-share discounting, the Coca-Cola Company and PepsiCo have often attempted to purchase the franchises and replace them with company-owned bottlers. Vending operations are very high margin businesses, and PepsiCo and Coca-Cola increasingly service vending machines directly from their company-owned bottlers. To date, little price competition has emerged in the vending channel, in part because independents must purchase from exclusive franchise bottlers in their areas.

Price competition is heating up, however, in the fountain drink side of the business. As more and more families eat more and more meals outside the household, the fountain drink channel accounted for 27 percent of total sales in 1996, up from 17 percent in 1993. Coca-Cola has long dominated the fountain drink business. At restaurants and soda shops in 1993, Coke enjoyed a 59 percent share to Pepsi's 27 percent. By 1996 Coca-Cola's market share was 64 percent to Pepsi's 21 percent. Recently, PepsiCo declared an intent to vigorously pursue fountain drink sales through discount pricing tactics if necessary. This development threatens continuing profitability in this important channel of the soft drink industry.

Sometimes price versus nonprice competition simply reflects the lack of product differentiation available in commodity-like markets (e.g., in selling cement). However, the incidence of price competition is also determined in part by the cost structure prevalent in the industry. Where fixed costs as a percentage of total costs are high, margins will tend to be larger. If so, firms are tempted to fight tooth and nail for incremental customers because every additional unit sale represents a substantial contribution to covering the fixed costs. All other things being the same, gain-share discounting will therefore tend to increase the greater the fixed cost is. For example, gross margins in the airline industry reflect the enormous fixed costs for aircraft leases and terminal facilities, often reaching 80 percent. Consider the following **break-even sales change analysis** for an airline that seeks to increase its total contributions by lowering its prices 10 percent:

Break-even Sales Change Analysis
A calculation of the percentage increase in unit sales required to justify a price discount, given the gross margin.

$$(P_0 - MC) Q_0 < (0.9 P_0 - MC) Q_1$$
$$< (0.9 P_0 - MC)(Q_0 + \Delta Q)$$

[10.1]

---

[14] Based on "Cola Wars Continue," Harvard Business School Case Publishing, 1994; "Pepsi Hopes to Tap Coke's Fountain Sales," *USA Today*, November 6, 1997, p. 3B; and "Antitrust Suit Focuses on Bottlers' Pricing and Sales Practices," *Wall Street Journal*, January 20, 1999, p. B7.

where revenue minus variable cost (*MC* times *Q*) is the *total contribution*. If discounting is to succeed in raising total contributions, the change in sales ΔQ must be great enough to more than offset the 10-percent decline in revenue per unit sale. Rearranging Equation 10.1 and dividing by P_0 yields

$$\frac{(P_0 - MC)\, Q_0}{P_0} < \left[\frac{P_0 - MC}{P_0} - 0.1\,\frac{P_0}{P_0}\right](Q_0 + \Delta Q)$$

$$pCM\, Q_0 < [pCM - 0.1]\,(Q_0 + \Delta Q)$$

where *pCM* is the price-cost margin percentage, often referred to as the contribution margin percentage. That is,

$$\frac{pCM}{[pCM - 0.1]} < \frac{(Q_0 + \Delta Q)}{Q_0}$$

$$\frac{pCM}{[pCM - 0.1]} < 1 + \frac{\Delta Q}{Q_0} \qquad\qquad [10.2]$$

Using Equation 10.2, an 80-percent price-cost margin implies that a sales increase of only 15 percent is all that one requires to warrant cutting prices by 10 percent. Here's how one reaches that conclusion:

$$\frac{0.8}{[0.8 - 0.1]} < 1 + \frac{\Delta Q}{Q_0}$$

$$1.14 \quad < 1 + \frac{\Delta Q}{Q_0}$$

$$1.14 \quad < 1 + 0.15$$

In contrast, in paperback book publishing, a price-cost margin of 12 percent implies sales must increase by better than 500 percent in order to warrant a 10-percent price cut—i.e., $0.12/0.02 < 1 + 5.0^+$. Because a marketing plan that creates a 15-percent sales increase from a 10-percent price cut is much more likely than one that creates a 500-percent sales increase from a 10-percent price cut, the airline industry is more likely to focus on pricing competition than the paperback book publishing industry.

Example

CONTRIBUTION MARGINS AT HANES DISCOURAGE DISCOUNTING

First-quality white cotton T-shirts and briefs have long been the mainstay of the Hanes Corporation. Selling these "blanks" to other companies that perform value-added finishing, dyeing, embroidering, or custom stitching, Hanes captures only the initial stages in the value chain. At a wholesale price of $1.25 and with $0.85 direct cost of goods sold, the gross margin for Hanes briefs of $0.40 must recover all fixed costs and distribution and selling expenses and earn a profit. With a $0.15 commission per unit sale as a selling expense, the contribution margin (*CM*) is $0.25, and the contribution margin percentage (*pCM*) is $0.25/$1.25 = 20%.

Because of very price-elastic demand, price discounted by as little as 15 percent can double unit sales. However, with margins (*pCM*) as low as 20 percent, the additional sales triggered by the discount are much less attractive than one might think. Break-even sales change analysis using Equation 10.2 confirms that a doubling of sales volume is less than the incremental sales change required to restore total contributions to the levels earned before the price cut:

Table 10.1   Hanes Sales Volume Required to Maintain Operating Profit with a
15-Percent Price Cut

	Given Data	With 15% Price Cut	Double Sales Volume	Triple Sales Volume	Quadruple Sales Volume
Price	1.25	1.0625	2.125	3.1875	4.25
DCGS (VC only)	−0.85	−0.85	−1.70	−2.55	−3.40
Commission	−0.15	−0.15	−0.30	−0.45	−0.60
CM	0.25	0.0625	0.125	0.1875	0.25

Note: All data are shown in U.S. dollars per unit sale.

$$pCM/(pCM - \Delta P) = 0.20/(0.20 - 0.15) = 4.0$$

The interpretation here is that unit sales must increase by 300 percent $(1 + 300\%\Delta Q)$ in order to restore total contributions to their pre-existing level. That is, the price reduction must more than *quadruple* unit sales in order to raise total contributions (operating profit). The data displayed in Table 10.1 demonstrate this conclusion in a spreadsheet format.

Barriers to exit increase the intensity of rivalry in a tight oligopoly. If remote plants specific to a particular line of products (e.g., aluminum smelting plants) are nonredeployable, tactics will be more aggressive because no competitor can fully recover its sunk cost should margins collapse. In addition to capital equipment, nonredeployable assets can include product-specific display racks (L'eggs); product-specific showrooms (Ethan Allen); and intangible assets that prove difficult to carve up and package for resale (unpatented trade secrets and basic research). Trucking companies, on the other hand, own very redeployable assets—i.e., trucks and warehouses. If a trucking company attacks its rivals, encounters aggressive retaliation, then fails and must liquidate its assets, the owners can hope to receive nearly the full value of the economic working life remaining in their trucks and warehouses. As a result, competitive tactics in the trucking industry are not as effective in threatening rivals, so competitive intensity is lower and profitability is higher.

Finally, industry demand growth can influence the intensity of rivalry. When sales to established customers are increasing and new customers are appearing in the market, rival firms are often content to maintain market share and realize high profitability. When demand growth declines, competitive tactics sharpen in many industries, especially if capacity planning has failed to anticipate the decline. Furniture companies discount steeply when housing demand slows. Airline prices and profits declined sharply when demand for air travel leveled off unexpectedly after the Gulf War. Between 1965 and 1975, soft drink consumption in the United States grew by 49 percent. Again, between 1975 and 1985, demand growth was 53 percent. However, from 1985 to 1995, U.S. demand grew by only 24 percent. Sales in the United States flattened out by 1992; annual consumption had reached a plateau of approximately 50 gallons per person (i.e., a gallon per week). Porter's model predicts that flat soft drink demand would lead to more intense rivalry and the lower profitability that PepsiCo Inc. and Coca-Cola Co. are beginning to experience. Recently, Coke has deflected many initiatives to its fast-growing international division in an attempt to reduce the likelihood of intense rivalry with PepsiCo here in the U.S.

INTENSITY OF RIVALRY AT NORTHWEST AIRLINES[15]

Example

http://

You can learn more about a recent U.S. Department of Transportation study of entry issues associated with fortress hubs at the following Internet site maintained by AirportNet:
http://www.airportnet.org/depts/publicat/express/1996htm/3-11-96.htm

The Minneapolis hub of Northwest Airlines is a very concentrated terminal facility; Northwest has over 80 percent of the flights. Thus, Northwest's market share is comparable to Microsoft's dominance of the operating system business with Windows XP. However, high indirect fixed costs for aircraft leases and facilities imply high margins that make it very tempting for airlines to attract incremental customers through price discounting. In contrast, Windows is seldom, if ever, discounted. Consequently, in one-stop flights from Minneapolis, Northwest is subject to intense price competition. Also, exit barriers are low in airlines but rather high in computer software, where massive sunk-cost expenses for research and development create largely unpatentable trade secrets that are not easily resold. Finally, industry demand growth is low in airlines but extremely high in computer software.

Frequent price competition, low exit barriers, and flat growth all imply tremendous rivalrous intensity in the airline industry and downward competitive pressure on Northwest Airline's profit margins. The opposite is true in Microsoft's OS software business. Windows XP is seldom discounted and remains extremely profitable. In short, airlines have industry characteristics that incline the performance results of even a dominant firm to be more nearly competitive, whereas a dominant firm in computer operating systems faces less intense rivalry.

The Myth of Market Share

In summary, the key to profitability in many businesses is to design a strategy that reduces the threat of substitutes, the power of buyers and suppliers, and the threat of entry. Then, firms must adopt tactics and elicit tactical responses from their rivals that do not erode away the profit potential in their effective business strategy. This often means forsaking gain-share discounting and other aggressive tactics that would spiral the industry into price wars. Price premiums reflecting true customer value are very difficult to win back once buyers have grown accustomed to predictably timed clearance sales or a pattern of deep discount rivalry between the competitors. Department store retailers and airlines are painfully aware of this tactical mistake.

More generally, discounting and excessive promotions designed to grab market share are seldom a source of long-term profitability and often result in lower capitalized value. 7-Up doubled and tripled its market share in the late 1970s largely because of discounting. Profits declined, and the company was eventually acquired by Cadbury Schweppes. Hon Industries makes twice the return on investment of Steelcase in the office equipment market even though Hon is one third of Steelcase's size. Boeing is much more profitable with a reduced output rate and more wide-bodied orders going to Airbus.

After the initial penetration of a new product or new technology into a relevant market, market share should never become an end in itself. Increasing market share

---

[15] Based on "Mergers, Monopolies, and the Soaring Cost of Flying," *The Margin,* March/April 1990, p. 19, and "Flying to Charlotte Is Easy," *Wall Street Journal,* June 14, 1995, p. S1.

is the means to achieve scale economies and learning curve-based cost advantages. But additional share points at any cost almost always mean a reduction in profits, not the reverse.

A CONTINUUM OF MARKET STRUCTURES

The relationship between individual firms and the relevant market as a whole is referred to as the industry's *market structure* and depends upon:

1. The number and relative size of firms in the industry
2. The similarity of the products sold by the firms of the industry; that is, the degree of product differentiation
3. The degree to which decision making by individual firms is independent, not interdependent or collusive
4. The conditions of entry and exit

Four specific market structures are often distinguished: pure competition, monopoly, monopolistic competition, and oligopoly.

Pure Competition

Pure Competition
A market structure characterized by a large number of buyers and sellers of a homogeneous (nondifferentiated) product. Entry and exit from the industry is costless, or nearly so. Information is freely available to all market participants, and there is no collusion among firms in the industry.

The **pure competition** industry model has the following characteristics:

1. A large number of buyers and sellers, each of which buys or sells such a small proportion of the total industry output that a single buyer's or seller's actions cannot have a perceptible impact on the market price
2. A homogeneous product produced by each firm; that is, no product differentiation, as with temporary typing services or AAA-grade January wheat
3. Complete knowledge of all relevant market information by all firms, each of which acts totally independently, such as the 117 home builders of standardized three-bedroom subdivision homes in a large city
4. Free entry and exit from the market; that is, minimal barriers to entry and exit

The single firm in a purely competitive industry is, in essence, a price taker. Because the products of each producer are perfect substitutes for the products of every other producer, the single firm in pure competition can do nothing but offer its entire output at the going market price. As a result, the individual firm's demand curve approaches perfect elasticity at the market price. It can sell nothing at a higher price because all buyers will rationally shift to other sellers. If the firm sells at a price slightly below the long-run market price, it will lose money.

For example, Figure 10.3 indicates the nature of the industry and firm demand curves under pure competition in tract home building. Line DD' represents the total industry or market demand curve for tract houses and $S'S$ is the market supply curve. At price \$108,000, the market price, a total of Q_{DI} houses will be demanded by the sum of all firms in the industry. Line dd' represents the demand curve facing each individual firm. The individual firm sells its entire output, Q_{DF}, at the market price \$108,000. By definition the quantity Q_{DF} represents only a small fraction of the total industry demand of Q_{DI}.

Figure 10.3   Pure Competition in Tract Home Building

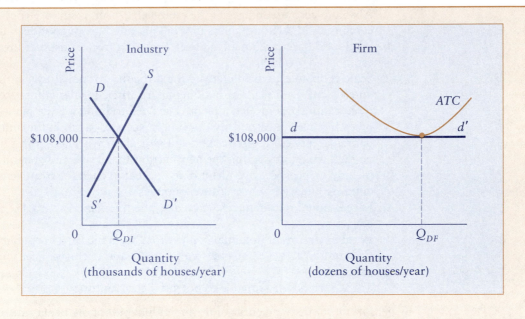

Why get involved in industries where revenues per sale ($108,000 in Figure 10.3) are just sufficient to cover fully allocated unit costs of $108,000 when the going market price is $108,000? The reason is that these "hairline margins" are the ticket to the occasional windfalls when demand increases and price rises enough to generate excess profits (for a few months in the tract home business, a few days in the wildcatter oil business, a few hours in the AAA Kansas City wheat business, or a few minutes in the T-bond resale market). Note that the timing and magnitude of these windfalls are not predictable. Otherwise the respective real estate development land, oil leases, and grain silos would rise in value, and the expected excess profit would again reduce to hairline break-even. Also, remember that at competitive equilibrium the business owner-manager is getting a salary or other return as great as could be received in his or her next best activity. In short, this is not the business environment where venture capital and entrepreneurial returns of 40 percent on invested capital occur when things go right, but it does provide perhaps a steady 12 percent with good managerial skills and cost controls. And occasionally in such a competitive setting, windfall profits erupt for a short time.

Monopoly

The **monopoly** model at the other extreme of the market structure spectrum from pure competition is characterized as follows:

Monopoly
A market structure characterized by one firm producing a highly differentiated product in a market with significant barriers to entry.

1. Only one firm producing some specific product line (in a specified market area), like an exclusive cable TV franchise.

2. Low cross-price elasticity of demand between the monopolist's product and any other product; that is, no close substitute products.

3. No interdependence with other competitors because the firm is a monopolist in its relevant market.

4. Substantial barriers to entry that prevent competition from entering the industry. These barriers may include any of the following:

   a. Absolute cost advantages of the established firm, resulting from economies in securing inputs or from patented production techniques.

   b. Product differentiation advantages, resulting from consumer loyalty to established products.

   c. Scale economies, which increase the difficulty for new firms in financing an efficient-sized plant or building up a sufficient sales volume to achieve lowest unit costs in such a plant. The need to build a large plant to compete effectively is also likely to lead to excess capacity in the industry, depressed prices, and reduced profits for all firms. These prices may not be high enough to permit the new entrant to survive and generate profits, and its prospect may deter many potential entrants from actually entering a market where scale economies are substantial.

   d. Large capital requirements, exceeding the financial resources of potential entrants.

   e. Legal exclusion of potential competitors, as is the case for public utilities, and for those companies with patents and exclusive licensing arrangements.

   f. Trade secrets not available to potential competitors.

By definition, the demand curve of the individual monopoly firm is identical with the industry demand curve, because the firm is the industry. As we saw in Chapter 9, the identity between the firm and industry demand curves allows decision making for the monopolist to be a relatively simple matter, compared to the complexity of rivalrous tactics with few close competitors in tight oligopoly groups.

Monopolistic Competition

Monopolistic Competition
A market structure very much like pure competition, with the major distinction being the existence of a differentiated product.

E.H. Chamberlin and Joan Robinson coined the term **monopolistic competition** to describe industries with characteristics both of competitive markets (i.e., many firms) and of monopoly (i.e., product differentiation).[16] The market structure of monopolistic competition is characterized as follows:

1. A few dominant firms and a large number of competitive fringe firms

2. Dominant firms selling products that are differentiated in some manner: real, perceived, or just imagined

3. Independent decision making by individual firms

4. Ease of entry and exit from the market as a whole but very substantial barriers to effective entry among the leading brands

By far the most important distinguishing characteristic of monopolistic competition is that the outputs of each firm are differentiated in some way from those of every other firm. In other words, the cross-price elasticity of demand between the products of individual firms is lower than among tract home builders, oil wildcatters, AAA January wheat suppliers, or T-bill resellers in purely competitive markets. Product differentiation may be based on exclusive features (Disney World), trademarks (Nike's swoosh), trade names (Bass Weejuns), packaging (L'Eggs hosiery), quality (Coach

---

[16] E.H. Chamberlin, *The Theory of Monopolistic Competition* (Cambridge: Harvard University Press, 1933), p. 56. See also Joan Robinson, *The Economics of Imperfect Competition* (New York: Macmillan, 1933).

handbags), design (Sony Walkman), color and style (Swatch watches), or the conditions of sale. These conditions may include such factors as credit terms, location of the seller, congeniality of sales personnel, after-sale service, warranties, and so on.

Because each firm produces a differentiated product, it is difficult to define an industry demand curve in monopolistic competition. Thus, rather than well-defined industries, one tends to get something of a continuum of products. Generally, it is rather easy to identify groups of differentiated products that fall in the same industry, like light beers, after-shave colognes, or perfumes.

Oligopoly

Oligopoly

A market structure in which the number of firms is so small that the actions of any one firm are likely to have noticeable impacts on the performance of other firms in the industry.

The **oligopoly** market structure of an industry describes a market having a few closely related firms. The number of firms is so small that actions by an individual firm in the industry with respect to price, output, product style or quality, terms of sale, and so on, have a perceptible impact on the sales of other firms in the industry. In other words, oligopoly is distinguished by a noticeable degree of *interdependence* among firms in the industry. The products or services that are produced by oligopolists may be homogeneous—as in the cases of air travel, 40-foot steel I-beams, aluminum, and cement—or they may be differentiated—as in the cases of automobiles, cigarettes, home appliances, cruise ships, colas, and cereals.

Although the degree of product differentiation is an important factor in shaping the single oligopolist's demand curve, the degree of interdependence of firms in the industry is of even greater significance. Primarily because of this interdependence, defining a single firm's demand curve is complicated. The relationship between price and output for a single firm is determined not only by consumer preferences, product substitutability, and level of advertising, *but also by the responses that other competitors may make to a price change by the firm.* A full discussion of rival response expectations will be deferred until Chapter 12.

PRICE-OUTPUT DETERMINATION UNDER PURE COMPETITION

As discussed above, the individual firm in a purely competitive industry is effectively a price taker because the products of every producer are perfect substitutes for the products of every other producer. This leads to the familiar horizontal or perfectly elastic demand curve of the purely competitive firm. Although we rarely find instances where all the conditions for pure competition are met, securities exchanges and the commodity markets approach these conditions. For instance, the individual wheat farmer or T-bill reseller has little choice but to accept the going price for wheat.

Short Run

A firm in a purely competitive industry may either make transitory profits (in excess of normal returns to capital and entrepreneurial labor) or operate at a loss in the short run.

In pure competition, the firm must sell at the market price (p_1 or p_2), and its demand curve is represented by a horizontal line (D_1 or D_2) at the market price, as shown in Figure 10.4. In the purely competitive case, marginal revenue MR is equal to price P, because the sale of each additional unit increases total revenue by the price of that unit (which remains constant at all levels of output). For instance, if

$$P = \$8/\text{unit}$$

then

$$\text{Total revenue} = TR = P \cdot Q$$
$$= 8Q$$

Marginal revenue is defined as the change in total revenue resulting from the sale of one additional unit, or the derivative of total revenue with respect to Q:

$$MR = \frac{dTR}{dQ} = \$8/\text{unit}$$

and marginal revenue equals price.

The profit-maximizing firm will produce at that level of output where marginal revenue equals marginal cost. Beyond that point, the production and sale of one additional unit would add more to total cost than to total revenue ($MC > MR$), and hence total profit ($TR - TC$) would decline. Up to the point where $MC = MR$, the production and sale of one more unit would increase total revenue more than total cost ($MR > MC$), and total profit would increase as an additional unit is produced and sold. *Producing at the point where marginal revenue MR equals marginal cost MC is equivalent to maximizing the total profit function.*[17]

The individual firm's supply function in Figure 10.4 is equal to that portion of the MC curve from point J to point I. At any price level below point J the firm would shut down because it would not even be covering its variable costs (i.e., $P < AVC$). Temporary shutdown would result in limiting the losses to fixed costs alone.

Example

PROFIT MAXIMIZATION IN PURE COMPETITION (SHORT RUN): ADOBE CORPORATION

This example illustrates the profit-maximization conditions for a firm operating in a purely competitive market environment in the short run. Assume Adobe Corporation faces the following total revenue and total cost functions:

$$\text{Total revenue } TR = 8Q$$
$$\text{Total cost } TC = Q^2 + 4Q + 2$$

Marginal revenue and marginal cost are defined as the first derivative of total revenue and total cost, or

$$\text{Marginal revenue } MR = \frac{dTR}{dQ} = \$8/\text{unit}$$

$$\text{Marginal cost } MC = \frac{dTC}{dQ} = 2Q + 4$$

---

[17] This can be proven as follows:

$$\pi = TR - TC$$
$$\frac{d\pi}{dQ} = \frac{dTR}{dQ} - \frac{dTC}{dQ} = MR - MC = 0$$

or, $MR = MC$ when profits are maximized.

Check for profit maximization by taking the second derivative of π with respect to Q, or $\frac{d^2\pi}{dQ^2}$. If it is less than zero, then π is maximized.

Figure 10.4   Firm in Pure Competition: Short Run

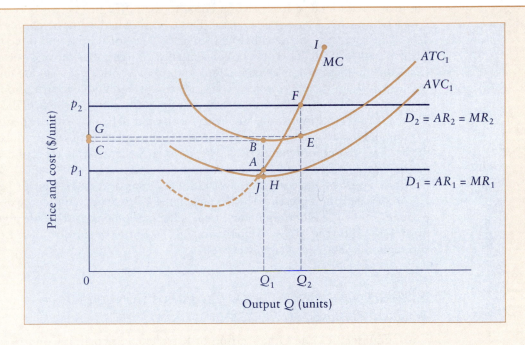

Similarly, total profit equals total revenue minus total cost:

$$\text{Total profit } (\pi) = TR - TC$$
$$= 8Q - (Q^2 + 4Q + 2)$$
$$= -Q^2 + 4Q - 2$$

To maximize total profit, we take the derivative of π with respect to quantity, set it equal to zero, and solve for the profit-maximizing level of Q. (It is also necessary to check the second derivative to be certain we have found a maximum, not a minimum!)[18]

$$\frac{d\pi}{dQ} = -2Q + 4 = 0$$
$$Q^* = 2 \text{ units}$$

But because $MR = \$8/\text{unit}$ and $MC = 2Q + 4 = [2(2) + 4] = \$8/\text{unit}$, when total profit is maximized, we are merely setting $MC = MR$.

---

[18] The check for profit maximization goes as follows:

$$\frac{d^2\pi}{dQ^2} = -2$$

Because the second derivative is negative, we know we have found a maximum value for the profit function.

Returning to Figure 10.4, if price $P = p_1$, the firm would produce the level of output Q_1, where $MC = MR$ (profits are maximized or losses minimized). In this case the firm would incur a loss per unit equal to the difference between average total cost ATC and average revenue or price. This is represented by the height BA in Figure 10.4. The total loss incurred by the firm at Q_1 level of output and price p_1 equals the rectangle p_1CBA. This may be conceptually thought of as the loss per unit (BA) times the number of units produced and sold (Q_1). At price p_1 losses are minimized, because average variable costs AVC have been covered and a contribution remains to cover part of the fixed costs (AH per unit times Q_1 units). If the firm did not produce, it would incur losses equal to the entire amount of fixed costs (BH per unit times Q_1 units). Hence we may conclude that in the short run a firm will produce and sell at that level of output where $MR = MC$, as long as the variable costs of production are being covered ($P > AVC$).

If price were p_2, the firm would produce Q_2 units and make a profit per unit of EF, or a total profit represented by the rectangle $FEGp_2$. The supply curve of the competitive firm is therefore often identified as the marginal cost schedule above minimum AVC (i.e., the MC schedule from J to I). Industry supply is the horizontal summation of these firm supply curves.

Example

NORTH SEA AND WEST TEXAS OIL FIELDS CONTINUED TO PRODUCE DESPITE PRICES BELOW ATC[19]

Throughout 1998, the Organization of Petroleum Exporting Countries (OPEC) attempted to cut production by 3.1 million barrels a day (roughly 10 percent of OPEC total production), and crude prices rose immediately from $13 per barrel to $17 per barrel. However, numerous quota violations by OPEC members and lower demand for energy from slumping Asian economies resulted in a price collapse to $9.96 per barrel. This lowest price range is typical of historical crude oil prices which hovered around an inflation-adjusted price of $10 for most of the 20th century—see Figure 10.5, Panel (a).

Oil in the Persian Gulf region is cheapest to find, develop, and extract at an average *total* cost of $2 per barrel. In contrast, Venezuelan oil breaks even at $7 per barrel, West Texas at $10 per barrel, and the North Sea fields necessitate offshore oil rigs and expensive extraction technology that generate $11-per-barrel average total cost. These producers and their associated output trace out a traditional upward-sloping long-run supply curve (here a step function) for the crude oil industry—see Figure 10.5, Panel (b). At $9.96 world-market oil prices, North Sea and West Texas fields may have ceased exploration and development for new oil but did not shut down operations in known fields.

Temporary shutdown is contemplated only when the market price falls below the average *variable* cost for these higher-cost fields, equal to about $4 per barrel. At $9.96 per barrel, both West Texas and North Sea wells lose less by operating (i.e., $10 − $9.96 = $0.04 and $11 − $9.96 = $1.04, respectively) than by shutting down, which would incur a loss of $6 and $7 average fixed cost, respectively. The decision to not shut down, interrupt deliveries, and threaten distribution relationships paid handsome dividends in 2000 as crude oil prices tripled to $34 per

---

[19] "OPEC Talks Tough Again," *Time*, March 22, 1999, p. 62; "Cheap Oil: The Next Shock?" *The Economist*, March 6, 1999, pp. 23–25; and "Poised to Strike," *The Economist*, September 9, 2000, pp. 17–18.

barrel—again see Figure 10.5, Panel (a). Even if the market price had remained as low as $9.96, West Texas and North Sea producers (as well as all the less expensive producing areas) would have been better off operating than shutting down.

Long Run

In the long run, all inputs are free to vary. Hence, no differentiation exists between fixed and variable costs. Under long-run conditions, average cost will tend to be just equal to price and all excessive profits will be eliminated (see Point A where $p_1 = AC_1$ in Figure 10.6). If not, and if, for example, a price above p_1 exceeds average total costs, more firms will enter, the industry supply will increase (as illustrated by the parallel shift outward to the right of the $\Sigma_{SR}S_{FIRM}$ along market demand D^2_{MKT} in Figure 10.6), and market price will again be driven down toward the equilibrium, zero-profit level p_1.

Figure 10.5   Crude Oil Prices and Costs

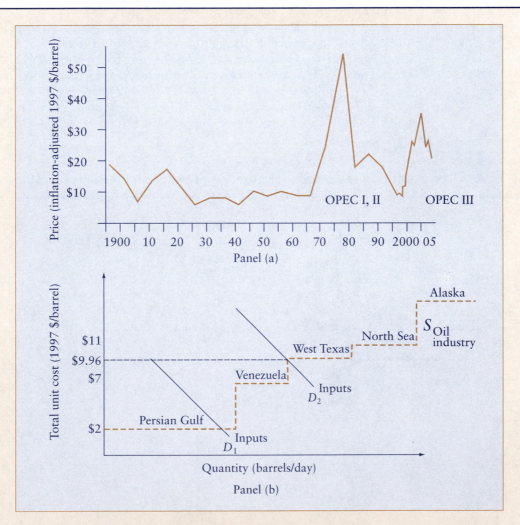

External Diseconomy of Scale

An increase in unit costs reflecting higher input prices.

In addition, as more firms bid for available factors of production (skilled labor, managerial talent), in some cases the cost of these factors will tend to rise. In that event, the entire cost structure of MC_1 and AC_1 will rise to reflect the higher input costs. This shift up in the firm's cost structure to AC_2 (see Figure 10.6) results in a two-way squeeze on excess profit and is referred to as an **external diseconomy of scale**. External scale diseconomies are distinguished from internal scale economies and diseconomies in that the latter reflect unit cost changes as the rate of output increases *assuming no change in input prices*, whereas the former reflect exactly the bidding up of input prices as the industry expands in response to an increase in market demand. Under a constant input price assumption, the long-run industry supply curve $_{LR}S_{IND}$ in Figure 10.6 would be flat, a so-called *constant-cost industry* like coal-fired electricity. However, with the rising input prices for crude oil depicted in Figure 10.5, Panel (b), the long-run supply curve $_{LR}S_{IND}$ for the downstream final product gasoline rises to the right, signifying an *increasing-cost industry,* as depicted in Figure 10.6. (It is quite possible to have downward-sloping long-run supply curves. A decreasing-cost industry occurred in the 1980s in calculators and again in the 1990s in PCs; computer chip inputs became less expensive as the personal computer market expanded, as shown in Figure 10.7.)

The net result is that in the long-run equilibrium, all purely competitive firms will tend to have identical costs, and prices will tend to equal average total costs (i.e., the average total cost curve AC will be tangent to the horizontal price line p_2). Thus, we may say that at the long-run profit-maximizing level of output under pure competition, equilibrium will be achieved at a point where $P = MR = MC = AC$. In long-run equilibrium, each competitive firm is producing at its most efficient (that is, its lowest unit cost) level of output.

Figure 10.6   Long-Run Equilibrium Under Pure Competition (Increasing Cost Industry)

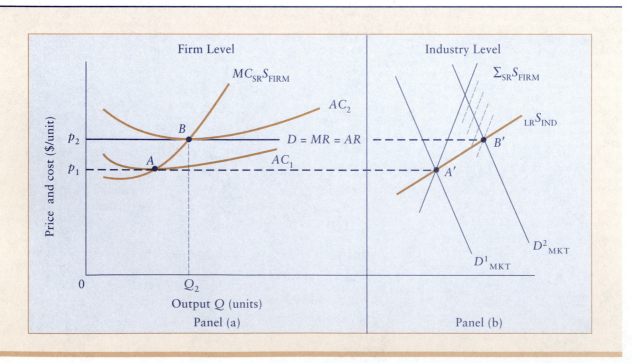

Figure 10.7   Computer Price Index and U.S. Final Sales of Personal Computers

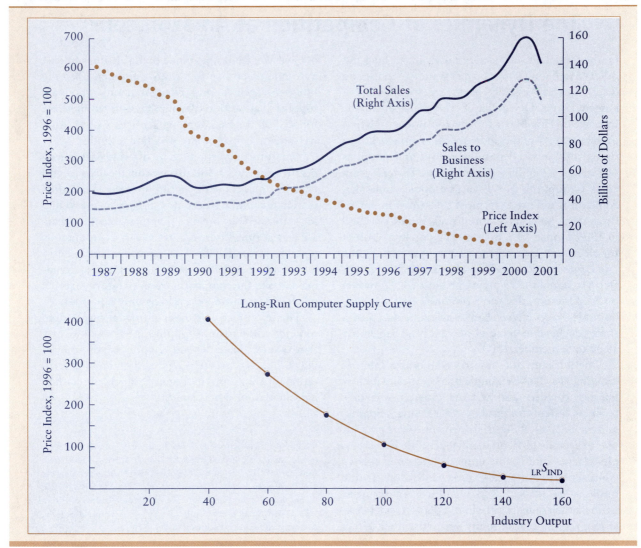

PRICE-OUTPUT DETERMINATION UNDER MONOPOLISTIC COMPETITION

Monopolistic competition is a market structure with a relatively large number of firms, each selling a product that is differentiated in some manner from the products of its fringe competitors, and with substantial barriers to entry into the group of leading firms.

Product differentiation may be based on special product characteristics, trademarks, packaging, quality perceptions, distinctive product design, or conditions surrounding the sale, such as location of the seller, warranties, and credit terms. The demand curve for any one firm is expected to have a negative slope and be extremely elastic because of the large number of close substitutes. The firm in monopolistic competition has limited discretion over price (as distinguished from the firm in pure competition) because of customer loyalties arising from real or perceived

WHAT WENT RIGHT   WHAT WENT WRONG

The Dynamics of Competition at Amazon.com[20]

On-line retailing started very slowly in clothing and other search goods that buyers want to "touch and feel," but it has excelled in one experience good—namely, books. One dollar of every $27 spent on the Internet in 1996 went to Amazon Books, the first on-line retailer in this industry. Amazon stocks less than 1,000 bestsellers but displays and provides reviews on 2.5 million popular titles. Using Ingram Book Group, the world's largest book wholesaler, Amazon is able to ship most selections in one to three days. Sales have doubled each half-year and in 1999 topped $1.6 billion. The potential growth for electronic booksellers is enormous because the two largest bookshop chains, Barnes and Noble and Borders, earned 1999 pretax profits of $217 million on $3.3 billion sales and $166 million on $3.0 billion sales, respectively. Nevertheless, Amazon.com shares declined in value 41 percent from September 1999 to September 2000.

One difficulty for Amazon.com is that Internet retailing is a classic example of a business with low barriers to entry and exit. As soon as Amazon's business systems for display, order taking, shipping, and payments stabilized, since profits were present, one expected substantial entry activity. For example, Barnes and Noble entered into an exclusive contract with America Online to pitch electronic book sales to AOL's 8.5 million subscribers. Borders then quickly announced plans to enter electronic retailing. And many specialist booksellers

of Civil War books, jet plane books, history books, auto books, and so forth, have flooded onto the Internet search engines. Even Amazon's wholesale supplier Ingram Book Group has entered the fray; for $2,500, Ingram support services will set up a web site on behalf of any new book retailer.

Amazon.com responded by offering customized notification and book discussion services to add value for readers with special interests. The information revolution has made relationship marketing to established customers a pivotal element in securing repeat purchases. Nevertheless, the numerous open opportunities for fast, easy, and cheap entry likely will erode the profits in electronic book retailing down to the competitive rates of return on time, talent, and investment, perhaps only 7 percent.

The imperfect consumer information, limited time for comparison shopping, and brand loyalty that retailers have depended upon are disappearing with Internet search engines, and retailing's traditionally slim profit margins are quickly becoming hairline thin or nonexistent.

---

[20] Based on "Web Browsing," *The Economist*, March 29, 1997, p. 71; "In Search of the Perfect Market: A Survey of Electronic Commerce," *The Economist*, May 10, 1997; "The Net: A Market Too Perfect for Profits," *BusinessWeek*, May 11, 1998, p. 20; "Comparison Shopping Is the Web's Virtue—Unless You're a Seller," *Wall Street Journal*, July 23, 1998, p. A1; and *Value Line, Ratings and Reports*, various issues.

---

product differences. Profit maximization (or loss minimization) again occurs when the firm produces at that level of output and charges that price at which marginal revenue equals marginal cost.

Short Run

Just as in the case of pure competition, a monopolistically competitive firm may or may not generate a profit in the short run. For example, consider a demand curve such as $D'D'$ in Figure 10.8, with marginal revenue equal to MR'. Such a firm will set its prices where $MR' = MC$, resulting in price P_3 and output Q_3. The firm will earn a profit of EC dollars per unit of output. However, the low barriers to entry in a monopolistically competitive industry will not permit these short-run profits to be earned for long. As new firms enter the industry, industry supply will increase, caus-

Figure 10.8   Long-Run Equilibrium in Monopolistic Competition

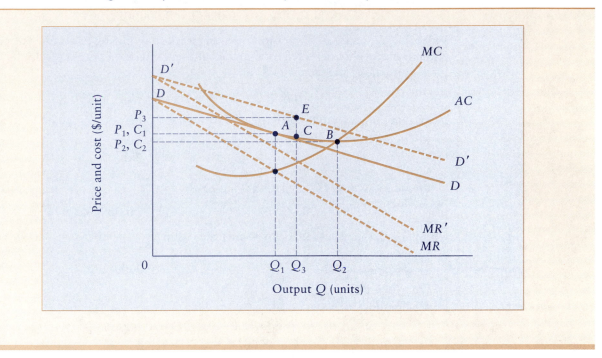

ing the equilibrium price to fall. This is reflected in a downward movement in the demand curve facing any individual firm.

Long Run

With relatively free entry and exit into the competitive fringe, average costs and a firm's demand function will be driven *toward* tangency at a point such as A in Figure 10.8. At this price, P_1, and output, Q_1, marginal cost is equal to marginal revenue. Hence a firm such as an airline is producing at its optimal level of output. Any price lower or higher than P_1 will result in a loss to the firm because average costs will exceed price.

Because the monopolistic competitor produces at a level of output where average costs are still declining (between Points A and B in Figure 10.8), monopolistically competitive firms produce with "excess" capacity. Of course, this argument overlooks the extent to which idle capacity may be a source of product differentiation. Idle capacity means a firm such as an airline can operate with high delivery reliability and change order responsiveness, which can be very important to business travelers on congested planes, and that warrants a price premium relative to competitive fringe airlines.

Example

LONG-RUN PRICE AND OUTPUT DETERMINATION: VIDEO MAGIC, INC.

The market for video rentals in Charlotte, North Carolina, can best be described as monopolistically competitive. The demand for video rentals is estimated to be

$$P = 10 - 0.004Q$$

where Q is the number of weekly video rentals. The long-run average cost function for Video Magic is estimated to be

$$LRAC = 8 - 0.006Q + 0.000002Q^2$$

Video Magic's managers want to know the profit-maximizing price and output levels, and the level of expected total profits at these price and output levels.

First, compute total revenue (TR) as

$$TR = P \cdot Q = 10Q - 0.004Q^2$$

Next, compute marginal revenue (MR) by taking the first derivative of TR:

$$MR = \frac{dTR}{dQ} = 10 - 0.008Q$$

Compute total cost (TC) by multiplying $LRAC$ by Q:

$$TC = LRAC \cdot Q = 8Q - 0.006Q^2 + 0.000002Q^3$$

Compute marginal cost (MC) by taking the first derivative of TC:

$$MC = \frac{dTC}{dQ} = 8 - 0.012Q + 0.000006Q^2$$

Next, set $MR = MC$

$$10 - 0.008Q = 8 - 0.012Q + 0.000006Q^2$$
$$0.000006Q^2 - 0.004Q - 2 = 0$$

Use the quadratic formula to solve for Q. Q^* is equal to 1,000.[21] At this quantity, price is equal to

$$P^* = 10 - 0.004\,(1{,}000)$$
$$= 10 - 4$$
$$= \$6$$

Total profit is equal to the difference between TR and TC, or

$$\pi = TR - TC$$
$$= 10Q - 0.004Q^2 - [8Q - 0.006Q^2 + 0.000002Q^3]$$
$$= 10(1{,}000) - 0.004(1{,}000)^2 - [8(1{,}000) - 0.006(1{,}000)^2$$
$$+ 0.000002(1{,}000)^3]$$
$$= \$2{,}000$$

The MR and MC at these price and output levels are \$2.

The fact that Video Magic expects to earn a profit of \$2,000 suggests that the firm can anticipate additional competition, resulting in price cutting, that will ultimately eliminate this profit amount.[22]

---

[21] The solution of the quadratic formula, $aQ^2 + bQ + c = 0$, is

$$Q = \frac{-b \pm \sqrt{b^2 - 4ac}}{2a} = \frac{-(-.004) \pm \sqrt{(-.004)^2 - 4(0.000006)(-2)}}{2(0.000006)}$$

$$= 1{,}000;\ -333.33$$

Only the positive solution is feasible.

[22] Recall that the TC function includes a "normal" level of profit. Hence this \$2,000 represents an economic *rent* above a normal profit level.

SELLING AND PROMOTIONAL EXPENSES

In addition to varying price and quality characteristics of their products, firms may also vary the amount of their advertising and other promotional expenses in their search for profits. This kind of promotional activity generates two distinct types of benefits. First, demand for the general product group may be shifted upward to the right as a result of the individual firm and industry advertising activities. The greater the number of firms in an industry, the more diffused will be the effects of a general demand-increasing advertising campaign by any one firm. In contrast, a monopolist such as an electric utility, or a highly concentrated oligopoly such as computer operating systems, will be more inclined to undertake an advertising campaign.

The second, more widespread incentive for advertising is the desire to shift the demand function of a particular firm at the expense of other firms offering similar products. This strategy will be pursued both by oligopolists like Philip Morris and General Mills and by firms in more monopolistically competitive industries like AT&T, MCI, and Sprint.

Determining the Optimal Level of Selling and Promotional Outlays

Selling and promotional expenses, often collectively referred to as advertising, are one of the most important tools of nonprice competition.

To illustrate the effects of advertising expenditures and to determine the optimal selling expenses of a firm, consider the case where price and product characteristics already have been determined, and all retailers are selling at the manufacturer's suggested retail price.

The determination of the optimal advertising outlay is a straightforward application of the marginal decision-making rules followed by profit-maximizing firms. Define MR to be the change in total revenue received from a one-unit increase in output (and the sale of that output). For fixed-price settings, MR just equals the price, P. Define MC to be the change in total costs of producing and distributing (but not of advertising) an additional unit of output. The marginal profit or contribution margin from an additional unit of output is (from Chapter 9):

$$\text{Contribution Margin } (pCM) = P - MC \qquad [10.3]$$

The marginal cost of advertising (MCA) associated with the sale of an additional unit of output is defined as the change in advertising expenditures (ΔAk) where k is the unit cost of an advertising message, A, or

$$MCA = \frac{\Delta Ak}{\Delta Q} \qquad [10.4]$$

The optimal level of advertising outlays is the level of advertising where the marginal profit contribution (pCM) is equal to the marginal cost of advertising, or

$$pCM = MCA \qquad [10.5]$$

As long as a firm receives a greater contribution margin than the MCA it incurs to sell an additional unit of output, the advertising outlay should be made. If pCM is less than MCA, the advertising outlay should not be made and the level of advertising should be reduced until $pCM = MCA$. This marginal analysis also applies to other types of nonprice competition like after-sale service and product replacement guarantees.

Example

OPTIMAL ADVERTISING: FLOW MOTORS FORD

The marginal profit contribution from selling Ford automobiles at Flow Motors averages $1,000 across the various models it sells. Flow Motors estimates that it will have to incur $550 of additional promotional expenses to increase its sales by one unit over the current level. Should the outlay for promotion be made?

Because $pCM > MCA$ (i.e., $1,000 > 550), Flow's profit will be increased by $450 if it incurs an additional $550 of promotional expenses. Flow should continue to make additional promotional outlays (which are likely to be less and less effective at triggering additional sales) up to the point where the marginal cost of advertising equals the expected marginal profit contribution.

If Flow were to find that MCA was greater than pCM, Flow should cut back on its promotional outlays until $pCM = MCA$.

Optimal Advertising Intensity

Optimal expenditure on demand-increasing costs like promotions, couponing, direct mail, and media advertising can be compared across firms. For example, the total contributions from incremental sales relative to the advertising cost of beer ads can be compared to the total contributions relative to the advertising cost of cereal ads. Advertising is often placed in five media (network TV, local TV, radio, newspapers, and magazines). The "reach" of a TV ad is measured as audience thousands per minute of advertising message; reach is directly related to the advertising message's cost (k). A manager should fully fund in the marketing budget any ad campaign for which

$$(P - MC)\,(\Delta Q/\Delta A) > k \qquad [10.6]$$

where $(P - MC)$ is the contribution margin and $(\Delta Q/\Delta A)$ is the increase in demand (i.e., a shift outward in demand) attributable to the advertising.[23]

Example

FORD AND P&G TIE AD AGENCY PAY TO SALES

Historically ad agencies have earned more income each time their clients buy another expensive 30-second slot on network TV (or other media), whatever the performance of the ad in generating incremental sales. In 1997, Ford and Procter and Gamble, two of the world's biggest advertisers, announced that henceforth all agency billings would need to be performance based. These incentive payment plans will include a fixed fee for designing ad campaigns plus incentive pay based on the incremental sales traceable to the ad. Ford and P&G believe this system will encourage agencies to search for database marketing, Internet, and event sponsorships that far exceed the marginal media buy in advertising productivity, $\Delta Q/\Delta A$.

Expanding Equation 10.6 identifies the two determinants of the optimal advertising expenditure per dollar sales or "advertising intensity." Ak/PQ is determined by the gross margin $(P - MC)/P$ and by the advertising elasticity of demand E_a:

$$\frac{Ak}{PQ} = \frac{(P - MC)}{P}\,\frac{A}{Q}\,(\Delta Q/\Delta A) \qquad [10.7]$$

---

[23] Sometimes, the price points at which the product can be sold change after a successful ad campaign. If so, the appropriate valuation of the incremental sales in Equation 10.6 is the new contribution margin.

$$\frac{Ak}{PQ} = \frac{(P - MC)}{P} E_a \qquad\qquad [10.8]$$

Both factors are important. With high margins (near 70 percent) and very effective ads, Kellogg spends 30 percent of every dollar of sales revenue on cereal advertising. In contrast, the jewelry industry has 92 percent margins, the highest of all four-digit industries, but Zales' advertising inserts in the weekend paper simply do not trigger many jewelry sales. The advertising elasticity of jewelry is low; consequently, a company like Zales spends less than 10 percent of sales revenue on advertising. Campbell Soup has relatively high advertising elasticity of demand given its strong brand name, but the margins on canned goods are very low (less than 5 percent); consequently, Campbell Soup spends just one tenth of what Kellogg spends on advertising as a percentage of sales revenue—just 3 percent of sales revenue.

OPTIMAL ADVERTISING INTENSITY AT KELLOGG AND GENERAL MILLS[24]

The ready-to-eat (RTE) cereal industry spends 55 percent of its sales revenue on marketing and promotion—30 percent on advertising alone. In part, this resource allocation decision reflects the fact that cereal demand is very sensitive to successful ad campaigns like Kellogg's Tony the Tiger or General Mills' Wheaties, The Breakfast of Champions. In addition, however, RTE cereal margins are among the highest of any four-digit industry. Kellogg's Raisin Bran sells for $4.49 and has a direct fixed plus variable manufacturing cost of $1.63. That calculates as a $(4.49 - 1.63)/4.49 = 70$ percent gross margin. Frosted Flakes' margin is 72 percent, and Fruit Loops' margin is 68 percent. These margins reflect brand loyalties built up over many years of advertising investments as well as Kellogg's 37-percent market share. In the highly concentrated RTE cereal industry, Quaker Oats (8 percent), Post (15 percent), General Mills (25 percent), and Kellogg control 85 percent of the market.

Until recently, advertising and retail displays were the predominant form of competition in cereals. Like Coca-Cola and PepsiCo, the dominant RTE cereal companies had concluded that price discounting would be mutually ruinous and ultimately ineffective. Therefore, each company decided independently to refrain from discounting prices to attempt to gain market share. However, in June 1996, 20-percent price cuts swept through the industry, in part in response to the growth of private-label cereals (e.g., Kroger Raisin Bran) which had collectively grabbed close to 10 percent of the market. Margins on some leading brand-name products fell to 50 percent with ingredients (15 percent), packaging (10 percent), wages (10 percent), and distribution (15 percent) accounting for the rest of the selling price. By late 1997, the price war had ended, and traditional advertising competition resumed.

The Net Value of Advertising

Traditional economic analysis has tended to conclude that the primary impacts of advertising are to raise prices to consumers and to lead to the creation and maintenance of monopoly power.[25]

---

[24] Based on "Cereals," *Winston-Salem Journal,* March 8, 1995, p. A1 and "Denial in Battle Creek," *Forbes,* October 7, 1996, pp. 44–46.

[25] Evidence in support of this view is presented in William Comaner and Thomas Wilson, *Advertising and Market Power* (Cambridge, MA: Harvard University Press, 1974).

George Stigler and Phil Nelson[26] used the theory of the economics of information to argue that by giving consumers price information, advertising is expected to reduce the price paid. The discovery of price information may be costly and time consuming in the absence of price advertising. If, for example, it costs a consumer $10 in time costs to discover the store that will offer a saving of $8 on the price of an item, the search for price information is not worthwhile. But if price advertising makes all consumers aware of the lowest price supplier of an item at an additional cost of only $1, then the great majority of consumers will be better off as a result of this advertising. For example, Benham[27] found the price of eyeglasses to be substantially lower in states that permitted price advertising than in those that prohibited such advertising. Similar results have been found for dental, medical, and legal services.

In addition, Nelson found that advertisers of all products have substantial incentives to provide useful and truthful information to customers. High-quality information can reduce the search cost for consumers as they seek to make a choice between alternative goods. Because consumers can assess the truthfulness of the information contained in an advertisement and because advertising creates brand awareness (both for good and inferior brands), advertisers who misrepresent their product will not be successful in generating future (and repeat) business.

COMPETITIVE MARKETS UNDER ASYMMETRIC INFORMATION

In competitive markets for newsprint, crude oil, auto rentals, and delivered pizza, both buyers and sellers have full knowledge of the capabilities and after-sale performance of the standard products. Equilibrium price just covers the supplier's cost of production for a product of known reliable quality. If suppliers were to charge more, rival offers and entry would quickly erode their sales. If suppliers were to charge less, they could not afford to stay in business. This has been the message so far of Chapter 10; in competitive markets under ideal information conditions, you get what you pay for. These markets differ enormously from competitive markets under asymmetric information, which are sometimes called "lemons markets." One prominent example of asymmetric information in a lemons market is used automobiles, in which the true quality of tires, mechanical repairs, or other features often is known only to the seller. Other such goods include house paint, mail-order computer components, and common cold remedies.

In a lemons market, the buyers discount all unverifiable claims by the sellers, who market only lower quality products as the reduced prices buyers are willing to offer. This disappearance of higher quality products from the marketplace illustrates the concept of adverse selection—i.e., the lower quality products are selected in and the higher quality products are adversely selected out. To resolve the marketing problems posed by adverse selection requires credible commitment mechanisms such as warranties, brand-name reputations, collateral, or price premiums for reliable repeat-purchase transactions.

---

[26] George J. Stigler, "The Economics of Information," *Journal of Political Economy* (June 1961), pp. 213–225; and Philip Nelson, "The Economic Consequences of Advertising," *Journal of Business* (April 1975), pp. 213–241.

[27] Lee Benham, "The Effect of Advertising on the Price of Eyeglasses," *Journal of Law and Economics* (October 1972), pp. 337–352.

Incomplete versus Asymmetric Information

One distinction that can sharpen our understanding of these complicating factors in competitive exchange is that between asymmetric information and **incomplete information.** Incomplete information is associated with uncertainty, and uncertainty is pervasive. Practically all exchanges, whether for products, financial claims, or labor services, are conducted under conditions of uncertainty. On the one hand, decision makers often face uncertainty as to the effect of random disturbances on the outcome of their actions. This uncertainty typically leads to insurance markets. On the other hand, decision makers are sometimes uncertain as to the payoffs or even types of choices they face. This condition typically leads to intentionally incomplete contracting. Chapter 15 addresses incomplete contracting.

Asymmetric information exchange, in contrast, refers to situations in which either the buyer or the seller possesses information which the other party cannot verify or to which the other party does not have access. For example, mail-order suppliers of computer components or personal sellers of used cars often have an informationally advantaged position relative to the buyers. The sellers know the machine's capabilities, deficiencies, and most probable failure rate, but these are difficult matters for the buyer to assess from reading magazine ads or kicking the tires. And the typical 90-day warranty does nothing to alter this information asymmetry. Both buyer and seller face uncertainty against which they may choose to insure, but one has more information or better information than the other.

Search Goods versus Experience Goods

http://

Read about American economist and Nobel Prize winner George Akerlof's seminal paper on asymmetric information and the market for used cars at the Internet site: http://www.cybersteering. com/cruise/feature/ indianautousers.html

In services, retailing, and many manufacturing industries, buyers generally search the market to identify low-price suppliers. Sometimes this search is accomplished by asking for recommendations from recent purchasers, by scouring the catalogs and ads, or by visiting showrooms and sales floors. In selecting a supplier, many customers are also intensely interested in multiple dimensions of product and service quality, including product design, durability, image, conformance to specifications, order delay, delivery reliability, change order responsiveness, and after-sale service. Customers often spend as much time and effort searching the market for the desired quality mix as they do searching for lowest price. Retailers and service providers understand this and often offer many quality combinations at various prices to trigger a purchase of these **search goods.** Consider, for example, the many price-quality alternatives available from your favorite clothing, sporting goods, or furniture store.

On the other hand, some products and services have important quality dimensions that *cannot* be observed at the point of purchase. Consider used cars and other resale machinery, nonprescription remedies for the common cold, house paint, and mail-order computer components. The quality of these items can be detected only through experience in using the products. Hence, products and services of this type are termed **experience goods** and are distinguished from search goods.

Ultimately the problem with experience goods in competitive market exchange is the unverifiability of asymmetric information. The seller knows how to detect the difference between high- and low-quality products (e.g., between lemons and cream puffs in the used-car market), but cannot credibly relay this information to buyers, at least not in chance encounters between strangers. Fraudulent sellers will claim high quality when it is absent, and realizing this, buyers rationally discount all such information. Because of the private, impacted nature of the product quality information, the seller's claims and omissions can never be verified without experiencing the reliability of the auto, the efficacy of the common cold remedy, the durability of the house paint, or the capability of the computer component.

All of this is not to say that the buyers of experience goods are without recourse or that the sellers are without ingenuity as to how to market their products. Warranties and investments in reputations provide mechanisms whereby the sellers of house paint and computer components can credibly commit to delivering a high-quality product. The essential point is that in the absence of these bonding or hostage mechanisms, the experience-good buyer will rationally disbelieve the seller's claims. Consequently, the honest seller of truly high-quality experience goods will find little market for his or her higher cost, higher priced product. The "bad apples drive out the good" in many experience-good markets.

Adverse Selection and the Notorious Firm

Suppose customers recognize that unverifiable private information about experience–good quality is present, yet knowledge of any fraudulent high-price sale of low-quality products spreads almost instantaneously throughout the marketplace. Is this extreme reputational effect sufficient to restore the exchange of high-quality/high-price experience goods? Or, can the notorious firm continue to defraud customers here and elsewhere? The answer depends on the conditions of entry and exit discussed earlier in this chapter, but not in the way you might expect.

Consider the cost structure and profits of such a notorious firm, depicted in Figure 10.9. If offered the low price P_l, the firm operates in competitive equilibrium at Q_1

Figure 10.9   Low-Quality Experience Goods Emerge from Competitive Markets

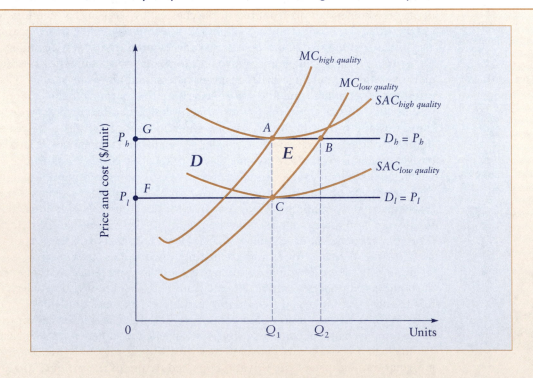

where the price just covers the marginal cost and average total cost ($SAC_{low\ quality}$) for Q_1 units of the low-quality product. Alternatively, if offered the high price P_h, the firm can either competitively supply Q_1 of the high-quality experience good and again just break even against the higher costs of $SAC_{high\ quality}$,[28] or the firm can deliver a low-quality experience good at Q_2 and continue to incur the lower costs $SAC_{low\ quality}$. The third alternative entails an expansion of output along $MC_{low\ quality}$ in response to the price rise and generates profits. That is, the incremental output ($Q_2 - Q_1$) earns incremental profit equal to the difference between P_h and $MC_{low\ quality}$—namely, the shaded area ABC (labeled bold E)—and in addition, the original output Q_1 earns a fraudulent rent of area $GACF$ (labeled bold D). Although the supplier observes his own cost directly and therefore detects the availability of $D + E$, the problem for the experience-good buyer is that in terms of point-of-sale information, high-price transactions at Point B on $MC_{low\ quality}$ and at Point A on $MC_{high\ quality}$ are indistinguishable. Both types of products have an asking price of P_h, and only the seller observes the output rate Q_1 versus Q_2.

Of course, the supplier is not indifferent between the two alternatives. The high-quality transaction offers a cash flow from operations just sufficient to cover capital costs and break even at Point A, whereas the fraudulent transaction (a low quality product at a high price at Point B) offers a net profit for at least one period. Table 10.2 depicts this interaction between experience-good buyers and a potentially fraudulent firm as a payoff matrix. The seller can produce either low- or high-quality, and the buyer can offer either low or high prices. The row player (the seller) gets the below-diagonal payoffs in each cell, and the column player (the buyer) gets the above-diagonal payoffs in each cell. The buyer prefers to cover the high cost of high-quality products (in the northwest cell) rather than pay less and only cover the lower cost of low-quality products (in the southeast cell). However, the buyer is worst off when the seller fails to deliver a high-quality product for which the buyer has paid a high price (in the southwest cell). The buyer also recognizes that getting more

Table 10.2   Experience-Good Payoff Matrix

		Buyer	
		Offer High Price	**Offer Low Price**
Seller	**High Quality**	Break even / Better	Loss (−D) / Best
	Low Quality	Profit (D + E) / Worst	Break even / Worse

Note: Column-player payoffs are above diagonal. Row-player payoffs are below diagonal.

---

[28] The minimum cost output for the plant configuration and cost structure associated with high quality could shift right or left, but to simplify, assume that the SAC just increases vertically from Point C to Point A.

than she pays for (in the northeast cell) would impose losses on the seller who would prefer to break even with a low-price/low-quality transaction in the southeast cell.

Each player in this business game attempts to predict the other's behavior and respond accordingly. Knowing that the seller prefers profits to breaking even at high prices and that the seller prefers breaking even to losses at low prices, the buyer predicts that low-quality product will be forthcoming irrespective of the price offered. Therefore, the buyer makes only low-price offers. Only those who wish to be repeatedly defrauded offer to pay high prices for one-shot transactions with strangers offering experience goods.

Adverse Selection
A limited choice of lower quality alternatives attributable to asymmetric information.

Lemons Market
Asymmetric information exchange leads to the low quality products and services driving out the higher quality products and services.

This reasoning motivates **adverse selection** by the rational seller in an experience-good market. Because sellers can anticipate only low-price offers from buyers, the sellers never produce high-quality products. That is, the market for experience goods will be incomplete in that not all product qualities will be available for sale. Anticipating that buyers will radically discount their unverifiable high-quality "cream puffs," individual sellers of used cars choose to place only low-quality **"lemons"** on the **market.** The "cream puffs" often are given away to relatives. Similarly, jewelers in vacation locations, anticipating that out-of-town buyers will radically discount high-grade, uncertified gemstones, choose to sell only lower quality gemstones. And unbranded mail-order computer components are inevitably of lower quality. Adverse selection always causes competitive markets with asymmetric information to be incomplete. Again, the bad apples drive out the good.

Insuring and Lending under Asymmetric Information: Another Lemons Market

This same adverse selection reasoning applies beyond experience-good product markets whenever asymmetric information is prominent. Consider the transaction between a bank loan officer and a new commercial borrower, or between an insurance company and a new auto insurance policyholder. Through an application and interview process and with access to various databases and credit references, the lender or insurer attempts to uncover the private, impacted information about the applicant's credit or driving history. Nevertheless, just as in the case of claims made by the itinerant seller of an experience good, verification remains a problem. The applicant has an incentive to omit facts that would tend to result in loan or insurance denial (e.g., prior business failures or unreported accidents), and knowing this, the lender may offer only higher rate loans and the insurer higher rate policies.

The problem is that higher rate loans and expensive insurance policies tend to affect the composition of the applicant pool resulting in adverse selection. Some honest, well-intentioned borrowers and good-risk insurance applicants will now drop out of the applicant pool because of concern about their inability to pay principal and interest and insurance premiums on time as promised. But other applicants who never intended to repay (or drive carefully), or more problematically, those who will try less hard to avoid default or accidents, are undeterred by the higher rates. The asymmetric information and higher rates have adversely selected out precisely those borrowers and drivers the lender and auto insurance company wanted to attract to their loan portfolio and insurance risk pool. Recognizing this problem, the creditors and insurers offer a restricted and incomplete set of loan and insurance contracts. Credit rationing that excludes large segments of the population of potential borrowers and state-mandated protection against uninsured motorists are reflections of the adverse selection problem resulting from asymmetric information in these commercial lending and auto insurance markets.

SOLUTIONS TO THE ADVERSE SELECTION PROBLEM

In both theory and practice, there are two approaches to eliciting the exchange of high-quality experience goods, commercial loans to new borrowers, or auto insurance policies to new residents. The first involves regulatory agencies such as the Federal Trade Commission, the Food and Drug Administration, and the Consumer Product Safety Commission. These agencies can attempt to set quotas (e.g., on minimum product durability, on minimum lending in "red-lined" underprivileged communities, or on minimum auto liability insurance coverage). They may also impose restrictions (e.g., on the sale of untested pharmaceuticals), enforce product safety standards (e.g., on the flammability of children's sleepwear), and monitor truth in advertising laws. We discuss public regulation at greater length in Chapter 17.

Mutual Reliance: Hostage Mechanisms Support Asymmetric Information Exchange

Reliance Relationship
Long-term, mutually beneficial agreements, often informal.

Hostage or Bonding Mechanism
A procedure for establishing trust by assigning valuable property contingent on your nonperformance of an agreement.

A second, quite different approach involves self-enforcing private solution mechanisms where each party relies on the other. Such **reliance relationships** often involve the exchange of some sort of hostage, such as a reputational asset, an escrow account, or a surety bond. In general, **hostage or bonding mechanisms** are necessary to induce unregulated asymmetric information exchange. For this second approach to the adverse selection problem to succeed, buyers must be convinced that fraud is more costly to the seller than the cost of delivering the promised product quality. Then and only then will the customers pay for the seller's additional expected costs attributable to the higher-quality products.

One simple illustration of the use of a hostage mechanism to support asymmetric information exchange is a product warranty, perhaps for an auto tire. Tires are an experience good in that blowout protection and tread wear life are product qualities not detectable at the point of purchase. Only by driving many thousands of miles and randomly encountering many road hazards can the buyer ascertain these tire qualities directly. However, if a tread wear replacement warranty and a tire blowout warranty make the sellers conspicuously worse off should they fail to deliver high-quality tires, then buyers can rely on that manufacturer's product claims. As a consequence, buyers will be willing to offer higher prices for the unverifiably higher-quality product.

Hostage mechanisms can be either self-enforcing or enforced by third parties. Like warranties, a seller's representations about after-sale service and product replacement guarantees are ultimately contractual agreements that will be enforced by the courts. However, other hostage mechanisms require no third party enforcement. Suppose DuPont's industrial chemicals division reveals to potential new customers the names and addresses of several satisfied current customers. This practice of providing references is not only to assist potential buyers in gauging the quality of the product or service for sale but also to deliver an irretrievable hostage. Once new customers have the easy ability to contact regular customers and blow the whistle on product malfunctions or misrepresentations, the seller has an enhanced incentive to deliver high quality to both sets of buyers. Connecting all suppliers and customers in a real-time information system is a natural extension of this familiar practice of providing references. The total quality movement's (TQMs) ISO 9000 standards recommend that companies insist on just such information links to their suppliers.

Example

CREDIBLE PRODUCT REPLACEMENT CLAIMS: DOONEY & BOURKE

The women's handbag market has a wide selection of brand names, prices, and qualities. Leather products have several search good characteristics in that one can touch and feel the material in order to assess the fineness or coarseness of the grain, the evenness of the tanning process, and the suppleness of the leather, etc. In these respects, one can search for just that quality for which one is willing to pay. However, the susceptibility to discoloring with age or exposure to the elements and the quality of the stitching is much harder to detect at the point of purchase. As a result, some aspects of handbag purchase are an experience good exchange. Therefore, one wonders how the wide variety of prices and qualities can be sustained. Dooney & Bourke resolved this question by offering an almost preposterous replacement guarantee. Like Revo sunglasses, Dooney & Bourke offered to replace any handbag for the life of the customer. Because each state attorney general will assist any customer in enforcing this promise, the commitment was credible, and the replacement guarantee provides a hostage that supports high-price, high-quality exchanges. In particular, customers can easily discern that Dooney & Bourke is better off producing an exceptionally high-quality handbag to deliver at the first transaction rather than an unlimited series of replacements.

Brand-Name Reputations as Hostages

A marketing mechanism that supports asymmetric information exchange is a brand-name reputation such as Sony Trinitron color televisions, Apple Macintosh computers, Pepperidge Farm snacks, and Toyota Lexus automobiles. Branding requires a substantial investment over extended periods of time. Moreover, brand names are capital assets that provide future net cash flows from repeat-purchase customers as long as the brand reputation holds up. To defraud customers by delivering less quality than the brand reputation promised would destroy the capitalized market value of the brand name. Buyers anticipate that value-maximizing managers will not intentionally destroy brand-name capital. Brand names therefore deliver a hostage, providing assurances to buyers that the seller will not misrepresent the quality of an experience good.

Ultimately, brand-name capital provides such a hostage because the disreputation effects on the brand name that result from delivering fraudulent product quality cannot be separated from the salable brand asset. Successful brands can be extended to sell other products; Nestlé's original hot chocolate brand can be extended to sell cereal-based candy bars, and Oreo cookies can be extended to sell ice cream. But the product failure of Texas Instruments (TI) personal computers means that now the TI brand name cannot be easily extended to other consumer electronic products. All the potential buyers have to figure out is whether the seller would be worse off sacrificing the value of the brand name but economizing on production expenses rather than simply incurring the extra expense to produce a high-quality product while retaining the brand value. A brand-name asset such as Pepperidge Farm may suggest one answer, whereas Joe's Garage suggests another.

Example

CUSTOMERS FOR LIFE AT SEWELL CADILLAC[29]

The most profitable luxury automobile dealership in the United States is operated in Dallas, Texas, by Carl Sewell. Several decades ago Mr. Sewell realized that the critical success factor in his business was establishing repeat-purchase transactions with regular customers. Many potential buyers shop for lowest price in the new automobile market, sometimes with no more inconvenience than the fingertip browsing of the Internet. And because the alternatives are many, and the information on posted prices is great, many dealerships spend several hundred dollars per car on personal selling costs with little prospect of repeat business. Carl Sewell decided instead to expend similarly large amounts attracting "customers for life." He began by making the apparently preposterous claim that he would dispatch Sewell Cadillac emergency roadside service to any Sewell Cadillac customer experiencing car trouble anywhere in the state of Texas. To economize on the need for such trips, Sewell developed an extensive dealer-based maintenance schedule and instituted one of the first total quality management (TQM) programs in his service department.

Because these policies introduced new process-based competitive advantages, they were difficult for other dealers to imitate. These process innovations cost plenty, but the word-of-mouth reputation effects every time the dealership delivered on its promise spread the name and quality image of Sewell Cadillac across North Texas. Soon customers were driving in from surrounding cities for the privilege of doing high-margin business with Carl Sewell. And even more importantly, these same customers came back time and time again with very little additional cost to the dealership.

If brand-name assets could be sold independent of their reputations (or disreputations), then this hostage mechanism would cease to support experience-good exchange. Assets that can be redeployed at the grantor's wish are not hostages in this reliance contracting sense. The implication is that easy entry and exit, which worked to ensure break-even prices just sufficient to cover costs in the normal competitive markets, may have undesirable consequences here in asymmetric information experience-good markets.

Price Premiums with Nonredeployable Assets[30]

Recall that if sellers are offered prices that just cover high-quality cost, sellers of experience goods prefer the profit from defrauding customers by delivering low-quality products. But suppose buyers offered reliable sellers a continuing price premium above the cost of high-quality products. At P_{hh} in Figure 10.10, the non-notorious firm produces Q_1' high-quality product and earns a continuous stream of profits $(IJAG + JKA)$, labeled $T + U$. This perpetuity may now exceed (in present value) the notorious firm's one-time-only fraudulent rent from production at Q_2'—namely, $D + T$, plus incremental profit $E + U + V$. That is,

$$(T + U)/d > [(D + T) + (E + U + V)]/(1 + d) \qquad [10.9]$$

where d is an appropriate discount rate (e.g., the firm's weighted average cost of capital, perhaps 12 percent). By Equation 10.9, lower discount rates or faster rising

[29] See Carl Sewell and Paul B. Brown, *Customers for Life* (New York: Simon & Schuster, 1992).

[30] See B. Klein and K. Leffler, "The Role of Market Forces in Assuring Contractual Performance," *Journal of Political Economy*, Vol. 89, Number 4, 1981, pp. 615–641.

marginal cost (i.e., a smaller incremental profit from the expansion of output, shaded area V in Figure 10.10) decreases the likelihood of fraudulent behavior. If reliable delivery of a high-quality product does in fact earn long-term net profit in excess of the one-time-only profit from fraud, sellers will offer both low- and high-quality products at P_l and P_{hh}, respectively, and some buyers will purchase in each market.

However, transitory profits alone do not allow an escape from adverse selection. Because profits attract entry in competitive markets, the price premiums will erode, and notorious firm behavior will then return. What is missing is a mechanism to dissipate the rent from the price premiums. If the sellers invest the high-quality price premiums in firm-specific assets, such as L'eggs retail displays for convenience stores or Ethan Allen's interiors for their showrooms, then new entrants will encounter a higher entry barrier than previously. Such barriers cause potential entrants to perceive much lower potential net profit and therefore deter entry. L'eggs or Ethan Allen's operating profits in excess of the production cost can then persist, and high-quality, high-price experience goods can survive in the marketplace.

The rent-dissipating investments must not be in generic retail sites easily redeployable to the next tenant or capital equipment easily redeployable to the next manufacturer (e.g., corporate jet aircraft). If that were the case, hit-and-run entry would recur each time high-quality prices rose above cost. New entrants would just move in on the business for a short time period and then sell off their assets in thick resale markets when profits eroded. Then, competitive equilibrium would again induce adverse selection in experience-good markets. Instead, the investment that dissipates the operating profit from high-quality products must be sunk cost investment in nonredeployable assets.

Figure 10.10   High-Quality Experience Goods Earn a Price Premium

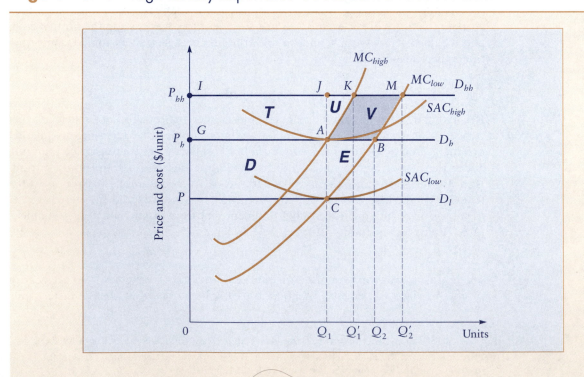

Nonredeployable Assets
Assets whose value in second-best use is near zero.

Asset Specificity
The difference in value between first-best and second-best use.

Nonredeployable assets are assets whose liquidation value in second-best use is low. Usually this occurs when the assets depend on a firm-specific input such as a L'eggs or Ethan Allen brand name. Without the brand name, no firm has a use for the egg-shaped retail racks designed for L'eggs original packaging or the lavish Ethan Allen showrooms. Many such nonredeployable assets have high value in their first best use. The difference between value in first best use and liquidation value is a measure of the **specificity of the asset.** Highly specific assets make the best hostages to convince customers that asymmetric information transactions will be nonfraudulent.

In summary, asymmetric information causes competitive markets for experience goods to differ rather markedly from the competitive markets for search goods. Long-run equilibrium for high-quality experience goods requires revenues in excess of total unit cost. These profits are invested by reliable sellers of experience goods in highly specific assets. Potentially notorious firms with redeployable assets attract only customers seeking low-price/low-quality experience goods. In experience-good markets, you get what you pay for when reputations matter or other hostage mechanisms establish the seller's credibility.

Example

EFFICIENT UNCUT DIAMOND SORTING: DEBEERS[31]

Another illustration of experience-good exchange is block booking by the DeBeers diamond cartel, which controls over 80 percent of the uncut wholesale diamond business. DeBeers offers groupings of diamonds of various grades to approved wholesale buyers. Because buyers are not allowed to cull the less valuable stones, the quality of the diamonds in any given grouping is unverifiable at the point of purchase—hence, the term *sights*. If these arrangements were one time only, no buyer would purchase high-price sights or agree to the culling restrictions. But because block booking economizes on the duplicatory assessments of rejected stones that would otherwise result, DeBeers can consistently offer its sights at net costs below the value at which the diamonds grade out. Buyers therefore have a reason for purchasing high-quality experience goods from DeBeers. If a competitor offered no culling restrictions and lower prices, the diamond merchants would carefully weigh the additional cost of sorting the diamonds themselves against the price premiums at DeBeers and might well decide to continue doing business with DeBeers. Knowing this, very few potential competitors ever enter the uncut diamond wholesale business to challenge DeBeers despite its high markups and margins. DeBeers' reputation for passing on its cost savings in diamond sorting to buyers is the hostage that brings buyers back time and time again.

SUMMARY

- Competitive strategy entails an analysis of the firm's resource-based capabilities, the design of business processes that can secure sustainable competitive advantage, and the development of a road map for innovation.
- Types of strategic thinking include industry analysis, competitor analysis, strategic positioning, and identification of core competencies derived from resource-based-capabilities.
- Sustainable competitive advantage may arise from product differentiation strategy (product capabilities, branding, and endorsements), from focused cost or cost leadership strategy, or from information technology strategy.

---

[31] Based on R. Kenney and B. Klein, "The Economics of Block Booking," *Journal of Law and Economics* 26 (1983), pp. 497–540.

- The choice of competitive strategy should be congruent with the breadth or narrowness of the firm's strategic focus.
- A successful competitive strategy includes an ongoing process of reinvention and reconfiguration of capabilities and business models.
- A relevant market is a group of economic agents that interact with each other in a buyer-seller relationship. Relevant markets often have both spatial and product characteristics.
- The Five Forces model of business strategy identifies threat of substitutes, threat of entry, power of buyers, power of suppliers, and the intensity of rivalry as the determinants of sustainable incumbent profitability in a particular industry.
- The threat of substitutes depends upon the number and closeness of substitutes as determined by the product development, advertising, brand-naming, and segmentation strategies of pre-existing competitors.
- The threat of entry depends upon the height of barriers to potential entrants including capital requirements, economies of scale, absolute cost advantages, switching costs, access to distribution channels, and trade secrets and other difficult-to-imitate forms of product differentiation.
- The bargaining power of buyers and suppliers depends upon their number, their size distribution, the relationship between industry capacity and industry demand, the uniqueness of the inputs, the potential for forward and backward integration, and the extent to which each party to the bargain has outside alternatives.
- The intensity of rivalry depends upon the number and size distribution of sellers in the relevant market, the relative frequency of price versus non-price competition, switching costs, the proportion of fixed to total cost, the barriers to exit, and the growth rate of industry demand.
- The *demand* for a good or service is defined as the various quantities of that good or service that consumers are willing and able to purchase during a particular period of time at all possible prices. The *supply* of a good or service is defined as the quantities that sellers are willing to make available to purchasers at all possible prices during a particular period of time.
- In general, a profit-maximizing firm will desire to operate at that level of output where marginal cost equals marginal revenue.
- In a purely competitive market structure, the firm will operate in the short run as long as price is greater than average variable cost.
- In a purely competitive market structure, the tendency is toward a long-run equilibrium condition in which firms earn just normal profits, price is equal to marginal cost and average total cost, and average total cost is minimized.
- In a monopolistically competitive industry, a large number of firms sell a differentiated product. In practice, few market structures can be best analyzed in the context of the monopolistic competition model. Most actual market structures have greater similarities to the purely competitive market model or the oligopolistic market model.
- Advertising expenditures are optimal from a profit-maximization perspective if they are carried to the point where the marginal profit contribution from an additional unit of output is equal to the marginal cost of advertising. The optimal level of advertising intensity (the advertising expenditure per sales dollar) varies across products and industries; it is determined by the marginal profit contribution from incremental sales and by the advertising elasticity of demand.
- Exchange under incomplete information and under asymmetric information differ. *Incomplete information* refers to the uncertainty that is pervasive in practically

all transactions and motivates insurance markets. *Asymmetric information,* on the other hand, refers to private information one party possesses that the other party cannot independently verify.

- Asymmetric information in *experience-good* markets leads to *adverse selection* whereby high-price/high-quality products are driven from the market by low-quality products whose low quality is indistinguishable at the point of sale. Buyers in such *lemons markets* refuse to offer prices high enough to cover the cost of high quality because under competitive conditions suppliers will predictably commit fraud, and then perhaps move on to conduct business with unsuspecting customers under other product or company names.

- To escape adverse selection and elicit high-quality experience goods necessitates either intrusive and expensive regulation or some sort of bonding mechanism to induce *self-enforcing reliance relationships* between buyers and sellers. Warranties, independent appraisals, leases with a high residual, collateral, irrevocable money-back guarantees, contingent payments, and brand names all provide assurance to buyers that the seller will not misrepresent the product quality. Hostage mechanisms support asymmetric information exchange.

- Another way to escape adverse selection is for buyers to offer price premiums and repeat-purchase transactions to firms that resist fraudulently selling low-quality experience goods for high prices. These profits are invested by reliable sellers in *nonredeployable, highly specific assets.* Potentially *notorious firms* with redeployable assets continue to attract only customers seeking low-price/low-quality products. Under asymmetric information, at best you get what you pay for, never more than that.

EXERCISES

1. The profitability of the leading cola syrup manufacturers PepsiCo and Coca-Cola and of the bottlers in the cola business is very different. PepsiCo and Coca-Cola enjoy an 81-percent operating profit as a percentage of sales; bottlers experience only a 15-percent operating profit as a percentage of sales. Perform a Porter's Five Forces analysis that explains why one type of business is potentially so profitable relative to the other.

2. Network television operating profit in 1997 varied from 45–55 percent at MTV and Nickelodeon to 12–18 percent at NBC and ABC. Provide a Porter Five Forces analysis of each type of network. Why is MTV so profitable relative to the major networks?

3. The costs of building a conventional hot-rolled steel mill have declined substantially as a result of the new minimill technology that requires only scrap metal, an electric furnace, and 300 workers rather than iron ore raw materials, enormous blast furnaces, rolling mills, reheating furnaces, and thousands of workers. What effect on the potential industry profitability would Porter's Five Forces framework suggest this new technology would have? Why?

4. What effect do you think a state law requiring gasoline stations to post their prices prominently will have on the average price of gasoline charged in the state? How can consumers benefit from such a law requiring the posting of gasoline prices?

5. At one point during the energy crisis of the 1970s, gasohol was viewed as one part of a solution to the problem of shortages of petroleum products. Gasohol

was made from a blend of gasoline and alcohol derived from corn. What would you expect the impact of this program to be on the price of corn, soybeans, and wheat?

6. If the government sets a price floor for milk, would you expect that a need would arise for restrictions on the number of cows farmers can milk? In the absence of these restrictions, what outcome would you expect?

7. The demand function for propane is

$$Q_D = 212 - 20P$$

The supply function for propane is

$$Q_S = 20 + 4P$$

a. What is the equilibrium price and quantity?
b. If the government establishes a price ceiling of $6, what quantity will be demanded and supplied?
c. If the government establishes a price floor (minimum price) of $9, what quantity will be demanded and supplied?
d. If supply increases to

$$Q'_S = 20 + 6P$$

what is the new equilibrium price and quantity?
e. If demand increases to

$$Q'_D = 250 - 19P$$

and the supply is as given in Part (d), what is the new equilibrium price and quantity?

8. Assume that a firm in a perfectly competitive industry has the following total cost schedule:

Output (Units)	Total Cost ($)
10	$110
15	150
20	180
25	225
30	300
35	385
40	480

a. Calculate a marginal cost and an average cost schedule for the firm.
b. If the prevailing market price is $17 per unit, how many units will be produced and sold? What are profits per unit? What are total profits?
c. Is the industry in long-run equilibrium at this price?

9. During several past wars, and more recently under programs designed to curb inflation, the government has imposed price ceilings on certain commodities. This is done to keep prices from rising to the natural level that would prevail under supply-demand equilibrium. The result is that the quantity that sellers are willing to supply at the ceiling price often falls short of the quantity demanded at that price. To bring supply and demand more into equilibrium, ration coupons are sometimes issued.

a. Show graphically, using both supply and demand curves, the effects of a ceiling price.

b. On the black market, how much would you be willing to pay for a ration coupon good for the purchase of one unit of the rationed commodity?

c. If the aggregate demand curve for Commodity X is $P = 100 - 5Q$, and the industry supply curve for that product is $P = 10 + 10Q$, calculate the following:

   (i) The equilibrium price and quantity for Commodity X.

   (ii) The quantity that will be sold if a ceiling price of $60 is established.

   (iii) The black market price of a ration coupon good for the purchase of one unit of X.

10. Royersford Knitting Mills, Ltd., sells a line of women's knit underwear. The firm now sells about 20,000 pairs a year at an average price of $10 each. Fixed costs amount to $60,000, and total variable costs equal $120,000. The production department has estimated that a 10-percent increase in output would not affect fixed costs but would reduce average variable cost by 40 cents.

The marketing department advocates a price reduction of 5 percent to increase sales, total revenues, and profits. The arc elasticity of demand with respect to prices is estimated at -2.

a. Evaluate the impact of the proposal to cut prices on (i) total revenue, (ii) total cost, and (iii) total profits.

b. If average variable costs are assumed to remain constant over a 10-percent increase in output, evaluate the effects of the proposed price cut on total profits.

11. The Jenkins Tool Company has estimated the following demand equation for its product:

$$Q_D = 12,000 - 4,000P$$

where

$$P = \text{price/unit}$$
$$Q_D = \text{quantity demanded/year}$$

The firm's total costs are $4,000 when nothing is being produced. These costs increase by 50 cents for each unit produced.

a. Write an equation for the total cost function.

b. Specify the marginal cost function.

c. Write an equation for total revenue in terms of Q.

d. Specify the marginal revenue function.

e. Write an equation for total profits, π, in terms of Q. At what level of output are total profits maximized (that is, find the maximum of the total profit function)? What price will be charged? What will total profit be?

f. Check your answers in Part (e) by equating marginal cost and marginal revenue and solving for Q.

g. What model of market pricing behavior has been assumed in this problem?

12. A firm operating in a purely competitive environment is faced with a market price of $250. The firm's total cost function (short run) is

$$TC = 6,000 + 400Q - 20Q^2 + Q^3$$

a. Should the firm produce at this price in the short run?

b. If the market price is $300, what will total profits (losses) be if the firm produces 10 units of output? Should the firm produce at this price?

c. If the market price is greater than $300, should the firm produce in the short run?

13. The Poster Bed Company believes that its industry can best be classified as monopolistically competitive. An analysis of the demand for its canopy bed has resulted in the following estimated demand function for the bed:

$$P = 1760 - 12Q$$

The cost analysis department has estimated the total cost function for the poster bed as

$$TC = \frac{1}{3}Q^3 - 15Q^2 + 5Q + 24{,}000$$

a. Calculate the level of output that should be produced to maximize short-run profits.

b. What price should be charged?

c. Compute total profits at this price-output level.

d. Compute the point price elasticity of demand at the profit-maximizing level of output.

e. What level of fixed costs is the firm experiencing on its bed production?

f. What is the impact of a $5,000 increase in the level of fixed costs on the price charged, output produced, and profit generated?

14. Assume that a firm sells its product in a perfectly competitive market. The firm's fixed costs (including a "normal" return on the funds the entrepreneur has invested in the firm) are equal to $100 and its variable cost schedule is as follows:

Output (Units)	Variable Cost Per Unit
50	$5.00
100	4.50
150	4.00
200	3.50
250	3.00
300	2.75
350	3.00
400	3.50

a. Find the marginal cost and average total cost schedules for the firm.

b. If the prevailing market price is $4.50, how many units will be produced and sold?

c. What are total profits and profit per unit at the output level determined in Part (b)?

d. Is the industry in long-run equilibrium at this price? Explain.

15. Exotic Metals, Inc., a leading manufacturer of zirilium, which is used in many electronic products, estimates the following demand schedule for its product:

Price ($/Pound)	Quantity (Pounds/Period)
$25	0
18	1,000
16	2,000
14	3,000
12	4,000
10	5,000
8	6,000
6	7,000
4	8,000
2	9,000

Fixed costs of manufacturing zirilium are $14,000 per period. The firm's variable cost schedule is as follows:

Output (Pounds/Period)	Variable Cost (Per Pound)
0	$0
1,000	10.00
2,000	8.50
3,000	7.33
4,000	6.25
5,000	5.40
6,000	5.00
7,000	5.14
8,000	5.88
9,000	7.00

a. Find the total revenue and marginal revenue schedules for the firm.

b. Determine the average total cost and marginal cost schedules for the firm.

c. What are Exotic Metals' profit-maximizing price and output levels for the production and sale of zirilium?

d. What is Exotic's profit (or loss) at the solution determined in Part (c)?

e. Suppose that the federal government announces it will sell zirilium, from its extensive wartime stockpile, to anyone who wants it at $6 per pound. How does this affect the solution determined in Part (c)? What is Exotic Metals' profit (or loss) under these conditions?

16. Wyandotte Chemical Company sells various chemicals to the automobile industry. Wyandotte currently sells 30,000 gallons of polyol per year at an average price of $15 per gallon. Fixed costs of manufacturing polyol are $90,000 per year and total variable costs equal $180,000. The operations research department has estimated that a 15-percent increase in output would not affect fixed costs but would reduce average variable costs by 60 cents per gallon. The marketing department has estimated the arc elasticity of demand for polyol to be −2.0.

a. How much would Wyandotte have to reduce the price of polyol to achieve a 15-percent increase in the quantity sold?

b. Evaluate the impact of such a price cut on (i) total revenue, (ii) total costs, and (iii) total profits.

17. Tennis Products, Inc., produces three models of high-quality tennis rackets. The following table contains recent information on the sales, costs, and profitability of the three models:

Model	Average Quantity Sold (Units/ Month)	Current Price	Total Revenue	Variable Cost per Unit	Contribution Margin per Unit	Contribution Margin*
A	15,000	$30	$ 450,000	$15.00	$15	$225,000
B	5,000	35	175,000	18.00	17	85,000
C	10,000	45	450,000	20.00	25	250,000
Total			$1,075,000			$560,000

*Contribution to fixed costs and profits.

The company is considering lowering the price of Model A to $27 in an effort to increase the number of units sold. Based on the results of price changes that have been instituted in the past, Tennis Products' chief economist has estimated the arc price elasticity of demand to be -2.5. Furthermore, she has estimated the arc cross elasticity of demand between Model A and Model B to be approximately 0.5 and between Model A and Model C to be approximately 0.2. Variable costs per unit are not expected to change over the anticipated changes in volume.

a. Evaluate the impact of the price cut on the (i) total revenue and (ii) contribution margin of Model A. Based on this analysis, should the firm lower the price of Model A?

b. Evaluate the impact of the price cut on the (i) total revenue and (ii) contribution margin for the entire line of tennis rackets. Based on this analysis, should the firm lower the price of Model A?

18. Jordan Enterprises has estimated the gross margin $(P - MC)/P$ for its Air Express model of basketball shoes to be 40 percent. Based on market research and past experience, Jordan estimates the following relationship between the sales for Air Express and advertising/promotional outlays:

Advertising/Promotional Outlays	Sales Revenue
$500,000	$4,000,000
600,000	4,500,000
700,000	4,900,000
800,000	5,200,000
900,000	5,450,000
1,000,000	5,600,000

a. What is the marginal revenue from an additional dollar spent on advertising if the firm is currently spending $1,000,000 on advertising?

b.   What level of advertising would you recommend to Jordan's management?

19.   Which of the following products and services are likely to encounter adverse selection problems: golf shirts at traveling pro tournaments, certified gemstones from Tiffany's, graduation gift travel packages, or mail-order auto parts? Why or why not?

20.   Without employing a tread wear warranty contract, how could the sellers of tires credibly commit to the delivery of high-quality products with long tread wear life?

21.   If a particular supplier in Table 10.2 succeeds in reducing the cost of low-quality products and now earns a profit on the low-price transactions, is the likelihood of fraud by that firm greater or less?

22.   If notorious firm behavior (i.e., defrauding a buyer of high-priced experience goods by delivering low-quality) becomes known throughout the marketplace only with a lag of three periods, profits on high-quality transactions remain the same, and interest rates rise slightly, are customers more likely or less likely to offer high prices for an experience good? Explain.

CASE EXERCISES

APPLE COMPUTER

Investigate recent developments at Apple's website; then, answer the following questions:

QUESTIONS

1.   Does easy access to distribution channels or small minimum efficient scale indicate high or low barriers to entry in the PC business? Why?

2.   Do suppliers appropriate little or most of the value in the PC value chain? Why?

3.   What factors determine the intensity of rivalry in an industry? Is the intensity of rivalry in the PC industry high or low? Why?

SAVING SONY MUSIC

Explore the crisis that Internet file-sharing of copyrighted music recordings has caused for Vivendi Universal, Sony Music, EMI, and AOL Time Warner Music, who together supply 70 percent of the global music industry.

Sony website:
http://www.dismal.com/

QUESTIONS

1.   How would the role of Internet Firms Napster and, more recently, Kazaa be reflected in a Porter Five Forces industry analysis?

2.   Why was the Internet a disruptive technology for Sony but not for Dell?

3.   What should be Sony's competitive strategy in response to this crisis? Include a discussion of resource-based capabilities, business opportunities, and a road map of future innovation.

4.   Is your competitive strategy for Sony Music a product differentiation strategy, a low-cost strategy, or an information technology strategy? What is your strategic focus?

Price and Output Determination: Monopoly and Dominant Firms

CHAPTER PREVIEW In this chapter we analyze the optimal price and output decision for dominant firms operating in monopoly or near-monopoly markets. The most important implication of such markets is that the dominant firm does not have to accept the market price as a given. Rather, dominant firms have substantial latitude in establishing price-cost markups. In addition to considering price and output determination for "unregulated" monopolies and near-monopolies, we also look at these decisions for regulated industries—electric power, natural gas distribution and transmission, and broadcast communications. With public debate focused on deregulation, it is imperative that reform be consistent with microeconomic principles to avoid some of the problems inherent in the current system of utility regulation.

MANAGERIAL CHALLENGE

Dominant Microprocessor Company Lagging Behind Next Trend[1]

With continuous innovation, ever-faster, more powerful chip designs, and a business plan riveted on supplying the $160-billion PC industry, Intel Corporation has dominated the high-end market in microprocessors. After being forced out of the dynamic random access memory (DRAM) chip business by Japanese rivals in 1986, Intel reinvented itself as the lead supplier of microprocessors. Intel has an 85-percent market share in the microprocessor chips that control most personal computer functions and process software instructions. In addition, Intel sells 90 percent of the chip sets that control the flow of data from the microprocessor to the display screens, modems, and graphical user interface. With market dominance have come enormous economies of scale in production and increasing returns to marketing expenditures that allowed Intel to beat out its smaller rivals. High markups and margins (for mass-produced electronics products) resulted; for example, the Pentium series and Intel 486 microprocessors earned 25-percent net profit margins.

Using tight nondisclosure agreements with its customers, Intel has managed to protect its proprietary trade secrets about chip design and manufacture. Intellectual property is the company's most important asset, and some buyers of Intel chips have found that the dominant firm withholds vital information about technical specifications required to fully integrate the chips into new products unless it gets access to its customers' new technologies.

Intergraph, a maker of high-end workstations for media applications, alleged recently that Intel withheld information about subtle bugs in some Intel chips until Intergraph agreed to license its graphical user interface technology to the chip supplier.

Although the worldwide PC market is expected to continue to grow at 15 percent per year, the penetration of PCs into U.S. households has stalled at 45 percent (versus TVs at 98 percent). Digital telephones, hand-held computers, video-game players, and set-top control boxes for digital televisions may prove to be a market even bigger than the PC market. Such devices require inexpensive computer chips that process data very fast, not high-end Intel chips designed to run Microsoft's complex software. Hitachi and Advanced Micro Devices (AMD) are likely leaders in this new chip segment.

Intel may have missed one of the "strategic inflection points" that Intel President Andy Grove says is so important to the success of any high technology company. Mr. Grove knows Intel must get prepared for streamlined lower end chip products that sell for under $40, despite the fact that Intel's chips have sold for $87 to $200.

---

[1] Based on "Hand-Held Combat," *Wall Street Journal,* February 12, 1998, p. A1; "Showdown Looms Over Chip Giant's Power," *Wall Street Journal,* June 8, 1998, p. B1; and "Intel Lags Behind in Cheap Chips," *Wall Street Journal,* March 1, 1999, p. C15.

MONOPOLY DEFINED

Monopoly is defined as a market structure characterized by one firm producing a highly differentiated product in a market with significant barriers to entry. Because there are no close substitutes for the product of a monopolist, the demand curve facing a monopolist will have a significant negative slope and be less price elastic than comparable demands where there are more substitutes. A monopoly market structure may be thought of as the opposite extreme from pure competition in terms of the range of market structures.

Just as purely competitive market structures (e.g., for AAA January wheat in Kansas City) are rare, so too pure monopoly markets are also rare. All goods and services have some substitutes available for them. The more distant the substitutes that are available, the closer a market is to being a pure monopoly.

Example

THE MICKEY MOUSE MONOPOLY: DISNEY

When it began, Disneyland in Anaheim, California, was unique. Other theme parks like Six Flags have since reduced Disney's monopoly power. Disney World in Orlando, Florida, was an attempt to resecure Disney's near-monopoly position in the market, but Universal Studios, SeaWorld and other attractions throughout the Orlando area quickly offered additional theme park experiences. Were they a complement or a substitute for Disney World? Negative cross-price elasticity of demand evidence suggests complementary relationships. Seventy percent of Disney World's business is repeat business; more variety inside or outside the park means more frequent returns for longer vacations. Anticipating these developments, Disney long ago became a major property owner throughout the Orlando area.

SOURCES OF MARKET POWER FOR A MONOPOLIST

http://
The following Internet site contains an amicus brief on the economics of intellectual property prepared for the U.S. Supreme Court case of *Lotus Development Corporation v. Borland International:*
http://www.panix.com/
~jesse/amicus/cover.html

Several sources of market power can be enjoyed by monopolists or near-monopoly dominant firms. First, a firm may possess a *patent* or *copyright* that prevents other firms from producing the same product. For example, Pharmacia & Upjohn, Inc., has a patent on the product Rogaine, the hair growth stimulator for balding men. The long and expensive governmental approval process for competing products creates a significant barrier to entry for potential competitors.

Second, a firm may *control critical resources*. De Beers Consolidated Mines Limited owns or controls the vast majority of diamond production in South Africa and until recently, had marketing agreements with other major diamond-producing countries, including the former Soviet Union. This control of raw materials enabled De Beers to maintain high world prices for cut diamonds for 65 years.

Example

IMPERMANENT CONTROL OF DENVER AIRPORT HUB: UNITED AIRLINES[2]

The market power attributable to the control of critical resources is typically quite transient. After the deregulation of airlines in 1979, some major carriers developed fortress hubs. In the mid-1980s, USAir (now US Airways), United, Delta, and

---

[2] "Air Fares Decline in Denver," *Wall Street Journal,* February 6, 1996.

Northwest controlled 78 percent, 70 percent, 72 percent, and 80 percent of the gates at their hubs in Charlotte, Denver, Atlanta, and Minneapolis, respectively. These dominant carriers effectively barred rival entry by entering into long-term leases with airport authorities. Local customer loyalty then supported 20- to 27-percent price premiums based on the delivery reliability, change order responsiveness, and nonstop scheduling convenience at these hubs.

By the mid-1990s, however, small start-up airlines threatened to break into the hubs of these market leaders. Delta encountered strong challenges from Kiwi and AirTran, whose presence in Atlanta caused margins on competing routes to dwindle. Frontier Airlines attracted discount and drive-in traffic at Denver. Consequently, United fares to and from Denver have declined substantially since 1995. In contrast, US Airways still controls fully 92 percent of the departures from Charlotte; high fares have induced the city council to approach Southwest Airlines and AirTran about a possible entry.

A third source of monopoly power may be a *government-authorized franchise*. In most U.S. cities, one firm is chosen to provide cable TV services to the community. Network Solution is authorized by the U.S. Bureau of Standards to serve as the sole registry for .com, .net, and .org domain names. The same type of monopoly power occurs when a government agency like the FDA or FCC adopts an industry standard that heavily favors one industry or one company over all others. The adoption of Motorola's proposed HDTV standards has often been criticized on this basis; the alternative standard is one proposed by Sony, a Japanese firm.

Monopoly power may also arise because there are significant *economies of scale* over a wide range of output. Thus, the first entrant firm will enjoy declining long-run average costs. Under these circumstances it is natural for there to be only one supplier of the good or service, because that one supplier can produce the output more cheaply than can a group of smaller competitors. These so-called natural monopolies are usually closely regulated by government agencies to restrict the profits of the monopolist.

Increasing Returns from Network Effects

Finally, *increasing returns in network-based businesses* can be a source of monopoly market power. When Microsoft managed to achieve a critical level of adoption for its Windows graphical user interface (GUI), the amount of marketing and promotional expenditure required to secure the next adoption actually began to fall.

Marketing and promotions are generally subject to diminishing returns, as depicted in the left most third of Figure 11.1. From 0- to 30-percent market share, the marketing required to achieve each additional share point has a diminishing effect on the probability of adoption by the next potential user (note the reduced slope of the sales penetration curve). Consequently, additional share points become more and more expensive over this range. But when the number of other users of a network-based device reaches a 30-percent share, the next 50 or so share points are cheaper to promote. That is, beyond the 30-percent inflection point, each additional share point of users connected to Windows leads to an increasing probability of adoption by another user; hence a decrease in the marketing expense required to secure another unit sale (note the increased slope of the sales penetration curve

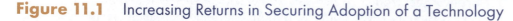

Figure 11.1   Increasing Returns in Securing Adoption of a Technology

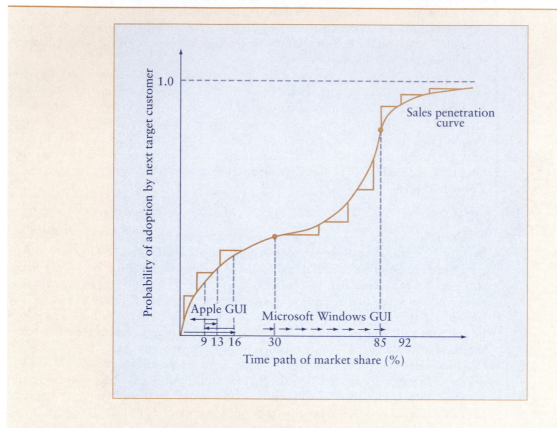

in this middle third of Figure 11.1) Then beyond 85 percent, in the rightmost third of Figure 11.1, diminishing returns again set in.

These network-based effects of compatibility with other users reflect increased value to the potential adopter. The same thing occurs when an ever-increasing number of independent software vendors (ISVs) write applications for an operating system like Windows that has achieved more than a 30-percent acceptance in the marketplace and has therefore effectively become an industry standard. Because of the inflection points in the sales penetration curve, Microsoft's increasing returns make an 85-percent monopoly control of the operating system market highly likely. Whatever customer relationships preexisted, once Microsoft achieved a 30-percent share, increasing returns in marketing its product offering introduced a disruptive technology **network effect** that displaced other competitors. Inexorably, Microsoft's share then grew and grew and grew to 92 percent. Netscape's Internet search engine experienced exactly this same sort of displacement by Microsoft's Internet Explorer when Microsoft achieved a 30 percent-plus penetration by bundling Internet Explorer with Windows, effectively giving away the search engine for free to reach the middle sales penetration range of increasing returns.

Network Effect
A source of unit cost reduction based on network value rather than scale of operations or volume purchase discounts.

Example

WHAT WENT RIGHT AT MICROSOFT BUT WRONG AT APPLE COMPUTER?[3]

Throughout much of its history, Apple Computer, discussed in the *Managerial Challenge* at the beginning of Chapter 10, has hovered around 7–10-percent market share in the U.S. personal computer market. Twice in its early history, Apple reached double-digit share points (16 percent in 1986 and 13 percent in 1993). At no time could Apple come close to achieving the inflection point (depicted at 30 percent in Figure 11.1). Apple therefore pursued increasing returns by attempting to become an industry standard in several personal computer submarkets like the desktop publishing, journalism, media-based advertising, and the entertainment industries. In addition, despite fiercely defending their graphical user interface (GUI) code for almost two decades with patent applications and trade secret infringement suits, in 1998–1999 Apple reversed course and began discussing broad licensing and alliance agreements with both Microsoft and IBM. Compatibility with other operating systems had been easy to achieve, but widespread adoption of Mac programming code by independent software vendors had not. Consequently, to obtain a critical mass of adoptions that would trigger ISVs to begin writing software applications for the Mac, Apple reversed its company policy on the closed architecture of its GUI. The GUI code at Apple was clearly technically superior to the early-generation Windows products. However, as with the adoption race between VHS and Betamax videos, the technically superior product lost out to the product that first reached increasing returns—namely, Microsoft Windows GUI running on IBM-clone PCs.

Netscape too once controlled 80 percent of the Internet browser market, but lost shares rapidly once Microsoft's Internet Explorer reached increasing returns. When Internet Explorer achieved 55 percent of the market share, Netscape made its browser services compatible and instead began positioning itself as a portal for Wintel machines to use in accessing the Net. Netscape was trying to avoid Apple's mistake of refusing to recognize an evolving industry standard and then finding itself buried by Microsoft's increasing returns.

Even with increasing returns set off by network effects, monopoly is far from inevitable. The reasons are three-fold. First, innovative new products can easily offset the cost savings from increasing returns to promotion spending. Second, network effects tend to occur in technology-based industries that are also experiencing external economies of scale—i.e., falling input prices. Figure 11.2 shows that between 1997 and 2002, the cost per megahertz for silicon computer chips fell from $2.00 to $0.10, and between 1998 and 2002, hard drive storage device cost per megabyte fell from $0.40 to $0.05, cost per month for a T1 highspeed data transmission line fell from $475 to $420, and even copper fell from $0.90 to $0.70 per pound. During the same period, Corning fiber-optic cable became essentially free to anyone who would carry it off. In short, as these input suppliers grew to serve the expanding product markets in computer equipment and telecom devices, they encountered new productivity from learning curves and innovative design breakthroughs that drove down their costs. And since the computer chip, memory device, and telecom

[3] Based on "Netscape to Woo Microsoft's Customers, *Reuters,* October 1, 1998, 10:21 A.M. EST; W. Brian Arthur, "Increasing Returns and the New World of Business," *Harvard Business Review,* July-August 1996; and "Sorting Out the Deal," *U.S. News and World Report,* August 18, 1997, p. 20.

Figure 11.2 Declining Component Costs Lead to External Economies of Scale in Computers and Telecoms

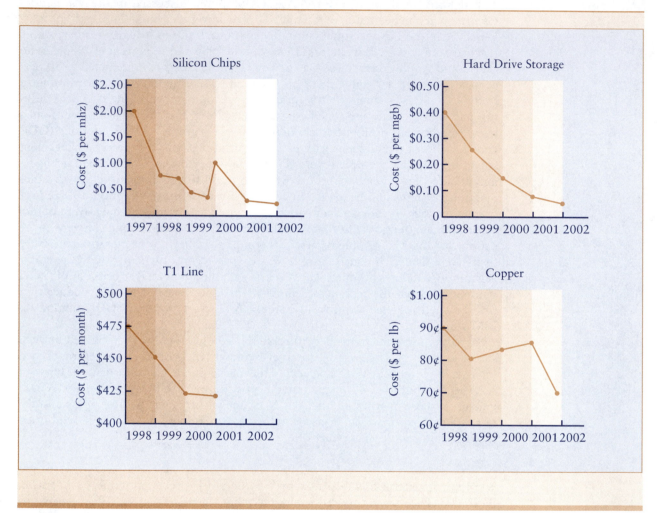

Source: *Wired,* March 2002, p. 55.

equipment markets tend to be highly competitive, the cost savings of input suppliers like AMD and Corning get passed along to the final product producers like Sun Computers, PC-assembler Compaq, cell phone manufacturer Nokia, and router manufacturer Cisco. Consequently, generally lower costs for all inputs have offset in large part the advantage from increasing returns in promotion and selling expenses for companies like Microsoft, Dell, and Palm.

Third, technology products whose primary value lies in their intellectual property—products like computer software, pharmaceuticals, and telecom networks—have revenue sources that are dependent on renewals of governmental licensures and product standards. Unlike autos or steel, once R&D costs have been recouped, the marginal cost of additional copies of the software, additional doses of the

WHAT WENT RIGHT   WHAT WENT WRONG

Pilot Error at Palm[4]

Palm Pilot, the once-dominant product in handheld computers, demonstrates how fragile is the position of even an industry leader with increasing returns to promotional spending in a technology business. Despite having 80 percent of the handheld operating system market and despite producing 60 percent of the handheld hardware at its peak in 2000, Palm Inc. has lost market share to rivals. Palm experienced growth so fast (165-percent year-over-year sales increases) that it gave little attention to operational issues such as managing the supply of inputs and forecasting demand. When in 2001 it mistimed the announcement of its m500 product upgrades, which were delayed by supply chain bottlenecks,

the customers stopped buying older models. Handspring, Sony, Hewlett-Packard, Microsoft's Pocket PC, and the popular Blackberry drove prices lower and offered newer product features. Almost overnight, excess Palm IV and V inventory piled up on shelves, and inquiries about Microsoft's Pocket PC shot way up. Customers were awaiting the new model, and Palm was forced to take a $300 million write-down on their inventory losses. The stock price fell from $25 to $2 a share.

[4] Based on "How Palm Tumbled," *Wall Street Journal*, September 7, 2001, p. A1.

medicine, or additional users on the wireless system are close to zero; every single unit sold thereafter is close to pure profit. Consequently, competitor firms who have incurred the up-front fixed costs but not succeeded in reaching the inflection point of increasing returns rationally spend enormous sums seeking to obtain these rents through the political process and in the courts. For example, Genentech's first commercial success was a multiple sclerosis drug that avoided direct challenge to a broad Schering-Plough Corporation patent by employing special FDA rule making. Xerox was forced to license its wet paper copier technology at low royalty fees. Netscape and Sun succeeded during Microsoft's long antitrust trial of 1997–2002 in placing conduct restrictions on their competitor—e.g., restrictions on Microsoft's installation agreements for Windows, and prohibition of Microsoft's refusal to deal with Windows licensees who install Netscape's competing web browser software.

How can firms get around the inflection point of Figure 11.1 and achieve increasing returns? Free trials for a limited period of use is one approach. Another is giving the technology away if it can be bundled with other revenue-generating product offerings. Microsoft was able to give Internet Explorer (IE) away for free without running the danger of a predatory pricing indictment because IE's variable cost was $0.004; that is, it rounded to zero. Another approach is to undertake consolidation mergers and acquisitions; this strategy underlaid IBM's acquisition of Lotus in 1995 and Oracle's hostile takeover of PeopleSoft in 2003. Some companies like Sun Microsystems also employ JAVA programming subsidies to independent software vendors whose applications will provide network effects as complements to Sun's JAVA-based OS. Finally, securing the mandatory adoption of an industry standard favorable to your own product is a path to increasing returns. Motorola continues to work toward this end with its HDTV standard for the U.S. market.

PRICE AND OUTPUT DETERMINATION FOR A MONOPOLIST

Recall that the demand curve facing a pure monopolist is the same as the industry demand curve because one firm constitutes the entire industry. The price-output decision for a profit-maximizing monopolist is illustrated in Figure 11.3.

Just as in pure competition, profit is maximized at the price and output combination where $MC = MR$. This corresponds to a price of P_1, output of Q_1, and total profits equal to BC profit per unit times Q_1 units. For a negative-sloping demand curve, the MR function is not the same as the demand function. In fact, for any linear, negatively sloping demand function, the marginal revenue function will have the same intercept on the P axis as the demand function and a slope that is twice as great as that of the demand function. If, for example, the demand function were of the form

$$P = a - bQ$$

then

$$\text{Total revenue} = TR = P \cdot Q$$
$$= aQ - bQ^2$$

and

$$MR = \frac{dTR}{dQ} = a - 2\,bQ$$

The slope of the demand function is $-b$, and the slope of the MR function is $-2\,b$.

Example

PROFIT MAXIMIZATION: MONOPOLY

Assume a monopolist is faced with the following demand function:

$$Q = 400 - 20P$$

and short-run total variable cost function:

$$TC = 5Q + \frac{Q^2}{50}$$

To maximize profits, it would produce and sell that output where $MC = MR$, and charge the corresponding price:

$$MC = \frac{dTC}{dQ} = 5 + \frac{Q}{25}$$

MR may be found by rewriting the demand function in terms of Q:

$$P = \frac{-Q}{20} + 20$$

and then multiplying by Q to find TR:

$$TR = P \cdot Q$$
$$= -\frac{Q^2}{20} + 20Q$$

$$MR = \frac{dTR}{dQ} = -\frac{Q}{10} + 20$$

Setting $MR = MC$ yields

$$-\frac{Q*}{10} + 20 = 5 + \frac{Q*}{25}$$

$$Q* = 107 \text{ units}$$

Substituting $Q*$ back into the demand equation, we may solve for $P*$:

$$P* = \frac{-107}{20} + 20$$

$$= \$14.65/\text{unit}$$

Hence the profit-maximizing monopolist would produce 107 units and charge a price of \$14.65 each. This yields a profit of

$$\pi* = TR - TC$$

$$= (P* \cdot Q*) - \left(5Q* + \frac{Q^{*2}}{50}\right)$$

$$= 14.65(107) - \left(5(107) + \frac{(107)^2}{50}\right)$$

$$= \$803.57$$

Figure 11.3   Price and Output Determination: Pure Monopoly

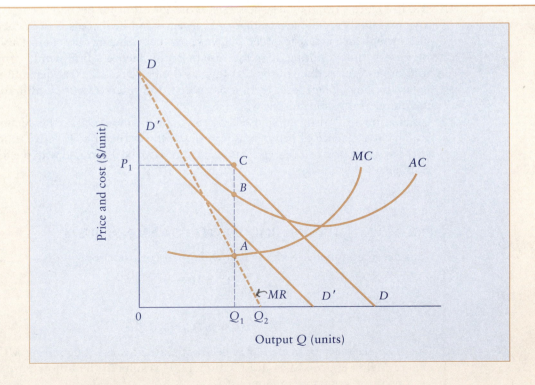

The Importance of Price Elasticity of Demand

Recall from Chapter 3 that marginal revenue (*MR*), the incremental change in total revenue arising from one more unit sale, can be expressed in terms of price (*P*) and the price elasticity (E_D), or

$$MR = P\left(1 + \frac{1}{E_D}\right) \tag{11.1}$$

Equating *MR* with *MC* (as shown in Figure 11.3) yields the profit-maximizing relationship in terms of price and price elasticity, or

$$MC = P\left(1 + \frac{1}{E_D}\right) \tag{11.2}$$

For the monopoly case, price will be greater than marginal cost. For example, if price elasticity $E_D = -2.0$, price will equal

$$MC = P\left(1 + \frac{1}{-2}\right)$$
$$MC = .5P$$
$$P = 2MC$$

Note from Equation 11.2 that a monopolist will never operate in the area of the demand curve where demand is price inelastic (i.e., $|E_D| < 1$). If the absolute value of price elasticity is less than 1 ($|E_D| < 1$), then the reciprocal of price elasticity ($1/E_D$) will be less than minus 1 and marginal revenue $\left[P\left(1 + \frac{1}{E_D}\right)\right]$ will be negative. In Figure 11.3, the inelastic range of output is output beyond level Q_2. A negative marginal revenue means that total revenue can be increased by reducing output (through an increase in price). But we know that reducing output must also reduce total costs, thus resulting in an increase in profit. Hence a firm would continue to raise prices (and reduce output) as long as the price elasticity of demand is in the inelastic range. Therefore, for a monopolist, the price-output combination that maximizes profits must occur where $|E_D| \geq 1$.

Equation 11.2 also can be used to show that the more elastic the demand (suggesting the existence of better substitutes), the lower the price (relative to marginal cost) any given firm can charge. This relationship can be illustrated with the following example.

Example

PRICE ELASTICITY AND PRICE LEVELS FOR MONOPOLISTS

Consider a monopolist with the following total cost function:

$$TC = 10 + 5Q$$

The marginal cost (*MC*) function is

$$MC = dTC/dQ = 5$$

The price elasticity of demand has been estimated to be -2.0. Setting $MC = MR$ (where *MR* is expressed as in Equation 11.1) results in the following price rule for a profit-maximizing monopolist:

$$MC = \$5 = P(1 + 1/-2.0) = MR$$
$$P = 5/(0.5) = \$10/unit$$

If, however, demand is more price elastic, such as $E_D = -4.0$, the profit-maximizing monopolist would set the price at

$$P = \$5/(0.75) = \$6.67/unit$$

OPTIMAL MARKUP, CONTRIBUTION MARGIN, AND THE CONTRIBUTION MARGIN PERCENTAGE

Sometimes it proves useful and convenient to express these relationships between optimal price, price elasticity, and marginal cost as a markup percentage or contribution margin percentage. Rearranging Equation 11.2 to solve for optimal price yields

$$P = \frac{E_D}{(E_D + 1)}MC \qquad [11.3]$$

where the multiplier term ahead of MC is 1.0 plus the percentage markup.[5] For example, the case of $E_D = -3$ is a product with a $-3/(-3 + 1) = 1.5$ multiplier—that is, a 50-percent markup. The optimal profit-maximizing price recovers the marginal cost and then marks up MC another 50 percent. If $MC = \$6$, this item would sell for $1.5 \times \$6 = \$9$ and the profit-maximizing markup is $3, or 50 percent more than the marginal cost.

Contribution Margin Percentage
The difference between the profit-maximizing price and marginal cost, often expressed as a percentage of the price. When more than one unit sale is involved, contribution margin is the difference between revenue and incremental variable cost.

The difference between price and marginal cost (i.e., the absolute dollar size of the markup) is often referred to as the **contribution margin** because having already covered incremental variable cost, these additional dollars are available to contribute to covering fixed cost and earning a profit. They are often expressed as a percentage of the total price. In the previous example, the $3 markup above and beyond the $6 marginal cost represents a 33-percent contribution to fixed cost and profit, that is, a 33-percent contribution margin on the $9 item. To summarize, an elasticity of -3.0 implies that the profit maximizing markup is 50 percent, and that 50-percent markup implies a 33-percent contribution margin. Using Equation 11.3 and $E_D = -3$,

$$\frac{(P - MC)}{P} = \frac{1.5\ MC - 1.0\ MC}{1.5\ MC}$$

Contribution Margin % = 0.5 / 1.5 = 33%

Price elasticity information therefore conveys implications for the marketing plan. Combining the contribution margin percentage (33 percent) with incremental variable cost information indicates what dollar markups and product prices to announce.

Example

MARKUPS AND CONTRIBUTION MARGINS ON CHANEL NO. 5, OLE MUSK, AND WHITMAN'S SAMPLER

Consider three products available at the typical drugstore counter: Chanel No. 5, Whitman's Sampler, and store brand fragrance Ole Musk. Chanel has a loyal following of regular buyers and a price elasticity of -1.1. Whitman's has some rather close substitutes but substantial name recognition and packaging familiarity; its price

---

[5] The symbol MC may be understood to refer to the accountant's narrow definition of *variable costs,* operating costs that vary with the least aggregated unit sale in the business plan.

elasticity measures −1.86. Finally, customers perceive many close substitutes for the generic fragrance Ole Musk, whose price elasticity is therefore −12.0.

Table 11.1 shows the optimal prices, markups, and contribution margins for these three products. Using Equation 11.3, the multiplier on MC for Chanel No. 5 is −1.1/(−1.1 + 1) = 11.0, and the optimal markup is therefore 1000 percent (i.e., ten times the incremental variable cost of the essences and the bottle). Because optimal price is 11.0 MC, the contribution margin percentage on Chanel No. 5 calculates as 10.0 MC/11.0 MC = 91%. Whitman's Sampler has a multiplier of −1.86/(−1.86 + 1) = 2.16, an optimal markup therefore of 116 percent and a contribution margin of 1.16 MC/2.16 MC = 54%. In contrast, Ole Musk with the greatest price elasticity has a multiplier of −12/(−12 + 1) = 1.09, a markup of 9 percent, and a contribution margin percentage of 0.09 MC/1.09 MC = 8%.

Thus, the more elastic the demand function for a monopolist's output, the lower the price that will be charged, *ceteris paribus*. At the limit, consider the case of a firm in pure competition with a perfectly elastic (horizontal) demand curve. In this case the price elasticity of demand approaches −∞; hence, 1 divided by the price elasticity approaches 0 and marginal revenue in Equation 11.1 becomes equal to price. Thus, the profit-maximizing rule in Equation 11.2 becomes "Set price equal to marginal cost" and the profit-maximizing markup in Equation 11.3 is zero—i.e., the marginal cost multiplier is 1.0. Of course, this is the same price-cost solution developed in Chapter 10 in the discussion of price determination under pure competition.

Components of the Gross Profit Margin

Gross Profit Margin Revenue minus the sum of variable cost plus direct fixed cost, also known as direct costs of goods sold in manufacturing.

Gross profit margin (or just "gross margin") is a term often used in manufacturing to refer to the contribution margin further reduced by *direct* fixed costs. For example, in a carpet plant the gross margin on each product line would be the plant's wholesale revenue minus the sum of variable costs plus machinery setup costs for the production runs involving that type of carpet. A manufacturer's income statement identifies variable costs plus direct fixed manufacturing cost as the "direct cost of goods sold" (DCGS). Thus, the gross margin is revenue minus direct cost of goods sold.[6]

Table 11.1   Optimal Prices, Markups, and Margins

	E_D	Price	Contribution Margin	Markup %	Contribution Margin %
Chanel No. 5 ($85/½ oz.)	−1.1	11.00 MC	10.00 MC	1000%	91%
Whitman's Sampler ($8/lb.)	−1.86	2.16 MC	1.16 MC	116%	54%
Ole Musk ($6/4 oz.)	−12.0	1.09 MC	0.09 MC	9%	8%

[6] The gross margin definition can be applied to retail firms but not to service firms whose direct cost of goods sold is undefined by accountants. In services, the contribution margin definition of unit profit is prevalent, and activity-based costing (ABC) determines what costs are variable to a product line or an account.

Gross profit margins differ across industries and across firms within the same industry for a variety of reasons. First, some industries are more capital intensive than others. Airlines have 70–80-percent gross profit margins, not because they are particularly profitable relative to other industries, but, because airlines have high fixed costs; the capital asset cost of the aircrafts are a large proportion of the total cost structure. An essential distinction arises, therefore, between operating profits (net income on an income statement) and net cash flow available to owners after interest and other fixed costs for capital assets have been paid. The first component of the gross profit margin percentage, then, is capital costs per sales dollar.

Second, differences in gross margins reflect differences in advertising, promotion, and selling costs. Leading brands in the ready-to-eat cereal industry have 70-percent gross margins but half of that price-cost differential (fully 35 percent of every sales dollar) is spent on advertising and promotion. The automobile industry also spends hundreds of millions of dollars on advertising but only 9 percent per sales dollar. The second component of the gross profit margin percentage is advertising and selling expenses per sales dollar.

Third, differences in gross margins arise because of differential overhead in some businesses. The pharmaceutical industry has very high gross margins, in large part because of the enormous expenditures on research and development to find new drugs. To conduct business in that product line, other pharmaceutical firms then incur patent fees and licensing costs which raise their overhead costs and set the industry-level prices. Overhead costs also may differ if headquarters salaries and other general administrative expenses are high in certain firms but not others.

Finally, after accounting for any differences in capital costs, selling expenses, or overheads, the remaining differences in gross margins do reflect differential profitability.

Example

COMPONENTS OF THE GROSS MARGIN AT KELLOGG CO.[7]

The largest box of Kellogg's Raisin Bran sells for $4.49 and has a variable-plus-direct fixed manufacturing cost of $1.63. That calculates as a (4.49 − 1.63)/4.49 = 70-percent gross margin. The margin on Frosted Flakes is 72 percent, on Fruit Loops 68 percent, and across all Kellogg's brands 55 percent. These high margins reflect brand loyalties built up over many years by massive and continuous advertising investments. On the leading brands, Kellogg spends 30 percent of each sales dollar on advertising, and adds another 5 percent on couponing, slot-in shelf space allowances, rebates, and other promotional expenses. Capital costs entail approximately 22 percent per sales dollar. Expenditures on headquarters, general administrative, R&D, and all other overheads total 8 percent. That leaves a net profit margin of about 5 percent.

Successful restaurants have almost twice the gross margin of convenience stores on food items sold (60 percent versus 32 percent), and much of that differential (perhaps 25 percent), reflects net profit. Not so in Kellogg's business where, as we have seen, most of its 70-percent gross margin goes to recover advertising, capital equipment, and other fixed costs. The much higher net profit margin in a successful restaurant is a reward for bearing high-failure risk. Long term, the incidence of success in restaurants is really quite low; three out of five lose money.

---

[7] Based on "Cereals," *Winston-Salem Journal*, March 8, 1995, p. A1, and "Denial in Battle Creek," *Forbes*, October 7, 1996, pp. 44–46.

Monopoly and Capacity Investment

Because monopolists do not face the discipline of strong competition, they install excess capacity or, alternatively, fail to install enough capacity. Indeed, a monopolist seeking to restrain entry of new competitors into the industry may install excess capacity that can be used to credibly threaten to flood the market with supply and lower prices, thus making entry less attractive to potential competitors. Even in regulated monopolies such as electric utility companies, considerable evidence shows that regulation often provides incentives for a firm to overinvest or underinvest in generating capacity. Because utilities are regulated so that they have an opportunity to earn a "fair" rate of return on their assets, if the allowed return is greater (less) than the firm's true cost of capital, there is an incentive to overinvest (underinvest) in new plant and equipment.

Limit Pricing

Maximizing *short-run* profits by setting marginal revenue equal to marginal cost in order to yield an optimal output of Q_1 and an optimal price of P_1 may not necessarily maximize the *long-run* profits (or shareholder wealth) of the firm. By keeping prices high and earning monopoly profits, the dominant firm encourages potential competitors to commit R&D or advertising resources in an effort to obtain a share of these profits. Instead of charging the short-run profit-maximizing price, the monopolist firm may decide to engage in *limit pricing*, where it charges a lower price, such as P_L in Figure 11.4, in order to discourage entry into the industry by potential rivals.

Figure 11.4   Limit-Pricing Strategy

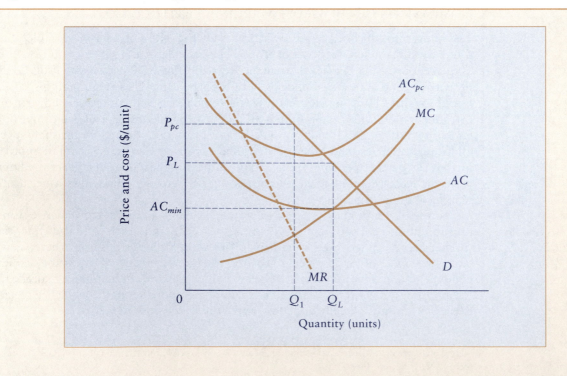

Figure 11.5   Effect of Pricing Strategies on Profit Streams as a Patent Expires

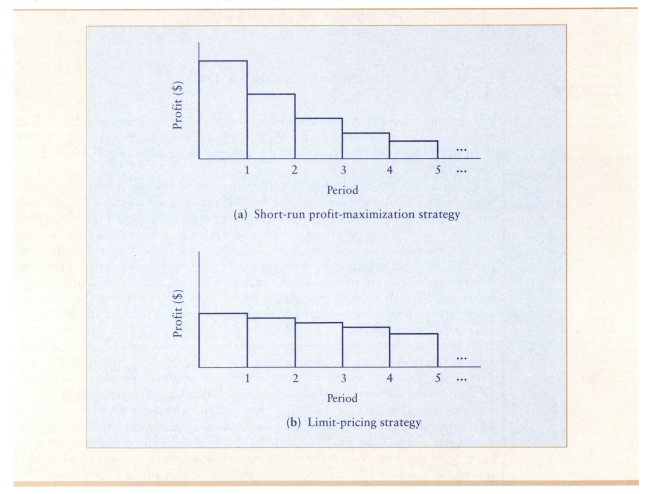

(a) Short-run profit-maximization strategy

(b) Limit-pricing strategy

With a limit-pricing strategy, the firm forgoes some of its short-run monopoly profits in order to maintain its monopoly position in the long run. The limit price, such as P_L in Figure 11.4, was set below the minimum point on a potential competitor's average total cost curve, (AC_{pc}). The appropriate limit price is a function of many different factors.[8]

The effect of the two different pricing strategies on the dominant firm's profit stream is illustrated in Figure 11.5. By charging the (higher) short-run profit-maximizing price, the firm's profits are likely to decline over time at a faster rate (Panel *a*) than by charging a limit price (Panel *b*). The firm should engage in limit pricing if the present value of the profit stream from the limit-pricing strategy exceeds the present value of the profit stream associated with the short-run profit-maximization rule of equating marginal revenue and marginal cost. Such a decision is more likely the higher the discount rate is. Choosing a high discount rate will place relatively higher weight on near-term profits in the calculation of present discounted value

---

[8] The limit-pricing model illustrates the importance of *potential* competition as a control device on existing firms. See D. Carlton and J. Perloff, *Modern Industrial Organization,* 3d ed. (New York: Harper-Collins, 1999), Chapter 10, for an expanded discussion of the limit-pricing concept.

and relatively lower weight on profits that occur further into the future. A high discount rate is justified when the firm's long-term pricing policy, and hence profits, are subject to a high degree of risk or uncertainty. The higher the risk, the higher is the appropriate discount rate.

LIMIT PRICING TO DISCOURAGE GENERIC DRUGS: BRISTOL-MYERS SQUIBB[9]

Patent protection is the key to financial success in the pharmaceutical industry. The typical patented drug emerges from tests on 250 chemical compounds, requires 15 years of research and FDA approval processes, and accumulates total costs of entry averaging $350 million.

Capoten is Bristol-Myers Squibb's (BMS) hypertension drug for use in reducing heart-attack risk. Rather than limit pricing, BMS maintained Capoten's 57-cents-per-pill price right to the end of its 20-year patent protection in February 1996. Competition from generics selling for 3 cents per pill was swift and disastrously effective. BMS introduced its own generic product which cannibalized sales of the branded product still further. By the fourth quarter of 1996, Capoten sales had collapsed to $25 million from $146 million the year before. BMS and other leading pharmaceutical companies are merging to realize economies of scale in R&D in the hope that a full pipeline of follow-on drugs with improved efficacy or reduced side effects can restore their profitability.

In contrast, Eli Lilly and Schering-Plough chose limit pricing and advertising for their leading medications, the antidepressant Prozac and the allergy treatment Claritin. Prozac lost patent protection in 2001, and Claritin in 2003. One reason Schering-Plough chose a different (limit) pricing strategy is that Claritin has no improved follow-on drug available, the FDA has demoted the prescription-only product to over-the-counter status at an identical dosage, and as a consequence $100-per-month-per-patient revenue was projected to decline to $9 if short-run profit maximization continued. At a gross profit margin of 79 percent, Schering-Plough was facing a monumental loss of $2.1 billion in operating profits on $2.7 billion in Claritin sales.

In general, new biotechnologies have allowed imitation pharmaceuticals to appear much faster in the 1990s than in earlier decades. Indeed, the first hypertension drug, Inderal, enjoyed almost a decade from 1968–1977 of pure monopoly sales before Capoten was introduced. Prozac, on the other hand, met competition from imitators within four years of its 1988 introduction. And Recombinate, a breakthrough drug for hemophiliacs newly patented in 1992, encountered copycat products by 1994. Tactics like limit pricing become all the more important in the presence of such quick and relatively easy imitation by fast-second competitors.

REGULATED MONOPOLIES

Several important industries in the United States operate as regulated monopolies. In broad terms, the regulated monopoly sector of the American economy includes **public utilities** such as electric power companies, natural gas companies, and communications companies. In the past, much of the transportation industry (airlines,

---

[9] Based on "Too Clever by Half," *The Economist,* September 20, 1997, p. 68; "Time's Up," *Wall Street Journal,* August 12, 1997, p. A1; "Industry Merger Wave Heads to Europe," *Wall Street Journal,* November 12, 1999, p. A15; "Wearing Off: Schering-Plough Faces A Future Without Claritin," *Wall Street Journal,* March 22, 2002, p. A1.

trucking, railroads) also were regulated closely, but these industries have been substantially deregulated over the past 10 to 25 years.

Electric Power Companies

http://
Access the Federal Energy
Regulatory Commission
Internet site at
http://www.ferc.gov/

Investor-owned electric power companies make up one large industry subject to economic regulation. Electric power is made available to the consumer through a production process characterized by three distinct stages. First, the power is generated in generating plants. Next, in the transmission stage, the power is transmitted at high voltage from the generating site to the locality where it is used. Finally, in the distribution stage, the power is distributed to the individual users. The complete process may take place as part of the operations of a single firm, or the producing firm may sell power at wholesale rates to a second enterprise that carries out the distribution function. In the latter case, the distribution firm often is a department within the municipal government serving the locality or a consumers' cooperative.

Firms producing electric power are subject to regulation at several levels. Integrated firms carrying out all three stages of production are usually regulated by state public utility commissions. These commissions set the rates to be charged to the final consumers. The firms normally receive exclusive rights to serve individual localities through franchises granted by local governing bodies. As a consequence of their franchises, electric power companies have well-defined markets within which they are the sole provider of output. Finally, the Federal Energy Regulatory Commission (FERC) has the authority to set rates on power that crosses state lines and on wholesale power sales. Some states are continuing to partially or totally deregulate the power production and transmission elements of this industry. The California crisis with deregulated electricity raises questions about the desirability of fully deregulated competition at the retail (distribution) level.[10]

Natural Gas Companies

A second energy industry with extensive regulation is the natural gas industry. The furnishing of natural gas to users also includes a three-stage process. The first stage is the production of the gas in the field. Transportation to the consuming locality through pipelines is the second stage. Distribution to the final user makes up the third stage. The FERC historically set the field price of natural gas that is to be moved out of the production stage. The regulation of natural gas prices at the wellhead has been effectively phased out. In addition, the FERC oversees the interstate transportation of gas by approving pipeline routes and by controlling the wholesale rates charged by pipeline companies to distribution firms. The distribution function may be carried out by a private firm or by a municipal government agency. In either event, the rates charged to final users also are controlled because the distribution firm often has a monopoly in its service area.

Communications Companies

In the communications industry, the most important activities are the provision of radio, cable, television, and telephone service regulated by the Federal Communications Commission (FCC). Local service in the intrastate markets, which may

[10] See M. Maloney, R. McCormick, and R. Sauer, *Consumer Choice, Consumer Value: An Analysis of Retail Competition in America's Electric Utility Industry,* Washington, DC, Citizens for a Sound Economy, 1996; "Electric Utility Deregulation Sparks Controversy," *Harvard Business Review,* May/June 1996; and A. Faruqui and K. Eakin, eds., *Pricing in Competitive Electricity Markets,* Boston: Kluwer, 2000.

WHAT WENT RIGHT   WHAT WENT WRONG

Public Service Company of New Mexico

The Public Service Company of New Mexico (PNM) provides electric power service (generation and distribution) and natural gas distribution services to the majority of the population of New Mexico. This monopoly position is regulated by the Public Service Commission of the State of New Mexico and, to a lesser extent, by the Federal Energy Regulatory Commission. These commissions determine the rates the company may charge its various classes of customers for the services that are provided. The rates are intended to be based on the cost of providing service, including a "fair return" on the capital invested.

PNM earned a 4.9 percent return on common equity during 1992, 8.0 percent on common equity during 1995, and 7.5 percent on common equity between 1997 and 1999. The industry average return on equity was 11 to 12 percent, according to *Value Line*. PNM earned extraordinarily low returns even though PNM is authorized by its regulatory commission to charge rates consistent with its earning a return of 12.5 percent on common equity. Why has this monopoly supplier of utility services (and many other utility companies) been unable to earn its authorized return?

During the 1970s, PNM experienced high growth in the demand for its services as the Sunbelt prospered and industry grew in the region. One large user of power was the growing uranium mining industry in New Mexico that was serving the needs of nuclear power plants being built by other electric utilities. Faced with rapid growth in demand and increasing costs for its traditional fuel, natural gas, PNM embarked on a major program to expand and modernize its power-generating capacity. As the managers of the utility planned for the future, they made projections of future demand. PNM's managers examined a number of alternatives to meet the growing demand, including purchasing power from nearby utilities, building large coal-fired plants close to New Mexico's abundant coal resources, and building nuclear power plants. The objective of PNM's management was to meet the projected demand at the lowest cost. Having seen what hap-

pened to the price of natural gas in the early 1970s, these managers also were aware of the desirability of having a diverse mix of fuel sources. PNM ultimately decided to participate with other regional utilities in the construction of several large coal-fired plants in the Four Corners region of northwest New Mexico, to build additional coal-fired plants of its own, and to participate with other utilities in the construction of a five-unit nuclear power plant called Palo Verde.

As time passed, load growth did not materialize as expected. In the aftermath of the disaster at Three Mile Island, demand for uranium ore declined and lower cost alternative sources were developed. The New Mexico uranium mining industry virtually shut down. The state of New Mexico required that expensive pollution control devices, called scrubbers, be installed at the coal plants being constructed, thereby dramatically increasing their cost and the cost of power produced from these plants. The Palo Verde project was plagued by cost overruns, delays, and extensive and costly safety modifications. Ultimately, two of the five units of Palo Verde were canceled. When the construction program was completed, PNM found itself with capacity nearly 80 percent in excess of peak demand (a 20-percent reserve margin is more normal).

The regulatory process facing utilities does not ensure that a company will earn its authorized returns. Consequently, the New Mexico state regulatory commission has refused to permit PNM to recover the costs of this excess capacity in rates charged to its present customers. Even in the absence of regulation, PNM would probably be unable to fully recover the costs of this excess capacity.

http://

Financial information on the Public Service Company of New Mexico, and on electric industry restructuring in New Mexico, is available on the following Internet site:
http://www.pnm.com/

be provided either by one of the former Bell System companies or by one of the so-called local telephone independents, is regulated by state commissions. Radio station ownership has become very concentrated; perhaps 70 percent of the stations in the top 100 markets are now controlled by two companies.

THE ECONOMIC RATIONALE FOR REGULATION

The preceding brief survey of the regulated sector reveals the crucial nature of the regulated industries: They furnish services that are critical to the functioning of the economy. Apart from this factor, do the regulated industries share any other common characteristics that account for the regulation imposed on them? This question can be answered by considering the major reasons cited as justifications for instituting economic regulation.

Natural Monopoly Argument

Natural Monopoly
An industry in which maximum economic efficiency is obtained when the firm produces, distributes, and transmits all of the commodity or service produced in that industry. The production of natural monopolists is typically characterized by increasing returns to scale throughout the range of output demanded by the market.

It is asserted frequently that the firms operating in the regulated sector are **natural monopolies,** indicating that a tendency exists for a single supplier to emerge because of a production process characterized by increasing returns to scale. Increasing returns to scale imply that as all inputs are increased by a given percentage, the average total cost of a unit of output decreases. Consequently, the long-run unit cost of output declines throughout the range of output levels that are relevant. This situation is illustrated in Figure 11.6 for a firm in long-run stable equilibrium.

Suppose that the market demand curve for output is represented by the curve DD in Figure 11.6. The socially optimal level of output would then be Q^*; at that level of output, price would be well below the average total cost per unit AC^* but equal to short-run and long-run marginal cost. A single producer is able to realize economies of scale that are unavailable to firms in the presence of competition. From a social perspective, competition would result in inefficiency in the form of costs like unit cost AC_C much higher than the monopoly unit cost AC_M, for a firm six times as large as the competitive comparison firm. It often is argued that if production relations exist like those in Figure 11.6, a single supplier will eventually emerge. Competing firms will realize that their costs decrease as output expands. As a consequence, they will have an incentive to cut prices as long as MR exceeds $LRMC$ to increase sales volume and spread the fixed cost. During this period, prices will be below average cost, resulting in losses for the producing firms. Unable to sustain such losses, the weaker firms gradually leave the industry, until only a single producer remains. Thus, competitive forces contribute to the emergence of the natural monopoly.

If a monopolistic position were to exist in the absence of regulation, the monopolist would maximize profit by equating marginal revenue and marginal cost at an output like Q_M, leading to a higher price P_M and lower output. Thus, intervention through regulation is required to achieve the benefits of the most efficient organization of production. In its simplest form, this is the explanation of regulation based on the existence of natural monopolies.

Example

ARE LARGE-SCALE ELECTRICITY GENERATING PLANTS BECOMING EXTINCT?

The electric utility industry in the United States long has been subject to intense regulation of its prices, service standards, and the choice of production technologies it employs. Regulation is provided by state utility commissions and the Federal Energy Regulatory Commission (FERC).

Figure 11.6   Natural Monopoly: Price-Output Determination

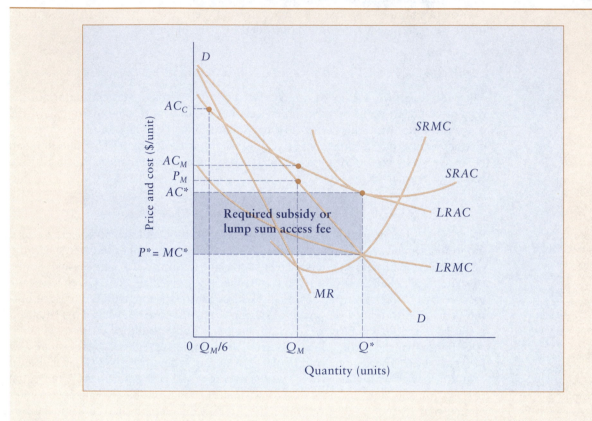

Many of the power plants constructed during the 1970s and 1980s were very large base-load generating plants using coal or nuclear energy as their fuel. During that time there was a belief that these larger plants would provide the lowest cost sources of power due to their economies of large scale. However, in some cases the final cost of these plants has greatly exceeded initial estimates.

As the electric utility industry has entered an era of deregulation and begun to face market competition, these old assumptions of economies of scale have been called into question. Independent power producers, who produce electricity for sale to utility companies or directly to end users, have built many smaller, less capital-intensive plants. These producers have realized substantial cost savings by substituting a cheap variable input, natural gas, for the expensive fixed capital equipment required in nuclear and coal-fired power plants.

Deregulation will likely accelerate this trend toward distributed generation of electricity in smaller plants with considerably less economies of scale.

Figure 11.6 illustrates one ever-present problem that arises in the presence of a genuine natural monopoly. Suppose that a regulatory agency succeeds in establishing the socially optimal price for output, P^*. As the cost curves indicate, this price would lead to losses for the producing firm, because price would be below the average total cost AC^*. This is obviously an unsustainable result. In this situation the regulating agency normally sets prices at average cost, ensuring revenues sufficient to cover all costs. The most efficient way to realize said revenue, however, is to charge a per-unit price equal to $LRMC$ (P^*) and collect the shaded deficit area in Figure 11.6 as a *lump sum* access fee, perhaps divided equally among the utilities customers. Alternatively, with time-of-day metering, the lump sum access fees can depend on when the customer uses power—higher lump sum access fees at peak periods like 4 P.M. to 8 P.M.

Peak-Load Utility Rates

When output cannot be stored in inventory, and the power utility ordinarily stands ready to satisfy whatever level of demand is imposed by users, the cost of producing a unit of output varies according to a time dimension. For simplicity, suppose that there are only two levels of demand, an afternoon peak period when the demand is high and the rest of the day (an off-peak period) when the demand is below the level of afternoon demand. Because of the way in which electricity is produced, the generating capacity required to produce power for the afternoon period stands idle for the remainder of the firm's operating cycle; that is, there is excess generating capacity except during the period when demand is at its peak. The firm can produce additional output during the morning, for instance, at a relatively low marginal cost associated with the cost of the additional fuel used. In contrast, to produce an additional unit of output during the afternoon period, the firm would have to install an additional unit of generating capacity, implying that the marginal cost of that unit of output would be quite high. Because expanding output in the peak period requires the expansion of productive capacity, the basic principle of equating prices to marginal costs suggests that peak and off-peak output be priced differently to reflect the differences in marginal cost.

To analyze what type of pricing policy is appropriate in the presence of peak loads, consider the situation shown in Figure 11.7 where two independent demand periods are assumed. In the peak period (late afternoon), demand is represented by curve D_1, whereas in the off-peak period, demand is shown by D_2. All units of output require the use of fuel at a constant rate, assumed to be b per unit. In addition, capital or generating capacity, which costs β per unit, is also required to produce all output; however, the capacity is not fully used except in the peak period.

The supply curve relevant for determining price and output during the late afternoon is the curve $b + \beta$, which reflects the marginal (and average) cost of supplying an additional unit of output during the peak period. At price $P_1 = b + \beta$, day users are just willing to pay the cost of producing a unit of output, so this is the appropriate price for peak service. At this price, Q_1 units of output are produced, implying that Q_1 is the level of capacity installed. At what price should off-peak output be sold? Given the existence of capacity Q_1, the appropriate price of off-peak output is P_2, equal to the marginal cost of fuel alone. Providing off-peak service imposes no other costs. As a result, the price should be no higher than b per unit at which Q_2 units of output are sold.[11]

---

[11] If base-load generation has high capital costs (i.e., if $\beta > b$), peak-load pricing can induce many consumers to shift their clothes drying and some cooking to off-peak times, for example, through the use of interruptible service, or highly efficient water heaters that allow customers to heat water at night, rather than on demand. If this occurs, the peak period may be shifted to the current off-peak period. Of course, under these circumstances, the original peak-load prices will be incorrect. The solution is to charge a fraction of the capital cost during each period.

Figure 11.7 Peak-Load Pricing

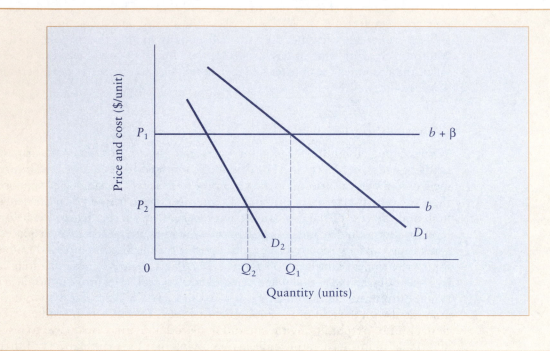

Peak-Load Pricing
The process of charging a higher price during those periods of time when demand is heaviest and lower prices when demand is light.

This simplified example illustrates the basic principles of **peak-load pricing.** This policy encourages the most efficient use of existing capacity. Notice that in the usual case, users would be expected to purchase both peak and off-peak output, since air conditioner use between 4 P.M. and 8 P.M. has very price inelastic demand.

SUMMARY

- Monopoly is a market structure with one firm producing a differentiated product in a market with significant barriers to entry.
- In a pure monopoly market structure, firms will generally produce a lower level of output and charge a higher price than would exist in a more competitive market structure. This conclusion assumes no significant economies of scale that might make a monopolist more efficient than a large group of smaller firms.
- The primary sources of monopoly power include patents and copyrights, control of critical resources, government "franchise" grants, economies of scale, and increasing returns in networks of users of compatible complementary products.
- Increasing returns from network effects are limited by input cost reductions among competitors, by innovative new product introductions, and by lobbying efforts.
- Monopolists will produce at that level of output where marginal cost equals marginal revenue if their goal is to maximize short-run profits.

- The price charged by a profit-maximizing monopolist will be in that portion of the demand function where demand is elastic (or unit elastic). The greater the elasticity of demand facing a monopolist, the lower will be its price relative to marginal cost, *ceteris paribus*.
- Contribution margins are defined as revenue minus incremental variable cost, or revenue minus marginal cost when only one unit is sold.
- *Contribution margins* and *markups* are inversely related to the price elasticity of demand.
- *Gross margins* are defined as revenue minus direct costs of goods sold (incremental variable cost plus direct fixed cost), and serve to recover capital costs, selling costs, and overhead as well as earn profits.
- Limit pricing is a strategy followed by some monopolists to discourage rivals from entering an industry. The monopolist prices its product below the short-run profit maximizing level to forestall new entry in the long run.
- Public utilities are a group of firms, mostly in the electric power, natural gas distribution, natural gas pipeline, and communications industries, that are closely regulated with respect to entry into the business, prices, service quality, and total profits.
- The rationales for public utility regulation are many. The *natural monopoly* argument is applied in cases where a product is characterized by increasing returns to scale. The one large firm can theoretically furnish the good or service at a lower cost than a group of smaller competitive firms. Regulators then set utility rates to prevent monopoly price gouging, ideally allowing the regulated firm to earn a return on investment just equal to its cost of capital.
- Price discrimination by utilities is often economically desirable on the basis of cost justifications and demand justifications.
- *Peak-load pricing* is designed to charge customers a greater amount for the services they use during periods of greater demand. Long-distance phone services typically have been priced on a peak-load basis.

EXERCISES

1. Information Resources, Inc. (IRI) collects data on consumer packaged goods at 32,000 scanner checkout counters and in panel surveys of 70,000 households. IRI records indicate that department store-brand pantyhose sell for a gross margin of 43 percent and a contribution margin of 29 percent, and the store inventory turns over 14 times per year.
    a. What expenses explain the difference between 43 percent and 29 percent?
    b. What percentage change in unit sales is required to increase total contributions if price is cut by 10 percent?
    c. Comparing the products in Table 11.1, why should Whitman's Sampler sell for a contribution margin of 54 percent when store-brand pantyhose sell for 29 percent?

2. You have been retained as an analyst to evaluate a proposal by your city's privately owned water company to increase its rates by 100 percent. The company has argued that at the present rate level, the firm is earning only a 2-percent rate of return on invested equity capital. The company believes a 16-percent rate of return is required in today's capital markets.

Assume that you agree with the 16-percent rate of return proposed by the company.

a.   What factors need to be considered when setting rates designed to achieve this objective?

b.   Would your analysis differ if you knew that individuals were prohibited by law from drilling their own wells? What impact would this have on the price elasticity of demand?

c.   Water companies have a large proportion of fixed costs as compared with variable costs. How does this fact influence your analysis?

3.   If the regulatory process is working effectively, the aggregate of all projects undertaken by a nondiversified electric utility firm should have a net present value that equals zero. Why is this true?

4.   California Electric has a cost of equity capital of 16 percent. The firm has consistently been authorized a return on equity capital below this cost. Also, the effects of regulatory lag and attrition have further reduced the realized return to the 13-percent range. If the utility expects this problem to continue, what actions would you expect Cal Electric to take or not take as a result?

5.   Ajax Cleaning Products is a medium-sized firm operating in an industry dominated by one very large firm—Tile King. Ajax produces a multiheaded tunnel wall scrubber that is very similar to a model produced by Tile King. Ajax has decided to charge the same price as Tile King to avoid the possibility of a price war. The price charged by Tile King is $20,000.

   Ajax has the following short-run cost curve:

$$TC = 800{,}000 - 5{,}000Q + 100Q^2$$

a.   Compute the marginal cost curve for Ajax.

b.   Given Ajax's pricing strategy, what is the marginal revenue function for Ajax?

c.   Compute the profit-maximizing level of output for Ajax.

d.   Compute Ajax's total dollar profits.

6.   One and Only, Inc., is a monopolist. The demand function for its product is estimated to be

$$Q = 60 - .4P + 6Y + 2A$$

where Q = quantity of units sold

   P = price per unit

   Y = per capita disposable personal income (thousands of dollars)

   A = hundreds of dollars of advertising expenditures

The firm's average variable cost function is

$$AVC = Q^2 - 10Q + 60$$

Y is equal to 3 (thousand) and A is equal to 3 (hundred) for the period being analyzed.

a.   If fixed costs are equal to $1,000, derive the firm's total cost function and marginal cost function.

b. Derive a total revenue function and marginal revenue function for the firm.

c. Calculate the profit-maximizing level of price and output for One and Only.

d. What profit or loss will One and Only earn?

e. If fixed costs were $1,200, how would your answers change for parts (a) through (d)?

7. The Lumins Lamp Company, a producer of old-style oil lamps, has estimated the following demand function for its product:

$$Q = 120,000 - 10,000P$$

where Q is the quantity demanded per year and P is the price per lamp. The firm's fixed costs are $12,000 and variable costs are $1.50 per lamp.

a. Write an equation for the total revenue (TR) function in terms of Q.

b. Specify the marginal revenue function.

c. Write an equation for the total cost (TC) function in terms of Q.

d. Specify the marginal cost function.

e. Write an equation for total profits (π) in terms of Q. At what level of output (Q) are total profits maximized? What price will be charged? What are total profits at this output level?

f. Check your answers in Part (e) by equating the marginal revenue and marginal cost functions, determined in Parts (b) and (d), and solving for Q.

g. What model of market pricing behavior has been assumed in this problem?

8. A monopolist faces the following demand function for its product:

$$Q = 45 - 5P$$

The fixed costs of the monopolist are $12 and the monopolist incurs variable costs of $5.00 per unit.

a. What is the profit-maximizing level of price and quantity for this monopolist? What will profits be at this price and output level?

b. If the government imposes a franchise tax on the firm of $10, what will be the profit-maximizing level of price, output, and profits?

c. If the government imposes an excise tax of 50 cents per unit of output sold, what is the impact on the profit-maximizing level of price, output, and profits?

d. If the government imposes a ceiling of $6 on the price of the firm's product, what output will the firm produce and what will be total profits?

9. Unique Creations has a monopoly position in the production and sale of magnometers. The cost function facing Unique has been estimated to be

$$TC = \$100,000 + 20Q$$

a. What is the marginal cost for Unique?

b. If the price elasticity of demand for Unique is currently -1.5, what price should Unique charge?

c. What is the marginal revenue at the price computed in Part (b)?

d. If a competitor develops a substitute for the magnometer and the price elasticity increases to -3.0, what price should Unique charge?

10. What motivation does a monopolist have to overinvest in plants and equipment? What factors might restrain the monopolist from such overinvesting?

11. The Public Service Company of the Southwest is regulated by an elected state utility commission. The firm has total assets of $500,000. The demand function for its services has been estimated as

$$P = \$250 - \$.15Q$$

The firm faces the following total cost function:

$$TC = \$25,000 + \$10Q$$

(The total cost function does not include the firm's cost of capital.)

a. In an unregulated environment, what price would this firm charge, what output would be produced, what would total profits be, and what rate of return would the firm earn on its asset base?

b. The firm has proposed charging a price of $100 for each unit of output. If this price is charged, what will be the total profits and the rate of return earned on the firm's asset base?

c. The commission has ordered the firm to charge a price that will provide the firm with no more than a 10-percent return on its assets. What price should the firm charge, what output will be produced, and what dollar level of profits will be earned?

12. A firm faces a demand function per day of

$$P = 29 - 2Q$$

and a total cost function of

$$TC = 20 + 7Q$$

a. Calculate the profit-maximizing price, output, and profit levels for this firm if it is not regulated.

b. If regulators set the maximum price the firm may charge equal to the firm's marginal cost, what output level will be produced and what will be the level of profits?

c. If regulators seek to equate total costs (including a fair return to invested capital) with total revenues, what output level will be produced and what price will be charged?

13. The Odessa Independent Phone Company (OIPC) is currently engaged in a rate case that will set rates for its Midland-Odessa area customer base. OIPC has total assets of $20 million. The Texas Public Utility Commission has determined that an 11-percent return on its assets is fair. OIPC has estimated its annual demand function as follows:

$$P = 3,514 - 0.08Q$$

Its total cost function (not including the cost of capital) is

$$TC = 2,300,000 + 130Q$$

a. OIPC has proposed a rate of $250 per year for each customer. If this rate is approved, what return on assets will OIPC earn?

b. What rate can OIPC charge if the commission wants to limit the return on assets to 11 percent?

c. What problem of utility regulation does this exercise illustrate?

14. In the text example "Profit Maximization: Monopoly" on page 484, show that the price elasticity of demand is in the elastic region at the profit-maximizing price and output levels of $14.65 and 107 units, respectively.

15. In this chapter you have learned about conditions that support the formation of a monopoly, as well as monopoly pricing behavior. Since 1890, monopolization of a market has been illegal in the U.S. if the monopoly power was obtained in ways that lessened existing or potential competition. Dominant firm market power obtained through better timing, ingenious business plans, innovative products, and good luck is not illegal. Read a variety of summaries of U.S. Supreme Court cases that have helped refine antitrust law on this issue at http://www.westbuslaw.com. What tests were developed by the Supreme Court to establish illegal monopolization?

http://
Monopoly and U.S. Antitrust Law

CASE EXERCISE

DIFFERENTIAL PRICING OF PHARMACEUTICALS: THE HIV/AIDS CRISIS[12]

The HIV/AIDS crisis has been called the worst pandemic since the 14th century Black Plague. The first incident of HIV/AIDS was discovered by the U.S. Centers for Disease Control in 1981. Over the next two decades, 60 million people would become infected, and 22 million would die. Most HIV/AIDS cases are reported in the developing world, where 95 percent of those with HIV live today. Beyond social welfare and humanitarian concerns, as a result of globalization and the fastest growing international business opportunities in China and India, AIDs is now everybody's business. Because the pharmaceutical industry especially relies upon governmental authority to approve formularies for reimbursement, to protect its monopoly patent rights, and to prevent importation of unauthorized, unlicensed imitation medicines, the question of how to price AIDS drugs is a very pubic issue.

Although no one has yet developed a cure for HIV, a number of companies have developed patented drugs that inhibit either the virus's ability to replicate or its ability to enter host cells. Without further drug discovery, however, the best that can be done at present once a person contracts HIV is to partially and temporarily suppress the virus, thus delaying progression of the infection. The drugs that suppress HIV are called anti-retrovirals, and the first, known as Retrovir (also known by its generic name zidovudine or AZT), was introduced in 1987 by Burroughs Wellcome (now GlaxoSmithKline) and was the only approved therapy available to treat HIV until 1991. Since then, several new anti-retrovirals have been developed by large pharmaceutical companies such as Abbott Labs, Bristol-Myers Squibb, Merck, Roche, and smaller biotech companies such as Agouron, Gilead Sciences, Triangle Pharmaceuticals, and Trimeris. Largely as a result of these drugs, the rate of increase of AIDS-related diseases (e.g., opportunistic infections) dramatically slowed in the United States from 1992–1995 and actually decreased in 1996 for the first time.

Yet, even in the early days of anti-retroviral drug development, HIV/AIDS drug pricing was a serious and contentious issue. Burroughs Wellcome faced an enormous wave of protest in the late 1980s in the U.S. and Europe over its pricing of AZT and subsequently reduced the drug's price by 20 percent in 1987 and by a further 20 percent in 1989. The core problem is the fact that the vast majority of HIV/AIDS

---

[12] E. Berndt, "Pharmaceuticals in U.S. Health Care: Determinants of Quality and Price," and M. Kremer, "Pharmaceuticals and the Developing World," *Journal of Economic Perspectives*, Fall 2002, pp. 45–90.

cases are outside what the UN classifies as "rich countries" such as the U.S. North America registered about 980,000 cases of individuals living with HIV/AIDS and fewer than 10,000 deaths due to AIDS in 2002, but the comparative numbers for sub-Saharan Africa were nearly 30 million cases and more than two million deaths in 2002. Similarly, the U.S. adult infection rate was estimated at slightly more than one half of a percent in 2002 versus almost nine percent in sub-Saharan Africa, with a high of 38.8 percent in Botswana (UN AIDS). If the affordability of HIV/AIDS drugs in the U.S. (with a GDP per capita in excess of $30,000) is a serious issue, the problem is even more acute in the hardest hit countries, whose GDPs per capita often are less than one tenth of the U.S. GDP, in many cases even below $1,000. Compounding the problem is the fact that many new AIDS drugs, especially those designed to attack the growth in drug-resistant HIV, grow ever more expensive. Trimeris and Roche introduced Fuzeon in early 2003, for example, at a wholesale price of €20,245 per annum, at least three times the price of any existing HIV/AIDS drug. The pricing decision sparked immediate protests in the U.S. and abroad. Even many providers of Medicaid, the state-based health assistance program for the indigent in the U.S. (and now the buyer of more than 50 percent of HIV/AIDS drugs in the U.S.), immediately suggested that they could not contemplate how they would possibly pay for such an expensive therapy.

GlaxoSmithKline and Roche, the leading HIV/AIDS drug manufacturers, and their cohorts now find they must balance the fiscal realities of their expensive, R&D-intensive business model against enlarged, global, corporate social responsibilities. A nation-state specific pricing policy across global markets has resulted in a tenfold differential between the highest priced market, the United States, and the price charged in the poorest countries. Glaxo and Roche management teams face many serious business-ethics issues in this highly charged environment. Is such a tenfold price differential sustainable? How does one manage the resulting problem of parallel importing and secure trade protection from unauthorized reimportation of export drugs? What should they do if even 90-percent price reductions still leave the therapies too expensive for the majority of patients in less developed countries? Will abrogation of intellectual property in the developing world threaten intellectual property protection at home? Will a public affairs backlash in high-priced markets force drug price discounts? If so, how can the massive R&D investment required for ongoing drug discovery and development be recovered? Are these companies facing such a public relations disaster that their corporate brand equity could be radically affected? What are big pharmaceutical companies corporate responsibilities in a public health crisis? Should Glaxo (or Roche) go it alone, or instead pursue collaborative strategies with other big pharmaceutical rivals?

QUESTIONS

1. Is the monopoly on patented pharmaceuticals secure? What barrier to entry prevents the reimportation into the U.S. of pharmaceuticals sold at lower prices abroad (say, in Canada)?

2. Analyze the contribution margin percentage on pharmaceuticals relative to ready-to-eat cereals. Identify three reasons why pharmaceutical margins are higher.

3. Suggest an approach to the big pharmaceutical company problem of differential pricing in the U.S., Western Europe, and Japan versus the less developed world.

12

Price and Output Determination: Oligopoly

CHAPTER PREVIEW The previous two chapters analyzed price and output decisions of firms that competed in relevant markets where there were either a large number of sellers (i.e., pure competition and monopolistic competition) or essentially no other sellers (i.e., monopoly). In pure competition, the firm made its price and output decisions independently of the decisions of other firms. The monopoly firm did not need to consider the pricing actions of rival firms, because it did not have any competitors. This chapter examines price and output decisions by firms in oligopoly market structures where there are a small number of competitors, and each firm's decisions are likely to evoke a response from one (or more) of these rival firms. To maximize shareholder wealth, each oligopoly firm must take into account these rival responses in its own decision making. Game-theoretic analysis is introduced to assist in the analysis and prediction of rival responses. In the next chapter, we extend the game-theoretic discussion to consider insights from best practice tactics.

MANAGERIAL CHALLENGE

Are Nokia's Margins on Cell Phones Collapsing?[1]

From a stodgy Finnish industrial conglomerate selling everything from rubber boots and wire cable to toilet paper and televisions, Nokia transformed itself into a relentlessly focused technology company. When Sweden's telecommunications-equipment giant Ericsson developed a cellular network across Scandinavia in the 1980s, Nokia provided the wireless but bulky radio telephones. Recognizing the strategic opportunity presented by mobile telephony, Nokia spun off other business in the 1990s to rivet its attention on the enormous market potential of a digital (not analog) cell phone. Nokia grew from 22-percent market share in 1985 (half of Motorola's 45 percent) to overtake the market leader in 1998 and sell 37 percent of the $58 billion in cell phones worldwide, relative to Motorola's 17 percent, by 2002. With huge scale economies and a snazzy branded product, Nokia's cell phone margins at 19 percent outstripped Motorola's 5 percent. Ericsson with margins at −30 percent decided to join a venture with Sony cell phones and instead focus its efforts on cell transmission towers and equipment. From 1997 to 2000, the share prices of Alcatel, Siemens, and Motorola all doubled, but Nokia's share price grew tenfold from $5 to $55.

In 2001, however, a disruptive new technology appeared. Third Generation (3G), a high-speed worldwide mobile phone network, rewrote the telecommunications landscape. European telephone company partners of Nokia went deeply into debt to pay $125 billion for 3G licenses and spent another $100 billion for 3G network equipment. Nokia's share price collapsed from $55 to $15 amidst concerns about cell phone margins.

First, the high-speed data-intensive 3G technology will allow the introduction of new wireless web products into the handset marketplace—i.e., handheld computers by Dell, pocket audiovisual terminals by Palm and Motorola, and game consoles

from Sony-Ericsson. Nokia, NEC, and Panasonic have introduced an innovative cell phone with a built-in digital camera. Second, it's not about voice messaging anymore; these enhanced mobil phones will create value principally through their software applications provided by third-party independent software vendors (ISVs). And the ISVs will want their share of the gross margins that have made Nokia so profitable. In contrast, the power of these ISV suppliers was virtually nonexistent in the voice-only mobile phone business. Third, the developed world is nearly saturated with wireless services, which are achieving 60 percent penetration in some North American and European markets, and demand will consequently be growing at only 10 percent over the next few years, despite Nokia's projections of 25 percent. Furthermore, the next growth spurt in sales will likely come from China and Latin America, where Nokia will have to compete against or ally itself with well-connected or even nationalized telephone companies. This increased power of buyers will also reduce gross margins relative to the situation in the fragmented markets of North America and Western Europe. Fourth, the threat of entry is very real; two Japanese consumer electronics manufacturers, NEC and Panasonic, have adapted the same 3G technology into the first wireless Internet devices. Finally, Nokia's very substantial brand equity is likely to pose a low barrier to entry with these new devices that will likely involve unobtrusive headsets and otherwise remain hidden in pockets.

Should Nokia invest heavily in 3G infrastructure and product design? If not, what should they do?

---

[1] Based on "Nokia: A Finish Tale," *The Economist*, October 14, 2000, pp. 83–85; "Is Nokia's Star Dimming?" *BusinessWeek*, January 22, 2001, pp. 66–72; and "Nokia Widens Gap," *Wall Street Journal*, August 20, 2002, p. B6.

OLIGOPOLISTIC MARKET STRUCTURES

An oligopoly is characterized by a relatively small number of firms offering a product or service. The product or service may be differentiated, as in soft drinks, cereals, and athletic shoes, or relatively undifferentiated, as in airlines, crude oil, aluminum, and cement. The distinguishing characteristic of oligopoly is that the number of firms is small enough that actions by any individual firm in the industry on price, output, product style or quality, introduction of new models, and terms of sale have a perceptible impact on the sales of other firms in the industry. Thus, the distinctive feature of oligopoly is the easily recognizable interdependence among the firms in the industry. Each firm is aware in its decision making that any new move, such as introducing a price cut or launching a large promotional campaign, is likely to evoke a countermove from its rivals.

In all oligopoly markets, rival response expectations are therefore the key to firm-level analysis. If rival firms are expected to match price increases and price cuts as in airlines, a share-of-the-market demand curve may characterize adequately the sales response to the pricing initiatives of one of the firms (such as Southwest Airlines); see Figure 12.1, Panel (a). On the other hand, if rival firms are slow to match price increases and cuts, oligopolists can discount to gain share and will lose share in response to price hikes. In some markets like I-beam steel, rivals match price cuts but ignore price increases. Consequently, Nucor faces a much more price elastic demand above the going equilibrium price than the share-of-the-market demand below that price. These asymmetric rival response expectations lead to kinked oligopoly firm demand schedules examined at length later in the chapter and illustrated in Figure 12.1, Panel (b).

Oligopoly in the United States: Relative Market Shares

Much of U.S. industry is best classified as oligopolistic in structure with a wide range of industry configurations. At one extreme are the markets for digital printers, tea, shaving razors, and athletic shoes where Hewlett-Packard (49 percent), Lipton

Figure 12.1   Rival Response Expectations Determine Firm Demand

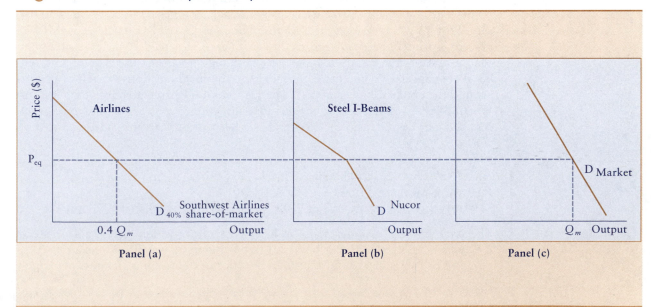

(37 percent), Gillette (70 percent), and Nike (47 percent) are all several times larger than their next largest competitors (see Table 12.1).

Example

HEWLETT-PACKARD DOMINANCE IN PRINTERS[2]

The computer industry has spawned three very evenly distributed share distributions in personal computers, computer storage devices, and database software, but in printers, Hewlett-Packard leads a pack of distant followers. At 49-percent market share, sales of HP printers are five times larger than their closest rivals Xerox and Lexmark, which have 10 percent and 8 percent of the market, respectively. The HP business plan for printers calls for a razor-and-blades approach of relatively inexpensive machines followed by a long period of selling lucrative ink and toner replacement cartridges. In 2001, HP printers and supplies made $410 million in operating profits on $5 billion in sales revenue. This represents two-thirds of HP's $647 million overall profit on only one-tenth of the $49 billion in sales. Despite vicious price wars for market share in the sub-$100 and sub-$200 segments, the printer business has clearly been a cash cow for HP. On the horizon for high-end products, HP plans to launch a digital printing press to replace the plates and film required today for commercial offset printing. In the mass market targeted by Lexmark, Canon, and Epson, penetration of PCs into American households and businesses has reached a plateau, but printing volume (and therefore demand for HP supplies) may continue to grow because of the printing of digital photographs and web pages.

In crackers, beer, soft drinks, candy, and databases, not one but two firms dominate. In snack foods, Nabisco's 45-percent market share and Keebler's 22 percent overshadow Pepperidge Farms' 7 percent. Similarly, Coke and Pepsi dominate the soft drink market, and Oracle and IBM dominate the database software market. These duopoly pairs of dominant firms often study complex tactical scenarios of moves and probable countermoves. In still other cases, three firms circle warily, planning their tactical initiatives and retreats: tires (Goodyear 28 percent, Bridgestone/Firestone 21 percent, Michelin 23 percent); batteries (Duracell 44 percent, Energizer 33 percent, Rayovac 11 percent); cereals (Kellogg 30 percent, General Mills 30 percent, Post 13 percent); long-distance telephone service (AT&T 43 percent, MCI 26 percent, Sprint 12 percent); and credit cards (Visa 51 percent, MasterCard 25 percent, and American Express 18 percent). Although no airline has a dominant market share nationally, a number of airlines have dominant positions at various airports around the country. For example, American has a 64-percent share at Dallas/Fort Worth, Northwest has an 80-percent share at Minneapolis/St. Paul and a 73-percent share at Detroit, and US Airways has a 94-percent share at Charlotte.

Example

AIRLINES DECONCENTRATE WHILE CABLE AND RETAIL GASOLINE FIRMS CONSOLIDATE: SOUTHWEST AIRLINES, AT&T BROADBAND, AND EXXON/MOBIL

The static market share distributions in Table 12.1 are seldom very stable. Instead, the dynamics of the share distribution often tell important insights. For example, over the ten-year period 1992–2002, the rank order of the leading airlines was largely

---

[2] Based on "HP Sees Room for Growth in Printer Market," *Wall Street Journal*, June 28, 2001, p. B10.

Table 12.1   Largest U.S. Market Shares in Oligopolistic Industries

Shaving Razors and Blades (2002)

Gillette	70%
Schick	20
Bic	5

Digital Printers (2001)

Hewlett-Packard	49%
Xerox	10
Lexmark	8
IBM	4
Canon	3

Athletic Shoes (1998)

Nike	47%
Reebok	16
Adidas	7

Tea (2001)

Lipton	37%
Celestial Seasonings	10
Bigelow	10
Tetley	10
Luzianne	6

Crackers (1998)

Nabisco	45%
Keebler	22
Pepperidge Farm	7
Private Label	6

Confectionary (2002)

Hershey	30%
Mars	17
Wrigley	7
Nestlé	7

Database Software (1999)

IBM	36%
Oracle	30
Microsoft	10

U.S. Beer (2001)

Anheuser-Busch	49%
Miller	20
Coors	11
Pabst	4
Heineken	3

Soft Drinks (2003)

Coca-Cola	44%
PepsiCo	32
Cadbury Schweppes	16

Tires (2003)

Goodyear/Sumitomo	28%
Michelin	23
Bridgestone/Firestone	21

Batteries (1999)

Duracell	44%
Energizer	33
Rayovac	11

Tobacco (2001)

Phillip Morris	49%
R.J. Reynolds	24
Brown and Williamson	15

Credit Cards (1999)

Visa	51%
MasterCard	25
American Express	18

Textbooks (2002)

Pearson	27%
Thomson	22
McGraw-Hill	13

Long-Distance Telephone (1999)

AT&T	43%
MCI/WorldCom	26
Sprint	12
Qwest	7

U.S. Autos (2001)

General Motors	28%
Ford	25
DaimlerChrysler	16
Toyota	10
Honda	8

Trucks (2001)

Freightliner	30%
International	17
Mack	13
Peterbuilt	12
Kenworth	11
Volvo Truck	10

Music Recording (2001)

Universal/Polygram	23%
Sony	15
EMI	13
Warner	12
BMG	8

Personal Computers (2000)

Dell	20%
Compaq	17
HP	11
Gateway	9
IBM	6

Computer Storage (2002)

EMC	34%
Compaq	21
IBM	16
Sun	11
HP	9

Wireless (2002)

Verizon Wireless	30%
Cingular Wireless	22
AT&T Wireless	20
Sprint PCS	14
Nextel	10
Voicestream	6

Sources: "Industry Surveys," *Net Advantage Database,* Standard & Poor's; and *Market Share Reports,* Gale Research, annual issues.

Market Share Distributions over Time in Airlines, Cereals, and Cell Phones

Airlines				Cereals				Cell Phones			
1992		**2002**		**1993**		**1999**		**1998**		**2002**	
American	21%	American	19%	Kellogg	35%	Kellogg	30%	Motorola	25%	Nokia	37%
United	20	United	17	General Mills	25	General Mills	30	Nokia	20	Motorola	17
Delta	15	Delta	15	Post/Nabisco	18	Post/Nabisco	13	Ericsson	15	Samsung	10
Northwest	14	Northwest	11	Quaker	8	Private Label	11	Samsung	6	Siemens	9
Continental	11	Continental	9	Private Label	6	Ralston	7	Panasonic	5	Sony/Ericsson	5
US Airways	9	Southwest	7	Ralston	5	Quaker	6	Siemens	5		

Sources: *Wall Street Journal,* December 21, 2001, p. A8; December 27, 1996, p. A3; October 16, 1998, p. B4; and August 20, 2002, p. B6.

unchanged, but every one of the major hub-and-spoke carriers (except Delta) lost two to three share points to the point-to-point discounters Southwest and America West (see data above). In cereals, General Mills' new product introductions continued to take share points from Kellogg during 1993–1999, but it was Post/Nabisco who was the big loser to private-label discount cereals (Kroger Raisin Bran) and their contract supplier Ralston/Purina. In cell phones, Nokia marched toward market share dominance during 1998–2002 while Motorola's slide continued, and Ericsson refocused on supplying cellular network equipment.

In cable systems and retail gasoline, consolidation occurred. The top six cable companies had 2 million to 11 million subscribers in 1995, whereas by 2001 the top six had 5 million to 16 million subscribers. See Figure 12.2. Although the total industry subscription base grew by 29 percent over this time period from 47 to 61 million, the top six grew by 65 percent from 32 to 53 million. Consequently, the top six cable operators were 66 percent of the total industry in 1995 and 87 percent of the total industry in 2001. Massive consolidation also occurred in retail gasoline, where company after company sought a large partner with whom to merge. Scale economies in exploration and development as well as the closing of duplicatory, redundant gas stations drove the trend.

Finally, on the right-hand side of Table 12.1, note several industries where the share distributions are more equal but where the strong interdependencies between leading firms, so characteristic of oligopoly, remain prominent in each firm's business planning. In telephone service, the regional phone companies created by the breakup of AT&T (SBC Communications, Verizon, Bell South, and Quest) have become larger in market value than the long-distance carriers AT&T, MCI/WorldCom, and Sprint who engage in nearly continuous price wars. Sales in the U.S. auto and truck markets are very dispersed across five or six companies. And in four industries heavily influenced by the disruptive technology of Internet computing (namely, music recording, PCs, computer file storage devices, and wireless system operators), the forces of competition have dispersed the shares across a half dozen firms.

INTERDEPENDENCIES IN OLIGOPOLISTIC INDUSTRIES

The nature of interdependencies in oligopolistic industries can be illustrated using an airline pricing example.

Figure 12.2   Relative Size in Cable and Gasoline

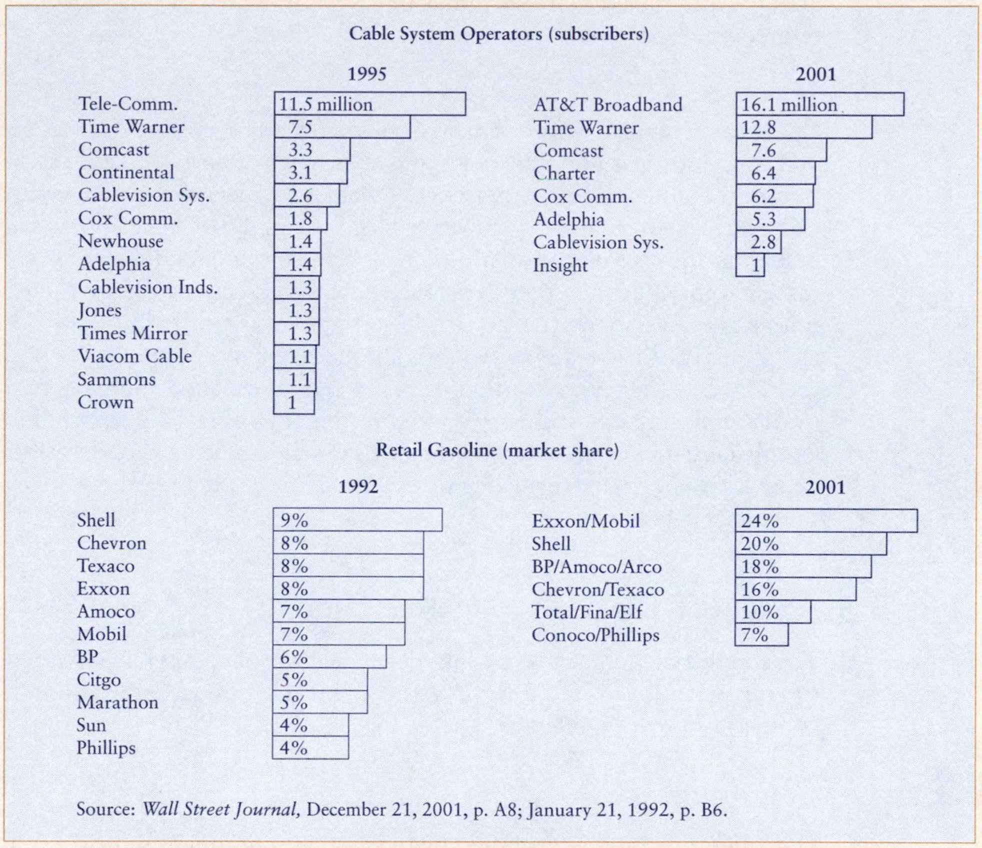

Cable System Operators (subscribers)

1995		2001	
Tele-Comm.	11.5 million	AT&T Broadband	16.1 million
Time Warner	7.5	Time Warner	12.8
Comcast	3.3	Comcast	7.6
Continental	3.1	Charter	6.4
Cablevision Sys.	2.6	Cox Comm.	6.2
Cox Comm.	1.8	Adelphia	5.3
Newhouse	1.4	Cablevision Sys.	2.8
Adelphia	1.4	Insight	1
Cablevision Inds.	1.3		
Jones	1.3		
Times Mirror	1.3		
Viacom Cable	1.1		
Sammons	1.1		
Crown	1		

Retail Gasoline (market share)

1992		2001	
Shell	9%	Exxon/Mobil	24%
Chevron	8%	Shell	20%
Texaco	8%	BP/Amoco/Arco	18%
Exxon	8%	Chevron/Texaco	16%
Amoco	7%	Total/Fina/Elf	10%
Mobil	7%	Conoco/Phillips	7%
BP	6%		
Citgo	5%		
Marathon	5%		
Sun	4%		
Phillips	4%		

Source: *Wall Street Journal,* December 21, 2001, p. A8; January 21, 1992, p. B6.

Source: *Wall Street Journal,* July 9, 1998.

Example

AIRLINE PRICING: THE PITTSBURGH MARKET

Consider the case of the airline route between Pittsburgh and Dallas. One can fly this route on a number of different airlines, but only American and US Airways offer nonstop service between these cities. (Flights on other airlines require a stopover and change of planes, which many travelers prefer to avoid, if possible.) Prior to the introduction of American's new fare, both airlines were charging $1,054 for a round-trip coach-class ticket. American's new fare was $640, a reduction of $414. US Airways was then faced with the decision of whether to maintain its current $1,054 fare (or some other fare above American's new fare), match American's new $640 fare, or undercut American's $640 fare. American's demand function (and revenues) in the Pittsburgh-Dallas market depended on the reaction of US Airways to the fare reduction. A decision by US Airways to charge a higher fare (e.g., the current $1,054 fare) would result in additional market share for American, because many travelers would choose American's lower-priced service. A decision by US Airways to match American's new fare would result in American retaining its existing market share on the Pittsburgh-Dallas route. However, depending on the price elasticity of demand and the mix of full fare and discounted tickets sold, the price reduction could actually increase American's revenues and profits. Finally, a decision by US Airways to undercut American's new $640 fare would lead to a lower market share and a likely further price reduction by American. The above analysis obviously can get much more complicated when there are more than two competitors under consideration.

These recognizable interdependencies can lead to varying degrees of competition and cooperation among the oligopolistic firms. At one extreme is the case of intense rivalry (i.e., no cooperation), where a firm may seek to drive its competitor(s) out of business. Alternatively, some form of informal, or tacit, cooperation may take place among the oligopolistic firms—"conscious parallelism of action"—with respect to pricing and other decisions.[3] NASDAQ security dealers have been accused of this type of cooperative pricing in setting bid-ask spreads.[4] At the other extreme is a formal collusive agreement among the firms to act as a monopoly cartel (like the OPEC oil cartel) by setting prices to maximize total industry profits. Because of the wide scope of industry configurations in Table 12.1 that fall under the oligopoly classification, several normative models can be used to describe oligopolists' competitive behavior regarding price, output, and other conditions surrounding the sale of their products.

IGNORING INTERDEPENDENCIES

The simplistic approach to the interdependency problem among oligopolists is merely to ignore it; that is, for a firm to act as if it does not exist at all and assume that competitors will do likewise.

Cournot Model

One oligopoly model, proposed by the French economist Augustin Cournot, asserts that each firm, in determining its profit-maximizing output level, *assumes that the other firm's output will not change.*

For example, suppose that two duopolists (Firms *A* and *B*) produce identical products. If Firm *A* observes Firm *B* producing Q_B units of output in the current period, then Firm *A* will seek to maximize its own profits assuming that Firm *B* will continue producing the same Q_B units in the next period. Firm *B* acts in a similar manner. It attempts to maximize its own profits under the assumption that Firm *A* will continue producing the same amount of output in the next period as Firm *A* did in the current period. In the Cournot model this pattern continues until long-run equilibrium is reached—a point where output and price are stable and neither firm can increase its profits by raising or lowering output. The following example illustrates the determination of the long-run Cournot equilibrium.

Example

COURNOT OLIGOPOLY SOLUTION: SIEMENS AND THOMSON-CSF

Suppose that two European electronics companies, Siemens (Firm *S*) and Thomson-CSF (Firm *T*), jointly hold a patent on a component used in airport radar systems. Demand for the component is given by the following function:

---

[3] See F.M. Scherer and David Ross, *Industrial Market Structure and Economic Performance*, 3d ed. (Chicago, IL: Rand McNally, 1990), pp. 339–346, for a discussion of the conscious parallelism doctrine.

[4] "U.S. Examines Alleged Price-Fixing on NASDAQ," *Wall Street Journal*, October 20, 1994, p. C1.

$$P = 1,000 - Q_S - Q_T \qquad [12.1]$$

where Q_S and Q_T are the quantities sold by the respective firms and P is the (market) selling price. The total cost functions of manufacturing and selling the component for the respective firms are

$$TC_S = 70,000 + 5Q_S + .25Q_S^2 \qquad [12.2]$$

$$TC_T = 110,000 + 5Q_T + .15Q_T^2 \qquad [12.3]$$

Suppose that the two firms act independently, with each firm seeking to maximize its own total profit from the sale of the component.

Siemens's total profit is equal to

$$
\begin{aligned}
\pi_S &= PQ_S - TC_S \\
&= (1,000 - Q_S - Q_T)\, Q_S - (70,000 + 5Q_S + .25Q_S^2) \\
&= -70,000 + 995\, Q_S - Q_T Q_S - 1.25 Q_S^2 \qquad [12.4]
\end{aligned}
$$

Note that Siemens's total profit depends on the amount of output produced and sold by Thomson (Q_T). Taking the partial derivative of Equation 12.4 with respect to Q_S yields

$$\frac{\partial \pi_S}{\partial Q_S} = 995 - Q_T - 2.50 Q_S \qquad [12.5]$$

Similarly, Thomson's total profit is equal to

$$
\begin{aligned}
\pi_T &= PQ_T - TC_T \\
&= (1,000 - Q_S - Q_T)\, Q_T - (110,000 + 5Q_T + .15Q_T^2) \\
&= -110,000 + 995 Q_T - Q_S Q_T - 1.15 Q_T^2) \qquad [12.6]
\end{aligned}
$$

Note also that Thomson's total profit is a function of Siemens's output level (Q_S). Taking the partial derivative of Equation 12.6 with respect to Q_T yields

$$\frac{\partial \pi_T}{\partial Q_T} = 995 - Q_S - 2.30 Q_T \qquad [12.7]$$

Setting Equations 12.5 and 12.7 equal to zero yields

$$2.50 Q_S + Q_T = 995 \qquad [12.8]$$

$$Q_S + 2.30 Q_T = 995 \qquad [12.9]$$

Solving Equations 12.8 and 12.9 simultaneously gives the optimal levels of output for the two firms—$Q_S^* = 272.32$ units and $Q_T^* = 314.21$ units. Substituting these values into Equation 12.1 yields an optimal (equilibrium) selling price of $P^* = \$413.47$ per unit. The respective profits for the two firms are obtained by substituting Q_S^* and Q_T^* into Equations 12.4 and 12.6 to obtain $\pi_S^* = \$22,695.00$ and $\pi_T^* = \$3,536.17$.

CARTELS AND OTHER FORMS OF COLLUSION

Cartel
A formal or informal agreement among firms in an oligopolistic industry. Cartel members may agree on such issues as prices, total industry output, market shares, and the division of profits.

Oligopolists may seek to reduce the inherent risk that exists because of the interdependencies of the industry structure by either formally or informally agreeing to cooperate or collude in decision making. Formal agreements of oligopolists are called **cartels**. In general, collusive agreements of any sort are illegal in the United States under the Sherman Antitrust Act of 1890; however, some important exceptions exist. For example, prices and quotas of various agricultural products (e.g., milk, oranges) are set by growers in many parts of the country with the approval of the federal government. The International Air Transport Association (IATA), composed of airlines flying transatlantic routes, sets uniform prices for these flights. And ocean shipping rates are set by hundreds of collusive "conferences" on each major transoceanic route.

Illegal collusive arrangements, however, have also arisen from time to time. One of the best-known modern documented cases of this type of illegal cooperation was in the electrical equipment manufacturing industry during the 1950s. Several large firms—including General Electric, Westinghouse, and Allis Chalmers—along with some of their top executives were convicted of engaging in agreements to fix prices and divide up the markets for such items as switch gear and circuit breakers.[5] Cement and paving companies as well as cardboard box manufacturers also are regularly indicted for price fixing. In a celebrated 1994 indictment, General Electric was accused of conspiring with De Beers Centenary AG to fix industrial diamond prices.[6] In the largest criminal price-fixing case ever, the grain-processing giant Archer-Daniels-Midland (ADM) pled guilty in 1996 to organizing an explicit quota and pricing system among five firms in the lysine market (see Figure 12.3); lysine is an amino acid food supplement that speeds the growth of livestock. ADM paid $100 million

Figure 12.3   Lysine Manufacturers Who Pled Guilty to Price Fixing

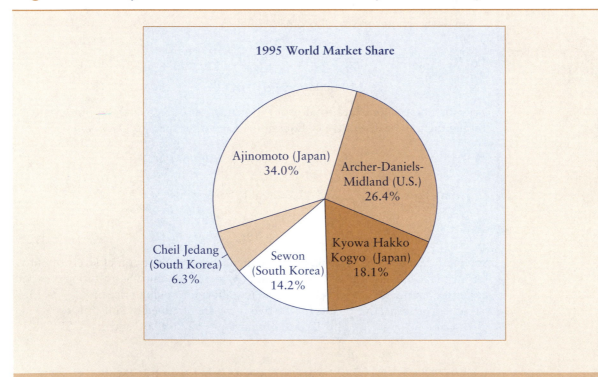

Source: *Wall Street Journal*, July 9, 1998.

[5] See "Collusion among Electrical Equipment Manufacturers," *Wall Street Journal*, January 10 and 12, 1962, reprinted in Edwin Mansfield, *Monopoly Power and Economic Performance* (New York: W.W. Norton, 1964).

[6] "GE Price-Fixing Case Won't Be Easy for Government," *Wall Street Journal*, October 20, 1994, p. B3.

in antitrust penalties, and ADM executives have gone to jail.[7] Roche and BASF, large Swiss and German industrial conglomerates in pharmaceuticals, chemicals, fragrances, and vitamins, agreed to pay $500-million and $225-million fines, respectively, to the U.S. Justice Department for their leadership of a price-fixing conspiracy in vitamin supplements. This 1999 antitrust settlement reduced Roche's profitability by 30 percent.[8] These severe penalties suggest that the inefficiencies arising from cartelization of an industry are indeed serious. Businesses that ignore the prohibition against price fixing do so at great peril.

Example

OCEAN SHIPPING CONFERENCES[9]

Since the Shipping Act of 1916, ocean freight companies have been exempted from the antitrust laws of the United States. Shipping rates on a transoceanic route are set jointly by 10 to 50 competitors acting as a "shipping conference." Two studies in 1993 and 1995 by the U.S. Agriculture Department and the FTC found that rates were 18 or 19 percent lower when ocean-shipping companies broke out of these conference arrangements and negotiated as independents. Nevertheless, the conferences maintain their market power by signing exclusive-dealing contracts with large volume customers. The enormous capacity of the shipping conferences allows more schedule frequency and greater reliability than the independents can offer. And liquidated-damages penalty clauses in these exclusive contracts remove much of the incentive for even price-sensitive cargo to seek out independent shippers. Instead, circuitous transportation plans avoid the highest rates. Polaroid, for example, ships film to Europe by first trucking 300 miles to the port of Montreal, despite the fact that the product is manufactured 20 miles from the port of Boston.

Factors Affecting the Likelihood of Successful Collusion

The ability of oligopolistic firms to engage successfully in collusion depends on a number of factors examined below:

Number and Size Distribution of Sellers   Effective collusion generally is more difficult as the number of oligopolistic firms involved increases. In the 1990s, the De Beers diamond cartel in Switzerland and South Africa was effective in part because Russia agreed in 1995 to sell 95 percent of its total wholesale supply through De Beers. De Beers's central selling organization and Russia alone accounted for over 75 percent of world supply at that time.[10]

Product Heterogeneity   Products that are alike in all significant physical and subjective characteristics are said to be homogeneous, and price is the only characteristic that matters. When products are *heterogeneous* (or differentiated), cooperation is more difficult because competition is occurring over a broad array of product

[7] "In ADM Saga, Executives Now on Trial," *Wall Street Journal,* July 9, 1998, p. B10.

[8] "Scandal Costs Roche," *Wall Street Journal,* May 25, 1999, p. A20.

[9] Based on "Making Waves," *Wall Street Journal,* October 7, 1997, p. A1; and J. Yong, "Excluding Capacity-Constrained Entrants through Exclusive Dealing: Theory and Applications to Ocean Shipping," *Journal of Industrial Economics,* Vol. 46, No. 2, June 1996; and "Shipmates," *Wall Street Journal,* February 20, 2003, p. A1.

[10] See "Disputes Are Forever," *The Economist,* September 17, 1994.

characteristics, such as durability, fashion timing, warranty, and after-sale policies. The state of Florida recently accused the leading producers of toilet tissue of illegally fixing prices for their homogeneous product. International cartels in toilet tissue are much less likely because the products are so heterogeneous around the world.

Cost Structures The more cost functions differ among competing firms, the more difficult it will be for firms to collude on pricing and output decisions. Also, successful collusion is more difficult in industries where fixed costs are a high percentage of total costs. Of course, a higher percentage of fixed costs implies higher contribution margins to recover those fixed costs. And, as we saw in Equation 10.2 in Chapter 10, higher margins imply a lower break-even sales change required to make discounting attractive. Therefore, breakdowns in collusively high prices are most notable in industries that employ highly capital-intensive production processes, such as petroleum refining, steel making, and airlines.

Size and Frequency of Orders Successful oligopolistic cooperation also depends on the size distribution over time of customer orders. Effective collusion is more likely to occur when orders are small, frequent, and received regularly. When large orders are received infrequently at irregular intervals as in the purchase of aircraft engines, it is more difficult for firms to collude on pricing and output decisions. Hence, Pratt & Whitney, Rolls-Royce, and General Electric have never colluded on jet engines, despite the fact that GE did collude with other manufacturers in hydroelectric power plant equipment.

Secrecy and Retaliation An oligopolistic firm will be less tempted to grant secret price concessions to selected customers if it feels that these price reductions will be detected, thereby provoking retaliation from other cartel members. The toilet tissue manufacturers' collusive agreement, mentioned earlier, allegedly operated through public bids for institutional customers like schools and hospitals. Sealed bids might have prevented the collusion, surprisingly.

Percentage of External Output[11] Most cartels contain the seeds of their own destruction. With increased prices and profits, cartels attract outside entry. Increased supply, external to the cartel, means larger restrictions on output for cartel members in order to sustain any given market price. At one point in 1999, De Beers had to purchase for its own inventory $3.96 billion in diamonds (in only an $8-billion market) in order to stabilize prices because so many Canadian, Australian, and Russian diamonds (external to the De Beers cartel) had entered the market.

Finally, in 2000, with 37 percent of total diamond supply outside the cartel, De Beers declared its 65-year cartel ended. Similar events led to the demise of the OPEC I cartel when Mexican, Venezuelan, and Norwegian oil flooded onto the market. Similarly, the ocean shipping prices are breaking down because the rate-setting "conferences" now control less than 70 percent of the $85-billion North Atlantic market and less than 50 percent of the $262 billion trans-Pacific market. External suppliers reduce the likelihood of successful collusion to stabilize prices above their competitive level.

---

[11] Based on "De Beers to Abandon Monopoly," *Wall Street Journal*, July 13, 2000, p. A20, and "Atlantic Ocean Shipping Cartel Makes Concessions," *Wall Street Journal*, February 7, 1997, p. A2.

Cartel Profit Maximization and the Allocation of Restricted Output

Under both legal cartels and secret collusive agreements, an attempt is made to increase prices and profits above the level that would prevail in the absence of collusion. The profit-maximization solution for a two-firm cartel, E and F, is shown graphically in Figure 12.4. The *industry* demand, D, marginal revenue, MR, and marginal cost, ΣMC, curves are shown in the last panel to the right. The industry marginal cost curve is obtained by summing horizontally across outputs the marginal cost curves of the individual firms in the center and left-hand panels—that is, $\Sigma MC = MC_E + MC_F$. Total industry profits are maximized by setting total industry output (and consequently price) at the point where industry marginal revenue equals industry marginal cost—i.e., Q^*_{Total} units of output at a price of P^* per unit.

If the cartel seeks to maximize its profits, the market share (or quota) for each firm should be set at a level such that the marginal cost of all firms is identical and at the level of the industry (summed) MC that just equates to MR. The optimal output allocation is for Firm E to produce a quota of Q^*_E units and for Firm F to produce a quota of Q^*_F units. If Firm E were producing at a level where its marginal costs exceeded Firm F's, cartel profits could be increased by shifting output from E to F until marginal costs were equal.[12]

Cartel pricing agreements are hard to reach, but the central problem for a cartel lies in monitoring these output shares or quotas. Detecting quota violations and effectively enforcing punishment schemes are nearly impossible. Consequently, most cartels are very unstable. The two longest running cartels are the Organization of Petroleum Exporting Countries (OPEC) and the De Beers diamond cartel. They have received enormous attention precisely because their longevity is so exceptional. Most cartels are like the price-fixing agreements among cardboard box manufacturers;

Figure 12.4   Price-Output Determination for a Two-Firm Cartel

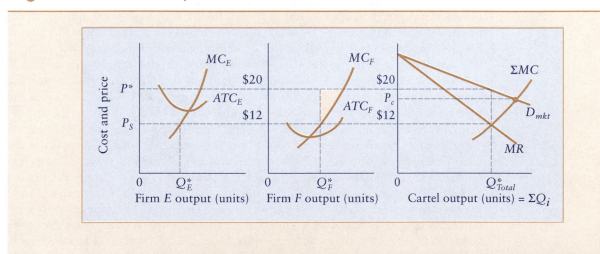

these collusive agreements form approximately once a quarter and break up within a few weeks. Let's return to Figure 12.4 and see why.

Suppose you are Firm *F* facing a cartel-determined price for crude oil P^* of $20 per barrel. Your marginal costs are presently running $12 per barrel at your assigned quota of Q_F/Q_{Total}. The Aramco pipelines, which once consolidated all your throughput from the production wells to shipping terminals, have now been superseded by numerous independent shipping terminals, many within your own nation. In addition, your crude is relatively undifferentiated from that of many other OPEC members. Should you abide by your quota commitment? Is it in your best interest to do so? The answer depends on whether your additional sales beyond quota are detectable and whether your additional output will increase total supply enough to place downward pressure on the cartel price. If the answer to both questions is no, then because a 40-percent profit margin ($8) awaits your selling another barrel, a profit maximizer will be tempted to expand output and capture the shaded area of incremental profit in the middle panel of Figure 12.4.

Of course, the problem is that other cartel members may think exactly the same way. If everyone takes the cartel price as given and independently profit maximizes, then cartel supply increases to ΣMC, and black market price must fall to the competitive level P_c of perhaps $17 just to clear the market. Enforcement of the ideal quotas Q_F and Q_E is the Achilles' heel of every cartel. In OPEC, Saudi Arabia plays a pivotal role in absorbing quota violations by other OPEC members and thereby stabilizing the cartel.

Example

OPEC MEMBERS ADOPT A NEW QUOTA AGREEMENT[13]

The high prices of the OPEC oil embargo in the early 1980s stimulated enormous increases in production in nontraditional oil-producing regions. Exploration and development took place in Mexico; Prudhoe Bay, Alaska; Russia; and the North Sea despite extraction costs three to five times higher than the $2-per-barrel exploration, development, and extraction cost in the Middle East (see Figure 12.5). In recent years, however, even OPEC members themselves have contributed to a crude oil glut on world markets. From 1987 to 2000, OPEC production rose from 18 million to 32 million barrels per day. With non-OPEC production also rising from 37 to 45 million barrels and yet consumption not increasing fast enough to absorb all these new supplies, crude oil traded in a narrow range around $24 for much of this period, but then finally plummeted to $10 in 1998–1999 (see Figure 12.6).

In an attempt to stabilize the declining prices, OPEC members agreed in March 1999 (and again in September 2000) to a production quota system. As in the cartel's heyday of the late 1970s, the largest cartel members agreed to larger cutbacks. Saudi Arabia, with a 30-percent share of OPEC output, accepted a 585,000-barrel-per-day cutback, which equals 7 percent of its February 1999 average daily production of 8.8 million barrels (see Table 12.2). Iran, with a 13-percent share, agreed to a 264,000-barrel cutback, which also equals a 7-percent reduction of its 3.6-million-barrel output. Venezuela accepted a 125,000-barrel-per-day cutback, which equals a 4-percent reduction of its 3.4-million-barrel output. Overall, these cuts plus other reductions by non-OPEC members Mexico

[13] Based on "Oil Nations Move Closer to a New Round of Cuts," *Wall Street Journal,* March 12, 1999, p. A3; "Crude Cuts: Will Oil Nations Stick or Stray?" *Wall Street Journal,* March 26, 1999, p. A19; "The Next Oil Shock," *The Economist,* March 6, 1999; "Standstill Britain," *The Economist,* September 16, 2000, p. 64; and "At OPEC Some Say There's Enough Oil," *Wall Street Journal,* September 12, 2000, p. A2.

Figure 12.5 Crude Oil Exploration, Development, and Extraction Costs, 1999 (U.S. Dollars per Barrel)

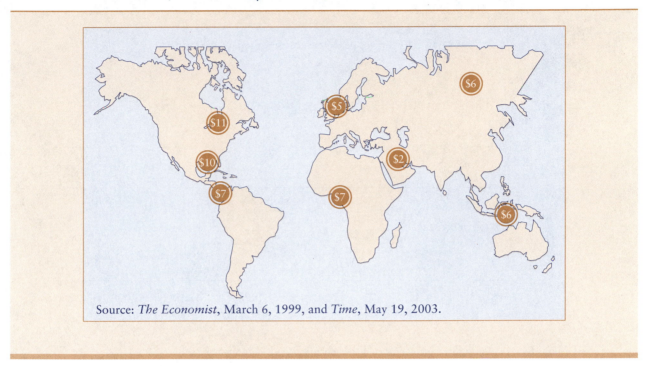

Source: *The Economist*, March 6, 1999, and *Time*, May 19, 2003.

and Norway reduced the supply on world markets by 2 million barrels per day of the 76-million-barrel-per-day world consumption. Crude oil prices responded almost immediately, rising over threefold from a $10 trough to $33 per barrel in 18 months (see Figure 12.6). The OPEC III cartel was in place.

It remains to be seen whether these cartel quotas will be violated. Since 1981, cheating has often destabilized the OPEC cartel. Saudi Arabia presently has over 2.7 million barrels per day excess capacity, and Iran, UAE, and Kuwait together have another 1.5 million barrels per day. In addition, Saudi Arabia has an enormous 262 billion barrels of known but untapped crude oil reserves, by comparison to only 30 billion barrels in the U.S. (see Table 12.2). Therefore, the Saudis prefer to discourage the emergence of energy conservation technologies in Western Europe and the United States. The last time crude prices spiked in the early 1980s, the United States responded with conservation and the development of alternative fuels, reducing energy dependency by almost half. U.S. spending on oil fell to 1.7 percent of GDP in 1995–1998 compared to 3.1 percent in 1975–1980.

Example

CARTEL PRICING AND OUTPUT DECISIONS: SIEMENS AND THOMSON-CSF

The determination of the profit-maximizing price and output levels for a two-firm cartel can also be determined algebraically when the demand and cost functions are given. Consider again the Siemens (Firm S) and Thomson-CSF (Firm T) example

Figure 12.6   Crude Oil Prices Affected by OPEC III Production Quotas

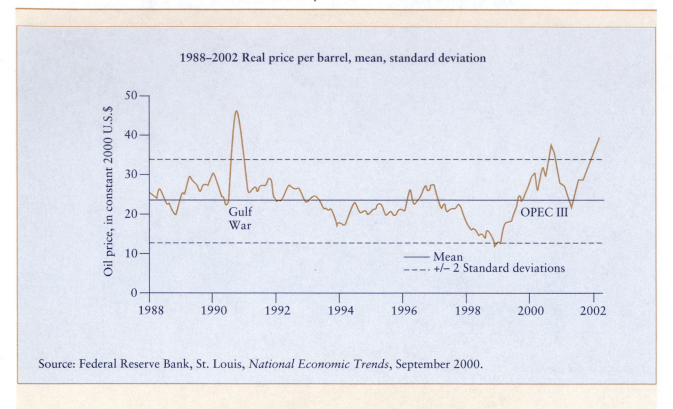

1988–2002 Real price per barrel, mean, standard deviation

Source: Federal Reserve Bank, St. Louis, *National Economic Trends*, September 2000.

discussed in the previous section. The demand function was given by Equation 12.1 and the cost functions for the two firms were given by Equations 12.2 and 12.3. Suppose that Siemens and Thomson decide to form a cartel and act as a monopolist to maximize total profits from the production and sale of the components.

Total industry profits (π_{Total}) are equal to the sum of Siemens's and Thomson's profits and are given by the following expression:

$$\pi_{Total} = \pi_S + \pi_T \qquad [12.10]$$
$$= PQ_S - TC_S + PQ_T - TC_T$$

Substituting Equations 12.1, 12.2, and 12.3 into this expression yields

$$\pi_{Total} = (1,000 - Q_S - Q_T)\,Q_S - (70,000 + 5Q_S + .25Q_S^2)$$
$$+ (1,000 - Q_S - Q_T)\,Q_T - (110,000 + 5Q_T + .15Q_T^2)$$
$$= 1,000Q_S - Q_S^2 - Q_SQ_T - 70,000 - 5Q_S - .25Q_S^2$$
$$+ 1,000Q_T - Q_SQ_T - Q_T^2 - 110,000 - 5Q_T - .15Q_T^2$$
$$= -180,000 + 995Q_S - 1.25Q_S^2 + 995Q_T$$
$$- 1.15Q_T^2 - 2Q_SQ_T \qquad [12.11]$$

To maximize π_{Total} take the *partial* derivatives of Equation 12.11 with respect to Q_S and Q_T:

Table 12.2   2001 Production, Market Share, and Known Reserves of OPEC and Non-OPEC Oil Producers

		Production (Million barrels/day)	Market Share	Reserves (Billion barrels)
O	Saudi Arabia	8.80	30%	262
P	Iran	3.65	13%	90
E	Venezuela	3.40	12%	78
C	Iraq	2.40	8%	113
	UAE	2.40	8%	98
M	Nigeria	1.98	7%	23
E	Kuwait	2.10	7%	97
M	Libya	1.43	5%	30
B	Indonesia	1.31	4%	5
E	Algeria	0.82	3%	9
R	Qatar	0.70	2%	4
S	Total	29.0 million	100%	806 billion
N	North America	14.0	31%	73.8
O	Canada	2.7	6%	4.9
N	Mexico	3.6	8%	26.9
–	United States	7.7	17%	30.4
O	Europe	6.75	15%	18.9
P	Pacific	0.8	2%	3.1
E	Russia	7.1	16%	48.6
C	Rest of World	15.80	36%	80.2
	Total	44.5 million	100%	203 billion

Source: *The Economist*, March 6, 1999; September 14, 2002, p. 26; and International Energy Agency.

$$\frac{\partial \pi_{Total}}{\partial Q_S} = 995 - 2.50 Q_S - 2 Q_T$$

$$\frac{\partial \pi_{Total}}{\partial Q_T} = 995 - 2.30 Q_T - 2 Q_S$$

Setting these expressions equal to zero yields

$$2.5 Q_S + 2 Q_T - 995 = 0 \qquad [12.12]$$
$$2 Q_S + 2.3 Q_T - 995 = 0 \qquad [12.13]$$

Solving Equations 12.12 and 12.13 simultaneously gives these optimal output levels: $Q_S^* = 170.57$ units and $Q_T^* = 284.39$ units.

Substituting these values into Equations 12.10 and 12.11 gives an optimal selling price and total profit for the cartel of $P^* = \$545.14$ per unit and $\pi_{Total}^* =$

$46,291.43, respectively. The marginal costs of the two firms at the optimal output level are equal to

$$MC_S^* = \frac{d(TC_S)}{dQ_S} = 5 + .50Q_S$$

$$= 5 + .50(170.57) = \$90.29$$

$$MC_T^* = \frac{d(TC_T)}{dQ_T} = 5 + .30Q_T$$

$$= 5 + .30(284.29) = \$90.29$$

As in the graphical solution illustrated earlier in Figure 12.2, the optimal output (or market share) for each firm in the cartel occurs where the marginal costs of the two firms are equal.

Comparison of Cartel Pricing and Cournot Equilibrium: Siemens-Thomson Example

Table 12.3 summarizes the results of the Siemens and Thomson example for the cases discussed above—(a) where the two companies acted independently to maximize their own company profits (Cournot equilibrium), and (b) where they formed a cartel to maximize total industry profits. Several conclusions can be drawn from this comparison. First, total industry output (Q^*_{Total}) is lower and selling price (P^*) is higher when the firms collude than when there is no collusion. Also, total industry profits (π^*_{Total}) are higher when the firms set prices and output jointly than when they act independently. Finally, although this may not be true in all collusive agreements, one firm's profits (i.e., Siemens's) are actually lower under the cartel solution than

---

Table 12.3   Comparison of Pricing, Output, and Profits for Siemens and Thomson

Optimal Value	(a) No Collusion: Siemens and Thomson Act Independently to Maximize Their Own Company's Profits	(b) Collusion: Siemens and Thomson Form a Cartel to Maximize Total Industry Profits
Q_S^* (Siemens's output)	272.32 units	170.57 units
Q_T^* (Thomson's output)	314.21 units	284.29 units
$Q_{Total}^* = Q_S^* + Q_T^*$ (Total industry output)	586.53 units	454.86 units
P^* (Selling price)	$413.47/unit	$545.14/unit
π_S^* (Siemens's profit)	$22,695.00	$14,858.15
π_T^* (Thomson's profit)	$3,536.17	$31,433.28
$\pi_{Total}^* = \pi_S^* + \pi_T^*$ (Total industry profit)	$26,231.17	$46,291.43

when it acts independently. Therefore, to get Siemens to participate in the cartel, Thomson probably would have to agree to share a significant part of the cartel's additional profits with Siemens.

The remainder of this section and the International Perspectives section below examine the history of two organizations that engage in collusion and effectively act as cartels.

Example

A Sports Cartel: Major League Baseball[14]

Major League Baseball (MLB), a cartel of professional team owners, has been exempted from the antitrust laws since a U.S. Supreme Court decision in 1922. MLB restricts entry, approves transfers of ownership, and regulates the selection and employment of apprentice players for their first six years in professional baseball. In 1975, Curt Flood of the St. Louis Cardinals successfully challenged baseball's restrictive labor practices (the "reserve clause") for major leaguers beyond their sixth year, and a collective bargaining agreement then granted such players free agency status. Experienced players were thereafter entitled to offer their services to the highest bidder whenever their contracts were due for renewal.

As a result, salaries skyrocketed, and star players concentrated in the biggest markets (like New York, Los Angeles, and San Francisco) where owners with larger ticket revenue, higher concession sales, and bigger television contract licensing fees offered to pay more. Even the average player profited from the end of baseball's reserve clause. Average salary for major leaguers rose in inflation-adjusted dollars from $160,000 in 1972 to $1,015,000 in 1992. Because owners spend fully 58 percent of team revenue on salaries and another 13 percent on the scouting system and the minor league apprentice teams, the MLB cartel intervened to preserve competition among the teams. When perceived competitive imbalance continued to plague the sport, MLB began a revenue-sharing system characteristic of cartels. Currently, the wealthiest teams are taxed 34 percent of total revenue to subsidize salaries for teams with a smaller fan base, either because of smaller markets (Minneapolis) or less success on the field (Montreal). One question is whether these subsidies, totaling more than $260 million in 2003, might actually provide incentives to cut payroll, rather than hire better players and attempt to attract more fans.

**International
Perspectives**

The Organization of Petroleum Exporting Countries (OPEC) Cartel

The Organization of Petroleum Exporting Countries (OPEC) was founded in 1960 by five Persian Gulf countries that were experiencing declining oil revenues as a result of the pricing practices of the integrated oil companies who had organized in 1947 as ARAMCO, a joint venture for exploration and development of the Mideast oil fields. At that time the international oil companies, which produced and marketed a large percentage of the world's oil, set the price and paid oil concession royalties. Under the terms of the ARAMCO agreement, the host nations were gradually acquiring the oil field assets at pre-arranged terms using royalty revenue, concluding their purchase in 1972.

---

[14] Based on "Let the Market Rule," *Wall Street Journal,* November 10, 1998, p. A22; "Just Not Cricket," *The Economist,* May 31, 2003, p. 34; and Gerald Scully, *The Market Structure of Sports* (Chicago: Chicago University Press, 1995).

Among OPEC's long-range goals, the most important was that member governments should determine oil prices. During 1973 and 1974, OPEC was able to achieve a unilateral fourfold increase in the world price of crude petroleum from $3 to $12 per barrel. In 1975 OPEC produced more than 80 percent of the oil traded on world markets, and its market dominance made this price increase possible. This era is often referred to as OPEC I.

OPEC is a price-fixing cartel in the sense that it sets prices at regular meetings of the oil ministers from the OPEC countries. Saudi Arabia is the most influential member of OPEC because of the tremendous size of its production capacity—almost one half of OPEC's total output at the inception of OPEC and still 30 percent of OPEC output today (see Table 12.2). All pricing decisions are voted on by the oil ministers and are supposed to be unanimous; however, during the early 1980s, the OPEC members were unable to agree on a uniform price. The price of oil ranged from $32 to $41 ($80 to $105 in 2003 dollars) per barrel among the various producing countries. OPEC I had clearly achieved its goal of restricting output enough to raise prices and profits. But Saudi Arabia and Kuwait, having large reserves expected to last well into the 22nd century, attempted to hold prices at the low end of this range to retard the development of substitute fuels. Other countries with lesser petroleum reserves (such as Libya and Iran), along with Algeria, priced their oil at the high end of the range in an attempt to maximize their returns before their oil ran out.

Rampant covert price cutting took several different forms. Nigeria, for example, engaged in secret price cutting by reducing royalties and income taxes for the oil companies working there. Other OPEC members bartered and extended payment terms for oil purchases, thereby reducing interest expenses on the funds required to finance the purchase. During the early 1980s, Saudia Arabia regularly stabilized declining oil prices by acting as a "swing producer," cutting its production to as low as 2 million barrels per day (from a high of 10 million barrels per day in 1980) when its authorized quota was 4.35 million. OPEC II ended effectively in October 1985, however, when Saudia Arabia changed its policy and began increasing its output to as much as 6 million barrels per day. Once, when the Saudis increased their output to its full capacity utilization level, prices fell to as low as $12 per barrel.[15]

OPEC now controls less than 45 percent of world oil output, and Venezuela has publicly challenged the role of Saudia Arabia as swing producer and price leader, especially in the Western hemisphere.[16] With 7-million-barrel-per-day production (see Table 12.2), Russia has posed the same challenge in other parts of the world. In spite of these problems, OPEC has managed to survive.

PRICE LEADERSHIP

Another model of price-output determination in some oligopolistic industries is **price leadership**. Many industries exhibit a pattern where one or a few firms normally set a price and others tend to follow, frequently with a time lag of a few days. In the case of basic steel products, for example, the price that prevails within a week is generally uniform from one producer to another.

Effective price leadership exists when price movements initiated by the leader have a high probability of sticking and no maverick or nonconforming firms exist. The

---

[15] *Wall Street Journal*, September 8, 1981 and "Why the Saudis Won't Back Down Soon," April 8, 1986; and J. Griffin and W. Xiong, "The Incentive to Cheat: An Empirical Analysis of OPEC," *Journal of Law and Economics*, Vol. 60, No. 2, 1997.

[16] *The Economist*, March 16, 1996, p. 68, and "Jump Start," *Wall Street Journal*, August 14, 1997.

http://

Read a speech by the Director of the Bureau of Economics, Federal Trade Commission, on horizontal price fixing and price leadership in cyberspace at the following Internet site: http://www.ftc.gov/ speeches/other/confbd4.htm

fewer the number of firms in the industry (that is, the greater the interdependencies of decision outcomes among firms), the more effective price leadership is likely to be. Two major price leadership patterns have been observed in various industries from time to time: These are *barometric* and *dominant price leadership*.

Barometric Price Leadership

In barometric price leadership, one firm announces a change in price that it hopes will be accepted by others. The leader need not be the largest firm in the industry. In fact, this leader may actually change from time to time. The leader must, however, be reasonably correct in its interpretation of changing demand and cost conditions so that suggested price changes will be accepted and stick. In essence, the barometric price leader merely initiates a reaction to changing market conditions that other firms find in their best interest to follow. These conditions might include such things as cost increases (or decreases) and sluggish (or brisk) sales accompanied by inventory buildups (or shortages) in the industry.

Example

BAROMETRIC PRICE LEADERSHIP: AMERICAN AIRLINES AND CONTINENTAL AIRLINES[17]

In the second week of March, 2002, American Airlines announced a de facto increase in business airfares. Three-day advance purchase fares were no longer available on many nonstop routes from American hubs. Instead, American returned to the old 7-day-advance-purchase requirement to obtain an initial discount of about 20 percent off full coach class (unrestricted Y class) fares of $1,629 from Dallas to New York or $1,684 from Dallas to Miami, for example. Other much cheaper Saturday overnight fares bought 7 days or even 14 days in advance were not affected since those prices are targeted primarily at leisure travelers.

American Airlines was hoping that its major competitors Continental, Delta, United, US Airways, and Northwest would take this opportunity to follow its lead and increase margins. Only Continental did so. Indeed, Northwest took advantage of the situation and promoted a steeply discounted $198 round-trip fare on exactly American's principal nonstop routes. Within a few days, American rolled back the 7-day requirement in most markets but retained them where it had a dominant hub, as at Dallas-Ft. Worth. In addition, American simultaneously announced a week of $198 fares on ten nonstop routes from United's Chicago hub, ten nonstop routes from Delta's Atlanta hub, ten nonstop routes from US Airways' Pittsburgh hub, and ten nonstop routes from Northwest's Minneapolis hub. Only Continental was spared.

Dominant Firm Price Leadership

In dominant firm price leadership, one firm establishes itself as the leader because of its larger size, customer loyalty, or lower cost structure in relation to other competing firms. The leader may then act as if it were a monopolist in its segment of the market. What is the incentive for followers to accept the established price? In some cases it may be a fear of cutthroat retaliation from a low-cost dominant firm that keeps smaller firms from attempting to undercut the prevailing price. In other cases, following a price leader may be viewed as simply a convenience.

---

[17] Based on "Airfare Skirmish Shows Why Deals Come and Go," *Wall Street Journal*, March 19, 2002, p. B1.

Figure 12.7   Dominant Price Leadership

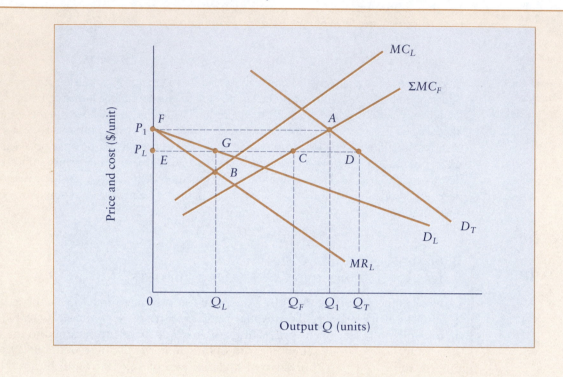

The price-output solution for the dominant-firm model is shown in Figure 12.7. D_T shows total market demand for the product, MC_L represents the marginal cost curve for the dominant (leader) firm, and ΣMC_F constitutes the horizontal *summation* of the marginal cost curves for the follower firms, each of which may well have costs higher than MC_L. In the following analysis, *assume that the dominant firm sets the price knowing that follower firms will sell as much output as they wish at this price. The dominant firm then supplies the remainder of the market demand; i.e., the residual demand in the dominant firm's segment of the market.*

Given that the follower firms can sell as much output as they wish at the price P_L established by the dominant firm, they are faced with a horizontal demand curve and a perfectly competitive market situation. The follower firms view the dominant firm's price P_L as their marginal revenue and maximize profits, producing that level of output where their marginal cost equals the established price. The ΣMC_F curve therefore shows the total output that will be *supplied* at various prices by the follower firms. The dominant firm's residual demand curve D_L is obtained by subtracting the amount supplied by the follower firms ΣMC_F from the total market demand D_T at each price. For example, at a price of P_L, Point G on the D_L curve is obtained by subtracting EC from ED. Other points on the D_L curve are obtained in a similar manner. At a price of P_1 the quantity supplied by the follower firms Q_1 is equal to total market demand (Point A), and the dominant firm's residual demand is therefore zero (Point F). The dominant firm's marginal revenue curve MR_L is then obtained from its residual demand curve D_L.

The dominant firm maximizes its profits by setting price and output where marginal cost equals marginal revenue. As shown in Figure 12.7, $MR_L = MC_L$ at Point B. Therefore, the dominant firm should sell Q_L units of output at a price of P_L per unit. At a price of P_L, total demand is Q_T units, and the follower firms supply $Q_T - Q_L = Q_F$ units of output.

The following example illustrates the application of these concepts.

Example

PRICE LEADERSHIP: AEROTEK

Aerotek and six other smaller companies produce an electronic component used in small planes. Aerotek (L) is the price leader. The other [follower (F)] firms sell the component at the same price as Aerotek. Aerotek permits the other firms to sell as many units of the component as they wish at the established price. The company supplies the remainder of the demand itself. Total demand for the component is given by the following function:

$$P = 10,000 - 10Q_T \qquad [12.14]$$

where

$$Q_T = Q_L + Q_F \qquad [12.15]$$

that is, total output (Q_T) is the sum of the leader's (Q_L) and followers' (Q_F) output. Aerotek's marginal cost function is

$$MC_L = 100 + 3Q_L \qquad [12.16]$$

The aggregate marginal cost function for the other six producers of the component is

$$\Sigma MC_F = 50 + 2Q_F \qquad [12.17]$$

We are interested in determining the output for Aerotek and the follower firms and the selling price for the component given that the firms are interested in maximizing profits.

Aerotek's profit-maximizing output is found at the point where

$$MR_L = MC_L \qquad [12.18]$$

Its marginal revenue function (MR_L) is obtained by differentiating the firm's total revenue function (TR_L) with respect to Q_L. Total revenue (TR_L) is given by the following expression:

$$TR_L = P \cdot Q_L \qquad [12.19]$$

Q_L is obtained from Equation 12.15:

$$Q_L = Q_T - Q_F \qquad [12.20]$$

Using Equation 12.14, one can solve for Q_T:

$$Q_T = 1,000 - .10P \qquad [12.21]$$

To find Q_F, we note that Aerotek lets the follower firms sell as much output (i.e., components) as they wish at the given price (P). Therefore, the follower firms are faced with a horizontal demand function. Hence

$$MR_F = P \qquad [12.22]$$

To maximize profits, the follower firms will operate where

$$MR_F = \Sigma MC_F \qquad [12.23]$$

Substituting Equations 12.22 and 12.17 into Equation 12.23 gives

$$P = 50 + 2Q_F \qquad [12.24]$$

Solving this equation for Q_F yields

$$Q_F = .50P - 25 \qquad [12.25]$$

Substituting Equation 12.21 for Q_T and Equation 12.25 for Q_F in Equation 12.20 gives

$$Q_L = (1,000 - .10P) - (.50P - 25)$$
$$= 1,025 - .60P \qquad [12.26]$$

Solving Equation 12.26 for P, one obtains

$$P = 1,708.3333 - 1.6667Q_L \qquad [12.27]$$

Substituting this expression for P in defining total revenue yields

$$TR_L = (1,708.3333 - 1.6667Q_L)Q_L$$
$$= 1,708.3333Q_L - 1.6667Q_L^2 \qquad [12.28]$$

Differentiating this expression with respect to Q_L, one obtains Aerotek's marginal revenue function:

$$MR_L = \frac{d(TR_L)}{dQ_L}$$
$$= 1,708.3333 - 3.3334Q_L \qquad [12.29]$$

Substituting Equation 12.29 for MR_L and Equation 12.16 for MC_L and equating the two gives the following optimality condition:

$$1,708.3333 - 3.3334Q_L^* = 100 + 3Q_L^* \qquad [12.30]$$

Solving this equation for Q_L^* yields

$$Q_L^* = 253.945 \text{ units}$$

or an optimal output for Aerotek of 253.9 units of the component. Substituting this value of Q_L into Equation 12.27 gives

$$P^* = 1,708.3333 - 1.6667 (253.945)$$
$$= \$1,285.083$$

or an optimal selling price of $1,285.08. The optimal output for the follower firms is found by substituting this value of P into Equation 12.25,

$$Q_F^* = .50 (1,285.083) - 25$$
$$= 617.542 \text{ units}$$

or an optimal output of 617.5 units.

THE KINKED DEMAND CURVE MODEL

Sometimes when an oligopolist cuts its prices, competitors quickly feel the decline in their sales and are forced to match the price reduction. Alternatively, if one firm raises its prices, competitors rapidly gain customers by maintaining their original prices and hence have little or no motivation to match a price increase. In a situation such as this, the demand curve facing an individual oligopolist would be far more elastic for price increases than for price decreases. If an oligopolist *raises* its price and others do not follow, the increase in price will lead to a declining share of the market. This is illustrated in Figure 12.8. Demand segment *KD'* is the *share-of-the-market demand curve* where all rivals match price and this firm's market share remains unchanged, perhaps at 21 percent. For price increases above *P*, however, if rival firms do not match price, the demand segment facing this firm is more elastic. For price increases, its market share declines, perhaps to 15 percent.

The oligopolist's demand curve is therefore represented by *DKD'*, with the prevailing price as *P* and output as *Q*. The marginal revenue curve is discontinuous because of the kink in the demand curve at *K*. Hence, marginal revenue is represented by the two line segments *MRX* and *YMR'*. If the marginal cost curve *MC* passes through the gap *XY* in the marginal revenue curve, the most profitable alternative is to maintain the current price-output policy.[18] The profit-maximizing level of price and output remains

Figure 12.8   The Kinked Demand Curve Model

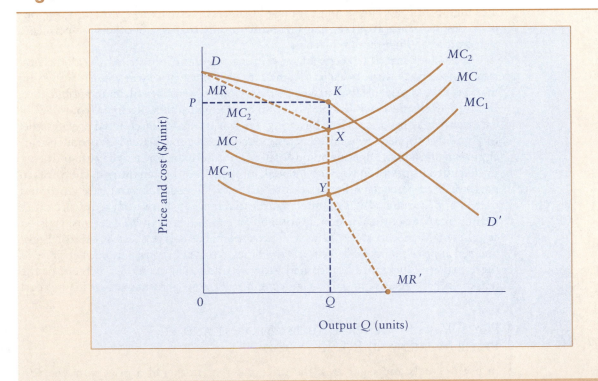

---

[18] Profit may not be increased by increasing price (and decreasing output) because *MR* > *MC*, and this difference would increase with a price increase. Similarly, profit may not be increased by decreasing price (and increasing output) because *MR* < *MC*, and this difference would also increase with a price decrease.

constant for the firm, which perceives itself to be faced with a fixed unit price, even though costs may change over a rather wide range (for example, MC_2 and MC_1). Similarly, shifts in the demand curve either to the right (an increase in demand) or to the left (a decrease in demand) may not change the price decisions of the firm. Because the kink is determined at the *prevailing price,* a shift in demand shifts the gap XY in the marginal revenue curve to the right or left. If MC still passes through the gap, the prevailing price is maintained, although output will either increase or decrease.

A number of criticisms have been made of the kinked demand curve model as a general model of oligopoly behavior. Although the model does provide a theoretical explanation for why stable prices have been observed to exist in some oligopolistic industries, it takes the prevailing price as given and offers no justification for why that price level rather than some other is the prevailing price. For this reason alone, the kinked demand model of oligopolistic pricing must be viewed as incomplete.

AVOIDING PRICE WARS

Knowing how to avoid a price war has become a critical success factor for many high-margin businesses in tight oligopolistic groups. Recall from our discussion of break-even sales change analysis in Chapter 10 that the higher the margin, the more tempted companies are to employ price discounting to increase incremental sales. Because each additional sale imposes few additional costs, high margins encourage price discounting to gain market share. So building a business plan or adopting a strategy that reduces the power of substitutes, entrants, buyers, and suppliers and thereby generates high profit margins is no guarantee of success. To sustain profitability, oligopoly firms also must avoid the gainshare discounting that would otherwise permeate the tactics in a high-margin business.

The ready-to-eat (RTE) cereal, beer, film, and cigarette industries have all recently experienced price wars. In each case, the catalyst for the price war was the fast rising market share of private labels in what had previously been a heavily branded category. Between 1989 and 1999, Kodak Gold film for 35mm cameras declined from a $3.49 list price to a $2 list price after a blistering series of attacks by discounted private-label films, many supplied by Fuji. Kodak responded with a good-better-best product strategy involving its own "fighting brand" of film, Funtime Film, for everyday use and heavily defended its brand equity with "Kodak moment" ads but, in the end, cut prices to preserve its 70-percent market share. Also, in the 1990s, generic cigarettes (e.g., a brand named appropriately "Basic") took substantial market share from many premium brands like Marlboro, Winston, Merit, and Salem. Similarly in RTE cereals, Ralston supplies many grocery store chains with private label cereals (e.g., Kroger Raisin Bran) that sell at price points 30 percent less than the premium brands. The market share of these private label store brands had grown rapidly, capturing 8.7 percent of the market in 1994 relative to only 5.6 percent in 1993, a 50-percent increase in one year!

Example

PRICE WARS AT GENERAL MILLS AND POST AND AT PHILIP MORRIS AND R.J. REYNOLDS[19]

In both cereals and cigarettes, the price cut that triggered a price war was 20-percent discount per unit. This amount represented a $1.00 price discount on the $4.80 average price for a full-size box of RTE cereal, and a $0.40 discount off

---

[19] Based on "Denial in Battle Creek," *Forbes,* October 7, 1996; "Cereal Thriller," *The Economist,* June 15, 1996; and P. Cummins, "Cereal Firms in Cost-Price Squeeze," Reuters News Service, May 15, 1996.

the $1.92 average price per pack of premium brand cigarettes. In cigarettes, the April 1993 price war was started by the price leader, Philip Morris, which controlled a 47-percent market share. The 1995 price war in cereals was started by Post Cereals, the distant third player in the industry with a 13-percent market share. At the same time, Quaker Oats with a 7-percent market share began selling branded cereals like Cap'n Crunch and Life in large "value-priced" bags for $3.50. Post had carefully analyzed the tactical situation and decided it could better maintain regular customers and compete for price-sensitive new customers if Kellogg and General Mills reduced advertising. Post believed they would do so only in response to a massive industrywide price cut.

General Mills was experiencing a slowly eroding 25-percent market share, while Kellogg faced a rapidly declining 35-percent market share. As recently as 1988, Kellogg had controlled 41 percent of the market. Every share point in the U.S. ready-to-eat cereal industry is worth $80 million in sales. In part because of a panic-stricken determination to arrest the erosion of their market shares, both Kellogg and General Mills quickly decided to match the Post price cut. Full-size boxes of branded products like General Mills' Wheaties and Kellogg's Frosted Flakes were cut in price from $4.80 to $3.88. Just as Post had predicted, each of the leading firms then scaled back their advertising campaigns. And cereals like Post Raisin Bran and Post Grape Nuts gained share rapidly, at least for a short time.

In contrast, the motives for the cigarette price war were less subtle. Philip Morris's largest competitor, R.J. Reynolds, had undergone a leveraged buyout (LBO) five years earlier. Reynolds was much less strapped for cash at the time of the price war (1993) than it had been at any time since the LBO. If Philip Morris had intended by its $1 price cut to ruin its competitor financially, 1987, 1988, or 1989 would have been a better time to do it. In 1987, fully 97 percent of the Reynolds company's projected future cash flow was committed to debt repayments. By 1993, the accelerated early paydown of the debt repayment schedule had brought the debt commitment at Reynolds down to 64 percent of the expected cash flow.

Instead, Philip Morris appears to have become persuaded that, at the all-time-high price of almost $2.00 per pack, the heavy smoker who quit had $35 extra per week with which to buy many attractive substitutes. Health clubs (some offering very effective smoker cessation programs) seldom cost that much. This motivation for the price cut is suggested by the fact that incremental sales of Marlboro rose by only 4.4 percent (from 21.6 percent to 26 percent). Break-even sales change analysis implies that 18.5 percent—i.e., $4.4/\frac{1}{2}(21.6 + 26.0) = 0.185$—was well below the increase in sales required to raise operating profits. For Marlboro with an 82 percent contribution margin, the 20 percent price cut necessitated a 32 percent ($0.82/(0.82 - 0.20) = 1.32$) increase in sales to achieve increased short-term profit.

One key to avoiding price wars in tight oligopolies is to recognize the ongoing nature of the pricing rivalry and attempt to mitigate the intensity of the price competition by growing the market. United Airlines cannot hope to get rid of American Airlines. Kodak foresees a perpetual rivalry with Fuji Film. And Pepsi is stuck with Coke. Consequently, each rival must anticipate retaliation for aggressive discounting designed to attract away the other company's regular customers. Far better to maintain high prices and expect your rivals to do the same. Then, each company can focus on opening new markets and selling more volume to established customers.

WHAT WENT RIGHT   WHAT WENT WRONG

Good-Better-Best Product Strategy at Kodak[20]

Marriott Corporation and Kodak have responded to the fierce price competition in their respective industries by introducing upscale, high-quality mid-range, and down-market product lines to their respective target customers. Ritz-Carlton, Court-yards by Marriott, and Fairfield Inns all operate as subsidiary hotel chains under the parent Marriott Corporation but as very distinct offerings.

Similarly, in the early 1990s, in response to declining perceived quality differentials, collapsing market share, and price pressure from private label film, Kodak introduced a new lineup that included Royal Gold, Kodak Gold Plus, and Funtime Film. Successful segmentation is the key to such a product strategy for avoiding ruinous price discounting. Funtime Film (and the Kodak disposable cameras that followed) are positioned for everyday use to capture the hundreds of events, posed people, and scenery that highly accessible cheap film sold through convenience store distribution channels make possible. These are, however, photo shots that customers will later find "lost" in great stacks in file cabinets, desk drawers, and old shoeboxes.

These films are not generally used to memorialize anything of significance. Instead, the snapshot accentuates the experiential event, as it happens.

"Kodak moments," however, pursue a very different set of value-drivers. Kodak Royal Gold provided exceptional picture resolution in many different light conditions. Although slower, Gold Plus is also able to memorialize subtleties of expressions of surprise, exhaltation, pride in fulfilling challenging tasks, etc. Kodak's marketing research had found that many of their customers would pay a price premium to memorialize a personal emotion (such as when a woman demonstrably triumphs amidst the worst rapids in the front right corner hazard seat of a whitewater raft filled with men). Heavy advertising and event marketing further established this product image.

---

[20] Based on "Film-War Spoils: A Buck a Roll?" *Wall Street Journal,* November 11, 1998, p. B1; Eastman Kodak Company: Funtime Film, Harvard Business School Publishing, 1998; and "Kodak Is Rolling Out Digital Photo Processing," *Wall Street Journal,* February 9, 1999, p. A4.

Coke Classic now sells an average of six servings per day to heavy Coke drinkers. In the last five years, Coke has introduced dozens of new soft drinks to countries throughout the world. As a result, the Coca-Cola concentrate syrup has never been discounted in 80 years.

Customer segmentation with differential pricing is another way to avoid price wars. If low-cost new entrants attack a major airline, one effective response that avoids initiating a price war with other major carriers involves matching prices to a very targeted customer segment and then carefully controlling how much capacity is released for sale to that segment. "Fencing" restrictions like 10-day advance-purchase requirements and Saturday night stay-overs prove crucial in segmenting the price-sensitive discretionary traveler from the regular business expense-account customer. The incumbent carriers can "meet the competition" in these restricted fare classes while reserving sufficient capacity for those who desire to pay for the reliability, convenience, and change order responsiveness of business class and full-coach seats. And most importantly, the incumbent's established competitors can maintain high prices on unaffected departures, segments, and routes. In Appendix 14A, we discuss how revenue management techniques can help accomplish these goals.

Example

WHAT WENT RIGHT AT INTERLINK SURGICAL STEEL?[21]

In the 1980s and early 1990s, Interlink sold replacement hypodermic syringes by the thousands to hospitals for 10 cents per syringe. Each time a catheter was changed, a new hypodermic syringe would be inserted into the patient's vein. A Japanese company entered the market with an identical product for 3 cents each. Interlink promptly introduced a replacement device that only needs insertion one time; that is, any new saline or pharmaceutical drip lines can be hooked directly to an Interlink syringe device that need not be removed and replaced. This new process reduces the risk of patient infection and the inherent hazard to the nursing staff of exposure to patient blood. Interlink again dominates the market, and prices have stabilized at high levels.

In addition to segmenting the target customers into more and less price-sensitive submarkets, product line extensions can also aid in avoiding gainshare price discounting by providing reference prices and framing effects that serve to help sell the mid-range product at full (undiscounted) price. Consumers of unbranded products tend to remember the last price they encountered on the shelf in deciding whether to purchase at the quoted price today. Branded products, however, trigger very long reference pricing. Discounting with a major branded item like Tide detergent or Kodak film tends to etch in the customer's mind a new lowball price that can be expected thereafter for many months. Therefore, what one really might like to do in the face of private-label discount competition is to introduce a super premium product offered at price points well above your traditional product. These highest reference prices too will be remembered by the regular brand loyal customers. And since opportunity losses in descending from mid-range to bargain-basement products (while saving $2, for example) tend to weigh more heavily upon consumers than the perceived satisfaction from moving upscale to super premiums (at an equal $2 cost), one can expect the mid-range products to sell even better in the presence of the framing provided by super premium products. In the late 1990s, Kodak introduced super premium digital photography with a product line called Picture CD. Max and Advantrix film were also introduced by Kodak at price points 15 percent above the Gold Films, now sold in discounted multipacks through Sam's Club, Wal-Mart, and Kmart. Max and Advantrix soon provided 38 percent of Kodak's sales with relatively little discounting.

Another way to avoid or at least mitigate the effects of price wars is to differentiate through innovation. Rather than matching price cuts, a higher-priced brand can call attention to the risks of disloyalty by highlighting conspicuous product innovations the discounters have missed. Sony's Mavica is an easy-to-use point-and-shoot digital camera that records the eye's images on a photo sensitive-electronic plate and translates them into binary data to be read onto a simple floppy disk. The floppy pops out of the camera and into any PC for easy and immediate printing. Digital cameras accounted for only 1.1 million of the 12 million cameras sold in the United States in 1999, but this segment is growing at an annual rate of 50 percent. While digital camera competitors Kodak and Casio were fixated on improving picture resolution to justify complicated expensive peripherals, Sony simplified the process and markedly increased customer value. As a result the competitor

---

[21] Based on "How to Fight a Price War," *Harvard Business Review,* March/April 2000, pp. 107–116, and "How to Escape a Price War," *Fortune,* June 13, 1994, pp. 82–90.

Figure 12.9   Segmented Oligopoly with Extreme Brand Loyalty

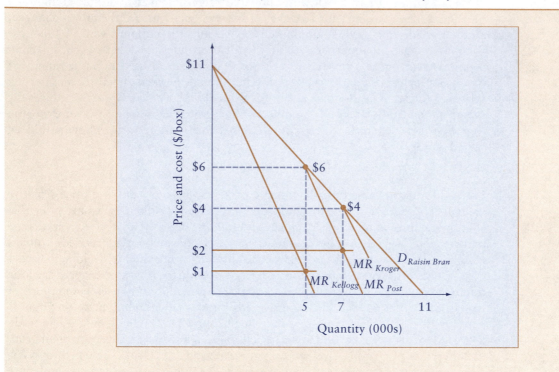

products fluctuate between $300 and $500, while Mavica earns a premium price of $665. Sony's innovation objective is to establish full connectivity between digital cameras, cell phones, and TVs.

Figure 12.9 illustrates how an oligopolistic market with extreme brand loyalty attributable to innovation, customer risk avoidance, or effective brand name advertising can be analyzed. Kellogg's Raisin Bran faces an inverse demand segment, ($11 − Q^d) = Price, that includes the highest willingness to pay customers. Setting MR in this segment, $11 − 2$Q^d$, equal to a marginal cost of $1, Kellogg's Raisin Bran maximizes operating profit at $Q^* = 5(000)$ and a price per box of ($11 − 5) = $6. Without as established a brand image, Post Raisin Bran must sell under $6 and accordingly faces a different segment whose inverse demand may be written as ($6 − Q^d) = Price—i.e., the line segment from $6 downward to the right along D in Figure 12.9. Setting MR at Post, $6 − 2Q$, equal to a higher $2 marginal cost per box yields a profit-maximizing output for Post of 2(000) at a profit-maximizing price of ($6 − $2) = $4 per box. These (5/11 = 45%) and (2/11 = 19%) market shares for Kellogg and Post, respectively, approximate their actual market shares in the ready-to-eat cereal market for raisin bran products. Additional firms with still less brand loyalty, like Kroger Raisin Bran, would supply the remaining segments illustrated still farther downward to the right.

Perhaps the best way to avoid a price war in a small oligopolistic rivalry group is to not start one in the first place. If someone else does start a price war, often the best response is simply to match the competition and then accentuate nonprice elements of the marketing mix by increasing services or advertising brands. Rather than furthering the downward price spiral, Reynolds matched the Philip Morris price cut on its premium brands, Winston and Salem, and ignored the discounting elsewhere. Kellogg matched the Post price cut on only two thirds of its premium brands. Two years later, cereal prices in the all-important grocery store distribution channel began to return to their 1995 pre-price-war levels.

Example

NONPRICE TACTICS IN A PRICE WAR: KELLOGG AND COORS[22]

Kellogg has the strongest brands in the cereals industry with 12 of the 15 top-selling cereals. Rather than match Post's price cuts in 1995, Kellogg might have poured not two but three scoops of raisins into every box of Kellogg's Raisin Bran. In the first two months after the price cuts by Post and General Mills, Kellogg lost three share points (from 35 percent to 32 percent) and Post gained four (from 16 percent to 20 percent). At $80 million per share point and 55-percent gross margins (on average across the affected brands), Kellogg's contributions on the lost sales totaled $132 million ($-3 \times \$80$ million $\times 0.55$). To retrieve that $132-million-per-year operating profit, Kellogg slashed prices 19 percent on two thirds of its brands, sacrificing more than $305 million ($-0.19 \times \$2.4$ billion sales $\times 0.66$). Market share continued to decline to 29 percent in 1999, and the capitalized value of Kellogg fell by $7 billion. Many observers have wondered whether expending $305 million (or half that much) on product innovation or on advertising would have accomplished more.

Coors implemented exactly the same nonprice response in the midst of a costly price war between Anheuser-Busch and Miller Brewing. As Miller and Bud products reduced the category to more and more of a commodity, Coors and Stroh's decided to realign their product positioning with Corona and Heineken. Amidst heavy advertising, Coors gained two share points despite prices $2-per-case higher than Miller and Bud.

A final key to avoiding price wars is to recognize the tactical insights often available from game-theoretic analysis of various actions. With effective competitor surveillance to identify a rival's payoffs, the response of a competitor to one's own price cuts is often predictable based on unilateral self-interest. In other circumstances, cooperative high-price outcomes may emerge from a convergence of mutual interest. In addition, simply recognizing the detailed structure of the pricing "game" can be a first step toward modifying the competitive environment to increase profitability. In the next section and the following chapter, we present game-theoretic techniques that have proven very useful for generating managerial insights into effective tactical decision making.

OLIGOPOLISTIC RIVALRY AND GAME THEORY

Most oligopolistic competition takes place today in product-line submarkets between a few rival incumbents, each with some market power over price. Consider Bayer Aspirin, Bufferin, Excedrin, and St. Joseph's in pain relievers; Pepsi and Coke in colas; Six Flags and Disney in theme parks; and United, Delta, US Airways, and American

http://

Learn more about game theory at Al Roth's game theory and experimental economics Internet site: http://www.economics. harvard.edu/~aroth/alroth. html

---

[22] Based on "Cereal Thriller," *The Economist,* June 15, 1996; and "Big Brewers Find Price War," *Wall Street Journal,* July 2, 1998, p. B6, and January 4, 1999, p. R6.

in air travel to Florida. Smaller competitors selling generic products are often present in fringe markets, but what distinguishes these oligopolists is the presence of some brand name or other barrier to effective entry. A small number of well-established, profitable, and highly interdependent incumbents is often the result. This oligopolistic market structure leads to some quite different forms of competition than we have previously encountered.

Recall that in a competitive industry, such as tract home building or video rentals, each competitor can and must act independently. Each atomistic competitor takes price as "given," that is, determined externally in the open market, because any decision to expand or embargo his or her own supply has no appreciable effect on the industry supply. Even if one firm were to purchase all the video rental outlets in a community, the barriers to entry are so low that any price above cost would surely attract enough new competitors to restore the competitive price-taking equilibrium. In contrast, each firm in an oligopolistic market must pay very close attention to the moves and countermoves of its rivals, and often it fiercely defends its market share. Ultimately, competitor surveillance is important in all market structures because quickly adaptive behavior is preferable to reactive behavior. But the intense interdependence of oligopolistic rivalry makes proactive behavior best of all. Each oligopolist must try to predict well in advance the actions, responses, and counterresponses of the rivals and then choose optimal strategies accordingly. Modern **game theory** was invented for precisely this purpose.[23]

A Conceptual Framework for Game-Theoretic Analysis

A general definition of a **strategy game** is any consciously interdependent choice behavior by purposeful individuals or hierarchical groups who share a common goal (e.g., tribes, sports teams, or value-maximizing companies). As such, strategy games have always been a part of human endeavors from the very beginnings of prehistory. Some of the earliest formal analyses of strategy games involve voting games, bargaining games, and games of defense. Pliny the Younger, a first-century historian, records the pivotal role of strategic voting in the trial of a Roman senator, whose suicide was assisted by several freedmen. The accused preferred death to banishment and almost won acquittal despite a majority in favor of the conviction. Only by strategically voting a second-choice punishment of banishment did those senators in favor of execution prevent a minority control of the agenda from obtaining the acquittal.

Another example suggests that private property rights for one's personal effects evolved from a strategy game in which prehistoric tribes of hunter-gatherers had to decide between guarding consolidated property or marauding against targets of opportunity. The private property consolidators won out; let's see why. In Table 12.4 two competing players (Randle and Kahn) compete for resources by selecting between two actions: Maraude, which occasionally yields unguarded windfall treasures, but leaves one's own possessions vulnerable to counterattack; or Guard, which frees time between defensive struggles for consolidating and multiplying the fruits of one's labors. Kahn has a tactical advantage against anything but strongly guarded positions, but knows too little about defense to be effective in guarding against attack. However, no matter what action Kahn decides to take, an examination of the payoff matrix in Table 12.4 reveals Randle is always better off selecting Guard. Guard is a **dominant strategy** for Randle in that Randle's outcomes from Guard exceed the outcomes from any alternative strategy, independent of the opponent's

Game Theory
A mathematical theory of decision making by the participants in a conflict-of-interest situation.

Strategy Game
A decision-making situation with consciously interdependent behavior between two or more of the participants.

Dominant Strategy
An action rule that maximizes the decision maker's welfare independent of the actions of other players.

---

[23] Two useful volumes on game theory are A. Dixit and S. Skeath, *Games of Strategy* (New York, Norton, 1999), and Eric Rasmussen, *Games and Information*, 2d ed. (Cambridge, MA: Basil Blackwell, 1993).

Table 12.4   Privitization of Personal Effects

		Randle			
		Guard		**Maraude**	
Kahn	**Guard**	Better	1st	Worst	4th
	Maraude	Worse	2nd	Best	3rd

Notes: Randle ranks outcomes from 1st to 4th. Kahn ranks outcomes from best to worst.

behavior. Knowing this or discovering it through trial and error, Kahn predicts his rival Randle will continue to Guard. On that condition, Kahn then prefers Guard himself. {Guard, Guard} therefore emerges as the strategic equilibrium—i.e., a *dominant strategy equilibrium.*

Components of a Game

The essential elements of all strategy games are present in the above example and include the following: players, actions, information sets, payoffs, an order of play, focal outcomes of interest, strategies, and equilibrium strategies. Let's illustrate with another example, taken this time from service quality competition. Suppose two *players,* Xerox and Sharp, must choose whether to discontinue copier repair service that is seven territories removed from their respective regional headquarters located in two different cities 200 miles apart. Six or seven territories of full service repair are the *actions.* The *payoffs* from the decisions, which must be announced simultaneously at next week's industrial trade show, are shown in Table 12.5. This payoff matrix is the **normal form of the game,** which is an appropriate way of representing any simultaneous-play (versus sequential-play) game.

Normal Form of the Game
A representation of payoffs in a simultaneous-play game.

Sharp finds that full service repair on demand in the more distant seventh territory is very expensive. Cutting back to six territories reduces cost by $15 per week per customer and raises Sharp's profit from $55 to $70 per week when Xerox also cuts back, and from $45 to $60 per week when Xerox does not. The improved effectiveness of Sharp's service in the remaining six territories lowers the prices rival Xerox can charge and reduces its profit from an initial $45 down to only $30 should Xerox continue servicing all seven territories. By cutting back to six territories itself, Xerox can restrict its losses to just $5 ($45 now to $40). The common *information set* known to both players includes knowledge of all these effects.

What strategy should Xerox adopt? First, using the concept of *dominant strategy* it is clear that Sharp will discontinue service in the seventh territory. Sharp is better off cutting back to six territories independent of what Xerox does. For Sharp, seven territories is *dominated* (unambiguously less preferred than six territories). Xerox wishes it were not so, because its most successful operation entails head-to-head, seven-territory competition against Sharp. Nevertheless, predictable reality lies elsewhere, and Xerox must predict six-territory behavior on the part of its rival and proceed to

Table 12.5   Six or Seven Territories?

		Sharp	
		Six Territories	**Seven Territories**
Xerox	**Six Territories**	$70 / $40	$55 / $35
	Seven Territories	$60 / $30	$45 / $45

Notes: **Payoffs are profits. Sharp payoffs are above the diagonal, and Xerox payoffs are below the diagonal.**

Iterated Dominant Strategy

An action rule that maximizes self-interest in light of the predictable dominant-strategy behavior of other players.

reexamine its remaining options. Having eliminated Sharp's dominated strategy in the second column, Xerox now has an unambiguously preferred *strategy* of providing full service repairs in only six territories itself. {Six, Six} is therefore the *equilibrium strategy* pair. That is, by applying the concept of a dominant strategy equilibrium to the prediction of its rival's behavior, Xerox can iterate back to analyze its own best action. {Six, Six} is therefore referred to as an **iterated dominant strategy** equilibrium.

The strategic equilibrium concept of eliminating dominated strategies in simultaneous games first appeared in *The Theory of Games and Economic Behavior* (1944) by John von Neumann and Oskar Morgenstern. Von Neumann and Morgenstern confined their analysis primarily to cooperative games, in which players can form coalitions, arrange side payments, and enter into binding agreements. John Nash, Reinhard Selten, and John Harsanyi won the 1994 Nobel Prize in economics for their extension of strategic equilibrium concepts to noncooperative games, sequential games, and games of imperfect information.

NOBEL GOES TO THREE GAME THEORISTS

Example
http://

Read more about Harsanyi, Nash, and Selten at the Nobel Prize Internet Archive:
http://www.almaz.com/nobel/economics/1994a.html

Nash, Selten, and Harsanyi won the 1994 Nobel Prize for their work on equilibrium strategies in sequential games ranging from chess and poker to central bank interventions, limit pricing to deter entry, research and development competitions, and the auctioning of the radio magnetic spectrum. Not infrequently, multiple equilibria arise in such games—e.g., when either duopoly competitor may initiate price cuts and find that the other party will neither match nor discount further. Another implication of their work is that the order of play can have determinate effects on strategic decisions. Moving first in a preemptive product development can often foreclose a later competitor's threatened entry. In other circumstances, making the last response in the endgame, as dynamic technology changes to a new direction, can secure a strategic advantage. In addition, under incomplete information about opponent types, behaving like a "crazy" firm, which predatorily prices below cost when there is no later chance of recovering the losses, may deter an opponent's entry. Distinguishing between these and other complex paths to the most profitable strategy is the role of equilibrium strategies.

Cooperative and Noncooperative Games

Cooperative Games
Game structures that allow coalition formation, side payments, and binding third-party enforceable agreements.

The fact that in a **cooperative game** players can form coalitions, make side payments, and communicate to one another their private information about their own prices, profit margins, or variable costs has limited the usefulness of cooperative game theory in business settings. An illustration of a side payment in cooperative games is the mandatory compensation scheme a manufacturer might impose when one sales representative violates another's exclusive territory. Or, suppose in the previous Xerox and Sharp example that the two firms got together to arrange a side payment for Sharp that would ensure a strategic equilibrium of {Seven, Seven}. Also in cooperative games, a cartel might decide to enter into binding (i.e., third-party enforceable) contracts to segment the demander nations involved in a global diamond, coal, or coffee market. As you may already suspect, most such cooperative game agreements between arms-length competitors to exchange price information or arrange side payments are per se violations of the antitrust laws in the United States and Western Europe.[24] For these reasons, business strategists paid relatively little attention to game theory until *noncooperative* strategic equilibrium concepts were developed.

Noncooperative Games
Game structures that prohibit collusion, side payments, and binding agreements enforced by third parties.

   Noncooperative games prohibit collusive communication, side payment schemes, and third-party enforceable binding agreements. Instead, such games focus on self-enforcing reliance relationships to characterize strategic equilibrium and predict rival response. One example we have already encountered in Chapter 10 is the mutual reliance between sellers with nonredeployable assets and buyers of high-priced experience goods. Other examples include computer companies who build operating systems to a common standard that can communicate across PC platforms or competing airlines who announce high fares day after day despite the quick but short-lived attraction of breaking out as a renegade discounter. Clearly, these noncooperative games differ from cooperative games in important ways that make them more applicable to business strategy. Chapter 13 is devoted to an analysis of noncooperative games, with particular attention given to sequential equilibrium concepts such as first-mover/second-mover advantages and credible threats/credible commitments.

Other Types of Games

Games are also classified according to the number of players involved, the compatibility of their interests, and the number of replays of the game. We analyzed both of the above games as *single-period ("one-shot") games*. Clearly, however, the ongoing rivalry between the players in "Guarder-Marauder" and in "Six or Seven Territories" is highly pertinent to the strategic situation. In the next chapter, we turn our attention to the distinct and somewhat paradoxical implications of so-called *repeated games*. In a *two-person game,* each player attempts to obtain as much as possible from the other player through whatever methods of cooperation, bargaining, or threatening are available. *N-person games* are more difficult to analyze because subsets of players can form coalitions to impose solutions on the rest of the players. Coalitions can be of any size and can break up and re-form as the game proceeds. Parliamentary government is the classic example of *n*-person games. Although the possibility of coalitions adds greatly to the richness of the types of situations that can be considered by game theory, coalition-proofness is an equilibrium concept that adds substantial complexity to the theory required to analyze such games.

---

[24] For example, the antitrust opinions in *U.S. v. National Gypsum*, 428 U.S. 422 (1978) and *U.S. v. Airline Tariff Publishing Co., et al.*, 92-52854 (1992) expressly prohibited the exchange of preannouncement price lists between competitors.

In a **two-person zero-sum game**, the players have exactly opposite interests; one player's gain is the other player's loss and vice versa. "Guarder-Marauder" serves as an intuitive example. Although a number of parlor games and some military applications can be analyzed with zero-sum games, the great preponderance of real-life conflict-of-interest situations do not fit within this model. In contrast, in a *two-person non-zero-sum game*, both players may gain or lose depending on the actions each chooses to take. "Six or Seven Territories" is a non-zero-sum game; limiting competition to six territories raises the total profit from the interaction to $110 rather than $90. In all such games at least one outcome is jointly preferred, and consequently, the players may be able to increase their payoffs through some form of cooperation. Perhaps the most famous generic structure for non-zero-sum games is the *Prisoner's Dilemma*. Many real-world conflict-of-interest situations, such as duopoly pricing between Pepsi and Coke, experience good transactions, urban renewal decisions among adjacent landowners, and bargaining policy with terrorists, can be represented as Prisoner's Dilemma games.

In a Prisoner's Dilemma, two suspects are accused of jointly committing a crime.[25] To convict the suspects, however, a confession is needed from one or both of them. They are separated and no information can pass between them, so this is a noncooperative game. If neither suspect confesses, the prosecutor will be unable to convict them of the crime and each suspect will receive only a short-term (1-year) prison sentence. If one suspect confesses (that is, turns state's evidence) and the other does not, then the one confessing will receive a suspended sentence and the other will receive a long-term (15-year) prison sentence. If both suspects confess, then each will receive an intermediate-term (6-year) prison sentence. Each suspect must decide, under these conditions, whether or not to confess. This conflict-of-interest situation can be represented in a game matrix such as the one shown in Table 12.6.

This game can be examined by using the concept of a security level, or minimum payoff. For Suspect 1, the minimum payoff of the two alternative actions "Not Confess" and "Confess" are a 15-year and a 6-year prison sentence, respectively. The

Table 12.6　Prisoner's Dilemma Payoff Matrix

		Suspect 2	
		Not Confess	**Confess**
Suspect 1	**Not Confess**	One-year prison term for each suspect	Fifteen-year prison term for Suspect 1; suspended sentence for Suspect 2
	Confess	Suspended sentence for Suspect 1; fifteen-year prison term for Suspect 2	Six-year prison term for each suspect

[25] This example is discussed in more detail in Luce and Raiffa, *Games and Decisions*, Section 5.4.

maximization of his security level would therefore motivate Suspect 1 to choose the second alternative action by confessing. Similar reasoning holds true for Suspect 2, and she also would be motivated to choose the alternative of confessing her guilt. Thus, the second alternative for each player (that is, "Confess") dominates the other strategy (that is, "Not Confess") and constitutes an equilibrium strategy pair and, in this sense, represents the solution of the game. A dominant strategy is one that provides a player with a larger payoff, regardless of what strategy the other player chooses. In this game both suspects would clearly receive a larger payoff (that is, a shorter sentence) if they both decided to choose their first alternatives ("Not Confess"). However, in seeking to maximize their predictable payoffs (or, more accurately, to maximize their security levels), the first alternative is not a rational choice for either suspect.

As discussed above, in cooperative games the players have complete freedom of communication with the opportunity to make threats and enter into binding and third-party enforceable agreements. Examining the Prisoner's Dilemma game again, assume that the two players (that is, suspects) are able to communicate with each other and are able to enter into a binding agreement on which strategy each player will choose. In this case, because the cooperative outcome associated with both suspects not confessing is preferred to the noncooperative solution, the suspects would have an incentive to enter into a binding agreement for each to choose the strategy of not confessing. Without strong legal or moral sanctions to force the suspects to adhere to the agreement, however, each suspect would be tempted to double-cross the other suspect by confessing his or her guilt. The suspect that breaks the agreement has the possibility of reducing his or her sentence from a six-year prison term to a suspended sentence, as can be seen in Table 12.6. In a cooperative game, however, all such agreements are binding and enforceable.

The analogy to pricing and output decisions among firms in oligopolistic industries is striking. In some instances, cooperation may take the form of price leadership, where one firm takes on the role of price leader and the other firms act as followers. In other instances, the firms may enter into illegal price-fixing agreements and form a cartel. However, just as each of the suspects in the Prisoner's Dilemma game has an incentive to double-cross the other suspect, firms in oligopolistic industries have an incentive to depart from agreed-upon prices or output quotas in any price-fixing agreement. As a result, these price-fixing agreements often break down quickly as one (or more) of the firms attempt(s) to increase its (their) profits through secret price reductions to customer(s). The Prisoner's Dilemma structure of many such pricing games predicts that the representative cartel member will have a dominant strategy to cheat on the cartel agreements.

Example

COFFEE CARTEL DISSOLVES[26]

In October 1991, the 17 top Colombian and Brazilian coffee producers announced an agreement to set up a coffee cartel. Each country and several African and Central American smaller producers agreed in principle to take millions of tons of coffee beans off the market in an effort to drive up wholesale prices. Brazilian producers would hold back 2 million bags of a projected 18-million-bag crop. Colombian producers would hold back 1.3 million bags. However, both countries opposed a formal quota system with assigned production ceilings, monitoring mechanisms, and penalization of violators. In July 1989, the previous International Coffee Agreement had collapsed over the refusal to accept assigned quotas.

[26] Based on "Non-Zero-Sum Strategic Game," *Financial Times*, July 2, 1995.

When the 1992 harvest proved more plentiful than expected, coffee bean prices plummeted. Prisoner's Dilemma is less a "game" than a paradox about cooperation. If all major coffee bean producers could rely upon one another to withhold production, all would have higher profitability. However, each cartel member maximizes self-interest by releasing excess supplies to the world market at just below the cartel official price. Because numerous fellow members think the same way, equilibrium market price will decline. Only dupes then continue to restrain output when world market prices collapse, signaling that other members are violating the agreement. Coffee bean producers observed market price dropping precipitously in 1992 and concluded correctly that the cartel agreements to restrain output had dissolved.

We shall see in the next chapter that raising the stakes from noncooperation or entering into a long-term, continuing relationship with opponent/cooperators can diminish this incentive to cheat. Nevertheless, most cartels are like the frequent price-fixing agreements that evolve several times a year among the manufacturer sales representatives for cardboard packaging. Within two or three weeks, the collusive uniform pricing across alternative regional suppliers breaks down, often before the ink on Justice Department indictments can dry.

Summary

- An *oligopoly* is an industry structure characterized by a relatively small number of firms in which recognizable *interdependencies* exist among the actions of the firms. Each firm is aware that its actions are likely to evoke countermoves from its rivals.

- In the *Cournot* model of oligopoly behavior, each of the firms, in determining its profit-maximizing output level, assumes that the other firm's output will remain constant.

- A *cartel* is a formal or informal agreement among oligopolists to cooperate or collude in determining outputs, prices, and profits. If the cartel members can enforce agreements and prevent cheating, they can act as a monopolist and maximize industry profits.

- A number of factors affect the ability of oligopolistic firms to engage successfully in some form of formal (or informal) cooperation. These include the number and size distribution of sellers, product heterogeneity, cost structures, size and frequency of orders, secrecy and retaliation, and the percentage of industry output external to the cartel.

- *Price leadership* is a pricing strategy in an oligopolistic industry in which one firm sets the price and, either by explicit or implicit agreement, the other firms tend to follow the decision. Effective price leadership exists when price movements initiated by the leader have a high probability of sticking and there are no maverick or nonconforming firms.

- In the *kinked demand curve* model, it is assumed that if an oligopoly firm reduces its prices, its competitors will quickly feel the decline in their sales and will be forced to match the reduction. Alternatively, if the oligopolist raises its prices, competitors will rapidly gain customers by maintaining their original prices and will have little or no motivation to match a price increase. Hence, the demand curve facing individual oligopolists is much more elastic for price increases than for price decreases and may lead oligopolists to maintain stable prices.

- In a *game-theoretic* analysis of oligopolistic firms' decision making, the firm assumes that its competitor(s) will choose its (their) optimal decision-making strategy. Based on this assumption about its competitor(s), the firm chooses its own best counterstrategy.

- Business strategy games may be classified as simultaneous-play or sequential-play, one-shot or repeated, zero-sum or non-zero-sum, two-player or *n*-player, and cooperative or noncooperative.

- *Cooperative games* allow communication, coalition formation, binding side payment agreements, and third-party enforceable contracts.

EXERCISES

1. Assume that two companies (*C* and *D*) are duopolists that produce identical products. Demand for the products is given by the following linear demand function:

$$P = 600 - Q_C - Q_D$$

where Q_C and Q_D are the quantities sold by the respective firms and *P* is the selling price. Total cost functions for the two companies are

$$TC_C = 25,000 + 100\,Q_C$$
$$TC_D = 20,000 + 125\,Q_D$$

Assume that the firms act *independently* as in the Cournot model (that is, each firm assumes that the other firm's output will not change).

   a. Determine the long-run equilibrium output and selling price for each firm.
   b. Determine the total profits for each firm at the equilibrium output found in Part (a).

2. Assume that two companies (*A* and *B*) are duopolists who produce identical products. Demand for the products is given by the following linear demand function:

$$P = 200 - Q_A - Q_B$$

where Q_A and Q_B are the quantities sold by the respective firms and *P* is the selling price. Total cost functions for the two companies are

$$TC_A = 1,500 + 55Q_A + Q_A^2$$

$$TC_B = 1,200 + 20Q_B + 2Q_B^2$$

Assume that the firms act *independently* as in the Cournot model (that is, each firm assumes that the other firm's output will not change).

   a. Determine the long-run equilibrium output and selling price for each firm.
   b. Determine Firm *A*, Firm *B*, and total industry profits at the equilibrium solution found in Part (a).

3. Consider Exercise 2 again. Assume that the firms form a *cartel* to act as a monopolist and maximize total industry profits (sum of Firm *A* and Firm *B* profits).

   a. Determine the optimum output and selling price for each firm.
   b. Determine Firm *A*, Firm *B*, and total industry profits at the optimal solution found in Part (a).
   c. Show that the marginal costs of the two firms are equal at the optimal solution found in Part (a).

4. Compare the optimal solutions obtained in Exercises 2 and 3. Specifically:
   a. How much higher (lower) is the optimal selling price when the two firms form a cartel to maximize industry profits, compared to when they act independently?
   b. How much higher (lower) is total industry output?
   c. How much higher (lower) are total industry profits?

5. Alchem (L) is the price leader in the polyglue market. All ten other manufacturers [follower (F) firms] sell polyglue at the same price as Alchem. Alchem allows the other firms to sell as much as they wish at the established price and supplies the remainder of the demand itself. Total demand for polyglue is given by the following function ($Q_T = Q_L + Q_F$):

$$P = 20{,}000 - 4Q_T$$

Alchem's marginal cost function for manufacturing and selling polyglue is

$$MC_L = 5{,}000 + 5Q_L$$

The aggregate marginal cost function for the other manufacturers of polyglue is

$$\Sigma MC_F = 2{,}000 + 4Q_F$$

   a. To maximize profits, how much polyglue should Alchem produce and what price should it charge?
   b. What is the total market demand for polyglue at the price established by Alchem in Part (a)? How much of total demand do the follower firms supply?

6. Chillman Motors, Inc., believes it faces the following segmented demand function:

$$P = \begin{cases} 150 - .5Q & \text{when } 0 \le Q \le 50 \\ 200 - 1.5Q & \text{for } Q > 50 \end{cases}$$

   a. Indicate both verbally and graphically why such a segmented demand function is likely to exist. What type of industry structure is indicated by this relationship?
   b. Calculate the marginal revenue functions facing Chillman. Add these to your graph from Part (a).
   c. Chillman's total cost function is

$$TC_1 = 500 + 15Q + .5Q^2$$

   Calculate the marginal cost function. What is Chillman's profit-maximizing price and output combination?
   d. What is Chillman's profit-maximizing price-output combination if total costs increase to

$$TC_2 = 500 + 45Q + .5Q^2$$

   e. If Chillman's total cost function changes to either

$$TC_3 = 500 + 15Q + 1.0Q^2$$

   or

$$TC_4 = 500 + 5Q + .25Q^2$$

what price-output solution do you expect to prevail? Would your answer change if you knew that all firms in the industry witnessed similar changes in their cost functions?

7. Suppose that two Japanese companies, Hitachi and Toshiba, are the sole producers (i.e., duopolists) of a microprocessor chip used in a number of different brands of personal computers. Assume that total demand for the chips is fixed and that each firm charges the same price for the chips. Each firm's market share and profits are a function of the magnitude of the promotional campaign used to promote its version of the chip. Also assume that only two strategies are available to each firm—a limited promotional campaign (budget) and an extensive promotional campaign (budget). If the two firms engage in a limited promotional campaign, each firm will earn a quarterly profit of $7.5 million. If the two firms undertake an extensive promotional campaign, each firm will earn a quarterly profit of $5.0 million. With this strategy combination, market share and total sales will be the same as for a limited promotional campaign, but promotional costs will be higher and hence profits will be lower. If either firm engages in a limited promotional campaign and the other firm undertakes an extensive promotional campaign, then the firm that adopts the extensive campaign will increase its market share and earn a profit of $9.0 million, whereas the firm that chooses the limited campaign will earn a profit of only $4.0 million.

a. Develop a payoff matrix for this decision-making problem.

b. In the absence of a binding and enforceable agreement, determine the dominant advertising strategy and minimum payoff for Hitachi.

c. Determine the dominant advertising strategy and minimum payoff for Toshiba.

d. Explain why the firms may choose not to play their dominant strategies whenever this game is repeated over multiple decision-making periods.

8. Consider the following payoff matrix:

		Player B Strategy	
		1	**2**
Player A Strategy	**1**	$2,000 / $1,000	−$1,000 / −$2,000
	2	−$2,000 / −$1,000	$1,000 / $2,000

a. Does Player A have a dominant strategy? Explain why or why not.

b. Does Player B have a dominant strategy? Explain why or why not.

9. Suppose that two mining companies, Australian Minerals Company (AMC) and South African Mines, Inc. (SAMI), control the only sources of a rare mineral used in making certain electronic components. The companies have agreed to form a cartel to set the (profit-maximizing) price of the mineral. Each company must decide whether to *abide* by the agreement (i.e., not offer secret price cuts to customers) or *not abide* (i.e., offer secret price cuts to customers). If both companies abide by the agreement, AMC will earn an annual profit of

$30 million and SAMI will earn an annual profit of $20 million from sales of the mineral. If AMC does not abide and SAMI abides by the agreement, then AMC earns $40 million and SAMI earns $5 million. If SAMI does not abide and AMC abides by the agreement, then AMC earns $10 million and SAMI earns $30 million. If both companies do not abide by the agreement, then AMC earns $15 million and SAMI earns $10 million.

a. Develop a payoff matrix for this decision-making problem.

b. In the absence of a binding and enforceable agreement, determine the dominant strategy for AMC.

c. Determine the dominant strategy for SAMI.

d. If the two firms can enter into a binding and enforceable agreement, determine the strategy that each firm should choose.

10. *Library Research Project.* Examine the literature on the price-fixing agreements that occurred in the electrical equipment industry during the 1950s. For example, see Richard Austin Smith, "The Incredible Electrical Conspiracy," *Fortune* (April/May 1961).

a. What firms and products were involved in the conspiracy?

b. What measures did the executives use to keep their meetings secret?

c. How did the companies determine who should get contracts and orders?

d. What market-sharing formulas (quotas) were used in allocating demand?

e. What were some of the problems encountered in maintaining the price-fixing agreements?

http://
Information-Sharing Among Oligopolists

11. It was observed in the chapter that collusion among oligopolists can be facilitated in part by information sharing. As a consequence, the sharing of price information among rival oligopolists can violate U.S. antitrust laws. You can see how the U.S. Supreme Court has interpreted antitrust law as it pertains to sharing price information by reading a summary of the case of *U.S.* v. *U.S. Gypsum Co. et al.* (438 U.S. 422), which is available at the following Internet site: http://www.ripon.edu/Faculty/bowenj/antitrust/usgypsum.htm.

In what manner was price information shared, and why did the court find this to be an antitrust violation?

CASE EXERCISE

CELL PHONES DISPLACE MOBILE PHONE SATELLITE NETWORKS

Motorola's Iridium, a go-anywhere mobile phone system that beamed signals down from 66 satellites, was called "the eighth wonder of the world" by Motorola CEO Chris Galvin. However, at $1,500 for a handset the size of a brick, consumers balked, and few business customers needed the security and reliability offered in remote corners of the globe like Katmandu. As a result, Motorola's 25-percent market share in cell phones declined steadily to 13 percent in 2001, and Motorola stock fell 16 percent from 1997–2001, during a period when the S&P 500 was up 76 percent.

QUESTIONS

1. Characterize the product space for analog mobile phones when Iridium began.

2. What trends did Nokia pursue as it designed mobile phone products in the late 1990s? Refer to the Managerial Challenge at the beginning of this chapter.

3. What might a more proactive Motorola have done differently had it correctly perceived the steps its rival Nokia would take?

13

Game-Theoretic Rivalry: Best-Practice Tactics

CHAPTER PREVIEW When incumbents and potential entrants in product-line submarkets compete against a few rivals, effective decision making necessitates effective tactics. Effective tactics in turn require methods for anticipating rival initiatives, rival response, and counterresponse. Most such predictions of rival behavior can be obtained by analyzing noncooperative sequential and simultaneous games. Prominent examples include entry deterrence and accommodation games, bidding games, manufacturer-distributor games, product development or research and development games, and pricing and promotion games.

All such noncooperative games prohibit side payments and binding contracts between rivals and instead depend on self-enforcing reliance relationships to secure strategic equilibrium. For example, each airline in a posted pricing game must decide whether it is in its own best interest to resist discounting to gain market share, in light of the best reply responses the airline anticipates from its rivals. In some circumstances, mutual discounting proves to be a dominant strategy that provides protection from the inroads of a renegade discounter, but forgoes the profits from all firms maintaining higher prices. This is the implication of the Prisoner's Dilemma pricing game of Chapter 12.

The order of play can matter in such games if credible threats and commitments influence the endgame outcomes. In this chapter we explore the role that first-mover and last-mover advantages, nonredeployable assets, credible punishment schemes, hostage mechanisms, matching price guarantees, and imperfect information can play in helping oligopolists escape the repeated Prisoner's Dilemma and secure higher prices. Appendix 13A explores capacity planning and pricing against a low-cost competitor with a case study of People Express and JetBlue pressuring Piedmont Airlines and United, respectively.

MANAGERIAL CHALLENGE

Price Differentials in Computers: IBM, Compaq, and Dell[1]

For a decade IBM and Compaq maintained a $1,000-or-more price differential over clone PC makers and second-tier firms such as Zenith, Dell, and AST. Both competitors always had the opportunity to attract sales away from their rivals by renegade discounting, but neither wished to start a price war. Predictably, any discounting would be matched, and both firms would then be worse off. Margins were large and profits high, but sales growth declined precipitously. PC assembly and retailing became subject to enormously effective grassroots entry, and the PC market fragmented. From 1987 to 1991 approximately 300 PC makers below the top 100 vendors increased their share of the market from 4 percent to 16 percent. That volume exceeded both IBM's 12 percent and Apple's 13 percent. IBM's much-lauded systems solutions for mainframe computing never proved effective in the PC market. Niche marketing to hospitals one day, to computer-aided design firms another day, and to airline revenue management systems a third day suited the small clone PC manufacturers who incurred very low overhead. Basically, these firms just buy components such as disk drives, motherboards, monitors, and memory chips on the spot market and assemble to order, one customer at a time.

In 1993–1994 Compaq and IBM slashed prices, promoted the discounts, and the price differential between the leading, second-tier, and clone companies all but disappeared. Even Apple followed suit. The growth of the clone segment stopped, and their share of the market declined to 12 percent. However, profitability at the leading firms plummeted, and Dell grabbed a larger and larger share of the business.

Should the leading firms adopt limit pricing and continue to deter new entrants, or should they accommodate the clone segment and return to higher prices? Longer term, can IBM and Compaq match the supply chain efficiency of a direct-to-the-customer operation like Dell, who holds almost no inventory and can convert purchase orders to cash in 36 hours? If not, should IBM exit the PC assembly business altogether? What then?

The following Internet site, maintained by PC Week, contains additional information on price competition in the PC industry:

http://www8.zdnet.com/pcweek/news/0714/17ecuts.html

---

[1] Based on "PC Giants' Price War Hurts Tiny Makers," *Wall Street Journal*, November 2, 1992, p. B1.

BUSINESS STRATEGY GAMES

In many oligopolistic industries today, change has become the norm. Correctly anticipating changes in entry and exit, technology, product development, pricing, and promotions several steps ahead of actual events and at least one step ahead of the competition is often the key to a successful business. Despite one's best efforts, sometimes a competitor takes the lead, and then quickly adaptive behavior is preferable to reactive behavior. Unquestionably, however, proactive behavior is best of all, and proactive behavior requires accurate and reliable predictions of rival initiatives and rival response. The managerial purpose of game theory is to provide these predictions of rival behavior. To execute defensive strategy as well as plan strategic initiatives, business managers must thoroughly understand game-theoretic reasoning.

The predictive capability of game theory proves valuable to Coca-Cola and PepsiCo, for example, in deciding whether to maintain high prices or announce discounts for their competing promotions each week in grocery and convenience stores. If both discount, they each earn $8,000, relative to the $12,000 per week per store that is available to each when they both maintain high prices. However, if one discounts while the other maintains high prices, the discounter earns $17,000, and the rival earns only $6,000. As a value-maximizing manager, what should you do? Think about it. Use the normal form of the game and the techniques of the last chapter to sketch out a strategy. Have you settled for a second-best outcome? Suppose the $6,000 were instead $9,000? Is there now a way to secure the win-win $12,000 outcome? The Prisoner's Dilemma facing PepsiCo and Coca-Cola is a noncooperative positive-sum game of coordination. In this chapter we will study how to escape the dilemma by changing the structure of such games.

Simultaneous Versus Sequential Games

In Chapter 12 we saw that strategy games can be classified into several types: cooperative versus noncooperative, two-person versus *n*-person, zero-sum versus non-zero-sum, and one-play versus repeated games. All strategy games can also be subdivided further into either **sequential games,** in which the order of play is specified and often pivotal to the strategic equilibrium, or **simultaneous games,** such as the airline fare announcements that take place concurrently on an electronic bulletin board at 7:00 A.M. each Wednesday morning. In this chapter we address both simultaneous and sequential games and continue our focus from Chapter 12 on noncooperative, self-enforcing relationships between arm's-length competitors.

To illustrate the importance of the sequential order of play in many tactical situations, consider a two-player coordination game that often arises between manufacturers and independent retail distributors. The payoffs for the promotion and sale of a heavy truck like those sold by Volvo-GM Truck are displayed in normal form in Table 13.1. Let's first examine the actions and payoffs in the left-hand column. The manufacturer wants the retail distributors to continue providing personal selling efforts and after-sales service, rather than discontinue these activities and thereby increase their retail margins. In return, the manufacturer agrees to advertise the product. If services continue and advertising occurs, the customers will tolerate the pass-through of a higher wholesale price. The manufacturer will also assist in the realization of this higher revenue by announcing an increase in the manufacturer's suggested retail price (MSRP). In that case, the retail distributor and the manufacturer can earn additional profits per sale of $2,000 and $5,000, respectively. However, if MSRP increases and retail services are discontinued (as in the northwest cell of Table 13.1), sales volume declines enough that neither party receives any incremental profit.

Independent distributors may feel tempted to deliver less service than they promise. Although sales will decline, their lack of reasonable efforts in personal selling may be difficult for the manufacturer to observe directly and therefore may be difficult to distinguish from bad luck. A few quarters of apparently bad luck at a substantially

Sequential Game
A game with an explicit order of play.

Simultaneous Game
A game in which players must choose their actions simultaneously.

http://

To learn about different game strategies used by corporations that have appeared in popular press articles, access the following Internet site:
http://www.gametheory.net/cgi-bin/viewnewsgame.pl#Seq

Table 13.1   Simultaneous Manufacturer/Distributor 1

		Truck Manufacturer	
		Price increase **Advertise**	**No price increase** **Do not advertise**
Retail Distributor	**Increase margins (Discontinue services)**	$0 / $0	$2,000 / $3,000
	Continue services	$5,000 / $2,000	$0 / $0

Note: Column-player payoffs are above the diagonal. Row-player payoffs are below the diagonal.

higher margin may be in the retail distributor's best interests. This outcome is represented in the northeast cell of Table 13.1. If retail services *are* discontinued, eventually the manufacturer will catch on, not advertise, and leave the MSRP unchanged. Since both parties would then incur fewer expenses, both would again realize incremental profit—i.e., $3,000 for the retailer but only $2,000 for the manufacturer. If the MSRP remains unchanged and the manufacturer does not advertise, but retailer services continue (i.e., the southeast cell), both parties barely cover variable plus direct fixed costs. Therefore, no incremental profit is available on an additional sale.

What would you do as the dealer/distributor in this situation? Would you try for the increased margin by economizing on selling expenses and after-sale services? Remember that your best payoff arises when the manufacturer anticipates your discontinuation of services and does not raise prices. And the manufacturer's best payoff occurs when you provide the expected dealer services and he raises prices. Perhaps you could take turns? One period you could cut services and he would maintain prices; the next period he could raise prices and you would maintain services. How would you coordinate this on again–off again business relationship, assuming that merging the two entities into one vertically integrated firm is infeasible? What if your reputation for sharp dealing and misleading manufacturers as to your reliability caused you to miss future distributorship or dealership opportunities? What if it didn't?

As these questions multiply, one quickly comes to the realization that the coordination of business activities in a simultaneous game can be a real challenge. In this chapter, we will analyze the optimal tactics for playing Manufacturer/ Distributor 1. And in Chapter 15, we will see how these coordination problems can be resolved by, and indeed motivate, private voluntary contracting and the social invention of default rules in the law of contracts. For now, simply note how much predictability of rival behavior emerges in this coordination game if we introduce a small but pivotal change in the structure of the game—in particular, a sequential order of play.

A Sequential Coordination Game

Now suppose the manufacturer (*M*) must commit first to either increase advertising or leave it unchanged. And suppose this decision is easily observable and irreversible. For example, suppose the advertising increase is tied to the release of a product update by the manufacturer. If the manufacturer updates the product, the retail distributor (*R*) can anticipate with certainty that manufacturer advertising will follow. No longer must the distributor wonder whether the business opportunity is best represented by the first or the second column of Table 13.1. If the product update is released, thereafter the retail distributor knows that the first column is in play. And the retail distributor then has an obvious choice—for example, to continue providing services and receive $2,000 rather than discontinue services and receive zero. That is, the mere introduction of a sequential order to the decision-making made it possible to predict the optimal strategic behavior by both parties and resolve the ambiguity present in the simultaneous game.

    The new structure of the game can be represented as Figure 13.1, which is referred to as a **game tree** or *decision tree*. The order of the decisions is read from left to right, and each circle represents a decision node. *Update* or *Not update* identifies possible *actions* that the Player *M* can take at the first decision node. The *payoffs* for the manufacturer and the retailer, respectively, associated with each sequence of possible actions are listed in the right-hand columns.

    Since the manufacturer can look ahead and foresee that an *Update* of the product will make it advantageous for the retail distributor to *Continue,* the manufacturer finds it in his own best interest to commit to an update, then increase wholesale and MSRP prices, and follow through with advertising. That is, the manufacturer can look ahead and analyze what subsequent choices are in the retail distributor's best interest (i.e., his *best reply responses*) and then reason back to detect what actions are in the manufacturer's own best interest). Each party in Figure 13.1 is

Game Tree

A schematic diagram of a sequential game.

Figure 13.1   A Sequential Coordination Game: Manufacturer/Distributor 1

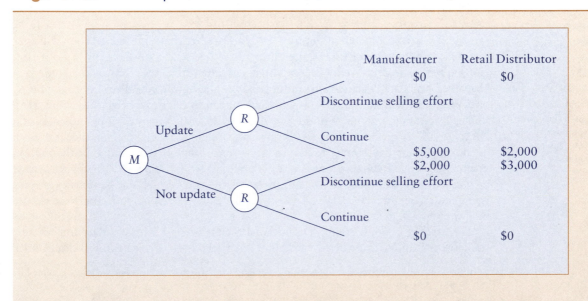

able to look ahead and reason back using the concept of best-reply response to predict the rival's behavior. None of this sequential reasoning was available in the simultaneous-play version of the game.

To take another example of sequential games, suppose two insurance companies, who manage employee benefit programs, are bidding for additional business in their area of expertise at a market rate of $200 per hour. The potential customers refuse to leave their current suppliers and award benefit management contracts to the new firms unless billing rates are cut by $50. Abbott, Abbott & Daughters (AA&D) decides to do just that. Your firm, Zekiel, Zekiel & Sons (ZZ&S), must decide whether to match the price cut and then allow customers to choose randomly between the two firms, or whether to lower rates still further to $100 per hour. Past experience suggests, however, that the price cutting may well not stop there. The clients will surely take their best current offer back and forth between the two firms, thereby forcing a downward price spiral. The question therefore is "How low will you go?" Importantly, in this game there is a penultimate stopping rule—i.e., at a price below your $40 cost, the additional business becomes unprofitable and must be refused.[2] AA&D has higher costs—namely, $66 per hour.

Again, your decision depends on an analysis of the sequence of predictable future events represented with a game tree or decision tree, such as in Figure 13.2. To simplify, assume that all rate cuts must be in $50 increments, that customers choose quickly between equal rate quotes using fair coin tosses (represented by capital letter *N* for *Nature*), that once a rate quote has been matched it cannot be lowered, and that many potential customers are present in the market. It is now your turn at node Z1 with rates at the $150-per-hour level. What should you do? Match rates or cut rates further?

First, as with all sequential games, ZZ&S needs to predict the subsequent best reply response of its rival at $100, look ahead to its own counter at $50, and finally analyze the endgame of prices below $50. Then ZZ&S will be in a position to reason back to the question at hand. **Endgame reasoning** always entails looking ahead to the last play in an ordered sequence of plays, identifying the player whose decisions will control the outcome of the endgame, and then predicting that player's most preferred choice.

Endgame Reasoning
An analysis of the final decision in a sequential game.

In this instance, knowing that AA&D would lose money at the $50 per hour rates in the lowest branch of Figure 13.2, you predict that at node A2 they will simply match your offer of $100 per hour and take their chances on a coin flip. Consequently, no decision by ZZ&S about a counter at $50 per hour will be required. However, your analysis is far from finished. Realizing all this allows you to employ **backwards induction** and rethink whether your plan to cut rates initially from $150 to $100 is, in fact, in your best interest. Because the endgame reasoning indicates that AA&D will quote a matching $100 rate and split the market at that price, why not on the previous play simply match their current offer of $150 and split the market at a higher price? Realizing that your own price cut from $150 to $100 will not attract new customers, but instead will simply lower the price at which the market is split, you decide to match AA&D's $150 offer, pass the customer a fair coin to toss, and be done with it.

Backwards Induction
Reasoning in reverse time sequence from later consequences back to earlier decisions.

The strategy pair for AA&D and ZZ&S that provides an equilibrium for this sequential bidding game is then {$150, Match}. That is, after the initial price cut to

---

[2] Alternatively, your customers may express shock and say, "If it's that inexpensive, why should I hire employee benefit consultants who usually are very pricey? Instead, I'll just employ someone to do the job on a regular basis in house." Neither outcome is desirable, and therefore at a price of $50 you encounter a stopping rule.

Figure 13.2   How Low Will You Go?

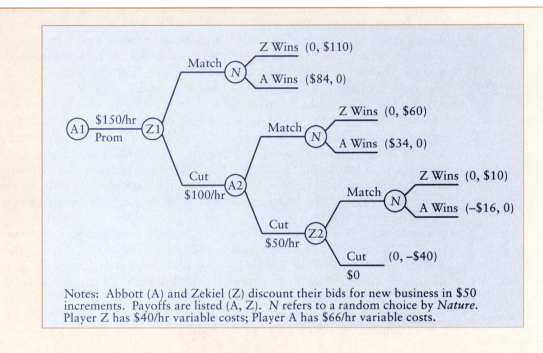

Notes: Abbott (A) and Zekiel (Z) discount their bids for new business in $50 increments. Payoffs are listed (A, Z). N refers to a random choice by *Nature*. Player Z has $40/hr variable costs; Player A has $66/hr variable costs.

elicit external business, the competitors in effect take turns selling their services at $150 per hour, each randomly winning 50 percent of the new business. This pricing strategy results in an expected profit of 0.5($150 − $40) = $55 per hour. Neither firm prefers the alternatives—namely, a 50-percent market share of the new business at $100 per hour, an expected value of $30 per hour—so, a noncooperative, self-enforcing agreement to share the market at higher prices emerges. Insurance companies, accountants, optometrists, and other suppliers of homogenous professional services seem to recognize that gainshare discounting even in the presence of a cost advantage often proves counterproductive.

Strategic Equilibrium in Sequential Games

Looking ahead to the rival's best-reply responses in the endgame and then reasoning back to each prior question is Reinhard Selten's concept of an equilibrium strategy for sequential games, a concept for which he and John Nash won the 1994 Nobel Prize in economics. Like many other pathbreaking ideas, this very intuitive strategic equilibrium concept is quite deceptive in its simplicity. A **Nash equilibrium strategy** is a decision maker's optimal action such that the payoff, when all other players make best-reply responses, exceeds that decision maker's payoff from any other action, again assuming best-reply responses. Selten applied this Nash equilibrium concept to sequential play and invented the concept of Nash equilibrium in a proper subgame. Selten's **subgame perfect equilibrium strategy** always involves looking ahead to the best-reply responses in all proper subgames and then reasoning back to your preferred strategy at earlier decision points.

Nash Equilibrium Strategy
An equilibrium concept for nondominant strategy games.

Subgame Perfect Equilibrium Strategy
An equilibrium concept for noncooperative sequential games.

As we saw in analyzing "How low will you go?" some nodes of a decision tree, such as Z2 in the bottom half of Figure 13.2 and the endgames thereafter, can be eliminated from consideration if they cannot be reached by best-reply responses. Such decision points are "off the equilibrium path." Selten's idea was that only in the proper subgame nodes would the Nash equilibrium concept hold. From Z2, AA&D need not consider the effect of ZZ&S matching $50 prices rather than discounting to zero. The reason is that AA&D's cutting rates to $50 in the first place is not a best-reply response for AA&D; that action at node A2 results in losses ($-$16) for AA&D with 0.5 probability and zero profits with 0.5 probability, whereas matching the $100 rate results in $34 or zero profits, each with a probability of 0.5—i.e., expected profits of $17. Consequently, the nodes beyond an AA&D price cut to $50 are not a proper subgame; they cannot be reached by best-reply responses.[3] Subgame perfect equilibrium strategy therefore entails analyzing the outcomes associated with actions and best-reply responses at A1 and Z1, the only proper subgame nodes of Figure 13.2.[4] Again, {$150, Match} proves to be the subgame perfect equilibrium strategy.

Sometimes this identification of proper and improper subgames can get quite complicated when there can be many possible endgames. To illustrate, consider the three-way comparative advertising duel in Exercise 3 at the end of this chapter. With varying degrees of success, three firms attack one another with comparative advertising in pairwise, sequential competitions until just one firm remains. It can take two complete rounds of advertising attacks and almost 20 endgames to analyze the subgame perfect equilibrium strategy for that problem.

BUSINESS GAMING AT VERIZON[5]

Former Verizon chairman Ray Smith employed the techniques, exercises, and lessons of game theory throughout his organization. In "war games," teams of Verizon managers assumed the role of major competitors and explored tactics that could defeat Verizon's business plans. Other teams detailed future contingencies in a large game tree that allowed Verizon to map its future moves and countermoves as well as uncover the competitive effects of new technological developments (like digital voice and video transmission) before they happened. Traditional planning models lock managers into assumptions the importance of which they can only gauge through sensitivity analysis. But sequential game analysis constantly reminds managers to shape the game, not just play it. That can mean reversing the order of play by highlighting the value of preemptive strikes in some circumstances (e.g., in merging with Nynex) but highlighting the value of "fast second" best reply responses in other circumstances (e.g., in basic research and product development by Lucent Technologies).

---

[3] By analogous reasoning, the subgame at A2 itself is eliminated because ZZ&S's best-reply response to the initial promotional discount is to match at $150 per hour, not to cut rates to $100. Thus, the decisions from Node A2 onward cannot be reached by best-reply responses and cannot therefore be involved in subgame perfect equilibrium strategy.

[4] The reader may wonder about the relevance of A2 and matching prices at $100 per hour if there is a miscommunication or strategic mistake by ZZ&S at Node Z1. These are valid questions because mistakes and miscommunication do happen in the reality of business rivalry. Indeed, a refinement of subgame perfect strategy allows for just such mistakes and describes equilibrium strategy for either player in this game less uniquely as {Match any price below $200}.

[5] Based on "Business as a War Game: Report from the Battlefront," *Fortune*, September 30, 1996, pp. 190–193.

In addition, Verizon has learned to recognize endgames that are unfavorable to the company and reshape the structure of the competitive rivalry in those businesses. Verizon recently redefined the scope of the telephone industry's local network strategy game by winning approval in the courts for telephone companies to own the content transmitted over their phone lines. Verizon managers are now hard at work analyzing the new larger game that includes business directories, digitized movies, and video production.

BUSINESS RIVALRY AS A SEQUENTIAL GAME

It is important to emphasize that the subgame perfect equilibrium concept is self-enforcing. It predicts stable rival response, not because of effective monitoring and third-party enforcement, but because each party would be worse off departing from the equilibrium strategy pair than it would be implementing it. Thus, Abbott, Abbott & Daughters and Zekiel, Zekiel & Sons have, in effect, made credible commitments to one another not to lower rates below the $150 per hour necessary to attract the new business. Credibility mechanisms are the key to securing subgame perfect strategies. And credibility can work both ways; credible commitments can also become credible threats. Let's see how.

Consider a well-established pharmaceutical manufacturer of ulcer relief medicine, who presently markets the only effective curative therapy possessing no known side effects and earns $100,000. This incumbent (let's call the firm "Pastense") faces an entry challenge from a small potential entrant new to the industry ("Potent" for short). Potent has discovered a new therapeutic process that also has the potential to cure stomach ulcers. Potent must decide whether to enter the monopoly market or stay out and license its trade secrets to any one of several interested buyers. Pastense must decide whether to maintain its present high prices, moderate its prices, or radically discount its prices. The payoffs are displayed in Table 13.2. If Potent enters,

Table 13.2   Payoffs (in Thousands) from Entry Deterrence for Accommodation in Ulcer Relief Pharmaceuticals

		Potent (the potential entrant)	
		Stay Out and License	Enter
Pastense (the incumbent)	Maintain High Price	$80 / $30	$0 / $80
	Moderate Price	$70 / $60	$35 / $50
	Discount Price	$40 / $20	$50 / $40

Note: Column-player payoffs are above diagonal. Row-player payoffs are below diagonal.

http://

Read a RAND article relating first-mover advantage to the decline of the U.S. machine tool manufacturing industry in the 1980s at the following Internet site:

http://www.rand.org/ publications/RB/RB1500/

and Pastense does not moderate or discount, suppose all the ulcer relief business goes to the new entrant and the incumbent realizes nothing. In contrast, with entry and discount prices, suppose the incumbent's product enjoys a slight cost advantage and earns a $10,000 greater payoff (i.e., $50,000 and $40,000 in the bottom right corner of Table 13.2). Moderate incumbent prices result in a $35,000 payoff for Pastense and a $50,000 payoff for Potent.

To prevent the reduction of its profit from $100,000 as a monopolist to $50,000 post-entry, Pastense itself might be a prime candidate for the purchase of Potent's trade secret. Realistically, however, it is liable to run up against antitrust constraints that restrict mergers between dominant incumbents and new entrants. Note also that what another established pharmaceutical manufacturer will pay to license the trade secret, with all the attendant technology transfer problems and yet significantly more extensive distribution and marketing experience, bears little correlation to what Potent itself could hope to earn upon entry. Potent receives its second highest payoff ($60,000) when it licenses its trade secret and Pastense maintains moderate prices. Potent earns the least (namely, $20,000) when it stays out and licenses, but Pastense discounts.

First-Mover and Fast Second Advantages

As is now obvious, "Who can do what, when?" is the essence of any such sequential strategy game. The order of play is pivotal, because it determines who initiates and who replies, and this determines the best-reply response in the endgame, and thus the strategic equilibrium. As is natural in the present case, suppose the new entrant must choose first whether or not to enter, and the incumbent selects a pricing response thereafter. Figure 13.3 displays the game tree for this order of play. The endgame appears in the two nodes to the right, each labeled I for Incumbent. If Potent enters, Pastense strongly

Figure 13.3   Entry Deterrence I: Incumbent Pricing (in Thousands) in Response to Entry Threat

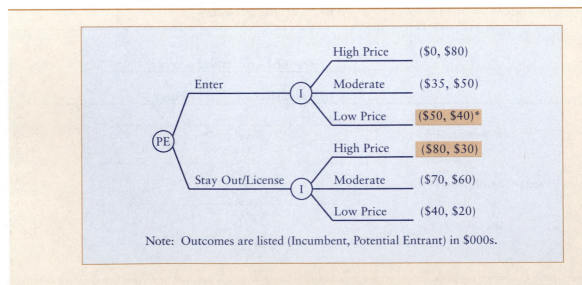

Note: Outcomes are listed (Incumbent, Potential Entrant) in $000s.

prefers a Low pricing response, because $50,000 far exceeds the zero or $35,000 outcomes from either the High or Moderate alternatives. This analysis of the incumbent's best-reply response allows Potent to predict that its own $80,000 and $50,000 outcomes should be eliminated from further consideration. Even though each is theoretically associated with its entry, neither can be obtained if Pastense does what is in its own best interest (i.e., makes a best-reply response in this proper subgame).

Similarly in the bottom endgame node, if Potent stays out, its royalty payoffs of $60,000 cannot be obtained, because Pastense will price High to secure $80,000 for itself rather than accept its lower $70,000 and $40,000 alternatives. This means

Focal Outcomes of Interest
Payoffs involved in an
analysis of equilibrium
strategy.

that there are only two **focal outcomes of interest** to Potent in making its entry decision: the shaded payoffs of $40,000 from entering and $30,000 from staying out. Being a value-maximizing firm, Potent decides to enter, predictably, and the events of the starred subgame perfect strategic equilibrium {Enter, Discount} then unfold. Notice that both players could be better off with the {$70,000, $60,000} outcome in the lower node, but Potent cannot expect Pastense to respond with Moderate rather than High prices should Potent stay out and try to secure the $60,000 payoff from licensing. Consequently, with the present structure of the game, a payoff of $40,000 from {$50,000, $40,000} is the best they can hope to do.

However, to illustrate the pivotal importance of the order of play, let's mix things up a bit. From the incumbent's point of view too, the outcomes {$50,000, $40,000} are not entirely satisfactory. Given its second-mover timing, Pastense did as well as could be expected. But the incumbent may wonder whether seizing the first-mover initiative would have worked to its advantage. The fact of the matter is that no general rule on this point exists; sometimes it will, and sometimes it will not. Each sequential game situation is in this way unique.

To analyze the question, in Figure 13.4 we reverse the order of play in Entry Deterrence II. Now, the potential entrant controls the endgame, and the incumbent

Figure 13.4   Entry Deterrence II: Entry Deterrence in Response to Incumbent Price Commitment (in Thousands)

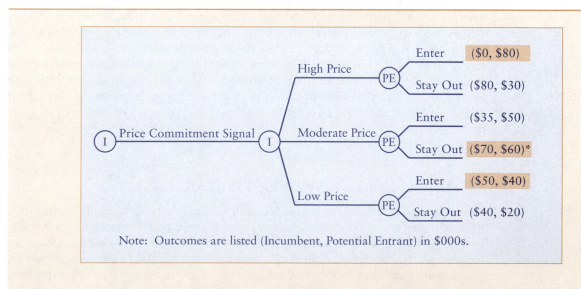

Note: Outcomes are listed (Incumbent, Potential Entrant) in $000s.

must announce irreversible pricing policies in advance. Saying they are irreversible does not make it so, but more on that in the next section. Analyzing the three endgame nodes, Pastense realizes that Potent will choose to enter when high prices are pre-committed, stay out when moderate prices are precommitted, or enter when discount prices are precommitted. Knowing this, Pastense prefers to announce a moderate pric-ing policy, and the starred {Moderate, Stay Out} strategic equilibrium eventuates. Not only has the potential entrant's behavior changed, but in addition, the payoff to Pastense has risen from $50,000 to $70,000. In this instance, a first-mover advantage proved to be just what the name implies.

Example

TECHNOLOGY LEADER OR FAST SECOND: IBM[6]

Whether to secure first-mover advantages in the development of new computing tech-nologies or instead engage in a pattern of quick imitation (i.e., a "fast second" strat-egy) poses a more difficult choice than one might think. In the absence of sunk-cost investments as a barrier to entry, hit-and-run entry often proves very effective. Apple computer commercialized the graphical user interface that Xerox invented. Microsoft quickly challenged Netscape's early dominance of Internet browsers. And Sun Microsystems developed the reduced instruction-set computing (RISC) that IBM pioneered.

By restraining up-front investments in basic research and focusing instead on the development of products, IBM has recently switched from a technology leader to a "first of a kind" systems problem solver for high-margin customers. One example has been the marriage of computer imaging and voice-recognition devices that allows hospital radiologists and surgeons to superimpose X-ray images and text on any PC throughout the local-area network in a medical center. Doctors speak to one another while viewing PC-based images, and the IBM hardware and software creates a dig-ital transcript of their diagnostic findings and expert opinions. Other examples would be IBM's wireless modem for the cellular industry and eraser-heads to replace the unwieldy and easily damaged trackball cursor controls in PCs.

On the other hand, IBM Microelectronics has recently leveraged the company's long-standing basic research effort in materials science into a breakthrough in sili-con chips. IBM's engineers have discovered how to form copper rather than aluminum circuits and yet prevent the copper atoms from bleeding into the surface of the sili-con. Copper is a more conductive material and therefore can be laid down in nar-rower circuits than aluminum. The more circuits etched on a square centimeter of silicon, the more powerful and cost effective the computer chip. IBM's breakthrough in copper-on-silicon circuitry promises to increase computing power 40 percent for any given size chip. Here, a company may well want patent protection of its first-mover advantage.

CREDIBLE THREATS AND COMMITMENTS

In multiperiod games, all threats and commitments derive their credibility ultimately from whether or not the threat maker or commitment maker successfully identifies and adopts subgame perfect strategies. In Entry Deterrence I (see Figure 13.3), Pastense's threat to discount the ulcer relief medicine if Potent entered was credible precisely because discounting was, in fact, a best-reply response. Any other response

---

[6] Based on "Einstein and Eraser-Heads," *Wall Street Journal*, October 6, 1997, p. 1.

Credible Threat
A conditional strategy the threat maker is worse off ignoring than implementing.

would have made Pastense worse off (i.e., lowered its payoff). A **credible threat** is therefore defined as a conditional strategy that the threat maker is worse off ignoring than implementing. By the same token, a commitment by Pastense to maintain high prices (i.e., not to discount and thereby spoil the royalty value of Potent's trade secret) if Potent would stay out of the market is a credible commitment. Again, this action is the incumbent's best-reply response to Potent's staying out and just earning royalties from the ongoing value of its trade secret. Therefore, without any monitoring or third-party enforcement whatsoever, one can fully rely on Pastense to honor its commitment, because it would not be in its own best interest to do otherwise.

In Figure 13.3, if Potent wanted to secure a commitment from Pastense to price at the *moderate* level in exchange for some portion of the much larger $60,000 royalties, Potent would need to employ a binding, third-party-enforceable contractual agreement. It is simply not in Pastense's best-reply-response interest to fulfill such a commitment otherwise.

You can now begin to see why purposeful individual behavior and a shared objective in groups is so critical to game-theoretic reasoning. To predict choices of highly interdependent players, one must know what makes them tick, what true goals they seek, and what the consequence of various actions is on those goals. Sometimes this is harder than it sounds. For example, performance-based incentives and takeover threats often align management objectives quite closely with stockholder value, but what motivates a closely held, family-run business is sometimes difficult to fathom. Moreover, consistently transmitted signals of business strategy are often jammed or misinterpreted by the receiver. Therefore, to ensure the effective communication of credible threats and credible commitments requires some guidelines. This can be illustrated by returning to the Entry Deterrence game.

As we have seen, Pastense found the switch to first-mover status highly advantageous. By promising to maintain moderate prices rather than discount, its profits increased from $50,000 to $70,000 when Potent sold out rather than entered. The question we must now reexamine, however, is "Why did Potent believe Pastense?" After all, it is clear from the original game tree in Figure 13.3 that once Potent licensed its trade secret to another less capable potential entrant (let's call the new firm "Impotent"), Pastense was better off raising its price back to the high level it had once enjoyed, thereby receiving the $80,000 payoff from high prices rather than a $70,000 payoff from moderate prices. Thus, Pastense's promise to maintain a moderate price was not a **credible commitment** because Pastense is worse off making good on the commitment than ignoring it. One might be inclined to respond that likewise Potent can renege on its commitment to stay out of the ulcer relief business. Licensing a trade secret for royalty revenue today need not preclude Potent's potential entry tomorrow. Indeed, such royalty agreements seldom include a no-competition clause. However, there is a difference. Potent's payoff is maximized by staying out! Its commitment to stay out if the incumbent maintains moderate prices *is* in Potent's own best interest. Staying out is a best-reply response; therefore it is a credible commitment.

Credible Commitment
A promise that the promise-giver is worse off violating than fulfilling.

Mechanisms for Establishing Credibility[7]

As second mover, Potent controls the endgame and therefore finds itself in a position to insist on the necessary assurances from Pastense. Several alternative mechanisms for establishing credibility present themselves. Pastense might establish a bond or contractual side payment, which would be forfeited if Pastense raised prices.

[7] This section relies heavily on A. Dixit and B. Nalebuff, *Thinking Strategically: The Competitive Edge in Business, Politics, and Everyday Life* (New York: Norton, 1991), especially Chapters 5 and 6.

Nonredeployable Reputational Asset
A reputation whose value is lost if sold or licensed.

Some such contracts, referred to as maximum resale price maintenance agreements, do exist between retailers and their suppliers. Another possible credibility mechanism would be for Pastense to invest heavily in its moderate price strategy to establish a reputation for moderate prices. Loss of this **nonredeployable reputational asset** would discourage reneging on its commitment to maintain moderate prices. Third, Pastense could short-circuit or interrupt the repricing process by preselling its ulcer relief medicine with forward contracts. Forward sale contracts would generally not be repriced because the courts generally refuse to excuse forward or future contract breach for any reason. Fourth, Pastense could enter into teamwork or an alliance relationship with Potent that would sufficiently dilute the rewards from reneging on its commitment, perhaps by taking an equity stake in Potent. Fifth, Pastense could change the structure of the game to require that both it and Potent only "take small steps." In the next section, we analyze leasing as a way to pursue this credibility mechanism.

Hostage Mechanism
A mechanism for establishing the credibility of a threat or commitment.

And finally and most practically in this situation, Pastense could arrange an irreversible and irrevocable **hostage mechanism**, whereby likely future customers were granted a moderate price guarantee. Sometimes referred to as "most favored nation" clauses, these price guarantees promise double refunds if the customer discovers any lower-price Pastense transaction during the next or the previous year. As long as Potent observed at least one moderate price transaction before licensing its trade secret, it could rest assured that Pastense had now offered a credible commitment not to raise prices. The resulting double refunds should Pastense raise prices and the sacrifice of future transactions with its own repeat-purchase customers should it renege on the refunds ensure that Pastense will finally be better off honoring its commitment to moderate prices than ignoring it. And again, notice that these are entirely self-enforcing agreements.

Example

http://

For a real-world example of a double-the-difference price guarantee related to textbook purchases, see the following Internet site:
http://www.uofabookstores.com/uaz/dept/textbooks/lowpriceguarantee.asp

DOUBLE-THE-DIFFERENCE PRICE GUARANTEES: CIRCUIT CITY

At times, Circuit City offers to rebate twice the differential purchase price of a VCR to preferred customers should those customers find the same VCR selling for less anywhere in the local area over the next three months. This rebate guarantee will be enforced by the courts. As in the simultaneous-play pricing game between PepsiCo and Coca-Cola, Circuit City normally would be better off discounting (maybe even steeply discounting) when competitors like Sound Warehouse maintain high prices. But in the face of this double-the-difference low-price guarantee, Circuit City would lose more money on rebates than it could possibly gain from any amount of incremental business it could reasonably expect to take away from Sound Warehouse. In effect, Circuit City has given its competitor a hostage that supports a commitment to maintain high prices.

In Figure 13.5, Circuit City provides a bond of its intentions to maintain high prices by preannouncing the double-the-difference price guarantee. Sound Warehouse must then decide whether to discount or maintain high prices in light of the Circuit City rebate program. Like all good hostage mechanisms, the hostage is worth more to the hostage giver than its value in use to the recipient. That is, Sound Warehouse *could* trigger double-rebate payments at Circuit City by discounting its own price. And harming a competitor is a reasonable secondary goal, but it's only secondary. Securing your own highest payoff perhaps through legal cooperation with a competitor is the primary goal. Because Circuit City would respond to a Sound Warehouse discount by matching the lower price point, Sound Warehouse would gain nothing by using the hostage in this way. Indeed, for the hostage recipient such a decision would lead to the payoff labeled "Worse" in the top right-hand corner of Figure 13.5.

Knowing that Circuit City controls the endgame and that it would be in Circuit City's best interest after announcing the rebate program to match a discount price, Sound Warehouse finds itself preferring to maintain high prices. Because Circuit City is also best off by maintaining high prices, the payoff {Best*, Better} results. Thus, by introducing a price guarantee that limited its own ability to take advantage of its opponent's vulnerability at high prices, Circuit City secured first-best outcomes when the alternative was Worse (i.e., compare the shaded and unshaded boxed payoffs in Figure 13.5). A hostage mechanism establishing one's credible commitment to maintain high prices if the rival maintains high prices will often elicit high prices from that rival. Thus, from the point of view of both companies, double-the-difference low-price guarantees are unambiguously preferred. Of course, consumer advocates will not prefer these high price outcomes, but complaining about double-the-difference price guarantees attracts few sympathizers to the consumer cause.

As we discussed in Chapter 10, all buyers rationally discount experience goods like used cars and computer components if they cannot verify independently at the point of purchase the seller's quality claims. A replacement guarantee or a product

Figure 13.5   Double-the-Difference Price Guarantees

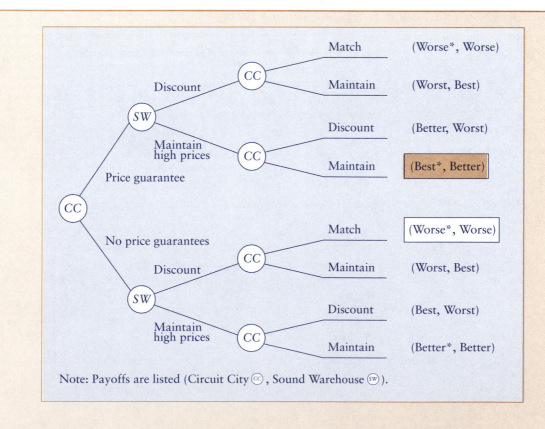

Note: Payoffs are listed (Circuit City ⓒⓒ, Sound Warehouse ⓢⓦ).

performance repair warranty are other good examples of hostage mechanisms—in this case, hostage mechanisms that establish the credibility of a seller's commitment to deliver high-quality components in goods it offers for sale. Should the seller violate his or her commitment, a third party (usually the courts) will impose on the seller monetary judgments that are larger than the incremental cost of upgrading from lower to higher quality inputs in the first place. Therefore, the buyer is assured of a higher quality machine when the seller offers to include a replacement guarantee or repair warranty for the same (or a slightly higher) price. These guarantees and warranties illustrate a *credible commitment* mechanism—i.e., third-party-enforceable promises that the promise-giver would be worse off violating than keeping.

What exactly constitutes a credible replacement guarantee when sellers indicted for mail fraud may be judgment-proof? Consider Figure 13.6. Claims by Dooney & Bourke handbags, Revo sunglasses, and Sewell Cadillac for lifetime repair or replacement provide credible commitments. Why? The key is repeat customer business. Because incremental sales to established or referral customers are much less expensive than attracting new customers, the customer-for-life relationships can provide a hostage mechanism. Dooney & Bourke's, Revo's, or Sewell Cadillac's normally preposterous replacement or service guarantees backed by a brand name, unique distribution channel, or other non-redeployable asset become credible because of the seller's dependence on repeat or referral business. In effect, Sewell Cadillac says "My sunk cost investments cannot be recovered (and, by definition, cannot be

Figure 13.6   An Illustration of a Non-Credible Lifetime Guarantee

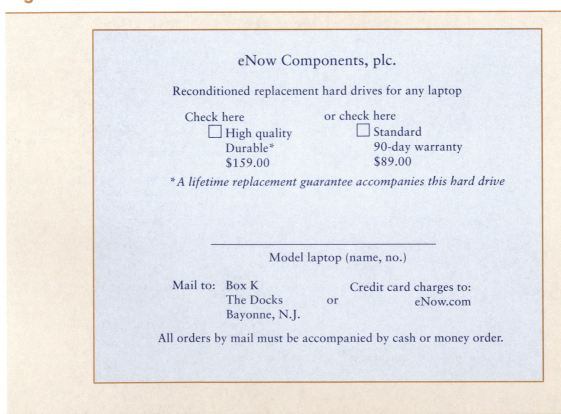

eNow Components, plc.

Reconditioned replacement hard drives for any laptop

Check here   or check here
☐ High quality   ☐ Standard
Durable*   90-day warranty
$159.00 $89.00

*A lifetime replacement guarantee accompanies this hard drive

_____
Model laptop (name, no.)

Mail to: Box K   Credit card charges to:
          The Docks   or   eNow.com
          Bayonne, N.J.

All orders by mail must be accompanied by cash or money order.

liquidated at anything near their historical cost) unless I earn your repeat business." Not so in the case of eNow Components, plc; this company is not likely to plan on more than one transaction with any customer. It may not even plan on doing business through its present post office box or e-business site for long.

Example

NONCREDIBLE COMMITMENTS: BURLINGTON INDUSTRIES

Classic examples of noncooperative business strategies that malfunction because of the absence of credible commitments include the quota "commitments" in a cartel and the "commitment" not to compete after purchasing surplus equipment in a declining industry. Burlington Industries has experienced many problems with its overseas sales of old textile looms, often acquired in mergers and then liquidated at scrap value. The foreign buyers restore the old equipment and then backship their production into the United States despite no-competition clauses in the equipment purchase contracts. Burlington has now begun to destroy old equipment, not just dismantle it, especially in declining product lines where it wishes to pursue a niche strategy as "the last iceman."[8] The idea is to preserve high margins as the last company to sell a particular textile product, block ice, manual typewriters (Smith Corona, Brother, or Olivetti), or mainframe computers by destroying excess capacity. IBM also bought up Amdahl Millenium and Hitachi Skyline mainframes and crushed them.

As to the quota commitments in a cartel, recall from Chapter 12 that in order to sustain monopoly cartel prices, every cartel member must restrain its output to the assigned quota, but commitments to do so are simply not credible commitments. As a consequence, despite many attempts to build teamwork, to secure hostages (both economic and political), and to employ other credibility mechanisms, almost all cartels prove to be highly unstable. The experience in the corrugated cardboard industry is typical. Price-fixing indictments suggest that cartels among the cardboard manufacturers within a sales region form approximately quarterly and break up usually within a week to 10 days. In this case, the inability to secure credible commitments serves a desirable public purpose.

Credible Commitments in Leasing and Renewable Licenses

What buyers will pay for a capital equipment purchase like a corporate jet, a mainframe computer, or a business license depends in part on how well the seller resolves some credible commitment issues. If a piece of equipment has working life that will extend over several market periods, an early adopter of a new model worries about obsolescence risk, uncertain product reliability, and falling prices. How well a manufacturer addresses these three perceived risks of buying early will determine the rate of adoption and the prices paid.

What competitive advantages IBM's newest mainframe or minicomputer might offer an information technology user like a direct marketer will be seriously compromised whenever IBM introduces a still newer model and makes the direct marketer's machine obsolete. In addition, other potential buyers who discern somewhat less advantage in the new equipment will likely receive the benefit of a reduced price from IBM at some later date. Knowing this, the first buyer hesitates, adopts later, and

---

[8] Kathryn Harrigan has written about this superficially very curious strategy in "Endgame Strategy," *Forbes,* July 1987, pp. 181–196.

offers to pay less than she otherwise would for the new technology. To overcome this persistent problem that will recur with every new generation of equipment, IBM must somehow credibly commit to maintaining high prices and to a planned rate of obsolescence that allows early buyers time to recover their investment costs.

In an industry with very slowly moving technology, a dominant firm could make contractual commitments to phase in new updated equipment only on a preset (delayed) schedule. At times, tractor-trailer trucks have been sold this way, and to a certain extent, the limited body style change from year to year in some automobile models reflects the same idea. However, in the computer industry, even IBM cannot afford such a straitjacket; technology simply moves too fast. So what alternatives remain? Buyers of updated capital equipment can't be expected to risk a lot of capital soon after the rollout of a new model; yet, companies producing computer equipment cannot lock themselves into delays.

Model Upgrades: The Practice of Versioning

One approach is to continuously upgrade the product at higher and higher prices, what Carl Shapiro and Hal Varian call "versioning."[9] Microsoft has adopted this model upgrade strategy with their Windows operating system. The buyer is told, in effect, don't hesitate; the next model will be even more expensive. But of course operating systems are not consumed on the spot, and they don't wear out. Like any durable goods monopolist, Microsoft's biggest competitor for Windows NT is Windows 2000, just as the best substitute for Windows 2000 was Windows 98. Another approach, therefore, is to ask buyers to take small steps by leasing the equipment one market period at a time. Although this fails to slow (and may quicken) the pace of new product introductions, buyers risk less up-front capital and therefore can be induced more easily to take on the new model and update their capital equipment more frequently *at higher prices*. IBM employed exactly this approach for many years by only offering to lease their mainframe computers.

Similarly, Dell Computer advertises "How many companies will let you return your computer when it becomes obsolete?" and leases its PCs for $99 per month with the opportunity to renew for a new updated computer two years later. And BMW auto leases provide bumper-to-bumper scheduled maintenance and unexpected repairs for the lifetime of the lease. So leasing mitigates obsolescence and maintenance risk. But what about the early adopters' risk of subsequent price reductions? How does leasing address that risk?

Example

LEASING OF DIGITAL MOVIEHOUSE PROJECTORS: HUGHES-JVC[10]

George Lucas's *Star Wars* movies are now filmed entirely on digital cameras. Cinema companies like General Cinema and Carmike much prefer digital film over the sixty-pound celluloid film prints that often reach diameters of five feet. Downloading compressed-signal digital films with high-speed secure data networks will allow the moviehouses much more flexibility in their scheduling. In addition, the sound and projection quality will no longer deteriorate after a few dozen showings. The movie production companies also like the new technology because a full national rollout of a celluloid movie requires 5,000 prints that cost approximately $2,000 each to

---

[9] See C. Shapiro and H. Varian, "Versioning: The Smart Way to Sell Information," *Harvard Business Review*, November-December 1998, pp. 106–118.

[10] Based on "Curtains for Celluloid," *The Economist*, March 27, 1999, p. 81.

produce, and it necessitates a large fleet of trucks to move the film canisters about the country.

The biggest hurdle to the fast adoption of this new technology is the $500,000 replacement cost for the new projectors in a small (five-screen) cinema. With the U.S. industry badly overbuilt (some estimates suggest as many as 10,000 more cinemas than the market demand requires), General Cinema, Carmike, and others are hesitant to commit this much additional capital. Each would like to wait for the discounted digital projector prices that they believe will come later. Hughes-JVC, who manufactures one of the projectors, and CineComm Digital Cinema plan to lease the projectors to cinemas. Distribution will be handled by satellite to cut operating costs enough that leasing fees for the projectors can be tied to actual showings. This allows lower revenue cinemas in overbuilt markets to participate in earlier adoption of the new technology.

The Tactical Advantage of Licensing and Leasing

Careful analysis of the manufacturer's asymmetric information in making planned obsolescence and price discount decisions reveals the tactical advantage of leasing. Because the manufacturer knows the marketing plans and can estimate the pace of technology and the risk of obsolescence much better than the end user, one would think lease terms can be more favorable when the seller undertakes to absorb the risk of price promotions and planned obsolescence. That is, in a competitive marketplace for capital equipment leases (like the corporate jet lease market), one would expect sellers to offer closed-end leases with residual values that reflect their very accurate estimates of what a two-year-old corporate jet will be worth. This residual value is what really establishes the credibility of the manufacturer's commitment over the lease period to refrain from discounting or introducing a new model that would render the current model obsolete. Were the leasewriter (the lessor) to violate this promise, the asset returned at the end of the lease would be worth less than the residual value at which the manufacturer-lessor has agreed to take it back. In effect, the manufacturer has given a hostage to the leaseholder (the lessee). By agreeing to take back the capital equipment for a preset amount and dispose of it in the resale market, the manufacturer-lessor has credibly committed to a limited set of price promotions and to a limited rate of planned obsolescence.

Example

NETJETS FRACTIONAL OWNERSHIP PLANS FOR LEARJET AND GULFSTREAM AIRCRAFT

LearJet, Inc., a division of Bombardier Aerospace, employs the same techniques in marketing their fractional jet ownership in frequent ads in the *Wall Street Journal*. FlexJets offers guaranteed access on four hours' notice to a fleet of Learjet and Challenger business aircraft for as little as $175,000 per year cost. Flightjets.com offers 100-percent availability, predictable fixed costs, and guaranteed liquidity should a client need to sell out. NetJets, a division of Warren Buffet's Berkshire Hathaway Company, offers fractional shares in "the world's largest and finest fleet of 450 Gulfstream aircraft with guaranteed availability, guaranteed costs, and guaranteed liquidity of your asset." These contractual arrangements are essentially operating leases.

One indication that these fractional ownership-leasing arrangements are designed to establish the credible commitment of the lessor is their price stability as luxury-goods sales collapsed in the stock market slump of 2000–2002. NetJets continues to offer a $44-million Gulfstream V_1, the top-of-the-line business jet, for $10 million up front and $678,000 per year plus operating costs of $3,118 per hour in flight, despite a collapse of the resale value of the plane NetJets takes back at the end of the lease. A used Gulfstream comparable to the lease-end aircraft in late 2002 sold for $18 million, when more normal resale prices would be $25–$28 million.[11] Again, someone (either lessor or lessee) must bear these repricing risks, but leasing offers a credible commitment from manufacturers to early adopters that such asset price collapses will not result from seller price promotions subsequent to an early adopter's purchase decision.

In contrast, deal making on luxury new car sales in 2003 drove the resale value of two-year-old Lexus LS 430s and Sabb 9-5s down by 23.4 percent from $53,500 to $41,000 in just one year, compared to a 14.7 percent reduction for two-year-old models one year earlier.

Of course, there still remains the risk of technological developments and competitor discounts that the manufacturer cannot control. The lessor and lessee have credibly committed some things and left others to chance. All such remaining risks will be priced into the terms of the residual value lease. As a result, over the lifetime of the equipment it will not be cheaper to lease rather than to buy. To draw an analogy, the buyer who insists on a product warranty imposes the estimable risk of product failure on the seller-lessor; therefore this risk allocation gets priced into a higher lease payment.

Closed-End Lease with Residual Values
A credible commitment mechanism for limiting the rate of planned obsolescence and establishing delays in price promotion.

Nevertheless, manufacturers need some way of credibly committing themselves to maintaining high asking prices and a limited rate of planned obsolescence over the buyer's holding period. Only then will early adopters pay the higher prices at which manufacturers wish to transact in the early mature phase of an upgraded product's life cycle. **Closed-end leases that declare a residual value** offer such a credible commitment because they demonstrate and certify just what the manufacturer's best estimates of forward value truly are. Such leases therefore shore up purchase prices paid by early adopters of durable equipment.

Example

LICENSING OF TAXI MEDALLIONS AND CELL PHONES

Similarly, by selling a taxi medallion or a cellular phone authorization as a renewable license, a municipality can credibly commit to a constrained increase in the supply of the city's transportation and communication infrastructure. If the city were to insist on an outright purchase, taxi and cellular entrepreneurs would be concerned that soon thereafter the city would flood the market with additional taxis and cell phone companies. Consequently, the amounts bid for the right to do business would decline substantially. For example, in Washington, D.C., the city council authorized essentially open entry, attracted 12 cabs for every 1,000 residents, and found that the equilibrium entry fee was $25. In contrast, New York City has restricted entry to 11,797 taxi medallions, 2 taxis per 1,000 residents, and as a result the New York taxi medallion asset transfers for $140,000.[12]

---

[11] "Prices on Private Planes Dive," *Wall Street Journal,* September 5, 2002, and "The Bargain Jaguar," March 20, 2003, p. D1.

[12] "New York Taxi Policy," *Wall Street Journal,* March 17, 1992, p. A14, and "Put the Brakes on Taxicab Monopolies," November 6, 1984, p. A20.

The point is not that potential license holders wish to avoid being duped, although of course all of us *are* motivated to choose tactics which avoid such embarrassments. Instead, it's that licenses authorizing a business are a property right that the license holders may need to resell. Random disturbances befall every company, and license holders cannot assume that they will be able to operate forever. Licenses are durable capital assets, and the preservation of their resale value is of no less concern than would be the case for an owner of a mainframe computer or corporate jet. Municipalities can raise more money, therefore, with renewable leases for all business licenses.

Exercise 13 at the end of the chapter provides some data for calculating the renewable lease amounts for a taxi medallion.

What occurs in business licensing by municipal and state governments also occurs in the licensing of trade secrets and patents. Again, credible commitments by seller-lessors to actions that will maintain forward asset values are the key to eliciting buyer-lessee willingness to pay. Certainly, at times, a patent holder will maximize value by retaining the patent for its own exclusive use. Manufacturing capacities can be expanded, advertising bought, and distribution systems built. Fungible capital is always available to support promising business plans, whatever the stage of development of the patented or patentable products. Nevertheless, the unique manufacturing capabilities, product designers, brand names, or distribution channels of another company may increase the capitalized value of a patent. Taking small steps through renewable leasing and offering residual values as hostages are the credible commitment mechanisms that maximize the value of many trade secrets and patents.

This section has argued that renewable licensing and leasing offers tactical advantages in establishing credible commitments not obtainable with outright sales. Again, this does *not* imply that leasing will be generally cheaper than buying. Any costs imposed on the seller by the credibility mechanisms (e.g., a higher residual value) will be priced into the lease. The point is simply that some credible commitments impose lower cost on the asymmetrically informed manufacturer as a lessor than would be the discount to the buyer required to achieve the same ends through an outright sale. Consequently, manufacturer profitability increases with renewable licensing and leasing, relative to the alternative profitability available from the outright sale of durable equipment, business licenses, or patents.

Entry Deterrence and Accommodation

In this section, we examine the tactical issues that arise when an incumbent firm faces an imminent threat of entry. We analyze whether to accommodate or attempt to deter the potential entrant and what capacity planning or limit pricing or sunk cost investment tactics to employ in that effort. At the end of the section, we characterize contestable markets as dependent on both entry and exit barriers. First, consider another type of credible threat or commitment, that can markedly influence the subsequent competition—namely, an investment in nonredeployable excess capacity. Irreversible investment in excess capacity credibly commits a high-priced incumbent to serve the price-sensitive new customers who might be attracted into the market by a potential entrant's discounting. If these and other regular customers can be expected to favor doing business with the incumbent, then excess capacity investment can substantially enhance the deterrent effect of an incumbent's threat to cut prices in response to entry.

Figure 13.7   Excess Capacity Enhances Credibility in Entry Deterrence Games

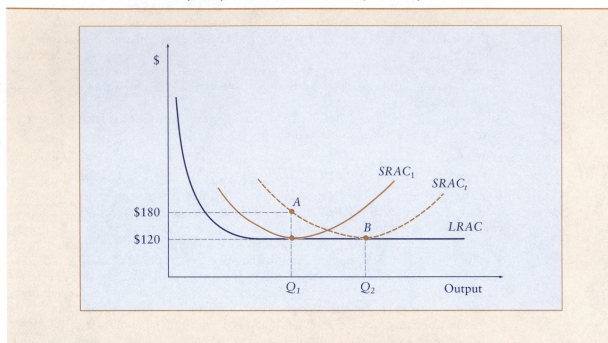

Why exactly does excess capacity enhance an incumbent's threat to reduce prices should low-price entrants appear in the market? Is it that the incumbent can thereby prevent the new entrant from acquiring a large market share? Is it that the incumbent can deny the new entrant a unique reputation for low prices? Is it that the incumbent can become more profitable than before the entry threat? The answer to all these questions is no. The sole reason any action or communication is credible is if it makes the threat-maker worse off ignoring the threat than carrying out the threat. In Figure 13.7, the competitive firm that invests in excess capacity by expanding from Plant 1 to Plant 2 is worse off with unchanged output Q_1 and unit costs of $180 at A than selling the larger output Q_2 with unit costs of $120 at B. A noncompetitive firm that must lower price to carry out a threat thereby increases sales and also moves from Q_1 to Q_2. Ignoring the threat would leave the incumbent worse off with higher unit costs at A now that Plant 1 has been replaced by Plant 2.

Example

EXCESS CAPACITY REACHES EPIC PROPORTIONS IN WORLD CAR MARKET: DAEWOO[13]

Sales in the three biggest and most profitable car markets in the United States, Europe, and Japan are stagnant at best. Yet, auto manufacturers around the world continue to expand. By 2002, the worldwide auto market grew to 57 million vehicles per year but exhibited 40-percent surplus capacity with 79 million vehicles being produced.

[13] Based on "Car Making in Asia: Politics of Scale," *The Economist*, June 24, 2000, pp. 68–69; "A Worldwide Glut Doesn't Sway Samsung," *Wall Street Journal*, September 18, 2000, p. A4; "The Kia Standard," *The Economist*, September 6, 1997, p. 62; and "In Asia, GM Pins Hopes on a Delicate Web," *Wall Street Journal*, October 23, 2001, p. A23.

Nissan and Mazda in Japan, Saab in Sweden, Renault in France, and Daewoo in Korea are all experiencing sizable losses. Why continue to add capacity?

Economies of scale do not seem to be involved. The GM-Opel-Fiat-Saab-Daewoo and Ford-Jaguar-Volvo-Land Rover-Mazda global alliances focus on designing common platforms for vehicle families so that multimillion-dollar body-stamping machines and assembly plants can produce Opel Astra sedans one week and Fiat Zafira seven-seat minivans the next. Increasingly, up to a dozen different vehicles will share the same assembly line. Even with less popular vehicles, minimum efficient scale has therefore become much less difficult to achieve.

A second explanation for continued capacity expansion highlights the location of the new capacity, much of which is appearing in Asia, especially South Korea and Thailand. Two thirds of the growth in new car sales between 2000–2010 is projected to come in the developing countries of China and India. In 2000, Japanese manufacturers in Thailand, Malaysia, the Philippines, and Indonesia, produced and sold fully 90 percent of all the autos in the Asian economic region, but not for long.

GM, Ford, and BMW all set up new plants during 1999 in Thailand. GM's $650-million new plant produces the Chevrolet Cruze, a light SUV designed especially for the Japanese market. South Korean auto capacity has now reached 6 million vehicles at Hyundai-Kia, Daewoo, Sangyoung, and Samsung despite the fact that domestic consumption is only 1.5 million vehicles and worldwide sales of the group are running only 3.5 million. The GM-Fiat alliance recently acquired Saab and Daewoo. The Korean conglomerate Samsung opened a new 500,000-vehicle-per-year robot-equipped plant at an investment of $5 billion. Predictably, local retail auto prices in Korea are being slashed as the looming overcapacity forces profit margins down to levels that no longer attract new auto industry investment.

But that may be exactly the idea. Incumbent manufacturers want to deter further entry into an economy that can easily ship throughout this new Asian growth market by precommitting to enough capacity that no potential entrant will doubt their threat to aggressively cut prices to defend market share. If this tactical initiative works and potential entrants stay out, the incumbent firms will never have to make good on their threat.

Excess Capacity Precommitments

To address the tactical ramifications of installing excess capacity, consider the capacity decision of a well-established hospital that faces an entry threat from an outpatient clinic specializing in obstetrics and elective plastic surgery. The hospital is constructing a new surgical wing. The hospital's business manager can build a facility to meet the future demand projected at their currently high prices, or she can expand the new facility plans to include some considerable excess capacity. Suppose that the birthing rooms and type of operating theater used in obstetrics and plastic surgery are not redeployable to general surgical or other specialized uses. Instead, the excess capacity, if built, will serve as a nonredeployable excess capacity precommitment by the hospital to compete for all the new price-sensitive business that a lower priced surgical clinic might attract into the market.

The structure of this game is presented in the decision tree in Figure 13.8. The hospital chooses excess capacity or not; the clinic chooses thereafter to enter or stay out, and the hospital then controls the pricing endgame. If the hospital builds excess capacity, it is more likely to cut prices in the face of entry, and the clinic is then better off staying out. If the hospital does not build excess capacity, it is more likely to accommodate the entrant by maintaining high prices, and the clinic is then better off entering. Therefore, looking ahead to predict the hospital and the clinic's best-reply responses in the various proper subgames and endgames, the hospital's likely choices narrow to two strategies shaded in Figure 13.8: {Excess Capacity, Stay Out, Limit Pricing} and {No Excess Capacity, Enter, Accommodate with Moderate Price}. Clearly, business as usual is no longer an option. In particular, the very profitable prior business with high prices, no excess capacity, and no competition in the top row of the game tree is no longer a focal outcome of interest. The entry threat may require that the incumbent hospital now maximize its remaining profit by precommitting itself to constructing some excess capacity. In that scenario, then, the clinic will consider hit-and-run entry, but probably decide instead to stay out and enter the same market in another community with less capacity present or projected.

In general, whether incumbents will choose to deter potential entrants (e.g., in the bottom half of the game tree in Figure 13.8) by the use of excess capacity pre-commitments or will actually prefer to accommodate (in the top half of the game tree) by retaining their smaller capacities and lowering prices is a complex question that depends on several factors. As we saw earlier, the answer depends in part on whether the incumbent can secure a first-mover advantage. Without it, in Entry Deterrence I, the incumbent discounted, but with it in Entry Deterrence II the incumbent moderated prices. This decision also depends on whether the post-entry competition will be in prices among differentiated product sellers, each with some market power over price, or in quantities among homogeneous product sellers with no market power over price. Finally, the decision to deter or accommodate depends on how old

Figure 13.8   Excess Capacity Precommitment Game

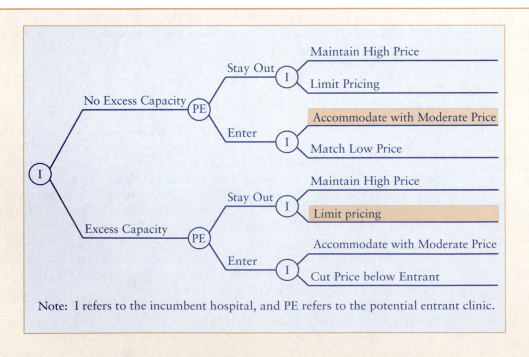

Note: I refers to the incumbent hospital, and PE refers to the potential entrant clinic.

and new customers in various segments of the market sort between an incumbent with excess capacity and a capacity-constrained lower priced entrant.

Customer Sorting Rules

Brand Loyalty
A customer sorting rule favorable to incumbents.

Efficient Rationing
A customer sorting rule in which high-willingness-to-pay customers absorb the capacity of low-price entrants.

Inverse Intensity Rationing
A customer sorting rule that assures that low-willingness-to-pay customers absorb the capacity of low-price entrants.

Random Rationing
A customer sorting rule reflecting randomized buyer behavior.

If the entrant attracts only new price-sensitive customers, that's one thing. If, on the other hand, the new entrant takes away high-willingness-to-pay regular customers of the incumbent, that's something else. Not surprisingly, the former situation more typically leads to accommodation; the latter often leads to deterrence.

Probably the simplest customer sorting pattern of all is extreme **brand loyalty** to incumbents. In this case, even in the face of differentially higher prices, customers reject the new entrant's offered capacity and instead backorder and reschedule when denied service at the incumbent. Inexorable competitive pressure from imitators normally erodes this degree of market power, but Microsoft might be an example of the exception. At the other extreme, **efficient rationing** allocates the fixed-priced capacity of new entrant discounters in a manner that achieves maximum consumer surplus. This customer sorting rule implies that those with the highest willingness to pay will exert the effort, time, and inconvenience to seek out, queue up, and order early to secure low-priced capacity. Of course, the obvious qualification is that these customers are also likely to have the highest opportunity cost of their time. A third alternative, then, is **inverse intensity rationing**, a much less threatening customer sorting pattern posed by new low-priced capacity in a segmented market. In this instance, the low-willingness-to-pay customers quickly absorb all the capacity of the low-priced entrant. Starting with that customer just willing to pay the entrant's low price, one proceeds up the demand curve only as far as required to stock out the new entrant. In this instance, the demand of the incumbent may be largely unaffected if the discounter's capacity remains relatively small. Finally, there is **random rationing** of the low-priced capacity. Under random rationing, all customers willing to pay the low prices—i.e., both regular customers of the incumbent and the new customers attracted into the market by the entrant's discounting—have an equal chance of securing the low-priced capacity. For example, if 70 customers were present in the market at the incumbent's original high price, and 30 additional customers appear in response to the discounts, the probability of any 1 of the 100 securing service from 40 units of low-priced capacity is $40/100 = 0.4$. Conversely, the probability of not being served is $(1 - 0.4) = 0.6$, and under random rationing the incumbent's expected demand falls as a result of the entry from 70 to $(70 \times 0.6) = 42$.

Because of the pivotal nature of these customer sorting rules and the decision timing in predicting deterrence versus accommodation behavior, game-theoretic analysis must often be intertwined with an industry study in order to discriminate among the many possible implications. Otherwise, the rational business decisions of incumbents in these models may vary over a wide range from the relatively passive acquisition of excess capacity all the way to the aggressive incumbent who occasionally predates by pricing below cost with no prospect of later recovering the loss. For the purpose of predicting rival behavior, this state of game-theoretic knowledge presents something of an embarrassment of riches. Hence, we reiterate the importance of doing sufficient field research to discover the particulars of the industry or firm-specific situation.

In Appendix 13A, we explore the entry deterrence and accommodation game between People Express and Piedmont Airlines and between United and Jet Blue. Detailed cost, price, and realized revenue data allow us to distinguish among several pricing and capacity choice implications of sequential game theory. The analysis lends support to the importance of customer sorting patterns in explaining why People Express met with little resistance and indeed was accommodated by incumbents in mid-Atlantic city-pair markets, but encountered effective deterrence from Piedmont in the Southeastern city-pair markets. Eventually, People Express was forced to withdraw and exit from all of its Southeastern routes.

A Role for Sunk Costs in Decision Making

In both theory and practice, sequential games of entry deterrence and accommodation have uncovered a very rich variety of strategic incumbent behavior in response to entry or potential entry. These include the excess capacity precommitments just discussed as well as the credible price discount threats of the previous section. However, they also include price discrimination and capacity allocation schemes. Such yield management or revenue management systems can provide incumbents with an effective way to deter new entrant discounters. We discuss revenue management in Appendix 14A. Finally, entry deterrence and accommodation strategy may also be expressed through advertising campaigns or other promotional investments in nonredeployable assets. Some examples would be reputational investments in company logos (such as Beatrice), or showrooms specially coordinated to enhance only Thomasville Furniture, or old L'eggs retail displays unusable for selling anything other than egg-shaped products. All three investments precommit the incumbent to aggressively defend market share and cash flow in order to recover the cost of these nonredeployable investments.

Nonredeployable investments are a reality in many industries. Industrial machinery is often specialized to the purpose at hand and sometimes even to a particular supplier. For decades, Sara Lee Hosiery bought twisted nylon fiber for their highest quality hosiery from a sole source supplier; the upstream nylon production equipment and the downstream hosiery spinning equipment were only usable in this one application. Much of the trade secret knowledge discovered by Microsoft programmers is not easily packaged and separated out for redeployment and sale to another firm. Even airplanes cannot be redeployed to routes and trip distances for which they are not designed. Markets in which nonredeployable, sunk cost assets are common will be markets whose cost conditions deter entry.

Contestable Market
An industry with exceptionally open entry and easy exit where incumbents are slow to react.

Contestable markets are strategic industry groups in which new firms can enter and exit on short notice without anticipating losses due to sunk costs. Even if only a few firms dominate such a market, prices seldom rise above break-even levels because of the constant "hit and run" tactics of the frequent entrants. Rival firms jump in and scallop off the profits whenever prices rise and then escape quickly once the profits are dissipated. This ensures little divergence from cost-covering competitive equilibrium. In the perfectly contestable markets scenario, incumbents react more slowly to entry threats than their regular customers who chase after the most inexpensive supplier of the moment.

In contrast, as we have seen in Figure 13.8, proactive incumbents invest in excess capacity and nonredeployable assets in order to deter entry. That may sound like sunk-cost reasoning, and indeed that is exactly what it is. Recognizing the sequential interdependence of rivalrous strategy and the role of credible threats and credible commitments therein has led to a rehabilitation of the role of sunk costs in managerial decision making. In fact, it is precisely because firms can do nothing about their sunk-cost investments, precisely because they are irreversible, irrevocable, and otherwise unrecoverable, that a particular threatened plan of action involving the use of these assets is credible. The player with sunk-cost investments has burned bridges; no better alternatives exist than to remain in the business of serving repeat customers, making credible commitments, and delivering on credible threats until the equipment becomes obsolete or wears out. Again, best-reply reasoning is the key to credibility, and credibility is the key to subgame perfect equilibrium strategy.

Example

CONTESTABLE MARKET IN BICYCLE HELMETS: BELL SPORTS[14]

Bell Sports began as a motorcycle helmet manufacturer with a small side-bet business in bicycle helmets and accessories. In 1986 sales in the bicycle line were $2 million per year. Today Bell has sales of bicycle helmets nearing $100 million, 85 percent of which occur in the United States. Nine states have initiated regulations making bicycle helmets mandatory for young riders. The potential growth in Europe, where Bell helmets have become a fashion statement, is even greater. Prices range from $29 for colorful hard-shell designs to $80 for ultra-lightweight infant helmets.

The trouble with running a fast-growing niche business is that without sunk-cost investments Bell inevitably attracts many new entrant competitors. Bicycle helmets are easy to fabricate and quickly sell themselves. All one needs is plastic molding machines and a foam extrusion process. These technologies are easily converted from many other industries, and more importantly, can be redeployed to those other uses upon exit. The product sells well in bike shops and such discount stores as Kmart and Wal-Mart without any significant sales force, point-of-sale actions, or after-sale service required of the retail distributors. Consequently, the bicycle helmet market is a classic case of *contestable markets*. Bell Sports is constantly subject to hit-and-run entry from other niche manufacturers—for example, American Recreation, Troxel Cycling, and Giro Sports.

The theory of contestable markets suggests that with no barriers to entry or exit and low customer costs of switching manufacturers, Bell Sports can never make more than a competitive profit in this business. As soon as prices rise above cost, temporary competitors enter the business, customers switch their allegiance, and Bell must lower prices. As a consequence, gross margins are low (averaging 8 percent) and fluctuate by as much as 50 percent from year to year. Bell's only alternatives are to outdo the hit-and-run entrants on new designs or to commit enough marketing investment dollars to establish a nonredeployable brand asset "Bell Helmets," known for safety with style. Until then, entry deterrence will prove infeasible, and entry accommodation must continue.

Brinkmanship and Wars of Attrition

Sometimes the question of tactical interest is not one of deterring or accommodating the entry of other firms but rather how long should your own firm stay in an obviously declining business. In competing to win an exclusive license (e.g., to host the Olympics), to define an industry standard (e.g., for digital HDTV), to earn FDA approval for a new class of drugs, or to capture the product loyalty of fickle customers with advertising, the bloodletting by multiple competitors may prevent profitability until someone concedes and drops out. The first period of a multiperiod sequential game representing these so-called "wars of attrition" is displayed on the left-hand side of Figure 13.9. Each period requires a $10 million "ante" at the start of the period

---

[14] Based on "Bell Sports," *Forbes*, February 13, 1995, pp. 67–68.

Figure 13.9 A War of Attrition for HDTV Industry Standard

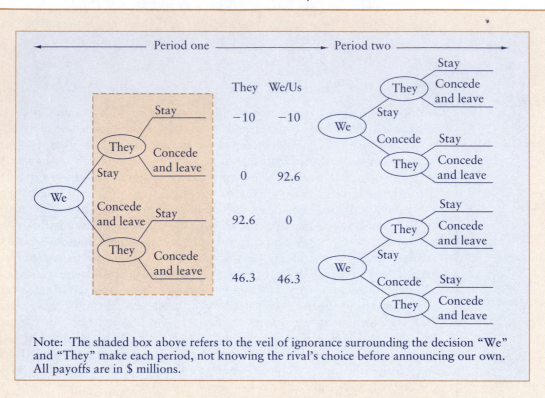

Note: The shaded box above refers to the veil of ignorance surrounding the decision "We" and "They" make each period, not knowing the rival's choice before announcing our own. All payoffs are in $ millions.

just to remain in the game, and no one knows her rivals' decision when deciding whether to "hold 'em or fold 'em." It's as though auction bids were sealed and then opened simultaneously. If either firm concedes and leaves, it pays nothing, and the other firm's $10 million ante is immediately recoverable by the firm who stays.

The market prize payoffs come at the end of the year and are equal to $100 million if one firm concedes and $50 million if both concede. These market prizes occur every year until the end of the game. If at the start of any period our rivals ("They") leave and concede the $100 million market to "Us," a payoff of [$100/(1 + r)] awaits—e.g., at 8 percent interest rates, ($100/1.08) − $10 + $10 = $92.6 million.[15] If "We" concede when "They" stay, $92.6 million awaits as their payoff. If both firms concede in their attempts to win the entire market prize, they immediately merge, and the market is split 50–50 with no further cost. If "They" hang tough and stay in competition, and "We" do the same, both firms lose $10 million, no one wins the prize that period, and "We" proceed to the decision as to whether to spend another $10 million ante to compete in the next period. The question is "How long should you stay?"

Consider the three-period game. If "We" leave now, the payoff is zero when "They" stay and $50 million when "They" concede. Let p be the probability that our

---

[15] In the discussion that follows, we ignore discounting to simplify the analysis. The payoff of $92.6 million therefore becomes $100 million.

opponent is a type who will concede immediately. Then the expected payoff from conceding immediately ourselves is just

$$\$50p + 0(1 - p) \geq 0 \qquad [13.1]$$

If we leave at the start of the second period, our expected payoff would be equal to

$$\$100p + \$50q - \$10 \geq 0 \qquad [13.2]$$

where q is the probability that our rival will concede at the start of the second period, and $(1 - p - q)$ is the probability "They" will stay until the third period, never conceding. If we stay to the end, our expected payoff is as follows:

$$\$200p + \$100q - \$20 \geq 0 \qquad [13.3]$$

Setting Equation 13.1 equal to 13.2 and 13.2 equal to 13.3, then solving simultaneously, yields the values of p and q that would leave "Us" just indifferent between conceding and hanging tough. Collecting terms and simplifying, we have

$$50p + 50q = 10 \qquad [13.4]$$
$$-100p - 50q = -10 \qquad [13.5]$$

which together imply $p = 0$, $q = 0.2$, and $(1 - p - q) = 0.8$.

In other words, "We" are indifferent as to conceding or hanging tough and paying $10 million each of the first two periods to stay until the endgame if and only if there is no less than a 20-percent chance "They" will leave in the second period and no more than an 80-percent chance "They" will stay until the endgame. We decide whether to stay or leave by assessing the actual situation and actual rival and then comparing these 20 percent and 80 percent derived probability break points against our subjective probability estimates of the actual situation.

Tactical Insights About Slippery Slopes

Slippery Slope
A tendency for wars of attrition to generate mutual losses that worsen over time.

Note that $p = 0$ implies that neither party concedes immediately. Instead, $q = 0.2$ indicates a middle ground strategy of opponent types who test the competitive waters before conceding at the start of Period 2. This positive probability of "middle grounders" is a reflection of a **slippery slope**. Once you enter into a war of attrition and make your own first "ante" of -10 (because the Bayesian probability of Hang Toughers was less than 0.8), the probability of middle grounders who will step on that slippery slope with you is NOT zero. Instead, the equilibrium probability of middle grounders in this game is 0.2. That is, there is a nontrivial probability of a sequence of mutual losses, a death spiral until the less deep pocket is empty. Hence, these so-called "brinkmanship" games have serious and largely uncontrollable consequences even for the player with an advantaged position.

What is a best-reply response in the n period game? Ignoring discounting of future cash flows for the moment to simplify the analysis, if we hang tough until the rivals leave and if the rivals leave in period t, we realize the $100 million market prize for $n - t$ periods and pay $10 million for t periods. Since if we leave now, $\$50p = 0$ is the payoff, the expected value of all other alternatives can be no worse than this; otherwise we'll just leave now. Combining these facts

$$(n - t)\$100 - t\,\$10 > 0 \qquad [13.6]$$
$$0.91n > t \qquad [13.7]$$

where 0.91 is the ratio of the $100-million prize to the sum of the periodic cost $10 million plus the $100 million prize. That is, for the parameters of the payoffs in this war of attrition, if "We" believe the rivals will stay 91 percent of the total time or less, we should stay. If we believe "They" will stay more than 91 percent (or, with discounting, 90.25 percent) of the total time, we should concede immediately and save our $10 million ante to invest in another competition. For the three-period case, if "We" believe the rivals will stay less than $0.9025 \times 3 = 2.71$ years, we should hang tough and stay to the end ourselves. Obviously, these calculations apply to the symmetrically positioned "They" as well, so wars of attrition quickly become a matter of bluffing and signaling. The most useful insight the above analysis offers in such games is that each player should assess the probability of his or her rivals' leaving in light of all the available evidence and should hinge his own decision on the ratio of the prize to the sum of the prize plus periodic cost. Very much like playing poker, you hold rather than fold the bigger the prize and the smaller the periodic cost of hanging tough and calling your rivals' bluff.

SIMULTANEOUS GAMES

Although sequential game reasoning is critical to the successful conduct of business strategy, some decisions must be made simultaneously with one's rivals. Consider offers in a multiround auction for Olympic hosting, mineral rights, cellular phone licenses, release dates for fashion clothing collections, sales territory assignments, contract bids for new business, promotional ads to meet a newspaper deadline, and posted price announcements. We have already seen one setting in which rival firms must reveal their prices quite literally one moment apart. Every morning at 7:00 A.M. each airline announces all its fares for all its routes at an electronic clearinghouse sponsored by the airline industry.

The same problem also exists for cruise ship operators. Suppose that two cruise lines, Carnival and Royal Caribbean, operate the only three-day Caribbean cruises from Miami. If each firm acts independently to maximize its own profits, the long-run (Cournot equilibrium) profit-maximizing price is $300 per person. If two firms act jointly (e.g., form a cartel) to maximize total industry profits, the profit-maximizing price is $450. Assume that these are the only two prices under consideration.

The payoffs or profits to each firm are shown in Table 13.3. The below-diagonal number in each cell is the payoff to Royal Caribbean, and the above-diagonal number is the payoff to Carnival. Each firm is reluctant to choose the (jointly) more profitable $450 price. If either firm reneges and discounts to $300, then the firm that charges $450 will earn significantly lower profits than the rival. This game has a typical Prisoner's Dilemma ordering of outcomes. As we have seen, only a sucker unilaterally cooperates by announcing high prices under such circumstances. For example, the payoff for Carnival from unilateral defection ($375,000) exceeds the payoff from mutual cooperation at high prices ($275,000), which itself exceeds the payoff from mutual defection at low prices ($185,000), which finally exceeds the payoff from unilateral cooperation ($60,000). This ensures that Carnival has a dominant strategy—i.e., to defect. Royal Caribbean (RC), on the other hand, has no such dominant strategy. However, because RC can predict Carnival's behavior, by eliminating the prospect of Carnival's dominated $450 strategy, RC can iterate to a preferable strategy itself. Therefore, Royal Caribbean's behavior is also quite predictable, and the iterated dominant strategy equilibrium proves to be {$300, $300} or {Defect, Defect} just as in Prisoner's Dilemma itself.

Note that both cruise ship companies could have had dominant strategies, but that is unnecessary for iterated dominant strategy equilibrium. The reason is that a dominant strategy requires no particular optimal or suboptimal response behavior on

---

Table 13.3   Monopoly Pricing (in Thousands) for
Cruise Ships with One Dominant Strategy

		Carnival	
		$450	**$300**
Royal Caribbean	**$450**	$350 / $275	$50 / $375
	$300	$320 / $60	$175 / $185

Notes: Column-player payoffs (in thousands) are above the diagonal. Row-player payoffs are below the diagonal.

---

the part of anyone else. It is defined as an action for player i that is an optimal action $\{a_i^*\}$ in the strong sense that no matter what other players do, the payoff for player i, $\Pi_i\{a_i^*, a_{-i}\}$ exceeds the payoff for player i from any other action, $\Pi_i\{a_i, a_{-i}\}$.[16]

$$\Pi_i\{a_i^*, a_{-i}\} > \Pi_i\{a_i, a_{-i}\} \qquad [13.8]$$

Consequently, one dominant strategy is quite enough to predict rival behavior and therefore strategic equilibrium in any two-person game. Once Carnival's dominant strategy (i.e., to defect and cut prices to $300) has been identified, Royal Caribbean's behavior (i.e., to also defect) is easily predictable. We have seen this twice before in "Six or Seven Territories?" and in "Marauder-Guarder." Recall that Kahn had no dominant strategy but was able to predict his rival's behavior based on her dominant strategy, and that was enough for him to identify an optimal strategic equilibrium response.

Nash Equilibrium Strategy

What about games without any dominant strategy? To examine this question we now return to the problem at the beginning of the chapter concerning PepsiCo and Coca-Cola. If unilateral defection by one's rival (i.e., low rival prices in the face of your high prices) should result in $6,000 payoffs, then the problem is simple and each firm has a dominant strategy to defect to the new lower prices. But what if that circumstance now pays off $9,000 for PepsiCo as in Table 13.4?[17] Then, there is no dominant strategy. PepsiCo wants to discount when Coca-Cola maintains higher prices ($14,000 > $12,000), but just as clearly PepsiCo wants to maintain higher prices when Coca-Cola discounts ($9,000 > $6,300). And, the same ambiguity is present for Coca-Cola. What criteria allow the prediction of rival behavior in this game of "Renegade Discounting"?

---

[16] A starred action refers to a maximizing choice—namely, here, an action that results from maximizing profit.

[17] The rest of the payoff matrix has been altered to more readily identify the moves and countermoves of each party. Nevertheless, the qualitative structure of the game's outcomes remains the same.

Table 13.4   Renegade Discounting in Soft Drinks with No Dominant Strategy

| | Coca-Cola | |
	Maintain High Prices	**Discount Low Prices**
PepsiCo **Maintain High Prices**	$12,000 / $13,000	$9,000 / $16,000
PepsiCo **Discount Low Prices**	$14,000 / $10,500	$6,300 / $8,000

Column-player payoffs (in thousands) are above the diagonal. Row-player payoffs are below the diagonal.

The answer lies in a reflexive application of the concept of best-reply response. If an action were the best reply to a rival's action, which in turn was the best reply to the original action, the parties would have identified an equilibrium strategy. More formally, a Nash equilibrium strategy is defined as an action for player i that is conditionally optimal $\{a_i^*\}$ in that the payoff for player i, given best-reply responses by rivals $\Pi_i \{a_i^*, a_{-i}^*\}$, exceeds the payoff for player i from any other action $\Pi_i \{a_i, a_{-i}^*\}$ given best-reply responses of rivals:

$$\Pi_i \{a_i^*, a_{-i}^*\} > \Pi_i \{a_i, a_{-i}^*\} \qquad [13.9]$$

In Renegade Discounting there are two such pure Nash equilibria: $\{$Maintain$_p^*$, Discount$_c^*\}$ and $\{$Discount$_p^*$, Maintain$_c^*\}$ where the subscripts refer to PepsiCo and Coca-Cola. Recall that here there is no order of play; we could have just as easily reversed the recording of the actions in these strategy pairs listing Coca-Cola rather than PepsiCo first. The actual rivals appear to have perceived precisely this point because, for 42 weeks in 1992, they took turns discounting their grocery store merchandise.

What is notable about these Nash strategies is that they are nonunique. The multiple equilibria occur because Nash equilibrium is weaker (i.e., easier to satisfy) than dominant strategy equilibrium. The latter requires that an action be optimal for every possible rival response, whereas Nash equilibrium requires only that an action be optimal for a best-reply rival response. That is a less demanding requirement of the equilibrium strategy set and therefore easier to satisfy. However, this knowledge does not help solve PepsiCo's problem as to what price to announce. Remember that each bottler is announcing its price without knowing until afterwards what its rival announced. If PepsiCo believed Coca-Cola would discount half the time and maintain half the time, the expected value of PepsiCo's maintaining is $10,500, whereas the expected value of PepsiCo's discounting is smaller (i.e., only $10,150). This would seem to suggest a preference for maintaining high prices, but again, predictably high PepsiCo prices allow Coca-Cola to unilaterally defect and earn $16,000, whereas PepsiCo would then realize only $9,000. So how can PepsiCo avoid tipping its hand and ending up with the $9,000 outcome rather than its own $14,000 defection outcome too often?

The answer lies in PepsiCo's randomizing the pricing process. PepsiCo must figure out what automated pricing response would make Coca-Cola indifferent between maintaining and discounting and thereby willing to randomize its own price announcement. That is, what probability of discounting by PepsiCo will equate Coca-Cola's expected payoff from maintaining high prices to its expected payoff from discounting? Interestingly, because the payoffs are asymmetrical, the desired probability is not 0.5. Let's see what the solution is. Using p and $(1 - p)$ to represent the probabilities of PepsiCo's maintaining and discounting, respectively, we calculate

$$(p)\ \$13,000 + (1 - p)\ \$10,500 = (p)\ \$16,000 + (1 - p)\ \$8,000 \quad [13.10]$$

where the Coca-Cola payoffs have been arranged to correspond to the columns of Table 13.4. The solution probabilities $p = 0.454$ and $(1 - p) = 0.546$ accomplish the objective of making Coca-Cola indifferent and therefore its choice unpredictably random.

Note, however, that there is a mirror-image Nash reflexivity associated with this solution concept. Coca-Cola faces a comparable payoff structure and strategy dilemma to that of PepsiCo, and presumably therefore would want to know what probabilities of maintaining and discounting would make PepsiCo indifferent between the two choices. Calculating as before

$$(p')\ \$12,000 + (1 - p')\ \$9,000 = (p')\ \$14,000 + (1 - p')\ \$6,300 \quad [13.11]$$

where the PepsiCo payoffs have been arranged to correspond to the rows of Table 13.4, we obtain $p' = 0.574$ and $(1 - p') = 0.426$. If randomized choice by PepsiCo is a best-reply response to randomness by Coca-Cola, and if Coca-Cola can then do no better, this renegade discounting game must have a third Nash equilibrium strategy—namely, {Maintain by PepsiCo with $p = 0.454$, Maintain by Coca-Cola with $p' = 0.574$}. This strategy pair is called a **mixed Nash equilibrium strategy**. A 0.454 probability weight on maintaining and a 0.546 probability weight on discounting by PepsiCo yields $11,634 expected value for each of Coca-Cola's price announcement strategies. Similarly, a 0.574 probability weight on maintaining and a 0.426 probability weight on discounting by Coca-Cola yields $10,720 expected value for each of PepsiCo's price announcement strategies. There are therefore two pure and one mixed Nash strategy in the strategic equilibrium solution for this game.[18]

The adoption of a conspicuous automated mechanism to implement this mixed Nash strategy (e.g., a computer mechanism to replicate the appropriate unfair coin toss) is a way of implementing the mixed strategy. In principle, however, none of these three Nash equilibrium strategies is preferable to any other. In a one-shot play of Renegade Discounting, all four cells in Table 13.4 still arise. The {$6,300, $8,000} outcome in the southeast cell and the {$12,000, $13,000} outcome in the northwest cell as well as the two asymmetric outcomes that correspond to our two pure Nash strategies will all sometimes arise. In a noncooperative simultaneous game incorporating no communication in advance, no side payments, and no binding agreements, there is simply no way to avoid this multiplicity of possible strategic equilibria. In practice, therefore, a one-shot play of any of the three Nash strategies in the Renegade Discounting game can work out very well or very badly.

Mixed Nash Equilibrium Strategy
A strategic equilibrium concept involving randomized behavior.

---

[18] The simultaneous manufacturer/distributor game in Table 13.1 also can be solved using mixed strategy. If the manufacturer increases prices with probability 0.60 and the retailer discontinues services with probability 0.71, the two companies will each have made their opponent's decision unpredictably random.

Of course, the {$12,000, $13,000} outcome is best of all. In the next section we will see how to secure this win-win outcome by introducing repeated plays, imperfect information, and credibility mechanisms to convert this simultaneous game to a sequential game.[19] In conclusion, Nash equilibrium strategies provide guidelines for optimal strategies when information about payoffs is complete and certain and when one player's actions cannot influence another player's choices. Sometimes business managers are simply stuck with those conditions.

Example

KODAK TAKES A PROMOTIONAL DISCOUNT[20]

To avoid price wars, Eastman Kodak Co. constantly rolls out new products and segments photographic film into several tiers. Kodak Regular film sells at one price point. Kodak Instacolor sells at a higher price point. And Kodak Gold sells at the highest price point. At Christmastime 1997, Kodak Gold was replaced by a new line called Family of Gold. Between September and Christmas, Kodak decided to discount the obsolete Kodak Gold film 10 percent in some distribution channels and 20 percent in others. Although the original list prices would have made more money for Kodak if competitor prices had remained high, Fuji Photo Film Co. correctly anticipated this short-term promotion of the product Kodak was retiring and proceeded to cut its prices 35 percent. Both companies perceived a one-shot Prisoner's Dilemma simultaneous pricing game.

A sequential product introduction game and the subsequent advertising and pricing responses of Sony and Kodak appear in Exercise 12 at the end of the chapter.

ESCAPE FROM PRISONER'S DILEMMA

In this section, we relax the assumptions of single-play, complete and perfect information games. Let's return to the Prisoner's Dilemma payoff structure of the opening situation posed in this chapter. Recall that both PepsiCo and Coca-Cola were in that case worst off if either unilaterally defected from maintaining high prices. The payoff matrix is presented again in Table 13.5. These are operating profits per week per store. Each soft drink bottler would like to pursue the $12,000 payoff, but the only way to avoid the vulnerability of a unilateral defection is by defecting oneself! Dominant strategy drives both players to discount their 12-packs in the one-shot game. However, surely PepsiCo and Coca-Cola recognize they are engaged in an ongoing competitive process, not a one-shot (i.e., single-play) game. Week after week, they will encounter one another in many future replays of this pricing game at grocery and convenience stores all across the nation. Consequently, tacit cooperation rather than dogmatic price cutting has a chance to evolve.

Suppose Coca-Cola begins the process by announcing a high price in Period 1. Coke's intention is to play that price continuously until PepsiCo defects and thereafter to never announce High again. This is a so-called **grim trigger strategy**. One perturbation by PepsiCo away from cooperative High pricing, and Coca-Cola's punishment is immediate and never-ending. Multiperiod punishment schemes are a key to inducing cooperation in Prisoner's Dilemma games, whether it is film prices,

Grim Trigger Strategy
A strategy involving infinitely long punishment schemes.

[19] Barry Nalebuff calls this "changing the nature of competition" and sharply distinguishes the conduct from "collusion" that would violate the antitrust laws. See "Businessman's Dilemma," *Forbes*, October 11, 1993, p. 107.
[20] Based on "Kodak Cuts Price on Film," *ABC News and Starwave Co.*, September 26, 1997.

Table 13.5   Repeated Prisoner's Dilemma in Soft Drinks (in Thousands)

		Coca-Cola	
		Maintain High Prices	**Discount**
PepsiCo	**Maintain High Prices**	$12,000 / $12,000	$6,000 / $17,000
	Discount	$17,000 / $6,000	$8,000 / $8,000

airline fare wars, or soft drink pricing. In this case, PepsiCo compares the perpetuity opportunity loss of ($12,000 − $8,000) discounted at the interest rate r per period to the one-time gain from defection of ($17,000 − $12,000):

$$\$4,000/r > \$5,000 \text{ if } r < 0.8 \qquad [13.12]$$

At any discount rate less than 80 percent, the forgone future gains from cooperatively maintaining high prices outweigh the one-time gains from defection. At any lower rate of discount, the dominant strategy to defect in one-shot games is no longer attractive. This calculation and conclusion reflect a generalizable **Folk Theorem**, which states that for any payoff structure, a discount rate always exists that is low enough to induce cooperation in an infinitely repeated Prisoner's Dilemma.

However, because companies do not last forever, the Folk Theorem raises an obvious question, "What about for shorter periods, say 20 weeks?" The 20-period calculation is easily done; r now must be less than 79 percent. But if 20 weeks, what about 10, and if 10, what about for 2 weeks? Suppose it is now the beginning of Week 2. We know we are out of this "cooperative" structure next week (i.e., Week 3), so our remaining incentive to maintain high prices is only $4,000/(1 + r)$, and our incentive to defect is $5,000. Now all of a sudden, for any discount rate, we're better off defecting. This, too, is a generalizable result. The last play of a finitely repeated Prisoner's Dilemma has the same incentives as a one-shot Prisoner's Dilemma; everybody defects. Therefore, one period away from the endgame of a finitely repeated play Prisoner's Dilemma, neither party has an incentive to maintain its reputation for cooperating.

Unraveling and the Chain Store Paradox

In fact, the prospects for cooperation in any finitely repeated Prisoner's Dilemma are very poor indeed. What is true for a 2-period game must be true by backwards induction for a 3-period game, a 4-period game, and even a 20-period game. Reinhard Selten investigated this **unraveling problem** for finitely repeated Prisoner's Dilemmas in the context of chain store incumbents facing repeated entry threats from rivals.[21]

Folk Theorem
A conclusion about cooperation in repeated Prisoner's Dilemma.

Unraveling Problem
A failure of cooperation in games of finite length.

---

[21] See J. Harsanyi and R. Selten, *A General Theory of Equilibrium Selection in Games* (Cambridge: MIT Press, 1988), or for a less technical treatment, E. Rasmussen, *Games and Information*, 2d ed. (Cambridge: Blackwell, 1994), Chapter 5.

In a Prisoner's Dilemma setting just like those we've been examining, the incumbent has a dominant strategy to accommodate the new entrant. But one's intuition says that in the face of enough repetitions of the chain store competition, the incumbent's reputation for fighting entry can pay off. And in the extreme, this intuition is absolutely correct. In **infinitely repeated games**, the Folk Theorem does apply. However, with any fewer repetitions, in even the enormous number of chain store competitions that might face a McDonald's or a Wal-Mart, the cooperative equilibrium unravels.

Infinitely Repeated Games
A game that lasts forever.

Selten invented the concept of subgame perfect strategic equilibrium to show this paradoxical result and to emphasize the sequential nature of reputation effects and the pivotal role of endgame reasoning. In Figure 13.10 we have a chain store Incumbent (I) who accommodates or fights in response to a Potential Entrant (PE) who stays out or enters. Accommodation forgoes $20,000 of the incumbent chain store's profit ($100,000 − $80,000) and induces future entry, but fighting the present entry to acquire a reputation for toughness in future possible entry situations entails actual losses now (−$10,000). Conceive of the displayed game tree as the last three encounters of a 20-chain store competition perceived by both players

Figure 13.10   The Chain Store Paradox

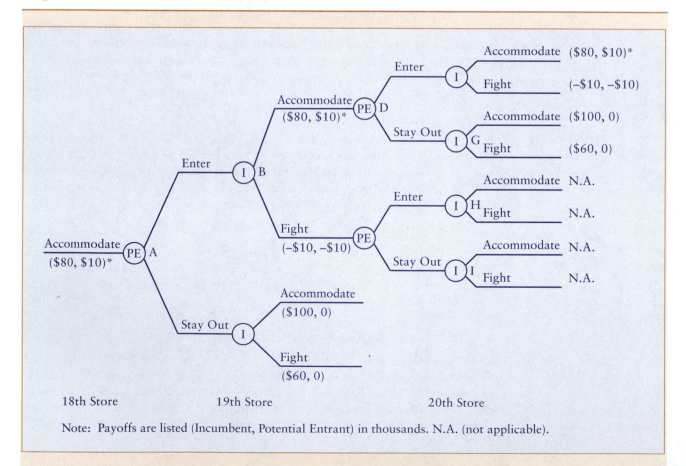

Note: Payoffs are listed (Incumbent, Potential Entrant) in thousands. N.A. (not applicable).

from the start. Looking ahead to the endgame, it is clear that the incumbent will accommodate in the last submarket where it is presently located or at least in the last submarket where it hopes to locate in the future. One hundred thousand dollars exceeds $60,000, and $80,000 exceeds −$10,000. More importantly, there is no future payoff thereafter to a tough reputation for fighting (or anything else). There is no thereafter! Because the Potential Entrant also knows this, entry will surely take place in that last submarket.

Now, in looking back to the previous submarket (i.e., the 19th store), the incumbent realizes that its rival's subsequent entry in the 20th submarket is certain and therefore that, again, there is no return to reputation for fighting in that 19th submarket. Accommodate is therefore the best-reply response in the proper subgame from Node B onward to the endgame. Because the entrant can predict this decision as well, entry occurs in the 19th submarket at Node A. But what is true of the 19th must therefore be true of the 18th, and the 17th, and so forth, right back to the start of the game.

Chain Store Paradox
A prediction of always-accommodative behavior by incumbents facing entry threats.

http://
Access a working paper on the chain store paradox at the Internet archive site at Washington University in St. Louis:
http://ideas.repec.org/p/wpa/wuwpmi/9701005.html

This is the backwards induction reasoning that leads to the **chain store paradox**. We can calculate in Submarket 1 that at reasonable rates of discount the incumbent has sufficient net present value profits from future deterrence to justify fighting now rather than accommodating. Yet, the credibility of the incumbent's present fighting is jeopardized by the predictability of its future accommodation. And because of that predictability of accommodation as a best-reply response all the way out to the endgame, the reputation effects of any present fighting unravel. Accommodation therefore occurs in every submarket or every period in the 20-submarket/20-period game just as we argued earlier it would in the 2-submarket/2-period game.

One's intuition tugs the other way, especially when a long line of potential entrants is waiting in the wings. Hence, the term chain store *paradox*. And, as we shall now see, changing some other features of the chain store decision problem can overturn this counterintuitive result.

Cooperative Equilibrium in Repeated Prisoner's Dilemma

One way to short-circuit the reasoning of the chain store paradox is to introduce an uncertain ending of the game. If the incumbent can never be sure whether future encounters beyond Submarket 20 will arise, then the reputational effect of fighting in the 19th period returns. Any positive probability that the game will continue is sufficient (again, at low enough discount rates) to restore the deterrent effect of fighting in Period 20. If fighting is rational in Period 20, then the incumbent is willing to fight in 19, 18, and so forth, back to Period 1. And if the incumbent is willing in Period 1, then it may not have to because the other firm will not enter. The analogous implication in a finitely repeated pricing game such as Repeated Prisoner's Dilemma in Soft Drinks (in Table 13.5) is that the rivals will cooperate by maintaining high prices as long as the endgame is uncertain. With one period remaining, we can then write Equation 13.13 as

$$\$4,000 + \$4,000 \times \frac{1}{(1+r)} \times p > \$5,000 \qquad [13.13]$$

where p is the probability of the game continuing beyond the next period. For $r = 0.1$, a probability as low as 0.28 is sufficient to elicit cooperation in maintaining high prices and a ($12,000, $12,000) northwest cell outcome in Table 13.5. Therefore, infinite repetition is not required to induce cooperation in Prisoner's Dilemmas; an uncertain ending will suffice.

Example

VIOLATION OF THE CHAIN STORE PARADOX: SEMICONDUCTOR PRICING AT INTEL, NEC, AND MOTOROLA[22]

These insights seem especially important in industries with fast-changing technology, such as computer chips and consumer electronics, where cost disadvantages that might end an incumbent's business are seldom permanent because the technology changes so often. One illustration is the semiconductor industry, where Intel and Motorola have recently returned to dominance after almost being displaced by Japanese firms such as Hitachi, NEC, and Toshiba ten years ago.

With each successive generation of chips (see Table 13.6), the market leaders practice life cycle pricing techniques. After a period of high target pricing and value-based pricing, Intel, with 26 percent of the worldwide market, limits price rather than accommodate NEC with 13 percent, Motorola with 10 percent and numerous small competitors. That is, chip prices are slashed in an attempt to deter entry by the imitators. Then, with uncertain timing, the whole process repeats itself. New chips are introduced at high prices, imitators reverse-engineer the design, and limit pricing again ensues. The uncertain endpoint of the successive chip generation games leads to a violation of the chain store paradox and increased likelihood of higher prices, just as in the soft drink pricing competition between Coca-Cola and PepsiCo.

Another ingenious escape from Prisoner's Dilemma incorporates the Bayesian probability concept of estimating opponent types based on the forecast provided by past events. If some irrational "crazies" who do not always maximize payoff profit are known to exist in the market, a perfectly sane incumbent may take actions that seem crazy. The intent of the incumbent is to secure an asymmetric information pooling equilibrium in which the incumbent is indistinguishable from the crazies.[23] An example would be an automobile manufacturing incumbent who predates—i.e., who prices

---

Table 13.6   Major Intel Microprocessor and Clock Speed

Year	Microprocessor	MHz
'79	8088	5
'82	286	6
'85	386	16
'89	486	25
'93	Pentium	60
'95	Pentium Pro	150
'97	Pentium II	233
'99	Pentium III	333
'02	Pentium IV	550

---

[22] Based on *Investor's Business Daily,* January 13, 1998, p. A8.

[23] See R. Gibbons, "An Introduction to Applicable Game Theory," *Journal of Economic Perspectives,* 11(1), Winter 1997, pp. 140–147, and Rasmussen, op. cit., pp. 352–356.

below variable cost—even though the operating losses from such a strategy may not be recoverable in excess profits later. Japanese automobile manufacturers are often accused of such "dumping" in the offshore auto markets, especially in Europe.

Example

PREDATION REPUTATION AT BROWN AND WILLIAMSON

The U.S. Supreme Court has addressed these issues in promulgating a new standard for judging predatory pricing behavior by U.S. firms. In *Brooke Group Ltd.* v. *Brown and Williamson Tobacco Company 113 U.S. 2578 (1993),* the Court held that pricing generic cigarettes below cost was not evidence of an undesirable predatory intent to monopolize a market because Brown and Williamson had no opportunity thereafter to earn excess profits and recoup its losses from the alleged predatory period. Whether the Court looked deeply enough into the long-term effect of deterring effective entry through a pricing policy that left Brown and Williamson indistinguishable from "crazies" is a hotly debated antitrust issue. This reputation effect of becoming known as a firm who might well price below cost is more valuable the higher are the costs of new entrants, the weaker is the brand loyalty to incumbents, and the larger is the number of potential entrants waiting in the wings. American Airlines dissuaded Vanguard, Sunjet, and Western Pacific from remaining as discounters in Dallas-Ft. Worth using such tactics. In May 2001, their indictment for predation was dismissed on the grounds that at no point did American lower price below its average variable cost.

Similarly in instant cameras, when in 1982 Kodak priced its Instamatic at $11.95 despite a $28 direct manufacturing cost, there was very little prospect of recovering the −$16.05 operating loss per camera at a subsequent date. Instead, this pricing tactic was generally seen as an attempt to clear inventory quickly before exiting the Instamatic submarket in 1985.

Winning Strategies in Evolutionary Computer Tournaments: Tit for Tat

We have seen that a grim trigger strategy can induce cooperation in an infinitely repeated Prisoner's Dilemma. Let's analyze what characteristics of multiperiod, but not perpetual, punishment schemes appear most successful at promoting cooperation. One transparent disadvantage of grim triggers is that cooperative outcomes cannot survive a single small mistake or miscommunication by either player. Selten's concept of a **trembling hand trigger strategy** seeks to improve on this issue by allowing one grace period misplay by the other party before the grim punishment of defection forever is imposed. Of course, a wily rival understanding this strategy will take advantage of its opponent by claiming just as many one-period "mistakes" of defection as it can get away with.

Robert Axelrod has been intrigued by the reasons why in long-term interactions, when people are ardently pursuing their own goals, they often end up cooperating with competitors.[24] He investigated the question of optimal strategy in repeated Prisoner's Dilemma by conducting a computer simulation in which 151 strategies competed against one another 1,000 times. He discovered that those strategies that

Trembling Hand Trigger Strategy
A punishment mechanism that forgives random mistakes and miscommunications.

[24] Robert Axelrod, *The Evolution of Cooperation* (New York: Basic Books, 1984). See also "Evolutionary Economics," *Forbes*, October 11, 1993, p. 110, and Jill Neimark, "Tit for Tat: A Game of Survival," *Success*, May 1987, p. 62.

http://
You can play an interactive online game of the prisoner's dilemma at the following Internet site:
http://www.princeton.edu/~mdaniels/PD/PD.html

finished highest in the computer tournament had several characteristics in common. First, winning strategies have great clarity to avoid fewer mistakes by their opponents; simpler is better. Second, winning strategies make unilateral attempts to cooperate; they are initiators of niceness. Third, as we would expect, all winning strategies are provokable; they have credible commitments to some punishment rule. But limited-duration punishment schemes displaying forgiveness won out over maximal-punishment grim trigger strategies. The reason seems to be that, fourth, winning strategies can recover from misperceptions and mistakes; reprisals need not be self-perpetuating. What types of actual strategies would you guess best fit these five criteria? Surprisingly, "Tit for Tat" won the tournament! Repeating what your opponent did on the last round is simple and clearly provokable, but consistent with initiating cooperation. And perhaps most importantly, "Tit for Tat" is forgiving. After a single-period punishment, it reverts to cooperating as soon as the opponent/cooperator does so.

For example, one possible approach to cooperation for cruise ship companies Carnival and Royal Caribbean (RC) in Table 13.7 is to follow a "Tit-for-Tat" (TFT) decision rule. Royal Caribbean, who has a dominant $300 strategy, could signal a **conspicuous focal point** by promoting "staterooms" (rather than smaller, less well-appointed "cabins") as an industry standard and then choosing the $450 pricing strategy in the first period. Thereafter, Royal Caribbean would select the same pricing strategy in the next period as Carnival chose in the previous period. For example, if Carnival charges $450 in the current period, then Royal Caribbean would do likewise in the next period. On the other hand, if Carnival defects and charges $300 in the current period, then Royal Caribbean would retaliate by charging the same $300 price next period. Through repeated plays, the participants may "learn" the "Tit-for-Tat" decision rule being applied by their competitor.

Conspicuous Focal Point
An outcome that attracts mutual cooperation.

Price-Matching Guarantees

How should Carnival respond to a "Tit for Tat" decision rule by Royal Caribbean? It is insightful to pursue the analogies between this limited duration punishment scheme and a matching price guarantee. In Table 13.7, a matching price guarantee

Table 13.7   Cruise Ship Pricing with Price Matching

Royal Caribbean Pricing Policy	Carnival Pricing Policy $450	Carnival Pricing Policy $300	Carnival Pricing Policy "Match"
$450	$350 / $275	$150 / $375	$350 / $275
$300	$320 / $160	$175 / $185	$175 / $185
"Match"	$350 / $275	$175 / $185	$350 / $275

Note: Column-player payoffs above the diagonal in $ thousands.

by Royal Caribbean substantially reduces the incentive of Carnival to attempt a gain-share discount down to $300 when RC has announced $450 prices. Under the heading "$300" in the second column, one sees that Carnival's $300 discounted price can no longer generate the $375,000 payoff of the first row but instead simply realizes the $185,000 payoff that arises under a matching price policy by RC. This is the same $185,000 payoff that arises in the middle cell of this column when both firms discount to $300. Since RC's customers will monitor and enforce RC's matching price guarantee by requesting rebates of ($450 − $300 =) $150 from RC, Carnival cannot hope to gain a significant share of RC's customers. To place Royal Caribbean in the same straitjacket, Carnival too will likely announce a matching price guarantee as protection in those times when RC might try a sneak discount attack on Carnival's market share. Assuming, as we did earlier, that Royal Caribbean initiates play with a $450 price announcement, both cruise companies will maintain $450 prices, effectively playing "Match, Match" and escaping the Prisoner's Dilemma by realizing the ($350,000, $275,000) payoff in the far northwest and far southeast cells. Like double-the-difference price guarantees, matching price guarantees increase the expected price level and hence the profitability in a tight oligopoly market.

Now, how does this outcome compare to "Tit for Tat"? Although let's now assume that there is no "Match" alternative in the game, Carnival should see Royal Caribbean's TFT decision rule as a delayed matching price guarantee. That is, with a one-period lag, Royal Caribbean is going to match any discount that Carnival tries and subsequently match (again with a one-period lag) any return to high prices as soon as Carnival returns. These payoff paths are certain; no amount of apologizing by Carnival about mistakes and miscommunications can prevent RC's one-period duration punishment scheme. Therefore, Carnival simply compares the profits from discounting unilaterally this period ($375,000 − $275,000) to a discounted opportunity loss from punishment next period ($275,000 − $160,000):

$$\$100,000 < \$115,000/(1 + r) \quad \text{iff } r < 0.15 \qquad [13.14]$$

As long as the discount rate is less than 15 percent and the continuation of this particular cruise route is certain for both firms, Carnival should not discount and thereby defect on the industry leader's pricing policy of $450. If the probability of continuance (p) falls below 1.0, a limited duration punishment scheme like "Tit for Tat" becomes much less effective immediately. For example, multiplying the future opportunity loss from punishment next period by just 10 percent less than certainty of continuance,

$$\$100,000 < \$115,000 \, (0.9)/(1 + r) = \$103,500/(1 + r) \qquad [13.15]$$

implies that Carnival will defect and discount to attempt to gain market share any time the interest rate is greater than 3.5 percent—i.e., almost anytime.[25] "Tit for Tat" therefore is a more effective coordination device for oligopolists that expect to encounter one another again and again with very high probability—e.g., PepsiCo and

---

[25] Equation 13.15 can also be written to highlight the interplay between p and r as
$$\$100,000 < \$115,000 \, (0.9)/(1 + r) = \$115,000/(1 + R)$$
where R is the effective rate of interest $1/(1 + R) = (p/(1 + r) = 0.9/(1 + r)$. In the above "Tit for Tat" example, because the probability of continuance is near 1.0, the effective rate of interest and the actual rate of interest are quite similar. For $r = 10$ percent and $p = 0.9$, $(p/(1 + r)) = 0.9/1.1 = 0.82$, and therefore the effective rate of interest is 22 percent—i.e., $1/(1 + 0.22) = 0.82$. As p gets smaller, the effective and actual rate of interest diverge exponentially. For example, for an actual interest rate of 10 percent and $p = 0.55$, $(p/(1 + r)) = 0.55/1.1 = 0.5$, and therefore the effective rate of interest is 100 percent—i.e., $1/(1 + 1.0) = 0.5$.

Coca-Cola, Nike and Reebok, United and American Airlines, Kodak and Fuji, Anheuser-Busch and Miller, and perhaps Carnival and Royal Caribbean.

Since the ($450, $450) actions yield $90,000 more for Royal Caribbean than the iterated dominant strategy equilibrium ($300, $300), Royal Caribbean may well initiate cooperation and thereafter play "Tit for Tat." With rational, unconfused, and well-informed competitors, communication of conspicuous focal points and multi-period punishment schemes can elicit conditional cooperation in repeated Prisoner's Dilemma. Perhaps for this reason, the Third Federal Circuit Court has prohibited airlines from signalling such coordination information to one another through their centralized reservation systems. Self-enforcing reliance mechanisms are often utilized to establish credible commitments between business rivals precisely because arm's-length competitors are limited by the antitrust statutes in their ability to contract to assure cooperation.

Example

Price Signalling
A communication of price change plans, prohibited by antitrust law.

SIGNALLING A PUNISHMENT SCHEME: NORTHWEST[26]

In the summer of 1989, America West announced a $50 fare reduction for 21-day advance purchase tickets on the busy Minneapolis–Los Angeles route. Rather than cutting its own $308 fare from its Minneapolis hub to match the America West $258 fare, Northwest announced a $40 reduction (from $208 to $168) for 21-day advance purchase tickets on the busy Phoenix–New York route. America West's hub is in Phoenix. This retaliatory fare was labeled on the Airline Tariff Publishing computer system as available for only the next 2 days, with possible renewal thereafter. Five days later, America West canceled its $50 promotion on West Coast travel.

Antitrust law makes it illegal for companies to conspire to fix prices. **Signalling** the particulars of a multiperiod punishment scheme in order to elicit cooperation in maintaining high prices is seen as a violation of the law. Northwest defended its actions as "competitive initiatives and responses consistent with independent self-interest" and therefore thoroughly legal. However, signalling limited-duration punishment schemes involving prices is not. *U.S. v. Airline Tariff Publishing Co. et al.,* 92-52854 (1992) expressly prohibited the preannouncement of price changes that might facilitate price coordination.

One reason is indicated by the pricing outcome in another of Northwest's routes (Detroit–Philadelphia) after a similar round of anticompetitive tactics. When Spirit Airline, a tiny discount carrier, entered that market in June 1996, one-way fares declined from $170 to $49 on all Northwest flights. Northwest increased flights and drove Spirit from the market. Subsequently, Northwest cut flights and returned in 1997 to $230 one-way fares.

Industry Standards and Regulatory Constraints

Unlike in chess or poker, in business strategy games the players are free to change the rules—i.e., the very structure of the game itself. Third-party enforcement of industry standards or regulatory constraints are often a way of changing the structure of a simultaneous-play business rivalry into a sequential-play game. Java programming language for the Internet and digital signal specifications

[26] Based on "Fare Game," *Wall Street Journal,* June 28, 1990, p. A1; "Fare Warning," *Wall Street Journal,* October 9, 1990, p. B1; and "Why Northwest Gives Competition a Bad Name," *Business Week,* March 16, 1998, p. 34.

for cellphones (CDMA, TDMA, GSM, and iDEN) or for high-definition television (Motorola versus Sony standard) are examples of industry standards used in this way. By restricting the flexibility of one another's best-reply responses, rivals can often secure an escape from the dominant strategy payoffs of a Prisoner's Dilemma and achieve more profitable outcomes.

Consider the business-to-business sale of electrical equipment illustrated in Figure 13.11. General Electric would like to manufacture and distribute a high specifications ("gold-plated") product, perhaps a large transformer for factories and hospitals. Unfortunately, however, the GE distributor has higher payoffs from not providing full installation. Under those circumstances, GE is better off manufacturing a transformer that meets only minimal specifications. Because of the distributor's dominant strategy, the two companies earn payoffs {Worse, Better} and find themselves in a Prisoner's Dilemma. They would both prefer the northwest cell {Better, Best}, but each would then be vulnerable to a defection by the other company, resulting in their Worst outcome. By enlisting third parties (TP) like Underwriters' Laboratory in specifying an installation standard or local building codes in enacting

Figure 13.11   Electrical Industry Standard Allows GE Distributor to Escape Prisoner's Dilemma

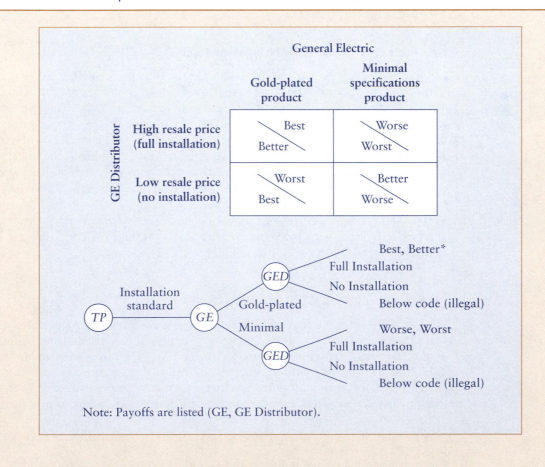

Note: Payoffs are listed (GE, GE Distributor).

an installation regulation, General Electric and its distributors can escape the Prisoner's Dilemma. Since a General Electric distributor would then be engaged in an illegal ("below code") sale should it provide anything less than full installation, General Electric can anticipate full installation and will therefore proceed to manufacture the high specifications product. The payoffs will then improve to {Better, Best}.

The same argument is often made by manufacturers who wish to limit the discounting of their distributors. Resale price maintenance (RPM) agreements prohibit retailers from cutting the price at which they resell the product below a manufacturer's suggested retail price. Most such restrictions on the vertical pricing relationship between manufacturers and distributors or distributors and retailers are illegal, especially when they appear motivated by the desire of competing retail dealers for less price competition. For example, Chevrolet dealers in Los Angeles once approached GM about using an RPM agreement to sanction the steep discounting of a "renegade" dealer who had markedly cut everyone's possible profit margins. In *United States* v. *GM* (1966), the Supreme Court declared this anticompetitive practice illegal per se.

Occasionally, however, a manufacturer or distributor can demonstrate a "legitimate manufacturer's interest" in regulatory or industry standards which place a floor under the resale prices of its products (e.g., a rare book distributor). When one of these special exceptions is made and an RPM agreement is allowed, the parties have succeeded in using a regulatory mechanism to escape a Prisoner's Dilemma analogous to Table 13.5.[27]

Example

RESALE PRICE MAINTENANCE AGREEMENT: STRIDERITE[28]

In the late 1990s, Nintendo, New Balance Athletic, and StrideRite all paid multi-million dollar fines to settle charges that the manufacturers cut shipments to retail outlets that refused to charge full list price. In StrideRite's case, leading retailers were cut off if they refused to sell six styles of women's Keds at MSRP prices from $20–$45. Although StrideRite insisted that it could suspend contracts with retailers who violated other company marketing policies and procedures, the government found that StrideRite had refused to deal with only those particular dealers who discounted Keds. The courts concluded this was an anticompetitive business practice because the suspended dealers had been pressured by StrideRite to raise prices. Vertical requirements contracting about matters *other than resale price* is widespread and perfectly legal. Such mechanisms are a standard business contracting solution to the Prisoner's Dilemma problem in Figure 13.11.

Hostages Support Cooperative Exchange

In Chapter 10 we encountered another noncooperative mechanism for securing cooperation in a repeated Prisoner's Dilemma. Potentially notorious firms selling low-quality experience goods (e.g., PC components) for high prices were identifiable in Table 10.4 as firms with entirely redeployable assets. That is, firms selling out of temporary locations, with unbranded products and no company reputation, were firms that one could reasonably expect to follow the dominant strategy of producing low

---

[27] See L. Telser, "Why Should Manufacturers Want Fair Trade II?" *Journal of Law and Economics*, 33, October 1990, pp. 409–417.

[28] Based on "StrideRite Agrees to Settle," *Wall Street Journal*, September 28, 1993, p. A5.

quality. Consequently, these were firms to whom no customer would offer a high price.

On the other hand, we argued that firms who asked high prices but also exhibited verifiable sunk-cost investments that dissipated the rent from such prices, were much better bets. Reputational advertising of nontransferable company logos (say, Apple) or investment in nonredeployable transaction-supporting assets, such as product-specific showrooms (Ethan Allen) and unique retail displays (L'eggs), presented a hostage to buyers.[29] Because sellers offering hostages are worse off if they fail to deliver on the promise of high quality, a buyer can rely on these credible commitments even if unable to verify quality at the point of purchase. Although the credible commitments are noncontractual in nature, the reliance relationships they establish are no less predictable than if these were enforceable contracts.

Finally, then, we have cooperative game mechanisms, involving binding (third-party-enforceable) agreements. In Chapter 15, we analyze coordination games designed to illustrate the role of private contractual agreements such as franchise agreements, escrow bonds, and refund guarantees. These contractual mechanisms can also allow escape from defection outcomes in a Prisoner's Dilemma. They, too, offer hostages that support win-win exchange despite a dominant strategy that would otherwise lead players to mutual defection. The key to the credibility of such mechanisms remains exactly the same as in noncooperative games. First, in the light of the warranty obligations, is the promiser better off fulfilling his or her promise than ignoring it? And second, is the warranty or bond *irrevocable* other than for just causes the promise-giver cannot control? If both features characterize the "hostage" given, then the commitments are credible (consistent with best-reply response), and the players in both cooperative and noncooperative games can allow themselves to be vulnerable to defection and yet escape the Prisoner's Dilemma.

SUMMARY

- Proactive oligopolists require accurate predictions of rival initiatives and rival response. The managerial purpose of game theory is to predict just such rival behavior.

- Simultaneous play games occasionally arise in pricing and promotion rivalry, but the essence of business strategy is sequential reasoning. The order of play matters in sequential games of coordination between manufacturers and distributors, entry deterrence and accommodation, service competition, R&D races, product development, and so on, because rivals must predict best-reply responses and counterresponses all the way out to an endgame. Endgame reasoning entails looking ahead to the last play in an ordered sequence of plays, identifying the player whose decisions control the available outcomes in the endgame, and then predicting that player's preferred action.

- Subgame perfect equilibrium strategy looks ahead to analyze endgame outcomes and then reasons back to prior best-reply responses. Credible threats and credible commitments are the key to endgame reasoning, and therefore credibility mechanisms are the key to subgame perfect equilibrium strategy.

- Nash equilibrium and dominant strategy equilibrium differ in important ways. Nash equilibrium strategy entails actions that maximize each decision maker's

---

[29] Recall that the buyers had easy access to information about fraud and punished violators with grim trigger strategies. Otherwise, customers sorted randomly across all the reliable firms.

payoff, given best-reply responses of the other players. In contrast, dominant strategy equilibrium entails actions that maximize at least one decision maker's payoff, no matter what any other player chooses to do.

- Advantages may accrue to either first-movers or fast-seconds in a business rivalry. The former can credibly threaten or credibly precommit and therefore preempt some outcomes, whereas the latter replies and can determine the best-reply response in the endgame. Which is more advantageous depends on the particulars of the tactical and strategic situation.

- Threats and commitments ultimately derive their credibility from the threat maker adopting subgame perfect strategy. A credible threat is a conditional strategy the threat maker is worse off ignoring than implementing. A credible commitment is an obligation the commitment maker is worse off ignoring than fulfilling.

- Mechanisms for establishing credibility include establishing a bond or contractual side payment, investing in a nonredeployable reputation asset, short-circuiting or interrupting the response process, entering into a profit-sharing alliance, taking small steps, or arranging an irreversible and irrevocable hostage mechanism.

- Closed-end leases with preset residual values are a mechanism for establishing a durable goods manufacturer's credible commitment to early buyers of new models not to discount deeply after the sale.

- Incumbents may seek to deter potential entrants through the use of excess capacity precommitments or credible threats of advertising campaigns and price discounts. Whether incumbents deter or accommodate potential entrants depends in general on the presence or absence of first-mover advantages, on the structure of competition in prices versus quantities, and on how customers sort across alternative firms when the low-priced capacity stocks out.

- Customer sorting patterns include the following: random rationing in which all customers are equally likely to obtain the low-priced capacity; efficient rationing in which the highest (then next highest) willingness-to-pay customers obtain the low-priced capacity until it is exhausted; extreme brand loyalty in which none of the regular customers seek the low-priced capacity; and inverse intensity rationing in which the lowest (then next lowest) willingness-to-pay customers obtain the low-priced capacity until it is exhausted. With inverse intensity rationing, the customer sorting implies a segmented market and is most likely to lead to accommodation of entry.

- In wars of attrition, whether to hang tough and stay in competition for a market price or concede defeat and leave depends on the ratio of the prize to the sum of the prize plus the periodic cost of competing.

- Nash equilibrium for simultaneous games identifies pure and mixed strategies. In both cases, players' choices reflect best-reply reactions of rivals and therefore provide stability.

- Most Nash equilibrium strategies are nonunique; multiple pure Nash strategies exist.

- Mixed strategy provides an optimal rule for randomizing one's actions among multiple Nash equilibrium strategies.

- Mutual cooperation in a repeated Prisoner's Dilemma game can be secured with the uncertain endgame timing, adoption of an industry standard, multiperiod punishment schemes like "Tit for Tat" or grim trigger strategy, and strategic hostage or bonding mechanisms for establishing credible commitments and threats.

- Cooperation in noncooperative games is more likely if strategies are clear, provokable, take cooperative initiatives unilaterally, and are forgiving so as not to perpetuate mistakes. The "Tit-for-Tat" strategy has these characteristics.
- Playing against "Tit for Tat" strategies necessitates comparing the additional profit from unilateral defection against the discounted opportunity loss from limited-duration certain punishment next period. As the probability of continued replay declines, "Tit for Tat" becomes a less effective coordination device for escaping the Prisoner's Dilemma than a matching price policy.

EXERCISES

1. Identify the dominant strategy equilibrium if PepsiCo and Coca-Cola each earn $12,000 per week per store when both maintain high six-pack prices, $8,000 per week per store when both promote a low discounted price, $17,000 per week per store for either party that defects successfully alone to low prices, and $6,000 per week per store for either party that maintains high prices when the other party defects. What pricing action will PepsiCo choose? What about Coca-Cola?

2. How does the analysis and the strategic equilibrium outcome differ in Figure 13.2 if the other firm enjoys a cost advantage—for example, $35 at AA&D? Then does the order of play (i.e., who goes first in making price cuts) matter in this bidding game with asymmetric costs?

3. Consider an ongoing sequence of pairwise marketing competitions between three companies with promotional campaigns of varying degrees of success. Each campaign involves comparative advertising belittling the target company. The company with the most loyal customers (call this firm Most) enjoys 100-percent success when it attacks either of the others. The company with the least loyal customers (i.e., Least) has a 30-percent success rate when it belittles either Most or More. More, itself, experiences an 80-percent success rate. The firms each launch their advertising attacks one at a time in an arbitrary sequence. Least goes first and can attack either Most or More. More attacks second, and Most attacks third. If more than one of the opponents survive the first round of competition, the order of play repeats itself: Least, then More, then Most. Any player can skip his or her turn; that is, the three actions available to Least to initiate the game are as follows: attack More, attack Most, or do nothing and pass the turn.

    Try to diagram the game tree and employ subgame perfect equilibrium analysis to identify the strategic equilibrium. What should the most vulnerable firm with the least loyal customers do to initiate play? What would be More's best-reply response if attacked and More survives? What if Least did nothing? What would Most do when and if its turn arose?

4. Why should the early adopters of an information technology system provided by IBM Systems Solutions be willing to pay more for a closed-end lease of the servers and other hardware required than for an outright purchase?

5. People who are regularly late often don't bother to carry watches. This would be a real problem except for the fact that other people tend to adjust to their tardiness by starting meetings ten minutes after they're scheduled, coming to lunch appointments ten minutes late, etc. Analyze the following coordination game and explain why.

		Harry	
		Be Punctual	**Always Late**
Tom	**Be Punctual**	100 \ 100	50 \ 70
	Always Late	70 \ 50	95 \ 95

6. Identify all the Nash equilibria for Simultaneous Manufacturer/Distributor I in Table 13.1. Calculate the mixed strategy equilibrium. Show your work.

7. The outcomes in the bottom half of the game tree describing the last (the 20th) submarket of the chain store paradox in Figure 13.10 are labeled N.A. (not applicable). Why? What specific equilibrium concept in sequential games rules out the applicability of these outcomes? Hint: How would you describe the game tree from Node E onwards as opposed to the game tree from Node D onwards?

http://

The Changing Antitrust Treatment of Resale Price Maintenance

8. The U.S. Supreme Court and other federal courts have ruled on a number of cases involving resale price maintenance. Access the following Internet site: http://www.stolaf.edu/people/becker.

    Find the section that summarizes antitrust cases, and read the summary for *Albrecht* v. *Herald Co.* (1968), and *State Oil* v. *Khan* (1997). Describe how the antitrust doctrine applied by the court to resale price maintenance has changed, and relate this change to the economic analysis of resale price maintenance in the chapter you have just read. What economic arguments did the Supreme Court use in overturning the earlier Albrecht decision?

9. What problems arise in PepsiCo's couponing customers every other week to try to attract additional business? Would mail-order segmentation of PepsiCo versus Coca-Cola customers help this process? How?

10. Suppose you have announced you will "meet the competition" in response to entry threats by a potential entrant who has done marketing research in your target market at a lower price point than you currently sell. What difference does it make, if any, if technology is moving very fast in the market so that this proves to be a one-time-only simultaneous-play game?

11. Nike and Adidas are facing the following coordination problem in trying to decide whether to conduct heavy or light combative advertising against the other firm. What should each firm do?

		Nike	
		Light Ads	**Heavy Ads**
Adidas	**Light Ads**	$12 M \ $10 M	$6 M \ $4 M
	Heavy Ads	$4 M \ $5 M	$9 M \ $8 M

12. Analyze the following sequential game and advise Kodak about whether they should introduce the new product Picture CD.

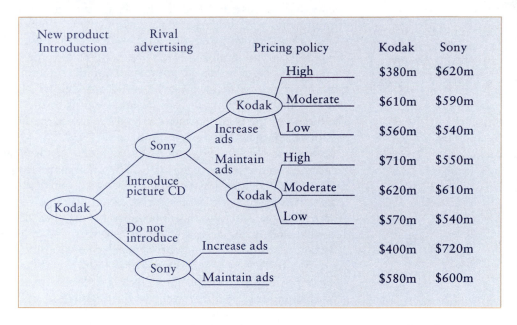

New product Introduction	Rival advertising	Pricing policy	Kodak	Sony
		High	$380m	$620m
		Moderate	$610m	$590m
	Increase ads	Low	$560m	$540m
	Maintain ads	High	$710m	$550m
		Moderate	$620m	$610m
		Low	$570m	$540m
	Increase ads		$400m	$720m
	Maintain ads		$580m	$600m

13. Calculate the 8-hour-shift costs of operating a taxi with a medallion license that cost $125,000 borrowed at 10-percent interest assuming two shifts for 365 days per year, plus a $25,000 car that depreciates 50 percent in one year, plus $22 for gas and maintenance per shift per day. Would you pay $60/shift for a taxi operator's license? Why or why not?

14. Explain how the concept of Nash equilibrium differs from Pareto efficient equilibrium in economics. (Hint: Does "gains from trade" imply a credible commitment to trade?)

15. A math graduate student explains to her friends how to approach a group of smart attractive guys who have brought along famous actor Russell Crowe. What should her friend do? Ignore Russell Crowe or fixate on Russell Crowe? Explain the equilibrium reasoning underlying your answer.

| | | Student 1 | |
		Ignore R.C.	Fixate on R.C.
Student 2	Ignore R.C.	No date tonight / No date tonight	Date with R.C. / Date with other guys
	Fixate on R.C.	Date with other guys / Date with R.C.	No date ever / No date ever

Note: Best payoff—date with R.C., Better—date with other guys, Worse—no date tonight, Worst—no date ever with any of these guys.

SUPERJUMBO DILEMMA[30]

Boeing and Airbus build wide-body commercial aircraft in several sizes at the rate of about one wide-body per day. Customers first pay a deposit of one third of $84–$127 million for a 767, one third of $134–$185 million for a 777, and one third of $165–$200 million for a 747. The second third is due after final assembly when the aircraft is described as a "white tail," and the final third is due at delivery. Final assembly requires 15–25 days, the entire production schedule is 11 months long, and of course, design modifications add months to the front end of each project. The largest of the Boeing planes carries 420 passengers or 300 plus freight; by comparison, the largest Airbus (the A320) carries 330.

As early as 1993, Boeing and Airbus entered into discussions to jointly develop a very large commercial transport (VLCT) with perhaps 1,000 seats. If each firm proceeded independently, the market for VLCTs is so small relative to the massive R&D costs that sizeable losses were assured. Either firm had superior profit available if it proceeded alone. Analyze this noncooperative product development game and predict what Boeing and Airbus would do and why.

In contrast, the two competitors decided to enter into a strategic alliance with the option to develop a superjumbo or withdraw and maintain a wide-body focus. Analyze Boeing's decision in light of its $45-million contribution margin on each 747 produced and sold. Net operating profit is about $15 million.

Boeing \ Airbus	Enter Strategic Alliance and Jointly Develop VLCT	Enter Strategic Alliance but Don't Agree to Develop VLCT
Enter Strategic Alliance and Jointly Develop VLCT	Reduced development risk / Cannibalize wide-body business	Loss from alliance costs / Max default risk, possibly net profit
Enter Strategic Alliance but Don't Agree to Develop VLCT	Max default risk, possibly a net profit / Loss from alliance costs but preserve wide-body business	Loss from alliance costs / Ongoing net profit of $15mm per wide-body plane

QUESTIONS

1. Why did Airbus go ahead with the A380 Superjumbo with its 800 seats, $10.7-billion development cost, and 250 planes required to break even by 2001?

2. If Boeing finds itself less profitable at 60 percent market share than at 45 percent, what is the likely impact on the Airbus-Boeing tactical competition?

---

[30] Based on M. Kretschmer, "Game Theory: The Developer's Dilemma, Boeing v. Airbus," Booz, Allen, and Hamilton, *Strategy & Business,* 2nd Quarter, 1998; "Towards the Wild Blue Yonder," *The Economist,* April 27, 2002, p. 67; and "Giving 'em Away," *Business Week,* March 5, 2001, pp. 52–55.

Appendix 13a

Capacity Planning and Pricing Against a Low-Cost Competitor: A Case Study of Piedmont Airlines and People Express

AIRLINE ENTRY STRATEGY

During early 1981 People Express (PX) became one of the first new entries into the deregulated interstate airline industry. PX's entry strategy was to offer a uniform low-price, no frills, high-frequency regionwide service to 13 peripheral mid-Atlantic cities using a hub and spoke system out of Newark, New Jersey. By unbundling all services, adopting quick turnaround times, working longer crew shifts, and converting all first-class and galley space into additional coach-class seats, PX achieved a 31-percent reduction relative to the industry average in direct fixed costs per flight (e.g., crew costs) and a 25-percent reduction in variable costs per seat (e.g., cabin service). Having secured the lowest operating cost structure in the industry, PX set out to attract customers who saw air travel as a commodity and would regularly fly rather than drive. The prototypical target customer was a manufacturer's trade representative who often needs to travel on short notice, but is seldom on the company expense account.

In essence, People Express had created a new segment of the market not previously served by much more expensive and infrequent Mohawk and Allegheny flights (the predecessors of US Airways). Importantly, inverse intensity rationing of the cheap capacity ensued. That is, the new low-willingness-to-pay customers attracted into the market by PX's discounting quickly secured all of PX's capacity, leaving almost none available to other air travelers. As a result, PX failed to take regular customers away from the higher priced incumbents. Figure 13A.1 displays the strategy game this entry presented to the mid-Atlantic regional airlines. The incumbents had to decide whether to match PX's deeply discounted fares or accommodate PX by maintaining high fares. PX had to decide whether to enter with a large-capacity 120-seat Boeing 737 or a small-capacity 30-seat deHavilland 128.

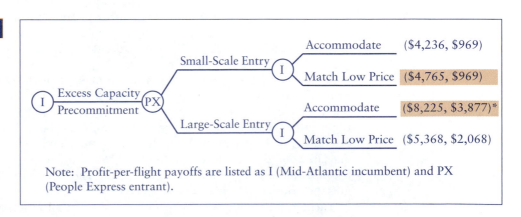

Note: Profit-per-flight payoffs are listed as I (Mid-Atlantic incumbent) and PX (People Express entrant).

LARGE-SCALE ACCOMMODATION

As in Entry Deterrence I in Chapter 13, the new entrant had to decide first, but prediction of the equilibrium strategy was easy because PX had a dominant strategy. No matter what the incumbents' pricing response in the mid-Atlantic markets, PX had higher payoffs from a large-capacity entry. PX's payoffs of $3,877 and $2,068 per flight with frequently scheduled larger capacity aircraft dominated $969 per flight with frequently scheduled small-capacity aircraft. Examining the payoffs resulting from large-capacity entry, the incumbents preferred to accommodate with $8,225 operating profit per flight rather than match and earn only $5,368 per flight. Even though by matching PX's discount, incumbents could pick up extra seats in overflow demand from People's customers, the loss of margin was sufficient to induce the incumbents to prefer to accommodate large-scale entry. {Large Capacity, Accommodate} therefore proved to be the subgame perfect equilibrium. Using leaseback purchases to leverage its modest start-up capital into 17 large-capacity planes, People Express intensively developed a dozen peripheral mid-Atlantic routes and thereby managed to avoid retaliation from either the regional or major carriers.

In the Southeast regional markets, the situation was entirely different. Piedmont Airlines was the second-fastest-growing airline in the post-deregulation era. By serving small- to medium-size cities ignored by the major carriers and by connecting through hubs with little or no competition, Piedmont retained a record 95 percent of its passengers on connecting flights. Piedmont knew that its reputation with business travelers was high and rising, but also knew that measuring tactical success against a new entrant would require hard data. Piedmont therefore proceeded to count and categorize every passenger on every PX flight into Piedmont cities. From these competitor surveillance data, Piedmont determined that several travel segments sorted randomly to the low-price supplier when substantial price differentials were present, but loyalty to the incumbent prevailed when prices were identical. This brand preference for the incumbent was almost universal at $79 prices, but remained strong even with the new lower-willingness-to-pay customers attracted into the market by People's discounting to $49, $39, $29, and even $19.

Large-Scale Entry Deterrence

Figure 13A.2 displays the entry deterrence and accommodation game with random rationing that presented itself to Piedmont and People Express in early 1985; the boxed data list the common information. On a typical 400-mile route, Piedmont had to decide whether to match PX's $49 one-way fares or accommodate the new entrant by maintaining its own $79 one-way fares. Again, PX had to decide whether to enter with a large capacity 120-seat Boeing 737 or a small capacity 30-seat deHavilland 128. And again, PX had to decide first; the incumbent's (i.e., Piedmont) pricing decision controlled the endgame.

Analysis of the subgame perfect equilibrium strategy is straightforward. First, let's examine the payoffs resulting from small capacity entry in the top half of the diagram. The incumbent (PI) prefers to accommodate with $6,979 operating profit per flight rather than match and earn only $5,365 per flight. Even if by matching PX's discount, the incumbent picks up 30 extra seats from People's customers, the loss of margin from ($79 − $16.69) to ($49 − $16.69) is sufficient to reduce the operating profit from $6,979 to $6,330. Consequently, the second row of endgame outcomes must be eliminated by PX from further consideration; Piedmont would never select it. Turning then to the large capacity payoffs, the situation is a bit different. With its 120-seat capacity, a 737 PX can satisfy all 64 new demanders attracted into the

FIGURE 13A.2   Matching Price Response with Random Rationing

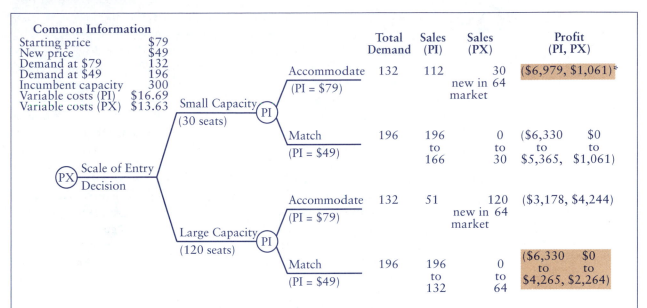

Notes: Payoffs are listed (Incumbent, Potential Entrant). PI refers to the incumbent airline (Piedmont) and PX refers to the potential entrant and actual entrant airline (People Express). The sales ranges and payoff ranges are described in the text.

market at price points between $79 and $49 and, in addition, can offer 56 seats of remaining capacity to the incumbent's price-sensitive customers. In PX's mid-Atlantic markets, this had not proven a problem for incumbents because inverse intensity rationing of PX's cheap capacity described the customer sorting pattern. In contrast, in Piedmont's Southeastern markets, PX's capacity was randomly rationed. With accommodative differential prices of $79 and $49, every customer willing to pay at least $49 would then have an equal probability of securing service from the low-price entrant. For large-scale entry, this meant that 120 seats would be rationed among 196 customers so each of the 132 customers willing to pay the incumbent's $79 accommodating price faces a $(1 - (196 - 120)/196) = 0.61$ chance of being served and a 0.39 chance of being denied service at the low-price entrant. Therefore, the expected demand at Piedmont from accommodating large-scale entry was $132 \times 0.39 = 51$ seats, which implied an expected operating profit of only $3,178.

Responding to the large-scale entry by matching prices offered the potential for much greater Piedmont profit (i.e., $6,330). Again, to ascertain the payoffs in the face of large-scale entry, the incumbent employed extensive competitor surveillance and tracking of target customers, such as the regional headquarters personnel flying regularly back and forth to corporate headquarters in New York. These data allowed Piedmont to conclude that at worst, with matching $49 prices, People Express would attract all 64 new customers who had entered the market in response to discounting, but none of Piedmont's regular customers. At worst, then, Piedmont would receive $(\$49 - \$16.69) \times 132 = \$4,265$ from matching PX's discount and only $3,178 from accommodating prices. Consequently, PX should have eliminated from further consideration its otherwise very attractive $4,244 per flight outcome associated with Piedmont's accommodation of PX's large-scale entry. Predictably, Piedmont would never go for it. Then, from People's perspective, the profit per flight from large capacity entry, using PX's lower incremental variable cost of $13.63, was at best ($49 − $13.63) × 64 = $2,264 and could go as low as zero. In contrast, the profit per flight from small capacity entry was a nearly certain $1,061. PX should have realized that the subgame perfect equilibrium was {Small Capacity, Accommodate}.

Instead, what actually happened was that People Express entered with the same large capacity employed in its peripheral mid-Atlantic routes. Piedmont was surprised, but of course matched prices, and a price war quickly ensued. At one point, the fares got down to $19, and residents of the Carolinas found themselves invited to "tavern lunches" at Tavern on the Green in New York. Eventually PX's operating profits fell so low it was forced to withdraw. People Express appears to have failed to recognize that with random rationing at differential prices and loyalty to the incumbent at matching prices, only small-scale entry could have induced accommodation and the sustainable $1,061-per-flight payoffs that were available in this market. This basic insight of several entry deterrence and accommodation games is sometimes humorously referred to as "judo economics." The subgame perfect strategic equilibrium in which mid-Atlantic incumbents were induced to accommodate large-scale entry presumed inverse intensity rationing, such as PX had experienced in its original markets. When the customer sorting pattern changed, the subgame perfect strategic equilibrium changed. People Express chose the right strategy, but for the wrong game and ended up being deterred. The fundamental and generalizable managerial insight here is that differences in customer sorting patterns alter the best-reply responses of incumbents facing entry.

EXERCISES

1. In the entry deterrence and accommodation game between Piedmont and People Express, explain why Piedmont's expected demand following small-scale entry in Figure 13A.2 is 112.

2. What customer sorting rules likely apply at the local airport where you reside? Do they differ in your estimation across destinations and target customer segments? Why or why not?

3. Why is knowing just one dominant strategy in the People Express entry game sufficient to predict rival behavior and identify the strategic equilibrium?

4. Today United Airlines and Delta Airlines face competition from discounters JetBlue and AirTran. One important difference, however, is that AirTran and Delta have virtually identical costs of 8.6 and 8.8 cents per available seat mile, whereas JetBlue, like People Express, has costs much lower than the incumbent. It costs United $23,690 to operate an Airbus 320 cross-country from Dulles in Washington, D.C., to Oakland, California, with exactly the same crew and equipment that JetBlue operates for only $14,454.[31] Booz Allen estimates that 39 percent of this huge cost differential is attributable to processes required by United's hub-and-spoke system as opposed to JetBlue's point-to-point operations with a single type of aircraft. Also, JetBlue pilot costs are 25.5 percent of total costs (lowest in the industry), whereas United's are 49.7 percent (highest in the industry). Devise an entry deterrence or accommodation strategy for Delta and for United.

---

[31] "Costly Race in the Sky," *Wall Street Journal,* September 9, 2002, p. B1.

14

Pricing Techniques and Analysis

CHAPTER PREVIEW This chapter builds on the price and output determination models developed in Chapters 10 through 13 as it considers more complex pricing issues. The first two sections examine a value-based pricing conceptual framework. Then we characterize differential pricing in directly segmented markets where different target customers are charged nonuniform prices for identical products or services at different times or places. Differential pricing in less segmented or indirectly segmented markets is accomplished with bundled pricing, tying, and nonlinear pricing using two-part tariffs (an access or entry fee combined with a user fee). Finally, we discuss the con-

cept of pricing throughout the product life cycle including penetration pricing, target pricing, limit pricing, price skimming, prestige pricing, and price lining. Together, the pricing practices presented in this chapter provide an extensive overview of the way managers actually apply pricing techniques to maximize shareholder wealth.

Appendix 14A develops the powerful revenue management systems that have revolutionized pricing and capacity allocation for multiproduct firms with perishable products or services like hotel rooms, rental cars, airline seats, satellite transmissions, and baseball games.

MANAGERIAL CHALLENGE

Pricing of Apple Computers: Market Share Versus Current Profitability[1]

Apple Computer manufactures and sells Macintosh, Powerbook, and iMac personal computers (PCs). Apple PCs compete against IBM, Toshiba, Compaq, Dell, and Packard Bell machines. Apple often uses microprocessor chips designed by Motorola as the "brains" of its PCs, whereas most of the other PC makers use Intel (or Intel clone) microprocessor chips in their machines.

Historically, Apple has priced its personal computers higher than similar models of other PC makers. For example, despite price cuts in early 1995 by both Apple and other PC companies, Macintosh systems were still priced $500 to $1,000 higher. Consequently, Apple's market share fell from 9.4 percent in 1993 to 8 percent in 1994. While industry shipments skyrocketed, Apple's margins increased (from 24 percent to 29 percent) on essentially flat unit sales.

By emphasizing current profit over market share, Apple discouraged independent software develop-

ers. Some observers believe that the company must increase its market share to about 20 percent to motivate software companies to write application programs for Apple PCs.

Ian Diery, Apple's sales vice president, defended the company's high prices, saying that Apple had to improve its balance sheet so that it could continue research and marketing efforts. This chapter focuses on a variety of different pricing strategies like Apple's decision to charge premium prices for its products.

http://

Access financial information on Apple Computer, including quarterly earning reports, at the following Internet site: http://www.apple.com/investor/

---

[1] Jim Carlton, "Apple's Choice: Preserve Profits or Cut Prices," *Wall Street Journal*, February 22, 1995, p. B1.

CONCEPTUAL FRAMEWORK FOR PROACTIVE, SYSTEMATIC-ANALYTICAL, VALUE-BASED PRICING

In the past, pricing decisions were often treated as an afterthought and made in ad hoc fashion as a reaction to competitor initiatives. When pricing rivalry was more stable, many firms would simply routinely mark up cost. Today, pricing proactively with systematic analysis of which orders to accept (and which to refuse) at many different value-based prices has become a critical success factor for many businesses.

Proactive pricing is tactically astute and internally consistent with operations strategy. A high-cost airline cannot slash prices dramatically even if 10- or 20-percent increases in market share in a high-margin segment are thereby achievable. It must instead anticipate a matching price reaction by its lower-cost rivals, perhaps followed by still further price cuts below its own cost. Knowing all this in advance renders gainshare discounting much less attractive despite the temptation of additional incremental sales in a high-margin business.

To take another example, in the men's aftershave industry, an incumbent recently encountered a new entrant whose product, Vibrance, was introduced with a penetration price 40 percent below the leading brand. The incumbent increased advertising but maintained its original price point and was astounded to observe a 50-percent decline in market share through its grocery store distribution channel. Only afterwards was systematic analysis completed. Estimations showed that demand was very price elastic and advertising inelastic. Pricing decisions must be systematic and analytical, based on hard facts instead of ad hoc hunches.

Finally, the appropriate conceptual framework for setting prices is an analysis of the determinants of customer value. What triggers a customer's purchase is value in excess of asking price or a ratio of value to price greater than a competitor's ratio. Firms must begin their pricing decisions by identifying the value-drivers in each customer segment. Business air travelers value delivery reliability, the ability to change itineraries on short notice (i.e., change order responsiveness), and schedule convenience more than the service characteristics of attentive flight attendants, wide seats, or quiet flights. Because such process-based value drivers are harder to imitate, sustainable price premiums are often associated with these operations processes rather than the product or service characteristics themselves.

On the other hand, Prestone and Zerex have leading anticorrosive radiator fluids whose product characteristics warrant a price premium. Under apparent price pressure, Zerex often simply meets the competition as long as competing prices on generic radiator fluid cover cost. A thorough value analysis reveals, however, that this reactive cost-based pricing fails to realize about one-third of Zerex's sustainable profit margin. Cost-based pricing has been called one of the "five deadly business sins" by Peter Drucker; what firms should do instead is "price-based costing." That is, firms should segment customers, perform extensive value analysis, and then develop products whose costs allow substantial profitability in each product line the firm chooses to enter. Each firm's marketing and operations capabilities are the key to then sustaining that profitability.

Costs are not irrelevant. Indeed, a key to effective revenue management is knowing with great precision just what activity-based costs are associated with each type of order from each customer segment. Knowledge of differential costs supports the adoption of differential pricing, and even more importantly, allows value-based pricing managers to discern *which orders to refuse*. But costs should be the consequence of a value-based pricing and product development strategy.

In sum, pricing decisions should be proactive and systematic-analytical, not reactive and ad hoc. And, most importantly, pricing should be value-based, not cost-based. This value-based conceptual framework leads naturally to a differential pricing environment in which mass-produced products or services are customized to the requirements of target customer classes and nonuniform pricing then ensues.

INTERTEMPORAL PRICING IN TARGET MARKET SEGMENTS

Value-based differential pricing implies identifying the different value drivers for various segments of the target market. Direct segmentation of target customers and the prevention of resale arbitrage between them can be accomplished with a variety of "fences." Two of the most frequent involve intertemporal pricing and pricing by delivery location.

http://
Read an article by Kevin M. Guthrie on value-based pricing at the following Internet site for the Andrew W. Mellon Foundation's recent Scholarly Communication and Technology conference:
http://www.arl.org/scomm/scat/guthries.html

Congestion-based pricing at peak demand periods on roadways, bridges, and subway systems is illustrated in Figure 14.1. Peak-period drivers place demands on a Los Angeles toll road between 6:00 A.M. and 9:00 A.M. far in excess of its carrying capacity (Q_C). Charging peak-period commuters a toll equal to just the minuscule cost of wear and tear maintenance—i.e., an off-peak marginal cost—(MC_{OP}) induces many more cars to enter the highway (Q_{PEAK}) than can be accommodated (i.e., $Q_P > Q_C$). The result is slowdowns, stoppages, and a markedly increased travel time for each commuter. Beyond Q_C, the traffic volume at which this congestion begins, MC_P represents the incremental fuel and time costs imposed (by one additional car) on all the other drivers along a 10-mile stretch of toll road. A congestion toll of ($P_P - MC_{OP}$) induces discretionary peak period travelers to switch to other travel times and alternative modes of transportation. If a toll road authority set peak-period prices just sufficient to cover this congestion cost, traffic volume would decline from Q_{PEAK} (P_{OP}) to Q_P, and the equilibrium differential prices P_P and P_{OP} would emerge. **Congestion pricing** accomplishes the goal of placing a true resource cost on the scarce transportation system capacity at peak travel times.

Congestion Pricing
A fee that reflects the true marginal cost imposed by demand in excess of capacity.

CONGESTION TOLLS IN ORANGE COUNTY, CALIFORNIA[2]

In 1985 the typical American spent 22 hours per year in traffic jams due to peak-period congestion. By 1995, this figure had doubled to over 40 hours per year. In California, total waiting time in traffic jams was projected to exceed 79 million hours in 2003, costly indeed. See the steeply rising MC_P in Figure 14.1. Is the answer simply more highways? One community in Southern California thinks not. Congestion tolls which charge commuters for the congestion their cars impose on other drivers have been adopted by a private toll road in Orange County, near Los Angeles. Every day, 24,000 drivers pay a peak-period congestion toll of $3.30 per trip for a 10-mile stretch of true expressway. Toll booths, which themselves cause delays, have been replaced by credit-card-size transponders mounted in dashboards from which overhead computers deduct tolls as the cars speed along. Although the congestion toll expenses of a typical commuter mount up quickly, the cost of additional vehicles on the peak-period road imposes the need for additional road capacity at a price as high as P'_P. And time is money, so faced with the slow commute on "freeways," many peak-period travelers are opting for the differential pricing of a toll road.

Example

http://

Read about urban transportation issues, including an article about driver support for congestion tolls, at the following Internet site maintained by Resources for the Future:

http://www.rff.org/ intersections/urb_transp. htm

Like peak–off-peak roadway pricing, many other examples of differential pricing entail charging differential prices for the same capacity at different times. Intertemporal pricing at matinee and evening movie theaters, for example, involves segmented demanders not in rivalry for the same theater seats. First-run movies and subsequent movie videos, hardback and later paperback editions of books, seasonal discounts in the resort and cruise ship businesses, and weekend discounts on airlines all represent effective intertemporal segmentation of different target customer classes. However, if two customer classes are in rivalry for the same capacity (e.g., the seats in coach class on a particular airplane flight), then differential pricing involves price discrimination, which is discussed below.

Direct segmentation of target customer classes can also be accomplished by geographic locations. Customers who arrive at the neighborhood rental counters of Hertz

---

[2] Based on "How to Make Traffic Jams a Thing of the Past," *Fortune*, March 31, 1997, p. 34, and "A Survey of Commuting," *The Economist*, September 5, 1998, p. 62.

Figure 14.1   Congestion Tolls with Peak–Off-Peak Demand

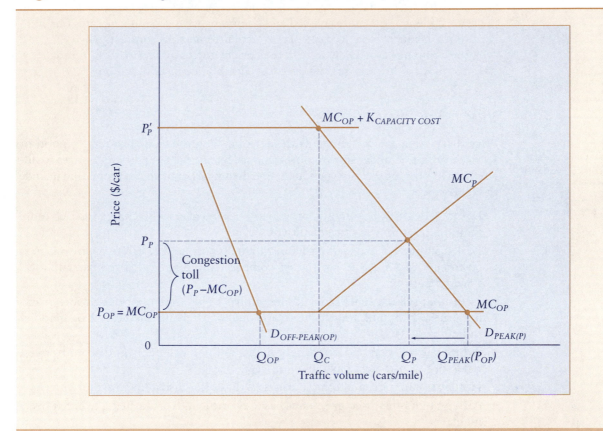

and Avis have flexibly timed, convenience-based uses for rental cars. Consequently, the neighborhood-location demand is much more price sensitive than the airport-location demand by business travelers. A recent study found that weekday rates for a midsize sedan were $43 in neighborhood rental locations versus $69 on average in airport rental locations.[3] Since round-trip taxi fares from airports to the neighborhood locations would typically far exceed the $26 price difference, Avis and Hertz customers are effectively segmented. Other examples of location-based segmentation would be electronic debits for driving in inner-city congestion zones (e.g., London has recently imposed a £5/day charge in and around Westminster), and fashion clothing from France's Arche or Ralph Lauren sold less expensively in discount outlets along interstate highways or in vacation resort locations. Outlet shoppers almost never overlap with the customers these companies find in their trendy downtown boutiques. Hence, geographic segmentation works.

Outlet shoppers will also buy a less costly, less durable version of the product (e.g., a lighter weight chemise cloth in Polo golf shirts), so in differential pricing, Ralph Lauren accomplishes more than just inventory clearance without any danger of cannibalizing full-price sales. Instead, such companies are "versioning" their product. Hal Varian and Carl Shapiro have argued that versioning is an especially good way

---

[3] "Playing the Car-Rental Game," *Wall Street Journal*, July 31, 2002, p. D3.

to sell information economy items like software.[4] A voice recognition package sells for $79 as general-purpose Voice ProPad, for $795 as Office Talk, and for $7,995 as Voice Ortho, a special-purpose medical transcriptor. All three versions derive from the same code, but the more enabled and comprehensive version generates one hundred times as much value to particular target customers. In contrast, when Amazon sells the *same* book or DVD at different prices to customers with different click streams, that's a different pricing practice. That's price discrimination.

PRICE DISCRIMINATION

Price Discrimination
The act of selling the same good or service, produced by a single firm, at different prices to different buyers during the same period of time.

Price discrimination is defined as the act of selling the same product (a good or service), produced under single control (that is, by one firm), at different prices to different buyers during the same period of time. Examples of price discrimination include the following:

- Doctors, dentists, hospitals, lawyers, and taxpreparers who charge the rich more than the poor for the same quality of service
- Dell Computer Corp. selling its ultralight laptop at $2,307 to small business customers, at $2,228 to health care companies, and at $2,072 to state and local governments
- Firms that sell the exact same product under two different labels at widely varying prices (Hotpoint and Kenmore appliances, Michelin and Sears Roadhandler radial tires)
- Athletic teams that sponsor family nights and ladies' nights at discount prices, while other customers pay the full price
- Hotels, restaurants, and other businesses that offer discounts to senior citizens
- Airlines that offer discounted fares based on the length of stay (e.g., over Saturday night)
- Korean TV manufacturers who sell products direct to the customer at a lower price in the United States than in Japan

Most differential pricing to a firm's retail customers is perfectly legal and it unambiguously raises profits. This happens because the satisfaction or utility gained from the purchase of the product exceeds that which is lost from paying a uniform price, and a *consumers' surplus* results. If a coffee aficionado were willing to pay $6.00 for a morning cup of java, but found that Starbuck's charged only $2.00, the consumers' surplus would be $4.00. Price discrimination transfers some of this consumers' surplus from the consumer to the seller.

Example

eBUSINESS CLICKSTREAMS ALLOW PRICE DISCRIMINATION: PERSONIFY[5]

Personify, an Internet service company, has created software that allows web businesses to categorize buyers based on their clickstream patterns. Relating these segments to their price sensitivity in past purchases, Virtual Vineyards, CDNow, and Amazon.com have begun charging different prices for the same wine, CD, or book. If it costs $200 to produce and stock a case of 20 bottles of wine, and if five customers

---

[4] C. Shapiro and H. Varian, "Versioning," *Harvard Business Review*, November/December 1998, pp. 106–114.

[5] Based on "I Got It Cheaper Than You," *Forbes*, November 2, 1998, pp. 83–84.

will pay $24 a bottle (for one bottle each) while another fifteen customers will pay $8 a bottle, uniform pricing will result in a loss, and the vineyard will stop producing this wine. At an $8 uniform price, all twenty customers buy, and the winery loses $40. At a $24 price, five customers buy, and the winery loses $80. But suppose the five customers pay $20 per bottle, while the fifteen are asked to pay $7. Each group paid less than their willingness to pay and less than their proposed uniform price, yet the winery makes a $5 profit.

In the limiting case of perfect price discrimination, the seller discovers the maximum each individual is willing to pay for each unit purchased, sometimes called the reservation price. The monopolist then charges all purchasers their own reservation prices and manages to capture the entire consumers surplus. For example, in the discriminatory descending price (Dutch) auction market for T-bills (discussed in Chapter 16), bidders each submit their entire demand schedule of bids at various quantities.

Example

PRICELINE IMPLEMENTS PERFECT PRICE DISCRIMINATION[6]

Priceline.com has taken this process one step further by inducing potential buyers to post their differential offer prices on a website. Buyers of airline tickets on Priceline.com, for example, don't get to specify their carrier, their departure time, or their number of stops. This "reverse auction" process imposes advance planning time costs, inconvenient trip itineraries, and the uncertainty as to whether any seller will accept the offer. However, for a deep enough discount some customers purchase seats that would otherwise go empty. Other customers see the time, inconvenience, and unreliability as justification for paying the airline's own much higher posted prices. In effect, each customer in the Priceline distribution channel pays a different mark-up and has no opportunity to resell to those with higher willingness to pay. In principle, Priceline's system allows perfect price discrimination.

Because the information required for such pricing is extremely rare, perfect price discrimination almost never occurs. Instead, firms usually attempt to price discriminate among classes of customers using intertemporal and geographic segmentation. Even that degree of differential pricing may, however, lead to adverse customer reactions. As a result, sellers have adopted several techniques of *indirect segmentation*: two-part tariffs, tying, and bundling.

Two-Part Tariff

One effective method of implementing price discrimination is to charge both a lump-sum entry fee and a user fee. Amusement parks, nightclubs, golf and tennis clubs, cellular phone providers, Internet access providers, and rental car companies often employ such pricing. Their revenue per unit sale is a nonlinear function of two parts: a lump-sum monthly or daily fee that provides access to the facility, phone, computer, or rental car independent of use, and a per-hour or per-minute or per-mile fee that varies with usage. Although the magnitude of user fees should be and

---

[6] Based on "Priceline Depends on Ignorance," *Pittsburgh Post-Gazette*, May 24, 2000, p. C-2.

often is reflective of marginal costs, heavy demanders pay more through higher user fees. Companies differ on whether to set uniformly high or low entry fees and whether to charge high or low user fees. AT&T Wireless and Gillette practically give away their cell phones and razors but then charge steep prices for the calls and blades. Golf and tennis clubs, in contrast, charge substantial membership fees and annual dues, but often adopt trivial user fees (e.g., $5 per court hour). Even within the same industry, some variation occurs; the Pebble Beach golf course and the Wimbledon tennis club have $350 greens fees for a round of golf or two sets of tennis.

Example

CALIFORNIA CONSUMERS PREFER TWO-PART TARIFFS FOR ELECTRICITY[7]

In principle, as experience has shown in Britain, Australia, and New Zealand, deregulation of electricity can work well if peak-load customers are asked to pay a price that reflects the marginal cost of the current. It has been estimated that as much as 55 percent of the variation in intraday cost is attributable to extraordinary transmission line fees and old inefficient plants fired up to meet the last 5 percent of peak demand. Running the dishwasher at 6 P.M. peak periods in August 2000 imposed wholesale costs on Pacific Gas and Electric of $220 per megawatt hour, relative to approximately $100 at 10 A.M. or 10 P.M. off-peak periods. April off-peak costs were only $20/mwh. However, U.S. consumers are averse to advanced metering systems and time-of-day pricing. One alternative is to charge uniform prices per kilowatt hour but add on access fees for interruptible (brownout) service far below those that hospital and computer system operators would pay for uninterruptible service. Industrial customers expect that such two-part pricing will lower their overall power costs by as much as 30 percent. The real success or failure of the deregulatory initiative in electricity will hinge on whether residential customers will conserve energy when the marginal cost is high or, alternatively, will pressure their politicians to cap the price of electricity and then over-burden the scarce capacity of underfunded electric companies.

Consider the two-part pricing depicted in Figure 14.2 on page 610 for separate customer segments with relatively elastic and relatively inelastic demand for rental autos. These might be young couples who are renting cars for vacationing (D_1) and manufacturers' trade representatives renting cars for making sales calls (D_2). The challenge is to find a uniform daily rate (the lump sum access fee) and a mileage charge that maximize profit and keep both segments in the market. One alternative would be to price the mileage at its marginal cost $(MC) = OA$ and elicit Q_1 and Q_2 usage while realizing from both customer segments the maximum daily rate (a lump sum access fee) that the price-sensitive D_1 demanders will pay (namely, hatched area AEF). Perhaps, however, a better alternative is available. Suppose the car rental agency raises the price to P^* and reduces the daily access fee to the hatched and shaded area P^*DF in Figure 14.2. Mileage will decline in both segments, and area P^*DEA will be net revenue lost by virtue of the reduced daily access fee in both segments. However, the additional net revenue from mileage charges (P^*DGA in one segment

[7] Based on "How To Do Deregulation Right," *BusinessWeek*, March 26, 2001, p. 112; "PG&E Gropes for a Way Out," *Wall Street Journal*, January 4, 2001, p. A1; and A. Faruqui and K. Eakin, eds., *Pricing in Competitive Electricity Markets*, New York: Kluwer, 2000.

WHAT WENT RIGHT   WHAT WENT WRONG

$19.95 for "Unlimited Access" at America Online[8]

In qualifying for and winning purchase orders, customer service and availability are often as important as low price. Internet on-line provider America Online (AOL) provides computer help by phone and downloadable help files as well as Internet access. Internet access is a limited-capacity service for which assured availability may be expensive. Most on-line providers have infrastructure costs for high-speed modems, routers, servers, and other equipment that run 80 cents to $1.30 an hour per customer. The larger the established customer base, the lower are these direct fixed costs of on-line access per customer. With 7 million subscribers, AOL had a direct fixed cost of only 25 cents per customer per hour for basic access. In contrast, help lines and other on-line customer support impose a variable cost of $25 to $30 per customer per hour. Neophyte users are therefore big money losers, whereas cyberspace veterans generate high profit margins.

To attract this high margin segment who require little customer support, in February 1996 AT&T WorldNet offered the first flat-rate access fee ($19.95 per month) with no user charge per hour. The rest of the industry (MCI Internet, Microsoft Network, CompuServe, AOL) quickly followed suit, and a battle for market share erupted. For $19.95 a month, AOL users became entitled to an unlimited amount of attempted access to the Net.

As customers quickly discovered, however, "unlimited access" did not mean unlimited use. The need to make 20 sign-on attempts before achieving an Internet connection led to frustrated customers and a "D" service rating from *PC World*. With this radical degradation of service quality and few ways to impose switching costs on veteran customers who sought access from other providers, AOL initially lost share and margins.

The solution was new pricing packages that tied the total customer expense to the desired degree of availability and intensity of use. MCI Internet offered $3 for 3 hours per month plus $1.80 for each additional hour. Prodigy offered $9.95 for 10 hours plus $2.50 for each additional hour. CompuServe offered 5 hours for $9.95 plus $2.95 for each additional hour, or $24.95 for 20 hours plus $1.95 for each additional hour. All these services have adopted two-part pricing—that is, a lump-sum access fee plus a user charge to cover variable cost and discourage trivial uses of the scarce capacity.

---

[8] Based on "Shopping for Web Access," *USA Today*, February 3, 1997, p. 8D; "Rivals Target AOL Users," *USA Today*, February 3, 1997, p. 1D; "Why Internet $19.95 Deals May Not Last," *Wall Street Journal*, December 24, 1996, p. B1; "Waiting for the Call," *The Economist*, April 5, 1997, p. 72; and "Net Firms Tinker with Service Pricing," *Investor's Business Daily*, April 4, 1998, p. A1.

and $P*HIA$ in the other segment) will more than offset the lost access fees. Consequently, in addition to charging positive lump-sum access fees, a price discriminating monopolist will adopt two-part tariffs that price usage above its marginal cost. The more similar the demands of target customer segments, the closer the optimal user fee should be to marginal cost. The more dissimilar the segment demands are, the higher the optimal unit price above *MC* should be.

Where capacity is insufficient to absorb peak demand, two-part pricing is an efficient way to recover capacity cost and provide for additional capital equipment investment. Using such mechanisms, CompuServe delivered Internet connection on the customers' first try 97 percent of the time. AOL then decided to offer a Light Usage Plan for $4.95 a month for the first three hours of Internet use plus $2.50 for each additional hour. Without at least a small user fee to discourage trivial use, excess demand would have continued to plague their business.

Figure 14.2   Optimal Two-Part Tariffs for Auto Rentals

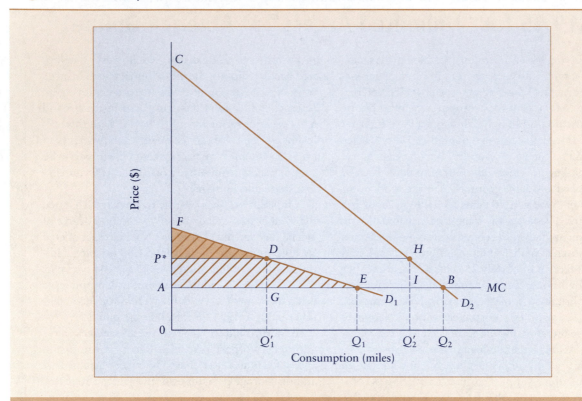

Bundling

Another highly effective pricing mechanism that sellers use to capture consumer surplus is bundling. Have you ever wondered why Time Warner Cable offers Showtime, the channel for popular first-run movies, only in a bundled package that includes the History Channel, which you usually ignore? One insight is that this particular bundle of product offerings occurs because someone else is a history buff who is wondering why the History Channel comes with a cable package that includes largely unwatched movies. That is, if sellers are restricted from quoting perfect price discriminating differential prices to every customer, the operating profit to a seller from bundling negatively correlated demands is always larger than the operating profit from selling equally costly products separately. Let's see why.

Suppose that two sets of customers have the following **reservation prices** for two cable channels, each of which incurs variable licensing fees of $1 for a single showing to a single household. Movie buffs would pay $9 for access to first-run movies and $2 for access to historical documentaries. History buffs would pay $8 for access to the History Channel and $3 for access to Showtime. If the channels are priced uniformly to both customer segments as separate products, Time Warner can realize at most $8 (or $9 – $1) on Showtime and $7 (or $8 – $1) on the History Channel for a total of $15 operating profit.[9] However, note that both types of customers would pay up to $11 for the combined pair of channels rather than do without. If Time Warner made them available only as a bundled package, sales revenue would be $22 minus $4 licensing fees for a total of $18 operating profit. The $18 profit exceeds $15 by quite a lot, and it turns out that this result is entirely general. As long as one

Reservation Price
The maximum price a customer will pay to reserve a product or service unto their own use.

customer is willing to pay more for an item that another customer wants less than some alternative item, the seller who is restricted to charging the two customers the same uniform price will always be better off bundling the two items, assuming all reservation prices exceed variable cost.

Now suppose the variable costs are higher at, say, $3. The History Channel valued at $2 by the movie buff is no longer a profitable sale. Pure bundling includes this unprofitable sale and generates the same $22 revenue but now incurs $12 of total variable cost, yielding a profit of only $10. Forgoing the sale of the History Channel to the movie buff by selling each product separately at a $9 price for Showtime and an $8 price for the History Channel generates $6 (or $9 – $3) on Showtime and $5 (or $8 – $3) on the History Channel, yielding a total of $11 operating profit. Quite intuitively, pure bundling will be less attractive than pricing separately when some of the bundled sales are unprofitable.

It is also easy to see why positively correlated demand across customers works against bundling. Figure 14.3 displays reservation prices along a "budget" line that our customers mentioned above are willing to spend on the two products.[10] The y-intercept is the total willingness-to-pay constraint for the two products—namely, $P_b + P_m = \$11$. With movie channel reservation prices on the vertical axis and History Channel reservation prices on the horizontal axis, each customer's mix of reservation prices lies along the line,

$$P_m = \$11 - 1\,(P_b) \tag{14.1}$$

The −1 in Equation 14.1 signifies the perfect negative correlation between the reservation prices (demand) of our movie buff and those of our history buff. But suppose Time Warner has a third type of customer whose reservation prices are positively correlated with those of the movie buffs—that is, a third type of customer who values Showtime at $8 and the History Channel at $5. These reservation prices are high when the movie buff's reservation price is high and low when the movie buff's reservation price is low. Such positively correlated demand lies above the budget constraint in Figure 14.3 because the total willingness to pay on the left-hand side of Equation 14.1 is no longer $11 but rather is now $13, as shown for Point 3.

With positively correlated demands across two of the three customer types, Time Warner could sell the Showtime-History Channel bundle to all three for $11 and earn $15 (= 3 × ($11 − $6)).[11] However, a better alternative is available. **Mixed bundling** sells the products both separately and as a bundle with the bundled price discounted below the sum of the two separate prices. In our three-customer-type example, Time Warner could sell Showtime for $9 and sell the History Channel for $8, while making the Showtime-History Channel bundle available for the package price of $13. The third type of customer would opt for the bundle, whereas each of the other types of customers would buy one product only. Revenue for this mixed bundling approach totals $30, but only four license fees are required, therefore earning $18 in profit. In general, pure bundling generates less profit than mixed bundling when positively correlated demands are involved.

Mixed Bundling
Selling multiple products both separately and together for less than the sum of the separate prices.

---

[9] In this example, selling both products separately to both customer segments does not pay because of the much lower prices required. Specifically, Showtime priced separately into both segments would have to sell for as little as $3, thereby earning operating profits of $4 (or $6 − $2), and the History Channel would have to sell for as little as $2, earning $2 (or $4 − $2). Thus, the total profit of $6 from selling all products to all customers at a uniform price would substantially diminish the potential profit $15 from selling each product to its target market alone. If the asymmetric demands in the two segments were not so different, this result could reverse, as long as all the reservation prices were greater than variable cost.

[10] This budget line is analogous to the budget line of a household making consumption decisions, except in this case it is the firm who is constrained by the maximum expenditure the customer is willing to make on the two goods.

[11] Here we are again assuming that variable costs are at the higher level, $3 per showing.

Figure 14.3   Reservation Prices for Three Customer Segments

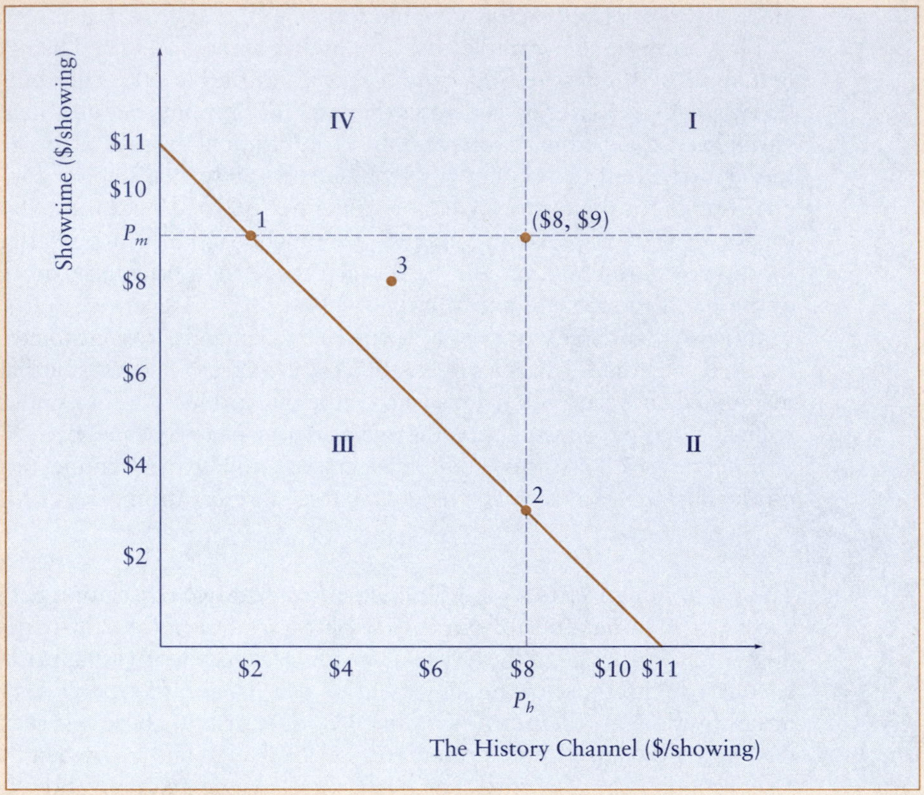

Figure 14.3 can be used to characterize the attractiveness of pure bundling for the seller. If all customers have perfectly negatively correlated demands, their reservation prices lie, as we have seen, along the $11 budget constraint. If customers have positively correlated demands, their reservation prices will lie above or below this reservation budget constraint. With separate product prices of $P_m = \$9$ and $P_h = \$8$, customers with reservation prices in Quadrant I will always buy both products rather than one of the separate products alone (Quadrants II and IV) while those in Quadrant III will never buy either product sold separately. In addition, however, we know that customers with reservation prices above the reservation budget constraint will buy the bundled package and those below will not. Optimally, Customer 3 will therefore purchase the bundle, Customer 1 will purchase Showtime alone, and Customer 2 will purchase the History Channel alone. Only mixed bundling can achieve this result.

Example

McDonald's Introduces Mixed Bundles as "Extra Value Meals"

In the U.S., fast food consumption skyrocketed in the 1980s and 1990s as 70 percent of households became two-worker households, and families began eating out several times a week. Beer and pizza or a soft drink, burger and fries became the standard supper for many high time-cost households. With greater health consciousness, however, not everyone who wanted a burger wanted the fries. In other cases, some consumers wanted the fries but not the burger, and preferred lower fat chicken sandwiches instead. McDonald's Corporation has done its best to respond to these customer trends by introducing "Extra Value Meals" that bundled sandwiches, fries and a medium soft drink and by introducing numerous chicken alternatives.

The 2003 prices for some of McDonald's most popular menu items are listed below:

Menu Item	Separate Price	Bundled Price	Total if Purchased Separately
Large French Fries	$1.39		
Medium Soft Drink	$1.09		
McGrill Chicken Sandwich	$2.69	$4.29	$5.17
Chicken McNuggets	$2.79	$4.29	$5.27
McChicken Sandwich	$1.00	$3.39	$3.48
Big and Tasty Burger	$1.59	$3.49	$4.07
Double Cheeseburger	$1.00	$3.39	$3.48
Big Mac	$2.19	$3.79	$4.67
Quarter Pounder	$2.19	$3.79	$4.67

Examining only the last two columns, which menu items demonstrate that McDonald's competition is "heating up" such that single-item specialty customers are getting almost as much of a per-item discount as the bundled "Extra Value Meal" customers?

We now investigate the optimal level at which price-discriminating prices should be set, returning to the simplest case of differential prices in directly segmented distribution channels.

OPTIMAL DISCRIMINATING PRICE LEVELS

To maximize profits, discriminating monopolists, such as the Blue Ridge Dairy Cooperative, must allocate their capacity shown in Figure 14.4 to produce output in such a way as to make identical the marginal revenue in all their segmented markets. If marginal revenue derived from the grocery store milk market exceeded marginal revenue derived from the school contract market, profits could be increased by transferring output from the school market to the store market. When the price rise in the school market (resulting from the output reduction) and the price decline in the store market (resulting from the output expansion) settle to such a level that MR is equal in both markets, the monopolist is at a profit-maximizing equilibrium allocation of capacity. The total capacity to be allocated among the two or more market segments is determined by setting the combined marginal revenue of all markets equal to marginal cost. This is illustrated in Figure 14.4. The marginal revenue curves for store milk sales (MR_1) and school contract sales (MR_2) are added together horizontally to yield the total marginal revenue curve $MR_1 + MR_2$. Total capacity is set at the point where total marginal revenue equals marginal cost (that is, Point A). Total capacity at this point is Q_T gallons of milk. Because marginal revenue must be equal in each market to achieve profit maximization, one can determine the price

Figure 14.4   Price Discrimination: Blue Ridge Dairy Cooperative

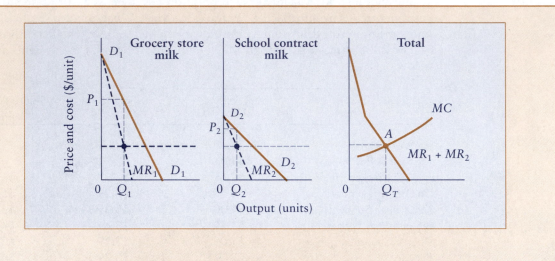

and output combination that will prevail in each market at the profit-maximizing level of marginal revenue. In the store milk market, output will be Q_1 gallons at a price of P_1, because this is the price-output combination that corresponds to the profit-maximizing level of marginal revenue required to cover the marginal cost of the last gallon sold. Similarly, in the school market, output equals Q_2 gallons at a price of P_2 (determined from the demand curve D_2D_2). The sum of the outputs in these two markets equals total output ($Q_1 + Q_2 = Q_T$). Not surprisingly, one finds that the price is higher in the less competitive store milk market, where the price elasticity of demand is less, than in the more competitive school market. As a general rule, one would expect to find an inverse relationship between the price elasticity of demand and price in markets served by discriminating monopolists.

Example

THIRD-DEGREE PRICE DISCRIMINATION TAKES HOLD IN LONG-DISTANCE MARKET: AT&T, MCI WORLDCOM, AND SPRINT[12]

AT&T, MCI WorldCom, and Sprint have competed aggressively for long-distance telephone customers with two-part tariffs. AT&T offered a Friends and Family plan that allowed unlimited wireless calls for $24.95 per month and long-distance land lines at 7 cents per minute plus $5.95 per month. Friends and Family are presumably price-sensitive in usage minutes relative to commercial customers but have substantial value from an access opportunity day or night if needed. MCI WorldCom segregated customers by peak and off-peak usage. Daytime peak hours cost 10 cents per minute plus $4.95 per month, whereas nighttime rate plans cost 5 cents per minute plus $5.95 per month. Sprint's "Nickel Anytime" offer is good for weekend and nighttime callers up to 35 hours per week after an $8.95 monthly fee. By segmenting the target market and preventing arbitrage with designated friends and family or time of day, these companies succeeded in lowering prices to price-sensitive segments while increasing their profitability overall with higher prices to other segments.

[12] Based on "WorldCom Increases Rates," *Wall Street Journal*, September 12, 2000, p. B6, and "AT&T Unveils 7-Cent Plan in Price War," *Wall Street Journal*, August 31, 1999, p. B4.

MATHEMATICS OF PRICE DISCRIMINATION

This section develops the mathematics of price discrimination using some numerical examples.

Price Discrimination and the Price Elasticity of Demand

An inverse relationship must exist between price and price elasticity in the separate markets served by a discriminating monopolist. Recall that marginal revenue must be equal in each market served by the monopolist and must equal total marginal cost for profits to be maximized. If the marginal revenues are not equal, total revenue could be increased (with no impact on total cost) by shifting sales from the low marginal revenue market to the high one. In Chapter 3 the relationship between marginal revenue (MR) and price (P) was shown to be the following (Equation 3.7):

$$MR = P\left(1 + \frac{1}{E_D}\right) \qquad [14.2]$$

where E_D is the price elasticity of demand. If there are two markets such that P_1, P_2, E_1, and E_2 represent the prices and price elasticities in the two markets, we may equate marginal revenue in each market:

$$MR_1 = MR_2 \qquad [14.3]$$

However, it must be the case that

$$MR_1 = P_1\left(1 + \frac{1}{E_1}\right) \quad \text{and} \quad MR_2 = P_2\left(1 + \frac{1}{E_2}\right)$$

Hence,

$$P_1\left(1 + \frac{1}{E_1}\right) = P_2\left(1 + \frac{1}{E_2}\right)$$

$$\frac{P_1}{P_2} = \frac{\left(1 + \dfrac{1}{E_2}\right)}{\left(1 + \dfrac{1}{E_1}\right)} \qquad [14.4]$$

Example

PRICE DISCRIMINATION AND THE PRICE ELASTICITY OF DEMAND: TRANS-AMERICA AIRLINES

Trans-America Airlines has determined that the price elasticity of demand for New York-to-Los Angeles unrestricted coach and Super Saver (stayover Saturday night required) coach services are -1.25 and -2.50, respectively. Determine the relative prices (P_1/P_2) that Trans-America should charge if it is interested in maximizing profits on this route. Substituting $E_1 = -1.25$ and $E_2 = -2.50$ into Equation 14.4 yields

$$\frac{P_1}{P_2} = \frac{\left(1 + \dfrac{1}{-2.50}\right)}{\left(1 + \dfrac{1}{-1.25}\right)}$$

$$= 3.0$$

or

$$P_1 = 3.0\, P_2$$

Thus the price of an unrestricted coach seat (P_1) should be 3.0 times the price of a Super Saver coach seat (P_2). We see that when the elasticity in Market 1 (unrestricted coach) is less (in absolute value) than that in Market 2 (Super Saver coach), the price in Market 1 will exceed the price in Market 2.

Price Discrimination and Profitability of the Firm

The advantages to a monopolist of engaging in price discrimination can be illustrated with the following example. Two cases are considered—Case I, where the firm charges different prices for the same product in the two different markets, and Case II, where the firm charges the same price in the two different markets (i.e., does not engage in price discrimination).

Example

PRICE DISCRIMINATION AND PROFITABILITY: TAIWAN INSTRUMENT COMPANY

Taiwan Instrument Company (TIC) makes computer memory chips in Formosa, which it ships to computer manufacturers in Japan (Market 1) and the United States (Market 2). Demand for the chips in the two markets is given by the following functions:

$$\text{Japan: } P_1 = 12 - Q_1 \qquad [14.5]$$
$$\text{United States: } P_2 = 8 - Q_2 \qquad [14.6]$$

where Q_1 and Q_2 are the respective quantities sold (in *millions* of units) and P_1 and P_2 are the respective prices (in dollars per unit) in the two markets. TIC's total cost function (in millions of dollars) for these memory chips is

$$C = 5 + 2\,(Q_1 + Q_2) \qquad [14.7]$$

Case I: Price Discrimination   TIC's total combined profit in the two markets equals

$$
\begin{aligned}
\pi &= P_1 Q_1 + P_2 Q_2 - C \qquad [14.8]\\
&= (12 - Q_1)Q_1 + (8 - Q_2)Q_2 - [5 + 2(Q_1 + Q_2)]\\
&= 12Q_1 - Q_1^2 + 8Q_2 - Q_2^2 - 5 - 2Q_1 - 2Q_2\\
&= 10Q_1 - Q_1^2 + 6Q_2 - Q_2^2 - 5 \qquad [14.9]
\end{aligned}
$$

To maximize π with respect to Q_1 and Q_2, find the partial derivatives of Equation 14.9 with respect to Q_1 and Q_2, set them equal to zero, and solve for Q_1^* and Q_2^*:

$$\frac{\partial \pi}{\partial Q_1} = 10 - 2Q_1 = 0$$

$$Q_1^* = 5 \text{ (million) units}$$

$$\frac{\partial \pi}{\partial Q_2} = 6 - 2Q_2 = 0$$

$$Q_2^* = 3 \text{ (million) units}$$

Figure 14.5   Demand and Cost Functions for Memory Chips: Taiwan Instrument Company

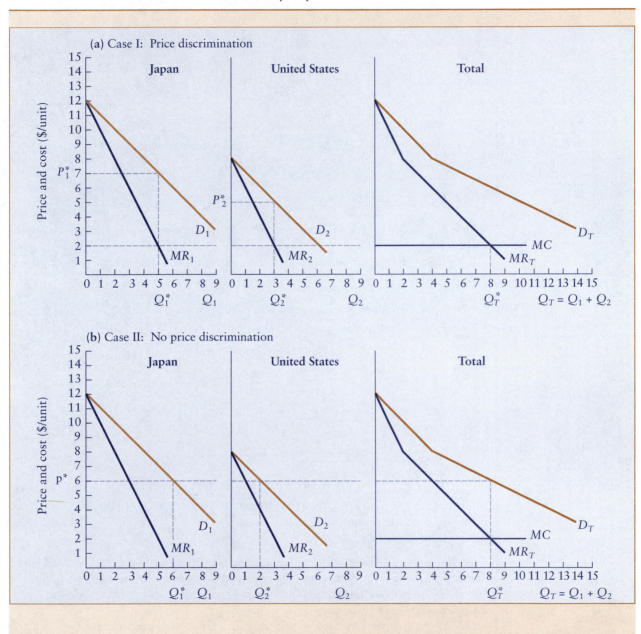

Substituting Q_1^* and Q_2^* into the appropriate demand and profit equations yields

$$P_1^* = \$7 \text{ per unit}$$
$$P_2^* = \$5 \text{ per unit}$$
$$\pi^* = \$29 \text{ (million)}$$

The optimal solution is illustrated graphically in Figure 14.5 (a).

Maximizing π with respect to Q_1 and Q_2 is equivalent to setting $MR_1 = MR_2$. The equivalence of MR_1 and MR_2 may be proved by taking the partial derivatives of the TR function with respect to Q_1 and Q_2:

$$\begin{aligned} TR &= P_1 \cdot Q_1 + P_2 \cdot Q_2 \\ &= (12 - Q_1)\, Q_1 + (8 - Q_2)\, Q_2 \\ &= 12Q_1 - Q_1^2 + 8Q_2 - Q_2^2 \end{aligned} \qquad [14.10]$$

and substituting the solution values, $Q_1^* = 5$ and $Q_2^* = 3$:

$$MR_1 = \frac{\partial TR}{\partial Q_1} = 12 - 2Q_1$$

$$MR_1^* = 12 - 2(5) = \$2 \text{ per unit}$$

$$MR_2 = \frac{\partial TR}{\partial Q_2} = 8 - 2Q_2$$

$$MR_2^* = 8 - 2(3) = \$2 \text{ per unit}$$

which equals the total marginal cost, that is, the derivative of Equation 14.7 with respect to $(Q_1 + Q_2)$.

The respective elasticities in the Japanese and U.S. markets at the optimal solution are

$$\begin{aligned} E_1 &= \frac{dQ_1}{dP_1} \cdot \frac{P_1}{Q_1} \\ &= -1\left(\frac{7}{5}\right) = -1.40 \end{aligned}$$

and

$$\begin{aligned} E_2 &= \frac{dQ_2}{dP_2} \cdot \frac{P_2}{Q_2} \\ &= -1\left(\frac{5}{3}\right) = -1.67 \end{aligned}$$

Hence we see that, as in the Trans-America Airlines example, when the elasticity of demand is less in Japan (Market 1) than in the United States (Market 2), the price in Japan is greater than in the United States.

Case II: No Price Discrimination   Suppose that protectionist trade laws in the United States prohibit foreign computer chip manufacturers from selling these products for less than the prices charged in Japan. In other words, assume that TIC is not permitted to engage in price discrimination.

To determine the profits TIC will earn if it does not discriminate between the two markets, solve the two demand equations for Q_1 and Q_2 and add them to get a total demand function:

$$\begin{aligned} Q_1 &= 12 - P_1 \\ Q_2 &= 8 - P_2 \\ Q_T &= Q_1 + Q_2 \\ &= 12 - P_1 + 8 - P_2 \end{aligned}$$

Because price discrimination is no longer possible, P_1 must equal P_2, and

$$Q_T = 20 - 2P$$

or

$$P = 10 - \frac{Q_T}{2}$$

Total profit is now

$$\pi = PQ_T - C$$

$$= 10Q_T - \frac{Q_T^2}{2} - 5 - 2Q_T$$

$$= 8Q_T - \frac{Q_T^2}{2} - 5 \qquad [14.11]$$

To find the profit-maximizing level of Q_T, differentiate Equation 14.11 with respect to Q_T, set it equal to zero, and solve for Q_T^*:

$$\frac{d\pi}{dQ_T} = 8 - Q_T = 0$$

$$Q_T^* = 8 \text{ (million) units}$$

Substituting Q_T^* into the appropriate equations yields

$$P^* = 10 - \frac{Q_T}{2} = \$6 \text{ per unit}$$

$$\pi^* = 8Q_T - \frac{Q_T^2}{2} - 5 = \$27 \text{ (million)}$$

$$Q_1^* = 12 - 6 = 6 \text{ (million) units}$$
$$Q_2^* = 8 - 6 = 2 \text{ (million) units}$$
$$MR_1^* = 12 - 2(6) = \$0 \text{ per unit}$$
$$MR_2^* = 8 - 2(2) = \$4 \text{ per unit}$$

The optimal solution is illustrated graphically in Figure 14.5 (b).

The two cases are summarized in Table 14.1. Note that TIC's profits are higher when it engages in price discrimination ($29 million) than when it does not engage in price discrimination ($27 million).

Table 14.1   Taiwan Instrument Company: Effects of Price Discrimination

	Case I Price Discrimination		Case II No Price Discrimination	
Market	1 (Japan)	2 (U.S.)	1 (Japan)	2 (U.S.)
Price P* ($/unit)	7	5	6	6
Quantity Q* (million units)	5	3	6	2
Marginal Revenue MR* ($/unit)	2	2	0	4
Profit π* ($ million)		29		27

The example developed above shows that by charging different prices to different groups of customers, monopolists may always increase their profits above the level achieved if no market segmentation is attempted, as long as the groups of customers have differing demand elasticities.

PRICING OF MULTIPLE PRODUCTS

Most firms produce or sell more than one product; therefore, we must reexamine the basic model of a one-product firm, which maximizes profits by setting the marginal cost of production for the item equal to the marginal revenue derived from its sale alone. This model breaks down if firms have the opportunity to produce completely new products, new models of existing products, or new and different styles and sizes, by reallocating their productive capacity. As long as the new product (or modification of an existing product) may be sold at a price that exceeds the true marginal cost of producing and selling it, the profitability of the firm will be enhanced by its adoption.

Of course, the decision to add new or different products or drop some existing lines may have an impact on the sales of a firm's remaining outputs. Most new products may well compete with existing ones, lowering the net marginal revenue of the new product. Let us examine the nature of these demand interdependencies in more detail.

Products with Interdependent Demands

Consider the case of a firm that produces only two products (A and B). Total revenue (sales) for the firm can be represented as

$$TR = TR_A + TR_B \tag{14.12}$$

where TR_A and TR_B are the respective revenues for the two products. Marginal revenue for each of the products is given by

$$MR_A = \frac{\partial TR}{\partial Q_A} = \frac{\partial TR_A}{\partial Q_A} + \frac{\partial TR_B}{\partial Q_A} \tag{14.13}$$

The MR_A formula (Equation 14.13) shows that the marginal revenue associated with a change in the quantity sold of Product A is composed of two parts. The first term, $\partial TR_A/\partial Q_A$, measures the change in total revenue for Product A associated with a marginal increase (or decrease) in the quantity sold of Product A. The second term, $\partial TR_B/\partial Q_A$, represents the demand interdependency between the two products —that is, the change in total revenue for Product B associated with a marginal increase (or decrease) in the quantity sold of Product A.

The interdependency second term, $\partial TR_B/\partial Q_A$ can be positive, negative, or zero. If the two products under consideration are *complements*, then this term will be *positive*; that is, an increase in the quantity sold of one product will result in an *increase* in total revenue for the other product—e.g., razors and blades. If the products are *substitutes*, then this second term will be *negative*, meaning that an increase in the quantity sold of one product will result in a *decrease* in total revenue for the other product. This phenomenon is often referred to as cannibalization— e.g., Sensor razor sales may cannibalize Trac II razor sales. Finally, if there are no demand interdependencies between the two products, then the second term will be equal to zero.

Example

INTERDEPENDENT DEMANDS: THE GILLETTE COMPANY

Table 14.2 lists many of the products sold by the Gillette Company. Although most of Gillette's products have independent demands, several demand interdependencies are likely to exist. For example, the interdependency terms between Waterman pens and Braun electric shavers would likely be equal to zero, indicating that changes in demand for one product would have no effect on the demand for the other. However, one would expect the interdependency terms between the Sensor and Trac II razors to be negative, because these products are substitutes for one another. Indeed, this is the case for these products. When Gillette introduced the Sensor in the United States in 1990, sales (total revenues) of the Trac II razor declined below the level of the previous year. Conversely, one would expect the interdependency terms between Foamy shaving cream and Gillette razors (and/or razor blades) to be positive, because these products are complements to one another.

As this example illustrates, managers must be aware of and take into account demand interdependencies when making price and output decisions. Failure to recognize these interdependencies may lead to decisions that do not maximize shareholder wealth.

Table 14.2   Gillette Company Products

Razors and Blades
Sensor
Atra
Trac II
Good News
Daisy Plus

Toiletries and Cosmetics
Deodorants/Antiperspirants
   Right Guard
   Dry Idea
Shaving Cream
   Foamy
Hair Care
   White Rain
Skin Care
   Jafra

Stationary Products
Writing Instruments
   Waterman
   Paper Mate
   Flair
Correction Fluid
   Liquid Paper

Braun Personal Care Appliance Products
Electric shavers
Electric hair epilators
Hair dryers
Electric curling wands
Electric toothbrushes
Oral irrigators

Braun Household Appliances
Steam irons
Travel/alarm clocks
Toasters
Coffee makers
Food processors
Hand blenders
Juicers

Oral-B Preventive Dentistry Products
Toothbrushes
Dental floss
Interdental brushes
Professional dental supplies

Interdependent Products with Separate Production

In this section we develop a model that can be used in allocating resources when a firm produces multiple products that are produced separately. This analysis assumes that the productive resources of the firm can be transformed rather easily from one product to another, facilitating adaption to changing market and product demands. The market conditions that the firm faces for each of its products may range from pure competition to a near monopoly. When the firm has excess personnel, organizational resources, and capacity, it may increase output with only a small additional cost. Instead of reducing prices and increasing output for an existing product, it may decide to penetrate new product markets where price is greater than marginal cost. New product markets are assumed to be invaded in order of their profitability.

Starting from a point where the firm is producing one product, marginal revenue equals marginal cost, and 20 to 30 percent of capacity is being used, we may now examine the decision to add additional products. Figure 14.6 illustrates a situation of a firm with five products, although that number might well be greater or less. D_1 represents the demand for Product 1, D_2 for Product 2, and so on. The number of units of Product 1 that are sold equals Q_1, of Product 2, $Q_2 - Q_1$, and so on. Profits are maximized when the firm produces and sells quantities of the five products such that marginal revenue is equal in all markets and equal to marginal cost. The line EMR represents *equal marginal revenue*, the firm's marginal revenue—i.e., the opportunity in other product lines. Because it is assumed that new product markets were entered in order of their profitability, the prices charged for the five products are

Figure 14.6   Multiple-Product Pricing

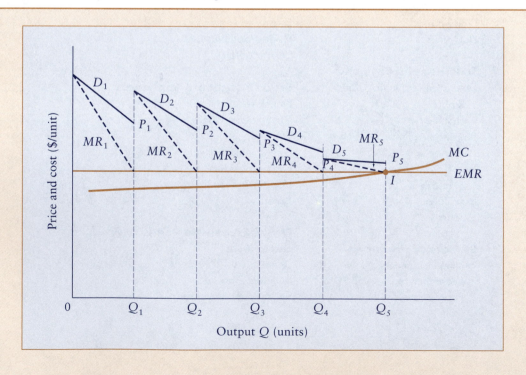

arranged in declining order, from P_1 to P_5, and the elasticity of demand increases from D_1 to D_5. The *EMR* line is determined by the intersection of the firm's marginal cost curve *MC* and the marginal revenue curve for the last product market that may be profitably served. Theoretically, this would be the one with the most elastic demand, D_5.

The equilibrium condition where there is virtually an equivalence between *P*, *MR*, and *MC* in the marginal market illustrates the well-known fact that nearly all firms produce some products that generate little or no profit and are on the verge of being dropped or replaced. In some cases, such as the railway and utility industries, zero-profit products may be produced to keep the organization intact.

Example

MULTIPLE-PRODUCT PRICING: SUPERMARKET PRICING

Supermarkets provide an illustration of this multiple-product pricing model. One of the primary productive resources of a supermarket is shelf space, which can be allocated among a wide variety of product categories—such as meat, dairy products, canned goods, frozen foods, and produce. Canned goods have only a 1- to 2-percent profit margin. Generally the markups and profit margins on staple items, such as bread, milk, and soap, are lower than on nonstaple items, such as imported foods and specialty items. In an effort to increase their overall profitability, many supermarkets have added higher profit-margin categories, such as delicatessens, in-store bakeries, fresh fish, and floral departments, to the mix of products they sell.[13] This can be accomplished either by reallocating existing shelf space through the reduction of the amount of shelf space assigned to lower profit-margin items or by expanding the overall size of the store. Expanding the size of the store may increase marginal costs whereas reallocating shelf space will unambiguously raise profitability if the newly added delicatessen demand is independent of preexisting fresh meat and cheese demand. If not, a careful analysis of the tradeoffs is warranted. Marginal revenue of the preexisting products lost should be subtracted from the projected marginal revenue of the new product.

PRICING IN PRACTICE

To this point, the pricing chapter has been concerned with firms that seek to maximize (short-run) profits. However, pricing is one of the areas where a longer-run life cycle view of the firm's decision making proves very helpful.

Product Life Cycle Framework[14]

In the early stages of **life cycle pricing**, the marketing, operations, and financial managers decide what the customer will value, how the firm can manage the supply chain to consistently deliver those characteristics, and how much it will cost, including the financing costs. If the value-based prices can cover this long-run full cost, the product becomes a prototype. Each proposed product or service then proceeds to marketing research, where the demand at various price points in several distribution channels usually is explored. Marketing research will identify a *target price*

http://
Read about the development of product life cycle theory by Conrad Jones at the following Internet site maintained by Booz Allen Hamilton:
http://www.bah.com/wcb/productlife.html

Life Cycle Pricing
Pricing that varies throughout the product life cycle.

---

[13] Allocation of shelf space within each product category also involves a consideration of profit margins when making decisions about stocking private-label versus national-brand canned goods, prepackaged versus fresh-cut meat, and so on.

[14] On the conceptual framework of value-based pricing over a product's life cycle, see T. Nagle, *The Strategy and Tactics of Pricing*, 2nd ed. (Englewood Cliffs, NJ: Prentice-Hall, 1995), Chapter 7.

that the cross-functional product manager or the general managers will know is required on average over the product life cycle in order for the new product to provide sufficient revenue to cover fully allocated cost.

Once a product or service rollout takes place (usually at target price levels), the marketing plan often authorizes promotional discounts. In this stage of the life cycle, the firm is interested in penetrating the market. To do so requires coupons, free samples, name recognition advertising, and slot-in allowances on retail shelves. *Penetration pricing* therefore characterizes an early stage of the product life cycle at which net prices to the manufacturer fall below the firm's target price, as shown in Figure 14.7.

In the mature stage of the product or service life cycle, the product managers focus on adding value in both product refinements and order management processes. These initiatives might include warranty service, brand-name advertising, product updates, or increased flexibility in accepting change orders from regular customers. Each decision at this mature stage is motivated by a desire to realize the highest *value-based pricing* allowed by the competitive conditions and potential entry threats. Although at times this view of pricing as a component of the product life cycle investment decision can be overwhelmed by short-term tactical firefighting, the product life cycle remains a planning framework to which the pricing manager often returns.

At a late mature stage of the product or service life cycle, product managers may decide to limit price, reducing it well below the value-based pricing level in order to deter entry. *Limit pricing* appears to be inconsistent with profit maximization but in fact is motivated by a long-term profitability objective.

Figure 14.7   Life Cycle of Price

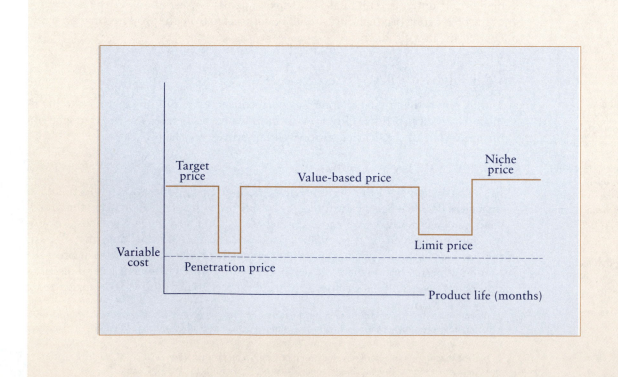

Example

LOSS OF PATENT PROTECTION LIMITS PRICE OF PROZAC: ELI LILLY

When brand-name pharmaceuticals reach the end of their twenty-year patent protection, sales may plummet unless prices are radically reduced. Some formerly patented drugs have lost as much as 80 percent of their sales in the *first year* after generic substitutes have been introduced. The ulcer relief medicine Zantac, Glaxo Wellcome's biggest seller, plummeted 51 percent in the first half year after loss of patent protection in July 1996. By year end, ten rival products were on the shelves. Zovinax, an antiherpes medication, lost 39 percent in the first six months after generics costing only 20 percent of Zovinax's price appeared in the marketplace. And sales of Bristol-Myers Squibb's Capoten, at 57 cents per pill, declined 83 percent the year that a 3-cents-per-pill substitute generic was introduced.

In light of these disastrous experiences throughout the pharmaceutical industry, Eli Lilly limited the price of the depression treatment Prozac to variable plus direct fixed costs in order to arrest or at least slow the onslaught of imitators into its antidepressants market.

Since competitors are constantly devising lower cost ways of imitating leading products, limit pricing often has only temporary success. If the entry threat materializes into a real live new entrant, many incumbent firms then decide to accommodate by raising prices in a particular high-price, high-margin market niche. This pricing practice is often referred to as *niche pricing*. Concluding that declining market share from entry into the mass market is inevitable, the incumbent moves upmarket and sells its experience and expertise at high prices in the top-end segments of the market, much as it did at the start of the product life cycle.

Example

NICHE PRICING OF NETPCS: IBM[15]

Traditional personal computers with ever larger hard drives and faster chips have become a commodity business dominated by component assemblers like Gateway and Dell. Recent product introductions by Dell, Compaq, and Hewlett-Packard suggest that the days of the $2,000 personal computer on every company desktop are numbered. Corporate America may be returning to a concept of networked computer terminals and timesharing pioneered by Hewlett-Packard and Dartmouth College in the late 1960s. These diskless machines are basically display terminals linked to a central server that sends them programs and data which then load and run locally. At $500–$750, these networked computers are much less costly to acquire and update than true PCs. Nevertheless, a niche market remains for desktop machines that include a hard disk and can still have some programs installed and run locally. IBM and other manufacturers intend to serve this niche market with NetPCs costing about $1,000. In addition to offering these network products and other high-priced system solutions like Internet security systems, IBM has announced its intent to exit low-end desktop PC manufacturing.

Full-Cost Pricing Techniques

Full-cost pricing requires that estimates be made of the variable costs of production and marketing. A charge to cover overhead, plus a percentage markup or margin, is then added to variable costs to arrive at a final price. Overhead or indirect costs

---

[15] Based on "NetPCs Having a Hard Time Booting Up," *BusinessWeek*, September 22, 1997, p. 102.

Full-Cost (or Cost-Plus) Pricing
A method of determining prices in which a charge to cover overhead, plus a percentage markup or margin, is added to variable production and marketing costs to arrive at a selling price.

may be allocated among a firm's several products in a number of ways. One typical method is to estimate total indirect fixed costs assuming the firm operates at a standard level of output, such as 70 to 80 percent of capacity. These standard overhead costs are then allocated among the various products on some basis such as unit sales as a percentage of total volume. For example, Wang Laboratories' average variable cost of producing and selling an early word processor was $500. The company added a charge of $600 to cover indirect or overhead charges. To this full average cost of $1,100, a markup of 20 percent was added, yielding a final price of $1,320. As IBM PCs took unit sales away from the Wang word processor, indirect charges rose. Rather than $600, $800, and then $1,000 were allocated to the word processor. Of course, steeper prices meant faster and faster declines in sales volume, implying still higher indirect charges.

Example

FULL-COST PRICING LOSES A BIG CONTRACT AT J.P. MORGAN: BRITISH TELEPHONE

This vicious circle of full-costing can be disastrous for a company facing stiff competition. British Telephone once found that its bid to provide secure long-distance microwave business communication for the investment bank J.P. Morgan ended up $4 million higher than a rival's bid of $9 million. When BT executives did a follow-up study to see why they had been so undercut by Sprint, they discovered that the vice president of the BT subsidiary in the United States had attempted to recover the entire annual overhead for the subsidiary headquarters from this one account. Needless to say, BT lost J.P. Morgan's business with a full-cost bid of $13 million when Sprint had offered to do essentially the same thing for $9 million. Full-cost pricing always runs the risk of such undercutting by rivals.

It is immediately apparent that full-cost pricing violates the marginal pricing rules of traditional theory, because fixed costs enter explicitly into the price determination formula. It has been argued, however, that when average (unit) costs remain nearly constant over the relevant output range, and when historical costs are adjusted to reflect costs actually incurred at the time prices are set, the use of cost-plus pricing may lead to nearly optimal decisions. These conditions are frequently encountered in the retail trades.

In addition, congestion-based pricing, which applies allocated costs for new capacity to wireless telephone customers who unexpectedly demand peak-period service, is another example of appropriate full-cost pricing techniques. One way to implement this pricing policy is with a target return on investment.

Under **target return-on-investment pricing**, or simply target pricing, the firm selects an acceptable profit rate on investment. This is usually defined as earnings before interest and depreciation divided by total gross operating assets. This return is then prorated over the number of units expected to be produced over the planning horizon. Target pricing rules may be expressed in equation form as

Target (or Target Return-on-Investment) Pricing
A method of pricing in which a target profit, defined as the desired profit rate on investment times total gross operating assets, is allocated to each unit of output to arrive at a selling price.

$$P = VC_l + VC_m + VC_{mk} + \frac{F}{Q} + \frac{\pi K}{Q} \qquad [14.14]$$

where P = price per unit
VC_l = unit labor cost
VC_m = unit material cost

VC_{mk} = unit marketing cost

F = total fixed or indirect costs

Q = number of units to be produced during the planning horizon

K = total gross operating assets

π = desired profit rate on investment

Full-Cost Pricing versus Incremental Contribution Analysis

Advocates of full-cost and target pricing argue that it is important to allocate all fixed costs among the various products produced by the firm and that each product should be forced to bear its fair share of the fixed-cost burden. In contrast, advocates of incremental pricing say that each product should instead be viewed in the light of its incremental contributions to covering fixed costs. The contribution analysis provides a sounder basis for considering whether the manufacture and sale of a product should be expanded, maintained, or discontinued in favor of some alternative that may make a greater contribution to covering company overhead and making a profit.

Example

FULL-COST PRICING VERSUS INCREMENTAL ANALYSIS: PHONEMATE COMPANY

If PhoneMate's model 7200 telephone answering machine accounts for 40 percent of sales but only 10 percent of the contribution to fixed costs and profits, the firm should seek ways to increase its contribution or replace it with a more profitable alternative. In this example, the full-cost pricing criteria might indicate that the product should be quickly discontinued because it is not covering its volume-weighted share of fixed costs. However, any contribution to fixed costs is more consistent with profit maximization in the short run than dropping the product and merely shifting the burden of covering fixed costs to the remaining products of the firm. A longer-run analysis *might* indicate that dropping the 7200 model will result in actual fixed-cost savings that are greater than the maximum fixed-cost contribution that the 7200 model may be expected to generate.

Every firm should have an effective control system in which a general manager continually monitors the overall contribution of the firm's complete product line. This person can then ensure that value-based prices are set sufficiently high in relation to both the variable cost of each product and the total fixed costs of the firm. Remember that target pricing must be met only on certain portions of the product's entire life cycle (see Figure 14.7).

The concept of **incremental analysis** is simple, but its application requires care. For instance, the decision to drop an item from the firm's product line requires that the loss in revenue from this action should be evaluated in the light of the total *actual* cost savings that may occur. The following questions must be addressed:

Incremental Analysis
The real-world counterpart to marginal analysis. Incremental analysis requires that an estimate be made of the changes in total cost and revenue that will result from a price change or from a decision to add or delete a product, accept or reject a new order, or undertake a new investment.

1. How much, if any, will sales of other items in the firm's product line increase because this item is dropped?
2. To what extent will some overhead or fixed costs be reduced?
3. Are there more profitable alternative uses for the firm's productive capacity?
4. What is the long-run sales and profit outlook for this item versus the alternatives being considered?

Example

INCREMENTALISM AT CONTINENTAL AIRLINES

At one point Continental was filling only about 50 percent of its available seats, or about 15 percent less than the industry average. Eliminating only 5 percent of its flights would have resulted in a substantial increase in this load factor, but would have reduced profits as well. The airline industry is characterized by extremely high fixed costs, which are incurred whether a plane flies or not. There are depreciation costs, interest charges, and the cost of maintaining ground crews, not to mention headquarters staff overhead. Consequently, Continental has found it profitable to operate a flight as long as it covers variable or out-of-pocket costs plus a small contribution to fixed costs.

The analysis of whether to operate a flight proceeds as follows: First, management examines the majority of scheduled flights to be certain that depreciation, overhead, and insurance expenses are met for this basic schedule. Then the possibility of scheduling additional flights is considered, based on their impact on corporate net profit. If revenues on a flight exceed *actual variable costs* plus direct fixed costs, the flight should be added. These relevant costs are determined by soliciting inputs from every operating department that specify exactly what extra expenses are incurred as a result of the additional flight's operation. For instance, if a ground crew that can service the additional flight is already on duty, none of the costs of this service are included in actual operating costs. If, on the other hand, overtime must be paid to service this flight, then that direct fixed cost varies with the decision to operate this flight and should be included among its costs.

Another example of such incremental analysis is the case of a late-night Continental flight from Colorado Springs to Denver and a very early morning return flight. Even though the flights often go without a passenger and very little freight, the cost of operating them is less than an overnight hanger rental in Colorado Springs. Hence the flights are maintained.

In performing this type of incremental analysis, two important points must be stressed. First, someone in management must have coordinating authority to ensure that overall objectives are met before facing decisions based solely on incremental analysis. In the case of Continental, the vice president of flight planning assumed this task. Second, every reasonable attempt must be made to identify *actual* incremental costs and revenues that are associated with a particular decision. Once this has been accomplished, incremental analysis becomes a useful and powerful tool in considering a wide range of decision problems facing the firm.

OTHER PRICING STRATEGIES

In addition to incremental and full-cost pricing strategies, several other pricing methods are used under particular circumstances addressed below. *Skimming* is often used in pricing new products. Also, some goods are deliberately priced very high to increase their prestige demand, especially in niche markets (see Figure 14.7). Finally, web-based pricing of goods and services sold over the Internet is considered.

Skimming

When a new product is introduced by a firm, pricing for that product is a difficult and critical decision, especially if the product is a durable good—one that has a relatively long useful life. The difficulty of pricing the new product arises from the fact that demand may not be known with confidence. If the price is initially set too low, some potential customers will be able to buy the product at a price below what they are willing to pay. These lost profits will be gone forever. This problem is accentuated when the firm initially has limited production capacity for the new product. In contrast, if the firm sets a high price and maintains this price over a long time period, new competition will be encouraged.

Skimming
A new-product pricing strategy that results in a high initial product price. This price is reduced over time as demand at the higher price is satisfied.

Under these circumstances, many firms have adopted a strategy of **skimming,** or pricing down along the demand curve. The initial price is set at a high level, even though the firm fully intends to make later price reductions. When the product is first introduced, there will be a group of fashion-conscious or technology-conscious early adopters who are willing to pay the high price established by the firm. Once this source of demand has been exhausted, the price is reduced and a new group of customers is attracted. This strategy is readily apparent in mainframe computers and explains the prevalence of capital leasing in that industry. As we discussed in Chapter 13, manufacturers who engage in a predictable pattern of price skimming need credibility mechanisms to assure early full-price customers that later discounting will be limited.

Example

APPLE iMAC COMPUTER

Since its initial introduction, several price reductions have been made on the iMac personal computer. This pricing strategy can be illustrated using Figure 14.8. Panel (a) shows the estimated demand curve DD and the marginal revenue curve MR for the iMac computer as well as the marginal cost curve MC. As a monopolist for the iMac, Apple would set price P_1 and produce output Q_1.

Suppose, however, that Apple chooses to follow the skimming strategy for its personal computer. It could initially set a price higher than P_1, such as P'. At that price, only Q' units would be demanded and sold. By setting the initial price at P', all consumers who are willing to pay that price or more will buy the product. Once

Figure 14.8   Example of Demand Skimming: iMac Personal Computer

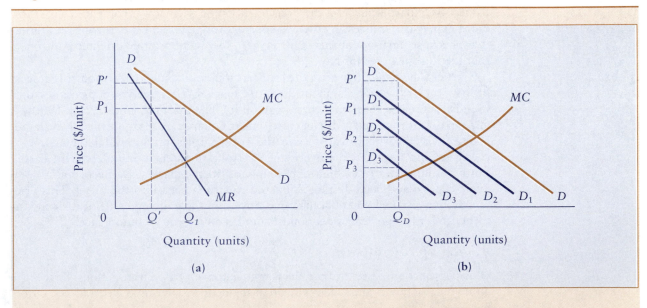

(a)

(b)

this has occurred, Apple can then lower the price to capture the demand from the next segment of customers.

Panel (b) shows new demand curves, such as D_1D_1. The new demand curve is less than the initial demand curve DD—it is shifted to the left—by an amount equal to the Q' units that have already been purchased at price P'. A new lower price is now established, such as P_1, and Q_D units are sold at this price. The new price P_1 may be set in such a manner that it approximately matches the firm's production capacity. When demand has been exhausted at this price, the price is lowered again, to a level such as P_2. The new demand curve D_2D_2 is lower and to the left of D_1D_1 by an amount equal to the Q_D units that were sold at the previous price. (Although Panel (b) shows quantity demanded to be the same amount for each price level, this is not necessary. The figure is merely drawn that way for ease of presentation.)

This strategy can be continued many times to capitalize on the unique product characteristics and availability until competition forces the firm to a "permanently" more competitive price level. The rate at which reductions are made may depend on production capacity, the speed of competitive product introductions, and the trade-off between receiving profits now and deferring them into the future by use of the skimming strategy. In the case of Apple and the original IBM machines, price reductions were strongly resisted until true IBM "clone" PCs became available from competitor firms such as Compaq, Packard-Bell, and Dell.

Prestige Pricing

Prestige Pricing
The practice of charging a high price for a product to enhance its perceived value.

Some products are priced to increase their perceived value to potential consumers. **Prestige pricing** is the practice of charging a high price so as to limit potential buyers and create the impression that the product is of higher quality than similar, mass market products. For example, in the automotive market the sporty European sedans, such as the Mercedes, Audi, and BMW, are priced in the $35,000 to $75,000 range. These cars have been highly successful in attracting a loyal, prestige-oriented clientele. At the same time, a car such as the Honda Accord has received wide acclaim from such impartial panels as the Consumers Union when it was compared with these more expensive vehicles. Its price is considerably less than the European alternatives, because it has not attracted the loyal following of prestige-oriented consumers that the European sedans have.

Cartier's in conjunction with the De Beers diamond cartel, which controls at least 80 percent of the world's uncut diamond market, effectively sets prices for diamonds by greatly restricting their availability. For example, in the early 1980s, it appeared that the South African cartel might collapse. A sharp decline in demand, coupled with the withdrawal of Zaire (the world's largest producer of diamonds) from the cartel and huge new discoveries in Australia threatened to undercut the cartel. But by holding nearly $1 billion in diamonds off the market, De Beers was able to avoid a price decline and bring Zaire and Australia back into the cartel. This pricing strategy assured potential diamond buyers of the ongoing value of their investment, and it has prevented diamonds from becoming too commonplace.

Pricing on the Internet[16]

eBusiness encounters several problems unique to web-based transactions. First is the anonymity of buyers and sellers who often are identified by only a web address. Offers

[16]An excellent survey of pricing strategy for Internet products is provided in John Figueiredo, "Finding Sustainable Profitability in Electronic Commerce," *Sloan Management Review,* Summer 2000, pp. 41–52. See also "The Click Here Economy," *Business Week,* June 22, 1998, pp. 122–126.

Table 14.3   Pricing Strategy for Various Internet Products

Commodity Products	Quasi-Commodity Products	Look-and-Feel Search Goods	Experience Goods Variable Quality
Crude oil Newsprint Sheet metal Paper clips	Books CDs Videos	Suits Homes New autos Toys	PCs Produce Tires Lumber
Low-cost, low-price strategy	Differentiate with reliable delivery and extra services	Employ differential pricing based on brands and time of adoption in fashion cycle	Customize and build to order with low- and high-price tiers

to buy (and sell) may be reneged; receivables may never arrive, and items delivered may not be what buyers thought they bought. The incidence of all these events is much greater in the virtual sales environment. As a result, offers are higher, and bids are lower. From another perspective, the bid-ask spread in an Internet transaction rises to cover the cost of fraud insurance.

A second problem that the Internet accentuates is the inability to confirm variable product quality with hands-on examination. Internet pricing of commodity products like crude oil, sheet metal, and newsprint paper on the left-hand side of Table 14.3 often pursues a low-cost strategy. The availability of quick resale at predictable commodity prices reassures buyers and sellers, and here Internet pricing at very tight bid-ask spreads proves quite efficient. However, as one moves to the right in Table 14.3, product quality becomes harder and harder to detect at the point of sale. Firms like Amazon and CDNow seek to substitute brand equity for the inability of customers to examine the product. America Online, Amazon, and Priceline have spent tens of millions of dollars establishing their brand equity.

In toys, suits, homes, and new autos, consumers search for that look-and-feel for which they're willing to pay. Brands again play an important role in certifying quality, but in this case it is product branding (Game Boy, Hart Schaffner Marx, Harris Tweed) that matters, not website brands. Customers rely on the hostage associated with the sunk cost investment in the product brand names to establish credibility in a relationship with the original equipment manufacturer, not the website reseller. Finally, with highly variable quality in tires, PCs, produce, and lumber, only strong warranties, escrow accounts, and replacement guarantees or deep discounts can replace the reputation effects that help sell these experience goods in nonvirtual settings. Internet sellers can add value and reduce some transaction costs in these markets by customizing and selling direct to the customer like Dell Computers, who provides order fulfillment and manufactures almost nothing. Perhaps this is why services have grown so quickly on the Net; the travel industry itself accounted for 35 percent of all online sales in 2002. Table 14.4 shows that the growth rate of services far surpassed growth in consumer products online.

In business-to-business (B2B) transactions, pricing is more complex than in the above business-to-consumer transactions. In B2B, multiple attributes come into play in the price negotiation. B2B customers haggle over date of shipment, delivery costs, warranty service times and locations, delivery reliability, and replacement

Table 14.4　Growth in Online Sales

	1997	2001	Compound Annual Growth Rate
Consumer Services			
Travel	$654 million	$ 7.4 billion	83%
Event Tickets	79 million	2 billion	124%
Financial Services	1.2 billion	5 billion	43%
Consumer Products			
Apparel	$ 92 million	$514 million	53%
Books/CDs	156 million	1.1 billion	63%
PCs	863 million	3.8 billion	45%
B2B	$ 8 billion	$183 billion	119%

Sources: *Business Week*, Forrester Research.

Dynamic Pricing
A price that varies over time based on the balance of demand and supply, often associated with Internet auctions.

guarantees. These additional considerations typically mean pricing is a part of a two- or three-step process. First, customers match their non-negotiable requirements to the suppliers with those attributes, and those firms become the order-qualified suppliers. Then, the remaining attributes may be negotiated away against demands for a lower price point. B2B Internet sales grew twentyfold from $8 billion in 1997 to $183 billion by the beginning of 2002; see Table 14.4.

Internet pricing in these B2B settings requires a matching process to qualify for an order and then a **dynamic pricing** algorithm to trade off the remaining attributes. Information technology complexity in these B2B transactions arises because customers are heterogeneous, and the attributes that qualify a firm to supply one group of customers may not match the requirements of other customers. In addition, as we shall see in Appendix 14A, delivery reliability—i.e., the probability of stockout and backorder—is a continuous variable that should be optimized with a revenue management solution, not a simple on-again/off-again attribute to promise or refuse a potential customer in exchange for a somewhat larger or smaller markup. Internet auctions may eventually allow the development of dynamic pricing tools to quote real-time opportunity costs for delivery reliability and change order responsiveness.

SUMMARY

- All pricing decisions should be proactive, systematic, and value based—for example, related to careful detailed assessment of customer value.
- *Price discrimination* is the act of selling the same good or service produced by a given firm at different prices to different customers. Two conditions are required for effective price discrimination:
  1. One must be able to segment the market and prevent the transfer of the product (or service) from one segment to another.

2. There must be differences in the elasticity of demand at a given price between the market segments.

- To maximize profits using price discrimination, the firm must allocate output in such a way that marginal revenue is equal in the different market segments.

- Price discrimination is often implemented through two-part pricing. Optimal *two-part prices* entail a lump-sum access fee and a user charge that exceeds marginal cost and varies per unit consumed.

- Bundling is another way to price discriminate while charging the same prices to different customers.

- For firms selling multiple products with interdependent demands, decisions to add or delete products in existing product lines may have (positive or negative) impacts on the sales of the firm's current outputs. In the analysis of such decisions, it is necessary to include the costs of these impacts in the marginal cost calculations.

- Pricing strategy varies throughout the product or service life cycle. A frequent pattern is target pricing, followed by penetration pricing, value-based pricing, limit pricing, and finally niche pricing.

- Many actual business pricing practices, such as *full-cost pricing* and *target pricing*, can be consistent with the marginal pricing rules of economic theory. *Incrementalism* is a widely applicable method of economic analysis that may help management to achieve a more efficient and profitable level of operation.

- When new products are introduced, firms may use the *skimming* strategy to price the product and increase total profits. *Prestige pricing* is often used in segmenting markets. Web-based pricing for products sold over the Internet requires different pricing strategies depending upon the type of product: commodity product, quasi-commodity product, search good, or experience good.

EXERCISES

1. Why does the phone company offer different pricing structures for business and personal phone lines? Compare this with the reasons why a bank has a different pricing structure for business and personal checking accounts.

2. DVDs and DVD players are no longer a niche product; 31 million players have been sold in the U.S. Sony sells both DVD players and DVDs. What should be Sony's approach to pricing? What difference will it make to Sony pricing if customers have now become dissimilar?

3. The price elasticity of demand for a textbook sold in the United States is estimated to be -2.0, whereas the price elasticity of demand for books sold overseas is -3.0. The U.S. market requires hardcover books with a marginal cost of $30; the overseas market is normally served with softcover texts, having a marginal cost of only $15. Calculate the profit-maximizing price in each market.

$$\left[\textit{Hint}: \text{Remember that } MR = P\left(1 + \frac{1}{E_D}\right). \right]$$

4. The price elasticity of demand for air travel differs radically from first-class (-0.3) to unrestricted coach (-0.4) to restricted discount coach (-0.9). What can one say about optimal prices (fares) on a cross-country trip with incremental variable costs (marginal costs) equal to $120?

5. American Export-Import Shipping Company operates a general cargo carrier service between New York and several Western European ports. It hauls two major categories of freight: manufactured items and semimanufactured raw materials. The demand functions for these two classes of goods are

$$P_1 = 100 - 2Q_1$$
$$P_2 = 80 - Q_2$$

where Q_i = tons of freight moved. The total cost function for American is

$$TC = 20 + 4(Q_1 + Q_2)$$

a. Determine the firm's total profit function.

b. What are the profit-maximizing levels of price and output for the two freight categories?

c. At these levels of output, calculate the marginal revenue in each market.

d. What are American's total profits if it is effectively able to charge different prices in the two markets?

e. If American is required by law to charge the same per-ton rate to all users, calculate the new profit-maximizing level of price and output. What are the profits in this situation?

f. Explain the difference in profit levels between the discriminating and nondiscriminating cases. To do this, one should calculate the point price elasticity of demand under the nondiscriminating price-output solution.

6. Phillips Industries manufactures a certain product that can be sold directly to retail outlets or to the Superior Company for further processing and eventual sale by them as a completely different product. The demand function for each of these markets is

$$\text{Retail Outlets: } P_1 = 60 - 2Q_1$$
$$\text{Superior Company: } P_2 = 40 - Q_2$$

where P_1 and P_2 are the prices charged and Q_1 and Q_2 are the quantities sold in the respective markets. Phillips's total cost function for the manufacture of this product is

$$TC = 10 + 8(Q_1 + Q_2)$$

a. Determine Phillips's total profit function.

b. What are the profit-maximizing price and output levels for the product in the two markets?

c. At these levels of output, calculate the marginal revenue in each market.

d. What are Phillips's total profits if the firm is effectively able to charge different prices in the two markets?

e. Calculate the profit-maximizing level of price and output if Phillips is required to charge the same price per unit in each market. What are Phillips's profits under this condition?

7. a. Many university bookstores offer to professors price discounts that are generally not available to students. What conditions make this sort of price discrimination feasible and profitable for the bookstores?

    b.   Similarly, students are often given discounts to attend cultural and athletic events, whereas professors do not receive these discounts. What conditions make this sort of price discrimination possible and desirable?

8. In the face of stable (or declining) enrollments and increasing costs, many colleges and universities, both public and private, have found themselves in progressively tighter financial dilemmas. This has led to a basic reexamination of the pricing schemes used by institutions of higher learning. One proposal advocated by the Committee for Economic Development (CED) and others has been for the use of more nearly full-cost pricing of higher education, combined with the government provision of sufficient loan funds to students who would not otherwise have access to reasonable loan terms in private markets. Advocates of such proposals argue that the private rate of return to student investors is sufficiently high to stimulate socially optimal levels of demand for education, even with the higher tuition rates. Others have argued against the existence of significant external benefits to undergraduate education to warrant the current high levels of public support.

    As with current university pricing schemes, proponents of full-cost pricing generally argue for a standard fee (albeit higher than at present) for all students. Standard-fee proposals ignore relative cost and demand differences among activities in the university.

    a.   Discuss several possible rationales for charging different prices for different courses of study.

    b.   What are the income-distribution effects of a pricing scheme that charges the same fee to all students?

    c.   If universities adopted a system of full-cost (or marginal cost) pricing for various courses, what would you expect the impact on the efficiency of resource allocations within the university to be?

    d.   Would you complain less about large lecture sections taught by graduate students if these were priced significantly lower than small seminars taught by outstanding scholars?

    e.   What problems could you see arising from a university that adopted such a pricing scheme?

9. General Medical makes disposable syringes, that it sells to hospitals and doctor supply companies. The company uses cost-plus pricing and currently charges 150 percent of average variable costs. General Medical has learned of an opportunity to sell 300,000 syringes to the Department of Defense if they can be delivered within three months at a price not in excess of $1 each. General Medical normally sells its syringes for $1.20 each.

    If General Medical accepts the Defense Department order, it will have to forgo sales of 100,000 syringes to its regular customers over this time period, although this loss of sales is not expected to affect future sales.

    a.   Should General Medical accept the Defense Department order?

    b.   If sales for the balance of the year are expected to be 50,000 units less because of some lost customers who do not return, should the order be accepted (ignore any effects beyond one year)?

10. Culinary Products, Inc. (CPI) performs a target return pricing calculation as part of its analysis of any proposed new products. CPI's research and

development department has provided the following information concerning a new food processor it has designed:

- Labor costs (per unit): $22
- Material costs (per unit): $11
- Marketing costs (per unit): $2
- Fixed overhead costs (per year): $1,500,000
- Gross investment (operating assets): $6,000,000
- Required rate of return on investment (per year): 25%

Determine the target price based on projected sales per year of:

a. 80,000 units
b. 100,000 units
c. 60,000 units

11. The Pear Computer Company has just developed a totally revolutionary new personal computer. It estimates that it will take competitors at least two years to produce equivalent products. The demand function for the computer has been estimated to be

$$P = 2,500 - .0005Q$$

The marginal (and average variable) cost of producing the computer is $900.

a. Compute the profit-maximizing price and output levels assuming Pear acts as a monopolist for its product.

b. Determine the total contribution to profits and fixed costs from the solution generated in Part (a).

Pear Computer is considering an alternative pricing strategy of sliding down the demand curve. It plans to set the following schedule of prices over the coming two years:

Time Period	Price	Quantity Sold
1	$2,400	200,000
2	2,200	200,000
3	2,000	200,000
4	1,800	200,000
5	1,700	200,000
6	1,600	200,000
7	1,500	200,000
8	1,400	200,000
9	1,300	200,000
10	1,200	200,000

c. Calculate the contribution to profit and overhead for each of the 10 time periods and prices.

d. Compare your results in Part (c) with your answers in Part (b).

e. Explain the major advantages and disadvantages of "sliding down the demand curve" as a pricing strategy.

http://

Congestion Pricing

12. During times of peak usage of network resources such as highways, main-frame computers, and power transmission lines, providing access to an additional user can have negative impacts on all other users. Congestion or peak-load pricing systems at least partially internalize the external costs of congestion. But while congestion pricing may make economic sense, how can charging commuters higher prices be made politically viable? Access the following Internet site maintained by the DOT: http://www.fhwa.dot.gov/policy/final.htm. Are there alternative solutions to the congestion problem? Also visit the Microsoft Research site at http://research.microsoft.com/research/network/disgame.asp and read the abstract *Congestion Pricing for Congestion Avoidance*.

Appendix 14a

Revenue Management

THE CONCEPT OF REVENUE MANAGEMENT[17]

Most competition takes place today in product-line submarkets between highly interdependent rivals, each with some market power over price. Consider Delta, Continental, and US Airways in air travel to Florida. To gain and sustain market share, each firm must secure competitive advantages by raising perceived value to customers or by lowering production, distribution, or selling cost. Then, by segmenting customers and preventing arbitrage, such firms may seek to raise revenue with price discrimination—for example, airlines charge larger markups for weekday business travelers who forgo fewer close substitutes than vacationers staying over a Saturday night.

Customer segmentation and price discrimination are frequently complicated by prohibitive stocking costs and capacity choices that must be made before demand is known. Consider an airline, printing business, or hospital, which must acquire and schedule capacity before the respective demands for the 11:00 A.M. flight, the press run next Thursday, or tomorrow's elective surgeries are known. Production scheduling and the marketing mix can influence the order flow of these businesses, but can never remove entirely the random character of their demand.

If no revenue can be realized after departure from empty airline seats, from underutilized printing presses, or empty surgical theatres, random customer arrivals force a firm with fixed capacity to choose between underutilizing excess capacity or imposing service denials and stockouts on regular customers. The "spoilage" from unsold capacity and the "spill" of high-margin repeat customers are serious problems that may affect the firm's financial success and indeed its survival. In Figure 14A.1, a reduction in capacity from Q^{d_1} to a level just sufficient to meet mean demand at P_0 reduces the spoilage for low demand events (Q^{d_2}) from AB to CD, but introduces spill (i.e., Spill$_2$) for high demand events (Q^{d_1}). Revenue or yield management (YM) is an integrated set of managerial economics techniques designed to deal with these pricing and capacity allocation problems under fixed capacity and random demand.

Example

SPILL AND SPOILAGE AT SPORT OBERMEYER[18]

The selling season in fashion retailing is short (lasting no more than several months), and customer demand at the product-line level is very fickle and hard to forecast. Consequently, buyers for retail merchants like Nieman-Marcus, Bloomingdale's, Saks Fifth Avenue, Rich's, and Marshall Field's must place orders far in advance of actual sales without really knowing which fashion trends will sell well and which will sell

---

[17] F. Harris and P. Peacock provide a thorough overview of YM techniques and potential industry applications in "Hold My Place Please: Yield Management Improves Capacity Allocation Guesswork," *Marketing Management*, 4(2), Fall 1995, pp. 34–46.

[18] Based on M. Fisher et al., "Making Supply Meet Demand in an Uncertain World," *Harvard Business Review*, May/June 1994, pp. 83–93.

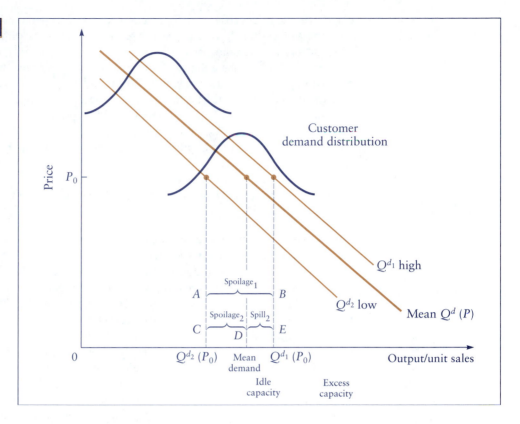

FIGURE 14A.1

Spill and Spoilage with Random Demand and Fixed Prices

poorly. Sport Obermeyer faces this problem with ski clothes. In a particular winter ski season, Pandora ski parkas may become a fashion statement and quickly sell out. If Pandora parkas go on back order, creating frustrated buyers, the store will lose that customer's goodwill and future sales. In addition, the lost retail contribution margin every time Sport Obermeyer "spills" one of these customers is $15.

On the other hand, Pandora's line of ski parkas may not "catch on" this season. Instead, they may end up as spoilage (i.e., a large inventory overhang of unsold winter clothes). The merchant would then incur losses on the unsold merchandise and forgo the opportunity to sell another Champion sweatshirt that could have occupied the ski parka's shelf space. Sport Obermeyer can use the tools of yield management to balance these costs of spill and spoilage and thereby determine how many parkas to order and what shelf space to devote to parkas versus sweatshirts.

A Cross-Functional Systems Management Process

Firms might respond to unanticipated demand fluctuations in the presence of capacity constraints by simply auctioning off their scarce product to the highest bidder or by holding massive clearance sales when faced with inventory overhang. Much to their detriment, department store retailers have taken this myopic marketing view of what mark-down prices can accomplish. Fashion-conscious customers shop numerous stores to "win" the trendy items and do so with little repeat purchase loyalty. Everyone else has become habituated to wait for the inevitable and deep discount sales. The proportion of department store revenue earned through transactions at clearance sale prices rose from 8 percent in 1970 to 55 percent in 2001.[19] Even regular customers of leading department stores report buying at discount prices almost as often (46 percent) as at regular prices (54 percent). Not surprisingly, profitability in department store retailing has collapsed, and consolidation mergers have taken some of the best known retailers out of business. What might these stores have done differently?

One alternative would be for the retail merchant's suppliers to develop flexible manufacturing systems (FMSs) so they could respond to demand fluctuations more quickly. If reorder cycles could occur several additional times within the fashion season, merchants could stockpile less inventory and yet experience fewer stockouts.

Example

TOYOTA PLANS TO ASSEMBLE CARS WITHIN FIVE DAYS OF A CUSTOM ORDER[20]

Toyota Motor Corp. has raised the bar in delivery service for custom-ordered vehicles. Using advanced information technology, direct marketing, just-in-time logistics, and an FMS, Toyota has reduced the time required to assemble a custom-ordered car to just 5 days. The industry average has fluctuated between 30 and 60 days in recent years. Production to order allows Toyota to reduce inventories 28 percent, substantially reducing costs. Whether unpredictable demand for certain types of models will overwhelm the limited surge capacity of this FMS system remains to be seen. This sounds almost too good to be true. An FMS is often too myopic an approach to the problem, one that attempts to use operations alone to solve a problem that is really cross-functional. Some manufacturing environments are simply inappropriate for the application of FMS technology. The economies from large production runs in textile manufacturing or metal working imply that designer jeans and refrigerator manufacturing operations should adopt transfer lines that minimize new setups in order to realize massive cost savings. A flexible manufacturing system will not provide the answer to unpredictable demand fluctuations in these types of production environments.[21]

Another alternative to resolve the problems posed by high-margin spill is simply to acquire more capacity. Of course, no company can afford to build additional capacity ad infinitum. Aggregate capacity planning incorporates a careful financial analysis of the capital budgeting problem that identifies the optimal fixed capacity for any line of business.

Reserving some of this fixed capacity for late-arriving high-margin customers is another key to successfully addressing the problem of demand fluctuations. Reserving capacity as the moment of delivery approaches should not be interpreted as "excess capacity" but rather as idle capacity that presents a sustainable revenue opportunity. This is one of the insights of yield management (sometimes called revenue management) analysis. Every company has some orders that it should refuse. **Yield management** (YM) is fundamentally an order acceptance and refusal process that links marketing decisions about demand creation and pricing with operations deci-

Yield Management
A cross-functional order acceptance and refusal process.

---

[19] B.P. Pashigian, "Demand Uncertainty and Sales," *American Economic Review,* 78(5), December 1993, pp. 936–953, and "Priced to Move," *Wall Street Journal,* August 7, 2001, p. A6.

[20] Based on "Toyota Develops a Way," *Wall Street Journal,* August 6, 1999, p. A4.

[21] For a more extensive discussion of yield management techniques and managerial insights applied to manufacturing, see F. Harris and J. Pinder, "A Revenue Management Approach to Demand Management and Order Booking in Assemble-to-Order Manufacturing," *Journal of Operations Management,* 12(4), December 1995, pp. 299–309.

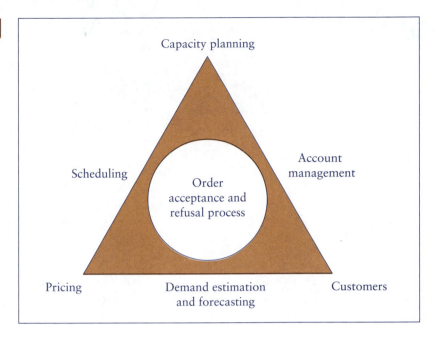

FIGURE 14A.2

Cross-Functional Revenue Management

sions about scheduling and financial decisions about capacity planning. The objective is to decide which orders to accept at particular prices and which to refuse. These relationships are depicted in Figure 14A.2 as a cross-functional triangle of account management, forecasting, and scheduling decisions.

Sources of Sustainable Price Premiums

Practitioners of yield management believe that the sources of sustainable price premiums lie in these cross-functional systems management processes. In this view, innovative products and successful advertising campaigns are quickly reverse engineered and readily imitated. Advertising and product design cannot therefore provide sustainable competitive advantage. Process advantages, on the other hand, prove much more difficult for competitors to imitate.

Yield management processes add conspicuous tangible value for which customers gladly pay higher prices. In most cases, the added value arises through customizing and optimizing the account and order management. In the airline industry, for example, some customers want extensive flexibility of reservations that allows frequent changes in departure and arrival times. If an airline has the operations capability and information technology to provide this service, business travelers with unconfirmed meeting schedules will offer large price premiums to secure this *change order responsiveness*. To take another example, Disney offers substantial price premiums to gift product suppliers who can deliver first quality on time as promised. When Disney order clerks submit an error-laden request that needs to be changed within the normal 30-day reorder cycle, Disney volunteers to pay even more. Such supplements to revenue go exclusively to firms that have the systems management processes that can handle extraordinary change order requests.

Firms compete on other aspects of order processing as well. Some customers want short *scheduling delays* (e.g., just-in-time retailers without warehouses). Others want high *delivery reliability* and a very small probability of being denied service in the event of a stockout (e.g., business executives traveling to a stockholders' meeting). Still others value *conformance to product or service specifications*. For time-sensitive

FIGURE 14A.3

Ratio of Business to
Leisure Fares and
Airline Market Shares
at Hub Airports

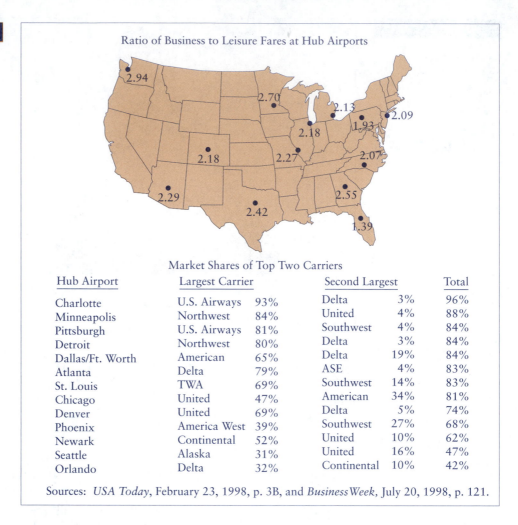

Ratio of Business to Leisure Fares at Hub Airports

Market Shares of Top Two Carriers

Hub Airport	Largest Carrier		Second Largest		Total
Charlotte	U.S. Airways	93%	Delta	3%	96%
Minneapolis	Northwest	84%	United	4%	88%
Pittsburgh	U.S. Airways	81%	Southwest	4%	84%
Detroit	Northwest	80%	Delta	3%	84%
Dallas/Ft. Worth	American	65%	Delta	19%	84%
Atlanta	Delta	79%	ASE	4%	83%
St. Louis	TWA	69%	Southwest	14%	83%
Chicago	United	47%	American	34%	81%
Denver	United	69%	Delta	5%	74%
Phoenix	America West	39%	Southwest	27%	68%
Newark	Continental	52%	United	10%	62%
Seattle	Alaska	31%	United	16%	47%
Orlando	Delta	32%	Continental	10%	42%

Sources: *USA Today*, February 23, 1998, p. 3B, and *BusinessWeek*, July 20, 1998, p. 121.

deliveries of organ transplants, for example, excellent on-time-service records warrant paying very high airfares. The alternative would be a much more expensive jet charter service. Manufacturers as well as service firms can establish sustainable price premiums based on these same order processing characteristics of change order responsiveness, minimal scheduling delay, delivery reliability, and conformance to specifications.

All of these sources of sustainable price premiums are prominent in airline services at "fortress hubs" where one carrier controls more than 65 percent of the seat departures at an airport. Figure 14A.3 displays the major hub airports in the continental United States and provides pricing and market share data for the top two carriers. In each of these cities, the dominant firm(s) have sufficient operating capacity and systems control to provide very high-quality service. At Dallas-Ft. Worth, for example, American Airlines has very high schedule convenience, with departures quite close to the time preferences of a DFW-origin traveler. Similarly, at this airport American can offer very high delivery reliability, schedule conformance to expectations, and change order responsiveness. Passengers, especially business travelers, will pay substantial premiums to secure these very high service quality characteristics because of the additional value such flights create in their own business activities. YM systems reserve idle capacity to meet these high-value demands when the late arrival of such requests is forecasted. When not, YM systems "protect" fewer seats and release more capacity to deep discount leisure segments of the market. Overall, fares per revenue

http://

To learn more about yield management, and to access information on yield management programs and expert systems, go to the following Internet site: http://www.mugc.cc. monash.edu.au/kfarrell/ iymrs/

passenger mile at a fortress hub like Atlanta (where Delta has a 70 percent share) are 84 percent higher than at Orlando, where Delta again is the leading carrier but has only 32 percent of the market.

REVENUE MANAGEMENT DECISIONS

Revenue or yield management (YM) can be divided into three decisions: (1) a proactive pricing and aggregate capacity planning decision, (2) an inventory or capacity reallocation decision, and (3) an overbooking decision. Figure 14A.4 places these decisions in a YM conceptual framework, showing a flow chart of the components of a revenue management process. What all three decisions have in common is a tactical focus heavily dependent on anticipated rival responses; a systems management philosophy integrating marketing, operations, and finance; and finally a multiproduct orientation that continuously reconfigures the firm's product offerings. We now address the managerial economics of each YM decision in turn.

Proactive Price Discrimination

Proactive price discrimination involves maximizing profits in the light of anticipated late-arriving demand and rival firm responses. In principle, computerized decision support systems (DSS) make it possible to reauction the remaining seats on a flight or the remaining runs on the printing press each time a new customer arrives on a reservation

FIGURE 14A.4

Revenue Management Flow Chart

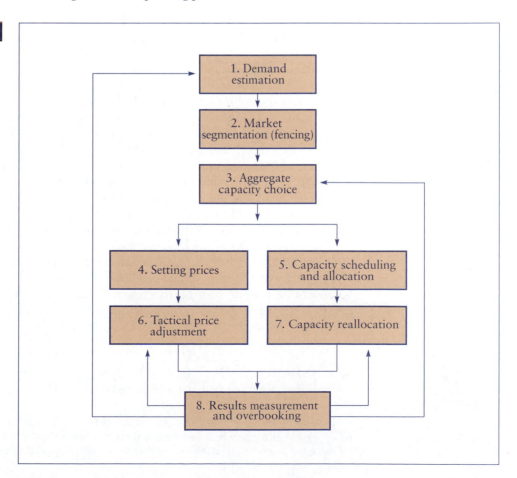

FIGURE 14A.5

Price Discrimination and Optimal Capacity Allocation (45 Days in Advance) for Thursday 11:00 A.M. Flight from Dallas to Los Angeles

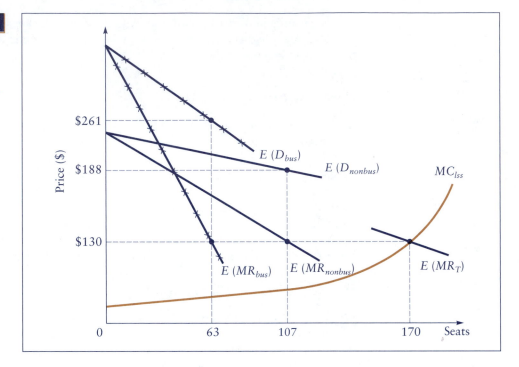

system. Conceivably, each customer would then experience first-degree price discrimination and pay a unique price reflecting his or her time of delivery, service costs, and price elasticity. Few YM practitioners have adopted bid price systems. Instead, most set prices and initially allocate capacity with the familiar techniques of marginal analysis.

Demand is estimated by market segment (e.g., for each of two customer classes—say, business and nonbusiness air travel). The expense account business traveler tends to make less flexible travel plans and reserve space later and thus faces fewer close alternatives than the nonbusiness traveler. Average revenue and marginal revenue schedules for business travelers therefore prove to be less elastic than for nonbusiness travelers, as indicated in Figure 14A.5. Previously, the airline's capacity planning department will have summed all the expected marginal revenues $E(MR)$ from the various segments and determined an optimal total capacity by setting summed marginal revenue $[\Sigma E(MR)]$ equal to the marginal cost of the last seat sold (MC_{lss}).[22] The result in Figure 14A.5 is that a plane with 170 seats should be scheduled for the Thursday 11:00 A.M. flight departure.

One may think of the optimal price discrimination decision as determining how this total capacity of 170 seats should be allocated across the customer segments. This is because at the margin a firm forgoes revenue unless the last customer in each segment contributes a marginal revenue equal to the marginal cost of the last seat sold (MC_{lss}), the optimal allocation results from equating the segment-level MRs to one another:

$$MR_{bus} = (MC_{lss}) = MR_{nonbus} \qquad \text{[14A.1]}$$

which in Figure 14A.5 is at $MR = \$130$. Consider a case in which this condition does not hold. Suppose the 62nd seat sold in the business class contributed $150 of marginal

---

[22] To find aggregate demand, remember that individual demands (and MRs) are horizontally summed for rivalrous goods that cannot be shared (such as airplane seats and bite-sized candy bars), whereas demands for nonrivalrous goods (such as outdoor statues, tennis courts, and national defense) are vertically summed.

revenue and the 108th seat sold in the nonbusiness class contributed $120. Clearly, one could raise $30 additional revenue for unchanged costs by selling one less seat in nonbusiness and one more in business, leaving both classes with, say, an $MR = \$130$.[23]

What prices can achieve the initial capacity allocation of 63 seats to the business class and 107 seats to the nonbusiness class? The answer is deceptively simple. Optimal price-discriminating prices are whatever asking prices will clear the market if the firm supplies 63 and 107 seats in these two fare classes. In Figure 14A.5 the answer appears to be $261 and $188 with some effective barrier or "fencing," that prevents resale from the lower to the higher fares. The trick, of course, is predicting demand sufficiently well to know what prices will have this effect for the 11 A.M. flight next Thursday.

OPTIMAL CAPACITY ALLOCATION: 11 A.M. FLIGHT TO LAX

Example

Table 14A.1 shows the data on which such a decision would be based in practice. The first three columns show number of seats demanded, fares, and marginal revenue for business-class travelers. For example, at a fare of $1,084, only one seat on the entire plane would be sold, and it would go to a business-class passenger. If the fare falls to $1,032, two seats are taken by business-class passengers. At a fare of $974, three seats are taken, and so on. Expected marginal revenue is the increase in total revenue realized from selling one more seat in the business class. For example, when a single seat is sold at $1,084, total revenue is also $1,084. When two seats are sold at a fare of $1,032, however, total revenue jumps to $2,064, and marginal revenue, which is the difference in total revenue realized from selling one more seat, is $2,064 minus $1,084, or $980. Similarly, the marginal revenue associated with the third seat sold is $2,922 minus $2,064, or $858.

Table 14A.1 also shows corresponding information for leisure class passengers. Note that the first leisure class seat is sold at $342, the second at $331, and so on. The last two columns depict total seats sold and marginal cost, which is the variable cost associated with serving one additional passenger in either class.

Using this simple two-booking-class example, marginal revenue equals rising marginal cost at $130 per seat. (Marginal cost increases by steps with the addition of flight attendants needed to serve additional passengers and the additional fuel consumed because of worsening aerodynamics at high load factors.) At $MC = \$130$, optimal fares are obtained by equating individual marginal revenues of both segments and the marginal cost of the last seat expected to be sold (the 170th seat in this example). Business and leisure traveler marginal revenues equal $130 at 63 and 107 seats, respectively, and fares of $261 and $188 are optimal at these seat allocation levels.

Capacity Reallocation

The second step in yield management is to *reallocate capacity* as delivery times approach in the light of advance sales and confirmed orders. Suppose you forecasted advance sales for business class on Thursday departures from Dallas to Los

---

[23] Note that the *MR* of each segment is not set equal to *MC*. Rather, the summed *MR* of all segments has been set equal to *MC*. The individual *MRs* are set equal to the *MC* of the last unit sold (i.e., $130), and therefore equal to one another.

TABLE 14A.1

Allocating Airline Capacity with Price-Discriminating Fares

Business Class			Leisure Class				
Expected Seat Demand	Fare	Expected Marginal Revenue	Expected Seat Demand	Fare	Expected Marginal Revenue	Total Seats	Marginal Cost
1	$1,084	$1,084				1	$87
2	1,032	980				2	87
3	974	858				3	87
4	907	705				4	87
5	835	550				5	87
10	613	390				10	87
			1	$342	$342		87
			2	331	320		95
			3	319	294		95
			4	311	288		95
20	456	280	5	305	280	25	95
			10	280	256		95
			20	260	240		95
30	381	230	30	250	230	60	100
			40	240	210		100
			50	231	194		100
40	331	180	60	222	180	100	112
			70	214	162		112
50	295	150	80	206	150	130	112
			90	198	140		120
60	268	133	100	192	133	160	125
63	261	130	107	188	130	170	130
			110	186	128		140
70	252	122	120	181	122	190	155
			130	176	115		170
80	235	110	140	173	110	220	190

Angeles in accordance with the exponential function (tickets purchased $= aB^t$) estimated in semilog form as

$$\ln(\text{tickets}) = \ln a + \ln B(t) = \alpha + \beta t \qquad [14A.2]$$

where t is a simple time trend variable. Similarly, suppose you forecasted all nonbusiness travel with a sales penetration function such as

$$\text{Tickets purchased} = e^{k_1 - k_2(1/t)} \qquad [14A.3]$$

estimated as

$$\ln(\text{tickets}) = k_1 - k_2(1/t). \qquad [14A.4]$$

where k_1 and k_2 are constants defining the rate of sales growth throughout the advance sales period. These forecasted business and nonbusiness "booking curves" are plotted in Figure 14A.6. Note that the curves exhibit the early- and late-arriving characteristics of demand in the nonbusiness and business markets, respectively.

The forecasted booking curves reflect new demand arrivals and cancellations and are, in that sense, net bookings. Moreover, assume they reflect substantial non-

FIGURE 14A.6

Advance Sales Forecasts, Bookings, and Threshold Curves

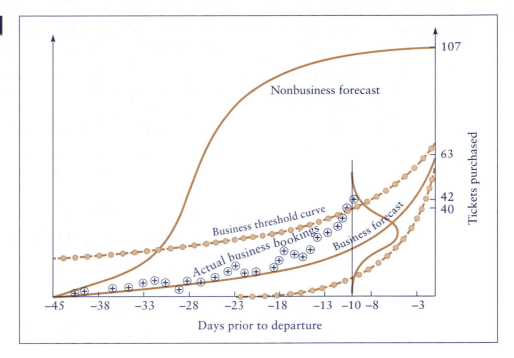

refundable deposits on advance sales and therefore imply realized revenue rather than just potential sales.[24] For the 11:00 A.M. flight to Los Angeles, the final demand target in Figure 14A.6 is 63 business and 107 nonbusiness passengers. This is an *initial* allocation of total capacity when customer reservations open 180, 120, 60, or in our case, 45 days prior to departure. It is subject to (and in fact often is) change(d) by the yield managers.

Confidence intervals based on the different demand arrival distributions are then used to determine when actual bookings have deviated so far from forecast as to warrant an exception report. For example, business travel appears to be above forecasted ticket sales at day $t - 10$ by a statistically significant amount. This violation of the **threshold sales curve** raises the question of whether to stop sales in the nonbusiness class where contribution margins $[(P_{nonbus} - MC) = (\$188 - \$130) = \$58]$ are clearly lower than in the business class segment, where $(P_{bus} - MC) = (\$261 - \$130) = \$131$.

The answer to this capacity reallocation question lies in applied statistics and in the initial profit-maximizing capacity choice under risk. Marginal capacity expansions are warranted as long as the expected incremental revenue minus marginal cost (i.e., the additional expected contribution to fixed cost) exceeds the incremental cost of additional capacity. In capacity reallocation, the cost of additional capacity in the business class is an opportunity cost—namely, the forgone contribution from selling one less seat in the nonbusiness class. At the margin, we would reallocate capacity as long as the expected contribution margin from allocating another seat to business travelers would exceed the lost contribution margin from a boarding denial in nonbusiness. That is,

$$(P_{bus} - MC)(Prob\ Shortage_{bus}) = (P_{nonbus} - MC)$$

$$\$131\ (Prob\ Shortage_{bus}) = \$58$$

[14A.5]

Threshold Sales Curve
A level of advance sales that triggers reallocation of capacity.

---

[24] In the last YM decision, we will consider the effect of no-shows on authorized overbookings.

where the *Prob Shortage*$_{bus}$ is the probability that the business class will in fact be full and, therefore, the probability that the extra business-class seat will realize its $131 marginal contribution.[25]

Using the preannounced prices and resulting contribution margins of $58 and $131, and solving Equation 14A.5, high yield spill should occur 44.1 percent of the time:

$$(\textit{Prob Shortage}_{bus}) = \$58/\$131 = 0.441$$

For any business-class demand distribution (say, normally distributed with a mean of 60 seats and a standard deviation of 20 seats), we can calculate the optimal capacity choice as

$$\mu_{seats} + z_\alpha \sigma_{seats} = 60 + 0.148 \times 20 = 63 \text{ seats} \qquad [14A.6]$$

where z_α is the absolute value of the standard normal critical value (z value) for one-tailed alpha from Table 1 in Appendix B. These calculations correspond to the initial situation in which business-class capacity was set at 63 seats (see Figure 14A.5). On this flight, 63 seats is often referred to as the **protection level** for business-class seats. Similarly, 107 seats is the **authorization level** for nonbusiness-class seats.

Now recall that at day $t{-}10$ in Figure 14A.6, we have received an exception report: it appears that the arrival distribution for next Thursday's flight is not normally distributed with mean 60 and standard deviation 20, that is, N(60,20). Instead, the exception report may indicate mean demand has increased such that the new demand distribution is N(62,20). Again, using the fact that with prices of $261 and $188 the optimal probability of stockout in business class is 0.441, we can calculate using Equation 14A.6 that the new optimal capacity allocation will be 62 seats + 0.148(20) seats = 65 seats. This implies that at present a stop-sales policy of 105 seats should apply to the bookings accepted in nonbusiness travel and that the extra two seats (107 − 105) should be reallocated to business class. Continued monitoring of bookings relative to the forecast thresholds may result in a return of these seats to nonbusiness class or a still further allocation toward business travelers.

The same questions and analyses we have examined in airlines apply in assemble-to-order manufacturing when a sport apparel manufacturer or a customized paper products manufacturer must decide which orders to accept and which to refuse (i.e., how to allocate fixed total capacity). As yield management moves out of the service sector (e.g., airlines, hotels, rental cars, advertising agencies, hospitals, professional services) and into manufacturing, these managerial economics techniques will become increasingly important.[26]

Protection Level
Capacity reserved for sale in higher margin segments.

Authorization Level
Capacity authorized for sale in lower margin segments.

Example

OPTIMAL PROBABILITY OF STOCKOUT AT SPORT OBERMEYER

Recall that Sport Obermeyer must allocate its fixed-retail shelf and display-rack space between Pandora parkas and Champion sweatshirts. The lost retail contribution margin every time Sport Obermeyer "spills" a Pandora parka customer is $15. The lost retail contribution margin on a Champion sweatshirt is $4. Knowing these margins and the relative sales effectiveness of particular shelf space, Sport Obermeyer can

---

[25] It is quite possible to have a positive probability of stockout on both sides of Equation 14A.5. Here, however, we assume an unlimited demand in the nonbusiness segment at the low fare of $188 for Dallas-Ft. Worth-LAX. That is, the probability of stockout is assumed to be 1.0 on the right-hand side.

[26] See F. Harris and J. Pinder, "A Revenue Management Approach to Order Booking and Demand Management in Assemble-to-Order Manufacturing," *Journal of Operations Management*, December 1995, pp. 299–309.

use the tools of yield management to balance the costs of spoilage and spill in order to decide the optimal incidence of stockouts in Pandora parkas. Using Equation 14A.5, Sport Obermeyer calculates that Pandora parkas should stock out 27 percent of the time—that is, *Prob (Shortage$_{parka}$) = 0.27*. With demand distribution data, Sport Obermeyer can calculate that a probability of shortage of $4/$15 = 0.27 requires stocking 85 size-8 parkas in each of its stores.

Optimal Overbooking

Optimal Overbooking
A marginal analysis technique for balancing the cost of idle capacity (spoilage) against the opportunity cost of unserved demand (spill).

The third and final yield management decision is an **optimal overbooking** decision. Here the airline authorizes the reservation clerks to sell more seats than are available on each departure to combat the lost revenue from "no-shows." Of course, many tickets entail discount fares that require advance purchase, but some business-class tickets are not purchased until check-in time. This means that a confirmed sale is not realized revenue until delivery time. In some industries orders can be canceled or shipments refused. At times the air carriers have experienced up to 35 percent no-shows in certain city-pair markets.

The optimal overbooking decision is an explicit illustration of marginal analysis in practice. Each airline seeks to minimize the summed costs of spoilage and spill. In Figure 14A.7, as expected demand of business travelers approaches planned capacity and the expected load factor approaches 100 percent, the total cost of spoilage (i.e., unsold seats × contribution$_{bus}$) declines geometrically toward zero. In contrast, as the expected load factor approaches 100 percent, the costs of high-yield spill rise for three reasons. First, oversales represent lost contributions, which might have been captured by other service offerings (e.g., later flights); that is, some customers balk and proceed to a competitor. Second, oversales necessitate out-of-pocket expenses to compensate passengers who board the airplane and then volunteer to give up their seats. And third, oversales and the resulting stockouts sacrifice customer goodwill and brand loyalty, thereby causing lost future sales. These rising total costs of high-yield spill also are depicted in Figure 14A.7.

Total summed costs are reduced when the load factor increases as long as the rising costs of oversales are more than offset by the falling cost of spoilage. From below 92- to 97-percent load factors, the declining cost of spoilage more than offsets the rising cost of oversales for nonbusiness travel. Beyond 97 percent, the rate of spoilage cost reduction is less than the rate of oversales cost increase. This may be seen in the lower diagram by comparing the $MC_{nonbusiness\ oversales}$ to the marginal benefit of reduced spoilage, $MB_{spoilage\ reduction}$, which is the MC of unsold seats *saved* by planning a higher load factor. For the nonbusiness class, the optimal planned load factor appears to be 97 percent. In contrast, in the business class the $MC_{business\ oversales}$ is so much higher as load factor increases that the optimal planned load factor is only 94 percent.

Both decisions are referred to as overbooking decisions because a 97-percent expected load factor for the 105 seats now allocated to nonbusiness travelers may necessitate actually booking not 0.97 × 105 = 102 seats, but rather 127 seats ((127 × (1 − 0.2) = 102) in periods when no-shows are averaging 20 percent. Similarly, optimal overbooking in business may imply confirming reservations not for 61 seats in heavy (35-percent) no-show periods, but rather for 94 seats (94 × 0.65 = 61). On average, 102 nonbusiness and 61 business travelers enplane for the Thursday 11:00 A.M. flight to Los Angeles. Of course, these 163 total passengers expected are only an average of actual passenger counts, which may vary on any particular departure from large spoilage to severe oversales.

Overbooking Decision
Minimizes Summed
Cost of Spoilage and
Spill

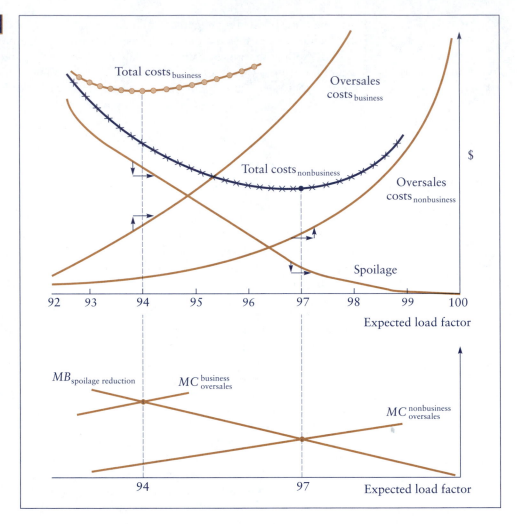

Example

PINPOINT BOOKING ACCURACY AT AMERICAN AIRLINES[27]

Price differentials on American Airlines' popular 5:30 P.M. flight (Flight 2015) from Chicago to Phoenix are huge, ranging from $238 to $1,404 round trip. American constantly adjusts the capacity allocation to each of seven fare classes as advance sales data deviate from forecast. Four weeks prior to a recent departure, American had already sold 69 of the 125 coach seats at Super Saver fares. With three weeks to departure, all three fare classes below $300 had reached their maximum authorization levels and were closed to further reservations. One day before departure, 130 passengers were booked on the 125-seat flight, but American was still authorizing up to five additional full coach reservations. The yield management computers predicted that cancellations and no-shows might go as high as 10. The next day Flight 2015 departed full with no one denied boarding. The systems management objective of YM is "to sell the right seat to the right customer at the right price at the right time" (Sabre Technology Solutions).

---

[27] Based on "High-Tech Pricing Boosts Business Fares," *Charlotte Observer*, November 9, 1997, p. 1D.

Yield management continuously reallocates capacity and adjusts these overbooking authorizations as advance sales data roll in. The incremental revenues from effective yield management can be significant. For example, American Airlines recently calculated its additional revenue from attending to these problems at $467 million per year. Marriott International estimates that revenue management contributes as much as $200 million each year to its revenue stream. And the Canadian Broadcasting Corporation realized a $2 million revenue gain the first two weeks after it adopted revenue management techniques.[28]

Example

REVENUE MANAGEMENT IN BASEBALL: THE BALTIMORE ORIOLES[29]

Recent applications of revenue management have taken the techniques out of travel services and into private-pay elective surgeries, radio and television advertising, opera and symphony concerts, law firms, consulting firms, golf courses, and now baseball. Like airlines, all these businesses have fixed capacity with perishable inventory; once the last out of the fifth inning has been called (or, some would say, the seventh inning stretch), empty seats offer no realizable value. Although season ticket holders are prominent in the planning of any professional sports franchise, single-game and three-game ticket packages remain a substantial source of revenue. And unstable demand makes prediction of sales in these more immediate segments a challenging and potentially very profitable process to do well, especially in baseball.

Most professional teams celebrate their sellouts, but some fail to realize that spare capacity (however slight) as game time approaches is a substantial revenue opportunity. Allowing discount ticket packages and promotions to displace last-minute walk-in customers often sacrifices high-margin repeat purchase business. At the same time, overall attendance in professional baseball remains below prestrike levels of the 1980s, and many games are played in ballparks only half full. The Baltimore Orioles revenue manager attempts to balance both of these errors of understocking and of overstocking. Single-game seats purchased well in advance are available at a discount. However, a substantial capacity of well-placed seats is protected in anticipation of late-arriving, high-willingness-to-pay, game-day-only customers. Advance sales are tracked, and variances are noted relative to previous sales histories for that home stand against similar opponents. As game day approaches, authorization levels for release of discount tickets gradually adjust to reflect the probability of stockout in higher-margin segments. Ideally, on game day, perhaps 97 percent of the seats are filled with fans in a variety of different segments paying a variety of different prices, each reflecting the location, customer responsiveness, reliability, timing, and other ticketing services that particular customers preferred, thereby adding maximum value.

SUMMARY

- Revenue or yield management (YM) consists of pricing and capacity allocation techniques for fixed-capacity manufacturers or service firms with perishable inventory and random demand.
- Flexible manufacturing systems and production-to-order just-in-time can seldom fully resolve the problem posed by YM.

---

[28] As cited in R. Cross, *Revenue Management: Hardcore Tactics for Market Domination* (New York: Broadway Books, 1997).

[29] Based on "Managing Baseball's Yield," *Barron's*, September 11, 1995, p. 50.

- YM provides an optimal order acceptance and refusal process with cross-functional resolution of account management, demand forecasting, and scheduling decisions.
- Proactive price discrimination equates the marginal revenue from different segments of the target market. It does so with differential value-based prices reflecting delivery reliability, change order responsiveness, scheduling convenience, conformance to expectations, and the value of these service quality characteristics to the particular class of customers (i.e., third-degree price discrimination).
- YM reallocates inventory or service capacity in accordance with the condition $(P - MC)_a$ $(Prob\ Shortage)_a = (P - MC)_b$. This procedure identifies optimal protection levels for high-margin segments, accounts, customers and an optimal authorization level for release of capacity to lower-margin segments, accounts, and customers.
- The optimal overbooking decision equates the declining marginal cost of spoilage as load factor or capacity utilization increases with the rising marginal cost of spill (i.e., oversales).

EXERCISES

1. Explain the effect on capacity reallocations of advance sales data implying mean demand of 55 rather than 60 during a slow travel week for business class, using the information in Figures 14A.5 and 14A.6 and Equation 14A.6.

2. Suppose the frequent-flyer program has raised the cost of high-yield spill twofold because business customers who are denied boarding now take their business to other carriers for several future trips, not just the current one. Reanalyze the overbooking decision in Figure 14A.7 under these circumstances. Will overbooking of business-class service increase or decrease?

3. An aircraft has 100 seats, extra passengers have $5 marginal cost, and there are two types of fares: full ($505) and discount ($105). While demand for discount tickets is unlimited, demand for full-fare tickets is estimated to be evenly distributed between 10 and 30 seats. How many seats should be protected for full-fare passengers?

4. What criteria should correlate to price premiums in capacity-constrained service businesses like accounting firms and advertising agencies?

5. Why is a long-haul trucking company not a good candidate for yield management techniques?

Pricing of Joint Products and Transfer Pricing

Chapter 14 addressed pricing decisions for firms that produce several alternative products that are technically independent in the production process. **Joint products,** in contrast, are interdependent in the production process; that is, a change in the production of one produces a change in the variable cost or the availability of the other. Many examples exist of joint products, including the production of liquid oxygen and nitrogen from air, beef and hides from steers, and gasoline and fuel oil from crude oil. In some cases, such as the production of beef and hides from cattle, the outputs are obtained in relatively fixed proportions. In other cases, such as the production of gasoline and fuel oil from crude oil, variable proportions of the outputs can be obtained through pressure and heat changes in the production process. Each of these cases is examined on the following pages.

JOINT PRODUCTS IN FIXED PROPORTIONS

When outputs are produced in fixed proportions, they should be analyzed as a *product package*. Because the products are jointly produced, all costs are incurred in production of the package and no conceptually correct method exists for allocating these costs to the individual products. Determination of the optimal output and prices of the products involves a comparison of the total marginal revenue from all the products with the marginal cost. In the following analysis, each unit of the product package consists of the output obtained from one unit of input. For example, the slaughtering of a steer might yield a product package consisting of 500 pounds of beef and one hide.

Figure 14B.1 (a) shows the demand functions and their respective marginal revenue functions for two products (A and B) that make up a product package, along with the marginal cost function for the production process. The total marginal revenue function (MR_T) for the product package is obtained by *vertically* summing the marginal revenue functions for the individual products (MR_A and MR_B). The net revenue gain to the firm of producing one more unit of the product package is the additional (marginal) revenue from Product A plus the inseparable additional (marginal) revenue from Product B. The intersection of the total marginal revenue function (MR_T) and the marginal cost function (MC) determines the optimal output of the product package (Q^*) along with the optimal prices of the two individual products (i.e., P_A^* and P_B^*).

Example

PRICING OF JOINT PRODUCTS: WILLIAMS COMPANY

Suppose the Williams Company is faced with the following demand functions for two joint products produced in fixed proportions:

$$P_1 = 50 - .5Q \qquad [14B.1]$$
$$P_2 = 60 - 2Q \qquad [14B.2]$$

FIGURE 14B.1   Optimal Price and Output Determination of Joint Products *A* and *B* Produced in Fixed Proportions

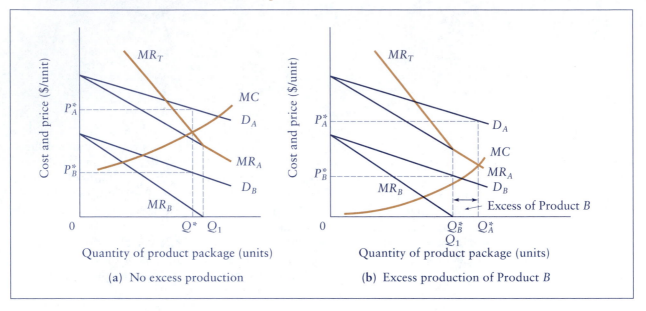

(a) No excess production

(b) Excess production of Product *B*

Furthermore, suppose that the marginal cost function for the joint products is

$$MC = 38 + Q \qquad [14B.3]$$

The two marginal revenue functions are obtained as follows:

$$TR_1 = P_1 Q = (50 - .5Q)Q = 50Q - .5Q^2$$

$$MR_1 = \frac{dTR_1}{dQ} = 50 - Q$$

$$TR_2 = P_2 Q = (60 - 2Q)Q = 60Q - 2Q^2$$

$$MR_2 = \frac{dTR_2}{dQ} = 60 - 4Q$$

Summing the two inseparable marginal revenue functions vertically yields

$$
\begin{aligned}
MR_T &= MR_1 + MR_2 \\
&= (50 - Q) + (60 - 4Q) \\
&= 110 - 5Q \qquad [14B.4]
\end{aligned}
$$

Setting the total marginal revenue function equal to the marginal cost function and solving for Q yields the optimal output

$$
\begin{aligned}
MR_T &= MC \\
110 - 5Q &= 38 + Q \\
72 &= 6Q \\
Q^* &= 12
\end{aligned}
$$

or 12 units of the product package. Substituting this value into the demand functions (Equations 14B.1 and 14B.2) gives the optimal prices of the two products:

$$P_1^* = 50 - .5(12)$$
$$= \$44 \text{ per unit of Product } A$$
$$P_2^* = 60 - 2(12)$$
$$= \$36 \text{ per unit of Product } B$$

One complication in the preceding analysis can occur if the marginal cost function (MC) intersects the total marginal revenue function (MR_T) at an output in excess of Q_1 in Figure 14B.1 (a). Above Q_1, the marginal revenue of Product B is negative and the firm would not want to sell more than Q_1 units of Product B. When this situation occurs, as shown in Figure 14B.1 (b), the optimal solution is to *produce* Q_A^* units of the product package. This is determined at the intersection of the MR_A and MC functions. Q_A^* units of Product A should be *sold* at a price of P_A^*. However, only Q_B^* $(= Q_1)$ units of Product B should be sold at a price of P_B^*. The *excess output* of Product B, namely $Q_A^* - Q_B^*$, should be destroyed or discarded so as not to depress the market price.

When solving a numerical problem, one can check to see if the marginal cost function intersects the total marginal revenue function at an output greater than Q_1 by substituting the optimal output (Q^*) into the MR_A and MR_B functions. If either marginal revenue value is negative, then the marginal cost function should be set equal to the marginal revenue function of the other product in determining the optimal price and output combination.[30] For example, if the MR_B function is negative, then one would use MR_A (rather than MR_T) to determine the optimal solution.

JOINT PRODUCTS IN VARIABLE PROPORTIONS

When the outputs can be produced in variable proportions, the analysis is somewhat more complex than the fixed proportions case.

PRICING OF JOINT PRODUCTS: SLUSSER CHEMICAL COMPANY

Example

The decision facing the Slusser Chemical Company is illustrated in Figure 14B.2. The quantities of two chemicals (X and Y) that may be produced are indicated on the vertical and horizontal axes. The isocost or production possibility curves (labeled TC) indicate the amounts of X and Y that may be produced for the same total cost. For instance, looking at the isocost curve labeled $TC = 8$, we see that the firm may produce Q_x units of X and Q_y units of Y, Q_x' units of X and Q_y' units of Y, or any possible combination along that curve at an equivalent total cost of $TC = 8$. Hence there are two ways of increasing the output of, say, Product X. One way is to move along the isocost curve, increasing the output of X at the expense of Y. The other is to increase the amount of the inputs or factors (e.g., capital and/or labor) in the production process; that is, move in a northeast direction to a higher isocost curve. The only requirement of isocost or production possibility curves is that they be concave to the origin, indicating an imperfect adaptability of the firm's productive resources in producing X and Y.

The isorevenue lines (labeled TR) take into account the prices received by Slusser for its two outputs. Each line is of equal revenue, indicating that any combination

---

[30] Note in the Williams Company example that when $Q^* = 12$, $MR_1 = 50 - 12 = \$38 > 0$ and $MR_2 = 60 - 4(12) = \$12 > 0$. Hence, no excess output of either product was being produced.

FIGURE 14B.2

Joint Products
Produced in Variable
Proportions: An
Optimal Price-Output
Mix—Slusser Chemical
Company

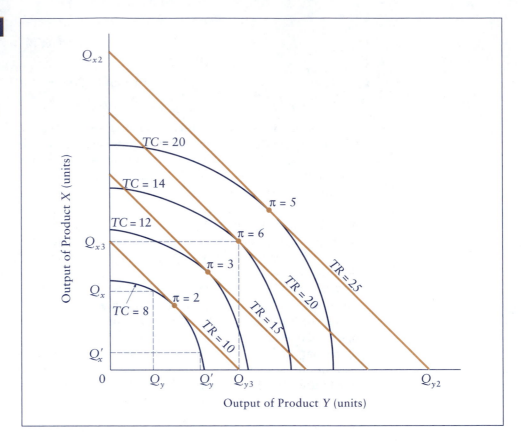

of X and Y along any particular line will yield the same total revenue. The *straight* isorevenue lines in Figure 14B.2 indicate that products X and Y are being sold in *purely competitive markets;* that is, the prices of X and Y do not change as output changes. (If this were not the case, the isorevenue lines would no longer be straight; nevertheless, the general tangency solution for an optimal output combination does not change.) Line $TR = 25$ is constructed such that Q_{y2} times the price of Y (P_y) equals Q_{x2} times the price of X (P_x). The slope of each isorevenue line is equal to $P_y \div P_x$, because the slope of $TR = 25$ equals $Q_{x2} \div Q_{y2}$, and $P_x(Q_{x2}) = P_y(Q_{y2})$; therefore

$$\frac{P_y}{P_x} = \frac{Q_{x2}}{Q_{y2}}$$

A whole family of isorevenue lines exists that is defined by the prices and levels of output for X and Y. The further one moves in a northeast direction, the greater the total revenue associated with any isorevenue line.

The solution for an optimum combination of outputs requires a point of tangency between the isocost and isorevenue curves. This may be illustrated with the $TC = 14$ isocost curve. Under the conditions depicted in Figure 14B.2 Slusser should produce Q_{x3} units of X and Q_{y3} units of Y because total profit, π (the difference between TR and TC), is maximized at that point. To produce any other possible output combination along the $TC = 14$ isocost curve, would result in the same costs (14), but would place the firm on a lower isorevenue curve, thereby reducing profit. Because profits are maximized at the point of tangency ($\pi = 6$), the marginal cost of producing each product must be exactly equal to the marginal revenue each product generates.

The analysis presented here could be expanded considerably by dropping some of the assumptions. For instance, the two-product case could be expanded to a more general n-product case. One could also assume a far greater number of variable factors of production than the one factor (or bundle of factors) implicitly assumed. In addition, the assumption that the prices of input factors are not a function of their use and the assumption that the prices of outputs are independent of the quantity produced could be dropped. Cases such as these may be analyzed with calculus,[31] but in many instances the simplified model presented provides an adequate framework for analysis. Linear programming also has proved to be an extremely useful tool for examining problems of allocating common productive facilities among two or more products to maximize profits.

In conclusion, the decision to add (or delete) products to (from) a firm's product line must consider true (net) marginal revenue and true (net) marginal cost. If a new product is a reasonably close substitute for an existing product, the addition of the new product is likely to cannibalize the sales of the existing product. This sales reduction must be considered in the marginal revenue analysis. In addition, complementarities in demand between two or more products (that is, when a lower price or increased availability of one product stimulates an increase in demand for another) must also be considered in a multiproduct firm's price and output decisions.

Finally, in deciding whether to add, delete, or change the relative output of any one product, the impact of that action on the cost of producing the firm's other outputs must be taken into consideration. Only after true marginal costs and benefits have been accounted for may optimal strategies about the makeup of a firm's product line be adopted.

TRANSFER PRICING

http://

Many articles and papers are available on transfer pricing and multinational firms at the Organization for Economic Cooperation and Development (OECD): http://www.oecd.org/eco/eco/

Associated with the tremendous growth in the size of corporations has been a trend toward decentralized decision making and control within these organizations. Because of the exceedingly complex coordination and communication problems within large multiproduct national or multinational firms, such firms typically are broken up into a group of semiautonomous operating divisions. Each division constitutes a profit center with the responsibility and authority for making operating decisions and an appropriate set of rewards and incentives to motivate profit-maximizing decisions. Because of the complexity of this problem, we limit the analysis below in several ways.

In practice, the external demand functions of two divisions are often interrelated. For example, a degree of dependence presumably exists between the demand functions of the Chevrolet and Pontiac divisions of General Motors. In the analysis of this section, however, it is assumed that the external demand functions of each division are independent.

The production processes of two divisions are also often cost dependent either through technological interdependence or through the effects of output changes on the costs of inputs employed in the production process. An example of the former type of interdependence would be the case of an oil refinery in which the mix of outputs (for example, gasoline, kerosene, heating oil, and lubricants) is limited by the production process. An example of the latter type would be two divisions that are bidding for a raw material (sheet metal) or labor skill in short supply and that are,

[31] Frederick Warren-Boulton, "Vertical Control with Variable Proportions," *Journal of Political Economy,* 1974, pp. 783–802.

as a result, causing the price to rise. In the ensuing analysis, it is assumed that the production processes are cost independent.

A third source of dependence, and the only one considered in this section, occurs whenever one division sells all or part of its output to another division of the same firm. For example, within the Ford Motor Company a multitude of internal transfers of goods and services takes place. The Engine and Foundry Division, Transmission and Chassis Division, Metal Stamping Division, and the Glass Division, among others, transfer products to the Automotive Assembly Division. The Automotive Assembly Division in turn transfers completed cars to the Ford and Lincoln-Mercury Sales and Marketing Divisions.

The price at which each intermediate good or service is transferred from the selling to the buying division affects the revenues of the selling division and the costs of the buying division. Consequently, the price-output decisions and profitability of each division will be affected by the transfer price.

A **transfer price** serves two sometimes competing functions in the decentralized firm. One function is to act as a measure of the *marginal* value of resources used in the division when making the price and output decisions that will maximize profits. The other is to serve as a measure of the *total* value of the resources used in the division when analyzing the performance of the division. It is sometimes possible for these functions to conflict.[32] The emphasis in this section is on determining the correct transfer price to use in making marginal decisions about product price and output of each division.

Transfer Price
The price at which an intermediate good or service is transferred from the selling to the buying division within the same firm.

PRICING OF INTERDEPARTMENTAL SERVICES AT BELL ATLANTIC[33]

Bell Atlantic (now Verizon) has taken the transfer pricing concept and applied it on an experimental basis to the pricing of interdepartmental services, such as information services, business research, medical services, and training and development. Each of 10 client-service departments charges other departments of the company for the services it renders. For example, a manager who uses an in-house speech writer would have to pay for this service out of his or her department's budget. The speech writer's department would then be credited with the amount charged for providing the service. From these revenues, each client-service department is expected to pay all its expenses, including salaries and benefits, rent, office equipment, and electricity. A department that fails to cover its costs could be faced with some difficult choices, such as replacing the manager, reducing its staff, or even possible elimination by giving the work to an outside vendor.

One of the most difficult problems in implementing such a transfer pricing system is determining the costs and market value of a department's services. Most departments at Bell Atlantic ended up pricing their services in line with what outside vendors charged. Some departments billed for their services on an hourly basis, whereas others charged a set amount for each project. To prevent overcharging by the client-service departments, in-house users were allowed to use outside vendors when they could obtain a better price from the vendor.

The benefits from such a pricing system are twofold. First, some client-service departments found that they were overstaffed and were required to reduce the scale

---

[32] See C. Horngren and G. Foster, *Cost Accounting: A Managerial Emphasis,* 10th ed. (Englewood Cliffs, NJ: Prentice Hall, 2000), Chapter 22.

[33] Based on "At Bell Atlantic, Competing Is Learned from the Inside," *Wall Street Journal,* July 12, 1989, p. B1.

of their operations. For example, the communications-services group eliminated 11 positions. Second, users of these services were forced to scale back their requests to more realistic levels if the price quote was too high. Under the old system, service requests were sometimes excessive because the costs were being borne by the department doing the work rather than by the clients. Annual savings with the new system of more than $4 million were reported for four of Bell Atlantic's client-service groups.

In the following analysis, assume that a decentralized firm consists of two separate divisions that form a two-stage process to manufacture and market a single product. The production division manufactures an intermediate product, which is sold internally to the marketing division at the transfer price. The marketing division converts the intermediate product into a final product, which it then sells in an imperfectly competitive (that is, monopolistic) external market.

Given the assumptions of demand and cost independence discussed above, there are three possible cases to consider:

- *No* external market for the intermediate product.
- *Perfectly competitive* external market for the intermediate product.
- *Imperfectly competitive* external market for the intermediate product.

The first two cases are examined in the remainder of this section. The third case of an imperfectly competitive external market can be analyzed using the third-degree price discrimination model discussed in the chapter. It leads to the counterintuitive result that optimal transfer prices may exceed external prices at which the manufacturer will sell to outside buyers. This price discrimination case is not reexamined here.

No External Market for the Intermediate Product

With no external market for the intermediate product, the production division would be unable to dispose of any excess units over and above the amount desired by the marketing division. Likewise, if demand for the final product should exceed the capacity of the production division, the marketing division would be unable to obtain additional units of the intermediate product externally. Therefore, the quantity of the product manufactured by the production division must necessarily be equal to the amount sold by the marketing division.[34] The determination of the profit-maximizing price-output combination and the resulting transfer price are shown in Figure 14B.3. The marginal cost per unit to the firm, MC, of any level of output is the sum of the marginal costs per unit of production, MC_p, and marketing, MC_m. By equating marginal cost MC to external marginal revenue MR_m (Point A), one obtains the firm's profit-maximizing decisions— P_m^* as the optimal price and Q_m^* as the optimal quantity of the final product to be sold by the marketing division in the external market. Therefore, the optimal transfer price P_t^* is set equal to the marginal production cost per unit MC_p at the optimum output level Q_p^* (Point B). This will cause each division, when seeking to maximize its own division profit, to maximize the overall profit of the firm. This result can be demonstrated in the following manner.

---

[34] This analysis assumes that all units produced during the period must be sold during the period; that is, no inventories of the intermediate product can be carried over into the next period.

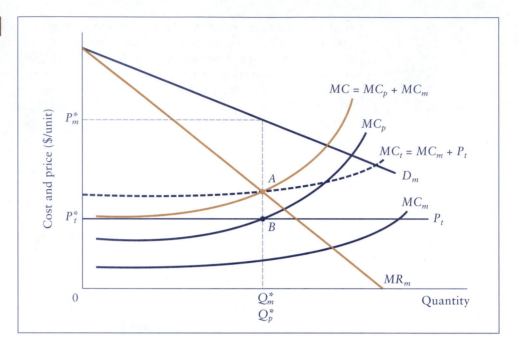

Once the transfer price is established, the production division will face a *horizontal* demand curve (and corresponding marginal revenue curve) at the given transfer price for the intermediate product. The profits of the production division will be maximized at the point where its divisional marginal cost equals divisional marginal revenue—in this case where the P_t line intersects the MC_p curve. This condition yields Q_p^* as the optimum quantity of the intermediate product, which is identical to the optimum quantity of the final product Q_m^* determined previously. Similarly, once the transfer price is established, the marketing division is faced with a marginal cost curve MC_t, which is the sum of the marginal marketing cost per unit MC_m and the given transfer price P_t. The profits of the marketing division will be maximized at the point where its divisional cost is equal to its divisional marginal revenue—in this case, where the MC_t and MR_m curves intersect. This condition yields the same optimal price and output decision (that is, P_m^* and Q_m^*) as was obtained previously in maximizing the overall profits of the firm.

Example

DETERMINING THE OPTIMAL TRANSFER PRICE: PORTLAND ELECTRONICS

The production division (p) of the Portland Electronics Company manufactures a component that it sells internally to the marketing division (m), which promotes and distributes the product through its own domestic retail outlets. Assume that there is no external market for this component (i.e., the production division cannot sell any excess production of the component to outside buyers and the marketing division cannot obtain additional components from outside suppliers). The marketing division's demand function for the component is

$$P_m = 100 - .001Q_m \qquad\qquad [14B.5]$$

where P_m is the selling price (in dollars per unit) and Q_m is the quantity sold (in units). The marketing division's total cost function in dollars (excluding the cost of the component) is

$$C_m = 300,000 + 10Q_m \qquad [14B.6]$$

The production division's total cost function (in dollars) is

$$C_p = 500,000 + 15Q_p + .0005Q_p^2 \qquad [14B.7]$$

where Q_p is the quantity produced and sold.

We are interested in determining the profit-maximizing outputs for the production and marketing divisions and the optimal transfer price for intracompany sales. The marginal cost per unit to the firm, MC, is equal to the sum of the marginal costs of production, MC_p, and marketing, MC_m:

$$MC = MC_p + MC_m \qquad [14B.8]$$

The marginal cost of the production division is equal to the first derivative of C_p (Equation 14B.7):

$$MC_p = \frac{dC_p}{dQ_p}$$
$$= 15 + .0010Q_p \qquad [14B.9]$$

The marginal cost of the marketing division is equal to the first derivative of C_m (Equation 14B.6):

$$MC_m = \frac{dC_m}{dQ}$$
$$= 10 \qquad [14B.10]$$

Substituting Equations 14B.9 and 14B.10 into Equation 14B.8 and recognizing that

$$Q_m = Q_p$$

we obtain

$$MC = 15 + .0010Q_m + 10$$
$$= 25 + .0010Q_m \qquad [14B.11]$$

The marketing division's total revenue function is equal to

$$TR_m = P_m Q_m$$
$$= (100 - .001Q_m)Q_m$$
$$= 100Q_m - .001Q_m^2 \qquad [14B.12]$$

Taking the first derivative of TR_m (Equation 14B.12) gives

$$MR_m = \frac{d(TR_m)}{dQ_m}$$
$$= 100 - .002Q_m \qquad [14B.13]$$

Setting Equation 14B.11 equal to Equation 14B.13 gives the optimal output for the marketing division:

$$MC = MR_m$$
$$25 + .0010Q_m = 100 - .002Q_m$$
$$Q_m^* = 25,000 \text{ units}$$

Because $Q_p = Q_m$, the optimal output for the production division is

$$Q_p^* = 25,000 \text{ units}$$

Therefore the optimal transfer price for intracompany sales of the component is equal to the marginal production cost per unit at the optimal output level of $Q_p^* = 25{,}000$ units, or

$$P_t^* = MC_p$$
$$= 15 + .0010(25{,}000)$$
$$= \$40 \text{ per unit}$$

Thus, to maximize profits, Portland's production division should produce and sell 25,000 units of the component to the marketing division. The marketing division should distribute 25,000 units of the component through its retail outlets. The optimal transfer price for intracompany sales is \$40—the production division's marginal cost per unit at an output of 25,000 units.

Perfectly Competitive External Market for the Intermediate Product

With an external market for the intermediate product, the outputs of the production and marketing divisions are no longer required to be equal. In the following analysis, assume that the external market for the intermediate product is perfectly competitive. Two different situations involving supply and demand for the intermediate product are examined below:

- *Excess internal supply.* The production division has the capacity to produce more of the intermediate product than is desired by the marketing division and sells the excess output externally in the competitive market.
- *Excess internal demand.* The marketing division requires more of the intermediate product than can be supplied internally by the production division and buys additional units externally in the competitive market.

Excess Internal Supply   The derivation of the optimal price-output decisions for the firm is shown in Figure 14B.4. With a perfectly competitive market for the intermediate product, the production division is faced with a horizontal external demand curve D_p for its output at the existing market price P_t. Setting divisional marginal revenue MR_p equal to the divisional marginal cost MC_p (Point C) yields a profit-maximizing output of Q_p^* units of the intermediate product. The marketing division, which must purchase the intermediate product either internally or externally at a price of P_t, will have a marginal cost curve MC_t, which is the sum of the marginal marketing cost per unit MC_m and the given transfer price P_t. Again, equating divisional marginal revenue MR_m to divisional marginal cost MC_t (Point D) shows that profits will be maximized when Q_m^* units of the final product are sold externally at a price of P_m^* per unit. The solution indicates that the production division should produce Q_p^* units of the intermediate product, sell Q_m^* units of its output to the marketing division, and sell the difference, $Q_p^* - Q_m^*$, externally, in the intermediate product market.

A clear-cut transfer price emerges from this analysis. The competitive market price P_t becomes the optimal transfer price (P_t^*) for intracompany sales of the intermediate product. The production division can sell as much output as it wishes externally at this price and therefore would have no incentive to sell internally to the marketing division at a price less than P_t^*.

FIGURE 14B.4

Determination of the
Transfer Price with a
Perfectly Competitive
External Market for the
Intermediate Product—
Excess Internal Supply

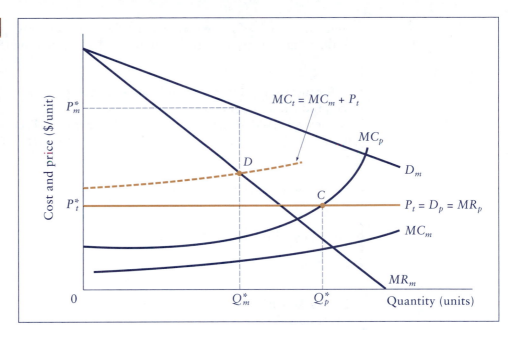

Example

DETERMINING THE OPTIMAL TRANSFER PRICE:
PORTLAND ELECTRONICS (continued)

Consider again the Portland Electronics Company discussed earlier. Suppose that the production division (p) of Portland Electronics Company manufactures a component that it can sell either internally to the marketing division (m), which promotes and distributes the product through its own domestic retail outlets, or externally in a perfectly competitive wholesale market to foreign distributors. The production division can sell the component externally to these distributors at $50 per unit.

The task is to determine the profit-maximizing outputs for the production and marketing divisions and the optimal transfer price for intracompany sales. The production division's optimal output occurs at the point where divisional marginal revenue equals divisional marginal cost. Because the production division can sell as much output as it wishes (externally) at the competitive market price of $50, its marginal revenue is equal to

$$MR_p = 50$$

As we saw earlier, the production division's marginal cost relationship is (from Equation 14B.9)

$$MC_p = 15 + .0010Q_p$$

Setting $MC_p = MR_p$ yields the optimal output for the production division:

$$15 + .0010Q_p = 50$$

$$Q_p^* = 35,000 \text{ units}$$

The marketing division's optimal output occurs where divisional marginal revenue equals divisional marginal cost. Marginal cost for the marketing division (MC_t) is equal to the sum of its own marginal marketing costs (MC_m) plus the cost per unit of the components purchased from the production division (P_t) or

$$MC_t = MC_m + P_t \qquad\qquad \text{[14B.14]}$$

Because the external wholesale market for the component is perfectly competitive, the production division would not be willing to sell components to the marketing division for less than the market price of $50 per unit. Therefore, the optimal transfer price (P_t^*) is the competitive market price of $50 per unit.

$$P_t^* = \$50 \text{ per unit}$$

As was shown earlier, marginal marketing costs (MC_m) were

$$MC_m = 10$$

Hence, by Equation 14B.14, MC_t is given by

$$MC_t = 10 + 50$$
$$= 60$$

The marketing division's marginal revenue function (MR_m) was given earlier as (from Equation 14B.13)

$$MR_m = 100 - .002Q_m$$

Setting $MR_m = MC_t$ yields the optimal output for the marketing division:

$$100 - .002Q_m = 60$$
$$Q_m^* = 20,000 \text{ units}$$

Thus to maximize profits, Portland's production division should produce 35,000 units of the component, sell 20,000 units internally to the marketing division, and sell the remaining 15,000 units (35,000 − 20,000) externally to other (foreign) distributors. The marketing division should distribute 20,000 units of the component through its retail outlets. The optimal transfer price for the intracompany sales is the competitive market price of $50 per unit.

Excess Internal Demand The derivation of the optimal price-output decisions for the firm under excess internal demand is shown in Figure 14B.5. Similar to the excess internal supply situation discussed above, the production division will attempt to maximize its profits by setting divisional marginal revenue MR_p equal to divisional marginal cost MC_p (Point E). This yields an optimal solution of Q_p^* units of the intermediate product. The marketing division, with a marginal cost curve MC_t equal to the sum of the marginal marketing costs per unit MC_m and the given transfer price P_t, will attempt to maximize profits by equating divisional marginal revenue MR_m to divisional marginal cost MC_t (Point F). This yields an optimal solution of Q_m^* units of the final product being sold externally at a price of P_m^* per unit. The solution indicates that the production division should produce and sell its entire output of Q_p^* units of the intermediate product to the marketing division. The marketing division should purchase an additional $Q_m^* - Q_p^*$ units of the intermediate product externally in the intermediate product market.

As in the situation of excess internal supply discussed earlier, the optimal transfer price (P_t^*) for intracompany transfers of the intermediate product is equal to the competitive market price P_t. The marketing division can purchase as much of

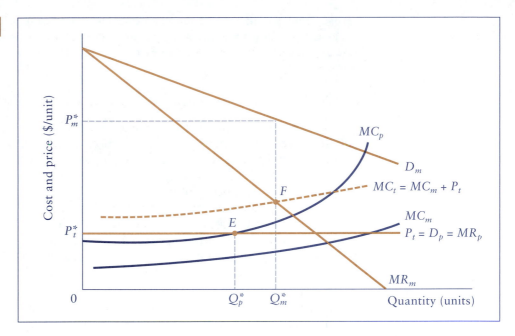

FIGURE 14B.5

Determination of the Transfer Price with a Perfectly Competitive External Market for the Intermediate Products—Excess Internal Demand

the intermediate product as it wishes externally at this price and therefore would be unwilling to make purchases from the production division at a price higher than P_t^*.

International Perspectives

TRANSFER PRICING, TAXES, AND ETHICS[35]

Multinational corporations have a great deal of flexibility in setting transfer prices, because there are often no external market standards for setting these intrafirm prices. In the absence of differential tax rates between the various countries in which a firm does business, the establishment of appropriate transfer prices involves application of microeconomic decision rules and cost accounting principles. However, because large multinational firms operate in several different countries, each with its own system of taxation and its own unique corporate income tax rates and policies, the use of transfer pricing to aggressively manage and reduce tax liabilities is common and profitable. For example, in 1991 the IRS charged Toyota with systematically overcharging its U.S. subsidiary for most of the vehicles and parts sold in the United States. The effect of these actions was to transfer profits that would have been booked (and taxed at high rates) in the United States to Japan, where tax rates are much lower. Toyota denied any wrongdoing but agreed to pay the IRS $1 billion in a settlement of these claims.

Westinghouse Electric booked 27 percent of its 1986 domestic profit in Puerto Rico, where it has very few sales. The corporate tax rate in Puerto Rico is set at 0 percent to stimulate the economy. Yamaha Motor Corporation's U.S. subsidiary paid only $5,272 in taxes in the early 1980s, whereas IRS accountants claim that proper accounting of transfer prices would have resulted in $127 million in taxes.

The issue of setting proper transfer prices is extremely complex. Many differences between company policies and IRS regulations arise because of the complexity of the issue. However, as can be seen above, the IRS has become increasingly aggressive in

---

[35] Based on L. Martz, "The Corporate Shell Game," *Newsweek,* April 15, 1991, pp. 48–49.

prosecuting blatant cases of abuse. Financial managers of multinational firms will have to give this issue greater attention in coming years, if they expect to achieve the goal of maximizing shareholder wealth within the bounds of legal and ethical standards of business practice.

SUMMARY

- *Joint products* are products that are technically interdependent in the production process; that is, a change in the production of one produces a change in the cost or availability of another. When the joint products are produced in *fixed proportions,* the optimal output of the product package (consisting of the individual products) and optimal prices of the individual products are found at the intersection of the total marginal revenue function and the marginal cost function of producing the product package. When joint products are produced in *variable proportions,* the optimal output occurs where the marginal cost of producing each product is equal to the marginal revenue of each product. This occurs at the point of tangency between the isocost and isorevenue curves for the products.

- A firm is often faced with the problem of pricing items that are produced and used internally in the firm. This is the emphasis of *transfer pricing* analysis. When the external market for the intermediate product is perfectly competitive, the firm should use the market-determined price on intracompany sales. In other cases an appropriate profit-maximizing transfer price is a function of the marginal costs and revenues of the respective divisions in the firm.

EXERCISES

1. Explain why you feel that the interdependency terms between each of the following pairs of products would tend to be either positive (complements), negative (substitutes), or zero (independent):

   a. Polaroid: Instant cameras and film
   b. Nabisco: Fleischmann's and Blue Bonnet margarine
   c. Nabisco: Ritz crackers and Oreo cookies
   d. Nabisco: Oreo cookies (regular size) and Mini Oreos
   e. Nabisco: Camel and Winston cigarettes
   f. General Motors: Saturn compact cars and Chevrolet compact cars
   g. General Motors: Buick full-size cars and Chevrolet compact cars

2. A company produces both oil and natural gas from a well in the panhandle of West Texas. If these products are produced from the well in fixed proportions, what would one expect the impact of an increase in the price of oil to be on the rate of gas production?

3. Refer to the Williams Company joint products example (Equations 14B.1–14B.4) discussed in the appendix:

   a. On a graph with quantity on the horizontal axis and price (and cost) on the vertical axis, plot the demand and marginal revenue functions for the two products and the marginal cost function for the product package.
   b. From the graph in Part (a), determine the optimal output and price for each of the two products. Compare the graphical solution with the algebraic solution in the chapter.

4. Referring again to the Williams Company joint products example (Equations 14B.1–14B.4) discussed in the appendix, assume that the marginal cost function (Equation 14B.3) is replaced with the following one:

$$MC = 22 + .5Q$$

Determine the optimal output and selling price for each of the two products.

5. Referring back to the Portland Electronics Company transfer pricing example discussed in the chapter, where there was a competitive external market for the intermediate product, complete the following table (based on the optimal solution):

	Production Division	Marketing Division
Total revenue		
Total cost		
Total profit		

6. Referring again to the Portland Electronics Company transfer pricing example discussed in the chapter, where there was a perfectly competitive external market for the intermediate product, assume that the company can buy (or sell) additional units of the component at $30 per unit. Determine the optimal price and output decisions for the production and marketing divisions and compare them with the solution obtained in the chapter.

7. Consolidated Sugar Company has two divisions: a farming-preprocessing (p) division and a processing-marketing (m) division. The farming-preprocessing division grows sugar cane and crushes it into juice, which it may sell to the processing-marketing division or sell externally in the perfectly competitive open market. The processing-marketing division buys cane juice, either from the farming-preprocessing division or externally in the open market, and then evaporates and purifies it and sells it as processed sugar.

    The processing-marketing division's demand function for processed sugar is

$$P_m = 24 - Q_m$$

where P_m is the price, in dollars per unit, and Q_m is the quantity sold, in units, and its cost function (excluding cane juice) is

$$C_m = 8 + 2Q_m$$

The farming-preprocessing division's total cost function for cane juice is

$$C_p = 10 + 2Q_p + Q_p^2$$

where Q_p is the quantity produced, in units. Assume that one unit of cane juice is converted into one unit of processed sugar. Furthermore, assume that the open market price for cane juice is $14.

    a. What is the profit-maximizing price and output level for the farming-preprocessing division?

    b. What is the profit-maximizing price and output level for the processing-marketing division?

    c. How much of its output (cane juice) should the farming-preprocessing division sell (i) internally to the processing-marketing division and (ii) externally on the open market?

    d. How much of its input (cane juice) should the processing-marketing division buy (i) internally from the farming-preprocessing division and (ii) externally on the open market?

    e. What is the minimum price at which the farming-preprocessing division would be willing to sell cane juice to the processing-marketing division? Explain.

    f. What is the maximum price that the processing-marketing division would be willing to pay to buy cane juice from the farming-preprocessing division? Explain.

    g. To maximize the overall profits of Consolidated Sugar, what price should the company use for intracompany transfers of cane juice from the farming-preprocessing division to the processing-marketing division?

CASE EXERCISE

TRANSFER PRICING

DeSoto Engine, a division of International Motors, produces automobile engines. It sells these engines to the automobile assembly division within the corporation. A dispute has arisen between the managers of the DeSoto division and the assembly division concerning the appropriate transfer price for intracompany sales of engines. The current transfer price of $385 per unit was arrived at by taking the standard cost of the engine ($350) and adding a 10-percent profit margin ($35), based on an estimated volume of 450,000 engines per year. The manager of the DeSoto division argues that the transfer price should be raised because the division's average profit margin on other products is 18 percent. The manager of the assembly division claims that the transfer price should be lowered because an assembly division manager at a competing automobile company indicated that engines cost his division only $325 per unit. The corporation's chief economist has been asked to solve this intracompany pricing problem.

    The economist collected the following demand and cost information. Demand for automobiles is given by the following function:

$$P_m = 10,000 - .01Q_m$$

where P_m is the selling price (in dollars) per automobile and Q_m is the number of vehicles sold. (Assume for simplicity that price is the only variable that affects demand.) The total cost function for the assembly division (*excluding* the cost of the engines) is

$$C_m = 1,150,000,000 + 2500Q_m$$

where C_m is the cost (in dollars). The DeSoto division's total cost function is

$$C_p = 30,000,000 + 275Q_p + .000125Q_p^2$$

where Q_p is the number of engines produced and C_p is the cost (in dollars).

QUESTIONS

Assume that no external market exists for these engines (that is, the DeSoto division cannot sell any excess engines to outside buyers and the assembly division cannot obtain additional engines from outside suppliers).

1. Determine the profit-maximizing output (vehicles) for the assembly division.

2. Determine the profit-maximizing output (engines) for the DeSoto division.

3. Determine the optimal transfer price for intracompany sales of engines.

4. Calculate (a) total revenue, (b) total cost, and (c) total profits for each division at the optimal solution found in Questions 1, 2, and 3.

    The manager of the DeSoto division is dissatisfied with the solution to the transfer-pricing problem. On further investigation, he finds that a *perfectly competitive external market exists for automobile engines,* with many automobile manufacturers and suppliers willing to sell or purchase engines at the going market price. Specifically, a large German automobile company (BW Motors) has offered to purchase all of DeSoto's engine output (up to 700,000 engines per year) at a price of $425 per unit.

5. Determine the profit-maximizing output for the assembly division.

6. Determine the profit-maximizing output for the DeSoto division.

7. Determine the optimal transfer price for intracompany sales of engines.

8. Determine how many engines the DeSoto division should sell (a) internally to the assembly division and (b) externally to BW Motors.

9. Calculate (a) total revenue, (b) total costs, and (c) total profits for each division at the optimal solution found in Questions 5, 6, 7, and 8.

V

Organizational Architecture and Institutional Economics

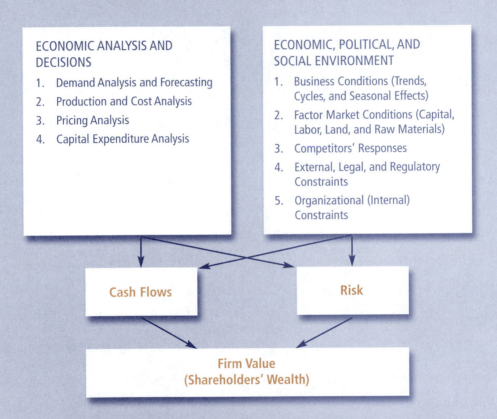

ECONOMIC ANALYSIS AND DECISIONS

1. Demand Analysis and Forecasting
2. Production and Cost Analysis
3. Pricing Analysis
4. Capital Expenditure Analysis

ECONOMIC, POLITICAL, AND SOCIAL ENVIRONMENT

1. Business Conditions (Trends, Cycles, and Seasonal Effects)
2. Factor Market Conditions (Capital, Labor, Land, and Raw Materials)
3. Competitors' Responses
4. External, Legal, and Regulatory Constraints
5. Organizational (Internal) Constraints

Cash Flows

Risk

Firm Value (Shareholders' Wealth)

Part V addresses the new institutional economics of designing an auction, providing incentives to managers, eliciting true cost revelation in a partnership, or vertically integrating to redraw the boundaries of the firm. Chapter 15 discusses the theory of business contracting, the principal-agent problem and corporate governance, vertical integration, and more generally the choice of organizational form. Chapter 16 explores optimal mechanism design in servic-

ing queues, in auction design, and in incentive-compatible revelation mechanisms for joint ventures and partnerships. Appendix 16A compares public sector to private market approaches for the control of externalities. Chapter 17 then addresses the economic regulation of business, including antitrust, patenting, and licensing, as well as regulatory quotas and approvals.

15

Contracting, Governance, and Organizational Form

CHAPTER PREVIEW This chapter explores the coordination and control problems faced by every business organization and the institutional mechanisms designed to solve these problems in a least-cost manner. The most important organizational decision is the determination of the boundary of the firm—i.e., the breadth of the span of hierarchical control. In dealing with external suppliers, outsource partners, internal divisions, authorized distributors, franchisees, and licensees, every firm must decide where the internal organization stops and where market transactions take over. Contracts between business organizations provide an *ex ante* framework defining these relationships, but all contracts are purposefully incomplete. Consequently, every firm must address the potential for postcontractual opportunistic behavior by business partners and then design governance mechanisms to reduce these contractual hazards.

Should Dell make or buy subassembly components for their PCs? Should Kodak license its digital camera technology for Internet distribution by AOL, or should it invest in a strategic partnership with AOL? Instead, should Kodak vertically integrate by buying an Internet service provider as Microsoft did in buying WebTV? Should Red Hat adopt open source architecture allowing its licensees to duplicate, modify, and redistribute its Linux-based software without charge?

We address these questions initially from the perspective of the coordination game between manufacturers and distributors using the game-theoretic techniques of Chapter 13. Vertical requirements contracts are introduced in the moral hazard framework of purposefully incomplete contracts. The principal-agent problem is explained and then resolved with incentive contracting and governance mechanisms. Thereafter, we develop extensively the choice of organizational form between relational contracting, joint ventures, alliances, and vertical integration with an application to the hosiery industry.

MANAGERIAL CHALLENGE

Controlling the Vertical: Ultimate TV[1]

Enormous business opportunities loom on the horizon for companies operating at the intersection of Web-based Internet services and the TV. Personal computers have penetrated into 70 percent of American households, but televisions are present in literally every household, with a measured penetration now reaching 98 percent. Over the next five to ten years, 220 million analog television sets may be replaced by $150 billion worth of television-enabled PCs and digital televisions. The lure for customers will be Internet-based interactive services and much higher digital picture quality.

Microsoft has invested heavily in digital entertainment programming for these "smart televisions" and television-enabled PCs. Their know-how and trade secret investments are largely nonredeployable and include the operating system and user interface backbone for everything from interactive museum tours to distance learning virtual courses to Web page construction. However, all these investments may be focused on the wrong distribution channel. WebTV Networks Inc. has perfected a system that allows consumers to surf the Internet through their low-end TVs.

The core of WebTV's (now MSN TV) product is a patented signal compression chip that crams the capabilities of a TV tuner, cable modem, and high-speed video modem into one $50 unit. MSN TV's technology has freed content providers of the bandwidth limitations that prevent the Net from transmitting high-speed Web images and video. It may also have freed consumers of the need to upgrade to digital TV. Most households are able to connect the device to their analog TV set and begin surfing the Internet within 15 minutes.

If twenty-first-century households will be able to cruise the Net and download video with inexpensive network PCs or old televisions, Microsoft's huge investment in digital entertainment will decline exponentially in value. Digital TV manufacturers quickly established partnerships with WebTV to assess the danger and perhaps take an equity stake. Consequently, in late 1997, Microsoft decided to vertically integrate and bought WebTV for $425 million. Microsoft intended to combine its one-way dependent and reliant digital entertainment assets with WebTV's technology to produce digital consumer products for cell phones, pagers, and handheld PCs. In addition, because cable companies appear most likely to trigger the adoption of "Ultimate TVs" through their leasing of set-top control boxes to residential customers, Microsoft sought to become a cable TV industry standard by investing over $10 billion in AT&T, Telewest, Comcast, and three European cable firms. The ensuing equity transfers of ownership upstream to the set-top software provider were the inception of Microsoft's vertical integration into interactive TV.

---

[1]Based on "Why Microsoft Is Glued to the Tube," *BusinessWeek*, September 22, 1997, p. 96; "Microsoft to Buy WebTV for $425 Million," *Wall Street Journal*, May 7, 1997, p. A8; "Microsoft's Blank Screen," *The Economist*, September 16, 2000, p. 74; and "Smart TV Gets Even Smarter," *BusinessWeek*, April 16, 2001, pp. 132–133.

INTRODUCTION

Organizational form and institutional arrangements play an extensive role in eliciting efficient behavior. Incentive contracts can motivate manager-agents to pursue the interests of owner-principals. Incentive-compatible revelation mechanisms can elicit true cost information to increase the market value of joint ventures between partners like IBM, Siemens, and Toshiba. On another front, allowing the freewheeling of electricity from one public utility to another or privatizing Conrail, British Telecom, Japan Air Lines, Telefonos de Mexico, and Societe Generale can improve the incentives to maximize capitalized value in these formerly bloated public monopolies. However, the role of institutions in motivating efficient behavior goes far beyond the design of incentive contracts and recent deregulation and privatization initiatives.

Institutional choices also involve the form of organization that companies adopt. For example, some firms like Volvo-GM Trucks, IBM, and Goodyear Tires develop franchise dealerships rather than attempt to contract over selling procedures and warranty service with the independent retailers preferred by manufacturers like Apple and Michelin. Other firms adopt stand-alone subsidiaries as independent divisions but centralize the production of common components (e.g., General Motors' Chevrolet, Cadillac, and Buick divisions all buy from Fisher Body Co.). Perhaps the most important application of these concepts occurs in deciding the boundary of the firm—i.e., whether it should vertically integrate throughout the supply chain like Exxon or outsource like Dell.

THE ROLE OF CONTRACTING IN COOPERATIVE GAMES

In Chapter 13, we saw that once a manufacturer commits to updating a product, distributors may find that their best-reply response is to continue extensive selling efforts and postsale services. If so, the required coordination of manufacturer and distributor actions can be achieved by a self-enforcing reliance relationship. At times, however, the payoffs are such that coordination requires something more than the voluntary, self-enforcing mechanisms that secure equilibrium in noncooperative games. Consider the decisions in Table 15.1. These are the same actions and payoffs with one exception. The distributor payoff in the northwest cell has been changed from break-even to $2,500 per truck. That is, the distributor is now better off discontinuing some of the selling effort associated with presale services. Sales volume declines, so the manufacturer is clearly worse off. But the distributor who economizes on selling costs may actually do better than with full effort in the southwest cell. Knowing that the distributor has a dominant strategy to defect and discontinue some selling effort, the manufacturer will decide not to cooperatively advertise either. The payoffs to the distributor now increase still further from $2,500 to $3,000, and the manufacturer earns $2,000.

However, this outcome is not value-maximizing. An advertised full-service product in the southwest cell generates profits summed across both players of $7,000—i.e., $2,000 more per truck than the dominant strategy equilibrium {Discontinue, Do not advertise}. To elicit full effort in either a one-shot or repeated version of Table 15.1 requires some sharing of this $2,000 cooperative surplus with the distributor. That is, rather than suspending shipments and changing distributors frequently as one after another pursues the dominant "Discontinue" strategy, the manufacturer may enter into a cooperative game of credible promises and sidepayments—i.e., a relational contract. For example, a franchise contract offering 40 percent of the $7,000 summed profits to the distributor (or penalizing the distributor $501 for non-

Table 15.1   Simultaneous Manufacturer/Distributor II

		Truck Manufacturer	
		Co-op advertising	**Do not advertise**
Retail Distributor	**Discontinue some selling effort**	$2,500 ⟍ 0	$3,000 ⟍ $2,000
	Continue all selling effort	$2,000 ⟍ $5,000	0 ⟍ 0

performance) can elicit a continuation of full selling effort. Since $0.4 \times \$7,000 = \$2,800$ exceeds the $2,500 profit from discontinuing selling effort, the manufacturer who offers such a contract can expect to realize both an acceptance from the chosen distributors and a ($2,800, $4,200) profit outcome.

Contracts are binding, third-party enforceable agreements designed to facilitate deferred exchange. A *promisee* undertakes some costly action (perhaps paying a consideration) in exchange for and relying upon the *promisor's* pledge of a subsequent performance. Here, recalling the sequential version of the above game from Chapter 13, the manufacturer updates the product, relying upon the retail distributor to subsequently perform presale selling efforts. In Figure 15.1 the manufacturer then decides about manufacturer-sponsored advertising that requires a coordinated ad investment by the retail distributor. With such delays in transaction comes the possibility of opportunistic behavior and an attendant increase in risk. Because the search costs, information costs, and negotiation costs of full contingent claims contracting is prohibitively expensive, all contracts will be purposefully incomplete. With incomplete contracts, distributors can appear to promise one thing and then deliver another. For example, the distributor may find that after the manufacturer commits to a product update, the discontinuance of some selling effort results in higher payoffs ($120,000) than result from continuing the full expected selling effort ($100,000). The retail distributor therefore selects "Discontinue" (as signified by the starred payoff in the top row of Figure 15.1). Knowing this, the manufacturer will "Advertise" to prevent a collapse of sales (the double starred payoff). When the distributor can be induced to make a credible commitment to continued selling efforts, the summed profits ($180,000 + $300,000) can be even higher. Vertical requirements contracts are one method of establishing such credibility.

Vertical Requirements Contracts

In the sequential game in Figure 15.1, the subgame perfect equilibrium strategy is {Update, Discontinue, Advertise} at the extreme top of the diagram. This odd combination of actions dominates all other sequential patterns and meets the conditions of best-reply response for each player at each proper subgame node in the decision tree. In particular, the manufacturer controls the endgame, preferring to Advertise when the distributor Discontinues and to Not Advertise when the distributor Continues. The payoffs for these choices are boxed in Figure 15.1. The unboxed payoffs are no longer

Figure 15.1   Vertical Requirements Contracting Is Required to Maximize Value

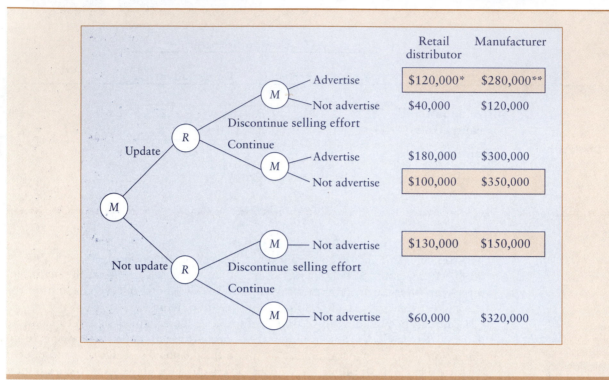

feasible payoff possibilities because they conflict with best-reply responses of the manufacturer in the endgame. Choosing from the feasible set of best-reply responses in the endgame, the retail distributor prefers the shaded $120,000 payoff from discontinuing services for an updated and advertised product, and the shaded $130,000 payoff from discontinuing services for a not-updated unadvertised product in the lower half of the decision tree. Therefore, moving by backward induction one more step (to the first node), the manufacturer will choose between the shaded outcomes consistent with best-reply responses of the distributor. Therefore, the manufacturer can be predicted to Update the product (i.e., the double-starred outcome).

The subgame perfect equilibrium strategy {Update, Discontinue, Advertise} generates total profits of $120,000 + $280,000 = $400,000. As in Simultaneous Manufacturer/Distributor II in Table 15.1, this self-enforcing strategic equilibrium is *not* value-maximizing. Since two alternatives generate more profit—i.e., {Update, Continue, Not Advertise} generates $450,000 total profits and {Update, Continue, Advertise} generates $480,000 total profits—one might expect some organizational form to emerge to realize this additional value. One alternative is vertical integration. By buying the distributor firm (for something slightly more than $120,000), the manufacturer could impose the value-maximizing actions and resolve coordination and control with internal monitoring and incentive systems within the consolidated firm.

Vertical Requirements Contract
A third-party enforceable agreement between stages of production in a product's value chain.

Alternatively, a **vertical requirements contract** that offers the distributor $120,000 plus half of the $80,000 cooperative surplus (i.e., $480,000 − $400,000) to provide full services if the manufacturer updates and advertises the product would increase the manufacturer's payoff from $280,000 to $320,000. Assuming alternative distributors were available, this contract would be accepted by the present distributor, and both players would be $40,000 better off than in the subgame perfect equilibrium {Update, Discontinue, Advertise}, which made no use of contracting. Again, as in our earlier discussion of contracting to maximize value in simultaneous Manufacturer/Distributor II, the contract here is likely to be structured around an offer of a percentage of the profits. By embracing ambiguity regarding the final product value, the manufacturer and distributor could agree to share this risk. A vertical requirements contract that offered to grant 33 percent of the summed profits ($160,000 of $480,000) to an authorized distributor in exchange for full selling effort and after-sale service of an updated product that was advertised by the manufacturer would maximize the value of this business opportunity.

Again, credible commitments are the key. Since postcontractual opportunism is available to the manufacturer who may promise to advertise but then not do so, the retail distributor may require escrow accounts for cooperative advertising. Alternatively, the parties could stipulate a $51,000 damage penalty should the manufacturer breach his duty to advertise after the distributor expended full effort in attempting to sell an upgraded product. In that event, referring again to Figure 15.1, the manufacturer would have $300,000 from advertising and $350,000 − $51,000 = $299,000 from not advertising. And since the retail distributor would then be better off continuing selling effort ($100,000 + $51,000) rather than discontinuing selling effort ($120,000), we could anticipate a value-maximizing {Update, Continue Effort, Advertise} outcome with a ($180,000 and $300,000) summed profit payoff.

Negotiating position may in the end reallocate some of the cooperative surplus back to the manufacturer. That is, for example, a profit-sharing franchise contract with the $51,000 stipulated penalty clause for manufacturer breach on advertising might start from the anticipated ($180,000 and $300,000) payoff and ask the distributor to pay a $50,000 franchise fee. On net, the distributor would receive updated products, $130,000, plus a stipulated damages agreement regarding advertising. The manufacturer would receive continued full selling effort by the distributor, $300,000, plus the $50,000 franchise fee.

The Function of Commercial Contracts

Expectation Damages
A remedy for breach of contract designed to elicit efficient precaution and efficient reliance on promises.

A contract provides a hostage beyond the mere reputational asset that prospective distributors might offer. In exchange for an agreed consideration, the promisee receives a credible promise. The promisor's commitment to perform is credible because the legal rules of contract interpretation and enforcement (in the courts) provide assurance that any expectations which the parties clearly spell out (i.e., stipulate) will be met. Although courts seldom order recalcitrant contractors to perform specifically as was promised, they are quick to award **expectation damages** that leave the parties no worse off than was anticipated under the contract. Standard contract remedies therefore provide incentives for efficient precaution by the promisor and for no more than efficient reliance on the promise by the promisee.

Example

CRANKSHAFT DELIVERY DELAY CAUSES PLANT CLOSING

The role of contract remedies as incentives is well illustrated by the famous case of *Hadley* v. *Baxendale, Court of Exchequer 1854, 9 Exch 341.* A mill owner ordered a replacement for a broken crankshaft from a machine shop that agreed to a standard repair and return of the mill owner's equipment. When return delivery was delayed because of poor road conditions, the mill owner sued for lost profits resulting from his extended plant closing. The court rejected this argument because the machine shop had taken the customary shipping precautions and would have been expected to do more (perhaps by arranging for an expedited delivery by express coach) only if the mill owner had stipulated the extraordinary damages that would arise from further delay. In other words, the machine shop was entitled to expect that the mill owner would not rely excessively on the promise of a three-day repair unless informed to the contrary. If the mill owner had time-sensitive business scheduled immediately thereafter and no temporary substitute crankshaft available, it was his responsibility to disclose those potentially destructive private facts, thereby eliciting a different level of precaution. Otherwise, the mill owner's reliance was excessive and inefficient, not deserving of the reinforcement that would have resulted from a court award of lost profit.[2]

This stipulation procedure works exceptionally well for fully anticipated events. Moreover, the rules of contract law summarized in the bottom half of Table 15.2 reduce the transaction costs of renegotiation and settlement when unanticipated events do occur. For example, the market price that can be realized on a truck can change dramatically between the time period of the reliance investment in a manufacturing facility to produce the updated truck and its subsequent promotion and sale.

Suppose the market price collapses because a competitor's new and improved substitute product is introduced. If the truck manufacturer and distributor agreed to a fixed-price contract six months earlier, the manufacturer will get the agreed-upon revenue because the distributor took that risk. On the other hand, if changes in the regulatory environment make it illegal to sell that model of truck, the frustration of purpose doctrine of the Uniform Commercial Code (UCC) will excuse the distributor from its contractual obligation to pay. Third, what if these two parties entered into a forward sales contract for diesel fuel to be used as a promotion to enhance the distributor's selling effort, and subsequently the price of diesel fuel tripled? The default rule of the UCC for forward sales contracts is non-excusal. If the manufacturer sold the distributor 100,000 gallons of diesel at $1.33 per gallon in June 2000 for delivery in December, and the December price is $4, the manufacturer took *that* risk. A pleading by the manufacturer that it would be ruinous financially to deliver as promised will have no effect; the manufacturer must either deliver the 100,000 gallons in December or face a swift and certain court judgement of ($4 − $1.33) × 100,000 = $267,000 awarded to the distributor. Every commercial contract must therefore stipulate the allocation of such risks or operate under these default rules that are intended to increase predictability and thereby reduce the transaction costs of business contracting.

Spot Market Transaction
An instantaneous one-time-only exchange of typically standardized goods between anonymous buyers and sellers.

In contrast to these deferred exchanges of a consideration for a promise, **spot market transactions** pose relatively few information and incentive problems. For example, buying electricity off the grid at quarter until the hour for delivery on the hour avoids pricing risk and the possibility of opportunistic behavior. Complete and certain information plus competitive entry and exit imply efficient markets. That is, all relevant information will be impounded immediately into equilibrium market prices that are fully informative in the sense that the best forecast of future prices is the

---

[2] An excellent extended discussion of the role of contract remedies as incentives for efficient reliance and efficient precaution against nonperformance appears in R. Cooter and T. Ulen, *Law and Economics*, 2nd ed. (Reading, MA: Addison-Wesley, 1997), pp. 214–232.

Table 15.2   A Spectrum of Alternative Contract Environments for Manufacturers and Distributors

	Spot Market Transactions	Vertical Requirements Contract	Relational Contract
Timing	Instantaneous, one-time-only	Deferred exchange; promise of future performance for immediate consideration	Repeat business
Players	Anonymous buyers/sellers	Contract partners	Well-known dealers/agents
Enforcement	Barter or consideration for a consideration	Enforced by impartial third parties	Self-enforcing; best-reply responses
Information	Perfect (complete and certain) information + competition leads to efficient markets	Purposefully incomplete contracts embrace ambiguity; governance mechanisms	Reputation; signaling/ bluffing games

Contracts facilitate deferred exchange by resolving problems arising from uncertain performance outcomes (the incomplete contract problem), unobservable effort in assuring performance (the moral hazard problem), and recontracting hazards (the hold-up problem) by

Basic Functions of Contract	Illustrative Contract Rule
1. Providing incentives for efficient precaution and efficient reliance	1. Award of expectation damages
2. Encouraging the development and exchange of asymmetric information	2. Required disclosure of destructive facts
3. Providing risk allocation mechanisms	3. Frustration of purpose doctrine
4. Reducing transaction costs	4. Nonexcusal in forward sales contracts

current price. However, these one-time-only transactions between anonymous buyers and sellers engaged in immediate delivery of standardized goods at fixed prices fail to solve several issues that arise in most contracting.

Table 15.2 summarizes these differences between spot market transactions, reputation-based relationships, and vertical requirements contracts between manufacturers and distributors. Contracts facilitate deferred exchange. Whenever one firm wishes to elicit a promise of future performance from another firm in exchange for an immediate consideration, the rules of contract law, as embodied primarily in the common law but also codified in statutes including the UCC, provide predictable outcomes at low transaction costs.

Many societies have a long and deep tradition of enforcing contract promises. What is less well understood is that promisors are seldom required to perform specifically as promised. Rather, the courts almost always impose a liability for expectation damages on parties that breach their contract promises. Expectation damages are often more efficient than obligating a promisor to specific performance because circumstances change, and cash flow expectations at the time of contract are often less onerous than being obligated to perform actions that may prove still more costly.

In some cases, contract promises are excused altogether. These excusals fall into two categories: exceedingly rare *formation excusals* and more frequent *performance excusals*. One formation excuse is that of mutual mistake. If Sam agrees to sell Harry what both parties think is an antique Mercedes-Benz, but the car turns out to be a Buick, the court will set aside the agreement to purchase. Similarly, if I sell you a damaged Learjet without disclosing the damage, you, the buyer, can ask to be excused. On the other hand, an astute buyer of a damaged jet who recognizes the potential for enhancing the value through inexpensive repair can profit from his or her asymmetric information without concern about whether the courts might later set aside the sales contract and restore the plane to its original owner. Requiring the disclosure of destructive facts without abating the incentive to develop asymmetric information that would enhance value (constructive facts) is a delicate balance which these contract rules of formation excusal seek to achieve.

In a typical performance excuse, contingent events may frustrate the purpose of a contract. If the city of New York hires retired policemen to provide additional security for a presidential visit to lower Manhattan, and if the president cancels such that the added security personnel are never scheduled, the city will be excused from its obligation to pay. In this case, the allocation of cancellation risk might have been stipulated by the parties but if not, the UCC default rule of frustration of purpose will set aside the contract. Both parties understand this in advance and plan accordingly, while saving the expense of negotiating the contingent outcomes.

Example

ENFORCEMENT AND EXCUSAL OF CONTRACT PROMISES: THE EXTRAORDINARY CASE OF 9/11[3]

Perhaps most extraordinary are contracts that are excused because an act of God or of war prevents performance. For example, on the morning of 9/11/2001, the bond trading house Cantor Fitzgerald on the 101st floor of the North Tower of the World Trade Center had contract promises to make markets in (i.e, set the price and execute trades in) U.S. Treasury, DuPont, and Eurodollar bonds. Over the next several hours, 658 of the firm's 960 employees died in the terrorist attack on the World Trade Center. Prices were not negotiated, some orders were lost, and some trades went unexecuted. Sellers lost money when the value of their assets plunged in the aftermath of the tragedy. Yet, few wondered whether the courts would hold Cantor Fitzgerald responsible for the expectation damages.

In a related example, Bank of New York was obligated to clear and provide cash settlements for about 84,000 government security transactions on 9/11. The client firms like Merrill Lynch & Co., Salomon Smith Barney, and J. P. Morgan Chase & Co. had invested large sums in real-time hard-wired data feeds and sophisticated telecommunications connections to Bank of New York. Yet, three of the bank's buildings in lower Manhattan were either damaged or forced to close because of the terrorist attack. At one point, Bank of New York owed Citigroup and J. P. Morgan Chase & Co. $30 million each on settlements the bank could not authorize for final clearance. Under other circumstances, each day said settlement was delayed could have

---

[3] Based in part on "Little Changes at Bank of New York," *Wall Street Journal,* March 8, 2002, p. C11.

resulted in a claim against the Bank of New York for expectation damages of approximately $(1/365) \times 2\% \times \$30$ million $= \$2,000$ per contract per day. With razor-slim margins on these clearing and settlement operations, such damages would have exhausted all profit. Yet, again, under these circumstances, an act of war had prevented performance of the contract, and the Bank of New York was entitled to a performance excuse.

These rules of the contract law evolve out of the complex interplay between sophisticated disputants in the courts; they are what Ludwig von Mises called "a result of human action rather than an act of human design." Whether or not contracts are enforced (and on what terms) determines the rate of economic growth across nations and the likelihood of foreign direct investment in developing and less developed countries.[4] In a social contract sense, the common law of contract provides a pivotal feature of the competition between nations and represents a crucial part of Western democracy's efficient institutional arrangements.

Incomplete Information, Incomplete Contracting, and Postcontractual Opportunism

Incomplete Information
Uncertain knowledge of payoffs, choices, etc.

Practically all such exchanges, whether for products, financial claims, or labor services, are conducted under conditions of **incomplete information**. On the one hand, decision makers often face uncertainty (incomplete information) as to the effect of random disturbances on the outcome of their actions. This uncertainty typically leads to insurance markets. On the other hand, decision makers are sometimes uncertain as to the payoffs or even types of choices they face. This type of incomplete information typically leads to intentionally incomplete contracting. Let's see why.

Potential losses from repetitive risks such as workplace injuries and weather hazards are often insured for a small periodic cash flow. Risk spreading is the primary purpose of insurance markets, which pool such casualty risks and thereby reduce the loss exposure to any individual business or household. Randomly occurring injuries at a consumer electronics assembly plant seldom coincide with injuries in a firm's delivery trucks or severe weather disruptions at a firm's mill. As a result, modest insurance premiums can cover the cost of the anticipated claims involving such diversifiable risk events. In this sense, uncertainty and incomplete information are routine business problems handled in routine ways by insurance contracting. Even oil pipelines, nuclear power plants, and skyscraper developers on earthquake faults can typically get insurance.

Full Contingent Claims Contract
An agreement about all possible future events.

However, incomplete information as to remote risks—i.e., what possible outcomes might occur—may prevent the parties at risk from writing insurance contracts that apportion the gains and losses under any and all contingencies. Consider the **full contingent claims contract** you and your surgeon would need to write before an organ transplant operation. Or alternatively, consider the full contingent claims contract two pharmaceutical companies would need before one licensed the rights to produce a pregnancy-related drug to the other. To develop all the accurate information required for a full contingent claims contract involving multigenerational cumulative health hazards is simply prohibitively expensive. Consequently, few transplant patients and few business partners attempt to negotiate full contingent claims contracts. The fact that information costs can be prohibitively large leads to the important insight that contracts are often incomplete by design.

---

[4] Douglas Cecil North, *The Rise of the Western World: A New Economic History* (Cambridge: Cambridge University Press, 1999).

Postcontractual Opportunistic Behavior Actions that take advantage of another party's vulnerabilities.

One immediate consequence of incomplete contracts is that after signing, one can expect to observe **postcontractual opportunistic behavior** not specifically prohibited by the restrictive covenants contained in the incomplete contract. Surgical patients may go fishing in swampy bacteria-infested water before their incisions fully heal. Employees who receive on-the-job training (OJT) may moonlight with their newly honed skills. Managers may reconfigure assets following a labor contract concession in ways their employees did not anticipate. Baseball players may attempt a hold out at the time of contract renewals just before a World Series. Knowing this, surgeons must defend against more injury suits, companies provide less OJT, workers agree to fewer wage concessions, and owners develop more farm team players than they otherwise would. So, the incompleteness of contracts results in inefficient behavior that is the inescapable consequence of costly and therefore incomplete information. To reduce these inefficiencies, companies adopt **governance mechanisms** to help resolve postcontractual disputes. Examples of corporate governance mechanisms include monitoring by independent directors, rank order tournaments for promotion, and mandatory arbitration agreements. In the next two sections, we explore the complementary roles of governance mechanisms and pay-for-performance incentive systems for managers.

Governance Mechanisms Processes to detect, resolve, and reduce postcontractual opportunism.

CORPORATE GOVERNANCE AND THE PROBLEM OF MORAL HAZARD

Whether manufacturers and distributors will decide to employ spot market transactions, relational contracting, fixed profit-share franchise contracts, or vertical integration depends on the relative transaction costs of coordination and control in the various contractual settings. In professing this transactions cost approach, Oliver Williamson has emphasized that contracts pose the *ex ante* framework but that **governance structures** provide the *ex post* implementation required to maximize value:

Governance Structure A mechanism that poses an alternative to incentives or direct monitoring for eliciting contractually-expected behavior.

> Transaction cost economics works out of an economizing perspective in which organization is featured and farsighted but incomplete contracting is projected. The parties to commercial contracts are thus held to be perceptive about the nature of the contractual relations of which they are a part, including an awareness of potential contractual hazards. However, because complex contracts are unavoidably incomplete—it being impossible or prohibitively costly to make provision for all possible contingencies *ex ante*—much of the relevant contractual action is borne by the *ex post* structures of governance.[5]

Hence a vertical requirements franchise contract between the manufacturer and distributor in Figure 15.1 will be only the beginning of their agreement. In addition, the firms will need to resolve two remaining coordination and control issues: (1) the inherent unobservability of selling effort on the part of the distributor, and (2) the enhanced effectiveness of advertising if the distributor shares its superior on-the-spot information about current trends in the marketplace. The information-sharing objective can be achieved through cooperative advertising allowances rebated back to the distributor out of the franchise fees.

Unobservable effort in fulfilling contract promises is a more difficult but standard business contracting problem—i.e., a "moral hazard" in all contractual agree-

---

[5] Oliver Williamson, "Economics and Organization: A Primer," *California Management Review*, Winter 1996, p. 136. See also Williamson's *The Mechanisms of Governance*, New York: Oxford University Press, 1996.

http://
To read about moral hazard issues in the news, access the following Internet site: http://radio.weblogs.com/0113343/categories/moralHazard/

Moral Hazard Problem
A problem of postcontractual opportunism that arises from unverifiable or unobservable contract performance.

ments. After securing terms to their liking, contract partners must be wary of the potential for post-contractual opportunistic behavior—i.e., shirking on the agreement in inconspicuous and hard-to-detect but potentially ruinous ways. This contractual issue is sometimes referred to as the problem of hidden action (or inaction) to distinguish it from the adverse selection (lemons market) problem of hidden asymmetric information. Nobel Prize winner Ronald Coase has emphasized that introducing creative and ingenious incentives into contracts can help resolve these moral hazard problems and induce self-enforcement of promises. For example, as discussed in the next section, the problem of providing incentives for unobservable managerial work effort can be at least partially solved with performance-based profit-sharing bonuses. Nevertheless, governance mechanisms continue to play an important role.

Consider the commercial lender's incentive contracting and **moral hazard problem** with eliciting unobservable borrower effort in selecting safe working capital projects. A known reliable borrower may approach a lender with a randomly occurring liquidity crisis that necessitates an extension of its bank line of credit.[6] The lender then offers terms for the loan renewal—i.e., an interest rate, principal amount, collateral requirements, and loan term. The situation is depicted in Figure 15.2. If the borrower decides to accept, a line of credit extension is granted. Then a random process intervenes presenting one of several uncertain business opportunities to the borrower. As in earlier chapters, we signify the role of uncertainty at a node in the decision tree with a large N for a choice by Nature. The possible business opportunities are a spectrum from the relatively safe investments in inventory during periods of backorders and stockouts to an extension of the company's receivables policy allowing customers to pay within 90 days rather than pay cash at the point of purchase. Because product sales may be very sensitive to credit terms such as "90 days same as cash," the latter use of working capital has a higher expected return but is very risky in that uncollected customer accounts may skyrocket.

The moral hazard problem for the lender is then motivated. The commercial bank wants the borrower to exercise great care, high effort, and good judgment in selecting projects on which to expend its newly granted working capital from the line of credit extension. However, banks must move carefully in setting the loan terms to elicit this largely hidden action. Remember, the bank does not know in advance what business opportunity the borrower will be facing; this is not a case of project financing where the commercial banker can take part in assessing the company's capital budgeting proposals and directly monitor its ROI. Instead, the bank makes the funds available and must then elicit subsequent borrower effort in appropriately screening projects that are randomly presented for possible investment.

What loan terms should the lender offer? Large loans with long repayment terms are most desired by the borrower to gain the most financial flexibility in the face of its current liquidity crisis. Having more funds and more time to straighten out a business plan that has gone awry is preferable from the point of view of the borrower. But do these terms elicit more or less effort in screening projects so as to prevent or contain a loss? Clearly, a high interest rate forces reliable borrowers to

---

[6] In other circumstances, lenders may face an adverse selection problem of detecting whether unknown borrowers are from a fraudulent or reliable subpopulation of loan applicants, and the offered terms of the loan will then affect the acceptance and refusals that determine the proportion of the loan portfolio from each group. Moderate interest rates and high collateral are intended in that situation to allow borrowers to signal their reliable intent to repay. In the situation examined here, we abstract from the hidden information problem of adverse selection (by assuming that the borrowers are known customers of the lending institution) to focus attention on the hidden action problem of moral hazard in commercial lending.

Figure 15.2   The Problem of Moral Hazard in Line-of-Credit Lending

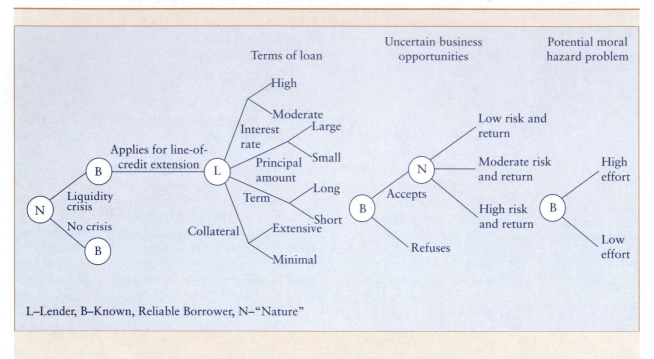

L–Lender, B–Known, Reliable Borrower, N–"Nature"

seek out the riskier working capital projects in order to secure higher expected returns and therefore be in a position to repay the loan. Moderate rates with extensive collateral pledges of security would seem to move the reliable borrower in the direction of more effort to find safer projects.

However, the most important aspect of the lender-borrower relationship may not involve these terms in the loan contract at all. The most effective way to manage the risks of default and nonpayment may be for the borrower to establish a frequent reassessment and renewal governance mechanism whereby the borrower must submit financial ratios on a regular basis to secure ongoing access to the extended line of credit. The more frequent, more convenient, and more audited these financial reports, the better the governance mechanism will work. In essence, a real-time governance mechanism whereby the bank becomes almost a project financing partner for every major use of its funds is the ideal way to elicit the desired care, effort, and judgment from the borrower. In the end, a project-by-project financing approval process is excluded by the definition of the problem, but the closer a governance mechanism can come to this result, the less likely a default will be.

The Need for Governance Mechanisms to Prevent Holdup

The hiring of managerial talent involves the three standard problems of all business contracts: (1) the allocation of residual risk problem because all contracts are purposefully incomplete, (2) the moral hazard problem because some actions with a bearing on contract performance (call it "effort") are always inherently unobservable, and (3) the holdup problem of postcontractual opportunism.

WHAT WENT RIGHT   WHAT WENT WRONG

Moral Hazard and Holdup at Enron and Worldcom[7]

Misaccounting for short-term business expenses as long-term capital investments required a $3.8-billion restatement of lower operating profits at WorldCom in fiscal year 2000. Enron executives depleted pension reserve accounts while heralding the attractiveness of employee stock option plans for retirement planning. Business news in 2002 made it abundantly clear that governance mechanisms are needed, but still the question remains, "Why, exactly?" Why don't debt contracts of bond holders, personal loan contracts that senior executives use to relocate their often lavish households, and performance-based incentive contracts aligning owner and managerial interests prevent these abuses? Is it just that too many gratuitous payments

have been extracted from compensation committees, too many executive loans have been forgiven, and too many deferred stock options have been reset to lower strike prices when stock prices fell? That is, are the incentives in all this incentive contracting just misaligned? The answer is decisively "No." There is a more basic, more fundamental problem. Incomplete contracts invite opportunistic behavior, requiring vigorous governing mechanisms.

[7] Based on "Taken for a Ride," *The Economist,* July 13, 2002, p. 64, and "WorldCom Aide Conceded Flaws," *Wall Street Journal,* June 16, 2002, p. A3.

There is the moral hazard problem of unobservable effort (possible shirking and devotion of one's creative ingenuity to entrepreneurial endeavors unrelated to one's job). There is the postcontractual opportunism problem of holdup (extracting large sums from the compensation subcommittee of the board of directors when managers have acquired unique skills and knowledge and the company has made specific investments not redeployable to others). And of course, finally, company performance whether measured by cash flows, earnings, or even sales is subject to random disturbances. Since it proves prohibitively expensive to contract in advance what the pay will be for every possible remote occurrence, one seldom if ever gets full contingent claims contracts. Instead, managerial contracts are purposefully incomplete; we misblame managers at times for poor performance and fail to acknowledge managerial merit at times for good performance.

"Incentive contracting" with a minimum salary guarantee and a performance-based bonus (like a stock option or restricted stock grant) is an efficient solution to the moral hazard and residual risk problems. But incentive contracting alone is insufficient because of postcontractual opportunism that may be small (e.g., numerous inconspicuous, but potentially ruinous, violations of duty) or large (e.g., postcontractual holdup and outright fraud). Governance mechanisms are the key to resolving this remaining problem of postcontractual opportunistic behavior. Table 15.3 provides a list of these interdependent implementation mechanisms of corporate governance.

The Principal-Agent Model

Many types of owner-principals hire manager-agents to stand in and conduct their business affairs in exchange for a claim on some of the residual income. Parent companies set up principal-agent relationships with subsidiaries. Manufacturer principals

Table 15.3   Implementation Mechanisms of Corporate Governance

- Internal monitoring by independent board of director subcommittees
- Internal/external monitoring by large creditors
- Internal/external monitoring by owners of large blocks of stock
- Auditing and variance analysis
- Internal benchmarking
- Corporate culture of ethical duties
- High employee morale supportive of whistle blowers

employ retail distributor and advertising agents. And most importantly, equity owners hire executives with managerial incentive contracts. The owners' objective in such principal-agent relationships is to preserve value-maximizing incentives while compensating risk-averse managers for a risky income stream and forgone alternative employment opportunities.

The Efficiency of Alternative Hiring Arrangements

Managerial hiring contracts may take on several pure or hybrid forms, including straight salary, wage rate, or profit sharing. In straight salary contracts, the manager and firm agree on a total compensation package and specific conditions of employment. In other contexts, such as consulting, the managerial consultant may receive an hourly wage rate equal to the best alternative employment opportunity in the competitive labor market for his or her type of consulting services. In Figure 15.3, the managerial consultant is hired for, say, 50 hours per week at wage rate W_a. D_l is the firm's input demand, which is the marginal revenue product of these labor services—namely, the marginal output of additional hours times the marginal revenue from selling the resulting additional output. Because each firm is atomistic in the labor market for these management consulting services, S_l is the perfectly elastic supply facing any given employer at the going market wage. Beyond 50 hours, the declining D_l no longer exceeds the incremental input cost along S_l.

Managers also may secure employment under a pure profit-sharing contract. Like pure commission-based salespeople or manufacturer's trade representatives, the manager may accept a percentage (say 40 percent) of the receipts directly attributable to his or her efforts in lieu of wage or salary income. Think of the percentage finder's fee sometimes offered for cost-saving suggestions in big corporations or the federal government. Again in Figure 15.3, we can represent this third alternative hiring arrangement as the ray AB, wherein the manager receives 40 percent of the owner's willingness to pay for each hour of management services. Initially, this profit share will exceed the wage rate alternative. For example, during the first 22 hours of work, the profit-sharing contract will overcompensate by area ADJ (shaded area O). Thereafter the profit share falls below the manager's market wage rate per hour.

If 40 percent proves to be an equilibrium profit share, the overcompensation (shaded area O) will just equal the undercompensation for the last 28 hours of work (shaded area DCF labeled U). This leaves both the owners and the manager indif-

Figure 15.3   Alternative Managerial Labor Contracts

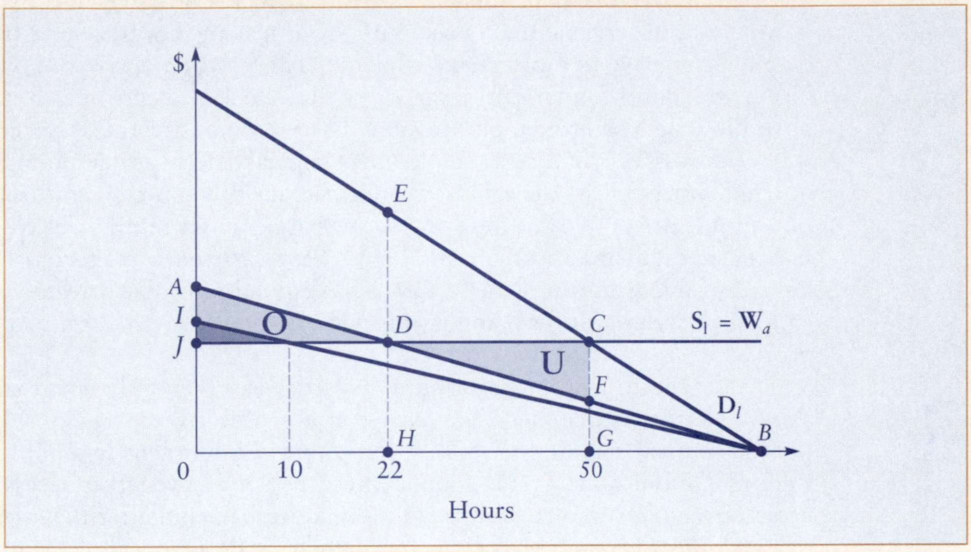

ferent between this hiring arrangement and the alternative 50-hour-per-week wage rate contract at W_a. If the profit share were reduced to, say, 35 percent (represented by the ray IB), the dark-shaded amount of overcompensation for the first 10 hours would fail to offset the massive undercompensation for hours 10 to 50. The manager would then reject the profit-sharing contract in favor of the wage rate offer. By raising the profit share back to 40 percent, the firm appears able to restore the attractiveness of each contract, at least for certain types of workers. In reality, as we shall now see, the situation in hiring managerial talent is often rather different.

Work Effort, Creative Ingenuity, and the Moral Hazard Problem in Managerial Contracting

Pure profit-sharing contracts contain the seeds of their own destruction. Suppose several individuals are involved in generating pharmaceutical sales, and the input that the profit sharer contributes to team production is largely unobservable. No time card can successfully monitor the input, perhaps because a measure of work effort rather than work hours is really what is required. This is an instance of truly "hidden actions" by an employee. The rational employee then considers his or her alternatives. As long as the profit-sharing compensation exceeds the alternative wage rate, he or she dedicates unobservable work effort to this job. Beyond 22 hours of work effort, however, the employee can earn more by working for someone else at the alternative wage rate W_a. Therefore, the disloyal (but rational) trade representative underworks the territory; he or she moonlights. This predictable response is another aspect of the *moral hazard problem*. Only a *moral* sense of duty to one's employer prevents this problem from becoming a real *hazard* to the business.

Predicting such behavior, the employer may decide to withdraw the offer of a pure profit-sharing contract. Let's see why. If the territory is underworked by 28 hours, the employer saves profit-sharing payments equal to area $DFGH$ in Figure 15.3, but loses output valued at $ECGH$ and therefore is out the net value [$ECGH - DFGH$ − the overpayment $ADJ = EDC$] relative to a wage contract that just paid piece rates for 50 hours of work at an implicit wage rate of W_a per hour. The fact that work effort is largely unobservable makes the pure profit-sharing contract unattractive to the employer relative to a piece-rate contract. This is not always so. For example, in hiring attendants for parking garages, the time clock and customer complaints (e.g., horn blowing and broken parking gate barriers) monitor the required input quite well. A dismissal policy in the employment contract making time-on-task a condition of employment elicits the required input. Similar time-on-task constraints and output quotas are employed in hiring sharecroppers and retail sales clerks. In these instances, the firms and their employees have evolved ways to resolve the moral hazard problem. Again, Ronald Coase has emphasized that private voluntary bargaining between principals and agents will often find ways to contract around such problems.[8]

The debilitating problem of moral hazard arises then only when an action such as work effort is unobservable except at a prohibitive cost. Consider again the pharmaceutical sales representative for whom appointment logbooks and random follow-up monitoring simply cannot detect the persuasive effort necessary to secure orders from physician customers. One could trail around after the sales representative and interview each physician after the sales calls were completed to try to detect the ingenuity and perseverance the sales rep displayed, but quite obviously, this monitoring practice would be prohibitively expensive. Instead, in the face of truly "hidden actions," the pharmaceutical company is more likely to jettison the pure profit-sharing contract in favor of some other performance-based incentive contract involving benchmarking. During a period of **benchmarking**, the employer reassigns previously low productivity sales territories to above-average trade representatives to see whether their effort can alter the success rate per sales call. If so, the employer concludes that lack of effort by prior sales representatives was responsible for the low sales. After several such benchmarkings, the employer is able to identify those sales representatives to be kept and those to be dismissed. Importantly, the "keepers" are then allowed to retain all the productive accounts they have developed.

For managerial jobs, however, the moral hazard problem is significantly harder to resolve. The input senior management contributes to team production is not time on task at the desk, but rather what we might call "creative ingenuity"—i.e., creative ingenuity in formulating and solving problems that may not even have arisen as yet. Managers are paid to think, and think hard about proactive problem solving, not to shuffle papers. The difficulty is that there is very little way to detect when creative ingenuity is being applied to the employer's business, rather than another business for whom the manager may be mentally moonlighting. Of course, eventually the difference will show up in performance, but over how long a period and how big a difference? These are tough questions to answer satisfactorily to stockholders after a senior manager has shirked his or her duties and has finally been let go.

More problematically, the shirking manager may never be let go, and the hardworking manager may never be rewarded. If random disturbances affect the company's performance, it is difficult even after the fact to separate unobservable shirking from negative random disturbances. How, then, are owners to know when to blame

Benchmarking
A comparison of performance in similar jobs, firms, plants, divisions, etc.

---

[8] This implication of the Coase Theorem is addressed at length in Appendix 16A. See also J. Farrell, "Information and the Coase Theorem," *Journal of Economic Perspectives* (Fall 1987), pp. 113–129.

senior managers for downturns in company performance and when to give them credit for upturns? One mechanism often employed to analyze these variances is the **company audit**. Managers are required to report on the sources and uses of funds in accordance with generally accepted accounting principles (GAAP). Independent auditors can then attempt to verify the managers' explanations for the period-to-period variances by sampling company records.[9] Despite dedicated efforts and substantial auditing fees, separating the effects of management decisions from random disturbances in company performance remains an elusive goal. That is, the moral hazard problem is much harder to solve when combined with the performance uncertainty most firms face.

Company Audit
A governance mechanism for separating random disturbances from variation in unobservable effort.

The Principal-Agent Problem

In isolation, neither hidden effort (unobservability) nor performance uncertainty pose any special difficulty for owner-principals hiring manager-agents. The moral hazard resulting from the unobservability of a manager's input is, by itself, resolvable by assigning the manager lagged residual income claims (e.g., deferred stock options or restricted stock). Settling up *ex post* with a manager, after all the effects of his or her effort and ingenuity have had time to influence performance, creates just the performance-based incentives that are required.

Example

INDEXED STOCK OPTIONS AT ADOBE SYSTEMS, DELL, AND CISCO[10]

To align managerial incentives with equity owner interests, most companies regularly award deferred stock options to their managers. These performance-based bonuses entitle the holder to purchase company stock at a slight discount to its current value. If the firm's performance subsequently improves, capitalized value rises and both shareholders and the managers stand to gain. To exercise their options, managers often must wait three to five years, but they sometimes realize gains of 50 to 80 percent or more. By 2000, CEO compensation in Fortune 500 companies averaged $13.1 million, fully 78 percent of which involved options-based compensation or for superior performance.

To acquire the stock for these deferred compensation programs, some companies dilute equity by issuing new shares, while other companies repurchase shares on the open market. To reduce the cost of these "buybacks," especially in a rising market, some companies like Adobe Systems index the exercise price for their deferred options to the average stock price of their industry. When all the related companies do well, the value of the option rises, but so does the exercise price. As a result, the managers do not exercise their options at that juncture and instead are motivated to outperform their peers in related companies in both good times and bad.

Another advantage of indexed options is that managers are not penalized for the unavoidable economic malaise that follows a disaster like 9/11. Some companies reset strike prices of executive options to lower levels in a period of stock market downturns. Because of the enormous power wielded by CEOs and the resulting potential for opportunistic "holdups" of the compensation committees of corporations, it is far better simply to index the executives' stock options. Between October 1999 and

---

[9] This audit mechanism is explored at greater length at the end of the chapter in the first Case Exercise.

[10] Based on "Stock Options That Don't Reward Laggards," *Wall Street Journal,* March 30, 1999, p. A26; "Corporate America Faces Declining Value of Options," *Wall Street Journal,* October 16, 2000, p. A1; and "The Gravy Train Just Got Derailed," *Business Week,* November 19, 2001, p. 118.

June 2000, managers at Cisco found their stock price performance compared to Microsoft, Compaq, and Intel, all of which declined substantially over this period. Cisco Systems share prices, for example, fell by only 27 percent, while Intel plunged 44 percent; Cisco managers should be rewarded a bit for reducing the losses.

Similarly, performance uncertainty taken alone creates a risk-allocation problem that may be easily resolved with insurance. Managers are somewhat less able to diversify than owners because of the specific human capital the former often invests in a long-term relationship with his or her corporate employer. This usually results in risk-averse owners and risk-averse managers structuring some sort of risk-sharing agreement to accomplish internally the manager's desire for at least partial insurance. A guaranteed baseline salary combined with a performance-based bonus is just such a risk-sharing agreement.

Example

P&G PAYS AD EXECUTIVES BASED ON PERFORMANCE

Procter and Gamble places over $3 billion per year in advertising through Saatchi & Saatchi, Leo Burnett, and other ad agencies. Traditionally, agencies earned flat-rate fees assessed as 15 percent of the ad dollars expended for the client. In the 1990s, Ford, Colgate-Palmolive, and P&G broke out of this flat-rate system and began paying a baseline fixed fee plus a performance bonus. Now, account executives at the agencies earn a fixed salary if their creative communications are less than compelling and P&G sales stay flat. On the other hand, a hugely successful ad campaign can earn multimillion dollar bonuses if P&G's sales growth can be attributed to the advertising. Both the clients, the ad agency owners, and the account execs now share in the risks of consumer whimsy, but a base salary provides a safety net should random misfortune occur.

Principal-Agent Problem
An incentives conflict in delegating decision-making authority.

The real difficulty for principal-agent contracting arises when both input unobservability and performance uncertainty are present simultaneously. The coexistence of these problems constitutes the so-called **principal-agent problem** most firms face. Settling up *ex post facto* with management teams then no longer creates the desired incentives. Some managers get unlucky and receive blame they did not deserve, and others get lucky and receive credit they did not earn. Many companies often attempt to address the problem of managerial moonlighting by benchmarking one manager against another (say, in comparable plants or geographic divisions). They hope that the effects of business cycle factors and random time-series disturbances will be highly correlated across plants and divisions, and that the manager's effort and creative ingenuity will therefore correspond with the plant or division's differential performance. Unfortunately, they are usually wrong. As a result, Japanese companies rely on intense loyalty-building exercises, peer pressure, and lifetime employment contracts to reduce mental moonlighting and other forms of shirking.

The principal-agent problem can be formalized as an optimization problem subject to dual constraints. The principal chooses a profit-sharing rate and a manager's salary guarantee to maximize the expected utility of the risk-averse owner-principals' profit where profit depends on the manager-agent's effort, on the cost of the mana-

Incentive Compatibility Constraint
An assurance of incentive alignment.

Participation Constraint
An assurance of ongoing involvement.

gerial incentives contract, and on random disturbances. An **incentive compatibility constraint** then aligns the effort chosen by the manager in response to the share and salary offer with that effort which maximizes the expected utility of the owner-principals. That is, an incentive-compatible profit share and salary elicit the managerial effort and creative ingenuity required to maximize the owner's value. Third and finally, the **participation constraint** ensures that the manager will reject his or her next best offer of alternative employment (e.g., at a known certain wage rate). In the next section, we illustrate the meaning of each of these three elements with a linear optimal incentives contract, which can solve the principal-agent problem. However, do not be misled; an optimal managerial incentives contract is easier to describe than to attain.[11] See the Case Exercise at the end of this chapter.

Screening and Sorting Managerial Talent with Optimal Incentives Contracts

Asymmetric information arises in all hiring decisions, but often plays an especially prominent role in managerial hiring decisions. Job applicants know all the information, but potential employers have access only to the information that applicants select for their resumés. Thus, among perhaps nineteen resumé facts that the personnel department might like to know, the applicant discloses only fourteen. Let's see how linear share contracts can be used to sort managerial talent based on one of these undisclosed characteristics—namely, a manager's risk aversion.

Suppose a large bank has two openings for which it desires managers of very different risk aversion. One position is the assistant vice president for commercial construction loans in a city with overbuilt office developments and, consequently, very high vacancy rates. The other position is an assistant vice president to manage the venture capital loan portfolio, to interact with owners of new start-up businesses, and to represent the bank at the entrepreneurship club of the city. As you might suspect, the bank has two rather different people in mind as ideal candidates for these openings. In the commercial construction area, the bank seeks an instinctively cautious and safety-conscious manager who will take every opportunity to reduce the very large default risk already present in this portion of the bank's business. Both jobs are simply listed as assistant vice president positions; no further details are given.

Two managers with the requisite training and experience apply for the bank positions. Their resumés are very similar. However, unbeknownst to the bank, one drives an old Porsche, not insured against collision damage, and has skydiving as an undisclosed former hobby. Instead of skydiving, this individual (let's call him Dashing) now prefers bungee jumping, which he understandably decides would be inappropriate to list as a hobby on an application for a bank job. The other individual (you guessed it, Smooth) drives a dealer-serviced Land Rover on which she carries the maximum auto insurance coverage. Despite never leaving town, Smooth keeps the Rover in four-wheel drive at all times to secure the extra traction. Once while attending a formal cocktail party with a few close friends, Smooth revealed that she spent her Christmas bonus on "more insurance, of course." Thinking none of this is of any real significance to the bank, she too omits the information from the job application.

---

[11] Even the solution we describe is limited to separable functions in effort and money income. The general principal-agent problem with risk-averse owners and managers has multiple solutions and requires *nonlinear* incentive contracts relating salary and profit share to company performance. See Jean Tirole, *The Theory of Industrial Organization* (Cambridge, MA: MIT Press, 1988), pp. 35–54, and David Kreps, *A Course in Microeconomic Theory* (Princeton, NJ: Princeton University Press, 1990), Chapter 16.

Linear Incentives Contract
A linear combination of salary and profit sharing intended to align incentives.

The bank's problem is to sort these two types of individuals, both of whom are well qualified, into the jobs appropriate for their very different risk aversions. In Figure 15.4, we display the guaranteed base salary and profit-sharing rate, the two components of a **linear incentives contract**. On the horizontal axis are various percentages that represent what additions to *or subtractions from* one's pay occur as a result of the profit-sharing agreement. A greater share rate initially elicits more effort and creative ingenuity and results in greater expected profit contribution from the manager's activities. Eventually, at still higher share rates the profit contribution actually declines. The two hill-shaped loci of points in Figure 15.4 represent expected profit-sharing payouts that would allow the firm to just break even on its incentive payments to the two managers. The lower expected profit hill corresponds to the commercial construction loans job, and the higher hill corresponds to the venture capital loans job.

Let's suppose that the company has expected sales of $100 million and a net cash flow from sales of 12 percent. Hence, expected profits available for distribution to owners and managers run $12 million. The bank first elicits responses to two tentative contract offers for their assistant vice president jobs. Contract A offers $48,000 salary plus or minus 0.1 percent of the net cash flow or $12,000, which implies a $36,000 to $60,000 possible range of income outcomes. Contract B offers $96,000 salary plus or minus 0.2 percent, or a $72,000 to $120,000 range. Contracts A and B are not equally attractive. One dominates the other in that minimum outcomes under Contract B exceed the maximum outcomes under Contract A. Because risk increases only modestly from 0.1 percent to 0.2 percent, both prospective employees are likely to select B, and therefore, contract B is said to result in a **pooling equilibrium**. Such an outcome is illustrated in Figure 15.4, where the indifference curves for both Smooth (I_S) and Dashing (I_D) indicate that Contract B would be preferred by both applicants.

Pooling Equilibrium
A decision setting that elicits indistinguishable behavior, etc.

To elicit a separation of the two applicants in accordance with their risk aversion necessitates withdrawing Contract B and instead introducing a more significant risk-return trade-off. We begin by indicating on Figure 15.4 the indifference curve for the more risk-averse applicant, Smooth (I_S), that establishes a line of demarcation between contracts to the northwest, which are more preferred than A, and those to the southeast, which are less preferred. To induce a revelation of the risk-aversion differences between Smooth and Dashing, the bank then offers a contract pair such as A and C. Contract C imposes a much larger 0.4 percent profit share and offers only $55,000 expected base salary, just $7,000 above Contract A. Smooth finds C much less preferred than the original Contract A and immediately says so. In contrast, less risk-averse (I_D) Dashing is so close to being risk neutral (i.e., with almost flat indifference curves between expected salary and profit share), that Dashing may well prefer Contract C. This **separating equilibrium** in which Smooth reveals her stronger risk aversion by rejecting C in favor of A, whereas Dashing does just the reverse, attains several of the employer's objectives. First, the linear profit-sharing contract has sorted Dashing as the manager to head up the venture capital personal banking group and Smooth as the manager for the commercial construction group. In addition, these profit-sharing contracts may be incentive-compatible contracts in that they elicit appropriate effort and creative ingenuity from both managers while maximizing the owner's value.

Separating Equilibrium
A decision setting that elicits distinguishable behavior.

However, one aspect of an optimal incentives contract remains unaddressed. The participation constraint has not yet been satisfied. An alternative employer can offer Contract D, which attracts Smooth with both more expected salary and lower profit risk while retaining the separating properties of the (A,C) contract pair. As long as

Figure 15.4   Sorting Managers with Linear Share Contracts

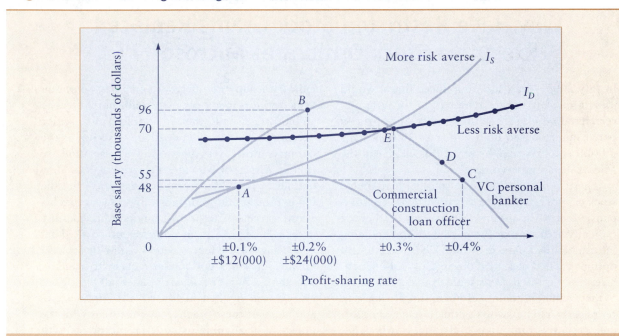

such improvements in both risk and return are possible, Smooth will continue to resign and move. Only with contract pair (*A*, *E*) will both the incentive compatibility and participation constraints be satisfied; Dashing selects Contract *E* while Smooth selects Contract *A*, and both remain in the bank's employ. In addition to resolving the sorting of managerial talent, if the incentives contract induces the appropriate effort from both managers and prevents their being bid away to alternative employment opportunities, this linear incentives contract constitutes a solution to the principal-agent problem in managerial contracting.

Contract Renewals and the Holdup Problem

Having used multiple incentive contracts and a separating equilibrium to solve the twin problems of (1) moral hazard associated with unobservable managerial work effort and (2) adverse selection associated with hidden, asymmetric information about managerial risk preferences, the stockholders face one final problem (a holdup problem) in their principal-agent relationships. Senior corporate officers often have specific company knowledge and experience that makes their institutional memory at least somewhat irreplaceable. Consequently, when it comes time to renew their contracts, senior managers often engage in postcontractual opportunism. Evidence of such holdups is rampant: massive executive "loans" are often forgiven, golden parachutes that will insure the manager's security even if removed in a hostile takeover are often negotiated, and option strike prices are often reset to lower levels in down markets. All these events suggest again that strong corporate governance is needed. Considerable effort to retain experienced senior managers is clearly value maximizing, but the compensation subcommittee of the board must be an independent body prepared to monitor, benchmark, and whistle-blow on these contract renewals if

WHAT WENT RIGHT   WHAT WENT WRONG

Why Have Restricted Stock Grants Replaced Executive Stock Options at Microsoft?[12]

In July 2003, Microsoft announced that it would join numerous other companies in granting restricted stock rather than stock options as a performance-based bonus to over 10,000 of its 30,000 employees. Why make this change in the Microsoft incentive contracts?

There seem to be several reasons. First, restricted stock cannot be sold if an executive leaves the company. Once stock options vest, in contrast, they are typically sold, and in the heyday of the booming information economy in the late 1990s, Microsoft's options created literally thousands of multimillionaires among Microsoft's senior ranks. Too many of these valuable human resources simply choose to retire early and move on to other pursuits; one former executive took up professional bowling. So, restricted stock is expected to enhance the retention of pivotal employees relative to granting options.

A second reason for preferring restricted stock is that boards of directors find it difficult to keep senior managers from extracting from compensation subcommittees option features that work against optimal incentive contracting. For example, few option exercise prices are indexed relative to the industry group or strategic competitors. So option value rewards mediocrity when all share prices in an industry rise together. In addition, most senior executive options are "reloaded." As soon as the option contracts vest (in two to five years) and are exercised, senior managers negotiate that new options be issued with new exercise prices but the old expiration date (of typically ten years). This allows executives to profit from induced volatility in their share prices; why not take out a corked bat and swing for the fences with a high-risk project? Finally, few stock option contracts restrict in any way the executive's ability to "unwind" his or her risk exposure by hedging the risks the options create. None of these practices is consistent with the objective of aligning managerial incentives with stockholder interests.

---

[12] "Microsoft Ushers Out Era of Options," *Wall Street Journal,* July 9, 2003, p. A1; Lucian Bebchuk et al., "Managerial Power and Rent Extraction in the Design of Executive Compensation," 69 *University of Chicago Law Review,* 751, Summer 2002; and B. Hall and K. Murphy, "The Trouble with Stock Options," *Journal of Economic Perspectives,* Summer 2003.

necessary. Table 15.3 listed this function of the board of directors as one among many mechanisms of effective corporate governance.

CHOICE OF EFFICIENT ORGANIZATIONAL FORM

http://

Find more on organizational architecture at http://www.ctiarch.com

Non-specific Investment
A fully redeployable asset.

Ultimately, the choice of organizational form—e.g., spot market transactions, relational contracting, franchise profit sharing, or vertical integration—depends upon what best suits the governance needs of the assets involved. Assets can be specific investments with little or no value in second-best use, like remote plants, or **non-specific investments** that are fully redeployable, like corporate jet aircraft. In addition, some assets are dependent on unique complementary investments (e.g., specially-designed computer hardware and closed-architecture software), while others are not dependent (e.g., a coal- or gas-fired power plant). One classic example of these asset-characteristic dichotomies is the hot-rolled steel-making process, which requires a blast furnace, converter, reduction furnace, and rolling mill. Because achieving the high temperatures of the molten steel intermediate products requires substantial energy, thermal economies of scope require locating these plants beside one another to avoid the reheating expense. However, the organization form question is not whether the operations will be physically integrated and in adjacent locations, but rather whether they will be jointly or separately owned and managed by companies like Bethlehem and U.S. Steel.

At one end of the spectrum, spot market recontracting is efficient for fully redeployable durable assets not dependent upon other complementary assets. Rental cars provide a good illustration of such assets that may be allocated through spot markets with no loss of efficiency, as shown in the top left-hand corner of Table 15.4. The limiting feature of this organizational form, however, is the potential for "holdup" inherent in the frequent renewal of spot market contracts. Should one party have nonredeployable assets (e.g., a steel mill's blast furnace or a major league sports franchise and stadium), spot market recontracting provides too many opportunities for metallurgical engineers or players with mobile skills and marketable talent to appropriate the surplus value in any business relationship. Should all parties have nonredeployable assets as in the hot rolled steel-making process, they all wish to avoid this holdup hazard.

Reliant assets are nonredeployable durable assets sold in thin markets for less than their value in first-best use. These assets are highly specific to their current use because of substantial unrecoverable sunk cost investments either in acquisition, distribution, or promotion. Specialized equipment in remote locations is the most common reliant asset. Where reliant assets are dependent on unique complements in order to achieve any substantial value added, one has the maximum potential for holdup in spot market recontracting. These dependency relations may be either one way or bilateral. Manufacturers with independent distributors are a good example of a bilateral dependent relationship involving reliant assets. Each party in a Volvo GM Heavy Truck Corporation manufacturer/distributor relationship is equally dependent on the other. In such cases, independent dealers often gravitate toward requirements contracts with a fixed profit share, as shown in the bottom right-hand corner of Table 15.4.

Reliant Assets
At least partially nonredeployable durable assets.

Table 15.4   Efficient Organizational Form Depends on Asset Characteristics

	Fully Redeployable Durable Assets	Nonredeployable Reliant Assets
Not Dependent on Unique Complements	Spot market recontracting	Long-term supply contracts + risk management
One-Way Dependent Assets	Relational contracts (alliances)	Vertical integration
Bilateral Dependent Assets	Relational contracts (joint ventures)	Fixed profit-sharing contracts

Example

http://

See a summary of the
*Continental T.V., Inc., et al.
v. GTE Sylvania Inc.* case at
http://www.ripon.edu/
Faculty/bowenj/antitrust/
cotvvsyl.htm

SCHWINN AND SYLVANIA DEALERS OFFERED EXCLUSIVE TERRITORIES[13]

The Schwinn and Sylvania companies sold their bicycles and TVs through authorized dealers who were prohibited from reselling to unauthorized bike shops and electronics stores. Although the dealers could carry other product lines, the resale restriction allowed dealers an exclusive territory. The U.S. Justice Department saw this vertical territorial restriction as anticompetitive, not as a transaction cost-reducing contractual alternative to the governance mechanisms that would otherwise be necessary to protect Schwinn and Sylvania's brand name capital. However, in *Continental T.V., Inc., et al. v. GTE Sylvania Inc., 433 U.S. 36 (1977)*, the Supreme Court disagreed. In this case the court explicitly recognized that brand capital is a specialized, nonredeployable asset that would be compromised if third-party dealers were allowed to sell the Sylvania product with unauthorized marketing plans. Exclusive territories therefore became subject to a rule of reason analysis whereby manufacturers could restrict resale if the territorial restriction was unrelated to preventing price discounting, but instead addressed other aspects of the presale selling effort and postsale services required to market the product successfully. Sylvania's fixed profit-sharing contracts with exclusive territories were seen as an efficient organizational form.

Relational Contracts
Promissory agreements of coordinated performance among owners of highly interdependent assets.

When assets are dependent on unique complements but not reliant because of their substantial redeployability, the parties often adopt long-term performance-based **relational contracts**. Redeployable corporate jets and pilots provide a good illustration. Pilots need not own the planes nor secure fixed profit-share contracts to operate the planes. Instead, as indicated in Table 15.4, the organizational form of a jet charter company is normally one of long-term relational contracts with standby pilots who report on short notice for piecemeal assignments. This alliance works well, and both the pilots and plane owners understand that the longevity and reliability of the relationship enhances value relative to spot market recontracting. To take a related example, Genentech's biotechnology is fully redeployable but one-way dependent on marketing behemoth partners like Pfizer or GlaxoSmithKline. As a result, in 1996, Genentech entered into 10 marketing partnerships, 20 licensing agreements, and numerous research alliances with larger drugmakers.

Example

YAHOO! AND MCI LAUNCH ALLIANCE FOR INTERNET ONLINE SERVICE

When Yahoo! built a widely-used Internet search engine, it clearly required a phone company to complement the website in providing on-line search services. However, just as clearly, Yahoo! was redeployable to more than one telecommunications provider (MCI, Sprint, AT&T). Consequently, although Yahoo! was dependent on telecom complements, there was little contractual hazard of *ex post* holdup. Since Yahoo! was one-way dependent but not reliant upon MCI, and MCI was neither dependent nor reliant on Yahoo!, a relational contract to establish an alliance between Yahoo! and MCI was the efficient organizational form. Another example of a relational contract between one-way dependent but not reliant assets is provided by the Kodak–AOL alliance to distribute digital photography online. AOL is fully redeployable to many other uses than providing online delivery of digital prints from film

---

[13] See S. Dutta, J. Heide, and M. Bergen, "Vertical Territorial Restrictions and Public Policy," *Journal of Marketing*, 63 (October 1999), pp. 121–134.

submitted to one of Kodak's 30,000 retail developing locations. Kodak believes, however, that it will soon be one-way dependent on an online partner as customers increasingly view, store, and share photos—and order reprints—over the Internet.

In contrast, consider the relational contract between a PC assembler and a chip supplier. This illustrates a bilateral dependency since without specially designed Motorola computer chips, Apple PCs have little value, and without Apple PCs, these Motorola chips have little value. Yet, each manufacturer makes reliance investments that are specific to the other partner's design decisions. Hence, as indicated in Table 15.4, a joint venture is the efficient organizational form.[14] Chapter 16 addresses incentive-compatible revelation mechanisms for joint ventures.

International Perspectives

ECONOMIES OF SCALE AND INTERNATIONAL JOINT VENTURES IN CHIP MAKING[15]

Approximately one dozen large electronics companies in the United States, Europe, and Japan were once involved in producing memory chips. Up-front costs for each item were staggering. For example, the cost of developing the 64-megabit memory chip design and production technology was estimated to range from $600 million to $1 billion. Once developed, memory chips then required investment of an additional $600 million to $750 million in a plant that produced up to 10 million chips a month.

Because of the massive scale economies that are available, many of the semiconductor companies involved in these research and development efforts formed international joint ventures to share the huge fixed costs and risks involved. Some of these partnerships include:

U.S. Company	Foreign Partner
AT&T	NEC (Japan)
Texas Instruments	Hitachi (Japan)
Motorola	Toshiba (Japan)
IBM	Siemens (Germany)

Initially these joint ventures took various forms. For example, AT&T and NEC agreed to swap basic chip-making technologies. Texas Instruments and Hitachi agreed to develop a common design and manufacturing process and then do low-volume production together, with mass production and marketing to be done separately by each company. Motorola and Toshiba entered into a partnership to comanufacture memory (and logic) chips. In the end, massive scale economies from production rates of millions per plant per month led to a consolidation of production in the Hitachi and Toshiba plants in Japan.

Finally, when reliant assets are one-way dependent on unique complementary resources, the most efficient organizational form is vertical integration. Remote

---

[14] The term *joint ventures* is often reserved for bilateral relationships that establish a separate corporate identity.

[15] Based on "The Costly Race Chipmakers Cannot Afford to Lose," *Business Week,* December 10, 1990, pp. 185–187, and "Two Makers of Microchips Broaden Ties," *Wall Street Journal,* November 21, 1991, p. 84.

WHAT WENT RIGHT   WHAT WENT WRONG

Cable Allies Refuse to Adopt Microsoft's WebTV as an Industry Standard[16]

Demand for interactive television with Internet surfing, web shopping, interactive sports, and e-mail has grown quickly in hotel and airport lounges but very slowly elsewhere. Cable companies like AT&T and Time Warner appear most likely to trigger the adoption of these smart TVs in households through their leasing of set-top control boxes to residential customers. After acquiring WebTV (now renamed MSN TV) for $425 million in 1997, Microsoft shifted to an alliance strategy to secure the adoption of its complex software by the cable TV operators. Microsoft's interactive WebTV product known as UltimateTV was fully redeployable across competing cable service companies, and the cable companies sought to remain fully redeployable across interactive TV software providers. Since Microsoft/WebTV was one-way dependent on cable providers, but cable had numerous other ways to generate value without Microsoft, an alliance was the efficient organizational form for these asset characteristics.

Microsoft's product offering required the cumbersome software architecture of Windows CE. Standard set-top control boxes don't have enough memory or fast enough microprocessors to support Microsoft's operating system. Consequently, between 1991–2000, Microsoft invested over $10 billion in codesigning digital entertainment networks and new set-top control boxes with seven cable companies worldwide (AT&T: $5 billion, Telewest Comm in the U.K.: $2.6 billion, Comcast: $1 billion, and another $1.2 billion in Rogers, NTL, and UPC in Canada and Europe). In return, AT&T Broadband and its subsidiary TCI promised forward sales contracts for a total of ten million set-top control boxes employing Microsoft CE software in a Motorola-built unit, the DCT5000.

Today, the first 250,000 DCT5000s sit idly stacked in a Seattle warehouse. Microsoft's software was simply too complex, too costly, and too late.

After Microsoft insisted on the exclusion of the simpler Sun Microsystems' OS, the full installation costs for the DCT5000 cable networks skyrocketed to $500 per control box. Yet marketing research showed that cable subscribers would willingly add only $5 per month to their cable bills in order to secure these enhanced services. Ongoing delays induced Europe's largest cable company, UPC, to order set-top digital entertainment software from Liberate, a Microsoft rival. By March 2002, even AT&T announced that it had no plans at present to deploy interactive WebTV software and that Microsoft would build only the replacement for the scrolling online TV guide. Microsoft's ehome Division has now refocused on delivering TV services, music, and digital photography through the PC rather than the other way around.

Had the cable companies allowed Microsoft/WebTV to become an industry standard, full-scale vertical integration would have been warranted. Microsoft's digital entertainment assets would then have been one-way dependent on cable service providers, whose assets would have been no longer redeployable. This is the classic case for vertical integration, shown in the middle of the right-hand column of Table 15.4. At one point in 1997, while Bill Gates was presenting UltimateTV as a possible industry standard, a cable company president Brian Roberts half-jokingly suggested that Microsoft buy the entire cable industry.

[16] Based on "Microsoft's Blank Screen," *The Economist*, September 16, 2000, p. 74, and "Set-Top Setback: Microsoft Miscues," *Wall Street Journal*, June 14, 2002, p. A1.

aluminum plants are one-way dependent on nearby bauxite mines. In contrast, because the bauxite can be shipped anywhere, the mine owners are not dependent on the local aluminum plant. Both assets entail substantial sunk cost investment, but only the remote aluminum plant is a nonredeployable durable asset—i.e., one with little value to other companies should the nearby bauxite source disappear. This is the situation in which upstream vertical integration by the manufacturer is required in order to prevent opportunistic holdup. Sometimes capitalized value is dependent on a downstream firm. eBay's huge success in attracting sellers of one-of-a-kind items to their network of auction buyers necessitated an electronic payments platform. PayPal captured that market, so in July 2002 eBay paid $1.4 billion to acquire PayPal and thereby vertically integrate downstream. PayPal had become a unique complement to nonredeployable eBay assets.

VERTICAL INTEGRATION

Search, bargaining, and holdup costs are all reduced when internal transfers and the monitoring and incentive systems within the firm replace the spot market contracting and recontracting necessitated by operating at arm's length with outside suppliers and independent distributors. As we have seen, Nobel laureate Ronald Coase and Oliver Williamson argue that these factors explain why the firm emerged as an organizational form despite the diseconomies of ever-wider spans of managerial control.[17] Another motive for a manufacturer to vertically integrate upstream to suppliers or downstream to retail distributors involves the inefficiency of successive monopolization (i.e., the presence of market power over price at more than one stage of production). For example, the transfer of WebTV's downstream equity to Microsoft (the upstream digital entertainment content provider in this interactive TV business model) is a method of precommitment by Microsoft to exercise upstream price restraint and not spoil the downstream market. We now illustrate these ideas further with a detailed study of vertical integration in the hosiery industry.

Consider, first, an upstream yarn supplier who operates in a competitive intermediate product market and a downstream hosiery manufacturer who enjoys the market power to markup the wholesale price for pantyhose above its marginal cost. Figure 15.5 illustrates the situation each firm faces when the yarn inputs are combined in fixed proportions with manufacturing labor and machinery to yield hosiery output. The outside demand curve and its marginal revenue capture the hosiery manufacturer's revenue opportunities in the wholesale pantyhose product market. Given the marginal cost of hosiery production (MC_h) and the competitive price of yarn ($P_y = MC_y$), the manufacturer sets summed marginal cost of hosiery production and yarn inputs ($MC_h + MC_y$) equal to hosiery marginal revenue (MR_h) at output Q^*. This proves to be a joint profit-maximizing output decision because the output that maximizes hosiery profits also sets the marginal cost of yarn equal to the net marginal revenue product of the yarn supplier. That is, subtracting the downstream marginal cost (MC_h) from the downstream marginal revenues (MR_h) leaves the *net* revenue opportunity available to the upstream yarn supplier—i.e., ($MR_h - MC_h$). Setting this derived demand for yarn inputs equal to upstream marginal costs (MC_y) identifies Q^* as the yarn supplier's preferred throughput rate as well as the hosiery manufacturer's preferred output rate. Thus, the upstream supplier who prices yarn

---

[17] For more extensive discussion of this topic, see S. Hamilton and K. Stiegert, "Vertical Coordination," *Journal of Law and Economics*, April 2000.

Figure 15.5   Hosiery Integration Analysis with Upstream Competitor

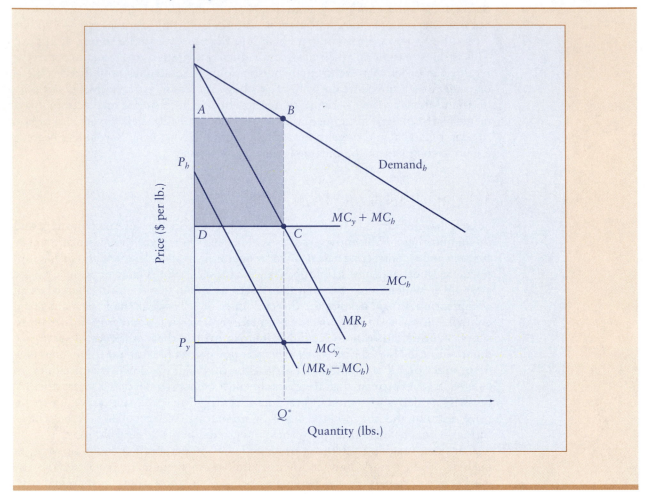

so as to just recover marginal cost imposes no throughput constraint on downstream hosiery operations.

Since the hosiery manufacturer in Figure 15.5 would change neither the yarn input prices, nor the wholesale output prices, nor the throughput quantity if the manufacturer were to vertically integrate upstream and operate the yarn supplier, vertical integration can only result in disadvantages associated with a wider span of managerial control. For profits $ABCD$ to remain unchanged, these disadvantages would need to be offset by some other factor like reduced transaction costs. In general, in the absence of other factors, we would conclude that in Figure 15.5, the hosiery manufacturer has no profit motive for backwards integration into the competitive yarn supplier's business.

In contrast, however, consider the case in which the yarn supplier has a proprietary process that is unique and adds substantial value to the hosiery manufacturing process. In Figure 15.6, the derived demand for the yarn input is again ($MR_h -$ MC_h) and everything else about the hosiery operations remains the same as in Figure 15.5, except that now the upstream firm has the market power to markup its own marginal cost (MC_y). Taking then a second marginalization of the revenue, sub-

Figure 15.6   Hosiery Integration Analysis with Upstream Market Power

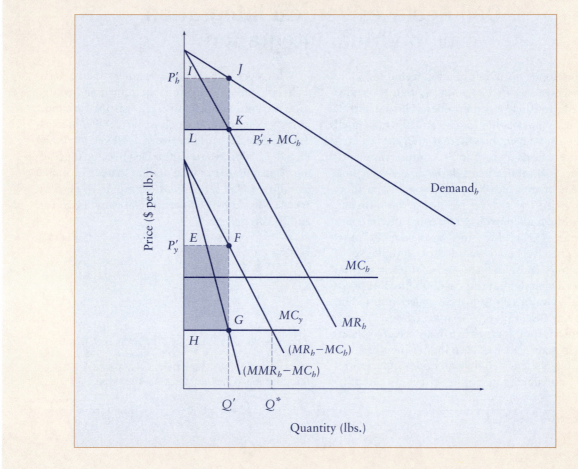

tracting off the hosiery production cost, and setting $(MMR_h - MC_h) = MC_y$, the yarn supplier maximizes upstream profits $EFGH$ by choosing a price P'_y at throughput Q'. Since P'_y exceeds the upstream marginal cost MC_y, the summed marginal cost facing the hosiery manufacturer is now higher, and consequently, the desired output declines from Q^* to Q'. Although hosiery prices rise to P'_h, the higher costs and smaller output of hosiery operations cause the profits of the downstream firm (the manufacturer) to decline—i.e., $IJKL$ in Figure 15.6 < $ABCD$ in Figure 15.5. That is, the presence of profit margins upstream results in a throughput constraint that unambiguously reduces downstream profitability.[18]

Backwards vertical integration by the hosiery manufacturer can squeeze out the margins upstream by simply setting an internal transfer price for yarn $P_y = MC_y$. This change will return the optimal throughput to Q^*, the profit-maximizing level for

[18] This implication holds without qualification here because of fixed proportions production, i.e., the efficient input mix remains unchanged despite the reduction in output. Under variable proportions, vertical integration may be motivated or not, depending on the input substitutability and possible cost savings.

WHAT WENT RIGHT   WHAT WENT WRONG

Dell Replaces Vertical Integration with Virtual Integration[19]

New developments in information technology, like the enterprise resource planning system SAP, have widened the efficient span of hierarchical control. But rather than enabling larger vertically integrated companies, SAP enables virtual integration. Dell Computers owns almost no PC component manufacturing operations. Instead, they outsource their requirements to several hundred supplier-partners who are tied together in a real-time monitoring, adaptation, and control system using the Internet. Their patented build-to-order business model must handle effectively an extraordinarily complex set of just-in-time component flows to support a final product assembly that ships 10,000 possible product configurations direct to a customer. Information technology clearly plays a key role in the governance mechanisms for this type of virtually integrated supply chain management. When this business model is successful, plant and equipment decline, inventories decline, and operating leverage rises substantially.

With less fixed capital investment than a vertically integrated competitor, the return on invested capital climbs accordingly. Dell was the fifth most quickly appreciating stock of the 1990s, increasing in value 297-fold between October 1990 and October 2000. By late 2000, Dell became the leading PC manufacturer with market shares distributed as follows: Dell 20 percent, Compaq 16 percent, Hewlett-Packard 11 percent, Gateway 9 percent, and IBM 6 percent.

http://

See what Michael Dell had to say about *virtual integration* at http://www.dell.com

---

[19] Based on "Identity Crisis," *Wall Street Journal,* October 10, 2000, p. C1; "Direct Hit," *The Economist,* January 9, 1999, pp. 55–58; and J. Margretta, "The Power of Virtual Integration," *Harvard Business Review,* March/April 1998, pp. 72–85.

---

the consolidated yarn and hosiery operations. That is, even after paying the upstream profits *EFGH* to secure the control rights from the yarn company, the downstream hosiery manufacturer has higher net profits ($ABCD - EFGH$) than its profit from independent operations *IJKL*. Consequently, we would expect these two firms to coordinate their operations either as a joint venture or as a vertically integrated firm.

LICENSING, PATENTS, AND TRADE SECRETS

Another choice of organizational form involves the decision as to whether to license patents and trade secrets to competitors. Think of Microsoft's machine code, Pfizer's drug discovery technology, and Disney's films and characters. Fifty years ago, 78 percent of the assets of U.S. nonfinancial corporations were tangible assets (real estate, inventories, and plant and equipment). Today that figure is just 53 percent; intangible assets such as patents, copyrights, and goodwill have grown to nearly dominate the account books. In addition, as the information economy comes center stage, intellectual property has become an all-important source of competitive advantage. By 1999, Microsoft held over 600 patents, and Sun Microsystems held 1,223, topping Thomas Edison's record 1,093. IBM Corporation was seeking patent protection at the

Table 15.5   Knowledge Capital, 1998 ($ billions)

	Sales	Book Value	Total Market Value	Market Value of Intangibles*
Merck	23.6	12.6	139.9	48.0
Bristol-MyersSquibb	16.7	7.2	107.0	30.5
Johnson & Johnson	22.6	12.4	92.9	29.7
DuPont	39.9	11.3	87.0	26.4
Dow Chemical	20.1	7.7	21.8	10.2
Monsanto	7.5	4.1	33.2	6.0

		Business Method Patents		
Patent Number	Date Issued	Device/Process	Inventors	Affiliate
5,797,127	8/18/98	Reverse auctions	Jay Walker et al.	Priceline.com
5,960,411	9/28/99	One-click buying	Jeff Bezos et al.	Amazon.com

*Estimated market value attributable to intangible, nonfinancial assets.
Source: Baruch Lev, *CFO*, February 1999, and *The Economist*, June 12, 1999, p. 62.

astounding rate of ten patent applications per working day.[20] Some of this activity is strategic patenting of technology portfolios where companies do not wish to make a new device immediately, but they can plausibly describe how they would make it, what the device is used for, and the novelty of the idea. These are the evidentiary requirements for obtaining a patent. Not just electronic devices, genetic engineering, and computer software, but also business process methods are "hot" current areas of patenting activity. Dell received a patent on the direct-to-the-consumer business model, and Walker Digital (parent of Priceline.com) received a patent on the Internet-based reverse auction in which buyers post prices that sellers can then "hit" to execute a sale. Patent attorneys believe the ATM machine, frequent flyer programs, and even credit cards could be patented as business processes if they were invented today.

Table 15.5 shows that the financial markets are definitely capitalizing this "knowledge capital" into the equity market value of companies with patents, trade secrets, and proprietary know-how. Almost half of the $22-billion market value of Dow Chemical and more than a third of the $140-billion market value of Merck is discounted cash flow from intangible assets, mostly intellectual property. Much of Amazon.com's $11-billion market value arises from licensing fees on their business methods patents. Between 1994 and 1999, IBM boosted its annual revenues from licensing its intellectual property by over 200 percent from $500 million to $1.6 billion. In consumer products too, Reebok recently paid $250 million in royalties to obtain a ten-year exclusive license to market National Football League-branded uniforms, hats, and equipment and to have its trademark on the players' apparel of all NFL teams. So, the revenue available from licensing is very substantial, but of course there are dangers from enlivening one's competitors.

---

[20] "The Knowledge Monopolies," *The Economist*, April 8, 2000, pp. 75–78; "Business Methods Patents," *Wall Street Journal*, October 3, 2000, p. B14; and "Mind Over Matter," *Wall Street Journal*, April 4, 2002, p. A1.

WHAT WENT RIGHT   WHAT WENT WRONG

Technology Licenses Cost Palm Its Lead in PDAs[21]

In 1996, Palm single-handedly created the personal digital assistant (PDA) craze. Like Apple, Palm builds its own software and hardware. Worldwide, Palm operating systems run three quarters of all handheld devices that are capable of surfing the Internet. Unlike Apple, Palm decided to license its OS technology to competing manufacturers Handspring and Sony. Within two short years, Handspring surpassed Palm in manufacturing sales of PDAs by offering expansion slots and peripheral equipment like phones and music players.

Licensing always entails such risks, but Palm really had little choice in the matter. Cell phone giant Nokia had licensed its Series 60 mobile-phone software to Siemens and Matsushita. The three firms together control 47 percent of the global cell-phone market. Series 60 technology enables a cell phone to send and receive digital camera pictures, e-mail, and, most importantly, to browse a stripped down version of the Net. If either Nokia or Palm succeeds in getting its OS adopted as an industry standard for hand-held Web surfing, it will set in motion a virtuous circle of increasing returns. Recently, Palm and Handspring have merged into palmOne to achieve a larger installed base.

---

[21] "Matsushita to Use Nokia's Cellphone Software," *Wall Street Journal,* December 20, 2000, p. B10, and "One Palm Flapping," *The Economist,* June 2, 2001, p. 65.

Much debate rages about the role of patent and trade secret protection in providing incentives for first-mover companies to innovate while stifling technological research by fast-second companies. Imitators often substantially advance some aspect of any new technology but must license the original patents or run the risk of defending themselves against patent infringement lawsuits. Jeff Bezos of Amazon.com has proposed that 20-year patent protection for computer software and business methods be reduced to only 3–5 years. Patent protection outside the U.S. is already diminished. In Europe, patent applications invite legal challenge, and a majority of initial patents have been overturned. The EU has also decided not to issue patents for either computer software or business methods. In this environment, trade secrets, proprietary know-how, and internal business practices take on added importance. Whether to "bury" the trade secrets or to acknowledge openly their existence and license them to competitors is a significant strategic decision about the firm's contracting and governance mechanisms. No less important is the decision as to whether, on the one hand, to attempt to develop know-how in house or, on the other, to license proprietary know-how from competitors.

Example

COMPETING BUSINESS PLANS AT CELERA GENOMICS AND HUMAN GENOME SCIENCES

Genomics has revolutionized drug discovery and development, with some respected industry analysts predicting that "all drug discovery efforts will be genomics-based by 2004."[22] Celera Genomics, the company that coannounced completion of the reading of the human genome sequence in 2000, expects to sell information, in effect to license its genome database, for as much as $90 million a year. It is hoped that comparing which genes are expressed and which remain recessive in various diseases will

---

[22] *BusinessWeek,* January 8, 2001, p. 113.

lead drug scientists to new blockbuster therapies and early detection of harmful side effects. However, an in-depth understanding of the biology of therapeutic mechanisms at the molecular level will also be key. Human Genome Sciences (HGS) has decided therefore to position itself as a drugmaker, attempting to patent drug processes, not simply license genetic information to traditional drug companies. HGS's first product, a wound healer, is in clinical trials.

In Table 15.6, Motorola and Lucent Technologies (the spinoff of Bell Labs from AT&T) are trying to decide whether to develop in house or license proprietary trade secrets in telecommunications engineering and software. Because of Lucent's long-term experience in this arena, if Motorola develops and patents the process and devices, Lucent expects to be very successful as an imitator earning $9 billion. Should licensing of some proprietary know-how prove necessary, Lucent believes an inexpensive limited license will be sufficient. Consequently, Motorola will be unable (in that circumstance) to recover its fully allocated research and development costs and will therefore lose money (i.e., the −$1 billion payoff in the southeast cell). In contrast, if Lucent undertakes to develop and patent the needed process, its first-mover advantage would yield substantial license fees from Motorola, whose solo attempts at imitation would render it unable to proceed without the proprietary knowledge gained through the trade secret license. Hence, the payoffs describing this situation are $4 billion/$3 billion in the northeast cell. To complete the description of the payoff matrix, if neither firm develops the process, no profits accrue to either party. And if they compete head to head in a patent race, we assume the development costs will rise such that total profits fall from $7 billion to $6 billion, divided $5 to $1 between the technology leader Lucent and follower Motorola. What should Lucent do?

If Lucent could be sure Motorola was proceeding, Lucent would most prefer to wait and play "fast second." $9 billion in the southwest cell is certainly attractive relative to $5 billion in the northwest cell. However, Motorola can be expected to avoid the development expense and attempt itself to wait, imitate, and license as required to fill in the gaps in its own trade secrets and proprietary know-how. Indeed, Motorola has a dominant strategy to wait, imitate, and license. Consequently, Lucent anticipates that the payoff ($4 billion/$3 billion) in the northeast cell will emerge as an iterated dominant equilibrium. Recall that an iterated dominant equilibrium

Table 15.6 To License or Develop Expertise in House? ($ billions)

		Motorola	
		Develop/Patent	Imitate/License
Lucent	Develop/Patent	$5 billion · · · $1 billion	$4 billion · · · $3 billion
	Imitate/License	$9 billion · · · −$1 billion	0 · · · 0

WHAT WENT RIGHT   WHAT WENT WRONG

Motorola: What They Didn't Know Hurt Them[23]

Motorola, Inc. was a pioneer in communications engineering with many of the early analog devices in radio, television, and military signal processing to its credit. More recently Motorola developed and successfully launched the first handheld cell phones and also took the lead in satellite-based wireless communications with Iridium, a global cellular network project. Ambitious future projects include a satellite-based, high-speed, high-security video conferencing network for corporate customers and a satellite-based transcontinental and transoceanic connection for land-based cell phone companies.

Network reliability problems began to arise, however, when Motorola insisted on slowly developing its own digital wireless proprietary know-how rather than licensing the needed trade secrets and patents from Lucent or QUALCOMM Incorporated. Motorola had little expertise in digital switches, computing equipment, and communications software. Yet, proprietary knowledge in these areas proved critical in attempting to integrate Motorola's satellite system with land-based cell phone networks. At one point, Motorola launched a cell phone system whose software essentially blocked any other user from simultaneously connecting through the same cell tower and receiving station. In effect, this device crashed the local cell

network anytime it was in use. Consequently, during a period in 1998 when QUALCOMM cell phones sold by the hundreds of thousands, Motorola was late to market with a competing product launch and even then announced a series of further delays. The operations problems were exacerbated by Motorola's lack of a common platform for its product configurations. Rather than mixing and matching standard components like Dell's operations strategy for assembling PCs, Motorola assembles cell phones from ten different platforms with few interchangeable components.

Perhaps it is not surprising that QUALCOMM and Lucent, a former division of AT&T, experienced less trouble adding know-how in wireless technology to their long-standing expertise in wire-based telecommunications networks than Motorola experienced trying to add know-how in digital switches and communications software to their long-standing expertise in analog wireless hardware. Motorola should have licensed the proprietary know-how rather than attempt to develop it in-house.

---

[23] Based on "Unsold State: Motorola Struggles to Regain Its Footing," *Wall Street Journal*, April 22, 1998, p. A1, and "How Motorola Roamed Astray," *Wall Street Journal*, October 26, 2000, p. B12.

---

strategy is a self-interest maximizing action by Lucent that is consistent with dominant-strategy responses of Motorola. Since at ($4 billion/$3 billion) in the northeast cell, neither party wishes to deviate to another action, (Develop$_{Lucent}$, License$_{Motorola}$) is a Nash equilibrium strategy, indeed the only Nash equilibrium in Table 15.6.

Although the numbers in Table 15.6 are only illustrative, thinking through the game-theoretic analysis can often prove very insightful in predicting rival reaction to company moves and countermoves. In this case, an analysis like Table 15.6 could well have helped because it clearly indicates the desirability of the licensing alternative rather than the in-house development Motorola actually pursued.

Whether or not to license depends in part on the availability of increasing returns and the enormous competitive advantage such cost reductions offer. In Europe, where few industry standards have emerged for information technology products and where patents are often successfully challenged, first-mover firms have licensed to competitors rather than simply watch their trade secrets and proprietary know-how be steadily eroded by imitators. The result has been markedly increased competition, lower prices for consumers, and a faster rate of technological adoption. For example, prices for some digital TV components (e.g., digital video broadcasting chips) keep dropping, and the digital technology is quickly being incorporated into related products like cell phones, pagers, and secure video business networks for corporate meetings. In the U.S., Red Hat uses a general public license to penetrate as quickly as possible into the operating system market with its Linux-based software that is intended to compete with Windows NT and eventually with Windows itself. Red Hat allows its suppliers and customers to copy, modify, and redistribute Red Hat software at no charge as long as they do so without charge. This open-source software strategy is an attempt to achieve the inflection point for increasing returns that other Microsoft competitors like Apple never reached.

A final tactical advantage of licensing comes from the analysis of recontracting hazards, as we saw earlier in Chapter 13. In purchasing high-end Alpha chips from Digital Equipment Corporation (now a division of Hewlett-Packard), many workstation manufacturers worry about the postcontractual opportunism to which they are vulnerable. At contract renewal, once their designs are optimized for the Alpha technology, the manufacturers worry that the price for these sole-source-supplied chips may rise steeply. Digital can credibly commit to more stable prices and thereby increase the rate of adoption for its product by licensing to AMD or Intel. Allowing customers to dual source the Alpha chip technology credibly commits Digital to renew its supply contracts without price gouging. Thus, Digital can discourage the development of the licensees' substitute products. Intel employed this licensing strategy itself while trying to establish the Pentium series of chips as an industry standard in PCs. IBM also licensed its operating system technology to Microsoft to speed the rate of adoption of DOS-based equipment. Apple Computers pursued the opposite non-licensing strategy, thereby effectively slowing the rate of adoption of Macs, and lost to IBM and Microsoft once those companies reached the level of product acceptance that established an industry standard and set off increasing returns.

SUMMARY

- Businesses make choices about organizational form that define the span of hierarchical control from the vertically integrated oil company at one extreme to the virtual manufacturer Dell, which outsources all manufacturing and assembly to supplier-partners.

- All external and internal business relationships require a solution to the twin problems of coordination and control. External business relationships can be organized through spot market transactions, long-term contracts, or reputation effects in relational contracting. These forms of organization differ in their timing, players, enforcement, and information structure.

- Long-term vertical requirements contracts provide an *ex ante* framework for resolving coordination and control problems between manufacturers, suppliers, and distributors. Because all contracts are purposefully incomplete, *ex post* opportunistic behavior requires governance mechanisms to reduce several types of contractual hazards. The *moral hazard problem* arises because of the unobservability of effort in assuring contract performance. The *postcontractual opportunistic behavior* called "holdup" presents another commonly occurring contractual hazard.

- Exchange under incomplete information and under asymmetric information differ. *Incomplete information* refers to the uncertainty that is pervasive in practically all transactions and motivates insurance markets. *Asymmetric information,* on the other hand, refers to private information one party possesses, that the other party cannot independently verify.

- Asymmetric information leads to the *problem of adverse selection.*

- Contracts are seldom complete because full *contingent claims contracting* is often prohibitively expensive. Intentionally incomplete contracting allows *postcontractual opportunistic behavior* and leads to the problem of holdup. Resolving the *holdup problem* in managerial contracting necessitates the use of *governance mechanisms.*

- Governance mechanisms include internal monitoring by director subcommittees and large creditors, internal/external monitoring by large block shareholders, auditing and variance analysis, benchmarking, an ethically dutiful corporate culture, and whistle-blowing.

- Managerial labor can be hired in several ways—for example, straight salary, wage rate, or profit sharing. Pure profit sharing results in moonlighting, however, because the manager's inputs—namely, effort and creative ingenuity—are largely unobservable. Unobservable effort leads to the *moral hazard problem,* which can be resolved by setting up *ex post facto* (e.g., with deferred stock options).

- In combination, random disturbances in firm performance and unobservable managerial effort present a more difficult *principal-agent problem* to resolve. Owner-principals do not know when to blame manager-agents for weak performance or give credit for strong performance. *Optimal incentives contracts* involving some guaranteed salary and a profit-sharing bonus can, in principle, resolve the principal-agent problem.

- Linear combinations of salary and profit sharing can also be used to elicit asymmetric information about managerial preferences, sort managers by their own personal risk aversion, and prevent adverse selection in managerial hiring. Boards of directors face a holdup problem in renewing senior executive contracts, necessitating governance mechanisms.

- What form of organization to adopt—e.g., spot market transactions, long-term vertical requirements contracts, relational contracts, or vertical integration—depends on the contractual hazards that need to be avoided. What contractual hazards arise in business relationships depends upon the asset characteristics, upon the redeployability or specificity of the fixed assets, and upon the relative dependence of those fixed assets on unique complementary assets.

- Vertical integration is an optimal organizational form when the assets are one-way dependent on complementary assets and are largely nonredeployable.

- Whether to develop and license or wait and imitate is an organizational form decision about the protection afforded by patents, the relative importance of proprietary know-how, the availability of industry standards, technological lock-in, value-enhancing complements, and other sources of increasing returns.

EXERCISES

1. If contract promises were not excused because of acts of God (like earthquakes in San Francisco) or acts of war (like the terrorist attack on the World Trade Center), what precautions would companies like Bank of New York have to

take to assure contract performance? How could one decide whether such precautions were deficient or excessive?

2. Again, if contract promises were not excused because of acts of God or acts of war, would the customers of Cantor Fitzgerald or Bank of New York change their behavior? If so, how? What reliance behavior would be considered efficient? What reliance behavior would be considered excessive?

3. For each of the possible loan terms the commercial lender might offer, identify what choices by the lender would be the worst for combating the moral hazard problem in Figure 15.2.

4. If coal mine tonnage can be shipped elsewhere cheaply, but an adjacent coal-fired power plant is not redeployable to other uses, what organizational form would be adopted by the power plant owners? Why?

5. Would warehouse operators insist on owning their own trucking companies? Why or why not? What coordination and control problems and contractual hazards would these companies encounter?

6. What organizational form would warehouse operators and truck hauling companies adopt?

7. In benchmarking sales representatives against one another, what problems arise from continuing to reassign the above-average trade representatives to previously unproductive sales territories?

8. Explain how the optimal incentives contract would differ if the less risk-averse bank officer (Dashing in Figure 15.4) had generated the smaller expected profit (i.e., the lower hill-shaped locus).

9. If the decision to develop and license or wait and imitate in Table 15.6 is a simultaneous-play repeated game between Lucent and Motorola for each new generation of technology, what happens if the Motorola payoff in the SE cell is positive $2 billion? How should Motorola "play" in this modified licensing game? How should Lucent play?

10. Analyze the pure Nash equilibrium and mixed Nash equilibrium strategies in the following manufacturer-distributor coordination game. How would you recommend restructuring the game to secure higher expected profit for the manufacturer?

		Manufacturer	
		Product Update/ Higher MSRP	No Update/ Same MSRP
Distributor	**Discontinue Special Selling Services**	0 / $1 M	$2 M / $4 M
	Continue Special Selling Services	$6 M / $2 M	0 / 0

BORDERS BOOKS AND AMAZON.COM DECIDE TO DO BUSINESS TOGETHER?

In 2001, Borders Books, the leading chain of bookshop retailers, entered into an agreement with Amazon.com, the online retailer, to fulfill Internet orders from the Border.com website. Using Table 15.4 and the questions below, what organizational form would you predict for this business relationship?

QUESTIONS

1. Are Amazon.com's warehouses, web pages, and one-click sales methods fully redeployable to other products? If so, name a few such products. If not, why not?

2. Are Borders' fixed assets fully redeployable? If so, suggest how. If not, why not?

3. Is Borders dependent on Amazon as a unique complement—i.e., is Amazon.com the only potential company that could process Internet-based orders for Borders?

4. Is Amazon dependent on Borders for referrals, or does it have its own Internet-based order flow?

5. Is your answer consistent with the multiyear fee-for-service contract between Borders and Amazon.com whereby Amazon processes the order, ships the book, records the sales, and pays Borders a referral fee? One Borders executive described this as a "low-risk, low return" approach to online sales while retaining Borders' focus on its core mission of running bookshops.

DESIGNING A MANAGERIAL INCENTIVE CONTRACT[24]

Specific Electric Co. asks you to implement a pay-for-performance incentive contract for its new CEO. The CEO can either work hard with a personal cost of $200,000 or reduce her effort, thereby avoiding the personal cost. The CEO faces three possible outcomes: her company experiences good luck with probability 0.3, medium luck with probability 0.4, or bad luck with probability 0.3. Although the management team can distinguish the three "states" of luck as the quarter unfolds, the Compensation Committee of the Board of Directors (and the shareholders) cannot do so. Sometime thereafter, the CEO decides to expend high or low work effort, and one of the observable shareholder values then results.

	Shareholder Value		
	Good Luck (30%)	Medium Luck (40%)	Bad Luck (30%)
High CEO Effort	$1,000,000,000	$800,000,000	$500,000,000
Low CEO Effort	$ 800,000,000	$500,000,000	$300,000,000

Assume 10 million shares and a $65 initial share price, implying a $650,000,000 initial shareholder value. Since the CEO's effort and the company's luck are unobservable to the owners and company directors, it is not possible upon observing a reduction to $50 share prices and $500,000,000 value to distinguish whether the

---

[24] An earlier version of this exercise was suggested by B. Ramy Elitzur of Tel Aviv University.

company experienced low CEO effort and medium luck, or high CEO effort and bad luck.

Answer the following questions from the perspective of a member of the Compensation Committee of the Board of Directors who is aligned with shareholder interests and is deciding on bonus plans for the CEO.

QUESTIONS

1.   What is the maximum amount it would be worth to shareholders to elicit high CEO effort all the time rather than low CEO effort all the time?

2.   If you decide to pay 1 percent of this amount (in Question 1) as a cash bonus, what performance level (what share price or shareholder value) in the table should trigger the bonus? Suppose you decide to elicit high CEO effort when and if medium luck occurs by paying the bonus for $800,000,000 outcomes. What criticism can you see of this incentive contract plan?

3.   Suppose you decide to elicit high CEO effort when and if good luck occurs by paying the bonus for $1,000,000,000 outcomes only. What criticism can you see of this incentive contract plan?

4.   Suppose you decide to elicit high CEO effort when and if bad luck occurs by paying the bonus for $500,000,000 outcomes. What criticism can you see of this incentive contract plan?

5.   In seeking to identify what share price to employ in triggering the payment of the bonus so as maximize shareholder value, how much would you, the Compensation Committee, be willing to pay an auditor who examines the expense and revenue flows in realtime and delivers perfect forecast information about the "luck" the firm is experiencing. Compare value with this perfect information relative to the best choice among the incentive contract plans in Questions 2, 3, and 4 above.

6.   Design a stock option-based incentive plan to elicit high effort. Show that this incentive contract improves shareholder value relative to the best of the cash-based incentive plans in Questions 2, 3, or 4.

7.   Design a restricted stock incentive plan to elicit high effort. Show that this incentive contract improves shareholder value relative to all prior alternatives.

8.   Financial audits are basically sampling procedures to verify with a predetermined accuracy the sources and uses of the company receipts and expenditures; the larger the sample, the higher is the accuracy. What's the maximum amount the Compensation Committee of the Board would be willing to pay for a perfect forecast if it were possible for the auditors to distinguish good from medium luck? medium from bad luck?

LIBRARY EXERCISE

VERTICAL INTEGRATION AT GM-FISHER BODY

Read the three papers by R. H. Coase, R. Freeland, and B. Klein in the April 2000 issue of the *Journal of Law and Economics,* and then explain the competing arguments as to why General Motors vertically integrated upstream to buy out Fisher Body Co.

16

Optimal Mechanism Design

CHAPTER PREVIEW   This chapter highlights the design of institutional mechanisms like the queuing procedures for ticket distribution to Disney World attractions or to a concert. Such institutional choices serve some explicit optimization goal. Sellers might, for example, design an auction mechanism to maximize revenue. Estate attorneys and their clients might design a procedural mechanism for the division of assets to maximize perceptions of fairness. And more generally, institutional mechanisms evolve in ways that maximize value by facilitating the capture of gains from trade. That is, efficient institutional mechanisms are likely to be those that persist and survive. Whether the result of human action (like the distillations of experience associated with social customs such as "no cutting in line") or the outcome of human design (like stratified lotteries for access to scarce kidney dialysis machines), the choice of institutional mechanisms can be analyzed with many of the standard tools of microeconomics.

We begin by using the game-theoretic tools of Chapter 13 to examine "fair division games" for the dissolution of assets in a partnership or an estate. Next we move to the choice of queue service rules designed to maximize seller revenue. With the same objective, we then examine auction design, including Internet auctions. Profit-sharing mechanisms to elicit true cost revelation in a partnership illustrate incentive-compatible mechanism design. Finally, in Appendix 16A, we discuss private contract bargaining as a mechanism to resolve certain kinds of externalities. This is the famous Coase Theorem whose qualifications lead to a discussion of public sector alternative mechanism designs.

MANAGERIAL CHALLENGE

Fidelity/W. R. Hambrecht Open Dutch Auction for IPOs[1]

The underwriting of new stock and bond issues in the United States is a lucrative business for investment banks (IBs). In 2001, Citicorp-Salomon, Morgan Stanley, and Goldman Sachs all earned more than $2 billion each in underwriting fees. The most lucrative new issue market is the initial public offering (IPO) market where these and other investment banks advise companies what initial value they should place on their shares. After agreeing upon an acceptable price, the investment banks then privately sell the shares in the new issue to long-term institutional customers and other preferred buyers chosen by the issuing firm.

However, Professor Jay Ritter estimates that in a random sample of 3,025 IPOs between 1990 and 1998, the typical IPO trades 1.9 million shares the first day after the issue, 120,000 shares per day one month after the issue, and 63,000 shares per day six months later. With so many shares changing hands the first day, this evidence suggests that the private placement process does not allocate the new issue to the highest-willingness-to-pay buyers. Indeed, the $68 million in average gross proceeds from the "private placement" of these IPOs is $9.1 million less than the average market value after the first day of trading. That is, the investment bank advisors underestimated the IPO values by an average of 14 percent. The issuing companies therefore left a total of $9.1 million × 3,205 = $27 billion on the table when they agreed to their underwriting deals. This $27 billion indirect cost of underwriting was twice as large as the already enormous underwriting fees.

A representative example in 2001 would be Prudential Financial, which raised $3.48 billion, but closed its first month of trading 19 percent above its offer price. Some IPOs are overpriced, and the investment banks share in this risk as well. HealthCentral.com, Inc. fell 44 percent from its offer price of $11 to $7.31 in the first month of trading. IB reputations with institutional customers are damaged by these overpriced deals.

W. R. Hambrecht & Co., an online investment bank, has decided there has to be a better way to determine what proceeds should go to the issuing company. With the backing of Fidelity Investments and its 3 million online investors, Hambrecht's "Open IPO" conducts a uniform-price Dutch auction. Potential investors place bids on the Internet for however many shares they want to demand at whatever price they desire to pay. Hambrecht aggregates these bids and allocates the stock to all bidders at the highest price that clears the market. Thus investors, not IB middlemen, select the price that is low enough to sell all the shares and get the deal done. In Hambrecht & Co.'s first IPO, Ravenswood Winery Inc. auctioned for $10.50 and sold for $10.88 on the first day of trading. Ninety-seven percent of the first-day trading value therefore went into the pockets of the issuing company; almost no proceeds were left on the table. Generally in auctions with substantial asymmetric information,

---

[1] Based on T. Loughran and J. Ritter, "Why Don't Issuers Get Upset About Leaving Money on the Table in IPOs?" 1999 NYSE Conference on U.S. Equity Markets in Transition, Phoenix, AZ; "IPO Scorecard," *Wall Street Journal*, December 30, 1999, p. A13; "Hoover's Online: IPO Central—Best and Worst Returns," http://www.hoovers.com, January 12, 2000; "Manager's Journal: IPOs Go Dutch and Small Investors Gain," *Wall Street Journal*, December 27, 1999, p. A18.

MANAGERIAL CHALLENGE

such Dutch auction methods increase the expected revenue to the seller relative to traditional English auction ascending price methods. Dutch auctions have often been used in times of similar information asymmetries to price stock buybacks.

Disclosed Fees from New Issue Underwriting				
	Gross Proceeds of Stock (billion)	Rank	Market Share (%)	Number of Issues	Stock and Bond Fees (million)
Goldman Sachs & Co.	$11.9	1	32	18	$2,090
Morgan Stanley Dean Witter	8.5	2	23	12	1,955
Merrill Lynch & Co., Inc.	5.5	3	15	15	1,622
Credit Suisse First Boston	4.5	4	12	8	2,395
Citicorp/Salomon Smith Barney	1.5	5	4	10	944
Lehman Brothers	1.4	6	4	14	1,885
UBS Warburg	0.7	7	2	7	871
JPMorgan Chase & Co.	0.6	8	2	4	1,027
Deutsche Bank	0.5	9	1	8	733
Bank of America Securities	0.4	10	1	4	464
Industry Totals	37.1	—	100.0	106	$4,159.8

Source: IPO Scorecard, Thomson Financial Securities Data, January 2002.

In this chapter, we discuss variations in the optimal mechanism design for auctions and other institutional procedures. Selling the radio magnetic spectrum in metropolitan zones to cellular phone companies using multiround open bidding simultaneous auctions illustrates the concept of optimal mechanism design. In contrast, the Federal Reserve has experimented with auctioning T-Bills using single-round, second-highest sealed bid auctions.

THE CONCEPT OF AN OPTIMAL MECHANISM DESIGN

In the previous chapter, we saw how performance-based linear incentive contracts can align the interests of owner-principals and manager-agents. In this chapter we will see how other institutional arrangements can align the interests of partners in a joint venture. Specifically, an "incentive-compatible contract" induces the partners to reveal their asymmetric information because each party incurs the cost of his or her own information revelation on the other party. That is, the contract imposes a mechanism design for sharing profits that aligns the self-interest of each partner with revelation of true and complete cost information to the other partner. This incentive-compatible revelation mechanism provides a complex example of the concept of optimal mechanism design.

In contrast, consider the apparently simpler question of how to divide a deceased individual's personal possessions fairly. Mechanism design focuses on the process or procedure that will create incentives to elicit the desired behavioral objective. In so-called **fair division games,** the key insight of mechanism design reasoning is the need for open communication and role reversal. This suggests letting one party divide the estate and the other choose which half he or she prefers. Under the incentives created by this procedure, the person dividing the estate will offer larger or more numerous possessions in one parcel if another parcel contains particularly valuable possessions. In short, the first party "cuts the cake" and the other party then chooses first which piece he or she wishes to consume.

Fair Division Games
Procedures for dividing assets by consensual agreement.

Fair Division of a Decaying Prize

The optimal mechanism design for fair division necessitates a tactical analysis when the prize is decaying with the passage of time as the players renegotiate. Suppose a partnership must divide $3 million between two partners. The only catch is that the partners must agree upon the dissolution of assets which declines by $1 million each time either party refuses the proposed division. Perhaps the assets are perishable pharmaceuticals or intellectual property that decays in value quickly. The two principals toss a coin to see who should make the first offer of how to split the $3 million. Suppose Joanne wins the toss. How much should she offer to Kathleen to secure her acceptance of the offer and forgo her rights of first refusal? Remember that Kathleen gets to structure a second-round offer should this first proposed division be refused, and she will also respond to Joanne's third and final offer should the second be refused. Notice that there definitely is a penultimate endgame to this problem in that after three rounds the assets are gone. Think about how little Kathleen would be willing to accept in the third and final round. Can Kathleen hold out for more than this in the second round? What, therefore, is the maximum Joanne needs to offer to trigger an acceptance in the first round? Does this game have a first-mover advantage, or is it better to play second and be the respondent in the third and final round?

These and related questions can be addressed with the sequential game techniques of Chapter 13. In Figure 16.1, Joanne makes the final offer at the far right but, as you may suspect, in one sense Kathleen's right of refusal controls this endgame. Since $100,000 is preferable to zero, Kathleen's best-reply response to an offer to split the final million as $900,000 for Joanne and $100,000 for Kathleen is to accept. This analysis implies that in the preceding (second) round, Kathleen can offer Joanne $1 million (i.e., $100,000 more than Joanne's endgame outcome), and Joanne's best-reply response is to accept. Stepping the backwards induction one more round back, this second-round analysis implies that if Joanne offers Kathleen $1.1 million in the first round (i.e., $100,000 more than Kathleen's second round outcome), Kathleen will accept. Note that we are short-circuiting threats and other modes of communication other than the proffering of the offers. Also note that we have assumed each party believes the other party is maximizing absolute gain, without regard to the relative distribution. In such circumstances, making the first *and the last* offer appears advantageous to Joanne.

Figure 16.1   Dissolution of Assets in a Partnership

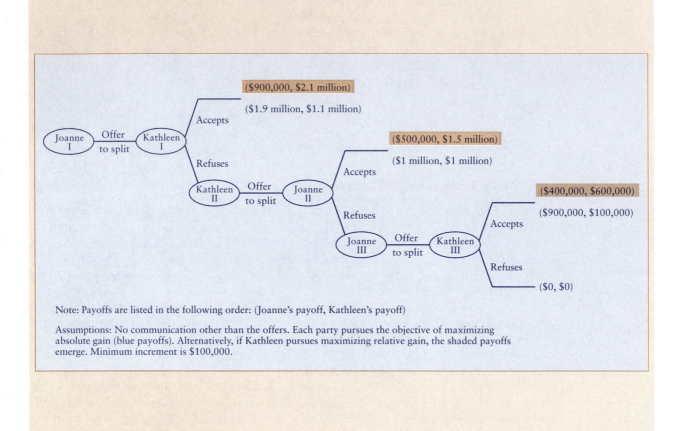

Note: Payoffs are listed in the following order: (Joanne's payoff, Kathleen's payoff)

Assumptions: No communication other than the offers. Each party pursues the objective of maximizing absolute gain (blue payoffs). Alternatively, if Kathleen pursues maximizing relative gain, the shaded payoffs emerge. Minimum increment is $100,000.

Mechanism design features of this problem include the rotating offer and right of refusal, the lack of communication about objectives and credible threats, and the coin toss to decide who offers first. Any of these could be changed, and it might make quite a difference. For example, suppose Kathleen was able to establish a reputational objective that she pursued relative wealth, not absolute wealth. In that event, the outcome (0, 0) would quite literally be preferable to the alternative of her partner Joanne going $800,000 up at ($900,000, $100,000). Even splitting the last million dollars ($500,000, $500,000) would not be preferable to ($0, $0). So only an asymmetric distribution *favoring* Kathleen (say, $400,000, $600,000 in shaded box) would elicit her acceptance. In earlier rounds, Joanne now knows that she must increase the unequal distribution in Kathleen's favor in order to secure Kathleen's acceptance. Given the $100,000 minimum increments, Kathleen reasons by backwards induction from the ($400,000, $600,000) outcome of Round 3 that she can offer ($500,000 $1.5 million) to secure Joanne's acceptance in Round 2. Finally, this intermediate outcome implies by the relative gain reasoning motivating Kathleen that Joanne can elicit Kathleen's acceptance at the start of the negotiations by offering a ($900,000, $2.1 million) split in Round 1. Comparing the blue and shaded offers in Round 1, it makes $1 million of difference whether or not the mechanism design allows communication or imposes closed bidding with unknown silent partners responding through intermediaries. Small institutional changes often make a large difference.

OPTIMAL QUEUE SERVICE RULES

A frequent business application of optimal mechanism design is the queue service rule for filling customer orders from those waiting to purchase. The traditional first-come first-served procedure induces an inefficient pattern of customer arrivals at, for example, a concert site. If the box office opens at 9:00 A.M. a few potential customers arrive three hours earlier or even the night before. Others stand on queue for two hours, and many more show up to wait in line at 8:00 A.M. What customers are willing to pay for tickets may be affected by the inconvenience of this wait. And the subpopulation of customers who have low opportunity cost of time (and are therefore willing to arrive the earliest, wait the longest, and obtain tickets with the greatest probability) may not be the subpopulation who will pay the most for tickets. This is why many ticket agencies have no objection to a wealthy patron paying someone with lower opportunity cost of time to stand on queue, purchase the ticket, and transfer it at face value to the higher-willingness-to-pay customer.[2] In any case, all this waiting time is time wasted; other queue service rules may be much more efficient.

First-Come First-Served versus Last-Come First-Served

As a provisional alternative, consider last-come first-served. Under this queue service rule, a customer has no incentive to stand on queue and wait. Indeed, any time a queue forms, all those in front of the last person to arrive have an incentive to leave and go about their other business, returning later when fewer people are likely to show up. In essence, the last-come first-served mechanism design has removed the incentives for inefficient behavior artificially created by first-come first-served. Customers do not prefer to arrive early and peak-load their demands. Instead, it was the nonoptimal queue service rule that artificially created incentives to arrive early, stand around, and wait. With last-come first-served, in contrast, customers have an incentive to spread their arrivals throughout the ticket window's normal hours of operation. Once a more or less uniform distribution of customer arrivals throughout the day can be established, the ticket agency can adjust its capacity and set its service rate to deal with the steady stream of customers who arrive and purchase with no waiting.

Example

CONTAINERIZED SHIPPING AT SEA-LAND

Historically, ocean shipping rates have been heavily regulated based on categories of cargo (e.g., paper, film, frozen fish) and shipping lanes (e.g., Rotterdam to New York, Liverpool to Jacksonville, Seoul to San Francisco). Conferences of ocean shipping companies announced common carrier shipping rates for first-come first-served

---

[2] Scalpers, of course, charge higher prices still, but note that such gray markets reveal to the ticket agency what those customers who are not willing to show up at the ticket window and wait are in fact willing to pay. This information helps the ticket agency set an optimal price.

customers. More than half the world's cargo still moves under publicly mandated ocean shipping contracts at these uniform shipping rates. With no ability to adjust prices, sales people maximized the volume of cargo. The only good ship was a full ship. Since empty slots on a container ship perish as a revenue opportunity the moment the ship sails and since a container ship like Regina Maersk has space above decks for over 700 containers, companies queued up large volumes of cargo in anticipation of each ship's departure. Waiting time became a substantial implicit cost totaling millions of dollars a day.

Today, deregulation is fast approaching the ocean shipping industry. Deregulation bills have been drafted, and a spot market for space in containerized ships has emerged to operate alongside the regulated contract cargo allocation rules of first-come first-served. The immediate consequence has been delays in low-priority shipments from one voyage to the next in favor of higher rate cargo. Shippers are no longer compelled to take a common carrier contract cargo of newsprint rolls instead of charging what the market will bear for an expedited delivery of perishable pharmaceuticals.

In response to this new business environment, Sea-Land Service, Inc., of Charlotte, North Carolina, has optimized the placement of their containers around the world. Each empty container at each freight terminal is assigned a forecasted net revenue opportunity at that location and at other potential locations along the shipping route. Balancing capacity at locations where it may be needed for increased demand or higher rate cargo has markedly reduced the waiting time of cargo in the Sea-Land system. Shippers who offer less waiting time can charge higher rates and earn higher profits in the deregulated ocean shipping industry of the near future. Last-come first-served policies may become widespread for certain high-margin cargo.

Few ticketing operations have adopted a last-come first-served queue service rule. One apparent reason and one subtle reason seem involved. First, the power of custom should not be underestimated. Customs like first-come first-served have evolved not randomly but rather to serve some useful purpose. One purpose may be to reduce the ill will created among those denied access when popular items sell out. If I can't observe the person who got the last ticket paying a premium market-clearing auction price higher than what I would have paid, some sense of fairness is provided by the first-come first-served queue service rule. And that sense of fairness may be important to prevent fighting in ticket lines. Customs often reduce precisely these kinds of inconspicuous but potentially ruinous transaction costs.

A second more subtle reason, however, is that still another queue service rule may be the optimal mechanism design. Under last-come first-served, recall that any customer should leave the queue whenever a later arrival preempts his or her priority ranking as last in line. But customers will not wish to return many times to the ticket window. Again, time is money. So, customers ahead in line are likely to offer side payments to late arrivals to induce *them* to leave. Predictably those with the highest opportunity cost of time will end up bribing those with lower opportunity cost to leave and return. This side payment system may again reduce the ticket agency's receipts because in many ways it has just replaced the inefficiency of arriving early and waiting with the inefficiency of arriving often, departing, and returning. The recipients of the side payments are no worse off since they voluntarily decide to leave and return later, but those who make the side payments now turn to the window and surely offer less than they otherwise would have paid to secure good seats.

Stratified Lotteries

How can the ticket agency's mechanism design deal with this subtle complication? One obvious answer is to employ advance reservations and price discrimination in segmented customer submarkets. Airline capacity subject to random demand arrivals is allocated in precisely that way, and we discuss using such revenue management schemes in Appendix 14A. Remember, however, that here the problem was one of allocating scarce capacity at uniform prices across all the customers for a particular type of seat. Lotteries and online auctions using the Internet may hold the key to an effective mechanism design. Online sales are cheaper than phone sales because there are no operators to pay, there are no toll-free-line charges, and customers will often accept an Internet or faxed ticket, thereby saving the ticketing agent's mailing expense. Only one in ten live entertainment tickets are distributed online, but this channel is growing much faster than industry sales as a whole.

Example

Stratified Lottery
A randomized mechanism for allocating scarce capacity across demand segments.

http://

To see how a stratified lottery works for allotting student housing, access the following Internet site: http://housing.sandiego. edu/stratified.html

STRATIFIED LOTTERY: TICKETMASTER[3]

Suppose rather than announcing in advance what position in the customer queue would be served first, the ticketing agency picked a position at random. In effect, that's exactly what a lottery for the right to purchase a ticket does. Anytime prior to the day of sale, a customer stops by an Internet website to pick up a lottery number. Since those customers with low willingness to pay are equally likely to get the winning lottery numbers as those with high willingness to pay, Ticketmaster and other companies adopt a **stratified lottery** scheme. Rights to purchase high-price seats are distributed in one lottery, medium-price seats in another, and low-price seats in a third. At a designated date, the winning numbers are chosen at random and posted on the website and public-access TV channels. Only those customers holding the winning lottery numbers arrive to buy tickets, and since seat availability is assured, there is no reason to arrive early, queue up, and wait. This lottery mechanism design does then optimally reduce waiting time while allowing the ticket agency to secure higher uniform prices for each class of seats.

Holding auctions online presents a conflict of interest with Ticketmaster's traditional business of adding a $3 to $5 convenience fee for computerized ticket distribution by mail and in music stores. As the exclusive ticketing agent for 70 million tickets worth $3 billion, Ticketmaster is wary of reselling tickets above face value. The sports teams, concert halls, and promoters would then suspect Ticketmaster of underpricing the original tickets to charge convenience fees on not one but two sales. Ticketmaster could, of course, simply insist that the arenas and promoters set the face value prices, but a better alternative may be available. Ticketmaster and competitor Advantix Inc., who owns tickets.com, are both advising arenas to conduct "official" Internet auctions themselves for some choice seats that would be held back from public sale.

AUCTION DESIGN AND INFORMATION ECONOMICS

Perhaps one of the most prominent applications of mechanism design theory has been in the design of auctions. Everything from *Monday Night Football* to mineral rights, forest land, airline tickets, used equipment, and the electromagnetic spectrum have

---

[3] Based on "Ticket Scalpers Find a Home on the Web," *Wall Street Journal,* February 4, 1999, p. B1; "A Winning Ticket," *The Economist,* August 22, 1998, p. 52; and S. Rosen and A. Rosenfeld, "Ticket Pricing," *Journal of Law and Economics* (40:2), 1997, pp. 351–377.

Table 16.1   A Comparison of Auction Mechanism Design Characteristics

eBay	Priceline
Sequential	Simultaneous
Minimum bid improvement	Continuous
Posted prices	Posted offers to buy (reverse auction)
Multiple rounds	One-time-only if seller "hits"
Open bidding	Credit card immediately authorized
Reserve	No reserve
Highest wins and pays	All accepted bids pay
First (highest) price	Whatever price was bid
English ascending price	Dutch discriminatory descending price
Consolidated feedback on seller	Seller anonymous

been allocated to their highest valued use through auctions. The choices in auction design are numerous, as illustrated in Table 16.1. Bidding can be *sequential* with rebid opportunities like most estate auctions or *simultaneous* like the sealed-bid auctions for newly issued government debt securities. Bid prices can be *continuous* or constrained by *minimum discrete bid* improvements. The New York Stock Exchange has recently switched to continuous decimalization of their auction prices from the one-eighth-tick size restrictions on minimum bid improvements. Bids may be *sealed,* revealed by *open outcry,* or *posted* anonymously as on eBay. Bidding can be *one-time only* or *dynamic,* repeated in multiple rounds with cancellation and amendment of prior bids allowed (so-called *open bidding*). Finally, owners can place a minimum reservation price (the *"reserve"*), below which the item will not sell, or allow an auction to proceed with *no minimum.*

Perhaps the most important design differences between major types of auctions are who pays, what amount, and how the winner is determined. In some auctions *all bidders pay*—e.g., on Priceline.com, credit card information must accompany all offers, and conceivably the seller could collect from all bidders if the prices were acceptable. Of course, most auctions adopt the *highest-wins-and-pays* allocation rule. What the winner pays (whether it is his or her own *highest bid* or, at times, the *second-highest bid*) and how the auctioneer arrives at the winning bid can differ. **English auctions** ascend to higher and higher prices with open outcry or posted bids until the last bidder to make an offer exceeding all other offers is declared the winner. **Dutch auctions** work in the opposite direction by identifying the first bidder to register an acceptance as the auctioneer announces a succession of descending asking prices. This is how the wholesale flower market in the Netherlands operates—hence, the term Dutch auction. In *ascending-price auctions* the winner takes all, but in *descending-price auctions* the winner is often given the opportunity to purchase less than the total capacity available for sale, and the auction then continues downward.

Which of these and other auction design characteristics maximize the revenue to the seller and which allocate resources to their highest-valued use are important business questions and public policy issues. One well-understood insight from mechanism design theory is that asymmetric information will lead to timid bidding in ascending price auctions because of the winner's curse. To illustrate the winner's curse,

English Auction
An ascending price auction.

Dutch Auction
A descending price auction.

consider the following auction situation:[4] You are developing a bidding strategy for an asset whose value to the seller is a random variable distributed uniformly between $0 and $100. The seller observes this value and desires some profit on the transaction to cover the auction expenses, but places no minimum reservation price on the auction. You anticipate that a rational seller will refuse all offers below his or her personal value. The asset might be a baseball player's labor contract or a set of maps of the subterranean geological formations in a petroleum-rich area. Because of different complementary assets and skill, your value is certain to be 50 percent higher than the seller's personal asset value. What offer should you make?

Winner's Curse in Asymmetric Information Bidding Games

If neither party knows the true value, an expected value of $50 plus a small premium (i.e., well below $75) is a reasonable offer that will be accepted. However, if the seller knows the true value, consider what reasonable offers will be accepted and what reasonable offers will be refused. To simplify the analysis, suppose just three offers and three realizations of the seller's value are possible: $0, $55, and $100. In Figure 16.2, we see that should the true value be zero, only offers that overpay for the asset will be accepted. These payoffs are shown in the shaded boxes to the right of the decision tree. Should the true value be $55, $55 offers will be refused and again only $100 offers that overpay (even relative to the $75 value to the bidder) will be accepted (see the lowest boxed payoff). If the assets have the maximum possible value to the seller of $100, offers of $0, $55, *and* $100 will be refused. In short, all reasonable offers will be refused. Therefore, surprisingly, you should offer nothing at all! If you win such an auction, you are cursed with having overpaid for the asset.

WINNER'S CURSE AT ABC[5]

When bids for the right to televise *Monday Night Football* reached $4 billion on an eight-year contract, NBC decided that the winner would be cursed with losses of $150 million to $175 million per year and dropped out of the bidding. ABC continued bidding and eventually won the "prize" for $4.4 billion. Since ABC has televised this show and sold its ad slots for 30 years, they were in the best position to know its true current value. However, ABC's bid of $4.4 billion is over $25 million per game, more than double their previous contract with the NFL. Viewership has tumbled 33 percent since the peak interest in professional football in the early 1980s. Although the new television rights do allow for more TV time-outs in which to sell commercials, $25 million per three-hour game works out to eighty-four 15-second spots (28 per hour), each costing $300,000 that will be required just to break even. Football can increase other prime-time ratings, as CBS demonstrated by successfully shifting the Sunday *NFL Game of the Week* audience right into their highest-rated show *60 Minutes*. When the Fox Broadcasting network won the rights to the Sunday NFL games, the *60 Minutes* audience share shrank from 30 percent to 22 percent. Nevertheless, we agree with NBC's assessment of the winner's curse. ABC may be hard pressed to come close to recovering their investment.

---

[4] Adapted from M. Bazeman and W. Samuelson, "I Won the Auction But Don't Want the Prize," *Journal of Conflict Resolution,* December 1983, pp. 618–634. See also R. McAfee and J. McMillan, "Auctions and Bidding," *Journal of Economic Literature,* September 1987, pp. 699–738.

[5] Based on "Thrown for a Loss By the NFL," *Time,* January 26, 1998, p. 52.

Figure 16.2   Winner's Curse in an Asymmetric Information Bidding Game

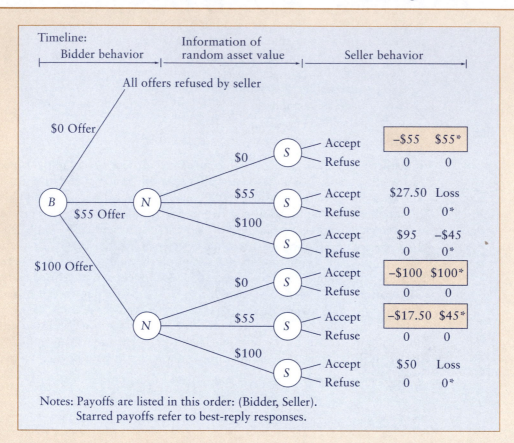

Notes: Payoffs are listed in this order: (Bidder, Seller).
Starred payoffs refer to best-reply responses.

Table 16.2 lists several auction price sequences for offshore oil tracts and FCC spectrum rights. The huge gaps between the winning bid and the second highest bid suggest that a winner's curse was present. The winning bidder for offshore oil in the Santa Barbara channel paid $11.4 million more than the second highest bid. Similarly, Wireless Co. paid $12.2 million more than GTE bid for the cell phone spectrum license in the Dallas Metro area. Bidding sequences for star players in professional sports look very similar.

Mechanism design theory reveals several insights about this asymmetric information bidding game. First, most bidders will figure out the winner's curse in an auction design like Figure 16.2 and therefore bid very timidly, if at all.[6] To induce more aggressive bidding in repeated, multiple-round versions of such asymmetric information games, sellers like De Beers find they must sort carefully their rough-cut diamonds, grading them into "sights." Reputation for reliability in grading the

---

[6] Notice that the same conclusion applies to a continuous-bid version of the auction, though experimental evidence suggests that most first-time players misperceive the asymmetric information nature of the seller's right of refusal and incorrectly bid $50 to $75. See C. Camerer, "Progress in Behavioral Game Theory," *Journal of Economic Perspectives,* 11(4), Fall 1997, pp. 167–188.

Table 16.2   Bids for Offshore Oil Contracts and FCC Spectrum Rights

| Offshore Oil[a] | | FCC Spectrum[b] | | |
Santa Barbara Channel	Alaska North Slope	Miami Metro Area	Dallas Metro Area	Bidder
$43.5	$10.5	$131.7	$84.2	Wireless Co.
32.1	5.2	126.0	72.0	GTE Inc.
18.1	2.1	125.5	68.7	Wireless Co.
10.2	1.4	119.4		
6.3	0.5	119.3		
	0.4	113.8		
		113.7		
		108.4		

[a]In millions, 1969 dollars.
[b]In millions, 1995 dollars.
Source: Adapted from Tables II and IV in R. Weber, "Making More for Less," *Journal of Economics and Management Strategy,* 6(3), Fall 1997, pp. 529–548.

sights more economically than the bidders could pick, cull, and resell the rejects is what brings De Beers' buyers back, auction after auction. De Beers then has a minimum participation rule that insists on a certain number of bids if one wishes to be asked back. Secondly, if the asymmetric information is discoverable by appraisals, marketing research, or other similar investments, another insight from auction design theory is that the seller should conduct a multiple-round auction with open bidding. Open bidding allows the bidders to react to asymmetric information revealed in prior rounds and therefore reduces the winner's curse. This idea was used by the Federal Communications Commission in the spectrum auctions for personal communication systems (PCS) like cell phones, mobile fax and data service, and voice-mail pagers.

Information Revelation in Common-Value Auctions

http://

Read the articles on common-value auctions at this site:
http://www.agorics.com/auctions/auction8.html

To illustrate this role of open bidding, consider two PCS bidders: Wireless Co., an alliance of Sprint and several large cable TV companies that spent $2.1 billion and won the rights to serve 145 million customers in 29 metropolitan service areas, and PCS PrimeCo., an alliance of three regional Bell companies that spent $1.1 billion and won the rights to serve 57 million customers in 11 metropolitan service areas. Several winning bids are listed in Table 16.3. For example, Wireless paid $46.6 million for the Louisville, Kentucky, service area. How did Wireless decide what to bid?

Suppose that both bidders know that the net present value of the rights to transmit PCS services in Louisville is a random variable uniformly distributed from $10 million to $60 million with six discrete values possible—for example, $10 million, $20 million, $30 million, $40 million, $50 million, and $60 million. Also assume

Table 16.3   Winning Bids in Broadband PCS Auction

Market	Population[a]	Winner	Second Highest	Bid[b]	Price/Pop.
New York	26.4	Wireless	Alaacr	$442.7	$16.76
San Francisco	11.9	PacTel	AmerPort	$202.2	$17.00
Charlotte	9.8	BellSouth	CCI	$70.9	$7.27
Dallas	9.7	Wireless	GTE	$84.2	$8.68
Houston	5.2	PrimeCo.	Wireless	$82.7	$15.93
New Orleans	4.9	PrimeCo.	Powertel	$89.5	$18.17
Louisville	3.6	Wireless	PrimeCo.	$46.6	$13.10
Salt Lake City	2.6	Wireless	GTE	$46.2	$17.95
Jacksonville	2.3	PrimeCo.	GTE	$44.5	$19.56

[a]In millions from the 1990 Census.
[b]Price paid for 30 MHz Block B spectrum rights, March 1995.
Source: P. Cramton, "The FCC Spectrum Auctions," *Journal of Economics and Management Strategy*, 6(3), Fall 1997, pp. 431–496.

Common-Value Auction
Auction where bidders have identical valuations when information is complete.

(provisionally) that both parties value the asset identically, a so-called **common-value auction.** The problem then from the bidders' point of view is to elicit sufficient information from the market environment and from the offers of other bidders to correctly identify the value and ensure a profit (i.e., not overpay for the asset). In advance, each company conducts marketing research experiments to narrow the possible outcomes and thereby better inform its own bid. Suppose Wireless Co.'s marketing research results are unable to exclude the two tails of the uniform distribution of possible values (i.e., $10 million and $60 million) but can exclude with certainty $20 million and $30 million as well as $50 million. Taken by itself, this information allows Wireless to narrow its probability assessments to $10 million, $40 million, and $60 million. Weighting each outcome equally yields an expected value bid of $36.7 million as follows:

$$\frac{1}{3} (\$10 \text{ million}) + \frac{1}{3} (\$40 \text{ million}) + \frac{1}{3} (\$60 \text{ million}) = \$36.7 \text{ million}$$

Similarly, PCS Prime Co. conducts its own marketing research which, let's assume, excludes $10 million, $30 million, and $50 million as possible outcomes for the Louisville service area. That is, PCS PrimeCo. has access to separate information that causes it to calculate a different expected value bid:[7]

$$\frac{1}{3} (\$20 \text{ million}) + \frac{1}{3} (\$40 \text{ million}) + \frac{1}{3} (\$60 \text{ million}) = \$40 \text{ million}$$

---

[7] The equally weighted probabilities of 1/3 are actually Bayesian probabilities of each possible remaining value based on a perfectly accurate forecast that $10 million, $30 million, and $50 million (the prime numbers in the set of possible asset values) have been ruled out. It is helpful if we think of the marketing research as identifying Prime and Not Prime numbers between one and six multiplied by one million. Then, the Bayesian probability ($20 million/Perfect Forecast of Not Prime) = (0.167 × 1.0)/(0.167 + 0.833 × 0.4) = 0.33 where 0.167 is the prior probability before the marketing research is conducted that $20 million will be the realized asset value. The number 1.0 is the accuracy of the forecasting instrument— for example, the conditional probability that when $20 million is the true value, the conclusion from the

These are the best estimates of the common value based on the asymmetric information available to the two firms. Consequently, in a simultaneous sealed-bid auction, the most a seller could hope to realize is $40 million. With sealed bids there is no information conveyed to the competitor, and an optimal bidding strategy is therefore simply to shade your bid slightly below the Bayesian expected value based on your own information set. PCS PrimeCo. would therefore bid something just under $40 (39.6) million and win the spectrum rights for the Louisville service area.

Bayesian Strategy with Open Bidding Design

Notice, however, from the seller's point of view *ex post facto* (after receiving the sealed bids) that the joint information set of the two parties suggests PCS PrimeCo. has underpaid. To review, the union of the two sets of marketing research outcomes excludes $10 million, $20 million, $30 million, and $50 million. Said another way, the *combined* marketing research results have narrowed the possible outcomes for the value of the Louisville service area to $40 million and $60 million. Neither firm has access to this much information. Each simply knows a subset of all the marketing research available. But as a seller in such a setting, the FCC wishes to elicit full revelation of *all* asymmetric information because it affects the winning bid. If $40 million and $60 million are equally likely, and the bidders can somehow discern this information, the Louisville service area is worth just under $50 million, not PCS PrimeCo.'s bid of just under $40 million.

One way to bring all the asymmetric information into play is to adopt a sequential open-bidding auction design in which each company is chosen at random to post its bid (in one round, then the random order of posting procedure is redone for Round 2, Round 3, etc.).[8] Then, whichever company bids first, the other company will deduce the first bidder's additional marketing research results and proceed to increase its bid in light of the more complete information available. For example, if PCS PrimeCo. bids first, and bids $40 million based on its own asymmetric information, Wireless Co. will then be in a position to deduce that PCS PrimeCo.'s marketing research excluded $10 million, $30 million, and $50 million as possible values. That's the only information that would be consistent with a bid of $40 million in a simultaneous sealed-bid auction over an asset with a uniform distribution from $10 million to $60 million with only these six possible outcomes. Knowing from its own marketing research that $20 million, $30 million, and $50 million have also been ruled out, Wireless will immediately place a winning bid of just under $50 million:

$$\frac{1}{2} (\$40 \text{ million}) + \frac{1}{2} (\$60 \text{ million}) = \$50 \text{ million}$$

---

marketing research will be that the value is Not Prime, meaning "not a prime number between one and six." The number 0.833 is the prior probability that the asset value will be something other than $20 million. And finally, the number 0.4 is the probability that when something other than $20 million is the true asset value, the perfectly accurate forecasting instrument will still say Not Prime. That happens with $40 million and $60 million—i.e., twice in five possibilities.

The analysis here is easily modified to incorporate less than perfect forecasts from the marketing research. That is fortunate indeed because imperfect forecasts are the reality of business. See E. Rasmussen, *Games and Information*, 2nd ed. (Cambridge: Basil Blackwell, 1993), Chapter 12, Section 4.

[8] Open bidding with a nonrandom, structured sequence of role reversals on multiple auctions allows bidders to signal and punish one another (e.g., with "tit for tat") and therefore increases the likelihood of tacit collusion.

With many bidders and other service areas in which Wireless Co. would be required to bid first and in which PCS PrimeCo. had a turn playing the fast second, this sequential open-bidding auction design would work well. Winning bids would rise to the Bayesian expected asset values reflecting all available information, and highest-value users would receive the assets.

Example

OPEN BIDDING SIMULTANEOUS AUCTION OF PCS SPECTRUM RIGHTS[9]

Thirty firms ultimately participated in the broadband spectrum auctions. The FCC specified two 30-MHz blocks for each of 51 metropolitan service areas. A special feature of these metropolitan service areas was strong interdependencies in providing service in contiguous service areas. Bidders were encouraged therefore to assemble and reassemble efficient bundles of licenses as the auction progressed. Consequently, multiple-round simultaneous auctions with open bidding were adopted by the FCC to allocate spectrum rights. Each bidder was told there would be several rounds of bidding, all bids in each round were announced, and each bidder was allowed to cancel or amend bids from round to round. All bids in every metro area remained open as long as any bidding activity continued in any service area. The auction lasted 112 rounds over a four-month period in early 1995. Using this auction design, the FCC raised $7.7 billion. AT&T paid $49.3 million and Wireless Co. paid $46.6 million for the A block and B block spectrum rights in Louisville.

As new technologies become available, the FCC intends to conduct additional auctions periodically to continue placing spectrum rights in the hands of the highest-value users. For example, in March 1998, 139 companies bid $578 million for UHF microwave transmission rights to broadcast wireless Internet access service, as we predicted.

Strategic Underbidding in Private-Value Auctions[10]

One serious drawback of English open outcry auctions is the strategic reticence (tendency to underbid) that bidders exhibit. If the bidders have common information but different valuations (i.e., a so-called **private-value auction**), those with high willingness to pay have an incentive to refrain from aggressive bidding in an attempt to just exceed the bid of the player with the second highest valuation. For example, in the FCC's spectrum auctions, the cellular phone incumbents already established in a metropolitan area had higher valuation than other bidders. In the early rounds of any such open bidding auction over private values, eventual high bidders hold back. Analysis of the FCC data suggests only 53 percent of the eventual winners were the high bidders after the early rounds. Sellers worry that this strategic reticence dampens the overall level of bidding throughout the auction and may well reduce final revenue.

Suppose two bidders each value a service or asset between $0 million and $10 million. No information about the actual net present values is known. That is, there is

Private-Value Auction
Auction where the bidders have different valuations when information is complete.

---

[9] Based on "Market Design and the Spectrum Auctions," A Special Issue of *Journal of Economics and Management Strategy,* 6(3), Fall 1997, and "Sale of Wireless Frequencies," *Wall Street Journal,* March 25, 1998, p. A3.

[10] Two excellent elaborations of this and the next topic are J. McMillan, "Bidding in Competition," *Games, Strategies, and Managers* (New York: Oxford University Press, 1992), Chapter 11, and E. Rasmussen, "Auctions," *Games and Information,* 2nd ed. (Cambridge, MA: Basil Blackwell, 1993), Chapter 12.

no common-value information, asymmetric or otherwise. This is a purely private value auction. The auction will last only one round, the bids are sealed, and the highest bid wins. Your valuation is $6 million—what should you bid?

With two bidders present, each must assume that the other will offer something less than his or her private value, say k times v where k is a proportion and v is the private value.[11] Any bids by Alice (P_a) that are greater than k times Bob's value (v_b) will win. That is, anytime $P_a/k > v_b$, Alice wins the auction and realizes a profit of $(v_a - P_a)$. With uniform density, the probability that Bob's value is any given number between $0 and $10 million is 1/10 million. Again, Alice wins when this value is between $0 and P_a/k dollars. Therefore, Alice's cumulative probability of winning is P_a/k events, each of which has a marginal probability of 1/10 million—i.e., Alice's cumulative probability of winning is $P_a/(k \times 10$ million). Alice's expected profit from the auction may therefore be written as follows:

$$\text{E(Profit}_a) = (v_a - P_a) \frac{P_a}{k \cdot 10,000,000} \qquad [16.1]$$

Differentiating Equation 16.1 with respect to P_a and setting the derivative equal to zero, Alice's expected profit from the auction is maximized when

$$(v_a - 2P_a) \frac{1}{k \cdot 10,000,000} = 0 \qquad [16.2]$$

—i.e., when $P_a = v_a/2$. That is, Alice will maximize her expected profit from participating in the auction, conditional on Bob's choosing a kv_b bidding rule, by choosing to reduce her own private value by 1/2. Since Alice and Bob are symmetrically situated in this bidding game, Bob too should reduce his private value by 1/2. With $k = 1/2$, the players are in a Nash equilibrium. Each maximizes self-interest, conditional on the other player's bidding $v/2$, by bidding half of his or her own private value. In a two-player, simultaneous, highest-price-wins-and-pays sealed-bid auction, the rational underbidding is fully 50 percent!

If there are five bidders, it is easy to show that a rational bidder should reduce true private value by 1/5, and if n bidders, by $1/n$.[12] Quite intuitively, therefore, the more bidders, the smaller is the rational underbidding. See Figure 16.3. Sellers understand this and therefore provide sorting services (in De Beers's case) and handsome catalogs and live exhibitions (in Christie's case) to draw bidders into the auction process. Paul Klemperer of Oxford University describes how this fundamental insight determined many of the auction design decisions for the British spectrum auctions. Thirteen different companies entered the bidding, resulting in the highest per-capita revenue raised by all the European and Asian 3G auctions.

Example

EXPONENTIAL VALLEY INC. AUCTIONS A CHIP PATENT[13]

Exponential Valley Inc., a Silicon Valley microprocessor start-up, has decided to auction its portfolio of 45 issued and pending patents rather than move into production. The computer chip patents include features that would allow a competitor to match forthcoming chip products from industry leader Intel Corp. Intel regularly

---

[11] This example relies on McMillan, *op. cit.*, pp. 138 and 208–209.

[12] See Rasmussen, *op. cit.*, p. 296, and Paul Klemperer, "Spectrum Auctions," *European Economic Review*, 46 (2002), pp. 829–845.

[13] Based on "An Auction of Chip Patents May Ignite Bidding War," *Wall Street Journal*, August 1, 1997, p. B5.

Figure 16.3   Strategic Underbidding Declines and Seller Revenue Rises with Bidder Entry in Private Value Auctions

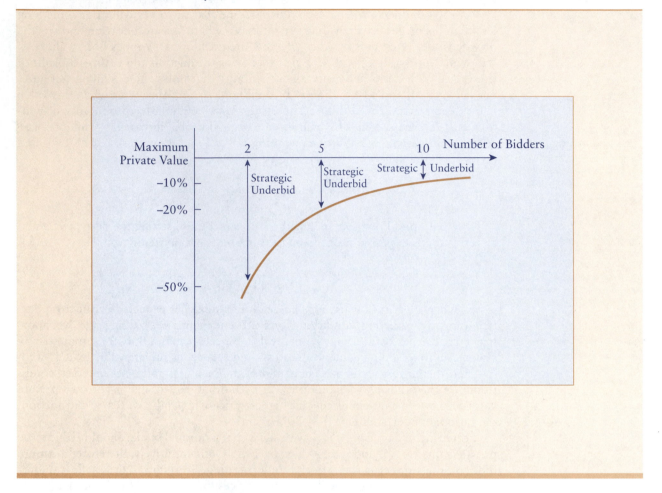

sues companies who make clones of their chips and has been very effective in deterring entry with this strategy. The Exponential Valley patents appear to offer an opportunity to provide protection from Intel's patent infringement suits. Digital Equipment, Advanced Micro Devices, and a division of National Semiconductor all expressed interest in bidding on the patents. At considerable expense, Exponential has developed a large prospectus of technical and bidding information that it targeted to other possible bidders: Rambus, Inc., Chromatic Research Inc., and Texas Instruments. Exponential Valley did so because the larger the number of bidders, the less the strategic underbidding will be.

If sellers expend enough resources to expand the pool of bidders, in the limit the seller can realize $(n-1)/n$ of the maximum private value (v_{max}). Five bidders implies 80 percent of v_{max}. Ten bidders implies 90 percent of v_{max}. Twenty bidders implies 95 percent of v_{max}. Increasing the number of bidders from two to five results in a 30-percent increase in value, doubling the number of bidders from five to ten results in a 10-percent increase in value, and doubling them again results in only a 5-percent increase in value. Diminishing returns to these efforts by sellers to expand the pool of bidders implies that the fundamental problem of strategic underbidding will be reduced but never eliminated.

Of course, underbidding in a private-value auction is rational only if bidders can be assured of winning in the final round. One way to reduce strategic underbidding in private-value auctions is to reduce the available information about other valuations by sealing the bids. A less extreme approach is to end the auction without warning, after several preliminary rounds, thereby in effect sealing the bids unpredictably. Of course, any mechanism that prevents communication may have a significant disadvantage when asymmetric information is present among the bidders as we saw in the previous section. Therefore, it can be in the seller's interest to induce the revelation of all such asymmetric information. In fact, sellers often have an incentive to preannounce expert appraisals of value (as Christie's and Sotheby's auction houses do) in order to reduce the winner's curse.

This concern is important in auction design, but not always controlling. The reason is that some asymmetrically held information can, if revealed, lower the rational bid (see the first Case Exercise at the end of the chapter). So, sealing bids is a design alternative that becomes more attractive the greater the variation in private values and the more symmetric the information pertaining to valuation among the bidders. Obviously, open bidding or preannouncing appraisals is more attractive whenever favorable information is known to the seller. However, even when the seller is in the dark, open bidding has a positive expected value for the seller because the exchange of common-value information always reduces the winner's curse.

Second-Highest Sealed-Bid Auctions: A Revelation Mechanism

Strategic underbidding is especially troubling, of course, if the seller is collecting bid revenue from all participants in the auction. A "seller" may be attempting to assess whether there exists sufficient total willingness to pay to justify investment in a new facility (e.g., a ballpark, a pool, a set of tennis courts, or a clubhouse). Each potential user is asked what he or she would pay for access. If sufficient demand exists, the facility manager then builds the facility and collects the highly divergent, discriminatory prices from each "bidder." The key to such an assessment is designing an **incentive-compatible revelation mechanism**. The same thing is true in designing a private-value auction. If, as an auction designer, one could remove the incentive to underbid and at the same time prevent a winner's curse, one could align incentives with true revelation of value. Think through the following illustration of an ingenious incentive-compatible auction mechanism that won William Vickery a considerable prize, the Nobel prize![14]

Following Vickery, rather than requiring the winning bidder to pay the high bid, what if the auction mechanism design specified in advance that the highest bid wins but that the winner would pay the second-highest bid? Notice that the winner's curse is no longer present. By definition, under the rules of a highest-pays-second-highest sealed-bid auction, the payment triggered by bidding one's true private value cannot exceed the next best alternative selling price. This use of a verifiable second opinion and exit option to shore up the bidder's protection from suffering a winner's

Incentive-Compatible Revelation Mechanism
A procedure for aligning incentives with revelation of true value.

[14] Every game theory and mechanism design theory book describes the Vickery auction, also known as the second-highest sealed-bid auction, or the uniform-price auction. Vickery's original article is also revealing and insightful; see W. Vickery, "Counterspeculation, Auctions, and Competitive Sealed Tenders," *Journal of Finance*, 16(8), 1961, p. 37.

Vickery Auction
An incentive-compatible revelation mechanism for eliciting sealed bids equal to private value.

curse was the key insight of William Vickery's incentive-compatible mechanism design. True revelation of maximum-willingness-to-pay proves compatible, through an ingenious mechanism design, with the bidder's desire to avoid the winner's curse.

To sum up, every bidder in a **Vickery auction** has no incentive to underbid. Reducing your bid below your private value has no effect on the payment due should you win. Instead, underbidding in a second-highest sealed-bid auction when you are the highest-willingness-to-pay participant simply increases the probability of losing an auction asset that it would have been possible to acquire for less than it is worth to you. And if someone else values the asset more than you, no payment is triggered by bidding up to your own private value. Therefore, for all possible cases, true revelation of private value dominates underbidding as a bidding strategy. And because bids are sealed and the auction lasts only one round, no strategic bidding, false carding, or signaling can have any effect on other participants in the auction. Therefore, No Underbidding is a dominant strategy equilibrium for all bidders.[15] Of course, realized revenue is still reduced by the full difference between first price and second-highest values, but at least the seller learns the true value.

Example

SECOND-HIGHEST SEALED-BID AUCTION: U.S. TREASURY BILLS[16]

Auction design decisions in security markets focus (appropriately) on which auction mechanisms raise the most revenue for the issuers. On this question, debate currently rages about the optimal design of Treasury bill new-issue security auctions. Denmark and Sweden adopt diametrically opposed designs. The Swedes sell government bills and bonds at discriminatory Dutch auction prices; the Danes sell at a uniform second-highest sealed-bid price. Given this diversity of expert opinion and practice, the U.S. Federal Reserve has authorized the New York Federal Reserve Bank to experiment with both designs for two-year and five-year notes. The preponderance of Treasury auctions in the United States (and indeed around the world) are discriminatory descending-price (Dutch) auctions; buyers pay whatever they bid for quantities of T-bonds along a demand schedule submitted by each bidder. If the market-clearing price implies a yield of 5.03 percent, a typical bidder may get $5 million worth of T-bonds at her highest submitted price yielding 5.00 percent, $7 million worth of T-bonds at a lower price yielding 5.02 percent, and perhaps another $10 million at the market-clearing (lowest) price yielding 5.03 percent.

Uniform price second-highest sealed-bid auctions are very different. Every bidder in this Vickery auction might pay the uniform-slightly-higher price associated with a yield of 5.02 percent, and the Treasury's marginal cost of raising debt capital will decline from 5.03 percent to 5.02 percent. However, some still higher-priced transactions no longer take place, and other lower-price transactions also no longer take place. Therefore it is unclear analytically what will happen to Treasury revenue; it depends on the interest rate elasticity of T-bill demand. The recent Vickery auction experiments have raised nearly identical revenue to the traditional Treasury auction methods. This result highlights the insight that the principal advantages of

---

[15] The bidder's degree of risk aversion has no bearing on this result. However, more risk-averse bidders do ensure against losing in winner-take-all first price sealed-bid auctions by increasing their bid relative to the seller revenue from a second-highest sealed-bid auction. We discuss the role of risk aversion further in the next section.

[16] Based on "Bidding Up Debt Auctions," *BusinessWeek*, September 8, 1997, p. 26, and S. Nandi, "Treasury Auctions: What Do the Recent Models and Results Tell Us?" *Federal Reserve Bank of Atlanta Economic Review*, Fourth Quarter, 1997.

second-highest sealed-bid Vickery auctions are not to raise seller revenue, but rather to minimize strategic underbidding, reveal true private valuations, and reduce bidder collusion among small numbers of bidders. In contrast, security markets are highly efficient, with numerous potential buyers willing to pay a common value of these T-bond and T-bill assets. Therefore, second-highest sealed-bid mechanism design is more appropriate for the private placement IPO market pioneered by Fidelity and W. R. Hambrecht and discussed at the start of this chapter in the Managerial Challenge. In sum, combining managerial insight about auction design with a careful analysis of the particulars of the business setting proves important.

What auction design to adopt is often a complex trade-off between the above results and the particulars of the business generating the asset value. In the U.S. broadband spectrum auctions discussed earlier, open bidding in multiple rounds with the winner paying his or her highest-price bid met the needs of the telecommunication companies to reconfigure their contiguous service areas as the auction proceeded. Careful analysis and application of the managerial insights from mechanism design reasoning can better inform these choices and increase capitalized value.

Revenue Equivalence of Alternative Auction Types[17]

Under particular circumstances, the four simplest types of auctions (English Ascending Price, Dutch Descending Uniform Price, First-Price Sealed-Bid, and Highest Pays Second-Highest Sealed Bid) yield equivalent revenue to the seller-auctioneer. For example, both First-Price Sealed-Bid auction participants and Dutch Descending Uniform Price auction participants must pay whatever they bid if their bids prove to be the winning market-clearing bids. In addition, participants in both types have no access to information about bidders with lesser valuations than themselves. Consequently, the optimal bidding strategy in a Dutch or First-Price Sealed-Bid auction is identical, and thus the winning bids will be identical (see Table 16.4).

Similarly, for private value auctions, as English auction participants learn more and more in the course of the bidding about the independent valuations of other bidders, the person with the highest valuation will ultimately offer an amount just in excess of the second highest bidder. Second-Highest Sealed-Bid auctions induce, as we have seen, true revelation of value from all bidders, but the winner also pays an amount just equal to the second highest bidder. Hence, an English Ascending Price auction and a Second-Highest Sealed-Bid auction yield essentially the same expected revenue to the seller in private value auctions. Indeed, it turns out that with risk-neutral bidders and private values, all four simple auction types result in the same expected revenue—i.e., an amount just equal to the highest value minus the full difference to the next highest bid. From a seller's perspective this Revenue Equivalence Theorem (RET) is a depressing result; one would hope to do better.

In several instances, one auction type does raise more expected revenue than another. These optimal mechanism design differences depend upon the risk preference of the bidders and upon the common-value or private-value nature of the item being auctioned. Continuing first with the private-value auctions, if bidders are risk averse and they are operating under the lack of information of a Dutch or First-Price Sealed-Bid design, they will seek to reduce the probability of losing the item when their valuation is highest. Consequently, relative to the situation in an English

---

[17] For a more extensive discussion of this topic, see A. Dixit and S. Skeath, *Games of Strategy* (New York: Norton) 1999, Chapter 15, and E. Rasmussen, *op. cit.*, Chapter 12.

or Second-Highest Sealed-Bid auction in which the winning bidder pays essentially the second highest bid, risk-averse Dutch or First-Price Sealed-Bid auction participants raise their bids in order to reduce the probability of being outbid by a close second valuation. Strategic underbidding to avoid the winner's curse is still present but it is mitigated by risk aversion. So, a seller-auctioneer can raise more revenue on average when the bidders are risk averse and the values are independent and private by conducting a Dutch or First-Price Sealed-Bid auction. These results for private-value auctions for items like patent licenses, sales territories, antiques, and fine art are summarized in the top section of Table 16.4.

As to common-value auctions for items that have thick resale markets like crude oil, mineral leases, forest logging rights, equity and debt securities, and easily redeployable surplus equipment such as commercial aircraft, the source of uncertainty in the valuation is an estimation risk. Every bidder knows that the true value at resale is identical across all auction participants; it's just that this true value is an unknown while the oil is still in the ground, the logs still in the forest, the IPOs yet unissued, etc. Each bidder must therefore assess this true value from his or her own forecast information in a Dutch Uniform Price or First-Price Sealed-Bid auction and from any additional information that can be gleaned from the sequence of bids in the English auction. Since Bayesian updating of the initial estimates (the "priors") in the sequential process of an English auction will tend to result in a pooling of the bidders' information, winning bids in the English auction will tend towards the mean estimate of the population of forecasts. As this is the best unbiased estimate of what value actually is the truly harvestable common value of the resource, strategic underbidding to avoid the winner's curse will be reduced to the maximum extent in the English auction.

Table 16.4   Seller Expected Revenue from Auction Types

	Private-Value Auctions (Patent License, Sales Territory, Estate Antiques)			
Risk-Neutral Bidders	Dutch = Uniform Price	First-Price Sealed-Bid	=	English = Second-Highest Sealed-Bid
Risk-Averse Bidders	Dutch = Uniform Price	First-Price Sealed-Bid	>	English = Second-Highest Sealed-Bid

	Common-Value Auctions (Mineral Lease, Logging Rights, Aircraft)			
Risk-Neutral Bidders	English >	Second-Highest Sealed-Bid	> Dutch = Uniform Price	First-Price Sealed-Bid
Risk-Averse Bidders	English >	Second-Highest Sealed-Bid	$\leq$ Dutch = Uniform Price	First-Price Sealed-Bid

Hence, as shown in the bottom section of Table 16.4, a seller-auctioneer can raise the most revenue with an English common-value auction. And since, as we saw in the previous section, Second-Highest Sealed-Bid designs can also substantially reduce the winner's curse in these common-value auctions, that auction design finishes second in projected revenue. And, for common-value auctions, these results go through whether bidders are risk neutral or not.[18]

INTERNET AUCTION DESIGN BECOMES A BIG e-BUSINESS DEBATE: eBAY VERSUS PRICELINE[19]

Online auctions have exhibited a truly explosive rate of Internet site development and attracted tremendous investor interest. Eight sites existed in July 1998; 400 existed in July 1999, and over 3,000 sites existed in July 2000. Some of the sites issued public shares and realized massive equity market value. By early 2000, eBay Inc. reached 10 million customers and achieved a market value of $21 billion. Shortly after its initial public offering in 1999, Priceline exceeded the *combined* market value of the major airlines (American, Delta, United) whose unsold last-minute tickets it offered to liquidate. In the information economy, online auctions are a key business model that may displace the two traditional price-setting processes: (1) one-on-one negotiation (haggling) and (2) a menu of fixed price quotes provided by the seller. Business-to-business (B2B) transactions may continue to require one-on-one negotiation over the many time, quality, availability, and delivery dimensions of the "deal," but in business-to-consumer transactions, auction prices themselves establish most of what is needed for a "deal."

In 2000, however, Priceline's share price fell 90 percent. Such peaks and troughs in capitalized value may simply reflect a speculative bubble in technology stocks in general and Internet-related stocks in particular. The share prices of eToys and E*Trade also collapsed 80 percent and 65 percent from their respective peaks. Although the speculative technology bubble of 1998–2000 provides a partial explanation, other factors seem involved in the roller coaster of auction site share prices. For one thing, Priceline failed to secure a broad patent for its reverse auction design. Public commentary suggests Priceline's patents will not protect the company from subsequent imitators. Priceline employs an ascending-posted-price highest-wins-and-pays auction mechanism design. Bids are listed anonymously to reduce collusion and posted continuously to mitigate the strategic underbidding that accompanies any private-value auction (i.e., the winner's curse). Bid payments must be guaranteed with a credit card at the time the buyers' offers are placed; subsequently, bids cannot be cancelled and are executed automatically if the offer is accepted.

eBay has a more transparent ascending-price auction design with minimum-increment-posted-prices and highest-wins-and-pays rules for declaring a winner. Rather than allowing sellers to remain anonymous until they decide to "hit" a Priceline buyer's posted offer, eBay consolidates feedback on the seller's past performance and hot-links it to the bidding site. Also unlike Priceline, eBay allows open bidding (i.e.,

---

[18] Risk aversion introduces the same complication into the analysis as earlier—i.e., Dutch Uniform Price and First-Price Sealed-Bid participants raise their bids to reduce the probability of losing an item to a close second competitor. Still, the benefits of information pooling tend to favor English or Second-Best Sealed-Bid designs for common value auctions.

[19] Based on "The Heyday of the Auction," *The Economist,* July 24, 1999, pp. 67–68; "Redesigning Business: Priceline," *Harvard Business Review,* Nov/Dec, 1999, pp. 19–21; "Dotty about dot.commerce?" *The Economist,* February 26, 2000, p. 24; "Going, Going, Gone, Sucker!" *Business Week,* March 20, 2000, pp. 124–125; and "Inside: Is Priceline Vulnerable?" *Harvard Business Review,* December 3, 1999, pp. 19–21.

offers are repeated in multiple rounds, and prior offers may be cancelled or amended). Open bidding proved especially effective in the spectrum rights auctions of bandwidth for PCS broadcast signals where the buyers were large telecommunications companies attempting to assemble networks of cellular phone licenses. Whether guaranteed offers or open bidding proves to be optimal for auctioning airline tickets, automobiles, and machinery will determine in part whether eBay or Priceline thrives.

A still larger auction design issue is whether to continue the traditional ascending-price (English) auction or adopt descending-price (Dutch) auction procedures. Basement.com and OutletZoo.com start prices high and drop them in increments until all the units for sale have been demanded. Clearly, sellers can realize more revenue in discriminatory Dutch auctions by charging differentially higher prices to the early bidders than can be realized in uniform-price Dutch or English auctions that identify a market-clearing price. Of course, sophisticated institutional and industrial buyers understand this as well, and this segment may well prefer a traditional nonauction website like Grainger.com where sellers post initial best offers and then focus on availability, delivery, installation, technical support, and other after-sale services. Establishing the value-in-use of these extras in the "total offering" may prove as critical as seller warranties and replacement guarantees to B2B customers.[20]

Contractual Approaches to Asymmetric Information in Online Auctions

In some ways Priceline.com is like couponing without the brand name as a guarantee of redemption security. Priceline's mechanism design does provide a way to price discriminate to the very price-sensitive customer segments without degrading one's brand identity. Perhaps this explains why Delta Airlines took a substantial equity stake in Priceline; Delta could liquidate its inventory without cannibalizing higher fare sales. But whether auctioning cars, hotel rooms, or airline trips, anonymous sellers offering unverifiable product or service claims must credibly commit to higher quality products if they hope to attract anything more than rock-bottom prices. As we have seen, hostage or bonding mechanisms are the key to credible commitments. We now discuss various contractual and organization design approaches to achieving credibility.

Appraisal
An estimate of value by an independent expert.

First, sellers can invest in and disseminate **appraisals** to try to distinguish their product offerings from fraudulently advertised products. Independent certified appraisals, like buy-back guarantees, place a floor under the value of the product offered for sale. Perhaps a tract of development land or the intellectual property in a patent lease is up for bids; the seller can pay for an appraisal about the range of values typically paid in resale markets for land or intellectual property assets with similar characteristics. Two drawbacks prevent the widespread adoption of this approach, however. Certified appraisals are expensive, and appraisals seldom establish maximum or unique asset value.

The second contractual approach sellers can adopt to establish credibility for their product claims is to signal their respective quality by offering *warranties and replacement guarantees*. These signaling features of the product offering are observable to the buyer at the point of sale and are highly correlated with the unobservable prod-

---

[20] See Ajit Kambil and Eric van Heck, *Making Markets* (Boston: HBS Press), 2002; James Anderson and James Narus, *Business Market Management* (New York: Prentice-Hall), 1999; and R. Oliva, "Sold on Reverse Auctions," *Marketing Management*, March/April 2003, p. 45.

uct or service quality at issue. Automobile tire manufacturers who take shortcuts vulcanizing the tire casings that embed steel wire belts in their tire treads will make shorter treadware warranties and guarantee against fewer blowout hazards. The buyer can therefore pay more for warrantied tires and feel assured that the tire quality is above that offered by nonwarrantied suppliers. Encouraging buyers to screen alternate suppliers in this way therefore achieves a separating equilibrium to the asymmetric information exchange that would be more costly for sellers to secure through independent appraisal of each potential tire. Warranty and replacement guarantee contracts with buyers necessitate conspicuous third-party enforcement, however, and therefore provide poor reasons to establish brand loyalty. As we have seen, investment in brand-name reputations can sometimes offer a more attractive hostage than these contract mechanisms.

Another way for sellers to credibly commit to the delivery of a high-quality durable product is to offer to lease rather than sell the product and then to offer *lease terms with a high residual value*. This feature of leasing offers a net advantage over buying in that sellers with informational advantages will credibly commit to forward value through the take-back provisions of the lease. If one seller says you can lease with a 60-percent residual at the end of 4 years and another quotes a 40-percent residual at the end of 4 years, all other things the same, the lease payments will recover depreciation only two thirds as great in the 60-percent residual lease. In that case, buyers may well be willing to lease a higher quality/higher priced product. Of course, such an approach to establishing credibility will not be adopted if sellers foresee substantial obsolescence risk. Therefore, high residuals seldom occur alone; usually other lease terms (e.g., financing charges, initial asset prices, or lease closing fees) adjust upward to "price in" the extra seller risk when residuals increase.

Finally, sellers can agree to accept **contingent payments**—that is, seller revenue dependent on the performance the buyer experiences. Suppose the due diligence required to establish clear value in an asset sale is prohibitively expensive. If a tract of development land has buried fuel tanks that are unknown to the seller but that necessitate substantial environmental remediation, the land seller can agree *ex ante* to pay *ex post* for the restoration of the land. If timberland sales or oil field leases prove particularly productive, the buyer and seller can agree to larger money payments than if the actual harvested timber and oil pumped prove disappointing. And these contingent payment contracts can be arranged as progress payments, so that the buyer and seller take small and continuous steps away from one another while money remains owed. Sometimes corporations employ contingent payments while exchanging hostages in an asset sale by requiring the seller to take a financial stake (perhaps 15 percent of the cash flow to equity owners) in the buyer's subsidiary spun off to manage the new assets. Given the low priority of an equity owner should the spin-off declare bankruptcy and need to liquidate, contingency payments increase the seller's incentives to reveal hidden features that determine the true cash flows realizable from the asset.

Contingent Payments
A fee schedule conditional on the outcome of uncertain future events.

INCENTIVE-COMPATIBLE REVELATION MECHANISMS

Perhaps the most powerful mechanism design tool for eliciting privately held asymmetric information is another variant of William Vickery's concept of self-enforcing revelation mechanisms—i.e., revelations that are consistent with an agent's objectives and therefore prove to be self-enforcing. Later, Edward Clarke and Ted Groves added the idea of multiple agents in group decision making such that the mechanism design objective became demand or cost revelation in a partnership that had to be compatible with the incentives of all the parties—hence, an "incentive-compatible (IC) revelation mechanism." Such IC revelation mechanisms have wide applicability in both the public and private sectors. Consider the following examples.

Example

INTEL AND ANALOG INC. FORM PARTNERSHIP TO DEVELOP DSP CHIP[21]

Intel Corp. has dominated the manufacture of semiconductor chips for computer microprocessors for more than a decade. With AMD and Siemens beginning to pose some threat in this traditional market, Intel formed a joint venture in 1999 with Analog Devices Inc. to move into the chip market for communications devices like cell phones, pagers, and wireless videophones. Intel and Analog will jointly develop a new line of digital signal processor (DSP) chips. DSP chips take analog signals like voice, photo images, and video and convert them to digital signals to be transmitted over wireless systems. Given the enormous growth in wireless communications, new signal compression and encryption capabilities of the Intel-Analog chip are expected to compete well against rival DSP suppliers Texas Instruments (TI) and Lucent Technologies. DSP chips also appear to have application in modems and other networking devices that provide high-speed access to the Internet. Speech recognition systems for machine-controlled applications are a complementary value-adding technology. By 2010, DSP chips will provide the functionality of a laptop computer on a thumbtack that fits into wristwatch-size devices. DSP chip sales growth has recently approached 30 percent per year, reaching total sales of $5.7 billion.

Groups of Intel and Analog engineers will collaborate on designing the core architecture of the chip, and the two companies will then separately develop and sell products based on the design. The contingent payoffs to each firm are therefore based in part on their cooperative design success and in part on their separate product development and marketing efforts. This joint venture contract provides incentives for continuing cooperation far beyond those generated by a simple profit-sharing agreement, yet it preserves each company's option to pursue some business plans privately.

Cost Revelation in Joint Ventures and Partnerships

When pivotal information in such partnerships is privately held and verification by third parties is infeasible or undesirable, the partners seek to adopt procedures to assure true revelation of this asymmetric information. Consider a joint venture to develop several new personal computer products between a PC designer-manufacturer, such as Apple Computer, and Motorola, a leading supplier of computer chips.[22] The Apple operating system depends on the capabilities of the Motorola chips, and the chips are produced in anticipation of the future requirements of the operating system. The partners believe they can better sustain a competitive advantage in this fast-moving technology by jointly developing new products. After the joint venture covers development and production costs, they agree to split the profits equally.

Each partner in the joint venture has private, impacted information about cost to which the other partner does not have access. For example, as it developed the

---

[21] Based on Intel Corporation and Analog Design Inc. joint press releases, February 3, 1999, and "TI Lays Out DSP Plans Until 2010," *Hardware Reviews and News* on the The-View.com, December 6, 1999.

[22] The general structure of this section relies on A. Dixit and B. Nalebuff, *Thinking Strategically* (New York: Norton, 1991), pp. 306–319. The illustration here is based on "Apple Wants Other PC Makers to Build Computers to Use Macintosh Software," *Wall Street Journal,* January 28, 1994, p. B5, and "IBM, Apple in PC Design Accord," *Wall Street Journal,* November 8, 1994, p. B5.

Power PC, Apple knows its operating system development costs, and Motorola knows its computer chip design and production costs. Although neither can independently verify the other partner's asymmetric information, the success of a joint venture often depends on each partner's ability to generate enough operating profits to recover development costs. This necessitates an accurate revelation of true costs. Let's see why and what can be done to achieve this goal.

The study of incentive-compatible revelation mechanisms can provide some answers. Each partner faces random disturbances in the determinants of its costs.[23] Sometimes software development is delayed by inconspicuous but debilitating bugs in the programming, which increase the cost from, say, $80 to $120 million. Similarly, sometimes chip development and production necessitates redesign (e.g., Intel's problems with the Pentium chip), increasing that cost from, say, $50 to $70 million. Neither partner can hope to discover and rectify all such problems in advance. However, each can detect early warning signals of cost overruns and, if need be, cancel that particular one of their several joint projects.

Cost Overruns with Simple Profit-Sharing Partnerships

When both cost overruns happen simultaneously, the product development joint venture should shut down, because the variable costs of proceeding to full-scale production ($120 million + $70 million) will exceed the projected revenue available, say, $180 million. These projectable operating profits and losses appear in Table 16.5. If Apple experiences $120 million cost (the column labeled High Costs), the partnership will cancel the project whenever Motorola also experiences high cost of $70 million (the row labeled High Costs) because proceeding would result in a $10-million operating loss. By the same token, when only one partner or neither partner experiences high costs, the joint venture project should go forward and realize profits of $30 million, $10 million, and $50 million, respectively. Only with correct operate and shutdown decisions can the joint venture generate its maximum value.

The incentive problem is that initially each partner has an incentive to overstate true costs in order to be overcompensated from the joint venture revenues. For example, in Table 16.5, if Apple reveals true costs of $80 million and Motorola claims costs

---

Table 16.5   Joint Profits (in Millions) from a Simple Profit-Sharing Partnership with $180 Million in Revenue

		Apple	
		Low Costs ($80)	High Costs ($120)
Motorola	Low Costs ($50)	$50	$10
	High Costs ($70)	$30	−$10

---

[23] Similar arguments can be made about asymmetric information regarding random disturbances in demand.

of $70 million when in fact its true costs are $50 million, Motorola's joint profit share declines by $10 million from one half of $50 million (top left cell) to one half of $30 million (lower left cell). But with $20 million extra reimbursement from overstating its cost, Motorola ends up with (1/2) $30 million + $20 million, which exceeds one half of $50 million by $10 million. Similarly, if Apple overstates its costs, the Apple profit share falls from $25 million to $5 million, but this decline is more than offset by the $40 million extra reimbursement for overstating its $80 million actual cost to $120 million.

If low cost and cost overruns are equally likely at Motorola and if the probability of a cost overrun at Apple is 0.3, then expected costs are $60 million at Motorola and $92 million at Apple. With true revelation of costs, expected net profit from the joint venture is then (0.5×0.7) $50 million + (0.5×0.3) $10 million + (0.5×0.7) $30 million + (0.5×0.3) $0 = $29.5 million—namely, $14.75 million for each partner.[24] However, if one or both partners overstate costs, the projects with mixed costs in the southwest and northeast cells of Table 16.5 will also be canceled, and the expected net profit from the joint venture then declines. For example, if Apple falsely reveals $120 million when low costs of $80 million are present, the joint development project is canceled whenever Motorola experiences $70 million cost. This cancellation results in the partners forgoing the $30 million profit on the mixed cost project in the southwest cell and reduces the expected value of the joint venture to $19 million—i.e., $9.5 million per partner.[25] Value-maximizing managers facing asymmetric information seek some revelation mechanism that will provide appropriate incentives to induce the revelation of true costs, thereby preserving and capturing the full $14.75-million-per-partner expected value of both the low cost and the mixed cost projects.

Clarke-Groves Incentive-Compatible Revelation Mechanism

One such revelation mechanism is known as the Clarke tax mechanism.[26] Edward Clarke's pathbreaking idea was that to create appropriate incentives for asymmetric cost (or demand) revelation in a partnership, each party's revelation should trigger an imposition of the expected costs on (and the forgone profit opportunity losses suffered by) the other partners. In this way, the maximizing incentives of each of the asymmetrically informed partners could be made compatible. For our PC product development example, Table 16.6 indicates the revenue shares each partner would receive under a Clarke tax mechanism. The row player Motorola gets the below-diagonal payoffs in each cell, and the column player Apple gets the above-diagonal payoffs in each cell.

After the other party's expected costs are covered, each partner's payoff is then recalculated as the residual or net revenue share from all noncanceled projects triggered by its own cost revelations. To illustrate, if Motorola reveals Low_m cost, the current project will proceed independent of Apple's cost, and Motorola will realize $88 million, which is $180 million total partnership revenue minus the $92 million expected cost of Apple:

[24] Note that the project in the southeast cell of Table 16.5 is canceled because of mutual early warnings of high cost and therefore a projected operating loss.
[25] This expected value is calculated as (0.5×0.7) $50 million + (0.5×0.3) $10 million = $19 million.
[26] This revelation mechanism is also referred to as the Clarke-Groves revelation mechanism after T. Groves, who formalized the concept, thereby showing a different connection to William Vickery's earlier work on incentive-compatible auction design.

Table 16.6   Individual Revenue Share (in Millions) Net of Partner Cost

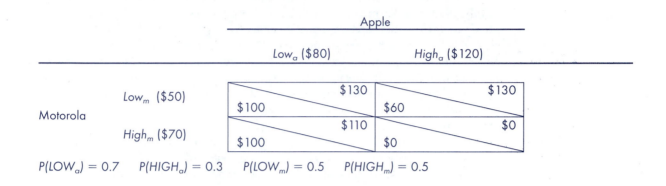

Note: Column-player payoffs are above diagonal. Row-player payoffs are below diagonal.

$$\text{Expected Net Revenue Share (Low for Motorola)}$$
$$= \$180 \text{ million} - (0.7 \times \$80 \text{ million} + 0.3 \times \$120 \text{ million})$$
$$= \$88 \text{ million}$$

This figure appears in the third column of Table 16.7. However, if Motorola announces $High_m$ cost, the project is canceled whenever Apple detects early warning signs that its own cost is $High_a$. Consequently, should Motorola decide to reveal high cost when low cost is present, its net revenue would fall from $88 million to 0.7 ($180 million − $80 million) + 0.0 ($180 million − $120 million) = $70 million, also listed in the third column of Table 16.7. Motorola's net revenue share declines because of a zero probability of realizing the $60-million revenue share in the northeast cell of Table 16.6. The false overstatement of cost by Motorola results in that project being canceled, and everyone loses. Under a Clarke tax mechanism, not just actions but information revelations themselves have consequences. And, as we shall see, these consequences can induce the true revelation of partnership costs.

Incentive-Compatible Revelation Mechanism
A procedure for eliciting true revelation of privately-held information.

The importance of the discovery of such **incentive-compatible revelation mechanisms** can hardly be overemphasized; they have led to many pathbreaking private sector and public policy applications. Clarke first developed the concept in the context of the true demand revelations needed in consumption partnerships to finance a jointly consumed park, pool, or playground.[27] The demand revelation problem in assessing an optimal tax share in a consumption partnership is analogous to the cost revelation problem in assessing an optimal profit share in a business partnership.

---

[27] To build the appropriate size urban park or swimming pool requires private, impacted information about use value and willingness to pay. But if one asks potential demanders who assume their answer will determine their tax share, the respondents will understate their willingness to pay. For more on the applications of revelation mechanisms, see R. Cornes and T. Sandler, "Clarke's Demand-Revealing Mechanism," *Theory of Externalities, Public Goods, and Club Goods* (New York: Cambridge University Press, 1986), pp. 105–108; Hal Varian, *Intermediate Microeconomics* (New York: Norton, 1999), pp. 622–627; or Edward Clarke, *Demand Revelation and the Provision of Public Goods* (Boston: Ballinger, 1980).

International Perspectives

JOINT VENTURE IN MEMORY CHIPS: IBM, SIEMENS, AND TOSHIBA[28]

After years of lobbying for nationalistic industrial policies that would subsidize the design and production of semiconductors in the United States, IBM entered into an agreement in July 1993 with Siemens and Toshiba to coproduce computer memory chips. At the same time, AMD and Intel announced similar joint ventures to develop flash memory chips with Fujitsu and Sharp, respectively. Flash chips retain the information needed to restart computer operating systems when the power is interrupted. In all three cases, the Japanese firm will contribute its superior manufacturing capability, and the American and German firms will contribute their design and innovative research capabilities.

The key question in such joint ventures is whether the Western companies will simply give away their technological knowledge while their Japanese partners deliver little asymmetric information in exchange. This happened once before in the computer chip industry of the 1960s and 1970s. To ensure a more evenly balanced partnership this time, the manufacturing know-how of the Japanese will be dissected as production cost information under various market conditions is revealed and analyzed by the joint venture partners. AMD and Fujitsu also undertook to establish a hostage mechanism by negotiating to purchase 5 percent of each other's stock.

An Optimal Incentives Contract

Optimal Incentives Contract
An agreement about payoffs and penalties that creates appropriate incentives.

To organize a joint venture or partnership around a Clarke-Groves revelation mechanism usually involves the implementation of a so-called **optimal incentives contract.** Each party agrees in advance to a set of partnership net revenue shares associated with the expected payoffs from a revelation mechanism (see the third column of Table 16.7). The important thing to appreciate is that the problem of independently verifying asymmetric information has not gone away. A third party attempting to enforce the contract (e.g., a U.S. district court) would still have just as much trouble verifying the claims for cost reimbursement arising under this contract as the parties had in trying to verify their own partner's cost. Entering into a partnership incentives contract does not define away the asymmetric information problem. Instead, the revelation mechanism creates incentives for a **self-enforcing reliance relationship** between the partners, not unlike the reliance relationship we described in Chapter 10 between repeat-purchase customers and high-reputation, premium-priced sellers of experience goods and the incentive-compatibility constraint we described in Chapter 15 as characterizing the optimal incentives contract between owner principals and manager agents.

Self-Enforcing Reliance Relationship
A noncontractual, mutually beneficial agreement.

That is, the structure of incentives underlying Table 16.7 is fully capable of inducing the partners to reveal their true costs; each would be worse off not doing so. We have already seen how Motorola would be worse off overstating its cost. Similarly, if Apple were to overstate its cost, profitable projects in the southwest cell of Table 16.6 would be canceled. Rather than realizing 0.5($130 million) + 0.5($110 million) = $120 million from the good fortune of incurring Low_a cost, Apple would instead realize only 0.5($130 million) = $65 million, which fails to cover its own low-cost realization of $80 million. In addition, this false overstatement of cost and the cancellation of the profitable project in the southwest cell reduces Apple's expected receipts from the partnership to just (0.5×0.7)($130 million) + (0.5×0.3)($130 million) = $65 million, whereas with true revelation it realizes $103.5 million =

[28] Based on "Pragmatism Wins as Rivals Start to Cooperate on Memory Chips," *Wall Street Journal*, July 14, 1993, p. B1.

Table 16.7   Expected Net Profit Shares (in Millions) with True Cost Revelation under an Optimal Incentives Contract

		Apple		
	Probability	Net Revenue Shares	Expected Costs	Net Profit Shares
Low_a	0.7	$120	$80	$28
$High_a$	0.3	$ 65	$60	$ 1.5
		$103.5	$74	$29.5
		Motorola		
	Probability	Net Revenue Shares	Expected Costs	Net Profit Shares
Low_m	0.5	$88	$50	$19
$High_m$	0.5	$70	$49	$10.5
		$79	$49.5	$29.5

(0.5 × 0.7)($130 million) + (0.5 × 0.7)($110 million) + (0.5 × 0.3)($130 million) = 0.7($120 million) + 0.3($65 million) = $103.5 million. Truth-telling dominates false revelation for both partners.

We can now also explain why both Apple and Motorola would adopt an optimal incentives contract that credibly commits each partner to a true revelation of asymmetric cost information. Apple realizes an expected net profit with true revelation of $103.5 million expected receipts minus expected costs of $74 million—i.e., $29.5 million, shown in the last column of Table 16.7. And similarly, Motorola realizes an expected net profit of $79 million expected receipts minus $49.5 million expected costs—i.e., $29.5 million. Each of these amounts equals the $29.5 million joint profits potentially available in the original simple profit-sharing contract of Table 16.5. However, recall that each party knows in advance that the other party will have private, impacted information about cost overruns. Each could therefore predict that the simple profit-sharing partnership would lead to cost overstatement, cancellation of the mixed cost projects, and loss of value. This proactive reasoning implies that only the mutual low-cost outcome in Table 16.5 will escape cancellation and actually generate profit. Therefore, only a much smaller expected profit is assured by the simple profit-sharing contract—i.e., just 0.5 × 0.7($50 million) = $17.5 million. This smaller amount from simple profit sharing is what rational parties choosing among partnership contracts would compare to the $29.5 million expected net profit from an optimal incentives contract.

The application of incentive-compatible revelation mechanisms and optimal incentives contracts has led to many exciting new types of asymmetric information partnerships. The same principles also underlie the concept of an efficient breach of contract in the economics of contract law—i.e., one partner's termination of a contractual relationship necessitates taking into account the opportunities forgone and expectation damage costs imposed on the partner who does not breach.[29] These concepts have become a key for achieving partnership or joint venture success in both small firms and large corporations under asymmetric information.

International Perspectives

Whirlpool's Joint Venture in Appliances Improves Upon Maytag's Outright Purchase of Hoover[30]

http://

To read about Whirlpool Corporation's worldwide acquisitions and ventures, access the following Internet site:

http://whirlpoolcorp.com/about/history/today.asp

Sometimes joint ventures are designed to increase the value of assets sold through a phased partnership rather than an immediate sale. As a potential buyer of Philips' European appliance division, Whirlpool sought access to more private information than due diligence by its merger and acquisition attorneys could uncover. Philips had a consumer franchise of nine appliance brands and a pan-European network of retail dealers who were second only to Electrolux in market share. But like other intangible assets (e.g., pivotal human resources and technical know-how), brands and distribution relationships are notoriously hard to value. In a new corporate organization and culture, could the Philips brands be redeployed without Philips' extremely strong reputation in European electronics? Would the fragmented network of independent dealers remain loyal once Whirlpool's name was substituted for Philips? And most important, what cost savings could be realized by sourcing all of the design, procurement, and production of Whirlpool and Philips components globally to achieve economies of scale?

These questions were best answered by a joint venture in which Philips retained a 47-percent ownership stake, and Whirlpool immediately assumed management control in exchange for $381 million. After both parties shared cost and demand information for three years and fully assessed potential value, the remainder of the business was sold to Whirlpool for $610 million.

In contrast, Maytag satisfied its strategic plan to enter the European market by purchasing outright Chicago Pacific Corporation, whose Hoover Appliance division had a substantial retail dealer network in Britain. However, Maytag knew little about the growing retail power of superstore chains near British shopping malls and still less about the marketing research on British households. Consequently, Maytag stumbled from one promotional blunder to another and eventually sold the Hoover European subsidiary at a $130 million loss. Again, with carefully designed incentives, a joint venture could have elicited the revelation of valuable asymmetric information to better ensure the success of Maytag's European initiative.

Implementation of IC Contracts

Incentive-compatible contracts are implemented with contingent claims contracting, a standard form instrument for sophisticated business attorneys. The parties agree on the projected probabilities for the various levels of cost, the likely auditable joint operating profit for the partnership, and the unobservable reimbursable cost to each party in each contingency. These agreements form the contract expectations and define the contract damages should unforeseen events induce either party to breach the contract.

---

[29] A good supplemental reading on efficient breach of contracts is R. Cooter and T. Ulen, *Law and Economics,* 4th ed. (Glenview, IL: Pearson Addison-Wesley, 2003).

[30] Based on A. Nanda and P. Williamson, "Use Joint Ventures to Ease the Pain of Restructuring," *Harvard Business Review,* November/December 1995, pp. 119–128.

The contract then elicits information revelation, and cancellation or go-ahead decisions are made. More generally, of course, there are consequences other than project cancellation versus go-ahead that can result from the information revelation of one partner. The information revealed by one partner more typically causes an expansion or contraction of the efforts (R&D efforts, prototype development efforts, marketing research efforts, etc.) of the other partner. And a revelation of misinformation fails to maximize what both can agree in advance would be the optimal course of action in each contingent state. It is those losses that the Clarke tax mechanism then deducts from joint profits to find IC contract receipts. This, of course, can prove quite a bit more complicated than the above example suggests; it presents a big challenge for the negotiating team of corporate attorneys.

In addition, you may have already noticed one further complication. The sum of the individual net revenue shares in every cell of Table 16.7 where the project goes ahead is greater than $180 million, the projected operating profit from the partnership. Specifically, if both parties declare high cost, each is entitled to an IC payout ($100 million in the case of Motorola and $130 million in the case of Apple) that together break the budget. To emphasize the generality of this result, the particular example has been constructed to exhibit "budget breaking" in each contingent event, except cancellation. More typically, some cells would exhibit surplus, and others would exhibit deficit. Still, the deficit cells may arise first. What is the partnership to do? What implementation procedure can handle this deficit budgeting problem?

Recall that both partners have substantially greater net profit shares under the IC contract ($29.5 million) than the expected profit from a simple profit-sharing agreement ($17.5 million). Eliciting true information revelation really does have value, and both parties therefore would be willing to make *ex ante* commitments to cover such a deficit. Examining the third column of Table 16.7 shows that Apple's expected net revenue share is $103.5 million, while Motorola's is $79 million. Consequently, $182.5 − $180 = $2.5 million per period (perhaps 2.5/0.05 = $50 million as a capital sum to cover the perpetual expected deficit) must be posted as a bond to implement the procedure. Each partner would be asked to establish credible commitment to the IC contract partnership by investing $25 million *ex ante* to achieve an increase in expected profit of $12 million ($29.5 − $17.5) per period.[31] Although complicated, these IC contracts clearly make sense for value-maximizing managers.

SUMMARY

- Incentive-compatible contracts for joint venture partners, fair division of a decaying prize, and the choice of queue service rules or auction designs all illustrate the concept of mechanism design. Optimal mechanism design seeks to elicit value-maximizing behavior while reducing transaction costs.

- Mechanism design features like first offer, right of first refusal, lack of communication, and credible threats in a dissolution of assets in a partnership can be analyzed as a sequential game.

- Small institutional changes often make a large difference in the outcome and distribution of payoffs.

---

[31] Technically, the investment to cover projected deficits will change an individual household's behavior unless we impose the restriction of quasi-linear preferences. In company settings, this assumption is plausible, however. See Varian, *op.cit.*, pp. 274–277.

- First-come first-served is a mechanism design for servicing a queue that reduces seller revenue because of predictable congestions and expected waiting time. Last-come first-served introduces leave-and-return transaction costs and also reduces seller revenue.

- Stratified lotteries can relieve congestion and reduce transaction costs in the queue, raising seller revenue.

- Auction design choices are multifaceted but at the simplest level always include who pays, what amount, and how the winner is determined. Simple auction types are English Ascending Price auctions, Dutch Descending Price auctions, First-Price Sealed-Bid auctions, and Second-Highest Sealed-Bid auctions.

- Auctions also differ in the resale opportunities available to the participants. Common-value auctions have thick resale markets where the items can be easily resold at a consensual fair market value. Private-value auction items have no common resale value and instead involve assets with differing valuations to the auction participants.

- The winner's curse implies that strategic underbidding is rational when the seller or other buyers have asymmetrically advantaged information about a common-value auction.

- Open bidding is a procedure for posting the offers in multiple rounds with cancellation and modification privileges to induce auction participants to pool their information about estimates of value. Open bidding reduces the winner's curse and raises expected auction revenue in common-value auctions.

- What simple auction types raise the greatest expected revenue for the seller-auctioneer depends upon the common-value or private-value nature of the item being auctioned and on the auction participants' risk aversion.

- Dutch auctions and First-Price Sealed-Bid auctions have identical information structures and identical bidding strategies, and therefore they generate identical expected revenue to the seller.

- Relative to Dutch or First-Price Sealed-Bid auctions, English Ascending Price and Second-Highest Sealed-Bid auctions raise the seller's expected revenue in common-value auctions for items like crude oil, forest logging rights, and aircraft because they encourage the most pooling of bidder information. In private-value auctions, bidders who are risk averse offer higher bids and therefore generate more auctioneer-seller revenue in Dutch and First-Price Sealed-Bid auctions.

- To escape adverse selection and elicit high-quality auction goods necessitates either intrusive and expensive regulation or some sort of bonding mechanism to induce *self-enforcing reliance relationships* between buyers and sellers. Warranties, independent appraisals, leases with a high residual, collateral, irrevocable money-back guarantees, contingent payments, and brand names all provide assurance to buyers that the seller will not misrepresent the product quality. Such hostage mechanisms support asymmetric information exchange.

- Joint ventures and partnerships face an asymmetric information problem in reimbursing each member for privately known costs that are unverifiable. As in demand revelation problems for funding public goods, so too in *cost revelation problems* for partnerships, each member has an initial incentive to falsely reveal (overstate) his or her private (cost) information.

- Both understatement of demand and overstatement of cost result in the cancellation of profitable partnership projects. Yet, each individual member may be better off with exaggerated cost reimbursement than with a simple profit share.

Preserving the maximum value of the partnership requires an *incentive-compatible revelation mechanism.*

- Under an incentive-compatible mechanism, cost revelations incur the expected costs imposed on and opportunities forgone by the other partners. Each partner agrees that not just actions, but information revelations themselves, have consequences for profit-share payout. Such a governance mechanism must be self-enforcing, however, because the asymmetric information problem has not disappeared. A court would have just as much trouble verifying the claims for reimbursement under this incentives contract as it would under the initial simple profit-sharing contract.

- Incentive-compatible revelation mechanisms do induce the true revelation of partnership costs.

- IC revelation mechanisms are implemented through contingent claims contracts and often require *ex ante* posting of a bond to solve the breaking-of-the-budget problem. Quasi-linear preferences are then required to assure a unique Clarke-Groves revelation mechanism solution for individual households. Business firms would, however, meet this condition without quasi-linear preferences.

EXERCISES

1. What auction design features reduce the winner's curse and therefore reduce strategic underbidding?

2. Why don't airlines and hotel chains worry about self-destructive cannibalization of their own higher-priced live sales when they list seats and rooms for sale in the virtual marketplace on Priceline.com?

3. What advantage does eBay's open bidding provide to sellers? Why?

4. Which two of the following are most clearly common-value auction items: Viper sports cars, electricity, patent licenses, T-bills, antiques, or fine art?

5. If some auction participants for crude oil field leases have estimates that the oil in the ground is worth $1.2 million, $1.3 million, or $1.5 million with certainty; and other auction participants have estimates that the same oil field lease is worth $1.1 million, $1.3 million, or $1.5 million with certainty; and a third group of auction participants have estimates that the same oil field lease is worth $1.1 million, $1.2 million, or $1.3 million, and all three forecasts contain the true common value, what is that value? How would you as auctioneer-seller design an auction to reduce strategic underbidding and realize this true value?

6. Distinguish common-value and private-value auctions; provide examples of each. Distinguish Descending Price (Dutch) auctions and Ascending Price (English) auctions; provide examples of each.

7. You are developing a bidding strategy for an ascending price sealed-bid auction of a crude oil field worth between $1 million and $51 million to the seller. Because your extraction costs are lower, your value is 20 percent greater than the seller's value. The seller faces transaction costs of conducting the sale and therefore will not accept an offer unless it exceeds her personal value. How much should you bid?

8. How can a second-highest sealed-bid ascending price auction design diminish the "winner's curse" and reduce the strategic underbidding that arises in highest-wins-and-pays typical ascending price auctions with sealed bids?

9. Some newly issued T-bills are auctioned by discriminatory pricing in Dutch auctions, whereas other newly issued T-bills are auctioned by uniform prices second-highest sealed-bid ascending price auctions. Which auction design is more like private placement of corporate newly issued bonds and IPO stock? Which auction design is more likely to increase seller revenue?

10. Fast Second and Speedo are trying to decide what to bid for a license in a cellular phone auction where the possible values of the new license are $10 million, $20 million, $30 million, $40 million, $50 million, and $60 million, each equally likely. The auction is single-round sequential, both parties have exactly the same value for the asset but neither knows its true value from the above distribution (i.e., a so-called common-value auction), and Fast Second gets to bid after Speedo.

    Each company has invested in marketing research about the value of the license which can come out one of two ways: possible values of $20, $30, or $50 million, or possible values of $20, $40, or $60 million. Whichever result arises is known to be 100 percent accurate—i.e., the license is worth one of the three identified amounts with certainty. Speedo proceeds with a bid of $33 million. Fast Second has marketing research saying that the value of the license is $20, $40, or $60. How much should Fast Second bid?

    Set up the Bayesian probability rule for Fast Second of BAYES PROB ($40 million value/Forecast of $33 million bid by Speedo).

11. Show that not just overstatement but also understatement of cost is dominated by truth-telling in the joint venture of Motorola and Apple.

12. What payoffs would be required under an optimal incentives contract like that in Table 16.7, if the cost overruns at Apple became as likely as those at Motorola?

Discussion Question

1. In this chapter we have assumed bidder's valuations are independent, but suppose they are affiliated. That is, suppose on eBay you wish to learn more about what a particular item is worth (a Beatles album) or you wish to affiliate with those who think Beatles albums are valuable and that affects your own personal valuation. How will this change from independent to affiliated valuations affect bidding strategy on eBay? Do you observe such behavior on the site?

CASE EXERCISES

SPECTRUM AUCTION

Continuing the analysis of broadband spectrum auctions from the chapter, suppose that two bidders know that the net present value of the rights to transmit PCS services in Louisville is a random variable uniformly distributed from $10 million to $60 million with six discrete values possible—i.e., $10 million, $20 million, $30 million, $40 million, $50 million, and $60 million. Also assume that both parties value the asset identically, making this a common-value auction. In advance, each company conducts marketing research experiments to narrow the possible outcomes and thereby better inform its own bid. Suppose Wireless Co.'s marketing research results exclude the two tails of the uniform distribution of possible values (i.e., $10 million and $60 million) as well as $40 million. Similarly, PCS PrimeCo. conducts its own marketing research which, let's assume, excludes $10 million, $30 million, and $50 million as possible outcomes for the Louisville service area.

a. What should Wireless Co. bid in a single-round sealed-bid common-value auction? What should PCS PrimeCo. bid in this same auction?

b. If Wireless goes first in a sequential posted price auction with multiple rounds to follow, what should PCS PrimeCo. respond in Round 2? In Round 3, will Wireless then wish to amend its earlier bid? Why or why not?

c. What auction design would be in the seller's best interest: single-round sealed-bid or multiple-round open bidding?

d. Identify other factors that could affect the optimal auction design.

DIVISION OF INVESTMENT BANKING FEES

You are the lead underwriter among a syndicate of five investment banks composed of yourself, the syndicate comanager, and syndicate members 3, 4, and 5. Your fivesome finds a deal worth $100 million in fees. You must submit a proffer as to how the fees should be divided, and the syndicate then votes by majority rule.

Your syndicate is rational and democratic in the sense that the division of fees will be decided based upon maximization of absolute gain in this single deal, and the members also have reputational reasons in future deals (where the lower ranked members hope to achieve more influence and get a higher ranked position) to abide by a majority decision.

If your proffer is rejected by vote of the syndicate, you are displaced as lead underwriter, removed altogether from the deal making, and replaced by the comanager who then makes a proffer to the remaining four. If his deal is rejected, he too is removed, and syndicate member 3 makes a proffer to the three firms remaining, and so on.

DISCUSSION QUESTION
1. What should you offer and to whom?

DEBUGGING COMPUTER SOFTWARE: INTEL[33]

Debugging has been a way of life in the computer industry from its inception. Indeed, the origin of the term *debugging* derives from the daily process of removing dead moths from the thousands of electronic tubes in the ENIAC, the first electronic computer. Every piece of computer hardware or software ever shipped has likely had logic faults. Indeed, most popular software programs contained thousands of known "bugs" in their first-generation products. In 1994, incomplete debugging of the floating point division calculator in the Pentium I computer chip caused a massive product recall that cost Intel $475 million dollars.

Why do computer component manufacturers release products with known bugs? One obvious answer is that delayed release may allow competitors to preempt the market with new technologies that render your product obsolete. Another important

---
[33] Based on "It's Not a Bug, It's a Feature," *Forbes,* February 13, 1995, p. 192.

answer is a central insight of managerial economics that everything worth doing is not necessarily worth doing well. Computer design and manufacturing firms face a rising marginal cost of correcting thousands of bugs detected by their beta testing process. At some point, each firm must balance the lost sales and replacement costs from product recalls against the ever-increasing cost of design perfection from continuously more debugging. A somewhat surprising third answer may, however, hold the key; fixing bugs in subsequent generations of software sells upgrades. Microsoft Windows 3.0 had a nasty bug that caused the program to crash with the finality of a hopeless error message—"unrecoverable application error." Microsoft fixed the bug in Version 3.1 and proceeded to sell millions of copies of the upgrade. Bugs in programs limit their durability, and in technology businesses the selling of upgrades is a part of the business plan.

DISCUSSION QUESTION

1. Discuss the practice of selling upgrades (sometimes called "versioning") as a mechanism design. What objective is being served? How well will this work, in the long run?

Externalities

In the normal course of business, every firm faces decisions influenced by externalities. This appendix analyzes the potential for resource misallocation with externalities, emphasing Ronald Coase's mechanism design for handling reciprocal externality problems. Other possible solutions are then considered, including regulatory directives, effluent or emission taxes (and subsidies), mergers, and the sale of pollution rights. Both managers and the public have a keen interest in least-cost implementation of the kinds of remedies society mandates for controlling externalities.

EXTERNALITIES AND BARGAINING

Externalities Defined

Externality
A spillover of benefits or costs from one production or utility function to another.

Externalities exist when a third party receives benefits or bears costs arising from an economic transaction in which he or she is not a direct participant. This occurs when producers or consumers provide benefits to third parties or impose costs on third parties for which the market system does not enable them to receive full payment in return.

A commuter, for example, may decide to drive rather than use public transportation to get to work in the morning. This results in additional road congestion and costs (in terms of the opportunity cost of lost time as well as greater operating expenses) to all those who had already entered the road. This commuter, however, looks only at personal operating costs and personal commuting time in deciding whether to drive or use public transportation. Another typical externality exists with pollution by-products of trucking deliveries that combine with certain atmospheric conditions to cause smog. In places like Los Angeles this problem may impose significant costs on asthmatic residents and businesses like the Pasadena Sightseeing Company. In short, externalities arise with any interdependency of household utility or firm production functions that is not reflected in market prices.

Pecuniary Externalities

Pecuniary Externality
A spillover that is reflected in prices and therefore results in no efficiency.

Only externalities that are not conveyed through the price system result in any inefficiency. Thus when mad cow disease causes preference for meat to shift from beef to chicken, the price of beef will fall and that of chicken will rise, making beef producers and chicken consumers worse off, and chicken producers and beef consumers better off, because of the price change. But all of these interdependencies have operated through the market price system, and they are therefore identified as **pecuniary externalities** that pose no inefficiency.

The legal doctrine of "coming to the nuisance" in *Spur Industries* v. *Del Webb Development,* S.C. Arizona, 1972 (108 Ariz. 178, 494 P.2d 700) illustrates the principle that pecuniary externalities result in no inefficiency. If the land you purchase for an eventual subdivision development is located next to a cattle feedlot, the price you pay per acre will reflect the stench. The reduced price of the land will internalize the spillover effects. Later, if residents of the subdivision complain about the stench and the feedlot is declared a pubic nuisance, you, the developer, may have to pay to relocate the cattle feeding business. Again, when external effects *are* reflected in prices, all affected parties directly participate in the transaction, and there is no inefficiency.

Externalities and Resource Misallocation

When nonpecuniary externalities are present, resources are likely to be misallocated by producers or consumers whether the externality is beneficial or harmful to its recipients. If producers or consumers make a contribution to society's well-being for which they are not compensated, they are less likely to engage in the action generating the external benefit than if they are fully reimbursed for all benefits generated. Similarly in the case of negative externalities, a producer or consumer will likely overallocate resources to some production or consumption activity if part of the cost if engaging in this activity is shifted to others. The reason for this likely misallocation of resources is that when nonpecuniary externalities exist, the price system fails to provide the correct signals to firms making output and resource-allocation decisions.

The general principle of how much of society's resources should be allocated to solving the externality problem is clear. An external cost, for example, should be reduced up to the point where the marginal spillover costs saved by any further reduction just equal the marginal lost profits from the externality-generating activity. Similarly, an action that generates external benefits should be expanded to the point where the marginal benefits to all of society from such an expansion just equal the societal marginal costs.

Coasian Bargaining for Reciprocal Externalities

In many cases, externalities arise because of incompatible uses of air, land, or water resources. For example, late-night takeoffs and landings by FEDEX jets may disturb sleep in houses around the airport. Feeding of thousands of animals in a small enclosed feedlot may create offensive odors in adjacent subdivisions. Agricultural land runoff of nutrient-rich water may adversely affect downstream intake by a bottled water plant. No adverse consequences would occur if either party were absent.

Reciprocal Externality
A spillover that results from competing incompatible uses.

Nobel prize winner Ronald Coase has argued that an efficient solution to such **reciprocal externalities** can generally be achieved if the generator and the recipient of the externality get together and reach an agreement through bargaining. Among the numerous examples in Coase's famous paper "The Problem of Social Cost," perhaps the most discussed is a reciprocal externality between a spark-throwing railroad and a farmer with adjacent flammable fields. Coase's ingenious and intriguing claim was that under certain conditions involving full information and low transaction costs, and answer to the question, "Who's liable and therefore who should pay damages?" had no effect on the resource allocation decisions of these parties. In particular, if the railroad had the property right to throw sparks along its right-of-way, the trains scheduled down this track and the acreage planted along it would be exactly the same as if the railroad had the liability for all spark-induced damages along its tracks.

Example

COASE'S RAILROAD

To see how this remarkable result aries through Coasian bargaining, consider the payoffs in Table 16A.1. If the railroad has the property right (i.e., Table 16A.1, Panel a), the farmer incurs $600 worth of crop destruction per train per 10 acres planted along the tracks. Initially, the railroad ignores these external spillover costs and chooses an activity level of trains that maximizes its own profits (i.e., two trains in the bottom row of Table 16A.1, Panel a). The farmer would plant 10 rather than 20 acres along the tracks in order to earn $300 and avoid losing $800 (in the extreme southeast cell). If there were substantial impediments to bargaining, no further action would take place in an unregulated *laissez-faire* market environment. Otherwise, a mutually beneficial private voluntary bargaining opportunity would exist.

In particular, if the railroad were to cut back to one train, the farmer's profit would rise from $300 to $900, while the railroad's profit would decline by $500 (from $1,500 to $1,000). Accordingly, $501 is a minimally sufficient bribe to elicit the lower train-activity level, and $600 is the savings in fewer crops burned. Thus, Coase predicted that if the parties have few impediments to bargaining, the farmer would offer a side payment sufficient to abate the incremental (second) train and its spark hazard, because the second train is worth less (to the railroad) than the incremental agricultural losses cost the farmer. Just how much the farmer will pay and how little the railroad will accept is not addressed, but one thing is clear. Potential gains from trade do motivate a bargain to reduce railroad activity from two trains to one and acreage planted from 20 to 10.

Now, consider the case in which the railroad has the liability for spark-induced crop damages. Initially, the farmer prepares to plant 20 acres along the tracks as this activity level maximizes his or her independent profit (at $1,600). However, no trains are profitable with this much acreage in production since $600 in damages per train per 10 acres (i.e., $1,200 altogether) is owed when the railroad has $1,000 gross profit with one train, and $2,400 in damages is owed when the railroad offers to compensate the farmer for not only crop damages, but also lost profit if the farmer would plant fewer acres. In particular, the railroad can offer the farmer $101 to plant 10 acres rather than 20 acres since the farmer's gross profit differs by only $100 (i.e., $1,500 versus $1,600). If the railroad then also compensates the farmer $600 for one train's crop damage on 10 acres, the railroad owes $701 and earns a gross profit of $1,000.

Table 16A.1, Panel b, displays the gross profits before crop damages have been compensated. Directing your attention to the middle row of Table A.1, Panel b, the railroad offers the farmer compensation in excess of $100—perhaps, $101—to scale back the acreage planted from 20 acres, where farmer gross profit is $1,600, to 10 acres, where farmer gross profit is $1,500. This reallocation of activities is worth $600 in damage savings to the railroad. Again, Coasian bargaining leads the parties to agree upon 1 train and 10 acres.

Coase Theorem
A prediction about the emergence of private voluntary bargaining in reciprocal externalities with low transaction costs.

The **Coase Theorem** states that reciprocal externality generators and recipients will choose efficient activity levels whatever the initial liability assignment. It makes no claim about the distributional consequences of reversing the direction of a liability assignment. Quite obviously, making the railroad liable in one instance and asking the farmer to cover his or her own crop losses from burned fields in the other result in quite different net profit outcomes. However, what the Coase Theorem does assert is that in reciprocal externality settings, resource allocation as to the

Coasian Bargaining

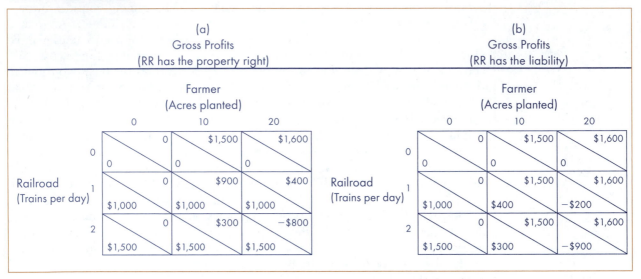

Source: Adapted from R. Coase, "The Problem of Social Cost," *Journal of Law and Economics*, 2 (October 1960), pp. 1–44.

externality-generating and externality-receiving activity levels will be unchanged independent of the initial liability assignment. One train will be scheduled, and 10 acres will be planted.

Qualifications of the Coase Theorem

Some powerful qualifications are in order, many of which Coase himself recognized. First, technical transaction costs of searching for and identifying the responsible owners and affected parties, of detecting violations of one's property rights, and of internally negotiating the side payments or bribes (say, within a group of claimants) must all remain low and be unaffected by the reversal of the liability assignment. Second, neither party can operate in a purely competitive market, for then the profits required for side payments and bribes would be nonexistent. And, third, and perhaps most important, one party quickly makes an offer the other is just willing to accept only when the information regarding the payoffs in Table 16A.1 (a) or Table 16A.1 (b) is complete, certain, and known to both parties. When information is incomplete and impacted, private voluntary bargaining need not lead to resource allocation that is invariant to the direction of liability assignment. And this asymmetric information qualification to the Coase Theorem holds even if property rights are fully specified, completely assigned, and enforced at no cost.

The problem presented by asymmetric information is present in all incompatible use situations where *reported* damages and the precautionary actions of the plaintiff and the defendant have some bearing on the assignment of liability. For example, the parties in Coase's railroad example would avoid liability in part by employing spark arresters or land setbacks as long as the benefit in crop-loss savings exceeded the cost. However, the problem posed by asymmetric information is that some aspects of precaution are inherently unobservable or unverifiable (e.g., attentiveness to subtle signals of impending hazard) while others are observable but affect accident avoidance in a nondeterministic way (e.g., good brakes may lock up on rain-slickened roads when less effective brakes would not). Uncertainty and unobservability together result in the problem of moral hazard, which we discussed in Chapter 15. There is no incentive-compatible mechanism that can both preserve the voluntary nature of the Coasian bargaining and also elicit true revelation of the unobservable damages. Therefore, contrary to the traditional understanding of the Coase Theorem, disputants in reciprocal externality conflicts might be expected not to engage in private voluntary bargaining alone, but rather to delegate the question of damage assessment and recovery to third-party court systems. Civil procedural rules in an impartial court system can be seen as credible commitment mechanisms by which potential disputants bind themselves to liability assignments and wealth transfer remedies that motivate efficient accident avoidance despite frequently asymmetric information. So, the implication of the Coase Theorem is sustained; externality disputants will contract their way to an efficient allocation of resource unless prohibitive transaction costs prevent the required bargaining.[1]

Impediments to Bargaining   Several impediments to private voluntary bargaining as a mechanism for resolving externalities are well recognized in the legal system. Prohibitive notification and search costs (to identify absentee owners and notify all the affected parties) are the justification for certifying **class action suits**. Class actions prove critical to reducing these transaction costs in the case of oil spills and other large-scale externalities affecting many claimants. Voluntary private bargaining about incompatible uses also may be impeded by the need for continuous monitoring of an unverifiable deal like the maximum rate of harvest of a deep sea fishery. However, unquestionably the most significant impediment to bargaining in large-numbers externality cases is the strategic holdout or strategic free-rider problem.

When a court grants an injunction against a polluter's operation, relief from the injunction may necessitate the polluter securing a unanimous waiver from the affected parties. If many claimants are certified as possessing such a right of waiver, each claimant has an incentive to hold out for more compensation than would be required to cover his or her damages. The predictable presence of **strategic hold-outs** in large-numbers externalities short-circuits the private voluntary bargaining hypothesized by the Coase Theorem to resolve the externality. In such cases, the courts therefore adopt other mechanisms involving liability rules and the payment of permanent damages.

Class Action Suits
A legal procedure for reducing the search and notification costs of filing a complaint.

Strategic Holdout
A negotiator who makes unreasonable demands at the end of a unanimous consent process.

Example

BOOMER V. ATLANTIC CEMENT CO., INC., 26 N.Y. 2D 219, COURT OF APPEALS, NY, 1970

In the early 1970s, a large cement plant valued at $45 million spewed cement dust regularly across a neighborhood of Albany, New York. Some of the affected households were unable to continue their laundry operations; others suffered the inconvenience of small airborne particulates that necessitated frequent washing and repainting of cars and homes. Asthmatics suffered more health problems. The Atlantic Cement plant was declared a public nuisance, and the court chose among three types of injunctions: (1) an order to cease operations until the air pollution could be abated, (2) an order to cease operations until a waiver could be obtained from each household in the affected neighborhood, or (3) an order declaring the cement plant liable for $185,000 in permanent damages and requiring a cessation of operations until these court-specified damages were paid. Since the first injunction hinged on undeveloped technology and the second created strategic holdouts, the New York Court of Appeals opted for the third alternative. Although the court, in effect, thereby licensed the ongoing nuisance for a one-time-only fee of $185,000, no private voluntary bargain to reduce the cement dust could have overcome the strategic

[1] See F. Harris, "Economic Negligence, Moral Hazard, and the Coase Theorem," *Southern Economic Journal*, 56 (3), January 1990, pp. 698–704.

free-rider/strategic holdout problem. And, as result of having to pay court-mandated damages, the plant's owners did begin to internalize the social cost of cement production when establishing new plants.

OTHER SOLUTIONS TO THE EXTERNALITY PROBLEM

Solution by Prohibition

One simplistic approach to solving externality problems is merely to prohibit the action that generates the external effects. A little reflection, however, should indicate that in most cases this is at least suboptimal and frequently impractical. Auto emissions could be cut to zero if autos were banned, but the effects of such a move, at least in the short run, would be disastrous. Pollution in the Houston Ship Channel or the Detroit River could practically be abolished if industries dumping waste products were prohibited from doing so. But employment would also grind to a halt if such a step were taken. Furthermore, an optimal solution does not require that externalities be completely eliminated, but rather that the *right amount* of them be eliminated. A strict zero-pollution policy often entails excessive pollution-abatement costs.

Solution by Regulatory Directive

Auto safety devices are a good example of a solution by regulatory directive. Recognizing that significant external benefits are to be gained from reducing serious automotive accidents, the federal government does not give the consumer the choice of regular inspection and maintenance of brakes, lights, and other safety equipment; it simply mandates inspection and repair for all vehicles. But how frequent the inspections and how extensive the repairs? Again, the problem of controlling externalities is to eliminate an externality up to the point where the marginal costs of further reductions are just equal to the marginal benefits derived therefrom. We have seen that outright prohibition will often be suboptimal, so another possibility that has been suggested is to let the government decide just how much of the externality may be produced (e.g., of air pollution emissions). Cancer-causing lead additives in gasoline and ozone shield-depleting chlorofluorocarbon (CFC) refrigeration gases have been massively reduced by regulatory directives (see Figure 16A.1).

One problem with this approach to setting an overall emissions standard arises when multiple sources of pollution are present, as in the acidification of rain by coal-fired power plants. Each of the polluting entities (each point source) must be directed as to how it should act. A simple proportionate distribution of "pollution rights" to each plant would overlook the dramatic difference in the cost of abatement from one plant to another. Instead, optimality requires that the marginal effectiveness of the last dollar spent on pollution abatement by each polluter be equated. So, a low-cost point source's regulatory permit should require more abatement than a permit for a high-cost point source. Yet, this sort of detailed point-source regulation is seldom achieved.

Solution by Taxes and Subsidies

Another potentially efficient solution to externality problems is to provide subsidies (either in the form of cash or tax relief) to those whose activities generate significant external benefits and to tax those whose activities create external costs. Such a

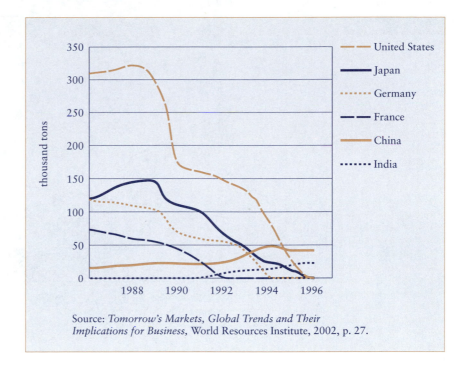

FIGURE 16A.1

CFC Production
(1986–1997)

Source: *Tomorrow's Markets, Global Trends and Their Implications for Business*, World Resources Institute, 2002, p. 27.

tax and subsidy scheme, however, requires a tremendous amount of information if it is to be administered in an optimal fashion.

Consider the analysis required for a per-unit pollution tax T* in Figure 16A.2. Demand per truck is the private willingness to pay (WTP) for trucking deliveries throughout the Los Angeles basin. Setting marginal private cost (MPC) equal to private WTP, the trucking company will put 50,000 miles a year on its typical delivery truck. Still more delivery miles are avoided by the managers because the price additional customers are willing to pay for deliveries is less than the MPC of operating the truck. The problem is that trucking mileage generates the by-product nitrous oxide (NO_2), which causes smog. Through careful environmental science, businesses like the Pasadena Sightseeing Co. and asthmatic citizens of LA estimate that the air pollution causes damages from lost tourist business as well as eyes, nose, and throat irritants of area BCD. Consequently, although marginal benefit (P_o) equals MPC at the private market equilibrium Point A, additional costs attributable to the NO_2 externality—namely, CB at 50,000 miles—suggest that full costs are substantially higher: namely, at Point E, MPC (AB) + MExC (CB) > P_o. With summed private plus external costs exceeding marginal benefits to the delivery truck's customers at 50,000 miles, the joint product trucking mileage/NO_2 is produced in excess of its optimal level. Fifty thousand miles per year is too much trucking. However, the question, as always, comes down to *how much less* trucking and associated pollution abatement is optimal.

In Figure 16A.2, the reduced mileage at which marginal social cost (MSC)—the sum of MPC + MExC—just equals marginal willingness to pay for trucking is 40,000 miles at Point F. Clearly, the smog victims have damages (area GHBC) great enough to compensate the trucking company for its lost profits (area FIA) associated with a 10,000-mile reduction in mileage. And the maximum side payment smog victims would offer for the next 10,000-mile reduction from 40K to 30K—namely, area JKHG—is smaller than the minimally sufficient bribe (area LMIF) that the trucking

FIGURE 16A.2

Optimal Per Unit
Pollution Tax

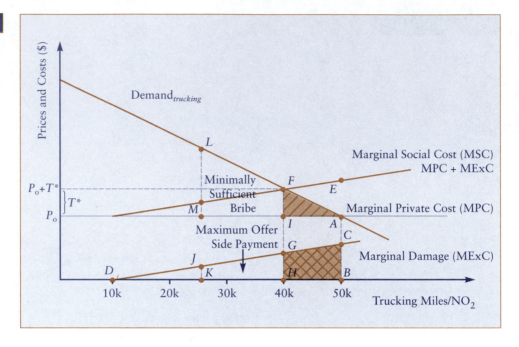

company would accept. But zeroing in on 40,000 miles as the optimal mileage (not 35K, 38K, 42K, or 45K) is very difficult because accurate marginal external cost information is so hard to come by. An optimal per-unit tax of T* levied on delivery truck mileage reduces the mileage chosen from 50,000 to 40,000 through user charges in the amount $P_o + T^*$ that reflect the marginal social cost of the (trucking/NO_2) joint product. But again, T* assumes heroically that the regulators know that 40,000 constitutes the optimal mileage.

In practice, a tax or emission charge would be placed on a firm's pollutants, such as pounds of particulate matter emitted from a delivery truck or power plant smokestack. A firm could continue to pollute if it pays the per-unit tax, or it could find that it is cheaper to buy pollution control equipment. If, after a reasonable period of time, a community still believes the level of particulate matter in the air is too high, the tax per pound of pollutant would be increased in a stepwise fashion until the community was satisfied with the result. The per-unit tax solution avoids the rigidity of all-or-nothing regulatory prohibitions or directives. And it induces firms to consider continuously the least-cost method of abating pollution.

An emissions tax approach has a number of problems of its own, however. First, only certain types of pollution can be measured easily with metering devices. Yet, an inexpensive method of accurately measuring pollutants is essential to such an emission-charge scheme. Second, although the tax scheme provides the possibility of building incentives for firms to move from densely to sparsely populated areas, this result is not likely to be greeted with universal acclaim by those living in the sparsely populated, relatively pollution-free areas. Third, the exact amount of an optimal effluent tax or emission tax is extremely difficult to estimate.

Solution by Sale of Pollution Rights

Another increasingly popular approach to the problem of pollution is the sale of pollution rights. Licenses could be sold that give the license holder a right to pollute up to some specific limit during a particular period of time. This is the approach that has been adopted under the 1990 Clean Air Act. The U.S. Environmental Protection Agency (EPA) sets a maximum level of some pollutant that may be safely emitted in an area. The federal government then sells, at auction, licenses to individual firms giving them the right to pollute up to a specified amount. The licenses could be freely traded in an organized market, permitting their price to fluctuate with market demands and abatement technology discoveries. The advantage of this approach is that it is essentially market oriented, forcing pollution costs to be internally recognized in all the price and production decisions of individual firms.

Example

PLANT EXPANSION REQUIRES PURCHASE OF OPEN-MARKET POLLUTION RIGHTS: TIMES MIRROR CO.

The United States has an active market for sulfur dioxide and nitrous oxide pollution rights (credits). An organized exchange (e.g., the Chicago Board of Trade) exists which allows electric utilities, trucking companies, and manufacturing firms to buy and sell pollution credits at periodic auctions. Also, a private placement market exists in which brokers, as well as some states, arrange customized contracts for pollution credits between companies that have excess credits to sell and companies that need credits to comply with environmental regulations. For example, the Times Mirror Company was able to complete a $120-million expansion of a paper-making plant near Portland, Oregon, after buying the right to emit 150 tons of additional hydrocarbons into the air annually. The pollution credits were acquired for $50,000 from the owners of two businesses that held surplus credits: a chemical plant that had gone out of business and a dry-cleaning firm that adopted a pollution-free cleaning fluid.

Solution by Merger

When the entities generating and absorbing the externalities are firms, merger is a very attractive way of internalizing externalities. If a paper mill is polluting a stream so that a chemical firm downstream must make large expenditures on water purification before using the water in its processes, the problem may be eliminated by a merger of the two firms. After the merger, it is in the best interests of the new consolidated firm to consider the chemical plant's water purification costs in determining what quality of effluent should be emitted from the paper mill. A similar example involving adjacent urban landowners is discussed below.

EXTERNALITIES AND URBAN RENEWAL

The theory of externalities can explain why blighted areas develop and persist in our cities and why urban renewal mechanisms can help if properly designed. Profit-maximizing landowners don't always find it in their best interest to keep their properties in good repair because the value of any particular property in a neighborhood is dependent not only on its size, design, and state of repair, but also on similar characteristics of the surrounding property. In short, real estate property value depends on three things: location, state of repair, and what the neighbors choose as their state of repair. Real estate maintenance therefore exhibits strong externalities.

The nature of this urban real estate interdependence may be illustrated with the Prisoner's Dilemma game from Chapter 12. Let us assume that two adjacent property owners, Smythe and Jones, have made an initial investment in their properties and are currently reaping a competitive return. Both are now faced with the

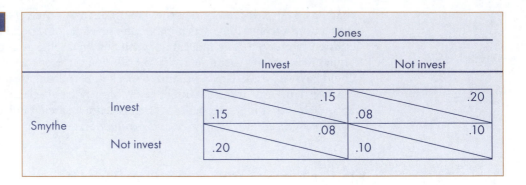

decision to make additional redevelopment investments. The return that each receives will be affected not only by his or her own investment decision but by the decision of the other landowner as well. This may be illustrated in Table 16A.2, which is read as follows: The entry below the diagonal in each cell represents the rate of return to Smythe from his action (Invest or Not invest) while the entry above the diagonal represents Jones's return from her action (Invest or Not invest). Beyond their initial investment, both Smythe and Jones have an additional amount available to invest in the properties. This additional sum is currently invested in corporate bonds yielding 10 percent. If neither Smythe nor Jones invests additional funds in real estate, they will continue to earn the 10-percent return, as is indicated in the "Not invest–Not invest" southeast cell. Alternatively, if both decide to invest and upgrade their properties, they will each earn a return of 15 percent, as indicated in the Invest-Invest northwest cell.

When Smythe invests and Jones does not, or vice versa, the one who redevelops earns only 8 percent because the new building is still in a predominantly old neighborhood, whereas the one who does not invest gets the benefits from the improvement in the neighboring property with no additional required outlay of funds. Let us see why this might occur. If Jones demolishes her old building and builds a new one complete with off-street parking and other attractions, this would mean that Smythe's tenants would, for example, have a better chance to find on-street parking spaces. In addition, Smythe's tenants might value living next door to some higher income people and having their children mix with each other. As a result Smythe may be able to raise his rents somewhat. Jones, however, is not so lucky, because potential renters would have to evaluate the neighborhood (including Smythe's old building). Consequently, Jones cannot charge the rents she would like. Thus Jones's return is only 8 percent, whereas Smythe gets a 20-percent return.

Being aware of the possible outcomes indicated in Table 16A.2, both Smythe and Jones could well decide not to invest. Let us examine the payoff matrix from Smythe's point of view. If Jones invests, Smythe can get a return of 15 percent if he also invests, but a 20-percent return by not investing. If Jones does not invest, the best Smythe can hope for is a 10-percent return by also not investing. Thus no matter what Jones does, Smythe is better off not investing. Similar logic follows for Jones. Each player, acting in his or her own self-interest in the absence of cooperation, will decide *not to invest* and will thus receive only a 10-percent return. But this solution is not optimal, because they could both receive a 15-percent payoff by getting together and agreeing to redevelop their properties. In the simple two-person case illustrated here, voluntary cooperation is likely, especially if the same two landowners replay the game again and again in each maintenance cycle (see the discussion entitled "Escape

from Prisoner's Dilemma" in Chapter 13). However, as the number of property owners increases, the chances of getting such voluntary cooperation diminish rapidly.

Perhaps the most obvious solution is for one landowner to buy out the other
(i.e., to merge). Another possibility is that some third party might step in, purchase
both properties (thereby internalizing the externalities), and receive the 15-percent
return on each. This does in fact happen quite often. For instance, Texas Eastern
Transmission purchased a 30-square-block area in Houston for redevelopment. But
without the public right of eminent domain, there is always the chance that some of
the property owners will refuse to sell in order to reap the externalities of development themselves, or they may hold out for such a high price that it appropriates all
the expected profits from the developer. In such cases, urban renewal including the
use of public condemnation orders and eminent domain seizure (with market-based
compensation as mandated by the "takings clause" of the U.S. Constitution) is
required to effect the optimal solution of mutual maintenance of all properties.

In this appendix we have examined several approaches for solving externalities
problems. It should be apparent that no one best solution exists for all cases. Because
of the great diversity of externality problems, appropriate policies must be tailored
to meet the specific problem while comparing the costs and benefits of alternative
solutions. Policymakers may then be guided in their decision making to choose that
abatement mechanism where net benefits are likely to be maximized and the social
costs are effectively internalized, forcing firms to treat social costs as a part of their
relevant costs for decision-making purposes.

SUMMARY

- Externalities exist when a third party receives benefits or bears costs arising from
  an economic transaction in which he or she is not a direct participant. The impact
  of externalities is felt outside of (external to) the normal market pricing and
  resource-allocation mechanism.
- Pecuniary externalities, in which spillover effects are reflected in the market pricing mechanism, result in no inefficiencies.
- Ronald Coase has shown that an efficient allocation of resources can generally
  be achieved in the case of small-numbers externalities by contractual bargaining
  between the creator and recipient of the externality.
- Impediments to private voluntary bargaining include prohibitive search and notification costs, internal negotiation costs among large numbers of affected parties, prohibitive monitoring costs, and an absence of the surpluses required for
  making side payments.
- Many possible solutions to problems of externalities exist. These include solution by voluntary side payment, governmental prohibition, regulatory directive,
  imposition of pollution taxes or subsidies, a sale of rights to create the externality, and merger.

EXERCISES

1. Discuss the problems of aircraft noise around an airport from an externality
   perspective and propose a possible solution if (a) housing existed in the airport area before the airport was built and (b) housing was built adjacent to
   the airport after the airport was built.

2. A sheep rancher has leased the mineral rights beneath her grazing land to an oil company. She fears that discharges from the oil wells will pollute her underground water resources. Consequently, the contract for the sale of mineral rights requires that the rancher and the oil company reach a mutually agreeable solution to the water contamination problem should it occur. If this bargaining fails to reach a conclusion acceptable to both sides, the mineral rights lease will be terminated automatically, and the rancher will be required to return a portion of the lease proceeds to the oil company. The portion that must be returned to the oil company is to be determined through a process of binding arbitration. Discuss likely outcomes should this problem arise.

3. Branding Iron Products, a specialty steel fabricator, operates a plant in the town of West Star, Texas. The town has grown rapidly because of recent discoveries of oil and gas in the area. Many of the new residents have expressed concern at the amount of pollution (primarily particulate matter in the air and waste water in the town's river) emitted by Branding Iron. Three proposals have been made to remedy the problem:

    a. Impose a tax on the amount of particulate matter and the amount of waste water emitted by the firm.

    b. Prohibit pollution by the firm.

    c. Offer tax incentives to the firm to clean up its production processes.

    Evaluate each of these alternatives from the perspectives of economic efficiency, equity, and the likely long-term impact on the firm.

4. Middlefield, Ohio, a town with a population of 50,000, is the home of Legco Steel. Legco employs about 20 percent of the town's workforce. Because of an increase in complaints from local environmentalists, the town's city council is considering taking action to reduce the firm's pollution. The following alternatives are being considered:

    • Pass an ordinance requiring the firm to reduce by 95 percent its discharge of particulates into the air.

    • Impose a tax of $5 per ton of particulates.

    • Maintain the status quo.

    The expected payoffs to the firm and the town are as follows:

Action	Firm (Impact on Profits)	Town (Impact on Employment)
Reduce discharge with ordinance	−50%	20% reduction in workforce employed in Middlefield
Tax the discharge	−10%	5% reduction in workforce employed in Middlefield
Do nothing	0%	0%

    a. What action do you think the town should take? Why?

    b. What other factors need to be considered?

    c. Why do you think the ordinance will have such a large impact on employment in Middlefield?

5. Lead Weight Refining, Inc., operates a large ore smelter in Junction City, Utah. The firm produces lead ingots that are later used to manufacture batteries for heavy-duty equipment. In the lead-refining process, a substantial amount of air pollution is generated. A local mothers' organization is concerned about the health hazards posed by the emissions of the firm. After consulting with local officials, the mothers convince the city to impose a pollution tax on the discharge of the firm.

Each unit of output, Q, is composed of one unit of lead, Q_L, and one unit of air pollution (particulates), Q_A. The total cost function of the firm is

$$TC = 25,000 + 8Q + 4Q^2$$

The demand for lead is

$$P_L = 4,522 - 4Q_L$$

The demand function for the firm's particulate pollution is derived from the use of these pollutants as an input in the battery production process. The demand function for these discharges is as follows:

$$P_A = 400 - Q_A$$

a. In the absence of any pollution tax, what price, quantity, and profit levels will prevail for the firm?

b. Compute the marginal revenue for lead output and for pollution output at this price and output level.

c. What is the minimum tax that must be charged to completely eliminate pollution by the firm?

d. Discuss the reasons why it is necessary to be able to measure the damage from pollution so the affected parties may reach an optimal solution through bargaining.

e. Is this same information also necessary to elicit the optimal amount of pollution abatement with a per-unit emissions tax? Why or why not?

6. The demand for specialty glue is given as follows:

$$P = 1,200 - 6Q$$

where P is the price per 100 pounds of specialty glue produced and Q is the amount produced and sold in hundreds of pounds.

The marginal cost of producing glue for the entire glue industry is as follows:

$$MPC = 700 + 2Q$$

a. What will industry output and price be in the absence of regulation?

b. The production of specialty glue results in the following marginal pollution costs:

$$MC = 200 + Q$$

What is the marginal *social* cost for the production of specialty glue?

c. If the firms in the industry attempt to achieve a *socially* optimal level of output, what price should be charged, and what should be the level of output?

Government Regulation

CHAPTER PREVIEW As managers make decisions designed to lead to the maximization of shareholder wealth, they are faced with many constraints. Some of these constraints are external social pressures that constitute the moral social responsibilities of business. Other constraints have been codified into legal obligations of all firms in a similar industry or class (e.g., to avoid anticompetitive trade practices). These statutory constraints are supplemented by a wide array of government regulations designed to ensure the smooth, efficient, and competitive functioning of the economy. To make wealth-maximizing price-output decisions, managers must fully understand the regulatory aspects of their environment. This chapter explores several types of regulatory issues: antitrust, business permits, licensing and patents, and quotas.

PHOTO ON PAGES 762 AND 763: © PHOTODISC, INC.

MANAGERIAL CHALLENGE

Deregulation and the Coase Theorem

The 1991 Nobel prize in economics was awarded to Professor Ronald Coase from the University of Chicago Law School. Professor Coase is best known for his work on the relationship among property rights, transaction costs, and the role of government. Coase challenged the prevailing view that economic externalities, such as water, air, and noise pollution, were "problems" in need of governmental action. It had been argued that firms will not consider these "external" costs when making choices regarding output levels and technology choices.

Coase argued that externalities should not be viewed as one party inflicting harm on another party. Rather, he viewed externalities as a problem of allocating a scarce resource. For example, a factory might use the surrounding buildings to absorb noise from its production process. The owners of a nearby amusement park might desire less noise so that they could attract more tourists. Coase claimed that this externalities problem would be resolved without government intervention if the transaction costs of arriving at the solution were kept low. The issue is one of arriving at the appropriate specification and assignment of property rights to noiselessness.

In air pollution control, this Coasian approach to allocating "rights to pollute" finally has been adopted on a widespread basis. Under the conditions of the Clean Air Act of 1990, the Environmental Protection Agency (EPA) is directed to set allowances for sulfur emissions from electric utility plants on a plant-by-plant basis.

Congress gave polluters the right to trade these rights among themselves. For example, if one firm already has emission levels at its plants that are within acceptable bounds, it can sell its excess rights to pollute to another firm. Depending on the price of these "pollution rights," firms that do not meet the emissions standards can choose either to buy the pollution rights at a market price, or to install the needed pollution control equipment—whichever is cheaper. The Chicago Board of Trade quickly created a market on which these pollution rights are actively traded. Such a development greatly reduces the transaction costs associated with the sale of tradeable pollution rights.

In the broadly defined arena of government regulation of business, there has been a resurgence of interest in allowing market forces to operate, rather than relying on governmental regulators. Deregulation of most aspects of the transportation industries is complete; natural gas pipelines and telephone companies have been greatly deregulated; and there is substantial movement toward deregulation of the electric utility industry. The trend toward greater deregulation will open new opportunities for future managers and confront them with new challenges.

http://

Read an autobiography of Ronald Coase at the following Internet site maintained by the Nobel Foundation:
http://www.nobel.se.edu/laureates/economy-1991-1-autobio.html

MARKET STRUCTURE, CONDUCT, AND PERFORMANCE

Antitrust regulation is designed to increase the incidence of competition by eliminating attempts to monopolize an industry, as well as by attacking certain patterns of market conduct that are believed to have harmful effects on a workably competitive market structure.

Market Performance

Ultimately what society would like from the producers of goods and services is a multidimensional performance concept which includes these elements:

1. Resources should be allocated in an *efficient* manner, sometimes labeled static efficiency.
2. Producers should be *technologically progressive;* that is, they should attempt to develop and adopt quickly new techniques that will result in lower costs, improved quality, or a greater diversity of new and better products. This concept is sometimes labeled dynamic efficiency. Smaller drug firms, for example, like AstraZeneca are often more innovative than the pharmaceutical industry giants like Schering-Plough, Bristol-Myers-Squibb, and Pfizer.
3. Producers should operate in a manner that encourages *full employment* of productive resources, including human capital.

Unfortunately, these elements of good market performance are not always completely compatible with one another or agreed on by everyone. This prevents the development of an unambiguous index that might be used to assess the performance characteristics of a firm or an industry. Consequently, research on market performance has tended to focus on certain specific, measurable aspects of market performance such as profit rates, price-cost margins, actual costs versus technologically possible costs, selling cost in relation to price or total costs, relative price flexibility, stability of employment throughout the business cycle, and improvements in the productivity of labor.

Market Conduct

With good performance as the ultimate objective, it is important to develop a conceptual model that will help explain the causes of good or bad performance. Joe Bain's structure-conduct-performance model of the factors influencing market performance is illustrated in Figure 17.1. Performance is viewed as dependent on the market conduct of firms in an industry. In general, market conduct includes the following patterns of behavior:

1. *Pricing behavior of the firm or group of firms*—This includes a consideration of whether prices charged tend to maximize individual profits, whether collusive practices in use tend to result in maximum group profits, or whether price discrimination is followed.
2. *Product policy of the firm or group of firms*—For example, is product design frequently changed (as with auto style changes)? Is product quality consistent or variable? What variety of products is made available?
3. *Sales promotion and advertising policy of the firm or group*—How important are sales promotions and advertising in the firm's or industry's market plans? How is the volume of this activity determined?

Figure 17.1   A Conceptual Market Structure-Conduct-Performance Model

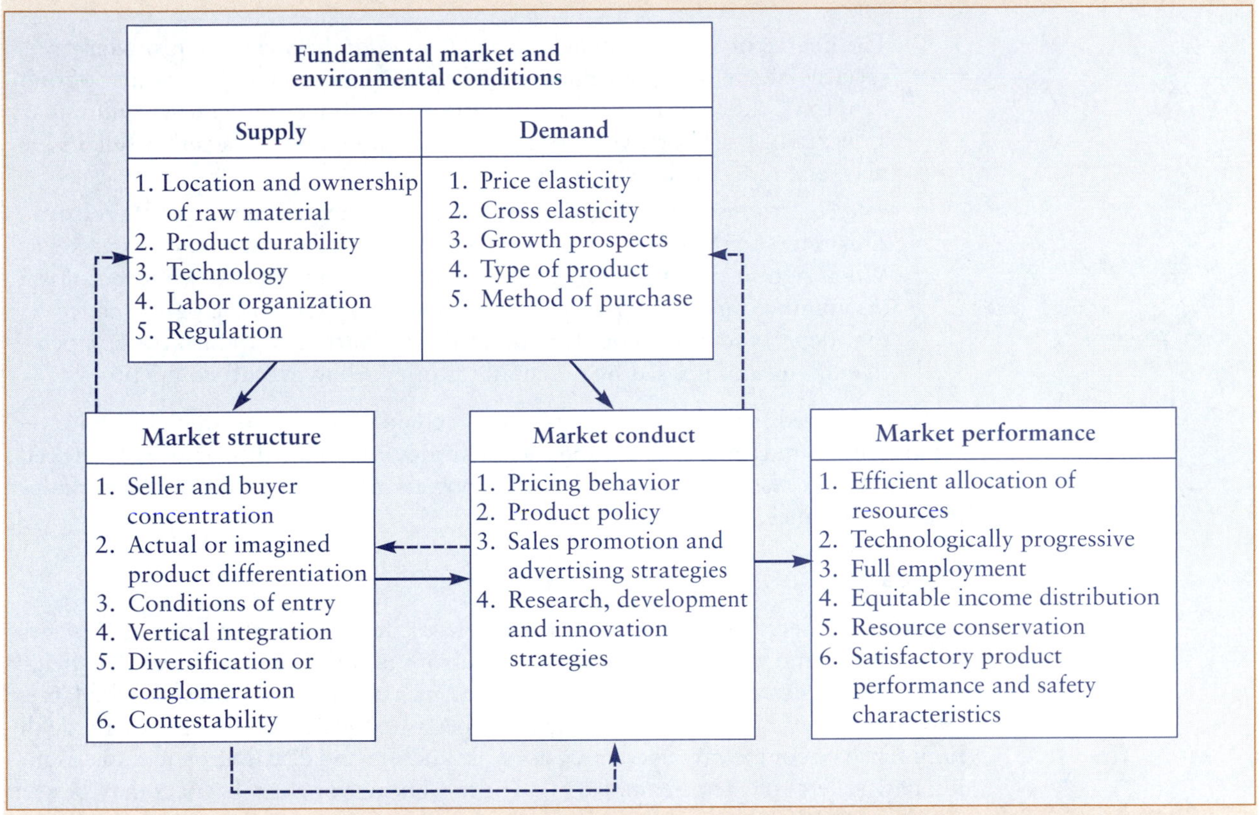

4. *Research, development, and innovation strategies employed by the firm or group*—How substantial are expenditures for these purposes? To what extent is new technology available to smaller firms? How quickly do leading firms adopt new technology?

Although the distinction between conduct and performance may sometimes be blurred, it is important to remember that performance refers to the *end results* of the policies or processes of adjustment pursued by a firm, whereas market conduct encompasses the *processes* whereby the end results are reached.

Market Structure

Market performance and market conduct are both dependent on the structure of a particular market. The concept of market structure refers to three main characteristics of buyers and sellers in a particular market:

1. The degree of *seller and buyer concentration* in the market, as well as the size distribution of these sellers or buyers—On the seller side, this determines whether an industry is classified as monopoly, oligopoly, pure competition, or some variant thereof. It is also important to know if there is a

significant "fringe" of potential competitors confronting the larger firms in a concentrated industry. Buyer concentration is also important because the bargaining power of buyers determines in part the gross margin sellers can earn.

2. The degree of actual or imagined *differentiation* between the products or services of competing producers—When buyers perceive the product of one firm to be different from that of another, these buyer preferences will impart a degree of market power to the seller that ultimately affects that seller's market conduct and performance.

3. The *conditions surrounding entry* into the market and later exit therefrom—This refers to the relative ease with which new sellers may enter a market. When significant barriers to entry exist, competition may cease to become a disciplining force on existing firms, and we are likely to see performance that departs from the competitive ideal. Exit barriers diminish the competitive discipline imposed by potential (as opposed to actual) competitors.

Other related aspects of market structure include the extent to which firms are vertically integrated back to their sources of supply or forward to the final markets, because that is also likely to impart market power and lead to unsatisfactory conduct and performance.

Threat of Entry

The threat of entry is a measure of the height of the barriers that exist against new competitors and that protect existing firms from potential competition. The height of the barriers to entry in an industry may be measured conceptually as "the largest percentage by which established sellers can persistently elevate their prices above the minimized or competitive average costs of production and distribution without inducing new sellers to enter the industry."[1] The importance of entry barriers may be seen in a patent entry barrier example. Consider the case of a monopolist who knows that raising prices above a level that just yields a normal rate of return on the investment will result in a large influx of new competitors in the industry. The monopolist may choose no competitors and normal profits in the short run to preserve a long-run position. Alternatively, when substantial barriers to entry exist or when entry is completely blocked, as in the case of the possession of patent rights, the monopolist may be expected to charge the highest price consistent with short-run profit maximization over the useful life of the patent. We can see that the relative ease or difficulty of entry for new firms in an industry can have a significant impact on industry performance.

When firms are able to raise their prices somewhat above those that would prevail under competition without inducing the entry of new firms, some barriers to new entry must exist. These may be classified into three types. These general types of entry barriers and how they arise are summarized on the left side of Table 17.1; the consequences of the entry barriers on new competitors are enumerated on the right.

Contestable Markets and the Structure-Performance Relationship

William Baumol, J. C. Panzar, and R. D. Willig[2] have developed a theory of *contestable markets* that provides additional useful insights into the structure, conduct, and performance relationship. The theory of contestable markets yields the

[1] Joe Bain, *Industrial Organization* (New York: John Wiley & Sons, 1968), p. 237.

[2] William J. Baumol, J. C. Panzar, and R. D. Willig, *Contestable Markets and the Theory of Industry Structure* (New York: Harcourt Brace Jovanovich, 1982).

Table 17.1   Type and Consequences of Barriers to Entry

Type	Consequences for New Entrants

A. Product differentiation barriers arise from
   1. Buyer preferences, conditioned by advertising, for established brand names
   2. Patent control of superior product designs by existing firms
   3. Ownership or control of favored distribution systems (for example, exclusive auto dealerships)
	A. 1. New entrants cannot sell their products for as high a price as existing firms can.
	   2. Sales promotion costs for new entrants may be prohibitive.
	   3. New entrants may be unable to raise sufficient capital to establish a competitive distribution system.

B. Absolute cost advantages of established firm's production and distribution arise from
   1. Control of superior production techniques by patent or secrecy
   2. Exclusive ownership of superior natural resource deposits
   3. Inability of new firms to acquire necessary factors of production (management, labor, equipment)
   4. Superior access to financial resources at lower costs
	B. 1. Costs of new entrants are higher than for existing firms. Hence, while existing firms may charge a price which results in above-normal profits, new entrants may be unable to make even a normal profit at that price.

C. Economies of large-scale production and distribution (or sales promotion) arise from
   1. Capital-intensive nature of industry production processes
   2. High initial start-up costs
	C. 1. The entry of a new firm at a sufficient scale will result in an industry price reduction and a disappearance of the profits anticipated by the new entrants.
	   2. New firms may be unable to acquire a sufficient market share to sustain efficient operations.

D. Limited access to distribution channel	D. Closed shelf-space or Internet portals will necessitate massive slot-in investments and may prohibit certain business models.

Source: Bain, *Industrial Organization*, pp. 237–265.

same results as the theory of perfect competition but requires substantially fewer assumptions. It explains the emergence of competitive performance in a market characterized by multiproduct economies and few firms.

A perfectly contestable market is one that is easily accessible to potential entrants and easy to escape because capital investments are redeployable (trucks, planes, information). The potential competitors use the incumbent firms' pre-entry price as the basis for evaluating the profitability of entry. With freedom of entry and exit, potential competitors need not fear the pricing reactions of incumbents. If profit potential disappears after initial entry, the new entrants can simply leave the industry. The possibility of hit-and-run profits by potential entrants will cause even a dominant incumbent firm to set prices equal to average cost, because at any higher price there will be an opportunity for profitable entry.

The theory of contestable markets has shifted the focus of attention in market structure, conduct, and performance relationships to the conditions of exit. The lower the barriers to entry *and exit,* the more nearly a market structure fits the perfectly contestable market model, and consequently, the more likely it is that the resulting set of prices and outputs will meet the perfectly competitive market norm of price equal to average unit cost.

<table>
<tr><td>*Example*</td><td>

ARE CITY-PAIR AIRLINES A CONTESTABLE MARKET?

Airplanes, of course, are the classic redeployable asset. However, there are several features of the airline business that do not meet the conditions of contestable markets. First, hub investments are sunk costs often not redeployable into other airline route structures. Second, costs of switching from one airline to another are often raised by frequent flyer programs, flight schedules, and ticket promotions that restrict interline transfers. Finally, airline incumbents change prices two or three times a day, adjusting to competitive threats much more quickly than hit-and-run entrants can move in and out of city pairs. So city-pair airlines are *not* a contestable market. Think of trucking or Internet search engines instead.

</td></tr>
</table>

Market and Environmental Conditions

Market structure, conduct, and ultimately performance are also influenced by certain *fundamental market and environmental conditions*. These may be divided into factors primarily influencing the *supply* or *input side* of the production equation and those whose primary impact is on the *demand side*. The supply side includes the location and ownership distribution of essential raw materials, the durability of the product, the available technology and production techniques commonly used, the degree to which labor inputs are readily available and organized (unionized), and the extent to which the firm's activities are regulated by government. On the demand side, such factors as the price elasticity of demand, the number of close substitutes that are available (measured by the cross elasticity of demand), the growth prospects of the industry, the type of good or service being produced (intermediate, consumer, specialty, convenience, and so on), and the method of purchase by buyers (list price acceptance, negotiation or haggling, sealed bid) must be included in an analysis of fundamental conditions influencing market structure, conduct, and performance.

The solid arrows in Figure 17.1 indicate flows that are primarily causal in the model, resulting ultimately in some observable market performance. As the dotted arrows indicate, however, some secondary and feedback flows are also involved. The major concern of studies in the field of market structure, conduct, and performance is to develop the capability to predict market performance, based either on observations of the fundamental market and environmental conditions, market structure, and market conduct, or on some contemplated and controllable changes in these factors.

We wish to emphasize one final point about the usefulness of this model in providing guidance for developing regulatory policies: There is no one place in the causal chain, from fundamental conditions to market performance, at which regulation (or deregulation) will always work best. In some cases, direct control of market structure (e.g., through failure to approve a proposed merger of satellite TV giants DIRECTV and EchoStar) may be effective. In other cases, direct control over certain business practices (that is, over market conduct) will be more effective.

Market Concentration

The purpose of measuring market concentration is to indicate the extent to which market exchanges take place in a competitive market structure. When industry sales, assets, or contributions to value added are concentrated in a few hands, market conduct and performance are less likely to be competitive in nature.

This is not always so; occasionally very concentrated industries are highly competitive. Intel has acquired most of its rivals, but two remaining firms compete vigorously. Figure 17.2 shows the dynamics of market share for Intel and AMD, who together control over 90 percent of the chip production for microprocessors in desktop PCs, where margins are very slim. However, in general, consolidation mergers rationalize excess capacity in an industry but accomplish little more. Risk-adjusted cumulative returns to acquiring-firm shareholders are consistently negative, offsetting many sizable premiums paid to target-firm shareholders.[3] Hence, efficiency gains from further consolidation in already concentrated industries are very few.

Market Concentration Ratio
The percentage of total industry output produced by the 4, 8, 20, or 50 largest firms.

One widely used index of market concentration is the **market** (or *industry*) **concentration ratio**. It may be defined as the percentage of total industry output (measured, for instance, in terms of sales, employment, value added, or value of shipments) attributable to the 4, 8, 20, or 50 largest companies. Data on market concentration ratios are regularly made available from the Bureau of the Census, based on the *Census of Manufacturers*. The Bureau of the Census defines industries in terms of SIC

Figure 17.2   Market Share Dynamics in Microprocessors for Desktop PCs

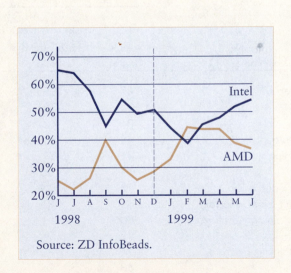

Source: ZD InfoBeads.

---

[3] See Robert Bruner, "Does M & A Pay?" *Journal of Applied Finance,* Spring/Summer 2002, pp. 45–68.

(Standard Industrial Classification system) product categories. Under this system, an industry is defined as a group of establishments producing a single product or a more or less closely related set of products. The SIC system consists of up to a seven-digit category code, indicating increasing specificity of industry and product as the number of digits increases. All manufacturing, for example, is specified by the first digit, food and kindred products by a two-digit category, candy and other confectionary products by a four-digit category, and sugar- or chocolate-coated nuts by a five-digit category.

It is necessary to use care in interpreting Bureau of the Census concentration ratios. In some cases the four-digit SIC industry designation will be too broad, including many products that do not serve the same function and hence are not substitutable. In other cases they are too narrow, failing to include ready substitutes. For example, metal, glass, and paper containers are classified as separate industries. Another problem with the census concentration ratios is that in some instances they understate the true level of concentration for bulky, low-value commodities that cannot be economically transported far from their places of production. This occurs in such industries as cement, milk supply, and concrete block and brick. Table 17.2

Table 17.2   Concentration Ratios and Herfindahl-Hirschman Index for Selected Industries

SIC	Industry Name	Share of Value Added Accounted for by the 4, 8, and 20 Largest Companies in Each Manufacturing Industry			Herfindahl-Hirschman Index
		4-Firm Ratio	8-Firm Ratio	20-Firm Ratio	
31123	Breakfast Cereals	87	95	99	2773
311511	Fluid milk	22	35	52	220
31511	Hosiery and socks	31	43	60	343
32561	Soap and detergents	68	80	87	1744
32411	Petroleum refining	41	57	84	625
32721	Flat glass	77	100	100	1829
327331	Concrete block and brick	12	18	29	73
331315	Aluminum sheet, plate, and foil	65	85	98	1448
333611	Turbine and turbine generator sets	80	91	97	2403
33511	Electric lamp bulbs	89	94	99	2849
32992	Sporting and athletic goods	24	31	45	191
33991	Silverware	68	76	88	2781

Source: 1997 *Census of Manufacturers*, MC92-S-2, U.S. Department of Commerce.

provides concentration ratios for selected industries. Some industries have become highly concentrated, such as breakfast cereals, turbine generators, light bulbs, and silverware. Some industries, such as hosiery and sporting goods, are very fragmented at the national level.

Herfindahl-Hirschman Index
A measure of market concentration equal to the sum of the squares of the market shares of the firms in a given industry.

Another important measure of market concentration is the **Herfindahl-Hirschman Index,** or *HHI*:

$$HHI = \sum_{i=1}^{N} S_i^2$$

where S_i is the market share of the *i*th firm and N is the number of firms in the industry. For example, in a revelant market consisting of just three firms like baby food (where Gerber has 70 percent, Beech-Nut has 16 percent, and Heinz has 14 percent market share), the *HHI* is $70^2 + 16^2 + 14^2$, which is equal to 5352. *HHI* has a maximum value of 10,000 and decreases as the number of firms (*N*) increases. The *HHI* is generally highly correlated with other measures of market concentration, such as the four-firm sales concentration ratio, but accentuates the potential influence of leading firms with asymmetrically large market shares. *HHI* values for selected industries are also shown in Table 17.2.

ANTITRUST REGULATION STATUTES AND THEIR ENFORCEMENT

Antitrust Laws
A series of laws passed since 1890 to limit monopoly power and to maintain competition in most American industries.

Since 1890, a number of federal laws have been passed with the intent of preventing monopoly and of maintaining competition in U.S. industry. The ultimate objective of these laws is to protect the public from the abuses and inefficiencies that are thought to flow from the possession of monopoly power. These laws have come to be known as **antitrust laws** because they were initially directed at the large stockholder trusts such as Standard Oil, American Tobacco, and several coal and railroad trusts. Under a trust agreement, the voting rights to the stock of a number of directly competitive firms were conveyed to a legal trust which managed the firms as if they were one big multiplant monopoly, thereby maximizing profits. Although extremely successful on the bottom line of the income statement, these trusts were viewed with increasing dismay because of the high price and restricted outputs that resulted. In this section we summarize the provisions of the most important of these antitrust laws and their effects on business decisions.

http://

An excellent source of information on antitrust on the Internet is found at the following address:
http://www.antitrust.org/
The Internet site for the Antitrust Division of the Department of Justice can be found at
http://www.usdoj.gov/atr/index.html
The following Internet site maintained by FindLaw provides a comprehensive set of links to antitrust resources on the Internet, including relevant U.S. Code, case summaries, journals, and access to the Federal Trade Commission and the Department of Justice:
http://www.findlaw.com/01topics/01antitrust/index.html

The Sherman Act (1890)

The Sherman Act was the first national antitrust law designed to regulate monopoly and the use of monopoly power. Its important provisions are brief, but they are wide ranging. First, it declares illegal

> every contract, combination in the form of a trust or otherwise, or conspiracy in restraint of commerce among the several States, or with foreign nations . . .

This provision applies only to agreements in which two or more persons are involved. The second important provision is more general, in that it also applies to individual efforts to monopolize. It declares that

> every person who shall monopolize, or attempt to monopolize, or combine or conspire with any other person or persons, to monopolize any part of the trade or commerce among the several States, or with foreign nations, shall be deemed guilty of a misdemeanor.

http://
You can read the full text of the Sherman Act, Clayton Act, and other laws pertaining to monopolies and the restraint of trade in Title 15 of the U.S. Code at the following Internet site maintained by Cornell University:
http://www.law.cornell.edu/uscode/15/ch1.html

This act turned the already existing common-law prohibitions against restraint of trade and monopolization into federal offenses requiring federal enforcement. In the years following the passage of the Sherman Act, dissatisfaction with the generality of its provisions, as well as with the lack of vigor with which it was enforced, led to pressure for additional legislation.

The Clayton Act (1914)

The Clayton Act enumerated four anticompetitive business practices that were prohibited in various circumstances:

1. *Price discrimination* between purchasers of commodities was illegal, except to the extent that it was based on differences in grade, quality, and quantity of the product sold. Lower prices were permitted only where they made "due allowances for differences in the cost of selling or transportation" and where they were offered "in good faith to meet competition." To discriminate otherwise in wholesale pricing was illegal if the effect was to substantially lessen competition or tend to create a monopoly.

2. Section 3 of the act forbade sellers from leasing or making "a sale or contract for the sale of . . . commodities . . . on the condition that the lessee or purchaser thereof shall not use or deal in the . . . commodity . . . of a competitor." This is commonly referred to as a prohibition against "exclusive dealing and *tying contracts*." As with the price discrimination section, the prohibition was not absolute, but only applied to the extent that the practice substantially lessened competition or tended to create a monopoly.

Example

WHY MILLER BEER IS SO HARD TO FIND IN MEXICO[4]

Mexico is the world's eighth largest beer market. Since the 1994 NAFTA agreement, Corona and Modelo beer exports grew fivefold to account for 11 percent of the U.S. market. Budweiser owns a 50-percent non-controlling stake of the Modelo brewer. The Miller Brewing Co. has attempted the same sort of penetration into the Mexican domestic market without any real success. Modelo and its rival Femasa have 99 percent of the market. For one thing, Femasa owns large convenience store channels in Mexico, and Miller is not stocked on their shelves. In other cases, bars are paid to deal exclusively with Modelo. As a consequence, a six-pack of Modelo Especial costs $4.60 in Mexico versus $1.80 for the best-seller in Brazil and $2.20 for the best-seller in Chile.

3. Section 7, the *antimerger* section, forbade any corporation engaged in commerce from acquiring the shares of a competing firm or from purchasing the stocks of two or more competing firms, where substantial damage to competition could be proven or where it tended to create a monopoly. Later, the Celler-Kefauver amendments extended this antimerger policy to include asset acquisitions.

4. *Interlocking Directorates,* defined as a case where the same person is on the board of directors of two or more firms, were declared illegal in Section 8 under these circumstances: (a) if the corporations competed with one

[4] Based on "Why Corona Is Big Here," *Wall Street Journal,* January 17, 2003, p. B1.

another; (b) if any one had capital, surplus, and undivided profits in excess of $1 million; and (c) if "the elimination of competition . . . between them would constitute a violation of any of the provisions of the antitrust laws."

The Federal Trade Commission Act (1914)

The Federal Trade Commission (FTC) Act was passed as a supplement to the Clayton Act. Its major antitrust provision, found in Section 5, merely states "that unfair methods of competition in commerce are hereby declared illegal." A determination of what constitutes unfair methods of competition beyond those specified in the Clayton Act is left to the Federal Trade Commission, which the act established as an independent government antitrust agency.

The Robinson-Patman Act (1936)

The Robinson-Patman Act can be discussed both as antitrust legislation aimed at controlling the pricing aspects of market conduct and as an expression of a government policy aimed at restricting certain forms of price competition, thereby benefiting a special group of sellers. The act's provisions are summarized below:

1. Section 2(a) makes it illegal to discriminate in price when selling goods of "like grade and quality" where the effect may be to "substantially lessen competition or tend to create a monopoly" or "to injure, destroy, or prevent competition."

   A seller who is charged with price discrimination has two legal defenses enumerated in Section 2(b): First, the "cost defense" permits differentials in price that "make only due allowance for differences in the cost of manufacture, sale, or delivery." Second, the "good faith defense" permits a lower price to be charged to meet "an equally low price of a competitor."

2. Sections 2(d) and 2(e) prohibit the seller from allowing discounts to a buyer for merchandising services rendered the seller by the buyer, unless similar discounts are offered to all buyers. Secret rebates were prohibited; advertising or promotional allowances, for example, must be made available to all buyers, not just a few selected large firms.

The Hart-Scott-Rodino Antitrust Improvement Act (1976)

The Hart-Scott-Rodino Act requires larger companies (i.e., those with assets and sales over $100 million and $10 million, respectively) that are planning to merge to provide notification and information concerning the proposed merger to the Antitrust Division of the Department of Justice and to the Federal Trade Commission. After notification of the proposed merger, a waiting period of 30 days ensues during which these government antitrust enforcement agencies review the information submitted by the companies and examine the competitive effects of the merger proposal. The initial waiting period often is extended by enforcement officials in order to seek additional documents from the companies. After reviewing the information submitted, the government can either challenge the proposed merger in federal court or allow the merger to be completed, possibly with some modifications. Companies can appeal rulings by the FTC, and private complainants can bring antitrust suits to the federal courts. State attorneys general can also initiate federal antitrust suits.

Example

CALIFORNIA'S CLASS ACTION SUIT AGAINST MICROSOFT SETTLES FOR $1.1 BILLION

Two and a half years after a U.S. district court found Microsoft guilty of maintaining a 92-percent monopoly of desktop operating system software by using anticompetitive practices (in January 2003), the defendant settled a class action lawsuit filed by the California Attorney General on behalf of 13 million California individuals and businesses. Microsoft has agreed to pay $5 to $29 vouchers for each California buyer who licensed either Windows 95 or Windows 98 between 1995 and 2001 as compensation for the alleged overcharges. The vouchers can be used for laptop, desktop, or tablet computers and for software from any computer company. If all 51 million vouchers are submitted, Microsoft stands to lose $1.1 billion.

Government antitrust agencies can use various methods to enforce the laws. Most antitrust cases are settled with *consent decrees* negotiated between the company and enforcement officials. Under a consent decree, a company agrees to take certain actions (or not engage in other actions) in return for the government agreeing not to seek additional penalties in the courts. In cases filed by antitrust agencies against a company, the courts may issue an *injunction* requiring (or prohibiting) certain actions by the company. The courts may also impose *fines* and, in certain instances, *prison sentences* if the defendants are found guilty of violating the antitrust laws. In cases involving charges of monopolization, the courts may require *divestiture* of certain assets by the company. Finally, in antitrust cases filed by private individuals and companies, the party filing the suit may be entitled to *treble damages* if the defendant is found guilty.

ANTITRUST PROHIBITION OF SELECTED BUSINESS DECISIONS

Collusion

Explicit agreements among competitors to fix prices along with other overt forms of collusion, such as market-sharing agreements, are illegal under the Sherman Act. The courts generally have ruled that such agreements are illegal, regardless of whether they cause injury to competitors. The legality of other less explicit forms of collusion is not as clear-cut. For example, in 1994 six major airlines agreed to settle price-fixing allegations that they used their jointly owned, computerized ticket information systems to provide advance notification of price changes to their competitors and thereby raise fares. On the other hand, other implicit forms of collusion, such as price leadership practiced in some industries, normally are not prosecuted under the antitrust laws. In a few cases, such as the sugar industry, producers have been legislatively exempted from the antitrust laws and are legally permitted to jointly set prices and allocate output (quotas).

Mergers That Substantially Lessen Competition

A number of difficult legal and economic issues are encountered in attempting to determine whether a proposed merger will be challenged by government antitrust agencies. First is the issue of what is meant by the term *substantially lessening competition*. Every horizontal merger reduces competition by eliminating at least one

http://

Read the full text of the 1992 horizontal merger guidelines issued by the U.S. Department of Justice at the following Internet site: http://www.usdoj.gov/atr/guidelines/merger.txt

competitor, by definition. The FTC and the Antitrust Division of the Department of Justice (DOJ) in 1997 reissued merger guidelines based on the Herfindahl-Hirschman Index (*HHI*) that they use in deciding whether to challenge a proposed merger:

1. For markets with an *HHI* above 1,800, the government is likely to challenge a merger that increases the index by 50 to 100 points, or more.
2. For markets with an *HHI* between 1,000 and 1,800, a merger challenge by the government is unlikely unless the index increases by 100 or more points.
3. For markets with an *HHI* below 1,000, the government is unlikely to challenge a merger.

A merger increases the *HHI* by 2 times the product of the market shares of the candidate firms. So when Beech-Nut and Heinz's baby food division wished to merge, the merger was challenged because the 5,352 point *HHI* changed as follows:

$$HHI \text{ before} = S^2_{\text{Gerber}} + S^2_{\text{Beech-Nut}} + S^2_{\text{Heinz}} = 5352$$
$$HHI \text{ after} = S^2_{\text{Gerber}} + (S_{\text{Beech-Nut}} + S_{\text{Heinz}})^2$$
$$= S^2_{\text{Gerber}} + (S^2_{\text{Beech-Nut}} + S^2_{\text{Heinz}} + 2S_{\text{Beech-Nut}}S_{\text{Heinz}})$$
$$= 70^2 + (16^2 + 14^2 + 2 \cdot 16 \cdot 14)$$
$$= 5,352 + \Delta HHI$$
$$= 5,352 + 448 = 5,800$$

The merger guidelines also list other factors that are considered in the analysis, including the ease with which competitors can enter the industry, likely failure of the to-be-acquired firm without the merger, and possible gains in efficiency for the (combined) firm.

A second important issue is the relevant product market to be used in computing statistics of market control, such as the *HHI*. Rather than measuring the cross-price elasticity of demand, the FTC and DOJ use a 5 percent price increase test—namely, what products, if not present in the market, would allow a monopolist to raise prices on a nontransitory basis by at least 5 percent? All such products should be included in the relevant market definition.

In addition to defining the relevant product market, the geographical market is also important in determining market control or power. Is the market local, regional, national, or international? Generally, a narrower definition of the market will heighten the measure of potential monopoly power and raise the probability of a merger substantially lessening competition. If the FTC or Antitrust Division comes to this conclusion, they will seek an injunction in federal court to stop the proposed merger.

Example

TRUSTBUSTERS REAPPEAR: MCI-WORLDCOM AND SPRINT MERGER PROPOSAL DISAPPROVED[5]

In the late 1990s, despite approving the $86-billion merger of Exxon and Mobil to create the largest institution in the integrated oil industry, the FTC and the Antitrust Division became more determined to stop mergers that result in highly concentrated

[5] Based on "Trustbusters," *Business Week,* June 1, 1998, p. 42; "Hanging Up on the WorldCom-Sprint Merger," *Knowledge at Wharton,* July 6, 2000; "Is the FTC Defending Goliath?" *Business Week,* December 18, 2000, pp. 160–162; and "Murdoch Wins DIRECTV," *Wall Street Journal,* April 10, 2003, p. B1.

industries becoming even more consolidated. In 1997, Staples and Office Depot were blocked from merging even though the combined firm would have controlled only 8 percent of the broadly-defined office products industry. After collecting and exhaustively analyzing demand data, the FTC staff persuaded the commission and a federal judge that prices were higher when only one office products superstore existed in a city. Apparently because of the convenience offered by full-line superstores, numerous smaller suppliers that necessitate multiple shopping trips were not seen by consumers as an effective substitute. Consequently, the relevant market was defined as office supply superstores and the prohibited merger would have controlled 76 percent of that market.

In the long-distance telecommunications market, the second-largest firm, MCI-WorldCom, with 28 percent market share was prohibited from merging with the third-largest firm, Sprint, with 17 percent market share. The FTC was riveted in this case on the 91-percent four-firm concentration of AT&T, MCI-WorldCom, Sprint, and Qwest-BellWest. Although GTE and Bell Atlantic's merger to create the fifth largest domestic U.S. long-distance company was approved, the $115 billion acquisition of Sprint by MCI-WorldCom was not.

Similarly, in July 2000 the FTC blocked a proposed merger between Heinz and Beech-Nut with 16 percent and 14 percent, respectively, of the baby food market. The rationale was that the Herfindahl-Hirschman index (*HHI*) for baby foods measured 5,352, relative to the 1,800-point presumptive benchmark that causes concern. But, in this case, the reason concentration is so enormous in baby food is that the behemoth Gerber has 70 percent of the market and is itself responsible for 4,900 of the 5,352 *HHI* points. The FTC did not accept the Heinz and Beech-Nut argument that together their two firms could realize scale economies, lower distribution and R&D costs, and thereby compete more effectively against the dominant firm.

Finally, in October 2001, Charlie Ergen's privately held EchoStar (DISH Network) launched a $31-billion bid for Hughes Electronics' (DIRECTV). DISH Network and DIRECTV were the top two satellite TV providers in the U.S.; Ergen argued that the relevant market included digital cable TV systems, with a combined industry share distribution as follows:

Comcast	33%
DIRECTV	17%
Time Warner	17%
DISH Network	13%
Charter Comm.	10%
Cox Comm.	10%
HHI	2036

The FTC and the Antitrust Division disagreed, defined the relevant market narrowly as satellite TV, and prohibited the merger. Even under the broader definition, ΔHHI for the proposed merger was 442 points, well beyond the 50-points safe harbor of the merger guidelines for an industry with *HHI* already in excess of 1800. Ergen's case, therefore, rested on potential efficiencies from the removal of duplicatory satellite transmissions, freeing bandwidth for additional channels.

Rather than filing a lawsuit to prevent a merger between large competing firms, antitrust enforcement agencies sometimes negotiate a consent decree that permits a merger to take place provided certain conditions are met to minimize the anticompetitive effects of the merger. For example, in the case of AT&T's $12.6-billion acquisition of McCaw Cellular (the largest U.S. cellular telephone company), the consent decree contained provisions requiring AT&T to operate McCaw as a separate subsidiary and allowing McCaw customers to pick any long-distance carrier to handle long-distance calls made on their cellular telephones. In another instance, the antitrust commission of the EU insisted that British Airways divest itself of 353 landing slots at London's Heathrow Airport if BA and American Airlines wished to merge. Rather than lose this many of its prized assets, BA decided to continue competing with American.

Monopolization

As we saw earlier, firms engaged in overt forms of collusion with other companies can be successfully prosecuted under the Sherman Act. Companies acting alone also can be charged under the act with illegally attempting to monopolize a market or engaging in monopolistic practices. However, proving such alleged violations of the laws often is quite difficult. Before the Microsoft case in 1998, the last large monopolization case brought by the antitrust enforcement officials resulted in the breakup of AT&T back in 1982.

Example

POTENTIALLY ANTICOMPETITIVE PRACTICES: MICROSOFT'S TYING ARRANGEMENTS[6]

More recently, it was alleged that dominant software maker Microsoft used its leading position in the market for computer operating systems to gain an unfair advantage in the market for applications software. Netscape had complained that Microsoft illegally tied its Internet access software (Microsoft Explorer) to sales of Windows 95, which provided the operating system for 92 percent of the personal computers in the U.S. Microsoft distributed Explorer free with every sale of Windows 95 to Compaq and Dell computers, priced Windows 95 without Explorer much higher, and threatened to remove the Windows 95 license if any Web browser other than Microsoft Explorer was preinstalled on the PCs Compaq shipped. Over four quarters in late 1996 and 1997, Microsoft's share of the Web browser market grew from 20 percent to 39 percent. By 1999, Netscape's share had fallen to 47%, and Microsoft's anticompetitive practices had resulted in a 53% share. Was this evidence of "substantial harm to competition," or just substantial harm to a particular competitor?

Tying arrangements that extend the monopoly power of a dominant firm in one market to another distinct product and relevant market are illegal per se. Because these sales practices precluded Netscape from selling its Web browser, Microsoft was required to unbundle the two products and change its pricing practices. Nevertheless, in May 1998, the Justice Department and twenty State Attorney General filed suit, alleging illegal tying arrangements and other anticompetitive practices. Microsoft vigorously defended itself for almost two years but in April 2000 was found guilty of the alleged violations.

---

[6] Based on "Browse This," *U.S. News & World Report,* December 5, 1997, p. 59; "U.S. Sues Microsoft Over PC Browser," *Wall Street Journal,* October 21, 1997, p. A3; "Knowing the ABCs of the Antitrust Case Against Microsoft," *Wall Street Journal,* October 30, 1997, p. B1; "Microsoft's Browser: A Bundle of Trouble," *The Economist,* October 25, 1997, p. 74; and "Microsoft on Trial," *Wall Street Journal,* April 4, 2000, p. A16.

Wholesale Price Discrimination

A large company that operates as a manufacturer or distributor in two (or more) different geographic (or product) markets and cuts wholesale prices in one market and not in the other market can be accused under the Robinson-Patman Act of engaging in illegal price discrimination. Differential pricing directly to final product customers is allowed (and often based on "what the market will bear") but not so in pricing to intermediate product resellers (wholesalers, distributors, etc.). For example, the publisher Penguin Books paid a large judgment to independent booksellers after it was proved that Penguin offered Barnes and Noble and Borders large-volume discounts and other trade promotions that were unrelated to the cost of serving those accounts. Similarly, six vending machine companies sued Philip Morris, alleging that other distributors and retail merchants received rebates, buybacks, and promotional allowances intended to lower costs and allow the favored distributors to drive the complainants out of business. This is the favoritism in wholesale trade that the Robinson-Patman Act was designed to prohibit.

Differentiating between the normal operation of a competitive market and illegal price cutting with the intent of eliminating current or potential competitors is a complex issue. Proving that a company has engaged in illegal price discrimination can be quite difficult because activity-based cost accounting is quite intricate.

Refusals to Deal

In general, a manufacturer can refuse to deal with any retail distributor who fails to follow company policies that are based on legitimate business justifications. However, there are three limitations on this authority. First, the orders of a renegade discounter can be refused if and only if the manufacturer acts independently of compliant dealers whose sales at higher price points are suffering because of the increased competition (*United States* v. *GM,* 1966). Second, an explicit well-justified policy must be in place in advance; the manufacturer cannot pressure individual dealers, threaten suspension of shipments of new "hot" products, or offer to reinstate if the offending discounters agree to raise their prices (*FTC* v. *Stride Rite,* 1996). Finally, manufacturers cannot lock in buyers of durable products by refusing to supply parts to independent service organizations (ISOs), especially if the ISO prices are far below the manufacturer's service prices. In *Eastman Kodak* v. *Image Technical Services* (1992), the Supreme Court argued that buyers of Kodak copiers might not fully estimate the life-cycle repair and maintenance costs of a Kodak-only service contract. Therefore, customers should be able to select independent service and nonwarranty repair well after the sale. Kodak's defense that ISO maintenance and repair failed to meet Kodak's quality standards was disproved by the evidence.

COMMAND AND CONTROL REGULATORY CONSTRAINTS: AN ECONOMIC ANALYSIS

Federal, state, and local governments are involved in the regulation of business enterprises. Table 17.3 contains a partial listing of the federal government agencies and departments, in addition to the Federal Trade Commission and Antitrust Division of the Department of Justice discussed earlier, that impose regulations on the operating decisions of firms. State regulations encompass a wide range of activities, including regulation of public utility companies and licensing of various businesses, such

Table 17.3   Partial Listing of Federal Government Regulatory Agencies

Department/Agency	Purpose
Environmental Protection Agency (EPA)	Regulates pollution of air, water, and land
Consumer Product Safety Commission (CPSC)	Protects against unreasonable risks of injury associated with consumer products
Equal Employment Opportunity Commission (EEOC)	Enforces laws on employment discrimination based on race, religion, and sex
Labor—Employment Standards Administration	Enforces minimum wage and overtime laws
Labor—Occupational Safety and Health Administration (OSHA)	Regulates safety and health conditions in the workplace
Labor—National Labor Relations Board (NLRB)	Regulates labor relations between employers and employees (and their unions)
Interstate Commerce Commission (ICC)	Regulates interstate surface transportation
Nuclear Regulatory Commission (NRC)	Regulates civilian use of nuclear energy
Securities and Exchange Commission (SEC)	Regulates issuance of new securities and trading of existing securities
Federal Communications Commission (FCC)	Regulates radio and television broadcasting and interstate telephone service
Federal Reserve System	Regulates commercial banks and bank holding companies
Agriculture—Food Safety and Inspection Service	Regulates meat and poultry industry for safety and accurate labeling
Health and Human Services—Food and Drug Administration (FDA)	Regulates safety of food, drugs, and cosmetics
Energy—Federal Energy Regulatory Commission (FERC)	Regulates interstate rates for transportation and sale of natural gas and transmission and sale of electricity
Transportation—Federal Aviation Administration (FAA)	Regulates safety of airplanes, airports, and airline operations
Transportation—National Highway Traffic Safety Administration (NHTSA)	Regulates safety of motor vehicles and tires
Labor—Mine Safety and Health Administration	Regulates safety and health in mines
Treasury—Office of Comptroller of the Currency	Regulates national banks
Treasury—Bureau of Alcohol, Tobacco, and Firearms (BATF)	Regulates manufacture and sale of alcoholic beverages, tobacco, explosives, and firearms

as health-care facilities, and numerous professions, such as law and accounting. Local governments frequently impose on businesses such regulations as zoning laws and building codes. Regulatory constraints can be imposed on individual firms, entire industries, or on all businesses. For example, the European Union prohibits direct-to-consumer advertising of prescription drugs. These constraints can affect a firm's operating costs (both fixed and variable), capital costs, and revenues. The following hypothetical example illustrates the scope and effect of environmental permits and command and control regulation by the EPA.

Example

THE PALLADIUM METAL-CASTING INDUSTRY

The palladium metal-casting industry is composed of about 25 firms that operate foundries engaged in making palladium castings. These foundries have been under attack because of the heavy pollution they cause in the communities where they operate. Consequently, the EPA proposed standards to force a reduction in particulate emissions.

The industry makes various sizes and shapes of castings; however, production levels in individual firms are measured by hundred-pound weights of castings poured, and prices and costs vary, roughly in accordance with the weight of the casting. Current industry employment is about 12,000 workers.

In an effort to assess the impact of proposed standards on the industry, the EPA has agreed to work with the trade association's economists to make these estimates. Industry demand has been estimated at

$$P = \$15,000 - .3Q$$

where P = price per hundred pounds of castings poured
Q = hundreds of pounds of castings poured

Hence, total revenue TR equals

$$TR = P \cdot Q$$
$$= \$15,000Q - .3Q^2$$

and marginal revenue MR equals

$$MR = \frac{dTR}{dQ}$$
$$= \$15,000 - .6Q$$

Similarly, the industry's total cost function TC has been estimated as

$$TC = \$100,000,000 + 6Q + .05Q^2$$

Hence marginal cost MC equals

$$MC = \frac{dTC}{dQ}$$
$$= 6 + .1Q$$

Because of a history of price leadership in the industry, the price-output solution that has generally evolved has been very close to that of a profit-maximizing monopoly. Consequently, price and output may be determined for the industry by equating marginal cost with marginal revenue and solving for Q:

$$MC = MR$$
$$6 + .1Q = 15,000 - .6Q$$
$$.7Q = 14,994$$
$$Q* = 21,420$$

Substituting in the demand equation, we find that

$$P* = 15,000 - .3(21,420)$$
$$= \$8,574$$

Given this price-output combination, total industry profits π are estimated as

$$\begin{aligned} \pi &= TR - TC \\ &= PQ - TC \\ &= (8,574)(21,420) - [100,000,000 + 6(21,420) + .05(21,420)^2] \\ \pi^* &= \$60,585,740 \end{aligned}$$

This profit of about $60.6 million represents a return on industry investment *(ROI),* estimated at about $840 million, of

$$ROI = \frac{\$60.6 \text{ million}}{\$840 \text{ million}} \times 100 = 7.2\%$$

This return is somewhat below average for U.S. industry, but this is merely an average return. Some firms are more efficient than others, thereby earning a higher return and vice versa.

To reduce smoke pollution within the proposed EPA limits, a total investment of $150 million would be required. This would increase total industry fixed costs by about $15 million (after-tax depreciation plus interest). If no variable costs were associated with the use of this pollution control equipment, the price-output solution would remain the same, but profits would drop by $15 million and the return on investment (assuming no required return on the pollution control investment) would decline to

$$ROI_1 = \frac{\$45.5 \text{ million}}{\$840 \text{ million}} \times 100 = 5.4\%^{\,7}$$

This is well below the U.S. industry average. If the $150 million pollution investment were considered in the asset base, the *ROI* would be even less impressive.

It is unrealistic, however, to assume that only fixed costs will change. Variable costs also increase because it is costly to operate and maintain the pollution control equipment. Hence industry economists estimated a new industry total cost function:

$$TC_1 = \$115,000,000 + 8Q + .1Q^2$$

and

$$MC_1 = \frac{dTC_1}{dQ} = 8 + .2Q$$

Equating MC_1 to MR, we get

$$\begin{aligned} MC_1 &= MR \\ 8 + .2Q &= 15,000 - .6Q \\ .8Q &= 14,992 \\ Q^* &= 18,740 \end{aligned}$$

Substituting in the demand equation yields

$$\begin{aligned} P^* &= 15,000 - .3(18,740) \\ &= \$9,378 \end{aligned}$$

Thus we see that output declines nearly 3,000 units and prices are increased by about $800. Under these circumstances, total industry profits π_2 equal

---

[7] Note that if the $150-million pollution control investment is added to the denominator, the computed *ROI* declines to 4.6 percent.

$$\pi_2 = TR - TC_1$$
$$= (9,378)(18,740) - [115,000,000 + 8(18,740) + .1(18,740)^2]$$
$$\pi_2^* = \$25,475,040$$

and return on investment (ignoring the pollution control investment) slips to

$$ROI_2 = \frac{\$25.5 \text{ million}}{\$840 \text{ million}} \times 100 = 3.0\%$$

Remembering that ROI_2 is an average figure, it is quite likely that some of the less efficient firms would close. Industry and EPA economists make an admittedly crude estimation that the new industry total cost and marginal cost functions, after the exit of some firms, would equal

$$TC_2 = \$85,000,000 + 15Q + .2Q^2$$
$$MC_2 = 15 + .4Q$$

The profit-maximizing output now becomes

$$MC_2 = MR$$
$$15 + .4Q = 15,000 - .6Q$$
$$Q^* = 14,985$$

and price equals

$$P^* = 15,000 - .3(14,985)$$
$$= \$10,504$$

Thus we see that output will decline about 4,000 more units (from 18,740 to 14,985) and price will increase by nearly $1,150.

New industry profits (π_3) will be

$$\pi_3 = TR - TC_2$$
$$= (10,504)(14,985) - [85,000,000 + 15(14,985) + .2(14,985)^2]$$
$$\pi_3^* = \$27,267,620$$

The resulting industry return on investment ROI_3 will be enhanced by both the increase in profits from $25 to $27 million and the reduction in total industry investment as a result of the departure of the inefficient firms. Total industry investment is now estimated to equal only $630 million. Hence

$$ROI_3 = \frac{\$27.2 \text{ million}}{\$630 \text{ million}} \times 100 = 4.3\%$$

It is also estimated that the departure of the industry's more inefficient firms will reduce total industry employment by about 3,000. The team of economists has determined that about one half of the output reduction (from 21,420 to 14,985) will be absorbed by shifting demands to substitute domestic metal firms, and the other half will result in a negative balance-of-payments drain. The current foreign price per hundred pounds of casting is about $10,300. Thus the balance-of-payments impact of the proposed environmental standard is

$$BOP \text{ impacts} = \frac{1}{2}(21,420 - 14,985)(\$10,300)$$
$$= \$33,140,250$$

Armed with this and other data, such as what the regional impacts of plant closings will be on both unemployment rates and overall regional economic development, the EPA is in a far better position to assess the effect of its proposed standards.

Perhaps the EPA will not decide on an across-the-board standard but may impose stricter limitations on firms located in densely populated areas than on those in sparsely inhabited areas. It may also decide to phase the standards in over time so their impacts will not be felt all at once. This would have the benefit of giving local communities, heavily dependent on the palladium foundries for employment, time to make necessary adjustments to expand the base of the area's economy, providing more stability in employment.

The preceding hypothetical example illustrates the insights that economic analysis can furnish in assessing the impact of operating controls on industry. Similar methods can be used to analyze nearly all the areas of operating constraints enumerated in Table 17.3.

The Deregulation Movement

http://
Read more about federal regulation of the energy industry at the following Internet site:
http://www.ferc.fed.us/

Beginning in the late 1970s and continuing through the 1980s and 1990s, sentiment has increased for relying less on government regulation and more on the marketplace to achieve desired economic objectives. This sentiment for increased deregulation has been felt most significantly in the price regulation of transportation services. Such pieces of legislation as the Airline Deregulation Act of 1978, the Railroad Revitalization Act of 1976, the Motor Carrier Act of 1980, and the Ocean Shipping Reform Act of 1998 have greatly increased the flexibility of airlines, railroads, ocean shippers, and the trucking industries to set prices and determine levels of service and areas of operation *outside* of the regulatory framework. The objectives of these pieces of legislation have been to give the affected industries greater pricing flexibility.

In the airline industry, deregulation has meant greater competition on many routes, with fare reductions and promotional fares becoming quite common. In the trucking industry, deregulation has been credited with a reduction in the rate of increase of trucking charges, and improvements in service in many areas. In the freight transportation industry, deregulation forced consolidation mergers such that 35 Class I freight railroads shrank to 9 between 1980 and 1996. Rates declined 45 percent over this period, one quarter of which was cost savings from the mergers. Long-haul freight saves the cost of sorting and exchanging freight cars. Increased density of freight and abandonment of duplicatory track has resulted in other rail cost savings. On May 1, 1999, ocean shipping rates were deregulated for the 40-foot containers that ship apparel, consumer electronics, autos, and ores from Asia to the United States and ship computer software, forest products, and grain back to Asia. The one-way cost of $3,500 for a 6,000-garment container will likely now decline.

After the FCC-Telcom Act of 1996, AT&T faced increased competition (primarily, but not exclusively) in the long-distance market from such firms as MCI and Sprint. Customers may also purchase their own phone equipment from a wide range of suppliers other than AT&T. The breakup of AT&T into seven independent regional phone companies and a long-distance company is an important step in deregulation of the telecommunications industry. The long-distance carriers may enter the local service telecom markets presently reserved for regional phone and cable companies. This should massively reduce the local access charges now embedded in the price of Internet service.

Deregulation has subjected electric power generation and transmission companies to additional competition. The National Energy Policy Act of 1992 mandated a more open transmission system, which will provide more power supply options to wholesale customers. For example, energy merchant Duke Power sells electricity throughout the nation, with new generating plants in New England, Mississippi, and California.

GOVERNMENTAL PROTECTION OF BUSINESS

Besides regulating business enterprises, numerous government programs and policies protect businesses by restricting the entry of competitors.

Restricting Competition

Many public policies pursued by the government have the effect, if not always the intent, of restricting competition. These policies take numerous forms, including the issuance of licenses and patents and the restrictions on price competition. Such import controls as tariffs and quotas have the same impact.

Licensing   When the government requires and issues a license permitting someone to practice a particular business, profession, or trade, it is by definition restricting the entry of some potential new competitors into that practice. Licensing is generally used to protect the public from fraud or incompetence in those cases where the potential for harm is quite large. Thus, doctors are required to meet certain educational standards of professional competence; restaurants need to meet public health standards; real estate agents must meet certain standards of professional knowledge; financial trustees must be bonded to ensure the public against fraud; and cab drivers are licensed with the intent of protecting the public from problem drinkers and accident-prone drivers. Nevertheless, the restricting of output by government licensure has tangible costs. Recently, Mecklenburg County, North Carolina, which surrounds Charlotte, learned that its role as a ground transportation hub was threatened because the smog permits authorized by the U.S. EPA and North Carolina regulatory agencies had foreclosed the construction of additional freight trucking terminals until some other dust-generating facility was closed.

Patent
A legal government grant of monopoly power that prevents others from manufacturing or selling a patented article.

http://
Access the U.S. Patent and Trademark Office at the following Internet site:
http://www.uspto.gov/

Patents   **Patents** are by definition a legal government grant of monopoly power. The holder of a patent may prevent others from manufacturing or selling a patented product or from using some patented process. The patent holder may grant a license permitting others to make limited use of the patent in exchange for some sort of royalty payment. The monopoly granted by a patent is not, however, an absolute one. First, it is limited to a 17-year period, and few renewals are permitted. Second, competing firms are not prohibited from engineering around an existing patent and bringing out a closely competing, alternative design. Third, many patents are successfully challenged by competitors, especially in the European Union, where patent applications are not kept secret. Even an unsuccessful legal challenge of a patent, particularly a challenge by a large firm on patents held by a smaller firm, may be successful in forcing the challenged firm to license its patent to pay for lengthy legal battles.

Society pays two definite costs when it grants monopoly power to an individual or firm. First, once an invention is made, it may cost very little for others to reverse engineer and duplicate it, except for the necessary production costs. Yet the monopoly grant entitles the inventor to receive a premium above the cost of production, either

WHAT WENT RIGHT   WHAT WENT WRONG

Aventis[8]

Generic drugs have become 42 percent of the U.S. prescription drug market. Generics usually enter the market at a 60–75-percent discount and eventually sell for as little as 20 percent of the original patented drug's price. When Eli Lilly's patent on Prozac was overturned in 2000, the firm lost 70 percent of its sales to generic rivals within one month. To prevent such disruptive shocks to the recovery of enormous fixed R&D costs, some pharmaceutical companies routinely file frivolous patent extensions that change simply the coating or the delivery system (tablet to liquid, for example). The White House proposed in late 2002 a 30-month extension on patents challenged by a generic substitute to reduce frivolous patenting. Of equal concern, Aventis (a Franco-German drug group headquartered in Strasbourg, France) is accused of bribing the American generic drug producer Andrix $90 million to delay the introduction of its cheaper substitute heart attack drug. Such sums suggest just how extensive the monopoly markup on patented pharmaceuticals must be.

---

[8] Based on "Don't Look Down," *The Economist*, January 6, 2001, p. 62; "Bloom and Blight," *The Economist*, October 26, 2002, p. 60; and "Protection Racket," *The Economist*, May 19, 2001, p. 58.

Best-Selling Patented Drugs, 2000

Drug	Patent Owner	Treatment	Drug	Patent Owner	Treatment
1. Losec	AstraZeneca	ulcers	6. Prozac	Eli Lilly	depression
2. Lipitor	Pfizer	cholesterol	7. Celebrex	Pfizer	arthritis
3. Zocor	Merck	cholesterol	8. Seroxat	GlaxoSmithKline	depression
4. Norvasc	Pfizer	high blood pressure	9. Claritin	Schering-Plough	allergies
5. Orgastro	Abbott Labs	erectile dysfunction	10. Zyprexa	Eli Lilly	schizophrenia

in the form of higher-than-competitive-level prices or royalty payments from licenses for a period of 17 years. It is possible that a shorter patent monopoly period would provide sufficient incentives to encourage a high level of inventive activity. Serious proposals suggest shortening the patent period to just four years for computer software, for example.

Second, it has been observed that critical patents frequently help create strong monopoly positions that remain long after the original patent expires, because of other barriers to entry that are built up in the interim. This has been the case in such industries as aluminum, shoe manufacturing, braking systems, rayon, cigarettes, metal containers, photographic equipment and supplies, and gypsum products.

Offsetting these monopoly costs is the increase in inventive activity that the patent monopoly is alleged to encourage. Unfortunately, it is impossible to assess this impact in any meaningful, quantitative manner. Although doubtlessly some reduction in inventive activity would occur if the patent right were abolished, firms may protect the profits from inventions in other ways, including the following:

1. By keeping the technical aspects of the invention secret (trade secrets)

2. By taking full advantage of the lead time over competitors that a new invention provides (first-mover advantages)

Patents are used quite extensively by some industries, such as electronics, drugs, and chemicals, whereas auto manufacturers, paper, machinery, and rubber processors use them very little, preferring first-mover advantage and trade secrets.

Import Quotas   Another major policy that has protected domestic businesses by restricting competition is the use of import quotas. Faced with tough competition from producers abroad, many U.S. industries have sought restrictions on imports of products from abroad. Most vocal among these industries have been the textile, sugar, steel, and automobile industries. These industries have argued that without restrictions on foreign competition, thousands of U.S. workers would lose their jobs and critical domestic industries could be faced with extinction.

Import quotas inevitably lead to higher prices being paid for goods subject to the import restrictions. For example, in the automobile industry, the U.S. International Trade Commission estimates that the Japanese auto import restrictions had the effect in the early 1980s of increasing the average price for a Japanese car by $1,300, or about 20 percent. Under the import restrictions, the supply of Japanese-made cars fell short of the demand and many dealers were able to charge as much as $1,000 more than the official sticker price for some of the most popular models. In addition, because of the higher prices being charged for Japanese-made vehicles, U.S. manufacturers were able to charge higher prices for their products.

International Perspectives

THE U.S. SUGAR IMPORT QUOTA[9]

Since 1982, the United States has imposed quotas on sugar imports to support a domestic price guarantee by the federal government that exceeds world market levels. The high price has stimulated U.S. sugar production and shifts in demand toward other sweeteners, which has necessitated large reductions in sugar import quotas in recent years.

Figure 17.3 illustrates some of the effects of the U.S. trade restrictions in 1983. The lines *SS* and *DD* are the U.S. supply and demand curves for sugar. The world price was 15 cents per pound, and U.S. purchases were assumed to have no effect on this price. With free trade, U.S. production, consumption, and imports would have been 6.14 billion pounds, 19.18 billion pounds, and 13.04 billion pounds, respectively. To raise the internal (U.S.) price to 21.8 cents per pound, a tariff of 2.8 cents per pound and a quota of 5.96 billion pounds were used. The value of the quota is 4.0 cents per pound, because 2.8 cents per pound of the 6.8 cents per pound differential between the U.S. price and the world price is due to the tariff.

The welfare effects of the trade restrictions are indicated by the areas *f*, *g*, *h*, *i*, and *j*. The price-increasing effects of the trade restrictions cause consumers to suffer a loss of consumer surplus equal to $1.266 billion, the sum of areas *f*, *g*, *h*, *i*, and *j*. Producers gain, in the form of producer surplus, area *f*, whose value in $616 million. The U.S. government also gains $167 million in tariff revenue, which is represented by area *i*. Consequently, the net effect for the United States is a loss of $483 million, which is the sum of areas *g*, *h*, and *j*. Area *g* is the loss due to inefficient production; area *h*, which is equal to $238 million, is the value of the import licenses received by foreign suppliers; and area *j* is the loss due to inefficient consumption. In other words, the quota entails a

http://

To learn more about the current U.S. sugar import quota, access the following Internet site maintained by the Foreign Agricultural Service (U.S. Department of Agriculture):
http://www.fas.usda.gov/itp/imports/sugar-import.html

---

[9] Adapted from C.C. Coughlin and G.E. Wood, "An Introduction to Non-Tariff Barriers to Trade," Federal Reserve Bank of St. Louis, January/February 1989, pp. 32–46.

Figure 17.3   The Effects of Trade Restrictions on the U.S. Sugar Market

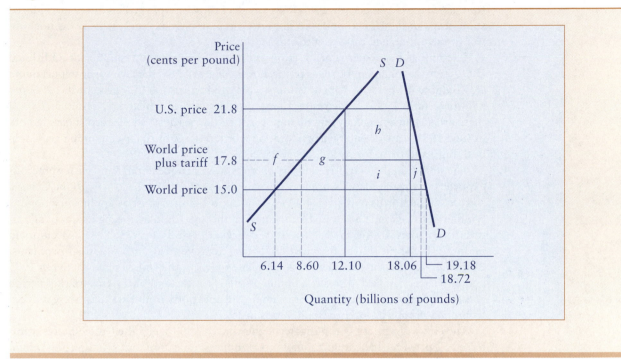

Source: P. Krugman and M. Obstfeld, *International Economics* (Glenview, IL: Scott, Foresman, 1988).

transfer from U.S. consumers to foreign producers of $238 million. In 1990, the lost consumer surplus remained high—$1.4 billion—and the net transfer abroad was $242 million.[10]

The preceding analysis, although effectively highlighting the winners and losers from the U.S. sugar program, is not the entire story. These estimates pertain to one year only. Because the U.S. sugar policy is ongoing, the losses are ongoing as well. In addition, important dynamic interrelationships between policy changes and production and trade changes exist.

There are a number of dynamic consequences of the U.S. sugar program, many stemming from the fact that sugar has several close substitutes. Corn sweeteners, noncaloric sweeteners, honey, and specialty sugars are all close substitutes. Higher sugar prices have induced the production of alternative sweeteners that compete with and, consequently, threaten U.S. sugar producers.

The fact that sugar is used in different goods has set in motion a number of adjustments. Examples abound of the distortions induced by the artificially high U.S. sugar price. For example, the large price differential between U.S. and foreign sugar provides a cost advantage to foreign, especially Canadian, food-processing firms. The sugar policy can be viewed as a tax on U.S. refiners and processors that was not levied on foreign firms.

Trade flows responded to these price changes as a rapid expansion in imports of sugar-containing goods ensued. In fact, the differential between U.S. and world sugar prices

---

[10] D. Appleyard and A. Field, *International Economics*, 3rd ed. (Boston: Irwin-McGraw-Hill, 1998), p. 296.

became so large at one time that sugar-containing goods were imported solely for their sugar content. For example, during 1985 world sugar prices declined so sharply that in June 1985, the U.S. sugar price was 776 percent of the world price. This difference induced some firms in the United States to import Canadian pancake mix, which was not subject to the quota, and process it to extract the sugar.

The induced changes in production and trade have forced a number of additional U.S. actions to maintain the sugar prices. For fiscal year 1985, the U.S. sugar import quota was reduced 17 percent. This was followed by reductions of 27.6 percent in 1986 and 45.7 percent in 1987. Trade restrictions on sugar substitutes also have resulted. Two of these are: (1) an emergency ban on imports of certain syrups and blended sugars in bulk in June 1983; and (2) emergency quotas on a broad range of sugar-containing articles in both bulk and retail forms in January 1985.

The increasingly restrictive import barriers have produced tensions with numerous exporters of sugar, most of whom are developing countries. To conform with the General Agreement on Tariffs and Trade (GATT), the import quotas must be applied in a nondiscriminatory fashion. The United States applied this provision by basing its quota allocation on imports during the relatively free-market period of 1975–1981. Attempts to maintain constant shares for most countries, however, ran into practical problems. Countries experiencing rapid growth in sugar exports to the United States between 1975 and 1981 were subjected to substantial cuts between the end of the free-market period and the beginning of the quotas. For example, sugar exports from Honduras were reduced from 93,500 tons in 1981 to 28,000 tons in 1983.

The effect of this cut was mitigated somewhat in 1983 when the United States transferred 52 percent of Nicaragua's quota to Honduras, an action that simultaneously punished the Sandinista regime and rewarded a neighboring state thought to be in danger from the Nicaraguan-supported rebellion. This action violated GATT rules and generated much criticism of the United States. Such a quota system increases the likelihood that trade policy is used for noneconomic reasons.

The lessons from the U.S. sugar program are straightforward. First, significant costs have been imposed on U.S. consumers. Second, the resulting distortions in economic incentives have harmed U.S. producers dependent on sugar. Third, economic responses to the legislation have revealed a number of loopholes that have necessitated additional restrictions and distortions so that U.S. sugar producers could continue to benefit.

SUMMARY

- *Market performance* refers to the efficiency of resource allocation within and among firms, the technological progressiveness of firms, the tendency of firms to fully employ resources, and the impact on the equitable distribution of resources.
- *Market conduct* refers to the pricing behavior; the product policy; the sales promotion and advertising policy; the research, development, and innovation strategies; and the legal tactics employed by a firm or group of firms.
- *Market structure* refers to the degree of seller and buyer concentration in a market, the degree of actual or imagined product differentiation between products or services of competing producers, and the conditions surrounding entry into the market.
- Contestable markets are assumed to have freedom of entry and exit for potential competitors, slow-reaching incumbents, and low switching costs for consumers. In a perfectly contestable market, the resulting set of prices and outputs approaches those expected under perfect competition.

- Measures of market concentration include:
  - the market concentration ratio, defined as the percentage of total industry output attributable to the 4, 8, 20, or 50 largest companies
  - the Herfindahl-Hirschman Index (HHI), which is equal to the sum of the squares of the market shares of all firms in an industry
- A group of antitrust laws has been passed to prevent monopoly and to encourage competition in U.S. industry. The most important of these acts are the Sherman Act of 1890, the FTC and Clayton Acts of 1914, the Robinson-Patman Act of 1936, the Celler-Kefauver Antimerger Act of 1950, the Hart-Scott-Rodino Antitrust Improvement Act of 1976, and Merger Guidelines of 1992 and 1997.
- Federal, state, and local governments all impose regulations on business enterprises. Regulatory constraints can affect a firm's operating costs (both fixed and variable), capital costs, and revenues.
- The current political and economic environment favors a significant reduction in the amount of government regulation and interference in the operation of the private sector of the economy. This has been observable in deregulation in the banking, transportation, natural gas pipeline, electric utility, and telecommunications industries.
- A number of regulatory policies are designed to restrict competition. These include licensing; issuing patents, trademarks, and copyrights; and using import controls, such as tariffs and quotas.

EXERCISES

1. Under what circumstances would you defend pure competition as the most efficient market structure? What arguments can you make to the contrary?

2. Discuss the proposition that corporate "raiders," such as T. Boone Pickens, Carl Icahn, and Saul Weinberg, are a valuable element in the efficient operation of the economy and that such takeover threats result in long-run benefits to shareholders and more efficient management.

3. An industry is composed of Firm 1, which controls 70 percent of the market, Firm 2 with 15 percent of the market, and Firm 3 with 5 percent of the market. About 20 firms of approximately equal size divide the remaining 10 percent of the market. Calculate the Herfindahl-Hirschman Index before and after the merger of Firm 2 and Firm 3 (assume that the combined market share after the merger is 20 percent). Would you view a merger of Firm 2 with Firm 3 as procompetitive or anticompetitive? Explain.

4. How can you justify the existence of government-granted monopolies for such public utilities as local telephone service, natural gas distribution, and electricity in the light of the traditional economic argument that the more competition there is, the more likely it is that an efficient allocation of resources will occur?

5. What are the major factors to be considered, for antitrust purposes, in determining the relevant market in which a firm competes?

6. Suppose an industry is composed of eight firms with the following market shares:

A	30%	E	8%
B	25	F	5
C	15	G	4
D	10	H	3

Based on the (revised 1997) merger guidelines, would the Antitrust Division likely challenge a proposed merger between

a. Firms C and D (assume the combined market share is 25 percent)?

b. Firms F and G (assume the combined market share is 9 percent)?
   Explain your answer.

7. Evaluate the importance of the concept of price elasticity of demand when attempting to identify the ultimate incidence of the impact of government regulations on business that (a) increase fixed costs and (b) increase variable costs.

8. Discuss the pros and cons of the regulation of oil and natural gas prices.

9. In this chapter you have learned about the circumstances under which a firm with market power would engage in price discrimination. Access the following Internet site at http://www.ripon.edu/Faculty/bowenj/antitrust/texvhasb. htm. This site contains the case of *Texaco, Inc.* v. *Ricky Hasbrouk* (490 U.S. 1105), which is particularly useful in illustrating the test applied by the U.S. Supreme Court for illegal price discrimination.

10. What economic arguments can be made in favor of mandatory seat-belt usage laws in automobiles and mandatory helmet laws for motorcycles?

11. What are the incentives to innovate for a monopoly firm as compared with a firm in a competitive market if patent protection is not available? Does your answer change if patent protection is available?

12. Would you consider the airline industry to be a contestable market? Explain.

13. Specific Motors Corporation is one of the Big Three auto manufacturers in Transylvania. Specific's share of the domestic auto market is 55 percent. The next two closest competitors control 25 and 15 percent of the market, respectively, and the rest may be accounted for by two small, specialized firms. Specific has been under pressure from Transylvania's Justice Department and the State Trade Commission for monopolistic practices. To discourage any attempts to break up Specific, management has decided to maintain its market share below 55 percent of the total domestic automobile sales revenues.

    Specific estimates that to stay within its constraint sales of 55 percent of the market, its total sales should not exceed $2.8 billion.
    The firm faces the following demand and cost functions:

$$P = 16,000 - .02Q$$
$$TC = 850,000,000 + 4,000Q$$

a. Calculate the unconstrained profit-maximizing level of price and output for Specific.

b. At this level, what will total sales revenues be? total profits?

c. If the firm constrains its sales revenue to $2.8 billion, calculate price, output, and profit levels under the constraint.

(*Hint:* Remember the quadratic formula: $x = \dfrac{-b \pm \sqrt{b^2 - 4ac}}{2a}$

based on the equation $ax^2 + bx + c = 0$.)

d. What is the cost to the firm of this market-share constraint?

14. Seidman Products, Inc. is a manufacturer of chocolate-flavored LTD tablets and aspirin. Each bottle of LTD costs the firm 50 cents in wages and 25 cents in materials to produce. In contrast, the wage and material costs per bottle of aspirin are 25 cents each. All LTD and aspirin that are produced in the period are sold on one-period credit terms. Labor and materials costs for the period must be paid in cash during that period. Liquid resources (cash, collections from previous periods, and bank credit), which are available to pay for labor and material expenses during the period, are expected to amount to $150. The firm has 60 hours of pill-manufacturing time available during the period and 25 hours of bottling time.

Each bottle of aspirin requires 9 minutes of manufacturing time and 6 minutes of bottling time. Each bottle of LTD requires 24 minutes of manufacturing time and 3 minutes of bottling time.

Because of the fear of misuse of the LTD if more is produced than is needed to meet pure medical research needs, the Food and Drug Administration has limited LTD output per period to a maximum of 100 bottles.

The selling price of a bottle of aspirin is $2.50. Each bottle of LTD sells for $4.75.

a. Formulate this problem in a linear-programming framework. Specify the objective function and all constraints.

b. Using the graphic method, solve for the optimal output mix between aspirin and LTD.

c. What is the cost to the firm of the FDA output restriction on LTD production?

d. As president of Seidman Products, what resources would you seek to increase to expand your firm's profits?

15. The industry demand function for bulk plastics is represented by the following equation:

$$P = 800 - 20Q$$

where Q represents millions of pounds of plastic.

The total cost function for the industry, exclusive of a required return on invested capital, is

$$TC = 300 + 500Q + 10Q^2$$

where Q represents millions of pounds of plastic.

a. If this industry acts like a monopolist in the determination of price and output, compute the profit-maximizing level of price and output.

b. What are total profits at this price and output level?

c. Assume that this industry is composed of many (500) small firms, such that the demand function facing any individual firm is

$$P = \$620$$

Compute the profit-maximizing level of price and output under these conditions (the industry's total cost function remains unchanged).

d. What are total profits, given your answer to Part c?

e. Because of the risk of this industry, investors require a 15-percent rate of return on investment. Total industry investment amounts to $2 billion. If the monopoly solution prevails (Parts a and b), how would you describe the profits of the industry?

f. If the competitive solution most accurately describes the industry, is the industry operating under equilibrium conditions? Why or why not? What would you expect to happen?

g. The Clean Water Coalition has proposed pollution control standards for the industry that would change the industry cost curve to the following:

$$TC = 400 + 560Q + 10Q^2$$

What is the impact of this change on price, output, and total profits under the monopoly solution?

h. Assume these standards are being proposed only in the state of Texas, which has 50 of the 500 producers. What impact would you expect the new standards to have on Texas firms? the rest of the industry?

16. A product you produce has the following annual demand function:

$$P = 90 - .003Q$$

The marginal cost of producing the product is $30. If the firm pays a fee of $50,000 to the General Drug Research Council, it can have its product's effectiveness certified. The demand function for a certified product is expected to be

$$P = 100 - .003Q$$

a. Calculate the price, output, and profit contribution if the product is not certified.

b. Calculate the price, output, and profit contribution if the product is certified.

c. Should the firm undergo the certification process?

17. Assume an industry produces a relatively homogeneous product, such that all sales must be made at approximately the same price. Assume also that the industry is dominated by one large firm, but a fringe of smaller, competitive firms exists. Fringe competitors and potential new entrants are so small in size that they have no perceptible influence on price.

Discuss graphically or verbally the pricing strategies available to the dominant firm:

a. If the profit-maximizing price charged by the dominant firm is below the lowest attainable average total cost (including normal profits) for the smaller existing competitive firms and potential entrants.

b. If the profit-maximizing price charged by the dominant firm exceeds the competitive fringe firms' lowest attainable average costs, including a normal profit. Would you expect a different strategy to be followed if the dominant firm sought to maximize short-run rather than long-run profits?

c. If the dominant firm is relatively unsure of the industry's future or perceives a rapidly changing technology in the industry such that an optimal scale of operation can be achieved with an increasingly small plant size. What strategy would you expect the dominant firm to follow?

d.   If the dominant firm adopts a long-run strategy to deter new entry. Explain how the use of full-cost pricing rules can lead to nearly maximum long-run profits.

18.   Public Service Company has been disappointed by its failure to be allowed to earn what it considers to be a fair return on its investment in utility assets. The firm has averaged a return on equity of 12 percent over the past 10 years, with a standard deviation of 3 percent. It is considering a series of acquisitions that, when complete, would roughly double the firm's size. The expected return on equity from these new activities is 19 percent, with a standard deviation of 7 percent. Based on past performance, the correlation between returns in the utility business and returns in the other businesses is expected to be $+0.3$.

a.   Calculate the expected return and risk of the returns for the Public Service Company before and after the acquisitions.

[*Hint:* A general formula for the risk (standard deviation) of two assets' returns is

$$\sigma_T = \sqrt{w_A^2 \sigma_A^2 + w_B^2 \sigma_B^2 + 2w_A w_B \rho_{AB} \sigma_A \sigma_B}$$

where w_A and w_B are the proportions invested in assets A and B, respectively, and $w_A + w_B = 1$; σ_A and σ_B are the standard deviations of returns for assets A and B, respectively; and ρ_{AB} is the correlation of returns from assets A and B.]

b.   Recalculate the expected return and risk of the Public Service Company after completing the acquisitions if the acquisitions are two times the size of the utility business of Public Service Company; that is, $w_A =$ proportion of utility assets $= 0.333$ and $w_B =$ proportion of acquired assets $= 0.667$.

c.   What other potential benefits can you see being derived from this program of diversification?

d.   What regulatory problems can you perceive when a utility diversifies outside of the regulated sector of the economy?

19.   An industry produces its product, Scruffs, at a constant marginal cost of $50. The market demand for Scruffs is equal to

$$Q = 75,000 - 600P$$

a.   What is the value to a monopolist who is able to develop a patented process for producing Scruffs at a cost of only $45?

b.   If the industry producing Scruffs is purely competitive, what is the maximum benefit that an inventor of a process that will reduce the cost of producing Scruffs by $5 per unit can expect to receive by licensing her invention to the firms in the industry?

20.   The demand curve in a competitive industry has been estimated to be

$$P = 1,500 - 9Q$$

The industry's short-run supply curve is

$$P = 80 + 3Q$$

A single firm emerges as the dominant firm in the industry and gradually acquires all of the other firms in the industry. The marginal cost curve for the monopolist becomes

$$MC = 50 + 3Q$$

as a result of effecting a number of operating economies.

a. Calculate the competitive market's price and output levels.

b. Calculate the price and output levels for the industry once the monopolist assumes control, assuming that industry demand remains unchanged.

c. If this monopolist is regulated so that the maximum price the monopolist is allowed to charge is $450, what is the benefit to consumers and the cost to the monopolist?

21. If OPEC agrees to raise the price of oil by $3 a barrel and if all other world oil prices increase by a similar amount, is the additional economic cost to consumers equal to $3 a barrel, something more, or something less?

CASE EXERCISES

PRICE FIXING OF AUCTION HOUSE COMMISSIONS

http://

Access the following Internet site: http://www.usdoj.gov/atr/cases/f6600/6653.htm. Read the case on *U.S.* v. *Sotheby's Holdings, Inc.* and the accompanying article regarding auction house collusion. What parallels do you see to the sellers on eBay and airline websites?

MICROSOFT TYING ARRANGEMENTS

a. Which of the following is a violation of the antitrust laws in the United States and why? (a) Microsoft monopolizes the market in PC operating systems with a 92-percent market share; (b) Microsoft attempts to monopolize the market in Internet portals with a pattern of anticompetitive tactics (tying arrangements, refusals to deal, etc.); (c) Microsoft sells Windows plus Microsoft Internet Explorer for less than Windows without Internet Explorer installed as the default browser; (d) Microsoft gives Internet Explorer away free to individual adopters with variable cost estimated at $0.0067; (e) Microsoft threatens to delicense Compaq and Dell, who would then be unable to preinstall Windows on PCs they ship unless Compaq and Dell exclude Netscape's Internet browser from the user interface.

b. What difference does it make to the tying arrangement issues if Internet Explorer is a functionally integrated component of Windows? What if it's more like a radio in an automobile than a steering post interlock device?

c. How should Microsoft market long-distance telephone services in the new wireless telecommunications devices that also include Internet portals?

MUSIC RECORDING INDUSTRY BLOCKED FROM CONSOLIDATING

Given the following market share distributions, the U.S. Antitrust Division blocked a merger of BMG and EMI in 2001, and the European Commission blocked a merger of Time Warner's music division and EMI in 2000. Analyze these decisions and present arguments both pro and con.

Market Shares in U.S.		Market Share in World	
Vivendi Universal	20%	Vivendi Universal	21%
Sony	20%	Sony	19%
BMG	15%	EMI	13%
Time Warner	13%	Time Warner	12%
EMI	11%	BMG	12%

What else should be involved in such merger policies?

VI
Long-Term Investment Decisions and Risk Management

ECONOMIC ANALYSIS AND DECISIONS

1. Demand Analysis and Forecasting
2. Production and Cost Analysis
3. Pricing Analysis
4. Capital Expenditure Analysis

ECONOMIC, POLITICAL, AND SOCIAL ENVIRONMENT

1. Business Conditions (Trends, Cycles, and Seasonal Effects)
2. Factor Market Conditions (Capital, Labor, Land, and Raw Materials)
3. Competitors' Responses
4. External, Legal, and Regulatory Constraints
5. Organizational (Internal) Constraints

Cash Flows

Risk

Firm Value
(Shareholders' Wealth)

This part of the book looks at the capital investment decision for a firm. Investments in new, long-term assets have a major impact on a firm's future stream of cash flows and the risk of those cash flows. As such, the long-term investment decision has a significant impact on the value of the firm. Capital investment decisions can be viewed as the link between the short-run price and output decisions made by managers of a firm and the long-run decisions made by those managers. A capital investment involves a change in the production technology used by the firm and/or a change in the scale of operations of the firm.

In Chapter 18, we introduce the concept of a project's net present value. The net present value of a project can be viewed as the increment to shareholder wealth that is expected to accrue as a result of undertaking a capital investment project. The same tools that are relevant to capital investment analysis by private sector managers also can be used, with minor modifications, by managers in public and not-for-profit enterprises. Chapter 19 examines decision making under risk and reviews the techniques for managing risk.

18

Long-Term Investment Analysis

CHAPTER PREVIEW   Investment analysis (capital budgeting) is the process of planning for the purchases of assets whose returns (cash flows) are expected to continue beyond one year. When making capital budgeting decisions, the managers of a firm are committing the firm's resources to the expansion of its productive capacity, an improvement in its cost efficiency, or a diversification in its asset base. Each of these decisions has important implications for the future cash flows the firm can be expected to generate and the risk of those cash flows. Capital expenditures are a bridge between the short-term price and output determination decisions facing managers daily and the longer-term strategic decisions that wealth-maximizing managers must make to remain competitive. Public sector managers use the techniques of cost-benefit analysis and cost-effectiveness analysis when analyzing many long-term resource-allocation decisions. These techniques also are presented in this chapter.

MANAGERIAL CHALLENGE

What Went Right? What Went Wrong? Are Fat Margins About to Plummet at Nokia?[1]

From a stodgy, old-economy conglomerate selling everything from rubber boots and wire cable to toilet paper and televisions, Nokia has transformed itself into a relentlessly focused technology company. When Sweden's giant telecommunications-equipment supplier Ericsson developed a cellular network across Scandinavia in the 1980s, Nokia provided the wireless but bulky radio telephones. Recognizing the strategic inflection point presented by mobile telephony, Nokia spun off other business in the 1990s to rivet its attention on the enormous market potential of a truly mobile cell phone. With a long-term investment gamble in digital cell phones, Nokia grew from half of Motorola's 45-percent share in 1995 to overtake the market leader and sell 32 percent of the cell phones worldwide in 2000, relative to Motorola's 18 percent. From 1997 to 2000, the share prices of Alcatel, Siemens, and Motorola all doubled, but Nokia's share price grew more than tenfold from $120 to $1,250.

A new disruptive technology is rewriting the telecommunications business landscape. Nokia's share price collapsed from $1,250 to $700 in 2001 per share amidst concerns that the gross margins on Nokia's cell phones were shrinking. The new data-intensive 3G cell phone networks are based on Internet-style packet switching technology rather than the circuit-switching technology of today's voice-only GSM cell phones. Again, Nokia must reinvent itself. Doing so necessitates another massive capital investment commitment, and such a decision necessitates projections of gross margins, sales, operating profits, and future net cash flows.

Porter's Five Forces analysis implies that the gross margins in the new 3G cell phones will be much smaller than in the GSM products. First, the 3G high-speed data-intensive technology allows the introduction of new substitute products into the handset marketplace, from handheld computers by Dell and pocket audio visual terminals by Palm and Motorola to game consoles from Sony. Second, these enhanced mobile phones create value principally through the software applications provided by third-party independent software vendors (ISVs). And the ISVs want their share of the gross margins that made Nokia so profitable. In contrast, the power of these ISV suppliers was virtually nonexistent in the voice-only mobile phone business. Third, the developed world is nearly saturated with wireless services at 60-percent penetration in some North American and European markets, and demand is forecasted to grow at only 10 percent over the next decade. The next growth spurt in sales will come from China and Latin America, where Nokia must compete against or ally themselves with well-connected local companies. This increased power of buyers will also reduce gross margins. Fourth, the threat of entry is very real; two Japanese consumer electronics manufacturers, NEC and Panasonic, have adapted the same 3G technology into wireless Internet devices. Finally, access to distribution channels has become much more expensive as wireless operators like AT&T Wireless and Alcatel expect vendor participation in the financing of the spectrum licenses for the 3G networks.

Should Nokia invest in 3G network infrastructure in competition with Ericsson and NTT? How

---

[1] Based on "Nokia: A Finnish Tale," *The Economist*, October 14, 2000, pp. 83–85.

THE NATURE OF CAPITAL EXPENDITURE DECISIONS

Previous chapters in the text have been primarily concerned with analytical tools and decision models that may assist managers in making the most efficient use of existing resources. This chapter considers decisions to replace or expand the capital resource base.

Decisions to replace assets have the effect of changing the technology employed by a firm. This leads to an alteration of the relevant production and cost functions. Most replacement decisions are made with the expectation that a sufficiently lower cost function will prevail after the replacement to justify the required outlays.

Decisions to expand a firm's asset base lead to an increase in the scale or size of the productive facilities. Expansion decisions are based on forecasts of future demand and costs after the expansion. If quantity demanded is suitably high or costs sufficiently low, the resulting profits may justify the expansion decision.

A **capital expenditure** is a cash outlay that is expected to generate a flow of future cash benefits lasting longer than one year. It is distinguished from a normal operating expenditure, which is expected to result in cash benefits during the coming one-year period. (The choice of a one-year period is arbitrary, but it does serve as a useful guideline.) **Capital budgeting** is the process of planning for and evaluating capital expenditures.

In addition to asset replacement and expansion decisions, other types of decisions that can be analyzed using capital budgeting techniques include research and development expenditures, investments in employee education and training, lease-versus-buy decisions, and mergers and acquisitions.

The importance of capital expenditures to a firm is derived from the fact that current capital outlays, by definition, have a long-range impact on the performance of the enterprise. These current outlays affect future profitability, and in aggregate they plot the future direction of the firm by determining products that will be produced, markets to be entered, the location of plants and facilities, and the type of technology (with its associated costs) to be used. Capital expenditures require careful analysis because they are both costly to make and difficult to reverse without incurring considerable costs.

Capital Expenditure
A cash outlay designed to generate a flow of future cash benefits over a period of time extending beyond one year.

Capital Budgeting
The process of planning for and evaluating capital expenditures.

http://
Read about the state of Rhode Island's experiences with capital budgeting at the following Internet site:
http://www.budget.ri.gov

A BASIC FRAMEWORK FOR CAPITAL BUDGETING

Recall from earlier chapters that the economic theory of the firm indicates that a firm should operate at the point where the marginal cost of an additional unit of output just equals the marginal revenue derived from that output. Following this rule will lead to profit maximization by a firm. As we saw in the Sara Lee example in Chapter 2, this principle may be applied to the capital budgeting decisions of the firm. In the context of capital budgeting, the marginal revenue may be thought of as the rates of return earned on successive investments. Marginal cost may be interpreted as the firm's weighted marginal cost of capital—that is, the cost of successive increments of capital acquired by the firm, weighted by the proportions in which these funds are expected to be used in the firm's capital structure.

Example

CAPITAL BUDGETING DECISION: CLARK CANDY COMPANY

This basic capital budgeting decision-making framework for the Clark Candy Company is illustrated in Figure 18.1. The company has nine investment projects under consideration, labeled *A, B, C, . . ., I*. The model assumes that all projects have the same risk. This schedule of projects often is called the *investment opportunity curve*. The projects are indicated by lettered bars on the graph. For example, Project *A* requires an investment of $2 million and is expected to generate a 24-percent rate of return. Project *B* will cost $1 million ($3 million minus $2 million on the horizontal axis) and generate a 22-percent rate of return, and so on. Graphically, the projects are arranged in descending order by their rates of return, indicating that no firm has a limitless number of possible investment projects that all generate very high rates of return. As new products are produced, new markets entered, and cost-saving technologies adopted, the number of highly profitable investment opportunities tends to decline. The *marginal cost of capital curve* represents the

Figure 18.1   A Simplified Capital Budgeting Model

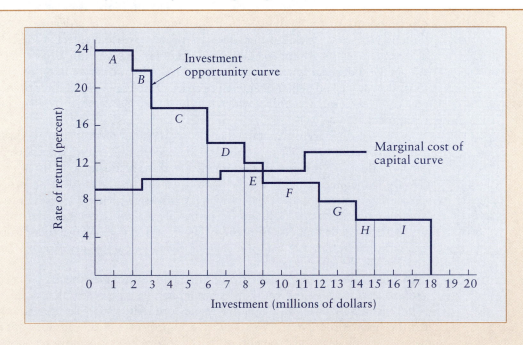

marginal cost of capital to the firm; that is, the cost of each additional dollar raised in the capital markets.

Using this basic model, the firm should undertake Projects *A*, *B*, *C*, *D*, and *E*, because their returns exceed the firm's marginal cost of capital. Although there are some practical difficulties in implementing this conceptual model, it furnishes a guideline for optimal decision making.

THE CAPITAL BUDGETING PROCESS

The process of selecting capital investment projects consists of the following important steps:

1. Generate alternative capital investment project proposals.
2. Estimate cash flows for the project proposals.
3. Evaluate and choose, from the alternatives available, those investment projects to implement.
4. Review the investment projects after they have been implemented.

Generating Capital Investment Projects

Ideas for new capital investments can come from many sources both inside and outside the firm. Proposals can originate at all levels in the organization, from factory workers all the way up to the board of directors. Most medium- and large-sized firms have departments whose responsibilities include searching for and analyzing capital expenditure projects. These departments include cost accounting, industrial engineering, marketing research, research and development, and corporate planning personnel.

Capital expenditure projects can be classified into various categories, depending on the nature of the benefits expected. One category includes projects that are designed to *reduce costs*. Like products that become obsolete, technological progress also renders plants, equipment, and production processes obsolete. Normal wear and tear make older plants and equipment more costly to operate due, for example, to more downtime and higher maintenance costs. Obsolescence and deterioration should generate proposals to replace older facilities with new, more efficient plants and equipment.

A second category of capital expenditures includes projects designed to *improve a firm's demand curve*, or to respond to changes in that curve. If increased demand for a product line is forecast, and if existing manufacturing and distribution facilities are inadequate to meet this demand, then the firm must develop proposals for expanding capacity. A firm also may make investments in advertising/product promotion campaigns in an attempt to positively influence the demand for its products. Although often not thought of as traditional capital expenditures, these promotional outlays have all the characteristics of capital investments and can be analyzed in the same way.

A third category of capital expenditure projects includes those that create *future growth options* for the firm. For example, investing in research and development (R&D) can be viewed as a capital expenditure that creates future growth options for the firm. Although any particular R&D project will be very difficult to justify using traditional capital expenditure analysis procedures, one must recognize that the traditional procedures normally do not consider the option value created by R&D outlays. These outlays give the firm the "option," but not the obligation, to make further outlays that are needed to bring a new product to market. Without the initial R&D outlays, the firm would not possess the option to make the second-phase expenditures and to reap the associated rewards.[2]

A fourth type of capital expenditure includes projects designed to *meet legal requirements and health and safety standards,* such as proposals for pollution control outlays, ventilation, employee safety, and fire-protection equipment. At first glance it may seem that these outlays are "simply required" and thus no analysis is needed. However, managers have the choice of not making these outlays and just shutting down a plant. The decision revolves around the question of whether the remaining cash flows in a project are sufficiently large to justify the additional outlays necessary to keep the plant operating.

CAPITAL EXPENDITURES AT CHRYSLER—THE GRAND CHEROKEE[3]

In early 1992 Chrysler Corporation introduced its new Grand Cherokee sport utility vehicle. The vehicle was developed using an unusual (for Chrysler) "platform team" approach. Instead of developing this new vehicle sequentially, passing it from market research to design to engineering to manufacturing, Chrysler assembled a team of 700 to 800 engineering, marketing research, and design personnel and told them to develop the new vehicle as a team. As a result, the new Cherokee was developed and brought to the market more quickly and at a lower cost than had been typical for other American auto companies. The new Grand Cherokee was developed and a new plant built in Detroit to produce it, all for about $1.1 billion. In comparison, in the early 1980s, General Motors spent $1 billion each just on the plants it built—not counting any new-product development costs. Chrysler planned to sell up to 175,000 of these vehicles each year, realizing a profit of $5,500 per unit.

The Grand Cherokee capital expenditures contain elements of both demand curve management and cost reduction. Chrysler saw sales of its older, smaller Jeep Cherokee decline from a peak of nearly 200,000 units per year to about 125,000, primarily because of stiff competition from the Ford-built Explorer. Chrysler hoped to regain much of this lost market share. In addition, the decision to build the Grand Cherokee in an efficient new plant in Detroit rather than in its older underutilized plant in Toledo reflected a commitment to hold costs of production at a minimum. Finally, it was Chrysler's intention to cut the price of its old Jeep Cherokee and market it aggressively as a low-cost, sporty utility vehicle alternative. Chrysler hoped that this strategy would permit it to expand export sales in Europe. Thus Chrysler created for itself the option either to retain the older model if it sold well at a lower price, or to phase out the older model and close the Toledo plant. Thus one can see that in many major capital expenditure projects there may be elements of cost reduction, demand management, and creation of strategic options to be considered in the evaluation process.

---

[2] See Nalin Kulatilaka and Alan Marcus, "Project Valuation under Uncertainty: When Does DCF Fail?" *Journal of Applied Corporate Finance* (Fall 1992), pp. 92–100; and Lenos Trigeorgis, "Real Options and Interactions with Financial Flexibility," *Financial Management* (Autumn 1993), pp. 202–224, for discussion of real options in capital budgeting.

[3] Based largely on "Iacocca's Last Stand at Chrysler," *Fortune,* April 20, 1992, p. 63ff.

Example

SARA LEE: CREATING STRATEGIC OPTIONS IN EASTERN EUROPE[4]

Sara Lee Corporation is a large, U.S.-based multinational manufacturer and marketer of branded high-quality consumer products. Among other items it produces and sells, Sara Lee is a major producer and marketer of coffee products in Holland, Belgium, Spain, France, and Denmark. During the 1990s, Sara Lee made a number of strategic acquisitions designed to enhance its long-term international position. With the opening of the economies of the former Soviet satellite states in Eastern Europe, Sara Lee embarked on a strategy designed to give it the needed "options" to expand into the Eastern European market. It acquired a 51-percent interest in Compack Trading and Packing Company, Hungary's largest coffee business. This acquisition gave Sara Lee an opportunity to develop experience operating a firm in the emerging, and somewhat peculiar, business climate of Eastern Europe. Although the acquisition of Compack was unlikely to provide immediate, positive returns to Sara Lee, it gave Sara Lee the expertise needed for considering other acquisitions and expansions in the Eastern European markets. On the basis of traditional capital investment criteria this acquisition was probably difficult to justify, but when the value of the strategic options it would create for making future investments in the region were considered, Sara Lee found this to be a very attractive acquisition.

Example

http://

You can read more about how stationary-source polluters can comply by scrapping older cars at the following Internet site maintained by the South Coast Air Quality Management District: http://www.aqmd.gov/ rules/html/r1610.html

ALTERNATIVE INVESTMENTS FOR CLEAN AIR[5]

The 1990 Clean Air Act placed strict new standards on air pollution. A California program provides polluting firms with a new investment alternative to meet the standards of the act. Prior to the implementation of the new market-based program in California, a polluting firm had two (legal) options—close the plant or make the capital investments needed to bring the plant up to acceptable emission standard levels. The California plan created a market for pollution rights. For example, suppose a factory must reduce its nitrogen oxide emissions by 130,000 pounds per year and it would cost the firm $1 million to install the necessary equipment. Under the California plan, the firm could buy 1,000 older cars, which emit an average of 130 pounds of nitrogen oxide a year, for a price of $700 per year each. The cars would be scrapped, removing them permanently from the roads, thereby reducing harmful emissions by the required 130,000 pounds. The company would save $300,000. In 1990, Unocal bought 8,376 pre-1971 cars for $700 each. These cars accounted for 13 million pounds of emissions per year, as much as the hydrocarbon emissions from 250,000 new cars or one large oil refinery. As this market-based approach spreads, financial managers will have one more investment alternative available when considering investments to meet pollution standards.

Estimating Cash Flows

One of the most important and difficult steps in the selection process is estimating the cash flows associated with investment projects. Because the cash flows will occur in the future, varying degrees of *uncertainty* exist about the values of these flows. We assume the decision maker is able to estimate cash flows with sufficient accuracy to use these estimates in deciding whether to undertake the capital investment. Another difficulty arises from the intentional or unintentional introduction of *bias*

---

[4] Based on Sara Lee Corporation, *1991 Annual Report.*

[5] Based on "Cold Cash for Old Clunkers," *Newsweek*, April 6, 1992, p. 61.

in cash-flow estimates. Individuals often have difficulty determining objective cash-flow estimates when they have a vested interest in seeing the project undertaken. The natural tendency is for some individuals to be overly optimistic in their estimates; that is, to underestimate the costs and to overestimate the benefits of an investment project. Therefore, it is helpful to have the estimates reviewed by someone outside the department or division proposing the expenditure.

Certain basic guidelines have been found helpful in approaching the analysis of investment alternatives. First, cash flows should be measured on an *incremental* basis. In other words, the cash-flow stream for the project should represent the difference between the cash-flow streams to the firm with and without acceptance of the investment project. Second, cash flows should be measured on an *after-tax* basis, using the firm's marginal tax rate. Third, all the *indirect effects* of the project throughout the firm should be included in the cash-flow calculations. If a department or division of the firm is contemplating a capital investment that will alter the revenues or costs of other departments or divisions, then these external effects should be incorporated into the cash-flow estimates. Fourth, *sunk costs* should not be considered when evaluating the project. A sunk cost is an outlay that has been made (or committed to be made). Because sunk costs cannot be recovered, they should not be considered in the decision to accept or reject a project. Fifth, the value of resources used in the project should be measured in terms of their *opportunity costs*. Recall from Chapter 8 that opportunity cost is the value of a resource in its next best alternative use. In the context of capital budgeting, opportunity costs of resources (assets) are the cash flows that these resources can generate if they are not used in the project under consideration.

For a typical investment project, an initial investment is made in year 0, which generates a series of yearly net cash flows over the life of the project (n). The net investment ($NINV$) of a project is defined as the initial net cash outlay in year 0. It includes the acquisition cost of any new assets plus installation and shipping costs and tax effects.[6]

The incremental, after-tax net cash flows ($NCFs$) of a particular investment project are equal to cash inflows minus cash outflows. For any year during the life of the project, these may be defined as the difference in net income after tax ($\Delta NIAT$) with and without the project plus the difference in depreciation (ΔD):

$$NCF = \Delta NIAT + \Delta D \qquad [18.1]$$

$\Delta NIAT$ is equal to the difference in net income before tax ($\Delta NIBT$) times ($1 - t$), where t is the corporate (marginal) income tax rate:

$$\Delta NIAT = \Delta NIBT(1 - t) \qquad [18.2]$$

$\Delta NIBT$ is defined as the difference in revenues (ΔR) minus the differences in operating costs (ΔC) and depreciation (ΔD):

$$\Delta NIBT = \Delta R - \Delta C - \Delta D \qquad [18.3]$$

Substituting Equation 18.3 into Equation 18.2 yields

$$\Delta NIAT = (\Delta R - \Delta C - \Delta D)(1 - t) \qquad [18.4]$$

---

[6] When the new asset is replacing an existing asset, one must also include in the net investment calculation the net proceeds from the sale of the existing asset and the taxes associated with its sale. See R. Charles Moyer, James R. McGuigan, and William J. Kretlow, *Contemporary Financial Management*, 8th ed. (Cincinnati: South-Western, 2001), pp. 316–319, for a discussion of the cash flow calculations for replacement decisions.

Substituting this equation into Equation 18.1 yields the following definition of net cash flow:

$$NCF = (\Delta R - \Delta C - \Delta D)(1 - t) + \Delta D \qquad [18.5]$$

Example

CASH-FLOW ESTIMATION: HAMILTON BEACH/PROCTOR-SILEX, INC.

To illustrate the cash-flow calculations, consider the following example. Suppose that Hamilton Beach/Proctor-Silex, a manufacturer of small electric appliances, has been offered a contract to supply a regional merchandising company with a line of food blenders to be sold under the retail company's private brand name. Hamilton Beach/Proctor Silex's treasurer estimates that the initial investment in new equipment required to produce the blenders would be $1 million. The equipment would be depreciated (using the straight-line method)[7] over five years with a zero (0) estimated salvage value at the end of the five-year contract period. Based on the contract specifications, the treasurer estimates that incremental revenues (additional sales) would be $800,000 per year. The incremental costs if the contract is accepted will be $450,000 per year. These include cash outlays for direct labor and materials, transportation, utilities, building rent, and *additional* overhead. The firm's marginal income tax rate is 40 percent.

Based on the information, *NINV* and *NCF* can be calculated for the project. The net investment (*NINV*) is equal to the $1-million initial outlay for the new equipment. The difference in revenues (ΔR) with and without the project is equal to $800,000 per year and the difference in operating costs (ΔC) is equal to $450,000 per year. The difference in depreciation (ΔD) is equal to the initial outlay ($1 million) divided by 5, or $200,000 per year. Substituting these values, along with $t = .40$, into Equation 18.5 yields the following:

$$NCF = (\$800,000 - \$450,000 - \$200,000)(1 - .40) + \$200,000$$
$$= \$290,000$$

Hamilton Beach/Proctor-Silex must decide whether it wants to invest $1 million now to receive $290,000 per year in net cash flows over the next five years. The next section illustrates two of the criteria used in evaluating investment proposals.

Evaluating and Choosing the Investment Projects to Implement

Once a capital expenditure project has been identified and the cash flows have been estimated, a decision to accept or reject the project is required. Acceptance of the project will result in a cash-flow stream to the firm; that is, a series of either cash inflows or outflows for a number of years into the future. Typically, a project will result in an initial (first-year) outflow (investment) followed by a series of cash inflows (returns) over a number of succeeding years. To compare and choose among alternative projects with their associated cash-flow streams, a measure of the desirability of each project must be obtained. The basic problem in measuring and comparing the desirability of investment projects is assessing the value of cash flows that occur at different points in time.

---

[7] This depreciation method is just one of several possible methods that can be used. See Moyer, McGuigan, and Kretlow, *op. cit.*, pp. 330–335, for a discussion of the various depreciation methods.

Internal Rate of Return (IRR)
The discount rate that equates the present value of the stream of net cash flows from a project with the project's net investment.

http://
Read more about internal rate of return in an article by consultant Ray Martin at the following Internet site maintained by RiskWorld:
http://www.riskworld.com/Nreports/

Example

http://
Access financial information on the Chrysler Corporation at the following Internet site: http://www.daimler chrysler.com

Various criteria can be employed to determine the desirability of investment projects. This section focuses on two widely used discounted cash-flow methods:[8]

- Internal rate of return *(r)*
- Net present value *(NPV)*

Internal Rate of Return   The **internal rate of return (IRR)** is defined as the discount rate that equates the present value of the net cash flows from the project with the net investment. The following equation is used to find the internal rate of return:

$$\sum_{t=1}^{n} \frac{NCF_t}{(1 + r)^t} = NINV \qquad [18.6]$$

where n is the life of the investment and r is the internal rate of return.

An investment project should be accepted if the internal rate of return is greater than or equal to the firm's required rate of return (cost of capital); if not, the project should be rejected.

CALCULATION OF INTERNAL RATE OF RETURN: HAMILTON BEACH/PROCTOR-SILEX

The internal rate of return for the Hamilton Beach/Proctor-Silex investment project is calculated as follows:

$$\sum_{t=1}^{5} \frac{290,000}{(1 + r)^t} = 1,000,000$$

$$\sum_{t=1}^{5} \frac{1}{(1 + r)^t} = \frac{1,000,000}{290,000} = 3.4483$$

The term $\left[\sum_{t=1}^{5} 1/(1 + r)^t \right]$ represents the present value of a \$1 annuity for five years discounted at r percent and is equal to 3.4483. Looking up 3.4483 in the *Period 05* row of Table 5 in Appendix B, this value falls between 3.5172 and 3.4331, which corresponds to discount rates of 13 and 14 percent, respectively. Interpolating between these values yields an internal rate of return of

$$r = .13 + \frac{3.5172 - 3.4483}{3.5172 - 3.4331} (.14 - .13)$$

$$= .1382$$

or 13.8 percent.

If Hamilton Beach/Proctor-Silex requires a rate of return of 12 percent on projects of this type, then the project should be accepted because the expected return (13.8 percent) exceeds the required return (12 percent). Later in this chapter we consider how to determine the required return (i.e., the firm's cost of capital).

Net Present Value   The **net present value (NPV)** of an investment is defined as the present value, discounted at the firm's required rate of return (cost of capital), of

---

[8] For those not familiar with discounting (present value) techniques, Appendix A at the end of this book provides a review of these concepts.

Net Present Value (NPV) The present value of the stream of net cash flows resulting from a project, discounted at the required rate of return (cost of capital), minus the project's net investment.

the stream of net cash flows from the project minus the project's net investment. Algebraically, the net present value is equal to

$$NPV = \sum_{t=1}^{n} \frac{NCF_t}{(1 + k)^t} - NINV \qquad [18.7]$$

where n is the expected life of the project and k is the firm's required rate of return (cost of capital).

An investment project should be accepted if the net present value is greater than or equal to zero and rejected if its net present value is less than zero. This is so because a positive net present value translates directly into increases in stock prices and increases in shareholder wealth.

Example

NET PRESENT VALUE CALCULATION: HERSHEY FOODS

Hershey Foods is considering an investment in a new wrapping machine for its "Kiss" candies. The machine has an initial cost (net investment) of $2.5 million. It is expected to produce cost savings from reduced labor and to generate additional revenues because of its increased reliability and productivity. Over its anticipated economic life of five years, the new "Kiss" wrapping machine is expected to generate the stream of net cash flows (NCF_t) listed below.

Year (t)	Net Cash Flow (NCF_t)
1	$600,000
2	800,000
3	800,000
4	600,000
5	250,000

If Hershey requires a return (k) of 15 percent on a project of this type, should it make the investment?

Hershey can solve this problem by computing the net present value of the cash flows from this project (using Equation 18.7) as follows:

Year (1)	Cash Flow (2)	Present Value Interest Factor at 15 Percent* (3)	Present Value (4) = (2) × (3)
0	($2,500,000)	1.00000	($2,500,000)
1	600,000	0.86957	521,742
2	800,000	0.75614	604,912
3	800,000	0.65752	526,016
4	600,000	0.57175	343,050
5	250,000	0.49718	124,295
			($379,985)

*Table 4, Appendix B

Because this project has a negative net present value, it does not contribute to the goal of maximizing shareholder wealth. Therefore, it should be rejected.

Table 18.1   Net Present Value vs. Internal Rate of Return for Mutually Exclusive Investment Projects

	Project X	Project Y
Net investment	$1,000	$1,000
Net cash flows		
Year 1	667	0
Year 2	667	1,400
Net present value at 5%	$240	$270
Internal rate of return	21.5%	18.3%

Net Present Value versus Internal Rate of Return   Both the net present value and the internal rate of return methods result in identical decisions to either accept or reject individual projects. This is true because the net present value is greater than (less than) zero if and only if the internal rate of return is greater than (less than) the required rate of return k. In the case of *mutually exclusive* projects—that is, projects where the acceptance of one alternative precludes the acceptance of one or more other alternatives—the two methods may yield contradictory results; one project may have a *higher* internal rate of return than another and, at the same time, a *lower* net present value.

Consider, for example, mutually exclusive projects X and Y shown in Table 18.1. Both require a net investment of $1,000. Based on the internal rate of return, Project X is preferred, with a rate of 21.5 percent compared with Project Y's rate of 18.3 percent. Based on the net present value with a discount rate of 5 percent, Project Y ($270) is preferred to Project X ($240). Thus it is necessary to determine which of the two criteria is the correct one to use in this situation. The outcome depends on what *assumptions* the decision maker chooses to make about the *implied reinvestment rate* for the net cash flows generated from each project. The net present value method assumes that cash flows are *reinvested at the firm's cost of capital,* whereas the internal rate of return method assumes that these cash flows are *reinvested at the computed internal rate of return.*[9] Generally, the cost of capital is considered to be a more realistic reinvestment rate than the computed internal rate of return because this is the rate the next (marginal) investment project can be assumed to earn. This can be seen in Figure 18.1. This last project invested in, Project E, offers a rate of return nearly equal to the firm's marginal cost of capital. Consequently, the net present value approach is normally superior to the internal rate of return when choosing among mutually exclusive investments. Table 18.2 summarizes the two techniques.

Reviewing Investment Projects after Implementation

A very important but often neglected step in the selection process is the review of investment projects *after* they have been implemented. The purpose of this review should be to provide information on the effectiveness of the selection process. In

[9] A more thorough discussion of this problem and the underlying assumptions is found in J. Hirshleifer, "On the Theory of the Optimal Investment Decision," *Journal of Political Economy* 66 (August 1958), pp. 95–103, and James H. Lorie and Leonard J. Savage, "Three Problems in Rationing Capital," *Journal of Business* 23 (October 1955), pp. 229–239.

Table 18.2   Summary of the Capital Budgeting Decision Criteria

Criterion	Project Acceptance Decision Rule	Benefits	Weaknesses
Net present value (NPV) method	Accept project if project has a positive or zero NPV; that is, if the present value of net cash flows, evaluated at the firm's cost of capital, equals or exceeds the net investment required	Considers the timing of cash flows Provides an objective, return-based criterion for acceptance or rejection; most conceptually accurate approach	Difficulty in interpreting the meaning of the NPV computation
Internal rate of return (IRR) method	Accept project if IRR equals or exceeds the firm's cost of capital	Easy to interpret the meaning of IRR Considers the timing of cash flows Provides an objective, return-based criterion for acceptance or rejection	Sometimes gives decision that conflicts with NPV; multiple rates of return problem*

*See Moyer, McGuigan, and Kretlow, *Contemporary Financial Management*, 8th ed., p. 347, for a discussion of the multiple internal rates of return problem.

http://

Ibbotson Associates publishes **Cost of Capital Quarterly,** which includes industry cost of capital analysis on over 300 industries, at the following Internet site:
http://www.ibbotson.com/content/cc_lvl1.asp

the review, the actual cash flows from an accepted project are compared with the estimated cash flows at the time the project was proposed. This type of analysis requires the firm to keep some additional information in its accounting records to be able to associate specific costs and revenues with various investment projects. Because estimating future cash inflows and outflows is uncertain, one would not expect the actual values to agree perfectly with the estimated values. The analysis therefore should be concerned with checking for any large or systematic discrepancies in the cash flow estimates by individual departments, plants, or divisions, and attempting to ascertain the reasons for these discrepancies. An analysis such as this will enable decision makers to make better evaluations of investment proposals submitted in the future.

ESTIMATING THE FIRM'S COST OF CAPITAL

A firm's cost of capital is an important input in the capital-budgeting analysis procedure. The theory and measurement of a firm's cost of capital is a complex topic that is more appropriately dealt with at length in financial management texts. The purpose of this section is to provide an introduction to the topic and to summarize some of its most important elements.

Cost of Capital
The cost of funds that are supplied to a firm. The cost of capital is the minimum rate of return that must be earned on new investments undertaken by a firm.

The **cost of capital** is concerned with what a firm has to pay for the capital—that is, the debt, preferred stock, retained earnings, and common stock—it uses to finance new investments. It also can be thought of as the rate of return required by investors in the firm's securities. As such, the firm's cost of capital is determined in the capital markets and is closely related to the degree of risk associated with new investments, existing assets, and the firm's capital structure. In general, the greater the risk of a firm as perceived by investors, the greater the return investors will require and the greater will be the cost of capital.

The cost of capital also can be thought of as the minimum rate of return required on new investments undertaken by the firm.[10] If a new investment earns an internal rate of return that is greater than the cost of capital, the value of the firm increases. Correspondingly, if a new investment earns a return less than the firm's cost of capital, the firm's value decreases.

The following discussion focuses on the two major sources of funds for most firms—debt and common equity. Each of these sources of funds has a cost. The cost of each of the various component sources of capital is an important input in the calculation of a firm's overall cost of capital.

Cost of Debt Capital

The pretax cost of debt capital to the firm is the rate of return required by investors. For a debt issue, this rate of return k_d equates the present value of all expected future receipts—interest I and principal repayment M—with the offering price V_0 of the debt security:

$$V_0 = \sum_{t=1}^{n} \frac{I}{(1 + k_d)^t} + \frac{M}{(1 + k_d)^n} \qquad [18.8]$$

The cost of debt k_d can be found by using the methods for finding the discount rate (that is, yield to maturity) discussed in Appendix A.

Most *new* long-term debt (in the form of bonds) issued by companies is sold at or close to par value (normally $1,000 per bond), and the coupon interest rate is set at the rate required by investors. When debt is issued at par value, the pretax cost of debt, k_d, is equal to the coupon interest rate. Interest payments made to investors, however, are deductible from the firm's taxable income. Therefore, the *after-tax* cost of debt is computed by multiplying the pretax cost by 1 minus the firm's marginal tax rate t:

$$k_i = k_d(1 - t) \qquad [18.9]$$

Example

COST OF DEBT CAPITAL: BELLSOUTH

To illustrate the cost of debt computation, suppose that BellSouth sells $100 million of 8.5-percent first-mortgage bonds at par. Assuming a corporate marginal tax rate of 40 percent, the after-tax cost of debt is computed as

$$k_i = k_d(1 - t)$$
$$= 8.5(1 - .40) = 5.1\%$$

Cost of Internal Equity Capital

Like the cost of debt capital, the cost of equity capital to the firm is the equilibrium rate of return required by the firm's common stock investors.

---

[10] Technically, this statement assumes that the risk of the new investments is equal to the risk of the firm's existing assets. Also, when used in this context, the cost of capital refers to a weighted cost of the various sources of capital used by the firm. The computation of the weighted cost of capital is considered in this chapter.

Firms raise equity capital in two ways: (1) *internally*, through retained earnings and (2) *externally*, through the sale of new common stock. The cost of internal equity to the firm is less than the cost of new common stock because the sale of new stock requires the payment of flotation costs.

The concept of the cost of internal equity (or simply "equity," as it is commonly called) can be developed using several different approaches, including the *dividend valuation model* and the *capital asset pricing model*.

Dividend Valuation Model
A model (or formula) stating that the value of a firm (i.e., shareholder wealth) is equal to the present value of the firm's future dividend payments, discounted at the shareholder's required rate of return. It provides one method of estimating a firm's cost of equity capital.

Dividend Valuation Model   Recall from Chapter 1 that shareholder wealth was defined as the present value, discounted at the shareholder's required rate of return k_e, of the expected future returns generated by a firm (see Equation 1.1). For the typical firm, these future returns can take two forms—the payment of dividends to the shareholder or an increase in the market value of the firm's stock (capital gain). For the shareholder who plans to hold the stock indefinitely, the value of the firm (shareholder wealth, according to the **dividend valuation model**) is

$$V_0 = \sum_{t=1}^{\infty} \frac{D_t}{(1 + k_e)^t}$$ [18.10]

where D_t is the dividend paid by the firm in period t.[11] If the shareholder chooses to sell the stock after n years, his or her wealth (V_0) is

$$V_0 = \sum_{t=1}^{n} \frac{D_t}{(1 + k_e)^t} + \frac{V_n}{(1 + k_e)^n}$$ [18.11]

where V_n is the market value of the shareholder's holdings in period n. However, Equation 18.11 can be shown to be identical to 18.10, because the value of the firm in Period n is based on the future returns (dividends) of the firm in Period $n + 1, n + 2, \ldots$.[12]

If the dividends of the firm are expected to grow *perpetually* at a *constant compound rate* of g per year, then the value of the firm (Equation 18.10) can be expressed as[13]

$$V_0 = \frac{D_1}{k_e - g}$$ [18.12]

where D_1 is the dividend expected to be paid in Period 1 and V_0 is the market value of the firm. If D_1 is the dividend *per share* (rather than total dividends) paid in Period 1, then V_0 represents the market price *per share* of common stock. Solving Equation 18.12 for k_e yields

$$k_e = \frac{D_1}{V_0} + g$$ [18.13]

---

[11] A profitable firm that reinvests all its earnings and never distributes any dividends would still have a positive value to stockholders. This is because its market value would be increasing, and shareholders could sell their stock and obtain a capital gain on their investment in the firm.

[12] The value of the firm in period n is

$$V_n = \sum_{t=n+1}^{\infty} \frac{D_t}{(1 + k_e)^{t-n}}$$

When this expression is substituted in Equation 18.11, Equation 18.10 is obtained.

[13] Equation 18.12 is often referred to as the *Gordon model*, for Myron J. Gordon, who pioneered its use. See Myron J. Gordon, *The Investment, Financing, and Valuation of the Corporation* (Homewood, IL: Irwin, 1962). More complicated forms of Equations 18.12 and 18.13 must be used if the constant growth assumption does not apply.

The following example illustrates how Equation 18.13 can be applied in estimating the cost of equity capital.

Example

COST OF INTERNAL EQUITY CAPITAL: FRESNO COMPANY

Suppose the current price of the common stock of Fresno Company (V_0) is $32. The dividend per share of the firm next year, D_1, is expected to be $2.14. Dividends have been growing at an average compound annual rate of 7 percent over the past 10 years, and this growth rate is expected to be maintained for the foreseeable future. Based on this information, the cost of equity capital is estimated as

$$k_e = \frac{2.14}{32} + .07 = .137$$

or 13.7 percent.

Capital Asset Pricing Model (CAPM)
A theory that formally describes the nature of the risk-required return tradeoff. It provides one method of estimating a firm's cost of equity capital.

Capital Asset Pricing Model   Another technique that can be used to estimate the cost of equity capital is the **capital asset pricing model (CAPM)**. The CAPM is a theory that formally describes the risk-required return trade-off for securities. According to the CAPM theory, the rate of return required by investors consists of a risk-free return r_f plus a premium compensating the investor for bearing the risk. The risk premium varies from stock to stock.

Obviously less risk is associated with an investment in a stable stock, such as BellSouth, than in the stock of a small, wildcat oil drilling firm W. As a result, an investor in the drilling stock requires a higher return than the BellSouth investor. Figure 18.2 illustrates the difference between required rates of return (or the cost of

Figure 18.2   The Security Market Line (SML)

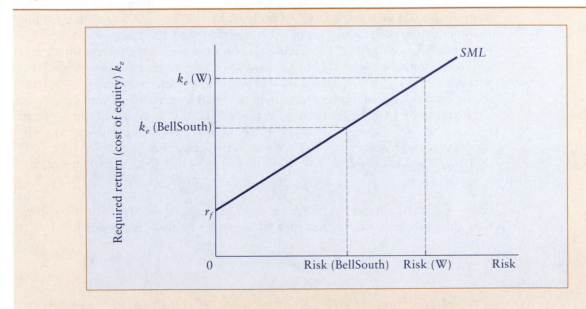

internal equity) for the two securities. The relationship illustrated in this figure is called the *security market line* (SML). The SML depicts the risk-return relationship in the market for all securities.

The cost of equity capital can be quantified using the CAPM. The CAPM assumes that a single risk-free rate exists, and the risk-required return trade-off for stocks is characterized by a straight line sloping upward from the risk-free rate. The required return can be obtained by calculating the risk associated with a stock.

Risk is defined as the variability of outcomes (e.g., returns). The variability of returns for individual stocks is closely related to the variability of stock prices. In the context of the CAPM and the SML, *total* variability of returns is not considered to be the relevant measure of risk, however. Instead, total variability can be divided into two components:

- The variability of returns that is *unique* to a security. This is called *unsystematic risk*. It includes return variability caused by such factors as differing management skills, strikes, natural disasters, effects of new competition, and so on.
- The variability of returns that affects *all* securities. This is called *systematic* or *non-diversifiable risk*. It is measured by the co-movement or covariation of a security's returns with the returns of the overall market. The overall market movement is usually measured by some broad market index such as the S&P 500 stock index. Systematic variability is caused by factors such as changes in the level of interest rates, the impact of recessions or business expansions, and so on.

If an investor holds a well-diversified portfolio of individual securities, the variability of returns arising from unique factors affecting individual securities can possibly be diversified away, leaving only systematic risk.

To use the SML to estimate the cost of equity, one must estimate the systematic risk of individual securities. One measure of the systematic risk of a stock is the stock's *beta,* β. (Beta is estimated as the slope of a regression line between an individual security's returns and the returns for a market index.)[14]

The stock market as a whole has a beta of 1.0; stocks whose prices fluctuate less than the market as a whole have betas of less than 1.0; and stocks with price fluctuations greater than the market have betas greater than 1.0. For example, if a stock has a beta equal to 1.0, a 5-percent increase (or decrease) in the returns on the market index would be expected to be associated with a 5-percent increase (or decrease) in that security's returns. If a stock has a beta of 2.0, a 5-percent increase (or decrease) in market returns would be expected to be associated with a 10-percent increase (or decrease) in that security's returns. Finally, a beta of 0.5 implies that a 5-percent increase (or decrease) in market returns would be expected to be associated with a 2.5-percent increase (or decrease) in that security's returns.

Thus, according to the CAPM, the cost of equity calculation can be illustrated as

$$k_e = r_f + \beta(k_m - r_f) \tag{18.14}$$

where k_m is the expected return on the market as a whole. This equation shows that the risk premium portion of a firm's cost of equity is proportional to its beta.

---

[14] See Moyer, McGuigan, and Kretlow, *Contemporary Financial Management*, 9th ed., Chapters 5 and 11, for a more detailed discussion of the CAPM theory and its use in calculating the cost of equity capital.

Example

COST OF INTERNAL EQUITY CAPITAL: MIDWESTERN POWER COMPANY

To illustrate the k_e calculation using the CAPM, suppose that the Midwestern Power Company common stock has a beta (β) of 0.8 and the present risk-free rate (r_f) is 7 percent. If the expected return on the market (k_m) is 13 percent, substituting these values into Equation 18.14 yields

$$k_e = 7.0 + 0.8(13.0 - 7.0)$$
$$= 11.8\%$$

Cost of External Equity Capital

The cost of external equity is greater than the cost of internal equity for the following reasons:

- Flotation costs associated with new shares are usually high enough that they cannot realistically be ignored.
- The selling price of the new shares to the public must be less than the market price of the stock before announcement of the new issue, or the shares may not sell. Before any announcement, the current market price of a stock usually represents an equilibrium between supply and demand. If supply is increased (all other things being equal), the new equilibrium price will be lower.

When a firm's future dividend payments are expected to grow forever at a constant per-period rate of g, the cost of external equity k'_e is defined as

$$k'_e = \frac{D_1}{V_{net}} + g \qquad [18.15]$$

where V_{net} is the net proceeds to the firm on a per-share basis.

Example

COST OF EXTERNAL EQUITY CAPITAL: FRESNO COMPANY

To illustrate, consider the Fresno Company example used in the cost of internal equity discussion, where $V_0 = \$32$, $D_1 = \$2.14$, $g = .07$, and $k_e = 13.7$ percent. Assuming that new common stock can be sold at \$31 to net the company \$30 a share after flotation costs, k'_e is calculated using Equation 18.15 as follows:

$$k'_e = \frac{2.14}{30} + 0.07$$
$$= 0.141 \text{ or } 14.1\%$$

Because of the relatively high cost of newly issued equity, many companies try to avoid this means of raising capital. The question of whether a firm should raise capital with newly issued common stock depends on the firm's investment opportunities.

Weighted Cost of Capital

Firms calculate their cost of capital to determine a discount rate to use when evaluating proposed capital expenditure projects. Recall that the purpose of capital expenditure analysis is to determine which *proposed* projects the firm should *actually* undertake. Therefore, it is logical that *the capital whose cost is measured and compared with the expected benefits from these proposed projects should be the next or marginal capital the firm raises.* Typically, companies estimate the cost of each capital component as the cost they expect to have to pay on these funds during the coming year.[15]

In addition, as a firm evaluates proposed capital expenditure projects, it normally does not specify the proportions of debt and equity financing for each individual project. Instead, each project is presumed to be financed with the same proportion of debt and equity contained in the company's target capital structure.

Thus the appropriate cost of capital figure to be used in capital budgeting is not only based on the next capital to be raised but also weighted by the proportions of the capital components in the firm's long-range target capital structure. This figure is called the *weighted,* or *overall, cost of capital.*

The general expression for calculating the weighted cost of capital k_a is as follows:

$$k_a = \begin{bmatrix} \text{equity} \\ \text{fraction} \\ \text{of capital} \\ \text{structure} \end{bmatrix} \begin{bmatrix} cost \\ of \\ equity \end{bmatrix} + \begin{bmatrix} \text{debt} \\ \text{fraction} \\ \text{of capital} \\ \text{structure} \end{bmatrix} \begin{bmatrix} cost \\ of \\ debt \end{bmatrix}$$

$$= \left[\frac{E}{D+E} \right] (k_e) + \left[\frac{D}{D+E} \right] (k_i) \qquad [18.16]$$

where D is the amount of debt and E the amount of equity in the target capital structure.[16]

Example

WEIGHTED COST OF CAPITAL: COLUMBIA GAS COMPANY

To illustrate, suppose that Columbia Gas has a current (and target) capital structure of 75-percent equity and 25-percent debt. (The proportions of debt and equity should be the proportions in which the firm intends to raise funds in the future.) For a firm that is not planning a change in its target capital structure, these proportions should be based on the current *market value weights* of the individual components (debt and common equity). The company plans to finance next year's budget with $75 million of retained earnings ($k_e = 12\%$) and $25 million of long-term debt ($k_d = 8\%$). Assume a 40-percent marginal tax rate. Using these figures, the weighted cost of capital being raised to finance next year's capital budget is calculated using Equation 18.16 as

$$k_a = 0.75 \times 12.0 + 0.25 \times 8.0 \times (1 - 0.40)$$
$$= 10.2\%$$

This is the discount rate that should be used to evaluate projects of average risk.

---

[15] Stated another way, the cost of the capital acquired by the firm in earlier periods—that is, the *historical* cost of capital—is *not* used as the discount rate in determining next year's capital expenditures.

[16] If the target capital structure contains preferred stock, a preferred stock term is added to Equation 18.16. In this case Equation 18.16 becomes

$$k_a = \left(\frac{E}{E+D+P} \right) (k_e) + \left(\frac{D}{E+D+P} \right) (k_i) + \left(\frac{P}{E+D+P} \right) (k_p)$$

where P is the amount of preferred stock in the target capital structure and k_p is the component cost of preferred stock.

Cost-Benefit Analysis
A resource-allocation model that can be used by public and not-for-profit sector organizations to evaluate programs or investments on the basis of the magnitude of the discounted benefits and costs.

COST-BENEFIT ANALYSIS

The remainder of this chapter is devoted to some techniques of analysis that may be used to assist in public and not-for-profit sector resource-allocation decisions. The primary analytical model examined is cost-benefit analysis, although cost-effectiveness studies are also discussed.

Cost-benefit analysis is an analytical tool used to evaluate programs and investments based on a comparison of all the benefits and costs arising from a particular program or project. Cost-benefit analysis is the logical public sector counterpart to the capital budgeting techniques discussed earlier. In the following sections of this chapter the focus is on the additional problems that arise in attempting to allocate resources and make other economic decisions in public and not-for-profit sector organizations. These include the measurement of benefits and costs, the determination of an appropriate discount rate, and the uses and limitations of the model.

Uses of Cost-Benefit Analysis

In general, cost-benefit analysis is a method for assessing the desirability of projects when it is necessary to take both a long and a wide view of the repercussions of a particular program expenditure or policy change. As in private sector capital budgeting, cost-benefit analysis often is used in cases where the economic consequences of a project or a policy change are likely to extend beyond one year in time. Unlike capital budgeting, however, cost-benefit analysis seeks to measure all economic impacts of the project; that is, side effects as well as direct effects.

Accept-Reject Decisions

Cost-benefit analysis may be used for a number of purposes, depending on the nature of the project, the constraints of public policy, and the requirements of the information user or decision maker. One use is to determine whether a specific expenditure is economically justifiable. For instance, one might examine a program designed to eradicate tuberculosis, considering the current costs of the disease that could be averted by a specific expenditure of funds. Benefits (averted costs) may be divided into four categories:

1. Expenditures on medical care, including physician and nurse fees, drug costs, and hospital and equipment charges
2. Loss of gross earnings during the disease
3. Reduction in gross earnings after the disease because of decreased employment opportunities resulting from the social stigma attached to the illness
4. The pain and discomfort associated with having the disease

Suppose a particular program designed to aid tuberculosis eradication is proposed that requires a one-time outlay of $250 million (Table 18.3). Assume that the total benefits (averted disease costs) of this one-year program are expected to accrue for a period of five years. If one accepts, for the moment, that an appropriate social discount rate is 15 percent for this project, the program may be evaluated in the net present-value analysis framework developed in the capital budgeting discussion. The decision rule is to accept the project if the (discounted) benefits are greater than or equal to the (discounted) costs. Because the program has a positive calculated net discounted benefit, in this case $81.83 million, it is an acceptable project.

Table 18.3   Net Benefit-Cost Analysis

End of Year (1)	Actual Dollar Benefit (Cost) (2)	Present Value Interest Factor at 15 Percent* (3)	Discounted Benefits and Costs ($ Million) (4) = (2) × (3)
0	($250,000,000)	1.000	($250.00)
1	150,000,000	.870	130.50
2	125,000,000	.756	94.50
3	100,000,000	.658	65.80
4	50,000,000	.572	28.60
5	25,000,000	.497	12.43
			Net benefits = $81.83

*Table 4, Appendix B.

Alternative decision-making criteria include the internal rate of return and the benefit-cost ratio. According to the internal rate of return criterion, a project is acceptable if the IRR is greater than or equal to the appropriate social discount rate. In the case of the tuberculosis eradication program, the IRR for the benefits and costs shown in Table 18.3 is 32.4 percent. Because this exceeds the social discount rate of 15 percent, the project is acceptable. According to the benefit-cost ratio criterion, a project is acceptable if the benefit-cost ratio is greater than or equal to 1.0, where the **benefit-cost ratio** is equal to the present value of the benefits (discounted at the social discount rate) divided by the present value of the costs (similarly discounted). For the tuberculosis eradication program, the benefit-cost ratio is equal to

Benefit-Cost Ratio
The ratio of the present value of the benefits from a project or program (discounted at the social discount rate) to the present value of the costs (similarly discounted).

$$\text{Benefit-cost ratio} = \frac{130.50 + 94.50 + 65.80 + 28.60 + 12.43}{250}$$

$$= 1.33$$

Because this ratio exceeds 1.0, the project is acceptable according to this criterion. All three decision criteria will give identical decisions to accept or reject individual projects.

Program-Level Analysis

In addition to being used to evaluate whether an entire program is economically justifiable, cost-benefit analysis may also be used to determine whether the size of an existing program should be increased (or reduced) and, if so, by what amount. This determination may be made using traditional marginal analysis as developed earlier in the text.

Returning again to the tuberculosis-control program, assume that, because of strong lobbying from the AMA, a number of expenditure levels beyond the originally proposed $250 million are being considered. Table 18.4 summarizes these proposed programs and their expected benefits. It can be seen that an analysis that looked in isolation at only one of these proposed program expenditure levels would have concluded that any of the program levels was worthwhile because each proposal generates positive expected net program benefits.

Table 18.4   Schedule of Program Benefits for Various Cost Levels

Program Cost (Millions of Dollars)	Discounted Program Benefits (Millions of Dollars)	Net Program Benefits (Millions of Dollars)
$250	$331.83	$ 81.83
300	496.00	196.00
350	540.00	190.00
400	565.00	165.00

Table 18.5   Marginal Analysis of Benefits and Costs

Program Cost (Millions of Dollars)	Marginal Cost (Millions of Dollars)	Discounted Marginal Benefits (Millions of Dollars)
$ 0	—	—
250	$250	$331.83
300	50	164.17
350	50	44.00
400	50	25.00

If these program levels are analyzed as a group, however, it becomes clear that there is a limit to the economically justifiable expenditure of funds for tuberculosis control. The required analysis is summarized in Table 18.5. A level of expenditure of $300 million is best because it generates an additional (marginal) $164.17 million in benefits, but the marginal program cost (in comparison to the $250 million program level) is only $50 million. To increase the program to $350 million would be counterproductive, because only $44 million in benefits are generated for the additional $50 million outlay (marginal costs exceed marginal benefits).

STEPS IN COST-BENEFIT ANALYSIS

The general principles of cost-benefit analysis may be summarized by answering the following set of questions:[17]

1. What is the objective function to be maximized?

---

[17] The next two sections of this chapter draw heavily on the review article by A.R. Prest and R. Turvey, "Cost-Benefit Analysis: A Survey," *Economic Journal* (December 1965), p. 683.

2. What are the constraints placed on the analysis?
3. What costs and benefits are to be included and how may they be valued?
4. What investment evaluation criterion should be used?
5. What is the appropriate discount rate?

The decision-making process in cost-benefit analysis may be traced in the flowchart presentation of Figure 18.3. Program objectives are set by the public through their political representatives. Alternatives are enumerated, explored, and revised in the light of constraints that may be operative in the system. These alternatives are then compared by enumerating and evaluating program benefits and costs in a present-value framework. Discounted benefits are compared with discounted costs, and intangibles are considered so a recommendation may be made about the merits of one or more alternative programs.

OBJECTIVES AND CONSTRAINTS IN COST-BENEFIT ANALYSIS

Cost-benefit analysis is merely an application of resource-allocation theory. As such, we need to examine it in the light of several criteria that have been proposed by welfare economists for evaluating the desirability of alternative social and economic states. One such criterion is Pareto optimality.[18] A change is said to be desirable or consistent with Pareto optimality if at least one person is made better off (in his or her own judgment) and no one is made worse off (in their own judgments). Although this criterion seems to be relatively value free, as well as potentially verifiable, it suffers from the severe weakness that few changes are likely to leave some individuals better off and *no one* worse off. In addition, it assumes that we know, *a priori*, how people affected by a program will evaluate its effects on them.

Cost-benefit analysis is tied to a weaker notion of social improvement, sometimes called the Kaldor-Hicks criterion, or merely the notion of a "potential" Pareto improvement. Under this criterion, a change (or an economic program) is desirable either (1) if it is consistent with the Pareto criterion or (2) if a potential Pareto improvement may be made by redistributing the gains such that all people in the community are at least as well off as they were before the change. This is the notion of cost-benefit analysis. A project is desirable if the benefits exceed the costs of the project because the project could be completed and the gainers *could* be made to compensate the losers. The fact that there is no compensation from gainers to losers is not a matter of direct consideration in cost-benefit analysis, but the income distributional impacts of a program are an extremely important side issue. All that cost-benefit analysis requires for a project to be acceptable is that total discounted societal benefits exceed the total discounted societal costs.

In addition to recognizing that the maximization of society's wealth is the primary objective function in cost-benefit analysis, it is also important to establish the constraints that may exist or be placed on the achievement of this objective. According to Otto Eckstein's classification system,[19] these include the following:

---

[18] A further discussion of the Pareto criterion is provided in W.J. Baumol, *Economic Theory and Operations Analysis*, 4th ed. (Englewood Cliffs, NJ: Prentice-Hall, 1977), Chapter 21.

[19] Otto Eckstein, "A Survey of the Theory of Public Expenditure Criteria," in *Public Finances: Needs, Sources and Utilization*, ed. James M. Buchanan (Princeton, NJ: Princeton University Press, 1961).

1. *Physical constraints*—The type of program alternatives considered is ultimately limited by the currently available state of technology and by the production possibilities derived from the relationship between physical inputs and outputs. For example, it is not yet possible to prevent cancer; hence, major emphasis, beyond research programs, must be directed toward early detection and treatment.

Figure 18.3   Schematic of the Cost-Benefit Analysis Process

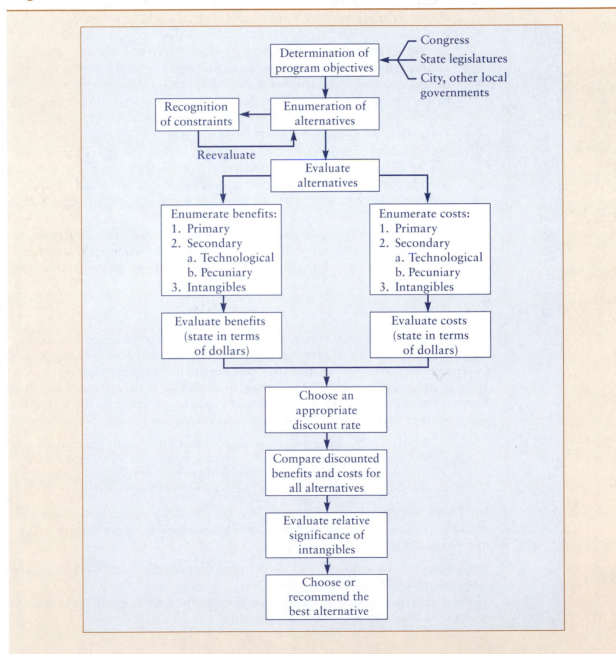

2. *Legal constraints*—These may include domestic as well as international laws relating to property rights, the right of eminent domain, due process, constitutional limits on a particular agency's activities, and so on.

3. *Administrative constraints*—Effective programs require that individuals are available, or can be hired and trained, to carry out the program objectives. Even the best-conceived program is worthless unless individuals with the proper mix of technical and administrative skills are available.

4. *Distributional constraints*—Programs affect different groups in different ways because gainers are rarely the same as losers. When distributional impacts are of concern, the objective of cost-benefit analysis might be presented in terms of maximizing total benefits less total costs, subject to the constraint that benefits-less-costs for a particular group reach a prespecified level.

5. *Political constraints*—What may be optimal may not be feasible because of the slowness and inefficiency of the political process. Many times what is *best* is tempered by what is *possible,* given the existence of strong competing interest groups as well as an often cumbersome political mechanism.

6. *Financial or budget constraints*—More often than not, agencies work within the bounds of a predetermined budget. This requires that the objective function be altered to the suboptimizing form of maximizing benefits given a fixed budget. Virtually all programs have some absolute financial ceiling above which the program may not be expanded, in spite of the magnitude of social benefits.

7. *Social and religious constraints*—It is futile to tell Indians to eat sacred cattle to solve their nutritional problems. This is just one example of the social and religious constraints which may limit the range of feasible program alternatives.

ANALYSIS AND VALUATION OF BENEFITS AND COSTS

Cost-benefit analysis is quite similar to traditional private sector profit-and-loss accounting. In the private sector the firm is guided by the criterion that private revenues must be equal to or exceed private costs over the long run for the firm to survive. In contrast, in cost-benefit analysis the economist asks whether society as a whole will be better off by the adoption or nonadoption of a specific project or by the acceptance of one project to the exclusion of alternatives. As Ezra Mishan points out:

> . . . For the more precise concept of the revenue of the private concern, the economist substitutes the less precise, yet meaningful, concept of the social benefit. For the costs of the private concern, the economist will substitute the concept of opportunity cost . . . or social value forgone elsewhere in moving factors into a projected economic activity.[20]

The starting point for evaluating benefits and costs of a project is the observable market valuations. This assumes that the following conditions are met (or at least approximately met):

• Consumers equate the value of the marginal unit of each commodity consumed to the value of forgone alternatives.

• Producers operate so that each commodity is produced in a manner that sacrifices the lowest value of forgone alternatives.

---

[20] Ezra J. Mishan, *Cost-Benefit Analysis: An Introduction* (New York: Praeger, 1971), pp. 7–8.

These are the conditions present in a competitive economy. With this assumption in mind, benefits may be measured by the market price of the outputs from a public program or by the price consumers would be *willing* to pay if they were charged. Similarly, costs are measured as the monetary expenditures necessary to undertake a project. When the assumed conditions of competition do not exist—for example, when externalities or economies of scale are present—then the estimate of benefits and costs must be modified to take account of this situation.

Direct Benefits

Benefits and costs may be categorized in a number of ways. *Primary* or *direct* benefits of a project consist of the value of goods or services produced if the project is undertaken compared to conditions without the project. The primary benefit of an irrigation project is the value of the additional crops produced on the irrigated land less the cost of seeds, labor, and equipment required to produce the crops. The primary benefits attributable to a college education might be considered as the increase in gross earnings of the graduate over what would have been earned without a college degree. In sum, the value of primary or direct benefits of a project may be taken as the total amount users pay (assuming pure competition) or would be willing to pay (total revenue if a charge is made, plus the consumers' surplus when pure competition does not prevail). Although this principle of evaluating direct benefits may be reasonably straightforward for irrigation projects, the estimation of direct benefits in the valuation of human life, as in health-care or accident prevention[21] programs, poses serious conceptual problems.

Direct Costs

Direct or *primary costs* are generally easier to measure than direct benefits. They include the capital costs necessary to undertake the project, operating and maintenance costs incurred over the life of the project, and personnel expenses. Once again the estimation of these costs is generally much easier for investments in physical assets—such as dams, canals, and so on—than it is for human resource investments. Remember that the costs being measured are opportunity costs, or the social value forgone elsewhere because factors of production have been moved into the projected area of activity. If a proposed project will draw 20 percent of the required labor from the ranks of the unemployed, the market cost (wage payments) of these workers' services will overstate the true social cost.[22] A similar conclusion applies for the use of idle land. With *no* alternative use, the opportunity cost of the use of this land is zero (for as long as no productive alternative uses exist), no matter what the government happens to actually pay its owner in compensation. Such compensation to the owner only affects the *distribution* of the benefits derived from land usage.

---

[21] For a summary of this problem, see Ezra J. Mishan, "Evaluation of Life and Limb: A Theoretical Approach," *Journal of Political Economy* (July/August 1971), pp. 687–705. See also *Journal of Risk and Uncertainty* 8, no. 1 (January 1994), for a series of articles dealing with cost-benefit analyses of health and safety regulations and the valuation of human life.

[22] A discussion of this issue is provided by Robert Haveman, "Evaluating Public Expenditures under Conditions of Unemployment," in *Public Expenditures and Policy Analysis,* eds. Robert Haveman and Julius Margolis (Chicago: Markham, 1970).

Indirect Costs and Benefits

In addition to the primary impacts of a project, government investment invariably creates *secondary* or *indirect* effects. Secondary costs and benefits may be of two types: *real* or *technological* effects, and *pecuniary* effects. Real secondary benefits may include reductions in necessary outlays for other government projects, as for example when an early glaucoma-detection campaign reduces the number of people who go blind, thereby reducing future government disability transfer payments. Similarly, an irrigation dam may reduce flooding and create a recreational area. These secondary benefits should be counted in a cost-benefit study. The same argument applies in accounting for secondary costs. For example, the Wallisville Dam Project in Texas was alleged to cause in excess of $500,000 in damages annually to saltwater fishing because of its impacts on the tidal marshlands. This real secondary cost should have been counted in the cost-benefit analysis of the Wallisville Project.

Pecuniary benefits should generally not be included in the enumeration of "countable" benefits in a study. They generally arise in the form of lower input costs, increased volumes of business, or changes in land values resulting from a project. For example, an improved highway may lead to greater business volume and profitability of gas stations, souvenir shops, and restaurants along that road, as well as higher land values and consequently higher rents to the landlords. Many of these benefits are purely distributional in nature because some business will be drawn from firms along other roads once the new road is completed.

If the economy is operating under conditions of full employment, secondary impacts of the multiplier effect and induced investment that may occur as a result of a particular government investment also should not be counted. Under full employment, these benefits must be presumed to occur whether the expenditure of funds is public or private. The objective of a regional project may be to induce local investment, generate multiplier effects, and reduce regional unemployment. Under special circumstances it may be appropriate to include some of these secondary effects in the analysis.

Intangibles

A final group of program benefits and costs is intangibles. These are recognizable impacts of a project for which it is either extremely difficult or impossible to calculate a dollar value. Intangibles may include such notions as quality of life, aesthetic contributions (or detriments), and balance-of-payments impacts. Intangibles may be merely listed if it proves impossible to translate them into reasonable estimates of dollar benefits and costs. Alternatively, they may be analyzed by making trade-offs against tangibles in such a manner that the cost of additional increments of intangible improvement, for instance, may be compared with the forgone tangible benefits of a project. An example of this sort of trade-off analysis can be seen in the U.S. Maritime program. One objective of the U.S. Maritime subsidies is to reduce the U.S. balance-of-payments deficit. A comparison of real program costs with balance-of-payments impacts can provide the basis for a choice among the commitment of various levels of real resources to gain foreign exchange savings. As one study of this matter concludes, "It is scarcely credible . . . that the Nation would have been willing to spend $1 to save $1 of foreign exchange."[23]

---

[23] Gerald R. Jantscher, "Federal Aids to the Maritime Industries," *The Economics of Federal Subsidy Programs,* Joint Economic Committee (Washington, DC: U.S. Government Printing Office, February 26, 1973).

The Appropriate Rate of Discount

Social Discount Rate
The discount rate to be used when evaluating benefits and costs from public sector investments.

When the benefits or costs of a program extend beyond a one-year time limit, they must be discounted back to some common point in time for purposes of comparison. This is so because most people prefer current consumption to future consumption. The **social discount rate** is used to adjust for this preference.[24] The choice of the appropriate discount rate to evaluate public investments is critical to the conclusions of any cost-benefit analysis. Projects that may appear to be justified at a low discount rate, say 5 percent, may seem to be a gross misallocation of resources at a higher rate, such as 15 percent. The choice of a discount rate is likely to have a profound impact on the type of projects to be accepted. A low rate favors investments with long lives, most of which will be of the durable "bricks and mortar" variety, whereas a high rate favors those whose benefits become available soon after the initial investment. When urgent public needs are apparent, a high rate will tend to be more appropriate. To take an extreme example, when deaths from automobile accidents are rising at an alarming rate, it does little good to invest in a dam, even though at a low rate of discount this may appear to be a better alternative than investing to reduce the automobile accident rate.

A higher rate may completely switch investment priorities. In spite of the fact that the choice of a discount rate may completely alter the outcome of a careful benefit-cost analysis, it is given little attention in many studies. In some cases the researcher may select a rate merely because it has been used in the past (probably with equally little justification). Other studies merely select some arbitrary rate, or rates, and perform the analysis, letting the reader decide which is best.[25]

The literature on the social discount rate is extensive and, in many cases, contradictory. Rather than attempt to synthesize and summarize the many points of view that have been expressed, the following discussion focuses on the opportunity cost criterion for estimating the social discount rate. This approach has been most clearly enunciated by Baumol.[26] Baumol's discussion is based on a recognition of the fact that resources invested in a particular manner in one sector could be withdrawn from that sector and invested elsewhere to yield either a higher or a lower rate of return.

Once it is recognized that the discount rate performs the function of allocating resources between the public and private sectors, then a discount rate should be chosen that will properly indicate when resources should be transferred from one sector to another. This simply means that if resources can earn 20 percent in the private sector, then they should not be transferred to the public sector unless they can earn something greater than 20 percent on the invested resources. As Baumol explains:

> The correct discount rate for the evaluation of a government project is the percentage rate of return that the resources utilized would otherwise provide in the private sector.[27]

---

[24] A review of discounting and present-value concepts is provided in Appendix A.

[25] Weisbrod, for example, used both 10 percent to represent the opportunity cost of capital in the private sector and 4 percent to represent the cost of government borrowing to perform his analysis. See Burton A. Weisbrod, *Economics of Public Health: Measuring the Economic Impact of Diseases* (Philadelphia: University of Pennsylvania Press, 1960).

[26] William J. Baumol, "On the Social Rate of Discount," *American Economic Review* (September 1968), pp. 788–802; "On the Discount Rate for Public Projects," in *Public Expenditures and Policy Analysis,* eds. Robert Haveman and Julius Margolis (Chicago: Markham, 1970), pp. 272–290; and "On the Appropriate Discount Rate for Evaluation of Public Projects," statement in *The Planning-Programming-Budgeting System: Progress and Potentials,* Subcommittee on Economy in Government, Joint Economic Committee, 90th Congress, 1st Session (Washington, DC: U.S. Government Printing Office, 1967).

[27] Baumol, *op. cit.,* "On the Discount Rate for Public Projects," p. 274.

In calculating the opportunity cost of funds withdrawn from the private sector, one should recognize that funds withdrawn from corporate investment will generally incur a higher opportunity rate than funds taken from consumption. If funds used by a firm generally yield a 20-percent rate of return *before taxes*,[28] then this is the opportunity cost to society of these funds. The cost of funds withdrawn from consumption may be estimated by reference to the rate of return on risk-free bonds, such as U.S. government securities. Consumers investing in such securities which pay, say, a 10-percent rate of interest, are actually indicating their preference between current consumption and future consumption. Those consumers who do not invest in these risk-free securities are indicating that they place a higher implied personal opportunity value on current consumption than the risk-free security rate. For non-bondholders, one must conclude that the opportunity cost of present consumption to them is at least as high, if not higher, than that of investors in risk-free securities.

We conclude, as does Baumol, that

> the correct discount rate for a project will be a weighted average of the opportunity cost rate for the various sectors from which the project would draw its resources, and the weight for each such sector in this average is the proportion of the total resources that would come from that sector.[29]

Example

COSTS AND BENEFITS OF A TOYOTA AUTOMOBILE PLANT IN KENTUCKY

Toyota built an assembly plant near Lexington, Kentucky, that is able to produce 200,000 automobiles annually. To get Toyota to locate the plant in Kentucky, the state agreed to invest approximately $325 million over a 20-year period. These expenditures include the following:

- Land and site preparation $ 33 million
- Local highway construction   47 million
- Employee training center and education of workers   65 million
- Education of Japanese workers and families   5 million
- Interest on economic development bonds   167 million

The returns to the state over the 20-year period are estimated at $632 million in income, sales, and payroll taxes from Toyota, its suppliers, and related businesses.

These numbers yield an internal rate of return of 25 percent, according to a University of Kentucky research team. Because the state's economic resources are limited, one must consider whether these resources should have been invested in other projects that would have generated even higher rates of return. However, as Brinton Milward, director of the university's center for business and economic research, explains, "Could you have put these funds into improvements in education and transportation and come up with a better benefit-cost ratio? My guess is no. Manufacturing has a pretty high multiplier" (in terms of the repeated turnover of money in the form of jobs and sales).

---

[28] The opportunity cost of funds withdrawn from corporate investment must be on a before-tax basis, because that is the true rate of return these resources generate. The fact that the corporate income tax may transfer up to 35 percent of this directly to the government is a distributional matter and not an efficiency consideration.

[29] Baumol, *op. cit.*, "On the Discount Rate for Public Projects," p. 279. Baumol raises a number of other important issues in his development of an appropriate social discount rate, such as the role of risk in public versus private investments, the problem of externalities not accounted for in both the public and private sectors, and income distribution issues. None of these, however, alters the fundamental arguments presented above.

COST-EFFECTIVENESS ANALYSIS

Although cost-benefit analysis may be beneficially applied in a wide range of areas, in many types of government activity it is simply not feasible because of the problems of measuring the value of program outputs. For instance, program analyses in the fields of defense, environmental protection, crime prevention, industry regulation, and income redistribution are more frequently conducted using the cost-effectiveness framework than the cost-benefit one. Cost-benefit analysis asks the questions: "What is the dollar value of program costs and benefits, and do the benefits exceed the costs by a sufficient amount, given the timing of these outcomes, to justify undertaking the program?" In contrast, the question asked by **cost-effectiveness analysis** is: "Given that some prespecified objective is to be attained, what are the costs associated with various alternative means for reaching that objective?" In essence, cost-effectiveness analysis *begins* with the premise that some identified program outputs are useful, and it proceeds to explore (1) how these outputs may be most efficiently achieved *or* (2) what the costs are of achieving various levels of the prespecified output.

In many governmental programs, the outputs can be specified and measured, but difficulty in evaluating these outputs in dollar terms precludes the use of cost-benefit analysis. For example, it is easy to measure or prespecify the number of families placed in adequate housing as a result of low-income housing programs. But it is far more difficult to evaluate the societal benefits accruing from this program because its major impacts are income redistributional. Cost-effectiveness analysis is widely applied in Department of Defense program studies. The benefits of most defense activities may be thought of as providing levels of deterrence. But for any specific program, such as the strategic nuclear bomber force, it is virtually impossible to quantify and evaluate benefits in dollar terms. In cases such as these, cost-effectiveness analysis may be useful.

Cost-Effectiveness Analysis
An analytical tool designed to assist public decision makers in their resource-allocation decisions when benefits cannot be easily measured in dollar terms, but costs can be monetarily quantified.

Constant-Cost Studies

With these general remarks about cost-effectiveness analysis in mind, three more specific types of these studies are examined. *Constant-cost studies* attempt to specify the output that may be achieved from a number of alternative programs, assuming all are funded at the same level (costs are constant between alternatives). In essence, constant-cost studies measure what may be acquired for a specific outlay of funds. Constant-cost studies differ from cost-benefit studies as there is no attempt to place dollar values on the outputs of alternative programs. The greatest use of constant-cost studies is in cases where program outputs have multiple dimensions (there may be income distribution effects, aesthetic effects, or impacts on future economic development). This is the case in many urban renewal programs. Decision makers may examine several alternatives for land provided by urban renewal. They might choose on the basis of what uses—industrial, commercial, or residential—offer the greatest potential profitability. Alternatively, an explicit attempt may be made to provide for planned development considering the esthetics of development, the impacts of current development on surrounding areas and future development potential, and the desire to provide a mix of different cultures and income groups within the city. For projects such as these, all one can do is attempt to spell out all the impacts of several alternative, equal-cost schemes. This in itself is likely to be a monumental task. With impacts clearly identified, it becomes the decision maker's responsibility to weigh (subjectively) the outputs of each alternative and to make a choice.

Least-Cost Studies

The second type of cost-effectiveness analysis is *least-cost studies*.[30] As might be expected, the emphasis of these studies is to identify the least expensive way of generating some quantity of an output. For instance, a city might decide that it wishes to reduce by 20 percent the number of burglaries occurring each year within its jurisdictional limits. One approach could be to expand the size of the police force, increase the number of foot patrol officers, and increase the number of squad cars on the streets at any one time. Another possibility might be to require builders to install security bars on the windows of all new homes and to provide cash or tax incentives for current homeowners to improve their personal security systems. A third alternative might be a community drive supporting Operation Identification, where individuals place permanent identifying marks on their belongings to make "fencing" of this merchandise more difficult. If it is recognized that drug addicts are responsible for many burglaries, a drug rehabilitation program may be considered. Combinations of these programs are also possible. Each of these alternatives is evaluated in terms of the expenditure required to achieve the desired objective—a 20-percent reduction in burglaries.

Objective-Level Studies

A third type of cost-effectiveness analysis is *objective-level studies*. These studies attempt to estimate the costs of achieving several alternative performance levels of the same objective. This may be illustrated with the case of reducing automobile emission levels. Table 18.6 provides some hypothetical data relating to various emission-control standards.

Table 18.6   Hypothetical Data Relating to the Cost of Achieving Various Levels of Auto Emission Reductions

Percentage of 1998 Emission Levels	Costs (Millions of Dollars— Including Fuel Consumption, More Frequent Maintenance, and Added New-Car Costs)
90	$200
70	250
40	500
20	2,500
10	7,500
5	38,000
1	140,000

[30] The discussion of both constant-cost and least-cost studies is based largely on Neil M. Singer, *Public Microeconomics* (Boston: Little, Brown & Co., 1972), Chapter 12.

In addition to the increased fuel and maintenance costs and the added new-car costs, other impacts of a program to reduce auto emissions must be considered. For example, what is the relative impact of such a program on various income groups? In areas where the automobile is a necessity, a program that substantially increases the cost of driving without simultaneously providing feasible alternative means of transportation could be disastrous. Given the current domestic energy situation, one must examine the effects of increased fuel consumption by less efficient engines on the balance of payments. Finally, in performing objective-level studies, we must be aware of the state of technology assumptions that are being made. Although the estimates in Table 18.6 may be realistic for the reciprocating engine, they may far overstate actual costs if alternative technology were assumed. Table 18.6 *does* illustrate that as the level of objective achievement increases, the associated costs frequently increase at a much more rapid rate. Objective-level studies do not directly measure program benefits, but they do measure intermediate program outputs or objectives. This may give the decision maker the information needed to make more rational decisions. For example, it may be clear that the $2.5 billion expenditure needed to reduce emissions to 20 percent of their 1998 levels is reasonable. It may be far less clear whether an additional 19-percent (from 20 percent to 1 percent) emissions reduction is worth the required incremental expenditure of $137.5 billion ($140 billion less $2.5 billion).

Thus, in comparison to cost-benefit analyses, cost-effectiveness analyses provide less positive inputs on which economic decisions can be made. They furnish decision makers with disciplined studies relating program costs with some measurable but unvalued estimates of program outputs.

SUMMARY

- A *capital expenditure* is defined as a current outlay of funds that is expected to provide a flow of future cash benefits.
- The capital expenditure decision process should consist of the following steps: generating alternative investment proposals, estimating cash flows, evaluating and choosing the projects to undertake, and reviewing the projects after implementation.
- The *internal rate of return (IRR)* is defined as the discount rate that equates the present value of the net cash flows from the project with the net investment. An investment project should be accepted (rejected) if its internal rate of return is greater than or equal to (less than) the firm's required rate of return (that is, cost of capital).
- The *net present value (NPV)* of an investment is defined as the present value of the net cash flows from the project, discounted at the firm's required rate of return (that is, cost of capital), minus the project's net investment. An investment project should be accepted (rejected) if its net present value is greater than or equal to (less than) zero.
- The *cost of capital* is defined as the cost of funds that are supplied to the firm. It is influenced by the riskiness of the firm, both in terms of its capital structure and its investment strategy.
- The after-tax cost of debt (issued at par) is equal to the coupon rate multiplied by 1 minus the firm's marginal tax rate.
- The cost of equity can be estimated using a number of different approaches, including the dividend valuation model and the capital asset pricing model.

- The weighted cost of capital is calculated by weighting the costs of specific sources of funds, such as debt and equity, by the proportions of each of the capital components in the firm's long-range target capital structure.
- *Cost-benefit analysis* is the public sector counterpart of capital budgeting techniques used in private sector resource-allocation decisions.
- Cost-benefit analysis involves the following steps:
  1. Determining the program objectives
  2. Enumerating the alternative means of achieving the objectives, subject to the legal, political, technological, budgetary, and other constraints that limit the scope of action
  3. Evaluating all primary, secondary, and intangible benefits and costs associated with each alternative
  4. Discounting the benefits and costs using a social discount rate to arrive at an overall measure of the desirability of each alternative (for example, benefit-cost ratio)
  5. Choosing (or recommending) the best alternative based on the overall measure of desirability and the relative magnitude of the nonquantifiable intangibles
- Because of the measurement problems arising from the intangible impacts and economic externalities of many public programs, cost-benefit analysis is most useful in comparing projects with similar objectives and similar magnitudes of intangibles and externalities.
- In cases where it is not feasible to place dollar values on final program outputs, *cost-effectiveness analysis* may be used. Cost-effectiveness analysis assumes *a priori* that the program objectives are worth achieving and focuses on the least-cost method of achieving them.

EXERCISES

1. A firm has the opportunity to invest in a project having an initial outlay of $20,000. Net cash inflows (before depreciation and taxes) are expected to be $5,000 per year for five years. The firm uses the straight-line depreciation method with a zero salvage value and has a (marginal) income-tax rate of 40 percent. The firm's cost of capital is 12 percent.
   a. Compute the following quantities:
      (i) Internal rate of return
      (ii) Net present value
   b. Should the firm accept or reject the project?

2. A machine that costs $12,000 is expected to operate for 10 years. The estimated salvage value at the end of 10 years is $0. The machine is expected to save the company $2,331 per year before taxes and depreciation. The company depreciates its assets on a straight-line basis and has a marginal tax rate of 40 percent. The firm's cost of capital is 14 percent. Based on the internal-rate-of-return criterion, should this machine be purchased?

3. A company is planning to invest $75,000 (before taxes) in a personnel training program. The $75,000 outlay will be charged off as an expense by the firm this year (Year 0). The returns estimated from the program in the form of greater

productivity and a reduction in employee turnover are as follows (on an after-tax basis):

Years 1–10: $7,500 per year

Years 11–20: $22,500 per year

The company has estimated its cost of capital to be 15 percent. Assume that the entire $75,000 is paid at time zero (the beginning of the project). The marginal tax rate for the firm is 40 percent.

Based on the net-present-value criterion, should the firm undertake the training program?

4. Alliance Manufacturing Company is considering the purchase of a new automated drill press to replace an older one. The machine now in operation has a book value of zero and a salvage value of zero. However, it is in good working condition with an expected life of 10 additional years. The new drill press is more efficient than the existing one and, if installed, will provide an estimated cost savings (in labor, materials, and maintenance) of $6,000 per year. The new machine costs $25,000 delivered and installed. It has an estimated useful life of 10 years, and a salvage value of $1,000 at the end of this period. The firm's cost of capital is 14 percent and its marginal income tax rate is 40 percent. The firm uses the straight-line depreciation method.

    a. What is the net cash flow in year zero (that is, initial outlay)?
    b. What are the net cash flows after taxes in each of the next 10 years?
    c. What is the net present value of the investment?
    d. Should Alliance replace its existing drill press?

5. Sam's Cleaners is considering opening a new store. The store will be owned by Sam and will cost $200,000 to build. It will be located on a piece of land that will be leased at a rate of $2,000 per year, payable at the end of each year. For planning purposes, the store is expected to have a maximum 20-year life. Cleaning equipment for the new store will cost an additional $40,000 and have an economic life of 20 years. The equipment will be depreciated on a straight-line basis to an estimated salvage value of $0 at the end of 20 years. The building will be depreciated on a straight-line basis to an estimated salvage value of $40,000.

    Operating revenues are expected to be $60,000 per year during the first 10 years. These revenues are expected to equal $100,000 per year for years 11–20. Cash operating costs, exclusive of lease payments, are expected to be $20,000 per year during the first 10 years of operation and to increase to $26,000 per year for years 11–20. The firm's marginal tax rate is 40 percent.

    a. Compute the net investment for the new cleaning store.
    b. Compute the annual net cash flows for the new cleaning store.
    c. Compute the project's net present value assuming a 12-percent cost of capital (required rate of return).
    d. Should Sam's Cleaners open the new store?

6. The Charlotte Hornets, a recent expansion basketball team, has been offered the opportunity to purchase the contract of an aging superstar basketball player from another team. The general manager of the Hornets wants to analyze the offer as a capital budgeting problem. The Hornets would have to pay the other team $800,000 to obtain the superstar. Being somewhat old, the basketball player is expected to be able to play for only four more years. The general

manager figures that attendance, and hence revenues, would increase substantially if the Hornets obtained the superstar. He estimates that *incremental* returns (additional ticket revenues less the superstar's salary) would be as follows over the four-year period:

Year	Incremental Returns
1	$450,000
2	350,000
3	275,000
4	200,000

The general manager has been told by the owners of the team that any capital expenditures must yield at least 12 percent after taxes. The firm's (marginal) income tax rate is 40 percent. Furthermore, a check of the tax regulations indicates that the team can depreciate the $800,000 initial expenditure over the four-year period.

a. Determine the following measures of the desirability of this investment:

  (i) Internal rate of return

  (ii) Net present value

b. Should the Hornets sign the superstar?

7. An acre planted with walnut trees is estimated to be worth $15,000 in 25 years. If you want to realize a 12-percent rate of return on your investment, how much can you afford to invest per acre? (Ignore all taxes and assume that annual cash outlays to maintain your stand of walnut trees are nil.)

8. Panhandle Industries, Inc. currently pays an annual common stock dividend of $2.20 per share. The company's dividend has grown steadily over the past 10 years at 8 percent per year; this growth trend is expected to continue for the foreseeable future. The company's present dividend payout ratio, also expected to continue, is 40 percent. In addition, the stock presently sells at eight times current earnings (that is, its "multiple" is 8).

Calculate the company's cost of equity capital using the dividend capitalization model approach.

9. Panhandle Industries, Inc. (see Exercise 8) stock has a beta, β, of 1.15 as computed by a leading investment service. The present risk-free rate is 7 percent, and the expected return on the stock market is 13 percent. Compute the company's cost of equity capital using the capital asset pricing model. How does this value compare with the one determined in Exercise 8 using the dividend capitalization model?

10. The Gordon Company currently pays an annual common stock dividend of $4.00 per share. Its dividend payments have been growing at a steady rate of 6 percent per year, and this rate of growth is expected to continue for the foreseeable future. Gordon's common stock is currently selling for $65.25 per share. The company can sell additional shares of common stock after flotation costs at a net price of $60.50 per share.

Based on the dividend capitalization model, determine the cost of

a. Internal equity (retained earnings)

b. External equity (new common stock)

11. Baker Manufacturing Company has a beta, β, estimated at 1.10. The risk-free rate is 6 percent and the expected market return is 12 percent. Compute the company's cost of equity capital.

12. The Williams Company has a present capital structure (that it considers optimal) consisting of 30-percent long-term debt and 70-percent common equity. The company plans to finance next year's capital budget with additional long-term debt and retained earnings. New debt can be issued at a coupon interest rate of 10 percent. The cost of retained earnings (internal equity) is estimated at 15 percent. The company's marginal tax rate is 40 percent.

    Calculate the company's weighted cost of capital for the coming year.

13. Several studies have reported very low private and social rates of return on an investment in securing (providing) graduate education in many disciplines. In spite of this evidence, an increasing number of schools have been offering advanced-level degrees. (Surprisingly, in spite of normative prescriptions of economic theory, economics falls into the category of these low-return disciplines.)

    a. How can you explain this seeming contradiction to an efficient allocation of societal resources?

    b. Can you suggest some alternatives that could help direct more resources away from low-return educational programs toward higher-return alternatives?

14. The state of Glottamora has $100 million remaining in its budget for the current year. One alternative is to give Glottamorans a one-time tax rebate. Alternatively, two proposals have been made for state expenditures of these funds.

    The first proposed project is to invest in a new power plant, costing $100 million and having an expected useful life of 20 years. Projected benefits accruing from this project are as follows:

Years	Benefits Per Year (Millions of Dollars)
1–5	$ 0
6–20	20

The second alternative is to undertake a job-retraining program, also costing $100 million and generating the following benefits:

Years	Benefits Per Year (Millions of Dollars)
1–5	$20
6–10	14
11–20	4

The state Power Department has argued that a 5-percent discount factor should be used in evaluating the projects, because that is the government's borrowing rate. The Human Resources Department suggests using a 12-percent rate, because that more nearly equals society's true opportunity rate.

a. What is implied by the various departments' desires to use different discount rates?

b. Evaluate the projects using both the 5-percent and the 12-percent rates.

c. What rate do you believe to be more appropriate?

d. Make a choice between the projects and the tax-refund alternative. Why did you choose the alternative you did?

15. The Department of Transportation wishes to choose between two alternative accident-prevention programs. It has identified three benefits to be gained from such programs:

- Reduced property damage, both to the vehicles involved in an accident and to other property (for example, real estate that may be damaged at the scene of an accident)
- Reduced injuries
- Reduced fatalities

The department's experts are willing to make dollar estimates of property damage savings that are expected to accrue from any program, but they will only estimate the number of injuries and fatalities that may be averted.

The first program is relatively moderate in its costs and will be concentrated in a large city. It involves upgrading traffic signals, improving road markers, and repaving some potholed streets. Because of the concentration and value of property in the city, savings from reduced property damage are expected to be substantial. Likewise, a moderate number of traffic-related deaths and injuries could be avoided.

The second program is more ambitious. It involves straightening long sections of dangerous rural roads and installing improved guardrails. Although the property damage savings are expected to be small in relation to total cost, the reduction in traffic-related deaths and injuries should be substantial.

The following table summarizes the expected costs and payoffs of the two programs:

Year	1	2	3	4	Total
Alternative #1					
Cost ($000)	200	200	100	50	550
Reduced property damage ($000)	50	100	250	100	500
Lives saved	60	40	35	25	160
Injuries prevented	500	425	300	150	1,375
Alternative #2					
Cost ($000)	700	1,800	1,100	700	4,300
Reduced property damage ($000)	150	225	475	300	1,150
Lives saved	50	75	100	125	350
Injuries prevented	800	850	900	900	3,450

Assume that a 10-percent discount rate is appropriate for evaluating government programs:

a. Calculate the net present costs of the two programs.

b. Generate any other tables that you may find useful in choosing between the programs.

c. Can you arrive at any unambiguous choice between the two alternatives? What factors are likely to weigh on the ultimate choice made?

16. One study completed for the American Enterprise Institute estimated the cost per life saved in several programs supported or mandated by the government. The following results were reported:

Estimates of cost per life saved	
Recommended for cost-benefit analysis by the National Safety Council for traffic safety	$37,500
Kidney dialysis at home	$99,000
Instructions to military pilots on when to crash-land airplanes	$270,000
Consumer Product Safety Commission's proposed lawn mower safety standards	$240,000 to $1,920,000
OSHA-proposed acrylonitrile exposure standard	$1,963,000 to $624,976,000
OSHA coke-oven emission standard	$4,500,000 to $158,000,000

Other analyses have indicated that a proposed plan to further reduce carbon monoxide auto emissions would cost $1 billion in increased costs of production and costs to the consumer and that the plan would prolong two lives in 20 years. This could be compared with the $200 it would cost to prevent each of 24,000 premature deaths per year by installing cardiac care units in ambulances.

Some studies of the value of a human life have computed an implicit value in the range of $200,000 to $700,000. These studies have examined wage differentials for hazardous jobs and provided estimates of what people are willing to pay for a small decrease in risk.

a. Given these estimates of the value of a human life, which of the programs discussed do you think should be pursued?

b. How can you explain the actions of a mine operator who may spend $5 million to free a trapped miner?

17. Capital budgeting has been discussed in the context of a profit-maximizing firm, and some argue that many of the same tools can be applied to government budget planning and analysis. To learn more about proposed legislation to utilize capital budgeting for the federal government, access the following Internet site: http://www.house.gov/wise/tcapbud.htm. What are the elements of HR 1233? How are the concepts of capital budgeting applied to government? In what ways are they different from those of a profit-maximizing firm? Can you see any possible controversies over what constitutes government investment?

http://
Capital Budgeting for the
Federal Government

CASE EXERCISES

COST-BENEFIT ANALYSIS[32]

The Michigan State Fairgrounds is centrally located in the Detroit Standard Metropolitan Statistical Area (SMSA), which consists of Wayne, Oakland, and Macomb counties. The population within the SMSA numbered 4,197,931 persons in 2000—over 47 percent of the state's total population. More than 59 percent and 75 percent of the state's population reside within 60 and 100 miles, respectively, of the fairground site. The site is located near an efficient freeway system that connects many areas of the state. The State Fairgrounds is operated by the Agriculture Department and is in a deplorable state of disrepair. Costs have exceeded revenues by a substantial margin every year in the recent past. A redevelopment program has been proposed for the fairgrounds that would serve several purposes:

1. Revitalization of the fairgrounds would prevent further economic deterioration of the existing facilities, increase attendance and consequently revenues, and perhaps make the fairgrounds an economically viable entity.

2. A further benefit to be realized would be an economic stimulus to the area resulting from increased employment from the initial construction program, as well as increased revenues realized from the additional business that the proposed new facilities would generate.

3. Finally, aesthetic value could be realized from the upgrading and redevelopment of what is currently a marginal area of the city.

The redevelopment program would consist of the overall rehabilitation of the grounds and buildings as well as the construction of several income-producing buildings, including a hotel and convention facility and a dog track (providing dog racing is legalized in Michigan and the fairgrounds can obtain the necessary license). Either a new coliseum would be constructed or the present one redesigned and refurbished. The cost of the redevelopment program would be $20 million. Construction would take three years with 50 percent of the cost incurred in year 0, 30 percent in year 1, and 20 percent in year 2. The redevelopment program would require funding by the state and/or federal government. The following estimated benefits would be derived from the project:

1. *Initial construction benefits.* Previous studies showed that 38 worker-years of employment are derived from each $1 million in construction. Assuming an hourly rate of $6, 40 hours per week, and 50 weeks per year, and relating this to the $20 million cost of the redevelopment program, results in $9,120,000 of economic benefit to be derived through increased employment. Like the construction costs, these benefits would be spread over three years ($4.560 million in year 0, $2.736 million in year 1, and $1.824 million in year 2).

2. *Coliseum.* An appropriate coliseum facility could generate, in excess of current levels, an additional $500,000 annually (years 3–20) from shows and events not currently available in the Detroit area.

3. *Increased state fair attendance.* With improved facilities (such as those planned in the redevelopment program), annual attendance at the state fair is expected to increase from 700,000 presently to 1,000,000 people. Assuming present per capita expenditures ($3.33) at the Michigan State Fair,

---

[32] Adapted from an unpublished paper by Eric Hartshom of Wayne State University, "Cost-Benefit Analysis Concerning the Proposed Redevelopment Program for the Michigan State Fairgrounds."

the increased attendance would result in an additional $1 million in revenue annually (years 3–20).

4. *Convention and hotel facility.* It is estimated that a 200-room hotel, convention, and dining facility located at the fairgrounds would generate nearly $1.5 million in additional revenue annually (years 3–20).

5. *Dog-racing track.* It is estimated that an average dog-racing facility will produce $1.5 million in revenue annually. However, it must be realized that dog racing is similar to horse racing, and it is expected that a portion of the revenues generated by a dog track would be realized owing to a transfer of funds from local horse-racing facilities. Because this transfer of funds should not be considered in the analysis, it would be assumed that one-third of the dog-racing revenues will result from the redistribution of funds from local horse-racing tracks. Consequently only $1 million in annual revenues (years 3–20) will be attributed to the proposed dog-racing track.

Type of Cost or Benefit	Year(s)	Annual Benefit (+) or Cost (−) ($ Million)
Construction outlay	0	$−10.000
Construction outlay	1	−6.000
Construction outlay	2	−4.000
Increased employment	0	+4.560
Increased employment	1	+2.736
Increased employment	2	+1.824
Coliseum	3−20	+0.500
State Fair attendance	3−20	+1.000
Convention and hotel facility	3−20	+1.500
Dog-racing track	3−20	+1.000

The costs and benefits of the proposed redevelopment are summarized in the above table. Assume that a 10-percent interest rate is appropriate for discounting the costs and benefits of the proposed project.

QUESTIONS

1. Determine the benefit-cost ratio (defined as the ratio of discounted benefits to costs) for the proposed fairground development.

2. Based on this analysis, should the redevelopment program be undertaken?

3. List some of the secondary benefits and costs, as well as intangibles, associated with the project.

   In calculating the benefits of the fairground redevelopment program, increased employment opportunities were included.

4. What assumption about employment in the Detroit area must be made in associating these benefits with the project?

5. Recalculate the benefit-cost ratio, assuming that these benefits are not included in the analysis. How does this affect the desirability of the project?

In calculating the benefits of the fairground redevelopment project, it was assumed that $1.5 million in additional annual revenue would be generated from the convention and hotel facility.

6. What assumption is being made about the effects of this facility on other hotel and convention facilities? Is this a realistic assumption?

7. Suppose that only $500,000 of the facility's annual revenues can be attributed to "new" convention and hotel business. Recalculate the benefit-cost ratio under this assumption (also exclude employment benefits). How does this affect the desirability of the project?

8. Suppose that the fairground is unable to obtain a license to operate a dog-racing track. Assume that construction costs are reduced by 15 percent if a dog-racing track is not built. Recompute the benefit-cost ratio under this assumption (also exclude employment and convention facility benefits). How does this affect the desirability of the proposed redevelopment project?

INDUSTRIAL DEVELOPMENT TAX RELIEF AND INCENTIVES

Tax relief competition between states seeking high-paying industrial jobs threatens to overpay for any conceivable net benefits. In 1993, Alabama paid over $300 million in highway, rail, sewer and other infrastructure investments to obtain a $300-million Mercedes plant with 1,500 jobs. In 1998, North Carolina agreed to build a new runway for $130 million and provide job training and tax breaks worth another $142.3 million to obtain a $300-million FedEx hub.

QUESTIONS

1. Assess the likely benefits of such a plant or hub and how one should go about analyzing them.

2. What form might a report to the Industrial Development Commission take? Outline the requisite components.

Decisions Under Risk and Uncertainty

CHAPTER PREVIEW   In Chapters 1 and 2, shareholder wealth was shown to be a function of both expected returns and risk. In general, investors will place a higher value on a more certain future stream of cash flows and devalue less certain cash flows. In this chapter we develop approaches for making decisions under risk and uncertainty, and examine techniques designed to manage risk. These techniques vary from, at one extreme, insurance and hedging, which lay off the risk to third parties for some certain prearranged cost, to, at the other extreme, scenario planning wherein companies make plans to gauge and absorb risk themselves.

MANAGERIAL CHALLENGE

Multigenerational Effects of Ozone Depletion and Greenhouse Gases[1]

The long-term effects of ozone depletion from chlorofluorocarbon (CFC) emissions and of CO_2 and other greenhouse gases from the burning of fossil fuels are controversial. Some scientists insist that the release of CFCs has opened a gaping hole in the ozone shield that provides protection from UV rays and that the increasing concentration of greenhouse gases has raised global temperatures. What is less controversial is that these environmental events have massive consequences for human health and wealth. Increasing incidence of skin cancers in Antarctica and Australia and a rising sea level imply tangible losses of catastrophic proportions—perhaps many billions of dollars annually. Some of these losses are immediate, but others are perhaps 250 years off. Benefit-cost analysis normally considers projects no more than 20 to 30 years long and employs discount rates of 2 percent to 7 percent. How should one discount such an uncertain and distant future as is involved in ozone depletion and greenhouse gases?

Assuming a constant discount rate equal to the rate of return on long-term government bonds (5.3 percent), the discount factor that should be applied to find the present value of projected benefits or losses avoided in year 250 would be $(1/1.053^{250})$ = .0000025 or $2.47 present value per million dollars of future losses avoided. Notice what happens, however, if uncertainty about the appropriate discount rate varies from 2 percent to 7 percent. The discount factor at 250 years would then vary from $(1/1.02^{250})$ = .00707875848 or $7,078 per million dollars for 2 percent, to as little as $(1/1.07^{250})$ = .00000005, one nickel per million dollars for 7 percent. The possibility of lower discount rates implies

that $707.8 million dollars should be spent today to avoid the projected $100 billion in delayed damage 250 years from now! Of course, the higher 7 percent rate implies spending just $500 to avoid the $100-billion future loss. This range of present value estimates from $500 to $707,875,848 is beyond what any analyst can work with in doing sensitivity analysis. What should a benefit-cost analyst conclude? And what should a business whose cash flows are dependent on "fun in the sun" recreation or physical assets built near sea level conclude?

One approach would be to assume that the outside estimates are equally likely and work with the average of the $500 and $707,875,848 estimates. Notice, however, that this implies a discount factor of (.00707876348/2) = .00353938174, or $353,938,174 per $100 billion, that reflects discounting with a surprisingly low 2.28 percent rate—i.e., $(1/1.022832^{250})$ = .0035393. That is, the equal probability of lower and higher discount rates implies a discount factor 1416 times bigger than the discount factor implied by a constant discount rate at 5.3 percent (i.e., .00353938174/ .0000025 = 1416). It's even 213 times bigger than the discount factor implied by a constant discount rate of 4.5 percent, the average of the 2 percent and 7 percent rates. How can this be, since any discount rate lower than average has an equally higher-than-average offsetting rate in the calculation? In

---

[1] Based on Richard Newell and William Pizer, "Discounting the Benefits of Climate Change Mitigation," Resources for the Future, December 2001, and Martin Weitzman, "Gamma Discounting," *American Economic Review,* March 2001.

MANAGERIAL CHALLENGE

short, the answer is that the higher rate scenarios discount themselves back to essentially zero and therefore enter the present value calculation with negligible weights, thereby guaranteeing that the lower-rate scenarios predominate in the calculation. The insight is that it's not the average discount rate (4.5 percent) that matters in such circumstances, just as the average depth of a pool does not determine the hazard to someone who cannot swim. Instead, the lowest applicable discount rate largely determines the present value of very long cash flow streams.

Martin Weitzman has calculated what discount factor is implied by assuming the discount rate begins at 4 percent and then follows a random path with equiprobable higher and lower rates and a standard deviation of 3 percent. The results led him

to recommend a constant sliding scale discount rate of 2 percent for 25- to 75-year cash flows, *and only 1 percent for 76- to 300-year cash flows* to account for discount rate uncertainty. The fact that higher and lower discount rates have such dramatically nonsymmetric effects on present value when very distant benefits are involved means that valuation may be much higher than previously thought. Richard Newell and William Pizer found that the value of reducing CO_2 emissions and other greenhouse gases rose from $6 to $10 per ton when a random walk procedure like Weitzman's was used to determine the appropriate discount rate. This 50-percent increase reflects the fundamental insight that the greater the proportion of distant future benefits in a cash flow stream, the more pivotal it is to account for discount rate uncertainty.

RISK AND DECISION ANALYSIS[2]

A commonly used classification scheme for decision analysis divides situations according to whether a decision is made by (i) an individual or (ii) a group, and according to whether it is made under conditions of (a) certainty, (b) risk, (c) uncertainty, or (d) unknowingness.

The distinction between an individual and a group is based on the compatibility of the objectives or interests of the participants in the decision-making situation. If all the participants share the same underlying objectives, then the decision problem can be analyzed *as if* the decision were going to be made by one individual. If, however, conflict exists between the objectives of two or more participants, then the decision-making situation would be analyzed as one of group decision making. A group decision-making situation is analyzed using the techniques of cooperative *game theory* discussed in Chapters 13 and 16.

The classification of decision-making problems among the certainty, risk, uncertainty, and unknowingness categories is determined by the players' knowledge of the possible outcomes. Define a situation to be decision making under

Risk
A decision-making situation in which the decision maker can specify the probabilities of occurrence of the various outcomes.

1. *Certainty* if each action is known to lead invariably to a specific outcome;
2. **Risk** if each action leads to one of a set of possible specific outcomes, each outcome occurring with a known probability;

---

[2] The next several paragraphs and the example appeared initially in the discussion of decision making under risk in Chapter 2. You may wish to review the measurement of risk, decision making under risk, and the concept of risk and return in that chapter.

Example

Auto Thefts of Jeep Wrangler Top Actuarial List[3]

The typical auto owner is averse to having his or her stream of consumption benefits from transportation wiped out. This risk of ruin cannot be offset by an equiprobable windfall gain. Consequently, risk-averse asset owners buy auto theft insurance—i.e., they pay a third-party insurer the expected loss plus a small sum for "bearing the risk." The actuarial profession arose to develop the probabilities required to calculate the size of this expected loss. For the average $15,000 American auto in 1998, the modest sum of $22.80 was sufficient to obtain annual auto theft insurance. This insurance premium implies that such cars were stolen approximately 1.5 times per 1000 per year ($0.00152 \times \$15,000 = \$22.80$). For some vehicles, however, the relative frequency of theft was much higher. The Jeep Wrangler sport utility vehicles were stolen with a relative frequency of 20.6 per 1000 per year or about one in fifty! Toyota Land Cruisers were stolen almost as often (17.4 per 1000 per year), and since the loss exposure was well over $30,000, Land Cruisers cost $530 per year to insure against theft. Extensive actuarial data on probabilities determines the amount required to cover the risk.

Uncertainty
A decision-making situation in which the decision maker is either unable or unwilling to specify the probabilities of occurrence of the possible outcomes of the decision.

3. **Uncertainty** if each action has as its consequence a set of possible specific outcomes, the probabilities of which are unknown; or
4. *Unknowingness* if each action has unknown consequences, the outcomes of which cannot be determined.

In this chapter, we present various approaches to decision making under risk; these approaches entail analyzing expected marginal utility, prospect theory, decision trees, risk-adjusted discount rates, scenario planning, and simulation models.

Expected Marginal Utility Approach

In decision problems whose uncertain possible outcomes constitute monetary payoffs (that is, dollars) with known probabilities of occurrence, it has been observed that a simple preference for higher dollar amounts is not sufficient to explain the choices made by many individuals. The classic example, known as the St. Petersburg paradox, was formulated by the 17th-century mathematician D. Bernoulli and illustrates the dilemma. The paradox consists of a gamble in which a "fair" coin—that is, a coin in which the probability of a head and tail is one half—is tossed until the *first head* appears. The player receives or wins 2^n dollars when the first head appears on the *n*th toss. The question is: How much should the player be willing to pay to participate in this gamble (that is, how much should the player be willing to wager)? The *expected monetary value* EMV of such a gamble is infinite.[4] Therefore, based on the criterion of expected monetary value, the individual should be willing to

---

[3] Based on Highway Loss Data Institute, *Report on Auto Theft 1998*.

[4] This statement can be demonstrated as follows:

$EMV = P(\text{1st head on 1st toss}) \times 2^1 + P(\text{1st head on 2nd toss}) \times 2^2 +$

$P(\text{1st head on 3rd toss}) \times 2^3 + \ldots$

$= \left(\frac{1}{2}\right)^1 \times 2^1 + \left(\frac{1}{2}\right)^2 \times 2^2 + \left(\frac{1}{2}\right)^3 \times 2^3 + \ldots$

$= 1 + 1 + 1 + \ldots$

EMV constitutes the sum of an infinite series of 1s.

wager everything he or she owns in return for the chance to receive 2^n dollars. Because most individuals refuse such all-or-nothing wagers, we conclude that the expected monetary value of the possible outcomes of the gamble is not the only objective. Other commonly observed examples of behavior that do not maximize expected monetary value are portfolio diversification and the simultaneous purchase of lottery tickets and insurance.

If we reject maximization of expected monetary value as a valid guide in decision problems involving risky outcomes, what then is the proper criterion? In their pioneering work, Von Neumann and Morgenstern constructed a framework based on the assessment of the "utilities" of the outcomes[5] which provides an answer to this question.[6] Within their framework it can be shown that the *maximization of expected utility* criterion will yield decisions that are in accord with the individual's true preferences. **Expected utility** is calculated by summing, over all the possible outcomes that may result from a decision, the product of the utility of each outcome, U_i, times its respective probability of occurrence, P_i, as follows:

Expected Utility
The product of the utility of each outcome times its respective probability of occurrence, summed over all possible outcomes.

$$E(U) = \sum_{i=1}^{n} U_i \times P_i \qquad\qquad [19.1]$$

http://

Access the Decision Analysis Society, a subdivision of the Institute for Operations Research and the Management Sciences, at http://www.fuqua.duke.edu/faculty/daweb

Let us illustrate how to use utilities and the maximization of expected utility criterion in decision problems involving risk. Suppose an entrepreneur has developed a new and untested product and is considering whether to invest some capital in an effort to market the product. Extensive studies of the marketing of products belonging to the same general category as this one have shown that 20 percent are successful and the remainder (that is, 80 percent) are failures. Because a subcontractor can be employed to manufacture the product, no investment in production facilities is required. The entrepreneur has determined that the cost of producing and marketing a batch of the product will be $40,000. If the marketing effort is successful, a profit of $160,000 will result. Suppose further that the product can be easily copied, and subsequent competition will therefore limit the profitable sales of the product to the initial production run. If the product is not initially successful and the marketing effort fails, the entrepreneur's loss will be limited to the initial $40,000 investment.

The basic characteristics of the decision problem can be summarized in a payoff table format such as Figure 19.1, where the various alternative actions (that is, decisions) are listed down the left-hand side of the payoff table, the various states of nature are listed across the top of the payoff table, and the various outcomes (that is, dollar payoffs) are listed in the payoff table for each action/state-of-nature combination. Note that the decision "Do Not Invest in Product" results in a zero return or payoff, regardless of the state of nature. The probability of occurrence of each state of nature is shown in the row below the payoff table.

The expected monetary value of the decision to "Invest in Product" is

$$EMV_1 = \$160,000 \times .20 + (-\$40,000) \times .80 = \$0$$

---

[5] *Utility* is defined as the satisfaction an individual receives from a good (or combination of goods). The term *good* can refer to a commodity (such as bread), a service (such as haircuts), or, as in the discussion in this section, wealth (money).

[6] See John von Neumann and Oskar Morgenstern, *Theory of Games and Economic Behavior*, 3d ed. (Princeton, NJ: Princeton University Press, 1953), pp. 15–30, especially pp. 26–27. Their framework consists of a series of axioms that imply the existence of a utility function. These axioms in turn yield a theorem concerning an individual's preferences for combinations of risky outcomes.

Figure 19.1   Payoff Table for Investment Decision Problem

		States of Nature	
		Product Is Successful	Product Is a Failure
Alternative Actions (Decisions)	Invest in Product	$160,000	–$40,000
	Do Not Invest in Product	0	0
	Probability of occurrence	.20	.80

and for the decision "Do Not Invest" it is

$$EMV_2 = 0 \times .20 + 0 \times .80 = \$0$$

Therefore, based on the maximization of expected monetary value criterion, the entrepreneur would be *indifferent* to the two alternative actions in this problem.

Let us now introduce the entrepreneur's utility function for wealth (money) into the decision-making framework and see how it affects preference for the two alternative actions.

Case I   Assume that the entrepreneur has a utility function (like Figure 19.2) that is characterized by *diminishing marginal utility* for money. *Marginal utility* measures the satisfaction the individual receives from a given incremental change in wealth. Marginal utility is given by the *slope* of the utility function at any point on the curve.

$$\text{Marginal utility} = \text{Slope} = \frac{\Delta U(M)}{\Delta M} \qquad [19.2]$$

Diminishing marginal utility indicates that the slope of the utility function is *decreasing* as the stock of money (that is, wealth) increases. It means that as an individual's wealth increases, that individual receives *less additional satisfaction* from each equal increment of wealth.

By Equation 19.2, the expected utility, based on the utility function in Figure 19.2 of the decision to "Invest in Product," is

$$E(U_1) = U(\$160,000) \times .20 + U(-\$40,000) \times .80$$
$$= .375 \times .20 + (-.50) \times .80 = -.325$$

and for the decision "Do Not Invest" it is

$$E(U_2) = U(0) \times .20 + U(0) \times .80$$
$$= 0 \times .20 + 0 \times .80 = 0$$

Figure 19.2   Utility Function Exhibiting Diminishing Marginal Utility

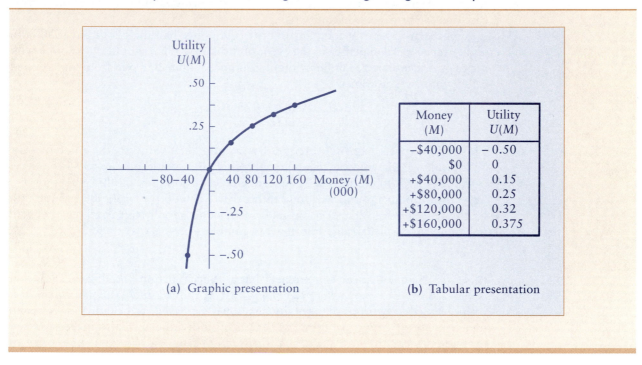

Money (M)	Utility U(M)
−$40,000	− 0.50
$0	0
+$40,000	0.15
+$80,000	0.25
+$120,000	0.32
+$160,000	0.375

(a) Graphic presentation   (b) Tabular presentation

The decision "Do Not Invest" has a higher expected utility. Therefore, based on the maximization of expected utility criterion, the entrepreneur would decide *not* to invest in the new product.

In terms of expected value, the investment is fair because, as was shown earlier, it has an expected monetary value of zero. An individual who, because of a diminishing marginal utility for money, exhibits a definite preference for *not* undertaking fair investments such as this one is said to be *risk averse*, or to have an aversion to risk.

Example

WHY BUY DISABILITY INSURANCE?

In some sense, life's always a gamble. When someone chooses the commercial jet pilot profession, the monetary rewards are great, but so too is the stress. Hour upon hour of routine boredom can be punctuated by momentary bouts of sheer terror. The stress causes health problems, any one of which can disqualify a pilot from flying. If jet pilots make a $260,000 salary with probability 0.8 and face permanent total disability and $40,000 of health care expenses with probability 0.2, then the *EMV* for pilots is $120,000. Referring to the table in Figure 19.2, the expected utility of the job and its health risks without (w/o) disability insurance is then

$$E(U_{w/o}) = 0.2 \times (-.50) + 0.8 \times (+.375)$$
$$= -.10 + .30$$
$$= .20$$

The pilot has an expected utility of 0.2, which is equivalent (again referring to the table in Figure 19.2) to a monetary value of, say, $68,000. That is,

$$MV(EU_{w/o}) = \$68,000 < \$120,000 = EMV$$

which reflects a risk-averse individual facing enormous income variation, in this case due to permanent disability risk.

Suppose an insurance company offers to guarantee half the pilot's pay ($80,000) and cover medical expenses in the event of disability. What would the pilot be willing to pay? The expected utility without insurance is quite different from the expected utility with (w/) insurance:

$$E(U_{w/}) = 0.2 \times (.25) + 0.8 \times (.375)$$
$$= 0.35$$

This 0.35 expected utility outcome has a monetary value to the pilot of, say, $145,000. So, to avoid the disability risk, this pilot would pay up to $145,000 − $68,000 = $77,000 to have a 20 percent chance of losing $80,000 (−$160,000 + $80,000 disability insurance payout) rather than $120,000 (−$160,000 + $40,000). Not only will risk-averse decision-makers reject actuarially fair gambles, they will pay more than is actuarially fair to avoid gambles—in this case, much more.[7]

Case II   Assume that the entrepreneur has a utility function (like Figure 19.3) that is characterized by *increasing marginal utility* for money. *Increasing marginal utility* indicates that the slope of the utility function is increasing as the individual's wealth increases. In other words, it means that as an individual's wealth increases, that individual receives *more additional satisfaction* from each (equal) increment of wealth.

Figure 19.3   Utility Function Exhibiting Increasing Marginal Utility

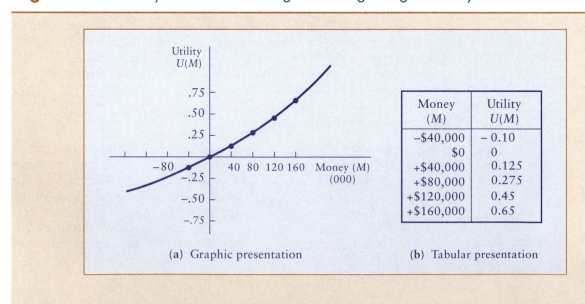

Money (M)	Utility U(M)
−$40,000	− 0.10
$0	0
+$40,000	0.125
+$80,000	0.275
+$120,000	0.45
+$160,000	0.65

(a) Graphic presentation   (b) Tabular presentation

[7] Nevertheless, competition in the disability insurance market will force the price of this policy down to something quite close to the expected cost of providing the insurance, $24,000.

Based on the utility function in Figure 19.3, the expected utility of the decision to "Invest in the Product" is

$$E(U_1) = U(\$160,000) \times 0.20 + U(-\$40,000) \times 0.80$$
$$= 0.65 \times 0.20 + (-0.10) \times 0.80 = +0.05$$

and for the decision "Do Not Invest," it is the same as in the preceding diminishing marginal utility case; that is, $E(U_2) = 0$. Therefore, the optimal decision, based on the maximization of expected utility criterion, would be *to invest* in the product.

An individual who, because of an increasing marginal utility for money, has a definite preference for undertaking actuarially fair investments such as this one is said to be a *risk preferrer* or to have a preference for risk. This individual undertakes, indeed seeks out, actuarially unfair gambles if the upside rewards are large enough (as in most lotteries).

Case III   Assume that the entrepreneur has a *linear* utility function (see Figure 19.4). In other words, the individual has a *constant marginal utility* for money, indicating that as wealth increases, the individual receives the *same additional satisfaction* from each given (equal) increment of wealth.

Although we will not illustrate the calculations for this case, it can be demonstrated that the expected utilities of the decisions to both "Invest in Product" and "Do Not Invest" are zero. Therefore, the entrepreneur with a linear utility function would be indifferent to the two alternative actions when seeking to maximize expected utility and would be said to be *risk neutral*. This individual makes decisions identical to those chosen by a person maximizing expected monetary value (EMV) alone.

In summary, we see that individuals' attitudes toward risk affect the shape of their utility functions and determine the alternatives that will be chosen in decision problems involving risk. Further analysis of utility theory has led to advances in marketing (prospect theory) and in auction design, which is discussed in Chapter 16.

Figure 19.4   Utility Function Exhibiting Constant Marginal Utility

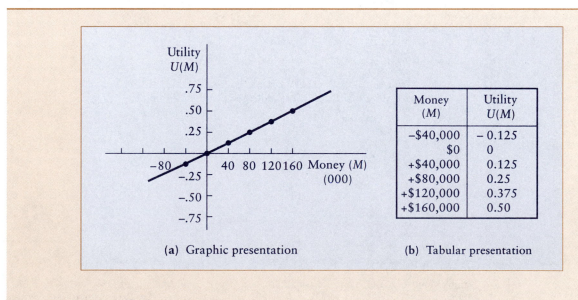

Money (M)	Utility U(M)
−$40,000	− 0.125
$0	0
+$40,000	0.125
+$80,000	0.25
+$120,000	0.375
+$160,000	0.50

(a) Graphic presentation   (b) Tabular presentation

Prospect Theory

Researchers have long noticed that several aspects of observed decision making under risk are inconsistent with any one of the above utility functions. For example, Milton Friedman and Leonard Savage suggested that some individuals buy both lottery tickets and disability insurance because of hybrid utility functions. Decision makers could be risk averse in some income ranges and risk preferring in others.

Social psychologists Daniel Kahneman and Amos Tversky hypothesized that decision makers were risk preferring at wealth levels below their current position and risk averse above (as in Figure 19.5).[8] This shape of the utility function agreed with the observation that the absolute value of utility losses was greater, often much greater, than an equal-value utility gain. Illustrated in a product category like minivans, the observation is that a household contemplating an SE model for $22,000 will perceive the decline in satisfaction or perceived value in dropping down to a $17,000 base model minivan (−160 utiles) as much greater than the increase in satisfaction (+100 utiles) associated with giving up another $5,000 to purchase a $27,000 LE model. The fact that perceived losses outweigh equal-value perceived potential gains reflects simply the diminishing marginal utility of income spent on the product above the current expenditure and the increasing marginal utility of money below the current expenditure. In short, anticipating prospective gains is less satisfying than avoiding losses.

Figure 19.5   Hybrid Utility Function Motivates Full-Line Forcing

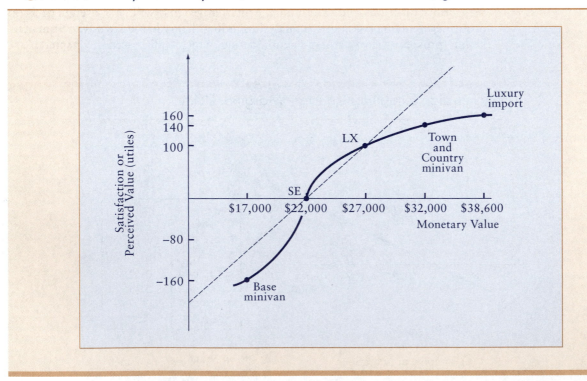

[8] Daniel Kahneman and Amos Tversky, "Prospect Theory: An Analysis of Decision under Risk," *Econometrica,* 47, no. 2 (March 1979), pp. 263–291; and Colin Camerer, "An Experimental Test of Several Generalized Utility Theories," *Journal of Risk and Uncertainty* 2, no. 1 (April 1989), pp. 61–104.

Many implications for marketing arise from this prospect theory. For one thing, firms are well advised to distribute trial products ("try now, pay later") because the utility loss if the consumer returns the product and owes nothing will be greater than the utility gained by prospective additional consumption with the money saved. Second, firms are well advised to ask consumers to forgo something prospective to pay for their product—i.e., a projected year-end bonus, tax refund, or frequent flyer award. Again, the payment in prospective additional consumption forgone will be perceived as less than an equivalent cash payment necessitating forgoing current consumption. Finally, firms with good-quality house brands should encourage premium brands in the channel, and those with premium brands should encourage the introduction of super-premium brands. If none exist, firms are advised to develop their own and force them into the channel.

Hanes, Kodak, Kroger, and many other firms pursue this "good, better, best" product strategy, sometimes called full-line forcing. Think of Marriott with its Fairfield Inns, Courtyard by Marriott, Marriott Resorts, and Ritz-Carlton properties. Let's return to Figure 19.5 to see why full-line forcing works. Auto dealers face an especially difficult competitive environment with mobile customers, innumerable substitute makes and models, and Internet search engines comparing price discounts by competing dealers on a real-time basis. Moving their repeat-purchase customers up along a base-car-to-luxury-car product spectrum across the "customer for life" cycle is one key to the business. Another key is to avoid selling only base automobiles.

In Figure 19.5, stepping down from an SE model Dodge minivan to a base model saves a customer $5,000 but sacrifices 50 percent of the perceived value of the minivan product line (-160 out of 320 total). Spending another $5,000 to step up to an LX (luxury) model garners 30 percent ($+100/320$) of the product line's perceived value. Although the unit sales of the dealership do not change, the mere presence of the LX model drives such a customer to justify spending $5,000 to avoid the greater disutility of the base model while congratulating himself or herself for avoiding spending another $5,000 for a smaller relative increase in satisfaction to the LX. After providing high quality (and high margin) service and maintenance for the SE over several years, the dealership then plans to see that same customer back in the showroom eyeing the LX models. Again, full-line forcing can encourage the "upsell" to the $27,000 LX model. Saving $5,000 by continuing to purchase SEs will result in a 30-percent disutility of ($-100/320$), whereas purchasing the $5,000-more-expensive Town and Country model (in Figure 19.5) would increase satisfaction by only 40 utiles, 12.5 percent. Again, the careful shopper, after comparing marginal benefits and marginal costs, decides to go with the LX, and the dealership rejoices.

Example

FULL-LINE FORCING IN PENS, ASPIRIN, AND MULTIVITAMINS AT REVCO AND ECKERD

Perhaps the most amazing aspect of prospect theory for marketing is the extent to which retail market shares can be altered by the practice of full-line forcing. Eckerd and Revco fully control the distribution channel policy in their own drug stores. In-house store brands can be sold beside national brands. Suppose Revco Aspirin at $2.89 for 100 80-mg tablets secures a 30-percent market share against a generic aspirin product selling 100 80-mg tablets at $1.50. Revco can allocate additional shelf space to non-store-brand painkillers and chooses between Bayer Aspirin at $2.89 and Tylenol at $5.29. Not surprisingly, Revco Aspirin's market share falls if the cheaper Bayer product is introduced. But what is astounding is that, in case after case, introducing the Tylenol product raises Revco Aspirin sales to a 40-percent market share, reduces generic aspirin from 70 to 40 percent, and raises Tylenol to 20 percent.

Since some people have side effects from aspirin but not from Tylenol, a fairer comparison perhaps is to investigate the same experiment with absolutely identical multivitamins. Revco multivitamins at $3.29 per 100 tablets might again secure 30 percent of the market relative to generic multivitamins at $1.99 with 70 percent market share. Introducing One-A-Day brand multivitamins at $5.19 into the channel will actually raise the market share of Revco's product. That is, with the good-better-best product strategy, market shares might distribute as follows: 40 percent generic, 40 percent Revco, and 20 percent One-A-Day. The disutility of lost perceived consumption outweighs equal-value utility gains.

Decision Tree Approach

Decision problems involving a sequence of alternative actions and random events can also be analyzed using *decision trees*. For the earlier investment decision, a sequential version can be represented in the decision tree shown in Figure 19.6. In a decision tree, decision nodes (diamonds) are used to represent points at which the decision maker must choose among several alternative actions, and random state-of-nature nodes (circles with an N) are used to represent possible state-of-nature outcomes. At decision node ◊ are two decision branches (alternative actions)—Invest and Do Not Invest in product. At the state-of-nature nodes are two state-of-nature branches (outcomes)—product is a Success and product is a Failure. The probabilities are shown along each state-of-nature branch. The outcome or payoff is shown at the end of the branch. Using this information, we can calculate the expected monetary value for each decision branch and then select the one with the *largest* expected value or use some other criterion.

When a decision tree is constructed with multiple periods, it is possible to recognize the feedback from each branch of the tree into each future period. For exam-

Figure 19.6 Decision Tree for Investment Decision Problem

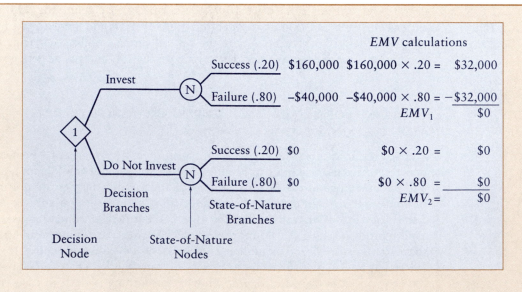

ple, if a firm invests in a new product, the success or failure of that product in Period 1 implies a great deal about its success or failure in future periods. If a product is successful during Period 1, the probability of future success is greatly enhanced. Accordingly, the prospect of success in Period 2 can be viewed as being closely correlated with the success in Period 1. Similarly, the prospect of success in Period 3 is enhanced if the product has been successful in Periods 1 and 2. These *conditional* probabilities can be explicitly incorporated into a multiperiod decision tree. The tools of sequential game theory from Chapter 13 can be especially valuable in these settings.[9]

Risk-Adjusted Discount Rate Approach

When making long-term capital budgeting (investment) decisions, the risk-adjusted discount rate approach is a commonly used method for dealing with the risk associated with future cash flow estimates. In the basic net present value decision-making model (which is described in more detail in Chapter 18), net present value (*NPV*) is defined as

$$NPV = \sum_{t=1}^{n} \frac{NCF_t}{(1 + k)^t} - NINV \qquad [19.3]$$

where NCF_t is the net cash flow in period t (for each of n periods). $NINV$ is the net investment, and k is the firm's *cost of capital*. An investment project is accepted if its NPV is greater than or equal to zero. In the risk-adjusted discount rate approach, the net cash flows for each project are discounted at a **risk-adjusted rate, k^***, rather than the firm's cost of capital (k). The magnitude of k^* depends on the risk of the project—the higher the risk, the higher is the risk-adjusted discount rate.

Risk-Adjusted Discount Rate
A discount rate that reflects the risk associated with a particular investment project.

The risk premiums (that is, $k^* - k$) applied to individual projects are commonly established *subjectively*. For example, some firms establish a small number of risk classes and then apply a different risk premium to each class. Average-risk projects, such as equipment replacement decisions, are evaluated at the firm's cost of capital; above-average-risk projects, such as facility expansions, might be assigned a risk premium of 3 percent above the firm's cost of capital; and high-risk projects, such as investments in totally new lines of business or the introduction of new products, might be assigned a risk premium of 8 percent above the firm's cost of capital. Because the risk premiums for each project are subjectively determined and no explicit consideration is given to the variation in cash flows of the project, this approach can lead to suboptimal decisions. In general, the risk-class method is most useful when evaluating relatively small projects that are frequently repeated. In these cases, much is known about the projects' potential returns, and it is probably not worth the effort to compute more "precise" risk premiums.

Example

RISK-ADJUSTED DISCOUNT RATE: HAMILTON BEACH/PROCTOR-SILEX, INC.

Hamilton Beach/Proctor-Silex has been offered a contract to supply private-label food processors to a regional discount store chain. The investment required for this project is $1 million. It is expected to produce annual net cash flows of $290,000 for a period of five years. Hamilton Beach/Proctor-Silex uses the risk-adjusted discount

---

[9] For more about what analytical tools are appropriate under risk, uncertainty, and unknowingness, see Hugh Courtney et. al., "Strategy Under Uncertainty," *Harvard Business Review,* November-December 1997, pp. 66–79.

rates shown in Table 19.1 when evaluating capital investment decisions. The risk premium (θ) for each risk class (determined subjectively) is added to the firm's cost of capital ($k = 12$ percent) to arrive at the risk-adjusted discount rate.

If the investment project (contract for food processors) is considered to be of average risk, then a risk-adjusted discount rate (k^*) of 12 percent is used in the discounted cash-flow analysis.

$$NPV = \sum_{t=1}^{5} \frac{\$290,000}{(1 + .12)^t} - \$1,000,000$$

$$= \$290,000(3.6048) - \$1,000,000$$

$$= +\$45,392$$

The *NPV* for the project at a discount rate of 12 percent is $45,392 and the project (contract) should be accepted.

However, if management decides that the project is of above-average risk and evaluates it at a rate (k^*) of 15 percent, the *NPV* is

$$NPV = \sum_{t=1}^{5} \frac{\$290,000}{(1 + .15)^t} - \$1,000,000$$

$$= \$290,000(3.3522) - \$1,000,000$$

$$= -\$27,862$$

Because the *NPV* of the project is negative at a 15-percent discount rate, it should *not* be accepted. Thus, the assessment of the project's risk affects its desirability (as measured by *NPV*) and determines whether it is accepted.

Simulation Approach

Simulation

A decision-making tool that models some event, such as cash flows from an investment project.

Computers have made it both feasible and relatively inexpensive to apply simulation techniques to economic decisions. **Simulation** is a planning tool that models some event. When simulation is used in capital budgeting, it requires that estimates be made of the probability distribution of each cash-flow element (revenues, expenses, and so on). If, for example, a firm is considering introducing a new product, the elements of a simulation might include the number of units sold, market price, unit

Table 19.1   Risk-Adjusted Discount Rates: Hamilton Beach/Proctor-Silex

Project Risk	Risk Premium (θ)	Risk-Adjusted Discount Rate ($k^* = k + \theta$)
Average risk	0%	12%
Above-average risk	3	15
High risk	8	20

production costs, unit selling costs, the cost of the machinery needed to produce the new product, and the cost of capital. These probability distributions are then put into the simulation model to compute the project's net present value probability distribution. In any period NCF_t may be computed as

$$NCF_t = [q(p) - q(c + s) - D](1 - t) + D \qquad [19.4]$$

where q is the number of units sold, p the selling price per unit, c the unit production cost (excluding depreciation), s the unit selling cost, D the annual depreciation, and t the firm's marginal tax rate. Using Equation 19.4 and the previously defined NPV equation (Equation 19.3), it is possible to simulate the net present value of the project. Based on the probability distribution of all the elements that influence the net present value, one value for each element is selected at random.

Example

INVESTMENT PROJECT SIMULATION: HOUSE OF CHOCOLATE, INC.

House of Chocolate is considering investing in a new mixing machine that costs $100,000 and has an expected life of 5 years. Annual depreciation (D) on the machine is $20,000 and the firm's marginal tax rate is 50 percent. Annual demand (q), selling price (p), unit production (c), and selling (s) costs are random variables.

Assume, for example, that the following values for the input variables are randomly chosen: $q = 20,000$; $p = \$10$; $c = \$2$; $s = \$1$. Inserting these values along with $D = \$20,000$ and $t = 50$ percent or 0.50 into Equation 19.4 gives the following:

$$
\begin{aligned}
NCF_t &= (20,000 \times \$10 - 20,000 \times \$3 - \$20,000)(1 - 0.50) + \$20,000 \\
&= (\$200,000 - \$60,000 - \$20,000) \times 0.50 + \$20,000 \\
&= \$80,000
\end{aligned}
$$

Given that the net investment is equal to the depreciable cost of the machinery ($100,000), that the net cash flows in each year of the project's life are identical, that $k = 10$ percent, and that the project has a 5-year life, the net present value of this particular iteration of the simulation can be computed as follows:

$$
\begin{aligned}
NPV &= \sum_{t=1}^{5} \frac{\$80,000}{(1 + 0.10)^t} - \$100,000 \\
&= \$80,000 \times 3.791 - \$100,000 \\
&= \$203,280
\end{aligned}
$$

In an actual simulation, an Excel computer program is run a number of different times using different randomly selected input variables in each instance. Thus the program can be said to be repeated, or *iterated*, and each run is termed an *iteration*. In each iteration the net present value for the project would be computed accordingly. Figure 19.7 illustrates a typical simulation approach.

The results of these iterations are then used to plot a probability distribution of the project's net present values and to compute a mean and a standard deviation of returns. This information provides the decision maker with an estimate of a project's expected returns as well as its risk. Given this information, it is possible to compute the probability of achieving a net present value that is greater or less than any particular value.

Figure 19.7   An Illustration of the Simulation Approach

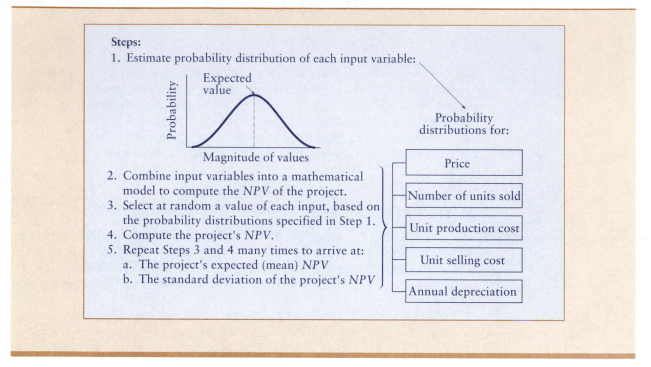

Steps:
1. Estimate probability distribution of each input variable:
2. Combine input variables into a mathematical model to compute the *NPV* of the project.
3. Select at random a value of each input, based on the probability distributions specified in Step 1.
4. Compute the project's *NPV*.
5. Repeat Steps 3 and 4 many times to arrive at:
   a. The project's expected (mean) *NPV*
   b. The standard deviation of the project's *NPV*

Probability distributions for:
Price
Number of units sold
Unit production cost
Unit selling cost
Annual depreciation

Example

INVESTMENT PROJECT SIMULATION: HOUSE OF CHOCOLATE, INC. (continued)

Assume that the simulation for the previously illustrated project results in a normal distribution with an expected net present value of $120,000 and a standard deviation of $60,000. The probability of the project having a net present value of $0 or less can now be found. The value of $0 is 2.0 standard deviations below the mean:

$$z = \frac{\$0 - \$120,000}{\$60,000}$$
$$= -2.0$$

It can be seen from Table 1 in Appendix B that the probability of a value less than 2.0 standard deviations below the mean is 2.28 percent. Thus there is a 2.28-percent chance that the actual net present value for this project will be negative. Figure 19.8 shows the probability distribution of this project's net present value. The shaded area under the curve represents the probability that the project will have a net present value of $0 or less.

The simulation approach is a powerful one because it explicitly recognizes all the interactions among the variables that influence the outcome. It provides both a mean and a standard deviation that can help the decision maker analyze trade-offs between risk and expected return. Unfortunately, considerable time and effort may be needed to gather the information for each of the input variables and to formulate the model correctly. This limits the feasibility of simulation to large projects. In

Figure 19.8   Illustration of the Probability That a Project's Returns Will Be Less Than $0; House of Chocolate, Inc.

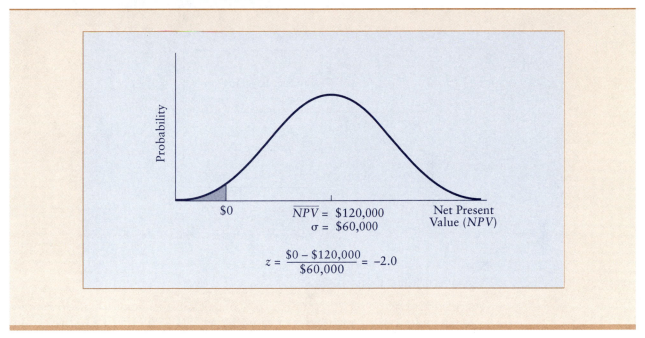

addition, the simulation example illustrated here assumed that the values of the input variables were independent of one another. If this is not true—if, for example, the price of a product has a large influence on the number sold—then this interaction must be incorporated into the model, introducing even more complexity.

DECISION MAKING UNDER UNCERTAINTY

Read about the history of decision making and decision analysis at the Arlington Software Corporation site: http://www.technology evaluation.com/arlingsoft. History_Decision_Making. pdf

Consider now a situation in which the decision maker is unable to specify the probabilities of occurrence for the various possible outcomes. Under these conditions, what is the appropriate decision criterion for choosing among the alternative actions in a decision problem? As we shall see in the following analysis, a number of different decision rules are available and no single best criterion can be specified.

To illustrate various proposed decisions criteria, consider again the investment decision example introduced earlier in the discussion of utility functions. Assume now that no information is available on the past success-failure rates for the marketing of similar types of products and that the entrepreneur is unable to furnish a subjective assessment of the chances of success and failure. Furthermore, assume that the entrepreneur's preferences for money are represented by the utility function shown in Figure 19.2. Using this utility function, the monetary payoffs of the investment decision problem shown in Figure 19.1 can be transformed into the utility values shown in Figure 19.9. The two decision criteria, which are illustrated in this section, are the *maximin* criterion and the *minimax regret* criterion.[10]

---

[10] Various other decision criteria have been proposed including investing optimally in additional information to resolve the uncertainty.

Figure 19.9   Utility (Payoff) Table for Investment Decision Problem

		States of Nature	
		S_1 Product Is a Success	S_2 Product Is a Failure
Alternative Actions	A_1 Invest in Product	.375	−.50
	A_2 Do Not Invest in Product	0	0

Maximin Criterion

The maximin criterion concentrates on the worst possible outcome (that is, *minimum* or smallest utility) across all states of nature associated with each alternative action. For Alternative A_1 ("Invest in Product"), the minimum utility in the first row of Figure 19.9 is −.50. Likewise, for Alternative A_2 ("Do Not Invest in Product"), the minimum utility in the second row is 0. With the maximin criterion, the alternative action having the *maximum* of these minimum utility values is chosen. Using this criterion, we would decide not to invest in the product (that is, Action A_2) because this alternative has the largest minimum utility value.

The maximin criterion is a very conservative decision-making rule because it evaluates alternative actions solely on the worst possible outcome associated with each action. Hypothetical decision problems can be constructed in which this criterion will yield choices that many critics find inappropriate or unreasonable.[11]

Minimax Regret Criterion

Regret measures the loss that results from choosing the incorrect alternative action for a given state of nature. The regret associated with an alternative action is the *difference* between the *best possible* payoff (or utility) that could have been received and the *actual* payoff (or utility) that is received. For example, consider the utility entries in Figure 19.9. Suppose S_1 is true (that is, the "Product Is a Success"). The regret associated with Alternative A_2 ("Do Not Invest In Product") is the difference between the largest utility in the S_1 column (that is, .375 for A_1) and the utility of A_2 in this column (that is, 0). Thus in the regret table shown in Figure 19.10, a value of .375 has been entered into the (A_2, S_1) positions. Clearly, there is no regret associated with Alternative A_1 ("Invest in Product"), because this is the correct decision when S_1 is true. Hence, a zero has been entered in the (A_1, S_1) position in Figure 19.10. Similar reasoning yields the regret values in the S_2 ("Product Is a Failure") column.

---

[11] See Luce and Raiffa, *op. cit.*, pp. 279–280, for an example of a decision-making situation that illustrates one of the problems associated with the maximin criterion.

Figure 19.10   Regret Table for Investment Decision Problem

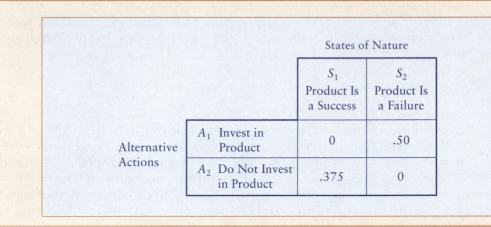

		States of Nature	
		S_1 Product Is a Success	S_2 Product Is a Failure
Alternative Actions	A_1 Invest in Product	0	.50
	A_2 Do Not Invest in Product	.375	0

Having specified the regret table, the *maximum* regret for each alternative action is determined. For A_1 the maximum regret (in Row 1) is .50. Similarly, for A_2 the maximum regret (in Row 2) is .375. The decision maker then chooses the alternative action having the *minimum* of these maximum regret values. In this case he or she would choose not to invest in the product (A_2), because this alternative has the smallest maximum regret value. Although this is the same action that was chosen previously using the maximin criterion, these two decision criteria often will not yield the same decisions in practice.

MANAGING RISK AND UNCERTAINTY

Many avenues are open to the manager who wishes to reduce the level of risk associated with a particular decision. In this section we briefly consider some of these strategies for managing risk and uncertainty.

Acquisition of Additional Information

http://
Read how the U.S. Department of the Interior applies risk management principles to mitigate risk to park visitors, employees, and public-trust resources at
http://www.mrps.doi.gov/

In many cases the uncertainty facing a manager arises because of a lack of information. For example, when making the decision to develop and market a new product, there is a considerable uncertainty regarding the market's acceptance of this new product. To reduce this decision to one involving risk, many firms will "test-market" the product in a limited area or present the product to panels of consumers for their evaluation. These surveys provide important information to the company as it seeks to assess the probable success of the new product in various product rollout scenarios.

Information can also be purchased from individuals or firms that possess the knowledge the decision maker seeks. For example, a wildcat oil drilling firm will employ the services of petroleum geologists as it attempts to determine where to drill exploratory wells. Similarly, companies that plan to sell new debt securities often pay to have their bonds "rated" by one of the bond rating services, such as Moody's or Standard and Poor's. The rating applied to the bonds reduce the risk of determining the yield that will have to be offered to investors when the bonds are sold.

Normally, additional information is costly. Hence, the wealth-maximizing firm is willing to pay for additional information as long as the marginal value of that information exceeds its marginal cost. For example, entering the Chinese perfume industry required Procter & Gamble to acquire valuable consulting expertise. Booz Allen Hamilton had the required knowledgeable personnel and was happy (for a price) to oblige.

Diversification

Diversification

The act of investing in a set of securities or assets having different risk-return characteristics.

Diversification is the act of investing in a set of securities or assets having different risk-return characteristics. By investing in diverse assets the firm can achieve a great deal more stability in returns than is possible by investing in a single asset. When a firm diversifies it holds a *portfolio* of assets or investments. *Portfolio risk* is the risk associated with collections of assets or securities. In the following examples we illustrate diversification through a portfolio of securities. The principles developed in these examples, however, are equally relevant to any collection of different assets. The diversification strategy has been used by many firms to reduce the risk associated with operating in a narrow line of business.

Expected Returns from a Portfolio   When two or more securities are combined into a portfolio, the expected return of the portfolio is equal to the weighted average of the expected returns from the individual securities. For example, assume a portfolio contains Acme Corporation (*A*) securities and Babbo Corporation (*B*) securities, which have expected returns of 12 percent and 8 percent, respectively. If a portion w_A of the available funds (wealth) is invested in Security *A*, and the remaining funds w_B are invested in Security *B*, the expected return of the portfolio $\hat{r}_p$ is as follows:

$$\hat{r}_p = w_A \hat{r}_A + w_B \hat{r}_B, \qquad\qquad [19.5]$$

where $\hat{r}_A$ and $\hat{r}_B$ are the expected returns for Securities *A* and *B*, respectively. Furthermore, $w_A + w_B = 1$, indicating that all funds are invested in either Security *A* or Security *B*.

The range of possible expected returns for a portfolio consisting of Securities *A* and *B* is 12 percent (if 100 percent of the portfolio is invested in Security *A* and 0 percent is invested in Security *B*) to 8 percent (if 100 percent is invested in Security *B* and 0 percent is invested in Security *A*). In addition, any linear weighted combination of returns for Securities *A* and *B* between 8 and 12 percent is also possible. For example, assume that 30 percent of this portfolio consists of Security *A*, and Security *B* constitutes the remaining 70 percent. In this case the expected return on the portfolio is computed as follows:

$$\hat{r}_p = 0.3(12\%) + 0.7(8\%) = 9.2\%$$

In general, the expected return from any portfolio of *n* securities or assets is equal to the sum of the expected returns from each security times the proportion of the total portfolio invested in that security:

$$\hat{r}_p = \sum_{i=1}^{n} w_i \hat{r}_i \qquad\qquad [19.6]$$

where $\Sigma\, w_i = 1$ and $0 \le w_i \le 1$.

Portfolio Risk   Although the expected returns from a portfolio of two or more securities can be computed as a weighted average of the expected returns from the individual securities, it is not sufficient merely to calculate a weighted average of the risk of each individual security to arrive at a measure of the portfolio's risk. Whenever the returns from the individual securities are not perfectly positively correlated, the risk of any portfolio of these securities may be reduced through the effects of diversification. Thus, diversification can be achieved by investing in a diverse set of securities that have different risk-return characteristics. The amount of risk reduction achieved through diversification depends on the degree of correlation between the returns of the individual securities in the portfolio. The lower the correlations among the individual securities, the greater the possibilities for risk reduction.

The risk for a two-security portfolio, measured by the standard deviation of portfolio returns, is computed as follows:

$$\sigma_p = \sqrt{w_A^2 \sigma_A^2 + w_B^2 \sigma_B^2 + 2 w_A w_B \, \rho_{AB} \sigma_A \sigma_B} \qquad [19.7]$$

where w_A is the proportion of funds invested in Security A; w_B is the proportion of funds invested in Security B; $w_A + w_B = 1$; σ_A^2 is the variance of returns from Security A (or the square of the standard deviation for Security A, σ_A); σ_B^2 is the variance of returns from Security B (or the square of the standard deviation for Security B, σ_B); and ρ_{AB} is the correlation coefficient of returns between Securities A and B.[12]

For example, consider a portfolio containing Securities A and B as described here:

	Acme (A)	Babbo (B)
Expected return	0.12	0.08
Standard deviation of returns	0.09	0.09
Proportion invested in each security	0.50	0.50

Given various values for the correlation between the securities' returns, the risk of a portfolio containing equal proportions of the two securities can be computed.

First, consider the case where $\rho_{AB} = +1.0$ (that is, perfect *positive* correlation). The portfolio's risk is calculated as follows:

$$\sigma_p = \sqrt{(0.5)^2(0.09)^2 + (0.5)^2(0.09)^2 + 2(0.5)(0.5)(+1)(0.09)(0.09)}$$

$$= \sqrt{0.002025 + 0.002025 + 0.00405}$$

$$= \sqrt{0.0081}$$

$$= 0.09 \text{ (or 9\%)}$$

When the returns from the two securities are perfectly positively correlated, the risk of the portfolio is equal to the weighted average of the risk of the individual securities (9 percent in this example). *Thus, no risk reduction is achieved when perfectly positively correlated assets are combined in a portfolio.*

The returns from most assets are not perfectly positively correlated; this allows for risk reduction through diversification. For example, consider next the case of a low

---

[12] The correlation coefficient measures the extent to which high (or low) values of one variable are associated with high (or low) values of another. Values of the correlation coefficient range from +1.0, for perfectly positively correlated variables, to −1.0, for perfectly negatively correlated variables. The *less* two variables are positively correlated, the *greater* are the potential benefits of portfolio risk reduction. See Chapter 4 for additional discussion of the meaning and measurement of the correlation coefficient.

Figure 19.11   Portfolio Risk versus Correlation of Security Returns*

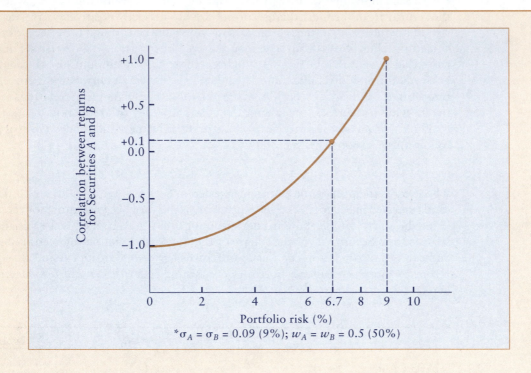

*$\sigma_A = \sigma_B = 0.09$ (9%); $w_A = w_B = 0.5$ (50%)

positive correlation of returns, such as $\rho_{AB} = +0.1$. The portfolio risk in this example is as follows:

$$\sigma_p = \sqrt{(0.5)^2(0.09)^2 + (0.5)^2(0.09)^2 + 2(0.5)(0.5)(+0.1)(0.09)(0.09)}$$

$$= \sqrt{0.002025 + 0.002025 + 0.000405}$$

$$= \sqrt{0.004455}$$

$$= 0.067 \text{ (or 6.7\%)}$$

In this case diversification reduces the portfolio risk from 9 percent (the weighted average of the individual security risks) to 6.7 percent.

Finally, consider the case of a perfect *negative* correlation $\rho_{AB} = -1.0$. In this example the portfolio risk is completely eliminated.[13]

Figure 19.11 graphs the relationship between the correlation of returns for Securities A and B and the risk (σ_p) of a portfolio containing equal proportions of Securities A and B ($w_A = w_B = 0.5$). This figure indicates that the relationship between portfolio risk and the correlation of security returns is not linear.

---

[13] When returns from two assets are perfectly negatively correlated, *some* combination of these two assets in a portfolio can completely eliminate portfolio risk. This risk-eliminating combination will only be $w_A = w_B = 0.5$ when the two assets have the same standard deviation of returns. When this is not the case, the weightings of w_A and w_B must be changed from 0.5 to fully eliminate portfolio risk.

WHAT WENT RIGHT   WHAT WENT WRONG

Conglomerate Diversification Misapplied: Gillette[14]

During the 1960s and 1970s many firms, such as ITT, Gulf + Western, Litton Industries, and LTV, attempted to reduce the risk of their operations by diversifying into a wide range of often unrelated industries. The rationale that was made for these far-flung acquisitions was to reduce the inherent operating risk of the enterprise. For example, U.S. Steel acquired Marathon Oil because of the cyclical risk in the steel industry. Ford Motor acquired a network of savings and loan institutions. Reynolds Tobacco diversified into food products, shipping, and oil and gas exploration. To make acquisitions in these unrelated businesses, the acquiring firms paid substantial premiums over the preacquisition market price of the acquired firms. Premiums of 20 to 75 percent or more were not uncommon.

In the late 1970s and early 1980s investors began to question the wisdom of these acquisitions. One issue involved the ability of the company's executives to manage effectively such a diverse collection of corporate assets. Indeed, the performance of many of the acquired firms suggested that they were less successfully managed as part of the conglomerate than when they were stand-alone enterprises. More importantly, the fundamental rationale for these acquisitions came under closer scrutiny. Why should a firm pay a premium to diversify itself when that same firm's stockholders can diversify at no premium by simply buying a portfolio of stock made up of diverse companies?

As the decade of the 1980s progressed, significant evidence suggested that these diversified firms were not maximizing the creation of shareholder value. It became evident that in many cases value could be created by acquiring these poorly run firms, selling off their diverse pieces, and refocusing the firm into its core business. This wave of restructuring often took the form of leveraged buyouts, where the firm was acquired in a highly debt-levered transaction, often with the managers of the firm taking a substantial ownership interest in the firm. The combination of the discipline of high required debt payments and the alignment of the interest of owners and managers produced dramatically better performance at many of these firms. On average, these transactions increased shareholder wealth by 50 percent or more.

After 32 straight quarters of double-digit growth in earnings per share (from 1990–1998), Gillette profitability stalled and even declined in the third quarter of 2000. Instead of focusing only on shaving products, diversification into White Rain shampoo, writing pens, Braun household appliances, and Duracell batteries proved largely unsuccessful. Management was unable to transfer their talents from shaving products to these far-flung businesses. By the end of 2000, Gillette's stock price had fallen 55% from its peak in early 1999.

---

[14] Based on "Most of Gillette's Bleeding Is Self-Inflicted," *BusinessWeek,* October 2, 2000, p. 56.

Diversification has been used by many firms to reduce the risks associated with operating in one narrow line of business. However, asset diversification for its own sake appears to reduce shareholder wealth in most cases because investors can typically diversify their portfolios more cheaply than firms can diversify their assets.

Hedge
A risk-reducing strategy of taking offsetting positions in the ownership of a derivative security and an underlying asset.

Hedging

A hedge is a transaction that limits the risk associated with market price fluctuations for a particular investment position. A **hedge** is accomplished by taking offsetting positions in the ownership of an asset or security through use of derivative

http://

Learn more about hedging and other economic reasons for commodity futures trading at the U.S. Commodity Futures Trading Commission site:
http://www.cftc.gov

securities, such as buying or selling a futures contract (or an option) to offset risk exposure in the cash market. A *futures contract* is a standardized contract, traded on an organized exchange, to buy or sell a fixed quantity of a defined commodity at a set price in the future. Hedging can also be accomplished using *forward contracts*. A forward contract is a contractual agreement between two parties to exchange a commodity at a set price in the future. The primary differences between futures contracts and forward contracts are that forward contracts are not actively traded on an organized exchange, such as the Chicago Board of Trade; normally forward contracts do not deal in standardized goods; and they carry the risk that one party to the contract may not perform as agreed. In contrast, futures contracts carry no such performance risk because they are essentially guaranteed by the exchange on which they are traded.

Futures and forward contracts create the legal obligation for the buyer (or seller) to purchase (or sell) the goods specified in the contract at the agreed-upon price at some future point in time. In contrast, an *option* gives the buyer the *right,* but not the obligation, to either buy or sell the underlying commodity. We will confine our discussion of hedging to futures contracts.[15]

Futures markets exist for many commodities, including minerals (such as copper, gold, silver, and crude oil), agricultural commodities (such as corn, wheat, live hogs, cotton, and cattle), and financial instruments (such as Treasury bills, Treasury bonds, foreign currencies, commercial paper, and broad-based common stock indexes such as *Standard and Poor's 500 Stock Index*). Any enterprise that normally buys or sells these commodities (or products closely related to these commodities) or is engaged in borrowing or lending operations can make use of futures contracts, forward markets, and options to eliminate, or at least largely offset, the risk of future price fluctuations.

Example

HEDGING BORROWING COSTS: WESTEX COMPANY

The corporate treasurer of Westex projects in late September that the company's cash flows will require a $3-million bank loan in mid-December. This loan is expected to be needed for three months. The contractual agreement between the corporate borrower and its bank establishes the rate on loans such as this to be 1.5 percentage points above the three-month Eurodollar rate (also referred to as the LIBOR—London Interbank Offer Rate). The current (September) LIBOR rate is 9.5 percent. The treasurer is concerned that this rate may increase over the next three months. Therefore, the treasurer wishes to "lock in" the current rate (11 percent) as her company's cost of borrowing in mid-December.

Eurodollar Time Deposit futures contracts are traded on the International Monetary Market (IMM), a division of the Chicago Mercantile Exchange. These Eurodollar contracts are for $1 million of three-month Eurodollar time deposits. The IMM has a pricing system that quotes these contracts on a discounted percentage basis; that is, the price of the contract is quoted as 100 minus the annualized interest rate on three-month Eurodollar time Deposits. For example, a contract price of 91 implies an annualized interest rate of 9 percent (100 minus 91 = 9 percent).

In September, the corporate treasurer observes that the December futures contract, which can be used to "lock in" the forward borrowing rate, is trading at 90.30, implying a forward Eurodollar rate of 9.7 percent (100.0 − 90.3). If the treasurer sells three

---

[15] More advanced treatments of hedging concepts are contained in Robert Jarrow and Stuart Turnbull, *Derivative Securities* (Cincinnati: South-Western), 1996.

December Eurodollar futures contracts ($1 million each) at 90.3, she can ensure that her cost of funds in December will be 11.2 percent (9.7-percent LIBOR rate plus the 1.5-percentage-points spread over LIBOR charged by the bank).

By mid-December the current Eurodollar rate has risen to 12.0 percent. The December futures price has declined to 88.00, reflecting the current 12-percent rate. Because of these higher rates, the company's quarterly interest payments to the bank are $100,250 ($3,000,000 × 13.5 percent × 0.25 years). The decline in the futures price, however, produces a profit for the corporate treasurer of $17,250 [(90.3 – 88.0) × $2,500 × 3 contracts]. (Each one percentage point increase in the price of a Eurodollar futures contract is equivalent to an increase in the value of that contract of $2,500 (that is, $1,000,000 × .01 × 0.25 years). Recall that the corporate treasurer sold three Eurodollar contracts in September at 90.3. The treasurer can cancel her position in the futures market by buying three contracts in December at the new lower price of 88.0.

Thus, the net interest cost to the corporate treasurer is $84,000 ($101,250 interest payment to the bank less $17,250 profit from the futures contracts), giving an effective annual rate of 11.2 percent.

In the example above, the treasurer has perfectly hedged her borrowing cost position. In practice, it is usually not possible to perfectly hedge one's position because of (1) differences in the size of standard future contracts and the amount of hedging desired by the firm; (2) the inability to find a futures contract in a commodity or financial instrument that has precisely the same pattern of price movements as the commodity or financial instrument in which the firm is dealing; (3) variations in the difference (called the basis) between the spot or cash market price for a commodity or financial instrument and the futures market price over the life of the futures contract; and (4) the inability to match a firm's period of risk exposure to the expiration time of the futures contract. In spite of these shortcomings, hedging can be used in many situations to reduce the risk of future price changes in goods or financial instruments. Over the past decade many new financial contracts have been developed that permit financial institutions and other firms to control their future financing cost and/or to guarantee their returns on anticipated future investments.

Other Approaches for Managing Risk and Uncertainty

In addition to hedging, acquiring additional information, and diversifying, several other techniques can be used to manage risk, such as purchasing insurance, gaining control over the operating environment, limiting the use of firm-specific assets, and scenario planning.

Insurance   When an individual makes a premium payment to an insurance company, that individual is exchanging the premium payment for protection against specified losses, up to the limits identified in the policy. Insurance is commonly available for losses due to fires, natural disasters, accidents occurring in the workplace, the death of key employees, fraud, product liability, and theft. Some financial instruments such as corporate bonds are backed by insurance that guarantees the payment of principal and interest. When deciding which risks should be insured externally, and which should be self-insured, managers are confronted with a trade-off between a certain, small, periodic cost (the payment of the insurance premium) and the uncertainty of bearing the full cost of a loss from time to time. The willingness of managers to assume some insurable risks, the cost of the insurance, and the severity of the consequences of experiencing an uninsured loss will determine whether insurance is purchased or not.

Gaining Control over the Operating Environment   Some business risks can be reduced by actions designed to gain control over the operating environment. For example, to ensure adequate outlets for its products, a firm may establish a network of exclusive dealerships. If access to raw materials is uncertain, a firm may integrate backwards toward the source of supplies. The use of patents and copyrights can protect a firm against immediate competition. Legal action can also reinforce its rights under patents and copyrights. For example, in 1993 Intel, a maker of computer microprocessor chips, filed a suit against a competitor, Advanced Micro Devices (AMD), charging that AMD's "clone" chip violated Intel copyrights. The lawsuit was viewed as an effort by Intel to create fear and uncertainty in the minds of AMD's customers and hence dissuade them from using ADM chips in their personal computers.[16]

Limited Use of Firm-Specific Assets   If a firm builds a plant that can be used only to produce its specific products, that firm has effectively limited its options should the product prove to be unsuccessful. The more general the purpose of the assets employed by a firm, the more flexibility that firm has to redeploy these assets to other uses. A trade-off exists between the use of firm- or product-specific assets, which are likely to be more efficient, and the use of more general-purpose assets, which give the firm increased future flexibility. When planning new investments, this trade-off must be carefully evaluated.

Scenario Planning   Finally, one tool that has proven useful for managing uncertainty is scenario planning. In the wake of the September 11, 2001, attack on the World Trade Center, the Wharton School at the University of Pennsylvania suggested that the future business environment was highly uncertain but divisible into four scenarios: paralysis, slow growth, thriving on chaos, and global growth.[17] In paralysis, companies would face unanticipated events and respond in a passive and reactive manner. In slow growth, events were forecastable, but response remained largely passive. In thriving on chaos, events would again be unanticipated, but nimble companies would respond opportunistically. In global growth, events would again be forecastable, and companies would aggressively identify paths to strategic success.

Classifying the company's strategic prospects under the various scenarios can prove very useful. Some company strategies will have positive payoffs under all scenarios. Other strategies will yield a significant positive payoff with upside potential under some scenarios and small negative payoffs in all others. Finally, some strategies will "bet the ranch" on one or a small number of scenarios and yield business-threatening negative payoffs in all others. Whether the company can take big bets like the third category or not depends on the irreversibility of the investment, the company's debt capacity, and the capital market's tolerance for a company reinventing itself in this business. Nokia survived such big bets fairly often in its telecommunications business, but in retailing Kmart did not.

---

[16] "Advanced Micro's 486-Chip Clones Violate Copyrights, Intel Charges," *Wall Street Journal,* April 29, 1993, p. B12.

[17] "Using Scenario Planning as a Weapon Against Uncertainty," *Knowledge @ Wharton,* November 8, 2001.

SUMMARY

- A decision problem consists of several basic elements—a decision maker, a set of objectives, two or more alternative actions that can possibly achieve the desired objectives, a state of doubt about which alternative is best in achieving the objectives, and an environment consisting of factors beyond the control of the decision maker.

- For purposes of exposition and analysis, decision making is divided into several parts: *individual decision making under certainty, risk, and uncertainty,* and *group decision making.* Decision making under risk refers to the situation where the probabilities of the possible outcomes can be specified by the decision maker. In decision making under uncertainty, the decision maker is either unwilling or unable to specify these probabilities. Decision making under unknowingness refers to situations in which outcomes cannot yet be identified. Group decision making refers to the situation where a conflict exists among the objectives of the participants.

- The decision maker's attitude toward risk affects the shape of his or her utility function and the choices he or she will make in the decision problem involving risk or uncertainty.

- Many different approaches are available for incorporating risk into the decision-making process. Five of these methods are the *expected marginal utility approach, prospect theory, decision tree approach, risk-adjusted discount rate approach,* and the *simulating approach.*

- The *maximin* and *minimax regret* decision criteria can be used to choose between alternatives in decision making under uncertainty.

- Perceived utility losses are often larger (in absolute value) than equivalent-value utility gains, implying a hybrid utility function suggested by prospect theory.

- Prospect theory implies sellers should distribute trial products, take prospective income in payment, and full-line force.

- Many techniques are available for managing risk, including investing in additional information, using derivative securities such as options and futures contracts to hedge a position in the cash market, using portfolio risk-reduction techniques when making investment decisions, purchasing insurance, investing in "flexible assets," making decisions designed to gain some control over the operating environment, and scenario planning.

EXERCISES

1. Suppose that a person is considering an investment in a new product. The cost of producing and marketing the product is estimated to be $6,000. Three possible outcomes can result from this investment:

    - The product can be *extremely successful* and yield a *net* profit of $24,000.
    - The product can be *moderately successful* and yield a *net* profit of $12,000.
    - The product can be *unsuccessful,* in which case the loss will be equal to the initial cost of producing and marketing the product (that is, $6,000).

    Additionally, assume that if the person does *not* invest in the new product, the $6,000 can be invested in another venture that is certain to yield a *net* profit of $1,500. Furthermore, suppose that he or she has assessed the chances of the product being extremely successful, moderately successful, and unsuccessful at .10, .20, and .70, respectively.

    a. Determine the decision alternatives.
    b. Determine the possible outcomes for each decision alternative.

c. Formulate the problem in a payoff table format (such as Figure 19.1) showing the net profit that will result from each alternative action/state-of-nature combination.

d. Determine the expected net profit of each decision alternative.

e. Assuming that the objective is to maximize expected monetary payoff, which alternative should be chosen?

2. Assume that the decision maker faced with the investment alternatives in Exercise 1 is risk averse in the sense of having a diminishing marginal utility for money (return). Suppose the utility function can be specified as follows:

Money M ($)	Utility U(M)
−6,000	−.75
0	0.0
+1,500	.09
+6,000	.225
+12,000	.375
+24,000	.525

a. Formulate Exercise 1 in a utility (payoff) table format (such as Figure 19.9), showing the utility that will result from each alternative action/state-of-nature combination.

b. Determine the expected utilities of each of the alternative actions.

c. Based on the maximization of expected utility criterion, which alternative should be chosen?

3. Consider Exercise 2 again. Suppose that the decision maker is either unable or unwilling to assess the probabilities of the product being extremely successful, moderately successful, or unsuccessful.

a. Based on the *maximin* decision criterion, which alternative should be selected?

b. Based on the *minimax regret* decision criterion, which alternative should be selected?

4. Shown below is an entrepreneur's utility function for money (return) along with two alternative investment projects (A and B). Assume that the entrepreneur has only enough funds to undertake one of these investments.

Utility Function		Investment			
Return	Utility	A		B	
		RETURN	PROBABILITY	RETURN	PROBABILITY
−$300,000	−4.00	−$300,000	.40	−$300,000	.10
0	0.0	1,500,000	.60	0	.20
300,000	.60			450,000	.40
450,000	.80			750,000	.30
750,000	1.00				
1,500,000	1.33				

  a. Calculate the expected monetary value of each investment.

  b. Assuming that the entrepreneur's investment objective is to maximize expected monetary value, which investment should be chosen?

  c. Calculate the expected utility of each investment.

  d. Assuming that the entrepreneur's objective is to maximize expected utility, which investment should be chosen?

  e. Explain why there is a difference in the alternatives chosen in Parts b and d.

5. A simulation model similar to the one described in the chapter has been constructed by the HNG Corporation to evaluate the largest of its new investment proposals. After many iterations of the model, HNG's management has arrived at an expected net present value of $4.2 million with a standard deviation of $2.4 million. The net present value probability distribution is approximately normal.

  a. Determine the probability that the project will have a negative net present value.

  b. Determine the probability that the net present value will be less than $1.0 million.

6. A bakery is considering how many dozen hamburger buns to stock on Saturdays. From past experience, the probabilities of selling 20, 25, 30, 35, or 40 dozen are know to be .15, .20, .30, .25, and .10, respectively. The selling price is $2 per dozen and the cost is $1 per dozen. Any hamburger buns unsold at the end of the day must be sold to a surplus baked goods store for $.30 per dozen, as they cannot be sold in the bakery the following day. The bakery must decide whether to stock 20, 25, 30, 35, or 40 dozen.

  a. Determine the alternative actions under consideration.

  b. Determine the states of nature.

  c. Formulate the problem in a payoff table format showing the net profit that will result from each alternative action/state-of-nature combination.

  d. Determine the expected profit of each alternative action.

  e. Based on the maximization of expected monetary value criterion, how many dozen hamburger buns should the bakery stock on Saturdays?

7. An investor is considering investing in two securities. Security A, the less risky security, has an expected return of 12 percent with a standard deviation of 3 percent. Security B has an expected return of 21 percent with a standard deviation of 11 percent. The correlation between the returns for Securities A and B is +0.3. The investor plans to put 60 percent of his wealth in A and 40 percent in B.

  a. Calculate the expected return from a portfolio made up of Securities A and B.

  b. What is the standard deviation of this portfolio's returns?

  c. What is the probability of receiving a portfolio return of less than 15 percent? (Assume that the distribution of portfolio returns is approximately normal.)

8. Mammoth Mutual Fund of New York has $10 million to invest in certificates of deposit (CDs) for the next 6 months (180 days). It can buy either a Pittsburgh National Bank (PNB) CD with an annual yield of 11 percent, or a Swiss bank

CD with a yield of 13.5 percent. Assume that the CDs are of comparable default risk. The analysts of the mutual fund are concerned about exchange rate risk. They were quoted the following exchange rates by the international department of a New York City bank:

Switzerland (Swiss Francs)	
Spot	$0.520
30-day futures	0.5190
90-day futures	0.5170
180-day futures	0.5155

a. If the Swiss bank CD is purchased and held to maturity, determine the net gain (loss) in U.S. dollars relative to the PNB CD, assuming that the exchange rate in 180 days equals today's spot rate.

b. Suppose the Swiss franc declines in value by 5 percent relative to the U.S. dollar over the next 180 days. Determine the net gain (loss) of the Swiss bank CD in U.S. dollars relative to the PNB CD for an uncovered position.

c. Determine the net gain (loss) from a covered position.

9. A corn producer can profitably produce a minimum of 10,000 bushels of corn if he is assured of a price of $2.90 per bushel at the time of planting. The corn will be harvested in late August. At the time of planting the farmer notes that the September futures price of corn is $2.90.

a. What action should the farmer take to hedge his position, that is, to "lock in" an effective price of $2.90 for his corn?

b. By late August the price of cash corn has dropped to $2.50. The September futures prices has also declined to $2.50. Ignoring commissions, compute the net profits and losses from the farmer's hedged position, after the farmer closes out the hedge.

c. How does your answer to Part b change if the late August cash price and the September futures price increase to $3.40?

10. Goody's Drug Company is considering an expansion into a new product line that is more risky than its existing product mix. The new product line requires an investment, *NINV,* of $10 million and is expected to generate annual net cash inflows of $2.0 million over a 10-year estimated economic life. Goody's weighted cost of capital is 12 percent, and the new product line requires an estimated risk-adjusted discount rate of 17 percent, based on the security market line and betas for comparable companies engaged in the contemplated new line of business.

a. What is the project's *NPV* using the company's weighted cost of capital?

b. What is the project's *NPV* using the risk-adjusted discount rate?

c. Should Goody's Drug adopt the project?

11. The managers of U.S. Rubber have analyzed a proposed investment project. The expected net present value (*NPV*) of the project, evaluated at the firm's weighted cost of capital of 18 percent, has been estimated to be $100,000. The company's managers have determined that the most optimistic *NPV* estimate of the project is $175,000 and the most pessimistic estimate is $25,000. The most optimistic estimate is a value that is not expected to be exceeded more than 10

percent of the time. The most pessimistic estimate represents a value that the project's *NPV* is not expected to fall below more than 10 percent of the time. What is the probability that this project will have a negative *NPV*?

http://

Accessing Decision Analysis Software

12. Decision and risk analysis is becoming increasingly sophisticated, and it is important for managers and business economists to have the necessary computer tools. There are a growing number of companies that provide decision analysis software. Many of them offer free demonstration software that can be used or downloaded from the Internet. Two such companies are Vanguard Software Corporation, maker of DecisionPro (http://www.vanguardsw.com/) and Arlington Software Corporation, maker of ERGO (http://www.arlingsoft. com). Access these or other similar sites, download their demonstration software, and compare their performance.

a The Time Value of Money

INTRODUCTION

Many economic decisions involve benefits and costs that are expected to occur at different future points in time. For example, the construction of a new office complex requires an immediate outlay of cash and results in a stream of expected cash inflows (benefits) over many future years. To determine if the expected future cash inflows are sufficient to justify the initial outlay, we must have a way to compare cash flows occurring at different points in time. Also, recall from Chapter 1 that the value of a firm is equal to the discounted (or present) value of all expected returns. These future returns are discounted at a rate of return that is consistent with the risk of the expected future returns. When future returns are more certain, the discount rate used is lower, resulting in a higher present value of the firm, *all other things being equal.* Conversely, when future returns are riskier or more uncertain, they are discounted at a higher rate, resulting in a lower present value of the firm, *all other things being equal.*

An explicit solution to the problem of comparing the benefits and costs of an economic transaction that occur at different points in time requires answers to the following kinds of questions: Is $1 to be received one year from today worth less than $1 in hand today? If so, why is it worth less? How much less is it worth?

The answers to these questions depend on the alternative uses available for the dollar between today and one year from today. Suppose the dollar can be invested in a guaranteed savings account paying a 6-percent annual rate of return (interest rate). The $1 invested today will return $1(1.06) = $1.06 one year from today. To receive exactly $1 one year from today, only $1/(1.06) = $.943 would have to be invested in the account today. Given the opportunity to invest at a 6-percent rate of return, we see that $1 to be received one year from today is indeed worth less than $1 in hand today, its worth being only $.943. Thus, the existence of opportunities to invest the dollar at positive rates of return makes $1 to be received at any future point in time worth less than $1 in hand today.[1] This is what is meant by the *time value of money.* The investor's required rate of return is called the *discount rate.*

PRESENT VALUE OF A SINGLE PAYMENT

We can generalize this result for any future series of cash flows and any interest rate. Assume that the opportunity exists to invest at a compound rate of *r* percent per

---

[1] In this analysis we are abstracting from price level considerations. Changes in the level of prices (the value of the dollar in terms of the quantity of goods and services it will buy) can also affect the worth of the dollar. In theory, future price increases (or decreases) that are *anticipated* by the market will be reflected in the interest rate.

annum. Then the *present value* (value today) of $1 to be received at the end of year *n*, discounted at *r* percent, is

$$PV_0 = \frac{1}{(1 + r)^n}$$ [A.1]

The term $1/(1 + r)^n$ is often called a Present Value Interest Factor, or $PVIF_{r,n}$. Table 4 in Appendix B contains PVIF values for various interest rates, *r*, and periods in the future, *n*.

PRESENT VALUE

Example

If an opportunity exists to invest at a compound rate of return of 12 percent, then the present value of $1 to be received four years ($n = 4$) from today is

$$PV_0 = \frac{1}{(1+.12)^4} = (PVIF_{12\%,4})$$

$$= \$1\,(0.6355)$$

$$= \$0.6355$$

As we see in Table A.1, investing $0.6355 today at an interest rate of 12 percent per annum will give $1 at the end of four years.

Alternatively, the PVIF factors from Table 4 in Appendix B could be used to find the present value of $1 expected to be received in four years ($n = 4$), assuming an interest rate of 12 percent ($r = 12\%$), as follows:

$$PV_0 = \$1(PVIF_{12\%,4})$$

$$= \$1(0.63552)$$

$$= \$0.6355$$

PRESENT VALUE OF A DEFERRED BEQUEST

Example

What is the present value of an expected bequest of $2 million to your university if the expected remaining life span of the donor is eight years and the university uses an interest rate of 9 percent to evaluate gifts of this type?

$$PV_0 = \$2,000,000(PVIF_{9\%,8})$$

$$= \$2,000,000(0.50187)$$

$$= \$1,003,740$$

TABLE A.1

Present Value of $1 to Be Received at the End of Four Years

Year	Return Received at End of Year	Value of Investment at End of Year	
0 (present)	—	$.6355	← Initial amount invested
1	.6355(.12) = $.0762	.6355 + .0762 = .7117	
2	.7117(.12) = .0854	.7117 + .0854 = .7971	
3	.7971(.12) = .0957	.7971 + .0957 = .8928	
4	.8928(.12) = .1072	.8928 + .1072 = 1.000	

Your university would be indifferent between receiving $1,003,740 today or $2 million in eight years.

Solving for the Interest or Growth Rate

Present value interest factors ($PVIF$) can also be used to solve for interest rates. For example, suppose you wish to borrow $5,000 today from an associate. The associate is willing to loan you the money if you promise to pay back $6,802 four years from today. The compound interest rate your associate is charging can be determined as follows:

$$PV_0 = \$6,802(PVIF_{r,4})$$

$$\$5,000 = \$6,802(PVIF_{r,4})$$

$$PVIF_{r,4} = \frac{\$5,000}{\$6,802}$$

$$= 0.735$$

Reading across the Period 04 row in Table B.4, 0.735 (rounded to three places for simplicity) is found in the 8% column. Thus, the effective interest rate on the loan is 8 percent per year, compounded annually.

Example

CALCULATION OF EARNINGS GROWTH RATES FOR HANAMAKER PAPER

Another common application of the use of $PVIF$ factors from Table B.4 is the calculation of the compound rate of growth of an earnings or dividend stream. For example, Hanamaker Paper Company had earnings per share of $2.56 in 2001. Security analysts have forecasted 2006 earnings per share to be $6.37. What is the expected compound annual rate of growth in Hanamaker Paper Company's earnings per share? We can use the $PVIF$ factors from Table 4 to solve this problem, as follows:

$$\$2.56 = \$6.37(PVIF_{r,5})$$

$$PVIF_{r,5} = 0.40188$$

Looking across the Period 5 row in Table B.4 we find a $PVIF$ equal to 0.40188 under the 20% column. Thus the compound annual growth rate of earnings for Hanamaker Paper Company is 20 percent. (Interpolation can be used for $PVIF$ values between the values found in the tables. In practice, financial calculators are normally used for these types of calculations.)

PRESENT VALUE OF A SERIES OF EQUAL PAYMENTS (ANNUITY)

The present value of a series of *equal* $1 payments to be received at the end of each of the next *n* years (an *annuity*), discounted at a rate of *r* percent, is

$$PV_0 = \frac{1}{(1 + r)^1} + \frac{1}{(1 + r)^2} + \cdots + \frac{1}{(1 + r)^n}$$

$$PV_0 = \sum_{t=1}^{n} \frac{1}{(1 + r)^t} \tag{A.2}$$

For example, the present value of $1 to be received at the end of each of the next four years, discounted at 12 percent, is

$$PV_0 = \sum_{t=1}^{4} \frac{1}{(1 + .12)^t}$$

$$= \frac{1}{(1 + .12)^1} + \frac{1}{(1 + .12)^2} + \frac{1}{(1 + .12)^3} + \frac{1}{(1 + .12)^4}$$

$$= .89286 + .79719 + .71178 + .63552 = \$3.0374$$

As shown in Table A.2, investing $3.0374 today at 12 percent will return exactly $1 at the end of each of the next four years, with nothing remaining in the account at the end of the fourth year. Again, rather than perform the present value calculations (Equation A.2), we can use a table to look up the values we need. Table B.5 in Appendix B contains the present values at various interest rates of $1 to be received at the end of each year for various periods of time. The values in Table B.5 are called Present Value Interest Factors for Annuities, or $PVIFA_{r,n}$, where r is the interest rate per period and n is the number of periods (normally years).

Using the $PVIFA$ factors from Table B.5, the present value of an annuity ($PVAN_0$) can be computed as

$$PVAN_0 = PMT(PVIFA_{r,n}) \qquad\qquad [A.3]$$

where PMT = the annuity amount to be received each period.

PRESENT VALUE OF AN ANNUITY

Example

You have recently purchased the winning ticket in the Florida lottery and have won $30 million, to be paid in equal $3 million increments ($PMT$) at the end of each of the next ten years. What are your winnings worth to you today using an interest rate of 8 percent? The $PVIFA$ factors from Table B.5 can be used to solve this problem as follows:

$$PVAN_0 = \$3,000,000(PVIFA_{8\%,10})$$
$$= \$3,000,000(6.7101)$$
$$= \$20,130,300$$

Thus, your $30-million winnings are worth only $20,130,300 to you today.

| TABLE A.2 | Present Value of $1 to Be Received at the End of Each of the Next Four Years |

Year	Return Received at End of Year	Amount Withdrawn at End of Year	Value of Investment at End of Year	
0 (present)	—	—	$3.0374	← initial amount invested
1	$3.0374(.12) = $.3645	$1.00	$3.0374 + .3645 − 1.00 = 2.4019	
2	2.4019(.12) = .2882	1.00	2.4019 + .2882 − 1.00 = 1.6901	
3	1.6901(.12) = .2028	1.00	1.6901 + .2028 − 1.00 = .8929	
4	.8929(.12) = .1071	1.00	.8929 + .1071 − 1.00 = .0000	

Solving for the Interest Rate

Present Value of an Annuity interest factors also can be used to solve for the rate of return expected from an investment. This rate of return is often referred to as the internal rate of return from an investment. Suppose the Big Spring Tool Company purchases a machine for $100,000. This machine is expected to generate annual cash flows of $23,740 to the firm over the next five years. What is the expected rate of return from this investment?

Using Equation A.3 we can determine the expected rate of return in this example as follows:

$$PVAN_0 = PMT(PVIFA_{r,5})$$
$$\$100,000 = \$23,740(PVIFA_{r,5})$$
$$PVIFA_{r,5} = 4.2123$$

From the Period 05 row in Table B.5, we see that a $PVIFA$ of 4.2123 occurs in the 6% column. Hence, this investment offers a 6-percent expected (internal) rate of return.

PRESENT VALUE OF A SERIES OF UNEQUAL PAYMENTS

The present value of a series of *unequal* payments ($PMT_t, t = 1, \ldots, n$) to be received at the end of each of the next n years, discounted at a rate of r percent, is

$$PV_0 = \sum_{t=1}^{n} \frac{PMT_t}{(1 + r)^t}$$
$$= \sum_{t=1}^{n} PMT_t(PVIF_{r,t}) \tag{A.4}$$

The $PVIF_{r,t}$ values are the interest factors from Table B.4. Thus, the present value of a series of unequal payments is equal to the sum of the present value of the individual payments.

Example

PROJECT EVALUATION FOR INTEL

Intel Corporation is evaluating an investment in a new chip-manufacturing facility. The facility is expected to have a useful life of five years and yield the following cash flow stream after the initial investment outlay:

End of Year t	Cash Flow PMT_t
1	+ $1,000,000
2	+ 1,500,000
3	− 500,000
4	+ 2,000,000
5	+ 1,000,000

The negative cash flow in Year 3 arises because of the expected need to install pollution control equipment during that year. The present value of this series of unequal payments can be computed using *PVIF* factors from Table B.4 and assuming a 10-percent interest (required) rate on the investment:

$$PV = \$1,000,000(PVIF_{10\%,1}) + \$1,500,000(PVIF_{10\%,2})$$
$$- \$500,000(PVIF_{10\%,3}) + \$2,000,000(PVIF_{10\%,4})$$
$$+ \$1,000,000(PVIF_{10\%,5})$$
$$= \$1,000,000(0.90909) + \$1,500,000(0.82645)$$
$$- \$500,000(0.75131) + \$2,000,000(0.68301)$$
$$+ \$1,000,000(0.62092)$$
$$= \$3,760,050$$

The present value of these cash flows ($3,760,050) should be compared to the required initial cash outlay to determine whether to invest in the new manufacturing facility.

b Tables

Values of the Standard
Normal Distribution
Function

Z	0	1	2	3	4	5	6	7	8	9
−3.	.0013	.0010	.0007	.0005	.0003	.0002	.0002	.0001	.0001	.0000
−2.9	.0019	.0018	.0017	.0017	.0016	.0016	.0015	.0015	.0014	.0014
−2.8	.0026	.0025	.0024	.0023	.0023	.0022	.0021	.0021	.0020	.0019
−2.7	.0035	.0034	.0033	.0032	.0031	.0030	.0029	.0028	.0027	.0026
−2.6	.0047	.0045	.0044	.0043	.0041	.0040	.0039	.0038	.0037	.0036
−2.5	.0062	.0060	.0059	.0057	.0055	.0054	.0052	.0051	.0049	.0048
−2.4	.0082	.0080	.0078	.0075	.0073	.0071	.0069	.0068	.0066	.0064
−2.3	.0107	.0104	.0102	.0099	.0096	.0094	.0091	.0089	.0087	.0084
−2.2	.0139	.0136	.0132	.0129	.0126	.0122	.0119	.0116	.0113	.0110
−2.1	.0179	.0174	.0170	.0166	.0162	.0158	.0154	.0150	.0146	.0143
−2.0	.0228	.0222	.0217	.0212	.0207	.0202	.0197	.0192	.0188	.0183
−1.9	.0287	.0281	.0274	.0268	.0262	.0256	.0250	.0244	.0238	.0233
−1.8	.0359	.0352	.0344	.0336	.0329	.0322	.0314	.0307	.0300	.0294
−1.7	.0446	.0436	.0427	.0418	.0409	.0401	.0392	.0384	.0375	.0367
−1.6	.0548	.0537	.0526	.0516	.0505	.0495	.0485	.0475	.0465	.0455
−1.5	.0668	.0655	.0643	.0630	.0618	.0606	.0594	.0582	.0570	.0559
−1.4	.0808	.0793	.0778	.0764	.0749	.0735	.0722	.0708	.0694	.0681
−1.3	.0988	.0951	.0934	.0918	.0901	.0885	.0869	.0853	.0838	.0823
−1.2	.1151	.1131	.1112	.1093	.1075	.1056	.1038	.1020	.1003	.0985
−1.1	.1357	.1335	.1314	.1292	.1271	.1251	.1230	.1210	.1190	.1170
−1.0	.1587	.1562	.1539	.1515	.1492	.1469	.1446	.1423	.1401	.1379
−.9	.1841	.1814	.1788	.1762	.1736	.1711	.1685	.1660	.1635	.1611
−.8	.2119	.2090	.2061	.2033	.2005	.1977	.1949	.1922	.1894	.1867
−.7	.2420	.2389	.2358	.2327	.2297	.2266	.2236	.2206	.2177	.2148
−.6	.2743	.2709	.2676	.2643	.2611	.2578	.2546	.2514	.2483	.2451
−.5	.3085	.3050	.3015	.2981	.2946	.2912	.2877	.2843	.2810	.2776
−.4	.3446	.3409	.3372	.3336	.3300	.3264	.3228	.3192	.3156	.3121
−.3	.3821	.3783	.3745	.3707	.3669	.3632	.3594	.3557	.3520	.3483
−.2	.4207	.4168	.4129	.4090	.4052	.4013	.3974	.3936	.3897	.3859
−.1	.4602	.4562	.4522	.4483	.4443	.4404	.4364	.4325	.4286	.4247
−.0	.5000	.4960	.4920	.4880	.4840	.4801	.4761	.4721	.4681	.4641

*Note: Table values give the probability of a value occurring which is *less than* Z standard deviations from the mean.
Note 1: If a random variable X is not "standard," its values must be "standardized": $Z = (X − \mu)/\sigma$. That is:

$$P(X \leq x) = N\left(\frac{x - \mu}{\sigma}\right)$$

Note 2: For $z \geq 4$, $N(z) = 1$ to 4 decimal places; for $z \leq −4$, $N(z) = 0$ to 4 decimal places.

TABLE B.1

Values of the Standard
Normal Distribution
Function (continued)

Z	0	1	2	3	4	5	6	7	8	9
.0	.5000	.5040	.5080	.5120	.5160	.5199	.5239	.5279	.5319	.5359
.1	.5398	.5438	.5478	.5517	.5557	.5596	.5636	.5675	.5714	.5753
.2	.5793	.5832	.5871	.5910	.5948	.5987	.6026	.6064	.6103	.6141
.3	.6179	.6217	.6255	.6293	.6331	.6368	.6406	.6443	.6480	.6517
.4	.6554	.6591	.6628	.6664	.6700	.6736	.6772	.6808	.6844	.6879
.5	.6915	.6950	.6985	.7019	.7054	.7088	.7123	.7157	.7190	.7224
.6	.7257	.7291	.7324	.7357	.7389	.7422	.7454	.7486	.7517	.7549
.7	.7580	.7611	.7642	.7673	.7703	.7734	.7764	.7794	.7823	.7852
.8	.7881	.7910	.7939	.7967	.7995	.8023	.8051	.8078	.8106	.8133
.9	.8159	.8186	.8212	.8238	.8264	.8289	.8315	.8340	.8365	.8389
1.0	.8413	.8438	.8461	.8485	.8508	.8531	.8554	.8577	.8599	.8621
1.1	.8643	.8665	.8686	.8708	.8729	.8749	.8770	.8790	.8810	.8830
1.2	.8849	.8869	.8888	.8907	.8925	.8944	.8962	.8980	.8997	.9015
1.3	.9032	.9049	.9066	.9082	.9099	.9115	.9131	.9147	.9162	.9177
1.4	.9192	.9207	.9222	.9236	.9251	.9265	.9278	.9292	.9306	.9319
1.5	.9332	.9345	.9357	.9370	.9382	.9394	.9406	.9418	.9430	.9441
1.6	.9452	.9463	.9474	.9484	.9495	.9505	.9515	.9525	.9535	.9545
1.7	.9554	.9564	.9573	.9582	.9591	.9599	.9608	.9616	.9625	.9633
1.8	.9641	.9648	.9656	.9664	.9671	.9678	.9686	.9693	.9700	.9706
1.9	.9713	.9719	.9726	.9732	.9738	.9744	.9750	.9756	.9762	.9767
2.0	.9772	.9778	.9783	.9788	.9793	.9798	.9803	.9808	.9812	.9817
2.1	.9821	.9826	.9830	.9834	.9838	.9842	.9846	.9850	.9854	.9857
2.2	.9861	.9864	.9868	.9871	.9874	.9878	.9881	.9884	.9887	.9890
2.3	.9893	.9896	.9898	.9901	.9904	.9906	.9909	.9911	.9913	.9916
2.4	.9918	.9920	.9922	.9925	.9927	.9929	.9931	.9932	.9934	.9936
2.5	.9938	.9940	.9941	.9943	.9945	.9946	.9948	.9949	.9951	.9952
2.6	.9953	.9955	.9956	.9957	.9959	.9960	.9961	.9962	.9963	.9964
2.7	.9965	.9966	.9967	.9968	.9969	.9970	.9971	.9972	.9973	.9974
2.8	.9974	.9975	.9976	.9977	.9977	.9978	.9979	.9979	.9980	.9981
2.9	.9981	.9982	.9982	.9983	.9984	.9984	.9985	.9985	.9986	.9986
3.	.9987	.9990	.9993	.9995	.9997	.9998	.9998	.9999	.9999	1.0000

Source: *Statistical Analysis: With Business and Economic Applications*, by Ya-lun Chou. Copyright © 1969 by
Holt, Rinehart and Winston, Inc. Reprinted by permission of Holt, Rinehart and Winston, Inc.

TABLE B.2*   Table of "Students" Distribution—Value of t

Degrees of Freedom	Probability												
	0.9	0.8	0.7	0.6	0.5	0.4	0.3	0.2	0.1	0.05	0.02	0.01	0.001
1	0.158	0.325	0.510	0.727	1.000	1.376	1.963	3.078	6.314	12.706	31.821	63.657	636.619
2	0.142	0.289	0.445	0.617	0.816	1.061	1.386	1.886	2.920	4.303	6.965	9.925	31.598
3	0.137	0.277	0.424	0.584	0.765	0.978	1.250	1.638	2.353	3.182	4.541	5.841	12.924
4	0.134	0.271	0.414	0.569	0.741	0.941	1.190	1.533	2.132	2.776	3.747	4.604	8.610
5	0.132	0.267	0.408	0.559	0.727	0.920	1.156	1.476	2.015	2.571	3.365	4.032	6.869
6	0.131	0.265	0.404	0.553	0.718	0.906	1.134	1.440	1.943	2.447	3.143	3.707	5.959
7	0.130	0.263	0.402	0.549	0.711	0.896	1.119	1.415	1.895	2.365	2.998	3.499	5.408
8	0.130	0.262	0.399	0.546	0.706	0.889	1.108	1.397	1.860	2.306	2.896	3.355	5.041
9	0.129	0.261	0.398	0.543	0.703	0.883	1.100	1.383	1.833	2.262	2.821	3.250	4.781
10	0.129	0.260	0.397	0.542	0.700	0.879	1.093	1.372	1.812	2.228	2.764	3.169	4.587
11	0.129	0.260	0.396	0.540	0.697	0.876	1.088	1.363	1.796	2.201	2.718	3.106	4.437
12	0.128	0.259	0.395	0.539	0.695	0.873	1.083	1.356	1.782	2.179	2.681	3.055	4.318
13	0.128	0.259	0.394	0.538	0.694	0.870	1.079	1.350	1.771	2.160	2.650	3.012	4.221
14	0.128	0.258	0.393	0.537	0.692	0.868	1.076	1.345	1.761	2.145	2.624	2.977	4.140
15	0.128	0.258	0.393	0.536	0.691	0.866	1.074	1.341	1.753	2.131	2.602	2.947	4.073
16	0.128	0.258	0.392	0.535	0.690	0.865	1.071	1.337	1.746	2.120	2.583	2.921	4.015
17	0.128	0.257	0.392	0.534	0.689	0.863	1.069	1.333	1.740	2.110	2.567	2.898	3.965
18	0.127	0.257	0.392	0.534	0.688	0.862	1.067	1.330	1.734	2.101	2.552	2.878	3.922
19	0.127	0.257	0.391	0.533	0.688	0.861	1.066	1.328	1.729	2.093	2.539	2.861	3.883
20	0.127	0.257	0.391	0.533	0.687	0.860	1.064	1.325	1.725	2.086	2.528	2.845	3.850
21	0.127	0.257	0.391	0.532	0.686	0.859	1.063	1.323	1.721	2.080	2.518	2.831	3.819
22	0.127	0.256	0.390	0.532	0.686	0.858	1.061	1.321	1.717	2.074	2.508	2.819	3.792
23	0.127	0.256	0.390	0.532	0.685	0.858	1.060	1.319	1.714	2.069	2.500	2.807	3.767
24	0.127	0.256	0.390	0.531	0.685	0.857	1.059	1.318	1.711	2.064	2.492	2.797	3.745
25	0.127	0.256	0.390	0.531	0.684	0.856	1.058	1.316	1.708	2.060	2.485	2.787	3.725
26	0.127	0.256	0.390	0.531	0.684	0.856	1.058	1.315	1.706	2.056	2.479	2.779	3.707
27	0.127	0.256	0.389	0.531	0.684	0.855	1.057	1.314	1.703	2.052	2.473	2.771	3.690
28	0.127	0.256	0.389	0.530	0.683	0.855	1.056	1.313	1.701	2.048	2.467	2.763	3.674
29	0.127	0.256	0.389	0.530	0.683	0.854	1.055	1.311	1.699	2.045	2.462	2.756	3.659
30	0.127	0.256	0.389	0.530	0.683	0.854	1.055	1.310	1.697	2.042	2.457	2.750	3.646
40	0.126	0.255	0.388	0.529	0.681	0.851	1.050	1.303	1.684	2.021	2.423	2.704	3.551
60	0.126	0.254	0.387	0.527	0.679	0.848	1.046	1.296	1.671	2.000	2.390	2.660	3.460
120	0.126	0.254	0.386	0.526	0.677	0.845	1.041	1.289	1.658	1.980	2.358	2.617	3.373
∞	0.126	0.253	0.385	0.524	0.674	0.842	1.036	1.282	1.645	1.960	2.326	2.576	3.291

*Note: Probabilities given are for two-tailed tests. For example, a probability of .05 allows for .025 in one tail of the distribution and .025 in the other.

Table 2 is taken from Table III of Fisher and Yates: *Statistical Tables for Biological, Agricultural and Medical Research,* published by Longman Group, Ltd., London (previously published by Oliver and Boyd, Edinburgh), and by permission of the authors and publishers.

TABLE B.3   The F-Distribution—Upper 5 Percent Points

δ_2 \ δ_1	1	2	3	4	5	6	7	8	9	10	12	15	20	24	30	40	60	120	∞
1	161.4	199.5	215.7	224.6	230.2	234.0	236.8	238.9	240.5	241.9	243.9	245.9	248.0	249.1	250.1	251.1	252.2	253.3	254.3
2	18.57	19.00	19.16	19.25	19.30	19.33	19.35	19.37	19.38	19.40	19.41	19.43	19.45	19.45	19.46	19.47	19.48	19.49	19.50
3	10.13	9.55	9.28	9.12	9.01	8.94	8.89	8.85	8.81	8.79	8.74	8.70	8.66	8.64	8.62	8.59	8.57	8.55	8.53
4	7.71	6.94	6.59	6.39	6.26	6.16	6.09	6.04	6.00	5.96	5.91	5.86	5.80	5.77	5.75	5.72	5.69	5.66	5.63
5	6.61	5.79	5.41	5.19	5.05	4.95	4.88	4.82	4.77	4.74	4.68	4.62	4.56	4.53	4.50	4.46	4.43	4.40	4.36
6	5.99	5.14	4.76	4.53	4.39	4.28	4.21	4.15	4.10	4.06	4.00	3.94	3.87	3.84	3.81	3.77	3.74	3.70	3.67
7	5.59	4.74	4.35	4.12	3.97	3.87	3.79	3.73	3.68	3.64	3.57	3.51	3.44	3.41	3.38	3.34	3.30	3.27	3.23
8	5.32	4.46	4.07	3.84	3.69	3.58	3.50	3.44	3.39	3.35	3.28	3.22	3.15	3.12	3.08	3.04	3.01	2.97	2.93
9	5.12	4.26	3.86	3.63	3.48	3.37	3.29	3.23	3.18	3.14	3.07	3.01	2.94	2.90	2.86	2.83	2.79	2.75	2.71
10	4.96	4.10	3.71	3.48	3.33	3.22	3.14	3.07	3.02	2.98	2.91	2.85	2.77	2.74	2.70	2.66	2.62	2.58	2.54
11	4.84	3.98	3.59	3.36	3.20	3.09	3.01	2.95	2.90	2.85	2.79	2.72	2.65	2.61	2.57	2.53	2.49	2.45	2.40
12	4.75	3.89	3.49	3.26	3.11	3.00	2.91	2.85	2.80	2.75	2.69	2.62	2.54	2.51	2.47	2.43	2.38	2.34	2.30
13	4.67	3.81	3.41	3.18	3.03	2.92	2.83	2.77	2.71	2.67	2.60	2.53	2.46	2.42	2.38	2.34	2.30	2.25	2.21
14	4.60	3.74	3.34	3.11	2.96	2.85	2.76	2.70	2.65	2.60	2.53	2.46	2.39	2.35	2.31	2.27	2.22	2.18	2.13
15	4.54	3.68	3.29	3.06	2.90	2.79	2.71	2.64	2.59	2.54	2.48	2.40	2.33	2.29	2.25	2.20	2.16	2.11	2.07
16	4.49	3.63	3.24	3.01	2.85	2.74	2.66	2.59	2.54	2.49	2.42	2.35	2.28	2.24	2.19	2.15	2.11	2.06	2.01
17	4.45	3.59	3.20	2.96	2.81	2.70	2.61	2.55	2.49	2.45	2.38	2.31	2.23	2.19	2.15	2.10	2.06	2.01	1.96
18	4.41	3.55	3.16	2.93	2.77	2.66	2.58	2.51	2.46	2.41	2.34	2.27	2.19	2.15	2.11	2.06	2.02	1.97	1.92
19	4.38	3.52	3.13	2.90	2.74	2.63	2.54	2.48	2.42	2.38	2.31	2.23	2.16	2.11	2.07	2.03	1.98	1.93	1.88
20	4.35	3.49	3.10	2.87	2.71	2.60	2.51	2.45	2.39	2.35	2.28	2.20	2.12	2.08	2.04	1.99	1.95	1.90	1.84
21	4.32	3.47	3.07	2.84	2.68	2.57	2.49	2.42	2.37	2.32	2.25	2.18	2.10	2.05	2.01	1.96	1.92	1.87	1.81
22	4.30	3.44	3.05	2.82	2.66	2.55	2.46	2.40	2.34	2.30	2.23	2.15	2.07	2.03	1.98	1.94	1.89	1.84	1.78
23	4.28	3.42	3.03	2.80	2.64	2.53	2.44	2.37	2.32	2.27	2.20	2.13	2.05	2.01	1.96	1.91	1.86	1.81	1.76
24	4.26	3.40	3.01	2.78	2.62	2.51	2.42	2.36	2.30	2.25	2.18	2.11	2.03	1.98	1.94	1.89	1.84	1.79	1.73
25	4.24	3.39	2.99	2.76	2.60	2.49	2.40	2.34	2.28	2.24	2.16	2.09	2.01	1.96	1.92	1.87	1.82	1.77	1.71
26	4.23	3.37	2.98	2.74	2.59	2.47	2.39	2.32	2.27	2.22	2.15	2.07	1.99	1.95	1.90	1.85	1.80	1.75	1.69
27	4.21	3.35	2.96	2.73	2.57	2.46	2.37	2.31	2.25	2.20	2.13	2.06	1.97	1.93	1.88	1.84	1.79	1.73	1.67
28	4.20	3.34	2.95	2.71	2.56	2.45	2.36	2.29	2.24	2.19	2.12	2.04	1.96	1.91	1.87	1.82	1.77	1.71	1.65
29	4.18	3.33	2.93	2.70	2.55	2.43	2.35	2.28	2.22	2.18	2.10	2.03	1.94	1.90	1.85	1.81	1.75	1.70	1.64
30	4.17	3.32	2.92	2.69	2.53	2.42	2.33	2.27	2.21	2.16	2.09	2.01	1.93	1.89	1.84	1.79	1.74	1.68	1.62
40	4.08	3.23	2.84	2.61	2.45	2.34	2.25	2.18	2.12	2.08	2.00	1.92	1.84	1.79	1.74	1.69	1.64	1.58	1.51
60	4.00	3.15	2.76	2.53	2.37	2.25	2.17	2.10	2.04	1.99	1.92	1.84	1.75	1.70	1.65	1.59	1.53	1.47	1.39
120	3.92	3.07	2.68	2.45	2.29	2.17	2.09	2.02	1.96	1.91	1.83	1.75	1.66	1.61	1.55	1.50	1.43	1.35	1.25
∞	3.84	3.00	2.60	2.37	2.21	2.10	2.01	1.94	1.88	1.83	1.75	1.67	1.57	1.52	1.46	1.39	1.32	1.22	1.00

TABLE B.3   The *F*-Distribution—Upper 1 Percent Points (continued)

δ_2 \ δ_1	1	2	3	4	5	6	7	8	9	10	12	15	20	24	30	40	60	120	∞
1	4052	4999.5	5403	5625	5764	5859	5928	5982	6022	6056	6106	6157	6209	6235	6261	6287	6313	6339	6366
2	98.50	99.00	99.17	99.25	99.30	99.33	99.36	99.37	99.39	99.40	99.42	99.43	99.45	99.46	99.47	99.47	99.48	99.49	99.50
3	34.12	30.82	29.46	28.71	28.24	27.91	27.67	27.49	27.35	27.23	27.05	26.87	26.69	26.60	26.50	26.41	26.32	26.22	26.13
4	21.20	18.00	16.69	15.98	15.52	15.21	14.98	14.80	14.66	14.55	14.37	14.20	14.02	13.93	13.84	13.75	13.65	13.56	13.46
5	16.26	13.27	12.06	11.39	10.97	10.67	10.46	10.29	10.16	10.05	9.89	9.72	9.55	9.47	9.38	9.29	9.20	9.11	9.02
6	13.75	10.92	9.78	9.15	8.75	8.47	8.26	8.10	7.98	7.87	7.72	7.56	7.40	7.31	7.23	7.14	7.06	6.97	6.88
7	12.25	9.55	8.45	7.85	7.46	7.19	6.99	6.84	6.72	6.62	6.47	6.31	6.16	6.07	5.99	5.91	5.82	5.74	5.65
8	11.26	8.65	7.59	7.01	6.63	6.37	6.18	6.03	5.91	5.81	5.67	5.52	5.36	5.28	5.20	5.12	5.03	4.95	4.86
9	10.56	8.02	6.99	6.42	6.06	5.80	5.61	5.47	5.35	5.26	5.11	4.96	4.81	4.73	4.65	4.57	4.48	4.40	4.31
10	10.04	7.56	6.55	5.99	5.64	5.39	5.20	5.06	4.94	4.85	4.71	4.56	4.41	4.33	4.25	4.17	4.08	4.00	3.91
11	9.65	7.21	6.22	5.67	5.32	5.07	4.89	4.74	4.63	4.54	4.40	4.25	4.10	4.02	3.94	3.86	3.78	3.69	3.60
12	9.33	6.93	5.95	5.41	5.06	4.82	4.64	4.50	4.39	4.30	4.16	4.01	3.86	3.78	3.70	3.62	3.54	3.45	3.36
13	9.07	6.70	5.74	5.21	4.86	4.62	4.44	4.30	4.19	4.10	3.96	3.82	3.66	3.59	3.51	3.43	3.34	3.25	3.17
14	8.86	6.51	5.56	5.04	4.69	4.46	4.28	4.14	4.03	3.94	3.80	3.66	3.51	3.43	3.35	3.27	3.18	3.09	3.00
15	8.68	6.36	5.42	4.89	4.56	4.32	4.14	4.00	3.89	3.80	3.67	3.52	3.37	3.29	3.21	3.13	3.05	2.96	2.87
16	8.53	6.23	5.29	4.77	4.44	4.20	4.03	3.89	3.78	3.69	3.55	3.41	3.26	3.18	3.10	3.02	2.93	2.84	2.75
17	8.40	6.11	5.18	4.67	4.34	4.10	3.93	3.79	3.68	3.59	3.46	3.31	3.16	3.08	3.00	2.92	2.83	2.75	2.65
18	8.29	6.01	5.09	4.58	4.25	4.01	3.84	3.71	3.60	3.51	3.37	3.23	3.08	3.00	2.92	2.84	2.75	2.66	2.57
19	8.18	5.93	5.01	4.50	4.17	3.94	3.77	3.63	3.52	3.43	3.30	3.15	3.00	2.92	2.84	2.76	2.67	2.58	2.49
20	8.10	5.85	4.94	4.43	4.10	3.87	3.70	3.56	3.46	3.37	3.23	3.09	2.94	2.86	2.78	2.69	2.61	2.52	2.42
21	8.02	5.78	4.87	4.37	4.04	3.81	3.64	3.51	3.40	3.31	3.17	3.03	2.88	2.80	2.72	2.64	2.55	2.46	2.36
22	7.95	5.72	4.82	4.31	3.99	3.76	3.59	3.45	3.35	3.26	3.12	2.98	2.83	2.75	2.67	2.58	2.50	2.40	2.31
23	7.88	5.66	4.76	4.26	3.94	3.71	3.54	3.41	3.30	3.21	3.07	2.93	2.78	2.70	2.62	2.54	2.45	2.35	2.26
24	7.82	5.61	4.72	4.22	3.90	3.67	3.50	3.36	3.26	3.17	3.03	2.89	2.74	2.66	2.58	2.49	2.40	2.31	2.21
25	7.77	5.57	4.68	4.18	3.85	3.63	3.46	3.32	3.22	3.13	2.99	2.85	2.70	2.62	2.54	2.45	2.36	2.27	2.17
26	7.72	5.53	4.64	4.14	3.82	3.59	3.42	3.29	3.18	3.09	2.96	2.81	2.66	2.58	2.50	2.42	2.33	2.23	2.13
27	7.68	5.49	4.60	4.11	3.78	3.56	3.39	3.26	3.15	3.06	2.93	2.78	2.63	2.55	2.47	2.38	2.29	2.20	2.10
28	7.64	5.45	4.57	4.07	3.75	3.53	3.36	3.23	3.12	3.03	2.90	2.75	2.60	2.52	2.44	2.35	2.26	2.17	2.06
29	7.60	5.42	4.54	4.04	3.73	3.50	3.33	3.20	3.09	3.00	2.87	2.73	2.57	2.49	2.41	2.33	2.23	2.14	2.03
30	7.56	5.39	4.51	4.02	3.70	3.47	3.30	3.17	3.07	2.98	2.84	2.70	2.55	2.47	2.39	2.30	2.21	2.11	2.01
40	7.31	5.18	4.31	3.83	3.51	3.29	3.12	2.99	2.89	2.80	2.66	2.52	2.37	2.29	2.20	2.11	2.02	1.92	1.80
60	7.08	4.98	4.13	3.65	3.34	3.12	2.95	2.82	2.72	2.63	2.50	2.35	2.20	2.12	2.03	1.94	1.84	1.73	1.60
120	6.85	4.79	3.95	3.48	3.17	2.96	2.79	2.66	2.56	2.47	2.34	2.19	2.03	1.95	1.86	1.76	1.66	1.53	1.38
∞	6.63	4.61	3.78	3.32	3.02	2.80	2.64	2.51	2.41	2.32	2.18	2.04	1.88	1.79	1.70	1.59	1.47	1.32	1.00

Source: E. S. Pearson and H. O. Hartley, *Biometrika Tables for Statisticians*, Vol. 1, Table 18 with permission.

TABLE B.4   Present Value of $1 (*PVIF*)

Period	1%	2%	3%	4%	5%	6%	7%	8%	9%	10%	Period
01	.99010	.98039	.97007	.96154	.95233	.94340	.93458	.92593	.91743	.90909	01
02	.98030	.96117	.94260	.92456	.90703	.89000	.87344	.85734	.84168	.82645	02
03	.97059	.94232	.91514	.88900	.86384	.83962	.81639	.79383	.77228	.75131	03
04	.96098	.92385	.88849	.85480	.82270	.79209	.76290	.73503	.70883	.68301	04
05	.95147	.90573	.86261	.82193	.78353	.74726	.71299	.68058	.64993	.62092	05
06	.94204	.88797	.83748	.79031	.74622	.70496	.66634	.63017	.59627	.56447	06
07	.93272	.87056	.81309	.75992	.71063	.66506	.62275	.58349	.54705	.51316	07
08	.92348	.85349	.78941	.73069	.67684	.62741	.58201	.54027	.50189	.46651	08
09	.91434	.83675	.76642	.70259	.64461	.59190	.54393	.50025	.46043	.42410	09
10	.90529	.82035	.74409	.67556	.61391	.55839	.50835	.46319	.42241	.38554	10
11	.89632	.80426	.72242	.64958	.58468	.52679	.47509	.42888	.38753	.35049	11
12	.88745	.78849	.70138	.62460	.55684	.49697	.44401	.39711	.35553	.31683	12
13	.87866	.77303	.68095	.60057	.53032	.46884	.41496	.36770	.32618	.28966	13
14	.86996	.75787	.66112	.57747	.50507	.44230	.38782	.34046	.29925	.26333	14
15	.86135	.74301	.64186	.55526	.48102	.41726	.36245	.31524	.27454	.23939	15
16	.85282	.72845	.62317	.53391	.45811	.39365	.33873	.29189	.25187	.21763	16
17	.84436	.71416	.60502	.51337	.43630	.37136	.31657	.27027	.23107	.19784	17
18	.83602	.70016	.58739	.49363	.41552	.35034	.29586	.25025	.21199	.17986	18
19	.82774	.68643	.57029	.47464	.39573	.33051	.27651	.23171	.19449	.16354	19
20	.81954	.67297	.55367	.45639	.37689	.31180	.25842	.21455	.17843	.14864	20
21	.81143	.65978	.53755	.44883	.35894	.29415	.24151	.19866	.16370	.13513	21
22	.80340	.64684	.52189	.42195	.34185	.27750	.22571	.18394	.15018	.12285	22
23	.79544	.63414	.50669	.40573	.32557	.26180	.21095	.17031	.13778	.11168	23
24	.78757	.62172	.49193	.39012	.31007	.24698	.19715	.15770	.12640	.10153	24
25	.77977	.60953	.47760	.37512	.29530	.23300	.18425	.14602	.11597	.09230	25

| TABLE B.4 | Present Value of $1 (*PVIF*) (continued) |

Period	11%	12%	13%	14%	15%	16%	17%	18%	19%	20%	Period
01	.90090	.89286	.88496	.87719	.86957	.86207	.85470	.84746	.84043	.83333	01
02	.81162	.79719	.78315	.76947	.75614	.74316	.73051	.71818	.70616	.69444	02
03	.73119	.71178	.69305	.67497	.65752	.64066	.62437	.60863	.59342	.57870	03
04	.65873	.63552	.61332	.59208	.57175	.55229	.53365	.51579	.49867	.48225	04
05	.59345	.56743	.54276	.51937	.49718	.47611	.45611	.43711	.41905	.40188	05
06	.53464	.50663	.48032	.45559	.43233	.41044	.38984	.37043	.35214	.33490	06
07	.48166	.45235	.42506	.39964	.37594	.35383	.33320	.31392	.29592	.27908	07
08	.43393	.40388	.37616	.35056	.32690	.30503	.28478	.26604	.24867	.23257	08
09	.39092	.36061	.33288	.30751	.28426	.26295	.24340	.22546	.20897	.19381	09
10	.35218	.32197	.29459	.26974	.24718	.22668	.20804	.19106	.17560	.16151	10
11	.31728	.28748	.26070	.23662	.21494	.19542	.17781	.16192	.14756	.13459	11
12	.28584	.25667	.23071	.20756	.18691	.16846	.15197	.13722	.12400	.11216	12
13	.25751	.22917	.20416	.18207	.16253	.14523	.12989	.11629	.10420	.09346	13
14	.23199	.20462	.18068	.15971	.14133	.12520	.11102	.09855	.08757	.07789	14
15	.20900	.18270	.15989	.14010	.12289	.10793	.09489	.08352	.07359	.06491	15
16	.18829	.16312	.14150	.12289	.10686	.09304	.08110	.07073	.06184	.05409	16
17	.16963	.14564	.12522	.10780	.09293	.08021	.06932	.05998	.05196	.04507	17
18	.15282	.13004	.11081	.09456	.08080	.06914	.05925	.05083	.04367	.03756	18
19	.13768	.11611	.09806	.08295	.07026	.05961	.05064	.04308	.03669	.03130	19
20	.12403	.10367	.08678	.07276	.06110	.05139	.04328	.03651	.03084	.02608	20
21	.11174	.09256	.07680	.06383	.05313	.04430	.03699	.03094	.02591	.02174	21
22	.10067	.08264	.06796	.05599	.04620	.03819	.03162	.02622	.02178	.01811	22
23	.09069	.07379	.06014	.04911	.04017	.03292	.02702	.02222	.01830	.01509	23
24	.08170	.06588	.05322	.04308	.03493	.02838	.02310	.01883	.01538	.01258	24
25	.07361	.05882	.04710	.03779	.03038	.02447	.01974	.01596	.01292	.01048	25

TABLE B.5   Present Value of an Annuity of $1 (*PVIFA*)

Period	1%	2%	3%	4%	5%	6%	7%	8%	9%	10%	Period
01	.9901	.9804	.9709	.9615	.9524	.9434	.9346	.9259	.9174	.9091	01
02	1.9704	1.9416	1.9135	1.8861	1.8594	1.8334	1.8080	1.7833	1.7591	1.7355	02
03	2.9410	2.8839	2.8286	2.7751	2.7233	2.6730	2.6243	2.5771	2.5313	2.4868	03
04	3.9020	3.8077	3.7171	3.6299	3.5459	3.4651	3.3872	3.3121	3.2397	3.1699	04
05	4.8535	4.7134	4.5797	4.4518	4.3295	4.2123	4.1002	3.9927	3.8896	3.7908	05
06	5.7955	5.6014	5.4172	5.2421	5.0757	4.9173	4.7665	4.6229	4.4859	4.3553	06
07	6.7282	6.4720	6.2302	6.0020	5.7863	5.5824	5.3893	5.2064	5.0329	4.8684	07
08	7.6517	7.3254	7.0196	6.7327	6.4632	6.2093	5.9713	5.7466	5.5348	5.3349	08
09	8.5661	8.1622	7.7861	7.4353	7.1078	6.8017	6.5152	6.2469	5.9852	5.7590	09
10	9.4714	8.9825	8.7302	8.1109	7.7217	7.3601	7.0236	6.7101	6.4176	6.1446	10
11	10.3677	9.7868	9.2526	8.7604	8.3064	7.8868	7.4987	7.1389	6.8052	6.4951	11
12	11.2552	10.5753	9.9589	9.3850	8.8632	8.3838	7.9427	7.5361	7.1601	6.8137	12
13	12.1338	11.3483	10.6349	9.9856	9.3935	8.8527	8.3576	7.9038	7.4869	7.1034	13
14	13.0088	12.1062	11.2960	10.5631	9.8986	9.2950	8.7454	8.2442	7.7860	7.3667	14
15	13.8651	12.8492	11.9379	11.1183	10.3796	9.7122	9.1079	8.5595	8.0607	7.6061	15
16	14.7180	13.5777	12.5610	11.6522	10.8377	10.1059	9.4466	8.8514	8.3126	7.8237	16
17	15.5624	14.2918	13.1660	12.1656	11.2740	10.4772	9.7632	9.1216	8.5435	8.0215	17
18	16.3984	14.9920	13.7534	12.6592	11.6895	10.8276	10.0591	9.3719	8.7556	8.2014	18
19	17.2201	15.2684	14.3237	13.1339	12.0853	11.1581	10.3356	9.6036	8.9501	8.3649	19
20	18.0457	16.3514	14.8774	13.5903	12.4622	11.4699	10.5940	9.8181	9.1285	8.5136	20
21	18.8571	17.0111	15.4149	14.0291	12.8211	11.7640	10.8355	10.0168	9.2922	8.6487	21
22	19.6605	17.6581	15.9368	14.4511	13.1630	12.0416	11.0612	10.2007	9.4424	8.7715	22
23	20.4559	18.2921	16.4435	14.8568	13.4885	12.3033	11.2722	10.3710	9.5802	8.8832	23
24	21.2435	18.9139	16.9355	15.2469	13.7986	12.5503	11.4693	10.5287	9.7066	8.9847	24
25	22.0233	19.5234	17.4181	15.6220	14.9039	12.7833	11.6536	10.6748	9.8226	9.0770	25

TABLE B.5   Present Value of an Annuity of $1 (*PVIFA*) (continued)

Period	11%	12%	13%	14%	15%	16%	17%	18%	19%	20%	Period
01	.9009	.8929	.8850	.8772	.8696	.8621	.8547	.8475	.8403	.8333	01
02	1.7125	1.6901	1.6681	1.6467	1.6257	1.6052	1.5852	1.5656	1.5465	1.5278	02
03	2.4437	2.4018	2.3612	2.3216	2.2832	2.2459	2.2096	2.1743	2.1399	2.1065	03
04	3.1024	3.0373	2.9745	2.9137	2.8550	2.7982	2.7432	2.6901	2.6386	2.5887	04
05	3.6959	3.6048	3.5172	3.4331	3.3522	3.2743	3.1993	3.1272	3.0576	2.9906	05
06	4.2305	4.1114	3.9976	3.8887	3.7845	3.6847	3.5892	3.4976	3.4098	3.3255	06
07	4.7122	4.5638	4.4226	4.2883	4.1604	4.0386	3.9224	3.8115	3.7057	3.6046	07
08	5.1461	4.9676	4.7988	4.6389	4.4873	4.3436	4.2072	4.0776	3.9544	3.8372	08
09	5.5370	5.3282	5.1317	4.9464	4.7716	4.6065	4.4506	4.3030	4.1633	4.0310	09
10	5.8892	5.6502	5.4262	5.2161	5.0188	4.8332	4.6586	4.4941	4.3389	4.1925	10
11	6.2065	5.9377	5.6869	5.4527	5.2337	5.0286	4.8364	4.6560	4.4865	4.3271	11
12	6.4924	6.1944	5.9176	5.6603	5.4206	5.1971	4.9884	4.7932	4.6105	4.4392	12
13	6.7499	6.4235	6.1218	5.8424	5.5831	5.3423	5.1183	4.9095	4.7147	4.5327	13
14	6.9819	6.6282	6.3025	6.0021	5.7245	5.4675	5.2293	5.0081	4.8023	4.6106	14
15	7.1909	6.8109	6.4624	6.1422	5.8474	5.5755	5.3242	5.0916	4.8759	4.6755	15
16	7.3792	6.9740	6.6039	6.2651	5.9542	5.6685	5.4053	5.1624	4.9377	4.7296	16
17	7.5488	7.1196	6.7291	6.3729	6.0472	5.7487	5.4746	5.2223	4.9897	4.7746	17
18	7.7016	7.2497	6.8389	6.4674	6.1280	5.8178	5.5339	5.2732	5.0333	4.8122	18
19	7.8393	7.3650	6.9380	6.5504	6.1982	5.8775	5.5845	5.3176	5.0700	4.8435	19
20	7.9633	7.4694	7.0248	6.6231	6.2593	5.9288	5.6278	5.3527	5.1009	4.8696	20
21	8.0751	7.5620	7.1016	6.6870	6.3125	5.9731	5.6648	5.3837	5.1268	4.8913	21
22	8.1757	7.6446	7.1695	6.7429	6.3587	6.0113	5.6964	5.4099	5.1486	4.9094	22
23	8.2664	7.7184	7.2297	6.7921	6.3988	6.0442	5.7234	5.4321	5.1668	4.9245	23
24	8.3481	7.7843	7.2829	6.8351	6.4338	6.0726	5.7465	5.4509	5.1822	4.9371	24
25	8.4217	7.8431	7.3300	6.8729	6.4641	6.0971	5.7662	5.4669	5.1951	4.9476	25

| TABLE B.6 | Durbin-Watson Statistic for 2.5% Significance (One-Tail) or 5.0% Significance (Two-Tail) |

	m = 1		m = 2		m = 3		m = 4		m = 5	
n	d_L	d_U	d_L	d_U	d_L	d_U	d_L	d_U	d_L	d_U
15	0.95	1.23	0.83	1.40	0.71	1.61	0.59	1.84	0.48	2.09
16	0.98	1.24	0.86	1.40	0.75	1.59	0.64	1.80	0.53	2.03
17	1.01	1.25	0.90	1.40	0.79	1.58	0.68	1.77	0.57	1.98
18	1.03	1.26	0.93	1.40	0.82	1.56	0.72	1.74	0.62	1.93
19	1.06	1.28	0.96	1.41	0.86	1.55	0.76	1.73	0.66	1.90
20	1.08	1.28	0.99	1.41	0.89	1.55	0.79	1.72	0.70	1.87
21	1.10	1.30	1.01	1.41	0.92	1.54	0.83	1.69	0.73	1.84
22	1.12	1.31	1.04	1.42	0.95	1.54	0.86	1.68	0.77	1.82
23	1.14	1.32	1.06	1.42	0.97	1.54	0.89	1.67	0.80	1.80
24	1.16	1.33	1.08	1.43	1.00	1.54	0.91	1.66	0.83	1.79
25	1.18	1.34	1.10	1.43	1.02	1.54	0.94	1.65	0.86	1.77
26	1.19	1.35	1.12	1.44	1.04	1.54	0.96	1.65	0.88	1.76
27	1.21	1.36	1.13	1.44	1.06	1.54	0.99	1.64	0.91	1.75
28	1.22	1.37	1.15	1.45	1.08	1.54	1.01	1.64	0.93	1.74
29	1.24	1.38	1.17	1.45	1.10	1.54	1.03	1.63	0.96	1.73
30	1.25	1.38	1.18	1.46	1.12	1.54	1.05	1.63	0.98	1.73
31	1.26	1.39	1.20	1.47	1.13	1.55	1.07	1.63	1.00	1.72
32	1.27	1.40	1.21	1.47	1.15	1.55	1.08	1.63	1.02	1.71
33	1.28	1.41	1.22	1.48	1.16	1.55	1.10	1.63	1.04	1.71
34	1.29	1.41	1.24	1.48	1.17	1.55	1.12	1.63	1.06	1.70
35	1.30	1.42	1.25	1.48	1.19	1.55	1.13	1.63	1.07	1.70
36	1.31	1.43	1.26	1.49	1.20	1.56	1.15	1.63	1.09	1.70
37	1.32	1.43	1.27	1.49	1.21	1.56	1.16	1.62	1.10	1.70
38	1.33	1.44	1.28	1.50	1.23	1.56	1.17	1.62	1.12	1.70
39	1.34	1.44	1.29	1.50	1.24	1.56	1.19	1.63	1.13	1.69
40	1.35	1.45	1.30	1.51	1.25	1.57	1.20	1.63	1.15	1.69
45	1.39	1.48	1.34	1.53	1.30	1.58	1.25	1.63	1.21	1.69
50	1.42	1.50	1.38	1.54	1.34	1.59	1.30	1.64	1.26	1.69
55	1.45	1.52	1.41	1.56	1.37	1.60	1.33	1.64	1.30	1.69
60	1.47	1.54	1.44	1.57	1.40	1.61	1.37	1.65	1.33	1.69
65	1.49	1.55	1.46	1.59	1.43	1.63	1.40	1.66	1.36	1.69
70	1.51	1.57	1.48	1.60	1.45	1.63	1.42	1.66	1.39	1.70
75	1.53	1.58	1.50	1.61	1.47	1.64	1.45	1.67	1.42	1.70
80	1.54	1.59	1.52	1.63	1.49	1.65	1.47	1.67	1.44	1.70
85	1.56	1.60	1.53	1.63	1.51	1.66	1.49	1.68	1.46	1.71
90	1.57	1.61	1.55	1.64	1.53	1.66	1.50	1.69	1.48	1.71
95	1.58	1.62	1.56	1.65	1.54	1.67	1.52	1.69	1.50	1.71
100	1.59	1.63	1.57	1.65	1.55	1.67	1.53	1.70	1.51	1.72

m = number of independent variables
n = number of observations
Source: From J. Durbin and G. S. Watson, "Testing for Serial Correlation in Least-Squares Regression," *Biometrika*, Vol. 38 (1951); 159–177. With the permission of the authors and the Trustees of *Biometrika*.

<table>
<tr><td rowspan="2">TABLE B.7

Critical Values for the
Dickey-Fuller Test</td></tr>
</table>

	Sample Size			
	25	50	100	∞
F ratio	7.24	6.73	6.49	6.25
AR(1) model	2.16	2.08	2.03	2.00
AR(1) model with constant	0.72	0.66	0.63	0.60
AR(1) model with constant and time trend	−0.15	−0.15	−0.28	−0.33

D. Dickey and W. Fuller, "Likelihood Ratio Tests for Autoregressive Time Series with A Unit Root," *Econometrica*, 49, 1981.

CHECK ANSWERS TO SELECTED END-OF-CHAPTER EXERCISES

CHAPTER 2

1. Budget = $875 million
2. c. $v = 0.067$
4. a. 0.0062

APPENDIX 2A

1. d. $Q^* = 8$
3. a. $100 - 12Q + 1.5Q^2$
5. b. $Q^* = 5$
8. a. 25 units newspaper advertising

CHAPTER 3

1. $Q_{A2} = 1,830$
3. 44%
5. a. -0.3
7. Chow: 11.528 million
9. $P = \$90$
11. a. $E_D = -0.59$
15. a. -3%
17. a. i. $E_D = -1.78$
19. -3%
22. a. $E_X = 1.34$
24. Week 2-3: $E_Y = 0.538$
28. $Q_{2000} = 5169$
30. c. $Q_2 = 505$
32. a. -0.375

CHAPTER 4

2. c. $Y = 11.148 + 1.492X$
4. d. $R^2 = 0.885$
6. a. Income coefficient = 5.9492
10. b. $E_A = 0.98$
13. c. 1.909
15. a. $E_X = d$
18. a. $Y' = 19.6325 + 1.2945X_1 + .3828X_2 - 2.5219X_3$

CASE EXERCISE— DEMAND ESTIMATION

7. $E_D = -0.167$

APPENDIX 4A

4. a. $R^2 = 0.93$
6. a. i. $S' = 247.644 + .3926A - .7339P$

CHAPTER 5

1. b. $S_{t+1} = 729,000$
4. b. GNP = 955
6. b. $+6\%$
8. a. $Q_D = 11,450$
10. b. $Y'_{10} = 259.03$
12. a. December 2005 = 468
14. a. $Q = 10,200(000)$

CHAPTER 6

1. Both increase
3. Outsource abroad and buy foreign assets
6. 50% decline. Relative purchasing power parity

CHAPTER 7

4. b. 10 or 11 men
6. b. $AP_x = 6X - .4X^2$
8. b. $Q^* = 44$
12. a. 4.88%
14. a. i. $\beta_L = 0.70$
16. a. Constant returns
17. a. Homogeneous of degree = 0.7

CASE EXERCISE

4. $E_K = 0.415$

APPENDIX 7A

1. d. $Q^* = 43.231$

CHAPTER 8

3. a. $10,000
8. a. $TC = 150 + 200Q - 9Q^2 + 0.25Q^3$
10. a. $Q^* = 10$
12. a. TC(one plant) = $4,275,000

CASE EXERCISE

1. $4.55

APPENDIX 8A

1. a. $L^* = 2.5$ units
3. a. $10

CHAPTER 9

3. a. $Q^* = \$574.08$ (million)
6. c. 8,000
8. a. p = 0.0062
11. a. $30,000,000

CASE EXERCISE— COST FUNCTIONS

5. $Q^* = 1,675$

CASE EXERCISE— CHARTER AIRLINE

3. 23,900

APPENDIX 9A

1. c. C = $803.51

CHAPTER 10

7. a. P = $8
9. c. iii. Ration coupon value = $15
11. d. $MR = 3 - Q/2,000$
13. b. $P^* = \$1,220$
15. d. $\pi = \$9,000$
17. b. i. $\Delta TR = +\$59,395$
18. b. $900,000 on advertising

CHAPTER 11

5. c. $Q^* = 125$
7. e. $\pi^* = \$263,625$
9. b. $P^* = \$60$
11. a. ROI = 14.2%
13. a. ROI = 12.98%

CHAPTER 12

2. a. $P^* = \$145$
   $Q^*_A = 30$
5. a. $P^* = \$9,666.70$
6. c. $P^* = \$125$
9. b. Dominant strategy for AMC is to "Not Abide"

CHAPTER 13

2. ($150, Match), No
3. Least should pass
6. P^r (continue) = 2/7, P^t (advertise) = 3/5

CHAPTER 14

3. $P_{US} = \$12$
5. a. $\pi = -20 + 96Q_1 + 76Q_2 - 2Q_1^2 - Q_2^2$
10. a. $P = \$72.50$

APPENDIX 14A

2. Decrease

APPENDIX 14B

4. $P_1^* = \$40.67$
7. c. i. $Q_m^* = 4$ units internally

CASE EXERCISE

1. $Q_m^* = 356,790$ units
5. $Q_m^* = 353,750$ units

CHAPTER 15

3. High interest rates, large principal, long term, unsecured
4. Vertical integration if power plant dependent on this type of coal. Otherwise, long-term supply contracts.
9. Take turns imitating and licensing the first, and thereafter, every other generation of products.

CASE EXERCISE— INCENTIVE CONTRACT

5. $1,200,000

CHAPTER 16

4. Electricity, T bills
5. $1.3 million. Use open bidding, multiple-rounds, highest-wins-and-pays
11. Apple's expected profit is $1.5 million less from understatement.

CASE EXERCISE— SPECTRUM AUCTION

b. PCS will bid $20 million

CASE EXERCISE—INVESTMENT BANKING FEES

1. Lead underwriter = $97 million
Syndicate Comanager = 0
Syndicate Member 3 = $1 million
Syndicate Member 4 = 0
Syndicate Member 5 = $2 million

APPENDIX 16A

5. c. $146

CHAPTER 17

6. a. HHI before = 1,964
13. a. $P^* = \$10,000$
15. b. $\pi^* = \$450$ million
18. a. σ_T (after) = 4.2%
20. b. $Q^* = 69.05$

CHAPTER 18

2. IRR = 9.1%
4. b. $NCF_{10} = \$5,560$
6. a. i. IRR = 14.94%
8. $k_e = 13.4\%$
10. b. $k'_e = 13\%$
12. $k_a = 12.3\%$
14. b. Power plant: $NPV_{@12\%} = -\$22.71$ million

CASE EXERCISE

1. B/C ratio = 1.90

CHAPTER 19

2. b. $E(U)$ for $A_1 = -0.3975$
4. a. $E(V_A) = \$780,000$
6. e. 30 dozen
8. c. $+\$32,620$
10. a. NPV = $1.31 million

A

Accounting cost, 347–349, 384
Accounting profit, 12
Acquisition cost, 349
Adverse selection, 460–462
Advertising
    intensity, 456–457
    net value, 457–458
Advertising elasticity, 104
Advertising expenses, 455–458
Agency costs, 16, 17
Agency relationships, 15–16
Airline Deregulation Act of 1978,
    783
Allocative efficiency, 319, 321
Analysis of variance, 146–149, 153
Annuity, present value of an, A-3,
    A-4
Antidumping sanctions, 267–268
Antitrust laws
    Clayton Act (1914), The, 772
    cross price elasticity of demand,
        102
    definition, 771
    enforcement, 774
    Federal Trade Commission Act
        (1914), The, 773
    Hart-Scott-Rodino Antitrust
        Improvement Act (1976),
        The, 773–774
    impact on business decisions,
        774–778
    Robinson-Patman Act (1936),
        The, 773
    Sherman Act (1890), The,
        771–772
Appraisals, 734
Arbitrage, 243
    covered interest, 289–290
    current, 254
    goods, 256–257
Arc cross price elasticity, 101
Arc elasticity, 85
Arc income elasticity, 98–99
Arc price elasticity, 82–84
Arithmetic scale, 418
Asset limitation, 864
Asset specificity, 467
Association and causation, 149–150
Asymmetric information
    adverse selection, 460–462
    application, 458
    auction design, 720
    experience goods, 459–460
    insuring and lending, 462–463

Internet auctions, 734–735
    screening and sorting, 691
    shareholder wealth-maximization,
        20–21
Attrition, wars of, 573–575
Auction design and information
    economics
    application, 719–720
    common-value auction, 723–725
    design differences, 720, 731–734
    Dutch auction, 720
    English auction, 720
    incentive-compatible auction
        mechanism, 729–731
    Internet auctions, 733–735
    open bidding, 725–726
    private-value auctions, 726–729
    second-highest bid sealed bid
        auctions, 729–731
    underbidding, strategic, 726–729
    Vickery Auction, 730
    winner's curse, 721–723
Authorization level, 648
Autocorrelation
    cyclical variation, 171
    definition, 170–171
    Durbin-Watson statistic, 171–172
    first-order autocorrelation, 171
    inferences, 171
    negative autocorrelation, 171–172
    positive autocorrelation, 171–172
    randomness, testing for, 172
    regression results, 173
    seasonal patterns, 171
    self-reinforcing trends, 171
    t-statistic application, 173
Average cost functions, 354–357
Average profit function, 33–34, 35
Axelrod, Robert, 585

B

Backwards induction, 552
Balance of payments, 279–283
Barometric forecasting techniques,
    204–205
    composite indexes, 207
    diffusion indexes, 207
    indicators, 205–207
    weaknesses, 206–207
Barometric price leadership, 525
Barriers to entry. See Entry, threat of
Baumol, William J., 825
Bayesian probability concept,
    584–585
Beecham v. Europharm, 278

Beggar thy neighbor trade policy,
    246–247, 266
Behavioral equations, 213
Benchmarking, 688
Benefit-cost ratio, 818
Best-reply response, 578
Binding agreements, 591
Blocs, trading, 262–263, 275
Bonding mechanisms, 463
Bonus plan, performance-based,
    3–4, 14–15
Brand loyalty, 257, 534, 571
Brand name, 464–465
Break-even analysis
    application, 394, 397–398
    business risk, 407–408
    contribution analysis comparison,
        397–399, 404–406
    definition, 397
    limitations, 405–406
    linear break-even analysis,
        399–404
    operating leverage, 406–407
    risk assessment, 408–409
Break-even sales change analysis,
    438–439
Brinkmanship, 573–575
Budget lines, 116, 118–119
Budgeting. See Capital budgeting
Bundling, 610–613
Business risk, 407–408

C

Cannibalization, 620
Capacity planning and pricing,
    597–600
Capacity reallocation decision,
    645–649
Capital account, 279–280
Capital asset pricing model,
    813–815
Capital assets, 349
Capital budgeting, 32
    cash flow estimates, 804–806
    classification, 802–804
    cost of capital (See Cost of capital)
    definition, 800
    evaluation, investment project,
        806–809
    internal rate of return, 807, 809
    model, 800–802
    net present value, 807–809
    post-implementation review,
        809–810
    selection process, 802–803

Capital expenditure, 800
Capital market, efficiency of, 37
Capital, cost of. *See* Cost of capital
CAPM. *See* Capital asset pricing
    model
Cartels, 513, 517–524, 541–542
Cash flows, 9, 12, 37, 805
Cause and effect relationship,
    149–150
Ceteris paribus, 82, 84, 99
Chainstore Paradox, 582–583
Change order responsiveness, 641
Clarke tax mechanism, 738–739
Class action suits, 753
Clayton Act (1914), The, 772
Closed-end lease with residual
    values, 566
Coase Theorem, 751–753, 763
Coase, Ronald, 683, 750
Cobb-Douglas production function
    expression, 297
    long-run cost function, 378–380
    production function, statistical
        estimation of, 326–330
Coefficient of determination, 147,
    148
Coefficient of variation, 45, 48
Coincident indicators, 205–207,
    208–209
Collusion, 513–516, 774
Common-value auction, 723–725
Comparative advantage, 264–266
Compensation, executive, 3–4,
    14–15, 690
Competitiveness
    asymmetric information, 458–459
    export pressure, increased, 234
    exports, 275–276, 282
    management in global economy,
        24–25
    regulation, government, 784–788
    strategy, 426–431
Complement strategy, 78–80
Complementary goods, 102
Complete markets, 19–20
Composite indexes, 207
Concentration market, ratio,
    769–771
Congestion pricing, 604–605
Conscious parallelism of action, 512
Consensus forecasting, 215–216
Conspicuous focal point, 586
Constant elasticity, 134
Constant elasticity demand, 181
Constant marginal impact, 133

Constant marginal utility, 52, 54,
    847
Constant rate of growth pattern,
    193, 194–195
Constraint, cost, 315–317
Consumer intentions surveys, 211
Contestable markets, 572, 573,
    766–768
Contingent payments, 735
Continuous probability distribution,
    44
Continuous variable, 305–306
Contracts, 675
    full contingent claims, 681
    incentive, 685
    incentive-compatible, 742–743
    linear incentives, 692
    optimal incentives, 740–742
    relational, 695–696
    renewal, 693–694
    vertical requirements, 675–677
Contractual expected returns, 22
Contribution analysis, 397–399,
    404–406
Contribution margin, 401, 439–440,
    487–488
Cooperative equilibrium, 583
Cooperative exchange, 590–591
Cooperative games, 539
Core competencies, 428
Corporate takeovers, managerial
    role in, 16
Correlation analysis, 131
    application, 148
    association and causation,
        149–150
    coefficient of determination, 147
    correlation coefficient, 145–146
    definition, 145
    variance, analysis of, 146–149
Correlation coefficient, 145–146
Cost analysis
    average cost functions, 354–357
    challenges, 347
    cost function, 352–359, 378–380
    definition, 347
    depreciation cost measurement,
        349
    diseconomies of scale
        (*See* Diseconomies of scale)
    economies of scale
        (*See* Economies of scale)
    explicit costs, 347
    fixed costs, 352
    implicit costs, 347

inventory valuation, 349–351
long-run cost function, 359–362
marginal cost functions, 355–357
opportunity costs, 347–349
optimal capacity utilization,
    359–360
production curve relationships,
    357–359
profitability measurement,
    347–348
relevant cost, 349–350, 351
short-run cost function, 351–359
total economic, 25
underutilized facilities, 350–351
variable costs, 352
Cost fixing, 437
Cost function, 352–359
    logarithmic, 395
    long-run (*See* Long-run cost
        function)
    short-run (*See* Short-run cost
        function)
    types, 383–384
Cost leadership strategy, 430
Cost of capital
    capital asset pricing model,
        813–815
    debt capital, 811
    definition, 810–811
    dividend valuation model,
        812–813
    external equity capital, 815
    internal economies of scale, 363
    internal equity capital, 811–812
    variability components, 814–815
    weighted cost of capital, 815–816
Cost overruns, 737–738
Cost-benefit analysis
    accept-reject decisions, 817–818
    application, 817
    benefit-cost ratio, 818
    classification system, 820–822
    constraints, 821–822
    definition, 817
    direct benefits, 823
    indirect costs, 824
    intangibles, 824
    Kaldor-Hicks criterion, 820
    model, 24
    Pareto optimality, 820
    pecuniary effects, 824
    primary benefits, 823
    program-level analysis, 818–819
    real effects, 824
    secondary effects, 824

steps, 819–820
technological effects, 824
valuations, market, 822–823
Cost-effectiveness analysis
  constant-cost studies, 827
  definition, 827
  least-cost studies, 828
  objective-level studies, 828–829
Cost-minimization process, 63–64
  allocative efficiency, 319, 321
  efficiency, production, 319–321
  input substitution effects, 321–323
  linear programming techniques,
    317–318, 340–344
  output constraint, 315–317
  output effect, 321–323
  overall production efficiency, 320
  process rays, 318–319
  production process, 318–319
  technical efficiency, 319, 321
Cost-of-capital
  direct costs, 823
  primary costs, 823
Costs
  accounting, 347–349, 384
  acquisition, 349
  agency, 16, 17
  average, 354–357
  direct, 385, 823
  economic, 6, 7, 347–349, 384
  explicit, 347
  fixed, 352, 403–404
  implicit, 347
  indirect, 824
  long-term cost function, 378–380
  marginal, 31, 355–357, 388
  marginal factor, 309
  operating, 405
  opportunity, 7, 347, 805
  primary, 823
  recontracting, 21
  relevant, 349–350, 351
  replacement, 349–350
  stranded, 394
  sunk, 350–351, 805
  switching, 437
  total, 399
  variable, 352, 405
Cournet Model, 512–513, 522–523
Covered hedges, 245
Covered interest arbitrage, 289–290
Creative ingenuity, 16, 688
Credibility
  closed-end lease with residual
    values, 566

commitment, credible, 558–559
credible threat, definition of, 559
establishment mechanisms,
  559–560
guarantees, 561–563
hostage mechanism, 560
importance, 552
leasing advantages, 563–567
licenses, advantages to renewable,
  563–567
organization form, 677
Credible commitment, 558–559
Credible threat, 558–559
Cross price elasticity of demand
  antitrust laws, 102
  arc cross price elasticity, 101
  definition, 101
  empirical estimates, 103–104
  interpretation, 102
  point cross price elasticity,
    101–102
Cross-functional systems management
  process, 639–641
Currency value. See Exchange rates
Current account, 279–280
Current arbitrage, 254
Cyclical variation, 171, 191–192

D
Debt capital, 811
Decision tree, 551, 850–851
Decision-making
  classification, 841, 842
  criterion, 855–857
  decision tree approach, 551,
    850–851
  example of, 4–5
  model, 5–6
  payoff table summarization, 844
  process, 6
  risk-adjusted discount rate,
    851–852
  simulation approach, 852–854
  sunk costs role, 572–573
Definitional equations, 213
Degree of operating leverage,
  406–407
Demand
  complementary goods, 78–80
  curves, 76–78, 87, 629–630
  derived demand, 80–81
  durable goods, 80–81
  estimation (See Estimation,
    demand)
  exchange rate considerations, 81

factors, 77
marginal utility, 75
price elasticity (See Price elasticity
  of demand)
producers' goods, 80–81
representation, 76–77
schedule, 74–75
shifts, 77, 78
substitute goods, 75–76
Demand function, 64, 76, 120–121,
  177, 179
Dependent variable, 132, 138
Depreciation, 385
Depreciation cost measurement, 349
Derivative markets, 20
Derivative of a function, 53–55
Derived demand, 80–81
Determinants
  Beggar thy neighbor trade policy,
    246–247
  grade flow role, 247
  growth rate role, 246–247
  inflation, 251
  real interest rates, 247–250
  trade-weighted exchange rate,
    259–260
Differential calculus
  optimization, 60–63
  relationship with marginal
    analysis, 52–55
Differential pricing, 603–606
Diffusion indexes, 207
Diminishing marginal returns,
  law of, 301–302
Diminishing marginal utility, 844
Direct (primary) benefits, 823
Direct (primary) costs, 823
Discount factor, 36
Discount rate, 11, 825–826, A-1
Diseconomies of scale, 366,
  367–368, 450
Diversification, 858
Dividend valuation model, 812–813
Dominant price leadership, 525–528
Dominant strategy, 536, 537,
  576–577
Double-log transformation,
  180–181
Dummy variables, 196–197
Durable goods, 80–81, 96
Durbin-Watson statistic, 171–172
Dutch auction, 720
Dynamic equilibrium (friction)
  theory of profit, 8
Dynamic pricing, 632

E

Eastman Kodak v. *Image Technical Services*, 778
Eckstein, Otto, 820, 822
Econometrics
   advantages, 211
   application, 131
   behavioral equations, 213
   comparative forecasting accuracy, 215–216
   definitional equations, 213
   dependent variable, 132
   endogenous variables, 213
   equations, 213
   exogenous variables, 213
   forecasting, 212
   independent variable, 132
   methodology, 131
   multiple-equation models, 213–215
   single-equation models, 211–212
   specification, model, 132
   structural equation models, 212–213
   structural equations, 213
   variable identification, 132
Economic cost, 6–7, 347–349, 384
Economic profit, 6, 7, 12, 25
Economic theory, 5
Economies of scale, 363–365, 367–368, 393–395, 450, 479, 697
Economies of scope, 364
Economy, global competitive, 24–25
Effect
   income, 75, 122
   substitution, 75–76, 120, 122
Effective exchange rate, 259
Efficiency
   market, 37
   objective, 24
Efficient rationing, 571
Elasticity
   advertising (*See* Advertising elasticity)
   cross price (*See* Cross price elasticity of demand)
   income (*See* Income elasticity of demand)
   price (*See* Price elasticity of demand)
Endgame reasoning, 552
Endogenous variables, 213
English auction, 720
Entry, threat of
   application, 567–568

capacity precommitments, excess, 568–571
large-scale deterrence, 598–600
Porter's five forces strategic framework, 432–433
pricing and output decisions, 434–435
regulation, government, 766
response to, 556–557
sorting rules, customer, 571–572
Equal payments, present value of, A-3, A-4
Equilibrium strategy, 553–554
Equimarginal criterion, 316
Estimation, demand
   constant marginal impact, 133
   consumer surveys, 129–130
   correlation analysis
      (*See* Correlation analysis)
   econometrics (*See* Econometrics)
   focus groups, 130
   Hawthorne effect, 130
   inverse demand function, 133
   least squares method, 139
   linear model, 133
   linear regression model, 136–138
   market experiment, 130, 131
   multiplicative exponential model, 133–134
   population regression coefficients, 139–140, 143–145
   predictions, regression equations role in, 142–143
   regression analysis
      (*See* Regression analysis)
   standard error of the estimate, 142
   statistical techniques, 128, 131
European Union, 270–271, 272, 275–277
Ex post implementation, 682
Exchange rates
   Beggar thy neighbor trade policy, 246–247
   current valuation, 240
   demand considerations, 81
   determinants (*See* Determinants)
   dollar market, U.S., 239
   equilibrium price, 240
   exposures, classification of, 237
   forwards, 245
   government transfers, 240–241
   hedges, 243–245
   import flows and transaction demand, 239–240
   import-export sales, 235–239

intervention, coordinated, 240–242
options, 245
purchase order requirements, export, 240
purchasing power parity (*See* Purchasing power parity)
real interest rates, 247–250
risk management, 243–244
sensitivities, 235–236
short-term fluctuations, 242–243
speculative demand, 240–241
spot, 292
sterilized intervention, 241
swaps, 245
trade-weighted, 259–260
transaction demand, 239–240
Executive compensation, 3–4, 690
   shareholder wealth-maximization, and, 14–15
Exogenous variables, 213
Expansion path, finding, 361–362
Expectation damages, 677
Expected marginal utility approach, 842–847
Expected monetary value (EMV), 842–843
Expected returns from portfolio, 858
Expected utility, 843
Expected value, 39–40
Expenditure plans, 210
Expenses, selling and promotional
   benefits, types of, 455
   capital advertising intensity, 456–457
   impacts of advertising, 458
   incentive sources, 455
   optimal level, determination of, 455–456
Experience goods, 459
Explicit costs, 347
Exponential smoothing, first-order, 201–203
Exports
   barriers, reduction of trade, 234
   Beecham v. *Europharm*, 278
   Beggar thy neighbor trade policy, 246–247, 266
   blocs, trading, 262–263
   capital account, 279–280
   comparative advantage, 264–266, 272–273
   competitiveness, 234, 275–276, 282
   currency advantages, single, 271–273

current account, 279–280
European Union, 270–271, 272, 275–277
exchange rate sensitivities, 235–239, 242–243
flows and transaction demand, 239–240
foreign exchange operating exposure, 237
free trade areas, 270–271
import controls, 266–267
increasing returns, 269–270
international trade flows, 260–262
maquiladora, 274
Mercantilist period, 266
Merck v. *Primecrown,* 278
mutual trade liberalization policies, 268
North American Free Trade Area, 270–271, 273–274, 275–277
operating risk exposures, 237
parallel imports, 277–278, 279
partners, trading, 273–275
payments, balance of, 279–283
perspectives, economic, 280–283
real terms of trade, 265
strategic policies, 268–270
trade deficits, 279–283
transaction risk exposure, 237
translation risk exposure, 237
twin deficits, 280, 282
Exposures, classification, 237
External equity capital, 815
Externalities
application, 749
class action suits, 753
Coase Theorem, 751–753
defined, 749
pecuniary externalities, 749–750
reciprocal nature, 750–752
resource allocation, and, 750
solutions, potential, 754–757
Spur Industries v. *Del Webb Development,* 749
strategic hold-outs, 753
urban renewal, 757–759

F

Fair division games, 715–717
Fast second advantages, 556–558
Feasible regions, 343
Federal Trade Commission Act (1914), The, 773
Financial hedges, 243–244

Firm-specific economies, 364–365
First derivative of a function, 53–55
First-mover advantages, 556–558
First-order autocorrelation, 171
First-order condition, 60–63, 64
First-order exponential smoothing, 201–203
Five forces strategic framework, 432–442
Fixed costs, 352
Fixed input, 298
Focal outcomes of interest, 557
Focus groups, 130
Folk theorem, 581
Forecasting
accuracy, evaluating model, 189
alternative methods, 190
barometric techniques (*See* Barometric forecasting techniques)
comparative forecasting accuracy, 215–216
composite indexes, 207
consensus, 215–216
diffusion indexes, 207
dummy variables, 196–197
Durbin-Watson statistic, 171–172
econometrics models (*See* Econometrics)
economic activity, 210
growth trends, declining rate of, 196
hierarchy, 188
indicators, 205–207, 208–209
input-output analysis, 220
least-squares method, 194
linear trend, 193, 194–195
Livingston survey, 215–216
models, elementary, 192–193
moving averages, 199–201
nonlinear trend, 193
operation risk exposures, 237
opinion polling techniques (*See* Survey and opinion polling techniques)
random walk variables, 218–219
ratio to trend method, 196
sales, 211
seasonal effects, 194, 196
secular trends, 190–191, 193
significance, 187–188
smoothing techniques (*See* Smoothing techniques)
stochastic time-series models, 216–219

survey and opinion polling techniques (*See* Survey and opinion polling techniques)
technique selection, 188–189
time-series analysis (*See* Time-series analysis)
Foreign exchange operating exposure, 237
Forward contract, 862
Forwards, 245
Fractional ownership, 565–566
Franchise, government-authorized, 479
Free trade, 97, 270–271
Freewheeling, 394
Friction theory of profit, 8
FTC v. *Stride Rite,* 778
Full contingent claims contract, 681
Full-cost pricing, 625–628
Full-line forcing, 848–850
Futures contract, 862

G

Gain-share discounting, 437
Game theory
application, 536, 549
business strategy, 548–555
components, 537–538
cooperative games, 539, 674–682
decision tree, 551
dominant strategy, 536, 537
game tree, 551
iterated dominant strategy, 538
Morgenstern, Oskar, 538
n-person games, 539
noncooperative games, 539
normal form of the game, 537–538
one-shot games, 539
Prisoner's dilemma game, 540, 541
repeated games, 539
rivalry, 535–541, 549
sequential games (*See* Sequential games)
simultaneous games (*See* Simultaneous games)
single-period games, 539
strategy game, 536–537
two-person game, 539
two-person zero-sum game, 540
von Neumann, John, 538
Game tree, 551
GDP, 281–282
international trade flows, 260–262

GNP, 280–282
Goods arbitrage, 256–257
Governance mechanisms, 682–685
Governance structure, 682
Gray markets, 277–278
Grim trigger strategy, 580–581
Gross domestic product. *See* GDP
Gross profit margin, 488–489
Growth rate role, 193–195
Guarantees, 561–563

H

Hart-Scott-Rodino Antitrust
    Improvement Act (1976),
    The, 773–774
Hawthorne effect, 130
Hedges, 243–245, 861–863
Herfindahl-Hirschman Index,
    770–771
Heteroscedasticity, 173
Holdup problem, 693–694
Homogenous production function,
    325
Hostage mechanisms, 463,
    464–465, 560, 590–591
Housing, 97

I

Identification problem, 177
Implicit costs, 347
Imports
    controls, 266–267
    export sales, 235–239
    exports, balance, 280–282
    flows and transaction demand,
        239–240
    international trade flows, 260–262
    regulation, government, 786–788
Incentive compatibility constraint,
    691
Incentive-compatible auction
    mechanism, 729–731
Incentive-compatible contracts,
    742–743
Incentive-compatible revelation
    mechanisms, 735–743
Incentive contracting, 685
Income effect, 75, 122
Income elasticity of demand
    arc income elasticity, 98–99
    ceteris paribus, 99
    combined effect with price
        elasticity, 105–106
    definition, 98
    empirical estimates, 100

interpretation, 99–100
    point income elasticity, 99
Income-superior goods, 99
Incomplete information, 459, 681
Increasing returns, 269–270
Incremental analysis, 627–628
Independent variable, 132
Indicators, 205–207, 208–209
Indifference curves
    budget lines, 118–119
    characteristics, 116–118
    demand function deviation,
        120–121
    income effects, 122
    optimal combination, 119–120,
        123
    substitution effects, 120, 122
Indirect costs, 824
Indirect segmentation, 607
Induction, backwards, 552
Inelasticity, 86, 87, 93
Inferior goods, 99–100
Infinitely repeated games, 582
Inflation, 251
Inflection point, 34
Information in advertising, 458–459
Information technology strategy,
    430–431
Innovation theory of profit, 8
Input classification, 298
Input substitution effects, 321–323
Input-output analysis, 220
Insurance, 863–864
Intangibles, 824
Interest rate determination, A-3, A-5
Interest rate parity, 290
Interest rates, 247–250
    forward, 290, 292
    real, 247–250
Internal equity capital, 811–812
Internal hedges, 243, 244
Internal rate of return, 807, 809
International Air Transport
    Association (IATA), 514
International Fisher effect, 290
Internet auctions, 733–735
Internet, pricing techniques, 630–632
Intertemporal pricing, 603–606
Inventory changes plans, 210
Inventory evaluation, 349–351
Inverse demand function, 133
Inverse intensity rationing, 571
Investment opportunity curve, 801
IRR. *See* Internal rate of return
Isocost lines, 313–315

Isoquants, production
    input substitution, 310–311
    marginal rate of technical
        substitution, 311–312
    perfect complements, 312–313
    perfect substitutes, 312–313
    representation, 309, 341–343
    returns to scale, 324
Iterated dominant strategy, 538

J

Joint products, 653–657
Joint ventures, 697, 735–736, 740,
    742

K

Kaldor-Hicks criterion, 820
Kinked demand curve model,
    529–530
Knockoffs, 277–278
Knowledge capital, 703

L

Lagging indicators, 205–207,
    208–209
Lagrangian multiplier technique, 338
Large-scale accommodation, 598–600
Law of comparative advantage,
    264–266
Law of demand, 75
Law of one price, 251
Leading indicators, 205–207,
    208–209
Learning curve
    application, 417
    characteristics, 417
    configurations, relationship,
        417–419
    effect, 363
    parameter estimation, 419
    percentage of learning, 420–421
Least-squares method, 94, 139, 419
Lemons markets, 458, 462–463
Licenses
    advantages, 563–567
    organization form, 702–707
    regulation, government, 784
Life-cycle pricing, 623–625
Limit pricing, 490–492, 624
Linear break-even analysis, 399–404
Linear incentives contract, 692
Linear model, 133
Linear programming, 317–319,
    340–344

Linear regression model, 131–132, 136–138
Linear trend, 193, 194–195
Livingston survey, 215–216
Logarithmic cost function, 389, 395
Logarithmic scale, 418
Long-run cost function
    cost analysis, 359–362
    engineering cost techniques, 396
    estimation, statistical, 391–392
    production, 299
    scale of operation, optimal, 392–393
    survivor technique, 396–397
Lotteries, stratified, 719

M

Macon Telegraph, The, 84–85
Macroeconomics, 5
Management strategies, risk
    acquisition of information, 857–858
    asset limitation, 864
    control of operational environment, 864
    diversification, 858
    hedging, 861–863
    insurance, 863–864
    portfolio, 858–861
    scenario planning, 864
Management, separation from ownership, 3, 14–15, 17
Managerial efficiency theory of profit, 8
Maquiladora, 274
Marginal analysis, 31–33, 48
    relationship with differential calculus, 52–55
Marginal benefit, 31, 32
Marginal cost functions, 355–357
Marginal costs, 31, 32, 388
Marginal factor cost, 309
Marginal product, 299–300, 301, 302
Marginal profit functions, 33–34, 35
Marginal rate of substitution, 120
Marginal rate of technical substitution (MRTS), 120, 311–312
Marginal return, 31
Marginal revenue, 88, 90–92, 445–447, 613–614, 801
Marginal revenue product, 308–309
Marginal utility, 52, 54, 75, 844–847

Mark-up, optimal, 487–488
Market
    conduct, 764–765
    environmental conditions, 768
    performance, 764
    structure of, 442–445, 765–766
Market demand curve, 76, 77
Market efficiency, 37
Market experiment, 130, 131
Market share, 441–442
Mass customization, 417
Maughan, Deryck C., 3
Maximum criterion, 856
Measurement errors, 174–175
Mercantilist period, 266
Merck v. Primecrown, 278
MERCOSUR, 264
Mergers to lessen competition, 757, 774–777
MES. *See* Minimum efficient scale
Microeconomics, 4, 5
Minimax regret criterion, 856–857
Minimum efficient scale, 368–369
Mixed Bundling, 611
Mixed Nash equilibrium strategy, 579
Money. *See* Time value of money
Monopolistic competition
    pricing and output decisions, 444–445, 451–454
Monopoly
    capacity investment, 490
    contribution margin, 487–488
    definition, 443
    gross profit margin, 488–489
    limit pricing, 490–492
    mark-up, optimal, 487–488
    market power, sources of, 478–483
    price and output determination, 484–485
    price elasticity, importance of, 486–487
    pricing and output decisions, 443–444
    pricing strategies, effect of, 490–492
    profit maximization, 484–485
    profit misconceptions, economic, 490
    regulation (*See* Regulation, government)
    theory of profit, 8
Moral hazard problem, 682–684, 687–688
Morgenstern, Oskar, 538

Motor Carrier Act of 1980, 783
Moving average forecasts, 199–201
MRTS. *See* Marginal rate of technical substitution
Multicollinearity, 176
Multiple linear regression model. *See* Regression analysis
Multiple-equation models, 213–215
Multiplicative exponential model, 133–134

N

n-person games, 539
NAFTA. *See* North American Free Trade Area
Nash equilibrium strategy, 553–554, 577–580, 705–706
National Energy Policy Act of 1992, 784
Natural monopoly, 495–497
Negative autocorrelation, 171–172
Net marginal return, 32
Net present value, 34–37, 48, 807–809
Network effect increasing returns, 479–483
NFP. *See* Not-for-profit organizations
Niche pricing, 625
Noncooperative games, 539
Nonlinear regression models, 180–181
Nonlinear trend, 193
Nonredeployable assets, 465–467, 572
Nonredeployable reputational asset, 560
Normal form of the game, 537–538
Normal goods, 99
Normal probability distribution, 41–42
North American Free Trade Area, 98, 270–271, 273–274, 275–277
Not-for-profit organizations, 23–24, 26
NPV. *See* Net present value

O

Obsolescence, planned, 565, 566
Oligopoly, 445
    barometric price leadership, 525
    cartels, 513, 517–524
    characteristics, 507
    collusion, 513–516

conscious parallelism of action, 512
Cournet Model, 512–513, 522–523
dominant price leadership, 525–528
game theory, 535–541
interdependencies, 510–512
kinked demand curve model, 529–530
output, 517
price leadership, 524–528
price wars, avoiding, 530–535
pricing and output decisions, 445
profit maximization, 517–519
relative market shares, 507–510
rigidity of price, 529–530
rivalry, 535–541
Sherman Act (1890), The, 513
OLS. *See* Ordinary least-squares
One price, law of, 251
One-shot games, 539
OPEC, 518–519, 523–524
Open bidding, 725–726
Operating leverage, 406–407
Operating risk exposures, 237
Opportunity cost, 7, 347, 805
Optimal capacity utilization, 359–360
Optimal incentives contract, 740–742
Optimal level, determination of, 455–456
Optimal output for the plant size, 360
Optimal plant size, 360
Optimal plant size for the output rate, 360
Optimal use determination, 307–309
Optimization and differential calculus, 60–63
Options, 245, 862
Ordinary least-squares, 155
Organization form
  alternative forms, 694–699
  application, 673–674
  auction design (*See* Auction design and information economics)
  Coase, Ronald, 683
  contracts, 675
  coordination and control issues, 682–683
  credibility, establishing, 677
  ex post implementation, 682
  fair division games, 715–717
  governance mechanisms, 682–685

  licensing, 702–707
  moral hazard problem, 682–684
  optimal mechanism design, 714–717
  patent protection, 702–707
  relational contracts, 695–696
  reliant assets, 695
  selection process, 674–675
  spot market transactions, 678–679
  trade secrets, 702–707
  vertical integration, 699–702
  vertical requirements contracts, 675–677
  Williamson, Oliver, 682
Organization of Petroleum Exporting Countries. *See* OPEC
Output effect, 321–323
Overall production efficiency, 320
Overbooking, optimal, 649–651
Ownership separation from management, 3, 14–15, 17

P
Paradox, St. Petersburg, 842
Parallel imports, 277–278, 279
Pari-mutuel betting, 86
Partial derivatives, 64–66
Participation constraint, 691
Partnerships, 735–736
Patent protection, 492, 625, 702–707, 784–786
Payoff table, 844
Peak-load pricing, 497–498
Pecuniary effects, 824
Pecuniary externalities, 749–750
Penetration pricing, 624
Perfect complements, 312–313
Perfect substitutes, 312–313
Perfectly elastic demand curve, 87
Performance bonus, 3–4
Planning horizon, 299, 405–406
Plant specific economies, 363–364
Point cross price elasticity, 101–102
Point income elasticity, 99
Point price elasticity, 85
Pollution rights, sale of, 756–757
Polynomial function, 182, 387–388
Polynomial transformation, 182
Pooling equilibrium, 692
Population regression coefficients, 139–140, 143–145, 151–152
Porter's five forces strategic framework, 432–442
Porter, Michael, 432

Portfolio risk, 858–861
Positive autocorrelation, 171–172
Postcontractual opportunistic behavior, 682
PPP. *See* Purchasing power parity
Prediction intervals, 143
Present value, 36, A-2
Present value interest factor (PVIF), 36
Prestige pricing, 630
Price differentiation, optimal, 613–615
Price discrimination
  price elasticity of demand, 615–616
  pricing techniques, 606–609
  profitability, firm, 616–620
  regulation, 778
Price elasticity of demand, 72, 81–82
  arc elasticity, 85
  arc price elasticity, 82–84
  budget, percentage of, 96
  ceteris paribus, 82, 84
  combined effect with income elasticity, 105–106
  durable goods, 96
  factors, 94–96
  free trade, 97–98
  housing, 97–98
  inelasticity, 86, 87, 93
  interpretation, 86–90
  Macon Telegraph, The, 84–85
  marginal revenue, 88, 90–92
  monopolistic importance, 486–487
  pari-mutuel betting, 86
  perfectly elastic demand curve, 87
  point price elasticity, 85
  pricing techniques, 615–616
  significance, 92
  substitutes, availability of, 94, 96
  time frame of analysis, 97
  unit elastic, 86–87
Price leadership, 524–528
Price premiums, 465–466
Price wars, avoiding, 530–535
Pricing and output decisions
  break-even sales change analysis, 438–439
  competitive strategy, 426–431
  cost fixing, 437
  entry, threat of, 434–435
  expenses, selling and promotional, 455–458
  long run, 449–450, 453–454
  market structures, 442–445

monopolistic competition, 444–445, 451–454
oligopoly, 445
Porter's five forces strategic framework, 432–442
power of buyers and suppliers, 436–437
pure competition, 442–443, 445–447
relevant market decision, 431–432
rivalry, intensity of, 437–441
short run, 445–448, 452–453
substitutes, threat of, 432–433
Pricing techniques
bundling, 610–613
by delivery location, 604–605
congestion pricing, 604–605
differential pricing, 277–278, 603–606
dynamic pricing, 632
full-cost pricing, 625–628
incremental analysis, 627–628
Internet, pricing on the, 630–632
intertemporal, 603–606
joint products, 653–657
life-cycle pricing, 623–625
limit pricing, 624
matching guarantees, 586–588
monopolistic, 577
multiple products, 620–623
niche pricing, 625
penetration pricing, 624
prestige pricing, 630
price differentiation, optimal, 613–615
price elasticity of demand, 615–616
pricing by delivery location, 604–605
proactive pricing, 602–603
profitability, firm, 616–620
resale price maintenance, 590
reservation price, 610–612
skimming, 628–630
supermarket pricing, 623
systematic-analytical, 602–603
target return-on-investment pricing, 623–624, 626–627
three-degree price discrimination, 612
transfer pricing, 657–666
two-part tariff, 607–610
value-based pricing, 602–603, 624
Primary benefits, 823
Primary costs, 823

Principal-agent
application, 685–686
benchmarking, 688
contract renewals, 693–694
creative ingenuity, 688
hiring arrangements, alternative, 686–687
holdup problem, 693–694
incentive compatibility constraint, 691
moral hazard problem, 687–688
participation constraint, 691
problems of, 15–16
work effort, 687–689
Prisoner's dilemma, 540, 541, 580–581, 583
Private-value auctions, 726–729
Proactive pricing, 602–603, 643–645
Probabilities
distributions, 39–42
risk assessment, 39–40
Process rays, 318–319, 341–343
Producer's goods, 80–81
Product differentiation, 436, 451
Product differentiation strategy, 428
Product specific economies, 363
Product, value of, 123–125
Production
average product, 300, 305–306
Cobb-Douglas production function (See Cobb-Douglas production function)
continuous variable, 305–306
cost-minimization process (See Cost-minimization process)
curve relationships, 357–359
decision formulation, 314
definition, 296
diminishing marginal returns, law of (See Diminishing marginal returns, law of)
elasticity, 300–301, 328
equimarginal criterion, 316
fixed input, 298
function, 296–299
increasing returns, 302–305
information economy, 305
input classification, 298
inputs, 296–297, 307
isocost lines, 313–315
Lagrangian multiplier technique, 338
linear programming, 318–319, 340–344
long run, 299, 378–380

marginal product, 299–300, 301, 302, 305–306
maximization, 317, 338, 340–344
objective, analysis, 299
optimal combination, 313–317
planning horizon, 299
process rays, 318–319, 341–343
requirements, 296
returns to scale (See Returns to scale)
short run, 299
stages, 307
theoretical development, 299
total product, 305–306
variable input (See Variable input)
virtuous circle, 305
Productivity law, diminishing. See Diminishing marginal returns, law of
Products
with interdependent demands, 620–621
with separate production, 622–623
Profit, 347–348
dynamic equilibrium (friction) theory of profit, 8
economic, 25
friction theory of profit, 8
function values, 33–34, 35
innovation theory of profit, 8
long-term, 490
managerial efficiency theory of profit, 8
maximization of, 9, 55–63, 446–448
monopoly theory of profit, 8
risk-bearing theory of profit, 7
short-term, 490
timing, 9
versus cash flows, 12
Promotional expenses, selling and, 455–458
Prospect theory, 848–850
Protection level, 648
Public good character, 23
Public sector, 23–24
Public utilities, 492, 494
Purchasing power parity, 251–252, 254–256
absolute version of, 251
cross-cultural differences, 254
implications, 251–252
inflation, 252–253
international, 289–292

international business role,
    254–259
relative, 252–253, 291–292
sensitivities, 254
trend assessment, application in,
    258–259
Pure competition, 442–443, 445–447

Q

Queue service rules, 717–719

R

Railroad Revitalization and
    Regulatory Reform Act of
    1976, 783
Random rationing, 571, 599
Random walk variables, 218–219
Rate of return, 807, 809
    required, 37
Ratio to trend method, 196
Rationing
    efficient, 571
    inverse intensity, 571
    random, 571, 599
Real rate of interest, 291
Real terms of trade, 265
Reciprocal transformation, 181–182
Recontracting costs, 21
Refusals to deal, 778
Regression analysis, 131
    application, 170
    assumptions, 136–138, 150
    autocorrelation
        (*See* Autocorrelation)
    computer calculations, 150–151
    Durbin-Watson statistic, 171–172
    forecasts, determination of,
        142–143, 151–152
    heteroscedasticity
        (*See* Heteroscedasticity)
    invalidation, potential, 174–175
    least-squares method, 194, 419
    linear regression model, 136–138
    measurement errors, 174–175
    multicollinearity, 176
    multiple, 386
    multiple linear regression model,
        150
    nonlinear regression models (*See*
        Nonlinear regression models)
    parameters, estimating, 140–141
    population regression coefficients,
        139–140, 143–145, 151–152
    predictions, role in determining,
        142–143

simultaneous equation
    relationship, 176–179
specification errors, 146–147,
    174–175
standard error of the estimate, 142
stochastic disturbance term, 137
variance, analysis of, 146–149,
    153
Regret, 856–857
Regulation, government
    Airline Deregulation Act of 1978,
        783
    antitrust issues (*See* Antitrust laws)
    Coase Theorem, 763
    communications companies, 493,
        495
    competition, restriction to,
        784–788
    concentration ratio, market,
        769–771
    constraints, analysis of, 778–783
    contestable markets, 766–768
    deregulation movement, 783–784
    Eastman Kodak v. *Image
        Technical Services,* 778
    electric power companies, 493
    entry, threat of, 766
    externality problem, 754
    FTC v. *Stride Rite,* 778
    Herfindahl-Hirschman Index,
        770–771
    import quotas, 786–788
    licensing, 784
    market conduct, patterns of,
        764–765
    monopolies, 492–495
    monopolization, 777
    Motor Carrier Act of 1980, 783
    National Energy Policy Act of
        1992, 784
    natural gas companies, 493
    natural monopoly argument,
        495–497
    patents, 784–786
    peak-load pricing, 497–498
    price discrimination, 778
    public utilities, 492, 494
    Railroad Revitalization and
        Regulatory Reform Act of
        1976, 783
    sequential games, 588–590
    third-degree price discrimination,
        612
    United States v. *GM,* 590, 778
Relational contracts, 695–696

Relative purchasing power parity,
    291–292
Relevant cost, 349–350, 351
Relevant market, 431–432
Reliance relationships, 463–464
Reliant assets, 695
Renegade discounting, 577–579
Repeated games, 539
Replacement cost, 349–350
Replacement guarantees, 734–735
Required rate of return, 37
Resale price maintenance, 590
Reservation price, 610, 612
Residual claimants, 22
Resource-allocation decisions, 12–13
Return risk relationships, 46–47
Returns
    constant, 379
    decreasing, 379
    increasing, 379–380, 479–483
Returns to scale, 379–380
    analysis, 323–324
    Cobb-Douglas production
        function, 326–330
    constant, 341
    coordination and control, 325–326
    definition, 323
    homogenous production function,
        325
    production functions, 324
    specialization of capital and labor,
        325
Revenue management
    auction types, 731–734
    authorization level, 648
    capacity reallocation, 645–649
    case study of, 30
    concept, 638
    cross-functional systems
        management process, 639–641
    overbooking, optimal, 649–651
    premiums, sources of sustainable
        price, 641–643
    price differentiation, 613–615
    price elasticity of demand, 86–88,
        90–92
    proactive price discrimination,
        643–645
    protection level, 648
    threshold sales curve, 647
    yield management, 640–641
Reverse auction, 607
Rigidity of price, 529–530
Risk, 48
    capital budgeting and, 814

decision analysis techniques, 841–842
evaluation of differential levels, 10
management strategies (*See* Management strategies, risk)
measurement, 45–46
net present value, and, 38
profitability, and, 7–8
return rate relationships, and, 46–47
Risk assessment, 38–42, 408–409
Risk neutral, 847
Risk preferrer, 847
Risk premium, 47
Risk return trade-offs, 47–48
Risk-adjusted discount rate, 851–852
Risk-bearing theory of profit, 7
Rivalry, 437–441, 555–556
Robinson-Patman Act, The, (1936), 773
Root mean square error (RMSE), 189

S

Sales expectation plans, 210
Sales force polling, 211
Sales forecasting, 211
Satisficing behavior, 18
Scenario planning, 864
Search goods, 459
Seasonal effects, 192, 196
Second derivative of a function, 63
Second-order condition, 62–63, 64
Secondary effects, 824
Secular trends, 190–191, 193
Security market line (SML), 814
Selection process, 674–675
Selection, adverse, 460–462
Self-enforcing reliance relationship, 740
Selling expenses, promotional and, 455–458
Selten, Reinhard, 553, 581, 582
Semilogarithmic transformation, 180
Separating equilibrium, 692
Sequential games
backwards induction, 552
Bayesian probability concept, 584–585
Chainstore Paradox, 582–583, 584
conspicuous focal point, 586
contestable markets, 572, 573
coordination of business activities, challenges to, 549–550

credibility mechanisms (*See* Credibility)
decision tree, 551
endgame reasoning, 552
equilibrium strategy, 553–554
fast second advantages, 556–558
first-mover advantages, 556–558
focal outcomes of interest, 557
Folk theorem, 581
game tree, 551
grim trigger strategy, 580–581
infinitely repeated games, 582
iterated dominant strategy, 576–577
mixed Nash equilibrium strategy, 579
Nash equilibrium strategy, 553–554
predictability of rival behavior, 549–550
price matching guarantees, 586–588
Prisoner's dilemma, 580–581
regulatory constraints, 588–590
rivalry, 555–556
subgame perfect equilibrium strategy, 553–554, 598–600
sunk costs, role for, 572–573
Tit-for-Tat decision rule, 585–586
trembling hand trigger strategy, 585
unraveling problem, 581–582
wars of attrition, 573–575
Shareholder wealth-maximization analysis, 17
asymmetric information, 20–21
complete markets, impact of, 19–20
decision rule specification, 34–35
developmental strategy, 17–18
fiduciary duty, 22–23
firm value determinants, 11
implications, 17–18
model, 9, 10, 12–13, 25
net present value, 36–37
objectives, 14–15
Sherman Act, The, (1890), 513, 771–772
Short-run cost function
analysis, cost, 351–359
cost-output data, altering, 386
definition and measurement differences, 384–385
estimation challenges, 384
estimation, statistical, 389–391

hypothesized cost-output relationships, 387–389
logarithmic function, 389
multiple regression analysis, 386
objectives, 385
polynomial function, 387–388
time period, selection of, 385–386
Simple linear regression model. *See* Regression analysis
Simulation techniques, 852–854
Simultaneous equation relationship, 176–179
Simultaneous games
application, 576–577
best-reply response, 578
Nash equilibrium strategy, 577–580
Prisoner's dilemma, 576
strategies, 576–580
Single payment, present value of, A-1, A-2
Single-equation models, 211–212
Single-period games, 539
Skimming, 628–630
Slippery slope, 575
Smoothing techniques, 198–204
Social discount rate, 825–826
Specification errors, 146–147, 174–175
Specificity, asset, 467
Speculation, 243
Speculative demand, 240–241
Spill and spoilage, 638–639
Spoilage and spill, 638–639
Spot market transactions, 678–679
Spur Industries v. *Del Webb Development*, 749
St. Petersburg Paradox, 842
Standard deviations, 40–42, 44–45, 48
Standard error of the estimate, 142
Standard normal probability function, 42
Statistical estimation of production function, 326–330
Sterilized intervention, 241
Stochastic disturbance term, 137
Stochastic time-series models, 216–219
Stock prices, factors affecting, 12–13
Strategic hold-outs, 753
Strategic positioning, 428
Strategy game, 536–537
Stratified lotteries, 719

Structural equation models, 212–213
Structural equations, 213
Subgame perfect equilibrium strategy, 553–554, 598–600
Substitute goods, 77, 94, 96, 102
Substitutes, threat of, 432–433
Substitution effect, 75–76, 120, 122
Sunk costs, 350–351, 805
  role for, 572–573
Supermarket pricing, 623
Survey and opinion polling techniques, 129–130, 207, 210
Survivor technique, 396–397
Swaps, 245
Switching cost, 437
Systematic risk, 814
Systematic-analytical pricing, 602–603

T

t-statistic application, 173
Target return-on-investment pricing, 623–624, 626–627
Tariffs, protective, 266–267, 270
Taxes and subsidies, 754–756
Technical efficiency, 319, 321
Technological effects, 824
Third-degree price discrimination, 612
Threshold sales curve, 647
Time depreciation, 385
Time value of money
  annuity, present value of, A-3, A-4
  application, A-1
  bequest, present value of deferred, A-2
  definition, A-1
  discount rate, A-1
  equal payments, present value of, A-3, A-4
  interest rate determination, A-3, A-5
  present value, A-2
  single payment, present value of, A-1, A-2
  unequal payments, present value of, A-5

Time-series analysis
  components, 190
  constant rate of growth pattern, 193, 194–195
  cyclical variations, 191–192
  dummy variables, 196–197
  growth trends, declining rate of, 196
  least-squares method, 194
  linear trend, 193, 194–195
  models, elementary, 192–193
  nonlinear trend, 193
  random fluctuations, 192
  ratio to trend method, 196
  seasonal effects, 192, 194, 196
  secular trends, 190–191, 193
Tit-for-Tat decision rule, 585–586
Total cost function, 352–354
Total product function, 300, 301
Total profit function, 33–34, 35
Total revenue, 6, 25, 397
Trade secrets, 702–707
Trade-offs, risk return, 47–48
Trade-weighted exchange rate, 259–260
Trading. *See* Exports
Transaction demand, 239–240
Transaction risk exposure, 237
Transfer pricing, 657–666
Translation risk exposure, 237
Trembling hand trigger strategy, 585
Twin deficits, 280, 282
Two-part tariff, 607–610
Two-person game, 539
Two-person zero-sum game, 540

U

Uncertainty, 405, 804, 842
  managing, 857–864
Underbidding, strategic, 726–729
Unequal payments, present value of, A-5
Unit elastic, 86–87
United States v. *GM*, 590
Unknowingness, 842
Unraveling problem, investigation of, 581–582
Unsystematic risk, 814

Use depreciation, 385
Utility maximization, 75–76

V

Value of new product, 123–125
Value-based pricing, 602–603, 624
Variable costs, 352
Variable identification, 132
Variable input
  average product, 300
  definition, 298
  elasticity of production, 300–301
  isoquants, production (*See* Isoquants, production)
  marginal factor cost, 309
  marginal revenue product, 308–309
  optimal use determination, 307–309
  total product function, 300, 301
Variable marginal product, 299–300, 301
Variable proportions, law of. *See* Diminishing marginal returns, law of
Variance, analysis of, 146–149, 153
Variation, coefficient of, 45, 48
Vector autoregression, 215
Versioning, 564, 605–606
Vertical integration, 699–702
Vertical requirements contracts, 675–677
Vickery auction, 730
Von Neumann, John, 538

W

Warranties, 734–735
Weighted cost of capital, 815–816
Williamson, Oliver, 682
Winner's curse, 721–723
World Trade Organization. *See* WTO
WTO, 267–269

Y

Yield management, 640–641

Profit Maximization: Monopoly

Price Elasticity and Price Levels for Monopolists

Markups and Contribution Margins on Chanel No. 5, Ole Musk, and Whitman's Sampler

Components of the Gross Margin at Kellogg Co.

Limit Pricing to Discourage Generic Drugs: Bristol-Myers Squibb

What Went Right/What Went Wrong: Public Service Company of New Mexico

Are Large-Scale Electricity Generating Plants Becoming Extinct?

Chapter 12: Price and Output Determination: Oligopoly

Managerial Challenge: Are Nokia's Margins on Cell Phones Collapsing?

Hewlett-Packard Dominance in Printers

Airlines Deconcentrate while Cable and Retail Gasoline Firms Consolidate: Southwest Airlines, AT&T Broadband, and Exxon/Mobil

Airline Pricing: The Pittsburgh Market

Cournot Oligopoly Solution: Siemens and Thomson-CSF

Ocean Shipping Conferences

OPEC Members Adopt a New Quota Agreement

Cartel Pricing and Output Decisions: Siemens and Thomson-CSF

A Sports Cartel: Major League Baseball

⊕ The Organization of Petroleum Exporting Countries (OPEC) Cartel

Barometric Price Leadership: American Airlines and Continental Airlines

Price Leadership: Aerotek

Price Wars at General Mills and Post and at Philip Morris and R.J. Reynolds

What Went Right/What Went Wrong: Good-Better-Best Product Strategy at Kodak

What Went Right at Interlink Surgical Steel?

Nonprice Tactics in a Price War: Kellogg and Coors

Nobel Goes to Three Game Theorists

Coffee Cartel Dissolves

Chapter 13: Game-Theoretic Rivalry: Best-Practice Tactics

Managerial Challenge: Price Differentials in Computers: IBM, Compaq, and Dell

Business Gaming at Verizon

Technology Leader or Fast Second: IBM

Double-the-Difference Price Guarantees: Circuit City

Noncredible Commitments: Burlington Industries

Leasing of Digital Moviehouse Projectors: Hughes-JVC

NetJets Fractional Ownership Plans for Learjet and Gulfstream Aircraft

Licensing of Taxi Medallions and Cell Phones

Excess Capacity Reaches Epic Proportions in World Car Market: Daewoo

Contestable Market in Bicycle Helmets: Bell Sports

Kodak Takes a Promotional Discount

Violation of the Chain Store Paradox: Semiconductor Pricing at Intel, NEC, and Motorola

Predation Reputation at Brown and Williamson

Signalling a Punishment Scheme: Northwest

Resale Price Maintenance Agreement: StrideRite

⊕ Case Exercise: Superjumbo Dilemma

Chapter 14: Pricing Techniques and Analysis

Managerial Challenge: Pricing of Apple Computers: Market Share Versus Current Profitability

Congestion Tolls in Orange County, California

eBusiness Clickstreams Allow Price Discrimination: Personify

Priceline Implements Perfect Price Discrimination

California Consumers Prefer Two-Part Tariffs for Electricity

What Went Right/What Went Wrong: $19.95 for "Unlimited Access" at America Online

McDonald's Introduces Mixed Bundles as "Extra Value Meals"

Third-Degree Price Discrimination Takes Hold in Long-Distance Market: AT&T, MCI WorldMom, and Sprint

Price Discrimination and the Price Elasticity of Demand: Trans-America Airlines

Price Discrimination and Profitability: Taiwan Instrument Company

Interdependent Demands: The Gillette Company

Multiple-Product Pricing: Supermarket Pricing

Loss of Patent Protection Limits Price of Prozac: Eli Lilly

Niche Pricing of NetPCs: IBM

Full-Cost Pricing Loses a Big Contract at J.P. Morgan: British Telephone

Full-Cost Pricing versus Incremental Analysis: PhoneMate Company

Incrementalism at Continental Airlines

Apple iMac Computer

Appendix 14A: Revenue Management

Spill and Spoilage at Sport Obermeyer

Toyota Plans to Assemble Cars Within Five Days of a Custom Order

Optimal Capacity Allocation: 11 A.M. Flight to LAX

Optimal Probability of Stockout at Sport Obermeyer

Pinpoint Booking Accuracy at American Airlines

Revenue Management in Baseball: The Baltimore Orioles

Appendix 14B: Pricing of Joint Products and Transfer Pricing

Pricing of Joint Products: Williams Company

Pricing of Joint Products: Slusser Chemical Company

Pricing of Interdepartmental Services at Bell Atlantic

Determining the Optimal Transfer Price: Portland Electronics

⊕ Transfer Pricing, Taxes, and Ethics

PART V: ORGANIZATIONAL ARCHITECTURE AND INSTITUTIONAL ECONOMICS

Chapter 15: Contracting, Governance, and Organizational Form

Managerial Challenge: Controlling the Vertical: Ultimate TV

Crankshaft Delivery Delay Causes Plant Closing

Enforcement and Excusal of Contract Promises: The Extraordinary Case of 9/11

What Went Right/What Went Wrong: Moral Hazard and Holdup at Enron and Worldcom

Indexed Stock Options at Adobe Systems, Dell, and Cisco

P&G Pays Ad Executives Based on Performance

What Went Right/What Went Wrong: Why Have Restricted Stock Grants Replaced Executive Stock Options at Microsoft?

Schwinn and Sylvania Dealers Offered Exclusive Territories